CASSELL'S NEW COMPACT
LATIN-ENGLISH
ENGLISH-LATIN
DICTIONARY

Compiled by

D. P. SIMPSON, M.A.

Assistant Master and formerly Head of
Classical Department at Eton College

FUNK & WAGNALLS COMPANY, INC.
New York

CASSELL'S NEW COMPACT LATIN-ENGLISH
ENGLISH-LATIN DICTIONARY

© Cassell & Co. Ltd, 1963
First published in the United States
in 1964 by Funk & Wagnalls Company, Inc.

Library of Congress Catalogue Card Number 64–11414
Printed in the United States of America

PREFACE

THE first Latin Dictionary published by Cassell appeared in 1854. It was the work of two Unitarian divines, J. R. Beard and his son Charles Beard, and consisted of two sections of equal length, Latin-English and English-Latin. The first of these sections was " revised, enlarged, and in part rewritten " for publication in 1886, by J. R. V. Marchant, who was for a short time a master at St. Paul's School, but later was called to the Bar, and became a County Court Judge. By 1892 the second section, English-Latin, had also been revised, and considerably shortened, by J. F. Charles, probably with help from Marchant. Charles had been a pupil, with Marchant, at the City of London School, and after graduating at London and Oxford he returned there as a master. The combined work of Marchant and Charles was reprinted at short intervals for the next sixty years. In 1927 a shortened version of it appeared, under the name of " Cassell's Compact Latin-English English-Latin Dictionary." This was prepared by Miss Millicent Thomas, M.A. (London), sometime Classics and Senior Mistress of Tottenham High School, and an assistant examiner in Classics for the University of London. She dispensed with most of the prolegomena printed by Marchant and Charles, and in her main text reduced both the length and the number of articles, leaving the rarer words out of account and removing the illustrative quotations from Latin authors. In her book, as in that of Marchant and Charles, the English-Latin section was little more than half as long as the Latin-English.

In 1959 Cassell published their " New Latin Dictionary." which was a complete revision by the present author of both sections of Marchant and Charles. The new " compact " dictionary follows as an abbreviation of this, the result of much the same process of selection and simplification as Miss Thomas applied to its predecessor.

This book resembles every other Latin dictionary so far produced by Cassell, in concerning itself with " classical " Latin, as used from about 200 B.C. to A.D. 100. It also conforms to the principle maintained since the time of Marchant and Charles, that the English-Latin section should be kept relatively short, in the hope that the user will refer from it to the Latin-English for fuller information. Both English and Latin words are treated in alphabetical order, except that adverbs appear under the adjectives from which they are derived, participles under verbs, and so on; certain synonyms, also, are grouped together within a single article. The spelling of Latin words is intended to correspond to what will be found in the more recent editions of Latin authors; I, i replaces J, j throughout, but V, v is retained. In the Latin-English section most vowels in Latin words are marked short (˘) or long (¯); in the English-Latin this has been done more sparingly, for the special purpose of distinguishing between words of similar form, or of indicating declension or conjugation.

D.P.S.

LIST OF SPECIAL TERMS

abbrev. abbreviated, abbreviation.
abl. ablative.
absol. absolute.
abstr. abstract.
acc. accusative.
act. active.
adj. adjective.
adv. adverb.
adversat. adversative.
architect. architectural.
class. classical.
coll. collective.
colloq. colloquial.
commerc. commercial.
compar. comparative.
concr. concrete.
conj. conjunction.
dat. dative.
dep. deponent.
dim. diminutive.
distrib. distributive.
e.g. exempli gratia (for example)
esp. especially.
etc. et cetera.
exclam. exclamatory.
f. feminine.
fig. figure, figurative.
foll. followed.
fut. future.
gen. general, generally.
genit. genitive.
gram., grammat. grammatical.
i.e. id est (that is).
imperf. imperfect.
impers. impersonal.
indecl. indeclinable.
indef. indefinite.
indic. indicative.
infin. infinitive.
interj. interjection.
interrog. interrogative.
intransit. intransitive.
logic. logical.

m. masculine.
medic. medical.
meton. by metonymy.
milit. military.
myth. mythological.
n. neuter.
naut. nautical.
neg. negative.
nom. nominative.
num. numeral.
obs. obsolete.
occ. occasionally.
opp. opposite (to).
partic. participle.
pass. passive.
perf. perfect.
pers. person.
personif. personified.
philosoph. philosophy, philosophical.
phr. phrase.
pl., plur. plural.
poet. poetical.
polit. political.
posit. positive.
prep. preposition.
pres. present.
pron. pronoun.
q.v. quod vide, quae vide (i.e. see article concerned).
reflex. reflexive.
relat. relative.
relig. religious.
rhet. rhetoric, rhetorical.
sc. scilicet (that is to say).
sing. singular.
subj. subjunctive.
subst. substantive.
superl. superlative.
t.t. technical term.
transf. transferred (i.e used in altered sense).
transit. transitive.
voc. vocative.

CASSELL'S LATIN-ENGLISH DICTIONARY

A

A, a, the first letter of the Latin Alphabet.

a, ah, interj. *Ah!*

a, ab, abs, prep. with abl. (1) of motion or measurement in space, *from, away from.* (2) of time, *from, after.* (3) of separation, difference, change, *from;* so of position or number, *counting from;* and of the relation of part to whole, *out of, of.* (4) or origin and agency; especially with passive verbs, *by, at the hands of, because of.* (5) *viewed from, on the side of:* a tergo, *in the rear;* hence *in connexion with, as regards.*

ăbăcus -i, m. *a square board;* hence *sideboard, counting-board, gaming-board, ceiling panel.*

ăbăliēnātĭo -ōnis, f. *transfer of property.*

ăbălĭēno -are, *to make alien, separate, estrange.*

ăbăvus -i, m. *great-great-grandfather.*

Abdēra -orum, n. pl., also -ae, f., *a town in Thrace, noted for the stupidity of its inhabitants.*

abdĭcātĭo -ōnis, f. *disowning, renunciation.*

¹abdĭco -are, *to renounce, reject;* esp. of magistracies, *to abdicate,* often with reflex. and ablative of office.

²abdĭco -dicĕre -dixi -dictum, in augury, *to disapprove of.*

abdo -dĕre -dĭdi -dĭtum, *to put away, withdraw, remove;* esp. *to secrete, hide.*

Hence partic. **abdĭtus** -a -um, *concealed, secret.* Adv. **abdĭtē.**

abdōmen -ĭnis, n. *belly;* hence *gluttony.*

abdūco -dūcĕre -duxi -ductum, *to lead* or *take away, detach, withdraw.*

ăbĕo -ire -ii -ĭtum, *to go away;* abi, *be off with you;* abi in malam rem, *go to the devil.* Transf., *to retire from office; to depart from life, die;* in discussion, *to digress;* in form, *to change;* of things, *to pass away, disappear, vanish; to pass over* from owner to owner.

ăbĕquĭto -are, *to ride off.*

ăberrātĭo ōnis, f. *escape, relief.*

ăberro -are, *to wander, deviate, escape.*

abhinc. (1) *hereafter.* (2) *ago:* abhinc annos tres, or annis tribus *three years ago.*

abhorreo -ēre, *to shrink back from;* hence *to be inconsistent with* or *opposed to;* a fide, *to be incredible.* Pres. part., as adj., *unseasonable, inappropriate.*

ăbĭcĭo -icĕre -iēci -iectum, *to throw down* or *away.* Transf., *to pronounce carelessly, break off abruptly; to get rid of, give up; to dash to the ground, weaken, dishearten.*

Hence partic. **abiectus** -a -um; of position, *low, common;* of character, *cowardly, mean;* of style, *without force, prosaic.* Adv. **abiectē,** *without spirit, meanly.*

abiectĭo -ōnis, f. *throwing away; animi, despondency, despair.*

ăbĭegnus -a -um, *of fir wood* or *deal.*

ăbĭēs ĕtis, f. *the silver fir;* meton., *anything made of deal,* such as *a ship* or *spear.*

ăbĭgo -ĕre -ēgi -actum, *to drive away;* of cattle, *to remove, steal.* Transf., *to banish, be rid of:* uxorem, *to divorce.*

ăbĭtĭo -ōnis, f. and **ăbĭtus** -ūs, m., *going away, departure; place of egress.*

abĭūdĭco -are, *to take away by a judgment.*

abiungo -iungĕre -iunxi -iunctum, *to unharness;* hence *to estrange, detach.*

abiuro -are, *to abjure, deny on oath.*

ablātīvus -a -um, *ablative.*

ablēgātĭo -onis, f. *sending away, banishment.*

ablēgo -are, *to send away, remove to a distance.*

ablĭgūrio -ire, *to lick away;* hence *to squander.*

ablūdo -ĕre, *to be out of tune.*

ablŭo -lŭĕre -lŭi -lūtum. *to wash clean; to wash away.*

abnĕgo -are, *to deny, refuse.*

abnĕpōs -ōtis, m. *great-great-grandson.*

abneptis -is, f. *great-great-granddaughter.*

abnocto -are, *to stay out all night.*

abnormis -e, *irregular, unconventional.*

abnŭo -nŭĕre -nŭi, fut. partic. -nūitūrus, *to refuse by a gesture, to deny.*

ăbŏleo -ēre -ēvi -itum, *to destroy, do away with.*

ăbŏlesco -ĕre -ēvi, *to perish.*

ăbŏlĭtĭo -ōnis, f. *removing, annulling, abolition.*

ăbolla -ae, f. *a cloak of thick woollen cloth.*

ăbōmĭno -are, and **ăbōmĭnor** -ari, dep. (1) *to deprecate:* quod abominor, *God forbid.* (2) *to hate, detest.*

ăbŏrĭor -ŏriri -ortus, dep.: of heavenly bodies, *to set;* poet., of the voice, *to fail.*

ăbŏriscor -i = aborior: q.v.

ăbortĭo -ōnis, f. *untimely birth, miscarriage.*

ăbortīvus -a -um, *prematurely born.*

ăbortus -ūs, m. *miscarriage.*

abrādo -radĕre -rāsi -rāsum, *to scrape off, shave.* Transf., *to squeeze out, to extort.*

abrĭpĭo -rĭpĕre -rĭpŭi -reptum *to, snatch away, drag off, remove, detach.*

abrōdo -rōdĕre -rōsi -rōsum, *to gnaw off.*

abrŏgātĭo -ōnis, f. *annulling, repealing.*

abrŏgo -are. *to repeal, annul, remove, take away.*

abrŏtŏnum -i, n. and **abrŏtŏnus** -i, m. *southern-wood.*

abrumpo -rumpĕre -rūpi -ruptum, *to break off, sever; to remove, dissociate; to break off prematurely, destroy.* Hence partic. **abruptus** -a -um, *steep, precipitous, abrupt, rough.* N. as subst., *a steep place.* Adv. **abruptē.**

abruptĭo -ōnis, f. *tearing away;* hence *divorce.*

abscēdo -cēdĕre -cessi -cessum, *to go away, depart, retire, desert.*

abscessĭo -ōnis, f. *going away, separation.*

abscessus -ūs, m. *going away, withdrawal.*

abscīdo -cīdĕre -cīdi -cīsum, *to cut off; to separate* or *take away.* Hence partic. **abscīsus** -a -um, *precipitous, abrupt, short.*

abscindo -scindĕre -scĭdi -scissum, *to tear off, wrench away;* venas, *to cut open the veins;* poet., abscissa comas, *with her hair torn.* Transf., *to divide* or *separate.*

abscondo -condĕre -condi (-condidi) -condĭtum (-consum), *to conceal; to lose sight of;* pass., of stars, *to set.* Adv. from partic., **absconditē,** *obscurely.*

absens -entis, *absent;* see also **absum.**

absentĭa -ae, f. *absence.*

absĭlĭo -ire, -ĭi or -ŭi, *to spring forth* or *away.*

absĭmĭlis -e, *unlike.*

absinthĭum -i, n. *wormwood.*

absisto -sistĕre -stĭti. *to go away from a place or person; to desist from an action.*

absŏlūtĭo -ōnis, f. (1) *acquittal.* (2) *perfection.*

absŏlūtōrĭus -a -um, *relating to acquittal.*

absolvo -solvĕre -solvi -sŏlūtum, *to loosen, to free:* of an accused person, *to acquit;* of a subject, *to dispose of, relate in full;* in gen. *to complete.* Hence partic. **absŏlūtus** -a -um, *perfect, complete; unfettered, unconditional.* Adv. **absŏlūtē,** *perfectly, completely.*

absŏnus -a -um, *inharmonious, discordant, disagreeing.*

absorbĕo -ēre -ŭi, *to swallow, gulp down;* hence *to carry away, engross.*

absque, prep. with abl. *without.*

abstēmĭus -a -um, *temperate, abstemious.*

abstergĕo -tergēre -tersi -tersum. *to wipe off, clean away.*

absterrĕo -ēre, *to frighten away.*

abstĭnentĭa -ae, f. *self-denial, temperance;* sometimes *fasting.*

abstĭnĕo -tĭnēre -tĭnŭi -tentum: transit., *to hold back;* intransit., *to abstain.* Hence present partic. **abstĭnens** -entis, *temperate.* Adv. **abstĭnenter.**

absto -are, *to stand aloof.*

abstrăho -trăhĕre -traxi, -tractum *to drag away;* hence *to remove, exclude, restrain.*

abstrūdo -trūdĕre -trūsi -trūsum, *to push away, hide.*

Hence partic. **abstrūsus** -a -um, *concealed, secret, abstruse;* of character, *reserved.*

absum, ăbesse, āfŭi. (1) *to be away, be absent* or *missing;* hence *to take no part in a thing, fail to help.* (2) *to be far away, be distant;* hence *to be far from doing a thing, to be free from a fault.*

absūmo -sūmĕre -sumpsi -sumptum, *to reduce, consume, waste, destroy.*

absurdus -a -um, *unmelodious, harsh.* Transf., *foolish, unreasonable, out of place;* of persons, *incapable.* Hence adv. **absurdē,** *harshly, discordantly; foolishly.*

ăbundantĭa -ae, f. *abundance, plenty; riches, wealth.*

ăbundē, *copiously, abundantly;* with est and genit., *there is plenty of a thing.*

ăbundo -are, *to overflow; to grow in abundance; to abound, be rich in,* esp. with abl. Hence partic. **ăbundans** -antis, *overflowing; abundant, numerous; abounding in;* adv. **ăbundanter,** *abundantly, copiously.*

ăbusquĕ, prep. with abl., *from.*

ăbūsus -ūs, m. *using up, wasting.*

ăbūtor -ūti -ūsus, dep., with abl. (1) *to make full use of.* (2) *to abuse, waste;* esp. *to use a word wrongly.*

ac; see atque.

Ăcădēmĭa -ae, f., *the Academy,* a grove near Athens where Plato taught; meton., *the Academic school of philosophy.* Hence adj. **Ăcădēmĭcus** -a -um; n. pl. **Ăcădēmĭca,** *Cicero's treatise on the Academic philosophy.*

ăcălanthis and **ăcanthis** -ĭdis, f., *a small bird, perhaps siskin.*

ăcanthus -i, m. (1) *bear's foot,* a plant. (2) *a thorny evergreen tree.*

Ăcarnānĭa -ae, f. *Acarnania, a country in western Greece.*

Acca Lārentĭa, *a Roman goddess;* **Lārentālĭa** or **Accālĭa** -ĭum, n. pl. *her festival at Rome in December.*

accēdo -cēdĕre -cessi -cessum, *to approach, come near;* of persons, *to enter upon a course;* ad rem publicam, *to begin public life;* of things, *to be added;* huc accedit ut, *it is also true that, moreover.*

accĕlĕro -are: transit., *to quicken, accelerate;* intransit., *to hasten.*

accendo -cendĕre -cendi -censum, *to kindle, set alight, set on fire.* Transf., *to fire, inflame, excite.*

accensĕo -censēre -censum, *to reckon in addition.* Hence partic. **accensus** -a -um, *reckoned with;* m. as subst., *an attendant;* in plural, **accensi,** *reserve troops, supernumeraries.*

acceptĭo -ōnis, f. *reception, acceptance.*

accepto -are, *to receive.*

acceptus -a -um, partic. from accipio; q.v.

accerso = arcesso; q.v.

accessĭo -ōnis, f. *a going* or *coming to; increase; a thing added, appendage.*

accessus -ūs, m. *approach, access; means of approach, entrance.*

¹**accīdo** -cīdĕre -cīdi -cīsum, *to hew* or *hack at;* hence *to weaken, ruin.*

²**accĭdo** -cīdĕre -cīdi, *to fall down;* ad pedes, *to fall at a person's feet.* Transf., *to happen, fall out.*

accĭĕo -ēre, obs. form of accio; q.v.

accingo -cingĕre -cinxi -cinctum, *to gird on a weapon; to equip, arm a person;* with reflex., or in pass., *to arm oneself,* hence *to make oneself ready.*

accĭo -ire -īvi (-ĭi) -ītum, *to call, summon.*

accĭpĭo -cĭpĕre -cēpi -ceptum, *to take, receive, accept.* Esp. with the senses, *to hear, feel,* etc.; with the understanding, *to grasp, to learn;* also *to take, interpret* in a certain sense; of persons, *to receive hospitably,* or *to treat* in any particular manner; in business, acceptum referre, *to enter on the credit side of an account book,* hence *to consider oneself indebted to someone for a thing.*
Hence partic. **acceptus** -a -um, *welcome, pleasant, agreeable.*

accĭpĭter -tris, m. *a hawk.*

accītus -ūs, m. *a summons.*

Accĭus -a -um, *name of a Roman gens;* esp. of L. Accius, tragic poet (170-c. 85 B.C.).

acclāmātĭo -ōnis, f. *a loud cry.*

acclāmo -are, *to cry out* (in approval or otherwise); with acc. of person, *to name by acclamation.*

acclāro -are, *to make clear, reveal.*

acclīnis -e, *leaning towards, inclined to.*

acclīno -are, *to lean towards, incline to.*

acclīvis -e, *inclined upwards.*

acclīvĭtās -ātis, f. *upward slope.*

acclīvus -a -um; = acclivis; q.v.

accŏla -ae, m. or f. *neighbour;* as adj. *living near, neighbouring.*

accŏlo -cŏlĕre -cŏlŭi -cultum, *to live near.*

accommŏdātĭo -ōnis, f. (1) *proportion* or *adjusting.* (2) *courteousness, complaisance.*

accommŏdātus -a -um, partic. from accommodo; q.v.

accommŏdo -are, *to fit, put on equipment,* etc.; *to make suitable, adjust, adapt.*
Hence partic. **accommŏdātus** -a -um, *adapted, suitable;* adv. **accommŏdātē**, *agreeably.*

accommŏdus -a -um, *fit, adapted.*

accrēdo -crēdĕre -crēdĭdi -crēdĭtum, *to believe* (with dat.).

accresco -crescĕre -crēvi -crētum, *to grow, increase;* with dat., *to be joined to a thing.*

accūbĭtĭo -ōnis, f. and **accūbĭtus** -ūs, m. *the act of reclining at table.*

accūbo -are, *to lie,* or *recline beside,* esp. at table; apud hominem, *to dine at a man's house.*

accumbo -cumbĕre -cŭbŭi -cŭbĭtum, *to lie down* or *recline,* esp. at table.

accŭmŭlātor -ōris, m. *one who heaps together.*

accŭmŭlo -are, *to heap up, accumulate; to heap things on a person, give in abundance; to ply, overwhelm a person with things; to increase.* Adv. from partic. **accŭmŭlātē**, *abundantly, copiously.*

accūrātĭo -ōnis, f. *accuracy, carefulness.*

accūro -are, *to take care of, prepare with care.*
Hence partic. **accūrātus** -a -um, *done with care, careful, exact, accurate.* Adv. **accūrātē**.

accurro -currere -curri (-cŭcurri) -cursum, *to run to;* of ideas, *to occur.*

accursus -ūs, m. *running, concourse.*

accūsābĭlis -e, *blameworthy.*

accūsātĭo -ōnis, f. *an accusation, indictment.*

accūsātor -ōris, m. *an accuser;* hence *an informer.*

accūsātōrĭus -a -um, *of* or *like an accuser;* adv. **accūsātōrĭē**.

accūsatrix -īcis, f. *a female accuser.*

accūso -are, *to accuse;* in gen., *to blame, find fault with.*

¹**ācer** -ĕris, n. *the maple tree* or *maple wood.*

²**ācer** -cris -cre, *sharp, cutting, keen.* Hence, to taste, *biting;* to touch, *sharp;* of sounds, *shrill;* of smells, *penetrating;* of sight, *keen;* of emotions, *painful;* of understanding or character, *quick, vigorous, energetic.* Adv. **ācriter**, *sharply, keenly.*

ācerbĭtās -ātis, f. *bitterness, harshness, painfulness;* in plur., *calamities.*

ācerbo -are, *to make bitter, to aggravate.*

ācerbus -a -um, *bitter.* Hence, of sounds, *harsh;* of looks, *dark, gloomy;* of speech or writing, *bitter;* of events, etc., *painful, severe;* of persons, *morose;* from the notion of unripeness, *premature.* Adv. **ācerbē**, *bitterly, harshly.*

ācernus -a -um, *made of maple wood.*

ācerra -ae, f. *a casket for incense.*

ācervatim, *by accumulation;* dicere, *to sum up.*

ācervo -are, *to heap up.*

ācervus -i, m. *a heap, mass;* in logic, *argument by accumulation.*

ācesco ācescĕre ācŭi, *to grow sour.*

ācētum -i, n. *vinegar.*

Achāĭa or **Achāĭa** -ae, f., *the Greek country of Achaia, in the Peloponnese,* or in gen. *Greece;* after 146 B.C., *the Roman province of Achaea.* Hence adj. and subst. **Achaeus** and **Achīvus**, *Achaean, an Achaean* (or *Greek*).

Achātes -ae, m. *friend of Aeneas.*

Achĕron -ontis, m. (older form **Achĕruns** -untis) *mythol. river in the lower world; the lower world itself.*

Achillēs s, and **Achillēūs** -ei, m. *a Greek hero, son of Peleus and Thetis.* Adj. **Achillēūs** -a -um.

Achīvus -a -um; see Achaia.

ācĭdus -a -um, *sharp, sour.*

ăcĭēs -ei, f. *keenness, edge*; of the mind, *penetration, insight*; of the eye, *a piercing look* or *keen vision*; sometimes *the pupil of the eye*, or *the eye itself*. Milit., *battle-line*; hence *battle, battlefield*.

ăcĭnăcēs -is, m. *a Persian sabre*.

ăcĭnus -i, m. and **ăcĭnum** -i, n. *a berry; the seed of a berry*.

ăcĭpenser -eris, also **ăcĭpensis** -is, m. *the sturgeon*.

ăclys -ўdis, f. *a small javelin*.

ăcŏnītum -i, n. *monk's hood, aconite*; in gen., *strong poison*.

acq- = adq-; q.v.

ăcrātŏphŏrum -i, n. *a vessel for unmixed wine*.

ăcrēdŭla -ae, f. *a bird*, perhaps *thrush, owl*, or *nightingale*.

ăcrĭcŭlus -a -um, *somewhat sharp in temper*.

ăcrĭmōnĭa -ae, f. *sharpness, keenness*.

ăcrĭtĕr, adv. from acer; q.v.

ăcrŏāmă -ătis, n. *an entertainment*, esp. *musical; an entertainer*, i.e. *reader, actor*, or *singer*.

ăcrŏāsis -is, f. *reading aloud, recitation*.

Ăcrŏcĕraunĭa -orum, n. pl. *part of the Ceraunian mountains*; hence *any dangerous place*.

¹acta -ae, f. *sea-shore, beach*; meton., *life at the seaside*.

²acta -orum -from partic. of ago; q.v.

Actaeon -ōnis, m. *a hunter turned into a stag by Diana, and killed by his hounds*.

actĭo -ōnis, f. *action, doing*; gratiarum, *giving of thanks*. Esp. *the action of a magistrate, a proposal*; in the theatre, *a plot*; at law, *an action* or *the bringing of it* or *right to bring it*; also *a legal formula* or *speech on an indictment*.

actĭto -are, *to be busy, in law-court* or *theatre*.

Actĭum -i, n. *a promontory in Acarnania*, near which Augustus conquered Antony and Cleopatra (31 B.C.). Adj. **Actĭăcus** and **Actĭus** -a -um.

actor -ōris, m. (1) *a driver*. (2) *a doer*; esp. *a dramatic actor, player; a public speaker; the plaintiff in an action; a manager of property*.

actŭărĭŏlum -i, n. *a small skiff*.

actŭārĭus -a -um, *swift*; actuaria (navis), *a fast-sailing vessel*.

actŭōsus -a -um, *active*; adv. **actŭōsē**.

actus -ūs, m. (1) *driving, movement*; esp. *of cattle*; hence *right of way for driving cattle*, etc. (2) *doing, action*, esp. *on the stage*; hence *the presentation of a piece on the stage*; also *a division of a piece, an act*.

actūtum, adv. *immediately, directly*.

ăcŭlĕātus -a -um, *provided with prickles* or *stings*; hence *pointed, stinging; hair-splitting, subtle*.

ăcŭlĕus -i, m. *sting, point*; fig., esp. in plur., *painful thoughts, cutting remarks*.

ăcūmen -ĭnis, n. *sharp point*; hence *the point of remarks*, etc.; *sharpness of intellect; cunning, trickery*.

ăcŭo -ŭĕre -ŭi -ūtum, *to sharpen, whet*;

to quicken, make expert; to inflame, encourage, incite.

Hence partic. **ăcūtus** -a -um, *sharpened, pointed, acute*; to the hearing, *shrill*; to touch, *piercing*; of events, etc., *sharp, painful*; of minds, *sharp, keen, intelligent*; of orators, *effective*. Adv. **acūtē**, *keenly, sharply*.

ăcus -ūs, f. *a needle, bodkin*; acu pingere, *to embroider*; acu rem tangere, *to hit the nail on the head*.

ăcūtŭlus -a -um *rather subtle*.

ăcūtus; see acuo.

ad, prep. with acc. (1) *of motion, towards*, to a person or place; ad Dianae (sc. aedem) *to Diana's temple*; ad me, *to my house*; often strengthened by usque. (2) *of rest, at* or *near*. (3) *of time*: either *to, until*, or *at, about*. (4) *of other relations*: *towards, for a purpose; concerning, bearing on; compared with, in addition to; in conformity with; approximating to, about; in consequence of* an event; *as far as, up to* a certain degree; ad summam, *on the whole*; ad verbum, *literally*.

ădactĭo -ōnis, f. *driving, compulsion*.

ădactus -ūs, m. *bringing to, application*.

ădaequē, *in like manner*.

ădaequo -are: transit., *to make equal*; hence *to compare*; intransit., *to match, come near to*.

ădămantēus -a -um, *hard as steel*.

ădămantĭnus -a -um, *made of steel*.

ădămas -antis, m. *the hardest steel, adamant*; poet., *anything firm, unyielding, durable*.

ădambŭlo -are, *to walk by* or *near*.

ădămo -are, *to fall in love with, find pleasure in*.

ădăpĕrĭo -ăpĕrire -ăpĕrui -ăpertum, *to open fully*.

ădauctus -ūs, m. *increase*.

ădaugĕo -ēre -auxi -auctum, *to increase, augment*.

ădaugesco, -ĕre, *to begin to increase*.

adbĭbo -bĭbĕre -bĭbi -bĭbĭtum, *to drink in*.

addenseo -ēre, and **addenso** -are, *to make thick* or *compact*.

addĭco -dicĕre -dixi -dictum, *to assent to*; in augury, *to promise well*; of a judge (especially the praetor), *to award*; of an auctioneer, *to knock down a lot*; of an owner, *to put up for sale*. Hence in gen., *to give up* or *over, doom, dedicate, surrender*; partic. **addictus**, *bound, pledged*.

addictĭo -ōnis, f. *a judge's award*.

addisco -discĕre -didĭci, *to learn in addition*.

addĭtāmentum -i, n. *an addition*.

addo addĕre addĭdi addĭtum. (1) *to give, bring, place*; of feelings, *to inspire, cause*. (2) *to add, join*; esp. in speech or writing; adde, *or* adde huc, *or* eo, *add to this, take also into consideration*.

addŏcĕo -ēre, *to teach in addition*.

addŭbĭto -are, *to begin to doubt*.

addūco -dūcĕre -duxi -ductum. (1) *to bring* or *lead to* a person, place, or condition; of persons, *to bring to a certain state of mind, to influence, induce.* (2) *to draw to oneself, pull in;* hence *to contract;* partic. **adductus** -a -um, *contracted, taut;* of persons, *strict.* Compar. adv. **adductius.**

ădĕdo -esse -ēdi -ēsum, *to nibble, gnaw; to consume, waste away.*

ădemptĭo -ōnis, f. *taking away.*

ădĕo, adv., *to that point, so far;* often strengthened by usque: of space, *so far;* of time, *so long;* of degree, *so much, so, to such an extent;* sometimes, *even, what is more;* enclitically, with pron. or conjunction, *just.*

ădĕo -ire -ii -itum, *to go or come to, approach, visit;* in ius, *to go to law;* of business, etc., *to undertake, undergo, incur;* adire hereditatem, *to enter on an inheritance.*

ădeps -ipis, c. *soft fat.*

ădeptĭo -ōnis, f. *attainment, obtaining.*

ădĕquĭto -are, *to ride to.*

ădesdum, or **ades dum,** *come hither.*

adfābĭlis -e, *easy to speak to, affable.*

adfābĭlĭtās -ātis, f. *affability.*

adfābrē, *in a workmanlike way.*

adfātim, *sufficiently, enough.*

adfātus -ūs, m. *address, speech.*

adfectātĭo -onis, f. *striving, eagerness.*

adfectātor -ōris, m. *a striver.*

adfectĭo -ōnis, f. *manner of being affected;* hence *relation* to a thing or person, or *change,* or *state, condition;* sometimes *favourable state of mind, good-will.*

adfecto -are, *to strive after, grasp at, aim at, aspire to;* polit. *to try to win over;* in literary style, *to affect;* partic. **adfectatus** -a -um, *studied.*

adfectus -ūs, m. *condition, disposition;* esp. of the mind, *a feeling;* often *friendly feeling, good-will.*

adfectus -a -um, partic. from adficio; q.v.

adfero adferre attŭli adlātum, *to carry to, bring to;* esp. of messages, and news; absol., *to bring news, report.* Transf., *to apply, bring to bear;* vim, *to offer violence; to cause, bring about; to bring forward by way of excuse or reason; to bring* by way of help, *contribute.*

adficĭo -ficĕre -fēci -fectum, *to influence, work upon;* with adverbs, *to affect;* with abl. of nouns, *to treat with, present with;* nominem sepultura, *to bury;* poena, *to punish,* beneficio adfici, *to be benefited;* absol., of the body, *to affect adversely, weaken.* Hence partic. **adfectus** -a -um, *affected, influenced;* with abl. *furnished with, treated with;* absol., of the body, *weakened, sick;* of undertakings, *worked upon,* and *so nearly finished.*

adfigo -figĕre -fixi -fixum, *to fasten to, affix;* litteram ad caput, *to brand;* adfigi animis, *to be imprinted.*

adfingo -fingĕre -finxi -fictum, *to form or invent in addition.*

adfinis -e *neighbouring;* hence *connected with, privy to;* also *related by marriage;* as subst., *a relative.*

adfinĭtās -ātis, f., *relationship by marriage;* meton., *relations by marriage;* in gen., *union.*

adfirmatĭo -ōnis, f. *positive assertion.*

adfirmo -are *to strengthen; to support a statement, to prove; to assert as true.* Adv. from partic., **adfirmātē,** *positively.*

adflatus -ūs, m. *blowing or breathing on, breath;* maris, *sea breeze.* Transf. *inspiration.*

adflĕo -flēre -flēvi -flētum, *to weep at.*

adflictātĭo -ōnis, f. *pain, torture.*

adflicto -are, *to agitate, knock about, harass, distress.*

adflictor -ōris, m., *a subverter.*

adfligo -flīgĕre -flixi -flictum, *to dash, knock down, knock about; to weaken, discourage, injure;* causam susceptam, *to drop.* Hence partic. **adflictus** -a -um, *damaged, shattered;* of spirits, *broken down, desponding;* of character, *vile, contemptible.*

adflo -are, *to blow on or breathe on.*

adflŭentĭa -ae, f. *overflow, abundance.*

adflŭo -flŭĕre -fluxi -fluxum. *to flow to, flow near;* of men, *to stream, to flock together.* Transf., *to flow freely, to be abundant,* with abl., *to abound in.* Hence partic. **adflŭens** -entis, *rich, abounding.* Compar. adv. **adflŭentius.**

adfor -ari, dep. *to accost, address;* esp. *to say farewell to the dead,* and *to pray to gods.*

adfulgĕo -fulgēre -fulsi, *to shine, glitter; to shine upon, favour,* with dat.

adfundo -fundĕre -fūdi -fusum, *to pour upon;* colonia amne adfusa, *washed by a river;* adfundere se, or adfundi, *to prostrate oneself.* Transf., *to throw in, add.*

adgĕmo -ĕre, *to groan at,* with dat.

adgĕro -gĕrĕre -gessi -gestum, *to carry to, bring up.*

adgestus -ūs, m. *carrying to, accumulation.*

adglŏmĕro -are, *to wind on a ball;* hence *to add.*

adglūtĭno -are, *to glue to, fasten to.*

adgrăvesco -ĕre, *to grow worse* (of sickness).

adgrăvo -are, *to make heavier;* hence, *to make worse.*

adgrĕdĭor -grĕdi -gressus, dep. *to go to, approach;* with words, *to address;* of enemies, *to attack;* of business, etc., *to begin, undertake, attempt.*

adgrĕgo -are, *to add to the flock; so to attach, associate.*

adgressĭo -ōnis, f. *the introduction to a speech.*

ădhaerĕo -haerēre -haesi -haesum, *to hang to, stick to, adhere;* of places, *to border on, be near;* fig., *to depend on, cling to.*

adhaeresco -haerescĕre -haesi -haesum, *to hang on to, adhere.* Transf., *to* *cling to, hang on, attach oneself;* in speaking, *to stick fast, stop.*

adhaesio -ōnis, f. and **adhaesus** -ūs, m. *adhering, clinging.*

ădhĭbĕo -ēre -ŭi -ĭtum, *to bring up to, apply, bring to bear;* of persons, *to invite, call in, employ* for a purpose; with adv., *to treat.*

ădhinnĭo -ire, *to neigh after, neigh at.*

ădhortātĭo -ōnis, f. *exhortation.*

ădhortātŏr -ōris, m. *one who exhorts.*

ădhortor -ari, dep. *to exhort, encourage* (esp. of soldiers).

ădhūc, of time, *hitherto, till now, till then; still, even now;* in gen., *besides, also;* with comparatives, *even, still.*

adiăcĕo -ēre, *to lie by the side of, be adjacent.* N. pl. of partic. as subst. **adiăcentĭa,** *the neighbourhood.*

adĭcĭo -icĕre -iēci -iectum, *to throw to;* hence *to cast, direct, apply;* also *to add;* at an auction, *to outbid.*

adiectĭo -ōnis, f. *addition, advance.*

adiectus -ūs, m. *addition.*

ădĭgo -ĭgĕre -ēgi -actum, *to drive, force, compel;* hominem ad iusiurandum, or iureiurando, *to put a man on his oath.*

ădĭmo -ĭmĕre -ēmi -emptum, *to take away.*
  Hence partic. **ădemptus** -a -um, poet., *dead.*

ădĭpatus -a -um, *fatty, greasy;* n. pl. as subst., *pastry.* Transf., o⁺ style, *bombastic.*

ădĭpiscor -ĭpisci -eptus, dep. *to come up to, overtake;* hence *to obtain.* Perf. partic. adeptus, used passively, = *obtained.*

ădĭtĭo -ōnis, f. *approach.*

ădĭtus -ūs, m. *approach, access;* hence also *right* or *possibility of entrance;* homo rari aditus, *difficult of access;* concr., *an entrance to a place, approach.* Transf., *opportunity of obtaining.*

adiūdĭco -are, *to award as a judge, assign, grant.*

adiūmentum -i, n. *help, assistance.*

adiunctĭo -ōnis, f. *joining, addition, union;* rhet. *a limitation,* or *repetition.*

adiunctor -ōris, m., *one who joins.*

adiungo -iungĕre -iunxi -iunctum, *to join to, connect;* adiunctus fundus, *neighbouring;* of immaterial things, *to associate, impart;* of persons, *to attach,* esp. as partner, friend, etc.
  Hence partic. **adiunctus** -a -um, *bound to, belonging to;* n. pl. as subst. *collateral circumstances.*

adiūro, -are, *to swear in addition; to swear to a thing, promise on oath.*

adiūto -are, *to be serviceable, help.*

adiūtor -ōris, m., *a helper, assistant, deputy.*

adiūtrix -īcis, f., of females and f. nouns, *an assistant, aid;* used of *reserve legions* under the empire.

adiŭvo -iŭvāre -iūvi -iūtum, *to help, assist, support.*

adlābor -lābi -lapsus, dep. *to glide to, flow to,* with dat or acc.

adlăbōro -are, *to labour at;* also *to add to by labour.*

adlacrĭmo -are, *to weep at.*

adlapsus -ūs, m., *a gliding approach.*

adlatro -are, *to bark at, rail at.*

adlaudābilis -e, *praiseworthy.*

adlecto -are, *to entice.*

adlēgātĭo -ōnis, f. *the sending of a person on a mission.*

adlēgo -are., *to send on private business, to commission;* adlegati, *deputies.* Transf., *to instigate, suborn; to adduce* or *allege in excuse.*

adlĕgo -lĕgĕre -lēgi -lectum, *to choose, elect.*

adlĕvāmentum -i, n., *a means of alleviation.*

adlĕvātĭo -ōnis, f., *a lifting up;* hence *alleviation.*

adlĕvo -are, *to lift up, erect;* hence *to lighten, alleviate;* pass., adlevari, *to be cheered.*

adlĭcĭo -lĭcĕre -lexi -lectum, *to allure, entice.*

adlīdo -līdĕre -līsi -līsum, *to strike against, dash against;* pass., adlidi, *to suffer damage.*

adlĭgo -are, *to tie to, bind to;* of wounds, *to bind up.* Transf., in gen., *to fetter, bind, confine;* esp. *to bind by friend-ship, obligations, promise,* etc.; pass., *to become an accomplice in, make oneself responsible for;* perf. partic. adligatus, *implicated, involved.*

adlĭno -lĭnĕre -lēvi -litum, *to smear on, bedaub.*

adlŏcūtĭo -ōnis, f. *an address;* esp. *a word of comfort.*

adlŏquĭum -i, n., *exhortation, encourage-ment, consolation.*

adlŏquor -lŏqui -lŏcūtus, dep. *to address;* esp. *to encourage, appeal to.*

adlūcĕo -lūcēre -luxi, *to shine at,* or *upon.*

adlūdo -lūdĕre -lūsi -lūsum, *to jest at, sport with;* of waves, *to play* or *dash upon.*

adlŭo -lŭĕre -lŭi, *to wash,* of the sea.

adlŭvĭēs -ēi, f., *a pool caused by flooding.*

adlŭvĭo -ōnis, f., *alluvial land.*

admātūro -are, *to hasten.*

admētĭor mētiri -mensus, dep. *to measure out to.*

Admētus -i, m. *husband of Alcestis.*

admĭnĭcŭlor -ari, dep. *to support, prop.*

admĭnĭcŭlum -i, n. *prop, support;* in gen., *aid, help.*

admĭnister -stri, m. *attendant, assistant.*

admĭnistra -ae, f. a (*female*) *helper.*

admĭnistrātĭo -ōnis, f. *the giving of help; direction, government.*

admĭnistrātŏr -ōris, m. *administrator, manager.*

admĭnistro -are, *to help, assist; to manage, direct, administer;* navem, *to steer.*

admīrābilis -e. *admirable; astonishing, strange.* Adv., **admīrābiliter.**

admīrābĭlĭtās -ātis, f. *admirableness; admiration.*

admīrātĭo -ōnis, f. *admiration;* plur. *outbursts of admiration; wonder, astonishment.*

admīror -ari, dep. *to admire; to be astonished, to wonder.* Hence gerundive **admīrandus** -a -um, *admirable.*

admiscĕo -miscēre -miscŭi -mixtum (-mistum), *to mix with, to join;* admisceri novis sermonibus *to become familiar with.*

admissārius -i, m. *stallion.*

admissĭo -onis, f. *audience,* esp. with kings, etc.

admitto -mittĕre -mīsi -missum, *to send to, admit;* esp. of horses, *to let go, put to a gallop.* Transf., *to allow; to admit a crime to one's record,* so *to commit;* hence n. of partic. as subst. **admissum** -i, *a crime.*

admixtĭo -ōnis, f. *an admixture.*

admŏdĕrātē, *appropriately.*

admŏdum, *up to the measure, up to the mark;* hence, *completely.* With adjectives and other parts of speech, *wholly, quite;* puer admodum, *a mere boy;* with numbers, *just about;* in affirmative answers, *certainly.*

admŏnĕo -ēre -ŭi -itum, *to admonish, remind, of a fact or duty.* N. of partic. as subst. **admŏnĭtum** -i, *an admonition.*

admŏnĭtĭo -ōnis, f. *a reminding;* esp. *a friendly admonition.*

admŏnĭtor -ōris, m. *one who reminds.*

admŏnĭtū, abl. sing. m., *by reminding, by warning.*

admordĕo -mordēre -morsum, *to bite at, gnaw;* fig. *to fleece.*

admōtĭo -ōnis, f. *moving to, application.*

admŏvĕo -mŏvēre -mōvi -mōtum, *to move to, bring up, apply;* manum operi, *to engage in a work;* manus nocentibus, *to lay hands on the guilty;* milit. *to bring up war-machines or soldiers.*

admūgĭo -ire, *to bellow after.*

admurmūrātĭo -ōnis, f. *murmuring.*

admurmŭro -are, *to murmur at.*

adnăto -are, *to swim to or beside.*

adnecto -nectĕre -nexŭi -nexum, *to bind to, connect with.*

adnexus -ūs, m. *binding, connexion.*

adnītor -nīti -nisus or -nixus, dep. *to press against, lean upon.* Transf., *to strive after.*

adno -are, *to swim to, or near, or beside.*

adnŏto -are, *to note, remark on.*

adnŭmĕro -are, *to count out, pay; to reckon in with,* with acc. and dat.

adnŭo -nŭēre -nŭi -nūtum, *to nod to; to indicate by nodding; to nod assent to;* in gen., *to agree;* also *to agree to give or do a thing.*

¹**ădŏlĕo** -ēre -ŭi, *to worship, offer sacrifice, burn a sacrifice; to sacrifice on* an altar; in gen., *to burn.*

²**ădŏlĕo** -ēre, *to smell.*

ădŏlescens = adulescens; q.v.

ădŏlescĕo -olescĕre -ŏlēvi (1) *to grow up, come to maturity.* (2) *to be heaped up, or perhaps to burn* (cf. adoleo). Hence partic. **ădultus** -a -um, *grown up, adult, mature.*

Ădōnis -is or -ĭdis, *a beautiful young man, beloved of Venus.*

ădŏpĕrĭo -ŏpĕrire -ŏpĕrŭi -ŏpertum, *to cover or close.*

ădŏpīnor -ari, dep. *to guess.*

ădoptātĭo -ōnis, f. *adopting.*

ădoptĭo -ōnis, f. *the adoption of a child.*

ădoptīvus -a -um, *adopted, connected with adoption;* of plants, *grafted.*

ădopto -are, *to choose for oneself;* esp. *to adopt, as child or grandchild;* of plants, *to graft.*

ădŏr -oris, n. *a species of grain, spelt.*

ădōrātĭo -ōnis, f. *praying to, adoration.*

ădōrĕus -a -um, *of spelt;* f. as subst. *a reward for valour* (originally a gift of corn).

ădŏrior -ōriri -ortus, dep. *to rise up at;* hence *to attack, set about, attempt, undertake.*

ădorno -are, *to prepare, furnish, provide; to adorn.*

ădōro -are, *to speak to;* esp. *to address a deity, in worship or entreaty;* sometimes *to ask a deity for a thing.*

adp-; see under app-.

adquĭesco -quĭescĕre -quĭēvi quĭētum, *to rest, repose, be undisturbed, find comfort.*

adquīro -quīrĕre -quīsīvi -quīsĭtum, *to acquire, get,* esp. *in addition to previous possessions.*

adrādo -rādĕre -rāsi -rāsum, *to scrape, shave.*

adrectus -a -um, partic. from adrigo; q.v.

adrēpo -rēpĕre -repsi -reptum, *to creep up, glide gently to.*

Adria = Hadria; q.v.

adrīdĕo -rīdēre -risi -risum, *to laugh to, to smile upon.* Transf., *to be favourable to; to please.*

adrĭgo rigĕre -rexi -rectum, *to erect, lift up;* hence *to excite, arouse.*

adrĭpĭo -rĭpĕre -rĭpŭi -reptum, *to seize, snatch, appropriate;* poet., terram velis, *to sail quickly to;* mentally, *to grasp, comprehend quickly;* legal, *to arrest, bring to court, accuse;* hence perhaps *to satirize.*

adrīsor -ōris, m. *a flatterer.*

adrōdo -rōdĕre -rōsi -rōsum, *to gnaw at.*

adrŏgans, partic. from adrogo; q.v.

adrŏgantia -ae, f. *assumption,* hence *pride, haughtiness.*

adrŏgo -are, polit., *to associate in office;* in gen., either *to take to oneself* (sibi), *to claim, assume,* or *to adjudge, grant to another* (dat.). Hence partic. **adrŏgans** -antis, *assuming, arrogant, haughty;* adv. **adrŏganter.**

adsc-; see under asc-.

adsectātĭo -ōnis, f. *respectful attendance.*

adsectātor -ōris, m. *a companion, follower.*

adsector -ari, dep. *to follow, attend respectfully.*

adsēcŭla (adsecla) -ae, m. *follower, servant, sycophant.*

adsensĭo -ōnis, *assent, agreement, applause;* philosoph. *belief in the reality of sensible appearances.*

adsensor -ōris, m. *one who assents or agrees.*

adsensus -ūs, m. *assent, agreement;* philosoph. *belief in the reality of sensible appearances;* poet., *echo.*

adsentātio -ōnis, f. *flattering assent or applause, flattery.*

adsentātiuncŭla -ae, f. *trivial flattery.*

adsentātor -oris, m. *a flatterer.*

adsentātōriē, *flatteringly.*

adsentio -sentire -sensi -sensum, and **adsentior** -sentiri, -sensus, dep. *to assent to, agree with.*

adsentor -ari, dep. *to assent constantly;* hence *to flatter.*

adsĕquor -sĕquı -sĕcūtus, dep. *to follow after; to reach by following, to come up to, attain;* mentally, *to grasp.*

¹**adsĕro** -sĕrĕre -sĕvi -sĭtum, *to plant at or near.*

²**adsĕro** -sĕrĕre -sĕrŭi -sertum, *to lay hold of a slave, and thereby either claim him or declare him free;* in gen. *to set free, protect, or to claim.*

adsertor -ōris, m. *one who asserts the freedom of another person or claims him as his own.*

adservio -ire, *to assist, help.*

adservo -are, *to preserve, watch.*

adsessio -ōnis, f. *a sitting by the side of one* (to console).

adsessor -ōris, m. *one who sits by, or assists.*

adsĕvērātio -ōnis, f. *earnestness, vehemence;* esp. *vehement assertion, asseveration.*

adsĕvēro -are, *to be earnest;* esp. *to assert confidently or strongly.* Adv. from partic. **adsĕvēranter,** *earnestly.*

adsĭdĕo -sĭdēre -sēdi -sessum, *to sit near, sit beside,* esp. *beside a person, to give comfort, advice,* etc.; usually with dat. Hence, *to devote oneself to; to approximate to;* milit., *to besiege, blockade.*

adsīdo -sĭdĕre -sēdi -sessum, *to sit down.*

adsĭdŭĭtās -atis, f. *continual presence, regular attention.* Hence *constancy; constant repetition;* epistularum, *regular correspondence.*

¹**adsĭdŭus** -a -um, *continuously in one place,* or *one occupation,* in gen. *constant, persistent.* Adv. **adsĭdŭē** and **adsĭdŭō,** *continuously, without remission.*

²**adsĭdŭus** -i, m. *a taxpaying citizen.*

adsignātio -ōnis, f. *assignment, allotment.*

adsigno -are. (1) *to assign, allot;* hence *to impute, ascribe.* (2) *to seal;* hence *to impress upon.*

adsĭlio -sĭlire -sĭlŭi, *to leap to,* or *on.*

adsĭmĭlis -e, *like, similar.*

adsĭmŭlo -are, *to make like; to compare.*

Hence partic. **adsĭmŭlatus** -a -um, *similar, pretended, simulated.*

adsisto adsistĕre adstĭti or astĭti, *to place oneself at, to stand by;* at law, *to defend.*

adsŏlĕo -ēre, *to be accustomed;* ut adsolet, *as is usual.*

adsŏno -are, *to answer with a sound.*

adsp-; see under asp-.

adsterno -ĕre, *to strew* or *spread upon.*

adstĭpŭlātor -ōris, m. *a supporter.*

adstĭpŭlor -ari, dep. *to agree with.*

adsto -stare -stĭti, *to stand up, stand by* esp. *to stand by to help, to assist.*

adstrĕpo -ĕre, *to make a noise at;* esp. *to applaud.*

adstringo -stringĕre -strinxi -strictum, *to tighten, draw together, contract, make fast;* in writing or speech, *to compress;* of persons, *to bind, oblige;* with reflex., se adstringere, *to commit oneself to, become guilty of.*

Hence partic. **adstrictus** -a -um, *tight, compressed, drawn together; close-fisted, avaricious;* of oratory, *concise;* adv. **adstrictē.**

adstrŭo -strŭĕre -struxi -structum, *to build to* or *near;* hence *to add to.*

adstŭpĕo -ēre, *to be astonished at,* with dat.

adsuēfăcio -făcĕre -fēci -factum, *to accustom a person to a thing.*

adsuesco -suescĕre -suēvi -suētum: intransit., *to grow accustomed:* adsuevi, *I am accustomed;* transit., *to accustom;* poet., *of things, to make familiar.*

Hence partic. **adsuētus** -a -um, *customary, usual; accustomed to.*

adsuētūdo -inis, f. *custom, use.*

adsuētus -a -um, partic. from adsuesco; q.v.

adsulto -are, *to leap violently upon; to attack, assault.*

adsultus -u, m. *leaping up, assault.*

adsum ădesse adfŭi, *to be present, to be at* or *near;* esp. *to be present and ready, to stand by;* hence, *to support, be favourable to;* sometimes *to be present for a special purpose,* esp. political or legal; of the mind, adesse animo *or* animis, *to attend;* of things, *to be near, at hand.*

adsūmo -sūmĕre -sumpsi -sumptum, *to take to oneself,* or *take in addition to* a person or thing; hence *to claim, appropriate, call in;* in logic, *to state the minor premises of a syllogism.*

adsumptio -ōnis, f. *choice, adoption;* in logic, *the minor premise of a syllogism.*

adsumptīvus -a -um, *deriving its defence from an extraneous cause.*

adsŭo -ĕre, *to sew on.*

adsurgo -surgĕre -surrexi -surrectum, *to rise up, stand up;* with dat., *to rise in the presence of* a person, *as a sign of respect:* of feelings, *to rise, be aroused;* of style, *to become elevated;* of material things, *to rise up.*

adt-; see under att-.

ădūlātio -ōnis, f. *fawning, cringing, flattery.*

ădūlātor -ōris, m. flatterer.

ădūlescens (ădŏlescens) -entis: as adj., *young, growing;* as subst., *a young man* or *young woman.*

ădūlescentia -ae, f. *youth.*

ădūlescentŭlus -i, m. *a young man.*

ădŭlo -are, *to fawn (upon)*.

ădŭlor -ari, dep. *to fawn*; with acc. or dat., *to flatter, cringe before*.

ădulter -eri, m., **ădultĕra** -ae, f. *an adulterer, adulteress*.

ădulter -era -erum, adj. *adulterous*.

ădultĕrīnus -a -um, *adulterous; not genuine, forged*.

ădultĕrĭum -i, n. *adultery*.

ădultĕro -are, *to commit adultery, to defile*. Transf. *to falsify, defile, corrupt*.

ădultus -a -um, partic. from adolesco; q.v.

ădumbrātim, *in outline*.

ădumbrātĭo -ōnis, f. *a sketch*.

ădumbro -are, *to shade in, to sketch*, esp. in words. Partic. **ădumbrātus** -a -um, *sketched*; hence *imperfect, shadowy, unreal*.

ăduncĭtās -ātis, f. *a bending, curvature*.

ăduncus -a -um, *bent in, crooked*.

ădurgĕo -ēre, *to press against*; poet., *to pursue closely*.

ădūro -ūrĕre -ussi -ustum, *to set fire to, kindle, singe*; of frost or wind, *to nip*. Hence partic. **ădustus** -a -um, *burnt*: hominum color, *sunburnt*.

ădusquĕ: prep. with acc., *as far as*; adv. *thoroughly, entirely*.

advectīcĭus -a -um, *brought from a distance, foreign*.

advecto -are, *to convey often*.

advectus -us, m. *conveying, carrying*.

advĕho -vĕhĕre -vexi -vectum, *to carry, bring, convey to a place*; pass., *to ride up, sail to*, etc.

advēlo -are, *to veil*.

advĕna -ae, c. *a stranger, foreigner*.

advĕnĭo -vĕnīre -vēni -ventum, *to come to, arrive*. Transf., of time, *to come*; of events, *to happen, come near, break out*; of property, *to come to an owner*.

adventīcĭus -a -um, *coming from without*; esp. *coming from abroad, foreign*.

advento -are, *to approach, come near*.

adventor -ōris, m. *a visitor, guest*.

adventus -ūs, m. *an arrival*.

adversārĭus -a -um. (1) *turned towards*; n. pl. as subst. *a day-book, journal, memorandum*. (2) *turned against, opposed, contrary*; as subst., m. and f. *an antagonist, rival*; n. pl., *the assertions of an opponent*.

adversor -ari, dep. *to oppose, resist*.

adversus -a -um, partic. from adverto; q.v.

adversus, adversum. Adv., *against, opposite*; adversum ire or venire, *go to meet*. Prep. with acc.: of place, *towards, opposite*; of action, etc., *against, in answer to*; of behaviour, *towards*; of comparison, *compared with*.

adverto (**advorto**) -vertĕre -verti -versum, *to turn towards*; of the senses, etc. *to direct towards an object*; esp. of the mind, animum (or mentem) advertere, *to direct one's attention to, to perceive*, and of offences, *to punish*; of the object of attention, *to attract*.

Hence partic. **adversus** -a -um, *turned towards, fronting, opposite*; solem adversum intueri, *to look straight at the sun*; adverso flumine, *against the stream*; venti adversi, *contrary winds*; hence, in gen., of persons and things, *opposed, unfavourable*; adversa valetudo, *ill health*; proelium, *unsuccessful*; n. as subst. *misfortune*.

advespĕrascit -avit, *evening approaches*.

advĭgĭlo -are, *to watch by, guard, be vigilant*.

advŏcātĭo -ōnis, f. *a calling to one's aid*; hence *legal assistance*; concr., *the bar*.

advŏco -are, *to summon, call*; esp. *to call to one's aid*: as legal t. t., *to call in as adviser, to consult an advocate*. M. of partic. as subst. **advŏcātus** -i, m. *one called in to help*, esp. in court as *witness* or *advocate*.

advŏlo -are, *to fly to*; hence *to hasten or rush to*.

advolvo -volvĕre -volvi -volūtum, *to roll to*; of suppliants, advolvi, or se advolvere, *to throw oneself down before a person*.

advors- advort- = advers-, advert-; q.v.

ădytum -i, n. *shrine*; poet., ex adyto cordis, *from the bottom of the heart*.

Aeăcus -i, m. *king of Aegina, grandfather of Achilles; after death a judge in the infernal regions*. Hence subst. **Aeăcĭdes** -ae, m. *a male descendant of Aeacus*.

aedēs (**aedis**) -is, f. *a building*; in sing., usually *a temple*; plur., *rooms*, or *a house*; of bees, *cells*.

aedĭcŭla -ae, f. *a small building*, esp. *a small temple* or *shrine*; in plur., *a little house*.

aedĭfĭcātĭo -ōnis. f.: abstr., *the act of building*; concr., *a building, structure*.

aedĭfĭcātor -ōris, m. *a builder, architect*.

aedĭfĭcĭum -i, n. *a building*.

aedĭfĭco -are, *to build, erect, establish; to create, frame*.

aedīlĭcĭus -a -um, *relating to the aediles*; m. as subst. *an ex-aedile*.

aedīlis -is, m. *an aedile, a public officer at Rome, in charge of streets, markets and public games*.

aedīlĭtās -ātis, f. *aedileship*.

aedĭtĭmus -i, and **aedĭtŭens** -entis, and **aedĭtŭus** -i, m. *keeper of a temple, sacristan*.

Aeēta and **Aeētēs** -ae, m., *king o Colchis, father of Medea*. Hence f. subst. **Aeētĭas** -ādis, and **Aeētīne** -es, = *Medea*.

Aegaeus -a -um, *Aegean*; n. as subst. **Aegaeum** -i, *the Aegean Sea*.

Aegātēs -um, f. pl. *three islands off the west coast of Sicily*.

aeger -gra -grum, *sick, ill*, physically or mentally; aeger consilii, *infirm of purpose*; aegris oculis, *with envious eyes*; politically *unsound, mutinous*. M. as subst. *an invalid*. Adv. **aegrĕ** *with pain, regret* or *difficulty*; hence *hardly, scarcely* (cf. vix).

Aegeus -ĕi, m., *king of Athens, father of Theseus.*

Aegīna -ae, f. *an island near Athens.*

aegis -ĭdis, f. *an aegis, or shield, esp. that of Jupiter or Minerva.* Transf., *a protection, bulwark.*

Aegisthus -i, m. *murderer of Agamemnon, afterwards husband of Clytemnestra.*

aegrē, adv. from aeger; q.v.

aegreo -ēre, *to be sick.*

aegresco -ēre, *to fall ill*; mentally, *to become troubled*; of bad things, *to become worse.*

aegrĭmōnĭa -ae, f., *grief, trouble of mind.*

aegrĭtūdo -ĭnis, f. *sickness,* esp. of the mind.

aegrōtātĭo -ōnis, f. *sickness,* of body or mind.

aegrōto -are *to be sick or ill,* in body or mind.

aegrōtus -a -um, *sick, ill,* in body or mind.

Aegyptus -i. (1) m., *a king of Egypt, brother of Danaus.* (2) f. *Egypt*; adj. **Aegyptĭus** and **Aegyptĭăcus** -a -um, *Egyptian.*

aelīnos -i, m. *a dirge.*

Aemĭlĭus -a -um, *name of an old patrician family at Rome.* Hence adj. **Aemĭlĭanus** -a -um, *relating to the gens Aemilia; a surname of Scipio Africanus minor.*

Aemōnĭa = Haemonia; q.v.

aemŭlātĭo -ōnis, f., *a striving after, emulation;* in bad sense, *jealousy, rivalry.*

aemŭlātor -ōris, m., *a rival, imitator.*

aemŭlor -ari, dep., *to rival, emulate;* with dat., *to envy.*

aemŭlus -a -um, *emulous, rivalling;* in bad sense, *jealous.* M. or f. as subst., *a rival,* esp. *in love.*

Aemus = Haemus; q.v.

Aenēās -ae, m., *son of Venus and Anchises, hero of Vergil's Aeneid.* Hence subst. **Aenēădēs** -ae, m., *a male descendant of Aeneas;* **Aenēis** -ĭdos, f. *Vergil's Aeneid.*

ăēnĕus and **ăhēnĕus** -a -um, *made of copper or bronze; hard as bronze, brazen.*

aenigma -ătis, n., *a riddle, mystery.*

ăēnĭpēs -pĕdis, *brazen-footed.*

ăēnus (**ăhēnus**) -a -um, *made of copper or bronze;* poet., *hard as bronze.* N. as subst., *a brazen vessel.*

Aeŏles -um, m. *the Aeolians, Greeks living in Greece and Asia Minor.* Hence adj. **Aeŏlĭcus** and **Aeŏlĭus** -a -um, *Aeolic.*

Aeŏlĭa -ae, f. *north part of the coast of Asia Minor.*

Aeŏlus -i, m. *ruler of the Aeolian islands and of the winds.*

aequābĭlis -e, *like, similar, equal.* Transf., *equal to itself, uniform, consistent; fair, impartial.* Hence adv. **aequābĭlĭter**, *equably, uniformly, fairly.*

aequābĭlĭtās -ātis, f., *uniformity, equability;* hence *evenness* in style, *impartiality* in law.

aequaevus -a -um, *of equal age.*

aequālis -e, *even;* of places, *level.* Transf., *equal;* esp. of time, *of the same age, contemporary, coexistent.* M. or f. as subst., *a comrade, person of the same age.* Adv. **aequālĭtĕr**, *evenly, equally.*

aequālĭtās -ātis, f., *evenness;* of places, *smoothness.* Transf., *equality,* esp. *equality of age.*

aequănĭmĭtās -ātis, f. *impartiality.*

aequātĭo -ōnis, f. *making equal;* bonorum, *communism.*

Aequi -orum, m. *a people of central Italy.*

aequĭlībrĭtās -ātis, f. *equal distribution of natural forces.*

aequĭnoctĭālis -e, *equinoctial.*

aequĭnoctĭum -i, n., *the equinox.*

aequĭpăro (**aequĭpĕro**) -are, *to compare; to equal.*

aequĭtās -ātis, f., *uniformity, evenness.* Transf., *equanimity;* also *impartiality, fairness, justice.*

aequo -are. (1) *to make level or equal.* (2) *to compare.* (3) *to equal, come up to.*

aequor -ōris, n., *a flat level surface;* esp. of a *plain,* or of *the sea;* rarely of *a river.*

aequŏrĕus -a -um, *belonging to the sea.*

aequus -a -um, adj. *equal.* (1) *equal in itself, even, level;* ex aequo loco loqui, *to speak in the senate;* milit., aequa frons, *a straight line.* (2) *equal to something else:* ex aequo, in aequo, *on even terms.* Transf., of places or times, *favourable, advantageous;* of battles, *even,* and so *indecisive;* of temper, *even, contented, easy;* aequo animo, *patiently, with resignation;* of behaviour, etc., *equal, impartial;* of persons, *fair;* aequum est, *it is just.* N. as subst. aequum -i, *level ground; fairness, equity.* Adv. **aequē**, *in like manner, equally; fairly, justly.*

āēr āĕris, m., *the lower air, the atmosphere.*

aerārĭus -a -um, *of or belonging to bronze or copper;* hence *belonging to (copper) money;* tribuni, *paymasters.* M. as subst. *a copper-smith;* in plur., aerarii, *the citizens of the lowest class in Rome.* N. as subst. *a treasury,* esp. *the public treasury at Rome.*

aerātus -a -um, *made of or fitted with copper or bronze;* hence *provided with money, rich.*

aerĕus -a -um, *made of or fitted with copper or bronze.*

aerĭfer -fĕra -fĕrum, *bearing brazen cymbals.*

aerĭpēs -pĕdis, *brazen-footed.*

āĕrĭus (**āĕrĕus**) -a -um, *belonging to the air, airy;* hence *high in the air, lofty.*

aerūgo -ĭnis, f., *the rust of copper, verdigris; rusty money.* Transf., *envy* or *avarice.*

aerumna -ae, f. *labour, toil, hardship.*

aerumnōsus -a -um, adj., *full of hardship.*

aes, aeris, n. *copper ore,* and *the alloy of copper, bronze.* Transf., *anything made of bronze; a vessel, statue,* *trumpet, kettle*; aera aere repulsa, cymbals; aes publicum, *public inscriptions.* Esp. *copper* or *bronze money*; aes grave, *the* as; aes signatum, *coined money*; also *money generally, pay*; aes alienum, *debt.*

Aeschўlus -i, m. *an Athenian tragic poet.*

Aescŭlāpĭus -i, m. *the god of medicine.* Hence subst. **Aescŭlāpĭum** -i, n. *a temple of Aesculapius.*

aescŭlētum -i, n., *an oak forest.*

aescŭlĕus -a -um, *relating to the* (*winter*) *oak.*

aescŭlus -i, f. *the winter or Italian oak.*

Aesōn -ŏnis, m., *a Thessalian prince, father of Jason.* Hence subst. **Aesōnĭdēs** -ae, m. *a male descendant of Aeson,* = *Jason*; adj. **Aesōnĭus** -a -um.

Aesōpus -i, m. *a Greek fabulist of Phrygia.*

aestās -ātis, f. *summer*; hence *summer weather, summer heat.*

aestĭfer -fĕra -fĕrum, *heatbringing.*

aestĭmābĭlis -e, *valuable.*

aestĭmātĭo -ōnis, f. *an appraising in terms of money*; litis, *assessment of damages.* Transf., in gen., *valuation, worth, value.*

aestĭmātor -ōris, m. *one who estimates, an appraiser.*

aestĭmo (**aestŭmo**) -are, *to appraise, rate, estimate the value of*; litem, *to assess the damages in a law-suit*; in a wider sense, *to value a thing or person*; hence, in gen., *to judge.*

aestīvus -a -um, *relating to summer.* N. pl. as subst. **aestīva** -orum, *a summer camp*, and hence, *a campaign; summer pastures for cattle.*

aestŭārĭum -i, n., *low ground covered by the sea at high water; a firth, creek.*

aestŭo -are, *to be agitated* or *hot*; of liquids, *to boil, seethe*; fig., of emotional excitement, *to burn*; of perplexity, *to waver.*

aestŭōsus -a -um, *hot, agitated*; adv. **aestŭōsē.**

aestus -ūs, m., *agitation, heat*; of liquids, esp. of the sea, *seething, raging*; also of the sea's *tide*, and *spray*; fig., of persons, *dizziness*; also *emotional excitement, heat, fury*, and *perplexity, anxiety.*

aetās -ātis, f., *age*: of human life, either *a lifetime* or *a time of life, age*; id aetatis, *of that age*; bona (or iniens) aetas, *flos aetatis, youth*; aetas ingravescens, or provecta, *old age.* Meton., *the persons of a particular age*: aetas puerilis, *boys.* In gen., *time, age, a period of time, epoch.*

aetātŭla -ae, f., *youth.*

aeternĭtas -ātis, f., *eternity, immortality.*

aeterno -are, *to make eternal, immortalize.*

aeternus -a -um, *eternal, everlasting*: aeternum, or in aeternum, *for ever.*

aether -ĕris, acc. -ĕra, m., *the upper air*; poet., *heaven*, or *the upper world.*

aethĕrĭus -a -um, *of the air* or *upper air*; aqua, *rain*; poet., *heavenly*, or *belonging to the upper world.*

Aethĭŏpĭa -ae, f., *Ethiopia*; adj. **Aethĭŏpĭcus** -a -um. and **Aethĭops** -ŏpis, *Ethiopian, Negro.*

aethra -ae, f., *the upper air, clear sky.*

Aetna -ae and **Aetnē** -ēs, f. *Etna, a volcano in Sicily*; adj. **Aetnaeus** -a -um.

Aetōlĭa -ae, f., *Aetolia, a country in the west of Greece*; adj. **Aetōlus, Aetōlĭcus, Aetōlĭus** -a -um.

aevĭtās -ātis, f. = aetas; q.v.

aevum -in, n., also **aevus** -i, m., *eternity.* Transf., *time, lifetime*, or *time of life*; flos aevi, *youth*; in gen., *a period of time.*

Āfĕr -fra -frum, adj. and subst., *African, from Africa*; esp. *from Carthage.* Hence subst. **Āfrĭca** -ae, f. *the continent of Africa*; esp. either *the country round Carthage* or *the Roman province of Africa.* Adj. **Āfrĭcānus** -a -um, *African, belonging to Africa*; esp. as a surname, conferred upon two of the Scipios. Also adj. **Āfrĭcus** -a -um; ventus Africus, *or simply* Africus, *the S.W. wind* (bringing rain and storms).

aff-; see under **adf-.**

Ăgămemnon -ŏnis, m. *leader of the Greek expedition to Troy.*

Ăgănippē -ēs, f. *a fountain in Boeotia, sacred to the Muses*; adj. **Ăgănippēus** -a -um, *sacred to the Muses.*

ăgāsō -ōnis, m. *a groom. lackey.*

ăgellus -i, m. *a little field.*

ăgēma -ātis, n. *a corps in the Macedonian army.*

Ăgēnor -ŏris, m. *father of Cadmus and Europa*; hence adj. **Ăgēnŏrĕus** -a -um, and subst. **Ăgēnŏrĭdēs** -ae, m. *a male descendant of Agenor.*

ăger, agri, m. *land, territory*; as cultivated, *a field; open country* (opp. towns); *land*, (opp. sea).

agg- (except agger and aggero); see **adg-.**

agger -ĕris, m. *heap, mound*; milit., *rampart*; poet., *any high place.*

aggĕro -are, *to form a mound, heap up, increase.*

ăgĭlis -e, *easily moved, light, nimble. active.*

ăgĭlĭtās -ātis, f. *quickness, agility.*

ăgĭtābĭlis -e, *easily moved, light.*

ăgĭtātĭo -ōnis, f., *movement, agitation, activity*; rerum magnarum, *management.*

ăgĭtātor -ōris, m. *driver*; esp. *charioteer.*

ăgĭto -are, *to put in motion, drive about* (cf. ago); of animals, *to drive* or *hunt*; of water, *to toss.* Transf. (1) *to vex, harry, trouble persons*, etc. (2) *to deal with, be engaged upon, argue, discuss, consider a subject; to maintain a state of affairs*; *to conduct a business; to keep a holiday; to spend time*; so, absol., *to live.*

Ăglāĭa -ae or **Ăglāĭē** -ēs, f. *one of the Graces.*

agmĕn -ĭnis, n. *a driving movement or a mass in (orderly)movement, a stream, band, train*; esp. milit., *an army on the march.*

agna -ae, f. *a ewe lamb.*

agnascor -nasci, -nātus, dep., of children, *to be born after their father's will.* M. of partic. as subst. **agnātus** -i, *a relation descended from a common ancestor in the male line; a child born into a family where a regular heir already exists.*

agnātio -ōnis, f. *relationship reckoned through males only.*

agnellus -i, m. *a little lamb.*

agnīnus -a -um, *of a lamb*; f. as subst., *lamb's flesh.*

agnĭtio -ōnis, f. *recognition*; in gen., *knowledge.*

agnōmen -ĭnis, n., *surname.*

agnosco -noscĕre -nōvi -nĭtum, *to know again, recognise; to know by inference or report, understand; to express knowledge, admit, acknowledge.*

agnus -i, m. *lamb.*

ăgo ăgĕre ēgi actum, *to set in motion, drive*; of animals, *to drive or hunt*; se agere, *to give up the ghost*; radices, *to strike root.* Transf., *to incite* to action; *to deal with, be engaged upon; to treat of* a subject; hoc agere, *to attend to the matter in hand*; pass., *to be concerned, be at stake*; actum est de, *it is settled about, so it is all over with*; bene agere cum homine, *to treat a person well*; grates, gratias, *to express thanks*; pacem, *to keep the peace*; of time, *to spend*; so absol., *to spend time, live*; on the stage, *to act, play*; primas partes, *to play the leading part*; legal and polit., *to take a matter up publicly*; agere (iure, or lege), *to go to law*; agere causam, *to plead a cause.* Pres. partic. **ăgens** -entis, as adj. *effective.*

ăgōn -ōnis, m. *a contest in the public games.*

ăgōnālĭa -īum and -orum, n. *a festival of Janus.*

agrārĭus -a -um, *relating to land*; m. pl. as subst., *the agrarian party*, aiming at a general distribution of public land.

agrestis -e, *belonging to the field or country; wild, rustic*; hence, *countrified, boorish, clownish.* M. as subst. **agrestis** -is, *a countryman.*

¹**agrĭcŏla** -ae, m. *farmer.*

¹**Agrĭcŏla** -ae, m. Gnaeus Julius, *governor of Britain, and father-in-law of Tacitus.*

agricult-; see under cult-.

Agrĭgentum -i, n.; also **Acrăgās** -antis, m.; *a Doric town in S.W. Sicily.*

agrĭpĕta -ae, m. *a land-grabber, squatter.*

Agrippa -ae, m. *a Roman family name.*

Agrippīna -ae, f. *the name of several Roman women,* esp. *Nero's mother.* Hence **Colonia Agrippinensis** (now Cologne).

ah or **a,** *ah! oh!*

Āhāla -ae, m., C. Servilius, *master of the horse under the dictator Cincinnatus,* 439 B.C.

ai, *ah!,* interjection of grief.

Āiax -ācis, m. *name of two Homeric heroes, sons of Telamon and of Oileus.*

āio, defective verb. *to say yes, to affirm, assert, state*; ain tu? *you don't say?* Hence pres. partic. **aiens** -entis, *affirmative.*

āla -ae, f. *a wing*; poet., of the *sails* or *oars* of a ship; of a man, *the armpit*; milit., *a wing, squadron.*

ălăbaster -stri, m., with pl. **ălăbastra,** *a perfume casket.*

ălăcer -cris -cre, and **ălacris** -e, *quick, lively, animated.*

ălacrĭtās -ātis, f. *quickness, eagerness, animation.*

ălăpa -ae, f. *a box on the ear,* given by a master to his slave when freeing him.

ālārĭus -a -um, and **ālāris** -e, *belonging to the wings* of an army; m. pl. as subst., *allied troops.*

ālātus -a -um, *winged.*

ālauda -ae, f. *a lark*; also *the name of a legion formed by Caesar in Gaul*; in pl. **Ālaudae** -arum, *the soldiers of this legion.*

Alba -ae, f., Alba Longa, *the oldest Latin town*; hence adj. **Albānus** -a -um.

albātus -a -um, *clothed in white.*

albĕo -ēre, *to be white.*

albesco -ĕre, *to become white.*

albĭco -are, *to be white.*

albĭdus -a -um, *whitish.*

Albĭon -ōnis, f. *old name of Great Britain.*

Albis -is, m. *the Elbe.*

albŭlus -a -um, *whitish*; f. as subst. **Albŭla** -ae (sc. aqua), *old name of the Tiber.*

album -i; *see* albus.

albus -a -um, *white, dead white*; hence *pale* or *bright*; sometimes *making bright*; fig., *fortunate.* N. as subst. **album** -i, *white colour; a white writing-tablet, a list.*

Alcaeus -i, m. *a Greek lyric poet* (about 600 B.C.).

alcēdo -inis and **alcўōn** -onis, f. *the kingfisher.* Hence n. pl. **alcēdōnĭa** -orum, *the kingfisher's time, quietness, calm.*

alces -is, f. *the elk.*

Alcestis -is, and **Alcestē** -ēs, f. *wife of Admetus, who saved her husband by dying for him.*

Alcēūs -ĕi and -ĕos, m. *grandfather of Hercules.* Hence subst. **Alcīdes** -ae, m. esp. of *Hercules.*

Alcĭbĭădēs -is, m. *an Athenian general, pupil of Socrates.*

Alcīnŏūs -i, m. *king of the Phaeacians, host of Odysseus.*

Alcmēna -ae, also **Alcmēnē** -ēs, f. *mother of Hercules.*

alcўōn = alcedo; q.v.

ălĕa -ae, f. *a game of dice, game of hazard*; hence *chance, risk, uncertainty.*

alĕātor -ōris, m. *dicer, gambler.*

aleātŏrĭus -um, *of a gambler.*

ālec = allec; q.v.

āles alĭtis, *winged; hence swift;* as subst., *a bird,* esp. *a large bird or bird of omen;* poet., *an omen, sign.*

ālesco -ĕre, *to grow up.*

Ālexander -dri, m. (1) = *Paris, son of Priam, king of Troy.* (2) *Alexander the Great* (356-323 B.C.), *king of Macedonia.* Hence **Alexandrīa** or **ēa** -ae, f. *a city founded by Alexander,* esp. *Alexandria in Egypt;* adj. **Ālexandrīnus** -a -um, *of Alexandria.*

alga -ae, f. *sea-weed.*

algĕo algēre alsi, *to be cold;* partic. **algens** -entis, *cold.*

algesco algescĕre alsi, *to catch cold.*

¹algĭdus -a -um, *cold.*

²Algĭdus -i, m. *a mountain in Latium;* adj. **Algĭdus** -a -um, *of Algidus.*

algor -ōris, m. *cold.*

algus -ūs, = algor; q.v.

ălĭās, see under alius.

ălĭbī. (1) *elsewhere, at another place;* alibi . . . alibi, *here . . . there.* (2) *otherwise, in other respects.*

ălĭca -ae, f. *spelt, or a drink prepared from spelt.*

ălĭcŭbi, *anywhere, somewhere.*

ălĭcundĕ, *from anywhere, from somewhere.*

ălĭēnātĭo -ōnis, f. *a transference, alienation;* mentis, *aberration of mind.*

ălĭēnĭgĕna -ae, m. *strange, foreign;* as subst., *a foreigner.*

ălĭēnĭgĕnus -a -um, *of different elements, heterogeneous.*

ălĭēno -are, *to make something another's, let go, transfer; to estrange* one person from another; *to put a thing out of one's mind, forget;* with mentem, etc., *to cause a person to lose his reason;* pass., alienari, *to go out of one's mind.*

ălĭēnus -a -um, *belonging to another;* aes, *another's money,* and so debt; in gen., *strange, foreign, unrelated;* esp. of persons, *not at home, unfamiliar,* or *estranged, unfriendly;* of things, *unfavourable.* M. as subst., **alienus,** *a stranger;* n. as subst. **alienum,** *another person's property.*

ālĭger -gĕra -gĕrum, *winged.*

ălĭmentārĭus -a -um, *relating to food.*

ălĭmentum -i, n. (1) *food.* (2) *maintenance.*

ălĭmōnĭum -i, n. *nourishment.*

ălĭo; see under alius.

ălĭŏquī and **ălĭŏquĭn.** (1) *otherwise, in other respects.* (2) *in general, in most respects.* (3) *else, in other conditions.*

ălĭorsum and **ălĭorsus.** (1) *in another direction, elsewhere.* (2) *in another manner.*

ālĭpēs -pĕdis, *having wings on the feet;* hence *swift;* m. pl. as subst., *horses.*

ălĭpta and **ălĭptēs** -ae, m. *the anointer in the wrestling-school* or *the baths.*

aliqua, aliquamdiu, aliquammultus; see under aliquis.

ălĭquando, *at any time, once; sometimes, occasionally; at last.*

ălĭquantŭlus -a -um, *little, small;* n. as adv. *a little.*

ălĭquantus -a -um, *of some size, moderate.* N. as subst. **ălĭquantum** -i, *a good deal;* acc. aliquantum, and (with compar.) abl. aliquanto, *somewhat, considerably.*

ălĭquātĕnus, *to a certain degree.*

ălĭqui, aliquae, or aliqua, aliquod, adj. *some.*

ălĭquis aliquid, pron. *someone, something; anyone, anything.* N. aliquid often with partitive genit., *a certain amount or number of;* as adv., *in any respect.* Transf., *somebody* or *something great* or *significant.* Hence adv. **ălĭquō,** *some whither, in some direction;* adv. **ălĭquā,** *by some road, in some way;* adv. **ălĭquamdiu,** *for some time;* adj. **ălĭquammultus,** *considerable in number or quantity.*

ălĭquot, indecl., *some, several.*

ălĭquŏtĭē(n)s, *several times.*

ălis, alid, old form of alius, aliud; q.v.

ălĭter; see under alius.

ălĭum or **allĭum** -i, *garlic.*

ălĭundĕ, *from some other direction:* alii aliunde, *from various directions.*

ălĭus -a -ud, adj. and pronoun, *another, other, different.* Distributively, *one, another:* alii . . . alii, *some . . . others;* alii alia censent, *some think one thing, some another.* In comparison, *other than,* followed by atque, quam, etc. Rarely, in plur., *all other, the rest;* in sing. = alter, *one of two.* Hence adv. **ălĭās.** (1) *at another time;* alias alias, *one person at one time, another at another.* (2) *otherwise.* Adv. **ălĭō,** *to another place;* alius alio *in various directions.* Transf., *to another person* or *object; for another end.* Adv. **ălĭtĕr.** (1) *otherwise, in another way;* alius aliter, *in different ways.* (2) *else, in other conditions.*

ălĭusmŏdi, *of another kind.*

all-, v. also under adl-.

allec or **ălec** -ēcis, n. *fish-pickle.*

Allecto or **Alecto,** *one of the three Furies.*

Allĭa (Alia) -ae, f. *river in Latium;* adj. **Alliensis** -e.

Allobrox -ŏgis, and pl. **Allobrŏges** -um, m. *the Allobroges, a Gallic people.*

almus -a -um, *nourishing, kind.*

alnus -i, f. *the alder;* meton, *a ship of alderwood.*

ălo ălēre ălŭi altum (or ălĭtum), *to nourish, support, rear, feed;* hence in gen., *to strengthen, increase, promote, advance.*

   Hence partic. **altus** -a -um, *grown, great.* As seen from below, *high,* hence, of the voice, *shrill;* of character, dignity, rank, *lofty, noble.* As seen from above, *deep;* hence of quiet, *deep;* of thoughts, *secret, deep-seated;* of time, *reaching far back, ancient.* N. as subst. **altum** -i, either *height* or *depth*. Adv. **alte**, *highly* or *deeply*.

ăŏlē -ēs, f., *the aloe; bitterness.*

Alpēs -ĭum, f. *the Alps;* adj. **Alpīnus** and **Alpĭcus** -a -um, *Alpine.*

Alphēus or **Alphēos** -i, m. *the chief river of the Peloponnese.*

alsĭus -a -um, *frosty, cold.*

altārĭa -ĭum, n. pl. *an erection upon an altar;* hence *high altars,* or *a high altar.*

alter -tĕra -tĕrum, *one of two, the one, the other;* as a numeral, *second;* unus et alter, *one or two;* in pl., of a *second set.* Hence of quality, *second, next best;* of similarity, *another, a second;* alter idem, *a second self;* of difference, *other, changed.*

altercātĭo -ōnis, f., *dispute, wrangling;* legal, *cross-examination.*

altercor -ari, dep. *to dispute, contend, quarrel;* legal, *to cross-examine, cross-question.*

alterno -are, *to do first one thing, then another:* transit, *to interchange;* intransit., *to alternate, waver.*

alternus -a -um, *one after the other, by turns, alternate, interchanging;* sermones, *dialogue;* of metre, *elegiac* (with hexameter and pentameter alternating).

altĕrŭter -utra -utrum, *one of two.*

altĭlis -e, *fattened, fed;* f. as subst. (sc. avis), *a fowl.*

altĭsŏnus -a -um, *sounding from on high; high-sounding, sublime.*

altĭtūdo -ĭnis, f. (1) *height;* hence *sublimity.* (2) *depth;* animi, *secrecy, reserve.*

altor -ōris, m, *nourisher, foster-father.*

altrix -īcis, f. *nurse, foster-mother.*

altus -a -um, **alte,** etc.; see under alo.

ălūcĭnor -ari, dep. *to wander in mind, dream, talk idly.*

ălumnus -a -um, adj. used as noun, *nursling, foster-child;* hence *pupil.*

ălūta -ae, f. *soft leather; a shoe, purse* or *patch.*

alvĕārĭum -i, n. *beehive.*

alvĕŏlus -i, m. *tray, trough, bucket; gaming-board.*

alvĕus -i, m. *a hollow, cavity, trough;* hence *boat;* also *the hold of a ship; bath-tub; bed of a stream; beehive; gaming-table.*

alvus -i, f. *belly, womb, stomach; hold of a ship, beehive.*

ămābĭlis -e, *amiable, lovely;* adv. **ămābĭlĭter.**

Ămalthēa -ae, f. either *a nymph, the nurse of Jupiter in Crete* or *the goat on the milk of which Jupiter was reared.*

ămandātĭo -ōnis, f. *a sending away.*

ămando -are, *to send away.*

ămans = partic. of amo; q.v.

ămănŭensis -is, m. *secretary, clerk.*

ămārăcĭnus -a -um, *made of marjoram;* n. as subst. *marjoram ointment.*

ămārăcus -i, c. and **ămārăcum** -i, n. *marjoram.*

ămārantus -i, m., *the amaranth.*

ămārĭtĭēs -ēi, f., *bitterness.*

ămārĭtūdo -ĭnis, f. *bitterness;* vocis, *harshness of voice.*

ămāror -ōris, m., *bitterness.*

ămārus -a -um, *bitter, pungent.* Hence, of things, *disagreeable, unpleasant;* of persons, *irritable;* of speech, *biting, acrimonious.* Adv. **ămārē**, *bitterly.*

ămātor -ōris, m. *a lover, friend, admirer;* esp. *the lover of a woman.*

ămātōrĭus -a -um, *loving, amorous;* n. as subst. *a love philtre.* Adv. **ămātōrĭē.**

ămātrix -īcis, f. *mistress, sweet-heart.*

Ămāzon -ōnis, f.; gen. in plur. **Ămāzŏnes** -um, myth., *nation of female warriors.* Hence subst. **Ămāzŏnis** -ĭdis, f. = Amazon; adj. **Ămāzŏnĭcus, Ămāzŏnĭus** -a -um.

ambactus -i, m. *vassal.*

ambāgēs, abl. -e, f. (of sing. only abl. found) *a roundabout way, winding.* Hence, in speech, etc., either *circumlocution* or *obscurity, ambiguity.*

ambĕdo -esse -ēdi -ēsum, *to eat round, consume.*

ambĭgo -ĕre, *to go about* or *round.* Transf., (1) *to doubt, hesitate;* ambigitur, impers., *it is in doubt;* (2) *to dispute, contend.*

ambĭgŭĭtās -ātis, f. *ambiguity.*

ambĭgŭus -a -um, *moving from side to side, doubtful, uncertain, insecure, unreliable;* of speech, *ambiguous, obscure;* n. as subst. *uncertainty, doubt, ambiguity.* Adv. **ambĭgŭē,** *ambiguously, indecisively.*

ambĭo -ire -ivi -or -ii -itum *to go round,* Hence (1) *to surround.* (2) *to go round from person to person, to approach, entreat, canvass* (for votes, help, etc.).

Ambĭŏrix -rĭgis, m. *chief of the Eburones in Gallia Belgica.*

ambĭtĭo -ōnis, f. *canvassing for office* (in a lawful manner); in gen., *desire for office, popularity* or *fame.*

ambĭtĭōsus -a -um, *going round;* esp. *active in seeking office, popularity* or *fame; ambitious, ostentatious.* Adv. **ambĭtĭōsē,** *ambitiously, ostentatiously.*

ambĭtus -ūs, m. *a going round, circuit, revolution.* Hence, of things, *border, edge* or *extent;* in speech, *circumlocution;* in relation to persons, *illegal canvassing for office, bribery, striving after popularity* or *effect.*

ambō -ae -ō, *both, two together.*

ambrŏsĭa -ae, f. *ambrosia, the food* or *unguent of the gods.*

ambrŏsĭus -a -um, *divine, immortal, ambrosial.*

ambūbāia -ae, f., *a Syrian flute-girl.*

ambŭlātĭo -ōnis, f. *a walk* or *place for walking.*

ambŭlātĭuncŭla -ae, f. *a little walk* or *place for walking, promenade.*

ambŭlo -are, *to walk, go for a walk, travel, march:* bene ambula, " *bon voyage*"; with acc., *to traverse.*

ambūro -ūrĕre -ussi -ustum, *to burn*

round, scorch; of cold, *to nip, numb*; in gen., *to injure.*

ămellus -i, m. *the purple Italian starwort.*

āmens -entis, *mad, insane, senseless.*

āmentĭa -ae, f. *madness, senselessness.*

āmento -are, *to furnish with a strap.*

āmentum -i, n. *a strap, thong.*

āmĕs -ĭtis, m. *a forked pole.*

ămĕthystĭnus -a -um, *amethyst-coloured*; n. pl. as subst., *dresses of amethyst colour.*

ămĕthystus -i, f. *an amethyst.*

amfractus = anfractus; q.v.

ămĭcĭo -ĭcīre -ĭcŭi or -ixi -ictum, *to clothe, wrap round, wrap up, cover, conceal.*

ămĭcĭtĭa -ae, f. *friendship*; in plur., concrete, = *friends.*

ămĭcĭtĭēs -ēi, f. = amicitia; q.v.

ămictus -ūs, m., *the putting on of a garment, esp. the toga.* Transf., *a garment, covering.*

ămīcŭla -ae, f. *a little mistress.*

ămĭcŭlum -i, n. *a mantle, cloak.*

ămīcŭlus -i, m. *a dear friend.*

ămīcus -a -um, *friendly, well-wishing, favourable.* M. as subst., ămīcus -i, *a friend*; in plur., *retinue*; f. as subst., ămīca -ae, *a friend or mistress.* Adv. ămīcē and ămīcĭter, *in a friendly manner.*

ămissĭo -ōnis, f. *loss.*

ămissus -ūs, m. = amissio; q.v.

ămĭta -ae, f. *a father's sister, aunt.*

ămitto -mittĕre -mīsi -missum, *to send away, let go, let slip*; hence, in gen., *to lose.*

Ammōn (Hammōn) (ōnis, m. *a Libyan deity,* worshipped at Rome under the name of Jupiter Ammon.

amnĭcŏla -ae, c. *dwelling by the river-side.*

amnĭcŭlus -i, m. *a little river.*

amnis -is, m. *a stream, river, torrent*; poet., *current, river water.*

ămo -are, *to love (passionately), be fond of*; amare se, *to be selfish or pleased with oneself*; amabo te, *or* amabo, *please, be so good*; with infin., *to like to do a thing*, also *to be wont, be accustomed.*

Hence partic. ămans -antis, *loving, fond*; as subst., *a lover.* Adv. ămanter, *lovingly.*

ămoenĭtās -ātis, f. *pleasantness, esp. of places.*

ămoenus -a -um, *pleasant, delightful,* esp. of places.

ămōlĭor -īri, dep. *to remove by an effort, set aside, get rid of*; amoliri se, *to take oneself off.*

ămōmum -i, n. *a shrub.*

ămor -ōris, m. *love, passion, fondness, desire*; meton., *an object of love, darling*; personified, *Love, Cupid.*

ămōtĭo -ōnis, f. *removal.*

ămŏvĕo -mŏvēre -mōvi -mōtum, *to move away, withdraw*; se amovere, *to depart*; in insulam, *to banish to an island*; of ideas or feelings, *to put aside.*

amphĭbŏlĭa -ae, f. *ambiguity, double meaning.*

Amphictўŏnes -um, m. plur., *the Amphictyons, religious representatives of the Greek states.*

Amphĭōn -ŏnis, m. *king of Thebes, husband of Niobe.*

amphĭthĕātrum -i, n. *amphitheatre.*

Amphitrītē -ēs, f. *wife of Neptune, goddess of the sea.*

amphŏra -ae, f. (1) *a two-handled jar.* (2) *a measure:* liquid, = about 7 gallons; of shipping, = about 1/40 of our ton.

amplector -plecti -plexus, dep., *to embrace, twine round, enclose, surround.* Transf., *to welcome, love, esteem*; in thought or speech, *to take in, consider, deal with*; *to include, comprise.*

amplexor -ari, dep. *to embrace; to welcome, love.*

amplexus -ūs, m. *encircling, embrace.*

amplĭfĭcātĭo -ōnis, f. *enlarging, heightening, amplification.*

amplĭfĭcātor -ōris, m. *one who enlarges.*

amplĭfĭco -are, *to enlarge, heighten, increase, magnify.*

amplĭo -are, *to enlarge, increase, magnify*; legal, *to adjourn a case.*

amplĭtūdo -ĭnis, f. *breadth; size; greatness, dignity, grandeur.*

amplus -a -um, *large, spacious, ample.* Transf., *great, important, honourable; eminent, distinguished*; amplissimi viri, *men of the highest position*; rhet., *grand, full.* Adv. amplē *and* amplĭter *fully, grandly.* Compar. adv. and n. subst., amplĭus, *more, further, besides*; with numerals, often = *more than.*

ampulla -ae, f. *flask, bottle.* Transf., *bombast.*

ampullor -ari, dep. *to speak bombastically.*

amputātĭo -ōnis, f. *cutting off, pruning.*

amputo -are, *to cut off,* esp. of trees, *to lop, prune*; of limbs, *to amputate*; hence, in gen., *to remove, diminish*; amputata loqui, *to speak disconnectedly.*

Āmūlĭus -i, m. *king of Alba Longa, brother of Numitor.*

ămurca -ae, f. *oil-lees.*

ămygdălum -i, n., *almond.*

Ămyntas -ae, m., *name of several Macedonian kings.*

ămystis -ĭdis, f., *the emptying of a goblet at a draught.*

ăn, conj.: in direct questions, *or*; in indirect questions, *or whether.*

ănăbathrum -i, n. *a raised seat.*

ănădēma -ătis, n. *a head ornament, fillet.*

ănagnostēs -ae, m. *reader.*

ănălecta -ae, m. *a dining-room slave.*

ănălŏgĭa -ae, f. *proportion, comparison, analogy.*

ănăpaestus -a -um: pes, *a metrical foot,* anapaest; n. as subst. *a poem in anapaestic verse.*

ănăphŏra -ae, f. in rhetoric, *the repetition of a word at the beginning of several sentences.*

ănas ănătis, f. *duck.*

ănătĭcŭla -ae, f. *little duck.*

ănătŏcismus -i, m. *compound interest.*

Ănaxăgŏras -ae, m. *a Greek philosopher of the fifth century B.C.*

anceps -cĭpĭtis, *two-headed; hence with two peaks or edges.* Transf., *coming on or from both sides; of two natures; ambiguous, uncertain, undecided;* hence *dangerous;* n. as subst., *danger.*

Anchīsēs -ae, m. *father of Aeneas.* Hence subst. **Anchīsĭădēs** -ae. m. *a male descendant of Anchises, Aeneas.*

ancīle -is, n., *a sacred shield, supposed to have fallen from heaven.*

ancilla -ae, f. *maid-servant, female slave.*

ancillāris -e *of a maid-servant.*

ancillor -ari, dep. *to serve (as a maid).*

ancillŭla -ae, f. *a little maid-servant.*

ancīsus -a -um, *cut round.*

Ancōn -ōnis, m., and **Ancōna** -ae, f. *a town on the Adriatic coast of Italy.*

ancŏra -ae, f. *an anchor;* ancoram tollere, *to weigh anchor.*

ancŏrāle -is, n. *a cable.*

ancŏrārĭus -a -um, *belonging to an anchor.*

Ancus (Marcius) -i, *fourth king of Rome.*

Ancyra -ae, f. *capital of Galatia, in Asia Minor.*

andrŏgȳnus -i, m. or **andrŏgȳne** -es, f. *hermaphrodite.*

Andrŏmăchē -ēs and **-cha** -ae, f. *wife of Hector.*

Andrŏmēdē -ēs, f. and **-da** -ae, f. *wife of Perseus.*

andrōn -ōnis, m., *corridor.*

Andrŏnīcus -i, m. L. Livius, *Roman dramatic and epic poet of the third century B.C.*

ānellus -i, m. *a little ring.*

ănēthum -i, n. *dill, anise.*

anfractus -ūs, m. *a turning, a bend;* solis, *revolution;* vallis, *winding.* Transf., *legal intricacies, circumlocution, digression.*

angellus -i, m. *a little corner.*

angĭportum -i, n. and **angĭportus** -ūs, m. *a narrow street.*

ango -ĕre, *to press tightly;* of the throat, *to strangle, throttle;* in gen., *to hurt, distress;* of the mind, *to torment, make anxious.*

angor -ōris, m. *compression of the throat, suffocation;* of the mind, *distress, anguish, trouble.*

anguĭcŏmus -a -um, *having snaky hair.*

anguĭfer -fĕra -fĕrum, *snake-bearing.*

anguĭgĕna -ae, m. *snake-born.*

anguilla -ae, f. *an eel.*

anguĭmănus -a -um, *snake-handed.*

anguĭnĕus -a -um, *of a snake, snaky.*

anguīnus -a -um, *snaky.*

anguĭpēs -pĕdis, *snake-footed.*

anguis -is, c. *a snake;* in astronomy, *the constellation Draco, or Hydra, or the Serpent.*

Anguītĕnens -entis, m., *the Snake-holder,* i.e. *the constellation Ophiuchus.*

angŭlātus -a -um, *angular, cornered.*

angŭlus -i, m. *a corner, angle;* esp.

either *a quiet corner, retired spot,* or, fig., *an awkward corner, strait.*

angustĭae -arum, f. pl. *narrowness;* hence, of space, *a strait, narrow place;* spiritūs, *shortness of breath;* of time, *shortness;* of supplies, *shortness, poverty;* of circumstances, *difficulty, distress;* of disposition, *narrow-mindedness;* of reasoning, *subtlety.*

angustus -a -um, *narrow, confined;* habenae, *tightly-drawn reins;* spiritus angustior, *constricted breath;* of time, *short;* of supplies, *short, scarce;* of circumstances, *precarious, critical;* of mind or speech, *narrow, petty, limited;* of style, *brief, simple.* N. as subst. **angustum** -i, *a narrow space.* Adv. **angustē,** *narrowly, sparingly, in a narrow, confined manner;* of speech, *briefly.*

ănhēlĭtus -ūs, m. *puffing, panting.* Transf., in gen., *breath; exhalaticn, vapour.*

ănhēlo -are, *to puff, pant;* transit., *to pant out words;* also *to pant for a thing, desire eagerly.*

ănhēlus -a -um, *puffing, panting;* febris, *causing to pant.*

ănĭcŭla -ae, f. *a little old woman.*

ănīlis -e *belonging to or like an old woman.* Adv. **ănīlĭter.**

ănīlĭtās -ātis, f. *old age (of women).*

ănĭma -ae, f. *breath, wind, air.* Transf., *the breath of life, vital principle, soul;* animam edere, *to give up the ghost;* poet., *life-blood;* meton., *a living being;* sometimes = *animus, rational soul.*

ănĭmadversĭo -ōnis, f. *perception, observation, notice;* esp. *unfavourable notice; censure, blame, punishment.*

ănĭmadversor -ōris, m. *an observer.*

ănĭmadverto (ănĭmadvorto) -vertĕre -verti -versum *to turn or give the mind to.* Hence *to take notice of, attend to; to perceive, observe.* Esp. *to take notice of a fault, blame, censure, punish.*

ănĭmăl -ālis, n. *a living being, animal.*

ănĭmālis -e. (1) *consisting of air, airy.* (2) *living.*

ănĭmans -antis, *living;* as subst., *a living being, animal.*

ănĭmātĭo -ōnis, f. *animating;* hence, *a living being.*

ănĭmo -are. (1) (anima), *to animate, give life to.* (2) (animus), *to endow with a particular disposition.* Hence partic. **ănĭmātus** -a -um. (1) *having life, alive.* (2) *having a disposition, inclined, disposed;* esp. *having courage, spirited.*

ănĭmōsus -a -um. (1) (anima), *full of breath, airy.* (2) (animus), *full of spirit or courage.* Adv. **ănĭmōsē,** *courageously.*

ănĭmŭla -ae, f. *a little soul, little life.*

ănĭmus -i, m. *the spiritual or rational principle of life in man.* More specifically: (1) *the seat of feeling, the heart;* animi causa, *for pleasure;* loc. (or genit.) animi, *at heart.* (2)

character, disposition; as a trait of character (esp. in plur.) *courage, spirit, vivacity*; also *pride, arrogance.* (3) *the seat of the will, intention*: habeo in animo, *I am resolved.* (4) *the seat of thought, intellect, mind, memory, consciousness.*

Ănĭo -ēnis, and poet. **Ănĭēnus** -i, m. *the Anio, a tributary of the Tiber.*

Anna -ae, f., *sister of Dido*; Anna Perenna, *an Italian goddess.*

annālis -e *lasting a year, or relating to a year.* M. as subst., usually plur. **annālēs** -ĭum, *yearly records, annals.*

anniversārĭus -a -um, *recurring every year.*

annōna -ae, f. *yearly produce, crop*, esp. of grain; *the price of provisions* (esp. corn), *the cost of living.*

annōsus -a -um, *full of years, long-lived.*

annŏtĭnus -a -um, *a year old, belonging to last year.*

annus -i, m. *a circuit of the sun, year*; exeunte anno, *at the end of the year*; annos LXX natus, *seventy years old*; habere annos viginti, *to be twenty*; esp. *year of office, or of eligibility for office*; poet., *time of year, season.*

annŭus -a -um, *lasting for a year*; *returning every year, annual.* N. plur. as subst. *a salary, pension.*

anquīro -quīrĕre -quīsīvi -quīsītum, *to seek carefully, inquire after, investigate*; legal, *to set an inquiry on foot.*

ansa -ae, f. *a handle*; hence, *occasion, opportunity.*

ansātus -a -um, *with a handle*; homo, *a man with arms akimbo.*

anser -ĕris, m. *goose.*

Antaeus -i, m. *a giant killed by Hercules.*

ante. Adv., *before*, of place or time. Prep., *before*, of place or time; ante urbem conditam, *before the founding of the city*; of preference, *sooner than, above.*

antĕā, *before, formerly.*

antĕambŭlo -ōnis, m. *a footman to clear the way ahead.*

antĕcăpĭo -căpĕre -cēpi -ceptum, *to seize beforehand*; hence *to anticipate, not to wait for*; philosoph., antecepta informatio, *an innate idea.*

antĕcēdo -cēdĕre -cessi -cessum, *to go before, precede*, in space or time; *to excel* (with dat. or acc.). Hence partic. **antĕcēdens** -entis, *preceding, antecedent.*

antĕcello -ĕre, *to be outstanding, excel* (with dat. or acc.).

antĕcessĭo -ōnis, f. *a preceding or going before*; philosoph., *the antecedent cause.*

antĕcursor -ōris, m. *a forerunner*; in pl., *pioneers.*

antĕĕo -īre -ii *to go before*, in space or time; hence *to excel* (with dat. or acc.).

antĕfĕro -ferre -tŭli -lātum, *to carry before.* Transf., *to prefer*; *to anticipate, consider before.*

antĕfixus -a -um, *astened in front*; n. as subst. *ornaments fixed on roofs.*

antĕgrĕdĭor -grĕdi -gressus, dep. *to*

go before; philosoph., *of antecedent causes.*

antĕhăbĕo -ēre, *to prefer.*

antĕhāc, *before this time, formerly.*

antĕlūcānus -a -um, *happening before daybreak.*

antĕmĕrīdĭānus -a -um, *before noon.*

antemitto -mittĕre -mīsi -missum, *to send before.*

antemna or **antenna** -ae, f. *a sail-yard.*

anteoccŭpātĭo -ōnis, f. *an exception.*

antĕpēs -pĕdis, m. *the forefoot.*

antĕpīlāni -orum, m. *front line soldiers* (i.e. *the* hastati *and* principes).

antĕpōno -pōnĕre -pŏsŭi -pŏsĭtum. *to place before, to prefer.*

antĕquam, conjunction, *before.*

antēs -ĭum, m. pl. *rows or ranks.*

antesignanus -i, m. usually plur., *soldiers chosen for a place in front of the standards*; hence, sing., *a leader.*

antesto (antisto) -stare -stĕti, *to stand before*; *to excel, surpass.*

antestor -ari, dep. legal, *to call as a witness.*

antĕvĕnĭo -vĕnire -vēni -ventum. *to come before, get the start of.* Transf., *to anticipate, prevent*; *to excel.*

antĕverto (-vorto) -vertĕre -verti -versum, *to come or go before, precede.* Transf., *to anticipate, prevent*; *to prefer.*

anticĭpātĭo -ōnis, f. *a preconception, innate idea.*

anticĭpo -are *to receive before, anticipate*; viam, *to travel over before.*

anticus -a -um, *forward, in front.*

antidea, antideo, antidhac; see antea, anteeo, antehac, of which they are old forms.

Antĭgŏnē -ēs, f. and **Antĭgŏna** -ae, f. *daughter of Oedipus, put to death for burying her brother.*

Antĭgŏnus -i, m., *name of several of the successors of Alexander the Great.*

Antĭŏchīa or **Antĭŏchēa** -ae, f. *Antioch, name of several Asiatic towns.*

Antĭpăter -tri, m. *name of several kings of Macedonia.*

antĭquārĭus -a -um *belonging to antiquity*; m. or f. as subst. *an antiquary.*

antĭquĭtās -ātis, f. *antiquity, ancient times*; *the history of ancient times*; in plur., *the ancients.*

antĭquĭtus v. antiquus.

antīquo -are, *to leave in its former state*; legem, *to reject a bill.*

antīquus -a -um, *coming before*; *previous, earlier*; absol., *old, ancient, primitive.* In compar. and superl., *preferred, more important.* M. pl. as subst. **antīqui** -orum, *the people of old time*, esp. *ancient authors.* Hence adv. **antīquē**, *in the ancient manner*; also **antīquĭtus**, *from of old or long ago.*

antistĕs -stĭtis, c. *a presiding priest* or *priestess.*

antistĭta -ae, f., *a presiding priestess.*

antisto, v. antesto.

antīthĕton -i, n. *antithesis, opposition.*

Antĭum -i, n. *an old town of Latium on the sea-coast.*

antlĭa -ae, f., *a pump.*

Antōnīnus -i, m. *name of several Roman emperors.*

Antōnĭus -a -um, *the name of a Roman gens.*

antrum -i, n. *a cave, hollow.*

Ănūbis -bis or -bĭdis, m. *an Egyptian god.*

ānŭlārĭus -a -um, *of a ring*: m. as subst. *a ring-maker.*

ānŭlus -i, m. *a ring*; anulus equestris, *the badge of knighthood at Rome.*

¹ānus -i, m. *the fundament.*

²ānus -ūs, f. *an old woman*; also used like adj., *old.*

anxĭĕtās -ātis, f., *anxiety, grief, anguish.*

anxĭfer -fĕra -fĕrum, *causing anxiety.*

anxĭtūdo -ĭnis, f. *anxiousness.*

anxĭus -a -um, *anxious, uneasy.* Transf., *causing anxiety.* Adv. **anxĭē.**

Anxŭr -ŭris, n. *an old town of the Volsci.*

Āŏnes -um, *the Boeotians*; **Āŏnĭa** -ae, f. *part of Boeotia, resort of the Muses*; hence **Āŏnĭdĕs** -um, f. *the Muses*; adj. **Āŏnĭus** -a -um.

Āornos -i, m., *the lake of Avernus.*

ăpăgĕ, interj. *away! be off!*

Āpellēs -is, m., *a Greek painter, friend of Alexander the Great.* Adj. **Āpellēus** -a -um.

ăper apri, m. *a wild boar.*

ăpĕrĭo ăpĕrīre ăpĕrŭi ăpertum. (1) *to uncover, lay bare*; hence in gen. *to reveal.* (2) *to open what was shut, open up*; ludum, *to open a school*; annum, *to begin the year.* Hence partic. **ăpertus** -a -um. (1) *uncovered, clear, unconcealed, manifest*; of speech, *clear, intelligible, frank*; of character, *frank, straight-forward, open.* (2) *unclosed, accessible, exposed.* N. as subst., *an open space.* Adv. **ăpertē**, *openly, frankly.*

ăpex -ĭcis, m. *the top*; esp. *the top of the conical cap of the Roman flamines, or the cap itself*; hence any *crown, tiara, helmet*; fig., *highest honour, crown*; gram., *the long mark over a vowel.*

aphractus -i, f. *a long undecked boat.*

ăpĭcātus -a -um, *wearing the priest's cap.*

ăpīnae -arum, f. pl. *trifles.*

ăpis or **ăpes** -is, f. *a bee.*

Āpis -is, m., *Apis, the ox-god of the Egyptians.*

ăpiscor apisci aptus, dep., *to attain, come to, come by.*

ăpĭum -i, n. *parsley or celery.*

aplustrĕ -is, n. generally plur. aplustria -ium, and aplustra -orum, *the carved stern of a ship.*

ăpŏdȳtērĭum -i, n. *the undressing-room in a bath.*

Āpollo -ĭnis, m. *Apollo, god of the sun, born at Delos*; ad Apollinis (sc. aedem), *to the temple of Apollo.* Adj. **Āpollĭnāris** -e, and **Āpollĭnĕus** -a -um.

ăpŏlŏgus -i, m. *a narrative, fable.*

ăpŏphŏrēta -orum, n. *presents given to guests.*

ăpōthēca -ae, f. *store-room.*

appărātē, adv. from apparo; q.v.

appărātĭo -ōnis, f. *preparation.*

appărātus -ūs, m.: abstr., *preparation, preparing*; concr., *provision, equipment, apparatus,* esp. on a pretentious scale; hence *splendour, magnificence, pomp, parade.*

appăreo -ēre -ŭi -ĭtum, *to become visible, appear, be manifest*; apparet, *it is clear*; sometimes *to appear as a servant, to serve* (with dat.).

appărĭo -ĕre, *to get, obtain.*

appărĭtĭo -ōnis, f. *waiting upon, serving*; meton., plur. *servants.*

appărĭtor -ōris, m. *a servant*; esp. *a public servant,* e.g. lictor.

appăro -are, *to prepare, get ready, provide.* Hence partic. **appărātus** -a -um, *prepared, well supplied or sumptuous.* Adv. **appărātē**, *sumptuously.*

appellātĭo -ōnis, f. *addressing, speech*; legal, *an appeal*; *a naming, name, title*; *pronunciation.*

appellātor -ōris, m. *an appellant.*

appellĭto -are, *to be accustomed to name.*

¹appello -are. (1) *to address, accost, speak to*; esp. *of asking favours, to approach, entreat, sue*; legal, *to appeal to.* (2) *to name, entitle*; hence, *to mention by name, make known.* (3) *to pronounce.*

²appello -pellĕre -pŭli -pulsum, *to drive to, bring to, apply*; nautical, *to bring to land*; huc appelle, *put in here.*

appendix -ĭcis, f. *appendage, addition.*

appendo -pendĕre -pendi -pensum, *to weigh to, deal out by weight.*

Appennīnus -i, m. *the chain of the Appennines.*

appĕtentĭa -ae, f. and **appĕtītĭo** -ōnis, f. *desire, longing.*

appĕtītus -ūs, m. *longing, appetite*; plur., *the passions.*

appĕto -ĕre -ivi or -ii -ītum, *to make for, grasp at, seek*; of places, *to make for or go to*; in hostile sense, *to attack*; intransit., of time, *to draw near.* Hence partic. **appĕtens** -entis, *eager, desirous, avaricious.* Adv. **appĕtenter**, *greedily.*

appingo -pingĕre -pinxi -pictum, *to paint to,* or *upon*; *to write in addition.*

Appĭus -i, m., **Appĭa** -ae, f. *a Roman praenomen common in the gens Claudia*; as adj. **Appĭus** -a -um, *Appian*: via, *the Appian Way, a road from Rome to Capua, afterwards extended to Brundisium*; also adj. **Appĭanus** -a -um, *belonging to an Appius, Appian.*

applaudo -plaudĕre -plausi -plausum. *to strike upon, clap.*

applĭcātĭo -ōnis, f. *attachment, application.*

applĭco -are -avi -atum, and -ŭi -ĭtum, *to apply to, place to* or *near*; corpora corporibus, *to close up the ranks*; naut., *to lay a ship to* or *beside*;

absol., *to land.* Transf. in gen., *to attach, connect;* with reflex. *to attach oneself, devote oneself.* Perf. partic. pass. **applĭcātus** -a -um, *situated near, built near.*

applōro -are, *to lament, deplore.*

appōno -pōnĕre -pŏsŭi -pŏsĭtum, *to place near, put to;* esp. *to serve, put on table; to appoint a person, to add a thing;* appone lucro, *reckon as gain.* Hence partic. **appŏsĭtus** -a -um, *placed near, lying near; approaching, near to; fit appropriate, apposite;* adv. **appŏsĭtē,** *appropriately.*

apporrectus -a -um, *extended near.*

apporto -are, *to carry, bring to.*

apposco -ĕre, *to ask in addition.*

apprĕcor -ari, dep. *to worship, pray to.*

apprĕhendo -prehendĕre -prēhendi -prehensum, and poet. **apprendo,** *to seize, lay hold of.*

apprĭmē, *above all, exceedingly.*

apprĭmo -prīmĕre -pressi -pressum, *to press to.*

approbātĭo -ōnis, f. *approval, assent;* in philosophy, *proof.*

approbātŏr -ōris, m. *one who approves or assents.*

approbo -are, *to approve of, assent to; to prove, establish; to make acceptable to another.*

apprōmitto -mittĕre -mīsi -missum, *to promise in addition.*

apprŏpĕro -are, *to hasten, hasten on.*

apprŏpinquātĭo -ōnis, f. *approach.*

apprŏpinquo -are, *to approach, draw near.*

appugno -are, *to assault, fight against.*

Appulia v. Apulia.

appulsus -ūs, m. *a driving towards;* hence *approach, influence;* naut. *landing.*

aprĭcātĭo -ōnis, f. *sun-bathing.*

aprĭcor -ari, dep. *to sun oneself.*

aprĭcus -a -um, adj. *open to the sun, sunny; loving the sun.*

Aprīlis -e *of April;* m. as subst. *the month of April.*

apto -are, *to fit, adapt, adjust; to make ready or fit.*

aptus -a -um. (1) as partic. *fitted, fastened, connected.* Transf., *depending on;* also *prepared, fitted out; fitted up with, equipped with,* with abl. (2) as adj. *suitable, appropriate, fitting.* Adv. **aptē.**

ăpŭd, prep. with acc. *at, near, by, with;* apud me, *at my house.* Of other relations: apud se, *in one's senses;* apud me valet, *it weighs with me;* apud patres *in our fathers' time;* apud Ciceronem, *in the works of Cicero.*

Āpŭlĭa or **Appŭlĭa** -ae, f. *Apulia, a region in S. Italy.* Adj. **Āpŭlĭcus** and **Āpŭlus** -a -um.

ăqua -ae, f. *water;* aqua et ignis, *the necessaries of life;* aqua et igni interdicere homini, *to banish a person;* aquam terramque poscere, *to demand submission.* Esp. *the water of the sea, a lake, a river,* or *rain;* in

plur. (medicinal) *springs;* often *water in the water-clock.*

aquaeductus -ūs, m. *an aqueduct; the right of conveying water.*

ăquārĭus -a -um, *belonging to water;* m. as subst. *a water-carrier* or *an inspector of conduits.*

ăquātĭcus -a -um, *living in water,* or *full of water, watery.*

ăquātĭlis -e, *living in water.*

ăquātĭo -ōnis, f. *a fetching of water;* meton., *a watering-place.*

ăquātŏr -ōris, m. *a water-carrier.*

ăquĭla -ae, f. *an eagle;* milit., *an eagle as the standard of a Roman legion;* architect, *gable* or *pediment.*

ăquĭlĭfer -fĕri m. *an eagle-* or *standard-bearer.*

ăquĭlo -ōnis, m. *the north wind; the north.*

ăquĭlōnĭus -a -um, *northern.*

ăquĭlus -a -um, *dark-coloured, blackish.*

Ăquītānĭa -ae, f. *Aquitania, the south-west part of Gaul.* Adj. **Ăquītānus** -a -um.

ăquor -ari, dep. *to fetch water.*

ăquōsus -a -um, *full of water, watery.*

ăquŭla -ae, f. *a little water, small stream.*

āra -ae, f. *altar;* hence *refuge, protection;* arae, plur., *name of certain rocks at sea.*

Ărăbĭă -ae, f. *Arabia.* Adj. **Ărăbĭus** and **Ărăbĭcus** -a -um, *Arabian;* adj. and subst. **Ărabs** -ăbis and **Ărăbus** -a -um *Arabian, an Arabian.*

Ărachnē -ēs, f. *a Lydian maiden turned into a spider by Minerva.*

ărānĕa -ae, f. *a spider;* menton., *the spider's web.*

ărānĕŏla -ae, f. and **ărānĕŏlus** -i, m. *a little spider.*

ărānĕōsus -a -um, *full of cobwebs.*

¹**ărānĕus** -i, m. *a spider.*

²**ărānĕus** -a -um, *of a spider;* n. as subst. *a cobweb.*

ărātĭo -ōnis, f. *ploughing, agriculture;* meton., *a ploughed field.*

ărātŏr -ōris, m. *ploughman, husband-man.*

ărātrum -i, n. *plough.*

arbĭter -tri, m. *a witness, spectator, legal, an umpire, arbitrator;* hence *any judge, ruler, master.*

arbĭtra -ae, f. *a female witness.*

arbĭtrārĭus -a -um, *arbitrary, uncertain.*

arbĭtrātus -ūs, m. *will, choice, decision.*

arbĭtrĭum -i, n. (1) *the presence of witnesses.* (2) *the decision of an umpire;* hence *any decision, judgment, authority;* arbitrio suo, *under his own control.*

arbĭtro -are, and **arbĭtror** -ari, dep. (1) *to witness, to bear witness.* (2) *to arbitrate, judge, decide.*

arbŏr (arbōs) -ŏris, f. *a tree;* also any wooden object, such as an *oar, mast, ship;* arbor infelix, *the gallows.*

arbŏrĕus -a -um, *relating to trees; treelike.*

arbustus -a -um, *planted with trees.*

N. as subst. **arbustum** -i, *a plantation, vineyard planted with trees.*

arbŭtĕus -a -um, *of the arbutus.*

arbŭtum -i, n. *the fruit, leaves, etc., of the wild strawberry or arbutus tree.*

arbŭtus -i, f. *the wild strawberry or arbutus tree.*

arca -ae, f. *a chest, box;* esp. *a money-box or coffin;* also *a cell.*

Arcādĭa -ae, f. *part of the Peloponnesus.* adj. **Arcădĭus** and **Arcădĭcus** -a -um.

arcānus -a -um, *shut, closed;* hence *silent, secret.* N. as subst. *a secret.* Adv. **arcāno,** *secretly.*

Arcăs -ādis, m. adj. and subst., *Arcadian, an Arcadian.*

arcĕo -ēre -ŭi. (1) *to shut in.* (2) *to keep at a distance, hinder, prevent, keep away.*

arcessĭtor -ōris, m. *a summoner.*

arcessītū abl. sing. m. *at the summons* (of a person).

arcesso (accerso) -ēre -īvi -ītum, *to fetch, call, summon;* legal, *to summon, bring before a court of justice;* in gen., *to fetch, derive, obtain.* Hence partic. **arcessītus,** *strained, far-fetched.*

archĕtȳpus -a -um *original.*

Archĭās -ae, m., Aulus Licinius, *a Greek poet defended by Cicero.*

archĭmăgīrus -i, m. *head cook.*

Archĭmēdes -is, m. *a mathematician and inventor, killed at the capture of Syracuse (212 B.C.).*

archĭpīrāta -ae, m. *chief pirate.*

architectōn -ōnis, m. *master-builder.*

architector -ari, dep. *to build, devise.*

architectūra -ae, f. *architecture.*

architectus -i, m. *an architect, master-builder, inventor, maker.*

archōn -ontis, m. *an archon, an Athenian magistrate.*

arcĭtĕnens -entis, *holding the bow.*

Arctŏs -i, f. *the Great and Little Bear;* hence *the north.*

arctōus -a -um, *belonging to the Bear;* hence, *northern.*

Arctūrus -i, m. *the brightest star of Bootes.*

arcŭla -ae, f. *a casket.* Transf., *rhetorical ornament.*

arcŭo -are, *to bend* or *shape like a bow.*

arcus -ūs, m. *a bow, arch, arc;* esp. *the rainbow.*

ardĕa -ae, f. *a heron.*

ardēlĭo -ōnis, m. *a busybody.*

ardĕo ardēre arsi, *to burn, glow, be on fire;* of bright objects, *to gleam;* of feeling (esp. of love), *to burn, smart;* of political disorder, *to be ablaze.* Hence partic. **ardens** -entis, *hot, glowing, burning, fiery, eager;* adv. **ardenter.**

ardesco -ēre *to take fire;* of bright objects, *to glitter;* of passions, *to become inflamed:* of strife, *to blaze up.*

ardor -ōris, m. *flame, burning, heat;* of bright objects, *gleam;* of feelings (esp. of love), *heat, eagerness;* meton., *an object of love, loved one.*

ardŭus -a -um, *steep, towering, lofty.*

Transf., *difficult to undertake* or *reach;* n. as subst., *difficulty.*

ārĕa -ae, f. *a level* or *open space, site, court-yard, threshing floor;* esp. *a playground;* hence, in gen., *play, scope.*

ārĕfăcĭo -făcĕre -fēci -factum, *to make dry.*

ārēna = harena; q.v.

ārĕo -ēre, *to be dry;* partic. **ārens** -entis, *dry, thirsty.*

Ārĕŏpăgus -i, m. *Mars' hill at Athens, where a court sat.* Hence **Ārĕŏpăgītes** -ae, m. *a member of the court.*

Ārēs -is, m. *the Greek god of war, Latin Mars.*

āresco -ēre *to become dry.*

ārĕtālŏgus -i, m. *a babbler about virtue.*

Ārĕthūsa -ae, f. *a fountain at Syracuse;* myth. *a nymph chased by the river Alpheus under the sea to Sicily.*

argentārĭus -a -um *relating to silver* or *money;* taberna, *a banker's stall.* M. as subst. *a money-changer, banker;* f. as subst., *the office* or *trade of a banker;* also *a silver mine.*

argentātus -a -um *ornamented with silver.*

argentĕus -a -um, *of silver.* Transf., *ornamented with silver;* *of the colour of silver;* *belonging to the Silver Age.*

argentum -i, n. *silver;* esp. *silver plate* or *silver coin;* hence, in gen., *money.*

Argīlētum -i, n. *the booksellers' district in Rome.*

argilla -ae, f. *white clay, potter's clay.*

Argō, Argūs, f. *the ship Argo.*

Argōnautae -arum, m. pl. *the Argonauts, the heroes who sailed in the Argo.*

Argŏs, n. and **Argi** -orum, m. pl. *Argos, capital of Argolis in the Peloponnese.* Adj. **Argēus** and **Argīvus** -a -um: plur. subst. **Argivi,** m. *the Argives* or *Greeks.* Hence f. subst. **Argŏlis** -ĭdis, *the district Argolis;* adj. **Argŏlĭcus** -a -um.

argūmentātĭo -ōnis, f. *the bringing forward of a proof.*

argūmentor -ari, dep. *to bring forward a proof, allege as a proof.*

argūmentum -i, n. *argument, proof; subject, contents, matter.*

argŭo -ŭĕre -ŭi -ūtum, *to put in clear light;* *to declare, prove;* *to accuse, blame, expose, convict.* Hence partic. **argūtus** -a -um: to the eye, *expressive, lively;* to the ear, *piercing, shrill, noisy;* of omens, *clear, significant;* of persons, *sagacious, cunning.* Adv. **argūtē,** *sagaciously.*

Argus -i, m. *the hundred-eyed guardian of Io.*

argūtĭae -arum, f. pl. *liveliness, animation;* of the mind, *cleverness, sagacity, cunning.*

argūtŭlus -a -um, *somewhat acute.*

Āriadna -ae and **Āriădnē** -ēs, f. *daughter of Minos of Crete.*

āridŭlus -a -um, *somewhat dry.*

āridus -a -um, adj. *dry, arid, thirsty;*

febris, *parching*; crura, *shrivelled*; of living conditions, *meagre*; intellectually *dry, jejune*; of character, *avaricious*. N. as subst., *dry ground*.

ărĭēs -ĭĕtis, m. *a ram; a battering ram; a prop, beam.*

ărĭēto -are, *to butt like a ram.*

Ărīōn -ōnis, m. *a cithara player, saved from drowning by a dolphin.*

Ariovistus -i, m. *a Germanic prince.*

ărista -ae, f. *the beard of an ear of grain*; hence *the ear itself*; also *a harvest.*

Ărĭstŏphănēs -is, m. *the Athenian comic dramatist.* Adj. **Ărĭstŏphănēus** -a -um.

Ărĭstŏtělēs -is and -i, m. *the Greek philosopher, pupil of Plato, founder of the Peripatetic school.* Adj. **Ărĭstŏtělēus** and **Ărĭstŏtělīus** -a -um.

ărĭthmētĭca -ae and -e -ēs, f.; also **ărĭthmētĭca** -orum, n. pl.; *arithmetic.*

arma -orum, n. pl. *defensive arms, armour, weapons of war*; hence *war; soldiers, military power; protection, defence*; in gen., *tools, equipment.*

armāmenta -orum, n. pl. *implements, tackle*, esp. of a ship.

armāmentārĭum -i, n. *an armoury.*

armārĭum -i, n. *a cupboard, chest.*

armātū, abl. sing. m. *with armour*; gravi armatu, *with heavy-armed troops.*

armātūra -ae, f. *equipment, armour*; meton., *armed soldiers.*

armentālis -e, *belonging to a herd.*

armentārĭus -i, m. *herdsman.*

armentum -i, n. *cattle for ploughing*; coll., *a herd.*

armĭfer -fĕra -fĕrum *bearing arms, warlike.*

armĭger -gĕra -gĕrum *bearing arms*; as subst., m. or f., *an armour-bearer.*

armilla -ae, f. *bracelet.*

armillātus -a -um *adorned with a bracelet.*

armĭpŏtens -entis *mighty in arms, warlike.*

armĭsŏnus -a -um *resounding with arms.*

armo -are, *to provide with arms, arm, equip, fit out.*

armus -i, m. *shoulder* or *shoulder-blade*; also, of an animal, *the side.*

Arnus -i, m. *chief river of Etruria (now Arno).*

ăro -are, *to plough, farm, cultivate.* Transf., *to furrow, wrinkle*; of ships, *to plough the sea.*

Arpīnum -i, n. *a Volscian hill-town, birthplace of Cicero*; adj. and subst. **Arpīnas** -atis; adj. **Arpīnus** -a -um.

arquātus -a -um, *relating to jaundice*; m. as subst., *a sufferer from jaundice.*

arr -; see also adr-.

arrha -ae, f. and **arrhăbo** -ōnis, m. *earnest money.*

ars -tis, f. (**1**) *skill, method, technique*; ex arte, *according to the rules of art.* (**2**) *an occupation, profession.* (**3**) *concrete*, in pl., *works of art.* (**4**) con-

duct, character, method of acting; bonae artes, *good qualities.*

Artaxerxēs -is, m. *name of several Persian kings.*

artērĭa -ae, f. *the wind-pipe; an artery.*

arthrītĭcus -a -um *gouty.*

artĭcŭlāris -e *of the joints*; morbus, *gout.*

artĭcŭlātim, *piecemeal, joint by joint, distinctly.*

artĭcŭlo -are, *to articulate, speak distinctly.*

artĭcŭlus -i, m.: in the body, *a small joint*; in plants, *a knob, knot*; of time, *a moment, crisis*; in gen., *a part, division, point.*

artĭfex -ficis, m. As adj.: act., *skilled, clever*; pass., *skilfully made.* As subst., *worker, craftsman, maker, creator, expert.*

artĭfĭciōsus -a -um. *skilful, accomplished; skilfully made*; hence *artificial.* Adv. **artĭfĭciōsē**, *skilfully.*

artĭfĭcĭum -i, n. *occupation, craft, art*; also *the theory, system of an art*; concr., *work of art*; in gen., *cleverness, skill, cunning.*

arto -are *to press together, reduce, abridge.*

artŏlăgănus -i, m. *a cake made of meal, wine, milk*, etc.

artopta -ae, m. *a baker; a bread pan.*

¹artus (**arctus**) -a -um, *narrow, tight, close*; somnus, *fast, sound*; of supplies, *small, meagre*; of circumstances, *difficult, distressing.* N. as subst. *a narrow space*; in gen., *difficulty, constraint.* Adv. **artē**, *narrowly, tightly, closely*; dormire, *soundly, fast*; artius appellare, *to cut a name short.*

²artus -ūs, m. normally plur., *the joints*; dolor artuum, *gout*: poet., *limbs.*

ārŭla -ae, f. *a little altar.*

ărund-; see harund-.

Aruns, *an Etruscan name for a younger son.*

arvīna -ae, f. *fat, lard.*

arvus -a -um, *ploughed.* N. as subst. **arvum** -i, *ploughed land, a field*; in gen., *a region.*

arx -cis, f. *fortress, citadel, stronghold, height*; fig., *bulwark, protection, headquarters.*

as, assis, m. *a whole, a unit*, divided into 12 parts (unciae); heres ex asse, *sole heir*; as a small coin, *the as*; as a weight, *a pound.*

Ascănĭus -i, m. *son of Aeneas.*

ascendo -scenděre -scendi -scensum *to mount, ascend, rise.*

ascensĭo -ōnis, f. *ascent*; oratorum *lofty flight.*

ascensus -ūs, m. *a going up, ascent*; meton., *a way up.*

ascĭa -ae, f. *a carpenter's axe; a mason's trowel.*

ascĭo -scire, *to take to oneself, adopt as one's own.*

ascisco asciscěre ascīvi ascītum, *to receive, admit*; of persons, *to adopt*; of things, *to take up, to approve.*

Hence partic. **ascītus** -a -um, *foreign, acquired.*

Ascra -ae, f. *town in Boeotia, home of Hesiod;* adj. **Ascraeus** -a -um.

ascrībo -scrībere -scripsi -scriptum: of things, *to write in, add in writing;* hence *to attribute, impute;* of persons, *to enrol, include, put on a list.*

ascriptīcius -a -um, *enrolled as member of a community.*

ascriptio -ōnis, f. *addition in writing.*

ascriptor -ōris, m. *one who approves.*

ăsella -ae, f. *she-ass.*

ăsellus -i, m. *ass.*

Ăsia -ae, f. (1) *a town and district in Lydia.* (2) *the continent of Asia.* (3) *the peninsula of Asia Minor.* (4) *the Roman province of Asia, formed in* 133 B.C. Hence adj. **Asiānus, Asiātĭcus** and **Asĭus** -a -um; subst. **Asĭs** -ĭdis, f., poet., *Asia.*

ăsīlus -i, m. *gad-fly.*

ăsīna -ae, f. *she-ass.*

ăsĭnus -i, m. *ass.*

ăsōtus -i, m. *sensualist, libertine.*

aspărăgus -i, m. *asparagus.*

aspargo, v. aspergo.

aspectābĭlis -e, *visible.*

aspecto -are, *to look at earnestly, look towards, observe, attend to.*

aspectus -ūs, m.: act., *looking, sight, range* or *power of vision;* pass., *sight, power of being seen, look, aspect, appearance.*

aspello -ĕre, *to drive away.*

asper -ĕra -ĕrum, *rough, uneven;* to the taste, *pungent, sour;* to the hearing, *harsh, grating;* of weather, *rough, stormy;* of character or circumstances, *rough, wild, harsh, difficult, severe.* N. as subst. *roughness, a rough place.* Adv. **asperē,** *roughly.*

¹**aspergo (aspargo)** -spergĕre -spersi -spersum, *to sprinkle upon* or *besprinkle with.*

²**aspergo (aspargo)** -ĭnis, f. *sprinkling, spray.*

aspĕrĭtās -ātis, f. *roughness, unevenness;* to the taste, *sourness;* to the ear, *harshness;* of character or circumstances, *harshness, fierceness, severity, difficulty.*

aspernātio -ōnis, f. *contempt.*

aspernor -ari, dep. *to despise, reject, spurn.*

aspĕro -are, *to make rough* or *sharp; to excite, arouse.*

aspersio -ōnis, f. *sprinkling.*

aspĭcio -spĭcĕre -spexi -spectum, *to look at, behold, survey, inspect, confront.* Transf., mentally, *to investigate, consider;* of places, *to look towards, face.*

aspīrātio -ōnis, f. *breathing, exhalation;* in speech, *pronunciation of the letter H, aspiration.*

aspīro -are: intransit., *to breathe, blow, exhale;* fig. *to be favourable, assist;* also *to climb up, reach towards a thing;* transit., *to blow air;* fig. *to infuse spirit,* etc.

aspis -ĭdis, f. *an adder, asp.*

asportātio -ōnis, f. *a taking away, carrying off.*

asporto -are, *to carry off, take away.*

asprēta -orum, n. pl. *rough, uneven places.*

asser -ĕris, m. *a stake, pole.*

assŭla -ae, f. *a shaving, chip.*

assus -a -um *dried, roasted;* n. pl. as subst. *a sweating bath.*

ast = at; q. v.

ast -; see also adst -.

astrŏlŏgĭa -ae, f. *astronomy.*

astrŏlŏgus -i, m. *an astronomer* or *astrologer.*

astrum -i, n. *a star,* or *constellation.* Transf., esp. plur., *the heights, glory, immortality.*

astu, n. *a city,* esp. *Athens.*

astus -ūs, m. *cleverness, cunning.*

astūtĭa -ae, f. *adroitness, craft;* in pl. *tricks.*

astūtus -a -um, *adroit, clever, crafty:* adv. **astūtē.**

ăsȳlum -i, n. *a sanctuary, place of refuge.*

ăsymbŏlus -a -um, *contributing nothing to the cost of an entertainment.*

at (ast), *but, yet, moreover;* sometimes introducing an imaginary objection, *but, you may say.*

ătăt, attat, attatae, attattatae, etc. interj. *oh! ah! alas!*

ătāvus -i, m. *a great-great-great-grandfather;* in gen., *an ancestor.*

Ătella -ae, f. *a city in Campania;* adj. **Ătellānus** -a -um; f. as subst. (sc. fabella) *a kind of popular farce;* m. as subst., *a player in these farces;* adj. **Ătellānĭus** or **Ătellānĭcus** -a -um, *of Atellane farces.*

āter atra atrum, *dead black, dark;* poet. *clothed in black.* Transf., *dark, gloomy, sad; malicious, poisonous.*

Ăthēnae -arum, f. pl. *Athens;* meton., *leaning.* Adj. **Ăthēnaeus** -a -um, *Athenian;* adj. and subst. **Ăthēnĭensis** -e, *Athenian, an Athenian.*

ăthĕos and **ăthĕus** -i, m. *an atheist.*

athlēta -ae, m. *wrestler, athlete.*

athlētĭcus -a -um, *relating to an athlete;* adv. **athlētĭcē,** *athletically.*

Atlās -antis, m. (1) *a mountain in Mauretania.* (2) *a mythical king and giant, changed into Mount Atlas.* Hence **Atlantĭădes** -ae, m. *a male descendant of Atlas;* **Atlantis** -ĭdis, f. *a female descendant of Atlas;* adj. **Atlantĭcus, Atlantēus** -a -um.

ătŏmus -i, f. *an atom.*

atque and **ac,** *and, and also, and indeed* In comparisons: of similarity, with such words as aequus or idem, *as;* of difference, with such words as alius or secus, *than, from.*

atquī, *nevertheless, but in fact;* sometimes confirmatory, *indeed, certainly.*

ātrāmentum -i, n. *black fluid, such as ink* or *shoemaker's black.*

ātrātus -a -um, *clothed in black, in mourning.*

Atreus -ei, m. *son of Pelops, father of*

Agamemnon and *Menelaus*. Hence
Ātrīdēs or **Ātrīda** -ae, m. *a son of
Atreus.*

ātriensis -is, m. *head slave, steward.*

ātrĭŏlum -i, n. *a little atrium, an antechamber.*

ātrĭum -i, n. *the hall or entrance room
in a Roman house temple or public
building.*

ătrōcĭtās -ātis, f. *frightfulness, cruelty,
harshness, barbarity.*

Atrŏpŏs -i, f. *one of the three Parcae
or Fates.*

atrox -ōcis, *terrible cruel, horrible*; of
human character, *harsh, fierce, severe.*
Adv. **ătrōcĭtĕr.**

attactū abl. sing. m., *by touch, by
contact.*

attăgēn -ēnis, m. and **attăgēna** -ae, f.
the black partridge.

Attălus -i, m. *name of several kings of
Pergamum*: adj. **Attălĭcus** -a -um.

attămen or at **tămen**, *but yet.*

attempĕro -are *to fit, adjust to*; adv.
from partic., **attempĕrātē**, *appropriately.*

attendo -tendĕre -tendi -tentum, *to
stretch to*; usually with animum
(animos), or absol., *to direct the
attention towards, attend to.*
Hence partic. **attentus**, *attentive,
careful*; adv. **attentē.**

attentĭo -ōnis, f. *attentiveness, attention.*

attento or **attempto** -are, *to try,
test, essay; to tamper with, try to
corrupt, or to attack.*

attĕnŭo -are, *to make thin, reduce,
weaken.*
Hence partic. **attĕnŭātus**, *made
weak; of style, abbreviated, over-
refined, or unadorned*; adv. **attĕnŭātē**,
simply, without ornament.

attĕro -tĕrĕre -trīvi (-tĕrŭi) -trītum,
to rub against, rub away; in gen., *to
weaken, ruin.*
Hence partic. **attrītus** -a -um,
rubbed away, worn out; fig., *frons,
shameless.*

attestor -ari, dep. *to attest, bear witness
to.*

attexo -texĕre -texŭi -textum, *to
weave or plait on or to*; hence, in
gen., *to add.*

Atthis -ĭdis, f. adj., *Attic, Athenian.*

Attĭca -ae, f. *Attica, the district of
Greece containing Athens.*

¹**Attĭcus** -a -um, *belonging to Attica or
Athens, Attic, Athenian*; adv. **Attĭcē**,
in the Attic or Athenian manner.

²**Attĭcus**, T. Pomponius, *the friend of
Cicero.*

attĭnĕo -tĭnēre -tĭnŭi -tentum: transit.,
to hold, keep, detain; intransit., *to
pertain to, or concern*, only in third
person: quod ad me attinet, *as far
as I am concerned*; nihil attinet, *it is
pointless.*

attingo -tingĕre -tĭgi -tactum, *to touch,
to reach*; of places, *to border upon*;
of enemies, *to attack, to strike.*
Transf., *to handle, manage, be concerned or connected with*; of feelings,

to affect a person; in writing or
speech, *to touch upon, to mention.*

attollo -tollĕre, *to raise, lift up.* Transf.,
to elevate, excite, exalt.

attondĕo -tondēre -tondi -tonsum, *to
cut, clip, prune*; in gen., *to diminish.*

attŏno -tŏnare -tŏnŭi -tŏnĭtum, *to
strike with thunder, stun.*
Hence partic. **attŏnĭtus** -a -um,
*struck by thunder; stunned, senseless;
inspired, frantic.*

attorquĕo -ēre, *to whirl, swing upward.*

attrăho -trăhĕre -traxi -tractum, *to
draw, drag, attract.*

attrecto -are, *to touch, handle, lay hands
on.*

attrĭbŭo -ŭĕre -ŭi -ūtum, *to allot,
assign, hand over.* Transf., in gen.,
to give, ascribe, add; of taxes, *to
impose.* N. of partic. as subst. **attrĭ-
būtum** -i, *a predicate, attribute.*

attrĭbūtĭo -ōnis, f. *the assignment of a
debt*; rhet. *an attribute.*

attrītus -a -um, partic. from attero;
q.v.

au, interj., *oh!*

auceps -cŭpis, m. *a fowler, bird-catcher;
a spy, eavesdropper,* or *caviller.*

auctĭficus -a -um, *increasing.*

auctĭo -ōnis, f. *an increasing;* hence,
from the bidding, *an auction.*

auctĭōnārĭus -a -um, *relating to an
auction.*

auctĭōnor -ari, dep. *to hold an auction.*

auctĭto -are and **aucto** -are, *to increase
very much.*

auctŏr -ōris, m. *one that gives increase.*
Hence (1) *an originator, causer, doer;
founder of a family; architect of a
building; author of a book; originator
of or leader in an enterprise; source of
or warrant for a piece of information.*
(2) *a backer, supporter, approver,
surety.*

auctŏrāmentum -i, n. *a contract;
wages.*

auctōrĭtās -ātis, f. (1) *support, backing,
lead, warrant*; polit., *sanction* (esp.
of the senate). (2) *power conferred,
rights, command; legal title.* (3)
in gen., *influence, authority, prestige;*
meton., *an influential person.*

auctōro -are, *to bind or hire for money.*

auctumnus = autumnus; q.v.

auctus -ūs, m. *increase, enlargement,
growth.*

aucŭpātĭo -ōnis, f. *fowling, bird-
catching.*

aucŭpĭum -i, n. *bird-catching, fowling;*
hence, in gen., *hunting, watching,
eavesdropping;* aucupia verborum,
cavilling, quibbling.

aucŭpor -ari, dep. *to catch birds;* in
gen., *to watch out for, lie in wait for.*

audācĭa -ae, f. *courage, daring;* in
bad sense, *audacity, impudence,
temerity;* in plur., *audacious deeds.*

audax -ācis, *bold* (in good or bad sense);
adv. **audācĭter** or **audācĭtĕr.**

audentĭa -ae, f. *boldness, courage.*

audĕo audēre ausus sum, *to be daring
to dare, venture, bring oneself to.*

Hence partic. **audens** -entis, *daring, bold*; compar. adv. **audentius**.

audientia -ae, f. *hearing, attention.*

audio -ire, *to hear, listen; to learn a thing by hearing; sometimes to listen to and believe* (or *obey*); *rarely to be called*; bene audire, *to be well spoken of.* Hence partic. **audiens** -entis, as adj., *obedient*; as subst., *a hearer.*

auditio -ōnis, f. *hearing, listening*; concr., *hearsay report.*

auditor -ōris, m. *a hearer, auditor, scholar.*

auditōrium -i, n. *a place of audience, lecture-room, court of justice*, etc.

auditus -ūs, m. *hearing, sense of hearing*; concr., *a report.*

aufĕro auferre abstŭli ablātum, *to carry away, remove*: in bad sense, *to make away with, carry off, steal.*

Aufidus -i, m. *a river in Apulia.*

aufūgio fŭgĕre -fūgi, *to flee, escape.*

augĕo augēre auxi auctum, *to enlarge, increase*; of rivers, in pass., *to be swollen*; in speech, *to extol, set forth*; with abl., *to enrich with, furnish with*; in transit. (rare), *to grow.* Hence partic. **auctus** -a -um, *increased, enriched.*

augesco -ĕre, *to increase, begin to grow.*

augmĕn -ĭnis, n. *increase, growth.*

augur -ŭris, c. *augur, soothsayer, seer.*

augŭrālis -e, *relating to an augur or augury*; n. as subst. **augŭrāle** -is, *part of the Roman camp, where auspices were taken.*

augŭrātio -ōnis, f. *divining, soothsaying.*

augŭrātus -ūs, m. *the office of augur.*

augŭrium -i, n., *the office and work of an augur, observation and interpretation of omens, augury*; in gen., *an omen, prophecy, presentiment.*

augŭrius -a -um, *relating to an augur.*

augŭro -are, *to act as an augur, take auguries*; locus auguratur, *the place is consecrated by auguries*; in gen., *to have a foreboding or presentiment.*

augŭror -ari, dep. *to act as an augur, foretell by auguries*; hence, in gen., *to foretell or to guess.*

Augusta -ae, f. *a name for any female elative of the Roman emperor, or town named after him.*

Augustālis -e, *belonging to or in honour of the Emperor Augustus.*

¹**augustus** -a -um, *consecrated, holy; majestic, dignified.* Adv. **augustē**, *reverently.*

²**Augustus** -i, m. *a name assumed by all Roman emperors.*

³**Augustus** -a -um, *relating to Augustus*; mensis, *August.*

aula -ae, f. *fore-court, court-yard*; poet = atrium, *an inner court.* Transf., *a palace, royal court*; meton., *courtiers.*

aula = olla; q.v.

aulaeum -i, n. usually plur., *embroidered work, tapestry curtains* (esp. of a theatre).

aulīcus -a -um, *of the court, princely.*

auloedus -i, m. *one who sings to the flute.*

aura -ae, *air*, esp. *air breathed or blowing, breath, wind*; poet., esp. plur., *upper air, heaven*; superas ad auras, *to the light of day*; ferre sub auras, *to make known*; poet. (rarely), *smell, glitter or echo.*

aurārius -a -um, *golden, of gold*; f. as subst., *a gold-mine.*

aurātus -a -um, *golden or adorned with gold.*

Aurēlius -a -um, *name of a Roman plebeian gens.*

aurĕŏlus -a -um, *golden, glittering, splendid.*

aurĕus -a -um, *golden, made of gold or adorned with gold*; poet., *of the colour of gold, and, in gen., excellent, beautiful.*

aurichalchum = orichalchum; q.v.

auricŏmus -a -um, *with golden hair or leaves.*

auricŭla -ae, f. *the lobe of the ear*; in gen., *the ear.*

aurifer -fĕra -fĕrum, *gold-bearing, gold-producing.*

aurifex -fĭcis, m. *a goldsmith.*

auriga -ae, c. *charioteer, driver*; of a ship, *helmsman*; as a constellation *the Waggoner.*

auriger -gĕra -gĕrum, *gold-bearing.*

aurigo -are, *to drive a chariot.*

auris -is, f. *the ear*; hence *hearing*; of a plough, *the earth- or mould-board.*

auritus -a -um, *long-eared*; hence *attentive.*

aurōra -ae, f. *dawn, break of day*; personified, *Aurora, goddess of morning*; meton., *the east.*

aurum -i, n. *gold; anything made of gold, gold plate, coin, a cup, ring, etc.; the golden age.*

Aurunca -ae, f. *a town in Campania.*

auscultātor -ōris, m. *a listener.*

ausculto -are, *to hear attentively, listen to*; sometimes also *to obey*; of servants, *to attend, wait.*

ausim, as subjunctive of audeo; q.v.

Ausŏnia -ae, f. *Ausonia, Lower Italy, and in gen., Italy*; adj. **Ausŏnius** -a -um.

auspex -ĭcis, c. *one who watches birds and divines from them*; esp. *an official witness of marriage contracts*: poet., in gen., *a leader.*

auspĭcium -i, n. *divination by means of birds, the taking of or right to take auspices.* Transf., *any omen or sign*; poet. *leadership, guidance.*

auspĭco -are, *to take the auspices.* Hence partic. **auspĭcātus** -a -um, *consecrated by auguries*; as adj., *favourable, auspicious.* Abl. abs. **auspĭcāto**, *after taking auspices*; hence *in a fortunate hour.*

auspĭcor -ari, dep., *to take the auspices*; hence *to begin favourably.*

auster -stri, m. *the south wind*; meton. *the south.*

austērĭtās -ātis, f., *harshness, strictness, severity.*

austērus -a -um, *sour, harsh, strict, severe, gloomy.* Adv. **austērē.**

austrālis -e, *southern.*

austrīnus -a -um, *southern.*

ausum -i, n. *a daring deed, undertaking.*

aut, *or, or else;* repeated, aut . . . aut . . ., *either . . . or . . .*

autem, *but, on the other hand, however, moreover, now.*

authepsa -ae, f. *a cooking-stove.*

Autŏmĕdōn -ontis, m. *charioteer of Achilles.*

autumnālis -e, *autumnal.*

¹**autumnus** -i, m. *autumn.*

²**autumnus** -a -um, adj., *autumnal.*

autŭmo -are, *to say, assert.*

auxĭliāris -e, *giving help, assisting:* m. pl. as subst., *auxiliary* or *allied troops.*

auxĭliārius -a -um, *helping;* milites, *auxiliary troops.*

auxĭliātŏr -ōris, m. *a helper.*

auxĭliātus -ūs, m. *help, assistance.*

auxĭlior -ari, dep., *to help, assist, support.*

auxĭlium -i, n. *help, aid, assistance;* milit., often plur., *auxiliary troops,* or in gen., *military power.*

ăvārĭtia -ae and **ăvārĭtiēs** -ēi f. *avarice, covetousness.*

ăvārus -a -um, *covetous, greedy;* adv. **ăvārē** and **ăvārĭtĕr.**

ăvĕho -vĕhĕre -vexi -vectum, *to carry off, bear away;* pass., *to ride* or *sail off.*

ăvello -vellĕre -velli and -vulsi (-volsi) -vulsum (-volsum), *to tear away, pluck away* (esp. with violence).

ăvēna -ae, f. *oats* or *wild oats;* hence *oaten pipe, shepherd's pipe;* in gen., *any stalk, straw.*

Ăventīnum -i, n. and **Ăventīnus** -i, m. *the Aventine, one of the seven hills of Rome.*

¹**ăvĕo** -ēre, *to long for, desire.*

²**ăvĕo** (**hăvĕo**) -ēre, *to be well;* found only in imperat. and infin.; ave, *hail!* or *farewell!*

Ăvernus -i, m. *a lake near Puteoli, said to be an entrance to the infernal regions;* meton., *the infernal regions;* adj **Ăvernus** -a -um, **Ăvernālis** -e.

ăverrunco -are, *to turn away, avert.*

ăversābĭlis, *from which one must turn away, horrible.*

¹**āversor** -ari, dep. *to turn away* (in shame, disgust, etc.); with acc., *to turn away from, avoid, shun.*

²**āversŏr** -ōris, m. *an embezzler.*

averto (**avorto**) -vertĕre -verti (-vorti) -versum (-vorsum), *to turn away, remove:* flumina, *to divert;* of feelings, *to estrange;* of property, *to carry off, appropriate embezzle;* poet., intransit., *to retire.*

Hence partic. **āversus** -a -um, *turned away, backward, behind;* of feeling, *disinclined, unfavourable, hostile.*

ăvĭa -ae. f. *a grandmother.*

ăviārĭum -i, *an aviary;* also *the haunts of wild birds.*

ăvĭdĭtās -ātis, f. *desire, longing;* esp. *desire for money, avarice.*

ăvĭdus -a -um, *desiring, longing for;* esp. *greedy for money, avaricious;* adv. **ăvĭdē.**

ăvis -is, f. *a bird;* often *a bird of omen,* and in gen., *an omen.*

ăvītus -a -um, *of a grandfather, ancestral.*

ăvĭus -a -um: of places, *out of the way, untrodden;* of persons, *wandering, astray, lost.*

ăvŏcātĭo -ōnis, f. *a calling away, diversion.*

ăvŏco -are, *to call away,* or *off, to withdraw, remove, divert.*

ăvŏlo -are, *to fly away, hasten away.*

ăvuncŭlus -i, m. *a mother's brother, uncle.*

ăvus -i, m. *a grandfather;* poet., in gen., *an ancestor.*

axis (or **assis**) -is, m. *an axle.* Hence (1) *a wheel;* meton., *a chariot, waggon.* (2) *the axis of the earth;* meton. *the north pole* or *the heavens;* sub axe, *in the open air.* (3) *a board, plank.*

B

B, b, *the second letter of the Latin Alphabet.*

băbae or **păpae**, interj. *wonderful!*

Băbўlōn -ōnis, f. *a city on the Euphrates;* **Băbўlōnia** -ae, f. *Babylonia, between the Euphrates and the Tigris;* adj. **Băbўlōnĭcus** and **Băbўlōnĭus** -a -um.

băca (**bacca**) -ae, f. *a berry, fruit; a pearl.*

băcātus -a -um, *set with pearls.*

baccar (**bacchar**) -āris, n. and **baccaris** -is, f. *a plant,* perhaps *sowbread.*

Baccha -ae, f. *a Bacchante, female worshipper of Bacchus.*

Bacchānal -is, n. *the place where Bacchus was worshipped;* plur. **Bacchānālĭa** -ium, *the (Greek) festival of Dionysus* or *Bacchus.*

bacchātĭo -ōnis, f. *revelling in Bacchanalian fashion.*

bacchor -ari, dep. *to celebrate the festival of Bacchus:* as passive, of places, *to be made the scene of Bacchic revels;* in gen., *to rage, rave like a Bacchante.* Partic. **bacchantes** = Bacchae; see Baccha.

Bacchus -i, m. *the god of wine:* meton., *the vine,* or *wine,* or *the Bacchic cry* (Io Bacche). Adj. **Bacchēus**, **Bacchĭcus,** and **Bacchĭus** -a -um.

bacĭfer -fĕra -fĕrum, *bearing berries.*

băcĭllum -i, n. *a little staff;* esp. *the lictor's staff.*

băcŭlum -i, n. and **băcŭlus** -i, m. *a staff, walking-stick.*

Baetis -is, m. *a river in Spain;* adj. **Baetĭcus** -a -um, *relating to the Baetis;* f. subst. **Baetĭca** -ae, f. *the*

Roman province of Baetica on the Baetis.

Baiae -arum, f. pl. *a holiday-resort on the coast of Campania*; adj. **Baiānus** -a -um.

băiŭlo -are, *to carry a burden.*

băiŭlus -i, m. *a porter.*

bălaena -ae, f. *a whale.*

bălănus -i, f. rarely m. *an acorn, ben-nut, chestnut or date.*

bălatro -ōnis, m. *buffoon, jester.*

bălātus -ūs, m. *the bleating of sheep or goats.*

balbus -a -um, *stammering*; adv. **balbē.**

balbūtĭo -ire, *to stammer, stutter*; hence in gen., *to speak obscurely.*

Bălĭāres (Bălĕāres) -ium, f. pl. *the Balearic Islands*; adj. **Bălĭāris** -e, **Bălĭārĭcus** -a -um.

bălĭnĕum or **balnĕum** -i, n. esp. in pl.; also heteroclite pl. **bălĭnĕae** or **balnĕae** -arum; *a bath, bathing place.*

ballista -ae, f. *a military engine for throwing large stones.*

balnĕae, v. balineum.

balnĕārĭus -a -um, *belonging to the bath*; n. pl. as subst. *baths, bathing-rooms.*

balnĕātor -ōris, m. *the keeper of a bath.*

balnĕŏlum -i, n. *a little bathroom.*

balnĕum, v. balineum.

bālo -are, *to bleat.*

balsămum -i, n. *the balsam-tree, or its gum.*

baltĕus -i, m. and **baltĕum** -i, n. *a girdle.*

bărathrum -i, n. *a pit, abyss*; esp. of *the lower world.*

barba -ae, f. *beard*; promittere barbam, *to let the beard grow.*

barbărĭa -ae and **barbărĭēs**, f. *a foreign country, as opposed to Greece and Rome*; *want of culture, rudeness, savagery.*

barbărĭcus -a -um, *foreign, i.e., not Greek or Roman.*

barbărus -a -um, *foreign, strange*; *uncultivated, rough, savage*; as subst., *a foreigner.* Adv. **barbărē**, *like a foreigner*; *roughly, barbarously.*

barbātŭlus -a -um, *with a slight beard.*

barbātus -a -um, *bearded.*

barbĭger -gĕra -gĕrum, *wearing a beard.*

barbĭtōs, m. and f. *a lyre.*

barbŭla -ae, f. *a little beard.*

bardŏcŭcullus -i, m. *a Gallic overcoat.*

bardus -a -um, *stupid, slow, dull.*

bāris -ĭdos, f. *an Egyptian barge.*

barītus (barrītus) -ūs, m. *a German war-cry.*

bāro -ōnis, m. *a blockhead, simpleton.*

barrus -i, m. *elephant.*

bascauda -ae, f. *a basket.*

bāsĭātĭo -ōnis, f. *kissing, a kiss.*

bāsĭātor -ōris, m. *a kisser.*

bāsĭlĭcus -a -um, *royal, kingly, princely.* M. as subst., *the best cast of the dice*; n. as subst., *a royal robe*; f. as subst., **băsĭlĭca** -ae, *a basilica, a building with double colonnades, where merchants met and courts were held.* Adv. **băsĭlĭcē**, *royally.*

băsĭo -are, *to kiss.*

băsis -is and -ĕos, f. *a pedestal, base*; villae, *foundation-wall*; tranguli, *base.*

bāsĭum -i, n. *a kiss.*

Bassăreus -ĕi, m. *a name of Bacchus.*

bătillum (or vătillum) -i, n. *a chafing-dish or shovel.*

battŭo (bātŭo) -ĕre, *to beat, knock.*

baubor -ari, dep., *to bark gently.*

bĕātĭtās -ātis, f. and **bĕātĭtūdo** -ĭnis, f. *happiness, blessedness.*

bĕātus -a -um, partic. from beo; q.v.

Belgae -arum, m. *the Belgae, a warlike people in the north of Gaul.*

bellārĭa -orum, n. pl. *dessert.*

bellātor -ōris, m. and **bellatrix** -īcis, f., *a warrior*; as adj. *warlike, courageous.*

bellātōrĭus -a -um, *warlike.*

bellĭcōsus -a -um, *warlike.*

bellĭcus -a -um, *of war, warlike.* N. as subst. **bellĭcum** -i, *the signal for march or attack.*

belliger -gĕra -gĕrum, *waging war, warlike.*

bellĭgĕro -are, *to wage war.*

bellĭpŏtens -entis, *mighty in war.*

bello -are and **bellor** -ari, dep. *to wage war, fight.*

Bellōna -ae, f. *the goddess of war.*

bellŭa, v. belua.

bellŭlus -a -um, *pretty, elegant.*

bellum -i, n. (old form, **duellum**), *war, fighting*; in bello, or loc., belli, *in time of war.*

bellus -a -um, colloq., *pretty, handsome*; adv. **bellē.**

bēlŭa -ae, f. *a beast, large animal*; as a term of reproach, *monster, brute, beast.*

bēlŭōsus -a -um, *full of monsters.*

Bēlus -j, m. *a king, founder of Babylon.* Hence f. pl. subst., **Bēlĭdes** -um, *the granddaughters of Belus, the Danaides.*

bĕnĕ, adv.; comp. **mĕlĭus**; superl. **optĭmē**; *well, rightly, properly*; bene rem gerere, *to succeed*; with adj. or adv., *thoroughly, very*; as an exclamation, *good, excellent*; bene facis, *I am obliged to you*; bene facta (or **benefacta**), *good deeds, benefits.*

bĕnĕfĭcentĭa -ae, f. *kindness.*

bĕnĕfĭcĭārĭus -a -um, *of a favour*; m. pl. as subst., *privileged soldiers.*

bĕnĕfĭcĭum -i, n. *a kindness, favour, service*; in political life, *favour, distinction, promotion, also privilege, exemption.*

bĕnĕfĭcus -a -um, comp. -entior, superl. -entissimus, *kind, generous, obliging.*

Bĕnĕventum -i, n. *a town in Samnium.*

bĕnĕvŏlens -entis, *well-wishing, obliging.*

bĕnĕvŏlentĭa -ae, f. *good-will, kindness.*

bĕnĕvŏlus -a -um, *kind, obliging, well disposed*; adv. **bĕnĕvŏlē.**

bĕnignĭtās -ātis, f. *kindness, generosity.*

bĕnignus -a -um, *kind, friendly, generous*; of things, *abundant, fruitful.* Adv. **bĕnignē**, *kindly, generously*; colloq., benigne dicis, *or* benigne, *much obliged* (accepting or refusing an offer).

cānĭtĭēs, acc. -em. *whitish-grey colour,* esp. of the hair; meton., *grey hair, old age.*

canna -ae, f. *reed.* Transf., *a reed-pipe; a small boat.*

cannăbis -is, and **cannăbum** -i, n. *hemp.*

Cannae -arum, f. pl. *town in Apulia, where Hannibal defeated the Romans* (216 B.C.). Adj. **Cannensis** -e.

căno cănĕre cĕcĭni cantum, *to sing* or *play.* Intransit. *to sing*; of cocks, *to crow*; of frogs, *to croak*; also (with abl.), *to play on an instrument*; canere receptui, *to sound the signal for retreat*; of instruments, *to sound.* Transit.: (1) *to sing with the voice.* (2) *to sing of, celebrate in song.* (3) *to sound* or *play an instrument.* (4) *to prophesy.*

cănor -ōris, m. *melody, song, sound.*

cănōrus -a -um, *melodious, harmonious, sweet-sounding*; n. as subst., *harmonious sound.*

Cantabria -ae, f. *a region in north-west Spain.*

cantāmen -ĭnis, n. *incantation.*

canthăris -ĭdis, f. *a beetle*: esp. *the Spanish fly.*

canthărus -i, m. *a tankard; a sea-fish, the black bream.*

canthērius -i, m. *a gelding, nag.*

canthus -i, m. *the tire of a wheel.*

cantĭcum -i, n. *a scene in Roman comedy, accompanied by music and dancing; a song; sing-song delivery in an orator.*

cantĭlēna -ae, f. *an old song, twaddle, chatter.*

cantĭo -ōnis, f. *a song; an incantation, enchantment.*

cantĭto -are, *to sing or play often.*

Cantĭum -i, n. *a district in Britain* (now Kent).

cantĭuncŭla -ae, f. *a flattering song.*

canto -are -avi -atum, *to sing or play.* Intransit., of persons, *to sing*; of cocks, *to crow*; also *to play on an instrument*; of instruments, *to sound.* Transit. (1) *to sing.* (2) *to sing of, celebrate, continually mention.* (3) *to predict.*

cantor -ōris, m. *a singer, poet, musician; an actor.*

cantus -ūs, m. *song, melody music, poetry; prophecy; incantation.*

cānus -a -um, *whitish-grey; hence aged*; m. pl. as subst., *grey hair.*

căpācĭtās -ātis, f. *breadth, capacity.*

căpax -ācis, *able to hold, broad, wide, roomy.* Transf., *receptive, able to grasp, capable, fit for.*

căpēdo -ĭnis, f. *a bowl used in sacrifices.*

căpella -ae, f. *a she-goat; a star in the constellation Auriga.*

Căpēna -ae, f. *a town in Etruria*; adj. **Căpēnus** -a -um; porta Capena, *a gate in Rome at the beginning of the Via Appia.*

căper -ri, m. *he-goat.*

căpesso -ĕre -īvi and -ĭi -ītum, *to seize, grasp eagerly*; of places, *to strive to reach, to make for*; of business, etc., *to take up, undertake*; rempublicam *to enter public life.*

căpillātus -a -um, *hairy, having hair.*

căpillus -i, m. *a hair*; usually pl., or collect. sing., *the hair of the head* or *beard.*

căpĭo căpĕre cēpi captum, *to take.* (1) in gen. *to take, seize*; of places, *to choose, reach,* or *take possession of*; of business, opportunities, etc. *to take up, take in hand, adopt*; of persons, *to choose.* (2) *to catch, take in a violent or hostile manner*; hence, *to attack, injure*; pass. capi, *to be injured* or *diseased*; oculis et auribus captus, *blind and deaf*; also *to charm, captivate, take in*; at law, *to convict.* (3) *to receive,* esp. of money; in gen., *to suffer, undergo, take on.* (4) *to take in, hold, contain, keep in*; mentally, *to grasp, comprehend.*

căpis -ĭdis, f. *a one-handled vessel.*

căpistro -are, *to fasten with a halter.*

căpistrum -i, n. *a halter.*

căpĭtālis -e, *relating to the head,* or *to life.* Transf., *deadly, mortal; first, chief, distinguished.* N. as subst. **căpital** and **căpĭtăle**, *a capital crime.*

căpĭto -onis, m. *a man with a large head.*

Căpĭtōlium -i, n. *the temple of Jupiter at Rome, the Capitol*; adj. **Căpĭtōlinus** -a -um; m. pl. as subst., *superintendents of games in honour of Jupiter Capitolinus.*

căpĭtŭlum -i, n. *a little head.*

Cappădŏcia -ae, f. *a district in Asia Minor.*

capra -ae, f. *a she-goat*; also *a star in the constellation Auriga.*

caprĕa -ae, f. *a roe.*

Caprĕae -arum, f. *small island off the Campanian coast* (now Capri).

caprĕŏlus -i, m. *a roebuck*; in plur., *props, supports.*

Capricornus -i, m. *Capricorn, a sign of the Zodiac.*

caprifĭcus -i, m. *the wild fig-tree,* and *its fruit.*

caprĭgĕnus -a -um, *born of goats.*

caprimulgus -i, m. *goat-milker*—i.e. *a countryman.*

caprīnus -a -um, *relating to a goat.*

caprĭpēs -pĕdis, *goat-footed.*

capsa -ae, f. *a box* or *case,* esp. *for books.*

capsārius -i, m. *a slave who carried his young master's satchel.*

capsŭla -ae, f. *a little chest.*

captātĭo -ōnis, f. *an eager seizing*; verborum, *quibbling.*

captātor -ōris, m. *one who eagerly seizes*; esp. *a legacy-hunter.*

captĭo -ōnis, f. (1) *a cheat, deception.* (2) *harm, loss.* (3) *a fallacy, sophism.*

captĭōsus -a -um, *deceitful; captious*; n. pl. as subst. *sophistries.* Adv. **captĭōsē.**

captĭuncŭla -ae, f. *fallacy, quibble.*

captīvĭtās -ātis, f. *captivity, capture*; collectively, *a number of captives.*

captīvus -a -um, *captured, taken,* esp. *in war.* Transf., *of a prisoner.*

M. and f. as subst., *a prisoner,
captive.*

capto -are, *to seize, catch at*; in gen.,
to strive after, desire, seek.

captus -ūs, m. *catching, taking*; hence
power or *manner of comprehension,
idea.*

Capŭa -ae, f. *chief town of Campania.*

căpŭlus -i, m. (1) *a coffin.* (2) *a
handle*; esp. *the hilt of a sword.*

căput -itis, n. *the head*; meton., *a
living individual,* esp. of human beings,
a person; also of a person's *life,
existence,* esp., in Rome, *a man's
political and social rights.* Transf.,
of lifeless things, *the top, summit,
extremity*; of rivers, etc., *the source*;
of persons and things, *the head,
leader, chief; headquarters, chief
point*; of places, *the capital.*

carbăsĕus -a -um, *made of canvas.*

carbăsus -i, f.; heteroclite pl.
carbăsa -orum, n.; *flax*; meton.,
anything made of flax, e.g. *garments,
curtains, sails.*

carbo -ōnis, m. *burning* or *burnt wood.*

carbōnārĭus -i, m. *a charcoal burner.*

carcer -ĕris, m. *prison, cell*; in plur.,
carceres, *the starting-place of a race-
course.*

carchēsĭum -i, n. *a goblet with handles.*
Transf., *the top of a mast, scuttle.*

cardĭăcus -a -um, *pertaining to the
stomach*; m. as subst., *one who suffers
from a disease of the stomach.*

cardo -ĭnis, m. *a hinge*; *any pole* or
pivot: cardo duplex, *the ends of the
earth's axis*; *a cardinal point, main
consideration.*

cardŭus -i, m. *thistle.*

cārectum -i, n. *a sedgy spot.*

cārĕo -ēre -ŭi, *to be without* (with abl)
of a place, *to absent oneself from.*

cārex -icis, f. *rush, sedge.*

cārĭes, acc. -em. abl. -e, f. *rottenness,
decay.*

cārīna -ae, f. *the keel of a ship*; meton.,
a ship, vessel.

cārĭōsus -a -um, *rotten, decayed.*

cāris -ĭdis, f. *a kind of crab.*

cārĭtās -atis, f. *dearness, high price*;
esp. *high cost of living.* Transf.,
affection, love, esteem.

carmen -ĭnis, n. *a song, tune,* vocal or
instrumental; *a poem, poetry, verse*;
*a prediction; an incantation; a
religious* or *legal formula.*

Carmentis -is, and **Carmenta** -ae, f.
a prophetess, mother of Evander;
adj. **Carmentālis** -e.

carnĭfex -fĭcis, m. *an executioner,
hangman.*

carnĭfĭcīna -ae, f. *the work of a hangman; execution, torture.*

carnĭfĭco -are, *to behead,* or *mangle.*

¹**cāro** -ĕre, *to card.*

²**cāro** carnis, f. *flesh.*

carpentum -i, n. *a two-wheeled carriage.*

carpo carpĕre carpsi carptum, *to pluck,
pull off, select, choose out*; and so *to
enjoy*; of animals, *to graze.* Transf.,
to proceed on a journey; *to pass over* a
place; *to carp at, slander* a person;

to weaken, annoy, harass an enemy;
to break up, separate, divide forces.

carptim, *in pieces, in small parts; in
different places; at different times.*

carptor -ōris, m. *one who carves food.*

carrūca -ae, f. *a four-wheeled carriage.*

carrus -i, m. *a four-wheeled baggage-
waggon.*

Carthāgo (**Karthāgo**) -ĭnis, f. (1) *the
city of Carthage in N. Africa.*
(2) Carthago (Nova), *a colony of the
Carthaginians in Spain* (now
Cartagena). Adj. **Carthāgĭnĭensis** -e.

cărunncŭla -ae, f. *a small piece of flesh.*

cārus -a -um, adj. *high-priced, dear
costly.* Transf., *dear, beloved.*

căsa -ae, f. *hut, cottage, cabin.*

cāsĕŏlus -i, m. *a little cheese.*

cāsĕus -i, m. *cheese.*

căsĭa -ae, f. (1) *a tree with an aromatic bark, like cinnamon.* (2) *the
sweet-smelling mezereon.*

Cassandra -ae, f. *a prophetess, daughter
of Priam.*

cassēs -ĭum, m. pl. *a net; a trap; snare;*
also *a spider's web.*

cassĭda -ae, f. = cassis; q.v.

Cassĭŏpē -ēs, f. *mother of Andromeda.*

cassis -ĭdis f. and **cassĭda** -ae, f. *a metal
helmet.*

Cassĭus -a -um, *name of a Roman gens*;
adj. **Cassĭānus** -a -um.

cassus -a -um, *empty, hollow*; with
abl., *devoid of.* Transf., *worthless,
useless, vain*; **in cassum** or **incassum** as adv., *in vain.*

Castālĭa -ae, f. *a spring on Mount
Parnassus, sacred to Apollo and the
Muses.*

castănĕa -ae f. *a chestnut* or *chestnut-
tree.*

castellānus -a -um, *relating to a fortress*; m. pl. as subst., *the garrison of
a fortress.*

castellātim, *in single fortresses.*

castellum -i, n. *a castle, fortress, fort;
a shelter, refuge.*

castīgātĭo -ōnis, f. *punishment, reproof.*

castīgātor -ōris, m. *one who reproves* or
corrects.

castīgo -are, *to reprove, chasten, punish;
to check, restrain.*
Hence partic. **castīgātus** -a -um,
restrained, orderly, neat.

castĭmōnĭa -ae, f. *purity.*

castĭtās -ātis, f. *chastity.*

¹**castor** -ōris, m. *the beaver.*

²**Castor** -ōris, m. *twin-brother of Pollux.*
Hence **ecastor** and **mecastor,** *By
Castor!*

castŏrĕum -i, n. *an aromatic secretion
obtained from the beaver.*

castrensis -e, *pertaining to a camp.*

castro -are, *to castrate, enervate,
weaken.*

castrum -i, n.: sing., *a castle, fort,
fortress*; plur. **castra** -orum, *a camp,
encampment*; aestiva, *summer quarters*;
hiberna, *winter quarters.* Transf.: *a
day's march; martial service; a party,
faction.*

castus -a -um, *clean, pure, chaste*;
with reference to religion, *pious,*

religious, holy. Adv. **castē**, *purely piously, religiously.*

căsŭla -ae, f. *a little hut, cottage.*

cāsus -ūs, m. *a falling, fall.* Transf.: (1) *what befalls, an accident, event, occurrence.* (2) *occasion, opportunity.* (3) *destruction, downfall, collapse*; and, in gen., *end.* (4) in grammar, *a case.*

cătăphractēs -ae, m. *a breastplate of iron scales.*

cătăphractus -a -um, *mail-clad.*

cătăplūs -i, m. *the arrival of a ship; a ship that is arriving.*

cătăpulta -ae, f. *an engine of war, a catapult.*

cătăracta (cătarracta) -ae, f. and **cătăractēs** -ae, m. *a waterfall; a sluice or flood-gate; a portcullis.*

cătasta -ae, f. *a stage upon which slaves were exposed in the market.*

cătēia -ae, f. *a kind of spear.*

¹cătellus -i, m. and **cătella** -ae, f. *a little dog, puppy.*

²cătellus -i, m. and **cătella** -ae, f. *a little chain.*

cătēna -ae, f. *a chain, fetter.* Transf., (1) *restraint.* (2) *a series.*

cătēnātus -a -um, *chained, bound, linked together*; *labores, continuous.*

căterva -ae, f. *crowd, troop, flock.*

cătervātim, *in troops, in masses.*

căthedra -ae, f. *a chair; esp. a soft one for ladies, or one occupied by a professor.*

Cătĭlīna -ae, m. L. Sergius, *a Roman noble, killed at the head of a conspiracy in 62 B.C.* Hence adj. **Cătĭlīnārius** -a -um.

cătillus -i, m. *a small dish or plate.*

cătīnus -i, m. *a deep dish or bowl.*

Căto -ōnis, m. *a cognomen belonging to members of the gens Porcia*; adj. **Cătōniānus** -a -um; subst. **Cătōnīni** -orum, m. *the party of M. Porcius Cato Uticensis, the younger Cato.*

Cătōnium -i, n. *the lower world* (with a play on the word Cato).

Cătullus -i, m. C. Valerius (c. 85-55 B.C.) *the Roman lyric and epigrammatic poet.*

cătŭlus -i, m. *a young animal, esp. a whelp, puppy.*

cătus -a -um, *sharp, cunning*; adv. **cătē**.

cauda (cōda) -ae, f. *the tail of an animal.*

caudex = codex; q.v.

Caudium -i, n. *an old city in Samnium, near the pass of the Caudine Forks.* Adj. **Caudīnus** -a -um.

caulae -arum, f. pl. *a hole, opening; a sheep-fold.*

caulis -is, m. *the stalk of a plant; esp. of a cabbage.*

caupo -ōnis, m. *a small shopkeeper or inn-keeper.*

caupōna -ae, f. *a tavern, inn.*

caupōnor -ari, dep. *to trade*

caupōnŭla -ae, f. *a little inn.*

Caurus (Cōrus) -i, m. *the north-west wind.*

causa (caussa) -ae, f. *a cause*, in all senses of the English word. (1) *a*

reason, motive, pretext. (2) *interest*; abl., causā, *on account of, for the sake of,* with genit., meā, etc. (3) *a case at law, law-suit, claim, contention*; causam dicere, *to plead.* (4) *situation, condition, case.*

causārius -a -um, *sickly, diseased*; m. pl., milit., *men invalided out of the army.*

causĭdĭcus -i, m. *an advocate, barrister* (often used contemptuously).

causor -ari, dep. *to give as a reason, or pretext; to plead, pretend.*

causŭla -ae, f. *a little cause or case.*

cautēs -is, f. *a rough sharp rock.*

cautĭo -ōnis, f. *caution, care, fore-sight, precaution; legal, security, bail, bond.*

cautor -ōris, m. *one who is on his guard, or who gives bail for another.*

cautus -a -um, partic. from caveo; q.v.

căvaedĭum -i, n. *an inner quadrangle.*

căvĕa -ae, f. *a hollow place, cavity.* Esp. *an enclosure, den, cage; the seats in a theatre.*

căvĕo căvēre căvi cautum, *to be on one's guard;* with acc. *to be on one's guard against:* cave ignoscas, *take care not to forgive;* with ut and the subj., *to take care that;* with dat. of person, *to take care for, provide for.* Commercial and legal, *to give security or to get security;* also *to provide, order,* in a will, treaty or law.
    Hence partic. **cautus** -a -um: of persons, etc., *cautious, wary, careful;* of property, *made safe, secured.* Adv. **cautē**, **cautim**, *cautiously or with security.*

căverna -ae, f. *a hollow place, cavern:* navis, *the hold;* caeli, *the vault of heaven.*

căvillātĭo -ōnis, f. *raillery, jesting, irony.* Transf., *sophistry.*

căvillātor -ōris, m. *a jester ˙oker.* Transf., *a quibbler.*

căvillor -ari, dep. *to jest, joke, satirize.* Transf., *to quibble.*

căvo -are, *to hollow out, excavate, pierce.*

căvum -i, n. and **căvus** -i, m. *a hollow, hole, cavity.*

căvus -a -um, *hollow, concave.*

-cĕ, *a demonstrative particle joined on to pronouns and adverbs*—e.g. hisce.

Cecrops -ōpis, m. *the mythical first king of Athens;* adj. **Cecrŏpius** -a -um, *Cecropian, Athenian.*

¹cēdo cēdĕre cessi cessum, *to go, proceed:* of things, *to turn out, happen; to fall to the lot of a person; to change into something else; to go away, withdraw, retire;* with dat., *to give ground to, submit to,* hence *to be inferior to;* transit., *to grant, yield.*

²cĕdŏ and plur. **cette**, colloquial imperat., *give, hand over, out with it!*

cedrus -i, f. *the cedar;* meton. *cedar-wood or cedar oil.*

cēlātor -ōris, m. *a concealer.*

cĕlĕber -bris -bre, *filled, crowded;* of places, *frequented;* of occasions, *well attended;* of sayings, *often repeated;*

of persons and things, *celebrated, famous, renowned.*

cĕlĕbrātĭo -ōnis, f. *a numerous assembly or attendance.*

cĕlĕbrātŏr -ōris, m. *one who praises.*

cĕlĕbrĭtās -ātis, f. *a crowd, multitude, numerous attendance*; of a festival, *celebration*; in gen., *fame, renown.*

cĕlĕbro -are, *to visit frequently, or in large numbers; to fill; to celebrate, solemnize; to publish, make known; to sing the praises of, to honour; to practise often, repeat, exercise.*
Hence partic. **cĕlĕbrātus** -a -um: of places, *much frequented*: of festivals, *kept solemn, festive*; in gen., *famous, celebrated.*

cĕlĕr -ĕris -ĕre, *swift, quick, rapid*; in a bad sense, *hasty, rash.* Adv. **cĕlĕrĕ** and **cĕlĕrĭtĕr.**

Cĕlĕres -um, m. *early name for Roman nobles,* esp. *the body-guard of the kings.*

cĕlĕrĭpēs -pĕdis, *swift-footed.*

cĕlĕrĭtās -ātis, f. *quickness, swiftness.*

cĕlĕro -are: transit., *to make quick, accelerate*; intransit., *to hasten.*

cella -ae, f. *a room*: esp. *a store-room or a garret, mean apartment*; in a temple, *the shrine of the god's image.*

cellārĭus -a -um, *of a store-room*; as subst. *a cellarer.*

cēlo -are, *to hide, conceal, keep secret.*

cĕlōx -ōcis, *swift, quick*; f. as subst. *a swift vessel, yacht.*

celsus -a -um, *upraised, high, lofty, elevated*; in bad sense, *proud, haughty.*

Celtae -arum, m. pl. *the Celts,* esp. those of Central Gaul. Adj. **Celtĭcus** -a -um.

Celtĭbĕri -orum, m. *the Celtiberians, a people in the middle of Spain.*

cēna -ae, f. *dinner, the main Roman meal*; meton., *a dish or course at a dinner.*

cēnācŭlum -i, n. *a garret, attic.*

cēnātĭo -ōnis, f. *a dining-hall.*

cēnātōrĭus -a -um, *relating to dinner*; n. pl. as subst. *clothes to dine in.*

cēnĭto -are, *to dine often.*

cēno -are: intransit., *to dine, sup*; transit, *to dine on, to eat.* Perf. partic., with middle meaning, **cēnātus,** *having dined, after dinner.*

censĕo censēre censŭi censum, *to estimate, to form or express an opinion or valuation* of a person or thing; esp. of the censor at Rome, *to take an account of the names and property of Roman citizens.* In gen., *to express an opinion, be of opinion, vote, advise, recommend*; of the senate, *to resolve.*

censor -ōris, m. *the sensor, a Roman magistrate.* Transf., *a severe judge, rigid moralist.*

censōrĭus -a -um, *relating to the censor*; homo, *an ex-censor*; tabulae, *the censor's lists.* Transf., *rigid, severe.*

censūra -ae, f. *the censor's office, censorship.* Transf., *judgment.*

census -ūs, m. *the census, an enrolment of names and assessment of property.* Transf., *the censor's list; the amount of property necessary for enrolment in a certain rank*; in gen., *property, wealth.*

centaurēum and **centaurĭum** -i, n. *the plant centaury.*

Centaurus -i, m. *a centaur,* i.e. *a monster of Thessaly, half man and half horse.*

centēni -ae -a (poet. also sing.), *a hundred together, a hundred each.*

centēsĭmus -a -um, *the hundredth.* F. sing. as subst. *the hundredth part*; hence *a tax of one per cent,* or as *interest on money, one per cent,* (reckoned at Rome by the month, therefore = 12 per cent. per annum).

centĭceps -cĭpĭtis, *hundred-headed.*

centĭens or **centĭēs,** *a hundred times.*

centĭmānus -a -um, *hundred-handed.*

cento -ōnis, m. *patchwork*; in war, *coverings to ward off missiles or extinguish fires.*

centum, *a hundred*; also *any indefinitely large number.*

centumgĕmĭnus -a -um, *hundred-fold.*

centumvĭrālis -e, *relating to the centumviri.*

centum vĭri or **centumvĭri** -orum, *a bench of judges dealing with civil suits.*

centuncŭlus -i, m. *a little piece of patchwork or a saddle-cloth.*

centuplex -ĭcis, *a hundred-fold.*

centŭrĭa -ae, f. *a division of* 100; *a company of soldiers; a century, a part of the Roman people, as divided by Servius Tullius.*

centŭrĭātim, *by centuries or companies.*

centŭrĭātus -ūs, m. *a division into companies or centuries; the centurion's office.*

¹centŭrĭo -are, *to divide into centuries*; comitia centuriata, *the assembly in which the whole Roman people voted in their centuries.*

²centŭrĭo -ōnis, m. *commander of a century, centurion.*

centŭrĭōnātus -ūs, m. *an election of centurions.*

cēnŭla -ae, f. *a little meal.*

cenum, see caenum.

cēra -ae, f. *wax; a waxen writing-tablet, wax seal,* or *waxen image.*

cērārĭum -i, n. *a fee for sealing a document.*

cĕrastēs -ae, m. *the horned snake.*

cĕrāsus -i, f. *a cherry-tree or a cherry.*

Cerbĕrus -i, m. *the dog guarding Hades.*

cercōpĭthēcus -i, m. *a kind of ape.*

cercūrus -i, m. *a species of vessel peculiar to Cyprus; a sea-fish.*

cerdo -ōnis, m. *a workman, artisan.*

cĕrebrōsus -a -um, *hot-tempered.*

cĕrebrum -i, n. *the brain; the understanding; hot temper.*

Cĕrēs -ĕris, *the Roman goddess of agriculture.* Transf., *bread, grain, corn.* Adj. **Cĕrĕālis** -e; n. pl. as subst. *the festival of Ceres on April* 10.

cērĕus -a -um, *waxen,* or *resembling wax*; m. as subst., *a wax taper.*

cērintha -ae, f. *the wax flower.*

cĕrīnus -a -um, *wax-coloured*: n. pl. as subst. *wax-coloured garments*.

cerno cernĕre crēvi crētum, *to separate, sift.* Transf., *to distinguish*, with the senses or with the mind; *to decide, resolve, determine.*

cernŭus -a -um, *falling headlong.*

cēro -are, *to smear or cover with wax.*

cērōma -ātis, n. *an ointment of oil and wax used by wrestlers.*

cērōmătĭcus -a -um, *anointed with the ceroma.*

cerrītus -a -um, *frantic, mad.*

certāmen -ĭnis, n. *contest, struggle.*

certātim, adv. *emulously, eagerly.*

certātĭo -onis, f. *contest, rivalry.*

certē and certō, adv. from certus; q.v.

certo -are, *to settle by contest*; hence *to contend, struggle, dispute.*

certus -a -um, adj. *settled, resolved, decided*, of projects and persons; *definite, certain, fixed; sure, to be depended on*; of things as known, *undoubted, sure*; certum scio, *I know for certain*; pro certo habeo, *I feel sure*; of persons *knowing, sure, certain*; certiorem facere, *to inform.* Adv. certē and certō, *certainly, assuredly.*

cērŭla -ae, f. *a little piece of wax.*

cērussa -ae, f. *white lead.*

cērussātus -a -um, *painted with white lead.*

cerva -ae, f. *hind*; poet., *deer.*

cervīcal -ālis, n. *cushion, pillow.*

cervīcŭla -ae, f. *a little neck.*

cervīnus -a -um, *relating to a stag.*

cervix -ĭcis, f. *the nape of the neck, the neck*; dare cervices, *to submit to the executioner.*

cervus -i, m. *stag, deer*; pl., milit., *stakes stuck in the ground as a palisade.*

cespes; see caespes.

cessātĭo -ōnis, f. *delaying, inactivity, laziness.*

cessātor -ōris, m. *one who loiters.*

cessĭo -ōnis, f. *a giving up, a cession.*

cesso -are, *to leave off, cease work, be idle, rest*; of things, *to be left alone, do nothing*; so of land, *to lie fallow.*

cestrosphendŏnē -ēs, f. *engine for hurling stones.*

¹cestus and cestos -i, m. *a girdle.*

²cēstus -us, m; see caestus.

cētārĭum -i, n. *a fish-pond.*

cētārĭus -i, m. *a fishmonger.*

cētĕrōquī or cētĕrōquĭn, *otherwise, else.*

cētĕrus -a -um, *the other, the rest*; usually plur., cētĕri -ae, -a; et cetera, *and so on.* Acc. n. sing. as adv. cētĕrum, *otherwise, moreover, but.*

Cĕthēgus -i, m. C. Cornelius, *a conspirator with Catiline, put to death by Cicero in 63 B.C.*

cētra; see caetra.

cette; see cedo.

cētus -i, m. and cētos n.; plur. cete; *any large sea-creature, such as whale, seal, dolphin.*

ceu, adv., *as, like as*; sometimes *as if.*

Chalcis -ĭdis or -ĭdos, f. *the chief city of Euboea.*

Chaldaei -orum, m. pl. *the Chaldaeans, famous as astrologers.*

chălybēĭus -a -um, *of steel.*

chălybs -ўbis, m. *steel*; an article made of steel, such as *a sword, a horse's bit, the tip of an arrow.*

chānē or channē -ēs, f. *the sea perch.*

Chāos, acc. Chaos, abl. Chao, n. *boundless empty space.* Hence *the lower world*; personified, *Chaos, the father of Night and Erebus*; the *shapeless mass out of which the universe was made.*

chara -ae, f. *an edible root.*

Chărĭtes -um, f. pl. *the Graces*, i.e. *Aglaia, Euphrosyne, and Thalia.*

Chăron -ontis, m. *Charon, who ferried souls over the Styx.*

charta -ae, f. *a leaf of Egyptian papyrus, paper; anything written on paper, a letter, poem, etc.*

chartŭla -ae, f. *a little paper, small piece of writing.*

Chărybdis -is, f. *a whirlpool opposite the rock Scylla.*

Chatti (Catti) -orum, m. *a Germanic people.*

Chauci -orum, m. *a Germanic people on the coast of the North Sea.*

chĕlÿdrus -i, m. *an amphibious snake.*

chĕlys, acc. -yn, f. *the tortoise*; hence, *the lyre made of its shell.*

chĕragra and chiragra -ae, f. *the gout in the hands.*

Cherrŏnēsus and Chersŏnēsus -i, f. *a peninsula*; esp. *of Gallipoli or the Crimea.*

chiliarchēs -ae, and chiliarchus -i, m. *a commander of 1,000 soldiers*; among Persians, *chancellor*, or *prime minister.*

Chimaera -ae, f. *a monster killed by Bellerophon.*

chimaerifer -fĕra -fĕrum, *producing the Chimaera.*

Chios or Chius -i, f. *an island in the Aegean Sea, famous for wine and marble.*

chirogrăphum -i, n. *an autograph, a person's own handwriting.*

chīrŏnŏmos -i, and chīrŏnŏmōn -ontis, m. *a gesticulator, a mime.*

chīrurgīa -ae, f. *surgery.*

chlăm`ydātus -a -um, *dressed in a chlamys.*

chlămys -ўdis, f. *a large upper garment of wool.*

chŏrāgĭum -i, n. *the training and production of a chorus.*

chŏrāgus -i, m. *he who pays for a chorus.*

chŏraulēs -ae, m. *a flute-player, accompanying the chorus.*

chorda -ae, f. *cat-gut*; usually as the *string of a musical instrument.*

chŏrēa -ae, f. *a dance in a ring.*

chŏrēus and chŏrīus -i, m. *the metrical foot afterwards called a trochee.*

chŏrus -i, m. *dance in a circle, choral dance.* Transf., *the persons singing and dancing, the chorus*; hence *a crowd, troop.*

Christus -i, m. *Christ*; **Christiānus** -i, m. *a Christian.*

chrŏmis -is, c. *a sea-fish.*

chrȳsanthus -i, m. *a flower*, perhaps *marigold.*

chrȳsŏlĭthos -i, m. and f. *chrysolite, or topaz.*

chrȳsophrys, acc. -yn. f. *a sea-fish.*

cĭbārĭus -a -um, *relating to food*; n. pl. as subst., *food, rations.* Transf. (*from the food of slaves*), *ordinary, common.*

cĭbātus -ūs, m. *food, nourishment.*

cĭbōrĭum -i, n. *a large drinking-vessel.*

cĭbus -i, m. *food, fodder, nourishment, sustenance.*

cĭcāda -ae, f. *a cicada*, or *tree cricket.*

cĭcātrix -īcis, f. *a scar*; on plants, *a mark of incision*; also a *patch on an old shoe.*

cĭcer -eris, n. *a chick-pea.*

Cĭcĕro -onis, M. Tullius, *Roman Statesman, orator, and writer* (106-43 B.C.); adj. **Cĭcĕrōnĭānus** -a -um.

cĭchŏrēum -i, n. *succory* or *endive.*

cĭcōnĭa -ae, f. *a stork.*

cĭcur -ŭris, *tame.*

cĭcūta -ae, f. *hemlock*; *poison extracted from the hemlock*; *a shepherd's pipe, made of hemlock stalk.*

cĭĕo cĭēre cĭvi cĭtum, *to move, stir, agitate.* Transf., *to give rise to, excite, arouse*; *to summon*; *to call by name.*
Hence partic. **cĭtus** -a -um, *quick, speedy.* Adv. **cĭtō**, *quickly*; citius quam, *sooner than, rather than.*

Cĭlĭcĭa -ae, f. *a region in Asia Minor.*

Cimber -bri, m.; usually pl. **Cimbri**, *the Cimbrians, a German tribe*; adj. **Cimbrĭcus** -a -um.

cīmex -īcis, m. *a bug.*

Cimmĕrĭi -orum, m. pl. (1) *a Thracian people, living on the Dnieper.* (2) *a mythical people, living in eternal darkness.*

cĭnaedus -i, m. *a wanton* or *shameless person.*

[1]**cincinnatus** -a -um, *having curled hair.*

[2]**Cincinnatus** -i, m. *a cognomen in the gens Quinctia.*

cincinnus -i, m. *curled hair, a lock of hair.* Transf., *artificial rhetorical ornament.*

Cincĭus -a -um, *name of a Roman gens.*

cinctūra -ae, f. *a girdle.*

cinctus -ūs, m. *a girding, a way of wearing the toga.* Transf., *a girdle.*

cinctūtus -a -um, *girded.*

cĭnĕfactus -a -um, *turned to ashes.*

cingo cingĕre cinxi cinctum, *to surround* or *equip the head* or *body*; pass., cingi, *to gird oneself*; in gen., *to surround*; esp. *to surround with hostile intent*, or *for protection*; of persons, *to escort, accompany.*

cingŭla -ae, f. *a girdle.*

cingŭlum -i, n. *a girdle, sword-belt.*

cingŭlus -i, m. *a girdle of the earth, zone.*

cĭnĭflo -onis, m. = cinerarius.

cĭnis -ĕris, m. rarely f. *ashes.*

Cinna -ae, m. *a Roman cognomen*, esp. of L. Cornelius Cinna, *supporter of Marius, noted for his cruelty.* Adj. **Cinnānus** -a -um.

cinnămōmum or **cinnămum** -i, n. *cinnamon.*

cippus -i, m. *a pale, stake*; esp. *a tombstone*; plur., milit., *palisades.*

circā. Adv., *around, round about.* Prep. with acc.: of space, *around, near*; of persons, *around* or *with*; of time or number, *about.*

circāmoerĭum -i, n. = pomerium; q.v.

Circē -ēs and -ae, f. *an enchantress, daughter of the Sun*; adj. **Circaeus** -a -um.

Circēïi -orum, m. pl. *a town in Latium.*

circensis -e, *belonging to the circus*; m. pl. as subst. (sc. ludi), *the circus games.*

circĭno -are, *to form into a circle* hence *to fly round.*

circĭnus -i, m. *a pair of compasses.*

circĭtĕr, adv., and prep. with acc., *about.*

circlus = circulus; q.v.

circŭeo; see circumeo.

circŭĭtĭo and **circŭmĭtĭo** -ōnis, f. *a going round, patrol.* Transf., *a roundabout way of speaking.*

circŭĭtus -ūs, m. *a going round in a circle, circuit.* Hence *a roundabout way, circuitous course*; also *compass, circumference, extent*; rhet., *a period.*

circŭlor -ari, dep. *to gather in groups*, or *collect a group around oneself.*

circŭlus (circlus) -i, m. *a circle, circular figure, circuit*; *any circular body*; *a circle* or *group for conversation.*

circum. Adv. *roundabout, around.* Prep. with acc. *round, around, round about, near.*

circŭmăgo -ăgĕre -ēgi -actum. (1) *to turn round*; esp. in the ceremonial manumission of a slave; of time, circumagi or circumagere se, *to pass away, be spent*; of the feelings, *to influence, bring round.* (2) *to drive about from one place to another*; *to distract.*

circŭmăro -are, *to plough round.*

circumcaesūra -ae, f. *the external outline of a body.*

circumcīdo -cīdĕre cīdi -cīsum, *to cut round, to cut, trim.* Transf., *to make less, by cutting, diminish.*
Hence partic. **circumcīsus** -a -um, of places, *abrupt, steep, inaccessible*; of style, *abridged, brief.*

circumclūdo -clūdĕre -clūsi -clūsum, *to shut in, enclose, surround.*

circumcŏlo -ere, *to dwell around, dwell near.*

circumcurso -are, *to run round.*

circumdo -dăre -dĕdi -dătum, *surround.* (1) *to put something round*, with acc. of the thing placed, and dat. of that round which it is placed. (2)

to surround with something, with acc. and abl. (rarely double acc.).

circumdūco -dūcĕre -duxi -ductum, *to lead round, move* or *drive round.* Transf., *to cheat; to extend, amplify.*

circŭmĕo (**circŭĕo**) -ire, -ii or -ivi, circŭitum, *to go round*; milit., *to surround; to go the rounds of, to visit*; hence *to canvass* or *solicit.* Transf., *to cheat, circumvent.*

circŭmĕquĭto -are, *to ride round.*

circumfĕro -ferre -tŭli -lātum, *to carry round, take round*; esp. of the eyes, *to turn all round*; in religion, *to lustrate, purify*, by carrying round consecrated objects. Transf., *to spread*, esp. *to spread news.*

circumflecto -flectĕre -flexi -flexum, *to bend round, turn about.*

circumflo -are, *to blow round.*

circumflŭo -flŭĕre -fluxi -fluxum, *to flow round.* Transf., *to overflow, abound*; with abl., *to abound in.*

circumflŭus -a -um: act., *flowing round, circumfluent*; pass., *flowed round, surrounded by water.*

circumfŏrānĕus -a -um. (1) *round the forum*: aes, *money borrowed from bankers.* (2) *attending at markets.*

circumfundo -fundĕre -fūdi -fūsum. (1) *to pour around*; in pass., or with reflexive, *to be poured round* = *to surround.* (2) act., *to surround, encompass*, and pass., *to be surrounded*; usually with instrumental abl.

circumgĕmo -ĕre, *to growl round.*

circumgesto -are, *to carry round.*

circumgrĕdĭor -grĕdi -gressus, dep., *to go round, travel round.*

circumiăcĕo -ĕre, *to lie round about, adjoin.*

circumicĭo -icĕre -iēci -iectum. (1) *to throw round, put round.* (2) *to surround* one thing with another. Hence partic. **circumiectus** -a -um, *thrown round, so surrounding, adjacent.*

circumiectus -ūs, m. *a surrounding, enclosing.*

circumĭtĭo = circuitio; q.v.

circumlĭgo -are. (1) *to bind round, bind to.* (2) *to bind round with* something.

circumlĭno -lĭnĕre -lĭtum. (1) *to smear one thing over another.* (2) *to besmear with, bedaub*; hence poet., *to cover.*

circumlŭo -lŭĕre, *to wash round, flow round.*

circumlŭvĭo -ōnis, f. *alluvial land.*

circummitto -mittĕre -mīsi -missum, *to send round.*

circummūnĭo -ire, *to wall round, to shut in by lines of circumvallation.*

circummūnītĭo -ōnis, f. *circumvallation.*

circumpădānus -a -um, *near the river Po.*

circumplector -plecti -plexus, dep. *to embrace, enclose, surround.*

circumplĭco -are, *to fold round, wind round.*

circumpōno -pōnĕre -pŏsŭi -pŏsĭtum, *to place* or *put round.*

circumrētĭo -ire, *to enclose in a net, ensnare.*

circumrōdo -rōdĕre -rōsi, *to gnaw round.* Transf., *to slander.*

circumsaepĭo -saepire -saeptum, *to hedge round, enclose.*

circumscindo -ĕre, *to tear off, round, to strip.*

circumscrībo -scrībĕre -scripsi -scriptum, *to describe a circle round, to enclose in a circular line.* Transf., (1) *to confine, define, limit, restrict.* (2) *to set aside, exclude.* (3) *to take in, ensnare, defraud*; vectigalia, *to embezzle.* Hence partic. **circumscriptus** -a -um, as rhet. t. t. *rounded, periodic*; also *concise.* Adv. **circumscriptē.** *in rhetorical periods, fully.*

circumscriptĭo -ōnis, f. *an encircling*; hence *circumference.* Transf., (1) *outline, boundary, limit*; in rhetoric, *a period.* (2) *swindling, defrauding.*

circumscriptor -ōris, m. *a cheat, swindler.*

circumsĕco -sĕcare -sectum *to cut round.*

circumsĕdĕo -sĕdĕre -sēdi -sessum, *to sit round*; esp. *to besiege, beleaguer.*

circumsessĭo -ōnis, f. *encircling, beleaguering.*

circumsĭdo -ĕre, *to besiege.*

circumsĭlĭo -ire, *to leap* or *jump round.*

circumsisto -sistĕre -stĕti or -stĭti, *to stand round, surround.*

circumsŏno -sonare -sonui: transit., *to sound all around* or *to make to resound*; intransit., *to resound, to echo.*

circumsŏnus -a -um, *sounding all around.*

circumspectĭo -ōnis, f. *looking about, circumspection, caution.*

circumspecto -are: intransit., *to look round repeatedly*; transit., *to look round at* or *for.*

¹circumspectus -a -um; see circumspicio.

²circumspectus -ūs, m. *looking round at*; hence *attention to; prospect, view all round.*

circumspĭcĭo -spĭcĕre -spexi -spectum: intransit., *to look round*, esp. *anxiously*; hence *to consider*; transit., *to look round at, survey*; hence *to consider carefully*; also *to look about for, seek for.* Hence partic. **circumspectus** -a -um: pass., of things, *deliberate, well considered*; act., of persons, *circumspect, cautious.*

circumsto -stare -stĕti: intransit, *to stand round* or *in a circle*; partic. as subst., circumstantes, *the bystanders*; transit., *to surround, beleaguer.*

circumstrĕpo -ĕre, *to make a loud noise around.*

circumsurgens -entis, *rising round.*

circumtĕro -tĕrĕre, *to rub against on all sides.*

circumtextus -a -um, *woven all round.*

circumtŏno -tŏnare -tŏnŭi, *to thunder round.*

circumtonsus -a -um, *shorn all round; of discourse, artificial.*

circumvādo -vādĕre -vāsi, *to attack from every side, to surround.*

circumvăgus -a -um, *wandering round, flowing round.*

circumvallo -are, *to blockade, beleaguer.*

circumvectĭo -ōnis, f. *a carrying round of merchandise*: portorium circumvectionis, *transit dues*; in gen., *circuit, revolution.*

circumvector -ari, *to ride or sail round; poet, to go through, describe.*

circumvĕhor -vĕhi -vectus, *to ride or sail round; poet., to describe.*

circumvēlo -are, *to veil round, envelop.*

circumvĕnĭo -vĕnire -vēni -ventum, *to come round, surround, encircle.* Transf., *to beset, assail; to cheat, defraud.*

circumvertor (-vortor) -verti, *to turn oneself round.*

circumvestĭo -ire, *to clothe all round.*

circumvŏlĭto -are, *to fly round, rove about.*

circumvŏlo -are, *to fly round.*

circumvolvo -volvĕre -volvi -vŏlūtum, *to roll round;* usually pass., *to revolve.*

circus -i, m. *a ring, circle, orbit:* candens, *the milky way;* also *an oval course for races.*

ciris -is, f. *a bird, into which Scylla was transformed.*

cirrātus -a -um, *curly-haired.*

Cirrha -ae, f. *a city near Delphi, sacred to Apollo;* adj. **Cirrhaeus** -a -um.

cirrus -i, m. *a lock, or ringlet of hair; the fringe of a garment.*

cis, prep., with acc., *on this side of, within.*

Cisalpīnus -a -um, *on this (the Roman) side of the Alps.*

cisĭum -i, n. *a light two-wheeled vehicle.*

Cisrhenānus -a -um, *on this (the Roman) side of the Rhine.*

cista -ae, f. *a chest, box.*

cistella -ae, f. *a little chest or box.*

cisterna -ae, f. *reservoir, cistern.*

cistŏphŏrus -i, m. *an Asiatic coin.*

cistŭla -ae, f. *a little chest or box.*

cĭtātus -a -um, partic. from ²cito; q.v.

cĭtĕr -tra -trum, *on this side;* usually compar., **cĭtĕrĭor** -us, genit. -oris, *on this side, nearer;* superl. **cĭtĭmus** -a -um, *nearest.*

cĭthăra -ae, f. *a stringed instrument, lyre, lute.*

cĭthărista -ae, m. *a player on the cithara.*

cĭthăristrĭa -ae, f. *a female player on the cithara.*

cĭthărĭzo -are, *to play the cithara.*

cĭthăroedus -i, m. *one who plays the cithara with voice accompanying.*

¹cĭtō, adv. from cieo; q.v.

²cĭto -are (1) *to put in motion, excite, start up.* (2) *to summon, call forward;* esp. *for legal, political or military purposes; hence to appeal to, point to authorities, etc.*

Hence partic. **cĭtātus** -a -um,

quick, speedy: citato equo, *at full gallop.* Adv. **cĭtātim.**

citrā (abl. f. from citer). Adv. *on this side, nearer.* Prep. with acc., *on this side of, nearer than; of time, since;* hence, in gen., *short of, without.*

cĭtrĕus -a -um, *belonging to the citrus-tree or citron-tree.*

citrō, adv. found only with ultro: ultro (et) citro, *up and down, hither and thither.*

citrus -i, m. (1) *the citrus, a kind of African cypress.* (2) *the citron-tree.*

cĭtus -a -um, partic. from cieo; q.v.

cīvīcus -a -um, *relating to a citizen, civic*: civica (corona), *the civic crown, awarded to one who had saved the life of a Roman in war.*

cīvīlis -e, *relating to a citizen, civic, civil;* esp. ius civile, *the Roman civil law or civil rights; befitting a citizen;* hence, *popular, affable, courteous; relating to public life or the state.* Adv. **cīvīlĭter**, *like a citizen; politely.*

cīvīlĭtās -ātis, f. (1) *the science of politics.* (2) *politeness, civility.*

cīvis -is, c. *citizen;* also *a fellow citizen*: under a king, *a subject.*

cīvĭtās -ātis, f.: abstr., *citizenship;* concr., *a union of citizens, state, commonwealth; the inhabitants of a city, townsfolk;* (rarely) *a city, town.*

clādēs -is, f. *destruction;* in gen., *disaster, injury, defeat.*

clam. Adv., *secretly, in secret*: esse, *to remain unknown.* Prep. with acc. or abl., *unknown to, without the knowledge of.*

clāmātor -ōris, m. *a shouter, noisy speaker.*

clāmĭto -are, *to cry aloud, shout violently.*

clāmo -are, *to call, shout, cry aloud;* with object, *to call to or upon a person, to shout something;* sometimes *to proclaim, declare.*

clāmor -ōris, m. *a loud shouting, cry;* poet., *of lifeless things, echo, reverberation.*

clāmōsus -a -um: act., *noisy, clamorous* pass., *filled with noise.*

clancŭlum. Adv. *secretly, in secret.* Prep. with acc., *unknown to.*

clandestīnus -a -um, *secret, clandestine;* Adv. **clandestīnō.**

clangor -ōris, m. *sound, clang, noise.*

clārĕo -ēre, *to be bright, to shine.* Transf., *to be evident; to be distinguished.*

clāresco clārescĕre clārŭi, *to become clear to the senses.* Transf., *to become evident; to become illustrious.*

clārĭgo -are, *to demand satisfaction,* used of the Fetialis.

clārĭsŏnus -a -um, *clearly sounding.*

clārĭtās -ātis, f. *clearness, brightness.* Transf., *clearness to the mind, plainness; fame, celebrity.*

clārĭtūdo -inis, f. *clearness, brilliancy.* Transf., *fame, celebrity.*

clāro -are, *to make bright or clear.* Transf., *to make plain to the mind; to make illustrious.*

clārus -a -um, *bright, clear, distinct*; poet., *of the wind, making clear, bringing fair weather.* Transf., to the understanding, *clear, evident, plain*; of reputation, *illustrious, distinguished*; in bad sense, *notorious.* Hence adj. **clārē**, *clearly, brightly, distinctly; illustriously.*

classiārius -a -um, *of the fleet*; m. pl. as subst., *marines.*

classicus -a -um. (1) *relating to the different classes of Roman citizens.* (2) *relating to the armed forces, esp. to the fleet*: m. pl. as subst., *marines*: n. sing. as subst., *the signal for battle or the trumpet giving this.*

classis -is, f. *a group as summoned, a division, class.* (1) *one of the classes into which Servius Tullius divided the Roman people.* (2) *the armed forces, esp. the fleet.* (3) in gen., *a class, group.*

clatri -orum, m. pl., *trellis, grating.*

claudĕo -ēre and **claudo** -ēre, *to limp, halt, be lame.*

claudicātio -ōnis, f. *a limping.*

claudīco -are, *to limp, be lame.* Transf., *to incline, be deflected; to halt, waver.*

Claudius (**Clōdius**) -a -um, *the name of two Roman gentes; esp. of the emperor Claudius* (10 B.C.-A.D. 54). Adj. **Claudiānus** -a -um, **Claudiālis** -e.

¹**claudo** claudĕre clausi clausum (and **clūdo**) *to close, shut up, make inaccessible*; of military positions, *to blockade, invest*; of prisoners, etc., *to shut in, confine.* Transf., *to conclude*; agmen, *to bring up the rear.* Hence partic. **clausus** -a -um, of character, *close, reserved*; n. as subst., *an enclosed place.*

²**claudo** = claudeo; q.v.

claudus -a -um, *limping, lame.* Transf., *crippled, defective*; poet. carmina alterno versu, *elegiac verse.*

claustrum -i, n., gen. plur., *a means of closing or shutting in: a bolt, bar; an enclosure, prison, den; a barricade, dam, fortress*; milit., *the key to a position.*

clausŭla -ae, f. *end, conclusion*: in rhetoric, *the close of a period.*

clāva -ae, f. *staff or cudgel.*

clāvārium -i, n. *an allowance to soldiers for buying shoe-nails.*

clāvīcŭla -ae, f. *the tendril by which the vine clings to its prop.*

¹**clāvĭger** -gĕri, m. *the club-bearer*, of Hercules.

²**clāvĭger** -gĕri, m. *the key-bearer*, of Janus.

clāvis -is, f. *a key*: claves adimere uxori, *to separate from one's wife.* Transf., *a stick for trundling a hoop.*

clāvus -i, m. (1) *a nail, spike.* (2) *a tiller, helm, rudder.* (3) *a stripe of purple on the tunic, worn broad by senators, narrow by knights.*

clēmens -entis, *mild, kind, merciful*; adv. **clēmenter**, *gentle.*

clēmentia -ae, f. *mildness, gentleness, mercy.*

Clĕŏpatra -ae, f. *the queen of Egypt and mistress of Antony, defeated with him at Actium.*

clēpo clēpere clepsi cleptum, *to steal*; se, *to conceal oneself.*

clepsydra -ae, f. *a water clock, esp. as used to measure the time allotted to orators.*

cliens -entis, m. *a client, dependent on a patronus* (q.v.); in gen., *a vassal or ally.*

clienta -ae, f. *a female client.*

clientēla -ae, f. *clientship, the relation between client and patron*; hence, in gen., *dependence.* Transf. (gen. plur.) *clients.*

clīnāmen -īnis, n. *inclination, swerving aside.*

clīnātus -a -um, *inclined, leaning.*

Clīo -ūs, f. *the Muse of history.*

clĭpĕātus -a -um, *armed with a shield*; m. pl. as subst., *soldiers with shields.*

clĭpĕus -i, m. and **clĭpĕum** -i, n. *a (round) shield.* Transf., *the disk of the sun; a medallion portrait.*

clītellae -arum, f. pl. *a pack-saddle, pair of panniers.*

clīvōsus -a -um, *hilly, steep.*

clīvus -i, m. *a slope, rise, gradient.*

clŏāca -ae, f. *a sewer, drain.*

Clŏācina -ae, f. *the cleanser, surname of Venus.*

Clōdius = Claudius; q.v.

Clōthō, f. *the spinner, one of the Parcae.*

clŭĕo -ēre, *I hear myself called, am named.*

clūnis -is, m. and f. *the buttocks.*

Clūsium -i, n. *a town of Etruria*; adj. **Clūsīnus** -a -um.

Clўtaemnestra -ae, f. *wife of Agamemnon who killed her husband, and was killed by her son Orestes.*

Cnīdus (-os), or **Gnīdus** (-os), -i, f. *a town in Caria, famous for the worship of Venus*; adj. **Cnīdius** -a -um.

Cnossus = Gnossus; q.v.

cŏācervātio -ōnis, f. *a heaping up.*

cŏācervo -are, *to heap up, accumulate.*

cŏācesco -ācescĕre -ācŭi, *to become sour.*

cŏacto -are, *to compel.*

cŏactor -ōris, m. *a collector of money*; coactores agminis, *the rear-guard.*

cŏactū, abl. sing. m. *by force, under compulsion.*

cŏactum -i, n. subst. from cogo; q.v.

cŏaedĭfĭco -are, *to build on.*

cŏaequo -are, *to level, make even.*

cŏagmentātio -ōnis, *a connexion, binding together.*

cŏagmento -are, *to join together*; pacem, *to conclude.*

cŏagmentum -i, n. *a joining joint.*

cŏagŭlum -i, n. *rennet or curds.*

cŏalesco -ālescĕre -ālŭi -ālĭtum, *to grow together; to take root, grow*; hence *to become established or firm.*

cŏangusto -are, *to limit, confine.*

cŏarcto, etc. = coarto, etc.; q.v.

cŏargŭo -ŭĕre -ŭi, *to show clearly,*

demonstrate fully; esp. *to prove wrong* or *guilty*.

cŏartātĭo -ōnis, f. *a confining in a small space.*

cŏarto -are, *to confine, draw together*; of discourse, *to compress*; of time, *to shorten.*

coccĭnātus -a -um, *clad in scarlet.*

coccĭnus -a -um, *scarlet-coloured*; n. pl. as subst., *scarlet clothes.*

coccum -i, n. *the berry of the scarlet oak*; hence *scarlet dye*; sometimes *scarlet cloth* or *garments.*

coclĕa (cochlĕa) -ae, f. *a snail* or *snail-shell.*

coclĕāre (cochlĕāre) -is, n. and coclĕārĭum -i, n. *a spoon.*

Cocles, *Roman cognomen*, esp. of Horatius Cocles, *the Roman who defended the bridge over the Tiber against Porsenna.*

coctĭlis -a, *baked*; muri, *made of burnt brick.*

Cōcȳtŏs and -us, -i, m. *a river of the lower world.*

cōda = cauda; q.v.

cōdex (older caudex) -dĭcis, m. *the trunk of a tree*; as a term of abuse, *dolt, blockhead.* Transf., *a book (made up of wooden tablets, covered with wax)*; esp. *an account-book, ledger.*

cōdĭcārĭus (caudĭcārĭus) -a -um, *made of tree trunks.*

cōdĭcillī -orum, m. *little trunks, logs.* Transf., *small tablets for memoranda*; hence *a letter, petition, codicil, rescript.*

coel-; see cael-.

cŏĕmo -ēmĕre -ēmi -emptum, *to buy up.*

cŏemptĭo -ōnis, f. *a form of marriage; a fictitious sale of an estate.*

coen-; see caen-.

cŏĕo -ire -ĭi -ĭvi -ĭtum, *to go* or *come together, assemble*; of enemies, *to engage*; of friends, etc., *to unite, combine*; transit., societatem coire, *to form an alliance*; of things, *to unite, come together*; of blood, *to curdle*; of water, *to freeze.*

cŏepĭo cŏepĕre, cŏepi cŏeptum (only the perfect-stem tenses are class.; see incipio), *to begin, commence.* N. of partic. as subst. cŏeptum -i, *a thing begun* or *undertaken.*

cŏepto -are, *to begin* or *undertake (eagerly).*

cŏeptus -ūs, m. (only in plur.), *a beginning.*

cŏerceo -cēre -cŭi -cĭtum, *to enclose, shut in, confine, restrain*; vitem, *to prune.*

cŏercĭtĭo -ōnis, f. *confining, restraint*; hence *punishment.*

cŏerŭlĕus = caeruleus; q.v.

cŏetus (cŏĭtus) -ūs, m. *meeting together, union, assemblage.*

cōgĭtātĭo -ōnis, f. *thinking, conception, reflection, reasoning*: sometimes a particular *thought, idea* or *intention.*

cōgĭto -are, *to turn over in the mind, to think, reflect*; sometimes *to intend, plan.*

Hence partic. cōgĭtātus -a -um, *considered, deliberate*: n. pl. as subst. *thoughts, reflections, ideas.* Adv. cōgĭtātē, *thoughtfully.*

cognātĭo -ōnis, f. *relationship, connexion by blood*; meton., *persons related, kindred, family*: in gen., *connexion, agreement, resemblance.*

cognātus -a -um, *related, connected by blood*; m. and f. as subst. *a relation either on the father's* or *mother's side.* Transf., *akin, similar.*

cognĭtĭo -ōnis, f. *getting to know, study, knowledge, acquaintance; recognition; legal inquiry, investigation*; in plur., *ideas, conceptions.*

cognĭtor -ōris, m. *a knower*; legal, *a witness* or *an attorney*; in gen., *a supporter.*

cognōmĕn -ĭnis, n. *a surname, family name.*

cognōmentum -i, n. *a surname, a name.*

cognōmĭnātus -a -um, *of the same meaning*; verba, *synonyms.*

cognōmĭnis -e, *having the same name.*

cognosco -gnoscĕre -gnōvi -gnĭtum, *to become acquainted with, get to know, learn*; in perf. tenses, *to know*; *to know again, recognize*; of judges, *to examine, hear, decide.*

Hence partic. cognĭtus -a -um, *known, proved.*

cōgo cōgĕre cŏĕgi cŏactum, *to bring, drive*, or *draw to one point, to collect*; *to bring close together, compress*: of liquids, etc. *to thicken, curdle*; milit., agmen cogere, *to bring up the rear.* Transf., *to restrict, confine*; *to compel.*

Hence partic., cŏactus, *constrained*: n. as subst., *thick cloth, felt.*

cŏhaerentĭa -ae, f. *coherence.*

cŏhaerĕo -haerēre -haesi -haesum: of a whole, *to cohere, hold together*; of one thing (or person), *to cling, adhere, be connected to* another.

cŏhaeresco -haerescĕre -haesi, *to hold together.*

cŏhērēs -ēdis, m. *a coheir.*

cŏhĭbĕo -ēre -ŭi -ĭtum, *to hold in, hold together*: hence *to confine, restrain, hold back, repress.*

cŏhŏnesto -are, *to do honour to.*

cŏhorresco -horrescĕre -horrŭi, *to shudder* or *shiver.*

cŏhors -tis, f. *an enclosure, yard.* Transf., *a troop, company, throng*; milit., *a cohort, the tenth part of a legion*; praetoria cohors, *the retinue of the governor of a province.*

cŏhortātĭo -ōnis, f. *exhortation, encouragement.*

cŏhortor -ari, dep. *to encourage, incite, exhort.*

cŏĭtĭo -ōnis, f. *a coming together, meeting*; *a faction, coalition, conspiracy.*

cŏĭtus -us, see coetus.

cŏlăphus -i, m. *a cuff, box on the ear.*

Colchis -ĭdis, f. *Colchis, a country on the Black Sea*; adj. Colchĭcus and

Colchus -a -um; f. adj. **Colchis** -ĭdis.

cōlĕus -i; see culeus.

cōlĭphĭa (**cōlўphĭa**) -orum, n. a food used by athletes.

cōlis = caulis; q.v.

coll-; see also conl-.

Collātĭa -ae, f. a town in Latium; adj. **Collātīnus** -a -um.

collīnus -a -um, hilly, relating to a hill: porta Collina, a gate of Rome near the Quirinal Hill.

collis -is, m. hill, high ground.

collum -i, n. (**collus** -i, m.) neck.

collўbus -i, m. exchange of money, or rate of exchange.

collўrium -i, n. eye-salve.

cōlo cōlĕre cōlŭi cultum, to cultivate, till, tend; to dwell in, inhabit a place; in gen., to take care of, attend to. foster, honour, worship, court. Hence partic. **cultus** -a -um, cultivated, tilled, planted; n. pl. as subst., cultivated land. Transf., physically, tidy, well-dressed, smart; mentally, refined. Adv. **cultē**, elegantly.

cōlŏcāsĭa -orum, n. pl. the Egyptian bean.

cōlōna -ae, f. a country-woman.

cōlōnĭa -ae, f. a farm, estate; a colony; meton., colonists.

cōlōnĭcus -a -um, relating to agriculture or to a colony.

cōlōnus -i, m. a farmer, sometimes a tenant farmer; a colonist, inhabitant of a colony.

cŏlor (**cŏlos**) -ōris, m. colour, tint, hue; esp. complexion; sometimes beautiful complexion, beauty. Transf., outward show, external appearance; cast, character, tone; an artful excuse.

cŏlōro -are, to colour; partic. **cŏlōrātus** -a -um, coloured: of complexion, tanned, dark.

cŏlossēus and **cŏlossĭcus** -a -um, colossal, gigantic.

cŏlossus -i, m. a colossus, statue larger than life; esp. that of Apollo at Rhodes.

cŏlŭber -bri, m. serpent, snake.

cŏlubra -ae, f. female serpent.

cŏlubrĭfer -fĕra -fĕrum, snake-bearing, snaky-haired (of Medusa).

cōlum -i, n. colander, sieve, strainer.

cŏlumba -ae, f. a pigeon, dove.

cŏlumbīnus -a -um, belonging to a pigeon.

cŏlumbus -i, m. a male dove or pigeon.

cŏlŭmella -ae, f. a little column.

cŏlŭmen -ĭnis, n. a height, summit, ridge; of buildings, roof, gable. Transf., chief, summit, crown; support, pillar.

cŏlumna -ae, f. a pillar, column; columnae, pillars as signs of book-sellers' shops in Rome; columnae Herculis, the pillars of Hercules. Transf., a support, pillar of the state; a water-spout.

cŏlumnārĭum -i, n. a tax on pillars.

cŏlumnārĭus, a rascal, thief.

cŏlurnus -a -um, of hazel-wood.

cŏlus -i and -ūs, f. or m., a distaff.

cŏma -ae, f. the hair of the head. Transf., leaves; rays of light.

cŏmans -antis, hairy; galea, crested; stella, a comet.

cŏmātus -a -um, hairy; Gallia Comata, a name for Transalpine Gaul: comata silva, in full leaf.

¹combĭbo -bībĕre -bĭbi, to drink in, suck up.

²combĭbo -ōnis, m. a comrade in drinking.

combūro -ūrĕre -ussi -ustum, to burn up; hence to ruin or consume.

cŏmĕdo -esse -ēdi -ēsum or -estum, to eat up, consume; of property, to waste, squander.

cŏmes -ĭtis, c. a fellow-traveller; hence a companion, comrade; sometimes attendant; in plur., comites, retinue.

cŏmētēs -ae, m. a comet.

cōmĭcus -a -um, of comedy, comic; esp. represented in comedy. M. as subst. an actor in comedy or writer of comedy. Adv. **cōmĭcē**, in the manner of comedy.

cŏmĭnus=comminus; q.v.

cōmis -e, courteous, kind, friendly, obliging; adv. **cōmĭter**.

cōmissābundus -a -um, revelling, rioting.

cōmissātĭo -ōnis, f. a revel, riotous procession.

cōmissātor -ōris, m. a reveller.

cōmissor -ari, dep. to revel.

cōmĭtās -ātis, f. courtesy, friendliness, civility.

cŏmĭtātus -ūs, m. train, retinue, following.

cŏmĭter, adv. from comis; q.v.

cŏmĭtĭa; see comitium.

cŏmĭtĭālis -e, relating to the comitia.

cŏmĭtĭātus -ūs, m. the assembly of the people in the comitia.

cŏmĭtĭum -i, n. a place of assembly, esp. one in the forum at Rome; plur. **cŏmĭtĭa**, the assembly of the Roman people for the election of magistrates, etc.; hence elections.

cŏmĭto -are, to accompany: esp. as partic. **cŏmĭtātus** -a -um, accompanied.

cŏmĭtor -ari, dep. to attend, accompany, follow.

commăcŭlo -are, to pollute.

commănĭpŭlāris -is, m. a soldier belonging to the same company.

commĕātus -ūs, m., free passage, going and coming; milit., leave of absence, furlough; also (often plur.) supply of provisions, food, forage.

commĕdĭtor -ari, dep. to practise, represent.

commĕmĭni -isse, to remember fully.

commĕmŏrābĭlis -e, worthy of mention, memorable.

commĕmŏrātĭo -ōnis, f. reminding, mention.

commĕmŏro -are, to call to mind, recollect; to remind another, so to mention, relate, recount.

commendābĭlis -e, commendable, praiseworthy.

commendātīcĭus -a -um, *giving recommendation.*

commendātĭo -ōnis, f. *recommendation; that which recommends, excellence.*

commendātŏr -ōris, m. and **commendātrix** -īcis, f., *one that commends.*

commendo -are, *to commit to the care or protection of anyone.* Hence, in gen., *to commit; to recommend; to set off, render agreeable.*

commensus, partic. of commetior; q.v.

commentārĭŏlum -i, n. *a short treatise.*

commentārĭus -i, m. and **commentārĭum** -i, n. *a memorandum, note-book;* as the title of a book, *a memoir* (usually plur.); legal, *a brief.*

commentātĭo -ōnis, f. *reflection, careful consideration; practice.*

commentīcĭus -a -um, *invented, fictitious.*

¹**commentor** -ari, dep. *to consider thoroughly; to practise, prepare; to invent, compose, write.*

²**commentor** -ōris, m. *an inventor.*

commĕo -are, *to go up and down, come and go.*

commercĭum -i, n. *trade, commerce;* meton. *the right to trade,* or *an article of traffic, merchandise,* or *a place of trade, depot.* Hence in gen., *intercourse, communication.*

commercor -ari, dep. *to buy up.*

commĕrĕo -ēre (also **commereor,** dep.) *to deserve fully; to commit a fault.*

commētĭor -mētiri -mensus, dep. *to measure:* sometimes *to measure one thing against another, compare.*

commĕto -are, *to go frequently.*

commigro -are, *to move in a body, migrate.*

commīlĭtĭum -i, n. *companionship in war or military service;* in gen., *fellowship.*

commīlĭto -ōnis, m. *a fellow-soldier.*

comminātĭo -ōnis, f. *threatening, threat.*

commingo -mingĕre -minxi -mictum, *to make water on, defile.*

commĭniscor -mīnisci -mentus, dep. *to think out, contrive, invent.* Perf. partic. in passive sense, **commentus** -a -um, *feigned, invented;* n. as subst. **commentum** -i, n. *a fiction, invention, contrivance.*

commĭnor -ari, dep. *to threaten.*

commĭnŭo -ŭĕre -ŭi -ūtum, *to make small, break up, diminish, weaken.*

commĭnus, *hand to hand,* esp. *in close combat;* in gen., *close up, close at hand.*

commiscĕo -miscēre -miscŭi -mixtum, *to mix together, mix up.*

commĭsĕrātĭo -ōnis, f. *pity;* rhet. *the exciting of pity.*

commĭsĕresco -ĕre, *to pity.*

commĭsĕror -ari, dep. *to pity, bewail;* of a speaker, *to excite pity.*

commissĭo -ōnis, f. *a setting together:* hence *the start of games, contests,* etc.

commissūra -ae, f. *a joining together, connexion, joint.*

committo -mittĕre -mīsi -um.miss (1) *to unite, connect, combine;* esp. *to bring together in a contest, to match:* hence *to compare.* (2) *to begin, set on foot, initiate:* with ut and the subj., *to bring it about that;* esp. of crimes, etc., *to commit, perpetrate,* and of penalties, *to incur.* (3) *to entrust, commit,* esp. with reflex. N. of partic. as subst. **commissum** -i. *an undertaking; a crime, fault; a trust, secret.*

commŏdĭtās -ātis, f. *proportion, fitness;* hence *a fit occasion,* also *convenience, advantage;* of persons, *kindness.*

commŏdo -are, *to make fit, adapt;* hence *to adapt oneself to a person, to please, oblige, serve;* with acc. *to furnish, lend, give.*

commŏdus -a -um, *to measure, in full, complete;* hence *proper, fit, appropriate;* of persons, character, etc., *friendly, obliging, pleasant.* N. as subst. **commŏdum** -i, *suitable time, opportunity, convenience; use, advantage, interest; remuneration; loan.* N. acc. as adv. **commŏdum,** *at the right time, opportunely; just then.* Adv. **commŏde,** *rightly, properly, fitly; pleasantly, comfortably, kindly.*

commōlĭor -iri, dep. *to set in motion.*

commŏnĕfācĭo -fācĕre -fēci -factum, *to remind, warn a person,* or *to call to mind a thing.*

commŏnĕo -ēre, *to remind, warn a person,* or *to call to mind a thing.*

commonstro -are, *to show fully.*

commŏrātĭo -ōnis, f. *delaying, lingering.*

commŏror -ari, dep. *to linger, stay;* transit., *to delay.*

commōtĭo -ōnis, *violent movement, excitement.*

commŏvĕo -mŏvēre -mōvi -mōtum, *to move violently, shake, disturb, carry about* or *away;* nummum, *to employ in commerce;* esp. of the mind or passions, *to excite, influence, upset;* of abstract things, *to start up, produce cause.*

Hence partic. **commōtus** -a -um, *insecure, unsteady; excited, upset.*

commūnĭcātĭo -ōnis, f. *communicating, imparting.*

commūnĭco -are (1) *to share out, give a share in;* hence *to communicate, impart a matter;* without object, *to take counsel, confer with a person.* (2) *to join, unite.* (3) *to take a share, participate.*

¹**commūnĭo** -ire, *to fortify thoroughly.*

²**commūnĭo** -ōnis, f. *sharing, mutual participation.*

commūnis -e, *shared, common, universal, public;* loca, *public places;* loci, *commonplaces;* of persons, *approachable, affable.* N. as subst. **commūnĕ,** *common property,* esp. *in plur.; state, commonwealth;* **in commūne,** *for the public good,* also *in general.* Adv. **commūnĭter,** *jointly, generally.*

commūnĭtās -ātis, f. *community, fellowship; sense of fellowship, affability.*

commurmŭror -ari, dep. *to mutter, murmur.*

commūtābĭlis -e, *changeable.*

commūtātus -ūs, m. *change, alteration.*

commūto -are, *to change, alter; to exchange, barter, interchange.*

cōmo cōmĕre compsi comptum, *to put together, make tidy, arrange, adorn;* esp. of the hair.
  Hence partic. **comptus** -a -um, *formed, framed; adorned, neat.*

cōmoedĭa -ae, f. *comedy.*

cōmoedus, *comic;* m. as subst., *a comic actor.*

cōmōsus -a -um, *hairy;* of plants, *leafy.*

compactĭo -ōnis, f. *joining together.*

compactum or **compectum** -i, n. *an agreement.*

compāgēs -is, f. *a joining together, connexion;* hence either *something that joins, a joint, seam,* or *something joined together, a structure.*

compāgo -ĭnis, f. *a joining together.*

compār -păris: as subst., *an equal, companion, mate;* as adj. *like, similar.*

compărābĭlis -e, *capable of comparison, comparable.*

¹compărātĭo -onis, f. *preparing, providing.*

²compărātĭo -onis, f. *a putting together;* hence, *comparison.*

compărātīvus -a -um, *relating to comparison, comparative.*

comparco (**comperco**) -parcĕre -parsi or -persi, *to scrape together, save up.*

compārĕo -pārēre -pārŭi *to appear, be visible; to be present, be in existence.*

¹compăro -are, *to prepare, get ready, provide;* hence *to arrange, settle.*

²compăro -are, *to couple together,* esp. for a contest, *to match.* Transf., *to liken, compare.*

compasco -pascĕre -pastum, *to feed* (cattle) *together.*

compascŭus -a -um, *of common pasturage.*

compellātĭo -ōnis, f. *accosting, rebuking.*

¹compello -pellĕre -pŭli -pulsum, *to drive together, collect; to force, compel.*

²compello -are, *to address, accost;* esp. *to reproach, rebuke;* legal, *to accuse before a court.*

compendĭārĭus -a -um *short;* f. and n. as subst., *a short cut.*

compendĭum -i, n. *saving, profit, advantage; shortening, abbreviation;* compendi facere, *to make short;* in plur. *short ways, short cuts.*

compensātĭo -ōnis, f. *balancing, compensation.*

compenso -are, *to weight together, balance.*

comperco = comparco; q.v.

compĕrendĭnātĭo -ōnis, f. and **compĕrendĭnātus** -ūs, m. *a putting off to the next day but one.*

compĕrendĭno -are, *to remand to the next day but one.*

complector -plecti -plexus, dep. *to embrace, surround, encompass.* Transf., *to hold fast, master; to attach oneself to, esteem;* of the mind, *to embrace, grasp, comprehend; to unite in oneself, to include.*

complēmentum -i, n. *a complement.*

complĕo -plēre -plēvi -plētum, *to fill up;* milit., *to man,* or *to bring up to strength;* of a sum, *to make up;* of fate, etc., *to fulfil;* of a task, *to finish.*
  Hence partic. **complētus** -a -um, *perfect, complete.*

complexĭo -ōnis, f. *connexion, combination;* in rhetoric, *a summary* or *a period;* in logic, *the statement of a syllogism* or *a dilemma.*

complexus -ūs, m. of persons, *embrace, grasp,* either in love or in combat; of things, *compass* or *connexion.*

complĭco -are *to fold together;* complicata notio, *confused, intricate.*

complōrātĭo -ōnis, f. and **complōrātus** -ūs, m. *lamentation.*

complōro -are, *to bewail, lament.*

complūres, -ĭum, *several.*

complŭvĭum -i, n. *roofless space in the centre of a Roman house.*

compōno -pōnĕre -pŏsŭi -pŏsĭtum. (1) *to put together;* esp. of unlike persons or things, either *to match as opponents,* or *to compare.* (2) *to make up a whole, compose.* (3) *to put in place, arrange, settle;* of enemies, *to reconcile.*
  Hence partic. **compŏsĭtus** -a -um. *constructed, put together; arranged in order, settled;* hence *adapted* to a purpose. Adv. **compŏsĭtē**, *in an orderly way.*

comporto -are, *to bring together, collect.*

compŏs -pŏtis, *having control of, possessed of, sharing in.*

compŏsĭtĭo -ōnis, f. *putting together;* of opponents, *matching; composing, compounding; orderly arrangement, settlement.*

compŏsĭtor -ōris, m. *an arranger, adjuster.*

compŏsĭtūra -ae, f. *connexion, joining.*

compŏsĭtus -a -um, partic. from compono; q.v.

compōtātĭo -ōnis, f. *drinking party.*

compōtor -ōris, m. and **compōtrix** -īcis, f. *a drinking-companion.*

compransor -ōris, m. *a dinner companion.*

comprĕcātĭo -ōnis, f. *(common) supplication.*

comprĕcor -ari, dep. *to pray to* or *for, supplicate.*

comprĕhendo -prĕhendere -prĕhendi -prĕhensum and **comprendo** -prendĕre -prendi -prensum, *to grasp; to take together, unite;* hence *to embrace, include; to take firmly, seize;* ignem, *to catch fire;* often of persons, *to capture, arrest;* of criminals, *to catch red-handed.* Transf., *to comprehend, perceive.*

comprĕhensĭbĭlis -e, *comprehensible.*

comprĕhensĭo -ōnis, f. (1) *a taking together, uniting;* rhet., *a period.* (2) *seizing, arrest.* Transf., *comprehending, comprehension.*

comprendo = comprehendo; q.v.

compressĭo -ōnis, f. *an embrace; compression of style, conciseness.*

compressū, abl. sing. m. *by pressing together; by embracing.*

comprĭmo -prĭmĕre -pressi -pressum, *to press together; to press tightly; hence to embrace; to check, restrain, suppress.* Hence compar. adv. **compressius,** *more (or rather) concisely.*

comprŏbātĭo -ōnis, f. *approval.*

comprŏbātŏr -ōris, m. *one who approves.*

comprŏbo -are (1) *to approve fully.* (2) *to confirm, prove, establish.*

comprōmissum -i, n. *reference to arbitrator.*

comprōmitto -mittĕre -mīsi -missum, *to agree to refer a cause to arbitration.*

¹**comptus** -a -um, partic. from como; q.v.

²**comptus** -ūs, m. *a head-dress; a band, tie.*

compungo -pungĕre -punxi -punctum, *to prick, puncture;* hence *to tattoo.*

compŭto -are, *to reckon together, calculate, compute.*

computresco -ĕre, *to rot, putrefy.*

Cōmum -i, n. *a lake-side town in Cisalpine Gaul (now Como).*

cōnāmen -mĭnis, n. *effort, endeavour;* concr., *a support.*

cōnātum -i, n. *an undertaking.*

cōnātus -ūs, m. *an exertion, effort;* sometimes *impulse, inclination; an undertaking.*

concaedēs -ium, f. pl. *a barricade of trees.*

concălĕfăcĭo -făcĕre -fēci -factum (pass. **concălĕfĭo**) *to warm thoroughly.*

concălesco -călescĕre -călŭi, *to become thoroughly warm.*

concallesco -callescĕre -callŭi, *to become thoroughly hard;* hence *to become practised or callous.*

concăvo -are, *to hollow out, make concave.*

concăvus -a -um, *hollow, vaulted, arched, concave;* aqua, *swelling.*

concēdo -cēdĕre -cessi -cessum: intransit., *to retire, withdraw;* concedere vita, *to die;* hence *to yield, submit, give way to,* with dat.; concedere naturae, *to die a natural death;* transit., *to yield, grant, give up;* of faults, *to pardon, overlook;* of actions, *to permit, allow.*

concĕlebro -are. *to visit often, or in large companies; to pursue an occupation eagerly; to celebrate a festivity; also to praise, extol a person or thing.*

concēnātĭo -ōnis, f. *supping together.*

concentĭo -ōnis, f. *singing together, harmony.*

concentus -ūs, m. *singing together, harmony;* hence *agreement, unity, concord.*

conceptĭo -ōnis, f. *conception, becoming pregnant; drawing up of legal formulae.*

conceptus -ūs, m. *conceiving, pregnancy; collecting, or a collection.*

concerpo -cerpĕre -cerpsi -cerptum, *to tear in pieces.* Transf., *to abuse.*

concertātĭo -ōnis, f. *contest, strife, dispute.*

concertātŏr -ōris, m. *a rival.*

concertātōrĭus -a -um, *relating to a contest.*

concerto -are, *to strive eagerly.*

concessĭo -ōnis, f. *yielding, granting.*

concessū, abl. sing. m. *by permission, with leave.*

concha -ae, f. *a sea-shell;* hence *a shell-fish,* esp. *mussel or pearl-oyster* or *the fish yielding purple dye;* poet., *a pearl or purple dye.* Transf., *a vessel like a shell,* e.g. *a salt-cellar or trumpet.*

conchȳlĭātus -a -um, *dyed with purple or dressed in purple.*

conchȳlĭum -i, n. *a shell-fish* esp. *a mussel or oyster, or the shell-fish which yielded the purple dye:* meton., *purple dye or a purple garment.*

¹**concĭdo** -cidĕre -cĭdi, *to fall down.* Transf., *to sink, perish;* of winds, *to subside;* of persons, *to be ruined, to fail,* esp. at law.

²**concīdo** -cidĕre -cĭdi, -cisum, *to cut up, cut down, destroy.* Transf., *to ruin, strike down.*

  Hence partic. **concīsus** -a -um, *cut up small, brief, concise.* Adv. **concīsē.**

concĭĕo -cĭēre -cīvi -cītum and **concĭo** -īre. (1) *to collect, bring together.* (2) *to move violently, excite, arouse, stir up.*

concĭlĭābŭlum -i, n. *a place of assembly.*

concĭlĭātĭo -ōnis, f. *a bringing together, uniting, conciliating, causing of goodwill;* sometimes *inclination.*

concĭlĭātŏr -ōris, m. *one who brings about a result.*

concĭlĭātrix -īcis, f. *she who unites;* hence *a match-maker.*

concĭlĭātū, abl. sing. m., *by union, by connexion.*

concĭlĭo -are, *to bring together, unite, reconcile, win over;* hence *of results, to bring about, cause.*

  Hence partic. **concĭlĭātus** -a -um, *won over, inclined, favourable.*

concĭlĭum -i, n. *bringing together, connexion, assembling, union;* esp. *an assembly for deliberation, a council.*

concinnĭtās -ātis, f. *elegance, harmony,* esp. of style.

concinnĭtūdo īnis, f. *elegance, harmony,* esp. of style.

concinno -are, *to put together carefully, to arrange:* hence *to produce, cause.*

concinnus -a -um, *well put together;* hence *pleasing, elegant, neat,* esp. of style. Adv. **concinnē,** *elegantly.*

concĭno -cinĕre -cĭnŭi: intransit., *to sing in chorus, play together;* hence *to agree in saying* and in gen. *to agree;* transit., *of songs, to sing together;* of festivals, *to celebrate;* of the future, *to prophesy.*

¹**concĭo** = concieo; q.v.

²**concĭo** -ōnis = contio; q.v.

concĭpĭo -cĭpĕre -cēpi -ceptum. (1) *to take together, contain, hold;* of ideas, *to express in a certain form of* *words.* (2) *to take completely in, absorb;* of fluids, *to suck in;* of fire, *to catch;* of air, *to draw in;* often also *to conceive.* Transf., *to take in, grasp* by senses or intellect; *to conceive, imagine;* of passions, *to begin to feel;* of action, *to devise,* esp. in bad sense.

concīsio -ōnis, f. *the breaking up of a clause into divisions.*

concīsus -a -um, partic. from ²concido; q.v.

concitātio -ōnis, f. *violent movement.* Hence *tumult, sedition;* also *disturbance of mind, passion.*

concitātor -ōris, m. *one who stirs up.*

concīto -are, *to move violently, stir up, excite;* equum calcaribus, *to spur to a gallop;* aciem, *to move forward the army.* Hence in gen., *to stir up, incite;* of results, *to cause, produce.* Hence partic. **concĭtātus** -a -um, *quick, rapid; excited, violent, passionate.* Adv. **concĭtātē,** *excitedly.*

concĭtor -ōris, m. *one who stirs up.*

conclāmātio -ōnis, f. *loud or combined shouting.*

conclāmo -are. (1) *to shout together or loudly;* with ut, *to demand loudly that;* with acc. of a dead person, *to bewail.* (2) *to call together.*

conclāve -is, n. *a room, chamber.*

conclūdo -clūdĕre -clūsi -clūsum *to shut up, enclose, confine.* Hence *to include, comprise; to bring to an end;* in logic, *to argue, infer.* Adv. from partic., **conclūsē,** *with well-turned periods.*

conclūsio -ōnis, f. *a shutting, closing;* milit, *a blockade.* Transf., *a close, conclusion;* rhet., *the conclusion of a speech, peroration,* or *a period;* in logic, *a conclusion, consequence.*

conclūsiuncŭla -ae, f. *a foolish inference.*

concŏlor -ōris, *similar in colour.*

concŏquo -cŏquĕre -coxi -coctum. *to boil or cook thoroughly;* hence *to digest.* Transf., *to bear, endure, stomach; to consider well, deliberate upon.*

concordia -ae, f. *agreement, union, harmony.*

concorditer, adv. from concors; q.v.

concordo -are, *to agree, be in harmony.*

concors -dis, *of one mind or opinion, agreeing, harmonious.* Adv. **concorditer.**

concrēbresco -brescĕre -brŭi *to increase.*

concrēdo -crēdĕre -crēdĭdi -crēdĭtum, *to entrust, commit.*

concrēmo -are, *to burn down, burn entirely.*

concrēpo -are -ŭi -ĭtum: intransit., *to rattle, creak, clash;* digitis concrepare, *to snap the fingers;* transit., *to rattle, strike upon.*

concresco -crescĕre -crēvi -crētum. *to grow, collect, be formed; to become stiff, congeal, harden.* Hence perf. partic. **concrētus** -a -um, *compounded; congealed, stiff.*

concrētio -ōnis, f. *a growing together, congealing; matter.*

concrūcio -are, *to torture violently.*

concŭbīna -ae, f. *a concubine.*

concŭbīnus -i, m. *a man living with a concubine.*

concŭbĭtus -ūs, m. *lying* or *reclining together;* hence *copulation.*

concŭbĭus -a -um, in the phrase concubia nocte, *at the time of first sleep, at dead of night.*

conculco -are, *to tread down, trample under foot.*

concumbo -cumbĕre -cŭbŭi -cŭbĭtum, *to lie* or *recline together* (at table); *to lie with, have intercourse with.*

concŭpisco -piscĕre -pīvi or -pĭi -pītum, *to desire eagerly, covet, aim at.*

concurro -currĕre -curri (or -cŭcurri) -cursum, *to assemble hurriedly, flock to one spot; to rush together, clash,* esp. *to meet in conflict, engage.*

concursātio -ōnis, f. *running together, concourse;* hence *coincidence;* in gen., *running about;* milit. *skirmishing.*

concursātor -ōris, m. *a skirmisher.*

concursio -ōnis, f. *running together, concourse;* rhet., *frequent repetition of a word.*

concurso -are, *to run about, rush to and fro;* milit., *to skirmish.*

concursus -ūs, m. *running together, concourse, union; a rushing together, clashing; a hostile encounter.*

concussŭ, abl. sing. m. *by shaking, by concussion.*

concŭtio -cŭtĕre -cussi -cussum *to shake together, agitate, disturb.* Hence, physically, *to shatter, impair;* of persons, *to shake the clothes of,* and so *to examine;* mentally, *to alarm, trouble, excite.*

condēcŏro -are, *to adorn carefully.*

condemnātor -ōris, m. *one who causes condemnation, an accuser.*

condemno -are, *to condemn;* of an accuser, *to urge* or *effect the condemnation of a person;* in gen., *to blame, disapprove.*

condenso -are and **condensĕo** -ēre, *to make thick, press close together.*

condensus -a -um, *dense, thick.*

condĭcio -ōnis, f. *an arrangement, agreement.* Hence (1) *a condition, stipulation, provision;* esp. *conditions of marriage, marriage contract.* (2) *state, condition, place, circumstances.*

condīco -dīcĕre -dixi -dictum, *to make arrangement, agree, fix, settle;* esp. *to agree to dine with a person.*

condignus -a -um, *very worthy;* adv. **condignē.**

condīmentum -i, n. *spice, seasoning, sauce, condiment.*

condĭo -ire; of fruits, etc., *to pickle, preserve;* of corpses, *to embalm;* in gen., *to season, temper.* Hence partic. **condītus** -a -um, *seasoned, savoury.*

condiscĭpŭlus -i, m. and **condiscĭpŭla** -ae, f. *a schoolfellow.*

condisco -discĕre -dĭdĭci, *to learn thoroughly.*

¹condĭtĭo = condicio; q.v.

²condĭtĭo -ōnis, f. *pickling or seasoning.*

condĭtor -ōris, m. *a founder*; hence, in gen., *contriver, composer, author.*

condĭtōrĭum -i, n. *the place in which a corpse or its ashes are preserved.*

condo -dĕre -dĭdi -dĭtum. (1) *to build, found; form, establish;* of literary work, *to compose, write* a poem, etc., and also *to write of* a subject. (2) *to put up, put away safely, store, to hide, withdraw;* of corpses, *to bury;* of time, *to pass, dispose of.*

condŏcĕfăcĭo -făcĕre -fēci -factum, *to train, instruct, teach.*

condŏlesco -dŏlescĕre -dŏlŭi, *to suffer severely, feel much pain.*

condōnātĭo -ōnis, f. *a giving away.*

condōno -are, *to give away, present, give up, sacrifice;* of debts, *to excuse;* of faults, *to overlook, forgive;* sometimes *to forgive* an injury *for the sake of* a third party (dat.).

condūco -dūcĕre -duxi -ductum: transit., *to bring or lead together, collect, unite, connect;* as commercial term, *to hire,* also *to contract for, farm;* intransit. (3rd person only), *to be of use, to profit, serve,* with dat.

conductīcĭus -a -um, *hired.*

conductĭo -ōnis, f. *a bringing together, uniting;* commerc., *hiring, farming.*

conductor -ōris, m. *one who hires; a contractor.*

condŭplĭco -are, *to double.*

condūro -are, *to harden.*

cōnecto -nectĕre -nexŭi -nexum, *to fasten, tie together, connect, join, unite.* Hence partic. **cōnexus** -a -um, *joined, connected;* n. as subst. *logical connexion.*

cōnexĭo -ōnis, f. *binding together; logical sequence.*

cōnexus -ūs, m. *connexion, union.*

confābŭlor -ari, dep. *to talk, converse.*

confarrĕātĭo -ōnis, f. *a Roman form of marriage.*

confarrĕo -are, *to marry by the ceremony of* confarreatio.

confătālis -e, *determined by the same fate.*

confectĭo -ōnis, f. (1) *production, completion;* tributi, *complete exaction.* (2) *consumption.*

confector -ōris, m. *one who produces or completes; a destroyer, consumer.*

confercĭo -fercire -fertum, *to press close together, compress, cram together;* usually in perf. partic. **confertus** -a -um, *compressed, dense;* of troops, *in close formation;* with abl., *stuffed with, full of;* adv. **confertim**, *compactly.*

confĕro -ferre -tŭli -lātum. (1) *to bring or put together, collect, concentrate;* of money, etc. *to contribute;* milit., *to bring into contact or collision;* pedem (cum pede), *to fight foot to foot;* signa conferre, *to engage;* of speech and ideas, *to interchange,*

discuss; of diverse things, *to compare.* (2) *to bring to* a particular place, sphere, task, etc.; se conferre, *to betake oneself,* or *to devote oneself;* in time, *to put off, postpone;* of responsibility, *to impute, attribute.*

confertus; see confercio.

confervĕfăcĭo -făcĕre, *to make very hot, melt.*

confervesco -fervescĕre -ferbŭi, *to begin to boil or glow.*

confessĭo -ōnis, f., *a confession, acknowledgment.*

confessus -a -um, partic. from confiteor; q.v.

confestim, *immediately, without delay.*

confĭcĭo -fĭcĕre -fēci -fectum. (1) *to finish, make ready, bring about, accomplish;* of arrangements, *to conclude, settle;* of time or space, *to complete, pass through;* of results, *to produce, cause.* (2) *to get together, obtain, win over.* (3) *to use up, exhause, consume:* of food, *to chew, eat* and also *to digest;* of property, *to waste;* of living creatures, *to destroy, kill;* in gen., *to weaken, wear out,* esp. of persons. Hence partic. **confĭcĭens** -entis *productive, efficient.*

confictĭo -ōnis, f. *a fabrication, invention.*

confīdens, confīdenter; see confido.

confīdentĭa -ae, f. *confidence;* in bad sense, *impudence, boldness.*

confīdo -fīdĕre -fīsus sum, *to have complete trust in, be assured.* Hence partic. **confīdens** -entis, *confident, self-reliant;* in bad sense *bold, self-assured;* adv. **confīdenter.**

confīgo -fīgĕre -fixi -fixum, *to fasten together;* *to pierce through, transfix, pin down.*

confingo -fingĕre -finxi -fictum, *construct, fashion, fabricate.*

confīnis -e. *having the same boundary, adjacent;* m. as subst. *a neighbour.* Transf., *closely allied, similar.*

confīnĭum -i, n. *a confine, boundary border.*

confirmātĭo -ōnis, f. *a thorough strengthening;* of an institution, *a securing, making firm;* of a person, *consolation, encouragement, support;* of a fact or statement, *confirmation, verification.*

confirmātor -ōris, m. *one who confirms.*

confirmo -are, *to make firm, strengthen, support;* se confirmare, *to recover strength;* polit. *to ratify;* of persons, *to strengthen in mind, encourage;* ot assertions, either *to corroborate, establish* or *to affirm, state positively.* Hence partic. **confirmātus** -a -um *encouraged, emboldened;* of things, *certain.*

confisco -are, *to lay up, preserve in a chest; to appropriate to the imperial treasury, to confiscate.*

confisĭo -ōnis, f. *confidence, assurance.*

confĭtĕor -fĭtēri -fessus sum, dep. *to confess, admit, acknowledge; to reveal, make known.*

Hence partic. **confessus** -a -um: in act. sense, *having confessed;* pass., *undoubted, acknowledged, certain.*

conflagro -are, *to blaze up, be well alight.*

conflictio -ōnis, f. *collision, conflict.*

conflicto -are, pass. or intransit., *to collide, contend;* transit., *to harass;* pass. *to be harassed* or *tormented.*

conflictū, abl. sing. m. *by striking together.*

confligo -flīgĕre -flixi, flictum: transit., *to strike* or *throw together; to bring together in order to compare;* intransit., *to collide, clash, come into conflict.*

conflo -are, *to blow up; blow into flame;* of metals, *to melt* or *forge;* of money, *to coin.* Transf., *to excite; to forge, fabricate, put together.*

confluo -flŭĕre -fluxi, *to flow, stream* or *flock together.* Partic. **confluens** -entis, *flowing together;* m. sing. or pl. as subst. *the confluence of two rivers;* as a place-name **Confluentes,** f. pl. *Coblenz.*

confodio -fŏdĕre -fōdi -fossum, *to dig thoroughly; to stab, pierce through.*

conformātio -ōnis, f. *form, shape;* vocis, *expression;* verborum, *arrange-ment;* philosoph., *an idea;* rhet., *a figure of speech.*

conformo -are, *to form, to put together, to adapt one thing to another.*

confrāgōsus -a -um, *rugged, uneven;* n. pl. as subst., *uneven places.*

confrāgus -a -um = confragosus; q.v.

confrĕmo -frĕmĕre -frĕmŭi, *to murmur, make a noise.*

confrico -fricāre -frīcŭi -frīcatum, *to rub hard.*

confringo -fringĕre -frēgi -fractum, *to break in pieces; to destroy.*

confūgio -fūgĕre -fūgi, *to fly, take refuge; to have recourse to.*

confūgium -i, n. *a place of refuge.*

confulcio -fulcire -fultus, *to prop up.*

confundo -fundĕre -fūdi -fūsum, *to pour; to pour together, mingle, mix, join;* hence *to confuse, throw into disorder, trouble, disturb, upset.*

Hence partic. **confūsus** -a -um, *disorderly, confused;* mentally, *em-barrassed, troubled.* Adv. **confūsē.**

confūsio -ōnis, f. *blending, union; confusion, disorder.*

confūto -are, *to check, repress;* by speech, *to put down, silence.*

congĕlo -are: transit., *to freeze, harden, thicken;* intransit., *to freeze up, become inert.*

congĕmino -are, *to redouble.*

congĕmo -gĕmĕre -gĕmŭi: intransit., *to sigh* or *groan loudly;* transit., *to bewail, lament.*

conger -gri, m. *a sea* or *conger eel.*

congĕriēs -ēi, f. *a heap, mass,* esp. of *wood;* rhet., *accumulation.*

congĕro -gĕrĕre -gessi -gestum, *to bring together, collect, pile up, accumu-late;* esp. *to build up;* in discourse, *to bring together, comprise;* of benefits, abuse, etc., *to heap upon a person.*

congestīcius -a -um. *heaped up.*

congestus -ūs, m. *a heaping together;* of birds, *the building of nests.* Transf., *a heap, mass.*

congiārium -i, n. *a donation (originally of wine, oil, etc.).*

congius -i, m. *a Roman liquid measure* (= *six* sextarii).

conglācio -are; intransit., *to freeze, be inert;* transit. *to turn to ice.*

conglŏbātio -ōnis, f. *a heaping* or *crowding together.*

conglŏbo -are, *to form into a ball, press tightly together.*

conglŏmĕro -are, *to roll, twist, entangle.*

conglūtinātio -ōnis, f. *cementing to-gether, connexion.*

conglūtino -are, *to cement together, connect, bind closely.*

congrātŭlor -ari, dep. *to wish joy to, congratulate.*

congrĕdior -grĕdi -gressus, dep. *to meet,* esp. *in conflict; in words, to dispute, argue.*

congrĕgābilis -e, *sociable, inclined to collect.*

congrĕgātio -ōnis, f. *an assembling, society, union.*

congrĕgo -are, *to collect into a flock* or *swarm;* of men, *to gather together;* with reflex., or in pass., *to swarm, assemble.*

congressio -ōnis, f. *meeting, inter-course, association.*

congressus -ūs, m. *a meeting;* either *a friendly meeting, social intercourse,* or *a hostile encounter, combat.*

congrŭentia -ae, f. *agreement, symmetry proportion.*

congrŭo -ŭĕre, -ŭi, *to run together, come together, meet; in time, to coincide; in gen., to be suited to, correspond with, agree.*

Hence partic. **congrŭens** -entis, *agreeing, fit, appropriate, suitable;* concentus, *harmonious, uniform;* clamor, *unanimous.* Adv. **congrŭen-tĕr,** *agreeably, suitably.*

congrŭus -a -um, *agreeing, fit, suitable.*

conicio -icĕre -iēci -ectum, *to throw together; to cast lots;* mentally, *to put two and two together, conjecture, guess; to interpret dreams etc.; in gen., to throw, hurl;* se conicere, *to betake oneself, flee;* of abstract things, *to bring up, bring in;* of money, *to throw away.*

coniectio -ōnis, f. *hurling, throwing; conjectural interpretation.*

coniecto -are, *to throw together;* hence *to put two and two together; conclude, infer, guess.*

coniector -ōris, m. *an interpreter.*

coniectūra -ae, f. *a guess, conjecture, inference; interpretation of dreams and omens, divination.*

coniectūrālis -e, *conjectural.*

coniectus -ūs, m. *a throwing* or *throwing together.*

cōnĭfer -fĕra -fĕrum and **cōnĭgĕr,** *cone-bearing.*

cōnītor -niti -nisus or -nixus, dep. *to ʾean* or *press hard; to make a great* *effort, physical* or *mental*; transit., of offspring, *to bring forth with difficulty.*

coniŭgālis -e, *of marriage, conjugal.*

coniŭgātĭo -ōnis, f. *etymological connexion of words.*

coniŭgātor -ōris, m., *one who connects.*

coniŭgĭālis -e, *of marriage, conjugal.*

coniŭgĭum -i, n., *a close connexion, union;* esp. *marriage, wedlock;* meton. *a husband* or *wife.*

coniŭgo -are, *to bind together, connect.*

coniunctĭo -ōnis, f. *uniting, joining together, connexion;* grammat., *a connecting particle, conjunction;* of persons, *union, association, connexion* (esp. by blood or marriage).

coniungo -iungĕre -iunxi -iunctum, *to join together, connect, unite;* amicitias, *to form;* esp. *to unite persons by marriage, friendship, alliance,* etc.
Hence partic. **coniunctus** -a -um, *connected, joined, agreeing, allied;* of place, with dat. *bordering on, near;* of time, *contemporary;* of persons, *connected* by blood or marriage or friendship. N. as subst., *an inherent property* or *quality;* rhet., *connexion.* Adv. **coniunctē**, *conjointly, in connexion; intimately, on friendly terms;* **coniunctim**, *conjointly, in common.*

coniunx (**coniux**) -iŭgis, c. *a husband* or *wife;* poet. *a betrothed virgin, bride.*

coniŭrātĭo -ōnis, f. *a union confirmed by an oath;* in bad sense, *conspiracy, plot;* meton., *conspirators.*

coniŭro -are, *to take an oath together;* in bad sense, *to plot, conspire;* perf. partic. (in act. sense) **coniŭrātus** -a -um, *sworn, united by oath;* m. pl. as subst. *conspirators.*

coniux = coniunx; q.v.

cōnīvĕo -nīvēre -nīvi or -nixi, *to close the eyes, wink, blink.* Transf. *to wink at, let pass.*

conlăbĕfăcto -are, *to cause to totter, to soften up.*

conlăbĕfīo -fĭĕri -factus, *to be made to totter, to be softened* or *broken.*

conlābor -lābi -lapsus, dep. *to fall* or *sink down, collapse; to fall down in a swoon* or *death.*

conlăcĕrātus -a -um, *much lacerated* or *torn.*

conlăcrĭmātĭo -ōnis, f. *a weeping together.*

conlăcrĭmo -are, *to weep together* or *weep much;* transit., *to weep for.*

conlactĕus -i, m., and **-a** -ae, f., *a foster-brother* or *sister.*

conlātĭo -ōnis, f. *a bringing together;* signorum, *a battle;* of money, *a contribution, collection.* Transf., *a comparison, simile, analogy.*

conlātus -a -um, partic. from confero; q.v.

conlaudātĭo -ōnis, f. *strong praise.*

conlaudo -are, *to praise very much.*

conlaxo -are, *to widen, extend.*

conlecta -ae, f. *a contribution in money*

conlectīcĭus -a -um, *gathered together;* exercitus, *quickly levied.*

conlectĭo -ōnis, f. *a gathering together,*

collection; rhet. *a brief recapitulation;* in logic, *a conclusion, inference.*

conlēga -ae, m. *a colleague, partner in office;* in gen., *an associate.*

conlēgĭum -i, n.; abstr., *colleagueship;* concr., *persons united as colleagues, a body, guild, corporation, college.*

conlībertus -i, m. *a fellow-freedman.*

conlĭbet or **conlŭbet** -bēre -bŭit or -bĭtum est, impers., *it pleases, is agreeable.*

conlīdo līdĕre -līsi -līsum, *to strike* or *dash together, to bring into hostile collision.*

conlĭgātĭo -ōnis, f. *a binding together connexion.*

¹**conlĭgo** -lĭgĕre -lēgi -lectum, *to gather* or *bring together, collect;* poet., *to gather into a smaller space, contract;* conligere se, or animum, or mentem, *to compose oneself , gain courage;* in the mind, *to put together,* hence *to infer, conclude.*

²**conlĭgo** -are, *to bind, tie, fasten together, connect;* sometimes *to detain, hinder, tie down.*

conlīnĕo are, *to direct in a straight line.*

conlĭno -lĭnĕre -lēvi -lĭtum, *to besmear, daub.*

conlĭquĕfactus -a -um, *liquefied melted.*

conlŏcātĭo -ōnis, f. *a placing, arrangement;* esp. *a giving in marriage.*

conlŏco -are, *to place, lay, set, arrange;* of time, money, etc. *to lay out, employ, spend;* of persons, *to settle, place;* of troops, *to billet, quarter;* of women, *to settle in marriage.*

conlŏcŭplēto -are, *to enrich.*

conlŏcūtĭo -ōnis, f. *conversation.*

conlŏquĭum -i, n., *talk, conversation, conference.*

conlŏquor -lŏqui -lŏcūtus, dep. *to speak to, converse with, to treat* or *negotiate with.*

conlūcĕo -ēre, *to shine on all sides, be completely illuminated.*

conlūdo -lūdĕre -lūsi -lūsum, *to play with; to have a secret understanding with, to act in collusion.*

conlŭo -lŭĕre -lŭi -lūtum, *to wash thoroughly, rinse.*

conlūsĭo -ōnis, f. *secret understanding.*

conlūsor -ōris, m. *a play-fellow; a fellow-gambler.*

conlustro -are, *to illuminate on all sides; to survey, look at on all sides.*

conlŭvĭo -ōnis and **conlŭvĭes** -ēi *collection of impurities, filth;* of people, *scum, rabble.*

conm-; see comm-.

conn-; see con-.

cōnōpēum or **cōnōpĭum** -i, n. *a mosquito net.*

cōnor -ari, dep. *to undertake, try, strive.*

conp-; see comp-.

conquassātĭo -ōnis, f., *a violent shaking.*

conquasso -are, *to shake thoroughly, shatter.*

conquĕror -quĕri -questus, dep. *to complain loudly (of).*

conquestĭo -ōnis, f. *a loud complaint.*

conquestŭ, abl. sing. m. *by loud complaint.*

conquiesco -quiēscĕre -quiēvi -quiētum, *to take rest, repose, be still, stop.*

conquīro -quīrĕre -quīsīvi -quīsītum, *to seek out, get together.* Hence partic. **conquīsītus** -a -um, *carefully sought out, chosen, costly.*

conquīsītĭo -ōnis, f. *search, collection;* of soldiers, *levying, conscription.*

conquīsītor -ōris, m., *a recruiting officer.*

conr-: see **corr-.**

consaepĭo -saepire -saepsi -saeptum, *to fence round, hedge in;* n. of partic. as subst. **consaeptum** -i, *an enclosure.*

consālūtātĭo -ōnis, f., *mutual salutation.*

consālūto -are, *to greet (mutually), hail, salute.*

consānesco -sānescĕre -sānŭi, *to become healthy, get well.*

consanguĭnĕus -a -um, *related by blood, brotherly, sisterly;* m. as subst., *brother;* f., *sister;* m. plur., *relations.*

consanguĭnĭtās -ātis, f., *relationship by blood, consanguinity.*

conscĕlĕro -are, *to defile with crime;* partic. **conscĕlĕrātus** -a -um, *villainous, depraved.*

conscendo -scendĕre -scendi -scensum, *to ascend, mount, go up;* equum, *to mount on horseback;* naut. (with or without navem, etc.), *to go on board ship, embark.*

conscensĭo -ōnis, f. *embarkation.*

conscientĭa -ae, f., *knowledge shared with others, "being in the know", joint knowledge; knowledge shared with oneself,* i.e. *consciousness,* esp. of right or wrong, *a good or a bad conscience.*

conscindo -scindĕre -scīdi -scissum, *to tear in pieces.*

conscĭo -ire, *to be conscious of guilt.*

conscisco -sciscĕre -scīvi and -scĭi -scītum, *to agree on, resolve, decree; to inflict upon oneself* (with or without sibi).

conscĭus -a -um. *sharing knowledge with others, privy to a thing, cognizant of;* m. or f. as subst., *an accomplice, fellow-conspirator; sharing knowledge with oneself,* i.e. *conscious,* esp. of right or wrong.

conscrībo -scrībĕre -scripsi -scriptum, *to enter on a list, enroll;* of troops, *to levy;* patres conscripti (patres et conscripti), *senators; to write, compose;* of physicians, *to prescribe; to write all over an object.*

conscriptĭo -ōnis, f. *writing, composition.*

consĕco -sĕcare -sĕcŭi -sectum, *to cut up, dismember.*

consĕcrātĭo -ōnis, f. *dedication, consecration;* of dead emperors, *apotheosis.*

consĕcro -are, *to consecrate;* sometimes *to dedicate to the gods below, to curse;* of persons, *to deify;* in gen., *to make holy or immortal.*

consectārĭus -a -um, *following logically,*

consequent; n. pl. as subst., *logical conclusions, inferences.*

consectātĭo -ōnis, f. *eager pursuit, striving after.*

consectātrix -īcis, f., *an eager pursuer, devoted friend.*

consectĭo -ōnis, f., *cutting to pieces.*

consector -ari, dep. *to follow, pursue eagerly; to make for, try to join, imitate, attain;* in hostile sense, *to chase, hunt.*

consĕcūtĭo -ōnis, f.: philosoph., *an effect, consequence;* rhet., *order, connexion, arrangement.*

consĕnesco -sĕnescĕre -sĕnŭi, *to become old, lose one's strength, decay.*

consensĭo -ōnis, f., *agreement, harmony, consent;* in bad sense, *plot, conspiracy.*

consensus -ūs m. *agreement, concord;* abl. consensu, *unanimously;* in bad sense, *secret agreement, conspiracy.*

consentānĕus -a -um, *agreeing, fit, suitable;* consentaneum est, *it is reasonable or suitable.*

consentĭo -sentire -sensi -sensum; of physical sensation, *to feel together;* of thought or sentiment, *to agree, assent, resolve unanimously;* with acc., bellum, *to resolve upon war;* in bad sense, *to plot, conspire;* of things, *to agree, harmonize.* Hence partic. **consentĭens** -entis, *harmonious.*

consēpĭo = consaepio; q.v.

consĕquentĭa -ae, f., *a consequence, succession.*

consĕquĭa -ae, f. = consequentia; q.v.

consĕquor -sĕqui -sĕcūtus, dep. (1) *to follow, go after;* in hostile sense, *to pursue; to follow in time, follow logically, result.* (2) *to follow right up, reach, obtain, catch, get;* of states and events, *to befall, happen to a person;* in speech or thought, *to understand, grasp.* Hence partic. **consĕquens** -entis, *appropriate, consequent;* n. as subst. *a logical consequence.*

¹consĕro -sĕrĕre -sēvi -sītum, *to sow, plant.* Transf., *to cover.*

²consĕro -sĕrĕre -sĕrŭi -sertum, *to connect, join, twine together;* milit., *to join in* conflict, esp. manum (or manus) conserere; *to engage.* Hence, from partic., adv. **consertē,** *connectedly.*

conserva -ae, f. *fellow slave.*

conservātĭo -ōnis, f. *preservation, keeping, laying up.*

conservātor -ōris, m., *preserver.*

conservo -are, *to keep, preserve, maintain.* Pres. partic. as adj. **conservans** antis, *preserving.*

conservus -i, m. *fellow slave.*

consessor ōris, m., *one who sits near, a neighbour;* in court, *an assessor.*

consessus -ūs m. *assembly.*

consīdĕrātĭo -ōnis, f., *consideration, contemplation.*

consīdĕro -are, *to look at, regard carefully, contemplate;* mentally, *to consider, reflect upon.*

Hence partic. **consīdĕrātus** -a -um; pass., *well weighed, deliberate;* act., of persons, *cautious, circumspect.* Adv. **consīdĕrātē**, *thoughtfully, carefully.*

consīdo -sīdĕre -sēdi -sessum, *to sit down, to settle;* esp. *to sit down in an assembly or court;* milit., *to take up one's position or encamp.* Transf.: of things, *to settle, sink, subside;* *to be overcome* or *neglected;* of ideas, *to sink in;* of feelings, *to subside.*

consigno -are, *to seal; to vouch for, authenticate; to record.*

consĭliārius -a -um, *deliberating;* m. as subst. *an adviser, assessor, interpreter.*

consĭliātŏr -ōris, m., *counsellor, adviser.*

consĭlĭor -ari, dep. *to consult, take counsel; to give counsel, advise.*

consĭlium -i, n. (1) *deliberation, consultation;* meton., *persons in consultation, an assembly, council;* as a quality, *judgment, understanding.* (2) *a resolution, plan;* abl., consilio, *intentionally, designedly.* (3) *advice, suggestion.*

consĭmĭlis -e, *exactly similar.*

consĭpio -sĭpĕre, *to be in one's right mind.*

consisto -sistĕre -stĭti -stĭtum, *to take one's stand, place oneself; to stand still, stop; to be posted or to halt.* Transf., of things, *to fall to, come upon, rest on; to stop, stay; to stand firm;* with abl. etc., *to consist, be formed of.*

consĭtĭo -ōnis, and **consĭtūra** -ae, f., *sowing, planting.*

consĭtor -ōris, m., *sower, planter.*

consōbrīnus -i, m. and **consōbrīna** -ae, f., *cousin (on the mother's side).*

consŏcĭātĭo -ōnis, f., *union, connexion.*

consŏcĭo -are, *to unite, connect, share, make common.*

Hence partic. **consŏcĭātus** -a -um, *united, harmonious.*

consōlābĭlis -e, *consolable.*

consōlātĭo -ōnis, f., *consolation, encouragement, alleviation;* *consoling words.*

consōlātŏr -ōris, m., *consoler.*

consōlātōrĭus -a -um, *consolatory.*

consōlor -ari, dep.: of persons, *to console, comfort, encourage;* of things, *to alleviate, lighten.*

consŏno -sŏnare -sŏnŭi. (1) *to sound together;* hence *to harmonize, agree.* (2) *to resound, echo.*

consŏnus -a -um, *sounding together, harmonious, accordant, suitable.*

consŏpĭo -ire, *to lull to sleep, stupefy.*

consors -sortis: act., *sharing in, partaking of;* as subst., *brother* or *sister;* as adj., *brotherly, sisterly;* pass., *shared.*

consortĭo -ōnis, f., *companionship, partnership.*

consortĭum -i, n., *partnership, participation.*

¹**conspectus** -a -um, partic. from conspicio; q.v.

²**conspectus** -ūs m.: act., *seeing, look,*

sight, view; hence *mental view, survey;* pass., *appearance.*

conspergo -spergĕre -spersi -spersum, *to sprinkle* or *moisten by sprinkling.*

conspĭcĭo -spĭcĕre -spexi -spectum, *to catch sight of, behold, perceive; to look at with attention, watch;* pass., conspici, *to attract notice, be gazed at.* Transf., *to see mentally, understand.*

Hence partic. **conspectus** -a -um, *visible; striking, remarkable, conspicuous.* Gerundive **conspĭcĭendus** -a -um, *worth looking at, notable.*

conspĭcor -ari, dep. *to catch sight of, perceive.*

conspĭcŭus -a -um, *visible; remarkable, striking, conspicuous.*

conspīrātĭo -ōnis, f., *blowing* or *breathing together; harmony, agreement, union;* in bad sense, *conspiracy, plot.*

conspīro -are, *to blow* or *breathe together;* of instruments, *to blow together, sound together.* Transf., *to agree, harmonize in opinion and feeling;* in bad sense, *to conspire.*

Hence partic. **conspīrātus** -a -um, *sworn together, united by oath;* m. as subst., *a conspirator.*

consponsor -ōris, m. *a joint surety.*

conspŭo -spŭĕre, *to spit upon.*

conspurco -are, *to cover with dirt, defile.*

conspūto -are, *to spit upon.*

constans -antis, partic. from consto; q.v.

constantĭa -ae, f., *steadiness, firmness.*

consternātĭo -ōnis, f., *fear, alarm, dismay, confusion; mutiny, tumult.*

¹**consterno** -sternĕre -strāvi -strātum, *to strew, scatter, cover by strewing.*

Hence partic. **constrātus** -a -um: esp. constrata navis, *a decked ship;* n. as subst., *flooring, deck.*

²**consterno** -are, *to throw into confusion, alarm, frighten; to stampede.*

constĭpo -are, *to press, crowd together.*

constĭtŭo -stĭtŭĕre -stĭtŭi -stĭtūtum, *to cause to stand, set up, place, establish, settle;* milit., *to post, station, arrange, bring to a halt; to settle people in homes or quarters; to found, set up buildings,* etc. Transf., *to appoint a person to an office; to settle, fix upon an amount, time, etc.; to decide about a fact, decide that; to decide on a course of action, decide to.*

Hence partic. **constĭtūtus** -a -um, *arranged, settled;* n. as subst., *anything arranged, settled* or *agreed upon.*

constĭtūtĭo -ōnis, f., *the act of settling; settled condition, disposition; a regulation, order, ordinance;* rhet., *the issue, point in dispute.*

consto -stare -stĭti -stātum. (1) *to stand together;* hence *to be composed, consist; to depend upon, rest upon; to correspond, be consistent (with dat.);* with abl., *to cost.* (2) *to stand firm, stand still; to remain the same, be unaltered;* of resolves, *to be fixed, firm;* of evidence, facts, etc., *to be* *established, sure, well-known*; impers. **constat,** *it is agreed*; in gen., *to exist.*

Hence partic. **constans** -antis, *steady, firm, unchanging, constant, consistent, resolute*; adv. **constantĕr,** *steadily, firmly.*

constringo -stringĕre -strinxi -strictum, *to bind together, bind fast, confine, restrain*; in speech, *to compress, abbreviate.*

constructio -ōnis, f., *putting together, building, construction.*

construo -struĕre -struxi -structum, *to heap up together; to construct, build up; to arrange.*

constuprātor -ōris, m. *ravisher, debaucher.*

constupro -are *to debauch, ravish, corrupt.*

consuāsor -ōris, m. *an adviser.*

consuēfācio -făcĕre -fēci -factum, *to accustom, habituate.*

consuesco -suescĕre -suēvi -suētum: transit., *to accustom, habituate*; intransit., *to accustom oneself*; in perf., consuevi, *I am accustomed*; cum homine, *to cohabit with a person.*

Hence partic. **consuetus** -a -um: of persons, *accustomed to*; of things, *accustomed, usual.*

consuētūdo -ĭnis, f., *custom, usage, habit*; of relations with persons, *intimacy, familiar acquaintance*; of lovers, *intrigue.*

consuētus -a -um, partic. from consuesco; q.v.

consul -sŭlis, m., *a consul*; plur., consules, *the consuls, the two chief magistrates at Rome under the Republic*; consul designatus, *consul elect*; pro consule, *an officer in the place of the consul, a proconsul, e.g. a governor of a province.*

consŭlāris -e. (1) *relating to a consul, consular.* (2) *having been a consul*; m. as subst., *an ex-consul, or provincial governor of consular rank.* Adv. **consŭlārĭtĕr,** *in a manner worthy of a consul.*

consŭlātus -ūs, m. *the office of consul, consulship.*

consŭlo -sŭlĕre -sŭlŭi -sultum. (1) *to reflect, consult, consider*; with dat., *to look to the interests of*; as a result of deliberation, *to come to a conclusion, to take measures*; boni (or optimi) consulere, *to take in good part.* (2) *to ask the advice of, consult.*

Hence partic. **consultus** -a -um: of things, *well considered, deliberated upon*; of persons, *experienced* (with genit). N. as subst. **consultum** -i: *the act of deliberation, reflection, consideration*; *the result of deliberation, a resolution, plan, decision*; esp. *a decree of the senate at Rome.* Abl. as adv. consulto, *deliberately, designedly.* Adv. consultē, *advisedly, after consideration.*

consultātĭo -ōnis, f., *a full consideration, deliberation; an asking for advice, inquiry.*

consulto -are. (1) *to consider maturely, weigh, ponder*; with dat., *to look to the interests of.* (2) *to consult, ask advice of.*

consultor -ōris, m. (1) *an adviser.* (2) *one who asks advice, esp. legal advice; a client.*

consummātĭo -ōnis, f. *a summing up, adding up; a finishing, completion.*

consummo -are, *to add together, sum up; to form a whole, complete, perfect.*

Hence partic. **consummātus** -a -um, *complete, perfect.*

consūmo -sūmĕre -sumpsi -sumptum, *to spend, employ on a purpose*; in gen., *to use up, finish, waste away, destroy.*

consŭo -sŭĕre -sŭi -sūtum, *to stitch or put together; to form.*

consurgo -surgĕre -surrexi -surrectum, *to rise up, stand up*, esp. *to speak, or as a mark of respect.* Transf.: of persons, *to be roused to action*; of things, *to arise, break out.*

consurrectĭo -ōnis, f., *a general standing up.*

contābesco -tābescĕre -tābŭi, *to waste away gradually.*

contăbŭlātĭo -ōnis, f., *planking, floor, storey.*

contăbŭlo -are, *to cover with boards, equip with floors or storeys.*

contactus -ūs, m., *contact, touching; contagion.*

contăgēs -is, f., *touch, contact.*

contăgĭo -ōnis, f., and **contăgĭum** -i, n., *touching, contact*; hence *contagion, infection.*

contāmĭno -are, *to pollute, infect*; of authors, *to blend (and so spoil) Greek plays.*

contĕgo -tĕgĕre -texi -tectum, *to cover, shield.*

contemno -temnĕre -tempsi -temptum, *to think meanly of, despise, contemn.*

Hence partic. **contemptus** -a -um, *despised; despicable, contemptible.*

contemplātĭo -ōnis, f., *surveying, contemplation.*

contemplor -ari, dep., *to mark out*; hence *to look at attentively, survey, regard; to consider carefully.*

contemptim, *contemptuously.*

contemptĭo -ōnis, f., *contempt, scorn, disdain.*

contemptor -ōris, m., **contemptrix** -rīcis, f., adj. and subst., *a despiser, contemptuous.*

¹**contemptus** -a -um, partic. from contemno; q.v.

²**contemptus** -ūs, m., *contempt, disdain.*

contendo -tendĕre -tendi -tentum, *to strain, stretch, exert*; of missiles, *to shoot, cast*; intransit., *to strive, strain, exert oneself, hasten*; of statements, *to assert with confidence, maintain.* In relation to another: transit., *to compare, contrast*; intransit., *to compete.*

Hence partic. **contentus** -a -um, *strained, stretched, tense; eager, zealous.* Adv. **contentē,** *eagerly, earnestly.*

¹**contentĕ**, adv. from contendo; q.v.

²**contentĕ**, adv. from contineo; q.v.

contentio -ōnis, f., *exertion, effort, straining, striving.* In relation to another, *contrast, comparison;* or *combat, contest, strife.*

¹**contentus** -a -um, partic. from contendo; q.v.

²**contentus** -a -um, *contented,* partic. from contineo; q.v.

contermĭnus -a -um, *bordering upon, adjacent, near.*

contĕro -tĕrĕre -trīvi -trītum, *to rub away, grind, pound;* in gen., *to wear away, destroy, obliterate;* of time, *to consume, spend.*

conterrĕo -ēre, *to terrify, frighten much.*

contestor -ari, dep. *to call to witness;* litem, *to start an action by calling witnesses;* partic. **contestātus** -a -um, in pass. sense, *witnessed to, approved.*

contexo -texĕre -texŭi -textum, *to weave* or *twine together, connect, unite, construct, form.*

Hence partic. **contextus** -a -um, *interwoven, connected, united.* adv. **contextĕ**, *in close connexion.*

¹**contextus** -a -um, partic. from contexo; q.v.

²**contextus** -ūs, m., *uniting, connexion.*

conticesco (conticisco) -ticescĕre -ticŭi, *to become silent, be stilled, abate.*

contignātĭo -ōnis, f., *floor of planks.*

contigno -are, *to floor with planks.*

contĭgŭus -a -um, *touching, contiguous, near;* with dat., *within reach of.*

continens -entis, partic. from contineo; q.v.

continentia -ae, f., *self-control, moderation, temperance.*

continĕo -tinēre -tinŭi -tentum. (1) *to hold together, keep together;* hence *to connect, join.* (2) *to keep in, surround, contain, confine;* hence *to include, comprise.* (3) *to hold back, restrain.* Hence pres. partic. **continens** -entis. (1) *lying near, adjacent.* (2) *hanging together, unbroken, continuous;* f. as subst., *a continent;* n. as subst., rhet., *a main point.* (3) *self-controlled, temperate, continent.* Adv. **continenter**, *without break, continuously; continently, temperately.* Partic. **contentus** -a -um, *contented, satisfied* (with abl.).

contingo -tingĕre -tĭgi -tactum: transit., *to touch, reach, grasp;* to touch *with* something, *smear* or *sprinkle* with; hence *to affect, infect* (esp. in perf. partic.); geograph. *to border on;* intransit., *to happen, befall,* usually of good luck (with dat.).

continŭātĭo -ōnis, f., *unbroken continuance* or *succession;* rhet., *a period.*

continŭĭtās -ātis, f., *continuity, unbroken succession.*

¹**continŭŏ**, adv. from continuus; q.v.

²**continŭo** -are, *to connect up, unite, make continuous, form into a series;* verba, *to make into a sentence;* magistratum, *to prolong.*

continŭus -a -um, *connected up, hanging together, continuous, uninterrupted.* N. abl. as adv. **continŭŏ**, *immediately, at once;* in argument, *necessarily, as an immediate consequence.*

contĭo -ōnis, f., *an assembly, public meeting.* Transf. *a speech made in such an assembly,* or *the speaker's platform.*

contĭōnābundus -a -um, *haranguing, speaking in public.*

contĭōnālis -e and **contĭōnārĭus** -a -um, *relating to a public assembly.*

contĭōnātor -ōris, m., *a popular orator, demagogue.*

contĭōnor -ari, dep., *to attend an assembly;* esp. *to speak in public before an assembly.*

contĭuncŭla -ae, f., *a short harangue.*

contorquĕo -torquēre -torsi -tortum *to twist, whirl, turn violently, contort; to whirl a spear,* etc., in throwing, and so *to hurl.*

Hence partic. **contortus** -a -um. (1) *intricate, confused, complicated.* (2) *whirling;* so *powerful, vigorous.* Adv. **contortĕ**, *intricately.*

contortĭo -ōnis, f., *whirling, twisting, intricacy.*

contra. Adv., *opposite, over against, on the opposite side;* of equivalence, *in return back;* of difference, *otherwise;* of opposition, *against.* Prep., with acc., *opposite to, over against; against, in opposition to.*

contractĭo -ōnis, f., *drawing together, contraction;* orationis, *abbreviation;* animi, *anxiety, depression.*

contractus -a -um, partic. from contraho; q.v.

contrādīco -dīcĕre -dixi -dictum, *to gainsay, contradict.*

contrādictĭo -ōnis, f., *a speaking against, contradiction.*

contrăho -trăhĕre -traxi -tractum. (1) *to draw together, collect, unite; to conclude* or *complete* any arrangement; in gen., *to cause, bring on, bring about;* aes alienum, *to contract debt.* (2) *to shorten, narrow, contract, reduce;* frontem, *to frown;* vela, *to furl one's sails;* of the spirits, *to depress.*

Hence partic. **contractus** -a -um, *contracted, narrow, straitened;* of persons, *retired quiet.*

contrārĭus -a -um, *opposite, opposed, contrary;* vulnera, *wounds in front;* with genit. or dat., *opposed to;* in gen., *hostile, injurious.* N. as subst. **contrārĭum** -i, *the opposite;* ex contrario, *on the other side.* Adv. **contrārĭē**, *in an opposite direction* or *manner.*

contrectātĭo -ōnis, f., *touching, handling.*

contrecto -are, *to touch, feel, handle;* of familiar handling, *to violate;* mentally, *to consider.*

contrĕmisco -trĕmiscĕre -trĕmŭi: intransit., *to tremble, quake;* transit, *to tremble before, be afraid of.*

contrĕmo -ĕre, *to tremble, quake.*

contrĭbŭo -tribŭĕre -tríbŭi -tríbūtum, *to brigade with, incorporate, unite*; of contributions, *to bring in.*

contristo -are, *to make sad* or *gloomy.*

contrītus -a -um, partic. from contero; q.v.

contrŏversĭa -ae, f., *a dispute* (esp. at law); sine controversia, *indisputably.*

contrŏversĭōsus -a -um, *strongly disputed.*

contrŏversus -a -um, *disputed, controverted.*

contrŭcīdo -are, *to cut in pieces, hew down, slay.*

contrūdo -trūdĕre -trūsi -trūsum, *to thrust, push together.*

contrunco -are, *to cut in pieces.*

contŭbernālis -is, c. (1) *a messmate, comrade.* (2) *a young staff-officer.*

contŭbernĭum -i, n. Concrete, *a soldiers' tent; the common dwelling of a male and female slave.* Abstract, *comradeship, companionship, intimacy; concubinage; junior staff duties.*

contŭeor -tŭēri -tŭĭtus, dep. *to see, survey, look at attentively;* mentally, *to consider, reflect upon.*

contŭĭtū (contūtū), abl. sing. m., *by surveying.*

contŭmācĭa -ae, f., *firmness, stubbornness, obstinacy.*

contŭmax -ācis, *firm, stubborn, obstinate;* adv. **contŭmācĭtĕr.**

contŭmēlĭa -ae, f. *outrage, physical violence;* of speech, *insult, affront.*

contŭmēlĭōsus -a -um, adj. *outrageous, insulting, abusive;* adv. **contŭmēlĭōsē.**

contŭmŭlo -are, *to bury, inter.*

contundo -tundĕre -tŭdi -tūsum, *to bruise, crush, pound, beat up, break up, demolish.*

contŭor -i = contueor; q.v.

conturbātĭo -ōnis f., *disorder, confusion.*

conturbo -are, *to throw into disorder, disturb, distress; to ruin, make bankrupt.*

contus -i, m. *a pole used in boating; a long spear or pike.*

cōnus -i, m., *a cone; the apex of a helmet.*

convălesco -vălescĕre -vălŭi, *to become strong, establish oneself;* esp. *to recover from a disease, get well.*

convallis -is, f., *an enclosed valley.*

convāso -are, *to pack up baggage.*

convecto -are, *to bring together, collect.*

convector -ōris, m. *a fellow-traveller.*

convĕho -vĕhĕre -vexi -vectum, *to bring together, carry into one place.*

convello -vellĕre -velli -vulsum, *to pluck up, pull away, wrench off;* milit., convellere signa, *to decamp;* in gen., *to weaken, overthrow, destroy.*

convĕna -ae, c.: adj., *coming together;* as subst., in plur., *a concourse, assembled multitude.*

convĕnĭentĭa -ae, f., *agreement, harmony, conformity.*

convĕnĭo -vĕnīre -vēni -ventum. (1) *to meet:* intransit., *to come to-gether, assemble;* legal, convenire in manum, of the wife, *to come into the power of her husband;* transit., *to visit, meet, call upon.* (2) *to fit, be suitable, be congenial;* impers. convenit, *it is fitting.* (3) *to agree;* usually in pass. sense, *to be agreed upon;* impers., convenit, *it is agreed.* Hence partic. **convĕnĭens** -entis, *agreeing, unanimous, concordant; fit, appropriate, suitable;* adv. **convĕnĭentĕr**, *agreeably, suitably.* N. of perf. partic. as subst., **conventum** -i, *an agreement, compact.*

conventĭcŭlum -i, n., *a coming together, assembly, association; a place of meeting.*

conventĭo -ōnis, f. *assembly; agreement, compact.*

conventum; see convenio.

conventus -ūs, m. *coming together, assembly, union, congress;* conventus agere, *to hold assizes;* in gen., *agreement.*

converro -verrĕre -verri -versum, *to sweep together, brush up; to beat thoroughly; to scrape together.*

conversātĭo -ōnis, f., *frequent use;* esp. *frequent sojourn in a place,* or *regular dealings with persons.*

conversĭo -ōnis, f. *a turning round, alteration,* or *periodical return;* rhet. *rounding off of a period,* or *repetition of word at the end of a clause.*

converso -are, *to turn round often;* pass. in middle sense, *to live, consort, have dealings.*

converto -vertĕre -verti -versum. (1) *to turn round, whirl round;* se convertere, *to revolve, to turn back;* milit., signa convertere, *to wheel round;* terga, or se, convertere, *to flee.* Transf., *to change, alter;* of books, *to translate.* (2) *to turn in any direction, direct;* conversus ad facing. Transf., *to direct, devote* (esp. with reflex.; rarely intransit.); pecuniam publicam domum, *to embezzle.*

convestĭo -ire, *to clothe; to cover, surround.*

convexus -a -um. (1) *vaulted, arched, convex;* n. as subst., arch. (2) *sloping downwards.*

convīcĭātor -ōris, m., *a railer, reviler.*

convīcĭor -ari, dep., *to rail, revile.*

convīcĭum n. *a loud cry, shout, clamour;* esp. *abuse, reproach, insult;* hence, in gen., *censure, reproof*

convictĭo -ōnis, f. *intercourse, familiarity;* meton., *familiar friends.*

convictor -ōris, m., *a constant associate.*

convictus -ūs, m. *living together, intercourse; entertainment, feast.*

convinco -vincĕre -vīci -victum, *to convict of a crime; to prove mistaken;* of things, esp. crimes or mistakes, *to prove conclusively, demonstrate.*

convīso -ere, *to examine carefully;* poet. *to beam upon.*

convīva -ae, m. *guest.*

convīvālis -e, *of a feast.*

convīvātor -ōris, m. *a host.*

convīvĭum -i, n. *a feast, entertainment, banquet;* meton., *the company assembled, guests.*

convīvo -vīvĕre -vixi -victum, *to live with, to feast with.*

convīvor -ari, dep. *to feast* (as a guest).

convŏcātĭo -ōnis, f. *calling together.*

convŏco -are, *to call together, assemble, convoke.*

convŏlo -are, *to fly together, run together.*

convolvo -volvĕre -volvi -vŏlūtum, *to roll together* or *roll round; to intertwine.*

convŏmo -ere, *to vomit all over.*

convulsus -a -um, partic. of convello; q.v.

cŏöpĕrĭo -ŏpĕrire -ŏpĕrŭi -ŏpertum, *to cover up, envelop, overwhelm;* lapidibus to stone to death.

cŏoptātĭo -ōnis, f., *election of a colleague, co-optation;* censoria, *filling up of the senate by the censors.*

cŏopto -are, *to choose, elect, co-opt.*

cŏŏrĭor -ŏriri -ortus, dep., *to arise, come forth together;* of things, *to appear, to break out;* of people, *to rise for insurrection* or *fight.*

cŏortus -ūs, m., *arising, breaking forth.*

Cŏos (Cŏus) = Cos; q.v.

cŏphĭnus -i, m., *basket, hamper.*

cōpĭa -ae, f., *plenty, abundance* (of persons or things); milit., *supplies, provisions;* also *troops, forces* (esp. plur.). Transf., *means, opportunity;* with genit. of person, *access to.*

cōpĭōsus -a -um, *richly provided, wealthy; plentiful, abundant;* of speech, *copious, eloquent.* Adv. **cōpĭōsē,** *abundantly, plentifully, copiously.*

cōpo, cōpōna = caupo, caupona; q.v.

cōpŭla -ae, f., *a link, bond, tie, connexion; a rope, a leash;* plur. *grapnels.*

cōpŭlātĭo -ōnis, f., *union, connexion.*

cōpŭlo -are, *to join together, connect, unite.*
Hence partic. **cōpŭlātus** -a -um, *connected, united, coupled.*

cŏquo cŏquĕre coxi coctum, *to cook, prepare food; to burn, ripen; to digest;* mentally: *to think of, meditate, contrive a thing; to harass a person.*

cŏquus (cŏcus) -i, m. and **cŏqua** -ae, f., *a cook.*

cŏr, cordis, n., *the heart;* often as seat of emotions or thought, *heart, mind, judgment;* meton., *a person.*

cōram, Adv., *personally, openly, face to face.* Prep., with abl., *in presence of.*

corbis -is, m. and f. *a wicker basket.*

corbīta -ae, f., *a slow-sailing merchant vessel.*

corcŭlum -i, n., *little heart.*

Corcȳra -ae, f., *Corcyra, an island in the Ionian Sea.*

cordātus -a -um, *prudent, wise;* adv. **cordātē.**

Cordŭba -ae, f. *a town in Hispania Baetica* (now *Cordova*).

Cŏrinthus -i, f. *Corinth, a city of Greece.*

Cŏrĭŏli -orum, m. pl. *a town of the Volsci in Latium;* adj. **Cŏrĭŏlānus** -a -um.

cŏrĭum -i, n. *hide, skin, leather; a leathern thong, strap.*

Cornēlĭus -a -um, *name of a Roman gens, including the Scipios.* Adj. **Cornēlĭānus** -a -um.

cornĕŏlus -a -um, *horny.*

¹cornĕus -a -um, *horny, made of horn; like horn, hard.*

²cornĕus -a -um, *of cornel-tree;* or *cornel-wood.*

cornĭcĕn -cĭnis, m., *a horn-blower.*

cornĭcŭlum -i, n. *a little horn; a horn-shaped decoration for soldiers.*

cornĭger -gĕra -gĕrum, *horned.*

cornĭpēs -pĕdis, *horn-footed, hoofed.*

cornix -īcis, f. *crow.*

cornū -ūs, n. *a horn;* fig., *strength, courage; anything made of horn,* esp. *a bow, trumpet, lantern; anything resembling a horn,* esp. *a hoof, beak, tip of a helmet, end of a stick* or *spar, end of a promontory, wing of an army.*

Cornūcōpĭa -ae, *the horn of Amalthea, symbol of plenty.*

cornum -i, n. *the cornel-cherry;* meton. *a spear of cornel-wood.*

cornus -i (and -ūs), f. *the cornel-tree;* hence *the wood of the cornel-tree, a spear of cornel-wood.*

cornūtus -a -um, *horned.*

cŏrolla -ae, f., *a little crown.*

cŏrollārĭum -i, n. *a garland of flowers; a present, gratuity.*

cŏrōna -ae, f. *garland, chaplet, crown;* sub corona vendere, *to sell into slavery prisoners of war* (*wearing chaplets*). Transf., *anything resembling a crown; a constellation; a circle of people, audience;* milit. *besiegers* (or *defenders*) of a city.

cŏrōnārĭus -a -um, *of a garland.*

cŏrōno -are, *to wreath, crown with a garland; to surround, enclose in a circle.*

corpŏrĕus -a -um, *of the body, bodily* or *of flesh.*

corpŭlentus -a -um, *fat, stout.*

corpus -pŏris, n. *body, substance, matter;* esp. *the body* of men and animals; *flesh, the trunk;* sometimes *a corpse.* Transf., *a person,* " *a body* "; the " *body politic* "; in gen., *the main mass* of a thing.

corpuscŭlum -i, n. *a little particle, atom; a small body.*

corrādo -rādĕre -rāsi -rāsum, *to scrape* or *rake together.*

correctĭo -ōnis, f., *straightening out, improvement, amendment.*

corrector -ōris, m. *improver, amender, corrector.*

correpo -rēpere -repsi -reptum, *to creep, slink, crawl.*

correptĭus, compar. adv. from corripio; q.v.

corrĭgĭa -ae, f. *a shoe-string, boot-lace.*

corrĭgo -rĭgĕre -rexi -rectum, *to put straight, set right, reform, amend.*

corrĭpĭo -rĭpĕre -rĭpŭi -reptum, *to seize, snatch up;* pecuniam, *to steal;*

viam, *to hasten on a journey*; se, *to hurry off*. Transf., of disease, etc., *to attack*; of the passions, *to overcome*; of persons, *to blame, rebuke, accuse, bring to trial*; in time, *to shorten*; hence, from partic., compar. adv. **correptius**, *more shortly*.

corrōbŏro -are, *to strengthen, invigorate.*

corrōdo -rōdere -rōsi, -rōsum, *to gnaw away.*

corrŏgo -are, *to get together, collect by begging.*

corrūgo -are, *to wrinkle up.*

corrumpo -rumpĕre -rūpi -ruptum.
(1) *to break up, destroy, annihilate.*
(2) *to spoil, make worse, weaken*; of documents, *to falsify*; of characters, *to corrupt*; corrumpere pecuniā, *to bribe.*
 Hence partic. **corruptus** -a -um, *spoilt, damaged, corrupt*; adv. **corruptē**, *corruptly, incorrectly.*

corrŭo -rŭere -rŭi: intransit. *to fall to the ground, sink down, be ruined*; transit., *to throw down, overthrow.*

corruptēla -ae, f., *corruption, bribery, seduction*; meton., *a corrupter.*

corruptio -ōnis, f. *corrupting; a corrupt state.*

corruptor -ōris, m. *corrupter, seducer, briber.*

corruptus -a -um, partic. from corrumpo; q.v.

cors = cohors; q.v.

Corsĭca -ae, f. *the island of Corsica*; adj. **Corsus** and **Corsĭcus** -a -um.

cortex -tĭcis, m. and f. *bark, rind, shell*; esp. *the bark of the cork tree, cork.*

cortina -ae, f. *a round kettle or cauldron*; esp. *the cauldron-shaped Delphic tripod*: cortina Phoebi, *the oracle of Apollo.*

cŏrŭlus = corylus; q.v.

cŏrus = caurus; q.v.

cŏrusco -are: transit., *to move quickly, swing, shake*; intransit., *to tremble, flutter*; of light, *to twinkle, flash.*

cŏruscus -a -um, *shaking, trembling*: of light, *twinkling, flashing.*

corvus -i, m. *a raven*; perhaps also *a rook.*

Cŏrybantes -ium, m. pl. *the priests of Cybele.*

cŏrycus -i, m. *a sand-bag, a punch-ball.*

cŏrylētum -i, n. *a hazel copse.*

cŏrylus -i, f. *a hazel tree.*

cŏrymbus -i, m. *a bunch of flowers or fruit, esp. a cluster of ivy berries.*

cŏryphaeus -i, m. *a leader, chief.*

cŏrytus or **cŏrytos** -i, m. *a quiver.*

¹cōs cōtis, f. *any hard, flinty stone*; esp. *a whetstone, grindstone.*

²Cōs or **Cŏus** (**Cŏos**) Coi, f. *a small island in the Aegean Sea*; adj. **Cŏus** -a -um; n. sing. as subst., *Coan wine*; n. plur., *Coan garments.*

cosmēta -ae, m. *a woman's valet.*

cosmĭcos -a -um, *of the world*; m. as subst. *a citizen of the world.*

costa -ae, f. *a rib or side.*

costum -i, n. *an eastern aromatic plant.*

cŏthurnātus -a -um, *in buskins*; hence *tragic, elevated.*

cŏthurnus -i, m. *a large hunting boot; a boot or buskin worn by tragic actors*; hence *tragedy, elevated style.*

cotid. = cottid.; q.v.

cottăna (**cotŏna, coctŏna, coctăna**) -orum, n. *a kind of small fig.*

cōturnix -īcis, f. *a quail.*

cŏvinnārĭus -i, m. *a soldier in a war chariot.*

cŏvinnus -i, m. *a war-chariot; a travelling-chariot.*

coxa -ae, f. *the hip-bone.*

coxendix -ĭcis, f. *the hip.*

crabro -ōnis, m. *a hornet.*

crambē -ēs, f. *cabbage.*

crāpŭla -ae, f. *drunkenness*; its *after-effects, "hangover".*

crās, *tomorrow.*

crassĭtūdo -ĭnis, f. *thickness, density.*

¹crassus -a -um, *thick, dense, solid*; aer, *misty, heavy*; of intellect, *dull or uneducated.* Adv. **crassē**, *roughly, rudely.*

²Crassus -i, m. *name of a family in the gens Licinia*; q.v.

crastīnus -a -um, *of tomorrow*; n. as subst. *the morrow.*

crātēra -ae, f. and **crātēr** -ēris, m. *a bowl, vase. for mixing wine with water; the crater of a volcano; a constellation, the Bowl.*

crātis -is, *a wicker frame, hurdle, a harrow*; milit. *fascines*; favorum, *honeycomb*; spinae, *the joints of the backbone.*

crĕātio -ōnis, f., *choice, election.*

crĕātor -ōris, m. and **crĕātrix** -īcis, f. *maker, founder; parent.*

crēber -bra -brum; of space, *thick, crowded together, close, numerous*; with abl., *crowded with, full of*; of time, *repeated, numerous, frequent*; of persons, to signify *repeated* action, e.g. creber pulsat, *he beats repeatedly.* Adv. **crēbrō**, *repeatedly, often.*

crēbresco (**crēbesco**) -escĕre -ŭi, *to become frequent, increase, gather strength.*

crēbrĭtās -ātis, f. *frequency.*

crēbrō, adv. from creber; q.v.

crēdĭbĭlis -e, *credible, worthy of belief*; adv. **crēdĭbĭlĭter**, *credibly.*

crēdĭtor -ōris, m., *a creditor.*

crēdo -dĕre -dĭdi -dĭtum, *to trust*: with acc. and dat., *to entrust, commit, esp.* of secrets and money; n. of perf. partic. as subst., creditum, *a loan*; with dat., *to trust in, rely upon*; also with dat., *to believe, give credence to*; with acc., *to believe as a fact, to accept as true*; in gen., *to believe, think, be of opinion.*

crēdŭlĭtās -ātis, f., *credulity.*

crēdŭlus -a -um, *believing easily, credulous, confiding.*

crĕmo -are, *to burn, consume with fire.*

crĕmor -ōris, m. *juice, pulp, cream.*

crĕo -are, *to make, create, produce; to elect to an office*; of parents, *to beget, bear.*

crĕpīda -ae, f. *sandal.*

crĕpīdātus -a -um, *wearing sandals.*

crēpīdo -ĭnis, f., *a base, foundation, pedestal; a quay, pier, dam.*

crĕpĭtācŭlum and crĕpĭtācillum -i, n. *a rattle.*

crĕpĭto -are, *to rattle, creak, crackle, rustle.*

crĕpĭtus -ūs, m. *rattling, creaking, rustling, clattering:* digitorum, *snapping of the fingers.*

crĕpo -are -ŭi -ĭtum: intransit., *to creak, rattle, rustle, crackle;* digiti crepantis signa, *a snapping of the fingers;* transit., *to make resound; to chatter about.*

crĕpundĭa -orum, n. pl. *a child's plaything; a rattle or amulet.*

crĕpuscŭlum -i, n. *twilight.*

cresco crescĕre crēvi crētum. (1) *to come into existence, spring forth, arise; past partic.* cretus, *sprung (from).* (2) *of what exists, to grow, grow up, increase in size, height, etc.;* luna crēscens, *waxing;* fig., *to increase in fame, power,* etc.

¹Crēta -ae, f. and Crētē -ēs, f. *Crete.* Hence m. adj. and subst. Crēs -ētis; f. adj. and subst. Cressa -ae; adj. Crētensis -e, and Crēticus -a -um, *Cretan.*

²crēta -ae, f. *chalk, or fuller's earth.*

crētātus -a -um, *chalked; hence in white.*

crētĭo -ōnis, f. *a declaration by an heir accepting an inheritance.*

crētōsus -a -um, *abounding in chalk.*

crētŭla -ae, f. *white clay for sealing.*

Crēūsa -ae, f. *wife of Aeneas.*

crībrum -i, n. *a sieve.*

crīmen -ĭnis, n. (1) *an accusation, charge:* esse in crimine, *to be accused;* meton., *an object of reproach.* (2) *fault, guilt, crime;* meton., *cause of crime.*

crīmĭnātĭo -ōnis, f. *accusation, calumny, charge.*

crīmĭnātor -ōris, m. *accuser, calumniator.*

crīmĭnor -ari, dep: with acc. of person, *to accuse, charge;* esp. *to calumniate;* with acc. of offence, *to complain of, bring up.*

crīmĭnōsus -a -um, *reproachful, calumnious, slanderous;* adv. crīmĭnōsē, *by way of accusation, reproachfully.*

crīnālis -e, *of or for the hair;* n. as subst. *a hair-band.*

crīnis -is, m. *hair;* esp. in pl.; *of a comet, the tail.*

crīnītus -a -um, *hairy, with long hair;* stella crinita, *a comet;* galea, *crested.*

crispĭsulcans -antis, *forked, wavy.*

crispo -are, *to curl; to move rapidly, brandish;* intransit. partic. crispans -antis, *curled, wavy.*

crispŭlus -a -um, *curly-haired, curly.*

crispus -a -um, *curly, curly-headed; trembling, quivering.*

crista -ae, f., *the crest, plume;* of a cock, *the comb.*

cristātus -a -um, *with a crest, plume or comb.*

crŏcĕus -a -um, *of saffron; saffron-coloured, golden, yellow.*

crŏcĭnus -a -um, *of saffron, saffron-*

coloured, yellow; n. as subst. *saffron oil.*

crŏcŏdīlus -i, m. *crocodile.*

crŏcŏtŭla -ae, f., *a saffron-coloured robe.*

crŏcus -i, m. and crŏcum -i n. *the crocus; saffron,* prepared from crocus; hence *the colour of saffron, yellow.*

Croesus -i, m., *a king of Lydia, famous for his wealth.*

crŏtălĭa -orum, n. *ear-rings.*

crŏtălistrĭa -ae, f. *a castanet-dancer*

crŏtălum -i, n. *a castanet.*

Crŏtōn -ōnis, c. *a Greek town near the "toe" of Italy.*

crŭcĭāmentum -i, n. *torture.*

crŭcĭātus -ūs, m., *torture, torment.*

crŭcĭo -are, *to torture, torment.*

crūdēlis -e, adj. *unfeeling, cruel;* adv. crūdēlĭter.

crūdēlĭtās -ātis, f., *cruelty, inhumanity.*

crūdesco -escĕre -ŭi, *to become hard or violent.*

crūdĭtās -ātis, f., *overloading of the stomach, indigestion.*

crūdus -a -um, adj. (1) *bleeding.* (2) *uncooked, raw;* of material, *fresh, not prepared;* of fruit, *unripe,* in gen. *green, fresh, immature, untimely;* of food, *undigested;* of persons, *stuffed, dyspeptic;* of feeling, etc., *hard, cruel;* of the voice, *harsh.*

crŭento -are, *to make bloody, stain with blood.*

crŭentus -a -um, *bloody, bloodthirsty; blood-red.*

crŭmēna -ae, f. *a pouch, purse; store of money, funds.*

crŭor -ōris, m. *blood shed, gore; murder, slaughter.*

crūs crūris, n. *the shin, shin-bone, leg;* of a bridge, *pier, support.*

crusta -ae, f. (1) *crust, rind, shell, bark.* (2) *inlaid work, bas-relief, embossing.*

crustŭlum -i, n. *a little cake.*

crustum -i, n. *bread, cake.*

crux crŭcis, f. *a cross;* hence *torment, trouble;* as a term of abuse, *gallows bird.*

crypta -ae, f. *covered gallery, vault, grotto.*

crystallĭnus -a -um, *of crystal;* pl. as subst., *crystal vases.*

crystallus -i, f. and crystallum -i, n. *crystal; a crystal drinking vessel; a precious stone looking like crystal.*

cŭbĭcŭlāris -e, *of a bedchamber.*

cŭbĭcŭlārĭus -a -um, *of a bedchamber;* m. as subst. *a chamber-servant.*

cŭbĭcŭlum -i, n. *bedroom.*

cŭbīle -is, n. *bed;* esp. *marriage-bed;* of animals, *lair, den, nest;* of bees, *hives;* in. gen., *seat, resting-place.*

cŭbĭtal -tālis, n., *an elbow cushion.*

cŭbĭtālis -e, *one cubit long.*

cŭbĭto -are, *to lie down often.*

cŭbĭtum -i, n. *the elbow; a cubit.*

cŭbĭtus -ūs, m. *lying down.*

cŭbo -are -ŭi -ĭtum, *to lie down, recline;* esp. at table or in bed; *to be ill in bed;* cubitum ire, *to go to bed;* of things, *to lie;* partic. cubans, *sloping.*

cŭcullus -i, m. *a hood, cowl.*

cŭcŭlus -i, m. *cuckoo.*

cŭcŭmis -mĕris, m. *cucumber.*

cŭcurbĭta -ae, f. *a gourd; a cupping-glass.*

cūdo -ĕre, *to beat, pound, thresh*; of metals, *to forge, stamp, coin.*

cūiās -ātis, *of what country?*

cuicuimŏdi *of whatever kind.*

cūius (quoius) -a -um: interrog., *whose?*; relat., *whose*; quoia causa, *wherefore.*

cūiuscĕmŏdi, *of whatever kind.*

cūiusdammŏdi, *of a certain kind.*

cūiusmŏdi, *of what kind?*

cūiusquĕmŏdi, *of every kind.*

culcĭta -ae, f. *bolster, pillow.*

cūlĕus = culleus; q.v.

cŭlex -ĭcis, m. *gnat, midge.*

cūlīna -ae, f. *kitchen*; meton., *food, fare.*

cullĕus (cūlĕus) -i, m. *a leather sack.*

culmen -ĭnis, n. *top, summit; the ridge of a roof; a stalk.*

culmus -i, m. *stalk, haulm, thatch.*

culpa -ae, f. *fault, blame*; esp. *the fault of unchastity*; meton., *a cause of error or sin.*

culpo -āre, *to blame, find fault with, disapprove.*

cultellus -i, m. *a little knife.*

culter -tri, m. *a knife; a ploughshare, coulter.*

cultĭo -ōnis, f. *cultivation, agriculture.*

cultor -ōris, m., *a cultivator, planter, husbandman*; with genit., *an inhabitant, occupier* of a place; *a friend, supporter* of a person; *a worshipper* of gods.

cultrix -īcis f. *she who tends or takes care; an inhabitant.*

cultūra -ae, f. *tilling, culture, cultivation, husbandry*; animi, *mental culture, cultivation*; potentis amici, *courting of.*

¹cultus -a -um, partic. from colo; q.v.

²cultus -ūs, m. *tilling, cultivation, tending*; in gen., *care, careful treatment*; deorum, *reverence*, animi, *training, education*; hence *refinement, culture, civilization.*

cūlullus -i, m. *a drinking-vessel.*

¹cum (older form quom) conj., *when; whenever; since; although*; cum . . . tum . . ., *both . . . and. . . .*

²cum, prep., with abl., *with, together with; at the same time as*; cum eo quod, ut, or ne, *on condition that.*

Cūmae -arum, f. *a city of Campania*; adj. Cūmānus and Cūmaeus -a -um.

cumba (cymba) -ae, f. *small boat, skiff.*

cŭmĕra -ae, f. *a corn-bin.*

cŭmīnum -i, n. *a herb, cummin.*

cumprimis, see primus.

cumque (cunque, quomque), adverb, usually found added to a relative, with the force of *-ever, -soever.*

cŭmŭlo -are, *to heap up, pile up, increase, heighten; to fill up, overload*; cumulatus laude, *loaded with praise*; also *to crown, bring to perfection.*

Hence partic. cŭmŭlātus -a -um: *heaped up, increased, enlarged; crowned*

perfected. Adv. cŭmŭlātē, *abundantly, fully.*

cŭmŭlus -i, m. *heap, pile, mass; addition, increase, finishing touch.*

cūnābŭla -orum, n. pl. *cradle.*

cūnae -arum, f. pl., *cradle*, of young birds, *nest.*

cunctābundus -a -um, *loitering, dilatory.*

cunctātĭo -ōnis, f. *delay, lingering hesitation.*

cunctātor -ōris, m. *one who delays.*

cunctor -ari, dep. *to delay, linger, hesitate*; of things, *to move slowly.*

Hence partic. cunctans -antis, *lingering, slow*; adv. cunctanter.

cunctus -a -um, *all, all collectively, the whole.*

cŭnĕātim, *in wedge formation.*

cŭnĕo -are, *to secure with wedges; to shape like a wedge.*

Hence partic. cŭnĕātŭs -a -um, *pointed like a wedge.*

cŭnĕus -i, m. *a wedge; troops in wedge formation; any triangular figure*; often of *the wedge-shaped compartments into which the seats of a theatre were divided.*

cŭnīcŭlōsus -a -um, *full of rabbits* (or *of caverns*).

cŭnīcŭlus -i, m. (1) *a rabbit, cony.* (2) *an underground passage*; milit. *a mine.*

cūpa -ae, f. *cask, butt.*

cŭpīdĭtās -ātis, f. *eager desire, passionate longing.* Esp. *ambition; avarice, factiousness, party spirit.*

cŭpīdo -ĭnis, f. and poet. m., *longing, desire.* Esp. *desire for power, ambition; avarice; physical desire, love.* Personified, Cŭpīdo -ĭnis, m. *Cupid, god of love*; plur. Cŭpīdĭnes, *Cupids*; adj. Cŭpīdĭnĕus -a -um.

cŭpīdus -a -um, *desirous, eager, keen.* Esp. *eager for power, ambitious; avaricious*; physically, *desirous, passionate*; towards persons, *attached, partial.* Adv. cŭpĭdē, *eagerly, passionately.*

cŭpĭo cŭpĕre cŭpīvi or -ĭi -ītum, *to desire, long for, wish for.*

Hence partic. cŭpĭens -entis *longing, eager*; as adj., with genit.; adv. cŭpĭenter.

cŭpītor -ōris, m. *one who desires.*

¹cuppēdĭa -ae, f. *taste for delicacies.*

²cuppēdĭa -orum, n. pl. *delicacies, tit-bits.*

cuppēdīnārius -i, m. *a confectioner.*

cuppēdo = cupido; q.v.

cŭpressētum -i, n. *a cypress wood.*

cŭpressĕus -a -um, *made of cypress wood.*

cŭpressĭfer -fĕra -fĕrum, *cypress-bearing.*

cŭpressus -i (-ūs), f. *the cypress; a casket of cypress wood.*

cūr (quor) *why? wherefore?*

cūra -ae, f. *care*: (1) *care taken, carefulness, pains, attention, minding of* things or persons; of *business, management, administration*; meton., *an object of care, or a guardian, care-*

taker. (2) *care felt, anxiety, worry, disquiet.*

cūrālĭum -i, n. *coral, esp. red coral.*

cūrātĭo -ōnis, f. *care, attention;* esp. medical *attention, healing, curing;* of business *management, administration;* frumenti, *commission to buy corn;* agraria, *commission to divide land.*

cūrātor -ōris, m. *guardian, overseer.*

cūrātus, partic. from curo; q.v.

curcūlĭo -onis, m. *a weevil, corn-worm.*

Cŭrēs -ium, f. *a town of the Sabines;* adj. **Cŭrensis** -e.

Cūrētes -um, m. *ancient inhabitants of Crete;* adj. **Cūrētis** -ĭdis = *Cretan.*

cūrĭa -ae, f. (1) *a curia, a division of the Roman patricians;* meton., *the meeting-place of a* curia. (2) *the meeting-place of the senate, senate-house;* at Athens, *the Areopagus.*

cūrĭālis -e, *belonging to the same curia.*

cūrĭātim, *by* curiae.

cūrĭātus -a -um, *relating to* curiae; comitia curiata, *the original assembly of the Roman people.*

cūrĭo -ōnis, m. *the priest of a* curia; *a herald, crier.*

cūrĭōsĭtās -atis, *inquisitiveness.*

cūrĭōsus -a -um. (1) *careful, attentive.* (2) *inquisitive.* (3) *wasted by cares.* Adv. **cūrĭōsē,** *carefully; inquisitively.*

cūris or **quĭris,** f. *a spear.*

cūro -are, *to care for, pay attention to, trouble about;* with gerundive, *to see to a thing being done;* of business, *to manage, administer;* physically, *to minister to, cure, rest;* in business, *to provide* or *procure* money; curare Romae, *to be in charge at Rome.*

Hence partic. **cūrātus** -a -um, *cared for; showing care.* Compar. adv. **cūrātĭus,** *more carefully.*

currĭcŭlum -i, n. *running; a contest in running, race; raceground, course lap; a racing chariot.*

curro currĕre cŭcurri cursum, *to run, hasten;* esp. *to run in a race;* at sea, *to sail;* of time, *to pass.*

currus -ūs, m. *a chariot, car;* esp. *one used in racing, or war, or at a triumph;* meton., *a triumph.* Transf., *a plough with wheels; a ship.*

cursim, *hastily, quickly.*

cursĭto -are, *to run up and down.*

curso -are, *to run hither and thither.*

cursor -ōris, m. *a runner; a courier, messenger; a running footman.*

cursus -ūs, m. *running, rapid motion; course, direction, movement, journey.*

curto -are, *to shorten, abbreviate.*

curtus -a -um, *shortened, mutilated, defective;* esp. *gelded.*

cŭrūlis -e, *relating to a chariot;* equi, *horses provided for the Circus;* (sella) curulis, *the curule chair,* official seat of consuls, praetors, and curule aediles.

curvāmen -ĭnis, n. and **curvātūra** -ae, f. *curving, arching.*

curvo -are, *to bend, arch, curve; to influence.*

curvus -a -um, *bent, bowed, arched, curved, winding;* morally, *crooked.*

cuspis -ĭdis, f. *point,* esp. *of a spear;* hence *a spear, lance; a trident; a spit.*

custōdĭa -ae, f. *watching, guarding, custody, care;* milit., *keeping guard, watch;* of prisoners, *custody, safe-keeping;* custodia libera, *house-arrest.* Transf., *persons guarding, guards, sentinels; the station of the guard, post, prison; persons guarded, prisoners.*

custōdĭo -ire, *to guard, watch, keep, take care of; to keep in sight, observe; to keep in prison, hold captive.*

custōs -ōdis, c. *guardian, watchman, keeper, attendant; a gaoler, sentinel, guard, spy.*

cŭtĭcŭla -ae, f. *skin, cuticle.*

cŭtis -is, f. *skin, hide, leather.*

cўathus -i, m. *a ladle for filling goblets with wine;* as *measure of capacity =* one-twelfth of a sextarius.

cўbaea -ae, f. (with or without navis), *a merchantman.*

Cўbĕlē or **Cўbēbē** -ēs, f. *a Phrygian goddess, worshipped at Rome.*

²**cyclas** -ădis, f., *a female robe of state.*

¹**Cyclas** -ădis, f., gen. plur., **Cyclădes,** *a group of islands in the Aegean Sea.*

cyclĭcus -a -um, *cyclic.*

Cyclops -clōpis, m. *a Cyclops,* gen. plur., **Cyclōpes,** *the Cyclopes, a gigantic one-eyed race;* adj. **Cyclōpĭus** -a -um.

cycnēus or **cygnēus** -a -um, *belonging to the swan.*

cycnus or **cygnus** -i, m. *the swan.*

cўlindrus -dri, m. *a cylinder; a roller.*

Cyllēnē -ēs and -ae, f. *a mountain in Arcadia, where Mercury was born.* Adj. **Cyllēnēus** -a and **Cyllēnĭus** -a -um.

cymba -ae, f. = cumba; q.v.

cymbălum -i, n. *a cymbal.*

cymbĭum -i, n., *a small drinking-vessel.*

Cўnĭcus -a -um, *Cynic, of the Cynic school.*

cўnŏcĕphălus -i, m. *the dog-faced baboon.*

cўnŏsūra -ae, f., *the constellation Ursa Minor.*

Cynthus -i, m. *a mountain in Delos, birth-place of Apollo and Diana;* hence adj. as subst., m. **Cynthĭus** -i, *Apollo,* f. **Cynthĭa** -ae, *Diana.*

Cўpărissus, f. = cupressus; q.v.

Cyprus or **Cypros** -i, f., *the island of Cyprus;* adj. **Cyprĭus** -a -um, *Cyprian;* f. as subst. *Venus.*

Cўrēne -es and **Cўrēnae** -arum, f. *a city of north-eastern Africa;* adj. **Cўrēnaeus** and **Cўrēnăĭcus** -a -um, *Cyrenaic;* m. pl. as subst., *the Cyrenaic philosophers.*

Cўthēra -orum, n., *the island Cythera, sacred to Venus;* adj. **Cўthĕrēus** and **Cўthĕrēĭus** -a -um, *Cytherean;* f. as subst. = *Venus.*

cўtīsus -i, c. *clover or lucerne.*

D

D, d the fourth letter of the Latin
alphabet.

Dācī -orum, m. *the Dacians, a warlike
people on the Lower Danube.* **Dācĭa**
-ae, f. *their country.*

dactylĭcus -a -um, *dactylic.*

dactylĭŏthēca -ae, f. *a casket for rings.*

dactylŭs -i, m. *a metrical foot, a
dactyl* (— ◡ ◡).

¹**daedălus** -a -um : act., *skilful;*
(natura) daedala rerum, *quaint
artificer;* pass., *curiously wrought,
variegated.*

²**Daedălus** -i. m., *mythical Athenian,
builder of the Cretan labyrinth;* adj.
Daedălēus and **Daedălĭus** -a -um.

Dalmātae (Delmătae) -arum, m. pl.,
*the Dalmatians, inhabitants of Dal-
matia.*

Dămascus -i, f. *Damascus, capital of
Syria;* adj. **Dămascēnus** -a -um.
Damascene; pruna, *damsons.*

damma (older **dāma**) -ae, f. or m. *a
fallow-deer, chamois, antelope;* as
meat *venison.*

damnātĭo -ōnis, f. *condemnation.*

damnātōrĭus -a -um, *condemnatory.*

damno -are, *to cause loss or injury to;*
at law, *to condemn, sentence, punish*
(offence usually genit., *punishment*
genit. or abl.); damnari inter sicarios,
to be condemned as an assassin; in
gen., *to condemn, disapprove of;* of
deities, damnare voti *or* voto, *to grant
a person's wish, and compel him to
discharge his vow;* also *to assign,
devote, make over.*

damnōsus -a -um: act., *causing loss or
damage, detrimental;* pass., *damaged,
injured;* middle sense, *self-injuring.*
Adv. **damnōsē,** *ruinously.*

damnum -i, n. *loss, damage injury;*
at law, *a fine.*

Dănăē -ēs, f. *mother of Perseus.*

Dănăus -i, m. *son of Belus, who left
Egypt for Argos;* adj. **Dănăus** -a -um,
Argive, Greek; m. pl. **Dănăi** -orum,
the Greeks; **Dănăĭdes** -um, f. *the
fifty daughters of Danaus.*

dănista -ae, m. *money-lender.*

dăno = old form of do; q.v.

Dānŭvĭus -i, m. *the Danube.*

Daphnē -ēs, f. *daughter of Peneus,
changed into a laurel-tree.*

daphnōn -ōnis, m. *a grove of laurels.*

daps, dăpis, f. *a sacrificial feast,
religious banquet;* in gen., *meal, feast,
banquet.*

dapsĭlis -e, *sumptuous, plentiful.*

Dardănī -orum, m. pl. *a warlike
Illyrian people.*

Dardănus -i, m. *son of Jupiter, mythical
ancestor of the royal family of Troy;*
adj. **Dardănus** and **Dardănĭus** -a
-um, *Trojan;* subst. **Dardănĭa** -ae,
f. = *Troy;* **Dardănĭdes** -ae, m. *a male
descendant of Dardanus;* **Dardănis**
-ĭdis, *a Trojan woman.*

Dārēus -i, m. *name of several Persian
kings.*

dătĭo -ōnis, f. *a giving;* legal, *right of
alienation.*

dătīvus -a -um, *to do with giving;*
(casus) dativus, *the dative case.*

dăto -are, *to give away.*

dător -ōris, m. *giver.*

Daunus -i, m. *a mythical king of
Apulia, ancestor of Turnus;* adj.
Daunĭus -a -um, *Daunian;* f. subst.,
Daunĭas -ădis, *Apulia.*

dē, prep., with abl. (1) in space,
down from, away from. Transf.,
coming from an origin; *taken from* a
class or stock, *made from* a material,
changed from a previous state; of
information, *from* a source. (2) in
time; *following from, after;* in the
course of, during. (3) *about* a subject;
on account of a cause; *acc rding to* a
standard.

dĕa -ae, f. *goddess.*

dĕalbo -are, *to whitewash, plaster.*

dĕambŭlo -are, *to take a walk.*

dĕarmo -are, *to disarm.*

dēbacchor -ari, dep. *to rave, revel
furiously.*

dēbellātor -ōris, m., *a conqueror.*

dēbello -are: intransit., *to fight to the
end, finish a war;* transit. *to fight out*
a fight; *to conquer* an enemy.

dēbĕo -ēre -ŭi -itum, *to owe.* Lit. of
money, etc.; n. of perf. partic. pass.
as subst., debitum -i, *a debt.* Transf.,
to be indebted to somebody for anything; with infin., *to be due to* do a
thing, *be morally bound to* or *be
bound by* logic or *necessity* or *law* to;
to have to pay because of fate, *to be
destined to give.*

dēbĭlis -e, *feeble, weak.*

dēbĭlĭtās -ātis, f. *weakness, feebleness.*

dēbĭlĭtātĭo -ōnis, f. *weakening, disabling.*

dēbĭlĭto -are, *to weaken, enfeeble,
disable;* to *enervate, break down.*

dēbĭtĭo -ōnis, f. *owing, debt.*

dēbĭtor -ōris, m. *one who owes, a debtor.*

dēbĭtum -i, subst. from debeo; q.v.

dēcanto -are: transit., *to sing or say
repeatedly;* intransit., *to leave off
singing.*

dēcēdo -cēdĕre -cessi -cessum. (1) *to
move away, withdraw, retire;* milit. *to
march away.* Transf., *to retire, give
up;* with dat., *to yield to, retire in
favour of,* esp. *to depart from life,* to
die. (2) of things, *to retire, abate
cease;* sol decedens, *setting.* (3) *to
go astray, deviate.*

dĕcem, indecl. *ten.*

Dĕcember -bris, adj. *of December*
(originally the tenth Roman month);
December (mensis), *December.*

dĕcempĕda -ae, f. *a ten-foot rule.*

dĕcempĕdātor -ōris, m. *a land-
surveyor.*

dĕcemprĭmi -orum, m. pl. *the ten
chief men in the senate of a municipium*
or *colonia.*

dĕcemvir -i, m.; usually plur., *a
board of ten commissioners at Rome* for
various purposes.

dĕcemvĭrālis -e *relating to the
decemvirs.*

dĕcemvĭrātus -ūs, m. *the office of
decemvir.*

dĕcennis -e, *of ten years.*

dĕcens -entis, partic. from decet; q.v.

dĕcentia -ae, f., *propriety, comeliness*

dĕcerno -cernĕre -crēvi -crētum, *to decide, determine; to settle that a thing is so; and of action, to decide to do or to give a thing; of a body, to decide, decree;* as a member of a body, *to move, propose;* of combatants, *to settle by fighting.* Hence partic. **dĕcrētus** -a -um; n. as subst. **dĕcrētum** -i, *a resolve, decree;* philosoph. *doctrine, principle.*

dĕcerpo -cerpĕre -cerpsi -cerptum, *to pluck off, pluck away.* Transf., *to gather; to derive; to take away.*

dĕcertātio -onis, f. *contest.*

dĕcerto -are, *to contend, fight to a finish.*

dĕcessio -ōnis, f., *a withdrawing, departure;* esp. *of a governor retiring from his province.* Transf., *deduction, diminution.*

dĕcessor -ōris, m., *one who retires from an office, a predecessor.*

dĕcessus -ūs, m. *withdrawal, departure.* Esp. *the retirement of an official; death;* of water, *ebb.*

dĕcet -ēre -ŭit, *it is proper, it is fitting* (physically or morally). Hence partic. **dĕcens** -entis, *proper, fit;* adv. **dĕcenter.**

¹dĕcido -cidĕre -cĭdi, *to fall down, to fall dead, die;* in gen., *to sink, fall.*

²dĕcido -cidĕre -cĭdi -cīsum, *to cut down, cut off; to cut short, to settle, to arrange.*

dĕciens and **dĕciēs,** *ten times.*

decim-; see also decum-.

dĕcimus (older **dĕcŭmus**) -a -um, *tenth;* decimum, *for the tenth time.*

dĕcipio -cipĕre -cēpi -ceptum, *to catch;* hence *to cheat, deceive, beguile* (esp. of time).

dĕcisio -onis, f. *a settlement, decision.*

Dĕcius -a -um, *name of a Roman gens;* adj. **Dĕciānus** -a -um.

dēclāmātio -ōnis, f., *loud, violent speaking, declamation; practice in oratory,* or *a theme for such practice.*

dēclāmātor -ōris, m. *a declaimer.*

dēclāmātōrius -a -um, *of declamation, rhetorical.*

dēclāmĭto -are, *to speak loudly, declaim;* esp. *to practise public speaking;* causas, *to plead for practice.*

dēclāmo -are, *to speak loudly;* esp. *to practise speaking in public;* with object, *to declaim.*

dēclārātio -ōnis, f. *making clear, open expression.*

dēclāro -are, *to make clear, explain, reveal, declare;* of appointments, *to proclaim a person as chosen.*

dēclīnātio -ōnis, f. *bending away, turning aside.* Transf., *an avoiding, declining;* rhet. *a digression;* grammat. *inflexion, declension.*

dēclīno -are: transit., *to bend aside, turn away, deflect.* Transf., *to avoid, to shun;* intransit. *to deviate, swerve, digress.*

dēclīvis -e, *inclined downwards, sloping;* n. as subst. **dēclīvĕ** -is, *a slope, declivity.*

dēclīvĭtās -ātis, f., *a declivity.*

dēcocta -ae, f. subst. from decoquo; q.v.

dēcoctor -ōris, m., *spendthrift, bankrupt.*

dēcollo -are, *to behead.*

dēcōlo -are, *to trickle away.*

dēcŏlor -ōris, *off-colour, pale.*

dēcŏlōrātio -ōnis, f. *discolouring.*

dēcŏlōro -are, *to discolour.*

dēcŏquo -cŏquĕre -coxi -coctum, *to boil thoroughly; to boil down, boil away;* of metals, *to melt away;* of property, *to waste;* commerc., *to ruin oneself, become bankrupt.* Hence partic. **dēcoctus** -a -um, *boiled down;* of style, *insipid;* f. as subst. *a cold drink.*

dĕcor -ōris, m. *grace, comeliness beauty.*

dĕcŏro -are, *to embellish, beautify, adorn.*

dĕcŏrus -a -um, physically, *graceful, beautiful, comely;* morally, *proper, fit, becoming.* N. as subst. **dĕcōrum** -i, *propriety, grace.* Adv. **dĕcōrē,** *fitly, becomingly.*

dēcrĕpĭtus -a -um, *infirm, decrepit.*

dēcresco -crescĕre -crēvi -crētum, *to grow down, become smaller, decrease.*

dēcrētum -i, subst. from decerno; q.v.

dĕcŭma (**dĕcĭma**) -ae, f. *a tenth part tithe* (as an offering, tax or largess).

dĕcŭmānus (**dĕcĭmānus**) -a -um, *of the tenth.* (1) *relating to the provincial tax of a tenth;* m. as subst. *the farmer of such a tax.* (2) *belonging to the tenth legion;* m. pl. as subst. *its members.* (3) *belonging to the tenth cohort.*

dĕcŭmātes -ium, pl. adj. *relating to tithes.*

dĕcumbo -cumbĕre -cŭbŭi, *to lie down, fall, fall down.*

dĕcŭmo (**dĕcĭmo**) -are, *to take a tithe;* milit. *to decimate troops.*

dĕcŭria -ae, f. *a body of ten men; a class, division,* esp. *of jurors; a party, club.*

dĕcŭriātio -ōnis, f. and **dĕcŭriātus** -ūs, m., *a dividing into decuriae.*

¹dĕcŭrio -are, *to divide into bodies of ten,* or *into classes in gen.*

²dĕcŭrio -ōnis, m., *head of a body of ten;* milit. *company-commander in the cavalry;* polit., *a senator of a municipium or colonia.*

dēcurro -currĕre -cŭcurri or -curri -cursum., *to run down, hasten down;* milit. *to move down* or *to manoeuvre.* Transf., *to run in a race;* transit. *to run through, traverse* a set course; *to have recourse to, take refuge in;* of ships. *to sail downstream* or *to land;* of water, *to run down.*

dēcursio -ōnis, f., milit., *a manoeuvre* or *charge.*

dēcursus -ūs, m. *a running down;* milit. *a manoeuvre, a charge, attack.* Transf., *the completion of a course;* rhet., *rhythmical movement.*

dēcurtātus -a -um., *mutilated (of style).*

dĕcŭs -ŏris, n. *distinction, honour, glory, grace*; moral *dignity, virtue*; of persons, *pride, glory*; plur., *decora, distinguished acts.*

dĕcŭtĭo -cŭtĕre -cussi -cussum, *to shake down, shake off, knock off.*

dēdĕcet -dĕcēre -dĕcŭit, *it is unbecoming, unsuitable, unfitting.*

dēdĕcŏro -are, *to dishonour bring shame upon.*

dēdĕcŏrus -a -um, *shameful, dishonourable.*

dēdĕcŭs -ŏris, n. *shame, dishonour, disgrace; a dishonourable action, crime, vice.*

dēdĭcātĭo -ōnis, f., *consecration.*

dēdĭco -are, *to dedicate, consecrate; to specify, indicate.*

dēdignor -ari, dep. *to think unworthy, scorn, reject.*

dēdisco -discĕre -dĭdĭci, *to unlearn, forget.*

dēdĭtīcius -a -um, *relating to surrender*; m. plur., dediticii, *subjects of Rome without rights.*

dēdĭtĭo -ōnis, *unconditional surrender, capitulation.*

dēdo dēdĕre -dĭdi -dĭtum, *to give up, surrender*; esp. of the conquered, *to give up, surrender.* Transf., *to give up to, dedicate, devote.* Hence partic. **dēdĭtus** -a -um, *devoted to, addicted to*; deditā operā, *intentionally.*

dēdŏceo -ēre, *to cause to unlearn, to unteach; teach not to.*

dēdŏlĕo -dŏlēre -dŏlŭi, *to make an end of grieving.*

dēdūco -dūcĕre -duxi -ductum, *to lead or bring down*; in time, from the past, *to trace downwards to the present*; in amount, *to reduce,* or, from an amount, *to subtract*; in gen., *to lead or draw away; to lead forth colonists, to found a colony; to escort a person to a place*; of persons and things, *to bring out of one state, opinion, etc. into another*; in weaving, *to draw threads*; hence, *to draw out, spin out* in speech or writing.

dēductĭo -ōnis, f. *a leading down; a reduction; a leading away* of colonists, etc.

dēerro -are, *to wander from the right path, go astray.*

dēfătīgātĭo -ōnis, f. *exhaustion, fatigue.*

dēfătīgo -are, *to weary, fatigue.*

dēfătiscor = defetiscor; q.v.

dēfectĭo -ōnis, f. *failure.* Hence *defection, rebellion; weakening, failing, vanishing.* Partic. **dēfectus** -a -um, *failing, deficient.*

dēfector -ōris, m. *rebel, deserter.*

¹dēfectus -a -um, partic. of deficio; q.v.

²dēfectus -ūs, m., *a failing, disappearing*; esp. *a failing of light, eclipse.*

dēfendo -fendĕre -fendi -fensum. (1) *to repel, repulse, ward off, drive away.* (2) *to defend, protect*; esp. *to defend in court*; in argument, *to maintain a proposition* or *statement; to sustain a part.*

dēfensĭo -ōnis, f. (1) *a warding off.* (2) *defence.*

dēfensĭto -are, *to defend frequently.*

dēfenso -are, *to defend vigorously.*

dēfensor -ōris, m. (1) *one who wards off* or *averts.* (2) *a defender, protector,* esp. in court.

dēfĕro -ferre -tŭli -lātum, *to bring down, carry down*; in gen., *to bring or carry away,* esp. *to a particular place*; deferre rationes, *to hand in accounts*; fig., *to offer, hand over, refer*; of news, *to communicate, report,* esp. *to authority*; legal, deferre nomen *to inform against a person, indict*: deferre crimen, *to bring a charge.*

dēfervesco -fervescĕre -fervi or ferbŭi, *to cease boiling*; of passion, *to cease to rage.*

dēfĕtiscor (dēfătiscor) -fētisci -fessus dep. *to become tired, grow weary*: esp. in perf. partic. **dēfessus** -a -um. *weary, tired.*

dēfĭcĭo -fĭcĕre -fēci -fectum: intransit. *to do less than one might, to fail*; hence, *to desert, rebel, revolt*; of things, *to fail, run short*; of sun or moon, *to become eclipsed*; of fire, *to go out*; of water, *to ebb*; of strength, etc., *to fail, become weak*; animo deficere, *to lose heart*; transit., *to abandon, leave, fail*; rarely pass. defici, *to be failed.* Hence partic. **dēfectus** -a -um, *feeble,* esp. *because of age.*

dēfīgo -fīgĕre -fixi, -fixum, *to fasten down, fix in*; in gen., *to secure, plant firmly*; of sight or thought, *to concentrate, fix upon*; of persons, *to fix, make motionless,* with astonishment, etc.; partic. defixus, *astounded*; of enchantment, *to bind by a spell.*

dēfingo -fingere -finxi, *to form, mould.*

dēfīnĭo -ire, *to limit, bound, mark out; to set limits to a thing, confine; to set as a limit, appoint, assign; to interpret* ideas or words in terms of each other, *to understand one thing by another*; in logic, *to define.* Hence partic. **dēfīnītus** -a -um, *definite, distinct*; adv. **dēfīnītē.**

dēfīnītĭo -ōnis, f., *limiting, prescribing*; in logic, *a definition.*

dēfīnītīvus -a -um, *definitive, explanatory.*

dēfit (as from defio), *fails.*

dēflăgrātĭo -ōnis, f. *burning, destruction by fire.*

dēflăgro -are, *to be burnt down, destroyed by fire*; in gen., *to be destroyed*; of passions, *to cease burning, abate, cool.* Partic. in pass. sense, **dēflăgrātus** -a -um, *burnt down, destroyed.*

dēflecto -flectĕre -flexi -flexum: transit., *to bend down* or *aside*; intransit., *to turn aside, turn away*; in speech, *to digress.*

dēflĕo -flēre -flēvi -flētum, *to bewail, weep for.*

dēfloccatus -a -um, *bald.*

dēflōresco -flōrescĕre -flōrŭi, *to shed blossom, fade, wither.*

dēflŭo -flŭĕre -fluxi. (1) *to flow down, slip down, descend;* abstr., *to come down,* esp. of the gifts of heaven. (2) *to flow away, disappear, be lost.*

dēfŏdĭo -fŏdĕre fōdi -fossum, *to dig down into;* to *form by digging, excavate; to dig in, cover, bury, conceal.*

dēformātĭo -ōnis, f. *deforming, disfiguring; degradation.*

dēformis -e. (1) *deformed, misshapen, ugly, disgusting.* Transf., *foul, shameful.* (2) *formless, shapeless.* Adv. **dēformĭter,** *in an ugly fashion.*

dēformĭtās -ātis, f. *deformity, ugliness; disgrace, dishonour.*

dēformo -are. (1) *to form, fashion; to delineate.* (2) *to put out of shape, disfigure; to disgrace, dishonour.*

dēfraudo (**dēfrudo**) -are, *to deceive, cheat;* genium suum, *to deprive oneself of pleasure.*

dēfrēnātus -a -um, *unbridled, unrestrained.*

dēfrico -frĭcare -frĭcŭi -frictum, *to rub down;* fig. *to satirize, lash.*

dēfringo -fringĕre -frēgi -fractum, *to break down, break off.*

dēfrŭtum -i, n. *new wine boiled down.*

dēfŭgĭo -fŭgĕre -fūgi: intransit., *to flee away;* transit., *to fly from, avoid.*

dēfundo -fundĕre -fūdi -fūsum, *to pour down, pour out.*

dēfungor -fungi -functus, dep. *to perform, discharge, have done with;* (vita) defungi, *to die.*

dēgĕner -ĕris, *fallen away from one's origin, unworthy of one's race, degenerate, unworthy, ignoble.*

dēgĕnĕro -are: intransit., *to become unlike one's kind, to fall off, degenerate;* transit., *to cause to degenerate,* or *disgrace by degeneracy.*

dēgĕro -ĕre, *to carry off.*

dēgo dēgĕre dēgi, *to pass time;* absol., *to live.*

dēgrandĭnat, impers., *it hails violently,* or (perhaps) *it ceases to hail.*

dēgrăvo -are, *to weigh down, bring down, lower.*

dēgrĕdĭor -grĕdi -gressus, dep., *to step down, march down.*

dēgusto -are, *to take a taste from, taste;* of fire, *to lick;* of a weapon, *to graze;* in gen., *to try, make a trial of, sound.*

dēhinc, *from here, hence; from this time, henceforth, immediately after that time, thereupon.*

dēhisco -ĕre, *to gape, open, split down.*

dehŏnestāmentum -i, n. *blemish, deformity disgrace.*

dehŏnesto -are, *to dishonour, disgrace.*

dehortor -ari, dep. *to discourage, dissuade.*

dēĭcĭo -ĭcĕre -ĭēci -ĭectum, *to throw, cast, hurl down;* with reflex., *to rush down;* of upright things, *to throw to the ground, fell;* of persons, *to kill, bring down.* In gen., *to fling away or*

aside; naut., deici, *to be thrown off course;* milit. *to dislodge; to eject, dispossess; to shift* a person from an opinion, attitude; *to disappoint.*

Hence partic. **dēĭectus** -a -um *low-lying; dispirited, dejected.*

dēĭectĭo -ōnis, f. *throwing down; eviction from property.*

¹**dēĭectus** -a -um, partic. from deicio; q.v.

²**dēĭectus** -ūs, m. *a throwing down; a declivity, steep slope.*

dēĭero -are, *to swear.*

dein; see deinde.

dĕinceps, *one after another, successively.*

dĕinde, and abbrev. **dĕin:** of space, *from that place;* of time, *thereafter, thereupon, then, afterwards;* in enumerations, *next, and then.*

Dēĭŏtărus -i, m. *a king of Galatia,* defended by Cicero.

dēĭungo -ĕre, *to disconnect.*

dēlābor -labi -lapsus, dep. *to glide down, fall down, sink;* of liquids, *to flow down.* Transf., *to sink to, come down to* circumstances, etc.; *to proceed from, be derived from* an origin; *to fall unawares among* people.

dēlăcĕro -are, *to tear to pieces.*

dēlāmentor -ari, dep. *to bewail, lament.*

dēlasso -are, *to weary, tire out.*

dēlātĭo -ōnis, f. *reporting, giving information against, denunciation.*

dēlātor -ōris, m., *an informer, denouncer.*

dēlectābĭlis -e, *delightful, pleasant.*

dēlectāmentum -i, n. *delight, amusement.*

dēlectātĭo -ōnis, f. *delight, pleasure.*

dēlecto -are, *to divert, attract, delight;* in pass., *with abl. to take delight in:* in pass. with infin., *to delight to.*

dēlectus -ūs, m. *choosing, choice.*

dēlēgātĭo -ōnis, f. *assignment of a debt.*

dēlēgo -are, *to transfer, commit, assign; to impute, attribute, ascribe.*

dēlēnīmentum -i, n. *what soothes or charms.*

dēlēnĭo (**dēlĭnĭo**) -ire, *to soften down; to soothe or charm.*

dēlēnītor -ōris, m. *one who soothes or cajoles.*

dēlĕo -lēre -lēvi -lētum, *to blot out, efface;* in gen., *to destroy, annihilate.*

dēlībĕrābundus -a -um, *carefully considering, deliberating.*

dēlībĕrātĭo -ōnis, f. *consideration, consultation.*

dēlībĕrātīvus -a -um, *relating to deliberation.*

dēlībĕrātor -ōris, m., *one who deliberates.*

dēlībĕro -are, *to weigh carefully, consider, consult about; to ask advice,* esp. of an oracle; as a result of deliberation, *to resolve.*

Hence partic. **dēlībĕrātus** -a -um. *resolved, determined.*

dēlībo -are, *to take a little from, to taste;* in gen., *to extract, derive; to take from so as to enjoy; to take from so as to lessen or spoil.*

dēlībro -are, *to peel the bark off.*

dēlībūtus -a -um, *steeped.*

dēlĭcātus -a -um, *soft, tender;* in bad sense, *luxurious* of things, *spoilt, effeminate* of persons; of tastes, *fastidious, dainty, nice.* Adv. **dēlĭcātē**, *luxuriously.*

dēlĭcīae -arum, f. pl. *allurements, charms, delights, fancies;* esse in deliciis, *to be a favourite;* concr., *darling, sweetheart.*

dēlĭcĭŏlae -arum, f. pl. *a darling.*

dēlictum -i, n. *a fault, crime.*

¹dēlĭgo -lĭgĕre -lēgi -lectum *to pick, pluck; to choose, select.*

²dēlĭgo -are, *to fasten, bind up.*

dēlingo -ere, *to lick off, lick up.*

dēlinquo -linquĕre -liqui -lictum, *to fail, be wanting,* esp. *to fail in duty, commit a crime.*

dēlĭquesco -lĭquescĕre -lĭcŭi, *to melt, dissolve; to vanish, disappear.*

dēlĭquo and **dēlĭco** -are, *to clarify; to explain.*

dēlīrātĭo -ōnis, f.. *folly, silliness, dotage.*

dēlīro -are, " *to go off the rails* " *act crazily, rave.*

dēlīrus -a -um, *silly, crazy, doting.*

dēlĭtesco -lĭtescĕre -lĭtŭi, *to conceal oneself, lie hid, take refuge.*

dēlītĭgo -are, *to scold furiously.*

Dēlos -i, f., *a small island in the Aegean Sea, birth-place of Apollo and Diana;* adj. **Dēlĭăcus** and **Dēlĭus** -a -um, *of Delos;* as subst. **Dēlĭus** -i, m. = *Apollo;* **Dēlĭa** -ae, f. = *Diana.*

Delphi -orum, m. *a town in Phocis, famous for its oracle of Apollo;* adj. **Delphĭcus** -a -um.

delphīnus -i and **delphīn** -īnis, m. *dolphin.*

dēlūbrum -i, n. *a shrine, temple.*

dēluctor -ari, dep. and **dēlucto** -are, *to wrestle.*

dēlūdo -lūdĕre -lūsi -lūsum, *to mock, cheat.*

dēlumbo -are, *to lame, enervate, weaken.*

dēmădesco -mădescĕre -mădŭi, *to become wet through.*

dēmando -are, *to entrust, commit.*

dēmens -mentis, *out of one's mind, insane, senseless;* adv. **dēmenter.**

dēmentĭa -ae, f., *senselessness, insanity;* in plur., *mad actions.*

dēmentĭo -ire, *to be mad, rave.*

dēmĕrĕo -ēre and **dēmĕrĕor** -ēri, dep. *to earn thoroughly; to deserve well of a person, to oblige.*

dēmergo -mergĕre -mersi -mersum, *to sink, plunge into, dip under;* aere alieno demersus, *over head and ears in debt.*

dēmētĭor -mētīri -mensus, *to measure out;* partic. **dēmensus** -a -um, in pass. sense, with n. as subst., *an allowance.*

dēmēto -mĕtĕre -messŭi -messum, *to mow, reap, cut down or off.*

dēmigro -are, *to emigrate, depart.* Transf., *to die.*

dēmĭnŭo -mĭnŭĕre -mĭnŭi -mĭnūtum, *to take away from, diminish, lessen;* capite se deminuere, *to suffer a loss of civil rights.*

dēmĭnūtĭo -ōnis, f. *lessening, diminution;* sui, *loss of prestige;* capitis, *loss of civil rights; right of alienation.*

dēmīror -ari, dep. *to wonder (at).*

dēmissĭo -ōnis, f., *sinking, lowering;* animi, *dejection.*

dēmītīgo -ari, *to make mild, soften.*

dēmitto -mittĕre -mīsi -missum, *to send down, lower, put down;* tunica demissa, *hanging loosely;* demissi capilli, *growing long;* milit., *to lead down;* naut., *to lower gear or bring a vessel downstream* or *to land.* Transf., *to sink, bury, plunge;* of spirits, *to lower.*
Hence partic. **dēmissus** -a -um, *hanging down;* of dress and hair, *long, loose;* of places, *low-lying.* Transf., *feeble, weak; unassuming, modest; down-cast, dispirited.* Adv. **dēmissē**, *low, near the ground.* Transf., *modestly, humbly meanly.*

dēmo dēmĕre dempsi demptum, *to take away, subtract.*

Dēmŏcrĭtus -i, m. *a philosopher of Abdera* (c. 460-370 B.C.). Hence adj. **Dēmŏcrĭtĭcus** -a -um.

dēmōlĭor -iri, dep. *to throw down, demolish.*

dēmōlītĭo -ōnis, f. *throwing down, demolition.*

dēmonstrātĭo -ōnis, f. *pointing out, indication, explanation, description;* rhet., *oratory concerned with praise and censure.*

dēmonstrātīvus -a -um, *demonstrative;* rhet., of oratory, *concerned with praise and censure.*

dēmonstrātor -ōris, m., *one who points out or indicates.*

dēmonstro -are *to indicate, explain, describe.*

dēmŏrĭor -mŏri -mortŭus, dep. *to die, die off;* with acc. of person, *to die for love of.*

dēmŏror -ari, dep.: intransit., *to delay, loiter;* transit., *to stop, delay, retard.*

Dēmosthĕnēs -is (also -i), *the Athenian orator* (384-322 B.C.).

dēmŏvĕo -mŏvēre -mōvi -mōtum, *to move away, remove;* hominem de sententia, *to make a person change his opinion.*

dēmūgītus -a -um, *filled with the noise of lowing.*

dēmulcĕo -mulcēre -mulsi, *to stroke down, caress by stroking.*

dēmum, of time, *at length, at last;* in enumerations, *finally, in short;* id demum, *that and that alone.*

dēmurmŭro -are, *to murmur or mutter over.*

dēmūtātĭo -ōnis, f., *change, alteration,* esp. for the worse.

dēmūto -are: transit., *to change, alter a thing,* esp. for the worse; intransit. *to change one's mind or become different.*

dēnārĭus -a -um, *containing ten;* denarius nummus, *or* denarius *alone, a Roman silver coin.*

dēnarro -are, *to narrate, tell, relate.*

dēnăto -are, *to swim down.*

dēnĕgo -are, *to deny, say no; to deny, refuse, reject a request.*

dēni -ae, -a, *ten by ten, ten at a time, by tens.*

dēnīcālis -e, *releasing from death;* feriae, *a funeral ceremony.*

dēnīquĕ: *in time, at last, finally;* in enumerations, *again, further or finally; in short, in fine.*

dēnōmĭno -are, *to name.*

dēnormo -are, *to make crooked.*

dēnŏto -are, *to mark out for another, designate precisely; to take note of.*

dens dentis, m. *a tooth.* Transf., of things resembling a tooth, e.g., *a mattock or sickle;* abstr., *of anything sharp, biting, destructive.*

denso -are, and densĕo -ēre, *to make thick, condense, press together.*

densus -a -um, *thick, close, dense;* in time, *frequent;* in degree, *intense, vehement;* in style, *of work or author, condensed.* Adv. densē, *densely;* of time, *frequently.*

dentālĭa -ĭum, n. pl. *the share-beam of a plough.*

dentātus -a -um, *provided with teeth, toothed; polished by teeth.*

dentĭo -ire, *to cut teeth;* of teeth, *to grow.*

dēnūbo -nūbĕre -nupsi -nuptum, *to be married off, to marry (of the woman),* esp. *beneath her.*

dēnūdo -are, *to lay bare, uncover, reveal.* Transf., *to rob, plunder.*

dēnuntĭātĭo -ōnis, f. *announcement, declaration, threat.*

dēnuntĭo -are, *to announce, give notice, declare, threaten;* bellum denuntiare, *to declare war;* legal, *to give notice, serve a summons.*

dēnŭo, *anew, again; a second time.*

deŏnĕro -are, *to unload, disburden.*

dēorsum *or* dēorsus, *downwards;* sursum deorsum, *up and down, backwards and forwards.*

dēpāciscor = depeciscor; q.v.

dēpactus -a -um, *fastened down, firmly fixed.*

dēpasco -pascĕre -pāvi -pastum and dēpascor -pasci, dep. *to feed off;* in gen., *to eat up, consume, reduce.*

dēpĕciscor -pĕcisci -pectus, dep. *to make a bargain for or about; to settle for, accept a condition.*

dēpecto -pectĕre -pexum, *to comb down;* in comedy, *to beat soundly.*

dēpĕcūlātor -ōris, m. *plunderer, embezzler.*

dēpĕcūlor -ari, dep. *to rob, plunder.*

dēpello -pellĕre -pŭli -pulsum, *to drive down, or away, expel, remove;* milit., *to dislodge;* naut., *to drive off course;* in gen., *to drive away, avert;* of persons, *to dissuade.*

dēpendĕo -ēre, *to hang down; to depend upon; to be derived from.*

dēpendo -pendĕre -pendi -pensum, *to weigh out and pay over.*

dēperdo -perdĕre -perdĭdi -perdĭtum, *to lose, waste, destroy;* esp. *of the effects of love.*

dēpĕrĕo -perire -pĕrĭi, *to perish or be ruined utterly; to be desperately in love.*

dēpĭlo -are, *to strip of hair or feathers.*

dēpingo -pingĕre -pinxi -pictum, *to paint, depict, portray.*

dēplango -plangĕre -planxi, *to bewail, lament.*

dēplexus -a -um, *clasping.*

dēplōro -are: intransit., *to weep bitterly, lament;* transit., *to lament, bewail; to regard as lost, give up.*

dēplŭit -plŭĕre, *rains down.*

dēpōno -pōnĕre -pŏsŭi -pŏsĭtum. (1) *to lay down, put down;* esp. *to lay as wager or prize.* (2) *for safe-keeping, to put down, deposit; to commit, entrust.* (3) *to lay aside, have done with.*

Hence partic. dēpŏsĭtus -a -um. (1) *laid out; dying, despaired of, dead* (2) *entrusted;* n. as subst. *a deposit.*

dēpŏpŭlātĭo -ōnis, f.. *laying waste, ravaging.*

dēpŏpŭlātor -ōris, m. *a ravager.*

dēpŏpŭlor -ari, dep.; also dēpŏpŭlo -are, *to lay waste, ravage, destroy.*

dēporto -are, *to carry down, carry off, take away; to bring home; to banish for life (with loss of rights and property).*

dēposco -poscĕre -pŏposci, *to demand,* usually *for a purpose,* esp. *for punishment.*

dēprāvātĭo -ōnis, f. *perverting, distorting;* animi depravity.

dēprāvo -are, *to make crooked, pervert, disfigure;* verbally, *to distort, misrepresent;* morally, *to spoil, corrupt.* Adv. from partic., dēprāvātē, *perversely.*

dēprĕcābundus -a -um, *earnestly entreating.*

dēprĕcātĭo -ōnis, f. (1) *an attempt to avert by entreaty, deprecating.* (2) *an entreaty against a person, for his punishment.*

dēprĕcātor -ōris, m. (1) *one that begs off, an intercessor.* (2) *one that pleads for.*

dēprĕcor -ari, dep. (1) *to try to avert by entreaty, to deprecate; to allege in excuse (so as to avoid punishment).* (2) *to entreat against a person, to curse.* (3) *to entreat for, beg for, intercede.*

dēprĕhendo and dēprendo -endĕre -endi -ensum, *to seize upon, catch hold of;* esp. *to surprise, catch, detect a person in a crime or fault; to discover, detect, observe a thing.*

dēprĕhensĭo -ōnis, f. *detection.*

dēprĭmo -prĭmĕre -pressi -pressum, *to press down, depress;* esp. *to plant deep in the ground, dig deep;* of ships, *to sink.*

Hence partic. depressus -a -um, *low-lying.*

dēproelĭans -antis, *struggling violently.*

dēprōmo -prōmĕre -prompsi -promptum, *to take down produce, fetch out.*

dēprŏpĕro: intransit, *to hasten;* transit., *to hasten over, produce in haste.*

dēpŭdet -pŭdēre -pŭdŭit, *ceases to be ashamed, loses all sense of shame.*

dēpugno -are, *to fight hard, fight it out.*

dēpulsĭo -ōnis, f. *driving away;* rhet. *defence.*

dēpulsor -ōris, m. *an averter.*

dēpŭto -are. (1) *to prune, cut off.* (2) *to count, estimate.*

deque; see susque deque.

dērĕlinquo -linquĕre -līqui -lictum, *to forsake, desert, abandon.*

dērĕpentĕ, *suddenly.*

dērēpo -rēpĕre -repsi, *to creep, crawl down.*

dērīdĕo -rīdēre -rīsi -rīsum, *to laugh at, mock, deride.*

dērīdĭcŭlus -a -um, *very laughable;* n. as subst. *ridicule;* esse deridiculo, *to be an object of ridicule.*

dērĭgo -rĭgĕre -rexi -rectum, *to set straight, direct;* (of placing also in form dirigo), *to order, dispose;* milit. *to draw up.* Transf., *to direct, aim, guide* abstr. things.

dērĭgŭi, perf., *grew quite stiff.*

dērĭpĭo -rĭpĕre -rĭpŭi -reptum, *to tear down, snatch away.*

dērīsor -ōris, m. *a mocker.*

dērīsus -ūs, m. *mockery, derision.*

dērīvātĭo -ōnis, f. *turning away or diversion of water.*

dērīvo -are, *to turn into another channel, to divert.*

dērŏgo -are, *to modify a law;* in gen., *to diminish, detract from.*

dērōsus -a -um, *gnawed away.*

dēruncĭno -are, *to cheat, fleece.*

dērŭo -rŭĕre -rŭi -rŭtum, *to cast down, make to fall.*

dēruptus -a -um, *broken off;* hence *precipitous, steep;* n. pl. as subst., *precipices.*

dēsaevĭo -ire -ĭi -ĭtum, *to rage violently.*

dēscendo -scendĕre -scendi -scensum, *to climb down, come down, descend;* milit., *to march down;* of things, *to sink, pierce, penetrate;* of mountains, *to slope down;* of the voice, *to sink.* Transf., of persons, *to lower oneself, stoop;* of things, *to sink in, penetrate.*

dēscensĭo -ōnis, f. *going down, descent;* Tiberina, *voyage down the Tiber.*

dēscensus -ūs, m. *going down, descent; way down.*

dēscisco -sciscĕre -scīvi or -scĭi -scĭtum, *to break away, revolt, withdraw, diverge.*

dēscrībo -scrībĕre -scripsi -scriptum. (1) *to transcribe, copy.* (2) *to describe, delineate, represent, portray.*

dēscriptĭo -ōnis, f. (1) *a copy.* (2) *a representation, figure, description.*

dēsĕco -sĕcare -sĕcŭi -sectum, *to hew off, cut off.*

dēsĕro -sĕrĕre -sĕrŭi -sertum, *to forsake, abandon, leave; to neglect, disregard.*

Hence partic. **dēsertus** -a -um, *forsaken, abandoned;* n. pl. as subst., *deserts, wildernesses.*

dēsertor -ōris, m. *one who forsakes,* milit., *deserter.*

dēservĭo -ire, *to serve zealously, be a slave to.*

dēsĕs -sĭdis, m. (nom. sing. not found), *idle, lazy, inactive.*

dēsīdĕo -sīdēre -sēdi -sessum, *to sit idle, be slothful.*

dēsīdĕrābĭlis -e, *desirable.*

dēsīdĕrātĭo -ōnis, f. *desire, longing.*

dēsīdĕrĭum -i, n. *desire or longing, grief for the absence or loss of a person or thing;* in gen., *a desire or request.*

dēsīdĕro -are, *to long for what is absent or lost, to wish for; to miss, find a lack of;* milit., *to lose.*

dēsīdĭa -ae, f. *idleness, inactivity, apathy.*

dēsīdĭōsus -a -um, *slothful, idle, lazy;* adv. **dēsīdĭōsē.**

dēsīdo -sīdĕre -sēdi, *to sink down, subside, settle.* Transf., *to deteriorate.*

dēsignātĭo -ōnis, f. *marking out, designation: appointment to an office.*

dēsignātor -ōris, m.=dissignator; q.v.

dēsignātor -ōris, m. = dissignator; q.v.

dēsigno -are, *to mark out, trace, plan;* in gen., *to point out, indicate, signify; to portray, delineate;* polit., *to nominate, elect;* partic. **dēsignātus,** *elected, designate.*

dēsĭlĭo -sĭlire -sĭlŭi -sultum, *to leap down;* ad pedes, *dismount.*

dēsĭno -sĭnĕre -sĭi -sĭtum: transit., *to cease, desist from;* intransit., *to cease, stop, end;* with in and acc., *to end in.*

dēsĭpĭentĭa -ae, f. *foolishness.*

dēsĭpĭo -sĭpĕre. *to be foolish, act foolishly.*

dēsisto -sistĕre -stĭti -stĭtum, *to stand away:* from a person, *to withdraw;* from action, etc., *to desist, leave off, cease.*

dēsōlo -are, *to leave solitary, forsake.*

dēspecto -are; *to regard from above, look down upon; to despise.*

¹dēspectus -a -um, partic. from despicio; q.v.

²dēspectus -ūs, m. *a looking down, downward view; an object of contempt.*

dēspērātĭo -ōnis, f. *hopelessness, despair.*

dēspēro -are: intransit., *to be without hope, despair;* transit., *to despair of, give up.* Adv. from pres. partic., **dēspēranter,** *despairingly, hopelessly.* Perf. partic. **dēspērātus** -a -um; in pass. sense, *despaired of;* in middle sense, *desperate.*

dēspĭcātĭo -ōnis, f. and **dēspĭcātus** -ūs, m. *contempt.*

dēspĭcĭentĭa -ae, f., *looking down upon; contempt.*

dēspĭcĭo -spĭcĕre -spexi -spectum, *to look down, regard from above; to look down upon, despise.* Pres. partic. act. **dēspĭcĭens,** *contemptuous.* Perf. partic. pass. **dēspectus** -a -um, *despised, contemptible.*

dēspĭcor -ari, *to look down upon, despise.* Perf. partic. in pass. sense **despĭcātus** -a -um, *despised, contemptible.*

dēspōlĭo -are, *to plunder, despoil.*

dēspondĕo -spondēre -spondi -sponsum, *to pledge, to promise,* esp. *to promise in marriage, betroth;* in gen., *to pledge, devote;* with animum *or* animos, *to lose heart, despair.*

dēspūmo -are. (1) *to skim off.* Transf., *to digest.* (2) *to drop foam.*

dēspŭo -spŭere, *to spit down, spit on the ground.* Transf., *to reject.*

dēsquāmo -are, *to take off the scales, to scale.*

dēsterto -stertĕre -stertŭi, *to finish snoring or dreaming.*

dēstillo -are, *to drip down, distil.*

dēstĭnātĭo -ōnis, f. *fixing, determining, appointment.*

dēstĭno -are, *to make fast, fix down; to fix, determine, settle, appoint;* with infin., *to resolve to do;* of persons, *to appoint* to an office; of things *to fix upon, intend to buy.*
  Hence partic. **dēstĭnātus** -a -um, *fixed, determined;* n. as subst., *an objective or intention;* (ex) destinato, *intentionally.*

dēstĭtŭo -stĭtŭĕre -stĭtŭi -stĭtūtum, *to set down, place;* esp. *to leave in the lurch, forsake, desert.*

dēstĭtūtĭo -ōnis, f. *forsaking, abandoning.*

dēstringo -stringĕre -strinxi -strictum. (1) *to strip;* esp. *to draw or bare a sword.* Transf., *to satirize, censure.* (2) *to touch lightly, graze.*
  Hence partic. **dēstrictus** -a -um, *severe.*

dēstrŭo -strŭĕre -struxi -structum, *to pull down, dismantle, destroy, ruin.*

dēsŭbĭto (or **dē sŭbĭto**), *suddenly.*

dēsūdo -are, *to sweat violently, exert oneself hard.*

dēsŭēfīo -fĭēri -factus sum, pass., *to be made unaccustomed.*

dēsŭesco -suescĕre -suēvi -suētum, *to become unaccustomed;* esp. partic. **dēsŭētus** -a -um: in pass. sense, *disused;* in middle sense, *unaccustomed, unused to.*

dēsŭētūdo -ĭnis, f. *disuse.*

dēsultor -oris, m. *a leaper, acrobat.* Transf., *an inconstant person.*

dēsultōrĭus -a -um, *relating to a desultor.*

dēsum -esse -fŭi, *to be down, fall short, fail, be missing or remiss.*

dēsūmo -sūmĕre -sumpsi -sumptum, *to take out, choose, select.*

dēsŭpĕr, *from above.*

dēsurgo -surgĕre -surrexi -surrectum, *to rise and go down or out.*

dētĕgo -tĕgĕre -texi -tectum, *to uncover, lay bare, disclose.*

dētendo -tendĕre -tensum, *to unstretch;* tabernacula, *to strike tents.*

dētergĕo -tergēre -tersi -tersum. (1) *to wipe off, clear away, brush off.* (2) *to cleanse by wiping.*

dētĕrĭor -ĭus, genit. -ōris, compar. (superl. deterrimus), *lower, inferior, poorer, worse.* Adv. **dētĕrĭus,** *worse.*

dētermĭnātĭo -ōnis, f., *boundary, end.*

dētermĭno -are, *to bound, fix the limits of, determine.*

dētĕro -tĕrĕre trīvi -trītum, *to rub away, wear out; to detract from, weaken.*

dētĕrrĕo -terrēre -terrŭi -territum, *to frighten away, deter, discourage.*

dētestābĭlis -e, *abominable, horrible.*

dētestātĭo -ōnis, f. (1) *a cursing, execration.* (2) *a warding off, averting.*

dētestor -ari, dep. (1) *to pray against: to pray for deliverance from* a person or thing, or *to curse, execrate.* (2) of the gods' action, *to avert, remove.*

dētexo -texĕre -texŭi -textum, *to make by plaiting; to finish, complete.*

dētĭnĕo -tĭnēre -tĭnŭi -tentum, *to hold back, detain; to prevent; to engage, occupy exclusively.*

dētondĕo -tondēre -tŏtondi *and* -tondi -tonsum, *to shear, clip.*

dētŏno -tŏnare -tŏnŭi *to cease to thunder or rage.*

dētorquĕo -torquēre -torsi -tortum. (1) *to turn away, bend aside.* (2) *to twist out of shape, distort.*

dētractĭo -ōnis, f. *drawing off, withdrawal, taking away; rhet., ellipsis.*

dētracto = detrecto; q.v.

dētractor -ōris, m., *detractor, disparager.*

dētrăho -trăhĕre -traxi -tractum. (1) *to draw down, drag down; to lower, humiliate.* (2) *to draw off, drag away, remove;* numerically, *to subtract;* in speech, *to detract from* a person, *disparage, slander.*

dētrectātĭo -ōnis, f. *refusal.*

dētrectātor -ōris, m. *disparager, detractor.*

dētrecto -are. (1) *to decline, refuse, shirk.* (2) *to disparage, detract from, depreciate.*

dētrīmentōsus -a -um, *detrimental, hurtful.*

dētrīmentum -i, n. *loss, damage, injury;* milit., *loss, defeat.*

dētrītus -a -um, partic. from detero; q.v.

dētrūdo -trūdĕre -trūsi -trūsum, *to push down, thrust down;* milit., *to dislodge;* legal, *to dispossess, eject.* Transf., of persons, *to force, compel;* of functions, *to put off, postpone.*

dētrunco -are, *to lop or cut off; to mutilate.*

dēturbo -are, *to force away, dash down;* milit., *to dislodge;* legal, *to eject, dispossess.*

Deucălĭōn -ōnis, m. son of Prometheus, *saved in an ark from a great flood, with his wife Pyrrha.*

deunx -uncis, m. *eleven-twelfths of a unit.*

deūro -ūrĕre -ussi -ustum, *to burn down;* of cold, *to destroy, nip.*

dĕus -i, m. *a god, a deity;* di meliora (ferant), *God forbid.*

dēvasto -are, *to lay waste, devastate.*

dēvĕho -vĕhĕre -vexi -vectum, *to carry away* or *down*; pass. devehi (sc. navi), *to sail*.

dēvello -vellere -velli -vulsum, *to pluck, tear away*.

dēvēlo -are, *to unveil, uncover*.

dēvĕnĕror -ari, dep. (1) *to worship, revere*. (2) *to avert by prayers*.

dēvĕnio -vĕnire -vēni -ventum, *to come to, arrive at, reach*.

dēverbĕro -are, *to thrash soundly*.

¹dēversor -ari, dep., *to lodge as a guest*.

²dēversor -ōris, m., *a guest*.

dēversōrĭŏlum -i, n. *a small lodging*.

dēversōrĭus -a -um, *fit to lodge in*; n. as subst. *an inn, lodging, refuge*.

dēvertĭcŭlum (dēvort-) -i, n. (1) *a by-way, by-path*; hence *digression*. (2) *an inn, lodging, refuge, resort*.

dēverto (dēvorto) -vertĕre -verti -versum; *to turn aside*; esp. *to turn aside to a lodging, to put up at, stay with*. Transf., *to digress*.

dēvexus -a -um, *moving downwards, descending, sinking*; of position, *sloping down, shelving, steep*; of tendency, *inclining to*.

dēvincio -vincire -vinxi -vinctum, *to bind, tie fast, attach, connect*. Hence partic. **dēvinctus** -a -um, *attached, devoted*.

dēvinco -vincĕre -vīci -victum, *to conquer thoroughly, subjugate, overcome*.

dēvītātĭo -ōnis, f. *avoiding*.

dēvīto -are, *to avoid*.

dēvĭus -a -um, *off the beaten track, out of the way, solitary, retired*; in mind, *erroneous, unreasonable*.

dēvŏco -are, *to call down* or *away*; devocare in dubium, *to bring into danger*.

dēvŏlo -are, *to fly down, hasten down*.

dēvolvo -volvĕre -volvi -vŏlūtum, *to roll down*; pass., *to roll down, fall headlong, sink back*.

dēvŏro -are, *to swallow, devour, seize upon*; of words, *to articulate badly, mispronounce*; of property, *to consume, waste*; of disagreeable things, *to swallow, accept, put up with*.

dēvortĭcŭlum; see deverticulum.

dēvortĭum -i, n., *a by-way, by-path*.

dēvōtĭo -ōnis, f. (1) *consecrating, devoting*. (2) *cursing*. (3) *enchantment, incantation*.

dēvōto -are, *to consecrate* or *devote to death*.

dēvŏvĕo -vŏvĕre -vōvi -vōtum, *to consecrate, devote*, esp. to a god, or to death; *to curse, execrate*; *to bewitch, enchant*; in gen., *to devote, give up*. Hence partic. **dēvōtus** -a -um, *devoted*; *accursed*; *attached to a person*; m. pl. as subst. *faithful followers*.

dextella -ae, f., *a little right hand*.

dexter -tĕra -tĕrum, or -tra -trum; compar. **dextĕrĭor** -ĭus, superl. **dextĭmus** -a -um; *right, on the right hand, on the right side*. Transf., *dexterous, skilful; propitious, favourable, opportune*. F. as subst., **dextĕra** or **dextra** -ae, *the right hand*; (a) dextra, *on the right*; esp. *the right hand as pledge of faith*; sometimes, in gen. *the hand*. Adv. **dextĕrē** or **dextrē**; compar. **dextĕrĭus** (*dexterously, skilfully*.

dextĕrĭtās -ātis, f., *skilfulness, readiness*.

dextrorsum and **dextrorsus**, *on the right, towards the right*.

Dīa -ae, f. *mother of Mercury*.

dĭădēma -ătis, n., *a royal headband, diadem*.

dĭaeta -ae, f. (1) *a way of living prescribed by a physician, regimen, diet*. (2) *a living-room*.

dĭălectĭcus -a -um, *of discussion, dialectical*; m. as subst., **dĭălectĭcus** -i, *a dialectician, logician*; f. **dĭălectĭca** -ae, and **dĭălectĭcē** -es, *the art of dialectic, logic*; n. pl. **dĭălectĭca** -orum, *dialectical discussion*; adv. **dĭălectĭcē**, *dialectically*.

dĭālis -e, *relating to Jupiter*; (flamen) dialis, *the priest of Jupiter*.

dĭălŏgus -i, m., *a philosophical conversation*.

Dĭāna (older **Dīāna**) -ae, f. *the virgin goddess of the moon and of hunting*; adj. **Dĭānĭus** -a -um, *belonging to Diana*.

dĭārĭa -orum, n. pl. *a day's allowance of food* or *pay*.

dĭbăphus (-a) -um, *double-dyed*; as f. subst. **dĭbăphus** -i, *the purple-striped robe of the higher magistrates in Rome*.

dīca -ae, f., *law-suit, action in a Greek court*.

dĭcācĭtās -ātis, f. *wit, satire, raillery*.

dĭcātĭo -ōnis, f. *settling as a citizen*.

dĭcax -ācis, *ready of speech; witty, satirical, sarcastic*.

dĭchŏrēus -i, m. *a double trochee*.

dĭcĭō -ōnis, f. *power, sovereignty, authority*.

dĭcĭs (genit.); dicis causa, dicis gratia, *for form's sake, for the sake of appearances*.

¹dīco -are, *to consecrate, dedicate, devote to the gods; to deify, place among the gods; to inaugurate*. Transf., *to devote, give up, set apart*; se civitati, or in civitatem, *to become a citizen*.

²dīco -dicĕre dixi dictum, *to indicate; to appoint; most commonly, to say, speak, tell, mention*; in pass. with infin., *to be said to*; impersonally, dicitur, *it is said that*; of ideas, *to express, put into words*; ius, *to administer law, give rulings*; of persons or things, *to mention, speak of, tell of, relate; to name, call; to mean, refer to*. N. of partic. as subst. **dictum** -i, *a word, saying, speech; a witty saying, a bon-mot; a prediction; an order, command*.

dĭcrŏtum -i, n. *a vessel with two banks of oars*.

dictamnus -i, f. *dittany, a plant*.

dictātor -ōris, m. *a dictator*; in Rome, *an extraordinary magistrate, elected* *in emergency and granted absolute power*; elsewhere, *a chief magistrate*.

dictātōrĭus -a -um, *belonging to a dictator, dictatorial.*

dictātūra -ae, f., *the ffice of dictator, dictatorship.*

dictĭo -ōnis, f. *saying, speaking, talk, oratory.*

dictĭto -are, *to say often, reiterate, assert repeatedly*; dictitare causas, *to plead frequently.*

dicto -are, *to say often; to say over, dictate a* thing to be written; hence *to get written down.*

dictum -i, n. subst. from ²dico; q.v.

¹Dīdō -ūs, f., *the founder of Carthage, also called Elisa or Elissa.*

²dīdo dīdĕre dīdĭdi dīdĭtum, *to divide, distribute, spread round.*

dīdūco -dūcĕre -duxi -ductum, *to draw apart, separate*; milit., *to divide, distribute,* also *to scatter, disperse.*

dĭēcŭla -ae, f. *a little day, a short time.*

dĭērectus -a -um, an abusive expression, like *go and be hanged!*

dĭēs -ēi, m. or f., *daytime, day; a day, period of twenty-four hours*; diem ex die, *from day to day*; in dies, *daily,* esp. of a continuing process of change; in diem vivere, *to live for the day*; meton., *the business or events of the day*; in gen., *time.* Esp. *a particular day, fixed date; a historic day; day of death; anniversary,* esp. *birthday.*

Dĭespĭter -tris, m. *a name for Jupiter.*

diffāmo -are, *to spread evil reports about, to defame.*

diffĕrentĭa -ae, f., *difference, distinction.*

diffĕrĭtās -ātis, f. *difference.*

diffĕro differre distŭli dīlātum. Transit., *to carry in different directions, spread abroad, scatter; to spread news; to harass, disturb, discredit* a person; in time, *to delay, postpone* business, *to put off* persons. Intransit., *to differ, be different*; nihil differt, *there is no difference.*

differtus -a -um, *stuffed full, crammed.*

diffĭcĭlis -e, *difficult;* of character, *hard to deal with, morose, obstinate.* Adv. **diffĭcĭlĭtĕr** and **diffĭcultĕr**, *with difficulty.*

diffĭcultās -ātis, f., *difficulty, need, trouble, distress;* of character, *obstinacy, moroseness.*

diffīdentĭa -ae, f., *want of confidence, distrust, despair.*

diffīdo -fīdĕre -fīsus sum, *to have no confidence, mistrust, despair*; partic. **diffīdens** -entis, *distrustful, diffident*; adv. **diffīdentĕr.**

diffindo -findĕre -fīdi -fissum, *to split, cleave, open*; legal, diem, *to postpone business.*

diffingo -ĕre, *to form again, forge anew*; fig., *to change.*

diffĭtĕor -ēri, dep. *to deny, disavow.*

difflo -are, *to blow apart.*

diffluo -flŭĕre -fluxi -fluxum, *to flow*

in different directions, to dissolve, melt away.

diffringo -fringĕre -fractum, *to shatter.*

diffŭgĭo -fŭgĕre -fūgi -fŭgĭtum, *to fly in different directions, to disperse.*

diffŭgĭum -i, n. *dispersion.*

diffundĭto -are, *to scatter.*

diffundo -fundĕre -fūdi -fūsum, *to pour in different directions, to spread out, diffuse, extend;* esp. *to make relax, brighten up, gladden.* Hence partic. **diffūsus** -a -um, *spread out, extensive, wide;* adv. **diffūsē,** *copiously, diffusely.*

diffūsĭlis -e, *capable of spreading, elastic.*

dīgĕro -gĕrĕre -gessi -gestum, *to carry in different directions, to separate, spread;* esp. in orderly fashion, *to arrange.*

dīgestĭo -ōnis, f. *arrangement, distribution.*

dīgestus -a -um, partic. from digero; q.v.

dīgĭtŭlus -i, m. *a little finger; the touch of a finger.*

dīgĭtus -i, m. (1) *a finger*; digitus pollex, *the thumb*; index, *the forefinger*; as a measure, *a finger's breadth, an inch.* (2) *a toe.*

dīglădĭor -ari, dep. *to flourish the sword; to fight, struggle fiercely;* in words, *to dispute.*

dignātĭo -ōnis, f. *esteem; dignity, reputation, honour.*

dignĭtās -ātis, f. *worth, worthiness, merit.* Transf., *dignified appearance or style; dignified position, esteem, honour;* esp. *official rank*; plur. dignitates, *persons of rank.*

digno -are, and **dignor** -ari, dep. *to consider worthy;* with infin., *to deign to.*

dignosco (dīnosco) -noscĕre -nōvi, *to recognize as different, to distinguish.*

dignus -a -um. (1) *worthy, deserving;* esp. of persons, usually with abl. or genit. (2) of things, *worth having, deserved, suitable, fittings;* dignum est, foll. by infin., *it is proper.* Adv. **dignē.**

dīgrĕdĭor -grĕdi -gressus, dep. *to go apart, depart, deviate;* in speech, *to digress.*

dīgressĭo -ōnis, f. and **dīgressus** -ūs, m. *separation, departure;* in speech, *digression.*

dĭiūdĭcātĭo -ōnis, f. *judging, decision.*

dĭiūdĭco -are. (1) *to judge between parties, to decide, determine.* (2) *to distinguish, find a difference between.*

dīiun-; see disiun-.

dīlābor -lābi -lapsus, dep., *to glide apart:* of solids, *to fall to pieces, fall down, melt, dissolve;* of liquids, gases, etc., *to flow apart, run away;* of persons in groups, *to break up, slip away;* in gen., *to break up, vanish* of time, *to go by.*

dīlăcĕro -are, *to tear in pieces.*

dīlāmĭno -are, *to split in two.*

dīlănĭo -are, *to tear in pieces.*

dīlăpĭdo -are, *to demolish.*

dīlargior -īri, dep. *to hand round, give liberally.*

dīlātĭo -ōnis, f. *putting off, postponing.*

dīlāto -are, *to spread out, extend; litteras, to pronounce broadly.*

dīlātor -ōris, m., *a dilatory person, loiterer.*

dīlātus, partic. from differo; q.v.

dīlaudo -are, *to praise highly.*

¹**dīlectus** -a -um, partic. from diligo; q.v.

²**dīlectus** -ūs, m.: in gen., *choosing, choice, selection;* milit., *a levy, recruiting of troops, conscription;* meton., *troops so raised.*

dīligens -entis, partic. from diligo; q.v.

dīligentia -ae, f., *carefulness, attentiveness, accuracy;* esp. *care in management, economy.*

dīligo -līgĕre -lexi -lectum, *to choose out; to prize, love, esteem highly.* Hence pres. partic. **dīligens** -entis, *attentive, careful;* esp. *careful in housekeeping, economical, saving;* adv. **dīligentĕr,** *attentively, carefully.*

dīlōrico -are, *to tear open.*

dīlūcĕo -ēre, *to be clear, evident.*

dīlūcesco -lūcescĕre -luxi, *to grow light, become day; to become clear.*

dīlūcĭdus -a -um, *clear, lucid, plain;* adv. **dīlūcĭdē.**

dīlūcŭlum -i, n., *the break of day, dawn.*

dīlūdium -i, n., *an interval, breathing-space.*

dīluo -lŭĕre -lŭi -lūtum, (1) *to wash apart, separate, dissolve;* of troubles, *to remove, resolve;* of puzzles, *to clear up.* (2) *to dilute, temper; to weaken, lessen, impair.*

dīlŭvĭes -ēi, f. *washing away, inundation.*

dīlŭvio -are, *to flood, inundate.*

dīlŭvium -i, n. *flood, deluge, inundation.*

dīmāno -are, *to flow in different directions, spread abroad.*

dīmensĭo -ōnis, f. *measuring.*

dīmētĭor -mētīri -mensus, dep. *to measure out.*

dīmēto -are and dep. **dīmētor** -ari, *to measure out.*

dīmĭcātĭo -ōnis, f., *a fight, struggle, battle.*

dīmĭco -are, -avi, *to brandish weapons;* hence *to fight, contend, struggle.*

dīmĭdĭātus -a -um, *halved, divided, half.*

dīmĭdĭus -a -um, *halved, divided in half;* dimidia pars, *half.* N. as subst. **dīmĭdĭum** -i, *half:* dimidio minus, *less by half.*

dīmĭnūtĭo; see deminutio.

dīmissĭo -ōnis, f. (1) *a sending out.* (2) *a dismissing, discharging.*

dīmitto -mittĕre -mīsi -missum, (1) *to send forth, send in different directions; without object, to send (word) round.* (2) *to send away, let go, let fall;* milit. *to disband or to detach;* of a gathering, *to break up, dismiss;* of places, *to*

give up, leave; of abstr. things, *to give up, renounce, abandon.*

dimminŭo -ĕre, *to dash to pieces.*

dīmŏvĕo -mŏvēre -mōvi -mōtum. (1) *to move asunder, part, divide.* (2) *to separate, remove, take away.*

dīnosco = dignosco; q.v.

dīnŭmĕrātĭo -ōnis, f. *enumeration.*

dīnŭmĕro -are, *to count,* esp. *to count money, to pay.*

dĭoecēsis -ĕos and -is, f., *a district under a governor.*

dĭoecētes -ae, m., *a revenue official or treasurer.*

Dĭŏmēdēs -is, m. (1) *a hero of the Trojan War, son of Tydeus.* (2) *king of the Bistones in Thrace.*

Dĭŏnē -ēs, f. and **Dĭōna** -ae, f. (1) *the mother of Venus.* (2) *Venus.* Adj. **Dĭōnaeus** -a -um.

Dĭŏnȳsus (-os) -i, m., *the Greek name of Bacchus.* Hence **Dĭōnȳsia** -orum, n. pl. *the feast of Dionysus.*

dĭōta -ae, f. *a two-handled wine-jar.*

dĭplōma -ătis, n. (1) *a letter of introduction given to travellers.* (2) *a government document conferring privileges.*

dīremptus -ūs, m. *a separation.*

dīreptĭo -ōnis, f. *plundering, pillaging.*

dīreptor -ōris, m., *plunderer, pillager.*

dīrĭbĕo -ēre -ĭtum, *to sort tablets when taken out of the ballot-box.*

dīrĭbĭtĭo -ōnis, f. *sorting of voting tablets.*

dīrĭbĭtor -ōris, m., *the officer who sorted voting tablets.*

dīrĭgo -rĭgĕre -rexi -rectum, *to arrange, direct.*
Hence partic. **dīrectus** -a -um, *straight, direct; straightforward, plain, simple.* Abl. as adv. **dīrecto** and adv. **dīrectē,** *straight, directly.* See also derigo.

dīrĭmo -ĭmĕre -ēmi -emptum, *to part, separate, divide.* Transf., *to break off, interrupt, stop* temporarily or permanently.

dīrĭpĭo -rĭpĕre -rĭpŭi -reptum, *to snatch apart, tear to pieces;* of spoil, *to divide,* hence, milit., *to pillage, lay waste; to tear away.*

dīrĭtās -ātis, f. *misfortune, disaster; cruelty, fierceness.*

dīrumpo -rumpĕre -rūpi -ruptum, *to break apart or to pieces, shatter;* of friendship, etc., *to sever, break up;* in pass., dirumpi, *to burst with envy, grief, anger.*

dīrŭo -rŭĕre -ŭi -ŭtum, *to pull apart, demolish, destroy, break up;* financially, *to ruin.*

dīrus -a -um, *fearful, horrible, frightful, cruel.* N. pl. **dīra** -orum, and f. pl. **dīrae** -arum, as subst., *unlucky omens, curses;* **Dīrae** -arum, as name for the Furies.

¹**Dīs,** Ditis, m. *a name of Pluto, god of the Lower World.*

²**dīs,** dītis (contracted from dives), *rich; having* or *containing* or *bringing wealth.*

discēdo -cēdĕre -cessi -cessum. (1) *to*

go asunder, part, separate. (2) to depart, go away; milit., to march away; discedere ab signis, to break the ranks; ab armis, to lay down arms; to come out of a contest, to come off; in gen., to depart, pass away; to deviate, swerve, digress; polit., of the senate, in sententiam discedere, to support a resolution.

disceptātio -ōnis, f. debate, discussion, controversy.

disceptātor -ōris, m. and disceptātrix -trīcis, f. an arbitrator.

discepto -are. (1) to decide, settle, determine. (2) to dispute, debate, discuss.

discerno -cernĕre -crēvi -crētum, to sever, separate, set apart. Transf., to distinguish, discern.

discerpo -cerpĕre -cerpsi -cerptum, to pluck to pieces, dismember.

discessio -ōnis, f. (1) going separate ways, separation; polit., voting, a division in the senate. (2) a going away, departure.

discessus -ūs, m. (1) parting, separation. (2) departure, going away; milit., marching off; banishment.

discīdium -i, n. tearing apart; separation, division; separation in feelings, disagreement.

discīdo -ĕre, to cut in pieces.

discindo -ĕre -scĭdi -scissum, to cleave asunder, split.

discingo -cingĕre -cinxi -cinctum, to take off the girdle, ungird. Partic. discinctus -a -um, ungirt; at ease, careless, dissolute.

disciplīna -ae, f., instruction, teaching; training, education; esp. military training. Transf., results of training, discipline, ordered way of life; that which is taught, learning, body of knowledge, science; a rhetorical or philosophical school or system.

discipŭla -ae, f., a female pupil.

discipŭlus -i, m. a pupil, apprentice.

disclūdo -clūdĕre -clūsi -clūsum, to shut away, separate, divide.

disco discĕre dĭdĭci, to learn, get to know; discere fidibus, to learn to play on the lyre; in gen., to receive information, find out; to become acquainted with, learn to recognize.

discŏlor -ōris, of different colours; in gen., different.

disconvĕnio -ire, to disagree, not to harmonize.

discordābĭlis -e, disagreeing.

discordĭa -ae, f. dissension, disagreement; milit., mutiny, sedition.

discordiōsus -a -um, full of discord, mutinous.

discordo -are, to be at discord, disagree, be opposed; milit., to be mutinous.

discors -cordis, disagreeing, inharmonious, opposed, different.

discrĕpantia -ae, f. disagreement, difference.

discrĕpātio -ōnis, f. disagreement, disunion.

discrĕpĭto -are, to be quite unlike.

discrĕpo -are -ŭi, to differ in sound, be

discordant; to disagree, be different. Res discrepat, or impers., discrepat, people are not agreed; with acc. and infin., it is inconsistent that.

discrībo -scrībĕre -scripsi -scriptum, to mark out, arrange, classify, define; to allot, fix, appoint. Hence partic. discriptus -a -um, classified, arranged; adv. discripte.

discrīmen -inis, n. (1) dividing line, distinction, difference, interval. (2) turning-point, critical moment; crisis, hazard, danger.

discrīmino -are, to separate, sunder, divide.

discriptio -ōnis, f. an arrangement definition, distribution.

discrŭcio -are, to torture, torment, esp. mentally.

discumbo -cumbĕre -cŭbŭi -cŭbĭtum. (1) to recline at table. (2) to go to bed.

discŭpio -cŭpĕre (colloq.), to long.

discurro -currĕre -cŭcurri and -curri -cursum, to run about, run to and fro.

discursus -ūs, m. a running about, running to and fro.

discus -i, m., a quoit.

discŭtio -cŭtĕre -cussi -cussum, to shatter. Transf., to disperse, scatter, break up.

dīsertus -a -um, eloquent, expressive; adv. dīserte and dīsertim.

dīsĭcio dīsĭcĕre dīsĭēci dīsiectum, to throw in different directions, cast asunder; of buildings, etc., to throw down; of military formations, to break up, disperse; of abstr. things, to break up, frustrate.

dīsiecto -are, to toss about.

¹dīsiectus -a -um, partic. from disicio; q.v.

²dīsiectus -us, m., scattering, dispersing.

dīsiunctio -ōnis, f. separation, estrangement; in logic, a disjunctive proposition.

dīsiungo (dīiungo) -iungĕre -iunxi -iunctum, to unbind, loosen, separate, remove, distinguish. Hence partic. dīsiunctus -a -um, separated, apart, distant, remote; of speech, disconnected; in logic, disjunctive. Compar. adv. dīsiunctĭus, rather in disjunctive fashion.

dispando -pandĕre -pandi -pansum, or -pessum, to expand, stretch out.

dispār -păris, unlike, dissimilar, unequal.

dispărīlis -e, unlike, dissimilar, unequal.

dispăro -are, to separate, part, divide; n. of partic. as subst. dispărātum -i, rhet., the contradictory proposition.

dispartio = dispertio; q.v.

dispello -pellĕre -pŭli -pulsum, to drive in different directions, to scatter.

dispendĭum -i, n. expenditure, expense loss.

dispenno = dispando; q.v.

dispensātio -ōnis, f., weighing out; management, administration; the office of a treasurer.

dispensātor -ōris, m. steward, bailiff treasurer.

dispenso -are, to weigh out or pay out; in gen., to distribute, to arrange.

disperdo -děre -dĭdi -dĭtum, to squander, ruin, spoil.

dispěrěo -ire -ĭi, to perish utterly, be squandered, ruined.

dispergo -spergěre -spersi -spersum, to scatter, disperse. Adv. from perf. partic. **dispersē**, dispersedly, here and there.

dispertĭo -ire, and dep. **dispertĭor** -iri, to separate, divide, distribute.

dispĭcĭo -spĭcěre -spexi -spectum, to see clearly, esp. by an effort; to make out, discern, perceive; to reflect upon, consider.

displĭcěo -ēre, to displease; displicere sibi, to be dissatisfied with oneself, be out of spirits.

displōdo -plōděre -plōsi -plōsum, to burst noisily.

dispōno -pōněre -pŏsŭi -pŏsĭtum, to put in different places, to distribute, put in order; milit., to station at intervals.

Hence partic. **dispŏsĭtus** -a -um, arranged, orderly; adv. **dispŏsĭtē**, in order, methodically.

dispŏsĭtĭo -ōnis, f. regular arrangement or order in a speech.

dispŏsĭtū abl. sing. m., in or by arranging.

dispŏsĭtūra -ae, f., arrangement, order.

dispŭdet -ēre -ŭit, it is a great shame.

dispŭtātĭo -ōnis, f. arguing, debate.

dispŭtātor -ōris, m. debater, disputant.

dispŭto -are, to reckon up; to debate, discuss, argue.

disquīro -ěre, to inquire into, investigate.

disquīsĭtĭo -ōnis, f. inquiry, investigation.

dissaepĭo -saepire -saepsi -saeptum, to hedge off, separate, divide; n. of perf. partic. as subst. **dissaeptum** -i, barrier, partition.

dissēco -sěcāre -sěcŭi -sectum, to cut up.

dissēmĭno -are, to spread abroad, disseminate.

dissensĭo -ōnis, f. difference in feeling or opinion; disagreement, variance, conflict, opposition.

dissensus -ūs, m. disunion, disagreement.

dissentānĕus -a -um, disagreeing, different.

dissentĭo -sentire -sensi -sensum, to be of different feeling or opinion, to be opposed, not to agree.

dissěrēnat -are, impers., it is clearing up all round, of the weather.

¹dissěro -sěrěre -sēvi -sĭtum, to scatter seed, sow; to spread.

²dissěro -sěrěre -sěrŭi -sertum, to set in order; hence to examine, treat of, discuss.

disserpo -ere, to creep about, spread.

dissertĭo -ōnis, f. a severance.

disserto -are, to treat of, discuss, argue.

dissĭděo -sīděre -sēdi -sessum, to sit apart, be distant, disagree, be opposed; of clothes, to sit unevenly.

dissīdo -sīděre -sēdi, to fall apart, disagree.

dissignātĭo -ōnis, f. arrangement.

dissignātor -ōris, m. one that arranges, a supervisor.

dissigno -are, to arrange, regulate, manage.

dissĭlĭo -sīlire -sĭlŭi, to leap apart, break asunder.

dissĭmĭlis -e, unlike, dissimilar; adv. **dissĭmĭlĭtěr**, differently.

dissĭmĭlĭtūdo -ĭnis, f. unlikeness, difference.

dissĭmŭlātĭo -ōnis, f. a concealing, dissembling, esp. of irony.

dissĭmŭlātor -ōris, m. dissembler, concealer.

dissĭmŭlo -are. (1) to dissemble, disguise, keep secret; pass. with middle force, dissimulata deam, concealing her divinity. (2) to ignore, leave unnoticed. Adv. from pres. partic. **dissĭmŭlantěr**, in a dissembling manner.

dissĭpābĭlis -e, that can be scattered.

dissĭpātĭo -ōnis, f. scattering.

dissĭpo or **dissŭpo** -are, to scatter, disperse; milit. to break up, rout; to break up, destroy, squander.

Hence partic. **dissĭpātus** -a -um, disconnected.

dissĭtus, partic. from dissero; q.v.

dissŏcĭābĭlis -e: act., separating; pass. unable to be united.

dissŏcĭātĭo -ōnis, f. separation, parting.

dissŏcĭo -are, to separate, sever, divide; in feeling, to estrange.

dissŏlūbĭlis -e, dissoluble, separable.

dissŏlūtĭo -ōnis, f. breaking up, dissolution, destruction; naturae, death; navigii, shipwreck; criminum, refutation; rhet., want of connexion.

dissolvo -solvěre -solvi -sŏlūtum, to loosen, break up, undo, destroy; glaciem, to melt; animam, to die; criminationem, to refute; of debts, to pay, discharge; to release a person from difficulties, to unravel, explain a difficulty.

Hence partic. **dissŏlūtus** -a -um, loose; navigium, leaky; of style, disconnected; of character, wanting in energy, lax; profligate, dissolute. Adv. **dissŏlūtē**, disconnectedly, loosely; carelessly, negligently, without energy.

dissŏnus -a -um, discordant, different, disagreeing.

dissors -sortis, having a different lot or fate.

dissuāděo suāděre -suāsi -suāsum, to advise against, oppose by argument.

dissuāsĭo -ōnis, f. advising to the contrary, speaking against.

dissuāsor -ōris, m. one who advises to the contrary, one who speaks against.

dissulto -are, to leap apart, burst asunder.

dissŭo -sŭěre -sŭi -sūtum, to unstitch, undo.

distaedet -ēre, causes boredom or disgust.

distantĭa -ae, f. distance, difference, diversity.

distendo (distenno) -tenděre -tendi -tentum, to stretch apart, expand, esp.

to *fill full, distend.* Transf., *to distract, perplex.*
Hence partic. **distentus** -a -um, *distended, full.*

distermĭno -are, *to separate by a boundary, divide.*

distĭchon distichi, n., *a poem of two lines, distich.*

distinctĭo -ōnis, f. *a distinction, difference; the finding of a difference, the act of distinguishing, discriminating*; rhet., *a division in a speech; a pause, stop.*

¹**distinctus** -a -um, partic. from distinguo; q.v.

²**distinctus** -ūs, m. *difference, distinction.*

distĭnĕo -tĭnēre -tĭnŭi -tentum, *to hold asunder, keep apart, separate.* Transf., *to divide in feeling; to distract; to keep away, prevent* a thing from happening.
Hence partic. **distentus** -a -um, *distracted, occupied.*

distinguo -stinguĕre -stinxi -stinctum, *to mark off, distinguish, divide.* Transf., *to separate, distinguish*; gram., *to punctuate; to set off, decorate, adorn.*
Hence partic. **distinctus** -a -um, *separate, distinct; set off, diversified, adorned.* Adv. **distinctē**, *clearly, distinctly.*

disto -are, *to be apart, be distant; to differ, be distinct*; impers., *distat, there is a difference.*

distorquĕo torquēre -torsi -tortum, *to twist apart, distort; to torture.*
Hence partic. **distortus** -a -um, *distorted, deformed; of speech, perverse.*

distortĭo -ōnis, f. *distortion.*

distractĭo -ōnis, f. *pulling apart, separation, disunion.*

distrăho -trăhĕre -traxi -tractum, *to pull apart or pull to pieces*; of associations, *to break up, dissolve*; of persons, *to draw away, estrange,* also *to distract*; of property, *to sell up*; gram., *to leave a hiatus in a verse.*

distrĭbŭo -ŭĕre -ŭi -ūtum, *to distribute, divide.* Adv. from partic. **distrĭbūtē**, *methodically, with logical arrangement.*

distrĭbūtĭo -ōnis, f. *division, distribution.*

distringo -stringĕre -strinxi -strictum, *to draw apart, stretch out, to engage at different points, divert, occupy.*
Hence partic. **districtus** -a -um, *busy, occupied, engaged.*

disturbātĭo -onis, f. *destruction.*

disturbo -are, *to drive apart in confusion; to destroy, raze to the ground; to bring to naught, frustrate, ruin.*

dītesco -ere, *to become rich.*

dīthyrambĭcus -a -um, *dithyrambic.*

dīthyrambus -i, m. *a dithyrambic poem* (originally in honour of Bacchus).

dītĭo, better **dicio**; q.v.

dītĭor, dītissĭmus; see dis.

dīto -are, *to enrich, make wealthy.*

dĭū, adv. (1) *by day.* (2) *for a long time.* (3) *a long time ago.* Compar. **dĭūtĭus**, *longer; too long.* Superl. **dĭūtissĭmē.**

dĭurnus -a -um, *belonging to a day* or *lasting for a day*; n. as subst. *a journal, account-book* or *a daily allowance.*

dīus -a -um, *divine, god-like*; hence *fine, noble*; also (apparently) *out of doors, in the open air.*

dĭūtĭnus -a -um, *lasting a long time, long*; adv. **dĭūtĭnē.**

dĭūtĭus, dĭūtissĭmē; see diu.

dĭūturnĭtās -ātis, f. *long duration.*

dĭūturnus -a -um, adj., *lasting a long time, of long duration.*

dīvārĭco -are, *to stretch apart, spread out.*

dīvello -vellĕre -velli -vulsum (-volsum), *to pluck apart, tear asunder, break up, destroy, interrupt; to distract, pull away, remove, separate.*

dīvendo -vendĕre -vendĭtum, *to sell in separate lots.*

dīverbĕro -are, *to strike apart, cleave, divide.*

dīverbĭum -i, n. *dialogue on the stage.*

dīversĭtās -ātis, f. *contrariety, contradiction; difference, diversity.*

dīversōrĭum; see deversorium.

dīverto (divorto) -vertĕre -verti -versum, *to turn different ways*; hence *to differ.*
Hence partic. **dīversus** -a -um, *turned away, turned in different directions*; of places, *out of the way, remote*; of character, *fluctuating, irresolute*; in gen., *different, unlike, opposed, hostile.* Adv. **dīversē**, *differently, diversely.*

dīves -vĭtis, *rich, wealthy*; with abl. or genit., *rich in.*

dīvexo -are, *to tear asunder*; hence *to destroy, plunder, to distract.*

dīvĭdĭa -ae, f. *division, trouble.*

dīvĭdo -vĭdĕre -vīsi -vīsum. (1) *to divide up, separate into parts*; esp. *to divide among persons, distribute, allot*; polit., *sententiam, to divide a resolution into parts so that each part can be voted on*; in music, *to accompany.* (2) *to separate from one another; to distinguish; to set off, to adorn.*
Hence partic. **dīvīsus** -a -um, *separate.*

dīvĭdŭus -a -um, *divisible; divided, parted*; fig., *distracted.*

dīvīnātĭo -ōnis, f. *the gift of prophecy, divination*; legal, *the selection of a prosecutor.*

dīvīnĭtās -ātis, f. *divine nature, divinity; the power of prophecy or divination; excellence, surpassing merit.*

dīvīnĭtŭs, *divinely, by divine influence; by inspiration, by means of divination; admirably, nobly.*

dīvīno -are, *to foretell, prophesy, forebode.*

dīvīnus -a -um. (1) *belonging or relating to a deity, divine; res divina, the service of the gods*; n. as subst. *a sacrifice,* in plur. *divine things* or *attributes.* (2) *divinely inspired, prophetic*; *vates, a poet*; m. as subst., *a seer.* (3) *noble, admirable.* Adv. **dīvīnē**, *divinely, by divine* *power; by divine inspiration, prophetically; admirably, excellently.*

dīvīsio -ōnis, f. *division, distribution.*

dīvīsor -ōris, m. *a divider; a distributor,* esp. *of lands; a hired bribery agent.*

dīvīsuī, dat. sing. m., *for division.*

dīvītiae -arum, f. pl. *riches, wealth; ornaments, rich offerings;* of soil, *richness.*

dīvortĭum -i, n. *divergence, separation;* of things, *a boundary, parting of the ways;* of persons, *separation, divorce.*

dīvorto; see diverto.

dīvulgo -are, *to make common, publish, spread abroad.*

Hence partic. **dīvulgātus** -a -um, *spread abroad, made common.*

dīvus -a -um: as adj., *divine* or *deified;* as subst., m. *a god* and f. *a goddess* (often as epithet of dead and deified emperors); **sub dīvo** (neuter), *in the open air.*

do dăre dědi dătum. (1) *to offer, give, grant, lend, bestow; to hand over, commit, devote;* of letters, *to give for dispatch;* **vela dare ventis,** *to sail;* **poenas,** *to pay a penalty;* **verba,** *to give words only,* i.e., *to cheat;* of news, *to tell, communicate.* (2) *to cause, bring about, put.*

dŏcĕo dŏcēre dŏcŭi doctum, *to teach, instruct* (with acc. of person and/or of thing); with clause, *to inform that* or *how;* **docere fabulam** *to teach a play to the actors, to bring out, exhibit.*

Hence partic. **doctus** -a -um, *taught; learned, instructed, well-informed; experienced, clever, shrewd.* Adv. **doctē,** *learnedly, skilfully; cleverly, shrewdly.*

dochmĭus -i, m. *a metrical foot, the dochmiac.*

dŏcĭlis -e, *teachable, docile.*

dŏcĭlĭtās -ātis, f. *teachableness, docility.*

doctor -ōris, m. *a teacher.*

doctrīna -ae, f. *teaching, instruction; knowledge, learning.*

doctus -a -um, partic. from doceo; q.v.

dŏcŭmen -ĭnis, n. and **dŏcŭmentum** -i, n., *example, pattern, warning, proof.*

dōdrans -antis, m. *three fourths;* as a measure of length, *nine inches.*

dogma -ătis, n. *a philosophical doctrine.*

Dolabella -ae, m. *a Roman family name in the gens Cornelia.*

dŏlabra -ae, f. *a pick-axe.*

dŏlĕo dŏlēre dŏlŭi, *to suffer pain,* physical or mental, *to be pained, to grieve;* of things, *to cause pain.*

Hence partic. **dŏlens,** *painful;* adv. **dŏlentĕr,** *painfully, sorrowfully.*

dōlĭum -i, n. *a wine-jar, cask.*

¹**dŏlo** -are, *to hew with an axe, to work roughly;* **caput fuste,** *to cudgel.*

²**dŏlo** or **dŏlōn** -ōnis, m. (1) *a pike, sword-stick.* (2) *a small foresail.*

dŏlor -ōris, m., *pain,* physical or mental; esp. *disappointment, resentment.* Transf., *cause of sorrow;* rhet., *pathos.*

dŏlōsus -a -um, *crafty, deceitful, cunning;* adv. **dŏlōsē.**

dŏlus -i, m. *a device, artifice; fraud, deceit, guile; a trap.*

dōmābĭlis -e, *tameable.*

dŏmestĭcus -a -um. (1) *belonging to house* or *family, domestic;* m. as subst., esp. plur., *members of one's family.* (2) *native; crudelitas, towards citizens;* bellum, *civil war.*

dŏmĭcĭlĭum -i, n. *place of residence, dwelling.*

dŏmĭna -ae, f. *mistress of a household; wife, mistress, lady;* of abstr. things, *ruler, controller.*

dŏmĭnātĭo -ōnis, f. *mastery, control, irresponsible power, despotism.*

dŏmĭnātor -ōris, m. *ruler, governor.*

dŏmĭnātrix -īcis, f. *a female ruler, mistress.*

dŏmĭnātus -ūs, m. *mastery, absolute power.*

dŏmĭnĭum -i, n. (1) *rule, power, ownership.* (2) *a feast, banquet.*

dŏmĭnor -ari, dep., *to rule, be supreme, domineer.*

dŏmĭnus -i, m. *master of a house, lord, master.* Transf. *husband* or *lover; a master, owner, possessor; employer; ruler, lord, controller.*

dŏmĭporta -ae, f. *one with her house on her back, the snail.*

Dŏmĭtĭānus -i, m. *son of Vespasian, brother of Titus, Emperor from* 81 *to* 96 A.D.

Dŏmĭtĭus -a -um, *name of a plebeian gens in Rome.*

dŏmĭto -are, *to tame, subdue, break in.*

dŏmĭtor -ōris, m, *tamer, conqueror, victor.*

dŏmĭtrix -īcis, f. *she who tames.*

dŏmĭtus -ūs, m. *taming.*

dŏmo dŏmāre dŏmŭi dŏmĭtum, *to tame, break in, conquer, subdue.*

dŏmus -ūs, f. *a house, home;* locative **domi,** *at home, in the house;* **domi habere,** *to have at home, to possess;* **domum,** *home, homewards;* **domo,** *from home.* Transf., *dwelling, abode; native country; household; philosophical school* or *sect.*

dōnārĭum -i, n. (1) *a temple, shrine, altar.* (2) *a votive offering.*

dōnātĭo -ōnis, f. *giving, donation.*

dōnātīvum -i, n. *an imperial largess.*

dōnĕc (older **donicum**). (1) *up to the time when, until.* (2) *so long as, while.*

dōno -are. (1) **rem homini,** *to give as a present, to present, grant, bestow, give up;* esp. *to remit a debt or obligation; to forgive, pardon.* (2) **hominem re,** *to present with.*

dōnum -i, n. *a gift, present;* **dono dare,** *to give as a present;* esp. *a votive offering.*

dorcas -ădis, f. *gazelle, antelope.*

Dōres -um, m., *the Dorians, one of the Hellenic tribes;* adj. **Dōrĭcus** and **Dōrĭus** -a -um, *Dorian, Greek.* F. **Dōris** -ĭdis: as adj., *Dorian;* as subst., *the country of the Dorians; the wife of Nereus;* meton., *the sea.*

dormĭo -ire, *to sleep; to rest, be inactive.*

dormīto -are, *to be sleepy, begin to sleep, nod; to dream, be lazy;* of a lamp, iam dormitante lucerna, *just going out.*

dormītōrius -a -um, *for sleeping.*

dorsum -i, n. *the back,* of men, animals or things; immane dorsum mari summo, *a reef; a mountain ridge, ' hog's back '.*

dōs dōtis, f., *a dowry, marriage portion; a gift, quality, endowment.*

dōtālis -e, *belonging to or forming a dowry.*

dōto -are, *to provide with a dowry, endow;* partic. **dōtātus** -a -um, *richly endowed.*

drachma (**drachŭma**) -ae, f., *a drachma, a small Greek coin.*

drăco -ōnis, m., *a kind of snake, dragon.*

drăcōnĭgĕna -ae, c. *dragon-born.*

drāpĕta -ae, m. *a runaway slave.*

Drĕpănum -i, n. and **Drĕpăna** -orum, plur., *a town on the west coast of Sicily.*

drŏmas -ădis, m. *a dromedary.*

Drŭentia -ae, f. *a river in Gaul (now Durance).*

Drŭidēs -um and **Drŭidae** -arum, m. *the Druids.*

Drūsus -i, m. *a cognomen of the gens Livia;* hence adj. **Drūsiānus** and **Drūsīnus** -a -um, *of Drusus:* subst. **Drūsilla** -ae, f. *name of several females of the* gens Livia.

Dryăs -ădis, f. *a wood nymph, Dryad.*

dŭbĭtābilis -e, *doubtful, uncertain.*

dŭbĭtātĭo -ōnis, f., *doubt, uncertainty; hesitation, irresolution.*

dŭbĭto -are. (1) *to doubt, waver in opinion, be uncertain.* (2) *to waver as to action, be irresolute, hesitate.* Adv. from partic., **dŭbĭtantĕr**, *doubtingly, hesitatingly.*

dŭbius -a -um, *doubtful.* (1) act., *wavering:* in opinion, *doubting; uncertain;* as to action, *hesitating, irresolute.* (2) pass., *uncertain, doubted, doubtful;* n. as subst.; in dubium vocare, *to call in question;* procul dubio, *without doubt.* (3) fig., *doubtful, dangerous, critical.* Adv. **dŭbĭē, dŭbĭē**, *doubtfully;* haud dubie, *certainly.*

dŭcēni -ae, -a, *a group of two hundred,* or *two hundred each.*

dŭcentēsima -ae, f. *the two hundredth part, one-half per cent.*

dŭcenti -ae, -a, *two hundred.*

dŭcentie(n)s, *two hundred times.*

dūco dūcĕre duxi ductum. (1) *to draw; to draw along or away;* hence *to shape anything long, to construct;* carmina, *to make verses;* of time, *either to spend or to delay, protract.* Transf., *to charm, influence, mislead; to derive.* (2) *to draw in;* aera spiritu, *to inhale;* pocula, *to quaff.* (3) *to lead;* in marriage, *to marry a wife;* milit., *either to lead on the march, or to command.* (4) *to calculate, count, reckon; to esteem, consider.*

ductim, *by drawing; in a stream.*

ductĭto and **ducto** -are, *to lead,* esp.

to lead home a wife. Transf., *to cheat.*

ductor -ōris, m. *a leader, commander; a guide.*

ductus -ūs, m. (1) *drawing, drawing off.* (2) *shaping, shape;* oris, *the lineaments of the face;* muri, *line of a wall.* (3) *leading, command, leadership.*

dūdum, *some time ago; a little while ago, not long since; a long while ago* or *for a long time.*

dŭellum, dŭellĭcus, dŭellātor = bellum, bellicus, bellator; q.v.

Dŭīlius -a -um, *name of a Roman gens.*

dulcēdo -ĭnis, f., *sweetness, pleasantness, charm.*

dulcesco -ĕre, *to become sweet.*

dulcĭcŭlus -a -um, *somewhat sweet.*

dulcis -e, *sweet;* unda, *fresh water;* in gen., *pleasant, delightful, agreeable;* of persons, *friendly, dear.* N. acc. **dulcĕ** and adv. **dulcĭter**, *sweetly.*

dulcĭtūdo -ĭnis, f. *sweetness.*

dum. (1) adv., *joined as an enclitic with other words;* nondum, *not yet;* vixdum, *scarcely yet;* nedum, *not to say;* age dum, *come now.* (2) conj.: *while, during the time that; while, throughout the time that; so long as, provided that; until.*

dūmētum -i, n. *a thorn brake, thicket.*

dummŏdo, *provided that, so long as.*

dūmōsus -a -um, *covered with thorn bushes, bushy.*

dumtaxat. (1) *at least, not less than.* (2) *at most, not more than.*

dūmus -i, m. *a thorn bush, bramble.*

dŭŏ -ae, -ŏ, *two.*

dŭŏdĕcĭe(n)s, *twelve times.*

dŭŏdĕcim, *twelve.*

dŭŏdĕcĭmus -a -um, *twelfth.*

dŭŏdēni -ae, -a, *twelve at a time* or *twelve each.*

dŭŏdēquādrāgēsimus, *thirty-eighth.*

dŭŏdēquādrāgĭnta, *thirty-eight.*

dŭŏdēquinquāgēsimus -a -um, *forty-eighth.*

dŭŏdētrīcĭe(n)s, *twenty-eight times.*

dŭŏdētrīgĭnta, *twenty-eight.*

dŭŏdēvīcēni -ae -a, *eighteen each.*

dŭŏdēvīginti, *eighteen.*

dŭŏetvīcēsĭmāni -orum, m. *soldiers of the 22nd legion.*

dŭŏetvīcēsĭmus -a -um, *twenty-second.*

duplex -plicis, *double, doubled, two-fold.* Transf. (1) plur., *both.* (2) *two-faced, deceitful, equivocal.* Adv. **duplĭcĭter**, *doubly.*

duplĭcārius -a -um: miles, *a soldier who gets double pay.*

duplĭco -are, *to double;* of words, *to repeat;* also *to form compound words.* Transf., *to bend double;* in gen., *to lengthen, increase.*

duplus -a -um, *twice as much, double;* n. as subst. *double,* esp. *a double penalty.*

dŭpondĭus -i, m., *a coin of two asses.*

dūrābĭlis -e, *lasting, durable.*

dūrāmen -ĭnis, n. *hardness.*

dūrătĕus -a -um, *wooden.*

duresco dūrescĕre dūrŭi, *to grow hard; of water, to freeze.*

dūrĭtās -ātis, f., *harshness, unfriendliness.*

dūrĭtĭa -ae, and **dūrĭtĭēs** -ēi, f., *hardness; fig., austerity, harshness, severity.*

dūro -are: transit., *to make hard or hardy, to inure;* intransit., *to become hard or dry; to be hard or callous; to endure, hold out; to last, remain, continue.*

dūrus -a -um, *hard, harsh; tough, strong, enduring;* in demeanour or tastes, *rough, rude, uncouth;* in character, *hard, austere, sometimes brazen, shameless;* of things, *hard, awkward, difficult, adverse.* Adv. **dūrē** and **dūrĭtĕr**, *hardly, hardily; roughly, rudely; harshly, unpleasantly, severely.*

dŭumvir and **dŭŏvir** -vĭri, m. usually pl., *a pair of magistrates, a commission of two.*

dux dŭcis, c. (1) *a guide, conductor.* (2) *a leader, ruler, commander.*

dÿnastēs -is, m. *ruler, prince.*

Dyrrhăchĭum -i, n. *a port in Illyria.*

E

E, e, the fifth letter of the Latin alphabet.

e, prep. = ex; q.v.

ĕā, adv. = abl. of is; q.v.

ĕādem, *by the same way, likewise.*

ĕātĕnus, *so far.*

ĕbĕnus -i, m. = hebenus; q.v.

ēbĭbo -bĭbĕre -bĭbi, *to drink up.*

ēblandĭor -iri, dep. *to obtain by flattery.*

ēbrĭĕtās -atis, f. *drunkenness.*

ēbrĭŏlus -a -um, *tipsy.*

ēbrĭōsĭtās -ātis, f. *love of drink, drunkenness.*

ēbrĭōsus -a -um, *drink-loving.*

ēbrĭus -a -um, *drunk, intoxicated.*

ēbullio -ire, *to boil up; to boast of.*

ēbŭlum -i, n. (or **-us** -i, m.), *the dwarf elder.*

ĕbur -ŏris, n. *ivory.* Transf. (1) *of things made of ivory.* (2) *the elephant.*

ĕburnĕŏlus -a -um, *made of ivory.*

ĕburnĕus or **ĕburnus** -a -um, *made of ivory, white as ivory.*

ēcastor, see Castor.

eccĕ, *behold! lo! see!*

eccĕrē, *there you are!*

ecclēsĭa -ae, f., *an assembly of the (Greek) people.*

ecdĭcus -i, m. *a solicitor for a community.*

Ēcĕtra -ae, f. *capital of the Volsci.*

ecf-; see eff-.

ĕchĕnēis -ĭdis, f., *a sucking fish, the remora.*

ĕchīnus -i, m. (1) *an edible sea-urchin.* (2) *a copper dish.*

ēchō -ūs, f. *an echo;* personif., *Echo, a wood-nymph.*

eclŏgārii -orum, m. pl. *select passages or extracts.*

ecquando, adv., *ever? at any time?*

ecqui, ecquae or ecqua, ecquod, interrog. adj., *is there any . . . that? does any . . .?*

ecquis, ecquid, interrog. pron., *is there any that? does anyone?* Hence **ecquid** or **ecqui,** *at all?* or *whether?* **ecquō,** *whither?*

ĕcŭlĕus i, m. *a little horse, colt; a rack, instrument of torture.*

ĕdācĭtās -ātis, f. *greediness, gluttony.*

ĕdax -ācis, f. *greedy, gluttonous; destructive, consuming.*

ĕdĕpol; see Pollux.

ēdīco -dīcĕre -dixi -dictum, *to announce, declare;* esp. of a magistrate, *to decree, ordain by proclamation.* Hence n. of partic. as subst. **ēdictum** -i, *a decree, edict.*

ēdictĭo -ōnis, f. *an edict.*

ēdicto -are, *to proclaim.*

ēdisco -discĕre -dĭdĭci, *to learn thoroughly.*

ēdissĕro -sĕrĕre -sĕrŭi -sertum, *to explain, set forth, relate fully.*

ēdisserto -are, *to explain exactly.*

ēdĭtīcĭus -a -um, *announced, proposed:* iudices, *jurors chosen by a plaintiff.*

ēdĭtĭo -ōnis, f. *the publishing of a book; a statement;* editio tribuum, *a proposal by a plaintiff for the choice of a jury.*

¹ĕdo ĕdĕre or esse ēdi ēsum, *to eat, devour, consume, waste.*

²ēdo -dĕre -dĭdi -dĭtum, *to put forth, give out;* animam, *to breathe one's last, die;* clamorem, *to utter.* Esp. (1) *to bring into the world, to bring forth, give birth to;* of things, *to produce.* (2) *to make known: of writings, to publish;* of ideas and information, *to divulge, spread;* officially, *to proclaim;* as legal t. t., *to fix, determine, nominate.* (3) *to bring about, cause, produce;* of magistrates, *to provide games for the people.* Hence partic. **ēditus** -a -um, *raised, high, lofty;* n. as subst. *a high place, eminence.*

ēdŏcĕo -dŏcēre -dŏcŭi -doctum, *to instruct thoroughly, inform fully.*

ēdŏmo -dŏmare -dŏmŭi -dŏmĭtum, *to tame thoroughly, entirely subdue.*

Ēdŏni -orum, *a Thracian people, famed for the worship of Bacchus;* adj. **Ēdōnus** -a -um, and **Ēdōnis** -nĭdis, f. *Thracian.*

ēdormĭo -ire, *to have one's sleep out;* transit., *to sleep off.*

ēdormisco -ĕre, *to sleep off.*

ēdŭcātĭo -ōnis, f. *bringing up, training, education.*

ēdŭcātor -ōris, m. *one who brings up; a foster-father or a tutor.*

ēdŭcātrix -īcis, f. *a foster-mother, nurse.*

¹ēdŭco -are, *to bring up, raise, rear, educate.*

²ēdŭco -dūcĕre -duxi -ductum. (1) *to draw out, lead out; of time, to spend;* milit., *to march troops out;* legal, *to bring before a court of law;* naut., *to take a ship out of port.* (2) *to raise up* (of persons and buildings); in astra, *to praise sky-high.* (3) *to bring up, rear.*

ĕdŭlis -e, *eatable.*

ēdŭro -are, *to last, endure.*

ēdūrus -a -um, *very hard.*

effarcĭo = effercĭo; q.v.

effātum -i, n. from partic. of effor; q.v.

effectĭo -ōnis, f. *practising.* Transf., *an efficient cause.*

effector -ōris, m. *one who produces, causes, originates.*

effectrix -trīcis, f. *she that causes or produces.*

¹effectus -a -um, partic. of efficio; q.v.

²effectus -ūs, m. *doing, execution, performance; effect, result.*

effēmĭno -are, *to make into a woman; in character, to make effeminate.*
　Hence partic. effēmĭnātus -a -um, *effeminate, womanish;* adv. effēmĭnātē.

effercĭo or effarcĭo -fercire, -fertum, *to stuff full;* partic. effertus, *stuffed.*

effĕrĭtās -ātis, f., *wildness, savagery.*

¹effĕro -are, *to make wild, make savage;* partic. effĕrātus -a -um, *wild, savage.*

²effĕro (ecfero) efferre extŭli ēlātum. (1) *to carry out, bring out;* efferre signa, *to march out.* Esp. *to carry to the grave, bury;* pass., efferri, *to be borne out, buried;* of the earth, *to bring forth, bear; to utter, express, publish* words or ideas. (2) *to carry off or away;* pass., efferri *to be carried away* by feelings. (3) *to raise up, lift up; to praise, extol;* efferri *or* se efferre, *to pride oneself, be puffed up.* (4) *to endure to the end.*
　Hence partic. ēlātus -a -um, *elevated, exalted;* adv. ēlātē, *loftily.*

effertus -a -um, partic. from effercio; q.v.

effĕrus -a -um, *wild, savage.*

effervesco -fervescĕre -fervi, *to boil up, effervesce;* of an orator, *to be passionate.*

effervo -ĕre, *to boil up or over; to swarm forth.*

effētus -a -um, *weakened* (by giving birth); *effete.*

efficācĭtās -ātis, f. *efficacy.*

efficax -ācis, *effective, efficient, efficacious;* adv. efficācĭtĕr.

efficĭens -entis, partic. from efficio; q.v.

efficĭentĭa -ae, f. *efficiency.*

efficĭo -ficĕre -fēci -fectum, *to do, produce, effect, make;* of results, *to bring about, cause* (esp. with ut and subj.); of numbers, *to make up, amount to;* philosoph. *to prove, show;* of appointments and changes, *to make.*
　Hence partic. efficĭens -entis, *effective:* causa, *efficient cause;* adv. efficĭentĕr, *efficiently, powerfully.*

effĭgĭēs -ēi, f. or effĭgĭa -ae, f. *an image, likeness, effigy; a shade, ghost; an ideal.*

effingo -fingĕre -finxi -fictum. (1) *to wipe.* (2) *to mould, form, fashion;* esp. *to form one thing like another, and so*

to *copy, represent, express* in words, *conceive* in thought.

effĭo (ecf-) -fĭĕri, old pass. of efficio; q.v.

efflāgĭtātĭo -ōnis, f., *an urgent demand.*

efflāgĭtātū abl. sing. m., *at an urgent request.*

efflāgĭto -are, *to ask earnestly, demand, entreat.*

efflīgo -ĕre -flixi -flictum, *to destroy.*

efflo -are, *to blow out, breathe out:* animam, *to die.*

efflōresco -flōrescĕre -flōrŭi, *to blossom, break into bloom.*

efflŭo (ecflŭo) -flŭĕre -fluxi, *to flow out.* Transf. (1) *to vanish, drop off.* (2) *to pass out of mind, be forgotten.* (3) *to come to light, become known.*

efflŭvĭum -i, n., *flowing out, outlet.*

effŏdĭo -fŏdĕre -fōdi -fossum. (1) *to dig out, gouge out.* (2) *to make by digging, to excavate.* (3) *to gut, to rummage.*

effor (ecfor) -fari -fatus, dep. *to speak out, express, speak:* in logic, *to state a proposition;* in religion, *formally to dedicate* a place.
　Hence partic. (in pass. sense) effātus -a -um, *pronounced; dedicated.*

effrēnātĭo -ōnis, f. *unbridled impetuosity.*

effrēno -are, *to unbridle, let loose;* partic. effrēnātus -a -um, *unbridled, unrestrained, violent;* adv. effrēnātē.

effrēnus -a -um, *unbridled, unrestrained.*

effringo -fringĕre -frēgi -fractum, *to break open.*

effŭgĭo -fŭgĕre -fūgi -fŭgĭtum: intransit., *to flee, fly away, escape, get off;* transit., *to escape from, avoid, shun.*

effŭgĭum -i, n. *a flying away, flight; means or opportunity of flight.*

effulgĕo -fulgĕre -fulsi, *to shine out, glitter; to be distinguished, conspicuous.*

effultus -a -um, *resting upon, supported by.*

effundo (ecf-) -fundĕre -fūdi -fūsum, *to pour out, pour forth, shed;* of solids, *to fling out, empty out;* with violence, *to throw off, fling down;* esp. of horses, *to throw their riders;* of weapons, *to discharge;* spiritum extremum, *to die;* se effundere and effundi, *to stream forth, pour forth,* also *to give oneself up to, indulge in:* of sounds, *to utter;* with ideas of generosity, waste, etc. *to pour out freely, squander;* habenas, *to slacken.*
　Hence partic. effūsus -a -um, *poured out;* hence *widespread, extensive; extravagant, wasteful; unrestrained;* adv. effūsē.

effūsĭo -ōnis, f. *a pouring forth; violent movement; extravagance, prodigality; exuberance of spirits.*

effūsus, partic. from effundo; q.v.

effūtĭo -ire, *to blab out, chatter.*

ēgĕlĭdus -a -um, *with the chill off; lukewarm, tepid.*

ĕgens -entis, partic. from egeo; q.v.

ĕgēnus -a -um, *needy, destitute*; with genit. or abl., *in need of*.

ĕgĕo -ēre -ŭi, *to want, be in need*; with genit, or abl. *to be in want of, to be without, not to have*; also *to desire, wish for, want*.
Hence partic. **ĕgens** -entis, *needy, destitute*; with genit., *in need of*.

Ĕgĕrĭa -ae, f. *a nymph, instructress of Numa Pompilius*.

ĕgĕro -gĕrĕre -gessi -gestum, *carry out or off*.

ĕgestās -ātis, f. *poverty, indigence, need*; with genit., *want of*.

ĕgestĭo -ōnis, f. *wasting*.

ĕgŏ, I; plur. nos. *we* (often used for sing.); alter ego, *my second self*; ad me, *to my house*; apud me, *at my house*, also *in my senses*.

ĕgrĕdĭor -grĕdi -gressus, dep.: intransit., *to go out, pass out*; milit., *to march out*; naut., egredi (ex) navi, *to disembark*; in speech, *to digress*; sometimes *to go up, ascend*; transit., *to go out of, pass beyond, overstep, pass*.

ĕgrĕgĭus -a -um, *not of the common herd; excellent, extraordinary, distinguished*; adv. **ĕgrĕgĭē**.

ĕgressus -ūs, m. *going out, departure*; esp. *landing from a ship, disembarkation*. Transf., *a passage out; the mouth of a river*; in speech, *digression*.

ehem, oho!

ēheu, alas! woe!

ēhŏ, hi!

ei (hei), ah! woe!

eiă and **heiă**: expressing joy or surprise, *well!*; in exhortation, *come on!*

ēiăcŭlor -ari, dep. *to throw out, hurl out*.

ēicĭo -īcĕre -iēci -iectum, *to throw out, cast out, eject*; vocem, *to utter*; armum, *to dislocate*; se eicere, *to rush out*; naut., *to bring to shore*; pass., *to be cast ashore, stranded*; eiectus, *a shipwrecked person*. Transf., *to drive out, expel, dispossess*; domo, *to divorce*; ex patria, *to banish*; of feelings *to cast out, put aside*.

ēiectāmentum -i, n. *that which is thrown up*.

ēiectĭo -ōnis, f. *banishment, exile*.

ēiecto -are, *to hurl out, eject*.

ēiectus -ūs, m. *casting out*.

ēiŭlātĭo -ōnis, f., and **ēiŭlātus** -ūs, m. *wailing, lamenting*.

ēiŭlo are, *to wail, lament*.

ēiūro and **ēiĕro** -are *to refuse or deny on oath*; bonam copiam, *to swear that one is insolvent*; forum sibi iniquum, *to declare that a court is partial*; magistratum, imperium, *to resign, abdicate*; in gen., *to give up, disown*.

ēiusdemmŏdi, *of the same kind*.

ēiusmŏdi, *of this kind, such, so*.

ēlābor -lābi -lapsus, dep. *to glide out, slip away, escape, disappear*.

ēlăbōro -are; intransit., *to labour hard, strive, take pains*; transit., *to labour on, work out, elaborate, esp. in partic.*

ēlăbōrātus -a -um, *elaborate, artificial*.

ēlāmentābĭlis -e, *very lamentable*.

ēlanguesco -guescĕre -gŭi, *to become weak, be relaxed*.

ēlātĭo -ōnis, f. *a lifting up*; fig., *exaltation*.

ēlātro -are, *to bark out, cry out*.

ēlātus -a -um, partic. from effero; q.v.

Ēlĕa or **Vĕlĭa** -ae, f. *town in Lucania, birth-place of Parmenides and Zeno, the founders of the Eleatic school of philosophy*; subst. **Ēlĕātes** -ae, m. Zeno; adj. **Ēlĕātĭcus** -a -um, *Eleatic*.

ēlectĭo -ōnis, f. *choice, selection*.

ēlectrum -i, n. *amber*; plur. *amber balls; an alloy of gold and silver, resembling amber*.

¹ēlectus -a -um, partic. from eligo; q.v.

²ēlectus -ūs, m. *choosing, choice*.

ēlĕgans -antis, *choice, fine, neat, tasteful*; in bad sense, *fastidious, fussy*; adv. **ēlĕgantēr**.

ēlĕgantĭa -ae, f. *taste, refinement, grace*; in bad sense, *fastidiousness*.

ēlĕgi -orum, m. pl. *elegiac verses*.

ēlĕgīa and **ēlĕgēa** -ae, f. *an elegy*.

ēlēmentum -i, n. *an element, first principle*; in plur., *physical elements; letters of the alphabet, beginnings, the elements of any science or art*.

ēlenchus -i, m. *a pearl pendant worn as an ear-ring*.

ēlĕphantus -i, c. *an elephant; ivory*.

ēlĕphās (-ans) -phantis, m. *an elephant; the disease elephantiasis*.

ēlĕvo -are, *to lift up, raise, elevate; to weaken, impair, disparage; to alleviate, lighten*.

ēlĭcĭo -lĭcĕre -lĭcŭi -lĭcĭtum, *to lure out, entice, call forth*; inferorum animas, *to conjure up*.

ēlīdo -līdĕre -līsi -līsum, (1) *to strike, knock, thrust out, expel*. (2) *to dash to pieces, shatter*.

ēlĭgo -lĭgĕre -lēgi -lectum, *to pick out, choose, select*; fig., *to root out*.
Hence partic. **ēlectus** -a -um, *chosen, select*; adv., **ēlectē**, *choicely*.

ēlīmĭno -are, *to carry out of doors*; dicta, *to blab*.

ēlīmo -are, *to file off, polish, elaborate, perfect*.

ēlinguis -e, *speechless or without eloquence*.

Ēlissa (Ēlisa) -ae, f. *another name of Dido*.

ēlixus -a -um, *boiled, sodden*.

ellĕbŏrus (hell-) -i, m. and **ellĕbŏrum (hell-)** -i, n. *hellebore, a plant considered a remedy for madness*.

ēlŏco -are, *to let, hire out*.

ēlŏcūtĭo -ōnis, f. *oratorical delivery, elocution*.

ēlŏgĭum -i, n. *a short saying, maxim; an inscription*; esp. on a gravestone, *epitaph; a clause in a will, codicil; a record of a case*.

ēlŏquentĭa -ae, f. and **ēlŏquĭum** -i, n., *eloquence*.

ēlŏquor -lŏqui -lŏcūtus, dep. *to speak out, express*; esp. *to speak eloquently*; partic. **ēlŏquens** -entis, *eloquent*; adv. **ēlŏquentēr**.

ēlūcĕo -lūcēre -luxi, *to beam forth, shine out, glitter*.

ēluctor -ari, dep: intransit., *to struggle out*; transit., *to struggle out of, surmount a difficulty*.

ēlūcubro -are, and **ēlūcubror** -ari, dep. *to compose by lamplight*.

ēlūdo -lūdēre -lūsi -lūsum: intransit., *to finish playing*, esp. of the waves of the sea; transit., *to pass over; to ward off, evade; to beat an opponent in play; to delude, mock*.

ēlūgĕo -lūgēre -luxi, *to mourn for the prescribed period*.

ēlumbis -e, *weak, feeble*.

ēlŭo -lŭēre -lŭi -lūtum, *to wash out, wash clean, rinse, cleanse*. Transf., *to squander; to wash away, efface, remove*.

Hence partic. **ēlūtus** -a -um, *washed out, watery, insipid*.

ēlŭvĭes -ēi, f. *a flowing out, discharge; a flowing over, flood*.

ēlŭvĭo -ōnis, f., *an inundation*.

Ēlȳsĭum -i, n., *Elysium, the abode of the blessed*; adj. **Ēlȳsĭus** -a -um; m. plur. as subst. *the Elysian fields*.

¹**em** = hem; q.v.

²**em**, interj. *here! hi!*

ēmācĭtās -ātis, f. *fondness for buying*.

ēmancĭpātĭo -ōnis, f. *emancipation or transfer*.

ēmancĭpo (-cŭpo) -are, *to release or emancipate a son from the patria potestas; to transfer or make over property; to give up persons*.

ēmāno -are, *to flow out; to arise, spring, emanate, spread abroad*.

Ēmāthĭa -ae, f. *a district of Macedonia*; adj. **Ēmāthĭus** -a -um, and f. **Ēmāthĭs** -ĭdis, *Macedonian*; Emathides, *the Muses*.

ēmātūresco -tūrescĕre -tūrŭi, *to become mature, to ripen; to become mild, be softened*.

ēmax -ācis, *fond of buying*.

emblēma -ătis, n. *inlaid or mosaic work*.

embŏlĭum -i, n. *a dramatic interlude*.

ēmendābĭlis -e, *that may be amended*.

ēmendātĭo -ōnis, f. *improvement, emendation, amendment*.

ēmendātor -ōris, m. and **ēmendātrix** -īcis, f. *amender, corrector*.

ēmendo -are, *to free from errors, correct, improve*; partic. **ēmendātus** -a -um, *free from mistakes, correct, faultless*; adv. **ēmendātē**.

ēmentĭor -iri -ītus, dep. *to devise falsely, feign, counterfeit*; absol., *to make false statements*.

ēmercor -ari, dep. *to buy up*.

ēmĕrĕo -ēre -ŭi -ĭtum and **ēmĕrĕor** -ēri -ĭtus, dep. *to obtain by service, earn completely; to deserve well of a person*; milit., *to earn pay, to serve, finish one's time*.

Hence partic. **ēmĕrĭtus** -a -um:

m. as subst., *a soldier that has served his time, a veteran*; as adj. *worn out, finished with*.

ēmergo -mergĕre -mersi -mersum: transit., *to cause to rise up*; emergere se *or* emergi, *to rise up, emerge, free oneself*; intransit., *to come forth, come up, emerge, free oneself, get clear; also to rise, come to the top; to come to light, appear*.

ēmĕrĭtus -a -um, partic. from emereo; q.v.

ēmētĭor -iri -mensus, dep., *to measure out*. Transf., *to pass over, traverse a distance*; partic. emensus -a -um in pass. sense, *traversed; to pass through, live through a period of time*.

ēmēto -ere, *to reap away*.

ēmĭco -micare -mĭcŭi -mĭcatum. (1) *to spring out, leap forth*. (2) *to gleam, shine forth, be conspicuous*.

ēmĭgro -are, *to move from a place, migrate*; e vita, *to die*.

ēmĭnentĭa -ae, f. *standing out, prominence; the lights of a picture*.

ēmĭnĕo -mĭnēre -mĭnŭi, *to project, stand out, be conspicuous, be remarkable*.

Hence partic. **ēmĭnens** -entis, *outstanding, projecting; distinguished, eminent*.

ēmĭnor -ari, *to threaten*.

ēmĭnus, *at a distance, from a distance*.

ēmĭror -ari, dep. *to wonder exceedingly, be astonished at*.

ēmissārĭum -i, n. *an outlet for water*.

ēmissārĭus -i, m. *an emissary, spy*.

ēmissĭo -ōnis, f. *sending forth, letting loose*.

ēmissus -ūs, m. *sending forth*.

ēmitto -mittĕre -mīsi -missum, *to send forth, send out*. Hence (1) *to dispatch, send on a chosen course*; of books, *to publish*. (2) *to let go, let loose, free, let slip*.

ēmo ēmĕre ēmi emptum, *to buy, purchase*; male *or* magno, *dear*; bene *or* parvo *cheap*. Transf., *to bribe, buy*.

ēmŏdĕror -ari, dep., *to moderate*.

ēmŏdŭlor -ari, dep., *to put to music*.

ēmŏlĭor -iri, dep., *to achieve by effort*.

ēmollĭo -ire -īvi -ītum, *to soften, make mild or effeminate*.

ēmŏlo -ĕre, *to grind away*.

ēmŏlŭmentum, -i, n. *result of effort; gain, advantage*.

ēmŏnĕo -ēre, *to warn, admonish*.

ēmŏrĭor -mŏri -mortuus, dep. *to die off, perish*.

ēmŏvĕo -mŏvēre -mŏvi -mōtum, *to move out or away, remove*.

Empĕdŏclēs -is, m. *a poet and philosopher of Agrigentum, of the fifth century* B.C.; adj. **Empĕdŏclēus** -a -um; n. pl. as subst. *the doctrines of Empedocles*.

empīrĭcus -i, m. *an unscientific physician, empiric*.

empŏrĭum -i, n. *a place of trade, market*.

emptĭo -ōnis, f. *buying, purchasing; a purchase*.

emptīto -are, *to buy up.*

emptor -ōris, m. *buyer, purchaser.*

ēmūgio -ire, *to bellow.*

ēmulgĕo -mulgēre -mulsum, *to drain out, exhaust.*

ēmungo -mungĕre -munxi -munctum, *to clean a nose*; with reflex. or in pass., *to wipe one's nose.* Transf. *to cheat a person.* Hence partic. **ēmunctus** -a -um: emunctae naris, *with a clean nose*, i.e. *shrewd, discerning.*

ēmūnĭo -ire, *to fortify, make safe*; *to build up*; paludes, *to clear up.*

ēn (sometimes **ĕm**) *lo! behold! see!* Interrog., *look, say*; with imperat., *come!*

ēnarrābĭlis -e, *that can be narrated or told.*

ēnarrātĭo -onis, f. *exposition; scansion.*

ēnarro -are, *to narrate or explain.*

ēnascor -nasci -nātus, dep. *to grow out, spring forth, arise.*

ēnāto -are, *to swim away, escape by swimming, to extricate oneself.*

ēnāvĭgo -are, *to sail away*; undam, *over the waves.*

endo; archaic = in.

endrŏmis -ĭdis, f. *a rough cloak worn after exercise.*

Endўmĭōn -ōnis, m. *a beautiful young man, loved by the Moon.*

ĕnĕco (**ēnĭco**) -necare -necŭi -nectum, *to kill off*; *to wear out, exhaust, torture.*

ēnervis -e, *powerless, weak.*

ēnervo -are, *to remove the sinews from; to weaken.* Hence partic. **ēnervātus** -a -um, *weakened, powerless.*

ēnĭco = eneco; q.v.

ĕnim, conj. *for; namely, for instance; indeed, truly, certainly*; at enim, *but you may object . . .* ; sed enim, *but indeed.*

ĕnimvēro, *to be sure, certainly.*

ēnĭtĕo -ēre -ŭi, *to shine out, shine forth, be conspicuous.*

ēnĭtesco -ĕre, *to gleam, shine forth.*

ēnītor -nīti -nīsus or -nixus, dep. *to work one's way up, struggle up, ascend*; with acc., *to climb*; in gen., *to strive, struggle, make an effort*; also transit., *to bring forth, bear.* Hence partic. **ēnixus** -a -um, *strenuous, eager*; adv. **ēnixē.**

Enna = Henna; q.v.

Ennĭus -i, m., Q. (239-169 B.C.), *the 'father of Roman poetry'.*

ēno -are, *to swim out, escape by swimming, flee.*

ēnōdātĭo -ōnis, f. *untying*; hence *explanation.*

ēnōdis -e, *without knots; clear, plain.*

ēnōdo -are, *to free from knots*; *to make clear, explain*; adv. from partic., **ēnōdātē**, *clearly, plainly.*

ēnormis -e, *irregular, unusual; very large, immense, enormous.*

ēnormĭtās -ātis, *irregular shape.*

ēnōtesco -nōtescĕre -nōtŭi, *to become known, be made public.*

ensĭfĕr -fĕra -fĕrum and **ensĭgĕr** -gĕra -gĕrum, *sword-bearing.*

ensis -is, m. *sword.*

enthўmēma -ātis, n., *a thought, line of thought, argument*; esp. *a kind of syllogism.*

ēnūbo -nūbĕre -nupsi -nuptum, *of a woman, to marry out of her rank.*

ēnuclĕo -are, *to take out the kernel*; hence *to explain in detail*; partic. **ēnuclĕātus** -a -um, *straightforward, simple, clear*; adv. **ēnuclĕātē.**

ēnŭmĕrātĭo -ōnis, f. *counting up, enumeration; recapitulation.*

ēnŭmĕro -are, *to reckon, count up, enumerate*; esp. *to pay out*; also *to recount, recapitulate.*

ēnuntĭātĭo -ōnis, f. *an enunciation, proposition.*

ēnuntĭo -are, *to tell, divulge, announce, express in words*; in logic, *to state a proposition*; also *to pronounce clearly.* N. of partic. as subst., **ēnuntĭātum** -i, *a proposition.*

ēnuptĭo -ōnis, f.: gentis, *a woman's marrying out of her gens.*

ēnūtrĭo -ire, *to nourish, rear, bring up.*

[1]ĕo ire īvi and ĭi ĭtum, *to go*; cubitum ire, *to go to bed*; milit., ire ad arma, *to fly to arms*; polit. (pedibus) ire in sententiam, *to support a motion.* Transf., *to pass, proceed*; in exclamations, i, *go to*; melius ire, *to go better*; ire in, with acc., *to be changed to.*

[2]ĕo. (1) old dat., *thither, to that point*; of degree, *so far, to such a pitch.* (2) locative, *there*; esp. with loci (partitive genit.). (3) abl., *for that, on that account.*

ĕōdem. (1) old dat., *to the same place*; *to the same point or person.* (2) locative, *in the same place*; *in the same condition.*

Ēōs, f. *dawn*; adj. **Ēōus** and **Ĕōus** -a -um, *belonging to the morning*, or *eastern.*

ēpastus -a -um, *eaten up.*

ēphēbus -i, m. *a young man between eighteen and twenty.*

ĕphēmĕris -ĭdis, f. *a journal, diary.*

ĕphippĭātus -a -um, *provided with a saddle.*

ĕphippĭum -i, n., *a horse-cloth, saddle.*

ĕphŏrus -i, m., *an ephor, a Spartan magistrate.*

ēpĭcōpus -a -um, *provided with oars.*

ĕpĭcrŏcus -a -um, *transparent, fine.*

Ĕpĭcūrus -i, m. *an Athenian philosopher, founder of the Epicurean school* (342-270 B.C.): adj. and subst. **Ĕpĭcūrēus** -a -um, *Epicurean, an Epicurean.*

ēpĭcus -a -um, *epic.*

ĕpĭdictĭcus -a -um, *for display.*

ĕpĭdīpnis -ĭdis, f., *dessert.*

ĕpĭgramma -ātis, n. *an inscription; an epigram.*

ĕpĭlŏgus -i, m. *a conclusion, peroration, epilogue.*

ĕpĭmēnĭa -orum, n. pl. *a month's rations.*

ĕpĭrēdĭum -i, n., *the strap by which a horse was fastened to a vehicle; a trace.*

Ēpīrus -i, f., *a region in north-west Greece*; adj. **Ēpīrensis** -e, *of Epirus*; subst. **Ēpīrōtes** -ae, m., *an Epirote*.

ēpistŏlĭum -i, n. *a little letter, note*.

ēpistŭla (or **ĕpistŏla**) -ae, f., *a written communication, letter, epistle*; ab epistulis, *to do with correspondence, of secretaries.* Transf., *sending of letters, post*.

ĕpĭtaphĭum -i, m. *a funeral oration*.

ĕpĭthălămĭum -i, n. *a nuptial song*.

ĕpĭthēca -ae, f. *addition*.

ĕpĭtŏma -ae and **ĕpĭtŏmē** -ēs, f. *abridgment, epitome*.

ĕpops -opis, m. *the hoopoe*.

ĕpos, n. *an epic poem*.

ēpōtus -a -um, *drunk up, drained.* Transf. (1) *spent on drink.* (2) *swallowed up*.

ĕpŭlae -arum, f. *food, dishes, a banquet, feast*.

ĕpŭlāris -e, *belonging to a banquet*.

ĕpŭlo -ōnis, m. *feaster*; Tresviri (later Septemviri) epulones, *a college of priests who had charge of sacrificial feasts*.

ĕpŭlor -ari, dep. *to feast, feast on*.

ĕpŭlum -i, n. *a banquet, feast, esp. on public occasions*.

ĕqua -ae, f. *a mare*.

ĕquĕs -ĭtis, m. *a horseman, rider, cavalryman*; polit., equites, *the knights, order between senate and plebs*; also collectively in sing.

ĕquester -stris -stre, *relating to horsemen, equestrian; relating to cavalry*; polit., *relating to the knights*.

ĕquĭdem *indeed, truly, for my part*; concessive, *of course, certainly, admittedly*.

ĕquīnus -a -um, *relating to horses*.

ĕquĭtātus -ūs, m. *cavalry*.

ĕquĭto -are, *to ride on horseback*; of winds, *to rush*.

ĕquŭlĕus = eculeus; q.v.

ĕquus -i, m. (older forms **ĕquos** and **ĕcus**) *a horse*; equus bellator, *a war-horse*; equis virisque, *with horse and foot, with all one's might*; ad equum rescribere, *to make a person a knight*.

ĕra -ae, f. *mistress, lady*.

ērādīco -are, *to root out*.

ērādo -rādĕre -rāsi -rāsum, *to scratch out; to destroy, get rid of*.

Ĕrătō, f. *the Muse of lyric and love-poetry*.

ercisco, **erctum** = hercisco, herctum; q.v.

Ĕrĕbus -i, m. *a god of the lower world*; hence *the lower world.* Adj. **Ĕrĕbēus** -a -um.

Ĕrĕchtheus -ĕi, m. a mythical king of Athens; adj. **Ĕrĕchthēus** -a -um, m. *Athenian*; subst. **Ĕrĕchthīdae** -arum, m. pl. *the Athenians*.

ērectus, partic. from erigo; q.v.

ērēpo -rēpĕre -repsi -reptum, *to creep out; to creep up or over*.

ēreptĭo -ōnis, f. *taking by force, seizure*.

ēreptor -ōris, m., *one who takes by force, a robber*.

ergā, prep. with acc., *towards, esp. of personal relations; more generally, about*.

ergastŭlum -i, n. *a workhouse for debtors* or *slaves*; in plur., *the inmates of an ergastulum*.

ergŏ: prep., preceded by genit., *because of, on account of*; adv., *therefore, accordingly, then*.

Ērichthŏnĭus -i, m. *a mythical king of Athens*; also *a mythical king of Troy*; adj. **Ērichthŏnĭus** -a -um, *Athenian* or *Trojan*.

ērĭcius -i, m. *hedgehog*; milit. *chevaux de frise*.

ērĭgo -rīgĕre -rexi -rectum, *to set up, place upright, erect, raise*; milit., *to march a body of soldiers up a height.* Transf., *to arouse, excite; encourage, cheer.*
Hence partic. **ērectus** -a -um, *raised, upright, erect; high, elevated, proud; alert, anxious, intent, with minds on the stretch; resolute, cheerful*.

ērīlis -e, *of a master or mistress*.

Ērīnys -ўos, f., *one of the Furies*; plur. Erinyes, *the Furies.* Transf., *scourge, curse*.

ērĭpĭo -rĭpĕre -rĭpŭi -reptum, *to snatch away, tear out*; in good sense, *to free, rescue.*
Hence partic. **ēreptus** -a -um, *snatched away* or *rescued*.

ērŏgātĭo -ōnis, f. *payment, expenditure*.

ērŏgo -are, *to ask for and obtain*; used in the sense *to pay out* money, esp. from public funds.

errābundus -a -um, *wandering*.

errāticus -a -um, *wandering, erratic*.

errātĭo -ōnis, f. and **errātus** -ūs m. *wandering, straying*.

¹erro -are, *to wander, stray, rove*; transit., *to wander over.* Transf., *to waver; to err, be mistaken.* N. of partic. as subst. **errātum** -i, *a fault, error, technically or morally*.

²erro -ōnis, m. *a wanderer, vagabond*.

error -ōris, m. *wandering about.* Transf., *wavering, uncertainty, error, mistake; source of error, deception*.

ērŭbesco -rūbescĕre -rūbŭi, *to grow red, blush*; with infin., *to blush to*; with acc., *to blush for, to respect*; gerundive **ērŭbescendus** -a -um, *of which one should be ashamed*.

ērūca -ae, f. *a colewort*.

ērructo -are, *to belch forth, throw up, vomit.* Transf. (1) *to talk drunkenly about.* (2) *to cast out, eject*.

ērūdĭo -ire, *to free from roughness; to instruct, teach, educate.*
Hence partic. **ērūdītus** -a -um, *instructed, educated*; adv. **ērūdītē**, *learnedly*.

ērūdītĭo -ōnis, f. *teaching, instruction; knowledge, learning*.

ērumpo -rumpĕre -rūpi -ruptum: transit., *to break open, cause to burst forth*; *to vent, discharge*; intransit., *to break out, burst forth*; milit., *to rush forth*.

ērŭo -rŭĕre -rŭi -rŭtum, *to tear out, dig up*; of buildings, *to raze, demolish*.

ēruptĭo -ōnis, f. *a bursting* or *breaking forth*; milit., *sally, attack.*

ěrus -i, m. *master, owner, lord.*

ervum -i, n. *bitter vetch.*

Ēryx -rȳcis or **Ěrȳcus** -i, m., *a mountain and city on the west coast of Sicily, with a famous temple of Venus.* Adj. **Ěrȳcīnus** -a -um; f. as subst. *Venus.*

esca -ae, f. *food, victuals, esp. as bait.*

escārĭus -a -um, *relating to food or bait.*

ēscendo -scendĕre -scendi -scensum: intransit., *to climb up, ascend; to go up from the sea-coast inland*; transit., *to ascend.*

ēscensĭo -ōnis, f., *a movement inland, esp. hostile.*

escŭlentus -a -um, *edible, esculent.*

escŭletum, escŭlus; see aesc-.

ēsĭto -are, *to keep eating.*

Esquĭlĭae -arum, f. *one of the seven hills of Rome, the Esquiline.* Hence adj. **Esquĭlĭus** and **Esquĭlīnus** -a -um, *Esquiline;* f. as subst. **Esquĭlīna** -ae, *the Esquiline gate.*

essĕdārĭus -i, m. *a fighter in a British* or *Gallic war-chariot.*

essĕdum -i, n. *a war-chariot used by Gauls and Britons.*

ēsŭ, abl. sing. m., *in the eating.*

ēsŭrĭo -ire, *to be hungry, desire food*: in gen., *to long for.*

ēsŭrītĭo -ōnis, f. *hunger.*

et; as adv., *also, even*; as conj., *and; and indeed*; in narrative, *and then*; occasionally adversative, *and yet*; after alius, idem, par, *as* or *than*; repeated et . . . et . . ., *both . . . and* . . .; so -que . . . et . . .; nec (neque) . . . et, *not only not . . . but.*

ětěnim, *for indeed.*

ětēsĭae -arum, m. pl. *winds which blow about the dogdays, Etesian winds.*

ēthŏlŏgus -i, m. *a mimic.*

ětĭam, (1) *as yet, still;* etiam atque etiam, *again and again.* (2) *also, besides, even;* non solum (or modo) . . . sed (or verum) etiam, *not only . . . but also;* with comparatives, *still.* (3) in answers, *yes, certainly.* (4) in questions, expressing incredulity, *actually? really?*

ětĭamnum and **ětĭamnunc**, *yet, still, till now.*

ětĭam-si, *even if, although.*

ětĭam-tum and **ětĭam-tunc**, *even then, till that time, till then.*

Etrūrĭa -ae, f. *a district in north-west Italy;* hence adj. and subst. **Etruscus** -a -um, *Etruscan,* an *Etruscan.*

et-si, *even if, although*; elliptically, *and yet, notwithstanding.*

ětȳmŏlŏgĭa -ae, f., *etymology.*

eu, *good! well done!*

Euan or **Euhan**, m. *a name of Bacchus.*

euans or **euhans** -antis, *shouting Euan,* of Bacchanals.

euge and **eugĕpae,** *well done!*

Euias or **Euhias** -adis, f., *a Bacchante.*

Euĭus or **Euhĭus** -i, m., *a name of Bacchus.*

Euměnĭdes -um, f., *Eumenides, the gracious ones,* euphem. for the Furies.

eunūchus -i, m., *a eunuch.*

euoe, euhoe, interj., *shout of the Bacchantes.*

Eurīpĭdes -is, m., *the Athenian tragic poet* (c. 485-406 B.C.); adj. **Eurīpĭdēus** -a -um.

Eurīpus -i, m. *a channel, strait,* esp. *the strait between Euboea and Boeotia; a canal* or *water-course.*

Eurōpa -ae, f. and **Eurōpē** -ēs, f.: myth., *daughter of Agenor, whom Jupiter, in the form of a bull, carried off to Crete;* geograph., *the continent of Europe.* Adj. **Eurōpaeus** -a -um, *belonging to Europa* or *to Europe.*

Eurus -i, m., *the south-east* or *east wind*; adj. **Eurōus** -a -um, *eastern.*

Euterpē -ēs, f. *Muse of harmony.*

Euxīnus -a -um, *an epithet of the Black Sea.*

ēvādo -vādĕre -vāsi -vāsum. Intransit., *to go out, go forth;* esp. *to climb up* or *out; to escape, get off.* Transf., *to turn out, result.* Transit., *to go out through, pass over; to climb up; to escape.*

ēvăgor -ari, dep.: intransit., *to wander out, stray away*; milit. *to wheel right and left, manoeuvre*; transit., *to overstep.*

ēvălesco -vălēscĕre -vălŭi, *to grow strong, prevail, come into vogue;* in perf., *to have power, be able.*

ēvānesco -vānēscĕre -vānŭi, *to vanish, disappear, pass away.*

ēvānĭdus -a -um, *vanishing, passing away.*

ēvasto -are, *to devastate, lay waste utterly.*

ēvěho -věhěre -vexi -vectum, *to carry out* or *up*; with reflex., or pass., of ships, *to sail away;* of riders, *to ride away.*

ēvello -vellěre -velli -vulsum, *to tear out, pluck out.*

ēvěnĭo -věnire -věni -ventum, *to come out.* Transf., *to turn out, result; to befall, happen, occur.* Hence n. of partic. as subst. **ēventum** -i, *issue, consequence, result; event, occurrence, experience.*

ēventus -ūs, m. *consequence, issue, result; event, occurrence, experience.*

ēverběro -are, *to strike violently.*

ēverrĭcŭlum -i, n., *a fishing-net, drag-net;* fig., *a clean sweep.*

ēverro -verrěre -verri -versum, *to sweep out; to plunder.*

ēversĭo -ōnis, f. *overturning, destruction, ruin.*

ēversor -ōris, m. *overturner, destroyer.*

ēverto -vertěre -verti -versum, *to turn out, dislodge, eject; to turn up, stir; to overturn, throw down, demolish destroy, ruin.*

ēvestīgātus -a -um, *tracked out, discovered.*

ēvīdens -entis, *visible, clear, plain, evident;* adv. ēvīdentĕr.

ēvīdentia -ae, f., *distinctness of language.*

ēvīgĭlo -are: intransit. *to wake up; to be awake, be vigilant;* transit., *to watch through, pass in watching; to work hard at, to elaborate.*

ēvīlesco -vīlescĕre -vīlŭi, *to become, contemptible.*

ēvincĭo -vincīre -vinxi -vinctum, *to bind, bind round.*

ēvinco -vincĕre -vīci -victum, *to conquer entirely, utterly subdue;* in gen., *to prevail over, get through, get over;* of results *to bring about;* of conclusions, *to prove irresistibly.*

ēviscĕro -are, *to disembowel, tear in pieces.*

ēvītābilis -e, *that can be avoided.*

ēvīto -are, *to avoid, shun.*

ēvŏcātor -ōris, m., *one who calls to arms.*

ēvŏco -are, *to call out;* esp. *to summon the spirits of the dead,* or *a deity;* milit. and polit. *to call out, call up, summon.* Transf., *to draw out, draw on;* *to call forth, produce.* M. pl. of partic. as subst. ēvŏcāti -orum, *veteran soldiers recalled to the colours.*

ēvoe; see euoe.

ēvŏlo -are, *to fly out, fly away;* *to come out quickly, rush forth, escape.*

ēvŏlūtĭo -ōnis, f., *the unrolling and reading of a book.*

ēvolvo -volvĕre -volvi -vŏlūtum. (1) *to roll out, roll forth;* of news, evolvi, *to spread.* (2) *to unroll, roll open;* esp. *to unroll a book to read it.* Transf., *to extricate, disentangle, detach; to unravel, disclose, explain.*

ēvŏmo -ĕre -ŭi -ĭtum, *to vomit forth, disgorge.*

ēvulgo -are, *to publish, make known.*

ēvulsĭo -ōnis, f. *pulling out.*

ex or ē, prep. with abl. (1) in space: *from* or *out of;* ex equo pugnare, *to fight on horseback* (operating *from* it); ex adverso *opposite.* (2) in time, *since,* esp. ex quo, *from which time, since;* also *immediately after;* aliud ex alio, *one thing after another.* (3) in other relations: *to denote origin, from, away from, out of, of;* ex animo, *heartily;* ex industria, *on purpose;* unus ex, *one of;* pocula ex auro, *gold cups;* *to denote cause or occasion, from, on account of, by reason of;* e vulnere mori, *to die of a wound;* *to denote correspondence, in accordance with;* ex re et ex tempore, *according to time and circumstance;* *to denote advantage,* e.g. e republica, *for the benefit of the state;* in gen., *in regard to, with respect to;* ex parte, *in part.*

exăcerbo -are, *to provoke, exasperate, embitter.*

exactĭo -ōnis, f. *driving out, expulsion; demanding, exacting,* esp. *collecting of debts, tribute,* etc.; in gen., *management, direction.*

exactor -ōris, m. *one who drives out; one who demands* or *exacts,* esp. *a collector of taxes;* in gen., *superinten-dent, overseer.*

exactus -a -um, partic. from exigo; q.v.

exăcŭo -ŭĕre -ŭi -ūtum, *to sharpen to a point, make sharp, intensify, stimulate.*

exadversum or exadversus, *opposite.*

exaedĭfĭcātĭo -ōnis, f. *building up.*

exaedĭfĭco -are *to build up, erect, finish.*

exaequātĭo -ōnis, f. *making equal, equality.*

exaequo -are. (1) *to make level* or *equal, level up, relate.* (2) *to equal, be like.*

exaestŭo -are, *to be hot, boil up, foam up.*

exaggĕrātĭo -ōnis, f., *heaping up;* hence *elevation, exaltation.*

exaggĕro -are, *to heap up; to enlarge, increase; to heighten, exalt, magnify.*

exăgĭtātor -ōris, m. *a censurer.*

exăgĭto -are, *to chase about; to harass, disquiet, disturb; to scold, blame, censure, criticize; to excite, irritate.*

exalbesco -bescĕre -bŭi, *to grow white, turn pale.*

exāmen -īnis, n. (1) *a swarm; a throng, crowd, shoal.* (2) *the tongue of a balance; testing, consideration.*

exāmĭno -are, *to weigh; to consider.*

exāmussim, *according to rule, exactly.*

exanclo -are, *to drain, exhaust; to bear to the end, endure.*

exănĭmālis -e, *dead; deadly.*

exănĭmātĭo -ōnis, f. *want of breath,* esp. *from fright.*

exănĭmis -e and exănĭmus -a -um, *lifeless, dead;* also (exanimis only), *breathless,* esp. *from fright.*

exănĭmo -are. (1) *to take away the breath of, to wind, stun, weaken.* (2) *to deprive of life, to kill.*

exantlo = exanclo; q.v.

exardesco -ardescĕre -arsi -arsum, *to blaze up, to become hot,* or *inflamed;* of disturbances, *to break out.*

exāresco -ārescĕre -ārŭi, *to dry, become dry* or *exhausted.*

exarmo -are, *to disarm, deprive of arms.*

exăro -are, *to plough up, dig up; to produce by ploughing;* hence *to write on waxen tablets.*

exaspĕro -are, *to make rough, to irritate.*

exauctōro -are, *to dismiss from military service, discharge, cashier.*

exaudĭo -ire, *to hear plainly; to hear favourably, listen to.*

exaugĕo -ēre, *to increase much.*

exaugŭrātĭo -ōnis, f. *profanation, desecration.*

exaugŭro -are, *to desecrate, profane.*

exauspĭco -are, *to take an augury from.*

excaeco -are, *to make quite blind; to stop up a channel.*

excalcĕo -are, *to take the shoes from;* in drama, *to take the tragic cothurnus from an actor.*

excandescentĭa -ae, f., *heat, irascibility.*

excandesco -descĕre -dŭi, *to become hot, to glow.*

excanto -are, *to charm out, bring forth by incantations.*

excarnĭfĭco -are, *to tear to pieces.*

excăvo -are, *to hollow out.*

excēdo -cēdĕre -cessi -cessum: intransit., *to go out, go away, pass out;* e vita, *to die; to go beyond a point or limit; to attain to, result in;* transit., *to leave, pass beyond, exceed.*

excellentĭa -ae, f. *eminence, distinction.*

excello -ĕre, *to stand out, excel, be distinguished;* partic. **excellens,** *high, lofty, eminent, remarkable;* adv. **excellentĕr,** *eminently.*

excelsĭtās -ātis, f., *height, elevation.*

excelsus -a -um, adj., *lofty, high, elevated, eminent.* N. as subst. **excelsum** -i, *a height, eminence.* Adv. **excelsē,** *loftily.*

exceptĭo -ōnis, f. *exception, restriction, limitation;* esp. *an exception by the defendant to the plaintiff's statement of a case.*

excepto -are. (1) *to take up, catch;* auras, *to snuff up.* (2) *to take in succession.*

excerno -cernĕre -crēvi -crētum, *to separate, sift, sort.*

excerpo -cerpĕre -cerpsi -cerptum, *to pick out; to gather out, choose; to put on one side, separate.* N. of partic. as subst. **excerptum** -i, *an extract.*

excessus -ūs, m. *departure; from life, i.e. death; from subject, i.e. digression.*

excetra -ae, f. *a snake, viper.*

excīdĭum -i, n. *overthrow, destruction.*

¹excīdo -cīdĕre -cĭdi, *to fall out, fall away, be lost; of words, to slip out unawares, escape; of ideas, to pass from memory or thought, be forgotten.*

²excīdo -cīdĕre -cĭdi -cīsum, *to cut out;* lapides e terra, *to quarry.* Transf. (1) *to destroy, demolish;* portas, *to force open.* (2) *to root out, banish.*

excĭĕo and **excĭo** -cīre -cīvi and -cĭi -cītum and cĭtum, *to call out, arouse;* esp. *to awaken from sleep or to summon to help;* in gen., *of persons, to excite, arouse; of feelings, to call forth, excite, produce; of material things, to stir, shake.*

excĭpĭo -cĭpĕre -cēpi -ceptum. (1) *to take out;* hence *to rescue; to except.* (2) *to take up, catch; to greet, welcome a person; to pick up news or ideas by listening; of events, to take people, come upon them.* (3) passively, *to receive; to take over from, follow, succeed, come later.*

excīsĭo -ōnis, *destruction.*

excĭto -are, *to arouse, rouse up; of things, to provoke, call forth, cause; of persons, to console, cheer, inspire; of buildings, to raise, erect; of fire, to kindle, inflame.*

Hence partic. **excĭtātus** -a -um, *lively, vigorous, loud.*

exclāmātĭo -ōnis, f. *exclamation.*

exclāmo -are, *to shout, cry aloud; to exclaim; to call somebody by name.*

exclūdo -clūdĕre -clūsi -clūsum, *to shut out, exclude, keep away;* of things, *to knock out;* of birds, *to hatch.*

exclūsĭo -ōnis, f. *shutting out, exclusion.*

excōgĭtātĭo -ōnis, f. *contriving, devising.*

excōgĭto -are, *to think out, devise, contrive, invent.*

excŏlo -cŏlĕre -cŏlŭi -cultum, *to tend or cultivate carefully; to adorn, polish, refine; to serve, honour a deity or person.*

excŏquo -cŏquĕre -coxi -coctum, *to boil down, boil away; to cook, bake, make hard;* fig., *to cook up.*

excors -cordis, *foolish, silly, without intelligence.*

excrēmentum -i, n. *excrement;* oris, *spittle.*

excresco -crescĕre -crēvi -crētum, *to grow up, spring up.*

excrētus -a -um, partic. of excerno, or of excresco.

excrŭcĭo -are, *to torture, torment.*

excŭbĭae -arum, f. pl. *lying out;* milit., *keeping watch, keeping guard.* Transf., *watchfires; watchmen, guard.*

excŭbĭtor -ōris, m. *sentinel, watchman, guard.*

excŭbo -bare -bŭi -bĭtum, *to lie or sleep out of doors;* milit., *to keep watch; to be watchful, vigilant.*

excūdo -cūdĕre -cūdi -cūsum, *to strike out, beat out;* esp. *to hammer, forge;* of birds, *to hatch.* Transf., of bees, *to mould;* of writers, *to compose.*

exculco -are, *to trample firm, tread hard.*

excūrātus -a -um, *carefully seen to.*

excurro -currĕre -cŭcurri and -curri -cursum *to run out, hasten forth;* milit., *to attack, make a sortie;* with acc., *to run over;* fig., *to run out, move freely;* of places, *to run out, to project.*

excursĭo -ōnis, f. *running out; movement forwards;* fig., *outset of a speech;* milit., *attack, assault, sally.*

excursor -ōris, m. *scout, skirmisher.*

excursus -ūs, m. *running out;* rhet., *digression;* milit., *attack, sally, assault.*

excūsābĭlis -e, *excusable.*

excūsātĭo -ōnis, *an excuse, plea, defence.*

excūso -are, *to exempt from blame or accusation; to excuse a person, to make excuses for a thing; to allege in excuse, to plead.*

Hence partic. **excūsātus** -a -um, *free from blame;* adv. **excūsātē,** *excusably.*

excŭtĭo -cŭtĕre -cussi -cussum. (1) *to shake out;* esp. *to shake out clothes to find anything hidden;* hence *to search, examine a person;* fig., *to investigate.* (2) *to strike off, throw out, knock away, shake off.*

exec-; see exsec-.

exĕdo -esse -ēdi -ēsum, *to eat up, devour, consume; to wear down, exhaust, destroy.*

exedra -ae, f. *a hall for conversation or debate.*

exemplāris -e, *serving as a copy*; n. as subst. **exemplar** -āris, *a copy, transcript; a likeness; a pattern, ideal.*

exemplum -i, n. (1) *a sample, example*; exempli causa (*or* gratia), *for instance; general character, manner, fashion* (as shown by examples); *an example to be followed, model; a precedent; an example of what may happen, warning, object-lesson;* hence *a punishment intended to deter.* (2) *a copy, transcript.*

exemptus -a -um, partic. of eximo; q.v.

exentĕro -are, *to torture, exhaust.*

exĕo -ire -ii (-īvi) -itum: intransit., *to go out, go away, go forth; to pass from state to state; to get out, to become known;* of time, *to come to an end, pass away;* transit., *to pass over;* also *to ward off.*

exeq-; see exseq-.

exercĕo -ēre -ŭi -ĭtum, *to keep at work, exercise, train, cultivate;* of abstr. things, *to employ, exploit;* of feelings, arts, and processes, *to practise, exercise;* of the mind, *to train;* hence *to overwork, harass, trouble.*

Hence partic. **exercĭtātus** -a -um, *trained, schooled; harassed; severe, vexatious.*

exercĭtātĭo -ōnis, f. *practice, exercise; experience.*

exercĭtĭum -i, n. *practice, exercise.*

exercĭto -are, *to train hard, keep at work.*

Hence partic. **exercĭtatus** -a -um, *trained, practised, exercised; troubled, harassed.*

¹**exercĭtus** -a -um, partic. of exerceo; q.v.

²**exercĭtus** -ūs, m. *training; a trained body of soldiers, army;* esp. *the infantry;* poet. in gen., *crowd, swarm.*

exēsor -ōris, m. *one who gnaws or eats away.*

exhālātĭo -ōnis, f. *exhalation, vapour.*

exhālo -are: transit., *to exhale, breathe out;* intransit., of things, *to steam;* of persons, *to expire.*

exhaurĭo -haurire -hausi -haustum. (1) *to draw out;* in gen., *to remove, take out, take away.* (2) *to drain dry, empty out, impoverish; to finish, bring to an end; to endure, suffer.*

exhērēdo -are, *to disinherit.*

exhērēs -ēdis, *disinherited.*

exhĭbĕo -hĭbēre -hĭbŭi -hĭbĭtum, *to produce, show, display, exhibit, present; to offer, allow; to produce by making, to cause.*

exhĭlăro -are, *to make cheerful.*

exhorresco -horrescĕre -horrŭi, *to shudder exceedingly, be terrified;* transit., *to tremble at, to dread.*

exhortātĭo -ōnis, f. *exhortation, encouragement.*

exhortātīvus -a -um, *of exhortation.*

exhortor -ari, dep. *to exhort, encourage.*

exĭgo -īgĕre -ēgi -actum. (1) *to drive out* or *away; to force out, exact, demand; to sell.* (2) *to drive through;* hence *to complete, finish; to determine, settle, adjust, regulate; to ascertain, decide.*

Hence partic. **exactus** -a -um, *accurate, precise, exact.*

exĭgŭĭtās -ātis, f. *littleness, smallness.*

exĭgŭus -a -um, *small, little, scanty:* of quantity, in size, *small;* in number, *scanty;* in time, *short;* of quality, *meagre.* N. as subst. **exĭgŭum** -i, *small extent.* Adv. **exĭgŭē**, *sparingly, scantily, scarcely.*

exīlis -e, *thin, slender, meagre;* in possessions, *poor;* with genit., *without;* of style, *dry, dreary.* Adv. **exīlĭter**, *thinly, poorly, meagrely.*

exīlĭtās -ātis, f. *thinness, meagreness, weakness.*

exīmĭus -a -um, *excepted;* hence *selected; exceptional, distinguished.* Adv. **exīmĭē**, *uncommonly, exceptionally.*

exĭmo -ĭmĕre -ēmi -emptum, *to take out, take away,* esp. off a list or out of a group; *to free, release; to take away, remove* an abstr. thing; of time, *to waste.*

exin = exinde; q.v.

exĭnānĭo -ire, *to empty;* gentes, *to plunder.*

exinde (**exin, exim**): in space, *thence, next;* in time, *thereupon, after that, then;* in logic, *consequently, accordingly.*

existĭmātĭo -ōnis, f. *the opinion that a man has, judgement; the opinion that others have of a man,* esp. morally, *reputation, good name, honour, character;* in finance, *credit.*

existĭmātor -ōris, m., *one who forms or gives an opinion, a critic.*

existĭmo (**-ŭmo**) -are, *to judge a thing according to its value;* in gen., *to judge, consider, regard.*

exĭtĭābĭlis -e, *deadly, destructive.*

exĭtĭālis -e, *destructive, fatal, deadly.*

exĭtĭo -ōnis, f. *going out.*

exĭtĭōsus -a -um, *destructive, fatal, deadly.*

exĭtĭum -i, n. *going out* or *away;* hence *destruction, ruin;* also *a cause of destruction.*

exĭtus -ūs, m. *going out, going forth; a means of going out, exit; end, finish; issue, result.*

exlex -lēgis, *bound by no law, lawless, reckless.*

exmŏvĕo = emoveo; q.v.

exobsecro -are, *to entreat earnestly.*

exŏcŭlo -are, *to deprive of eyes.*

exōdĭum -i, n., *a comic afterpiece.*

exōlesco -ōlescĕre -ōlēvi -ōlētum, *to grow old and weak, decay, fade out;* partic. **exōlētus** -a -um, *worn out;* m. as subst. *a dissolute person.*

exŏnĕro -are, *to unload, disburden;* in gen., *to free, release, relieve.*

exopto -are, *to desire eagerly, long for;*

partic. **exoptātus** -a -um, *desired, longed for.*

exōrābilis -e, *able to be entreated, placable.*

exōrātor -ōris, m., *one who entreats successfully.*

exordior -ordiri -orsus, dep. *to begin to weave;* in gen., *to begin.* Partic. in pass. sense **exorsus** -a -um, *begun.*

exordium -i, n., *the warp of a web;* in gen., *a beginning;* esp. *the beginning of a speech.*

exōrior -ŏriri -ortus, dep. *to rise, spring up, issue, appear, come forward.*

exornātio -ōnis, f., *adorning, ornament.*

exornātor -ōris, m., *one who adorns, an embellisher.*

exorno -are, *to furnish, provide plentifully;* also *to ornament, adorn.*

exōro -are, *to entreat successfully, obtain* a thing *by entreaty, prevail upon* a person.

¹**exorsus** -a -um, partic. of exordior; q.v.

²**exorsus** -ūs, m., *a beginning.*

exortus -ūs, m., *a rising; the East.*

exōs -ossis, *without bones.*

exosculor -ari, dep. *to kiss.*

exosso -are, *to bone, take out the bones.*

exostra -ae, f. *a theatrical machine, revealing the inside of a house to the spectators.*

exōsus -a -um, *hating exceedingly.*

exōticus -a -um, *foreign, outlandish, exotic.*

expallesco -pallescĕre -pallŭi, *to become very pale;* with acc., *to dread.*

expalpo -are, *to coax out.*

expando -ĕre, *to stretch out, expand, spread out.* Transf., *to explain.*

expăvesco -păvescĕre -pavi, *to grow very frightened;* with acc. *to dread exceedingly.*

expĕdio -ire -ivi and -ii -itum, *to free from a snare, disengage, disentangle, set free; to get things ready for action;* fig., *to release, clear, set free, set straight;* in speech, *to clear up* a point, *explain;* res expedit, or impers. expedit, *it is expedient, useful, advantageous.*
Hence partic. **expĕditus** -a -um, *unshackled, unimpeded;* milit., *lightly equipped;* in gen., *free, ready;* n. as subst. *clear ground;* of abstr. things, *clear, settled, ready.* Adv. **expĕdītē** *freely, easily.*

expĕditio -ōnis, f., *a military operation, expedition.*

expello -pellĕre -pŭli -pulsum, *to drive out, expel, thrust away.*

expendo -pendĕre -pendi -pensum, *to weigh out;* esp. *to weigh out in payment, pay out, put down;* sometimes *to pay* a penalty. Transf., *to value, rate;* in gen., *to weigh up, consider.*
Hence partic. **expensus** -a -um, *weighed out,* hence *paid out;* ferre homini expensum, *to note a thing as paid* to a person, *charge* to. N. as subst. **expensum** -i, *payment.*

expergēfăcio -făcĕre -fēci -factum, *to awaken, rouse, excite.*

expergiscor -pergisci -perrectus, dep. *to wake up, arouse oneself.*

expergo -pergĕre -pergi -pergĭtum, *to awaken.*

expĕrientia -ae, f., *trial, testing, attempt; knowledge gained by experience.*

expĕrimentum -i, n. *experience; proof from experience.*

expĕrior -pĕriri -pertus, dep. *to try, test, prove, put to the test;* experiri ius, *to go to law;* in perf., *to know by having tried, know by experience; to try to do* a thing. Pres. partic. **expĕriens** -entis, *enterprising, venturesome.* Perf. partic. **expertus** -a -um: pass., *tested, tried, approved;* act., *with experience, experienced.*

experrectus -a -um, partic. of expergiscor; q.v.

expers -pertis, *having no part in, not sharing in; wanting in, destitute of.*

expertus -a -um, partic. from experior; q.v.

expĕtesso -ere, *to desire, wish for.*

expĕto -ĕre -ii and -ivi -itum: transit., *to desire, strive after, make for;* of things due, *to demand, require;* with infin., *to seek to do;* intransit., *to fall upon.*

expiātio -onis, f. *atonement, expiation.*

expilātio -ōnis, f. *plundering, robbing.*

expilator -ōris, m., *plunderer, robber.*

expilo -are, *to plunder, rob.*

expingo -pingĕre -pinxi -pictum, *to paint over;* fig., *to describe, depict in writing.*

expio -are, *to propitiate, appease* an offended or threatening power; *to purify* what is defiled; *to atone for* an offence.

expiscor -ari, dep. *to fish out; to search out, find out.*

explānātio -ōnis, f. *making clear, explanation;* rhet., *illustration,* also *clear articulation.*

explānātor -ōris, m., *one who explains; an interpreter.*

explāno -are, *to make level, smooth out;* hence *to explain, make clear: to set out clearly,* or *articulate clearly.*

explaudo = explodo; q.v.

explēmentum -i, n., *filling, stuffing.*

explĕo -plēre -plēvi -plētum, *to fill, fill up; to complete* a required amount; *to make good* losses, etc.; in quality, *to complete, perfect;* of time, *to complete, finish;* of duties, *to fulfil, discharge;* of wants, *to satisfy, quench, appease.*
Hence partic. **explētus** -a -um, *perfect, complete.*

explētio -ōnis, f., *satisfying.*

explicātio -ōnis, f. *unfolding, uncoiling.* Transf., *explanation, interpretation.*

explicātor -ōris, m. and **explicātrix** -īcis, f. *interpreter, explainer.*

¹**explicātus** -a -um, partic. from explico; q.v.

²**explicātus** -ūs, m. *explanation, exposition.*

explico -are -avi -atum and -ŭi -itum, *to unfold, unroll, disentangle;* in gen.

to *spread out, extend, expand*; milit.,
to *extend ranks, deploy.* Transf., *to
disentangle, put in order*; of a debt,
to *pay off*; to *explain, expound, interpret*; to *set free.*
    Hence partic. **explĭcātus** -a -um,
ordered, arranged; made plain, clear;
also **explĭcĭtus** -a -um, *straight-
forward, easy*; adv. **explĭcātē,**
plainly.

explōdo (-plaudo) -plōdĕre -plōsi
-plōsum, to *hiss an actor off the stage*;
in gen., to *scare off, reject.*

explōrātĭo -ōnis, f. *investigation.*

explōrātor -ōris, m. *explorer, scout,
spy.*

explōro -are, to *search out, investigate,
explore*; milit., to *spy out, reconnoitre*;
to *test, try, put to proof.*
    Hence partic. **explōrātus** -a -um,
established, confirmed, certain; ex-
ploratum habeo, *I am sure*; adv.
explōrātē, *certainly, surely, definitely.*

expōlĭo -ire -ĭi and -ivi -itum, *to
smooth, polish, refine*; partic. **expōlītus**
-a -um, *smooth, polished.*

expōlĭtĭo -ōnis, f. *smoothing, polishing.*

expōno -pōnĕre -pŏsŭi, pŏsĭtum. (1) *to
put outside, cast out*; *to expose a
child*; naut. to *land, disembark.* (2) *to
put on view, display, show*; in words,
to *set forth, exhibit, explain.*
    Hence partic. **expŏsĭtus (expostus)**
-a -um, *exposed, open, accessible*; of
persons, *affable*; in bad sense,
vulgar.

exporrĭgo -rĭgĕre -rexi -rectum, *to
stretch out, expand, smooth out.*

exportātĭo -ōnis, f., *exportation.*

exporto -are, to *carry out*; esp. to
export.

exposco -poscĕre -pŏposci, to *implore,
entreat earnestly*; esp. to *demand the
surrender of a person.*

expŏsĭtĭo -ōnis, f. *putting out*; hence
statement, exposition, narration.

expostŭlātĭo -ōnis, f. *complaint, ex-
postulation.*

expostŭlo -are. (1) to *demand earnestly,*
esp. to *demand the surrender of a
person.* (2) to *make a claim or complaint, to expostulate.*

expōtus = epotus; q.v.

exprĭmo -prĭmĕre -pressi -pressum.
(1) to *press out, force out*; to *extort.*
(2) to *mould or form one thing in
imitation of another*; hence to *copy,
express, portray, represent*; esp. to
express in words, describe; to *translate; to articulate.* (3) to *raise up.*
    Hence partic. **expressus** -a -um,
made clear, prominent, distinct.

exprŏbrātĭo -ōnis, f. *reproach, upbraiding.*

exprŏbro -are, to *reproach*; to *bring up
a thing against a person.*

exprōmo -prōmĕre -prompsi -promp-
tum, to *bring forth, produce, exhibit,
display*; to *disclose, set forth, state,
utter.*

expugnābĭlis -e, *that may be taken by
storm.*

expugnātĭo -ōnis, f., *the taking of a
place by storm.*

expugnātor -ōris, m. *taker, capturer*;
pudicitiae, *violator.*

expugno -are, to *take by storm, capture*;
hence to *overcome, subdue*; to *gain
forcibly, extort*: with ut and the subj.,
bring it about that.

expulsĭo -ōnis, f., *driving out, expulsion.*

expulsor -ōris, m. and **expultrix**
-trīcis, f. *one who drives out.*

expungo -pungĕre -punxi -punctum,
to *prick out*; hence to *cancel, expunge.*

expurgātĭo -ōnis, f. *vindication, justification.*

expurgo -are, to *cleanse, purify.* Hence
to *cure*; to *purify*; to *justify, defend.*

expūtesco -ĕre, to *rot away.*

expūto -are, to *lop away*; hence to
consider; to *comprehend.*

exquīro (-quaero) -quīrĕre -quīsivi
-quisitum. (1) to *search for, look for,
ask for.* (2) to *search through, examine.*
    Hence partic. **exquīsītus** -a -um,
*carefully sought or worked out, choice,
exquisite, artificial.* Adv. **exquīsītē,**
accurately, carefully.

exsaevĭo -ire, to *rage to an end, cease
to rage.*

exsanguis -e, *bloodless, without blood*;
deathly pale; act., *making pale.*

exsarcĭo -sarcire -sartum, to *patch up,
make good, repair.*

exsātĭo -are, to *satisfy thoroughly,
satiate.*

exsātūrābĭlis -e, *that can be satiated.*

exsātūro -are, to *satisfy, satiate.*

exscen-; see escen-.

exscindo -scindĕre -scĭdi -scissum, to
tear out; to *destroy utterly.*

exscrĕo -are, to *cough out.*

exscrībo -scrībĕre -scripsi -scriptum,
to *write out*; to *copy*; to *note down,
register.*

exsculpo -sculpĕre -sculpsi -sculptum,
to *scratch out, erase*; to *carve or
scoop out.*

exsēco -sĕcare -sĕcŭi -sectum, to *cut
out, cut away.*

exsĕcrābĭlis -e, *cursing, execrating.*

exsĕcrātĭo -ōnis, f. *curse, execration;
an oath containing an imprecation.*

exsĕcror -ari, dep. to *curse, execrate*;
to *swear with an imprecation*; partic.
in pass. sense, **exsĕcrātus** -a -um,
cursed, execrated.

exsectĭo -ōnis, f. *cutting out.*

exsĕcūtĭo -ōnis, f. *performance, accomplishment*; executio Syriae, *administration*; of speech, *a discussion.*

exsĕquĭae -arum, f. pl. *a funeral
procession.*

exsĕquĭālis -e, *belonging to a funeral
procession.*

exsĕquor -sĕqui -sĕcūtus, dep. to
follow to the grave; in gen., to *follow
to the end*; to *maintain, keep up, to
carry out, accomplish, execute*; to
avenge, punish; to *relate, describe,
explain a matter*; to *suffer, endure.*

exsĕro -sĕrĕre -sĕrŭi -sertum, to
stretch out, thrust out; hence to *put*

forth, assert. Perf. partic. **exsertus** -a -um, *bared, protruding.*

exserto -are, *to stretch out.*

exsĭbĭlo -are, *to hiss out;* esp. *to hiss* an actor *off the stage.*

exsicco -are, *to dry thoroughly; to drain dry, to empty* by drinking. Hence partic. **exsiccātus** -a -um, of style, *dry, jejune.*

exsigno -are, *to mark out.*

exsĭlĭo -sĭlire -sĭlŭi, *to leap out* or *up.*

exsĭlĭum -i, n. *banishment, exile.* Transf., *place of exile;* plur. = exsules, *exiles.*

exsisto (existo) -sistĕre -stĭti -stĭtum, *to stand forth, appear; to spring forth, arise, come into existence.*

exsolvo -solvĕre -solvi -sŏlūtum. (1) *to loosen, untie, unbind, open;* glaciem, *to dissolve;* of persons, *to disentangle, free;* of things, *to explain.* (2) *to pay off; to discharge* any obligation, *perform* anything due.

exsomnis -e, *sleepless, wakeful.*

exsorbĕo -ēre, *to suck up, suck dry.*

exsors -sortis, *without lot; for which no lot has been cast, specially chosen; having no share in, deprived of,* with genit.

exspătĭor -ari, dep. *to deviate from the course;* fig., *to digress.*

exspectābĭlis -e, *that is to be expected, probable.*

exspectātĭo -ōnis, f. *waiting, looking for, expectation* (with objective genit.).

exspecto -are, *to look out for, wait for, await, wait to see;* esp. *with longing, fear, desire,* etc., *to hope for, dread.* Hence partic. (with compar. and superl.) **exspectātus** -a -um, *awaited, wished for, welcome.*

exspergo -spergĕre -spersum, *to sprinkle, scatter.*

exspēs, *without hope, hopeless.*

exspīrātĭo -ōnis, f. *exhalation.*

exspiro -are: transit., *to breathe out, exhale, emit;* intransit., *to blow forth, rush forth; to give up the ghost, to die.*

exspŏlĭo -are, *to plunder, rob, despoil.*

exspŭo -spŭĕre -spŭi -spūtum, *to spit out; to get rid of, cast away.*

externo -ēre, *to frighten, terrify.*

exstĭllo -are, *to drop moisture, drip, trickle.*

exstĭmŭlātor -ōris, m. *inciter, instigator.*

exstĭmŭlo -are, *to goad, excite, instigate.*

exstinctĭo -ōnis, f. *annihilation, extinction.*

exstinctor -ōris, m. *one who extinguishes, destroys, annihilates.*

exstinguo -stinguĕre -stinxi -stinctum, *to put out, extinguish;* of persons, *to kill;* in gen., *to abolish, destroy, annihilate.*

exstirpo -are, *to root out, extirpate.*

exsto (exto) -are, *to stand out, project; to be visible, show itself, appear; to be still in existence, be extant.*

exstructĭo -ōnis, f. *building up, erection.*

exstrŭo -strŭĕre -struxi -structum, *to heap up, pile up, build up.*

exsuctus -a -um, partic. of exsugo; q.v.

exsūdo -are; intransit., *to come out in sweat, exude;* transit., *to sweat out, sweat through, perform with great labour.*

exsūgo -sūgĕre -suxi -suctum, *to suck out, suck dry.*

exsul -sŭlis, c., *a banished person, an exile.*

exsŭlo (exŭlo) -are, *to be banished, live in exile.*

exsultātĭo -ōnis, f. *leaping up; exultation, excessive rejoicing.*

exsultim, adv. *friskingly.*

exsulto (exulto) -are, *to leap up frequently* or *violently.* Transf., *to rejoice exceedingly, exult, triumph;* of orators, etc., *to run riot, range freely.*

exsŭpĕrābĭlis -e, *that can be overcome.*

exsŭpĕrantia -ae, f., *superiority, pre-eminence.*

exsŭpĕro -are: intransit., *to mount up, appear above; to be prominent, excel;* transit., *to surmount; to surpass, exceed, overcome.*

exsurdo -are, *to deafen;* of taste, *to make dull* or *blunt.*

exsurgo -surgĕre -surrexi, *to rise up, lift oneself up, stand up; to regain strength.*

exsuscĭto -are, *to awaken from sleep;* of fire, *to kindle* or *fan;* mentally, *to excite, arouse;* so exsuscitare, *to make an effort.*

exta -orum, n. pl. *entrails of animals,* esp. *the heart, lungs, liver,* used by Romans for divination.

extābesco -tābescĕre -tābŭi, *to waste away entirely; to vanish, disappear.*

extāris -e, *used for cooking.*

extemplo (-tempŭlo), *immediately, forthwith.*

extempŏrālis -e, *extemporary, unrehearsed.*

extendo -tendere -tendi -tensum and -tentum, *to stretch out, expand, extend;* milit., *to extend in order of battle;* in gen., *to increase, extend;* in time, *to extend, prolong; to strain, exert.* Hence partic. **extentus** -a -um, *wide, extensive.*

extento -are, *to stretch out, strain.*

extĕnŭātĭo -ōnis, f. *thinning; as a* figure of speech, *diminution, lessening.*

extĕnŭo -are, *to make thin* or *small, to reduce, diminish;* milit., *to extend;* in gen., *to lessen, weaken, diminish;* in speech, *to disparage, depreciate.* Hence partic. **extĕnŭātus** -a -um, *weak, poor, slight.*

exter and **extĕrus** -a -um, *outward, foreign, strange;* compar. **extĕrĭor** -ius, genit. -ōris, *outer;* superl. **extrēmus** -a -um, *outermost;* n. as subst. *outer edge, extreme;* in time, *last;* n. as subst. *an end;* extremum, acc., *for the last time;* ad extremum, *to the end* or *at the end;* in degree or quality, *extreme;* esp. *lowest, worst;* extremum bonorum, malorum, *the* *highest good, evil;* superl. **extīmus** -a -um, *outermost.*

extĕrebro -are, *to bore out, extract by boring.*

extergĕo -tergēre -tersi -tersum, *to wipe off, wipe clean; to strip clean, plunder.*

extĕrĭor, exterius; see exter.

extermĭno -are, *to drive out, expel, banish; to put aside, remove.*

externus -a -um, *outside, external, foreign, strange;* m. as subst. *a foreigner, stranger;* n. pl. as subst. *outward or foreign things.*

extĕro -tĕrĕre -trivi -tritum, *to rub out; to wear away.*

exterrĕo -terrēre -terrŭi -terrĭtum, *to frighten badly, scare, terrify.*

extĕrus; see exter.

extexo -ĕre, *to unweave; to cheat.*

extĭmesco -tĭmescĕre -tĭmŭi: intransit. *to be terrified;* transit., *to be greatly afraid of, to dread.*

extĭmus; see exter.

extispex -spĭcis, m., *a soothsayer predicting from the entrails of victims.*

extollo -ĕre, *to lift up, raise up;* of buildings, *to raise, erect;* of spirits, etc., *to elevate, exalt;* in words, *to praise or exaggerate;* sometimes *to adorn; to defer, postpone.*

extorquĕo -torquēre -torsi -tortum, *to twist out, wrest away, wrench out, dislocate.* Transf., *to obtain by force, extort.*

extorris -e, *driven from the country, exiled, banished.*

extrā: adv. *outside;* extra quam, extra quam si, *except, unless;* prep., with acc., *beyond, outside of; without; except for;* extra iocum, *joking apart.*

extrăho -trăhĕre -traxi -tractum, *to draw out, drag out, extract, remove, extricate;* sometimes *to bring forward;* in time, *to draw out, prolong, protract.*

extrānĕus -a -um, *outside, extraneous; foreign, strange;* m. as subst. *a foreigner, stranger.*

extrăordĭnārĭus -a -um, *extraordinary, anomalous, irregular, unnatural;* milit. equites, cohortes, *picked troops of the auxiliary forces.*

extrārĭus -a -um, *outward, external, extrinsic; strange, unrelated, foreign.*

extrēmĭtās -ātis, f. *end, farthest portion, extremity.*

extrēmus -a -um; see exter.

extrīco -are, *to disentangle, extricate; to clear up, unravel.*

extrinsĕcus, *from without, from the outside; on the outside, outwardly.*

extrūdo -trūdĕre -trūsi -trūsum, *to push out, thrust forth;* merces, *to get sold.*

extundo -tundĕre -tūdi -tūsum. (1) *to form by beating with a hammer; to invent, devise.* (2) *to beat out violently, drive away; to extort.*

exturbo -are, *to drive away, thrust out;* mentem, *to agitate.*

exūbĕro -are, *to grow thickly, abound.*

exul; see exsul.

exulcĕro -are, *to make worse, aggravate; to irritate, embitter.*

exŭlŭlo -are, *to howl out, howl loudly;* partic. **exŭlŭlātus** -a -um, *invoked with howlings.*

exundo -are, *to overflow, to flow out or over, to abound.*

exŭo -ŭĕre -ŭi -ūtum. (1) *to lay aside, put off, put away.* (2) *to strip, deprive of a thing.*

exūro -ūrĕre -ussi -ustum, *to burn out, burn up, consume;* also *to dry up, warm, heat.*

exustĭo -ōnis, f. *burning up, conflagration.*

exŭvĭae -arum, f. pl. *that which is taken off;* of men *dress; spoils taken from the enemy, arms,* etc.; *the skin, slough,* or *hide of animals.*

F

F, f, the sixth letter of the Latin Alphabet.

făba -ae, f. *the broad bean.*

făbālis -e, *of beans.*

făbella -ae, f. *a little story, fable or drama.*

făber -bra -brum, *ingenious, skilful.* M. as subst. **făber** -bri, *a worker, craftsman;* faber tignarius, *a carpenter;* ferrarius, *a blacksmith;* milit. fabri, *the engineers;* also *a fish,* perhaps dory. Adv. **fabrē,** *skilfully.*

Făbĭus -a -um, *name of a Roman gens.*

fabrēfăcĭo -făcĕre -fēci -factum, *to make or fashion skilfully.*

fabrĭca -ae, f. *the art of a* faber; *a device, trick, a workshop.*

fabrĭcātĭo -ōnis, f., *making, framing, construction.*

fabrĭcātor -ōris, m. *maker, artificer.*

Fabrĭcĭus -a, -um, *name of a Roman gens.*

fabrĭco -are, and **fabrĭcor** -ari, dep., *to form, make, forge.*

fabrīlis -e, *relating to an artificer;* n.pl. as subst., *tools.*

făbŭla -e, f. (1) *talk, conversation:* fabulam fieri, *to get talked about.* (2) *a tale, story, fable, drama, myth;* fabulae! *nonsense!*

făbŭlor -ari, dep. (1) *to talk, converse, chatter.* (2) *to tell an untruth.*

făbŭlōsus -a -um, *renowned in story, fabled.*

făcesso făcessĕre făcessi făcessītum: transit., *to do eagerly, perform, fulfil, accomplish;* homini negotium, *to give trouble to;* intransit., *to make off, go away, depart.*

făcētĭa -ae, f.; sing., *wit;* plur., *wit, drollery, humour.*

făcētus -a -um, *fine, elegant; witty, facetious.* Adv. **făcētē,** *elegantly; wittily, humorously.*

făcĭēs -ēi, *shape, form, figure, outward appearance;* esp. *face, countenance.* Transf., *character, nature; seeming, pretence.*

făcĭlis -e, *easy to do; easy to manage,*

convenient, favourable; of movements, *easy, mobile*; of persons, *facile, dexterous, clever*; of character, *affable, easy, good-natured*. N. acc. as adv. **făcĭlĕ,** *easily, without difficulty; indisputably, certainly*; haud facile, *not easily, hardly*; facile pati, *to bear willingly*.

făcĭlĭtās -ātis, f. *easiness, ease*; of character, *willingness, friendliness, affability, good-nature*.

făcĭnŏrōsus -a -um, *wicked, criminal*.

făcĭnus -ŏris, n., *a deed, action*; esp. *a bad deed, crime, villainy*; hence *instrument of crime*; in plur., *criminals*.

făcĭo făcĕre fēci factum (the pass. is fio; q.v.). Transit., *to make, form, do, perform*; of feelings and circumstances, *to cause, bring about*; esp. copiam or potestatem, *to give a chance, grant permission*; with clause as object, esp. with subj., e.g. fac sciam, *let me know*; facere non possum quin, *I cannot but*; of troubles, *to experience, suffer*; with double acc., *to make, appoint, change into*; with genit., *to make something the property* of a person or thing, *to bring into the power of*, or mentally *to put into a category, to regard, to esteem, value*; with acc. and infin., *to take it, assume* or *to make out, represent* that a thing is so. Intransit., *to act*; with adverbs, *to behave*; facere cum, or ab, homine, *to act on the side of, support; to sacrifice*; *to be serviceable, to suit, help, be of service*; used instead of repeating another verb, *to do so*.
Hence partic. **factus** -a -um, *done, wrought*; n. of compar., factius, *nearer to achievement*; n. of positive as subst. **factum** -i, *a deed, act, exploit*.

factĭo -ōnis, f. (1) *a making, doing*; also *the right of making or doing*. (2) *a party, group*; esp. *a political party, faction, side*.

factĭōsus -a -um, *busy; factious, associated with a faction*.

factĭto -are. (1) *to practise, be accustomed to make or do*. (2) *to appoint openly*.

factus -a -um, partic. from facio; q.v.

făcŭla -ae, f., *a little torch*.

făcultās -ātis, f. *feasibility, opportunity, power, means; capacity, ability; resources, stock, abundance*.

făcundĭa -ae, f., *eloquence, readiness of speech*.

făcundus -a -um, *eloquent, fluent, ready of speech*; adv. **făcundē**.

faecŭla -ae, f. *lees of wine*.

faenebris -e, *relating to interest*.

faenērātĭo -ōnis, f. *lending at interest, usury*.

faenĕrātor -ōris, m. *money-lender, usurer*.

faenĕror -ari, dep. and **faenĕro** (**fenĕro**) -are, *to lend at interest; provincias, to despoil by usury; beneficium to trade in benefits*.

faenĕus -a -um, *of hay*; homines, *men of straw*.

faenĭlia -ĭum, n. pl. *hay-loft*.

faenĭsĕca -ae, m., *a mower; a country-man*.

faenum (**fēnum**) -i, n. *hay*.

faenus (**fēnus**) -ŏris, n. *interest on money; pecuniam dare faenore, to lend at interest; accipere faenore, to borrow*. Transf., *debt, indebtedness; capital, usury*.

Faesŭlae -arum, f. *town in Etruria*, (now *Fiesole*); adj. **Faesŭlānus** -a -um.

faex faecis, f. *the dregs* or *lees of liquid*, esp. *of wine*; fig. socially, *the dregs, the lower orders*.

fāgĭnĕus and **fāgĭnus** -a -um, *of beech*.

fāgus -i, f. *beech-tree*.

fāla (**phāla**) -ae, f. *a wooden tower* or *pillar*.

fālārĭca (**phălārĭca**) -ae, f. *a missile covered with tow and pitch*.

falcārĭus -i, m., *a sickle-maker*.

falcātus -a -um, *furnished with sickles; sickle-shaped*.

falcĭfer -fĕra -fĕrum, *carrying a scythe* or *sickle*.

Fălernus ăger, *the Falernian country, in Campania*; n. of adj. as subst. **Fălernum** -i, *Falernian wine*.

fallācĭa -ae, f. *deceit, trick, fraud*.

fallax -ācis, *deceitful, treacherous, false*; adv. **fallācĭter**.

fallo fallĕre fĕfelli falsum, *to deceive, lead astray, cause to be mistaken*; nisi fallor, *unless I am mistaken*; of abstr. things, *to disappoint, fail in*; poet., *to beguile, wile away; to escape the notice of, be concealed from*; impers. non fallit me, *I am not unaware*.
Hence partic. **falsus** -a -um. (1) *wrong, mistaken, misled*; n. as subst., *a mistake*; abl. as adv., falso, *falsely, mistakenly*. (2) *false, untrue, spurious*. (3) *deceitful, lying*; n. as subst. *a lie*; abl. as adv., falso, *falsely, fraudulently*. Adv. **falsē**.

falsĭdĭcus -a -um, and **falsĭlŏquus** -a -um, *lying*.

falsus -a -um, partic. from fallo; q.v.

falx falcis, f. *a sickle, bill-hook, pruning-hook*; *a sickle-shaped implement of war*.

fāma -ae, f. *talk, report, rumour, tradition*; fama est, *there is a rumour; public opinion; standing in public opinion, repute, good or bad*.

fămēlĭcus -a -um, *hungry, famished*.

fămes -is, f. *hunger, famine; insatiable desire; poverty of expression*.

fāmĭgĕrātor -ōris, m. *rumour-monger*.

fămĭlĭa -ae, f. *a household* (*of slaves*), *establishment*; pater familias or pater-familias, *the head of the household*; materfamilias, *a married woman* or *an unmarried woman whose father was dead*; filiusfamilias, *a son still under his father's power*. Transf., *a family estate; a family*, as a subdivision of a gens; *any fraternity, group, sect*.

fămĭlĭāris -e. (1) *belonging to the*

slaves of a house; as subst. **fămĭlĭārĭs** -is, m. *a servant, slave.* (2) *belonging to a family or household; known in the house or family, intimate, friendly*; m. and f. as subst. *a familiar friend.* (3) in augury, fissum familiare, *or* pars familiaris, *the part of the entrails relating to the persons sacrificing.* Adv. **fămĭlĭārĭter**, *familiarly, intimately.*

fămĭlĭārĭtās -ātis, f. *confidential friendship, intimacy*; meton., *familiar friends.*

fămōsus -a -um: pass., *much spoken of, renowned*; in bad sense, *infamous, notorious*; act., *libellous, defamatory.*

fămŭl, fămŭla; see famulus.

fămŭlārĭs -e, *relating to servants or slaves.*

fămŭlātus -ūs, m. *servitude, slavery, service*; meton., *an establishment of slaves.*

fămŭlor -ari, dep. *to be a servant, to serve.*

fămŭlus -a -um, *serving, servile*; as subst. m. **fămŭlus (fămŭl)** -i, *a servant, slave, attendant*; f. **fămŭla** -ae, *a female slave, handmaid.*

fănātĭcus -a -um, *inspired, enthusiastic, frenzied.*

fănum -i, n. *a temple with the land round it, a holy place.*

făr farris, n. *spelt, grain, meal.*

farcĭo farcire farsi fartum, *to fill full, stuff full.*

fărīna -ae, f., *meal, flour.*

farrāgo -inis, f. *mixed fodder for cattle, mash; a medley, mixture.*

farrātus -a -um, *provided with grain; made of corn.*

farrĕus -a -um, *made of spelt or corn.*

fartim (fartem), acc. sing., *stuffing, mincemeat.*

fartor -ōris, m. *a fattener of fowls.*

fās, n. *divine command, divine law*; sometimes *fate, destiny*; in gen. *right, that which is allowed, lawful*; fas est, *it is allowed, is lawful.*

fascĭa -ae, f. *a bandage, band, girdle, girth.*

fascĭcŭlus -i, m., *a little bundle or packet*; florum, *a nosegay.*

fascĭno -are, *to bewitch; to envy.*

fasciŏla -ae, f., *a little bandage.*

fascis -is, m. *a bundle, packet*; plur., fasces, *bundles of sticks with an axe projecting, carried by lictors before the chief Roman magistrates*; hence *high office*, esp. *the consulate.*

fasti -orum, m.; see fastus -a -um.

fastīdĭo -ire, *to loathe, feel distaste for, dislike.*

fastīdĭōsus -a -um, *squeamish, nice, dainty, fastidious*; with genit., *sick of, disgusted with, impatient of*; in act. sense, *disgusting, loathsome.* Adv. **fastīdĭōsē**, *fastidiously, with disgust.*

fastīdĭum -i, n. *loathing, squeamishness, disgust, dislike*; hence *scorn, haughtiness, disdain.*

fastīgātus -a -um, *pointed or sloping down*; adv. **fastīgātē**, *slantingly.*

fastīgĭum -i, n. *the gable end, pediment of a roof*; hence *a slope*, either up or down; *of measurements looking up, height*; *looking down, depth*; abstract, *high rank, dignity; principal point* in a subject.

¹fastus -ūs, m. *pride, haughtiness, arrogance.*

²fastus -a -um: dies fastus, plur. dies fasti, *or* simply fasti, *days on which the praetor could administer justice, court-days.* Transf., *a list of these days, with festivals*, etc., *the Roman calendar*; *a register, record*; *a list of magistrates.*

fātālĭs -e, *relating to destiny or fate; fated, destined by fate*; in bad sense, *deadly, fatal.* Adv. **fātālĭter**, *according to fate.*

fătĕor fătēri fassus, dep., *to confess, admit, allow; to reveal, make known.*

fātĭcănus and **-cĭnus** -a -um, *prophetic*; m. as subst. *a prophet.*

fātīdĭcus -a -um, *announcing fate prophetic*; m. as subst. *a prophet.*

fātĭfer -fĕra -fĕrum, *deadly, fatal.*

fătīgātĭo -ōnis, f. *weariness, fatigue.*

fătīgo -are, *to weary; fatigue; to vex, harass; to tease, importune, worry.*

fātĭlŏqua -ae, f. *a prophetess.*

fātisco -ere and **fātiscor** -i, dep., *to gape, crack, open; to become weak, droop.*

fătŭĭtās -ātis, f. *foolishness, silliness.*

fātum -i, n., *an utterance*, esp. *a divine utterance*; hence *destiny, fate; the will of a god*; personif. Fata, *the Parcae or Fates; doom, fate, natural death, misfortune, ruin, calamity.*

fătŭus -a -um, *foolish, idiotic, silly.*

Faunus -i, m. *a mythic deity of the forests.*

faustĭtās -ātis, f., *prosperity.*

faustus -a -um, *favourable, lucky, auspicious*; adv. **faustē.**

fautor -ōris, m. *patron, promoter, partisan.*

fautrix -trīcis, f., *a patroness.*

faux, f.; usually plur. **fauces** -ĭum, *gullet, throat, jaws.* Transf., *a chasm, gorge, defile; an isthmus, neck of land; straits.*

făvĕo făvēre făvi fautum, *to favour, be favourable to, help, support*, with dat.; with infin., *to be inclined to do.* Esp. as religious t. t., *to speak no words of bad omen*; hence *to be silent.*

făvilla -ae, f. *glowing ashes*, esp. *of the dead; a spark.*

făvĭtor -ōris, m. = fautor; q.v.

Făvōnĭus -i, m. = Zephyrus, *the west wind.*

făvor -ōris, m., *favour, good-will, support, inclinaton*; esp. *applause at the theatre, acclamation.*

făvōrābĭlis -e, *in favour, popular.*

făvus -i, m. *honeycomb.*

fax făcis, f. (1) *a torch*, esp. as carried at weddings and funerals. (2) *a fire-brand*; of persons, *instigator*; of things, *stimulus.* (3) *light, flame*, esp. *of heavenly bodies*; fig., *brilliance or passion.*

febrĭcŭla -ae, f., *a slight fever, feverishness.*

febris -is, f. *fever.*

Februārĭus -i, m. or **Februārĭus Mensis**, *the cleansing month, February;* Kalendae Februariae, *the 1st of February.*

februum -i, n. *religious purification;* **Februa** -orum, pl. *the Roman feast of purification on the 15th of February.*

fēcĭālis = fetialis; q.v.

fēcundĭtās -ātis, f. *fruitfulness, fecundity.*

fēcundo -are, *to fructify, fertilize.*

fēcundus -a -um, *fruitful, prolific; abundant, full, plentiful;* with genit., *rich in, abounding in;* act., *making fruitful.*

fel fellis, n. *the gall-bladder, gall, bile; poison, venom; bitterness.*

fēles -is, f. *a cat;* hence *a thief.*

fēlĭcĭtās -ātis, f. *happiness, good fortune, success;* personif., *Good Fortune* as a goddess.

fēlix -īcis, *fruitful, fertile.* Transf., of good omen, favourable, bringing good luck; fortunate, lucky, successful; Felix, *the Lucky One,* surname of Sulla. Adv. **fēlīcĭter**, *fruitfully; auspiciously, favourably; luckily, successfully.*

fēmella -ae, f. *young woman, girl.*

fēmen = femur; q.v.

fēmĭna -ae, f. *a female, woman;* of animals, *the female.*

fēmĭnĕus -a -um, *female, feminine; womanish, effeminate.*

fĕmur -ŏris or -ĭnis, n. *the thigh.*

fĕnestra -ae, f. *a window; a breach, loophole.*

fĕra -ae, f.; see ferus.

fērālis -e, *relating to the dead, funereal; deadly, fatal; mournful;* n. pl. as subst. *the festival of the dead,* in February.

fērax -ācis, *fruitful, fertile, prolific;* compar. adv. **fērācĭus**, *more fruitfully.*

fercŭlum -i, n. *a frame, litter, bier, tray;* of food, *a course or dish.*

fĕrē. (1) *almost, nearly;* with negatives, *scarcely, hardly.* (2) *just, exactly.* (3) *as a rule, generally, usually.*

fĕrentārĭus -i, m. *a light-armed soldier.*

fĕretrum -i, n., *a bier for carrying a corpse.*

fērĭae -arum, f. pl. *festivals, holidays.*

fērĭātus -a -um, *keeping holiday, idle, at leisure.*

fĕrīnus -a -um, *relating to a wild beast, wild;* f. as subst. *flesh of wild animals, game.*

fĕrĭo -ire, *to strike, knock, smite, hit;* esp. *to strike dead, slay, kill;* colloq., *to cheat.*

fĕrĭtās -ātis, f. *wildness, savageness.*

fermē. (1) *almost, nearly;* with negatives, *hardly, scarcely.* (2) *usually.*

fermentum -i, n. *leaven, yeast; a kind of beer.* Transf., *anger, passion.*

fĕro ferre, with perf. tŭli, supine latum. (1) *to bear, bring, carry;* prae se ferre, *to display, make public;* often *to endure, submit to;* esp. with adv.; ferre aegre, *to take ill, be vexed at.* (2) *to bring orth, produce.* (3) *to bring to* a place or person, *fetch, offer;* suffragium, sententiam, *to vote;* legem, *to propose a law;* ferre ut, *to propose that;* commercial, expensum ferre, *to set down in an account-book as paid; to cause, bring about; to report to others, spread abroad, speak of;* fama fert, *the story goes;* esp. *to publish* a person's *praises.* (4) *to bear away, carry off;* ferre et agere, *to plunder.* Transf., *to win, get;* centuriam, tribus, *to gain the votes of.* (5) *to bear along, move forward, put in motion;* milit., signa ferre, *to march.* Transf., *to move, impel, carry away;* without object, *to lead, tend.*

fĕrōcĭa -ae, f. *high spirit, courage;* in bad sense, *arrogance, ferocity.*

fĕrōcĭtās -ātis, f. *courage, untamed spirit;* in bad sense, *arrogance.*

fĕrox -ōcis, *courageous, high-spirited, warlike;* in bad sense, *wild, unbridled, arrogant;* adv. **fĕrōcĭter.**

ferrāmenta -orum, n. pl. *tools made of, or shod with, iron.*

ferrārĭus -a -um, *of iron;* m. as subst. *a blacksmith;* f. pl. as subst., *iron-mines.*

ferrātĭlis -e, *in irons;* of slaves.

ferrātus -a -um, *furnished or covered with iron;* servi, *in irons;* m. pl. as subst. *soldiers in armour.*

ferrĕus -a -um, *of iron; made of iron or like iron; hard, unfeeling, cruel; immovable, firm.*

ferrĭtērĭum -i. n. = ergastulum; q.v.

ferrūgĭnĕus and **ferrūgĭnus** -a -um, *rust-coloured, dusky.*

ferrūgo -ĭnis, f. *iron rust; the colour of rust.*

ferrum -i, n. *iron;* hence *any iron instrument;* plough, axe, scissors, and esp. *sword.*

fertĭlis -e, *fruitful, fertile, productive; fertilizing, making fruitful.*

fertĭlĭtās -ātis, f. *fruitfulness, fertility.*

fertum (fērctum) -i, n. *a sacrificial cake.*

fērŭla -ae, f. (1) *the herb fennel.* (2) *a stick, cane,* esp. *to punish slaves and children.*

fĕrus -a -um, *wild, uncultivated, uncivilized, rough, cruel;* m. and f. as subst., *a wild animal.*

fervĕfăcĭo -făcĕre -fēci -factum *to make hot, boil, melt.*

fervĕo fervēre ferbŭi (and **fervo** fervĕre fervi) *to be boiling hot, to boil, seethe, glow.* Transf., *to be in quick movement, to seethe; to be excited by passion, rage.* Hence partic. **fervens** -entis, *glowing, hot, heated;* of character or feeling, *heated, fiery.* Adv. **ferventer**, *hotly, warmly.*

fervesco -ĕre, *to become hot, begin to glow or boil.*

fervĭdus -a -um, *boiling, seething*

foaming; of character or feelings, *fiery, passionate, excited.*

fervo = ferveo; q.v.

fervor -ōris, m. *boiling heat, seething, foaming; ardour, passion.*

Fescennia -ae, f. *a town in Etruria famous for verse dialogues.* Adj. **Fescennīnus** -a -um.

fessus -a -um, *weary, tired, exhausted; fessa aetas, old age;* res fessae, *distress.*

festīnātĭo -ōnis, f. *haste, speed, hurry.*

festīno -are: intransit., *to hasten, hurry;* transit., *to hasten, accelerate.* Hence adv. **festīnanter** and **festīnātō,** *hastily.*

festīnus -a -um, *hastening, hasty.*

festīvĭtās -ātis, f. *gaiety, jollity;* of speech or writing, *cheerfulness, humour.*

festīvus -a -um, *of a holiday, festive; merry, good-humoured, cheerful;* adv. **festīvē.**

festūca -ae, f. *a stalk, straw, stem.* Transf., *a rod used in the manumission of slaves.*

festus -a -um, *of a holiday, festive;* of people, *keeping holiday;* n. as subst. *a feast.*

fētĭālis -s, m. *one of a college of priests responsible for formally making peace or declaring war;* as adj. = *belonging to the fetiales.*

fētūra -ae, f. *the bringing forth of young, breeding;* meton. *brood, offspring.*

¹**fētus** -a -um. (1) *pregnant; fruitful, fertile: teeming with, full of.* (2) *that has brought forth, newly delivered.*

²**fētus** -ūs, m. *the bringing forth or hatching of young;* of the soil, *bearing, producing.* Transf., *that which is brought forth: offspring, brood;* of plants, *fruit, produce, shoot.*

fibra -ae, f. *a fibre, filament; the entrails of an animal.*

fībŭla -ae, f. *a buckle, brooch, clasp; an iron clamp.*

fĭcēdŭla -ae, f. *a small bird, the becafico.*

fictĭlis -e, *shaped;* hence *earthen, made of clay;* n. as subst., esp. pl., *earthenware, earthen vessels.*

fictĭo -ōnis, f. *forming, feigning; assumption.*

fictor -ōris, m. *an image-maker, a moulder;* in gen., *maker, contriver.*

fictrix -īcis, f. *she that forms or fashions.*

fictūra -ae, f. *forming, fashioning.*

fictus, partic. from fingo; q.v.

fĭculnus and **fĭculnĕus** -a -um, *of the fig-tree.*

fīcus -i, and -ūs, f. *a fig-tree; a fig.*

fĭdēĭcommissum -i, n. legal, *a trust.*

fīdēlĭa -ae, f. *an earthenware pot or vase.*

fĭdēlis -e, *trusty, steadfast, faithful;* m. as subst., esp. pl., *confidants, faithful friends.* Adv. **fĭdēlĭter,** *faithfully; securely, without danger.*

fĭdēlĭtās -ātis, f., *faithfulness, trust, fidelity.*

Fĭdēnae -arum, and **Fĭdēna** -ae, f. *a town in Latium;* adj. **Fĭdēnas** -ātis.

fīdens -entis, partic. from fido; q.v.

fīdentia -ae, f. *confidence, boldness.*

¹**fĭdes** -ei, f., *trust, confidence, reliance, belief, faith;* fidem facere, *to create confidence, cause belief;* as mercantile t. t., *credit.* Transf., *that which produces confidence; faithfulness, conscientiousness;* fidem praestare, *to be loyal;* (ex) bona fide, *in good faith, sincerely;* of things, *credibility, actuality, fulfilment; a promise, assurance, word of honour, engagement;* fidem fallere, *to break a promise;* servare, *to keep a promise;* fide mea, *on my word of honour;* fides (or fides publica) *a promise of protection, safe-conduct;* hence, in gen., *faithful protection, constant help.*

²**fĭdes** -is, f., usually plur. *a gut-string for a musical instrument;* hence *a lyre, lute, harp.*

fĭdĭcen -cinis, m., *a player on the harp, lyre, lute;* poet., *a lyric poet.*

fĭdĭcĭna -ae, f. *a female player on the lute or harp.*

fĭdĭcĭnus -a -um, *of lute-playing.*

fĭdĭcŭla -ae, f., usually plur. *a little lyre or lute; an instrument for torturing slaves.*

Fĭdĭus -i, m., *a surname of Jupiter;* esp. in phrase, medius fidius! *So help me God!*

fīdo fīdĕre fīsus sum, *to trust, believe, confide in;* with dat. or abl.
Hence partic. **fīdens** -entis, *without fear, confident, courageous;* adv. **fīdenter.**

fīdūcĭa -ae, f. (1) *confidence, trust, assurance;* with sui, or absol., *self-confidence, self-reliance, courage.* (2) *fidelity.*

fīdūcĭārĭus -a -um, *entrusted, committed.*

fīdus -a -um, *trusty, true, faithful, sure;* superl. adv. **fīdissimē.**

fīgo fīgĕre fixi fixum. (1) *to fix, fasten, make fast, attach, affix;* esp. with oculos, *to fix the gaze.* (2) *to thrust home a weapon, etc. so as to stick fast.* (3) *to transfix.*
Hence partic. **fixus** -a -um, *fixed, firm, immovable.*

fĭgŭlāris -e, *of a potter.*

fĭgŭlus -i, m., *a worker in clay, potter.*

fĭgūra -ae, f. *form, shape, figure, size; an atom; shade of a dead person;* the abstr., *kind, nature, species;* rhet., *a figure of speech.*

fĭgūro -are, *to form, mould, shape;* rhet. *to adorn with figures.*

fīlātim, *thread by thread.*

fīlĭa -ae, f. *daughter.*

fĭlĭcātus -a -um, *adorned with ferns; embossed with fern leaves.*

fīlĭŏla -ae, f. *little daughter.*

fīlĭŏlus -i, m. *little son.*

fīlĭus -i, m. *son.*

fĭlix -īcis, f. *fern.*

fīlum -i, n. *a thread,* pendere filo (tenui), *to hang by a thread; a woollen fillet.* Transf., *form, shape;* of speech or writing, *texture, thread.*

fimbrĭae -arum, f. pl., *fringe, border edge.*

fimbriātus -a -um, *fringed.*

fīmus -i, m. and **fīmum** -i, n. *dung, dirt.*

findo findĕre fīdi fissum, *to split, cleave, divide, halve.* Hence partic. **fissus** -a -um, *split, cloven;* n. as subst., *a split, cleft;* in augury, *a divided liver.*

fingo fingĕre finxi fictum, *to shape, fashion, form, mould;* also *to arrange, put in order; to represent, imagine, conceive; to feign, fabricate, devise;* fingere vultum, *to put on an artificial expression.* Hence partic. **fictus** -a -um, *feigned, false;* n. as subst. *a falsehood.*

fīnio -ire, *to bound, limit, enclose, restrain; to define, determine, appoint; to put an end to, conclude, finish;* esp. *to finish speaking,* or *to die;* pass., *to end, cease.* Perf. partic. **fīnītus** -a -um; *of a phrase, well-rounded;* adv. **fīnītē**, *moderately, within bounds.*

fīnis -is, m. (sometimes f.) *boundary, limit, border; summit, end; object, aim;* in pl. *enclosed area, territory.*

fīnĭtĭmus and **fīnĭtŭmus** -a -um, *neighbouring, adjacent; related to, resembling, similar.* M. pl. as subst. *neighbours.*

fīnītor -ōris, m., *one who determines boundaries, a land surveyor.* Transf., *the horizon.*

fīo fĭĕri factus sum, used as pass. of facio. (1) *of persons and things, to be made, come into existence;* with predicate, *to become, be appointed;* with genit., *to be valued at.* (2) *of actions, to be done; of events, to happen;* with abl., quid illo fiet? *what will happen to him?* fieri ut, *to come about that;* fieri non potest quin, *it must be that.*

firmāmen -ĭnis, n. *support, prop.*

firmāmentum -i, n., *a means of support, prop; the main point in an argument.*

firmātor -ōris, m., *one who makes firm or establishes.*

firmĭtās -ātis and **firmĭtūdo** -dĭnis, f., *firmness, stability; strength of mind, constancy.*

firmo -are, *to make firm, strengthen; to make durable, make secure;* of spirits, *to encourage, cheer, animate;* of ideas, *to prove establish,* also *to assert, maintain.*

firmus -a -um, *firm, strong, stout; lasting, valid; morally strong.* Adv. **firmē** and **firmĭter**, *firmly, strongly, steadfastly.*

fiscella and **fiscīna** -ae, f., *a small basket.*

fiscus -i, m. *a basket; hence a money-bag, purse; the state treasury;* under the empire, *the emperor's privy purse* (opp. aerarium, *the state treasury*).

fissĭlis -e, *that can be split;* also *split.*

fissĭo -ōnis, f. *splitting, cleaving, dividing.*

fistūca -ae, f. *a rammer, mallet.*

fistŭla -ae, f. *a water-pipe; a reed-pipe;* *shepherd's pipe;* eburneola, *a pitch-pipe of ivory.*

fistŭlātor -ōris, m., *one who plays the reed-pipe.*

fixus -a -um, partic. from figo; q.v.

flābellum -i, n. *a small fan.*

flābĭlis -e, *airy.*

flābra -orum, n. pl. *blasts of wind, breezes.*

flaccĕo -ēre, *to be flabby; to fail or flag.*

flaccesco flaccescĕre flaccŭi, *to begin to flag, become flabby.*

flaccĭdus -a -um *flabby; weak, languid.*

flaccus -a -um, *flabby;* of men, *flap-eared.*

Flaccus; see Horatius, and Valerius.

flăgello -are, *to whip, scourge, beat.*

flăgellum -i, n. *a whip, scourge; the thong of a javelin; a young sprout, vine-shoot;* plur. *the arms of a polypus;* fig., *the sting of conscience.*

flăgĭtātio -ōnis, f., *an earnest demand or entreaty.*

flăgĭtātor -ōris, m., *one who earnestly demands or entreats.*

flăgĭtĭōsus -a -um, *shameful, disgraceful, infamous;* adv. **flăgĭtĭōsē**.

flăgĭtĭum -i, n. *a disgraceful action, shameful crime; shame, disgrace;* meton., *scoundrel, rascal.*

flăgĭto -are, *to entreat, ask, demand earnestly; to demand to know; to summon before a court of justice.*

flagrantĭa -ae, f. *burning, blazing, glittering.*

flagritrība -ae, m., *one that wears out whips, a whipping boy.*

flagro -are, *to blaze, burn, glow, flame,* also *to glitter.* Transf., *to glow or burn with passion; to suffer from,* with abl. Hence partic. **flagrans** -antis, *blazing, burning, glittering.* Transf., *passionate, ardent.* Adv. **flagranter**.

flagrum -i, n. *scourge, whip.*

¹**flāmen** -ĭnis. m. *the priest of some particular god.*

²**flāmen** -ĭnis, n. *a blowing, blast.*

flāmĭnĭca -ae, f. *the wife of a flamen.*

Flāmĭnīnus, *a surname in the patrician Gens Quinctia;* see Quinctius.

flāmĭnĭum -i, n., *the office of a flamen.*

Flāmĭnĭus -a -um, *name of a Roman gens.*

flamma -ae, f., *a flame, blazing fire.* Transf., *a source of light, torch, star, lightning; lustre, glitter; the fire or glow of passion; devouring flame, destruction.*

flammĕŏlum -i, n., *a small bridal veil.*

flammesco -ĕre, *to become inflamed.*

flammĕus -a -um, *fiery, flaming; flashing, fiery-red;* n. as subst. **flammĕum** -i, *a (flame-coloured) bridal veil.*

flammĭfer -fĕra -fĕrum, *flaming, fiery.*

flammo -are: intransit., *to flame, blaze, burn;* transit., *to set on fire inflame.*

flammŭla -ae, f. *little flame.*

flātus -ūs, m. *blowing, blast, breathing.*

Transf., *haughtiness, arrogance,* gen. plur.

flāvens -entis, *yellow* or *gold-coloured.*

flāvesco -ĕre, *to become yellow* or *gold-coloured.*

Flāvĭus -a -um, *name of a Roman gens to which the emperors Vespasian, Titus, and Domitian belonged.*

flāvus -a -um, *gold-coloured, yellow.*

flēbĭlis -e: pass., *lamentable, wretched, deserving tears;* act., *tearful, doleful.* Adv. **flēbĭlĭter.**

flecto flectĕre flexi flexum, *to bend.* (1) *to alter the shape of, to bow, twist, curve.* Transf., *to change, alter, influence.* (2) *to alter the direction of, to turn, wheel;* vocem, *to modulate.*

flĕo flēre flēvi flētum: intransit., *to weep; to drip, trickle;* transit., *to weep for, lament, bewail;* flendus, *to be lamented.*

¹**flētus** -a -um, partic. of fleo; q.v.

²**flētus** -ūs, m. *weeping, bewailing.*

flexĭbĭlis -e, *that can be bent, flexible;* of speech or the voice, *adaptable;* in bad sense, *fickle, changeable.*

flexĭlis -e, *flexible, pliant, supple.*

flexĭlŏquus -a -um, *equivocal, ambiguous.*

flexĭo -ōnis, f. *bending;* vocis, or modorum, *modulation of the voice;* deverticula flexionesque, *twists and turns.*

flexĭpēs -pĕdis, *crooked-footed, twining.*

flexŭōsus -a -um, *full of windings and turnings, crooked.*

flexūra -ae, f. *bending.*

¹**flexus** -a -um, partic. of flecto; q.v.

²**flexus** -ūs, m. *bending, turning;* of the voice, *modulation.* Transf., *change, alteration.*

flictus -ūs, m. *striking together, dashing against.*

flīgo -ere, *to beat* or *dash down.*

flo flare flavi flatum, *to blow;* intransit., of winds, persons and instruments; transit., *to blow, blow forth; to blow on* an instrument; *to cast metals, to coin.*

floccus -i, m. *a flock of wool;* flocci non facere, *to think nothing of.*

Flōra -ae, f., *the goddess of flowers, and Spring;* adj. **Flōrālis** -e, *belonging to Flora;* n. pl. as subst. *the festival of Flora.*

Flōrentĭa -ae, f. *a town in Etruria* (now *Florence*); adj. **Flōrentīnus** -a -um.

florĕo -ēre -ŭi, *to bloom, flower.* Transf., *to be in one's prime, to prosper, flourish, be in repute;* with abl., *to abound in, swarm with.* Hence partic. **flōrens** -entis, *blooming, flourishing.*

flōresco -ĕre, *to begin to blossom* or *flourish.*

florĕus -a -um, *made of flowers; rich in flowers, flowery.*

flōrĭdus -a -um, *flowery, blossoming; made of* or *rich in flowers;* of age, *fresh, blooming;* of speech, *flowery, florid.*

flōrĭfer -fēra fērum, *flower-bearing.*

flōrĭlĕgus -a -um, *culling flowers.*

flōs flōris, m. *a flower, blossom.* Transf., *the prime, flower of anything, the best,* *the pride;* on the face, *first beard, down;* vini *bouquet;* of speech, *ornament.*

floscŭlus -i, m., *a little flower.* Transf., *best part, pride;* of speech, *ornament.*

fluctĭfrăgus -a -um, *wave-breaking.*

fluctŭātĭo -ōnis, f. *moving backwards and forwards, fluctuation; indecision.*

fluctŭo -are, *to be wave-like, move up and down;* sometimes of a *glittering effect;* of persons and passions, *to be tossed about, to waver.*

fluctŭor -ari -atus, dep. *to toss about, waver.*

fluctŭōsus -a -um, *full of waves, stormy.*

fluctus -ūs, m. *a streaming, flowing.* Transf., *commotion, disturbance.*

flŭentum -i, n., *running water, a stream.*

flŭĭdus -a -um, *flowing, fluid.* Transf., *lax, languid; relaxing.*

flŭĭto -are, *to flow hither and thither, to float, swim, sail, move up and down, be tossed about.* Transf. *to flutter; to waver, vacillate.*

flūmen -ĭnis, n. *flowing;* hence *a river, stream;* flumine secundo, *down-stream;* flumine adverso, *upstream;* fig., *a stream of blood, tears, words, etc.*

flūmĭnĕus -a -um, *of a river.*

flŭo flŭĕre fluxi fluxum: of fluids, *to flow;* of a solid object, *to flow, drip with any liquid.* Transf., in gen., *to flow, stream, pour;* of abstr. things, *to proceed, issue, spread;* of circumstances, *to tend;* of language, *to flow; to sink, droop.* Hence pres. partic. **flŭens** -entis, *flowing;* hence *lax;* of speech, *fluent* or *diffuse;* adv. **flŭenter,** *in a flowing manner.* Past partic. **fluxus** -a -um, *flowing;* hence *leaky;* of solid objects, *waving, fluttering, loose;* of character, *lax, loose, weak;* of abstr. things, *fleeting, unstable.*

flūto -are, *to flow, float, swim.*

flŭvĭālis and **flŭvĭātĭlis** -e, *of a river.*

flŭvĭdus -a -um, *flowing, fluid.*

flŭvĭus -ĭi, m., *flowing water; a stream, river.*

fluxus -a -um, partic. from flŭo; q.v.

fōcāle -is, n. *a wrapper for the neck.*

fōcillo -are, *to warm up, refresh by warmth.*

fōcŭla -orum, n pl. *stoves.*

fōcŭlus -i, m. *a brazier.*

fōcus -i, m. *a fireplace, hearth;* meton., *house, family, home;* sometimes *altar-fire* or *funeral pyre.*

fŏdĭco -are, *to dig, jog;* latus, *to dig in the ribs.*

fŏdĭo fŏdĕre fōdi fossum, *to dig;* also *to dig out; to excavate.* Transf., *to prick, prod, jog.*

foecundus, **foecundo** = fecundus, fecundo; q.v.

foedĕrātus -a -um, *confederate, allied.*

foedĭfrăgus -a -um, *treaty-breaking.*

foedĭtās -ātis, f. *foulness, filthiness.*

foedo -are, *to make foul, make filthy, defile, disfigure;* morally, *to dishonour, disgrace.*

¹**foedus** -a -um, *foul, filthy, horrible, disgusting;* adv. **foedē.**

²**foedus** -ĕris, n. *a league* between states; *a compact, covenant, agreement.* Transf., *a law.*

foen-; see **faen-**.

foetĕo -ēre, *to have a bad smell.*

foetĭdus -a -um, *having a bad smell, stinking.*

foetor -ōris, m. *a bad smell, stink.*

foetus; see **fetus**.

fŏlĭātus -a -um, *leafy;* n. as subst. *a salve* or *oil of spikenard leaves.*

fŏlĭum -i, n. *a leaf.*

follĭcŭlus -i, m. *a little sack* or *bag.*

follis -is, m. *a leather bag; a pair of bellows; a purse; a puffed-out cheek.*

fōmentum -i, n. *poultice, fomentation.* Transf., *alleviation.*

fōmĕs -ĭtis, m. *touchwood, tinder.*

fons fontis, m. *a spring, fountain; fresh* or *spring water.* Transf., *spring, origin, source.*

fontānus -a -um, *of a spring* or *fountain.*

Fontēius -a -um, *name of a Roman gens.*

fontĭcŭlus -i, m. *a little fountain* or *spring.*

for fāri fātus, dep. *to speak, say;* also *to speak of.*

fŏrābilis -e, *that can be bored through, penetrable.*

fŏrāmen -ĭnis, n. *hole, opening, aperture.*

fŏras, *out of doors, forth, out;* (scripta) foras dare, *to publish.*

forceps -cĭpis, m. and f. *a pair of tongs, pincers.*

forda -ae, *a cow in calf.*

fŏre, **fŏrem**, used as fut. infin. and imperf. subj. of sum; q.v.

fŏrensis -e, *relating to the market* or *forum;* hence *of the business of the Roman forum,* esp. *legal.*

forfex -fĭcis, f. *a pair of shears* or *scissors.*

¹**fŏris** -is, f. *a door;* plur. fores, *folding-doors.* Transf., *any opening, entrance.*

²**fŏris**, adv. (1) (situated) *out of doors, outside, without;* sometimes, *abroad, outside Rome.* (2) *from without, from abroad.*

forma -ae, f. *form, figure, shape; beautiful shape, beauty; image, likeness; a shape serving as model,* e.g. *a shoemaker's last; a mould, stamp;* abstr., *form, manner, type;* in logic, *species; outline, general notion.*

formālis -e, *formal, having a set form.*

formāmentum -i, n. *conformation.*

formātor -ōris, m. *a fashioner.*

formātūra -ae, f. *forming, shaping.*

Formĭae -arum, f. *town on the coast of Latium;* adj. **Formĭānus** -a -um.

formīca -ae, f. *an ant.*

formīdābilis -e, *fearful, formidable.*

¹**formīdo** -are, *to be terrified, to dread.*

²**formīdo** -ĭnis, f. *dread, terror;* meton., *source of fear, dreadfulness, awfulness; a scarecrow.*

formīdŏlōsus -a -um: act., *causing dread, terrible, fearful;* pass. *fearful, timid.* Adv., **formīdŏlōsē**, *dreadfully, terribly.*

formo -are, *to form, shape, fashion; to arrange, order, regulate, dispose.*

formōsĭtās -ātis, f. *beauty.*

formōsus -a -um, *beautifully formed, beautiful;* adv. **formōsē**.

formŭla -ae, f. *physical beauty;* legal, *set form, formula;* esp. *the form of an alliance;* in gen., *rule, principle.*

fornācālis -e, *of an oven.*

fornācŭla -ae, f., *a little oven.*

fornax -ācis, f. *oven, furnace, kiln;* Aetnae, *the crater.*

fornĭcātus -a -um, *arched, vaulted.*

fornix -ĭcis, m. *arch, vault; arcade;* milit. *an arched sallyport.*

fornus = furnus; q.v.

fŏro -are, *to bore, pierce.*

fors, *chance, luck;* in nom. **fors**, also **forsit** (fors sit), **forsăn** (fors an), and **forsĭtăn** (fors sit an), *perhaps, perchance;* abl. **fortĕ**, *by chance, accidentally, as it happened.*

fortassĕ (**fortassis**), *perhaps.*

fortĕ; see **fors**.

fortĭcŭlus -a -um, *fairly bold.*

fortis -e, physically, *strong, powerful, robust;* morally, *brave, courageous, steadfast;* fortes fortuna adiuvat, *fortune favours the brave;* in bad sense, *bold, audacious.* Adv. **fortĭter**, *strongly, bravely.*

fortĭtūdo -ĭnis, f. *physical strength, moral bravery, courage;* plur., *deeds of bravery.*

fortŭĭtus -a -um, *accidental, casual, fortuitous, unpremeditated;* n. pl. as subst. *chance occurrences.* Abl. sing. as adv. **fortŭĭto**, *by chance, fortuitously.*

fortūna -ae, f. *chance, fate, lot, luck, fortune;* fortuna prospera, secunda, *good fortune;* adversa, *misfortune.* Transf., *lot, condition, state, mode of life; property, possessions.*

fortūno -are, *to make happy, bless, prosper.*

Hence partic. **fortūnātus** -a -um, *blessed, lucky, fortunate; well off, wealthy, rich.* Adv. **fortūnātē**, *happily, fortunately.*

fŏrŭli -orum, m., *a bookcase.*

fŏrum -i, n. *an open square, market-place;* forum bovarium, or boarium, *the cattle-market;* forum holitorium, *vegetable-market;* forum piscarium, or piscatorium, *fish-market;* in gen., *a place of public business,* commercial, political and judicial esp. in Rome. Transf., *of the business transacted in a forum;* forum agere, *to hold an assize;* forum attingere, *to apply oneself to public business.*

fŏrus -i, m. *the gangway of a ship; a block of seats in the theatre;* plur., *tiers of cells* in a beehive.

fossa -ae, f. *ditch, trench, channel.*

fossĭo -ōnis, f. *digging, excavation.*

fossor -ōris, m. *a digger, delver; a boor, clown.*

fossūra -ae, f. *digging.*

fōtus, partic. of foveo; q.v.

fŏvĕa -ae, f. *a pit,* esp. *as a trap for game, a pitfall.*

fŏvĕo fŏvēre fōvi fōtum, *to warm,*

keep warm, caress: fig., *to stay constantly in* a place; in gen., *to foster, cherish, support, encourage.*

fractus -a -um, partic. from frango; q.v.

frāga -orum, n. pl. *strawberries.*

frăgilis -e, *crackling; easily broken, fragile.* Transf., *fleeting, transitory; weak, feeble.*

frăgilĭtās -ātis, f., *frailty, weakness.*

fragmen -mĭnis, n. *a breaking;* hence, usually plur., *fragments, remains, ruins.*

fragmentum -i, n. *a piece broken off, fragment.*

frăgor -ōris, m., *a breaking; a noise of breaking, crack, crash.*

frăgōsus -a -um, *crashing, roaring; fragile; broken, rough.*

fragro -are, *to emit a smell,* esp. *a sweet smell;* pres. partic. **fragrans** -antis, *sweet-smelling, fragrant.*

frāgum; see fraga.

frango frangĕre frēgi fractum, *to break, break in pieces, shatter;* gulam laqueo, *to strangle;* fruges saxo, *to grind;* diem morantem mero, *to shorten;* of persons, passions, etc., *to master, subdue, humble;* frangi animo, *to be discouraged.*
   Hence partic. **fractus** -a -um, *broken, humbled, enfeebled.*

frāter -tris, m. *a brother;* frater germanus, *own brother;* fratres, *brothers and sisters;* also *a cousin* or *a brother-in-law.* Transf., *a comrade, compatriot, ally.*

frātercŭlus -i, m. *little brother.*

frāternĭtās -ātis, f. *brotherhood, fraternity.*

frāternus -a -um, *of a brother, brotherly, fraternal;* sometimes *of a cousin.* Transf., *of a related person; of some thing related to another.* Adv. **frāternē,** *in a brotherly manner, like a brother.*

frātrĭcīda -ae, m. *one who kills a brother, a fratricide.*

fraudātĭo -ōnis, f. *deceit, fraud, swindling.*

fraudātor -ōris, m. *deceiver, swindler.*

fraudo -are, *to cheat, defraud, swindle; to steal, embezzle.*

fraudŭlentĭa -ae, f. *deceitfulness.*

fraudŭlentus -a -um, *deceitful, fraudulent.*

fraus, fraudis, f.: act., *deceit, fraud;* sine fraude, *honourably;* in gen., *a crime, offence; delusion, error; damage, harm;* sine fraude, *without harm.*

fraxĭnĕus and **fraxĭnus** -a -um, *of ashwood, ashen.*

fraxĭnus -i, f. *an ash-tree;* meton., *a spear* or *javelin, with a shaft of ashwood.*

Frĕgellae -arum, f. *town of Volsci, in Latium.*

frĕmĕbundus -a -um, *roaring, murmuring.*

frĕmĭtus -ūs, m. *roaring, murmuring, growling.*

frĕmo -ĕre -ŭi -ĭtum, *to roar, murmur, growl;* with acc. *to murmur out something, grumble, complain.*

frĕmor -ōris, m. *roaring, murmuring.*

frendo -ĕre: intransit., *to gnash the teeth;* transit., *to crush, bruise, grind.*

frēni -orum, m.; see frenum.

frēno -are, *to bridle, curb, restrain, check.*

frēnum -i, n., usually plur. **frēna** -orum, n.; also **frēni** -orum, m. *bridle, reins, bit, curb.* Transf., *restraint.*

frĕquens -entis, *crowded, numerous, full;* of places, *full, frequented, populous;* of time, *repeated, frequent, constant;* of persons, *often doing a thing;* of things, *often done* or *used.* Adv. **frĕquenter,** *in large numbers; frequently, often.*

frĕquentātĭo -ōnis, f., *frequency, crowding.*

frĕquentĭa -ae, f.: of persons, *a large concourse, numerous assembly, population;* of things, *a large number, abundance.*

frĕquento -are, *to crowd;* of number *to collect in large numbers; to fill a place with people or things; to do a thing in crowds* or *with a crowd;* of time, *to do* or *use a thing frequently:* domum, *to visit often;* Hymenaee! frequentant, *they repeat.*

frĕtum -i; n. *a strait, sound, estuary, firth, channel;* fretum Siciliae, fretum Siciliense, or fretum, *the Straits of Messina;* *the sea* in gen., usually plur.: fig., *disturbance, turmoil.*

¹frĕtus -a -um, *relying on, confiding in,* with abl.

²frĕtus -ūs, m. *a strait; an interval, difference.*

frĭco frĭcare frĭcŭi frictum and frĭcātum, *to rub, rub down.*

frĭgĕo -ēre, *to be cold; to be inactive, lifeless, dull;* colloq., *to be coldly received, fall flat.*

frĭgesco -ĕre, *to become cold* or *dull.*

frĭgĭdŭlus -a -um, *somewhat cold* or *faint.*

frĭgĭdus -a -um, *cold, cool, chilly;* f. sing. as subst. *cold water.* Transf., in act. sense, *chilling, causing cold;* fig., *cold, dull, lifeless;* of speech, *flat.* Adv. **frĭgĭdē,** *coldly; languidly, feebly.*

frĭgo frĭgĕre frixi frictum, *to roast, parch.*

frĭgus -ŏris n. *cold, coolness; the cold of winter; a cold place; the cold of death* or *fright.* Transf., *coldness in action, dullness, indolence; a cold reception, coolness, disfavour.*

frĭguttĭo -ire, *to stammer.*

frĭo -are, *to rub, crumble.*

frĭtillus -i, m. *a dice-box.*

frīvŏlus -a -um, *trifling, worthless;* n. pl. as subst. *sticks of furniture.*

frondātor -ōris, m. *a pruner of trees.*

frondĕo -ēre, *to be in leaf, be leafy.*

frondesco ĕre, *to come into leaf, put forth leaves.*

frondĕus -a -um, *leafy.*

frondĭfer -fĕra -fĕrum, *leaf-bearing, leafy.*

frondōsus -a -um, *full of leaves, leafy.*

¹frons frondis, f. *a leaf, foliage*; meton., *a chaplet* or *crown of leaves.*

²frons frontis, f. *the forehead, brow*; frontem contrahere, *to frown.* Transf., in gen., *the front, forepart*; milit., *the van; the outside end of a book roll; frontage* (in measuring land).

frontālia -ĭum, n. pl. *the frontlet of a horse.*

fronto -ōnis, m., *a man with a broad forehead.*

fructŭārĭus -a -um, *fruit-bearing, fruitful.*

fructŭōsus -a -um, *fruitful, fertile.*

fructus -ūs, m.: abstr., *enjoyment, enjoying*; concr., *proceeds, profit, produce, income*; esp. *the fruits of the earth.*

frūgālis -e, *frugal, economical, honest*; adv. **frūgālĭter.**

frūgālĭtās -ātis, f., *frugality, economy, honesty*; of style, *restraint.*

frūgi; see frux.

frūgĭfer -fĕra -fĕrum, *fruitful, fertile; profitable, advantageous.*

frūgĭfĕrens -entis, *fruitful, fertile.*

frūgĭlĕgus -a -um, *collecting grain.*

frūgĭpărus -a -um, *fruitful, prolific.*

frūmentārĭus -a -um, *of grain* or *corn*; res, *the supply of corn*; m. as subst. *a corn-merchant.*

frūmentātĭo -ōnis, f. *a foraging; a distribution of corn.*

frūmentātŏr -ōris, m. *a forager* or *a provider of corn.*

frūmentor -ari, dep., *to forage, fetch corn.*

frūmentum -i, n., *corn, grain.*

frŭor frŭi fructus and frŭĭtus, dep., *to have the benefit of, to enjoy,* usually with abl.: votis, *to obtain one's wishes;* as legal t. t., *to have the use and enjoyment of.*

frustillātim, *bit by bit.*

frustrā, *in error:* frustra esse, *to be deceived, mistaken.* Transf., *in vain, without effect; wantonly, without reason.*

frustrāmen -ĭnis, n. *deception.*

frustrātĭo -ōnis, f. *deception, disappointment, frustration.*

frustro -are, and **frustror** -ari, dep. *to disappoint, deceive, trick.*

frustum -i, n. *a bit, piece, morsel.*

frŭtex -tĭcis, m. *a shrub, bush;* as a term of reproach, *blockhead.*

frŭtĭcētum -i, n., *a thicket.*

frŭtĭco -are and **frŭtĭcor** -ari, dep. *to shoot out, become bushy.*

frŭtĭcōsus -a -um, *bushy* or *full of bushes.*

frux frūgis, f., usually plur. **frūges** -um, *fruits of the earth;* in gen., *fruits, success;* ad bonam frugem se recipere, *to improve oneself.* Dat. sing. **frūgi,** used as adj., *useful, honest, discreet, moderate.*

fūco -are, *to colour, paint, dye;* fig., *to colour, embellish.*

Hence partic. **fūcātus** -a -um, *painted; counterfeited, simulated.*

fūcōsus -a -um, *painted; simulated; counterfeited.*

¹fūcus -i, m., *red* or *purple dye; red* or *purple colour; rouge;* in gen., *paint, dye of any colour; bee-glue.* Transf., *deceit, pretence.*

²fucus -i, m. *a drone bee.*

Fūfius -a -um, *name of a Roman gens.*

fŭga -ae, f. *flight, running away;* esp. *flight from one's country, exile, banishment.* Transf., *swift course, speed; avoiding,* with genit.

fŭgax -ācis, *ready to flee, flying; speeding, fleeting, transitory;* with genit., *avoiding.* Hence compar. adv. **fŭgācius.**

fŭgĭo fŭgĕre fūgi fŭgĭtum, *to flee.* Intransit., *to take to flight, run away; to pass away, disappear.* Transit., *to flee from, run away from, avoid;* with infin., fuge quaerere, *do not seek;* of things, *to escape the notice of a person.*

Hence partic., **fŭgĭens** -entis, *fleeing; avoiding,* with genit.; *fleeting, deteriorating.*

fŭgĭtīvus -a -um, *flying, fugitive;* m. as subst., *a fugitive,* esp. *a runaway slave.*

fŭgĭto -are, *to flee;* transit., *to fly from, avoid, shun.*

Hence partic. **fŭgĭtans** -antis, *fleeing;* with genit., *avoiding.*

fŭgo -are, *to put to flight, chase away; to drive into exile, to dismiss, avert.*

fulcīmen -ĭnis, n., *a prop, support, pillar.*

fulcĭo fulcīre fulsi fultum, *to prop up, support; to strengthen, secure;* morally *to support, stay, uphold.*

fulcrum -i, n., *the post* or *foot of a couch.*

fulgĕo fulgēre fulsi, *to flash, to lighten;* in gen., *to shine, gleam, glitter;* fig., *to be distinguished; to shine.*

fulgĭdus -a -um, *shining, gleaming, glittering.*

fulgo -ĕre = fulgeo; q.v.

fulgor -ōris, m., *lightning;* in gen., *glitter, brightness;* fig., *brightness, glory.*

fulgur -ŭris, n. *a flash* or *stroke of lightning;* sometimes *an object struck by lightning;* in gen., *brightness.*

fulgŭrālis -e, *relating to lightning.*

fulgŭrātŏr -ōris, m., *a priest who interpreted omens from lightning.*

fulgŭrītus -a -um, *struck by lightning.*

fulgŭro -are, *to lighten; to shine, be brilliant.*

fŭlĭca -ae, f. *a coot.*

fūlīgo -ĭnis, f. *soot; powder for darkening the eyebrows.*

fullo -ōnis, m. *a cloth-fuller.*

fullōnĭca -ae, f. *the art of fulling.*

fulmen -ĭnis, n. *a stroke of lightning, a thunderbolt.* Transf. *a crushing calamity; mighty* or *irresistible power.*

fulmĭnĕus -a -um, *of lightning; like lightning, rapid* or *destructive.*

fulmĭno -are, *to lighten.*

fultūra -ae, f., *support, prop, stay.*

Fulvĭus -a -um, *name of a Roman gens.*

fulvus -a -um, *tawny, yellowish brown,*

fūmĕus and **fumĭdus** -a -um, *smoky, full of smoke.*

fūmĭfer -fĕra -fĕrum, *smoky.*

fūmĭfĭcus -a -um, *causing smoke.*

fūmo -are, *to smoke, steam, reek.*

fūmōsus -a -um, *smoked.*

fūmus -i, m. *smoke, steam, vapour.*

fūnālis -e, *attached to a rope.* N. as subst. **fūnāle** -is, *the thong of a sling; a wax-torch.*

fūnambŭlus -i, m. *a rope-dancer.*

functĭo -ōnis, f. *performance, execution.*

funda -ae, *a sling; a sling-stone; a casting-net.*

fundāmen -inis, n. and **fundāmentum** -i, n. usually plur., *a foundation, basis.*

fundātor -ōris, m. *founder.*

fundĭto -are, *to sling.*

fundĭtor -ōris, m. *a soldier with a sling, a slinger.*

fundĭtus, *from the bottom; completely, entirely; at the bottom, below.*

¹**fundo** -are, *to lay the foundation of, to found; also to make firm, to strengthen.*
  Hence partic. **fundātus** -a -um, *founded, firm.*

²**fundo** fundĕre fūdi fūsum: of liquids, *to pour, pour out;* of metals, *to melt, cast.* Transf., *to pour out, shower, give abundantly; to squander;* se fundere, *to rush, stream;* of sounds, *to utter;* with emphasis on distribution, *to spread, extend, scatter;* milit. *to rout, defeat, scatter, put to flight.*
  Hence partic. **fūsus** -a -um, *spread out, extended;* crines, *flowing free;* of speech, *diffuse;* adv. **fūsē**, *widely, copiously.*

fundus -i, m. *ground; the bottom or base of anything; a farm, estate.*

fūnebris -e, *of a funeral funereal; deadly, destructive.*

fūnĕrĕus -a -um, *of a funeral, funereal; fatal, ill-omened.*

fūnĕro -are, *to bury solemnly, inter with funeral rites;* partic. **fūnĕrātus** -a -um, *done to death.*

fūnesto -are, *to defile or pollute with death.*

fūnestus -a -um: pass., *filled with mourning, defiled by death;* act., *fatal, disastrous, deadly.*

fungĭnus -a -um, *of a mushroom.*

fungor fungi functus, dep. *to occupy oneself with anything, to perform, execute, undergo,* usually with abl.; absol. in special sense, *to be affected, suffer.*

fungus -i, m. *a mushroom, fungus; a dull, stupid fellow; a 'thief' in the wick of a candle, a candlesnuff.*

fūnĭcŭlus -i, m. *thin rope, cord, string.*

fūnis -is, m. *rope, cord, line.*

fūnus -ĕris, n. *a funeral, burial.* Transf., *the corpse; death; destruction, ruin; a cause of ruin.*

fŭo fŭi fŭtūrus, etc.; see sum.

fūr fūris, c. *a thief.*

fūrax -ācis, *inclined to steal, thievish.* Hence superl. adv. **fūrācissimē**, *most thievishly.*

furca -ae, f., *a (two-pronged) fork, a pitch-fork; a fork-shaped prop or pole; an instrument of punishment, with two prongs to which the arms were tied;* geograph., *a narrow pass.*

furcĭfer -fĕra -fĕrum, *carrying the furca as a punishment;* applied to slaves, *gallows-bird.*

furcilla -ae, f., *a little fork.*

furcillo -are, *to support.*

furcŭla -ae, f. *a little fork; a fork-shaped prop;* geograph., *a narrow pass,* esp. of the Caudine forks.

furfur -ŭris, m. *bran; scales, scurf on the skin.*

fŭrĭa -ae, f., usually plur. *rage, frenzy, madness, passion;* personif., of the mythological Furies, *avenging deities;* fig., of persons.

fŭrĭālis -e, *furious, raging, frenzied; belonging to the Furies;* **fŭrĭālĭter** *furiously, madly.*

fŭrĭbundus -a -um, *raging, furious; inspired.*

fŭrĭo -are, *to make furious, madden;* partic., fŭrĭātus -a -um, *raging.*

fŭrĭōsus -a -um, *raging, raving, mad, furious;* adv. **fŭrĭōsē.**

Fūrĭus -a -um, *name of a Roman gens.*

furnus -i, m. *an oven, bakehouse.*

fŭro -ĕre, *to rage, rave, be mad;* often of impassioned persons, *to rave, be frantic;* furere aliquā, *to be madly in love with.* Adv. from partic., **fŭrenter**, *furiously.*

¹**fūror** -ari, dep., *to steal, pilfer;* fig., *to steal away, withdraw; to counterfeit, personate.*

²**fŭror** -ōris, m. *madness, raving, insanity; furious anger, martial rage; passionate love; inspiration, poetic or prophetic frenzy;* meton., *an object of passion.*

furtĭfĭcus -a -um, *thievish.*

furtim, adv. *by stealth, stealthily.*

furtīvus -a -um, *stolen; secret, concealed, furtive.* Adv. **furtīvē.**

furtum -i, n. *theft, robbery;* in plur., *stolen property;* fig., *underhand methods, trick, deceit,* esp. *secret or stolen love.*

fūruncŭlus -i, m. *a sneak thief, pilferer.*

furvus -a -um, *dark-coloured, black.*

fuscĭna -ae, f. *a three-pronged fork, trident.*

fusco -are, *to darken, blacken.*

fuscus -a -um, *dark-coloured;* of the voice, *indistinct.*

fūsĭlis -e, *molten, liquid, soft.*

fūsĭo -ōnis, f. *pouring-out, out-pouring.*

fustis -is, m. *a stick, cudgel, club.*

fustŭārĭum -i, n. *cudgelling to death.*

¹**fūsus** -a -um, partic. from fundo; q.v.

²**fūsus** -i, m. *a spindle.*

fūtātim, *abundantly.*

futtĭlis and **fūtĭlis** -e, *brittle; vain, worthless, good for nothing.*

futtĭlĭtās and **fūtĭlĭtās** -ātis, f. *worthlessness, folly, silliness.*

fŭtūrus -a -um used as future partic. of sum; q.v.

G

G, g, the seventh letter of the Latin alphabet, originally represented by C.

Gābĭi -orum, m. *an ancient city of Latium*; adj. **Gābīnus** -a -um.

Gābīnĭus -a -um, *name of a Roman gens.*

Gādēs -ium, f. *a town in Hispania Baetica* (now *Cadiz*); adj. **Gādītānus** -a -um.

gaesum -i, n. *a long heavy javelin.*

Gaetūli -orum, m. pl. *a people in north-west Africa.*

Gāius, abbrev. C., *a Roman praenomen*; fem. **Gāia.**

Gălătae -arum, m. *a Celtic people settled in Asia Minor, the Galatians.*

Galba -ae, m. *a cognomen of the Sulpician gens*; esp. of Ser. Sulpicius, Roman emperor A.D. 68-69.

galbănĕus -a -um, *of galbanum*; q.v.

galbănum -i, n., *the resinous sap of a Syrian plant.*

galbĭnus -a -um, *greenish-yellow.*

gălĕa -ae, f. *helmet.*

gălĕo -are, *to cover with a helmet*; partic., **gălĕātus** -a -um, *helmeted.*

gălērĭcŭlum -i, n. *skull-cap; wig.*

gălērītus -a -um, *wearing a hood or skull-cap.*

gălērum -i, n. and **gălērus** -i, m. *skull-cap; wig.*

galla -ae, f. *oakapple.*

Galli -orum, m. pl. *the Gauls, a Celtic people, to the west of the Rhine and in the north of Italy*; **Gallĭa** -ae, f. *Gaul, the land of the Gauls*; Cisalpina = *Northern Italy*; Transalpina = *France*; adj. **Gallĭcānus** and **Gallĭcus** -a -um, *Gaulish*; f. as subst., gallĭca, *a slipper.*

gallĭambus -i, m. *a song of the priests of Cybele.*

gallĭca; see **Galli.**

gallīna -ae, f. *hen.*

gallīnācĕus -a -um, *of poultry*; gallus, *a poultry-cock.*

gallīnārĭus -a -um, *of poultry*; m. as subst., *poultry-farmer.*

¹**gallus** -i, m. *cock.*

²**Gallus,** *a Gaul*; see **Galli.**

³**Gallus** -i, m. *usually plur.* **Galli** -orum, m. *a priest of Cybele.*

gănĕa -ae, f. and **gănĕum** -i, n. *a brothel or a low eating-house.*

gănĕo -ōnis, m. *a debauchee.*

Gangēs -is, m., *the river Ganges in India.* Adj. **Gangētĭcus** -a -um; f. adj. **Gangētis** -ĭdis = *Indian.*

gannĭo -ire, *to yelp, snarl, growl.*

gannītus -ūs, m. *yelping, snarling.*

Gănўmēdēs -is, m. *the cup-bearer of Jove.*

garrĭo -ire, *to chatter, prate, babble.*

garrŭlĭtās -ātis, f. *chattering.*

garrŭlus -a -um, *talkative, chattering, babbling, noisy.*

gārum -i, n. *fish-sauce.*

Gărumna -ae, f. *a river in Gaul* (now *Garonne*); **Gărumni** -orum, m.pl. *a people living on the Garonne.*

gaudĕo gaudēre gāvīsus sum, *to rejoice, be glad*; with abl. of cause, *to delight in*; in sinu gaudere, *to rejoice in secret.*

gaudĭum -i, n. *joy, gladness, delight; a source of delight.*

gausăpĕ -is, and **gausăpum** -i, n. *woollen cloth with a long nap, frieze.*

gāza -ae, f. *the royal treasure of Persia;* in gen., *treasure, riches, wealth.*

gĕlāsīnus -i, m. *dimple.*

gĕlĭdus -a -um, *cold, frosty, icy*; in act. sense, *chilling*; f. as subst. **gĕlĭda** -ae, *cold water.* Adv. **gĕlĭdē,** *coldly, feebly.*

gĕlo -are, transit., *to cause to freeze*; intransit., *to freeze.*

gĕlu -ūs, n. (earlier **gĕlus** -ūs, m. and **gĕlum** -i, n.), *frost, chill.*

gĕmĕbundus -a -um, *groaning, sighing.*

gĕmellĭpăra -ae, f. adj. *twin-bearing.*

gĕmellus -a -um, *twin, paired, double*; m. as subst., *a twin.*

gĕmĭnātĭo -ōnis, f. *doubling.*

gĕmĭno -are: transit., *to double; to join together, strike together, repeat*; partic. **gĕmĭnātus** -a -um, *doubled*; intransit., *to be double.*

gĕmĭnus -a -um, *twin, double; paired or half-and-half; similar, like*; m. pl. as subst. **gĕmĭni** -orum, *twins,* esp. *Castor and Pollux.*

gĕmĭtus -ūs, m., *a sigh, groan*; of things, *groaning, roaring.*

gemma -ae, f. *a bud or eye of a plant.* Transf., *a jewel, gem, precious stone; a jewelled goblet; a seal-ring, seal; a literary gem.*

gemmātus -a -um, *set or adorned with jewels.*

gemmĕus -a -um, *made of or set with jewels; bright.*

gemmĭfer -fĕra -fĕrum, *bearing or producing jewels.*

gemmo -are, *to bud*; pres. partic. **gemmans** -antis, *set with jewels, glittering like jewels.*

gĕmo gĕmĕre gĕmŭi gĕmĭtum: intransit., *to sigh, groan*; of lions, *to roar*; of doves, *to coo*; of things, *to creak*; transit., *to sigh over, lament, bemoan.*

gĕna -ae, f. usually plur., *cheek, cheeks and chin.* Transf., *eye-socket, eye.*

Genāva -ae, f. *a town of the Allobroges* (now *Geneva*).

gĕnĕălŏgus -i, m. *a genealogist.*

gĕner -eri, m. *a son-in-law; a grand-daughter's husband; a brother-in-law.*

gĕnĕrālis -e. (1) *belonging to a kind, generic.* (2) *universal, general.* Adv. **gĕnĕrālĭter,** *in general, generally.*

gĕnĕrasco -ĕre, *to be produced, come to birth.*

gĕnĕrātim. (1) *according to kinds or classes.* (2) *in general, generally.*

gĕnĕrātor -ōris, m. *begetter, producer*

gĕnĕro -are, *to beget, produce, bring to life.*

gĕnĕrōsus -a -um, *of noble birth, noble, well-bred*; of a place, *producing well.* Transf., of character, *noble, mag-nanimous.* Adv. **gĕnĕrōsē,** *nobly.*

gĕnĕsis -is, f. *the constellation which presides over one's birth.*

gĕnĕtīvus -a -um, *inborn, innate*; nomina, *family names*; casus, *the genitive case.*

gĕnĕtrix -trīcis f. *one who brings forth, a mother.*

gĕniālis -e. (1) *relating to marriage.* (2) *relating to enjoyment; joyful, gay.* Adv. **gĕniālĭter**, *jovially, gaily.*

gĕnĭcŭlātus -a -um, *knotty, full of knots.*

gĕnista (**gĕnesta**) -ae, f. *the plant broom.*

gĕnĭtābĭlis -e, *fruitful, productive.*

gĕnĭtālis -e, *creative, fruitful*; dies, *birthday*; of Diana, *presiding over births.* Adv. **gĕnĭtālĭter**, *in a fruitful manner.*

gĕnĭtīvus; see genetivus.

gĕnĭtor -ōris, m. *a begetter, father, producer.*

gĕnĭtūra -ae, f. *begetting, engendering*; in astrology, *nativity.*

gĕnĭus -i, m. *the guardian spirit of a man* or *place, a genius*; esp. *as a spirit of enjoyment, one's taste, inclination*; genium curare, *to enjoy oneself.* Transf., *talent, genius.*

gĕno = gigno; q.v.

gens gentis, f. *a clan, stock, people, tribe, nation.* Transf., *an offspring, descendant*; *a district, country*; esp. in partitive genit.: ubi gentium? *where in the world?*; plur., gentes, *foreigners.*

gentĭcus -a -um, *a nation, national.*

gentĭlīcĭus -a -um, *of a particular gens.*

gentīlis -e, *of a gens*; *of a country, national.*

gentīlĭtās -ātis, f. *the relationship between the members of a gens.*

gĕnu -ūs, n. *the knee.*

Gĕnŭa -ae, f. *coast-town in Liguria (now Genoa).*

gĕnŭālĭa -ium, n. pl. *garters.*

¹gĕnŭīnus -a -um, *natural, innate.*

²gĕnŭīnus -a -um, *belonging to the cheek* or *jaw*; dentes, *the jaw-teeth*; m. as subst. *a jaw-tooth.*

¹gĕnus -ĕris, n. *birth, descent, origin*; *race, stock, family, house*; hence *offspring, descendant(s); sex*; in gen., *class, kind, variety, sort*; in logic, *genus*; of action, etc., *fashion, manner, way.*

²gĕnus -ūs = genu; q.v.

gĕōgrăphĭa -ae, f. *geography.*

gĕōmetres -ae, m. *a geometer.*

gĕōmetrĭa -ae, f. *geometry.*

gĕōmetrĭcus -a -um, *geometrical*; m. as subst., **gĕōmetrĭcus** -i, *a geometer*; n. pl. **gĕōmetrĭca**, *geometry.*

gĕorgĭcus -a -um, *agricultural*; n. pl. as subst. **Gĕorgĭca** -orum, *the Georgics of Vergil.*

Germāni -orum, m. pl. *the Germans*; adj. **Germānus** -a -um, *German*; f. subst. **Germānĭa** -ae, *Germany*; adj. **Germānĭcus** -a -um, *German*; m. as subst. **Germānĭcus** -i, *a*

surname assumed after victories in Germany.

germānĭtās -ātis, *the relationship between brothers* or *sisters; brotherhood, sisterhood.*

¹germānus -a -um, *having the same parents*; m. or f. as subst. *own brother, own sister.* Transf., *brotherly, sisterly; genuine, real, true.* Adv. **germānē**, *faithfully, honestly.*

²Germānus -a -um; see Germani.

germen -ĭnis, n. *an embryo; a bud, shoot* or *graft*; fig., *germ.*

germĭno -are, *to sprout forth.*

¹gĕro gĕrĕre gessi gestum. Lit. (1) *to carry, bear*; esp. *to wear.* (2) *to bear, give birth to.* Transf., *to carry about, display* an appearance; personam gerere, *to act a part*; se gerere, *to conduct oneself* (with adv.); *to carry about, entertain* a feeling; *to carry on, conduct, manage business*; res gestae, *exploits*, esp., *warlike exploits.*

²gĕro -ōnis, m., *a carrier.*

gerrae -arum, n. pl. *wattled twigs.* Transf., *trifles, nonsense.*

gerro -ōnis, m. *a trifler, idler.*

gĕrŭlus -i, m. *porter, carrier.*

Gēryōn -ōnis, and **Gēryŏnēs** -ae, m. myth., *a king in Spain with three bodies, killed by Hercules.*

gestāmen -ĭnis, n. *that which is carried; that by which anything is carried, a carriage* or *litter.*

gestĭcŭlātĭo -ōnis, f. *pantomime, gesticulation.*

gestĭcŭlor -ari, dep. *gesticulate.*

gestĭo -ōnis, f., *management, performance.*

gestĭto -are, *to carry often, wear often.*

gesto -are, *to carry, bear about*; pass. *to ride about.*

gestor -ōris, m. *a tale-bearer, gossip.*

gestus -ūs, m. *carriage of the body, posture*; esp. *the gestures of an actor* or *orator.*

Gĕtae -arum, m. pl. *a people of Thrace living near the Danube.* Adj. **Gĕtĭcus** -a -um, *Thracian*; adv. **Gĕtĭcē**, *after the Getic fashion.*

Gĕtūlus, etc. = Gaetulus, etc.; q.v.

gibba -ae, f. *hump, hunch.*

gibber -ĕra, -ĕrum, *hump-backed.*

gibbus -i, m. *hump, hunch.*

Gĭgas -gantis, m. *a giant*; adj. **Gĭgantēus** -a -um.

gigno gignĕre gĕnŭi gĕnĭtum, *to beget, bear, bring forth*; *to cause.*

gilvus -a -um, *pale yellow.*

gingīva -ae, f. *gum* (of the mouth).

glăber -bra -brum, *bald*; m. as subst., *a page.*

glăcĭālis -e, *icy.*

glăcĭēs -ēi, f. *ice.* Transf., *hardness.*

glăcĭo -are, *to freeze.*

glădĭātor -ōris, m. *one hired to fight at public shows, a gladiator*; hence *bandit, brigand*; gladiatoribus, *at a show of gladiators.*

glădĭātōrĭus -a -um, *of gladiators, gladiatorial*; n. as subst., *gladiators' pay.*

glădĭātūra -ae, f. *the profession of gladiator.*

glădĭus -i, *sword.*

glaeba = gleba; q.v.

glaesum (glesum) -i, n. *amber.*

glandĭfer -fĕra -fĕrum, *acorn-bearing.*

glandĭum -i, n. *a delicate glandule in meat.*

glans glandis, f. *mast; an acorn, chestnut,* etc. Transf., *a bullet.*

glārĕa -ae, f. *gravel.*

glārĕōsus -a -um, *gravelly full of gravel.*

glaucōma -atis, n. (also -ae, f.) *a disease of the eye, cataract.*

glaucus -a -um. *bluish- or greenish-grey.*

glēba (glaeba) -ae, f. *a lump or clod of earth;* hence *land, soil; a piece, lump* of anything.

glēbŭla -ae, f., *a little clod* or *lump; a little farm* or *estate.*

glēsum = glaesum; q.v.

glīs glīris, m. *dormouse.*

glīsco -ĕre, *to grow up, swell up, blaze up.*

glŏbo -are, *to form into a ball* or *mass.*

glŏbōsus -a -um, *spherical.*

glŏbus -i, m. *a ball, globe, sphere; a troop, crowd, mass of people.*

glŏmĕrāmen -ĭnis, n. *a round mass, globe.*

glŏmĕro -are, *to form into a sphere,* or *rounded heap;* in gen., *to gather together, collect, amass.*

glŏmus -ĕris, n. *clue, skein, ball of thread.*

glōrĭa -ae, f. *fame, renown, glory.* Transf., of a member of a group, *the pride, the glory; desire of glory, ambition, boastfulness;* plur., *glorious deeds.*

glōrĭātĭo -ōnis, f. *glorying, boasting.*

glōrĭŏla -ae, f. *a little glory.*

glōrĭor -ari, dep. *to glory, boast, pride oneself.*

glōrĭōsus -a -um, *famous, glorious; ambitious, pretentious, boastful.* Adv. **glōrĭōsē,** *gloriously; vauntingly, boastingly.*

glūbo -ĕre, *to peel.* Transf., *to rob.*

glūtĕn -tīnis, n. *glue.*

glūtĭnātor -ōris, m., *one who glues books, a bookbinder.*

glūtĭo (gluttĭo) -ire, *to swallow, gulp down.*

glūto (glutto) -onis, m. *glutton.*

Gnaeus -i, m. *a Roman* praenomen, shortened Cn.

gnārĭtās -ātis, f. *knowledge.*

gnārus -a -um; act., *knowing, aquainted with, expert;* pass., *known.*

Gnātho -ōnis, m. *a parasite in the Eunuchus of Terence;* in gen. *parasite.*

Gnātĭa = Egnatia; q.v.

gnātus, gnāvus = natus, navus; q.v.

Gnĭdus = Cnidus; q.v.

Gnossus (Gnōsus) -i, f., *an ancient city of Crete, the residence of Minos;* adj. **Gnōsĭus** and **Gnōsĭăcus** -a -um, *Gnosian; Cretan;* f. adj. **Gnōsĭas** -ādis, and **Gnōsĭs** -ĭdis, *Cretan* and, as subst., *Ariadne.*

gōbĭus (cōbĭus) -i, and **gōbĭo** -ōnis, m. *a gudgeon.*

gonger; see conger.

Gorgō -gōnis, f. *also called Medusa, slain by Perseus;* adj. **Gorgŏnĕus** -a -um.

Gortŷna -ae, f. *an ancient city in Crete.*

grăbātus -i, m. *a low couch, camp-bed.*

Gracchus -i, m. *a cognomen in the Gens* Sempronia, esp. of Tiberius and Gaius, the 'Gracchi'. Adj. **Gracchānus** -a -um.

grăcĭlis -e, *slender, thin, slim;* of style, etc., *simple, without ornament.*

grăcĭlĭtās -ātis, f. *thinness, slenderness.*

grācŭlus -i, m. *jackdaw.*

grădārĭus -a -um, *going step by step.*

grădātim, adv. *step by step, by degrees.*

grădātĭo -ōnis, f., in rhetoric, *climax.*

grădĭor grădi gressus, dep. *to step, walk.*

Grădīvus -i, m. *a surname of Mars.*

grădus -ūs, m. *a step.* (1) *a step as made, a pace;* suspenso gradu, *on tiptoe;* gradum facere, *to step;* gradum inferre, *to advance;* hence in gen., *an approach.* (2) *a step as climbed, a stair;* hence *any tier, gradation; a braid of hair;* abstr., *degree, stage; rank, position;* milit. *station, post.*

Graeci -orum, m. *the Greeks;* sing. **Graecus** -i, m. *a Greek;* as adj. **Graecus** -a -um, *Greek;* adv. **Graecē,** *in the Greek language;* f. subst. **Graecĭa** -ae, f. *Greece;* Magna Graecia, *the Greek colonies in the south of Italy;* dim. **Graecŭlus** -i, m. *a little Greek.*

graecisso -are, and **graecor** -ari, dep. *to imitate the Greeks.*

Grāĭi -orum, m. = Graeci, *the Greeks;* adj. **Grāĭus** -a -um, *Greek.*

Grāĭŭgĕna -ae, m. *a Greek by birth.*

grallātor -ōris, m. *one that walks on stilts.*

grāmen -ĭnis, n. *grass, turf; any plant* or *herb.*

grāmĭnĕus -a -um, *grassy, of grass;* also *of cane* or *bamboo.*

grammătĭcus -a -um, *literary, grammatical;* as subst., m. *a philologist, grammarian;* f. sing. and n. pl. *grammar, philology.*

grammătista -ae, f. *a teacher of grammar* or *languages.*

grānārĭum -i, n. *granary.*

grandaevus -a -um, *very old.*

grandesco -ĕre, *to become great, grow.*

grandĭcŭlus -a -um, *rather large.*

grandĭfer -fĕra -fĕrum, *producing great profits.*

grandĭlŏquus -a -um, *speaking grandly; boastful.*

grandĭnat -are, impers. *it hails.*

grandĭo -ire, *to increase.*

grandis -e, *full-grown, great, large;* in stature, *tall;* in years, *old.* Transf., *great, important;* of style, *lofty, grand, sublime.*

granditās -ātis, f. of style, *loftiness. sublimity.*

grando -ĭnis, f. *hail, hail-storm.*

grānĭfer -fĕra -fĕrum, *grain-carrying.*

grānum -i, n. *grain, seed.*

grăphĭcus -a -um, *concerned with painting;* hence *masterly, skilful;* adv. **grăphĭcē.**

grăphĭum -i, n. *a stilus, a pointed instrument for writing on wax.*

grassātor -ōris, m. *an idler; a footpad.*

grassor -ari, dep. *to walk about, to loiter; to go about an undertaking; to proceed against somebody.*

grātes, f. pl. *thanks;* grates agere, *to express thanks;* habere, *to feel gratitude.*

grātĭa -ae, f. (1) *charm, attraction, pleasantness;* personif., of *the three Graces* (Euphrosyne, Aglaia, Thalia). (2) *favour* with others; *esteem, regard, popularity.* (3) *a favour done, service, kindness;* abl. gratiā, *on account of;* meā gratiā, *for my sake.* (4) *thankfulness, thanks;* in sing. and plur.: gratias agere, with dat., *to express thanks;* gratias habere, *to feel grateful;* abl. plur. **grātĭis** or **grātis,** *without recompense, for nothing, gratis.*

grātĭfĭcātĭo -ōnis, f. *complaisance, obligingness.*

grātĭfĭcor -ari, dep. *to oblige, gratify, do a favour to.*

grātĭōsus -a -um, *favoured, beloved; showing favour, complaisant.*

grātis; see gratia.

grātor -ari, dep. *to wish joy, to congratulate; to give thanks.*

grātŭītus -a -um, *not paid for or not provoked, gratuitous, spontaneous;* abl. sing. n. as adv. **grātŭīto,** *gratuitously.*

grātŭlābundus -a -um, *congratulating.*

grātŭlātĭo -ōnis, f. *wishing joy, congratulation; a thanksgiving festival.*

grātŭlor -ari, dep. *to wish a person joy, congratulate* (with dat.); *to give solemn thanks,* esp. to the gods.

grātus -a -um, adj. (1) *pleasing, welcome, agreeable;* gratum facere, *to do a favour.* (2) *thankful, grateful.* Adv. **grātē,** *willingly, with pleasure; thankfully.*

grăvanter and **grăvātē;** from gravo.

grăvātim, *reluctantly.*

grăvēdĭnōsus -a -um, *subject to colds.*

grăvēdo -ĭnis, f. *cold in the head, catarrh.*

grăvĕŏlens -lentis, *strong-smelling, rank.*

grăvesco -ĕre, *to become heavy; to grow worse.*

grăvĭdĭtās -ātis, f. *pregnancy.*

grăvĭdo -are, *to load, burden; to impregnate.*

grăvĭdus -a -um, *heavy; laden, filled, full; pregnant.*

grăvis -e. (1) *heavy;* of sound, *low, deep;* fig., *weighty, important;* of character, *elevated, dignified, serious;* of style, *elevated, dignified.* (2) *burdened, laden, weighed down;* esp. *pregnant.* (3) *burdensome, oppressive; grievous, painful, unpleasant.* Adv. **grăvĭter,** *heavily, weightily, reluctantly; grievously, painfully.*

grăvĭtās -ātis, f. (1) *weight;* fig., *consequence, importance;* of character,

dignity, authority, seriousness. (2) heaviness; pregnancy; dullness, faintness. (3) pressure; fig., unpleasantness.

grăvo -are, *to load, burden; to heighten, exaggerate, increase; to oppress, burden, trouble;* pass., *to feel burdened or troubled* by a thing, or *to make heavy weather of* doing it. Adv. **grăvanter,** and **grăvātē,** *reluctantly.*

grĕgālis -e, *of a herd* or *flock; common, ordinary;* m. pl. as subst., *companions, associates, accomplices.*

grĕgārĭus -a -um, *of a herd* or *flock;* miles, *a private soldier.*

grĕgātim, *in troops or crowds.*

grĕmĭum -i, n. *lap, bosom; womb.*

gressus -ūs, m. *a step;* of a ship, *course.*

grex grĕgis, m. *a herd, flock, drove;* of people, *a troop, band,* esp. *a philosophical sect* or *troop of soldiers;* grege facto, *in close order.*

grunnĭo (grundĭo) -ire, *to grunt like a pig.*

grunnītus -ūs, m., *the grunting of a pig.*

grus grŭis, m. and f. *a crane.*

grȳ, n. indecl. *scrap, crumb.*

gryllus -i, m. *cricket, grasshopper.*

gryps, grȳpis, m. *griffin.*

gŭbernācŭlum (-āclum) -i, n. *rudder; helm;* hence *direction, management, government.*

gŭbernātĭo -ōnis, f. *steering; direction, government.*

gŭbernātor -ōris, m. *helmsman, steersman, pilot; director, governor.*

gŭbernātrix -icis, f. *she that directs.*

gŭberno -are, *to steer a ship, be at the helm;* in gen., *to steer, direct, govern.*

gŭbernum -i, n. = gubernaculum; q.v.

gŭla -ae, f. *gullet, throat;* hence *greediness, gluttony.*

gŭlōsus -a -um, *gluttonous.*

gurges -itis, m. *whirlpool, eddy;* in gen., *troubled water, a stream, flood, sea;* fig., *abyss, depth.*

¹**gurgŭlĭo** -ōnis, f. *windpipe.*

²**gurgŭlĭo** -ōnis, m.; see curculio.

gurgustĭum -i, n. *hut, hovel.*

gustātus -ūs, m. *taste; appetite, flavour.*

gusto -are, *to taste, take a little of; to partake of, enjoy.*

gustus -ūs, m. *tasting; taste, flavour, a whet or relish.*

gutta -ae, f. *a drop; a spot or mark.*

guttātim, *drop by drop.*

guttŭla -ae, f. *a little drop.*

guttur -ŭris, n. *the windpipe, throat; gluttony.*

guttus -i, m. *a jug.*

Gȳăros -i, f. and **Gȳăra** -orum, n. *a barren island in the Aegean, used as a place of exile under the empire.*

Gȳgēs -is and -ae, m. *a king of Lydia, famous for his ring;* adj. **Gȳgaeus** -a -um.

gymnăsĭarchus -i, m. *the master of a gymnasium.*

gymnăsĭum -i, n. *school of gymnastics, gymnasium;* also *a place for philosophical discussion.*

gymnastĭcus and **gymnĭcus** -a -um, *gymnastic.*

gӯnaecēum (and **-īum**) -i, n. *the women's apartments in a Greek house.*

gypso -are, *to cover with gypsum;* partic. **gypsātus** -a -um, *covered with gypsum, whitened.*

gypsum -i, n. *gypsum;* meton., *a plaster figure.*

gӯrus -i, m ,*a circle, ring;* esp. *a course for training horses;* in gen., *orbit, circuit.*

H

H, h, the eighth letter of the Latin Alphabet.

ha! hahae! hahahae! exclamations of joy or amusement.

hăbēna -ae, f. *a strap; a bridle, reins* (esp. in plur.); **habenas dare**, *to loosen the rein;* **adducere**, *to tighten it.*

hăbĕo -ēre -ŭi -ĭtum, *to have, hold; to have about one, carry, wear; to contain;* more generally, *to possess, have power over;* absol., *to possess property, be wealthy;* of places, *to own, inhabit, or rule over;* of persons, *to keep,* esp. in a certain state, or relation. Transf., **habere in animo**, *to have in mind, intend;* **habes consilia nostra**, *you know of;* **habeo dicere**, *I have it in my power to say;* **bonum animum habere**, *to be of good courage;* **odium**, *to cherish hatred;* **invidiam**, *to experience ill-will;* **misericordiam**, *to involve or cause pity;* **concilium**, *to hold a council;* **orationem**, *to make a speech;* with reflex., *to keep oneself, be, in a condition;* **graviter se habere**, *to be ill;* **ut nunc res se habet**, *as things now are;* intransit., **bene habet**, *all right;* with adv., rarely, *to use, manage, treat;* with double acc., or dat., or pro and abl., *to hold, consider, regard in a certain light.* Perf. partic. **hăbĭtus** -a -um, *disposed; in a certain condition* (physical or mental).

hăbĭlis -e, *easily managed, handy; suitable, fit, convenient.*

hăbĭlĭtās -ātis, f. *aptitude, suitability.*

hăbĭtābĭlis -e, *habitable.*

hăbĭtātĭo -ōnis, f. *dwelling, habitation.*

hăbĭtātor -ōris, m. *inhabitant.*

hăbĭto -are: transit., *to inhabit;* intransit., *to dwell.*

hăbĭtūdo -ĭnis, f. *condition.*

¹**hăbĭtus** -a -um, partic. from habeo, q.v.

²**hăbĭtus** -ūs, m. *condition, habit, bearing;* of dress, *style;* of places, *lie of the land;* abstr., *nature, character, disposition, attitude.*

hāc, adv. from hic; q.v.

hactĕnus, *as far as this, so far (and no farther); hitherto; up to this point.*

Hadrĭa -ae; f. *a town in the north of Italy;* m. *the Adriatic Sea.* Adj. **Hadrĭăcus** and **Hadrĭātĭcus** -a -um, *Adriatic.*

Hadrĭānus -i, m., P. Aelius, Roman emperor from A.D. 117 to 138.

haedīlĭa -ae, f. and **haedillus** -i, m., *a little kid.*

haedīnus -a -um, *of a kid.*

haedŭlus -i, m. *a little kid.*

haedus -i, m. *a kid, young goat.*

Haemōnĭa -ae, f. *an old name of Thessaly;* adj. **Haemōnius** -a -um, *Thessalian;* f. subst. **Haemōnis** -nĭdis, *a Thessalian woman.*

haerĕo **haerēre haesi haesum**. (1) *to stick, cleave, adhere, hang on to a person or thing.* (2) *to come to a standstill, get stuck; be embarrassed.*

haeresco -ĕre, *to adhere, stick.*

haesĭtantĭa -ae, f. *faltering;* **linguae**, *stammering.*

haesĭtātĭo -ōnis, f.: in speech, *hesitation, stammering;* mentally, *hesitation, indecision.*

haesĭto -are, *to stick fast, to hesitate;* in speech, *to stammer;* mentally, *to be undecided, be at a loss.*

hālec; see alec.

hălĭaeĕtos -i, m. *sea-eagle, osprey.*

hālĭtus -ūs, m., *breath, vapour.*

hallex -īcis, m. *thumb or big toe.*

hālo -are, *to breathe out, exhale.*

hālūc-; see aluc-.

hăma (ăma) -ae, f. *bucket,* esp. *fireman's bucket.*

Hămādrӯas -ădis, f., *a wood-nymph, hamadryad.*

hāmātus -a -um, *provided with hooks, hooked; curved like a hook, crooked.*

Hămilcăr -căris, m. *father of Hannibal.*

hāmĭōta -ae, m., *an angler.*

Hammon; see Ammon.

hāmus -i, m. *a hook,* esp. *a fish-hook; a talon; a thorn.*

Hannĭbăl -bălis, m. *leader of the Carthaginians in the second Punic war.*

hăra -ae, f. *a pen or coop; a pig-sty.*

hărĭŏlor -ari, dep. *to utter prophecies.* Transf., *to talk nonsense.*

hărĭŏlus -i, m. and **hărĭŏla** -ae f. *a soothsayer, prophet.*

harmŏnĭa -ae, f. *melody, concord, harmony.*

harpăgo -ōnis, m., *a large hook, drag, grappling-iron.*

harpē -es, f. *a curved sword, scimitar.*

Harpӯiae (trisyll.) -arum, f. pl., *the Harpies, mythical monsters.*

hăruspex -spĭcis, m. *soothsayer;* a seer, prophet.

hăruspĭcīnus -a -um, *concerned with divination;* f. as subst. *divination.*

hăruspĭcĭum -i, n. *inspection of entrails, divination.*

Hasdrŭbăl (Asdrŭbăl) -bălis, m. *the brother of Hannibal.*

hasta -ae, f. *a spear, pike, javelin;* milit., and in ceremonial use, at public auctions and weddings.

hastātus -a -um, *armed with a spear* m pl. as subst. **hastāti** -orum, *the front rank of a Roman army when drawn up for battle.*

hastīle -is, n., *the shaft of a spear; a spear; a prop for vines,* etc.

hau, oh!

haud (haut), *not, not at all, by no means.*
hauddum, *not yet.*
haudquāquam, *by no means, not at all.*
hauriŏ haurire hausi haustum, *to draw up, draw out or in; to drink up, absorb, swallow; to shed* blood; *to drain, empty a receptacle;* in gen., *to derive, take in;* also *to exhaust, weaken, waste.*
haustrum -i, n. *a pump.*
haustus -ūs, m. *drawing of water;* legal, *the right to draw water;* of air, *inhaling;* of drink, *drinking, a draught;* of solids, *a handful.*
haut = haud; q.v.
hăvĕo; see aveo.
hebdŏmas -ădis, f. *seventh day of a disease* (supposed critical).
Hēbē -ēs, f. *the cup-bearer of the gods.*
hĕbĕnus -i, f. *the ebon-tree; ebony.*
hĕbĕo -ēre, *to be blunt, dull, heavy, inactive.*
hĕbĕs -ĕtis, *blunt, dull;* faint, sluggish, weak; mentally, *dull, heavy, stupid.*
hĕbesco -ĕre, *to become dull, blunt, dim.*
hĕbĕto -are, *to make blunt or dull, to deaden, dim.*
Hebraeus -a -um, *Hebrew, Jewish.*
Hebrus -i, m., *the chief river of Thrace.*
Hĕcătē -ēs, f. *goddess of magic and enchantment,* adj. **Hĕcătēïus** -a -um and f. **Hĕcătēïs** -ĭdis, *Hecatean, magical.*
hĕcătombē -ēs, f. *a hecatomb.*
Hector -tŏris, m. *son of Priam, husband of Andromache;* adj. **Hectŏrĕus** -a -um.
Hĕcŭba -ae, and **Hĕcŭbē** -ēs, f. *wife of Priam.*
hĕdĕra -ae, f. *ivy.*
hĕdychrum -i, n. *a fragrant ointment.*
hei, interj. = ei; q.v.
Hĕlĕna -ae, and **Hĕlĕnē** -ēs, f. *wife o Menelaus, carried off by Paris to Troy.*
Hĕlĭce -ēs, f. *a constellation, the Great Bear.*
Hĕlĭcon -ōnis, m., *a hill in Boeotia, sacred to Apollo and the Muses;* adj. **Hĕlĭcōnĭus** -a -um; subst. **Hĕlĭcōnĭădes** and **Hĕlĭcōnĭdes** -um, f. *the Muses.*
Hellē -ēs, f. *a girl drowned in the Hellespont, so named after her.*
hellĕborus; see elleborus.
Hellespontus -i, m., *the Hellespont, Dardanelles.*
hellŭo (hēlŭo) -ōnis, *glutton, squanderer.*
hellŭor (hēlŭor) -ari, dep. *to guzzle, gormandize.*
hĕlops (ĕlops, ellops) -ŏpis, m. *a fish, perhaps sturgeon.*
helvella -ae, f. *a small pot-herb.*
Helvĕtii -orum, m. *the Helvetii, a people in what is now Switzerland.*
hem, interj. *well! just look!*
hĕmĕrodrŏmus -i, m. *a special courier, express.*
hēmĭcillus -i, m. *mule.*
hēmĭcyclĭum -i, n. *a semi-circle* (of seats).
hēmĭna -ae, f. *a measure of capacity, about half a pint.*

hendĕcăsyllăbi -orum, m. pl. *verses of eleven syllables, hendecasyllables.*
Henna (Enna) -ae, f. *city of Sicily, with a temple of Ceres;* adj. **Hennensis** -e and **Hennaeus** -a -um.
heptēris -is, f. *a galley with seven banks of oars.*
hĕra = ĕra; q.v.
Hēra -ae, f., *the Greek goddess identified with the Roman Juno;* **Hēraea** -orum, n. pl., *her festival.*
herba -ae, f. *vegetation; a green plant; a blade or stalk,* esp. *of corn or grass.*
herbesco ĕre, *to grow into blades or stalks.*
herbĭdus -a -um, and **herbĭfer** -fĕra -fĕrum, *grassy.*
herbōsus -a -um, *grassy.*
herbŭla -ae, f. *a little herb.*
hercisco (ercisco) -ĕre, *to divide an inheritance.*
Hercle; see Hercules.
herctum -i, n. *an inheritance;* herctum ciere, *to divide an inheritance.*
Hercŭlănĕum -i, n. *town in Campania destroyed by an eruption of Vesuvius.*
Hercŭles -is and -i, m. *the son of Jupiter and Alcmena;* voc. **Hercŭles** or **Hercŭle** or **Hercle**, *used as an oath, by Hercules;* so also **Mĕhercŭles, Mĕhercŭle, Mĕhercle;** adj. **Hercŭlĕus** and **Hercŭlānĕus** -a -um.
Hercўnĭa silva -ae, f. *the Hercynian forest, in central Germany.*
hĕrĕ = heri; q.v.
hērēdĭtārĭus -a -um, *of an inheritance; inherited, hereditary.*
hērēdĭtās -ātis, f. *inheritance.*
hērēdĭum -i, n. *patrimony.*
hērēs (haerēs) -ēdis, c. *an heir, heiress, successor; an owner.*
hĕrī (hĕrē), *yesterday.*
hērĭfŭga = erifuga; q.v.
hērĭlis -e = erilis; q.v.
hermaphrŏdītus -i, m. *hermaphrodite.*
Hermes or **Herma** -ae, m. *the god Hermes, identified with the Roman Mercury.*
Hērō -ūs, f., *a priestess at Sestos, loved by Leander.*
Hērōdes -is, m. *Herod;* esp. *Herod the Great.*
Hērŏdŏtus -i, m. *the Greek historian, born 484 B.C.*
hērōĭcus -a -um, *relating to the heroes, heroic.*
hērōĭna -ae and **hērōĭs** -ĭdis, f. *a demigoddess, heroine.*
hērōs -ōis, m. *a demigod, hero.*
hērōus -a -um, *a hero, heroic;* m. as subst. *a hexameter.*
hĕrus = ĕrus; q.v.
Hēsĭŏdus -i, m. *an early Greek poet of Boeotia.*
Hespĕrus or **-os** -i, m. *the Evening Star;* adj. **Hespĕrĭus** -a -um, *western;* f. as subst. **Hespĕrĭa** -ae, *the western land; Italy or Spain;* f. adj. **Hespĕrĭs** -ĭdis, *western;* f. subst. **Hespĕrĭdes** -um, *daughters of Hesperus, living in the extreme west.*
hesternus -a -um, *of yesterday.*

hĕtairīa -ae, f. *a secret society.*

heu! *oh! alas!*

heus! *hallo! ho, there! hark!*

hexămĕter -tri, m.: adj., *with six feet* (of metre); as subst., *a hexameter.*

hexēris -is, f. *a galley with six banks of oars.*

hiātus -ūs, m. *a cleft, opening; the opening of the mouth, open jaws;* hence *gaping after, desire for;* gram. *hiatus.*

Hibēr -ēris, m. *an Iberian, Spaniard;* plur. Hibēres -ērum, and Hibēri -orum, m. *Spaniards;* Hibērus -i, m. *the river Ebro;* Hibēria -ae, *Spain;* adj. Hibērĭcus -a -um and Hibērus -a -um, *Spanish.*

hīberna -orum, n.; *see hibernus.*

hībernācŭlum -i, n.: in pl., *tents or huts for winter quarters.*

Hibernīa -ae, f. *Ireland.*

hīberno -are, *to winter, spend the winter.*

hībernus -a -um, *wintry, of winter; like winter, cold or stormy, wintering, for the winter;* n. pl. as subst. *winter quarters.*

hībiscum -i, n. *marsh-mallow.*

hibrīda (hybrīda) -ae, *a hybrid.*

¹hīc, haec, hōc, *this, this one; this present;* in court, *my client;* strengthened form hīce, haece, hōce; interrog. hīcĭnĕ, haecĭnĕ, hōcĭnĕ.

²hīc (and heic) *here; in this place, in this matter; hereupon;* strengthened hīce and interrog. hīcĭnĕ.

hiĕmālis -e, *of winter; wintry, stormy.*

hiĕmo -are. (1) *to winter, spend the winter.* (2) *to be stormy.*

hiems (hiĕmps) -ĕmis, f. *winter; the cold of winter; stormy weather, storm.*

Hiĕrŏsŏlўma -orum, n. pl. *Jerusalem.*

hīlăris -e and hīlărus -a -um, *cheerful, merry, gay;* n. acc. sing. as adv. hīlărĕ, *cheerfully.*

hīlărĭtās -ātis, f. *cheerfulness, gaiety.*

hīlăro -are, *to make joyful, to cheer up.*

hīlărŭlus -a -um, *gay, cheerful.*

hillae -arum, f. pl. *intestines of animals; a kind of sausage.*

Hīlōtae and Īlōtae -arum, m. pl., *the Helots, slaves of the Spartans.*

hīlum -i, n. *a trifle;* with neg. *not a whit, not in the least.*

hinc, adv., *from here, hence;* hinc atque illinc, *on this side and on that;* of causation, *hence, from this cause;* of time, *henceforth, or thereupon.*

hinnĭo -ire, *to neigh, whinny.*

hinnītus -ūs, m. *neighing.*

hinnŭlĕus -i, m. *a young roebuck, fawn.*

hinnus -i, m. *a mule.*

hĭo -are, *to open, stand open; to gape,* esp. *in astonishment or longing;* of speech, *to hang together badly;* with acc. object, *to pour forth.*

hippăgōgi -orum, f. pl. *transports for cavalry.*

Hippĭas -ae, m. *son of Pisistratus, tyrant of Athens.*

hippŏcentaurus -i, m. *a centaur.*

Hippŏcrătēs -is, m. *a physician of Cos* (flourishing about 430 B.C.).

Hippŏcrēnē -ēs, f. *a fountain on Mount Helicon.*

hippŏdrŏmos -i, m., *a hippodrome racecourse.*

Hippŏlўtus -i, m. *son of Theseus.*

hippŏtoxŏta -ae, m. *a mounted archer.*

hippūrus -i, m. *a fish,* perhaps *goldfish.*

hircīnus and hircōsus -a -um, *of a goat; goatlike.*

hircus -i, m. *a he-goat.*

hirnĕa -ae, f. *a can or jug.*

hirsūtus -a -um, *hairy, shaggy, rough; unadorned.*

Hirtīus -a -um, *name of a Roman gens.*

hirtus -a -um, *hairy, shaggy, rough, uncultivated.*

hīrūdo -ĭnis, f. *leech.*

hīrundo -ĭnis, f. *swallow.*

hisco -ĕre, *to open, split open, gape; to open the mouth.*

Hispāni -orum, m. pl. *the Spaniards;* Hispānīa -ae, f. *the whole of the Spanish peninsula;* adj. Hispāniensis -e and Hispānus -a -um.

hispĭdus -a -um, *rough, hairy, bristly.*

¹hister = histrio; q.v.

²Hister (Ister) -tri, m. *name of the lower part of the Danube.*

histōrĭa -ae, f. *inquiry; the results of inquiry; learning; historical narrative, history;* in gen., *narrative, a story.*

histōrĭcus -a -um, *of history, historical;* m. as subst., *a historian.*

histrĭcus -a -um, *of actors.*

histrĭo -ōnis, m. *an actor.*

histrĭōnālis -e, *of actors.*

hĭulco -are, *to cause to gape, to split.*

hĭulcus -a -um, *gaping, cleft, open; gaping with desire, longing;* of speech, *badly put together;* adv. hĭulcē, *with hiatus.*

hŏdĭē, *today; at present, still, even now; at once.*

hŏdĭernus -a -um, *of today.*

hŏlitor -ōris, m. *a kitchen-gardener.*

hŏlĭtōrĭus -a -um, *of herbs;* forum, *vegetable-market.*

hŏlus (ŏlus) -ĕris, n. *vegetable, pot-herb.*

Hŏmērus -i, m. *Homer, the Greek epic poet;* adj. Hŏmērĭcus -a -um.

hŏmĭcīda -ae, c. *a murderer, murderess, homicide.*

hŏmĭcīdĭum -i, n. *murder, homicide.*

hŏmo -ĭnis, c. *a human being, man, mortal;* in pl., *men, people, the world;* used like a pronoun, *he, him;* milit. in pl., *infantry.*

hŏmullus -i, and hŏmuncĭo -ōnis, and hŏmuncŭlus -i, m. *a little man, manikin.*

hŏnestās -ātis, f. (1) *honour, repute, respectability;* in pl., *notabilities.* (2) *worth, virtue, probity.* (3) *beauty.*

hŏnesto -are, *to honour, adorn, dignify.*

hŏnestus -a -um. (1) *honoured, in good repute, respectable.* (2) *honourable, proper, virtuous;* n. as subst., *morality, virtue.* (3) *fine, beautiful.* Adv. hŏnestē, *respectably; honourably; properly.*

hŏnor = honos; q.v.

hŏnōrābĭlis -e, *respectful.*

hŏnŏrārĭus -a -um, *done or given as an honour.*

hŏnŏrĭfĭcus -a -um, *causing honour, honouring*; adv. hŏnŏrĭfĭcē.

hŏnōro -are, *to honour, show honour to, adorn, dignify*; partic. hŏnōrātus -a -um, *honoured, distinguished, respected,* or in act. sense, *conferring honour*; adv. hŏnōrātē.

hŏnōrus -a -um, *honourable.*

hŏnōs and hŏnŏr -ōris, m. *honour, a mark of honour* or *respect, distinction;* honoris causa, *with due respect,* or *to honour,* or *for the sake of*; personif., *Honour*; frequently, *an office of dignity, a public office*; also *an offering to the gods, sacrifice*; poet., *beauty, grace.*

hoplŏmăchus -i, *a gladiator.*

hōra -ae, f. *an hour, the twelfth part of a day or night*; hora quota est? *what's o'clock?* in horam vivere, *to live for the moment*; in gen., *time, season*; in plur. *a clock, dial*; personif. *the Hours, goddesses who presided over the seasons.*

Hŏrātĭus -a -um, *name of a Roman gens.*

hordĕum -i, n. *barley.*

hŏrĭa -ae, f. *a small fishing-boat.*

hornōtĭnus and hornus -a -um, *of this year, this year's*; adv. hornō, *this year.*

hŏrŏlŏgĭum -i, n. *a clock; a sundial or water-clock.*

horrĕo -ēre, *to bristle, be rough*; of the hair, *to stand on end*; of persons, *to shudder, dread.* Gerundive as adj. horrendus -a -um, *horrible, dreadful; awful, worthy of reverence.*

horresco horrescĕre horrŭi, *to stand on end, bristle, be rough*; of persons, *to tremble, shudder, begin to dread.*

horrĕum -i, n. *a barn, granary, store-house.*

horrĭbĭlis -e, *horrible, frightful, dreadful*; colloq., *astonishing, wonderful.*

horrĭdŭlus -a -um, *somewhat rough, unadorned.*

horrĭdus -a -um, *rough, shaggy, bristly; shivering with cold.* Transf., *wild, savage; unpolished, uncouth; frightful, horrible.* Adv. horrĭdē, *roughly.*

horrĭfer -fĕra -fĕrum, *causing shudders of cold* or *fear.*

horrĭfĭco -are, *to make rough;* to *terrify.*

horrĭfĭcus -a -um, *causing terror, dreadful*; adv. horrĭfĭcē.

horrĭsŏnus -a -um, *sounding dreadfully.*

horror -ōris, m. *bristling, shuddering; roughness of speech; dread, fright,* esp. *religious dread, awe*; meton., *object of dread, a terror.*

horsum, *in this direction.*

hortāmen -ĭnis, n. and hortāmentum -i, n. and hortātĭo -ōnis, f. *exhortation, encouragement, incitement.*

hortātīvus -a -um, *of encouragement.*

hortātor -ōris, m. *an inciter, encourager.*

hortātus -ūs, m. *incitement, encouragement.*

Hortensĭus -a -um, *name of a Roman gens.*

hortor -ari, dep. *to exhort, incite, encourage*; esp *to harangue troops.*

hortŭlus -i, m. *a little garden*: plur. *grounds, a small park.*

hortus -i, m. *a garden*; in plur. *grounds, park.*

hospĕs -pĭtis, m. and hospĭta -ae, f. (1) *a host, hostess.* (2) *a guest.* (3) *a guest-friend, friend.* (4) *a stranger*; used also like adj. *foreign.*

hospĭtālis -e, *of a guest* or *host; friendly, hospitable*; adv. hospĭtālĭter.

hospĭtālĭtās -ātis, f. *hospitality.*

hospĭtĭum -i, n. *hospitality;* meton., *a guest-chamber, inn, quarters.*

hostĭa -ae, f. *an animal slain in sacrifice, a victim.*

hostīcus -a -um, *foreign*; but usually of *the enemy, hostile*; n, as subst. *enemy territory.*

hostīlis -e, *of, by* or *for the enemy; like an enemy, unfriendly, hostile*; adv. hostīlĭter.

Hostīlĭus -a -um, *name of a Roman gens.*

hostīmentum -i, n. *compensation, requital.*

hostĭo -ire, *to requite, recompense.*

hostis -is, c. *a stranger*; but esp. *an enemy, foe, opponent.*

hūc, *hither, to this place*; huc (atque) illuc, *hither and thither.* Transf., *in addition to this; to this pitch,* or *degree*; interrog. hūcĭnĕ?

hŭi, *exclamation of surprise, eh! hallo!*

hūiusmŏdi or hūiuscĕmŏdi, *of this kind.*

hum-; *see also um-.*

hūmānĭtās -ātis, f. *humanity, human nature, human feeling; kindness; refinement, education, culture.*

hūmānĭtŭs, *after the manner of men;* also *kindly.*

hūmānus -a -um, *human, of human beings*; m. as subst. *a human being;* of good qualities, *humane, kind, educated, civilized, refined.* Adv. hūmānē and hūmānĭtĕr, *humanly, politely, courteously, kindly.*

hŭmātĭo -ōnis, f. *burying, interment.*

hŭmĭlis -e, *on* or *near the ground, low, shallow.* Transf., of rank, etc., *humble, poor, insignificant*; of character, *abject* or *submissive*; of language, *mean, without elevation.* Adv. hŭmĭlĭtĕr, *humbly, meanly, abjectly.*

hŭmĭlĭtās -ātis, f. *nearness to the ground; lowness; shallowness.* Transf., *insignificance, obscurity; submissiveness, abjectness.*

hŭmo -are, *to cover with earth, bury; to perform any funeral rites over a corpse.*

hŭmus -i, f. *ground, earth, soil*; humi, *on the ground*; meton., *land, country.*

¹Hyăcinthus (-os) -i, m., *a beautiful youth, accidentally killed by Apollo.*

²**hўăcinthus** -i, m. *a flower, perhaps the martagon lily.*

Hўădes -um, f. *the Hyades, seven stars in the constellation Taurus.*

hўaena -ae, f. *hyena.*

hўălus -i, m. *glass;* colour *glassgreen.*

Hydra -e, f. *many-headed water-snake, slain by Hercules;* also *a constellation.*

hydraulus -i, m. *a water organ.*

hydria -ae, f. *an urn, jug.*

hydrōpĭcus -a -um, *dropsical.*

hydrops -ōpis, m. *the dropsy.*

hydrus -i, m. *a water-snake.*

Hўlās -ae, m. *companion of Hercules.*

Hўmēn -ēnis and **Hўmēnaeos** or **-us** -i, m. *Hymen, the god of marriage; the marriage song; a wedding* (esp. in plur).

hўperbătŏn -i, n. *transposition of words.*

hўperbŏlē -ēs, f. *exaggeration.*

Hўperbŏrĕi -ōrum, m. pl. *a people in the extreme north;* adj. **Hўperbŏrĕus** -a -um = *northern.*

hўpŏdĭdascălus -i, m. *an under-teacher.*

hўpomnēma -mătis, n. *a memorandum, note.*

I

i, the ninth letter of the Latin alphabet, used both as a vowel and as a consonant, formerly written j.

Iacchus -i, m. *name of Bacchus;* meton., *wine.*

iacĕo iacēre iacŭi, *to lie, be situated; to lie low, be flat; to lie sick or over-thrown or killed;* of hair or clothes, *to hang loosely;* fig., *to be neglected, or despised; to be overthrown; to be cast down, dejected.*

iăcĭo iăcĕre iēci iactum. (1) *to lay.* (2) *to throw, cast, hurl; to fling away, shed; to scatter, diffuse; to let fall in speaking, utter.*

iactantia -ae, f. *boasting, bragging.*

iactātĭo -ōnis, f. *a tossing, shaking.* Transf., *violent emotion; boasting, ostentation.*

iactātor -ōris, m. *boaster, braggart.*

iactātus -ūs, m. *shaking, quick movement.*

iactĭto -are, *to toss about; to bandy.*

iacto -are, *to throw, cast, toss, fling away* or *about; to diffuse, spread, scatter; to harass, disturb a person; to broadcast* words; *to bring up, discuss a subject; to keep bringing up, to boast of.* With reflex, or in pass., *to gesticulate;* also *to " throw one's weight about ", make oneself conspicuous.* Pres. partic. **iactans** -antis, *boastful;* adv. **iactanter.**

iactūra -ae, f. *throwing away; loss, sacrifice.*

iactus -ūs, m. *cast, throw;* intra iactum, *within range.*

iăcŭlābĭlis -e, *able to be thrown.*

iăcŭlātor -ōris, m. *a thrower;* esp. *a javelin-man, light-armed soldier.*

iăcŭlātrix -īcis, f. *the huntress (Diana).*

iăcŭlor -ari, dep. *to throw a javelin;*

to shoot at a target; to throw, cast, hurl a missile. Transf., *to make a verbal attack; to aim at, strive after; to utter.*

iăcŭlum -i, n. (1) *a dart, javelin.* (2) *a casting-net.*

iăcŭlus -a -um, *thrown, darting.*

iam, adv. *now, by now, already;* of future time, *immediately, presently, soon; henceforth; further, moreover; just, indeed;* iam diu, iam dudum, iam pridem, *now for a long time.*

iambēus -a -um, *iambic.*

iambus -i, m. *an iambus, a metrical foot (˘ ‾); an iambic poem.*

iamdūdum, iampridem; see iam.

Iānĭcŭlum -i, n. *a hill west of Rome.*

iānĭtor -ōris, m. *door-keeper, porter.*

iānĭtrix -īcis, f. *portress.*

ianthĭnus -a um, *violet-coloured.*

iānŭa ae, f. *door; entrance, approach.*

iānus -i, m. *a covered passage, arcade;* personif., **Iānus, Janus,** *an old Italian deity with two faces;* adj. **Iānālis** and **Iānŭālis** -e; hence also adj. **Iānŭārius** -a -um, *of Janus* or *of January;* Ianuarius (mensis), *January.*

Iăpyx -pȳgis, m. *a west-north-west wind.*

Iāsōn -ōnis, m. *leader of the Argonauts;* adj. **Iāsŏnĭus** -a -um.

iaspis -ĭdis, f. *jasper.*

ibēr-; see hiber-.

ĭbĭ, adv. *there, at that place; then; thereupon; therein, in that matter* or *person.*

ĭbĭdem, adv. *in the same place; at that moment; in that matter.*

ibis, genit. ĭbis and ĭbĭdis, f. *the ibis.*

ibiscum -hibiscum; q.v.

Icărus -i, m. *son of Daedalus, drowned whilst flying with wings made by his father;* adj. **Icărĭus** -a -um, *of Icarus.*

iccirco -idcirco; q.v.

Icēni -orum, m. *a British people in East Anglia.*

ichneumon -ŏnis, m. *the ichneumon.*

īcĭo or **īco** īci ictum, *to strike, hit, smite;* esp., *to strike* a bargain.

ictērĭcus -a -um, *jaundiced.*

ictus -ūs, m. *a blow, stroke;* in music, *beat.*

Ida -ae and **Idē** -ēs, f. *name of two mountains, one in Crete, one in Phrygia, near Troy;* adj. **Idaeus** -a -um.

idcirco (iccirco), *on that account; for that reason* or *purpose.*

ĭdem, ĕădem, ĭdem, *the same;* with dat., or ac, et, etc., *the same as;* by way of addition, *also;* of contrast, *yet;* alter idem, *a second self.*

ĭdentĭdem, *repeatedly, again and again.*

ĭdĕo, adv. *on that account, therefore; for that reason* or *purpose.*

ĭdĭōta -ae, m. *an ignorant, uneducated man.*

īdōlon -i, n. *a spectre.*

ĭdōnĕus -a -um, *fit, appropriate, suitable;* adv. **ĭdōnĕē.**

Ĭdūmaea -ae, f. *a district in Palestine.*

Īdūs -ŭum, f. pl. *the Ides, a day in the Roman month; the fifteenth day in March, May, July, October; the thirteenth in other months.*

iĕcur, iĕcŏris and iŏcĭnĕris, n. *the liver; supposed seat of the passions.*

iĕcuscŭlum -i, n. *a little liver.*

iēiūnĭtās -ātis, f. *hungriness, emptiness; of style, etc., poverty, meagreness.*

iēiūnĭum -i, n. *fast, abstinence, hunger; hence, leanness.*

iēiūnus -a -um, *fasting, hungry, thirsty; of objects, poor, scanty; of spirit, poor, mean: of style, meagre, weak.* Adv. **iēiūnē,** of style, *meagrely.*

ientācŭlum -i, n. *breakfast.*

iento -are, *to breakfast.*

igĭtur, *therefore, then; so, as I was saying; to emphasize, I say.*

ignārus -a -um: act., *ignorant, inexperienced in* (with genit.); pass., *unknown.*

ignāvĭa -ae, f. *idleness, listlessness; cowardice.*

ignāvus -a -um. (1) *idle, listless, inactive, inert, sluggish.* (2) *cowardly;* m. as subst. *a coward.* Adv. **ignāvē** and **ignāvĭtĕr,** *lazily, without spirit.*

ignesco -ĕre, *to kindle, catch fire; to glow with passion.*

ignĕus -a -um, *fiery, burning, glowing, ardent.*

ignĭcŭlus -i, m. *a little fire, flame, spark.*

ignĭfĕr -fĕra -fĕrum, *fire-bearing, fiery.*

ignĭgĕna -ae, m. *born of fire.*

ignĭpēs -pĕdis, *fiery-footed.*

ignĭpŏtens -entis, *ruler of fire.*

ignis is, m. *fire, conflagration; a watch-fire, beacon; a firebrand; lightning; in gen., glow, glitter.* Transf., *a fire-brand* (of war); *glow of passion; the beloved.*

ignōbĭlis -e, *unknown, obscure; of humble birth.*

ignōbĭlĭtās -ātis, f. *obscurity; humble birth.*

ignōmĭnĭa -ae, f. *degradation, disgrace, dishonour.*

ignōmĭnĭōsus -a -um: of persons, *disgraced;* of things, *ignominious, disgraceful.*

ignōrābĭlis -e, *unknown.*

ignōrantĭa -ae, and **ignōrātĭo** -ōnis, f. *ignorance.*

ignōro -are, *to be ignorant of, not to know;* rarely, *to neglect, ignore.*

ignosco -noscĕre -nōvi -nōtum, *to overlook, forgive, pardon.*

ignōtus -a -um: pass., *unknown; ignoble, obscure;* act., *ignorant.*

īlĕ -is, n., plur. **īlĭa** -ĭum, *intestines, guts; loin, flank;* ilia ducere, *to become broken-winded.*

Īlerda -ae, f. *a town in Spain* (now Lerida).

īlex -ĭcis, f. *holm-oak.*

Īlĭa -ae, f. *mother of Romulus and Remus.*

Īlĭăcus; see Ilion.

īlĭcet. (1) *a formula, it is all over.* (2) *immediately, forthwith.*

īlĭcētum -i, n. *ilex-grove.*

īlĭco (illĭco), *on the spot; immediately.*

īlignus -a -um, *of ilex or holm-oak.*

Īlĭŏn or **Īlĭum** -i, n. and **Īlĭŏs** -i, f. *Troy;* adj. **Īlĭus** and **Īlĭăcus** -a -um, *Trojan;* **Īlĭensēs** -ĭum, m. pl. *Trojans;* **Īlĭădēs** -ae, *a son of Troy;* **Īlĭăs** -adis, f. *a Trojan woman, or the Iliad of Homer.*

ill-, for words compounded from in/l . . ., see in-.

illā, *by that way.*

illāc, *by that way, there;* illac facere, *to belong to that party.*

illĕ, illa, illŭd (older forms **olle** and **ollus**), pron., *that, that yonder, that one;* emphatically, *that well-known;* in contrast with hic, *the former* (sometimes *the latter*); ille qui, *he who, the one who.*

[1]**illĭc, illaec, illŭc,** *that one;* interrog. illicine?

[2]**illĭc** or **illī,** *there, at that place; therein, in that matter.*

illim, *from that place or person.*

illinc, *from that place; on that side.*

illō, *thither, to that place; to that matter or point.*

illūc, *thither, to that place; to that matter or person.*

Illyrĭi -ōrum, m. pl. *a people on the Adriatic.*

īmāgĭnārĭus -a -um *imaginary.*

īmāgĭnātĭo -ōnis, f. *imagination, fancy.*

īmāgĭnor -ari, *to imagine, conceive, picture to oneself.*

īmāgo -ĭnis, f. *an image, copy, likeness; any representation, portrait, statue;* in plur. *waxen figures, portraits of ancestors; the shade or ghost of the dead; an echo; a mental picture, idea, conception;* rhet., *metaphor, simile, image;* abstr., *mere form, appearance, pretence.*

imbēcillĭtās -ātis, f. *weakness, feebleness.*

imbēcillus -a -um, *weak, feeble.* Compar. adv. **imbēcillĭus,** *somewhat weakly.*

imbellis -e, *unwarlike, not fighting, indisposed or unable to fight;* hence *feeble, peaceful, quiet.*

imber -bris, m. *a shower or storm of rain, pelting rain; a rain-cloud; water or any fluid; a shower of missiles.*

imberbis -e and **imberbus** -a -um *beardless.*

imbĭbo -bĭbĕre -bĭbi, *to drink in;* mentally, *to conceive; to resolve, determine.*

imbrex -ĭcis, c. *a hollow tile used in roofing.*

imbrĭfĕr -fĕra -fĕrum, *rain-bringing.*

imbŭo -ŭĕre -ŭi -ūtum, *to wet, steep, saturate;* fig., *to stain, taint;* mentally, *to accustom, initiate, instruct.*

imĭtābĭlis -e, *that can be imitated.*

imĭtāmĕn -ĭnis, n. *an imitation;* plur., *an image.*

imĭtāmentum -i, n. *imitating, imitation.*

imĭtātĭo -ōnis, f. *imitation; pretence.*

imĭtātor -ōris, m. and **imĭtātrix** -ĭcis, f. *an imitator.*

īmĭtor -ari, dep. *to imitate, copy; to depict; to be like, act like.*

immādŭi, infin. -isse, *to have become moist.*

immānis -e, *enormous, immense, monstrous; of character, savage, horrible, inhuman.*

immānĭtās -ātis, f. *savagery, frightfulness.*

immansuētus -a -um, *untamed, wild.*

immātūrĭtās -ātis, f. *immaturity; untimely haste.*

immātūrus -a -um, *unripe, immature; untimely.*

immĕdĭcābĭlis -e, *incurable.*

immĕmŏr -mŏris, *unmindful, forgetful, heedless.*

immĕmŏrābĭlis -e, *indescribable; unworthy of mention; silent, uncommunicative.*

immĕmŏrāta -orum, n. pl. *things not related.*

immensĭtās -ātis, f. *immensity.*

immensus -a -um, *immense, vast, boundless;* n. as subst., *immense size, immensity.*

immĕrens -entis, *not deserving, innocent.*

immergo -mergĕre -mersi -mersum, *to dip in, plunge in, immerse.*

immĕrĭtus -a -um: act., *not deserving (punishment), innocent;* pass., *undeserved;* adv. **immĕrĭtō,** *undeservedly.*

immersābĭlis -e, *that cannot be sunk.*

immētātus -a -um, *unmeasured.*

immigro -are, *to move away into*

imminĕo -ēre, *to project, overhang; in time, to be imminent, hang over; to threaten; to be on the watch or look out.*

imminŭo -ŭĕre -ŭi -ūtum, *to lessen, diminish; to weaken, infringe.*

imminūtio -ōnis, f. *diminishing, weakening;* rhet. *meiosis.*

immiscĕo -miscēre -miscŭi mixtum, *to mix in, intermingle; to join with, unite.*

immĭsĕrābĭlis -e, *unpitied.*

immĭsĕrĭcors -cordis, *unmerciful;* adv. **immĭsĕrĭcordĭter.**

immissĭo -ōnis, n. *letting grow.*

immītis -e, *unripe, sour; harsh, cruel, stern.*

immitto -mittĕre -misi -missum. (1) *to send in, put in, work in; to engraft.* (2) *to let loose; esp. to let grow.* (3) *to let go against, launch against;* se in hostes, *to attack; of feelings, to instil.*

immixus, partic. from immisceo; q.v.

immo, *on the contrary; yes indeed, no indeed; say rather.*

immōbĭlis -e, *immovable or hard to move; inexorable.*

immŏdĕrātĭo -ōnis, f. *excess.*

immŏdĕrātus -a -um, *immeasurable, endless; immoderate, unrestrained;* adv. **immŏdĕrātē.**

immŏdestĭa -ae, f. *want of restraint.*

immŏdestus -a -um, *unrestrained, extravagant;* adv. **immŏdestē.**

immŏdĭcus -a -um, *immoderate,*

excessive; unrestrained, unbridled; adv. **immŏdĭcē.**

immŏdŭlātus -a -um, *inharmonious.*

immoenis; see immunis.

immŏlātĭo -ōnis, f. *sacrificer.*

immŏlātor -ōris, m. *a sacrifice.*

immŏlītus -a -um, *built up, erected.*

immŏlo -are, *to sacrifice; to devote to death, to slay.*

immŏrĭor -mŏri -mortuus, *to die in or over.*

immŏror -ari, *to remain in; to dwell on a subject.*

immorsus -a -um, *bitten; stimulated.*

immortālis -e, *deathless, immortal, imperishable.* Adv. **immortālĭter,** *infinitely.*

immortālĭtās -ātis, f., *immortality; everlasting renown; extreme happiness.*

immōtus -a -um, *unmoved, motionless; undisturbed, calm; firm, steadfast.*

immūgĭo -ire, *to bellow in or on.*

immulgĕo -ēre, *to milk into.*

immundus -a -um, *impure, foul.*

immūnĭo -ire, *to fortify.*

immūnis -e, *without duty free, exempt;* in gen., *not working or not contributing; not sharing in, devoid of; stainless.*

immūnĭtās -ātis, f. *exemption from offices or burdens; immunity.*

immūnītus -a -um, *unfortified; unpaved.*

immurmŭro -are, *to murmur at.*

immūtābĭlis, -e *unchangeable.*

immūtābĭlĭtās -ātis, f., *immutability.*

immūtātĭo -ōnis, f. *change, alteration;* rhet., *metonymy.*

¹**immūtātus** -a -um, *unchanged.*

²**immutatus** -a -um, partic. from immuto; q.v.

immūto -are, *to change, alter;* immutata oratio, *allegory.*

impācātus -a um, *restless.*

impallesco -pallescĕre -pallŭi, *to turn pale.*

impār -păris, *unequal, uneven; unlike, discordant; ill-matched; of numbers, odd;* modi impares, *hexameter and pentameter.* Adv. **impărĭtĕr,** *unevenly, unequally.*

impărātus -a -um *unprepared, unprovided.*

impart-; see impert-.

impastus -a -um, *unfed, hungry.*

impătĭbĭlis = impetibilis; q.v.

impătĭens -entis *unable to endure, impatient;* adv. **impătĭenter.**

impătĭentĭa -ae, f. *impatience, inability to endure.*

impăvĭdus -a -um, *fearless, undaunted;* adv. **impăvĭdē.**

impĕdīmentum -i, n. *hindrance, impediment;* in plur., *the baggage of an army or traveller.*

impĕdĭo -ire, *to entangle, ensnare, obstruct, surround; to embarrass, hinder, prevent.*

Hence partic, **impĕdītus** -a -um, *entangled, hindered;* milit., *hindered by baggage;* of places, *impassable, blocked;* in gen., *embarrassed, obstructed; awkward, complicated.*

impēdītīo -ōnis, f. *hindrance.*

impello -pellĕre -pŭli -pulsum. (1) *to drive against, strike upon.* (2) *to set in motion; to incite, urge on, impel; esp. to push over one already slipping.*

impendĕo -ēre, *to hang over, overhang; to threaten, be close at hand.*

impendĭum -i, n. *expenditure, outlay, cost; interest on money.* Abl. as adv. **impendĭō**, colloq., *by much, very much.*

impendo -pendĕre -pendi -pensum, *to weigh out; hence to expend, lay out;* partic. **impensus** -a -um, of price, *considerable, great;* in gen., *strong, vehement.* Adv. **impensē**, *at great cost; urgently, eagerly.*

impĕnetrābĭlis -e, *impenetrable.*

impensa -ac, f. *expense, outlay.*

impĕrātor -ōris, m. *commander, leader;* milit., *the commander-in-chief;* also of the Roman emperors.

impĕrātōrĭus -a -um, *of a general; imperial.*

impĕrātrix -īcis, f. *a female commander.*

imperceptus -a -um *unperceived, unknown.*

impercussus -a -um, *not struck.*

imperdĭtus -a -um, *not lain, undestroyed.*

imperfectus -a -um, *incomplete, unfinished.*

imperfossus -a -um *unstabbed, unpierced.*

impĕrĭōsus -a -um, *commanding; sibi, master of oneself;* in bad sense, *imperious, tyrannical.*

impĕrĭtĭa -ae, f. *inexperience, ignorance.*

impĕrĭto -are, *to command, be in command, give an order.*

impĕrītus -a -um, *unskilled, inexperienced, ignorant;* adv. **impĕrītē.**

impĕrĭum -i, n. *an order, a command; the right to order, power, mastery, command; esp. political power, authority, sovereignty;* in imperio esse, *to hold office;* meton. *empire,* and in plur., *persons in authority.*

imperĭūrātus -a -um, *by which no one swears falsely.*

impermissus -a -un, *forbidden.*

impĕro -are, *to impose;* hence *to requisition, order a thing; to order an action to be done, give orders to a person; to rule over, govern, command.*

imperterrĭtus -um, *undaunted, fearless.*

impertĭo -ire, *to give a person a share in; to share a thing with a person, to impart, bestow.*

imperturbātus -a -um, *undisturbed, calm.*

impervĭus -a -um, *impassable.*

impĕtĭbĭlis -e, *insufferable.*

impĕto -ĕre, *to make for, attack.*

impetrābĭlis -e: pass., *obtainable;* act., *successful.*

impetrātĭo -ōnis, f. *obtaining by request.*

impetrĭo -ire, *to seek by favourable omens.*

impetro -are, *to get, accomplish, effect; esp. to obtain by asking.*

impĕtus -ūs, m. *an attack, onset; any rapid motion;* mental *impulse, passion, force.*

impexus -a -um *uncombed; rude, uncouth.*

impĭĕtās -ātis, f. *undutifulness; impiety unfilial conduct, disloyalty.*

impĭgĕr -gra -grum, *diligent, active,* adv. **impĭgrē.**

impĭgrĭtās -ātis, f. *activity.*

impingo -pingĕre -pēgi -pactum, *to thrust, dash, drive against;* fig., *to press upon, bring upon a person.*

impĭus -a -um, *undutiful, disloyal; godless, unfilial, unpatriotic;* adv. **impĭē.**

implācābĭlis -e, *implacable;* compar. adv. **implācābĭlĭus.**

implācātus -a -um, *unappeased, unsatisfied.*

implĕo -plēre -plēvi -plētum, *to fill in, fill up, complete; to satisfy, content a person; to fulfil, perform; to contaminate.*

implexus -a -um *involved, entwined.*

implĭcātĭo -ōnis, f. *entwining, interweaving; embarrassment.*

implĭco -are, -āvi -ātum and -ŭi -itum, *to enfold, entwine, entangle, involve; to associate, unite;* partic. **implĭcātus** -a -um, *confused, entangled;* adv. **implĭcĭtē,** *confusedly.*

implōrātĭo -ōnis, f. *an imploring for help.*

implōro -are, *to call upon with tears, to beseech, implore; to call for, beg for.*

implūmis -e, *unfledged.*

implŭo -plŭĕre -plŭi, *to rain upon.*

implŭvĭum -i, n. *an opening in the roof of a Roman house, or the basin for rain-water below it.*

impŏlītus -a -um, *rough, unpolished;* adv. **impŏlītē.**

impollūtus -a -um, *undefiled.*

impōno -pōnĕre -pōsŭi -pŏsĭtum, *to put, lay, place in or upon;* naut. *to put on board ship, to embark;* fig., *to lay or put upon, impose; to put over as master; to impose upon, cheat, deceive* (with dat.).

importo -are, *to bring in, import. introduce; to bring upon, cause.*

importūnĭtās -ātis, f. *self-assertion, inconsiderateness, insolence.*

importūnus -a -um, *unsuitable, ill-adapted, unfavourable; troublesome, tiresome;* of character, *assertive, inconsiderate.*

importŭōsus -a -um, *without harbours.*

impŏs -pŏtis, *having no power over.*

impŏsĭtus -a -um, partic. from **impono;** q.v.

impŏtens -entis, *feeble, powerless;* with genit., *not master of;* esp. *unable to command oneself, violent, unrestrained.* Adv. **impŏtentĕr,** *weakly; intemperately, passionately.*

impŏtentĭa -ae, f. *poverty; lack of self-restraint, violent passion.*

impraesentĭārum, *in present circumstances, for the present.*

impransus -a -um, *without breakfast, fasting.*

imprĕcor -ari, dep. *to invoke harm upon, to call down upon.*

impressĭo -ōnis, f. *physical pressure an attack, assault;* rhet., *distinct expression, emphasis;* philos., *sense-data, the impressions of the senses.*

imprīmīs, *especially, first of all.*

imprĭmo -prīmĕre -pressi -pressum, *to press upon* or *into; to seal, chase, emboss; to make by pressing, imprint.*

imprŏbātĭo -ōnis, f. *disapproval, blame.*

imprŏbĭtās -ātis, f. *badness, depravity.*

imprŏbo -are, *to disapprove, blame, reject.*

imprŏbŭlus -a -um, *somewhat wicked.*

imprŏbus -a -um, *inferior, bad; morally bad, perverse, wilful; bold, persistent, mischievous;* m.pl. as subst., *the unpatriotic.* Adv. imprŏbē, *badly, wickedly; impudently, boldly.*

imprŏcērus -a -um, *small, low of stature.*

imprōdictus -a -um, *not postponed.*

impromptus -a -um, *not ready.*

imprŏpĕrātus -a -um, *unhurried, slow.*

improspĕr -ĕra -ĕrum, *unfortunate;* adv. improspĕrē.

imprŏvĭdus -a -um, *without forethought, improvident;* adv. imprŏvĭdē.

imprōvīsus -a -um, *unforeseen, un-expected;* (ex)improviso, *unexpectedly.*

imprūdens -entis, *not foreseeing, not expecting; not knowing, unaware; unwise, rash, imprudent.* Adv. imprūdentĕr, *without forethought; unawares; unwisely.*

imprūdentĭa -ae, f., *lack of foresight or knowledge; ignorance; lack of wisdom, imprudence.*

impūbēs -bĕris and -bis. (1) *youthful;* genae, *beardless;* plur. as subst. *boys.* (2) *unmarried.*

impŭdens -entis, *shameless, impudent;* adv. impŭdentĕr.

impŭdentĭa -ae, f. *shamelessness, impudence.*

impŭdīcĭtĭa -ae, f. *incontinence, un-chastity.*

impŭdīcus -a -um *shameless;* esp. *unchaste.*

impugnātĭo -ōnis, f. *assault, attack.*

impugno -are, *to attack, assail.*

impulsĭo -ōnis, f. *pressure;* fig., *impulse, instigation.*

impulsor -ōris, m. *instigator.*

impulsus -ūs, m. *pressure, impulse; incitement, instigation.*

impūnĕ, *with impunity, unpunished, safely.*

impūnĭtās -ātis, f. *impunity, exemption from punishment.*

impūnītus -a -um, *unpunished, exempt from punishment; unrestrained;* adv. impūnītē.

impūrātus -a -um, *vile, infamous.*

impūrĭtās -ātis, f. *moral impurity.*

impūrus -a -um, *unclean, foul; morally, impure, vile, infamous.* Adv. impūrē.

¹impŭtātus -a -um, *unpruned, untrimmed.*

²impŭtātus -a -um, partic. from imputo; q.v.

impŭto -are, *to lay to a charge, enter*

in an account; to reckon as a merit or *fault in someone, to impute to; to reckon as a service done* or *gift given to someone.*

īmus -a -um, superl. from inferus; q.v.

¹in, prep. (1) with acc., *into, on to, towards, against;* of time, *until;* in omne tempus, *for ever;* in diem vivere, *to live for the moment;* of tendency or purpose, *for;* in adverbial phrases, indicating manner or extent: in universum, *in general;* in vicem, in vices, *in turn.* (2) with abl., *in, on, among;* of time, *in, at, within; in relation to* a person, *in the case of.*

²in-, inseparable particle, *without, not.*

ĭnaccessus -a -um, *inaccessible.*

ĭnācesco -ăcescĕre -ăcŭi, *to become sour.*

Ĭnăchus (Ĭnăchŏs) -i, m. *mythical king of Argos, father of Io, after whom the river Inachus in Argolis was named.*

ĭnadfectātus -a -um, *natural, un-affected.*

ĭnadsuētus -a -um, *unaccustomed.*

ĭnădustus -a -um, *unsinged.*

ĭnaedĭfĭco -are *to build in* or *upon; to build up, block up, barricade.*

ĭnaequābĭlis -e, *uneven, unequal;* adv. ĭnaequābĭlĭter.

ĭnaequālis -e. *uneven, unequal, various; making unequal, disturbing.* Adv. ĭnaequālĭtĕr, *unevenly.*

ĭnaequālĭtās -ātis, f. *unevenness.*

ĭnaequo -are, *to make even, level up.*

ĭnaestĭmābĭlis -e, *that cannot be estimated; hence priceless, inestimable; also having no value.*

ĭnaestŭo -are, *to boil, rage (in).*

ĭnaffectātus, see inadf-.

ĭnămābĭlis -e, *unlovely, hateful.*

ĭnămāresco -ĕre, *to become bitter.*

ĭnambĭtĭōsus -a -um, *unpretentious, down.*

ĭnambŭlātĭo -ōnis, f. *walking up and down.*

ĭnambŭlo -are, *to walk up and down.*

ĭnămoenus -a -um, *unlovely, dismal.*

ĭnănĭmus -a -um, *lifeless, inanimate.*

ĭnānĭo -ire, *to empty, make void.*

ĭnānis -e, *empty, void;* equus, *riderless;* navis, *unloaded;* corpus, *soulless;* with genit. or abl., *empty of;* of persons, *empty-handed, poor;* fig., *vain, hollow, idle.* N. as subst., *empty space, emptiness, vanity.* Adv. ĭnānĭtĕr, *vainly, uselessly.*

ĭnānĭtās -ātis, f. *emptiness, empty space; uselessness.*

ĭnărātus -a -um, *unploughed, fallow.*

ĭnardesco -ardescĕre -arsi, *to catch fire, burn, glow.*

ĭnāresco -ārescĕre -ārŭi, *to become dry.*

ĭnassuētus; see inadsuetus.

ĭnattĕnŭātus, *undiminished, unimpaired.*

ĭnaudax -ācis, *timid, fearful.*

ĭnaudĭo -ire, *to hear;* esp. *to hear as a secret.*

ĭnaudītus -a -um, *unheard* (esp. of accused persons); *unheard of, unusual.*

ĭnaugŭro -are: intransit., *to take the auguries;* transit., *to consecrate, install, inaugurate;* **inaugŭrātŏ,** *after taking the auguries.*

ĭnaures -ĭum, f. pl. *earrings.*

ĭnauro -are, *to cover with gold, gild, enrich.*

ĭnauspĭcātus -a -um, *without auspices;* **ĭnauspĭcātŏ,** *without consulting the auspices.*

ĭnausus -a -um, *not dared, not attempted.*

incaedŭus -a -um, *not cut, unfelled.*

incălesco -călescĕre -călŭi, *to glow, become warm or passionate.*

incalfăcĭo -făcĕre, *to heat, warm.*

incallĭdus -a -um, *ingenuous, unskilful;* adv. **incallĭdē.**

incandesco -candescĕre -candŭi, *to begin to whiten,* esp. *with heat.*

incānesco -cānescĕre -cānŭi, *to become grey.*

incanto -are, *to enchant.*

incānus -a -um, *quite grey.*

incassum, *in vain.*

incastĭgātus -a -um, *unchastised.*

incautus -a -um, adj. *incautious, careless, unwary; unguarded; not guarded against, unforeseen.* Adv. **incautē.**

incēdo -cēdĕre -cessi -cessum, *to walk, step, march; to proceed, come on;* of feelings, with dat., *to come over.*

incēlebrātus -a -um, *not spread abroad.*

incēnātus -a -um, *without dinner.*

incendĭārĭus -a -um, *fire-raising, incendiary.*

incendĭum -i, n. *a conflagration, fire; a torch, firebrand;* of passion, *fire, glow, heat:* in gen., *destruction, ruin.*

incendo -cendĕre -cendi -censum, *to kindle, set fire to, burn; to make bright, illumine; to fire with passion, excite, incense.*

incensĭo -ōnis, f. *burning.*

incensus -a -um, *not enrolled by the censor, unassessed.*

incensus, partic. from incendo; q.v.

inceptĭo -ōnis, f. *a beginning; an enterprise.*

incepto -are, *to begin; to attempt, undertake.*

inceptor -ōris, m. *a beginner.*

inceptum -i, n. of partic. of incipio; q.v.

incerno -cernĕre -crēvi -crētum, *to sift.*

incēro -are, *to cover with wax.*

incertus -a -um, *uncertain, doubtful, not sure.* (1) *as to fact:* act., of persons, *not knowing, doubting;* pass., of things, *not known, obscure;* n. as subst. *uncertainty.* (2) *as to action, hesitating, irresolute, undecided;* in-certam securim, *not surely aimed.*

incesso -cessĕre -cessīvi, *to attack, assail.*

incessus -ūs, m. *march, walk; manner of walking, gait; attack, assault; entrance, approach.*

incesto -are, *to defile, pollute, dishonour.*

¹incestus -a -um, *impure, defiled; sinful, unchaste;* n. as subst. *unchastity, incest.* Adv. **incestē.**

²incestus -ūs, m. *unchastity, incest.*

inchŏo; see incoho.

¹incĭdo -cīdĕre -cĭdi -casum, *to fall in or upon; to fall in with;* in hostem, *to attack;* in aes alienum, *to run into debt;* in mentionem, *to happen to mention;* of abstr. things, *to occur, happen,* " *crop up.*"

²incido -cīdĕre -cĭdi cīsum, *to cut into, cut open; to inscribe, engrave an inscription; to make by cutting; to cut through;* fig., *to cut short, bring to an end, break off.*

Hence, from partic., n. subst. **incīsum** -i, = incisio, q.v.; adv. **incīsē,** = incisim, q.v.

incīlĕ -is, n. *a ditch, trench.*

incĭlo -are, *to blame, scold.*

incingo -cingĕre -cinxi -cinctum, *to surround.*

incĭno -ĕre, *to sing.*

incĭpĭo -cĭpĕre -cēpi -ceptum (cf. coepi), *to take in hand, begin, commence; sometimes, to begin to speak.* N. of partic. as subst. **inceptum** -i, *a beginning; an attempt, enterprise.*

incĭsim, *in short clauses.*

incīsĭo -ōnis, f. *a clause of a sentence.*

incĭtāmentum, -i, n. *inducement, incentive.*

incĭtātĭo -ōnis, f.: act., *inciting, instigating;* pass., *violent motion, excitement, vehemence.*

incĭto -are, *to put into rapid motion, urge on, hasten;* in pass., or with reflex., *to quicken one's pace, hasten.* Transf., *to excite, spur, inspire; to incite against, stir up; to increase.*

Hence partic. **incĭtātus** -a -um, *rapid, vehement;* equo incitato, *at full gallop;* compar. adv. **incĭtātĭus,** *more violently.*

¹incĭtus -a -um, *in rapid motion.*

²incĭtus -a -um, *unmoved.*

inclāmo -are, *to call upon loudly;* esp., *to scold.*

inclāresco -clārescĕre -clārŭi, *to become famous.*

inclēmens -entis, *unmerciful, harsh, rough;* adv. **inclēmentēr.**

inclēmentĭa -ae, f. *unmercifulness, harshness.*

inclīnātĭo -ōnis, f. *leaning, bending, inclination;* in gen., *movement, tendency, change; good-will, liking.*

inclīno -are: transit., *to bend, incline, turn, change,* sometimes *for the worse;* in pass., *to fall back, waver;* intransit., *to take a turn, verge, incline, change;* milit., *to waver, yield.*

Hence partic. **inclīnātus** -a -um, *inclined, prone; sinking;* of the voice, *low, deep.*

inclūdo -clūdĕre -clūsi -clūsum, *to shut in, enclose;* esp. *to block, obstruct, confine.*

inclūsĭo -ōnis, f. *shutting up, confinement.*

inclŭtus, inclĭtus -a -um, *celebrated famous, renowned.*

¹incoctus -a -um, *uncooked, raw.*

²incoctus -a -um, partic. from incoquo; q.v.

incōgĭtābĭlis -e, and **incōgĭtans** -antis, *inconsiderate, thoughtless.*

incōgĭtantĭa -ae, f. *thoughtlessness.*
incōgĭtātus -a -um: pass., *unstudied*; act., *inconsiderate.*
incōgĭto -are, *to contrive, plan.*
incognĭtus -a -um, *unexamined, unknown; unrecognized,* so *unclaimed.*
incŏho -are, *to take in hand, begin.* Hence partic. **incŏhātus** -a -um, *only begun, not finished.*
incŏla -ae, c. *an inhabitant, native;* sometimes *a foreign resident.*
incŏlo -cŏlĕre -cŏlŭi, *to inhabit, dwell (in).*
incŏlŭmis -e, *uninjured, safe and sound.*
incŏlŭmĭtās -ātis, f., *safety, preservation.*
incōmĭtātus -a -um, *unaccompanied, without retinue.*
incommendātus -a -um, *not entrusted;* hence *without protector.*
incommŏdĭtās -atis, f. *inconvenience, disadvantage, unseasonableness.*
incommŏdo -are, *to be unpleasant or troublesome.*
incommŏdus -a -um, *inconvenient, troublesome, disagreeable, annoying;* n. as subst., *inconvenience, disadvantage;* incommodo tuo, *to your disadvantage;* adv. **incommŏdē,** *inconveniently.*
incommūtābĭlis -e, *unchangeable.*
incompărābĭlis -e, *incomparable.*
incompertus -a -um, *unknown.*
incompŏsĭtus -a -um, *not in order, irregular;* adv. **incompŏsĭtē.**
incomprēhensĭbĭlis -e, *impossible to catch; incomprehensible.*
incomptus -a -um, *unkempt, untrimmed; rude, rough.*
inconcessus -a -um, *not allowed, forbidden.*
inconcinnus -a -um, *awkward, inelegant, absurd.*
inconcussus -a -um, *unshaken, firm.*
incondĭtus -a -um, *not arranged, disorderly, confused;* adv. **incondĭtē.**
incongrŭens -entis, *not agreeing, inconsistent.*
inconsīdĕrātus -a -um, *thoughtless, inconsiderate;* pass. *unadvised, reckless.* Adv. **inconsīdĕrātē,** *without consideration.*
inconsōlābĭlis -e, *inconsolable; incurable.*
inconstans -stantis, *changeable, inconsistent;* adv. **inconstantĕr.**
inconstantĭa -ae, f. *changeableness, inconsistency.*
inconsultus -a -um: pass., *not consulted;* act., *without asking advice, unadvised;* hence *inconsiderate, imprudent.* Adv. **inconsultē,** *indiscreetly.*
inconsumptus -a -um, *unconsumed, undiminished.*
incontāmĭnātus -a -um, *unpolluted.*
incontentus -a -um, *not stretched;* fides, *untuned.*
incontĭnens -entis, *incontinent;* adv. **incontĭnentĕr.**
incontĭnentĭa -ae, f. *incontinence.*

inconvĕnĭens -entis, *not suiting, dissimilar.*
incŏquo -cŏquĕre -coxi -coctum, *to boil in or with; to dye.*
incorrectus -a -um, *unamended, unimproved.*
incorruptus -a -um, *not corrupted, untainted, unspoilt, unimpaired;* adv. **incorruptē.**
increbresco -ĕre -crebrŭi and **increbesco** -ĕre -crebŭi, *to become strong* or *frequent; to increase, prevail.*
incrēdĭbĭlis -e, *not to be believed, incredible;* adv. **incrēdĭbĭlĭtĕr.**
incrēdŭlus -a -um, *incredulous.*
incrēmentum -i, n. *growth, increase;* meton, *the makings of anything,* also *offspring.*
increpĭto -are, *to call loudly to; to reproach, chide.*
increpo -are -ŭi (-āvi) -ĭtum (ātum), *to rustle, make a noise; to be noised abroad;* transit., *to cause to sound.* Of persons, *to chide, rebuke.*
incresco -crescĕre -crēvi, *to grow (in or on).*
incrētus -a -um, partic. from incerno; q.v.
incrŭentātus and **incrŭentus** -a -um, *bloodless.*
incrusto -are, *to cover with rind, encrust.*
incŭbo -are -ŭi -ĭtum, *to lie in or on or over; to watch over; to hang over, lie heavily upon; to dwell in.*
inculco -are, *to trample in, press in, force upon, impress upon.*
inculpātus -a -um, *unblamed, blameless.*
¹incultus -a -um, *uncultivated, untilled;* n. pl. as subst. *wastes, deserts;* of dress, etc., *neglected, untidy;* in gen., *unpolished, rude.* Adv. **incultē.**
²incultus -ūs, m. *neglect, want of cultivation.*
incumbo -cumbĕre -cŭbŭi -cŭbĭtum, *to lie upon, put weight on, lean over, overhang; to apply oneself to, concentrate upon a thing; to incline to, favour, further a cause or movement.*
incūnābŭla -orum, n. pl. *swaddling-clothes;* hence *infancy; birthplace;* in gen., *source, origin.*
incūrātus -a -um, *uncared-for, unhealed.*
incūrĭa -ae, f. *carelessness, neglect.*
incūrĭōsus -a -um: act., *careless, negligent;* pass., *neglected.* Adv. **incūrĭōsē,** *carelessly.*
incurro -currĕre -curri (cŭcurri) -cursum, *to run into;* milit., *to assail, attack, make a raid into.* Transf., *to attack with words, inveigh against; to come upon, fall in with;* in space, *to extend into;* in time, *to coincide with.*
incursĭo -ōnis, f. a *clash, onset; collision;* milit., *attack, raid, invasion.*
incurso -are, *to run against, strike against, attack.*
incursus -ūs, m. *an attack, assault;* of the mind, *efforts, impulses.*
incurvo -are, *to bend, curve, make crooked.*

incurvus -a -um, *bent, curved, crooked.*
incūs -cūdis, f. *anvil.*
incūsātīo -ōnis, f. *blame, reproach, accusations.*
incūso -are, *to accuse, blame, find fault with.*
incussū, abl. sing. m., *by a clash.*
incustōdītus -a -um: pass., *unwatched, unguarded;* act., *incautious, imprudent.*
incūsus -a -um, *forged, fabricated.*
incūtio -cŭtĕre -cussi -cussum, *to dash, beat against; to strike into the mind, inspire with.*
indāgātio -ōnis, f. *investigation.*
indāgātor -ōris, m. and **indāgātrix** -tricis, f. *investigator, explorer.*
¹**indāgo** -are, *to track down,* as hounds hunting; *to explore, investigate.*
²**indāgo** -ĭnis, f. *surrounding and driving of game.*
indĕ, *thence, from there;* hinc . . . inde, *on this side . . . on that; from that cause, for that reason; from that time, thereafter; thereupon, then.*
indēbĭtus -a -um, *not owed, not due.*
indĕcens -centis, *unbecoming, unseemly, unsightly;* adv. **indēcenter.**
indēclīnātus -a -um, *unchanged, firm.*
indĕcor -ris or **indĕcŏris** -e, *unbecoming, shameful,*
indĕcŏro -are, *to disgrace, dishonour.*
indĕcŏrus -a -um, *unbecoming, unseemly, unsightly; disgraceful.* Adv. **indĕcŏrē.**
indēfensus -a -um, *undefended, unprotected.*
indēfessus -a -um, *unwearied, indefatigable.*
indēflētus -a -um, *unwept.*
indēiectus -a -um, *not thrown down.*
indēlēbĭlis -e, *imperishable.*
indēlībātus -a -um, *uninjured, undiminished.*
indemnātus -a -um, *uncondemned.*
indēplōrātus -a -um, *unwept, unlamented.*
indēprensus -a -um, *undiscovered.*
indēsertus -a -um, *not forsaken.*
indēstrictus -a -um, *untouched, unhurt.*
indētonsus -a -um, *unshorn.*
indēvītātus -a -um, *unavoided.*
index -dĭcis, m. *an informer; a sign, token; the forefinger; a title; a touchstone.*
Indi -orum, m. pl. *the Indians;* sing. **Indus** -i, m. *an Indian,* or *Ethiopian; an elephant-driver, mahout.* Adj. **Indus** and **Indĭcus** -a -um, *Indian;* subst. **India** -ae, f. *India.*
indĭcentĕ, abl. sing., *not saying:* me indicente, *without my saying a word.*
indĭcium -i, n. (1) *information, evidence; leave to give evidence; a reward for giving evidence.* (2) *any mark, sign, token.*
¹**indĭco** -are, *to make known, show, indicate; esp. to inform against, give evidence about; to put a price on, value.*
²**indīco** -dīcĕre -dixi -dictum, *to make publicly known, proclaim;* bellum, *to declare war.*

¹**indictus** -a -um, *not said, unsaid:* indictā causā, *without a hearing.*
²**indictus** -a -um, partic. from ²**indico**; q.v.
indĭdem, *from the same place or matter.*
indiffĕrens -entis, *indifferent; neither good nor bad; unconcerned.* Adv. **indifférentĕr.**
indĭgĕna -ae, *native.*
indĭgentia -ae, f. *want, need; desire.*
indĭgĕo -ēre -ŭi, *to want, need, require;* also *to long for.* Hence partic. **indĭgens** -entis, *in need.*
indĭges -gĕtis, m. *native, indigenous.*
indĭgestus -a -um, *disordered, confused, unarranged.*
indignābundus -a -um, *filled with indignation.*
indignātio -ōnis, f. *indignation; matter for indignation;* rhet., *the exciting of indignation.*
indignĭtās -ātis, f. *unworthiness, vileness; unworthy behaviour or treatment of others, indignity; indignation at unworthy treatment.*
indignor -ari, dep. *to consider unworthy, take as an indignity, be offended.* Hence partic. **indignans** -antis, *offended.*
indignus -a -um: of persons, *unworthy, not deserving* (with abl. or genit.); of things, *unworthy; hence disgraceful, shameful.* Adj. **indignē,** *unworthily, dishonourably; impatiently, indignantly.*
indĭgus -a -um, *needing, in want of.*
indīlĭgens -entis, *negligent;* adv. **indīlĭgentĕr.**
indīlĭgentia -ae, f. *carelessness, negligence.*
indĭpiscor -dīpisci -deptus, dep., and **indĭpisco** -ĕre, *to reach, obtain; to attain, get.*
indīreptus -a -um, *unpillaged.*
indiscrētus -a -um, *unsevered, undivided; undistinguished; indistinguishable.*
indīsertus -a -um, *not eloquent;* adv. **indīsertē.**
indispŏsĭtus -a -um, *disorderly, confused.*
indissŏlūbĭlis -e, *indissoluble.*
indissŏlūtus -a -um, *undissolved.*
indistinctus -a -um, *not separated; indistinct, obscure; unpretentious.*
indivĭdŭus -a -um, *indivisible, inseparable;* n. as subst. *an atom.*
indo -dĕre -dĭdi -dĭtum, *to put in or on;* of names, *to give, confer;* of abstr. things, *to introduce, cause, occasion.*
indŏcĭlis -e, *unteachable, untaught; ignorant, rude, artless;* of subjects, *unable to be learned.*
indoctus -a -um, *untaught, untrained, unskilled;* adv. **indoctē.**
indŏlentia -ae, f. *freedom from pain.*
indŏlēs -is, f. *native constitution or quality; nature, disposition, character, talents.*
indŏlesco -dŏlescĕre -dŏlŭi, *to be pained or grieved (at).*
indŏmĭtus -a -um, *untamed, wild.*

indormĭo -ire -īvi -itum, *to sleep on or over; to be negligent about*, with dat. or in.

indōtātus -a -um, *without dowry*; *corpora, without funeral honours*; *ars, unadorned, poor.*

indŭ, archaic form of in; q.v.

indŭbĭtātus -a -um, *undoubted, certain.*

indŭbĭto -are, *to feel doubt of*, with dat.

indŭbĭus -a -um, *not doubtful, certain.*

indūcĭae = indutiae; q.v.

indūco -dūcĕre -duxi -ductum. (1) *to draw over, spread over so as to cover*; also *to cover one thing with another; to put on clothing or arms; to erase writing*, and hence *to revoke, make invalid.* (2) *to lead* or *bring in, to introduce; to enter in an account-book; to lead on, induce, persuade*; with animum, or in animum, *to decide to do*, or *decide that a thing is so.*

inductĭo -ōnis, f. *leading* or *bringing in, introduction*; animi, *resolve, intention*; erroris, *misleading*; in logic, *induction.*

inductū, abl. sing. m., *by instigation.*

indulgentĭa -ae, f. *tenderness, indulgence.*

indulgĕo -dulgēre -dulsi: intransit., *to be forbearing, patient, indulgent*; fig., *to give oneself up to, indulge in*; transit. *to grant, allow, concede.*

Hence partic. **indulgens** -entis, *kind, tender, indulgent*; adv. **indulgentĕr.**

indŭo -dŭĕre -dŭi -dūtum, *to put on*, esp. of dress. Transf., *to clothe, surround, cover; to put on, assume, take up, engage in*; se, with dat. or in, *to fall into, fall on; to entangle.*

indūresco -dūrescĕre -dūrŭi, *to become hard or firm.*

indūro -are, *to make hard or firm.*

industrĭa -ae, f. *industry, diligence*; de (or ex) industria, *on purpose, intentionally.*

industrĭus -a -um, *diligent, painstaking, industrious*; adv. **industrĭē.**

indūtĭae -arum, f. pl. *truce, armistice, suspension of hostilities.*

indūtus -ūs, m. *a putting on, clothing.*

īnēbrĭo -are, *to intoxicate; to saturate.*

īnĕdĭa -ae, f. *fasting, abstinence from food.*

īnēdĭtus -a -um, *not published, unknown.*

īnēlĕgans -antis, *not choice, tasteless*; adv. **īnēlĕgantĕr.**

īnēluctābĭlis -e, *from which one cannot struggle free.*

īnēmŏrĭor -emori, dep. *to die in or at.*

īnemptus -a -um, *unbought.*

īnēnarrābĭlis -e, *indescribable, inexpressible*; adv. **īnēnarrābĭlĭtĕr.**

īnēnŏdābĭlis -e, *inextricable; inexplicable.*

īnĕo -ire -ĭi -ĭtum: intransit., *to go* or *come in, to enter*; of time, *to begin, commence*; transit., *to go* or *come into; to enter upon, start, begin*; consilium, *to form a plan*; numerum, or rationem, *to go into figures, make a calculation.*

īneptĭa -ae, f. *foolish behaviour, silliness, absurdity.*

īneptĭo -ire, *to talk foolishly.*

īneptus -a -um, *unsuitable, tasteless, silly*; adv. **īneptē.**

īnermis -e and **īnermus** -a -um, *unarmed, defenceless, helpless.*

īnerrans -antis, *not wandering, fixed.*

īnerro -are, *to rove about in.*

īners -ertis, *untrained, unskilful; inactive, lazy, idle, calm; cowardly; ineffective, dull, insipid.*

īnertĭa -ae, f. *unskilfulness; idleness.*

īnērūdītus -a -um, *illiterate, ignorant.*

īnesco -are, *to allure, entice, deceive.*

īnēvītābĭlis -e, *unavoidable.*

īnexcĭtus -a -um, *unmoved, quiet.*

īnexcūsābĭlis -e, *without excuse; inexcusable.*

īnexercĭtātus -a -um, *untrained, unpractised.*

īnexhaustus -a -um, *unexhausted.*

īnexōrābĭlis -e, *not to be moved by entreaty, stern, severe.*

īnexperrectus -a -um, *not awakened.*

īnexpertus -a -um: act., *inexperienced in, unacquainted with*; pass., *untried, untested, unattempted.*

īnexpĭābĭlis -e, *inexpiable; implacable irreconcilable.*

īnexplēbĭlis -e, *insatiable.*

īnexplētus -a -um, *unfilled, insatiate.*

īnexplĭcābĭlis -e, *that cannot be untied; intricate, difficult; inexplicable, beyond explanation; inconclusive, without result.*

īnexplōrātus -a -um, *unexplored, uninvestigated*; abl., **īnexplōrātō,** *without reconnoitring.*

īnexpugnābĭlis -e, *unconquerable, impregnable.*

īnexspectātus -a -um, *unlooked-for, unexpected.*

īnexstinctus -a -um, *unextinguished, inextinguishable.*

īnexsŭpĕrābĭlis -e, *insurmountable.*

īnextrĭcābĭlis -e, *that cannot be disentangled* or *unravelled.*

īnfabrē, *unskilfully.*

īnfabrĭcātus -a -um, *unwrought, unfashioned.*

īnfăcētĭae (**īnfĭc-**) -arum, f. pl. *crudity.*

īnfăcētus and **īnfĭcētus** -a -um, *dull, crude, without humour* or *wit*; adv. **īnfăcētē** (**īnfĭc-**).

īnfācundus -a -um, *not eloquent.*

īnfāmĭa -ae, f. *dishonour, disgrace*; also *a cause of disgrace.*

īnfāmis -e, *disgraced, disreputable.*

īnfāmo -are, *to put to shame, disgrace.*

īnfandus -a -um, *unutterable, abominable.*

īnfans -fantis, *speechless, unable to speak*; esp. of children; as subst., *a little child.* Transf., *tongue-tied, embarrassed; youthful, fresh; childish, silly.*

īnfantĭa -ae, f. *inability to speak; slowness of speech; infancy.*

īnfarcĭo (**īnfercĭo**) -ire, *to stuff in, cram in.*

īnfătŭo -are *to make a fool of.*

īnfaustus -a -um, *unlucky, unfortunate,*

infector -ōris, m. *a dyer.*

iinfectus -a -um, *unworked, unwrought; not done, unfinished, incomplete;* reddere infectum, *to make void, revoke; impracticable, impossible.*

²infectus, partic. from inficio; q.v.

infēcunditās -ātis, f. *barrenness, sterility.*

infēcundus -a -um, *barren, sterile.*

infēlicitās -ātis, f. *ill-luck, misfortune.*

infēlix -icis, *unfruitful, barren;* arbor, *the gallows.* Transf., *unhappy, unlucky;* act. sense, *causing unhappiness.* Adv. **infēlicitĕr**, *unluckily.*

infenso -are, *to attack, ravage.*

infensus -a -um, *hostile, aggressive;* of weapons, *aimed, ready;* in spirit, *embittered, dangerous.* Adv. **infensē.**

infĕr -a -um, **infĕri** -orum; see inferus.

infĕriae -arum, f. *offerings in honour of the dead.*

infercĭo; see infarcio.

infĕrior, infĕrius; see infra and inferus.

infernē, *on the lower side, beneath.*

infernus -a -um, *below, coming from below; of the lower world, infernal.* As subst., m. pl. **inferni**, *the shades;* n. pl. **infernă,** *the lower world.*

infĕro inferre intŭli inlātum, *to carry in, to put or place on;* templis ignes inferre, *to set fire to;* milit., signa in hostem, *to attack, charge;* bellum, with dat., *to make war on;* se inferre, and pass. inferri, *to betake oneself, to go;* of abstract things, *to bring on, introduce, occasion;* in accounts, *to enter;* in logic, *to infer, conclude.*

infĕrus -a -um, *below, lower, southern; o the lower world.* M. pl. as subst., **infĕri** -orum, *the dead, the lower world.* Compar. **infĕrior** -ius, *lower,* ex inferiore loco dicere, *to speak from the body of the court;* of time, *later, junior;* of number, rank, etc. *lower, inferior.* Superl. (1) **infĭmus** (**infŭmus**) -a -um, *lowest;* ab infima ara, *from the bottom of the altar;* of rank, etc., *lowest, meanest.* Superl. (2) **imus** -a -um, *lowest;* n. as subst., *the bottom;* of tone, *deepest, lowest;* of time, *last;* n. as subst., *the end.*

infervesco -fervescĕre -ferbŭi, *to begin to boil, grow hot.*

infesto -are, *to attack, disquiet.*

infestus -a -um; act., *aggressive, hostile, dangerous;* pass., *infested, beset, unsaᵉe.* Adv. **infestē,** *in a hostile manner.*

inficĕtus, inficĕtē = infacetus, infacete; q.v.

inficio -ficĕre -fēci -fectum. (1) *to tinge, dye, stain; to steep, imbue.* (2) *to poison, taint, corrupt.*

infidēlis -e, *untrue, disloyal, faithless;* adv. **infidēlitĕr.**

infidēlitās -ātis, f. *disloyalty.*

infidus -a -um, *untrue, disloyal.*

infigo -figĕre -fixi -fixum, *to fix, fasten or thrust in; to imprint, impress.*

infimus -a -um, superl. of inferus; q.v.

infindo -findĕre -fīdi -fissum, *to cut into.*

infinitās -ātis, f. *infinity, endlessness.*

infinitio -ōnis, f. *infinity.*

infinitus -a -um, *infinite, unbounded, immense;* n. as subst., *infinite space;* of time, *endless, unceasing;* of number, *countless;* also *indefinite, general.* Adv. **infinitē,** *infinitely, endlessly.*

infirmātio -ōnis, f. *weakening; refuting, invalidating.*

infirmitās -ātis, f. *weakness, feebleness; instability, fickleness.*

infirmo -are, *to weaken, impair, shake; to refute; to annul.*

infirmus -a -um, *weak, feeble; timorous.* Adv. **infirmē,** *weakly, faintly.*

infit, defective, *he (or she) begins;* esp *begins to speak.*

infitiālis -e, *negative, containing a denial.*

infitiās ire, *to deny.*

infitiātio -ōnis, f. *denying.*

infitiātor -ōris, m. *a denier;* esp. *one who denies a debt or deposit.*

infitior -ari, *to deny;* esp. *to deny a debt, refuse to restore a deposit.*

inflammātio -ōnis, f. *setting fire;* animorum, *inspiration.*

inflammo -are, *to kindle, set fire to; to inflame, excite.*

inflātio -ōnis, f. *inflation, flatulence.*

inflātus -ūs, m. *a blowing into, blast; inspiration.*

inflecto -flectĕre -flexi -flexum, *to bend, bow, curve.* Transf., *to warp, change; to sway, affect; to modulate the voice.*

inflētus -a -um, *unwept, unlamented.*

inflexio -ōnis, f. *bending, swaying.*

inflexus -ūs, m. *bending, curving.*

infligo -flīgĕre -flixi -flictum, *to strike, knock, dash against; to inflict a blow, cause damage.*

inflo -are, *to blow into; to play on wind instruments; to give a blast; to blow out, puff out.* Transf., *to inspire; to puff up, elate.* Hence partic., **inflātus** -a -um, *inflated, swollen; puffed up, pompous;* of style, *turgid.* Compar. adv. **inflātius,** *too pompously; on a grander scale.*

inflŭo -flŭĕre -fluxi -fluxum, *to flow in.* Transf., *to steal in, to stream in, rush in.*

infŏdĭo -fŏdĕre -fōdi -fossum, *to dig in, bury.*

informātio -ōnis, f. *conception, idea.*

informis -e, *formless, shapeless; deformed, hideous.*

informo -are, *to give form to, to shape, fashion;* mentally, *to form, dispose; to form an idea or conception of.*

infortūnātus -a -um, *unfortunate, miserable.*

infortūnium -i, n. *misfortune, ill luck; punishment.*

infrā. Prep., with acc., *below, under,* in position, size, rank; in time, *later than.* Adv., *below, underneath; in the lower world; to the south; in rank, lower.* Compar., **infĕrius,** *lower down.*

infractĭo -ōnis, f. *breaking*; animi, *dejection*.

infrăgĭlis -e, *unbreakable, strong*.

infrĕmo -frĕmĕre -frĕmŭi, *to growl*.

infrēnātus -a -um, *without bridle*, see also infreno.

infrendĕo -ēre, *to gnash with the teeth*.

infrēnis -e and **infrēnus** -a -um, *without bridle, unbridled*.

infrēno -are, *to bridle, rein ın, to restrain, check*.

infrĕquens -entis, *scanty, thin, not crowded*; of places, *not full, scantily populated*; of time, *infrequent*; of persons, *not doing a thing often*.

infrĕquentia -ae, f. *fewness, scantiness thinness*; of places, *emptiness, loneliness*.

infringo -fringĕre -frēgi -fractum, *to break*; *to weaken, impair, discourage*. Hence partic. **infractus** -a -um, *broken, weakened, impaired*.

infrons -frondis, *leafless*.

infructŭōsus -a -um, *unfruitful, unproductive*.

infūcātus -a -um, *coloured*.

infŭla -ae, f. *a band, bandage*; esp. *a fillet, a headband worn by priests, suppliants*, etc.

infundo -fundĕre -fūdi -fūsum, *to pour in or on*; with dat., *to pour out for*, hence *to administer*; se infundere, or pass. infundi, *to pour over*.

infusco -are, *to make dark, blacken; to disfigure, stain*.

ingĕmĭno -are: transit., *to redouble, repeat*; intransit., *to be redoubled, to increase*.

ingĕmisco -gĕmiscĕre (-escĕre) -gĕmŭi, *to sigh or groan over*.

ingĕmo -ĕre, *to sigh, groan over* (with dat.).

ingĕnĕro -are, *to implant, generate*.

ingĕnĭōsus -a -um, *talented, able*, of things, *requiring talent or naturally fit, adapted*. Adv. **ingĕnĭōsē,** *cleverly*.

ingĕnĭum -i, n. *nature, natural quality, constitution, character*, esp. *mental power, ability, genius*; meton., *a man of genius, or a clever invention*.

ingens -entis, *monstrous, vast, enormous*.

ingĕnŭĭtās -ātis, f. *free birth; noble-mindedness, uprightness, frankness*.

ingĕnŭus -a -um, *native, natural, innate; free-born, of free birth, worthy of a free man, noble, honourable, frank*. Adv. **ingĕnŭē.**

ingĕro -gĕrĕre -gessi gestum, *to carry or put in or upon; to press upon, force upon*; of abuse, *to heap on a person*.

ingigno only in perf. indic. **ingĕnŭi,** *I implanted,* and perf. partic. **ingĕnĭtus** -a -um, *implanted*.

inglōrĭus -a -um, *without fame, inglorious, undistinguished*.

inglŭvĭes -ēi, f. *crop, maw*; meton., *gluttony*.

ingrātĭīs or **ingrātĭs,** *unwillingly*.

ingrātus -a -um. (1) *unpleasant,*

unpleasing. (2) *unthankful, unrewarding.* Adv. **ingrātē,** *unwillingly; ungratefully.*

ingrăvesco -ĕre, *to become heavy; to become a burden, or become weary*; poet., *to become pregnant*.

ingrăvo -are, *to weigh down; to aggravate*.

ingrĕdĭor -grĕdi -gressus, dep. *to step in, enter, go in; to walk*. Transf., *to enter upon, begin on*; with infin., *to begin to*.

ingressĭo -ōnis, f. *an entering, going in; walking, gait, pace*. Transf., *beginning*.

ingressus -ūs, m. *going in, entering, entry*; milit., *an inroad; walking, stepping, movement*. Transf., *beginning*.

ingrŭo -ŭĕre -ŭi, *to fall upon, assail, attack*.

inguĕn -guĭnis, n. *the groin*.

ingurgĭto -are, with reflex., *to plunge oneself, or to glut, gorge oneself, gormandize*.

ingustātus -a -um, *untasted*.

inhăbĭlis -e, *unmanageable; unfit, ill-adapted*.

inhăbĭtābĭlis -e, *uninhabitable*.

inhăbĭto -are, *to inhabit*.

inhaerĕo -haerēre -haesi -haesum, *to stick in, cling to, cleave to*.

inhaeresco -haerescĕre -haesi -haesum, *to adhere to, begin to cling to*.

inhālo -are, *to breathe upon*.

inhĭbĕo -ēre -ŭi -ĭtum. (1) *to hold in, check, restrain*; naut., inhibere remis, navem retro inhibere, *to back water*. (2) *to practise, use, employ*.

inhĭbĭtĭo -ōnis, f. *restraining*; remigum, *backing water*.

inhĭo -are, *to gape*; hence *to covet, desire, long for*.

inhŏnesto -are, *to disgrace*.

inhŏnestus -a -um: morally, *degraded, dishonoured*; of things, *dishonourable, shameful*; physically, *ugly, unsightly*. Adv. **inhŏnestē,** *dishonourably*.

inhŏnōrātus -a -um, *not honoured; unrewarded*.

inhŏnōrus -a -um, *dishonoured*.

inhorrĕo -ēre, *to bristle*.

inhorresco -horrescĕre -horrŭi, *to begin to bristle, to bristle up; to shudder, quiver*, esp. from fright.

inhospĭtālis -e, *inhospitable*.

inhospĭtālĭtās -ātis, f. *want of hospitality*.

inhospĭtus -a -um, *inhospitable*.

inhūmānĭtās -ātis, f. *cruelty, inhumanity; incivility, discourtesy; stinginess, niggardliness*.

inhūmānus -a -um, *cruel, barbarous, inhuman; rude, uncivil; uncivilized*. Adv. **inhūmānē,** *inhumanly*; **inhūmānĭtĕr,** *uncivilly*.

inhŭmātus -a -um, *unburied*.

inĭbī, adv., *therein, in that place*; of time, *near at hand*.

inĭcĭo -ĭcĕre -ĭēci -iectum. (1) *to throw in, put in or into*. Transf., *to cause, inspire, occasion*; in conversation, *to throw in*. (2) *to throw on or over*;

manum inicere, *to lay hands on,
appropriate, take possession of.*
Transf., *to impose, lay on.*

iniectio -ōnis, f. *laying on.*

iniectus -ūs, m. *throwing on or over.*

inimicitia -ae, f. *enmity.*

inimico -are, *to make hostile, set at
variance.*

inimicus -a -um, *unfriendly, adverse,
hostile;* of things, *hurtful, prejudicial;*
m. or f. as subst., *enemy, foe.* Adv.
inimicē, *in an unfriendly manner.*

iniquitās -ātis, f. *unevenness; unfavourableness, difficulty; unfairness, injustice,
unreasonableness.*

iniquus -a -um, *uneven, unequal.*
Transf., of things, *excessive,
unbalanced, adverse, disadvantageous;*
of contests, *ill-matched;* of terms,
unfair; of persons, etc. *unkind,
unfavourable; perverse, disgruntled;*
animo iniquo ferre, *to take badly;*
m. pl. as subst. *enemies.* Adv.
iniquē, *unequally; unfairly, adversely.*

initio -are, *to initiate.*

initium -i, n. *a beginning;* ab initio,
from the start; initio, *at the start.*
Transf., in plur. *elements, first
principles; auspices; the beginning of
a reign; a secret worship, mysteries.*

initus -ūs, m. *an entrance; a beginning.*

iniucunditās -ātis, f. *unpleasantness.*

iniucundus -a -um, *unpleasant.*
Compar. adv. iniucundius.

iniudicātus -a -um, *undecided.*

iniungo -iungĕre -iunxi -iunctum,
*to join, attach, fasten to; to inflict
upon, bring upon.*

iniurātus -a -um, *unsworn.*

iniuria -ae, f. *injury, injustice, wrong;*
iniuriā, *wrongly.* Transf., *a
possession wrongfully obtained; revenge
for an affront.*

iniuriōsus -a -um, *doing wrong, unjust;
harmful.* Adv. iniuriōsē, *wrongfully.*

iniurius -a -um, *wrongful, unjust.*

iniussū, abl. sing. m. *without orders.*

iniussus -a -um, *unbidden, spontaneous.*

iniustitia -ae, f. *injustice; severity.*

iniustus -a -um, *unfair, unjust; harsh,
oppressive;* n. as subst. *injustice.*
Adv. iniustē.

inlābefactus -a -um, *unshaken, firm.*

inlābor -lābi -lapsus, dep. *to glide into,
fall into or upon.*

inlābōro -are, *to labour at.*

inlăcessītus -a -um, *unattacked, unprovoked.*

inlacrimābilis -e, *unwept; not to be
moved by tears, pitiless.*

inlacrimo -are, and inlacrimor -ari,
dep. *to weep over, bewail.*

inlaesus -a -um, *unhurt, uninjured.*

inlaetābilis -e, *gloomy, cheerless.*

inlăquĕo -are, *to entrap, ensnare.*

inlaudātus -a -um, *unpraised, obscure;
not to be praised, bad.*

inlautus = inlotus; q.v.

inlĕcebra -ae, f. *allurement, attraction,
charm; a decoy bird.*

inlĕcebrōsus -a -um, *attractive, enticing;* adv. inlĕcebrōsē.

¹inlectus -a -um, *unread.*

²inlectus -ūs, m. *enticement.*

³inlectus -a -um, partic. of inlicio;
q.v.

inlĕpĭdus -a -um, *inelegant, rude,
unmannerly;* adv. inlĕpĭdē.

¹inlex -licis, c. *a decoy, lure.*

²inlex -lēgis, *lawless.*

inlībātus -a -um, *undiminished, unimpaired.*

inlībĕrālis -e, *unworthy of a free man,
ungenerous, sordid, mean;* adv.
inlībĕrālĭtĕr.

inlībĕrālĭtās -ātis, f. *stinginess, meanness.*

inlicio -licĕre -lexi -lectum, *to entice,
allure, decoy.*

inlicĭtātor -ōris, m. *a sham bidder at
an auction, puffer.*

inlicĭtus -a -um, *not allowed, illegal.*

inlido -lidĕre -lisi -lisum, *to strike
beat, dash against.*

inlĭgo -are, *to bind, tie, fasten, attach
connect; to entangle, impede.*

inlimis -e, *free from mud, clean.*

inlĭno -linĕre -lēvi -lĭtum, *to smear,
daub; to spread something on a
surface or to spread a surface with
something.*

inlĭquĕfactus -a -um, *molten, liquefied.*

inlittĕrātus -a -um, *ignorant, illiterate.*

inlōtus (-lautus, -lūtus) -a -um,
unwashed, unclean.

inlūcesco (-isco) -lūcescĕre -luxi,
to become light, begin to shine; inlu-
cescit, *it grows light, is daylight.*

inlūdo -lūdĕre -lūsi -lūsum, *to play
with, sport with; to mock, laugh at,
ridicule; to maltreat.*

inlūmino -are, *to light up, illuminate;
to make clear, set off, adorn.* Adv.
from perf. partic. inlūmĭnātē,
luminously, clearly.

inlūsio -ōnis, f. *irony.*

inlustris -e, *light, bright, brilliant;
clear, plain, evident; distinguished,
famous.* Compar. adv. inlustrius,
more clearly, more distinctly.

inlustro -are, *to light up, make bright;
to bring to light, make clear; to make
illustrious, do honour to.*

inlŭviēs -ēi, f. *inundation, flood; mud,
dirt.*

inm-; see imm-.

innābilis -e, *that cannot be swum in.*

innascor -nasci -nātus, dep. *to be born
in, arise in or upon.*
Hence partic. innātus -a -um,
innate, inborn.

innăto -are, *to swim into; to swim or
float in or upon.*

innecto -nectĕre -nexŭi -nexum, *to tie
in, fasten, weave together;* fig., *to
put together, connect, entangle, implicate.*

innītor -nīti -nixus dep. *to lean upon,
support oneself by.*

inno -nare, *to swim in or on; to flow over;
to sail over, navigate.*

innŏcens -entis, *harmless, inoffensive,
blameless;* adv. innŏcentĕr.

innŏcentia -ae, f. *harmlessness, innocence, integrity.*

innŏcŭus -a -um: act., *innocuous, harmless, blameless*; pass., *unhurt, unharmed.* Adv. **innŏcŭē**, *harmlessly.*

innōtesco -nōtescĕre -nōtŭi *to become known or noted.*

innŏvo -are, *to renew.*

innoxius -a -um: act., *harmless, innocent*; pass., *unhurt, unharmed.*

innūba -ae, *unmarried, without a husband.*

innūbilus -a -um, *unclouded, clear.*

innūbo -nūbĕre -nupsi -nuptum, *to marry into.*

innŭmĕrābilis -e, *countless, innumerable*; adv. **innŭmĕrābilitĕr.**

innŭmĕrābilĭtās -ātis, f. *an infinite number.*

innŭmĕrālis -e, and **innŭmĕrus** -a -um, *countless, innumerable.*

innŭo -nŭĕre -nŭi -nūtum, *to give a nod to, make a sign to.*

innupta -ae, *unmarried*; as subst., *a maiden.*

innūtrĭo -ire, *to bring up in or among.*

ĭnoblītus -a -um, *mindful.*

ĭnobrūtus -a, -um, *not overwhelmed.*

ĭnobservābĭlis -e, *imperceptible.*

ĭnobservantĭa -ae, f. *negligence, carelessness.*

ĭnobservātus -a -um, *unperceived.*

ĭnoccĭdŭus -a -um, *never setting.*

ĭnoffensus -a -im, *not struck, not stumbling*; *unhindered, unobstructed.*

ĭnoffĭcĭōsus -a -um, *undutiful, disobliging.*

ĭnŏlens -entis, *without smell.*

ĭnŏlesco -ŏlescĕre -ŏlēvi, *to grow in or on.*

ĭnōmĭnātus -a -um, *inauspicious, unlucky.*

ĭnŏpĭa -ae, f. *want of means, need, poverty; helplessness.*

ĭnŏpīnans -antis, *not expecting, unawares*; adv. **ĭnŏpīnantĕr.**

ĭnŏpīnātus -a -um; pass., *unexpected, unlooked for*; (ex) inopinato, *unexpectedly*; act., *not expecting.*

ĭnŏpīnus -a -um, *unexpected, unlooked for.*

ĭnops -ŏpis, *poor, helpless, in need*; of language, *weak, poor.*

ĭnōrātus -a -um, *not brought forward and heard.*

ĭnordĭnātus -a -um, *disorderly, in confusion*: n. as subst. *disorder.*

ĭnornātus -a -um, *unadorned, plain; unpraised, uncelebrated.*

inp-; see **imp-**.

inquam, inquis, inquit, etc.; perf., inquii; *say.*

inquĭēs -ētis, *unquiet, restless.*

inquĭēto -are, *to disturb.*

inquĭētus -a -um, *unquiet, restless.*

inquĭlīnus -i, m. *tenant, lodger.*

inquĭno -are, *to befoul, pollute, stain, corrupt.* Hence partic. **inquĭnātus** -a -um, *dirty, foul, polluted*; adv. **inquĭnātē.**

inquīro -quīrĕre -quīsīvi -quīsītum, *to search for; to investigate, inquire into*; legal, *to search for evidence against anyone.*

inquīsītĭo -ōnis, f. *looking for, search*; esp. *search for evidence against; a looking into, investigation, inquiry.*

inquīsītor -ōris, m. *an inquirer; investigator*; legal, *one who searches for evidence to support an accusation.*

inrāsus -a -um, *unshaved.*

inraucesco -raucescĕre -rausi, *to become hoarse.*

inrēlĭgātus -a -um, *unbound.*

inrēlĭgĭōsus -a -um, *irreligious, impious*; adv. **inrēlĭgĭōsē.**

inrĕmĕābĭlis -e, *from which there is no return.*

inrĕpărābĭlis -e, *that cannot be restored, irrecoverable.*

inrĕpertus -a -um, *not discovered.*

inrēpo -rēpĕre -repsi -reptum, *to creep, crawl in; to insinuate oneself.*

inreprĕhensus -a -um, *unblamed, blameless.*

inrĕquĭētus -a -um, *restless, troubled.*

inrĕsectus -a -um, *uncut.*

inrĕsŏlūtus -a -um, *not loosed, not slackened.*

inrētĭo -ire, *to catch in a net, entangle.*

inrĕtortus -a -um, *not turned or twisted back.*

inrĕvĕrens -entis, *disrespectful*; adv. **inrĕvĕrentĕr.**

inrĕvĕrentĭa -ae, f. *want of respect, irreverence.*

inrĕvŏcābilis -e, *that cannot be called back, irrevocable; unalterable, implacable.*

inrĕvŏcātus -a -um, *not called back.*

inrīdĕo -rīdēre -rīsi -rīsum, *to laugh at, mock, ridicule.*

inrīdĭcŭlē, *without wit or humour.*

inrīdĭcŭlo, predicative dat., *for a laughing-stock.*

inrĭgātĭo -ōnis, f. *watering, irrigation.*

inrĭgo -are, *to conduct any liquid, to diffuse; to water, irrigate, inundate, flood over.*

inrĭgŭus -a -um: act., *watering, irrigating; refreshing*; pass., *watered, soaked.*

inrīsĭo -ōnis, f. *laughing at, mocking, derision.*

inrīsor -ōris, m. *a laugher, mocker, derider.*

inrīsus -ūs, m. *laughter, mockery, derision*; dat. inrisui, *for a laughing-stock.*

inrītābĭlis -e, *irritable, easily roused.*

inrītāmen -ĭnis, n. *incitement, inducement.*

inrītāmentum -i, m. *incitement, incentive.*

inrītātĭo -ōnis, f. *stirring up, provoking, incitement.*

inrīto -are, *to stir up, stimulate, incite, excite.*

inrītus -a -um, *void, invalid; vain, ineffectual, useless.*

inrŏgātĭo -ōnis, f. *the imposing of fine or penalty.*

inrŏgo -are, *to propose a measure against anyone; to inflict, impose.*

inrŏro -ae, *to moisten (with dew); to trickle down upon.*

inrumpo -rumpĕre -rūpi -ruptum, *to break in, burst in, rush in.*

inrŭo -rŭĕre -rŭi: transit., *to fling in*; intransit., *to rush in.*

inruptĭo -ōnis, f. *bursting in irruption.*

inruptus -a -um, *unbroken, unsevered.*

insălūbris -e, *unhealthy.*

insălūtātus -a -um, *ungreeted*

insānābĭlis -e, *incurable.*

insānĭa -ae, f. *madness, frenzy, senseless excess, extravagance; poetical rapture or inspiration.*

insānĭo -ire, *to be made, rage, rave; to be inspired.*

insānĭtās -ātis, f. *disease, unsoundness.*

insānus -a -um, *of unsound mind, mad, raving, senseless;* of poets, *inspired;* of things, *raging, stormy.* Adv. **insānē**, *madly.*

insătĭābĭlis -e: pass., *insatiable:* act., *that does not satiate, uncloying.* Adv. **insătĭābĭlĭtĕr**, *insatiably.*

insătŭrābĭlis -e, *insatiable;* adv. **insătŭrābĭlĭtĕr.**

inscendo -scendĕre -scendi -scensum, *to climb on, ascend, mount.*

inscĭens -entis, *not knowing fact, unaware;* in gen., *ignorant.* Adv. **inscĭentĕr.**

inscĭentĭa -ae, f. *ignorance, inexperience.*

inscĭtĭa -ae, f. *inexperience, want of skill, ignorance.*

inscītus -a -um, *ignorant, unskilful, stupid;* adv. **inscītē.**

inscĭus -a -um, *ignorant, not knowing.*

inscrībo -scrībĕre -scripsi -scriptum, *to write in or on, inscribe; to mark, impress; to entitle, mark as something; to ascribe, mark as belonging to.*

inscriptĭo -ōnis, f. *writing in or upon.*

¹inscriptus -a -um, *unwritten.*

²inscriptus -a -um, partic. from inscribo; q.v.

insculpo -sculpĕre -sculpsi -sculptum, *to cut or carve in, engrave.* Transf., *to impress.*

insĕco -sĕcare -sĕcŭi -sectum, *to cut into, notch.*

insectātĭo -ōnis, f. *close following, hot pursuit.* Transf., *abuse.*

insectātor -ōris, m. *pursuer, persecutor.*

insecto -are and **insector** -ari, dep. *to follow closely, pursue, harry; to harry with abuse, rail at, reproach.*

insĕdābĭlĭtĕr, *incessantly.*

insĕnesco -sĕnescĕre -sĕnŭi, *to grow old at or among.*

insensĭlis -e, *without sensation.*

insĕpultus -a -um, *unburied.*

insĕquor -sĕqui -sĕcūtus, dep., *to follow after, follow on;* in time, *to succeed; to pursue a subject; to pursue a person, to censure, reproach;* in gen., *to attack, assail.*

¹insĕro -sĕrĕre -sēvi -sĭtum, *to graft in, implant.* Hence partic. **insĭtus** -a -um, *implanted, innate; incorporated.*

²insĕro -sĕrĕre -sĕrŭi -sertum, *to let in, introduce, insert;* in gen., *to connect, put in or among.*

inserto -are, *to insert, put into.*

inservĭo -ire, *to be a slave, to serve; to be devoted to.*

insībĭlo -are, *to hiss, whistle in.*

insĭdĕo -ēre, *to sit in or on; to dwell, remain.*

insĭdĭae -arum, f. pl. *an ambush; a trap, plot.*

insĭdĭātor -ōris, m. *a man in ambush; a spy, waylayer.*

insĭdĭor -ari, dep., *to lie in ambush, lie in wait; to plot against, watch for.*

insĭdĭōsus -a -um, *deceitful treacherous;* adv. **insĭdĭōsē.**

insīdo -sīdĕre -sēdi -sessum, *to sit, settle, perch upon;* milit., *to occupy, beset;* of ideas, etc., *to sink in.*

insignĕ -is, n. *a distinguishing mark, token; badge, decoration, medal;* pl. as abstr., *distinctions, beauties.*

insignĭo -ire, *to mark, distinguish.* Hence partic. **insignītus** -a -um, *marked; conspicuous, clear;* adv. **insignītē**, *remarkably.*

insignis -e, *distinguished, remarkable, extraordinary;* adv. **insignĭtĕr.**

insīlĭa n. pl. *the treadles of a loom, or perhaps leash-rods.*

insĭlĭo -sĭlire -sĭlŭi, *to leap, spring, jump in or on.*

insĭmŭlātĭo -ōnis, f. *accusation, charge.*

insĭmŭlo -are, *to charge, accuse, esp. falsely.*

insincērus -a -um, *tainted.*

insĭnŭātĭo -ōnis, f., rhet. t. t., *gaining the favour of the audience.*

insĭnŭo -are, *to introduce by turning, to insinuate;* with (and occasionally without) reflex., *to penetrate, work one's way in.*

insĭpĭens -entis, *foolish;* adv. **insĭpĭentĕr.**

insĭpĭentĭa -ae, f. *foolishness.*

insisto -sistĕre -stĭti. (1) *to set foot on, tread on; to enter on a journey, road, etc., to set about a task;* with dat., *to follow hard upon, pursue.* (2) *to stand still in or on; to halt, stop, pause; to hesitate, doubt; to dwell upon a subject; to persist in a course.*

insĭtĭo -ōnis, f. *grafting.*

insĭtīvus -a -um, *grafted; spurious.*

insĭtor -ōris, m. *a grafter.*

insĭtus -a -um, partic. from insero; q.v.

insŏcĭābĭlis -e, *unable to combine.*

insōlābĭlĭtĕr, *inconsolably.*

insŏlens -entis, *contrary to custom.* Hence (1) *unaccustomed, unused.* (2) *unusual, excessive, extravagant; arrogant, insolent.* Adv. **insŏlentĕr**, *unusually, contrary to custom; excessively, extravagantly; haughtily, arrogantly.*

insŏlentĭa -ae, f. (1) *inexperience.* (2) *unusual character, novelty, extravagance, excess; pride, arrogance.*

insŏlesco -escĕre, *to become haughty or insolent.*

insŏlĭdus -a -um, *soft, tender.*

insŏlĭtus -a -um. (1) *unaccustomed.* (2) *unusual, strange, uncommon.*

insomnĭa -ae, f. *sleeplessness, loss of sleep.*

insomnis -e, *sleepless.*

insomnĭum -i, n. *a bad dream.*

insŏno -sŏnare -sŏnŭi, *to make a noise in or with; to sound, resound, bless.*

insons -sontis, *innocent, guiltless, harmless.*

insōpītus -a -um, *unsleeping, watchful.*

inspectĭo -ōnis, f. *scrutiny, consideration.*

inspecto -are, *to look at, observe.*

inspĕrans -antis, *not hoping, not expecting.*

inspĕrātus -a -um, *unhoped-for, unexpected.*

inspergo spergĕre -spersi -spersum, *to sprinkle in or on.*

inspĭcĭo -spĭcĕre -spexi -spectum. (1) *to look into, see into.* (2) *to view, examine, inspect; to consider.*

inspīco -are, *to sharpen to a point.*

inspīro -are, *to breathe upon, blow upon, inspire.*

inspŏliātus -a -um, *not plundered.*

instăbĭlis -e. (1) *unstable, unsteady, inconstant.* (2) *not supporting, insecure.*

instans -antis, and **instantĕr**; *from* insto; q.v.

instantĭa -ae, f. *presence; perseverance.*

instăr, n. (only nom. and acc. sing.), *an image, likeness;* usually with genit., in the sense *corresponding to, like.*

instaurātĭo -ōnis, f. *repetition, renewal.*

instaurātīvus -a -um, *renewed, repeated.*

instauro -are. (1) *to set up, establish.* (2) *to renew, restore;* hence *to repay, requite.*

insterno -sternĕre -strāvi -strātum, *to spread over, cover over;* equus instratus, *saddled.*

instĭgātor -oris, m. and **instĭgātrix** -tricis, f. *an instigator.*

instīgo -are, *to goad, incite, stimulate.*

instillo -are, *to drop in, pour in by drops, instil.*

instĭmŭlātor -ōris m. *an instigator*

instĭmŭlo -are, *to incite.*

instinctor -ōris, m. *an instigator.*

instinctū, abl. sing. m. *by instigation.*

instinctus -a -um, *instigated, incited, impelled.*

instĭta -ae, f. *border or flounce on a robe.*

instĭtĭo -ōnis, f. *standing still.*

instĭtor -ōris, m. *a hawker, pedlar.*

instĭtŭo -ŭĕre -ŭi -ūtum, *to put in place, set in order; to set up, make ready, build, construct;* abstr. *to establish, introduce, arrange; to settle on a course, to undertake, resolve, determine; to appoint* a person; *to instruct educate, train.*

instĭtūtĭo -ōnis, f. *arrangement; regular method; education, instruction.*

instĭtūtum -i, n. *an undertaking, purpose; an arrangement, institution, plan; an instruction, precept.*

insto -stare -stĭti. (1) *to stand in or on.* (2) *to be close to, follow closely, pursue eagerly; to devote oneself, persist, persevere; to insist, ask pressingly;* of time or events, *to approach, impend.*
    Hence partic. **instans** -antis,

present; pressing, urgent; adv. **instanter**, *urgently.*

instrēnŭus -a -um, *inactive, lazy.*

instrĕpo -ere -ŭi -ĭtum, *to rattle, clatter, creak.*

instructĭo -ōnis, f. *drawing up in order.*

instructor -ōris, m. *a preparer.*

instructus -ūs, m. *provision; matter* (in a speech).

instrūmentum -i, n. *equipment, tool, implement; dress; store, stock: any means to an end.*

instrŭo -strŭĕre -struxi -structum, *to build in or into; to set up, construct; furnish,* hence *to train* a person; *to prepare, provide;* milit., *to draw up in order of battle.*
    Hence partic. **instructus** -a -um, *equipped, supplied;* of persons, *trained, instructed.*

insuāvis -e, *unpleasant, disagreeable.*

Insubres -ium, *the Insubrians, a people in Cisalpine Gaul;* as adj. **Insŭbĕr** -bris -bre, *Insubrian.*

insūdo -are, *to sweat in or at.*

insuēfactus -a -um, *accustomed to.*

insuesco -suescĕre -suēvi -suētum; intransit., *to become used to;* transit., *to accustom, habituate anyone to.*

[1]insuētus -a -um: of persons, *unaccustomed, unused to;* of things, *unaccustomed, unusual.*

[2]insuētus -a -um, partic. from insuesco; q.v.

insŭla -ae, f. *an island.* Transf., *a detached house or block of flats.*

insŭlānus -i, m. *an islander.*

insulsĭtās -ātis, f. *tastelessness, absurdity.*

insulsus -a -um, *unsalted, insipid; tasteless, foolish;* adv. **insulsē.**

insulto -are, *to leap, prance in or on; to triumph over, insult.*

insum -esse -fŭi, *to be in or on; to be contained in, belong to.*

insūmo -sūmĕre -sumpsi -sumptum, *to take for a purpose, to expend.*

insŭo -sŭĕre -sutum, *to sew in, sew up.*

insŭpĕr: adv. *above, overhead; over and above, in addition, besides;* prep., with abl., *besides.*

insŭpĕrābĭlis -e, *insurmountable, impassable; unconquerable.*

insurgo -surgĕre -surrexi -surrectum, *to rise up, raise oneself up; to increase in power or force;* with dat., *to rise up against.*

insŭsurro -are, *to whisper, whisper in the ear.*

intābesco -tābescĕre -tābŭi, *to melt or wither away gradually.*

intactĭlis -e, *that cannot be touched.*

[1]intactus -a -um, *untouched; untried unspoilt, unhurt, virgin.*

[2]intactus -ūs, m. *intangibility.*

intămĭnātus -a -um, *unstained.*

[1]intectus -a -um, *uncovered, unclothed; open, frank.*

[2]intectus -a -um, partic. from intego; q.v.

intĕgellus -a -um, *more or less pure, undamaged.*

intĕger -gra -grum. (1) *complete,*

whole, entire, intact; fresh, sound, unexhausted; in integrum restituere, *to restore to its former condition.* (2) in quality, *unspoilt, pure, fresh;* morally, *innocent, uncorrupted:* in thought or feeling, *balanced, unbiased, impartial;* of matters for discussion or action, *unprejudiced, undecided;* integrum est mihi, *I am at liberty.* (3) *renewed, begun afresh.* Hence adv. **integrē** *wholly; honestly, uprightly, impartially;* of style, *purely, correctly.*

intĕgo -tĕgĕre -texi -tectum, *to cover, protect.*

integrasco -ĕre, *to break out afresh.*

integrātio -ōnis, f. *renewing.*

integritās -ātis, f. *unimpaired condition, soundness, health; uprightness, integrity;* of style, *purity, correctness.*

integro -are, *to make whole, heal, refresh; to renew, begin afresh.*

intĕgŭmentum -i, n. *a covering, cloak, disguise.*

intellectus -ūs, m. *understanding, comprehension.*

intellĕgentia -ae, f. *perception; understanding, knowledge, taste; capacity for understanding, intelligence.*

intellĕgo -lĕgĕre -lexi -lectum, *to discern, perceive; to understand, grasp; to understand* character, *judge, appreciate; to understand by a term, take as its meaning.*
Hence partic. **intellĕgens** -entis, *intelligent, understanding; having good sense* or *taste.* Adv. **intellĕgentĕr.**

intĕmĕrātus -a -um, *unspotted, undefiled.*

intĕmpĕrans -antis, *extravagant, unrestrained, intemperate;* adv. **intempĕrantĕr.**

intĕmpĕrantia -ae, f. *want of restraint, extravagance, excess.*

intĕmpĕrātus -a -um, *intemperate, immoderate;* adv. **intempĕrātē.**

intĕmpĕriēs -ēi, f. *wildness, lack of restraint, excess.*

intĕmpestīvus -a -um, *unseasonable, untimely; immoderate.* Adv. **intempestīvē,** *unseasonably.*

intĕmpestus -a -um, *unwholesome, unhealthy:* intempesta nox, *the dead of night.*

intemptātus -a -um, *untried.*

intendo -tendĕre -tendi -tentum. (1) *to stretch, strain;* abstr., *to maintain, try to prove.* (2) *to extend, aim, direct;* esp. *to direct one's course; to apply the mind, direct the thoughts; to intend, aim at.*
Hence partic. **intentus** -a -um, *stretched, tense, taut;* of thought or feeling, *anxious, intent;* of speech, *earnest;* in gen, *thorough, strict, rigorous.* Adv. **intentē,** *earnestly, attentively.*

¹**intentātus** -a -um; = intemptatus; q.v.

²**intentatus** -a -um, partic., from intento; q.v.

intentio -ōnis, f. *stretching, straining;* of the mind, *effort, exertion, attention; an attack, accusation.*

intento -are, *to stretch towards* or *against,* esp. *threateningly.*

¹**intentus** -ūs, m. *stretching out.*

²**intentus** -a -um, partic. from intendo; q.v.

intĕpesco -tĕpescĕre -tĕpui, *to become lukewarm.*

inter, prep. with acc. *between, among, amid; during, in the course of a* period; with pronouns, inter se, inter nos, etc., *between one another, mutually.*

intĕrāmenta -orum, n. pl. *woodwork of a ship.*

intĕrāresco -ĕre, *to become dry, decay.*

intercălāris -e and **intercălārius** -a -um, *inserted, intercalary.*

intercălo -are, *to insert;* esp. *to intercalate a day* or *month in the calendar.*

intercăpēdo -ĭnis, f. *interval, pause, respite.*

intercēdo -cēdĕre -cessi -cessum, *to go between, come between, intervene;* legal, *to interpose, stand surety; to step between, withstand, protest against.*

interceptio -ōnis, f. *taking away.*

interceptor -ōris, m. *one who takes away, an embezzler.*

intercessio -ōnis, f. legal, *becoming surety, going bail;* polit., *an exercise by the tribunes of their veto.*

intercessor -ōris, m. legal, *surety, bail;* polit., *one who opposes, an obstructor.*

¹**intercido** -cīdĕre -cīdi -cīsum, *to cut asunder, to demolish,* Hence adv. **intercīsē,** *piecemeal.*

²**intercido** -cĭdĕre -cĭdi. (1) *to fall between, intervene.* (2) *to drop out, be lost, be forgotten, perish.*

intercino -ere, *to sing between.*

intercĭpio -cĭpĕre -cēpi -ceptum, *to take by the way, intercept; to embezzle, appropriate;* through death, *to cut off, carry off prematurely;* of roads, *to block.*

interclūdo -clūdĕre -clūsi -clūsum, *to shut off, block, hinder; to enclose, shut in.*

interclūsio -ōnis, f. *stopping* or *blocking up; parenthesis.*

intercŏlumnium -i, n. *the space between two columns.*

intercurro -currĕre -cŭcurri -cursum, *to run between, to run through; to intercede; to be among, mingle with; to hasten in the meanwhile.*

intercurso -are, *to run between, run among.*

intercursū, abl. sing. m. *by running between, by the interposition.*

intercŭs -cŭtis, *under the skin:* aqua, *the dropsy.*

interdīco -dīcĕre -dixi -dictum. (1) *to stop by interposition, forbid, prohibit;* interdicĕre aqua et igni, with dat., *to outlaw.* (2) *to make an injunction, to order.*

interdictio -ōnis, f. *forbidding, prohibition:* aquae et ignis, *outlawing.*

interdictum -i, n. *a prohibition; a praetor's interdict* or *provisional order.*

interdĭū (interdĭus), *in the daytime, by day.*

interdo -dăre -dătum, *to put between or among, distribute.*

interductus -ū, m. *interpunctuation.*

interdum, *sometimes, now and then.*

interdŭo = interdo; q.v.

intĕrĕā, *meanwhile*; sometimes *nevertheless, notwithstanding.*

intĕremptor -ōris, m. *a murderer.*

intĕrĕo -ire -ii -ĭtum, *to be lost, to perish.*

intĕrĕquĭto -are, *to ride between.*

interfātĭo -onis, f. *speaking between, interruption.*

interfātur -fāri -fātus, dep. forms, *to speak between, interrupt.*

interfectĭo -ōnis, f. *slaying.*

interfector -ōris, m. *murderer.*

interfectrix -trīcis, f. *murderess.*

interfĭcĭo -fĭcĕre -fēci -fectum, *to do away with, destroy, put an end to, kill.*

interfĭo -fĭĕri, *to perish.*

interflŭo -flŭĕre -fluxi -fluxum, *to flow between.*

interfŏdĭo -fŏdĕre -fōdi -fossum, *to dig into, pierce.*

interfor; see interfatur.

interfŭgĭo -fŭgĕre, *to flee between.*

interfulgens -entis, *shining or gleaming among.*

interfūsus -a -um, *poured between, flowing between*; maculis interfusa, *stained here and there.*

interĭăcĕo -ēre, *to lie between or among.*

interĭăcĭo = interĭcĭo; q.v.

intĕrĭbi, *meanwhile.*

interĭcĭo -icere -ieci -iectum, *to throw, cast, put, among or between*; anno interiecto, *after an interval of a year.*

interiectĭo -ōnis, f. *interjection or parenthesis.*

interiectus -ūs, m. *throwing between*; of time, *an interval.*

intĕrim, *meanwhile*; sometimes *however.*

intĕrĭmo -ĭmĕre -ēmi -emptum, *to take away, destroy, make an end of; to put out of the way, kill.*

intĕrĭor -ĭus, genit. -ōris, *inner, interior*; *remote from the sea, inland, nearer*; in racing, *on the inside.* Transf., *more secret, more intimate.* Superl. **intĭmus** -a -um; q.v. Adv. **interĭus**, *more inwardly*; *short, not far enough.*

intĕritĭo -ōnis, f. *destruction, ruin.*

intĕrĭtus -ūs, m. *destruction, ruin.*

interiungo -iungĕre -iunxi -iunctum, *to join together, connect*; also *to unyoke.*

intĕrĭus; see interior.

interlābor -lābi -lapsus, dep. *to glide, flow between.*

interlĕgo -ĕre, *to pluck here and there.*

interlĭno -linĕre -lēvi -lĭtum, *to daub between*; *to erase, falsify by erasure.*

interlŏquor -lŏqui -lŏcūtus, dep. *to interrupt a person speaking.*

interlūcĕo -lūcēre -luxi, *to shine or gleam between*; *to be transparent, let light through gaps.*

interlūnĭum -i, n. *change of moon, time of new moon.*

interlŭo -lŭĕre, *to wash between.*

intermenstrŭus -a -um, *between two months*; n. as subst. *the time of the new moon.*

¹**intermĭnātus** -a -um, *unbounded, boundless.*

²**intermĭnātus** -a -um, partic. from interminor; q.v.

intermĭnor -ari, dep. *to threaten, forbid with threats*; perf. partic. in pass. sense, *forbidden with threats.*

intermiscĕo -miscēre, -miscŭi -mixtum, *to mix with, intermix.*

intermissĭo -ōnis, f. *leaving off, interruption.*

intermitto -mittĕre -mīsi -missum: transit., *to leave a space between, leave free*; in space, *to separate, break off*; in time, *to let pass*; in gen., *to discontinue, interrupt*; vento intermisso, *the wind having dropped*; intransit., *to cease, leave off.*

intermŏrĭor -mŏri -mortuus, dep. *to die off, perish suddenly*; partic. **intermortŭus** -a -um, *swooning, half-dead*; fig., *lifeless.*

intermundĭa -ōrum, n. pl. *spaces between the worlds.*

intermūrālis -e, *between walls.*

internascor -nasci -natus, dep. *to grow between or among.*

internĕcĭo -ōnis, f. *extermination, massacre.*

internĕcīvus (-nĕcīnus) -a -um, *murderous, deadly.*

internĕco -are, *to exterminate.*

internecto -ĕre, *to bind together, bind up.*

internōdĭum -i, n. *the space between two knots or joints.*

internosco -noscĕre -nōvi -nōtum, *to distinguish between.*

internuntĭa -ae, f. *a female messenger or go-between.*

internuntĭo -are, *to send messengers between parties.*

internuntĭus -i, m. *a messenger, mediator, go-between.*

internus -a, -im., *inward, internal; domestic, civil.*

interpellātĭo -ōnis, f. *interruption.*

interpellātor -ōris, m. *interrupter, disturber.*

interpello -are, *to interrupt, disturb, impede, obstruct.*

interpŏlo -are, *to furbish, vamp up; to falsify.*

interpōno -pōnĕre -pŏsŭi -pŏsĭtum, *to place between or among, interpose*; spatio interposito, *after an interval*; fidem, *to pledge one's word*; rarely, *to falsify*; with reflex., *to engage in, interfere with.*

interpŏsĭtĭo -ōnis, f. *putting in, insertion, introduction*; rhet. *parenthesis.*

interpŏsĭtū, abl. sing. m. *by putting between, by interposition.*

interprĕs -prĕtis, c. (1) *a negotiator, mediator, messenger.* (2) *an expounder, explainer; prophet, prophetess; interpreter; translator.*

interprĕtātĭo -ōnis, f., *explanation, interpretation; translation.* Transf., *meaning, signification.*

interprĕtor -ari, dep. (1) *to put an interpretation upon, understand in a certain sense.* (2) *to translate.*

interpunctio -ōnis, f. *punctuation.*

interpungo -pungĕre -punxi -punctum, *to punctuate;* partic. **interpunctus** -a -um, *well-divided.*

interquiesco -quiescĕre -quiĕvi -quiĕtum, *to pause between.*

interregnum -i, n. *a period between two reigns, interregnum.*

interrex -rēgis m. *a regent, temporary king* or *chief magistrate.*

interritus -a -um, *undaunted.*

interrŏgātio -ōnis, f. *questioning, interrogation:* esp. legal, *examination of witnesses;* in logic, *an argument, syllogism;* gram., *interrogation.*

interrŏgo -are, *to ask, question, interrogate;* esp. *to examine* a witness, or *to accuse, bring an action against.*

interrumpo -rumpĕre -rūpi -ruptum, *to break in the middle, sever, interrupt, disturb.* Adv. from partic. **interruptē**, *interruptedly, disconnectedly.*

intersaepio -saepire -saepsi -saeptum, *to enclose, hem in, block up.*

interscindo -scindĕre -scīdi -scissum, *to cut open, cut off, tear apart.*

interscribo -ĕre, *to write between.*

¹**intersĕro** -sĕrĕre -sēvi -sītum, *to sow* or *plant between.*

²**intersĕro** -sĕrĕre -sĕrŭi, *to put* or *place between.*

interspīrātio -ōnis, f. *breathing between, taking breath.*

interstinctus -a -um, *spotted, speckled.*

interstinguo -ĕre, *to extinguish.*

interstringo -ĕre, *to squeeze tight.*

intersum -esse -fŭi, *to be between; to be among, be present at, take part in* (with dat.); in time, *to intervene;* abstr., *to be between as a difference;* rarely *to differ, be different.* Hence impers. **intĕrest**, *it makes a difference, it concerns;* magni (or multum) meā interest, *it makes a great difference to me.*

intertextus -a -um, *interwoven.*

intertrīmentum -i, n. *loss, damage.*

interturbātio -ōnis, f. *disturbance, disquiet.*

intervallum -i, n. *distance between, interval* (of time or space); *difference, unlikeness.*

intervĕnio -vĕnire -vēni -ventum, *to come between, intervene; to interrupt* (with dat.) *to delay* (with acc.)

interventor -ōris, m. *an interrupting visitor.*

interventus -ūs, m. *intervention, interference.*

interverto (**-vorto**) -vertĕre -verti -versum, *to intercept; to embezzle, purloin; to cheat, rob.*

intervīso -vīsĕre -vīsi -vīsum, *to look in at, visit from time to time.*

intestābilis -e, *disqualified, dishonoured, infamous.*

intestātus -a -um, *having made no will, intestate;* n. abl. as adv. intestato, *intestate.*

intestīnus -a -um, *inward, internal;*

n. as subst., sing. and plur. *the intestines.*

intexo -texĕre -texŭi -textum, *to weave in, plait in, interweave; to weave around, wind around.*

intībum -i, n. *endive, succory.*

intĭmus (**intŭmus**) -a -um, superl. (compar. interior; q.v.), *innermost, inmost; most profound, most secret, intimate;* m. as subst., *an intimate friend.* Adv. **intĭmē**. *intimately; cordially, strongly.*

intingo (**-tinguo**) -tingĕre -tinxi -tinctum, *to dip in.*

intŏlĕrābĭlis -e, *unbearable, intolerable.*

intŏlĕrandus -a -um, *unbearable, unendurable.*

intŏlĕrans -antis: act. *impatient, unable to bear;* pass., *unbearable, intolerable.* Adv. **intŏlĕrantĕr**, *immoderately, impatiently.*

intŏlĕrantĭa -ae, f. *insufferable conduct, insolence.*

intŏno -tŏnare -tŏnŭi, *to thunder, thunder forth* (esp. of speakers).

intonsus -a -um, *unshorn, with long hair* or *beard;* hence of persons *rude, rough;* of country, *wooded, not cleared.*

intorquĕo -torquēre -torsi -tortum, *to twist* or *turn round;* of weapons, *to hurl;* partic. **intortus** -a -um, *twisted, tangled.*

intrā: adv. *inside;* prep., with acc. *inside, within, less than, short of.*

intrābilis -e, *that can be entered, accessible.*

intractābilis -e, *unmanageable, intractable.*

intractātus -a -um, *not handled; unattempted.*

intrĕmisco -trĕmiscĕre -trĕmŭi, *to begin to tremble.*

intrĕmo -ĕre, *to tremble, quake.*

intrĕpidus -a -um, *unconfused, calm;* adv. **intrĕpidē**, *calmly.*

intrīco -are, *to confuse, entangle.*

intrinsĕcus, *inside, inwardly, inwards.*

¹**intrītus** -a -um, *not worn away, unexhausted.*

²**intrītus** -a -um, partic. from intero; q.v.

¹**intrō**, *inwards, within.*

²**intro** -are, *to go into, enter.*

intrŏdūco -dūcĕre -duxi -ductum, *to introduce, bring in, bring forward, present, suggest.*

intrŏductĭo -ōnis, f. *bringing in, introduction.*

intrŏĕo -ire -ĭi -ĭtum, *to go into, enter.*

intrŏfĕro -ferre -tŭli -lātum, *to carry in.*

intrŏgrĕdĭor -grĕdi -gressus, dep. *to enter.*

intrŏĭtus -ūs, m. *an entrance; means of entrance; passage;* in gen., *beginning, introduction.*

intrōmitto -mittĕre -mīsi -missum, *to send in, allow to enter.*

introrsŭs (**-orsum**), *inwards, inwardly internally.*

intrōrumpo -rumpĕre -rūpi -ruptum, *to break into, enter by force.*

introspĭcĭo -spĭcĕre -spexi -spectum,

io look into, look inside, observe, examine.

intŭbum -i, n., see intibum.

intŭĕor -tŭēri -tūtus, dep. *to look at attentively, gaze at; to consider, contemplate, look to.*

intŭmesco -tŭmescĕre -tŭmŭi, *to swell, swell up; to increase; to swell with anger.*

intŭmŭlātus -a -um, *unburied.*

intŭor -i, dep. = intueor; q.v.

inturbĭdus -a -um, *undisturbed, quiet.*

intŭs, adv. *within, inside; to or from the inside; inwardly.*

intūtus -a -um. (1) *unprotected.* (2) *unsafe, dangerous.*

inŭla -ae, f. *the plant elecampane.*

inultus -a -um. (1) *unavenged.* (2) *unpunished.*

inumbro -are, *to shade, overshadow.*

inundātĭo -ōnis, f. *inundation, flood.*

inundo -are: transit., *to overflow, inundate, stream over;* intransit., *to overflow with.*

inungo -ungĕre -unxi -unctum, *to anoint.*

inurbānus -a -um, *rude, unpolished;* adv. **inurbānē.**

inurgĕo -urgēre -ursi, *to push, thrust against.*

inūro -ūrĕre -ussi -ustum, *to burn in or on, brand, imprint; to inflict; to crimp, curl, adorn.*

inūsĭtātus -a -um, *unusual, strange, uncommon;* adv. **inūsĭtātē.**

inūtĭlis -e, *useless, unserviceable, unprofitable; injurious, harmful.* Adv. **inūtĭlĭtēr.**

inūtĭlĭtās -ātis, f. *uselessness, unprofitableness; harmfulness.*

invādo -vādĕre -vāsi -vāsum. (1) *to go in, enter, get in; to undertake.* (2) *to attack, fall upon, assail, usurp, seize.*

invălesco -vălescĕre -vălŭi, *to gather strength, become strong.*

invălĭdus -a -um, *weak, powerless.*

invectĭo -ōnis, f. (1) *importation.* (2) *invective.*

invĕho -vĕhĕre -vexi -vectum, *to carry in, introduce;* pass., or with reflex., *to drive, ride or travel,* esp. *to advance against, attack;* of verbal attack, *to inveigh.*

invĕnĭo -vĕnīre -vēni -ventum, *to come upon, find, meet with, discover; to invent, devise; to procure, get, earn;* pass., or with reflex., *to show oneself.*

Hence partic., **inventus** -a -um, *discovered;* n. as subst. *an invention, discovery.*

inventĭo -ōnis, f. *inventing, invention; the inventive faculty.*

inventor -ōris, m. and **inventrix** -trīcis, f. *inventor.*

invĕnustus -a -um, *not charming, unattractive; unhappy in love.*

invĕrēcundus -a -um, *shameless, impudent.*

invergo -ĕre, *to tip or pour upon.*

inversĭo -ōnis, f. *irony; transposition; allegory.*

inverto -vertĕre -verti -versum *to*

turn over, turn about; to transpose, alter, pervert. Hence partic. **inversus** -a -um, *overturned, upside down.*

invespĕrascit -ĕre, impers. *it grows dark.*

investīgātĭo -ōnis, f. *inquiry, investigation.*

investīgātor -ōris, m. *inquirer, investigator.*

investīgo -are, *to search out, track out.*

invĕtĕrasco -ascĕre -avi, *to become old; to become obsolete; to become established, fixed, rooted.*

invĕtĕrātĭo -ōnis, f. *inveterateness, permanence.*

invĕtĕrātus -a -um, *of long standing, established.*

invĭcem, *in turn, alternately; mutually, reciprocally.*

invictus -a -um, *unconquered, unsubdued; unconquerable, invincible.*

invĭdentĭa -ae, f. *envying, envy.*

invĭdĕo -vĭdēre -vĭdi -vīsum, *to envy, grudge, be envious of.*

Hence partic. **invīsus** -a -um: pass., *hated;* act., *hostile.*

invĭdĭa -ae, f.: act., *envy, jealousy, ill-will;* pass., *odium, unpopularity.* Transf., *a source of ill-will.*

invĭdĭōsus -a -um, *envious; causing envy, envied; hateful.* Adv. **invĭdĭōsē,** *jealously, bitterly.*

invĭdus -a -um, *envious, grudging.*

invĭgĭlo -are, *to watch over* (with dat.).

invĭŏlābĭlis -e, *unassailable.*

invĭŏlātus -a -um, *uninjured, unhurt; inviolable.* Adv. **invĭŏlātē,** *inviolately.*

invīsĭtātus -a -um, *not seen; unusual, strange.*

invīso -vīsĕre -vīsi -vīsum, *to go to see, visit; to inspect, look at.*

¹**invīsus** -a -um, *unseen, secret.*

²**invīsus** -a -um, partic. from invideo; q.v.

invītāmentum -i, n. *invitation, attraction.*

invītātĭo -ōnis, f. *invitation, inducement.*

invītātū, abl. sing. m. *by invitation.*

invīto -are, *to invite, summon; to receive, entertain; to induce, allure;* with reflex., *to treat oneself.*

invītus -a -um, *unwilling, against one's will;* abl. absol., me invito, *against my will.* Adv. **invītē,** *unwillingly, against one's will.*

invĭus -a -um, *impassable, impenetrable;* n. pl. as subst., *trackless places.*

invŏcātĭo -ōnis, f. *calling upon, invocation.*

¹**invŏcātus** -a -um, *uncalled, uninvited.*

²**invŏcātus** -a -um, partic. from invoco; q.v.

invŏco -are, *to call in, call upon for help, invoke.*

invŏlātū, abl. sing. m., *by the flight.*

invŏlĭto -are, *to float or wave over.*

invŏlo -are, *to fly at, seize or pounce upon.*

invŏlūcrum -i, n. *a wrap, cover.*

invŏlvo -volvĕre -volvi -vŏlūtum, *to roll in or on; to envelop, wrap up, cover.* Hence partic. **invŏlūtus** -a -um, *rolled up; involved.*

invulgo -are, *to give information.*
invulnĕrātus -a -um, *unwounded.*
¹ĭō, interj., *hurrah! hi!*
²Ĭō (Ĭōn) -ūs (-ōnis), f. *an Argive girl, loved by Jupiter and changed into a cow;* adj. **Iōnīus** -a -um, *Ionian, of the sea between Italy and Greece, across which Io swam.*
iŏcātĭō -ōnis, f. *joke, jest.*
iŏco -are and iŏcor -ari, dep. *to joke, jest.*
iŏcōsus -a -um, *humorous, merry, facetious;* adv. **iŏcōsē.**
iŏcŭlāris -e, *jocular, laughable;* adv. **iŏcŭlārĭtĕr.**
iŏcŭlārĭus -a -um, *laughable, droll.*
iŏcŭlātor -ōris, m. *joker.*
iŏcŭlor -ari, dep. *to joke, jest.*
iŏcus -i, m. (plur. ioci and iŏca), *a joke, jest.*
Iŏnes -um, m. *the Ionians;* **Iōnĭa** -ae, f. *their country in Asia Minor;* adj. **Iōnĭăcus** and **Iōnĭcus** -a -um, *Ionian.*
Iphĭgĕnĭa -ae, f. *daughter of Agamemnon.*
ipse -a -um, *self;* ego ipse, *I myself; the very, actual;* with numbers, etc., *just, exactly;* of action, *by oneself, of one's own accord.*
ira -ae, f. *wrath, anger, rage;* meton., *cause of anger.*
īrācundĭa -ae, f. (1) *angry disposition, irascibility.* (2) *state of anger, fury, wrath.*
īrācundus -a -um, *inclined to anger, irascible;* adv. **īrācundē**, *wrathfully.*
īrascor -i, dep. *to grow angry* (with dat.); partic. **īrātus** -a -um, *angry.*
Īris -rĭdis, f. *messenger of the gods, and goddess of the rainbow.*
īrōnĭa -ae, f. *irony.*
irr-; see in-.
īs, ĕa, ĭd, *he, she, it; this* or *that (person* or *thing);* with qui (or ut), *one (of those) who, such . . . as;* with et, -que, etc., *and that too, and what is more;* in sing. id, *on that account;* id temporis, *at that time;* in eo est, *the position is such,* or, *it depends on this;* id est, *that is,* in explanation.
Īsis -is and -ĭdis, f., *the Egyptian goddess Isis.*
istāc, *by that way.*
iste ista istŭd, demonstr. pron. or adj. *that of yours, that beside you;* in speeches, referring to parties opposed to the speaker (opp. to hic, *my client);* often contemptuous.
Ister = Hister; q.v.
Isthmus (-os) -i, m., *the Isthmus of Corinth.*
¹istic istaec istōc or istŭc, *that of yours.*
²istic, adv. *over there, there by you; therein, in that.*
istinc, *from over there, thence.*
istīusmŏdī or istīus mŏdī or istĭmŏdī, *of that kind, such.*
istō, adv., *thither, to that place* or *thing.*
istōc and istŭc, *thither.*
Istri; see Histri.
ĭtă, *so, thus;* interrog., itane? *really?*

in answers, *certainly;* in narration, *and so;* with adj. or adv., *so, so very;* ita . . . ut, with subjunc., *in such a way that,* or *only to the extent that, only on condition that.*
Ītăli -orum and -um, m. *the Italians;* **Ītălĭa** -ae, f. *Italy;* adj. **Ītălĭcus** and **Ītălus** -a -um, *Italian;* f. adj. **Ītălis** -ĭdis.
ĭtăquĕ, *and so; therefore, for that reason.*
ĭtem, *also, likewise.*
ĭtĕr, ĭtĭnĕris, n. *going, way, direction; journey, march; right of way, permission to march;* concr., *way, road;* fig., *way, course, method.*
ĭtĕrātĭo -ōnis, f. *repetition, iteration.*
ĭtĕro -are, *to do a second time, repeat, renew.*
ĭtĕrum, *again, a second time;* iterum atque interum, *again and again.*
Ĭthăca -ae and Ĭthăcē -ēs, f., *an island in the Ionian Sea, home of Ulysses.*
ĭtĭdem, *likewise.*
ĭtĭo -ōnis, f. *going, travelling.*
ĭto -are, *to go.*
ĭtus -ūs, m. *movement, going, departure.*
¹iŭba -ae, f. *mane, crest.*
²Iŭba -ae, m. *name of two Numidian kings.*
iŭbăr -ăris, n. *beaming light, radiance; a heavenly body,* esp. *the sun.*
iŭbātus -a -um, *having a mane, crested.*
iŭbĕo iŭbēre iussi iussum, *to order, command, bid;* salvere iubere, *to greet;* polit. *to ratify an order.* Hence, from perf. partic. **iussum** -i, n., *an order, command.*
iūcundĭtās -ātis, f., *pleasantness, delightfulness, pleasure.*
iūcundus -a -um, *pleasant, agreeable, delightful;* adv. **iūcundē.**
Iūdaea -ae, f. *Judea* or *Palestine;* adj. and subst. **Iūdaeus** -a -um, *Jewish* or *a Jew.*
iūdex -ĭcis, m. *a judge;* in plur., *a panel of jurors.*
iūdĭcātĭo -ōnis, f. *judicial investigation; judgment, opinion.*
iūdĭcātus -ūs, m., *the office* or *business of a judge.*
iūdĭcĭālis -e and iūdĭcĭārĭus -a -um, *of a court of justice, judicial.*
iūdĭcĭum -i, n., *a trial, legal investigation; a law-court; jurisdiction; judgment, considered opinion, decision; power of judging, discernment, understanding, good judgment.*
iūdĭco -are, *to be a judge, judge, decide, declare;* perf. partic. **iūdĭcātus** -a -um, *of persons, condemned;* of things, *decided.*
iŭgālis -e, *yoked together;* m. pl. as subst. *a team of horses.* Transf., *matrimonial, nuptial.*
iŭgātĭo -ōnis, f. *the training of vines on a trellis.*
iŭgĕrum -i, n. *a measure of land,* about two-thirds of an English acre.
iŭgis -e, *perpetual, continuous,* esp. of water.
iŭglans -glandis, f., *a walnut* or *walnut-tree.*

iŭgo -are, *to bind together, connect, couple.*

iŭgōsus -a -um, *mountainous.*

iŭgŭlo -are, *to cut the throat of, to butcher; to ruin, destroy.*

iŭgŭlum -i, n. and **iŭgŭlus** -i, m. *the throat.*

iŭgum -i, n. (1) *a yoke or collar.* Transf., *a team of oxen or horses; a pair, couple; a chariot; any bond, union; the bond of love, marriage-tie; the yoke of slavery.* (2) *a cross-bar;* esp. *the yoke under which the vanquished were sent; the beam of a pair of scales; a ridge between mountains;* plur., poet., *mountain heights.*

Iŭgurtha -ae, m. *a king of Numidia;* adj. **Iŭgurthīnus** -a -um.

Iūlĭus -a -um, *name of a Roman gens; including the family of the Caesars; mensis Iulius or Iulius, the month of July.*

Iūlus -i, m., *son of Aeneas.*

iūmentum -i n. *a beast of burden.*

iuncĕus -a -um, *made of rushes; like a rush.*

iuncōsus -a -um, *full of rushes, rushy.*

iunctĭo -ōnis, f. *joining, connexion.*

iunctūra -ae, f., *a joining, joint; relationship; combination, putting together.*

iuncus -i, m. *a rush.*

iungo iungĕre iunxi iunctum, *to join, unite, connect; to yoke, harness; to mate; amicitiam, to form.*
Hence partic. **iunctus** -a -um, *connected, united, associated.*

iūnĭor; see iuvenis.

iūnĭpĕrus -i, f. *the juniper-tree.*

Iūnĭus -a -um, *the name of a Roman gens; mensis Iunius or Iunius, the month of June.*

Iūno -ōnis, f. *the goddess Juno, Greek Hera, sister and wife of Jupiter;* adj. **Iūnōnĭus** -a -um, *Junonian.*

Iuppĭter, Iŏvis, m. *Jupiter, the Roman supreme god;* sub Iove, *in the open air.*

iūrātor -ōris, m. *a sworn assessor.*

iūrēiŭro -are, *to swear an oath.*

iūrĕpĕrītus = iurisperitus; q.v.

iurgĭum -i, n., *altercation, quarrel, brawl.*

iurgo -are: intransit., *to quarrel, brawl;* transit., *to scold.*

iūrīdĭcĭālis -e, *relating to right or justice.*

iūrisconsultus -i, m. *one learned in law, a lawyer.*

iūrisdictĭo -onis, f. *the administration of justice; judicial authority.*

iūrispĕrītus or **iūrĕpĕrītus** -i, m. *skilled or experienced in the law.*

iūro -are, *to swear, take an oath,* in verba, *to swear after a prescribed formula;* perf. partic. in act. sense **iūrātus** -a -um, *having sworn, under oath;* also *having been sworn.*

¹iūs iūris, n. *broth, soup.*

²iūs iūris, n. *right, law; a court of justice; jurisdiction; right as conferred by law;* iure, *rightly.*

iusiūrandum iūrisiūrandi (or in two words), n. *an oath.*

iussū, abl. sing m., *by order, by command.*

iussum -i, n. subst. from iubeo; q.v.

iustĭtĭa -ae, f. *justice, airness, equity.*

iustĭtĭum -i, n. *a suspension of legal business;* in gen., *pause, cessation.*

iustus -a -um, *just, equitable, fair; lawful, justified, proper; regular, perfect, complete, suitable.* N. as subst., sing. iustum -i, *justice, what is right;* plur. **iusta** -orum, *due forms and observances,* esp. *funeral rites.* Adv. **iustē,** *justly, rightly.*

¹iŭvĕnālis -e, *youthful.*

²Iŭvĕnālis -is, m., D. Iunius, *a Roman writer of satires.*

iŭvencus -a -um, *young;* m. as subst., **iŭvencus** -i, *a young man, or young bullock;* f. **iŭvenca** -ae, *a young woman, or young cow, heifer.*

iŭvĕnesco iŭvĕnescĕre iŭvĕnŭi, *to come (or come back) to the prime of life.*

iŭvĕnīlis -e, *youthful;* adv. **iŭvĕnīlĭtĕr,** *youthfully.*

iŭvĕnis -is, adj., *young, youthful;* as subst. *a young man, young woman.*

iŭvĕnor -ari, dep. *to act like a youth, be impetuous.*

iŭventa -ae, f. *youth.*

iŭventās -ātis, f. *youth.*

iŭventūs -ūtis, f. *youth, the prime of life (between the ages of 20 and 45);* meton., *young men.*

iŭvo -are iūvi iūtum, (1) *to help, assist, aid.* (2) *to delight, please, gratify.*

iuxtā: adv. *close by, near; in like manner, equally;* prep., with acc., *close to, near to;* in time, *just before;* in gen., *near to, just short of.*

iuxtim, *near, close by; equally.*

Ixīōn -ōnis, m. *king of the Lapithae in Thessaly, bound to a perpetually revolving wheel in Tartarus.*

J

Unknown in classical Latin; invented by Italian humanists to represent the consonantal **i**, but now rarely used in classical texts.

K

The letter K, k, corresponding to Greek kappa (κ) belonged to the Latin Alphabet, but in some words was replaced by C.

Kălendae (Călendae) -arum, f. *the first day of a Roman month.*

Karthāgo = Carthāgo; q.v.

L

L, l, the eleventh letter of the Latin Alphabet.

lābasco -ĕre, *to totter; to give way.*

lābēcŭla -ae, f.. *a little stain, slight disgrace.*

lăbĕfăcĭo -făcĕre -fēci -factum, pass. lăbĕfīo -fīĕri -factus sum, *to shake, loosen, impair.*

lăbĕfacto -are, *to shake violently, weaken, disturb.*

¹lābellum -i, n., *a little lip.*

²lābellum -i, n. *a small washing-vessel.*

lābēs -is, f. *a stain, blemish; infamy, disgrace.*

lābĭa -ae, f., and lābĭum -i, n., *a lip.*

Lābĭenus -i, m., T. *an officer of Julius Caesar, who went over to Pompey.*

lăbĭōsus -a -um, *with large lips.*

lābĭum -i, n. = labia; q.v.

lābo -are, *to totter, waver, be about to fall, begin to sink.*

¹lābor lābi lapsus, dep. *to glide, slide, flow; to slip, fall down, fall away, decline; to make a mistake.*

²lăbor (lābos) -ōris, m. (1) *work, toil, effort, industry, capacity for work; feat, work, result of labour.* (2) *hardship, fatigue, distress;* labores solis, *eclipse of the sun.*

lābōrĭfer -fĕra -fĕrum, *bearing toil.*

lăbōrĭōsus -a -um: *of things, toilsome, laborious;* of persons, *industrious, toiling.* Adv. lăbōrĭōsē, *laboriously, with toil.*

lăbōro -are: intransit., *to work, toil, strive: to be troubled or anxious, to care; to suffer, be distressed or afflicted;* luna laborat, *is eclipsed;* transit., *to work out, elaborate, prepare, form.*

lābos -ōris, m. = labor; q.v.

¹lăbrum -i, n. *lip; edge, rim.*

²lăbrum -i, n. *basin, tub; a bathing-place.*

lābrusca -ae, f. *the wild vine.*

lābruscum -i, n. *the wild grape.*

lăbўrinthus -i, m. *a labyrinth.*

lăc lactis, n. *milk; milky sap; milk-white colour.*

Lăcaena -ae, f. adj. *(female) Spartan.*

Lăcĕdaemon -ŏnis, f. *the city Lacedaemon or Sparta;* adj. Lăcĕdaemŏnĭus -a -um, *Lacedaemonian.*

lăcer -cĕra -cĕrum, *torn, mangled;* act., *tearing to pieces.*

lăcĕrātĭo -ōnis, f. *tearing, mangling.*

lăcerna -ae, f. *a mantle worn over the toga.*

lăcĕro -are, *to tear to pieces, maim, mangle; to squander* money; *to slander, pull to pieces a character.*

lăcerta -ae, f. *a lizard; also a sea-fish.*

lăcertōsus -a -um, *muscular, powerful.*

¹lăcertus -i, m., *the upper arm with its muscles;* in gen., *vigour.*

²lăcertus -i, m. = lacerta; q.v.

lăcesso -ĕre -īvi and -ĭi -ītum, *to provoke, exasperate, excite, induce.*

Lăchĕsis -is, f., *one of the three Parcae or Fates.*

lăcĭnĭa -ae, f. *the flap of a garment.*

Lăcō (Lăcōn) -ōnis, m., *a Spartan, Lacedaemonian;* adj. Lăcōnĭcus -a -um and f. adj. Lăcōnis -ĭdis, *Spartan.*

lacrĭma (lacrŭma) -ae, f. *a tear; exudation from certain plants;* Heliadum, *amber.*

lacrĭmābĭlis -e, *deplorable, woeful.*

lacrĭmābundus -a -um, *breaking into tears, weeping.*

lacrĭmo (lacrŭmo) -are, *to weep, shed tears; to exude, to drip.*

lacrĭmōsus -a -um: *tearful, shedding tears; causing tears, mournful, piteous.*

lacrĭmŭla -ae, f., *a little tear.*

lacrŭma, etc.; see lacrima, etc.

lactans -antis, *giving milk.*

lactātĭo -ōnis, f. *enticement.*

lactens -entis. (1) *sucking milk;* plur. as subst., *sucklings, unweaned animals.* (2) *milky, juicy, full of sap.*

lactesco -ĕre, *to be changed into milk.*

lactĕus -a -um, *milky, of milk; milk-white.*

lacto -are, *to allure, wheedle.*

lactūca -ae, f. *lettuce.*

lăcūna -ae, f. *a cavity, hollow, dip;* esp. *a pool, pond.* Transf., *gap, deficiency, loss.*

lăcūnar -āris, n. *a panelled ceiling.*

lăcūno -are, *to work in panels, to panel.*

lăcūnōsus -a -um, *full of hollows or gaps.*

lăcus -ūs, m. *a hollow;* hence *a lake, pool, trough, tank, tub.*

laedo laedĕre laesi laesum, *to strike, knock;* hence *to hurt, injure, damage; to offend, annoy; to violate, outrage.*

laena -ae, f. *cloak.*

Lăertēs -ae, m. *father of Ulysses.*

laesĭo -ōnis, f. *an oratorical attack.*

laetābĭlis -e, *joyful, glad.*

laetātĭo -ōnis, f. *rejoicing, joy.*

laetĭfĭco -are, *to fertilize; to cheer, gladden, delight.*

laetĭfĭcus -a -um, *gladdening, joyous.*

laetĭtĭa -ae, f. (1) *fertility;* hence *richness, grace.* (2) *joy, delight.*

laetor -ari, dep. *to rejoice, be joyful.*

laetus -a -um, *fat, rich, fertile; glad, joyful, happy;* of style, *rich, copious, fluent.* Adv. laetē.

laevus -a -um, *left;* f. as subst., *the left hand, the left;* n. as subst., *the left side.* Transf., *left-handed, foolish, silly; unlucky, unpropitious;* but in augury, *favourable.* Adv. laevē, *on the left hand; awkwardly.*

lăgănum -i, n., *a cake.*

lăgēos -ei, f., *a Greek kind of vine.*

lăgoena *a large earthen jar with handles.*

lăgōis -ĭdis, f. *a bird, perhaps heathcock or grouse.*

lăguncŭla -ae, f. *a little bottle.*

Lāĭus -i, m. *father of Oedipus.*

lāma -ae, f. *a bog, slough.*

lambo lambĕre lambi, *to lick;* of rivers, *to wash.*

lāmenta -orum, n. pl. *wailing, weeping.*

lāmentābĭlis -e *lamentable, deplorable; expressing sorrow, mournful.*

lāmentātĭo -ōnis, f. *weeping, wailing.*

lāmentor -ari, dep. *to weep, wail, lament;* transit., *to bewail.*

lămĭa -ae, f. *a witch, vampire.*

lāmĭna, lammĭna, and lamna -ae, f. *a plate or thin piece of metal, marble,* etc.; *knife-blade; coin; nutshell.*

lampăs -pădis, f. *a torch*; hence *brightness*, esp. *of the sun*; also *a meteor*.

lāna -ae, f., *wool*; also *the down on leaves, fruit*, etc.

lānātus -a -um, *wool-bearing, woolly*.

lancĕa -ae, f. *a light spear* or *lance*.

lancĭno -are, *to tear to pieces*; *to squander*.

lānĕus -a -um, *of wool, woollen; soft as wool*.

languĕfăcĭo -făcĕre, *to make weak* or *faint*.

languĕo -ēre, *to be faint, weak, weary; to droop, flag*; partic. **languens** -entis, *faint, languid*.

languesco languescĕre langŭi, *to become faint, soft* or *listless*.

languĭdŭlus -a -um, *somewhat faint, limp*.

languĭdus -a -um, *faint, weak, limp; of wine, mild, mellow;* adv. **languĭdĕ**.

languor -ōris, m. *faintness, weariness, inactivity*.

lănĭātus -ūs, m. *mangling, tearing*.

lănĭēna -ae, f. *a butcher's shop*.

lānĭfĭcus -a -um, *working in wool*.

lānĭger -gĕra -gĕrum, *wool-bearing; woollen;* m. *as subst. a ram;* f., *a sheep*.

lănĭo -are, *to tear to pieces, mangle, lacerate*.

lănista -ae, m. *a trainer of gladiators; an instigator to violence, inciter*.

lānĭtĭum -i, n. *wool*.

lānĭus -i, m. *butcher*.

lanterna -ae, f. *lantern, lamp*.

lanternārĭus -i, m. *lantern-bearer*.

lānūgo -ĭnis, f. *down, of plants* or *on the cheeks*.

Lānŭvĭum -i, n. *a town in Latium*.

lanx lancis, f. *a plate, platter; the scale of a balance*.

Lāŏcŏōn -ontis, m. *a Trojan priest*.

Lāŏmĕdōn -ontis, m. *a king of Troy, father of Priam*.

lăpăthum -i, n. and **lăpăthus** -i, f. *sorrel*.

lăpĭcīdīnae -arum, f. *stone quarries*.

lăpĭdātĭo -ōnis, f. *throwing of stones*.

lăpĭdātor -ōris, m. *thrower of stones*.

lăpĭdĕus -a -um, *of stone*.

lăpĭdo -are, *to throw stones at;* impers. lapidat, *it rains stones*.

lăpĭdōsus -a -um, *full of stones, stony*.

lăpillus -i, m. *a little stone, pebble; a precious stone, gem*.

lăpis -ĭdis, m. *a stone*.

Lăpĭthae -arum, m. pl. *the Lapithae, a mountain race in Thessaly, famous for their fight with the Centaurs*.

lappa -ae, f. *a burr*.

lapsĭo -ōnis, f. *gliding; inclination, tendency*.

lapso -are, *to slip, stumble*.

lapsus -ūs, m. *gradual movement; gliding, sliding, fall; a fault, error*.

lăquĕārĕ -is, n., esp. plur., *a panelled ceiling*.

lăquĕātus -a -um, *with a panelled ceiling*.

lăquĕus -i, m. *a noose, halter, snare, trap*.

Lār Lăris, m., usually plur. **Lăres**, *Roman tutelary deities*, esp. *household deities*; meton., *hearth, dwelling, home*.

lardum (lārĭdum) -i, n. *bacon fat, lard*.

Lārentĭa -ae, f., or **Acca Lārentĭa**, *the wife of Faustulus, who brought up Romulus and Remus*.

Lăres; see Lar.

largĭfĭcus -a -um, *bountiful, liberal*.

largĭflŭus -a -um, *flowing freely*.

largĭor -iri, dep. *to give abundantly, lavish, bestow, grant; to condone*.

largĭtās -ātis, f. *liberality*.

largĭtĭo -ōnis, f. *free giving* or *spending, lavishing; granting, bestowing*.

largĭtor -ōris, m. *a liberal giver* or *spender; a briber; a waster*.

largus -a -um, *of things, abundant, plentiful, numerous;* with genit., *rich in;* of persons, *liberal, bountiful*. Adv. **largē**, *plentifully, liberally;* **largĭtĕr**, *abundantly, much*.

lārĭdum -i, n. = lardum; q.v.

larva (lārŭa) -ae, f. *a ghost, spectre; a mask*.

lascīvĭa -ae, f. *playfulness, sportiveness; wantonness, licentiousness, insolence*.

lascīvĭo -ire, *to sport, play; to wanton, run riot*.

lascīvus -a -um, *playful, wanton, licentious, insolent*. Adv. **lascīvē**.

lāserpīcĭum -i, n. *a plant from which asafoetida was obtained*.

lassĭtūdo -ĭnis, f., *weariness, exhaustion*.

lasso -are, *to make weary, exhaust*.

lassŭlus -a -um, *rather tired*.

lassus -a -um, *weary, tired, exhausted*.

lătebra -ae, f. *a hiding-place, retreat; a subterfuge, loophole*.

lătebrōsus -a -um, *full of hiding-places, secret;* pumex, *porous*. Adv. **lătebrōsē**, *secretly*.

lătĕo -ēre, *to lie hid, be concealed; to live in obscurity* or *safety; to be unknown*. Hence partic. **lătens** -entis, *concealed, hidden;* adv. **lătentĕr**, *secretly*.

lăter -tĕris, m. *a brick, tile*.

lătĕrāmen -inis, n. *pottery*.

lătercŭlus -i m. *a small brick* or *tile; a biscuit*.

lătĕrĭcĭus -a -um, *built of brick*.

lăterna; see lanterna.

lătesco -ĕre, *to hide oneself*.

lătex -tīcis, m. *fluid, liquid*.

lătĭbŭlum -i, n., *a hiding-place*.

lātĭclāvĭus -a -um, *having a broad purple stripe (as a distinction)*.

lātĭfundĭum -i, n. *a large landed estate*.

Lătīnĭtās -ātis, f. *pure Latin style; Latin rights*.

¹Lătīnus -a -um; see Latium.

²Lătīnus -i, m. *king of the Laurentians, host of Aeneas*.

lātĭo -ōnis, f. *bringing;* legis, *proposing, bringing forward*.

lătĭto -are, *to lie hid, be concealed*.

lātĭtūdo -ĭnis, f. *breadth, extent;* verborum, *broad pronunciation, brogue*.

Lătĭum -i, n. *a district of Italy, in which Rome was situated;* adj. **Lătĭus** and **Lătīnus** -a -um, *Latin;* adv. **Lătīnē**, *in Latin*.

Lătō -ūs, f. and Lătōna -ae, f. *the mother of Apollo and Diana.*

lātor -ōris, m. *the proposer of a law.*

lātrātor -ōris, m. *a barker.*

lātrātus -ūs, m. *barking.*

¹lātro -are, *to bark, bay; to rant, rumble, roar;* transit., *to bark at or for.*

²latro -ōnis, m. *a hired servant or mercenary soldier; a robber, bandit, brigand; a hunter; a piece on a draught-board.*

latrōcĭnĭum -i, n. *mercenary service; highway robbery, brigandage, villainy, roguery;* meton., *a band of robbers.*

latrōcĭnor -ari, dep. *to serve as a mercenary; to practise robbery.*

latruncŭlus -i, m. *a highwayman, bandit; a piece on a draught-board.*

¹lātus -a -um, partic. from fero; q.v.

²lātus -a -um, *broad, wide, extensive;* of style, *diffuse, full, rich.* Hence adv. **lātē,** *broadly, widely, extensively;* longe lateque, *far and wide.*

³lātus -ĕris, n. *the side, flank;* of persons, in pl., *the lungs;* milit., *a latere, on the flank.*

lātuscŭlum -i, n. *a little side.*

laudābĭlis -e, *praiseworthy, laudable;* adv. **laudābĭlĭtĕr.**

laudātĭo -ōnis, f. *praise, commendation; a testimonial; a funeral oration.*

laudātor -ōris, m. *a praiser;* esp. *one who delivers a testimonial or funeral oration.*

laudātrix -īcis, f. *a (female) praiser.*

laudo -are, *to praise, extol, commend; to name, mention, cite, quote;* partic. **laudātus** -a -um, *praiseworthy, esteemed.*

laurĕātus -a -um, *crowned with laurel;* litterae, *bringing news of victory.*

laurĕŏla -ae, f. *a laurel branch, laurel crown;* meton., *a triumph, victory.*

laurĕus -a -um, *of laurel;* f. as subst., **laurĕa,** *laurel tree or laurel crown.*

lauricŏmus -a -um, *covered with laurel-trees.*

laurĭfer -fĕra -fĕrum, and laurĭger -gĕra -gĕrum, *crowned with laurels.*

laurus -i, f. *the laurel or bay-tree;* meton., *triumph, victory.*

laus laudis, f. *praise, fame, glory, commendation.* Transf., *a praiseworthy action or quality.*

lautĭa -orum, n. pl., *entertainment given to foreign ambassadors at Rome.*

lautĭtĭa -ae, f. *splendour, elegance, sumptuous living.*

lautŭmĭae (lātŏmĭae) -arum, f. *a stone-quarry.*

lautus -a -um, partic. from lavo; q.v.

lăvabrum -i, n. *a bath.*

lăvātĭo -ōnis, f. *washing, bathing; bathing apparatus.*

Lāvīnĭa -ae, f. *daughter of Latinus, wife of Aeneas.*

lăvo lăvare or lăvĕre lāvi lautum or lōtum or lăvatum, *to wash, bathe; to moisten, wet; to wash away.*

Hence partic. **lautus** -a -um, *washed;* hence *fine, elegant, sumptuous, refined;* adv. **lautē.**

laxāmentum -i, n. *widening, extending; relaxing, mitigation, respite.*

laxĭtās -ātis, f. *wideness, roominess.*

laxo -are, *to widen, loosen, extend, enlarge; to undo, slacken, relax, relieve; to release, set free.*

laxus -a -um, *wide, loose, spacious;* of time, *later, postponed; loose, lax, relaxed.* Adv. **laxē,** *widely, loosely, without restraint.*

lĕa -ae, and lĕaena -ae, f. *a lioness.*

Lĕander -dri, m. *a youth who swam nightly across the Hellespont to visit Hero, till drowned in a storm.*

lĕbēs -ētis, m. *a bronze pan, cauldron, or basin.*

lectīca -ae, f. *a litter; a bier.*

lectĭcārĭus -i, m. *litter-bearer.*

lectĭcŭla -ae, f. *a small litter or bier; a settee.*

lectĭo -ōnis, f. *a picking out, selection, reading, perusal;* lectio senatus, *a calling over of the names of the senators.*

lectisternĭum -i, n. *a feast offered to the gods.*

lectĭto -are, *to read often or eagerly.*

lector -ōris, m. *a reader.*

lectŭlus -i, m. *a small bed, couch.*

¹lectus -a -um, partic. from lego; q.v.

²lectus -i, m. *a bed, couch.*

Lēda -ae, and Lēdē -es, f. *mother of Castor, Pollux, Helen, and Clytemnestra.*

lēgātārĭus -i, m. *a legatee.*

lēgātĭo -ōnis, f. *delegated authority;* polit., *the office of an ambassador, an embassy, legation;* milit., *the post of subordinate commander;* esp. *the command of a legion.*

lēgātor -ōris, m. *testator.*

lēgātum -i, n. and lēgātus -i, m., from lego; q.v.

lēgĭfer -fĕra -fĕrum, *law-giving.*

lēgĭo -ōnis, f. *a choosing; a chosen body;* esp. *a legion, a division of the Roman army.*

lēgĭōnārĭus -a -um, *belonging to a legion.*

lēgĭtĭmus (lēgĭtŭmus) -a -um, *lawful, legitimate; right, proper, appropriate.* Adv. **lēgĭtĭmē,** *lawfully, properly.*

lēgĭuncŭla -ae, f. *a small legion.*

¹lēgo -are, *to ordain, appoint;* of persons, *to make a deputy, delegate authority to;* of property, *to bequeath, leave as a legacy.* M. of partic. as subst. **lēgātus** -i, *a deputy;* polit., *an ambassador, envoy, or the deputy of a magistrate;* milit., *a subordinate commander,* esp. *commander of a legion.* N. **lēgātum** -i, *a legacy, bequest.*

²lĕgo lĕgĕre lēgi lectum, *to collect, gather, pick, pick up;* fila, *to wind up, spin;* vela, *to furl;* of places, *to pass through, traverse, coast along;* with the eyes, *to survey, scan, read, peruse;* out of a number, *to pick out, choose, select.*

Hence partic. **lectus** -a -um, *chosen, selected; choice, excellent.*

lēgŭlēius -i, m. *a pettifogging lawyer.*

lēgūmen -ĭnis, n. *pulse; the bean.*

Lĕmannus -i, m. *the Lake of Geneva.*

lembus -i, m. *a boat, cutter, pinnace.*

lemma -ătis, n. *theme, title; an epigram.*

lemniscātus -a -um, *ribboned.*

lemniscus -i, m. *a ribbon.*

Lemnos (-us) -i, f. *the island of Lemnos in the Aegean Sea;* adj. **Lemnĭus** -a -um, *Lemnian.*

lĕmŭrēs -um, m. pl. *ghosts, spectres;* **Lĕmŭrĭa** -orum, n. pl. *a festival held in May to expel ghosts.*

lēna -ae, f. *a procuress, bawd.*

Lēnaeus -a -um, *Bacchic.*

lēnĭmen -ĭnis, n. *means of alleviation.*

lēnīmentum -i, n. *mitigation, alleviation.*

lēnĭo -ire, *to make mild, mitigate, relieve.*

lēnis -e, *smooth, mild, gentle;* vinum, *mellow;* n. acc. as adv. **lēnĕ**, *gently;* adv. **lēnĭtĕr**, *smoothly, gently, mildly.*

lēnĭtās -ātis, f. and **lēnĭtūdo** -ĭnis, f. *gentleness, mildness, smoothness.*

lēno -ōnis, m. *a procurer, a go-between.*

lēnōcĭnĭum -i, n. *the trade of a procurer; enticement, allurement; of dress, finery; of style, 'purple patch'.*

lēnōcĭnor -ari, dep. *to work as a procurer; to make up to, to flatter; to advance, promote.*

lens lentis, f. *lentil.*

lentesco -ĕre, *to become pliant, soft, sticky; to weaken, slacken.*

lentiscus -i, f. and **lentiscum** -i, n. *the mastic-tree.*

lentĭtūdo -ĭnis, f. *slowness, sluggishness, apathy.*

lento -are, *to bend.*

¹**lentŭlus** -a -um, *somewhat slow.*

²**Lentŭlus** -i, m. *the name of a family in the patrician gens Cornelia.*

lentus -a -um, *tough, resistant, inert; sticky, tenacious; supple, pliant; inactive, apathetic; slow, lingering;* in dicendo, *drawling.* Adv. **lentē**, *slowly, calmly, coolly, deliberately.*

¹**lēnuncŭlus** -i, m. *a little procurer.*

²**lēnuncŭlus** -i, m. *a small boat or skiff.*

lĕo -ōnis, m. *lion.*

lĕōnīnus -a -um, *of a lion, leonine.*

Lĕontīni -orum, m. *a town on the east coast of Sicily.*

lĕpās -ădis, f. *a limpet.*

¹**lĕpĭdus** -a -um, *pleasant, charming, elegant, witty;* adv. **lĕpĭdē**.

²**Lĕpĭdus** -i, m. *name of a family in the patrician gens Aemilia.*

lĕpor and **lĕpos** -ōris, m. *pleasantness, charm, wit.*

lĕpus -ŏris, m. *hare.*

lĕpuscŭlus -i, m. *a young hare.*

Lesbos (-us) -i, f. *an island in the Aegean Sea, birth-place of Alcaeus and Sappho.*

lētālis -e, *deadly, mortal.*

lēthargĭcus -i, m. *a drowsy, lethargic person.*

lēthargus -i, m. *drowsiness, lethargy, coma.*

Lēthē -ēs, f. *the river of forgetfulness in the underworld.*

lētĭfer -fĕra -fĕrum, *deadly.*

lēto -are, *to kill, slay.*

lētum -i, n. *death; ruin, annihilation.*

leucaspis -ĭdis, f. *having white shields.*

lĕvāmen -ĭnis, n. and **lĕvāmentum** -i, n. *alleviation, mitigation, solace.*

lĕvātĭo -ōnis, f. *alleviation, mitigation; diminution.*

lĕvĭcŭlus -a -um, *rather vain, light-headed.*

lĕvĭdensis -e, *thin, slight, poor.*

¹**lĕvis** -e, *light;* milit., *light-armed;* in movement, *rapid, swift;* in value, *light, trifling, unimportant;* in character, *fickle, capricious, unstable.* Adv. **lĕvĭtĕr**, *lightly, softly, slightly.*

²**lēvis** -e, *smooth, polished, slippery; beardless, bald.*

lĕvĭsomnus -a -um, *lightly sleeping.*

¹**lĕvĭtās** -ātis, f. *lightness; levity, fickleness, inconstancy; groundlessness.*

²**lēvĭtās** -ātis, f. *smoothness, polish.*

¹**lĕvo** -are, *to raise, lift up; to make light, relieve, ease; to diminish, weaken, impair.*

²**lēvo** -are, *to make smooth, polish.*

lēvor -ōris, m. *smoothness.*

lex lēgis, f. *a set form of words, contract, covenant, agreement;* leges pacis, *conditions of peace;* esp. *a law, proposed by a magistrate as a bill, or passed and statutory;* legem ferre, rogare, *to propose a bill;* legem iubere, *to accept* or *pass a bill;* in gen., *a precept, rule.*

lībāmen -ĭnis, n. *a libation, offering to the gods; a sample, specimen.*

lībāmentum -i, n. *a libation, offering to the gods.*

lībātĭo -ōnis, f. *a libation.*

lībella -ae, f. (1) *a small coin, a tenth of a denarius; a farthing, mite.* (2) *a carpenter's level, plummet-line.*

lībellus -i, m. *a little book, note-book, diary; a memorial, petition; programme, placard; letter.*

lībens and **lŭbens** -entis, partic. from libet; q.v.

¹**līber** -ĕra -ĕrum, *free, independent, unrestrained; free from, exempt.* Adv. **lībĕrē**, *freely, without restraint, frankly, openly, boldly.*

²**līber** -bri, m. *the inner bark of a tree;* from the use of this in writing, *a book, volume, catalogue, letter.*

³**Līber** -ĕri, m. *an Italian deity, identified with Bacchus.*

lībĕrālis -e, *of freedom; worthy of a free man, gentlemanlike, courteous, generous;* adv. **lībĕrālĭtĕr**.

lībĕrālĭtās -ātis, f. *courtesy, kindness, generosity.* Transf. *a grant.*

lībĕrātĭo -ōnis, f. *setting free, release, acquittal.*

lībĕrātor -ōris, m. *a liberator.*

lībĕri -ĕrōrum and -ĕrum, m. pl. *children.*

lībĕro -are, *to set free, liberate, release, exempt;* of obstacles, *to lift, raise.*

liberta -ae, f.; see libertus.

lībertās -ātis, f. *freedom, liberty, independence; freedom of speech, frankness, candour.*

lībertīnus -a -um, *of the class of freed-man*; as subst. m. **lībertīnus** *a freed-man*, f. **lībertīna**, *a freedwoman.*

lībertus -i, m. *a freedman*; **līberta** -ae, f. *a freedwoman.*

lībet (**lŭbet**) -bēre -bŭit or -bĭtum est, impers., *it pleases, is agreeable* (with dat. of person).
Hence partic. **lĭbens** (**lŭbens**) -entis, *willing, with pleasure, pleased*; me libente, *with my good-will*; adv. **lĭbenter** (**lŭbenter**), *willingly, with pleasure.*

lībīdĭnōsus -a -um, *wilful, arbitrary, capricious; passionate, lustful.* Adv. **lībīdĭnōsē**, *wilfully, arbitrarily.*

lībīdo (**lŭbīdo**) -inis, f. *violent desire, longing*; esp. *irrational whim, caprice*; or *immoderate passion, lust.*

Lībītīna -ae, f. *goddess of the dead.*

lībo -are, *to take away from, remove, derive; to taste, touch, impair, diminish; to give a taste of, offer to the gods.*

lībra -ae, f. (1) *a balance, pair of scales*; aes et libra, *a fictitious form of sale.* (2) *the Roman pound of 12 oz.*

lībrāmentum -i, n. (1) *weight as a source of power* or *for balancing.* (2) *a horizontal plane.*

lībrāria -ae, f *a female who weighed out wool to slaves.*

lībrārius -a -um, *of books*; m. as subst., *a transcriber of books, a copyist,* or *a bookseller*; n. as subst., *a bookcase.*

lībrīlis -e, *of a pound weight.*

lībrītor -ōris, m. *an artilleryman.*

lībro -are, *to balance, hold up, poise*; of weapons, *to swing, level, brandish*; hence, *to hurl.*

lībum -i, n. *a cake, offered to the gods.*

Lĭburni -orum, m. *the Liburnians, a people of Illyria*; f. of adj. as subst. **Lĭburna** -ae, *a light vessel, galley.*

Lĭbўa -ae and **Lĭbўē** -ēs, f. *Libya*

lĭcens -centis, and **lĭcentĕr** from licet; q.v.

lĭcentia -ae, f. *freedom, leave, liberty; licentiousness.*

lĭcĕo -ēre -ŭi -ĭtum, *to be on sale, be valued at.*

lĭcĕor -ēri, dep. *to bid* or *bid for, offer a price.*

lĭcet lĭcēre lĭcŭit or lĭcĭtum est, impers., *it is allowed, one can* or *may*; as conjunction, *granted that, although.* Hence pres. partic. **lĭcens** -entis, *free, unrestrained, unbridled*; adv. **lĭcentĕr**; perf. partic. **lĭcĭtus** -a -um, *allowed, permitted.*

Lĭcīnius -a -um, *name of a Roman gens.*

lĭcītātĭo -onis, f. *bidding at a sale* or *auction.*

lĭcĭtus -a -um, partic. from licet; q.v.

lĭcĭum -i, n.: in weaving, *the thrum* or perhaps *a leash*; in gen., *a thread.*

lictor -ōris, m. *a lictor, attending the chief Roman magistrates.*

lĭgāmen -ĭnis, n. *string tie, bandage.*

lĭgāmentum -i, n. *bandage.*

Lĭgĕr -gēris, m. *a river* (now the *Loire*).

lignārius -i, m. *a carpenter.*

lignātĭo -ōnis, f. *wood-cutting.*

lignātor -ōris, m. *wood-cutter.*

lignĕŏlus -a -um, *wooden.*

lignĕus -a -um, *made of wood, wooden.*

lignor -ari, dep. *to cut* or *get wood.*

lignum -i, n. *wood, timber*; esp. *fire-wood.*

¹lĭgo -are, *to bind, bandage, harness; to bind together, connect, unite.*

²lĭgo -ōnis, m. *a mattock.*

lĭgŭla (**lingŭla**) ae, f. *a tongue of land, promontory; a shoe-strap.*

Lĭgŭrēs -um, m. pl. *the Ligurians, a people on the north-west coast of Italy.*

lĭgŭrio (**lĭgurrĭo**) -ire, *to lick, lick up; to gloat over; long for.*

lĭgŭrītĭo (**lĭgurr-**) -ōnis, f. *daintiness.*

lĭgustrum -i, n. *privet.*

līlium -i, n. *a lily*; milit. *a fortification consisting of pits and stakes.*

Lĭlўbaeon (**-baeum**) -i, n. *a promontory and town at the western end of Sicily.*

līma -ae, f. *a file; polishing, revision of a composition.*

līmātŭlus -a -um rather *polished, refined.*

limbus -i, m. *a border, hem, fringe.*

līmen -ĭnis, n. *threshold, doorway, entrance; home, house, dwelling; any entrance or border* or *beginning*; esp. *the starting-point in a race-course.*

līmes -ĭtis, m. *a by-way, path; a course, track*; esp. *a boundary-path, a boundary-line; a distinction, difference.*

līmo -are, *to file, polish, finish off; to investigate accurately; to file down, pare down, to diminish.* Partic. **līmātus** -a -um, *refined elegant*; compar. adv. **līmātĭus.**

līmōsus -a -um, *slimy, miry, muddy.*

limpĭdus -a -um, *clear, limpid.*

¹limus -a -um, of the eyes, *sidelong, looking sideways.*

²limus -i, m. *slime, mud, mire.*

³limus -i, m. *a priest's apron.*

līnĕa -ae, f. *a linen thread, string; a fishing-line, plumb-line*; ad lineam, *perpendicularly.* Transf., *a geometrical line; a boundary-line, goal.*

līnĕāmentum -i, n. *a line drawn with pen* or *pencil*; plur., *drawing, sketch, outline*; in gen., *a feature, lineament.*

līnĕo -are, *to make straight.*

līnĕus -a -um, *of flax* or *linen.*

lingo lingĕre linxi linctum, *to lick.*

lingua -ae, f. *a tongue; speech, language: a tongue of land, promontory.*

lingŭlāca -ae, f. *a chatterbox.*

līnĭger -gēra -gērum, *clothed in linen.*

līno linĕre līvi and lēvi lĭtum, *to smear one thing upon another*; or *to besmear one thing with another*; *to rub out writing*; *to befoul, dirty.*

linquo linquĕre lĭqui, *to leave, abandon, forsake*; pass., linqui, *to faint.*

lintĕātus -a -um, *clothed in linen.*

lintĕo -ōnis, m. *a linen-weaver.*

linter -tris, f. *a boat, skiff; a trough, tub, vat.*

lintĕus -a -um, *of linen*; n. as subst. *linen cloth, linen,* esp. *a sail.*

līnum -i, n. *flax, linen; a thread, line; a rope, cable.*

lippio -ire, *to have sore eyes, be bleareyed.*

lippĭtūdo -ĭnis, f. *inflammation of the eyes.*

lippus -a -um, *blear-eyed; half-blind.*

liquĕfăcio -făcĕre -fēci -factum, pass. **liquĕfīo** -fiĕri -factus sum, *to melt, dissolve; to decompose; to make weak, enervate.*

liquesco -ĕre -lĭcŭi, *to become fluid, melt, melt away, to putrefy; to become effeminate.*

liquĭdus -a -um. (1) *fluid, flowing, liquid*; n. as subst. *a liquid.* (2) *clear, bright, serene, calm, pure, evident, certain*; n. as subst. *certainty*; abl. sing. **liquĭdō** and adv. **liquĭdē**, *clearly, plainly.*

liquo -are, *to make liquid, melt; to strain, clarify.*

¹liquor -i, dep. *to be fluid, flow, melt: to melt away*; partic. **liquens** -entis, *flowing.*

²liquor -ōris, m. *fluidity; a liquid, fluid.*

līs, lītis, f. *a legal controversy, action, suit*; in gen., *contention, strife, quarrel.*

litātio -ōnis, f. *successful sacrifice.*

litĭgātor -ōris, m. *a party in a law-suit, litigant.*

lītĭgĭōsus -a -um, *of persons, fond of dispute, litigious; of things, full of dispute, contested at law.*

litĭgo -are, *to go to law*; in gen., *to quarrel, dispute.*

līto -are: intransit., *to bring an acceptable offering, and so to obtain favourable omens*; transit., *to sacrifice successfully.*

lītŏrālis -e, and **lītŏrĕus** -a -um, *of the shore.*

littĕra (**lītĕra**) ae, f. *a letter of the alphabet; a letter, dispatch, epistle*; plur., *written records, documents, deeds; literature, letters, scholarship.*

littĕrārius -a -um, *of reading and writing.*

littĕrātor -ōris, m. *a philologist, grammarian, critic.*

littĕrātūra -ae, f. *the alphabet, grammar.*

littĕrātus -a -um, *lettered, inscribed with letters; learned, liberally educated.* Adv. **littĕrātē**, *in clear letters, legibly; literally, word for word; learnedly.*

littĕrŭla -ae, f. *a letter* (of the alphabet) *written small*; plur., *a little letter, a note, a smattering of literature.*

littus, etc.; see **litus**, etc.

lītūra -ae, f. *an erasure, correction; a passage erased; a blot.*

lītus -ōris, n. *sea-shore, beach, strand, coast; the shore of a lake or river.*

lĭtŭus -i, m. *an augur's curved staff; a curved cavalry trumpet, clarion.*

lĭvĕo -ēre, *to be bluish in colour; to be envious, envy*; partic. **līvens** -entis, *bluish, livid; envious.*

līvesco -ĕre, *to become bluish.*

līvĭdŭlus -a -um, *rather envious.*

līvĭdus -a -um, *bluish, livid, black and blue; envious, spiteful.*

Līvius -a -um, *name of a Roman gens.*

līvor -ōris, m. *bluish colour, a livid spot; envy, spite.*

lixa -ae, m. *a sutler, camp-follower.*

lŏcātio -ōnis, f. *placing; hence a leasing, contract, lease.*

lŏcātōrius -a -um, *concerned with leases.*

lŏco -are, *to place, put, set; esp. to give in marriage*; commerc., *to let out on hire, farm out, lease, invest; to contract for work to be done.* N. of partic. as subst. **lŏcātum** -i, *a lease, contract.*

lŏcŭlus -i, m. *a little place*; plur., *loculi, a money-box; a school satchel.*

lŏcŭplēs -plētis, *with landed property, wealthy, rich; also trusty, sufficient, satisfactory.*

lŏcŭplēto -are, *to enrich.*

lŏcus -i, m. (plur., loci, *single places*; loca, *region*), *a place*; milit., *position, ground, post*; in time, *a period, or moment; position, situation, rank; occasion, cause; passage in a book.*

¹lŏcusta -ae, f. *a locust; a kind of lobster.*

²Lŏcusta -ae, f. *a notorious poisoner, accomplice of Nero.*

lŏcūtio -ōnis, f. *speech; pronunciation.*

lŏdix -dīcis, f. *blanket, rug.*

lŏgĭcus -a -um, *logical*; n. pl. as subst. *logic.*

lŏgŏs (**-us**) -i, m. *a word; a joke, jest, bon mot.*

lŏlĭum -i, n. *darnel.*

lollīgo -ĭgĭnis, f. *cuttle-fish.*

lōmentum -i, n. *face-cream.*

Londīnium -i, n. *London.*

longaevus -a -um, *aged, old.*

longinquĭtās -ātis, f. *length, distance, remoteness; of time, duration.*

longinquus -a -um, *long, distant, far, remote, foreign; of time, long, distant.*

longĭtūdo -ĭnis, f. *length.*

longŭlus -a -um, *rather long*; adv. **longŭlē**, *rather far, at a little distance.*

longūrius -i, m. *a pole, rod, rail.*

longus -a -um, *long; navis, a man-of-war*; poet., *spacious; of time, long, of long duration: esp. too long, tedious; of persons, prolix, tedious.* Adv. **longē**, *a long way off, far, at a distance; by far*; in time, *long, at length*; adv. **longĭter**, *far.*

lŏquācĭtās -ātis, f. *talkativeness.*

lŏquācŭlus -a -um, *rather talkative.*

lŏquax -quācis, *talkative, garrulous; babbling, noisy*; adv. **lŏquācĭter**.

lŏquella (**lŏquēla**) -ae, f. *speech, language.*

lŏquor lŏqui lŏcūtus, dep. *to speak* (in conversation); *to tell, say, talk of, mention.*

lōrātus -a -um, *bound with thongs.*

lōrīca -ae, f. *cuirass, corselet, breast plate; breastwork, parapet.*

lōrīcātus -a -um, *wearing a cuirass.*

lōrĭpēs -pēdis, *bandy-legged.*

lōrum -i, n. *a strap or thong of leather*; plur., *reins, bridle; scourge, whip.*

lōtŏs (-us) -i, f. *the name of several plants; esp. of an African tree and its fruit.*

¹lōtus -a -um, partic. from lavo; q.v.

²lōtus -i, f. = lotos; q.v.

lŭbet; lŭbīdo, etc. = libet, libido, etc.; q.v.

lŭbrĭco -are, *to make slippery.*

lŭbrĭcus -a -um, *slippery, smooth; quickly moving, uncertain, insecure, perilous, deceitful.*

Lūcāni -orum, m. pl. *a people in Southern Italy.*

Lūcānus -i, m., M. Annaeus, *author of the poem* Pharsalia.

lūcar -āris, n. *a forest-tax, used for paying actors.*

lŭcellum -i, n. *little profit, small gain.*

lūcĕo lūcēre luxi, *to be bright, shine, glitter; to be clear, evident;* impers., lucet, *it is light, it is day.*

Lucĕrēs -um, m. *one of the three patrician tribes.*

lŭcerna -ae, f. *lamp.*

lūcesco (lūcisco) lūcescĕre luxi, *to begin to shine;* impers., lucescit, *it grows light, day is breaking.*

lūcĭdus -a -um, *shining, bright; clear, lucid;* adv. lūcĭdē.

lūcĭfer -fĕra -fĕrum, *light-bearing, light-bringing;* m. as subst., *the morning star.*

lūcĭfŭgus -a -um, *shunning the light.*

Lūcĭlius -a -um, *name of a Roman gens.*

Lūcīna -ae, f. *the goddess of births.*

lūcisco = lucesco; q.v.

Lūcĭus -i, m. *Roman* praenomen (abbreviated to L.).

Lūcrētĭus -a -um, *name of a Roman gens.*

lucrĭfăcĭo -făcĕre *to gain, receive as profit.*

Lūcrīnus -i, m. *a lake on the coast of Campania, near Baiae, famous for oysters.*

lucror -ari, dep. *to gain, profit, win.*

lucrōsus -a -um, *gainful, profitable.*

lucrum -i, n. *gain, profit, advantage; love of gain, avarice.*

luctāmen -ĭnis, n. *effort, toil.*

luctātĭo -ōnis, f. *wrestling; a struggle contest.*

luctātor -ōris, m. *wrestler.*

luctĭfĭcus -a -um, *causing grief, baleful.*

luctĭsŏnus -a -um, *sad-sounding.*

luctor -ari, dep (and lucto -are), *to wrestle, struggle, strive, contend.*

luctŭōsus -a -um, (1) *causing sorrow, doleful.* (2) *feeling or showing sorrow, mourning.* Compar. adv. luctŭōsĭus.

luctus -ūs, m. *sorrow expressed, lamentation, mourning; mourning clothes.*

lūcŭbrātĭo -ōnis, f. *work done by night or lamp-light, nocturnal study.*

lūcŭbro -are, *to work by night;* in perf. partic. lūcŭbrātus -a -um, *done at night or spent in work.*

lūcŭlentus -a -um, *shining, bright, brilliant, splendid;* adv. lūcŭlentē and lūcŭlentĕr, *splendidly.*

Lūcullus -i, m. *name of a family in the gens Licinia.*

Lŭcūmo (Lŭcŏmo, Lucmo) -ōnis, m. *title given to Etruscan princes and priests.*

lūcus -i, m. *a (sacred) grove or wood.*

lūdĭa -ae, f. *an actress or female gladiator.*

lūdĭbrĭum -i, n. *derision, mockery; an object of derision, laughing-stock, plaything.*

lūdĭbundus -a -um, *playful, sportive.*

lūdĭcer -cra -crum, *sportive, done for sport; esp. of the stage.* N. as subst. lūdĭcrum -i, *a trifle, plaything; a theatrical performance.*

lūdĭfĭcātĭo -ōnis, f. *deriding, deceiving.*

lūdĭfĭco -are and lūdĭfĭcor -ari, dep. *to make game of, deride, delude, cheat, frustrate.*

lūdĭo -ōnis, m. and lūdĭus -i, m. *an actor.*

lūdo lūdĕre lūsi lūsum, *to play, sport; to play at or with; to imitate, banter, deceive, delude.*

lūdus -i, m. *play, game, sport, pastime;* plur., ludi, *public games or spectacles.* Transf., *a trifle, jest, joke;* ludum dare, *to give free play to; a training establishment, school.*

lŭella -ae, f. *expiation.*

lŭēs -is, f. *plague, pestilence, calamity.*

Lugdūnum -i, n. *a city in Gaul* (now Lyons). Adj. Lugdūnensis -e.

lūgĕo lūgēre luxi: intransit., *to mourn, be in mourning;* transit., *to bewail, lament, wear mourning for.*

lūgubris -e, *of mourning, mournful; plaintive; grievous.* N. pl. as subst. *mourning clothes.*

lumbus -i, m. *loin.*

lūmen -ĭnis, n. *light; a light, lamp; the light of day, day; the light of life; the light of the eye, the eye; an opening, a light in a building;* fig., *clearness, insight; a shining light, glory, ornament.*

lūmĭnārĕ -āris, n. *a window-shutter window.*

lūmĭnōsus -a -um, *bright.*

lūna -ae, f. *the moon; night, a month; a crescent-shaped ornament.*

lūnāris -e, *of the moon, lunar.*

lūno -are, *to bend into a crescent;* perf. partic. lūnātus -a -um, *crescent-shaped.*

lŭo lŭĕre lŭi lŭĭtūrus, *to loose; to expiate, atone for, make good;* luere poenam, *to pay a penalty;* of trouble, *to avert.*

lŭpa -ae, f. *a she-wolf; a prostitute.*

lŭpātus -a -um, *provided with iron spikes;* m. or n. pl. as subst., *a curb with jagged spikes.*

Lŭpercus -i, m. *an Italian pastoral deity, or one of his priests;* subst. Lŭpercal -cālis, n. *a grotto, sacred to* Lupercus; Lŭpercālĭa -ĭum and -iōrum, n. pl., *the festival of Lupercus, celebrated in February.*

¹lŭpīnus -a -um, *of a wolf, wolfish.*

²lŭpīnus -i, m. and lŭpīnum -i, n., *the lupin.*

lŭpus -i, m. *a wolf; a voracious fish,*

the pike; a horse's bit with jagged
points; a hook.

lūrĭdus -a -um, pale yellow, lurid,
ghastly.

lūror -ōris, m. ghastliness, paleness.

luscīnĭa -ae, f. nightingale.

luscĭōsus and **luscĭtĭōsus** -a -um,
purblind, dim-sighted.

luscus -a -um, one-eyed.

lūsĭo -ōnis, f. play, game.

Lūsĭtānĭa -ae, f. the modern Portugal,
with part of Spain.

lūsor -ōris, m. a player; a playful
writer; a mocker.

lustrālis -e, relating to expiation or
to a period of five years.

lustrātĭo -ōnis, f. purification by sacrifice; a going round, traversing.

¹lustro -are, to brighten, illumine.

²lustro -are, to purify, cleanse by sacrifices; to go round, go over, traverse;
to review, observe, examine.

¹lustrum -i, n., usually plur., the den
of a wild beast, woodlands; brothels,
debauchery.

²lustrum -i, n. an expiatory sacrifice;
a period of five years.

lūsus -ūs, m. playing, game, sport;
dalliance.

lūtěŏlus -a -um, yellow.

Lūtētĭa -ae, f. a town in Gallia (now
Paris).

¹lūtěus -a -um, saffron-yellow.

²lūtěus -a -um, of mud or clay; dirty.

lūto -are, to smear with mud.

lūtŭlentus -a -um, muddy, dirty,
filthy, impure.

¹lŭtum -i, n. a plant used for dyeing
yellow; yellow colour.

²lŭtum -i, n. mud, mire, dirt; clay.

lux, lūcis, f. light; esp. daylight, day;
a day; the light of life or of day;
the eye, eyesight; illustration, eluci-
dation; hope, encouragement; ornament.

luxŭrĭa -ae and **luxŭrĭēs** -ēi, f. rank-
ness, exuberant growth; excess, dissipation, extravagance.

luxŭrĭo -are and **luxŭrĭor** -ari, dep.,
to be luxuriant, rank, grow fast; to
frisk, sport, run riot.

luxŭrĭōsus -a -um, luxuriant, rank;
immoderate, excessive; luxurious, dissolute, extravagant. Adv. **luxŭrĭōsē**,
luxuriously.

luxus -ūs, m. luxury, excess, extravagance.

Lyaeus -i, m. surname of Bacchus;
wine.

lychnūchus -i, m. lamp-stand, candelabrum.

lychnus -i, m. lamp.

Lўcĭa -ae, f. a country of Asia Minor.

Lȳdĭa -ae, f. a country of Asia Minor;
ad. **Lȳdĭus** and **Lȳdus** -a -um,
Lydian.

lympha -ae, f. water, esp. clear spring
or river water.

lymphātĭcus and **lymphātus** -a -um,
raving, mad, frantic.

lynx -cis, c. lynx.

lȳra -ae, f. the lyre or lute, a stringed
instrument; lyric poetry, song.

lȳrĭcus -a -um, of the lyre, lyric.

M

M, m. the twelfth letter of the Latin
Alphabet.

Măcĕdō (-ōn) -ŏnis, m. a Macedonian;
subst. **Măcĕdŏnĭa** -ae, f.; adj.
Măcĕdŏnĭcus, Măcĕdŏnĭus -a -um.

măcellum, -i, n. a provision-market.

măcer -cra -crum, lean; thin, poor.

măcĕrĭa -ae, f. a wall, esp. garden-wall.

măcĕro -are, to soften; to make weak,
reduce; to torment, tease, vex.

măchaera -ae, f. a sword.

māchĭna -ae, f. a machine, contrivance;
a crane, windlass, catapult, ballista.
Transf., fabric; a device, trick,
stratagem.

māchĭnāmentum -i, n. machine,
instrument.

māchĭnātĭo -ōnis, f. contrivance,
machinery, mechanism; device, machination.

māchĭnātor -ōris, m. a maker of
machines, engineer; a deviser, contriver.

māchĭnor -ari, dep. to contrive, invent,
devise.

măcĭēs -ēi, f. leanness, thinness,
poverty, barrenness.

macresco -ĕre, to grow lean, become
thin.

macrŏcollum -i, n. paper of the
largest size.

mactābĭlis -e, deadly.

mactātū, abl. sing. m. by a sacrificial
stroke.

macte; see ¹mactus.

¹macto -are, to magnify, honour,
glorify.

²macto -are, to slay, smite; to afflict,
punish.

¹mactus -a -um, glorified, honoured;
used only in voc. m. **mactē**, well
done! bravo! good luck!

²mactus -a -um, smitten.

măcŭla -ae, f. a spot, mark, stain;
sometimes the mesh of a net; a moral
stain, blemish, fault.

măcŭlo -are, to spot, stain, defile,
pollute.

măcŭlōsus -a -um, spotted, speckled,
stained, polluted.

mădĕfăcĭo -făcĕre -fēci -factum, and
pass. **mădĕfīo** -fiĕri, to mak ˛wet,
moisten, soak.

mădĕo -ēre, to be wet, to stream; to
be drunk; to be boiled. Transf., to
be steeped in, abound in.

mădesco mădescĕre mădŭi, to become
wet.

mădĭdus -a -um, moist, wet; drunk;
boiled soft; dyed, steeped. Adv.
mădīdē, drunkenly.

mădor -ōris, m. moisture, wetness.

Maeandĕr and **Maeandrŏs (-us)** -dri,
m. a river of Asia Minor, proverbial
for its winding course; a winding.

Maecēnās -ātis, m. C. Cilnius, the
patron of Horace and Vergil.

maena (mena) -ae, f. a small sea-fish.

Maenās -ădis, f. a bacchante; a
prophetess.

maerĕo -ēre: intransit., to grieve,

mourn, lament; transit., *to lament, bewail.*

maeror -ōris, m. *mourning, grief, sorrow.*

maestĭtĭa -ae, f. *sadness, dejection, gloom.*

maestus -a -um, *sad, dejected, gloomy;* adv. **maestĭtĕr.**

măgālĭa -ium, n. pl. *huts.*

măgĕ; see magis.

măgĭcus -a -um, *magical.*

măgĭs (or **măgĕ**), *more, to a greater extent; rather, for preference;* non magis . . . quam, *not more* . . . *than, just as much* . . . *as;* quo magis . . . eo magis, *the more* . . . *the more.* Superl. **maxĭmē (maxŭmē),** *in the highest degree, most of all, especially, very much so;* quam maxime, *as much as possible;* with tum, cum, just, *precisely.*

măgister -tri, m. *master, chief, head, director;* populi, *dictator;* equitum, *master of the horse, the dictator's lieutenant;* magister (ludi), *a schoolmaster, teacher;* societatis, *director of a company;* elephanti, *driver;* navis, *master* or *helmsman.* Transf., *instigator, adviser, guide.*

măgistĕrĭum -i, n. *directorship, magistracy; direction, guidance.*

măgistra -ae, f. *a mistress, directress.*

măgistrātus -ūs, m. *a magistracy, official dignity, office.* Transf., *a magistrate, state official.*

magnănĭmĭtās -ātis, f. *greatness of soul, magnanimity.*

magnănĭmus -a -um, *high-minded, magnanimous.*

magnĭfĭcentĭa -ae, f. *loftiness of thought and action; grandeur, magnificence, splendour;* in bad sense, *boasting, pomposity.*

magnĭfĭco -are, *to prize highly, esteem.*

magnĭfĭcus -a -um, compar. **magnĭfĭcentĭor;** superl. **magnĭfĭcentissĭmus;** *grand, splendid, fine;* in bad sense, *boastful, pompous.* Adv. **magnĭfĭcē.**

magnĭlŏquentĭa -ae, f. *lofty* or *elevated language; pompous, boastful language.*

magnĭlŏquus -a -um, *lofty* or *elevated in language; pompous* or *boastful.*

magnĭtūdō -ĭnis, f. *greatness; animi, magnanimity.*

magnŏpĕrĕ and separately **magnō ŏpĕrĕ,** *greatly, very much.*

magnus -a -um; compar. **māior,** maius; superl. **maxĭmus (maxŭmus)** -a -um; *great, large;* of sound, *loud;* of price or value, *high;* magno and magni, *at a high price, dear, highly.* Transf., of time, *long, old;* of standing, *great, mighty, powerful, important;* m. pl. of compar. as subst. **māiōres,** *ancestors;* in maius, *to a higher degree;* see magnopere; for **maxĭmē,** see magis.

Măgō (-ōn) -ōnis, m. *brother of Hannibal.*

¹măgus -i, m. *a learned Persian; a magician.*

²măgus -a -um, *magical.*

Māia -ae, f. *the daughter of Atlas, mother of Mercury,* adj. **Māius** -a -um, *of Maia:* (mensis) Maius, *the month of May.*

māiestās -ātis, f. *greatness, grandeur, dignity, majesty;* crimen maiestatis, *treason.*

māior, māiōres; see magnus.

Māius -a -um, adj. from Maia; q.v.

māiuscŭlus -a -um, *somewhat greater* or *older.*

māla -ae, f. *cheek-bone, jaw-bone; jaw, cheek.*

mălăcĭa -ae, f. *a calm at sea.*

mălăcus -a -um, *soft, pliable; effeminate, delicate.*

mălĕdīco -dīcĕre -dixi -dictum (sometimes separately, male dico), *to speak ill, abuse;* pres. partic., **mălĕdīcens** -entis, *abusive;* n. of perf. partic. as subst. **mălĕdictum** -i, *cursing, abusive language.*

mălĕdictĭo -ōnis, f. *reviling, abuse.*

mălĕdĭcus -a -um, *abusive, scurrilous;* adv. **mălĕdĭcē.**

mălĕfăcĭo -făcĕre -fēci -factum (sometimes separately, male facio), *to injure;* n. of perf. partic. as subst. **mălĕfactum** -i, *an ill deed, injury.*

mălĕfactor -ōris, m. *an evil-doer.*

mălĕfĭcĭum -i, n. *wrongdoing; mischief.*

mălĕfĭcus -a -um, *evil-doing, mischievous;* adv. **mălĕfĭcē.**

mălĕsuādus -a -um, *ill-advising, seductive.*

mălĕvŏlens -entis, *spiteful, ill-disposed.*

mălĕvŏlentĭa -ae, f. *ill-will, spite, malice.*

mălĕvŏlus -a -um, *ill-disposed, spiteful, malicious.*

mālĭfer -fĕra -fĕrum, *apple-bearing.*

mălignĭtās -ātis, f. *ill-nature, malignity, spite; stinginess.*

mălignus -a -um, *ill-disposed, wicked;* esp. *stingy, niggardly; barren, unfruitful; stinted, scanty.* Adv. **mălignē.**

mălĭtĭa -ae, f. *badness, wickedness, vice;* esp. *craft, cunning, malice.*

mălĭtĭōsus -a -um, *wicked; crafty, roguish, knavish;* adv. **mălĭtĭōsē.**

mallĕŏlus -i, m. *a little hammer; a kind of fire-dart.*

mallĕus -i, m. *a hammer, mallet, pole-axe.*

mālo malle mālŭi, *to wish rather, prefer;* with dative of person, *to be more favourable to.*

mălōbathrum -i, n. *a plant, from which ointment was prepared.*

¹mălum -i, n.; see ¹malus.

²mălum -i, n. *an apple,* or other similar fruit.

¹mălus -a -um; comp. **pēior** -us; superl. **pessĭmus** -a -um; *bad, evil* (physically or morally); *unfavourable, unsuccessful, ugly.* N. as subst. **mălum** -i, *an evil; harm, disaster; punishment;* as a term of abuse, *scoundrel.* Adv. **mălē,** compar. **pēius;** superl. **pessĭmē,** *badly, ill;* male audire, *to be ill spoken of; unsuccessfully, unfortunately;* with words bad in sense, *bitterly, excessively*; with words of favourable sense, with negative force, e.g., **male gratus**, *unthankful*.

²**mālus** -i, f. *an apple-tree.*

³**mālus** -i, m. *the mast of a ship; an upright, pole.*

malva -ae, f. *the mallow.*

Māmers -mertis, m. *the Oscan name of Mars; hence* **Māmertīni** -orum, m. *the name assumed by certain mercenary troops.*

mămilla -ae, f. *breast, teat.*

mamma -ae, f. *breast.*

mānābĭlis -e, *flowing, penetrating.*

manceps -cĭpis, m. *a purchaser, farmer, contractor.*

mancĭpĭum (mancŭpĭum) -i, n. *a formal purchase of anything.* Transf., *a slave acquired by* mancipium.

mancĭpo (mancŭpo) -are, *to sell formally; to give up.*

mancus -a -um, *maimed, crippled, imperfect, defective.*

mandātū abl. sing. m. *by order.*

mandātum -i, n. subst. from mando; q.v.

¹**mando** -are, *to commit, entrust; of actions, to order, command, commission.* N. of partic. as subst., **mandātum** -i, *a commission charge, order.*

²**mando** mandĕre mandi mansum, *to chew, masticate, champ; to eat, consume.*

mandra -ae, f. *a stall, cattle-pen; a herd of cattle; a draughtboard.*

mānĕ, indecl. n.: as subst., *morning*; adv., *in the morning, early.*

mănĕo mānēre mansi mansum: intransit., *to remain, stay; to stay the night; to endure, last; promissis, to abide by*; transit., in gen., *to wait for, await.*

mānēs -ĭum, m. pl. *the shades of the departed, spirits of the dead*; poet., *the lower world, infernal regions; corpse, ashes, remains.*

mango -ōnis, m. *a salesman, esp., slave dealer.*

mănĭca -ae, f. *a sleeve, serving as a glove; handcuffs, manacles.*

mănĭcātus -a -um, *having long sleeves.*

mănĭcŭla -ae, f. *a little hand.*

mănĭfesto -are, *to show clearly, reveal.*

mănĭfestus -a -um, *palpable, clear, visible, evident; caught out, detected.* Abl. sing. n. as adv. **mănĭfestō**, *clearly*; compar. **mănĭfestĭus.**

Mānīlĭus -a -um, *name of a Roman gens.*

mănĭpŭlāris (mănĭplāris) *belonging to a maniple*; m. as subst. *a private soldier; a fellow-soldier.*

mănĭpŭlātim, *in bundles; in maniples.*

mănĭpŭlus (poet, mănĭplus) -i, m. *a handful, bundle*; milit. *a company of infantry, a division of the Roman army.*

Manlĭus -a -um, *name of a Roman gens.*

mannŭlus -i, m. *a pony.*

mannus -i, m. *a pony, cob.*

māno -are, *to flow, drip, spread*; with abl., *to drip with*; with acc., *to exude.*

mansĭo -ōnis, f. *stay, sojourn; station, stage.*

mansĭto -are, *to abide, stay.*

mansuēfācĭo -făcĕre -fēci -factum, pass. **mansuēfĭo** -fĭĕri -factus sum, *to tame; to soften, pacify, civilize.*

mansuēs -is or -ētis, *tame.*

mansuesco -suescĕre -suēvi -suētum: transit., *to tame*; intransit., *to grow tame or soft.* Hence partic. **mansuētus** -a -um, *tame, mild, soft*; adv. **mansuētē.**

mansuētūdo -ĭnis, f. *tameness: mildness, gentleness.*

mantēlē -is, n. *towel, napkin.*

mantēlum -i, n. *covering, cloak.*

mantĭca -ae, f. *wallet, knapsack.*

manto -are, *to remain, wait, wait for.*

Mantŭa -ae, f. *a town in north Italy.*

mănŭālis -e, *fitted to the hand.*

mănŭbĭae -arum, f. *money from the sale of booty, esp. the general's share; spoils, profits.*

mănŭbrium -i, n. *haft, handle.*

mănūf-; see manif-.

mănŭlĕus -i, m. and **mănŭlĕa** -ae, f. *a long sleeve.*

mănūmissĭo -ōnis, f. *the emancipation of a slave.*

mănūmitto -mittĕre -mīsi -missum (or as two words, manu mitto), *to manumit, emancipate a slave.*

mănŭprĕtĭum (mănĭpr-) -i, n. *wages, hire, reward.*

mănŭs -ūs, f. *hand*; manus dare, *to surrender*; in manibus, *on hand, in preparation*; servus ad manum, *a secretary*; abl. manu, *by hand, artificially.* Transf., *the strong arm, fist, force, effort; power, jurisdiction; the hand or touch of artist or craftsman; a band or body of men; an elephant's trunk*; manus ferrea, *grappling-iron.*

māpālĭa -ĭum, n. *huts, hovels.*

mappa -ae, f. *a table-napkin.*

Marcellus -i, m. *the cognomen of a family of the gens Claudia.*

marcĕo -ēre, *to wither, droop, be feeble.*

marcesco -ĕre, *to begin to droop, grow feeble.*

marcĭdus -a -um, *withering, drooping, enfeebled.*

marcor -ōris, m. *rottenness, decay.*

marcŭlus -i, m. *a small hammer.*

Marcus -i, *a Roman praenomen*, abbreviated M.

mărĕ -is, n. *the sea*; mare nostrum, *the Mediterranean*; superum, *the Adriatic*; inferum, *the Tyrrhenian Sea.*

margărīta -ae, f. and **margărītum** -i n. *a pearl.*

margĭno -are, *to border.*

margo -ĭnis, m. and f. *a border, edge, boundary.*

mărīnus -a -um, *of the sea, marine*: ros, *rosemary.*

mărītālis -e, *conjugal, matrimonial.*

mărītĭmus (mărĭtŭmus) -a -um, *of*

or *on the sea, marine*; praedo, *a pirate*; n. pl. as subst. *the sea-coast*.

mărĭto -are, *to marry, give in marriage*; of vines, *to bind* to a tree, *to train*.

mărĭtus -a -um, *matrimonial, nuptial*; of plants, *tied* or *trained together*; As subst. **mărĭtus** -i, m. *husband. lover, suitor*; **mărĭta** -ae, f. *wife*.

Mărĭus -a -um, *the name of a Roman gens*.

marmor -ŏris, n. *marble statue; stone; the white foamy surface of the sea*.

marmŏrĕus -a -um, *of marble, like marble*.

Măro -ōnis, m. *the cognomen of the poet P. Vergilius*.

marra -ae, f. *a hoe*.

Mars Martis, m. (old form, **Mavors**) *Mars*, *god of agriculture and of war*. Transf., *war, battle, fight*. Adj. **Martĭus** and poet. **Māvortĭus** -a -um, *of Mars*; Martius (mensis), *the month of March; warlike*. Adj. **Martĭālis** -e, *of Mars*; m. as subst. *a priest of Mars* or *soldier of the Legio Martia*.

Marsi -ōrum, m. *an ancient people of Latium*; adj. **Marsĭcus** and **Marsus** -a -um; Marsicum bellum, *the Social War*.

marsuppĭum -i, n. *purse, pouch*.

[1]Martĭālis -e, adj. from Mars; q.v.

[2]Martĭālis -is, m. M. Valerius, *Martial*, *the writer of epigrams*.

Martĭgĕna -ae, m. *offspring of Mars*.

Martĭus -a -um, adj. from Mars; q.v.

mas măris, m. *the male; manly, vigorous*.

mascŭlus -a -um, *male; manly, bold*.

Măsĭnissa -ae, m. *king of Numidia*.

massa -ae, f. *a lump, mass*.

massĭcum -i, n. *Massic wine*.

Massĭlĭa -ae, f. *a town in Gallia Narbonensis* (now *Marseilles*); adj. **Massĭlĭensis** -e.

mastīgĭa -ae, m. *a scoundrel*.

mastrūca -ae, f. *a sheepskin*.

matăra -ae, and **matăris** -is, f. *a pike, lance*.

mătellĭo -ōnis, m. *a small pot, vessel*.

māter, mātris, f. *mother; source, origin*.

mătercŭla -ae, f. *little mother*.

mātĕrĭa -ae, and **mātĕrĭes** -ēi, f. *matter, material, stuff; timber*. Transf., *subject-matter; occasion, cause; natural disposition*.

mātĕrĭo -are, *to construct of wood*.

mātĕrĭor -ari, dep. *to fell wood*.

mătĕris = matara; q.v.

māternus -a -um, *of a mother, maternal*.

mātertĕra -ae, f. *maternal aunt*.

māthēmătĭcus -a -um, *mathematical*; m. as subst. *a mathematician* or *astrologer*; f. **māthēmătĭca** -ae, *mathematics* or *astrology*.

mātrĭcīda -ae, c. *a matricide*.

mātrĭcīdĭum -i, n. *slaying of a mother, matricide*.

mātrĭmōnĭum -i, n. *marriage*.

mātrĭmus -a -um, *having a mother still living*.

[1]mātrōna -ae, f. *a married woman, matron*.

[2]Mātrōna -ae, m. *a river in Gaul* (now *the Marne*).

mātrōnālis -e, *of a married woman, matronly*; n. pl. as subst. **Mātrōnālĭa** -ĭum, *a festival held by Roman matrons*.

matta -ae, f. *a mat of rushes*.

mattĕa (**mattÿa**) -ae, f. *a dainty dish*.

mātūresco mātūrescĕre mātūrŭi, *to ripen, become ripe*.

mātūrĭtās -ātis, f. *ripeness, maturity; the right moment, fullness of time*.

mātūro -are: transit., *to make ripe, ripen; to quicken, hasten, accelerate; to anticipate, do too soon*; intransit., *to hasten, make haste*.

mātūrus -a -um, *ripe, mature, grown up, developed, perfect; timely, quick, speedy, early*. Adv. **mātūrē** *at the right time, seasonably, opportunely: in good time, betimes, early; too soon, prematurely*.

mātūtīnus -a -um, *early in the morning, of morning*.

Mauri -orum, m. *the Moors*; adj. **Maurus** -a -um; subst. **Maurītānĭa** -ae, f. *Mauritania*.

māvŏlo = malo; q.v.

Māvors -vortis, m. archaic and poet. for Mars; adj. **Māvortĭus** -a -um.

maxilla -ae, f. *jaw-bone, jaw*.

maxĭmĭtās -ātis, f. *greatness, size*.

maxĭmus, superl. of magnus; q.v.

māzŏnŏmus -i, m. or **māzŏnŏmon** -i, n. *a charger, large dish*.

mĕātus -ūs, m. *a going, motion; a way, path*.

Mēcastor; see Castor.

meddix -īcis, m. *an Oscan magistrate*.

Mēdēa -ae, f. *an enchantress, who helped Jason to obtain the golden fleece*.

mĕdĕor -ēri, dep. *to heal, to cure, assist, alleviate*; pres. partic. as subst. **mĕdens** -entis, m. *a physician*.

Mēdi -orum, m. *the Medes*; poet. = the *Persians*.

mĕdĭastīnus -i, m. *a drudge*.

mĕdĭca -ae, f. *lucerne, clover*.

mĕdĭcābĭlis -e, *curable*.

mĕdĭcāmen -ĭnis, n. *a drug, medicine, remedy; poison: dye, rouge*.

mĕdĭcāmentum -i, n. *a drug, medicine, remedy; a magic potion; poison; embellishment*.

mĕdĭcātus -ūs, m. *means of enchantment, charm*.

mĕdĭcīnus -a -um, *of the art of healing*; f. as subst. **mĕdĭcīna** -ae, *the art of healing; medicine; cure*.

mĕdĭco -are, *to drug; to dye*; partic. **mĕdĭcātus** -a -um, *steeped, drugged*.

mĕdĭcor -ari, dep., *to heal, cure*.

mĕdĭcus -a -um, *healing, medicinal*; m. as subst. **mĕdĭcus** -i, *a doctor, physician*.

mĕdimnum -i, n. and **mĕdimnus** -i, m. *a Greek measure of capacity*.

mĕdĭocris -e, *moderate, middling, ordinary*; adv. **mĕdĭocrĭter** *moderately, tolerably; with moderation*.

mĕdĭocrĭtās -ātis, f. *moderation*,

*medium, the mean; mediocrity, in-
significance.*

Mědiŏlānum and **-lānĭum** -i, n. *a
town in Cisalpine Gaul (now Milan).*

měditāmentum -i, n. *preparation,
practice.*

měditātĭo -ōnis, f. (1) *a thinking over,
contemplation.* (2) *practice, exercise,
preparation.*

měditerrānĕus -a -um, *inland*: n. pl.
as subst., *inland country.*

měditor -ari, dep. (1) *to think over,
consider;* esp. *to think about doing, to
meditate, intend.* (2) *to practise.*
Perf. partic. in pass. sense **měditātus**
-a -um, *meditated, considered, prepared;* adv. **měditātē,** *thoughtfully,
thoroughly.*

mědĭus -a -um, *middle, midmost, mid;
intervening, central, neutral, intermediate.* N. as subst. **mědĭum** -i,
*the middle; the public eye, everyday
life; the community, common good.*
Adv. **mědĭē,** *moderately.*

mědĭus fīdĭus; see fidius.

mědulla -ae, f. *the marrow of the bones.*

Mēdus; see Medi.

Mědūsa -ae, f. *one of the Gorgons, slain
by Perseus.*

Měgăra -ae, f. (and -orum, n. pl.).
(1) *a town in Greece.* (2) *a town in
Sicily.*

měgistānes -um, m. *grandees, mag-
nates.*

měhercŭle, měhercle; see Hercules.

měl mellis, n. *honey; sweetness,
pleasantness.*

mělanchŏlĭcus -a -um, *having black
bile, melancholy.*

mělānūrus -i, m. *small edible sea-fish.*

mělĭcus -a -um, *musical; lyrical, lyric.*

mělĭlōtŏs -i, f. *a species of clover.*

mělĭmēla -orum, n. pl. *honey-apples.*

mělĭor -us, compar. of bonus; q.v.

mělisphyllum and **mělissophyllŏn**
-i, n. *balm.*

Mělĭta -ae, f. *ine island of Malta;* adj.
Mělĭtensis -e, *of Malta.*

mělĭuscŭlus -a -um, *somewhat better;*
adv. **mělĭuscŭlē,** *somewhat better,
pretty well* (in health).

mellifer -fěra -fěrum, *producing honey.*

mellitus -a -um, *honeyed; sweet as
honey.*

[1]**mělōs,** n. *a tune, song.*

[2]**Mēlŏs** -i, f. *an island in the Aegean Sea.*

Melpŏmēnē -ēs, f. *the Muse of tragic
poetry.*

membrāna -ae, f. *a thin skin, film,
membrane; prepared skin, parchment.*

membrātim, *limb by limb; piecemeal,
singly; in short sentences.*

membrum -i, n. *a limb, member, part
(of the body); a clause in a sentence.*

měmĭni -nisse, perf. with sense of
present, *to remember, recollect.* Transf.
to make mention of, to mention.

měmor -ŏris, *mindful, remembering;
with a good memory; grateful, thoughtful, prudent; reminiscent, reminding.*

měmŏrābĭlis -e, *remarkable, worthy of
mention, memorable.*

měmŏrandus -a -um, gerundive from
memoro; q.v.

měmŏrātor -ōris, m. *a narrator.*

měmŏrātus -ūs, m. *mention.*

měmŏrĭa -ae, *memory, the capacity for
remembering, remembrance; record of
the past, tradition, history.*

měmŏrĭŏla -ae, f. *memory.*

měmŏrĭter, *by heart, from memory.*

měmŏro -are, *to mention, call to mind,
relate;* gerundive **měmŏrandus** -a
-um, *notable, memorable.*

Memphis -is and -īdos, f. *a city of
Egypt.*

Mĕnander -dri, m. *a Greek comic poet.*

menda -ae, f.; see mendum.

mendācĭum -i, n. *lie, falsehood.*

mendax -ācis, *lying, mendacious, false.*

mendīcĭtās -atis, f. *beggary.*

mendīco -are and **mendĭcor** -ari,
dep. *to beg, go begging; beg for.*

mendīcus -a -um, adj. *poor as a beggar,
beggarly; paltry, pitiful;* m. as subst.
mendĭcus -i, *a beggar.*

mendōsus -a -um, *full of faults,
inaccurate, making mistakes;* adv.
mendōsē, *faultily.*

mendum -i, n. and **menda** -ae, f. *a
fault, defect, blemish, mistake.*

Měnēlāus -i, m. *brother of Agamemnon,
husband of Helen.*

mens mentis, f. *mind, understanding,
intellect, judgment; feelings, disposition; courage; opinion, thoughts;
intention, resolve.*

mensa -ae, f. *a table, counter, altar; a
course at a meal.*

mensārĭus -i, m. *a financial com-
missioner.*

mensĭo -ōnis, f. *measuring.*

mensis -is, m., *a month.*

mensor -ōris, m., *a measurer, surveyor;
an architect.*

menstrŭus -a -um, *monthly; lasting a
month;* n. as subst. *rations for a
month, a month in office.*

mensūra -ae, f. *measuring; measure,
standard, capacity; amount, proportion.*

menta (mentha) -ae, f. *the herb mint.*

mentĭo -ōnis, f. *mention.*

mentĭor -iri, dep. *to lie; to deceive,
mislead, disappoint; to say falsely,
invent; fabricate; to counterfeit,
put on, assume.* Hence pres. partic.
mentĭens -entis, *lying;* m. as subst. *a
fallacy, sophism;* perf. partic. **men-
tītus** -a -um, *lying, fictitious.*

mentum -i, n. *the chin.*

měo měare, *to go, pass.*

měphītis -is, f. *a noxious exhalation,
malaria;* personif., *the goddess who
protects against malaria.*

měrācus -a -um, *pure, unmixed.*

mercābĭlis -e, *that can be bought.*

mercātor -ōris, m. *a merchant, whole-
sale trader.*

mercātōrĭus -a -um, *relating to trade.*

mercātūra -ae, f. *trade, traffic; merchandise.*

mercātus -ūs, m. *trade, traffic, business;
a market, fair, place of business.*

mercēdŭla -ae, f. *low wages or rent.*

mercennārĭus (mercēnārĭus) -a -um, *hired, paid;* m. as subst. *a hired servant.*

mercēs -ēdis, *hire, pay, wages; a bribe; cost, punishment; interest, rent, income.*

mercĭmōnĭum -i, n. *goods, merchandise.*

mercor -ari, dep. *to carry on trade, to traffic; to buy.*

Mercŭrĭus -a -m. *Mercury, messenger of the gods;* adj. Mercŭrĭālis -e, *of Mercury;* m. pl. as subst. *a corporation of traders at Rome.*

merda -ae, f. *excrement.*

mērenda -ae, f. *a luncheon.*

mĕrĕo -ēre -ŭi, ĭtum, and mĕrĕor ēri -ĭtus, dep. *to deserve, earn, obtain;* esp., *to earn pay as a soldier, serve as a soldier.* Hence perf. partic. mĕrĭtus -a -um, *deserving;* in pass. sense, *deserved.* N. as subst. mĕrĭtum -i, *desert, merit; a good action, benefit, service; blame, fault, grounds, reason.* Abl. as adv. mĕrĭtō, *deservedly, rightly.*

mĕretrīcĭus -a -um, *of a harlot;* adv. mĕretrīcĭē.

mĕretrīcŭla -ae, f. *a little harlot.*

mĕretrix -īcis, f. *a harlot.*

mergae -arum, f. *a two-pronged fork.*

mergēs -gĭtis, f. *a sheaf of corn.*

mergo mergĕre mersi mersum, *to dip, plunge into liquid, immerse, sink, overwhelm.*

mergus -i, m. *a sea-bird, esp. a gull.*

mērĭdĭānus -a -um, *of midday, meridian; southern.*

mērĭdĭātĭo -ōnis, f. *midday sleep, siesta.*

mērĭdĭēs -ēi, m., *midday, noon; the south.*

mērĭdĭo -are, *to take a siesta.*

¹mĕrĭto -are, *to earn regularly.*

²mĕrĭto, adv. from mereo; q.v.

mĕrĭtōrĭus -a -um, *hired;* n. pl. as subst., *lodgings.*

mĕrĭtum -i, n., subst. from mereo; q.v.

mĕrops -ōpis, f., *a bird, the bee-eater.*

merso -are, *to dip in, immerse.*

mĕrŭla -ae, f. *a blackbird; a fish, the sea-carp.*

mĕrus -a -um, *pure, unmixed; complete, sheer;* esp. of wine, *undiluted;* n. as subst. mĕrum -i, *wine unmixed with water.*

merx (mers) mercis, f. *merchandise, goods, wares.*

Mĕsŏpŏtămĭa -ae, f. *the country between the Euphrates and the Tigris.*

Messāna -ae, f. *a town in Sicily on the straits between Italy and Sicily.*

messis -is, f. *harvest, crop; time of harvest, harvest-tide.*

messor -ōris, m. *a reaper, mower.*

messōrĭus -a -um, *of a reaper.*

mēta -ae, f. *a pyramidal column* used as a turning-post or winning-post; *any turning-point; a goal, end, boundary.*

mĕtallum -i, n. *a metal; a mine, quarry* (esp. plur.).

mĕtămorphōsis -is, f. *transformation;*

plur. Mĕtămorphōsēs -ĕōn, *the title of a poem by Ovid.*

mĕtăphŏra -ae, f. *metaphor.*

mētātor -ōris, m. *a measurer, one who marks out.*

Mētaurus -i, m. *a river in Umbria.*

mētĭor mētiri mensus, dep., *to measure; to traverse, pass over; to estimate, judge.*

mĕto mĕtĕre messŭi messum, *to reap, mow, gather harvest; to mow down, cut off.*

mētor -ari, dep. (and mēto -are) *to measure off, lay out.*

metrēta -ae, f. *a Greek liquid measure.*

metrum -i, n. *a measure; metre.*

mĕtŭcŭlōsus -a -um, *timid; frightful.*

mĕtŭo -ŭĕre -ŭi -ŭtum, *to fear, be afraid.*

mĕtus -ūs, m. *fear, dread; reverence, awe.*

mĕus -a -um, *my, mine;* Nero meus, *my friend Nero.*

mīca -ae, f. *a crumb, morsel, grain.*

mĭco -are -ŭi, *to move rapidly to and fro, vibrate, flicker; to shine, glitter, sparkle.*

Mĭdās (Mĭda) -ae, m. *a king of Phrygia, who turned to gold everything that he touched.*

mĭgrātĭo -ōnis, f. *removal, change of home.*

mĭgrātū, abl. sing. m., *in transport.*

mĭgro -are: intransit., *to migrate, depart; to change;* transit., *to move, transport; to transgress.*

mīlēs -ĭtis, c. *a soldier; a private soldier, infantryman;* coll. *soldiery.*

mīlĭtāris -e, *of a soldier, military;* m. as subst. *a soldier;* adv. mīlĭtārĭtĕr, *in a soldierly manner.*

mīlĭtĭa -ae, f. *military service, warfare;* domi militiaeque, *at home and abroad, at peace and in war;* meton., *the military, soldiery.*

mīlĭto -are, *to serve as a soldier, be a soldier.*

mĭlĭum -i, n. *millet.*

millĕ, *a thousand;* plur. mīlĭa (millĭa) -ĭum, *thousands;* mille passuum, *a thousand paces, a Roman mile.*

mille(n)sĭmus -a -um, *thousandth.*

millĭārĭum (mīlĭārĭum) -i, n. *a mile-stone.*

millĭārĭus (mīlĭārĭus) -a -um, *containing a thousand.*

millĭē(n)s, *a thousand times.*

mīlŭīnus (milvīnus) -a -um, *of a kite; kite-like.*

mīlŭus (milvus) -i, m. *a kite; a fish, the gurnard.*

mīma -ae, f. *an actress.*

mīmĭcus -a -um, *farcical;* adv. mīmĭcē.

mīmŭla -ae, f., *a little actress.*

mīmus -i, m. *a mimic actor; a mime, farce.*

¹mīna, f. *smooth, hairless.*

²mīna -ae, f. *a Greek weight;* also *a Greek coin.*

mĭnae -arum, f. *battlements, parapets.* Transf., *threats, menaces.*

mĭnātĭo -ōnis, f. *threatening, menace.*

mĭnax -ācis, f. *projecting, overhanging.* Transf., *threatening.* Adv. **mĭnācĭtĕr,** *threateningly.*

mĭnĕo -ēre, *to project, overhang.*

Mĭnerva -ae, f. *goddess of wisdom and patroness of arts and sciences.* Transf., *wit, skill, art*; esp. *working in wool.*

mĭniātus -a -um, *coloured with red lead, painted vermilion.*

mĭnĭmē; see parum.

mĭnĭmus; see parvus.

mĭnister -tri, m. and **mĭnistra** -ae, f. *servant, attendant, assistant.*

mĭnistĕrĭum -i, n. *service, attendance, employment*; in plur., *attendants, retinue.*

mĭnistra -ae, f.; see minister.

mĭnistrātor -ōris, m., **mĭnistrātrix** -īcis, f. *a servant, attendant, assistant.*

mĭnistro -are, *to serve, wait,* esp. *at table; to attend to, take care of, direct; to serve, supply, provide.*

mĭnĭtābundus -a -um, *threatening.*

mĭnĭto -are and **mĭnĭtor** -ari dep. *to threaten.*

mĭnĭum -i, n. *native cinnabar; red-lead, vermilion.*

¹**mĭnor** -ari, dep. *to jut out, project.* Transf., *to threaten, menace* (with dat.). Adv. from partic. **mĭnantĕr,** *threateningly.*

²**mĭnor** -ōris, compar. of parvus; q.v.

Mĭnōs -ōis and -ōnis, *king of Crete; after his death, a judge in Tartarus.*

Mĭnōtaurus -i, m. *a monster, half-bull, half-man, slain by Theseus.*

mĭnŭmē and **mĭnŭmus**; see minim-.

mĭnŭo -ŭĕre -ŭi -ūtum, *to make smaller, lessen, diminish; to cut to pieces.* Hence partic. **mĭnūtus** -a -um, *small, petty, insignificant;* adv. **mĭnūtē.**

mĭnus; see parvus.

mĭnuscŭlus -a -um, *rather small.*

mĭnūtal -ālis, n. *a dish of mincemeat.*

mĭnūtātim, *bit by bit, gradually.*

mĭnūtĭa -ae, f. *smallness.*

mĭnūtus -a -um, partic. from minuo; q.v.

mīrābĭlis -e *wonderful, extraordinary, unusual;* adv. **mīrābĭlĭtĕr.**

mīrābundus -a -um, *wondering.*

mīrācŭlum -i, n. *a wonderful thing, prodigy, miracle; wonder, surprise.*

mīrātĭo -ōnis, f. *wonder, astonishment.*

mīrātor -ōris, m. *an admirer.*

mīrātrix -īcis, f. adj. *wondering.*

mīrĭfĭcus -a -um *causing wonder, wonderful, astonishing;* adv. **mīrĭfĭcē.**

mirmillo (murm-) -ōnis, m. *a kind of gladiator.*

mīror -ari, dep. *to wonder, be astonished (at); to admire, look on with admiration;* gerundive **mirandus** -a -um, *wonderful.*

mīrus -a -um, *wonderful, astonishing, extraordinary;* adv. **mīrē.**

miscellānĕa -ōrum, n. pl., *a hash, hotchpotch.*

miscĕo miscēre miscŭi mixtum, *to mix, mingle; to combine, unite; to prepare by mixing; to confuse, confound.*

mĭsellus -a -um, *miserable, wretched, little.*

Mĭsēnus -i, m. *the trumpeter of Aeneas*; **Mĭsēnum** -i, n. *a promontory and town in Campania.*

mĭser -ĕra -ĕrum, *wretched, unhappy, sad;* adv. **mĭsĕrē.**

mĭsĕrābĭlis -e, *sad, wretched, mournful, plaintive;* adv. **mĭsĕrābĭlĭtĕr.**

mĭsĕrātĭo -ōnis, f. *pity, compassion; a pathetic speech or tone.*

mĭsĕrĕo -ēre and **mĭsĕrĕor** -ēri, dep. *to pity* (with genit.); **ƒ** impers. **mĭsĕret** and dep. **mĭsĕrētur,** *it excites pity, one pities.*

mĭsĕresco -ĕre, *to pity, have compassion on* (with genit.).

mĭsĕrĭa -ae, f. *wretchedness, unhappiness, distress.*

mĭsĕrĭcordĭa -ae, f. *pity, compassion, mercy; an appeal to pity.*

mĭsĕrĭcors -cordis, *pitiful, compassionate.*

mĭsĕror -ari, dep. *to bewail, deplore; to pity, have compassion on*; gerundive **mĭsĕrandus** -a -um, *pitiable, lamentable.*

missĭcĭus -a -um, *discharged from military service.*

missĭlis -e, *that can be thrown;* n. as subst., *a missile.*

missĭo -ōnis, f. *a sending off, letting go, releasing, discharge; cessation, termination.*

missĭto -are, *to send repeatedly.*

¹**missus** -ūs, m. *a letting go, sending, throwing; a shot, the distance shot;* in races, *a course, heat.*

²**missus** -a -um, partic. from mitto; q.v.

mītesco -ĕre, *to become mild, soft, or ripe; to be allayed, to subside.*

Mithrĭdātes -is, m. *name of several kings of Pontus.*

mītĭgātĭo -ōnis, f. *assuaging, appeasing.*

mītĭgo -are, *to make mild, or ripe; to soothe, appease, pacify.*

mītis -e, *mild, soft, ripe; gentle;* of style, *mellow;* compar. adv. **mītĭus;** superl. **mītissĭmē.**

mitra -ae, f. *a head-dress, turban.*

mitrātus -a -um, *wearing the mitra.*

mitto mittĕre mīsi missum, *to send, dispatch; to send as a gift; to fling; to shed; to utter; to let go, release, give up; to dismiss, discharge; to pass over a subject.*

mītŭlus (mȳtŭlus, mūtŭlus) -i, m. *an edible mussel.*

mixtūra -ae, f. *a mixing, mixture.*

mna = ²**mina**; q.v.

Mnemŏnĭdĕs -um, f. pl. *the Muses.*

Mnēmŏsўnē -ēs, f. *Mnemosyne, mother of the Muses.*

mnēmŏsўnum -i, n. *a souvenir, memorial.*

mōbĭlis -e, *movable, easy to move; pliable, flexible; active, rapid; changeable, inconstant.* Adv. **mōbĭlĭtĕr,** *quickly, easily.*

mōbĭlĭtās -ātis, f. *mobility; inconstancy, changeableness.*

mōbĭlĭto -are, *to set in motion.*

mŏdĕrābĭlis -e, *moderate, restrained.*

mŏdĕrāmen -ĭnis, n. *means of guiding;* rerum, *management, government.*

mŏdĕrātim, *moderately, gradually.*

mŏdĕrātĭo -ōnis, f. *moderating, restraining; moderation, restraint.*

mŏdĕrātor -ōris, m. *a governor, controller, manager;* equorum, *a driver.*

mŏdĕrātrix -īcis, f. *she that governs or controls.*

mŏdĕror -ari, dep. (and mŏdĕro -are), *to keep within bounds; to regulate, restrain; to control, govern, direct.* Hence, from pres. partic. adv. mŏdĕrantĕr, *with controlling force;* perf. partic. mŏdĕrātus -a -um, *restrained, controlled;* adv. mŏdĕrātē, *with restraint.*

mŏdestĭa -ae, f. *moderation; restraint, propriety, orderliness; respect, obedience to authority.*

mŏdestus -a -um, *moderate, within bounds; orderly, restrained;* adv. mŏdestē.

mŏdĭcus -a -um, *moderate, within bounds, limited; temperate; ordinary, undistinguished.* Adv. mŏdĭcē, *moderately; to a limited extent; temperately, with restraint.*

mŏdĭfĭcātus -a -um, *measured.*

mŏdĭus -i, m. *a Roman corn-measure;* pleno modio, *in full measure, abundantly.*

mŏdŏ, *by measure; hence only, merely, but, just;* si modo, modo si, or modo alone with subj., *provided that, if only;* modo ne, *provided that . . . not;* modo non, *all but, nearly;* non modo . . . sed etiam, *not only . . . but also.* Of time, *just, lately; soon, directly;* modo . . . modo . . ., *at one time . . . at another. . . .*

mŏdŭlātĭo -ōnis, f. *rhythmical measure.*

mŏdŭlātor -ōris, m. *a musician.*

mŏdŭlor -ari, dep. *to measure; in music, to modulate, to sing to the accompaniment of an instrument; to play an instrument.* Adv. from partic. mŏdŭlātē, *in time* (of music).

mŏdŭlus -i, m. *a little measure.*

mŏdus -i, m. *a measure, standard of measurement; in music, rhythm, measure, time;* in plur., *strains, numbers.* Transf., *limit, boundary; rule; manner, mode, way, method;* servorum modo, *after the manner of slaves;* eius modi, *in that manner, of that kind.*

moecha -ae, f. *an adulteress.*

moechor -are, dep. *to commit adultery.*

moechus -i, m. *an adulterer.*

moenĕra=munera; see munus.

moenĭa -ĭum, n. pl. *the walls or fortifications of a city, ramparts, bulwarks;* poet., *castle, dwelling.*

Moesi -ōrum, m. pl. *a people between Thrace and the Danube;* Moesĭa -ae f., *their country.*

mŏla -ae, f. *a mill-stone;* plur., *a mill.* Transf., *grits, coarse meal or flour.*

mŏlāris -e, *of a mill, to do with grinding;* m. as subst. *a millstone; a molar tooth, grinder.*

mōlēs -is, f. *a shapeless mass,* e.g. *of rock; a massive construction,* e.g. dam, *mole, large building;* moles belli, *large military machines.* Transf., *a mass of men; greatness, might, power; trouble, difficulty.*

mŏlestĭa -ae, f. *annoyance, troublesomeness;* of style, *affectation, stiffness.*

mŏlestus -a -um, *burdensome, troublesome, irksome;* of style, *affected, laboured.* Adv. mŏlestē, *with annoyance;* moleste fero, *I take it badly, am annoyed;* of style, *affectedly.*

mōlīmen -ĭnis, n. and mōlīmentum -i, n. *great effort, exertion, endeavour.*

mōlĭor -iri, dep.: transit., *to stir, displace, work at; to construct laboriously, build, erect, contrive; to strive after; to destroy laboriously undermine;* intransit., *to toil, struggle, exert oneself.*

mōlītĭo -ōnis, f. *effort, laborious undertaking; demolition.*

mōlītor -ōris, m. *a builder, contriver.*

mollesco -ĕre, *to become soft or gentle.*

mollĭcŭlus -a -um, *soft, tender; effeminate.*

mollĭo -ire, *to make soft, pliable, supple; to make gentle or effeminate; to alleviate trouble; to ease a gradient.*

mollĭpēs -pĕdis, *soft-footed.*

mollis -e, *soft, tender, pliant, supple;* of weather, *mild;* of gradients, *easy;* of character, *tender, gentle, sensitive, or effeminate;* of circumstances, *easy, mild, pleasant;* of speech, *tender, moving.* Adv. mollĭtĕr, *softly, easily, gently, mildly; effeminately.*

mollĭtĭa -ae, and mollĭtĭes -ei, f. *softness, flexibility; tenderness, mildness, sensibility; effeminacy.*

mollĭtūdo -ĭnis, f. *softness, pliability; tenderness, sensibility.*

mōlo -ĕre -ŭi -ĭtum, *to grind in a mill.*

Mŏlossi -orum, m. *a people in Epirus.* Adj. Mŏlossus -a -um, pes, *a metrical foot, consisting of three long syllables;* m. as subst. *a Molossian hound.*

mōly -ўos, n. *the herb moly.*

mōmen -ĭnis, n. *movement; a moving mass; momentum, impulse.*

mōmentum -i, n. *movement, motion; change, alteration; a cause of motion, impulse;* mental *impulse, influence; weight, importance;* of time, *a turning-point, minute, moment.*

Mŏna -ae, f. *the Isle of Man; also the Isle of Anglesey.*

mŏnēdŭla -ae, f. *jackdaw.*

mŏnĕo -ēre, *to remind, admonish, warn, advise, instruct.* N. pl. of partic. as subst. mŏnĭta -ōrum, *warnings; prophecies.*

mŏnēris -is, f. *a vessel with one bank of oars.*

Mŏnēta -ae, f. (1) *the mother of the Muses.* (2) *a surname of Juno.* (3) *the mint; money.*

mŏnētālis -e, *of the mint.*

mŏnīle -is, n. *necklace, collar.*

mŏnĭmentum = monumentum; q.v.

mŏnĭtĭo -ōnis, f. *reminding, warning.*

mŏnĭtor -ōris, m. *one who reminds or prompts; an adviser, instructor.*

mŏnĭtus -ūs, m. *warning, admonition.*

mŏnŏgrammos or **-us** -i, m. adj. *sketched, shadowy.*

mŏnŏpŏdĭum -i, n. *a table with one foot.*

mons, montis, m. *a mountain; a mass; a great rock.*

monstrātor -ōris m. *a pointer-out; an inventor.*

monstro -are, *to show, point out; to ordain, appoint; to inform against, denounce.*

monstrum -i, n. *a wonder, portent.*

monstrŭōsus (monstrōsus) -a -um *strange, wonderful;* adv. **monstrŭōsē.**

montānus -a -um, *of a mountain, or mountainous;* m. as subst. *a mountaineer;* n. pl. as subst. *mountainous country.*

montĭcŏla -ae, c. *a highlander.*

montĭvăgus -a -um, *wandering over mountains.*

montŭōsus (montōsus) -a -um, *mountainous.*

mŏnŭmentum (mŏnĭmentum) -i, n. *a memorial, monument; a commemorative building; written memorials, annals, memoirs.*

¹mŏra -ae, f. *delay, hindrance; any space of time.*

²mŏra -ae, f. *a division of the Spartan army.*

mŏrālis -e, *moral, ethical.*

mŏrātor -ōris, m. *a delayer, retarder; an advocate who talks against time.*

¹mŏrātus -a -um, *having certain manners or morals; adapted to a character, in character, characteristic.*

morbĭdus -a -um, *sickly, diseased, unwholesome.*

morbus -i, m. *disease, sickness.*

mordax -ācis, *biting, snappish; stinging, pungent; satirical.* Compar. adv. **mordācius,** *more bitingly.*

mordĕo mordēre mŏmordi morsum, *to bite; to cut into; to nip, sting; to vex, hurt, pain.*

mordĭcus, *with the teeth, by biting.*

mŏrētum -i, n. *a salad.*

mŏrĭbundus -a -um, *dying, expiring; subject to death, mortal; causing death, deadly.*

mōrĭgĕror -ari, dep. (and **mōrĭgĕro** -are) *to comply with, gratify.*

mōrĭgĕrus -a -um, *compliant, accommodating.*

mŏrĭor mŏri mortŭus mŏrĭtūrus, dep. *to die; to die away, wither away, decay.* Hence partic. **mortŭus** -a -um, *dead; decayed, extinct; half-dead;* m. as subst. *a corpse.*

mŏrŏlŏgus -i, m. *talking like a fool.*

¹mŏror -ari, dep. *to delay:* intransit., *to linger, loiter, stay;* transit., *to retard, detain, hinder;* nihil (nil) morari, *to care nothing for.*

²mŏror -ari, dep. *to be foolish.*

mŏrōsĭtās -ātis, f. *peevishness, fretfulness.*

mŏrōsus -a -um, *peevish, captious, fretful;* adv. **mŏrōsē.**

Morphēus -ĕos, m. *god of dreams.*

mors mortis, f. *death; a corpse; a cause of death or destruction.*

morsus -ūs, m. *a bite, biting; pungency; a verbal attack;* in gen. *pain, vexation.*

mortālis -e, *subject to death, mortal; transitory, perishable; human, earthly;* m. as subst. *a mortal man.*

mortālĭtās -ātis, f. *liability to death.*

mortĭfer or **mortĭfĕrus** -fĕra -fĕrum, *causing death, fatal, deadly;* adv. **mortĭfĕrē.**

mortŭālĭa -ium, n. *funeral songs, dirges.*

mortŭus -a -um, partic. from morior; q.v.

mōrum -i, n. *a mulberry; a blackberry.*

¹mōrus -i, f. *a mulberry tree.*

²mōrus -a -um, *silly, foolish.*

mōs, mōris, *the will, inclination; morem homini gerere, to humour a person; custom, usage, wont, rule;* in plur., *ways, conduct, character, morals.*

Mōsa -ae, f. *a river in Gaul (now Meuse).*

Mōsella -ae, f. *a river in Gaul (now Moselle).*

mōtĭo -ōnis, f. *movement.*

mōto -are, *to move about.*

¹mōtus -a -um, partic. from moveo; q.v.

²mōtus -ūs, m. *motion, movement; terrae, an earthquake; mental activity, emotion; political movement, rebellion, rising, riot.*

mŏvĕo mŏvēre mōvi mōtum, *to move, set in motion, stir; to remove, dispossess, dislodge;* se movere, and in middle sense, moveri, *to move (one-self):* milit., movere signa, movere castra, *to march away; to move mentally, influence, affect, excite; to cause a result; to change, shake;* politically, *to arouse, disturb.*

mox, *soon, presently; then, thereupon.*

mūcĭdus -a -um, *snivelling; mouldy, musty.*

Mūcĭus -a -um, *name of a Roman gens;* adj. **Mūcĭānus** -a -um.

mucro -ōnis, m. *a sharp point or edge; a sword.*

mūcus -i, m. *mucous matter.*

mūgĭl (mūgĭlis) -is, m. *a fish, perhaps mullet.*

mūgĭnor -ari, dep. *to loiter, dally.*

mūgĭo -ire, *to bellow, low, roar, rumble, groan.*

mūgītus -ūs, m. *lowing, bellowing, rumbling, groaning.*

mūla -ae, f. *a female mule.*

mulcĕo mulcēre mulsi mulsum, *to stroke; to soothe, appease, charm.*

Mulcĭber -ēris and -ēri, m. *surname of Vulcan;* meton., *fire.*

mulco -are, *to thrash; to handle roughly.*

mulctra -ae, f., **mulctrārĭum** -i, n., and **mulctrum** -i, n. *milk-pail.*

mulgĕo mulgēre mulsi, *to milk.*

mŭlĭēbris -e, *of a woman, feminine; effeminate;* adv. **mŭlĭēbrĭter.**

mŭlĭer -ĕris, f. *a woman; a wife, matron.*

mŭlĭĕrārĭus -a -um, *womanish.*

mŭlĭercŭla -ae, f. *a little woman.*

mŭlĭĕrōsĭtās -ātis, f. *love of women.*

mŭlĭĕrōsus -a -um, *fond of women.*

mŭlīnus -a -um, *of a mule, mulish.*

mūlĭo -ōnis, m. *a mule-keeper, mule-driver.*

mūlĭōnĭus -a -um, *of a muleteer.*

mullus -i, m. *the red mullet.*

mulsus -a -um, *honeyed; as sweet as honey;* n. as subst. *wine sweetened with honey, mead.*

multa -ae, f. *a fine, mulct.*

multangŭlus -a -um, *many-cornered.*

multātīcĭus -a -um, *relating to a fine.*

multātĭo -onis, f. *fining.*

multēsĭmus -a -um, *very small.*

multĭcāvus -a -um, *porous.*

multĭcĭa -orum, n. pl. *finely woven garments.*

multĭfārĭam, *on many sides, in many places.*

multĭfĭdus -a -um, *cloven into many parts.*

multĭformis -e, *having many shapes.*

multĭfŏrus -a -um, *pierced with many holes.*

multĭgĕnĕris -e and **multĭgĕnus** -a -um, *of many kinds.*

multĭiŭgus -a -um, and **multĭiūgis** -e, *yoked many together; manifold, of many sorts.*

multĭlŏquax -ācis, *talkative.*

multĭmŏdis, *in many ways, variously.*

multĭplex -plĭcis, *having many folds, winds or turnings; having many parts, manifold, many-sided, versatile; many times as large.*

multĭplĭco -are, *to increase many times, multiply.*

multĭtūdo -ĭnis, f. *a large number, multitude, crowd; common people, mob.*

multo -are, *to punish.*

multus -a -um: sing., *much, great;* plur., *many, numerous;* multi, *the common herd;* ne multa, *briefly, in brief;* ad multum diem, *till late in the day;* in re multus, *prolix on a subject, busy in a matter;* occ., in sing., *many a;* n. acc. sing. as adv. multum, *much, greatly;* abl. multo, *by much, by far.* Compar. plus: in sing., n. only, *more;* genit. of value plūris, at *a higher price, of more value;* in plur. plūres, plūra, *more numerous, several, many.* Superl. plūrimus, *most, very many:* in sing., *of a large number,* like the English *full many a;* of energy, etc., *strong;* genit. of value plūrimi, *at the highest price or value.*

mūlus -i, m. *a mule.*

Mulvĭus pons, *a bridge across the Tiber.*

Mummĭus -a -um, *name of a Roman gens.*

Munda -ae, f. *town in Hispania Baetica.*

mundānus -i, m. *a citizen of the world.*

mundĭtĭa -ae, and **mundĭtĭēs** -ēi, f. *cleanness, neatness, spruceness, elegance.*

¹mundus -a -um, *clean, neat, elegant.*

²mundus -i, m. (1) *toilet-things, adornment.* (2) *the universe, world; mankind.*

mūnĕro -are and **mūnĕror** -ari, dep. *to give, present.*

mūnĭa -iōrum, n. pl., *duties, functions;* esp. *official.*

mūnĭceps -cĭpis, c. *the citizen of a municipium; a fellow-citizen, fellow-countryman.*

mūnĭcĭpālis -e, *belonging to a municipium, municipal.*

mūnĭcĭpĭum -i, n. *a borough, free town, municipal town.*

mūnĭfĭcentĭa -ae, f. *generosity.*

mūnĭfĭco -are, *to present generously.*

mūnĭfĭcus -a -um, *generous, liberal;* of wealth, *splendid;* adv. **mūnĭfĭcē.**

mūnīmen -ĭnis, n. *a protection, defence.*

mūnīmentum -i, n. *a fortification, defence, protection.*

mūnĭo (moenĭo) -ire, *to build,* esp. *to build a wall;* also *to surround with a wall; to fortify; to secure, defend, protect.* Hence partic. **mūnītus** -a -um, *fortified, secured.*

mūnītĭo -ōnis, f. *fortifying, building up, paving, bridging;* concr., *a fortification.*

mūnīto -are, *to pave, make passable.*

mūnĭtor -ōris, m. *a builder of fortifications, sapper, engineer.*

mūnus (moenus) -ĕris, n. *an office, function, duty; a charge tax; a service, favour, gift, present; a public show,* esp. *of gladiators: a public building.*

mūnuscŭlum -i, n. *a small gift.*

mūrālis -e, *of a wall, mural;* corona, *the crown given to the first man over the wall of a besieged city.*

¹mūrēna (muraena) -ae, f. *a sea-fish, the murry or lamprey.*

²Mūrēna -ae, m. *a cognomen in the gens Licinia.*

mūrex -ĭcis, m. *the purple-fish; purple dye; a sharp stone, projecting rock.*

mūrĭa -ae, f. *brine, pickle.*

murmillo=mirmillo; q.v.

murmur -ŭris, n. *a murmur, humming, roaring, rumbling, crashing.*

murmŭro -are, *to murmur, roar, crash.*

¹murra (myrrha) -ae, f. *the myrrh-tree; myrrh.*

²murra (myrrha) -ae, f. *a mineral, perhaps fluorspar.*

¹murrĕus (myrrhĕus) -a -um, *perfumed with myrrh; myrrh-coloured.*

²murrĕus (myrrhĕus) -a -um, *made of fluorspar.*

mūrus -i, *a wall, bank or dyke;* fig., *protection, defence.*

mūs, mūris, c. *a mouse or rat.*

Mūsa -ae, f. *a muse; a goddess of music literature and the arts.*

mūsaeus -a -um, *poetical, musical.*

musca -ae, f. *a fly.*

muscārĭum -i, n. *a fly-trap.*

muscĭpŭla -ae, f. and **muscĭpŭlum** -i, n. *a mouse-trap.*

muscōsus -a -um, *mossy.*

muscŭlus -i, m. *a little mouse; a sea-mussel*; milit., *a shed, mantelet.*

muscus -i, m. *moss.*

mūsēus -a -um = musaeus; q.v.

mūsĭcus -a -um, *belonging to poetry or music, musical*; m. as subst. *a musician*; f. sing. **mūsĭca** -ae and **mūsĭcē** -ēs, *music, poetry, learned studies*; adv. **mūsĭcē.**

mussĭto -are: intransit., *to grumble, mutter*; transit., *to keep quiet about a thing.*

musso -are, *to murmur, mutter, whisper; to keep quiet about a thing; to be at a loss.*

mustācĕum -i, n. and **mustācĕus** -i, m., *a must-cake, a sort of wedding-cake.*

mustēla (mustella) -ae, f. *a weasel.*

mustus -a -um, *young, new, fresh*; n. as subst. *new wine, must.*

mūtābĭlis -e, *changeable, variable, inconstant.*

mūtābĭlĭtās -ātis, f. *changeableness.*

mūtātĭo -ōnis, *changing, change, alteration; mutual change, exchange.*

mŭtĭlo -are, *to maim, mutilate, cut off; to curtail, diminish.*

mŭtĭlus -a -um, *maimed, mutilated.*

Mŭtĭna -ae, f. *town in Cisalpine Gaul* (now *Modena*).

mūtĭo (muttĭo) -ire, *to mutter, mumble.*

mūto -are: transit., *to move, shift; to change, alter; to exchange, barter*; with abl., *to give* or *to get one thing in exchange for another*; intransit., *to change, alter.*

mūtŭātĭo -ōnis, f. *borrowing.*

mūtŭor -ari, dep. *to borrow.*

mūtus -a -um, *inarticulate, dumb, mute, silent, still, quiet.*

mūtŭus -a -um. (1) ˈnterchanged, mutual, reciprocal*; n. as subst. *reciprocity, equal return*; abl. as adv. **mūtŭō,** *mutually, reciprocally.* (2) *borrowed, lent:* pecuniam dare mutuam, *to lend*; n. as subst., *a loan.*

mўŏpăro -ōnis, m. *a small piratical galley.*

mўrīcē -ēs, f. and **mўrīca** -ae, f. *the tamarisk.*

myrtētum (murtētum) -i n. *a grove of myrtle-trees.*

myrtĕus (murtĕus) -a -um, *of myrtle; adorned with myrtle.*

myrtum -i, n. *myrtle-berry.*

myrtus -i and -ūs, f. *the myrtle-tree; also a myrtle shaft.*

mystăgōgus -i, m. *a priest who showed sacred places to strangers.*

mystērĭa -orum, n. pl. *mysteries, secrets*, esp. of worship.

mystēs or **mysta** -ae, m. *a priest at the mysteries.*

mystĭcus -a -um, *secret, mystic.*

N

N, n, the thirteenth letter of the Latin Alphabet.

nablĭum -i, n. *a kind of harp* or *lyre.*

nae = ¹nē; q.v.

naenĭa = nenia; q.v.

Naevĭus -a -um, *name of a Roman gens*; esp. of Cn. Naevius, *a poet of the third century B.C.*

naevus -i, m. *a mole on the body.*

Nāĭăs -ădis and **Nāĭs** -ĭdis (-ĭdos); f. *a water-nymph, Naiad*; adj. **Nāĭcus** -a -um.

nam and **namquĕ**, conj., *for.*

nanciscor nancisci nactus *and* nanctus, dep. *to light upon, obtain, meet.*

nānus -i, m. *a dwarf.*

Narbo -ōnis, m. *town in southern Gau* (now *Narbonne*); adj. **Narbōnensis** -e.

Narcissus -i, m. *Narcissus, a beautiful young man changed into the flower of the same name.*

nardus -i, f. and **nardum,** -i, n. *nard.*

nāris -is, f. usually plur. **nāres** -ĭum, *the nostrils, nose.*

narrābĭlis -e, *able to be told.*

narrātĭo -ōnis, f. *telling, relating; a narrative.*

narrātĭuncŭla -ae, f. *a short narrative.*

narrātor -ōris, m. *a relater, narrator.*

narrātus -ūs, m. *narration, narrative.*

narro -are, *to make known; to say speak.*

narthēcĭum -i, n. *a box for perfumes and medicines.*

nārus = gnarus; q.v.

nascor -i, natus (and gnatus), dep. *to be born; to come into existence, arise, be produced.*

Hence partic. **nātus** -a -um, *born, naturally fitted* or *constituted*; pro re nata, *under present circumstances*; annos prope xc natus, *almost ninety years old.* As subst., m. *a son*; f. *a daughter.*

Nāsĭca -ae, m. *name of a family of the Scipios.*

Nāso -ōnis, m. *cognomen of the poet P. Ovidius.*

nassa -ae, f. *a basket for catching fish; a trap, snare.*

nasturcĭum -i, n. *a kind of cress.*

nāsus -i, m. *the nose*; naso suspendere adunco, *to turn up the nose at, ridicule, mock.*

nāsūtus -a -um, *having a large nose; acute, sagacious, satirical.*

nātālīcĭus -a -um, *relating to birth*; n. pl. as subst. *a birthday party.*

nātālis -e, *relating to birth, natal*; m. as subst., *a birthday*; plur. *birth, origin.*

nătātĭo -ōnis, f. *swimming.*

nătātor -ōris. m. *swimmer.*

nātĭo -ōnis, f. *being born, birth; a tribe, race, people*, esp. *uncivilized; a species, stock, class.*

nătis -is, f., usually plur. **nătēs** -ĭum, *the rump, buttocks.*

nātīvus -a -um, *born; native, natural; inborn, innate.*

năto -are, *to swim, float; to stream, flow; to swim with, be full of* (with abl.); f. pl. of partic. as subst. natantes, *fishes.*

nātrix -icis, f. *a water-snake.*

nātū, abl. sing. m. *by birth*; maior natu, *older*.

nātūra -ae, f. *birth; nature, natura qualities* or *disposition, character; an element, substance, essence*; rerum natura, *nature, the world* or *universe*.

nātūrālis -e, *natural, relating to nature*; adv. **nātūrālĭtĕr**, *naturally, by nature*.

nātus -a -um, partic. from nascor; q.v

nauarchus -i, m. *captain of a ship*.

nauclērus -i, m. *the master of a ship*.

naucum -i, n. *a trifle*; in genit. non nauci habere, *to think nothing of*.

naufrăgĭum -i, n. *shipwreck; wreckage; ruin, loss*; naufragium facere, *to suffer shipwreck*.

naufrăgus -a -um, pass., *shipwrecked*; act., *causing shipwreck*.

naulum -i, n. *fare, passage-money*.

naumăchĭa, ae, f. *a naval battle performed as a show*.

nausĕa -ae, f. *sea-sickness, nausea*.

nausĕo -are, *to be sea-sick; to cause disgust, nauseate*.

nausĕŏla -ae, f. *squeamishness*.

nauta -and **nāvĭta** -ae, m. *sailor, mariner*.

nautĭcus -a -um, *of a sailor, nautical*; m. pl. as subst. *sailors*.

nāvālis -e, *of ships, naval, nautical*; n. as subst. **nāvālĕ** -is, *a station for ships*; plur. *a dockyard*, or *materials for ship-building*.

nāvĭcŭla -ae, f. *a little ship, boat*.

nāvĭcŭlārĭus -a -um, *of (small) ships*; f. as subst. *the business of a ship-owner*; m. as subst. *a ship-owner*.

nāvĭfrăgus -a -um, *causing shipwreck*.

nāvĭgābĭlis -e, *navigable*.

nāvĭgātĭo -ōnis, f. *sailing, voyage*.

nāvĭger -gĕra -gĕrum, *ship-bearing, navigable*.

nāvĭgĭum -i, n. *a vessel, ship*.

nāvĭgo -are: intransit., *to sail, voyage, go by sea; to swim*; transit., *to sail over, sail through, navigate*.

nāvis -is, f. *a ship, vessel*; navis longa, *a man-of-war*; oneraria, *a transport*; praetoria, *flag-ship*.

nāvĭta = nauta; q.v.

nāvĭtās (gnāvĭtās) -atis, f. *energy, zeal*.

nāvo -are, *to do energetically*.

nāvus (gnāvus) -a -um, *zealous, energetic*. Adv. **nāvĭtĕr (gnāvĭtĕr)**, *energetically; completely*.

¹nē (nae), used before pronouns, *indeed, truly*.

²nē, *not, that not, lest*; ne . . . quidem, *not even, not . . . either*.

³-nĕ (sometimes **n'**) interrog., enclitic particle.

Nĕăpŏlis -polis, f. (1) *part of Syracuse*. (2) *a sea-port* (now *Naples*).

nēbŭla -ae, f. *vapour, fog, mist, cloud*.

nēbŭlo -ōnis, m. *a good-for-nothing fellow*.

nēbŭlōsus -a -um, *misty, foggy*.

nĕc and **nĕquĕ**, *not; and not, nor*; rarely *not even*; neque enim, *for . . . not*; nec non, *and also*; nec tamen, *and yet . . . not*; nec . . . nec, neque . . . neque, *neither . . . nor*.

necdum (nĕquĕ dum), *and not yet*.

nĕcessārĭus -a -um, *necessary, unavoidable, inevitable; pressing, urgent; closely connected*; as subst. *an intimate friend* or *relative*; n. abl. **nĕcessārĭō**, and adv. **nĕcessārĭē**, *necessarily, unavoidably*.

nĕcessĕ, indecl. adj. n., used with esse and habere; *necessary, unavoidable, inevitable, indispensable*.

nĕcessĭtās -ātis, f. *inevitability, necessity, urgency*; plur. *requirements, necessary expenses*. Transf., *intimate connexion, friendship, relationship*.

nĕcessĭtūdo -ĭnis, f. *necessity, inevitableness; need, want*. Transf., *close connexion, intimate friendship*; plur., *intimate friends, near relations*.

nĕcessum = necesse; q.v.

necnĕ, *or not*.

necnōn (nĕquĕ nōn); see nec.

nĕco -are, *to kill, slay, put to death*.

nĕcŏpīnans -antis, *not expecting, unaware*.

nĕcŏpīnātus (nĕc ŏpīnātus) -a -um *unexpected*; adv. **nĕcŏpīnātō**.

nĕcŏpīnus -a -um; pass., *unexpected*; act., *not expecting*.

nectar -āris, n. *nectar, the drink of the gods; honey, milk, wine*.

nectărĕus -a -um, *of nectar*.

necto nectĕre nexŭi *and* nexi nexum, *to tie, bind, fasten; to fetter, enslave; to affix, attach; to put together, devise*.

nĕcŭbi, *lest anywhere, that nowhere*.

nĕcundĕ, *lest from any quarter, that from no direction*.

nēdum, *not to say; after* (implied) negative, *much less, still less*; after affirmative, *much more*.

nĕfandus -a -um, *not to be spoken of; abominable*.

nĕfārĭus -a -um, *impious, abominable*; adv. **nĕfārĭē**.

nĕfās, n. indecl., *what is contrary to divine command; sin, crime, abomination*; per fas et nefas, *by fair means or foul*; as interj. *monstrous! dreadful!*

nĕfastus -a -um, *forbidden, unholy; unlucky; sinful*; dies nefasti, *days on which no public business could be transacted*.

nĕgātĭo -ōnis, f. *denying*.

nĕgĭto -are, *to persist in denying*.

neglectĭo -ōnis, f. *neglect*.

neglectus -ūs, m. *neglect, disregard*.

neglĕgentĭa -ae, f. *carelessness, negligence*.

neglĕgo -lĕgĕre -lexi -lectum, *to neglect, disregard; to make light of, overlook, omit*.
      Hence partic. **neglĕgens** -entis, *careless*; adv. **neglĕgentĕr**.

nĕgo -are, *to say no; to deny, say that . . . not; to deny a request, refuse to give* or *do*.

nĕgōtĭālis -e, *relating to business*.

nĕgōtĭātĭo -ōnis, f. *bankers' business*.

nĕgōtĭātor -ōris, m. *a business-man; esp. banker*.

nĕgōtĭŏlum -i, n. *a little business*.

nĕgōtĭor -ari, dep. *to carry on business*;

esp. as *a banker*; m. of partic. as subst.
negōtǐans -antis, *a businessman.*

negōtǐōsus -a -um, *full of business, busy.*

negōtǐum -i, n. *business, occupation, employment, task; pains, trouble, difficulty; a matter, piece of business.*

Nĕmĕa -ae, and **Nĕmĕē** -ēs, f. *a valley in Argolis*; adj. **Nĕmĕaeus** -a -um, subst. **Nĕmĕa** -orum, n. pl., *the Nemean games.*

nēmo -inis, c., *no one, nobody*: nemo non, *everyone*; non nemo, *some or many.*

nĕmŏrālis -e and **nĕmŏrensis** -e, *of woods or groves; sylvan.*

nĕmŏrōsus -a -um, *full of groves; thickly leaved, full of foliage.*

nempĕ, *truly, certainly, to be sure.*

nĕmus -ŏris, n. *a wood, grove.*

nēnǐa -ae, f. *a funeral song, dirge; an incantation; nursery ditty, lullaby.*

nĕo nēre nēvi nētum, *to spin; to interweave.*

nĕpa -ae, f. *a scorpion; a crab.*

¹nĕpōs -ōtis, m. *a grandson, a nephew; a descendant; a spendthrift.*

²Nĕpos -pōtis, m., C. Cornelius, *a Roman historian, friend of Cicero.*

neptis -is, f. *a grand-daughter.*

Neptūnus -i, m. *Neptune, god of the sea*; adj. **Neptūnǐus** -a -um.

nēquam, indecl.; compar. **nēquǐor**, superl. **nēquissǐmus**; *worthless, good for nothing, bad*; adv. **nēquǐtĕr**.

nēquāquam, *by no means, not at all.*

nēquĕ = nec; q.v.

nēquĕdum = necdum; q.v.

nēquĕo -ire, īvi and -ǐi -ǐtum, *to be unable.*

nēquīquam (**nēquicquam**), *in vain to no purpose; without good reason.*

nēquīta -ae, and **nēquǐtǐēs** -ēi, f. *worthlessness, badness; esp. extravagance.*

Nerēūs -ĕos and -ĕi, m. *a sea-god.*

Nēro -ōnis, m. *a cognomen in the gens Claudia*; esp. C. Claudius Nero, *fifth Roman emperor* (54–68).

nervōsus -a -um *sinewy, nervous, strong, vigorous*; adv. **nervōsē**.

nervǔlus -i, m., *nerve, strength.*

nervus -i, m. (usually plur.), *sinew, tendon*; fig. *strength, vigour, energy; a string,* esp. *of an instrument; a strap, thong, fetter.*

nescǐo -ire -īvi and -ǐi -ītum, *not to know, to be ignorant; to fail to recognise*; with infin. *to be unable to do*; nescio quis, quid, etc., *I know not who* or *what, somebody, something.*

nescǐus -a -um: act., *not knowing, ignorant, unaware; not knowing how, unable,* with infin.; pass., *unknown.*

Nestŏr -ŏris, m. *the most experienced of the Greek heroes at Troy.*

neu = neve; q.v.

neuter -tra -trum, *neither.* Transf., *of neither sex, neuter.* Adv. **neutrō**, *in neither direction, towards neither side.*

neutǐquam (ne ǔtǐquam), *by no means, not at all.*

nēvĕ or **neu**, *and not, or not, nor* (esp. following ut or ne).

nēvis, nēvult = nonvis, nonvult; see nolo.

nex, nĕcis, f. *death*; usually *violent death, murder.*

nexǐlis -e, *tied together, plainted.*

nexum -i, n. *an arrangement by which a debtor pledged his liberty as security for debt.*

nexus -ūs, m. *a tying together, connecting, restraining*; also in the sense of nexum, q.v.

nī (**nei**) and **nīvĕ**, *if not, unless*; also in the sense of ne, q.v.; quid ni? *why not?*

nīcētērǐum -i, n. *reward of victory, prize.*

nicto -are, *to wink.*

nīdor -ōris, m. *vapour, reek.*

nīdǔlus -i, m. *a little nest.*

nīdus -i, m. *a nest.*

niger -gra -grum, *black, dark-coloured; blackening; bad, unlucky*; n. as subst. *a black spot.*

nigresco nigrescĕre nigrǔi, *to become black, grow dark.*

nigro -are, *to be black*; partic. **nigrans** -antis, *black, dark.*

nigror -ōris, m. *blackness.*

nihǐl and contr. **nīl**, *nothing*; nihil non, *everything*; non nihil, *something*; nihil, *as internal acc.,* or *adv., not at all.*

nihildum, *nothing as yet.*

nihǐlum (**nīlum**), *nothing*; as adv., *not at all*; nihilominus, *nevertheless.*

nīl = nihil; q.v.

Nīlus -i, m. *the river Nile*; adj. **Nīlǐăcus** -a -um.

nimbǐfer -fĕra -fĕrum, *stormy.*

nimbōsus -a -um, *rainy, stormy.*

nimbus -i, m. *cloud, mist*; esp. *a black rain-cloud; a storm, shower.*

nīmīrum, *undoubtedly, certainly, of course* (often ironical).

nǐmis, *very much; too much, excessively.*

nǐmǐus -a -um, *very great; too great, excessive; intemperate, immoderate.* N. as subst. *a great deal, much*; also *excess, too much.*

ningo (**ninguo**) ningĕre ninxi, *to snow*; impers., ningit, *it snows.*

ninguēs -ǐum, f. pl. *snow.*

Nǐŏbē -es, f. and **Nǐŏba** -ae, f. *daughter of Tantalus, wife of Amphion.*

nǐsi, *if not, unless*; after negatives and questions, *except*; nisi quod, *except that.*

¹nīsus (**nixus**) -ūs, m. *pressing, straining, effort.*

²nīsus -a -um, partic. from nitor; q.v.

nītēdǔla -ae, f. *dormouse.*

nǐtĕo -ēre, *to shine, glitter, be bright; to glow, be sleek, flourish.* Hence partic. **nǐtens** -entis, *shining, bright, sleek, blooming.*

nǐtesco -ēre, *to begin to shine; to grow sleek.*

nǐtǐdus -a -um, *bright, shining; sleek, fat; flourishing, blooming.* Transf.,

spruce, elegant; refined, polished.
Adv. **nĭtĭdē.**

¹**nītor** nīti nīsus or nixus, dep. (1) *to rest, lean, support oneself (on); to trust (in), depend (on).* (2) *to strive, exert oneself, make an effort;* of movement, *to press on, climb up.*

²**nĭtor** -ōris, m. *brilliance, brightness, splendour, glow, elegance.*

nĭvālis -e, *of snow, snowy.*

nĭvĕ = ni, q.v., or neve, q.v.

nĭvĕus -a -um, *of snow, snowy.*

nĭvōsus -a -um, *snowy.*

nix, nĭvis, f. *snow.*

nixor -ari, dep. *to lean upon; to strive, strain.*

¹**nixus** = ¹nisus; q.v.

²**nixus;** see ¹nitor.

no nāre nāvi, *to swim.* Transf., *to sail, flow, fly.*

nōbĭlis -e, *known; celebrated, renowned, infamous, notorious; of noble birth, highly bred;* of things, *fine.*

nōbĭlĭtās -ātis, f. *fame, celebrity; noble birth, nobility;* meton., *the aristocrats, the nobility;* in gen., *excellence, worth.*

nōbĭlĭto -are, *to make known, make famous* or *notorious.*

nŏcĕo -ēre, *to hurt, injure, harm* (with dat.); partic. **nŏcens** -entis, *hurtful, injurious, guilty, wicked;* as subst., *a guilty person.*

noctĭlūca -ae, f. *the moon.*

noctĭvăgus -a -um, *wandering by night.*

noctū, abl. from nox; q.v.

noctŭa -ae, f. *owl.*

noctŭābundus -a -um, *travelling by night.*

nocturnus -a -um, *by night, nightly, nocturnal.*

nŏcŭus -a -um, *hurtful, injurious.*

nōdo -are, *to knot, tie in a knot.*

nōdōsus -a -um, *full of knots, knotty.*

nōdus -i, m. *a knot; a girdle; any tie, bond, connexion, obligation; a knotty point, difficulty.*

nōlo nolle nōlŭi, *to be unwilling, wish not to, refuse.*

nŏmăs -ădis, c. *a nomad,* esp. *a Numidian.*

nōmen -ĭnis, n. *a name;* nomen dare, *to go for a soldier, enlist;* nomen (hominis) deferre, *to give information against, accuse;* nomina solvere, *to pay debts;* nomen Romanum, *the Roman power;* nomine meo, *in my name, on my behalf.*

nōmenclātor -ōris, m. *a slave who reminded his master of names.*

nōmĭnātim, *by name, expressly.*

nōmĭnātĭo -ōnis, f. *nomination to a public office.*

nōmĭnĭto -are, *to call regularly by name.*

nōmĭno -are, *to name, give a name to, call; to mention, speak about; to make famous; to appoint, nominate to an office; to denounce, give information against.*
Hence partic. **nōmĭnātus** -a -um, *well-known, celebrated.*

nŏmisma -mătis, n. *a coin.*

nōn (old forms noenum, noenu), *not;* non nihil, *something;* nihil non,

everything; non quod, non quo, *not that, not because;* non ita, *not very, not particularly;* in questions = nonne? q.v.; in commands = ne; in answers, *no.*

nōnae -arum, f. *the nones; the fifth day in all months, except March, May, July and October, when it was the seventh.*

nōnāgēsĭmus (-ensĭmus) -a -um, *ninetieth.*

nōnāgĭēs (-ĭens), *ninety times.*

nōnāgintā, *ninety.*

nōnānus -a -um, *belonging to the ninth legion.*

nondum, *not yet.*

nongenti -ae -a, *nine hundred.*

nonnē, interrog. adv., asks a question to which an affirmative answer is expected.

nonnēmo, nonnĭhil; see nemo, nihil.

nonnullus (nōn nullus) -a -um, *some;* in plur., *several.*

nonnumquam (nōn numquam), *sometimes.*

nōnus -a -um, *ninth;* f. as subst., *the ninth hour* (roughly 3 p.m.).

nōnusdĕcĭmus -a -um, *nineteenth.*

Nōrĭcum -i, n. *Noricum, a country between the Alps and the Danube;* adj. **Nōrĭcus** -a -um.

norma -ae, f. *a rule, standard.*

nōs, plur. of ego; q.v.

noscĭto -are, *to get to know, investigate, observe, perceive;* or *to recognize.*

nosco noscĕre nōvi nōtum, *to become acquainted with, get to know;* hence, in perfect tenses, *to be acquainted with, know.* Transf., *to inquire into, investigate;* or *to recognize; to approve, acknowledge.*
Hence partic. **nōtus** -a -um, *known; famous; notorious, familiar, customary;* m. pl. as subst. *friends, acquaintances.*

noster -tra -trum, *our, ours;* of us, *to us, for us;* m. pl. nostri, *our people.*

nostrās -ātis, adj. *of our country, native.*

nŏta -ae, f. *a mark, token, note, sign;* in writing, *a letter, character; a distinguishing mark, brand;* hence *sort, quality;* also *mark of disgrace, stigma* (esp. as imposed by the censor).

nŏtābĭlis -e, *remarkable, striking;* adv. **nŏtābĭlĭtĕr.**

nŏtārĭus -i, m. *secretary* or *shorthand writer.*

nŏtātĭo -ōnis, f. *marking, noting, choice; the stigma of the censor.*

nōtesco nōtescĕre nōtŭi, *to become known.*

nŏthus -a -um, *illegitimate, bastard; hybrid, mongrel;* in gen., *spurious.*

nōtĭo -ōnis, f. *an examination, investigation; an idea, notion, conception.*

nōtĭtĭa -ae, and **nōtĭtĭēs** -ēi, f.: pass., *being known, fame, celebrity;* act., *knowledge, acquaintance;* hence *idea, notion, conception.*

nŏto -are, *to mark, mark out, distinguish, denote; to observe; to write; to stigmatize* (esp. of the censor).

¹**nŏtus** -a -um, partic. from nosco; q.v.

²**nŏtus** (**-ŏs**) -i, m. *the south wind.*

nŏvācŭla -ae, f. *a sharp knife or razor.*

nŏvālis -is, f. and **nŏvālĕ** -is, n. *fallow land; a cultivated field; crops.*

nŏvātrix -icis, f. *she that renews.*

nŏvellus -a -um, *new, young; fresh, unfamiliar.*

nŏvem, *nine.*

Nŏvember and **Nŏvembris** -bris, m. *of the ninth month of the Roman year, of November;* m. as subst., *November.*

nŏvendĕcim, nŏvemdĕcim, *nineteen.*

nŏvendiālis -e, *of nine days; happening on the ninth day; lasting nine days.*

nŏvēni -ae -a, *nine each, nine at a time;* poet., *nine.*

Nŏvensĭles dīvi, *gods whose worship had been introduced from foreign countries.*

nŏverca -ae, f. *step-mother.*

nŏvercālis -e, *of or like a step-mother.*

nŏvīcĭus -a -um, *new, fresh;* esp. *of persons new to slavery.*

nŏvĭēs (-ĭens), *nine times.*

nŏvĭtās -ātis, f. *newness, novelty, strangeness; the condition of a novus homo (see novus), newness of nobility;* in pl. *new acquaintances.*

nŏvo -are, *to make new, renew, revive; to change, alter; to invent;* novare res, *to make a revolution.*

nŏvus -a -um, *new, fresh, young; fresh, inexperienced; revived, refreshed; novel, unusual, extraordinary;* novus homo, *the first of a family to hold curule office;* novae res, *political changes, a revolution;* novae tabulae, *new account-books* (i.e. *a cancellation of debts*). N. as subst., *a new thing, news, a novelty.* Adv. **nŏvē,** *in a new or unusual way.* Superl., **nŏvissĭmus** -a -um, *latest, last, extreme;* agmen, *the rear;* adv. **nŏvissĭmē,** *lately, lastly, in the last place.*

nox noctis, f. *night;* meton., *sleep, darkness, gloom, death.* Abl. form as adv. **noctū,** *by night.*

noxa -ae, f. *harm, injury, damage; a fault, offence; punishment.*

noxĭa -ae, f. *fault, offence, crime.*

noxĭus -a -um, *hurtful, injurious; culpable, guilty.*

nūbēcŭla -ae, f. *a little cloud; a troubled expression.*

nūbes -is, f. *a cloud;* fig., *any dense mass; gloom; veil, concealment.*

nūbĭfer -fĕra -fĕrum, *cloud-bearing.*

nūbĭgĕna -ae, c. *born of a cloud.*

nūbĭlis -e, *marriageable.*

nūbĭlus -a -um, *cloudy, overcast; dark, gloomy;* n. sing. as subst., *cloudy weather;* n. pl., *clouds.*

nūbo nūbĕre nupsi nuptum, *to cover, veil; of a bride, to be married to, to marry* (with dat.); f. of partic. **nupta,** *married,* or, as subst., *a bride.*

nŭclĕus -i, m. *the kernel of a nut, the stone of fruits.*

nūdĭus, *it is now the . . . day since* (always with ordinal numerals); nudius tertius, *the day before yesterday.*

nūdo -are, *to make bare, strip, uncover;* milit. *to leave undefended; to strip, spoil, divest, deprive.*

nūdus -a -um, *naked, bare, uncovered; defenceless, deprived; unadorned, plain; bare, mere, alone, only.*

nūgae -arum, f. pl., *trifles, nonsense, stuff.*

nūgātor -ōris, m. *a trifler, humbug.*

nūgātōrĭus -a -um, *trifling, frivolous, futile.*

nūgax -ācis, *trifling, frivolous.*

nūgor -ari, dep. *to trifle, talk nonsense; to trick, cheat.*

nullus -a -um, *no, none, not any; non-existent, ruined;* nullo modo, nullo pacto, *by no means;* as a strong negative, *not at all;* as subst., esp. genit. and abl., *no one.*

num, interrog. particle, introducing a direct question, to which a negative answer is expected, or an indirect question, in the sense *whether.*

Nŭma -ae, m., Pompilius, *the second king of Rome.*

Nŭmantĭa -ae, f. *a town in Spain.*

nūmen -inis, n. *nodding, a nod; as an expression of will, command, consent; of a deity, divine will, divine command;* hence, in gen., *divine majesty, divinity, deity.*

nŭmĕrābĭlis -e, *able to be counted.*

nŭmĕro -are, *to count;* esp. *to count out money, to pay; to count over possessions,* i.e. *to own; to reckon, consider.*

Hence partic. **nŭmĕrātus** -a -um, *counted out; in hard cash, in ready money;* n. as subst. *hard cash, money down.*

nŭmĕrōsus -a -um. (1) *numerous.* (2) *rhythmical, metrical, melodious.* Adv. **nŭmĕrōsē.**

nŭmĕrus -i, m. (1) *a number, reckoning, total; a mass; a mere number, cypher; a category, band, class; rank, position, regard, consideration.* (2) *measure, part, respect;* in music, *metre, number, time.* Abl. sing. as adv. **nŭmĕrō,** *exactly, at the right time; too quickly, too soon.*

Nŭmĭda -ae, m. *a Numidian.*

Nŭmĭtor -ōris, m. *king of Alba, grandfather of Romulus and Remus.*

nummārĭus -a -um, *belonging to money; bribed with money, venal.*

nummātus -a -um, *provided with money, rich.*

nummŭlārĭus -i, m. *a money-changer.*

nummŭlus -i, m. *a little piece or sum of money.*

nummus -i, m. *a piece of money, coin;* esp. *the sesterce, a coin of small value.*

numquam = nunquam; q.v.

nunc, *now, at present; as things are;* of past or future time, *then, already.*

nuncŭpātĭo -ōnis, f. *naming, pronouncement.*

nuncŭpo -are, *to name, call by name to pronounce solemnly.*

nundĭnae -arum, f. pl. *market-day; the market-place; traffic, trade, business.*

nundĭnātĭo -ōnis, f. *the holding of a market, trade, business.*

nundĭnor -ari, dep. *to transact business, trade, traffic; to buy,* esp. *corruptly; to be present in great numbers.*

nundĭnum -i, n. *market-time.*

nunquam (numquam), *never;* numquam non, *always;* non numquam, *sometimes.*

nuntĭātĭo -ōnis, f. *a declaration made by the augur.*

nuntĭo -are, *to announce, give notice.*

nuntĭus -a -um, *announcing, bringing news.* M. as subst. **nuntĭus** -i: (1) *a messenger.* (2) *a message, news;* esp. *an official notice.*

nūper, *lately, not long ago.*

nupta -ae, f. subst. from nubo; q.v.

nuptĭae -arum, f. pl. *marriage, a wedding.*

nuptĭālis -e, *of marriage.*

nŭrus -us, f. *a daughter-in-law; any young married woman.*

nusquam, *nowhere, at* (or *to*) *no place; in nothing, on no occasion; to* or *for nothing;* nusquam esse, *not to exist.*

nūto -are, *to nod, keep nodding; to sway, waver.*

nūtrīcĭus -i, m. *a tutor, guardian.*

nūtrīco -are and **nūtrīcor** -ari, dep. *to suckle, nourish; to support, sustain.*

nūtrīcŭla -ae, f. *nurse, nanny.*

nūtrīmen -ĭnis, n. *nourishment.*

nūtrīmentum -i, n. *nourishment; support, training.*

nūtrĭo -ire and **nūtrĭor** -iri, dep. *to suckle, nourish, bring up; to make good, support, sustain.*

nūtrix -īcis, f. *a nurse, foster-mother.*

nūtus -ūs, m. *a nod; command, will; gravitation, downward movement.*

nux nŭcis, f. *a nut; a nut-tree.*

nympha -ae, and **nymphē** -es, f. *a bride;* Nymphae, *the Nymphs.*

O

O, o, the fourteenth letter of the Latin Alphabet.

o! interj. *oh!*

ob, prep. with acc., *in front of, before; in return for; because of, on account of;* ob rem, *to the purpose, with advantage.*

ŏbaerātus -a -um, *in debt;* as subst., *a debtor.*

ŏbambŭlo -are, *to walk up and down, walk about near.*

ŏbarmo -are, *to arm.*

ŏbăro -are, *to plough up.*

obbrūtesco -ĕre, *to become stupid or dull.*

obc-; see occ-.

obdo -dĕre -dĭdi -dĭtum, *to place before, put against;* fores, *to shut the door.*

obdormisco -dormiscĕre -dormīvi, *to go to sleep.*

obdūco -dūcĕre -duxi -ductum, (1) *to draw over, draw in front; of persons, to bring forward.* (2) *to cover, close over;* venenum, *to swallow;* frontem, *to wrinkle; of time, to pass, spend.*

obductĭo -ōnis, f. *covering, veiling.*

obdūresco -ĕre, *to become hard, harden.*

obdūro -are, *to be hard* (*against*); *to stand out, hold out, persist.*

ŏbēdĭo = oboedio; q.v.

ŏbĕo -ire -īvi and -ĭi -ĭtum. Intransit., *to go to, go to meet, go against;* of heavenly bodies, *to set;* of the living, *to die.* Transit., *to go to, go over, traverse; to go over, encompass,* by looking or speaking; *to enter upon, engage in, perform, execute* a task; with diem or mortem, *to die.*

ŏbĕquĭto -are, *to ride up to.*

ŏberro -are, *to wander about, go astray.*

ŏbēsus -a -um, *fat, plump; swollen; coarse.*

ŏbex -īcis, m. and f. *bolt, bar, barrier, barricade.*

obf-; see off-.

obg-; see ogg-.

ŏbhaeresco -haerescĕre -haesi -haesum, *to stick fast, adhere to.*

ŏbĭăcĕo -ēre, *to lie at, lie against.*

ŏbĭcĭo -icĕre -ĭēci -iectum, *to throw in the way, to expose; to inspire, cause, produce; to put before, hold before, as protection or obstacle; to bring up* anything as a reproach, *to throw in a person's teeth.*

  Hence partic. **obiectus** -a -um, *lying near, opposite to; exposed to; brought up against* a person; n. pl. as subst., *charges.*

obiectĭo -ōnis, f. *a reproach.*

obiecto -are, *to throw in the way, expose; to set against; to bring up* anything as a reproach, *to throw in a person's teeth.*

¹obiectus -a -um, partic. from obicio; q.v.

²obiectus -ūs, m. *placing against, putting opposite.*

ŏbīrascor -irasci -īrātus, dep. *to grow angry at.*

ŏbĭtĕr, *on the way, by the way, in passing.*

ŏbĭtus -ūs, m. *an approach;* of heavenly bodies, *setting;* of the living, *death, downfall, destruction.*

obiurgātĭo -ōnis, f. *scolding, reproving.*

obiurgātor -ōris, m. *a scolder, reprover.*

obiurgātōrĭus -a -um, *reproachful, scolding.*

obiurgo -are, *to scold, reprove, blame, chastise.*

oblanguesco -languescĕre -langui, *to become weary.*

oblatro -are, *to bark at; to scold.*

oblectāmen -ĭnis, n. *delight, pleasure.*

oblectāmentum -i, n. *delight, amusement, pastime.*

oblectātĭo -ōnis, f. *delighting, amusing.*

oblecto -are, *to please, amuse; to pass time pleasantly, while away time.*

oblīdo -līdĕre -līsi -līsum, *to crush.*

oblĭgātĭo -ōnis, f. *a bond, tie.*

oblĭgo -are, *to tie, bind up, bandage.* Transf., *to bind, make liable, oblige; to make liable to punishment, make guilty.* Hence partic. **oblĭgātus** -a -um, *bound, under an obligation.*

oblīmo -are, *to cover with slime or mud.*

oblĭno -linĕre -lēvi -lĭtum, *to smear, daub, besmear; to stain, defile;* perf. partic. **oblĭtus** -a -um, *overloaded.*

oblīquo -are, *to turn sideways, turn aside.*

oblīquus -a -um, *slanting, sideways, on one side;* of speech, *indirect, covert; looking askance, envious.* Adv. **oblīquē,** *sideways, aslant; indirectly, by implication.*

oblītesco -lītescĕre -lītŭi, *to conceal oneself.*

oblittĕro -are, *to cancel, blot out.*

oblīvĭo -ōnis, f. *forgetfulness, oblivion.*

oblīvĭōsus -a -um, *oblivious, forgetful; causing forgetfulness.*

oblīvĭscor oblīvisci oblītus, dep. *to forget.*

oblīvĭum -i, n., usually plur., *oblivion, forgetfulness.*

oblongus -a -um, *oblong.*

oblŏquor -lŏqui -lŏcūtus, dep. *to speak against, answer back, contradict, abuse, interrupt;* in music, *to accompany.*

obluctor -ari, dep. *to struggle against.*

obmōlĭor -iri, dep. *to build against* (as barrier or defence).

obmurmŭro -are, *to roar against.*

obmūtesco -mūtescĕre -mūtŭi, *to become dumb; to cease.*

obnātus -a -um, *growing on.*

obnītor -niti -nixus, dep. *to press against, strive against; to take up a stand, maintain a firm position;* adv. from partic., **obnixē,** *firmly, vigorously.*

obnoxĭōsus -a -um, *submissive, compliant.*

obnoxĭus -a -um, with dat., *liable, addicted to, guilty of; indebted, obliged, dependent on; subject to, exposed to.*

obnūbo -nūbĕre -nupsi -nuptum, *to cover.*

obnuntĭātĭo -ōnis, f. *the announcement of an unfavourable omen.*

obnuntĭo -are, *to report an unfavourable omen.*

ŏboedĭentĭa -ae, f. *obedience, compliance.*

ŏboedĭo -ire, *to obey, comply with, listen to* (with dat.); partic. **ŏboedĭens** -entis, *obedient, compliant;* adv. **ŏboedĭentĕr.**

ŏbŏrĭor -ŏrīri -ortus, dep. *to arise, appear.*

obrēpo -rēpĕre -repsi -reptum, *to creep up to; to steal upon, come on by surprise.*

obrētĭo -ire, *to catch in a net.*

obrĭgesco -rĭgescĕre -rĭgŭi, *to become stiff,* esp. *to freeze.*

obrŏgo -are, *to amend or repeal a law by introducing another.*

obrŭo -rŭĕre -rŭi -rŭtum; fut. partic. -rŭitūrus. Intransit., *to fall, collapse.* Transit., *to cover, bury, swamp, drown; to overwhelm, destroy, obliterate.*

obrussa -ae, f. *assay; test.*

obsaepĭo -saepire -saepsi -saeptum, *to fence in, block up, render inaccessible.*

obsătŭro -are, *to stuff, choke.*

obscēnĭtās (obscaen-) -ātis, f. *impurity, indecency.*

obscēnus (obscaenus) -a -um, *foul, filthy;* morally, *impure, indecent; ill-omened.* Adv. **obscēnē.**

obscūrātĭo -ōnis, f. *darkening; disappearance.*

obscūrĭtās -ātis, f. *darkness;* of language, *obscurity;* of condition, *obscurity, low birth.*

obscūro -are, *to cover, darken, obscure; to veil, conceal, suppress.*

obscūrus -a -um, *covered, dark, obscure;* n. as subst., *darkness;* of language, *obscure, unintelligible;* of origin, etc., *unknown, obscure;* of character, *secret, reserved, close.* Hence adv. **obscūrē,** *darkly; unintelligibly; secretly.*

obsecrātĭo -ōnis, f. *earnest entreaty, supplication; public prayer to the gods.*

obsecro -are, *to beseech, implore, entreat.*

obsĕcundo -are, *to comply with.*

obsēpĭo = obsaepio; q.v.

obsĕquella -ae, f. *compliance.*

obsĕquens -entis, partic. from obsequor; q.v.

obsĕquentĭa -ae, f. *complaisance.*

obsĕquĭum -i, n. *compliance, submission; indulgence, pliancy.*

obsĕquor -sĕqui -sĕcūtus, dep. *to comply with, yield to, obey;* partic. **obsĕquens** -entis, *compliant, obedient; favourable;* adv. **obsĕquentĕr.**

¹**obsĕro** -are, *to bolt, bar.*

²**obsĕro** -sĕrĕre -sēvi -sĭtum, *to sow thickly, cover with seeds, etc.;* partic. **obsĭtus** -a -um, *full of, covered with, beset by* (with abl.).

observantĭa -ae, f. *respect, attention.*

observātĭo -ōnis, f. *observing, watching; care, accuracy, circumspection.*

observātor -ōris, m. *observer, watcher.*

observĭto -are, *to watch carefully.*

observo -are, *to watch, regard, attend to;* of rules, *to keep, regard;* of persons, *to respect.*

Hence partic. **observans** -antis, *attentive, respectful.*

obses -sĭdis, c. *a hostage; a surety, security, pledge.*

obsessĭo -ōnis, f. *blockade.*

obsessor -ōris, m. *one who besets, haunts, or besieges.*

obsĭdĕo -sĭdēre -sēdi -sessum: intransit., *to sit down near;* transit., *to beset, haunt, frequent;* esp. *to blockade, besiege; to watch over, be on the look-out for.*

obsĭdĭo -ōnis, f. *blockade, siege.*

¹**obsĭdĭum** -i, n. *blockade, siege.*

²**obsĭdĭum** -i, n. *the condition of a hostage.*

obsīdo -sīdĕre -sēdi -sessum, *to blockade, besiege, invest.*

obsignātor -ōris, m. *one who seals; a witness to a will.*

obsigno -are, *to seal;* of a witness, *to sign and seal; to stamp, impress.*

obsisto -sistĕre -stĭti -stĭtum, *to place oneself before or in the way of; to oppose, withstand, resist.*

obsĭtus -a -um, partic. from ²obsero; q.v.

obsŏlĕfĭo -fĭĕri -factus, *to become worn out; to be degraded.*

obsŏlesco -escĕre -ēvi, -ētum, *to go out of use, decay, wear out;* partic. **obsŏlētus** -a -um, *worn out, decayed; obsolete; threadbare, poor;* compar. adv. **obsŏlētius,** *more shabbily.*

obsōnātor -ōris, m. *a caterer.*

obsōnium -i, n. *what is eaten with bread;* e.g., *vegetables, fruit, fish.*

¹obsōno -are and **obsōnor** -ari, dep., *to buy food, cater, provide a meal.*

²obsōno -are, *to interrupt by noise.*

obsorbĕo -ēre -ŭi, *to swallow, gulp down.*

obstetrix -icis, f. *midwife.*

obstinātio -onis, f. *persistence, firmness, obstinacy.*

obstino -are, *to persist, be resolved.*
Hence partic. **obstinātus** -a -um, *persistent, firm, obstinate;* adv. **obstinātē.**

obstĭpesco = obstupesco; q.v.

obstīpus -a -um, *leaning to one side; bent back* or *down.*

obsto -stare -stĭti -stātūrus, *to stand before* or *in the way, to oppose, resist, obstruct* (with dat.); n. pl. of partic. as subst. **obstantia,** *hindrances, obstacles, impediments.*

obstrĕpo -strĕpĕre -strĕpŭi -strĕpĭtum, *to make a noise, clamour at, disturb, interrupt* (with dat.); in pass., *to be drowned by noise* or *filled with noise.*

obstringo -stringĕre -strinxi -strictum, *to bind up, tie fast; to entangle, involve, put under an obligation.*

obstructio -ōnis, f. *hindrance, obstruction.*

obstrūdo = obtrudo; q.v.

obstrŭo -strŭĕre -struxi -structum, *to build against; to block up, close, stop.*

obstŭpĕfăcio -făcĕre -fēci -factum, *to astound, stupefy, render senseless;* pass. **obstŭpĕfīo** -fīĕri -factus.

obstŭpesco (obstĭp-) -stŭpescĕre -stŭpŭi, *to become senseless, be astounded.*

obsum ŏbesse obfŭi, *to be in the way, be prejudicial to* (with dat.).

obsŭo -sŭĕre -sŭi -sūtum, *to sew on; to sew up, close up.*

obsurdesco -descĕre -dŭi, *to become deaf; to turn a deaf ear.*

obtĕgo -tĕgĕre, -texi -tectum, *to cover up; to protect; to conceal;* partic. **obtĕgens** -entis, *concealing.*

obtempĕrātio -ōnis, f. *compliance, obedience.*

obtempĕro -are, *to comply with, submit to* (with dat.).

obtendo -tendĕre -tendi -tentum. (1) *to stretch before, spread before.* Transf., *to put forward as an excuse, plead, allege.* (2) *to cover, conceal.*

¹obtentus -ūs, m. *stretching* or *spreading before.* Transf., *pretext, pretence, excuse.*

²obtentus -a -um, partic. from obtineo; q.v.

³obtentus -a -um, partic. from obtendo; q.v.

obtĕro -tĕrĕre -trīvi -trītum, *to trample, crush, destroy.*

obtestātio -ōnis, f. *a calling of gods to witness; an entreaty in the name of the gods.*

obtestor -ari, dep. *to call as witness; to adjure, implore, entreat in the name of the gods.*

obtexo -texĕre -texŭi, *to cover.*

obtĭcĕo -ēre, *to be silent.*

obtĭcesco -tĭcescĕre -tĭcŭi, *to become silent.*

obtĭnĕo -tĭnēre -tĭnŭi -tentum: transit., *to hold, possess, keep, maintain;* esp. *to maintain an assertion;* also *to take hold of, grasp;* intransit., *to hold, obtain, continue.*

obtingo -tingĕre -tĭgi, *to happen, befall.*

obtorpesco -torpescĕre -torpŭi, *to become stiff, numb, insensible.*

obtorquĕo -torquēre -torsi -tortum, *to wrench, twist round.*

obtrectātio -ōnis, f. *disparagement, detraction.*

obtrectātor -ōris, m. *detractor, disparager.*

obtrecto -are, *to disparage, detract from.*

obtrūdo (obstrūdo) -trūdĕre -trūsi -trūsum. (1) *to gulp down, swallow down.* (2) *to force, obtrude.*

obtrunco -are, *to cut down.*

obtundo -tundĕre -tŭdi -tūsum and tunsum, *to beat upon, thump; to make blunt, dull, weaken, weary.*
Partic. **obtūsus** and **obtunsus** -a -um, *dull, blunt, blurred, insensible.*

obturbo -are, *to disturb, confuse, distract, harass.*

obturgesco -ĕre, *to swell up.*

obturo -are, *to stop up.*

obtūsus -a -um, partic. from obtundo; q.v.

obtūtus -ūs, m. *gaze, contemplation.*

ŏbumbro -are, *to overshadow, obscure; to conceal, protect, cover.*

ŏbuncus -a -um, *bent inwards, hooked.*

ŏbustus -a -um, *burnt, hardened in the fire.*

obvallo -are, *to surround with a wall, wall round.*

obvĕnio -vĕnire -vēni -ventum, *to come in the way of, to meet; to occur, happen, fall to a person's lot.*

obversor -ari, dep. *to move before, appear before.*

obverto (-vorto) -vertĕre -verti -versum, *to turn towards, direct against.* Partic. **obversus** -a -um, *turned towards;* m. pl. as subst., *opponents.*

obviam, *in the way, on the way;* hence, *with dat., towards, against, to meet;* obviam ire, with dat., *to go to meet, to oppose;* also *to help, remedy.*

obvius -a -um, *in the way, meeting* (with dat.); *exposed; ready at hand; affable, easy of access.*

obvolvo -volvĕre -volvi -vŏlūtum, *to wrap up, cover all round.*

occaeco -are, *to make blind, to blind, to darken; to conceal, make invisible, to make dull* or *numb.*

occallesco -callescĕre -callŭi, *to become thick-skinned, hard* or *unfeeling.*

occăno -cănĕre -cănŭi, *to sound.*

occāsĭo -ōnis, f. *a favourable moment, opportunity.*

occāsus -ūs, m. *the setting of heavenly bodies;* hence, *the west;* in gen., *fall, destruction.*

occātĭo -onis, f. *harrowing.*

occēdo -cēdĕre -cessi -cessum, *to go towards, meet.*

occento -are, *to sing a serenade to; to sing a lampoon against.*

occepto -are, *to begin.*

occĭdens -entis, m.; subst. from ²occido; q.v.

occīdĭo -ōnis, f. *slaughter, destruction, extermination.*

¹occĭdo -cīdĕre -cĭdi -cīsum, *to strike down, beat to the ground; to kill, slay; to plague to death, torment.*

²occĭdo -cīdĕre -cĭdi -cāsum, *to fall, fall down;* of heavenly bodies, *to set;* of the living, *to die, perish, be ruined.* Hence pres. partic. occĭdens -entis, *setting;* m. as subst. (sc. sol), *the setting sun, the west.*

occĭdŭus -a -um, *setting, sinking;* hence, *westerly, westerly.*

occĭno -cĭnĕre -cĕcĭni and -cĭnŭi, *to sing inauspiciously.*

occĭpĭo -cĭpĕre -cēpi -ceptum, *to begin.*

occĭpĭtĭum -i, n. and occĭput -ĭtis, n. *the back of the head, occiput.*

occīsĭo -ōnis, f. *killing, slaughter.*

occīsor -ōris, m. *slayer, murderer.*

occlūdo -clūdĕre -clūsi -clūsum, *to shut up, close up.*

occo -are, *to harrow.*

occŭbo -are, *to lie down,* esp. *to rest in the grave.*

occulco -are, *to trample, tread down.*

occŭlo -cŭlĕre -cŭlŭi -cultum, *to cover, hide.*

Hence partic. occultus -a -um, *hidden, concealed, private;* of persons, *close, reserved.* N. as subst., *concealment, secrecy, a secret.* Adv. occultē, *secretly, obscurely.*

occultātĭo -ōnis, f. *hiding, concealment.*

occultātor -ōris, m. *hider, concealer.*

occulto -are, *to hide, conceal.*

occultus -a -um, partic. from occulo; q.v.

occumbo -cumbĕre -cŭbŭi -cŭbĭtum, *to fall down, sink down;* esp. *to fall down dead.*

occŭpātĭo -ōnis, f. *seizing, taking possession; anticipation; business, employment, occupation.*

occŭpo -are, *to take possession of, seize, occupy, master; to fall upon, attack; to take up, employ; to invest money; to anticipate, get a start on a person, be first to do a thing.* Hence partic. occŭpātus -a -um, *busy, engaged, occupied.*

occurro -currĕre -curri -cursum, *to run to meet; to fall upon, attack; to work against, oppose, counteract;* of things, *to crop up, occur, come to mind.*

occursātĭo -ōnis, f. *attention, officiousness.*

occurso -are, *to run to meet; to oppose;* of things, *to occur, come to mind.*

occursus -ūs, m. *meeting, falling in.*

Ŏcĕănus -i, m. *the ocean, the sea which encompasses the earth;* personif., *the father of the Nymphs.*

ŏcellus -i, m. *a (little) eye; a darling.*

ōcĭor, ōcĭus, compar. adj., *swifter, quicker;* adv. ōcĭus, *more swiftly;* serius, ocius, *sooner or later;* sometimes = *swiftly only.*

ocrĕa -ae, f. *a greave.*

ocrĕātus -a -um, *wearing greaves.*

Octāvĭus -a -um, *name of a Roman gens;* esp. of *C. Octavius,* the *Emperor Augustus;* adj. Octāvĭānus -a -um.

octāvus -a -um, *eighth;* octavum, *for the eighth time;* f. as subst. octāva -ae, *the eighth hour.*

octāvusdĕcĭmus -a -um, *eighteenth.*

octĭēs (-ĭens), *eight times.*

octingentēsĭmus -a -um, *eight hundredth.*

octingenti -ae -a, *eight hundred.*

octĭpēs -pĕdis, *having eight feet.*

octō, *eight.*

Octōber -bris, *belonging to the eighth month of the Roman year,* reckoning from March; *of October;* m. as subst., *October.*

octōdĕcim, *eighteen.*

octōgēnārĭus -a -um, *consisting of eighty.*

octōgēni -ae -a, *eighty each, eighty at a time.*

octōgēsĭmus -a -um, *eightieth.*

octōgĭēs (-ĭens), *eighty times.*

octōgintā, *eighty.*

octōĭŭgis -e, *yoked eight together.*

octōnārĭus -a -um, *consisting of eight together.*

octōni -ae -a, *eight each, eight at a time, eight together.*

octōphŏros -on, *borne by eight;* n. as subst. octōphŏron -i, *a litter carried by eight bearers.*

octŭplĭcātus -a -um, *increased eight-fold.*

octŭplus -a -um, *eight-fold;* n. as subst. *an eight-fold penalty.*

octussis -is, m. *a sum of eight asses.*

ŏcŭlātus -a -um, *having eyes; catching the eye, conspicuous.*

ŏcŭlus -i, m. *the eye;* esse in oculis, *to be visible; an ornament, treasure; a bud or eye of a plant.*

ōdi odisse; fut. partic. ōsūrus, *to hate, detest, dislike.*

ŏdiōsus -a -um, *hateful, troublesome, annoying;* adv. ŏdiōsē.

ŏdĭum -i, n. *hatred; an object of hatred;* esse odio, with dat., *to be hated by.*

ŏdor (older ŏdōs) -ōris, m. *a smell, odour, scent; a scent, suspicion, inkling, presentiment;* in plur., *perfumery, spices.*

ŏdōrātĭo -ōnis, f. *smelling, smell.*

¹ŏdōrātus -ūs, m. *smelling; the sense of smell.*

²ŏdōrātus -a -um, partic. from odoro; q.v.

ŏdōrĭfer -fĕra -fĕrum, *having a pleasant smell; producing perfumes.*

ŏdōro -are, *to make odorous;* partic. ŏdōrātus -a -um, *sweet-smelling.*

ŏdōror -ari, dep. *to smell; to smell out, snuff at;* hence *to aim at, aspire to; to search into, investigate; to get an inkling* or *smattering of.*

ŏdōrus -a -um. (1) *sweet-smelling.* (2) *keen-scented, tracking by smell.*

ŏdōs = odor; q.v.

Ŏdyssēa -ae, f. *the Odyssey.*

oecŏnŏmĭa -ae, f. *arrangement, division.*

oecŏnŏmĭcus -a -um, *relating to domestic economy; orderly, methodical.*

Oedĭpūs -pŏdis and -i, m. *king of Thebes, son of Laius and Jocasta, fated to kill his father and marry his mother.*

Oenōnē -ēs, f. *a Phrygian nymph, loved and deserted by Paris.*

oenŏphŏrum -i, n. *a basket for wine.*

oenus = unus; q.v.

oestrus -i, m. *the gad-fly, horse-fly; inspiration, frenzy.*

oesus = usus; q.v.

oesȳpum -i, n. *a cosmetic.*

ŏfella -ae, f. *a bit, morsel.*

offa -ae, f. *a pellet, mass, lump; a swelling.*

offendo -fendĕre -fendi -fensum: transit., *to strike against, knock; to hit upon, fall in with; to shock, offend, displease;* intransit., *to knock, strike; to run aground; to stumble, make a mistake, to give offence* (with dat.); also *to take offence.*

Hence partic. offensus -a -um, *injured, hurt; offensive.*

offensa -ae, f. *a striking, knocking against; injury; displeasure, offence.*

offensĭo -ōnis, f. *a striking, knocking, hitting against;* pedis, *a stumbling.* Transf., *a misfortune, setback, indisposition; displeasure, disfavour, aversion, offence.*

offensĭuncŭla -ae, f. *a slight displeasure* or *check.*

offenso -are, *to strike, knock, stumble.*

¹offensus -a -um, partic. from offensus; q.v.

²offensus -ūs, m. *shock, collision; offence, dislike.*

offĕro offerre obtŭli oblātum, *to bring forward, place before, present, offer, expose; to inflict, occasion* trouble; se offerre, and pass., offerri, *to present oneself, appear.*

officīna -ae, f. *a workshop, factory.*

officĭo -fĭcĕre -fēci -fectum, *to act against; to get in the way of, impede, hinder, injure* (with dat.).

officĭōsus -a -um, *obliging, courteous, attentive; dutiful;* adv. officĭōsē.

officĭum -i, n. *dutiful* or *respectful action; attendance, service, duty; sense of duty, respect, courtesy; submission, allegiance.*

offīgo -ĕre, *to fix in, fasten.*

offirmo -are, *to make firm, to fasten;* with reflex. or intransit., *to be determined, persevere;* partic. offirmātus -a -um, *firm, resolute.*

offūcĭa -ae, f. *paint, rouge; deceit.*

offulgĕo -fulgēre -fulsi, *to shine upon.*

offundo -fundĕre -fūdi -fūsum, *to pour over, spread round; to overspread, cover, conceal; to overwhelm; to bring trouble, etc., upon a person.*

oggannĭo -ire, *to growl at.*

oh, interj. *oh! ah!*

ōhē, interj. *ho! hi!*

oi, interj. *oh!*

ŏlĕa -ae, f. *olive, olive-tree.*

ŏlĕāgĭnus -a -um, *of the olive-tree.*

ŏlĕārĭus -a -um, *of* or *for oil.*

ŏlĕaster -tri, m. *the wild olive-tree.*

ŏlĕo -ēre, *to emit an odour; to smell of, smack of;* partic. ŏlens -entis, *smelling; fragrant* or *stinking.*

ŏlĕum -i, n. *olive-oil, oil.*

olfacĭo -făcĕre -fēci -factum, *to smell; to scent out, detect.*

ŏlĭdus -a -um, *smelling.*

ōlim, *at that time; of the past, formerly, once; of the future, hereafter, one day; with a present, for a long time now; at times, often.*

ŏlit-; see holit-.

ŏlīva -ae, f. *olive; olive-tree; olive-wreath; staff of olive-wood.*

ŏlīvētum -i, n. *an olive-grove.*

ŏlīvĭfer -fĕra -fĕrum, *olive-bearing.*

ŏlīvum -i, n. *olive-oil, oil.*

olla -ae, f. *jar, pot.*

ollus, olle, obsolete form of ille; q.v.

ŏlo = oleo; q.v.

ŏlor -ōris, m. *swan.*

ŏlōrīnus -a -um, *of a swan.*

ŏlus; see holus.

Ŏlympĭa -ae, f. *a city in Elis, where the Olympic games were held.*

Ŏlympus -i, m. *a mountain range between Macedonia and Thessaly, supposed to be the abode of the gods.*

ŏmāsum -i, n. *bullocks' tripe.*

ōmen -ĭnis, n. *an omen, sign, prognostication.*

ōmentum -i, n. *fat; entrails, bowels.*

ōmĭnor -ari, dep. *to presage, prophesy, predict.*

ōmĭnōsus -a -um, *foreboding, ominous.*

ōmitto -mittĕre -mīsi -missum, *to let go, let fall; to give up, lay aside; to disregard;* in speaking, *to leave out, omit;* with infin., *to cease.* Hence partic. ŏmissus -a -um, *negligent, remiss.*

omnĭfer -fĕra -fĕrŭm, *bearing everything.*

omnĭgĕnus -a -um, *of all kinds.*

omnĭmŏdīs, *in every way, entirely.*

omnīnō, *altogether, entirely, wholly; in general, in all; certainly, admittedly.*

omnĭpārens -entis, *all-producing.*

omnĭpŏtens -entis, *almighty.*

omnis -e, *all, every, whole; of all kinds;* in sing., *each,* or *the whole of* one person or thing.

omnĭtŭens -entis, *all-seeing.*

omnĭvăgus -a -um, *wandering everywhere.*

ŏnăger and ŏnagrus -i, m. *wild ass.*

ŏnĕrārĭus -a -um, *of burden; freight;* iumenta, *beasts of burden;* (navis) oneraria, *a merchant* or *transport ship.*

ŏnĕro -are, *to load, burden; to fill, weigh down; to oppress, overwhelm; to make worse, aggravate.*

ŏnĕrōsus -a -um, *heavy, burdensome; troublesome.*

ŏnus -ĕris, n. *a load, burden, weight; a trouble, charge; a public burden, tax.*

ŏnustus -a -um, *laden, loaded; full.*

ŏnyx -ўchis, m. and f. *onyx; a casket of onyx.*

ŏpācĭtās -ātis, f. *shadiness.*

ŏpāco -are, *to shade, overshadow.*

ŏpācus -a -um, *shaded, shady; dark, shadowy, obscure.*

ŏpella -ae, f. *a little labour or trouble.*

ŏpĕra -ae, f. *trouble, pains, exertion;* operam dare, with dat., *to work hard at;* est operae pretium, *it is worth while;* opera mea, *thanks to me.* Transf., *time for work; work done;* in pl., *labourers, workmen,* also *mobsmen, gangsters.*

ŏpĕrārĭus -a -um, *relating to work;* m. **ŏpĕrārĭus** -i, *a labourer, workman.*

ŏpercŭlum -i, n. *a lid, cover.*

ŏpĕrīmentum -i, n. *a cover, covering.*

ŏpĕrĭo -pĕrīre -ĕrŭi -pertum, *to cover, bury, conceal; to close, shut up; to overwhelm;* n. of partic. as subst. **ŏpertum** -i, *a secret place, or secret.*

ŏpĕror -ari, dep. *to work, labour, be busy;* esp. in perf. partic. **ŏpĕrātus** -a -um, *engaged, busy* (esp. *engaged in worship*).

ŏpĕrōsus -a -um: act., *laborious, painstaking, industrious;* pass., *toilsome, difficult.* Adv. **ŏpĕrōsē,** *laboriously.*

ŏpertum -i, subst. from operio; q.v.

ŏpes; see ops.

Ŏpīcus -a -um, *Oscan.* Transf., *stupid, philistine.*

ŏpĭfer -fĕra -fĕrum, *helpful.*

ŏpĭfex -fĭcis, c. *a maker, framer; a workman, artisan.*

ŏpĭfĭcīna = officina; q.v.

ŏpīlĭo and **ŭpīlĭo** -ōnis, m. *shepherd.*

ŏpīmus -a -um, *rich, fruitful, fertile; lucrative; wealthy; sumptuous, abundant, copious;* of speech, *overloaded;* spolia opima, *spoils taken by a general from the enemy's general in single combat.*

ŏpīnābĭlis -e, *conjectural.*

ŏpīnātĭo -ōnis, f. *supposition, conjecture.*

ŏpīnātor -ōris, m. *one who supposes or conjectures.*

[1]**ŏpīnātus** -a -um, partic. from opinor; q.v.

[2]**ŏpīnātus** -ūs, m. *conjecture, supposition.*

ŏpīnĭo -ōnis, f. *opinion, conjecture, supposition; repute, rumour, report.*

ŏpīnĭōsus -a -um, *set in opinion.*

ŏpīnor -ari, dep. and **ŏpīno** -are, *to be of opinion, suppose, conjecture.* Partic. **ŏpīnātus** -a -um, in pass. sense, *supposed, fancied.*

ŏpīpărus -a -um, *splendid, rich, sumptuous;* adv. **ŏpīpărē.**

ŏpĭtŭlor -ari, dep. *to help, aid* (with dat.).

ŏportet -tēre -tŭit, impers., *it is proper, one should, one ought.*

oppēdo -ĕre, *to mock, insult.*

oppĕrĭor -pĕriri -pertus, dep. *to wait or wait for.*

oppĕto -ĕre -īvi and -ĭi -ĭtum, *to go to meet, encounter;* esp. *to encounter death, to die.*

oppĭdānus -a -um, *of a town;* sometimes *provincial, ' small-town ';* m. pl. as subst., *the inhabitants of a town.*

oppĭdo, *quite, very much;* in answers, *certainly.*

oppĭdŭlum -i, n. *a little town.*

oppĭdum -i, n. *a town;* in Britain, *a fortified wood.*

oppignĕro -are, *to pledge, pawn, give in pledge.*

oppĭlo -are, *to stop up, block up.*

opplĕo -plēre -plēvi -plētum, *to fill up, block.*

oppōno -pōnĕre -pŏsŭi -pŏsĭtum, *to put opposite or before; to pledge against, mortgage for; to set against, oppose, interpose; to allege as an objection; to contrast.* Hence partic. **oppŏsĭtus** -a -um, *standing against, opposite.*

opportūnĭtās -ātis, f. *convenience, fitness; a fit time, opportunity; advantage.*

opportūnus -a -um, *opportune, fit, suitable, convenient;* of time, *favourable;* with dat., sometimes, *exposed, liable to.* Adv. **opportūnē,** *seasonably, conveniently.*

oppŏsĭtĭo -ōnis, f. *opposing, opposition.*

[1]**oppŏsĭtus** -a -um, partic. from oppono; q.v.

[2]**oppŏsĭtus** -ūs, m. *placing against, opposing, interposition.*

oppressĭo -ōnis, f. *pressing down, oppression; suppression; seizure.*

[1]**oppressus** -ūs, m. *pressing down, pressure.*

[2]**oppressus** -a -um, partic. from opprimo; q.v.

opprĭmo -prīmĕre -pressi -pressum, (1) *to press upon, press down; to crush, smother, stamp out.* (2) *to catch, take by surprise, occupy forcibly.*

opprŏbrĭum -i, n. *reproach, scandal, disgrace; a verbal reproach, taunt; a cause of disgrace.*

opprŏbro -are, *to taunt, reproach.*

oppugnātĭo -ōnis, f. *an assault on a town;* in gen., *an attack.*

oppugnātor -ōris, m. *an assailant, attacker.*

oppugno -are, *to attack, assault.*

Ops ŏpis, f.: in nom. sing., *the goddess of abundance;* other cases **ŏpem, ŏpis, ŏpĕ,** *might, power,* esp. *power to aid; help, support;* plur. **ŏpēs,** *resources, means, wealth.*

ops-; see obs-.

optābĭlis -e, *desirable, to be wished for.*

optātĭo -ōnis, f. *a wish.*

optĭmās -ātis, *one of the best, aristocratic;* m. pl. as subst. **optĭmātēs,** *the aristocratic party, the aristocrats.*

optĭmus (optŭmus) -a -um, superl. of bonus; q.v.

[1]**optĭo** -ōnis, f. *choice, option.*

[2]**optĭo** -ōnis, m. *a helper, assistant.*

optīvus -a -um, *chosen.*

opto -are, *to choose, select; to wish for, desire.* Hence partic. **optātus** -a

-um, *wished for, desired, welcome*; n. as
subst. **optātum**, *a wish*; abl. **optātō**,
according to one's wish.
ŏpūlens, -entis; see opulentus.
ŏpūlentĭa -ae, f. *wealth, riches, opulence;
the power, greatness of a state.*
ŏpūlento -are, *to make wealthy, enrich.*
ŏpūlentus -a -um, also **ŏpūlens** -entis,
adj. *rich, wealthy; powerful, mighty;
splendid, sumptuous; lucrative.* Adv.
ŏpūlentē and **ŏpūlentĕr**, *richly,
splendidly.*
ŏpus -ĕris, n. *work, labour; work done,
a finished work; a building; a literary
work or a work of art*; plur. milit.
works, lines, siege-engines.
    ŏpus est (or **sunt**), *there is work, there
is need; one needs, it is necessary* (with
nom., abl., or genit. of what is needed).
ŏpuscŭlum -i, n. *a little work.*
ōra -ae, f. *edge, rim, boundary*; esp.
coast-line, coast; in gen., *region,
clime, country; the people of a district;
a hawser, cable reaching to shore.*
ōrācŭlum (ōrāclum) -i, n. *a solemn
utterance, oracle, divine response,
prophecy;* also *the place where an
oracle is given.*
ōrātĭo -ōnis, f. *speaking, speech; language, style;* esp. *a set speech;
eloquence; prose; an imperial message.*
ōrātĭuncŭla -ae, f. *a little speech, short
oration.*
ōrātor -ōris, m. *speaker; spokesman,
envoy; orator.*
ōrātōrĭus -a -um, *of an orator, oratorical;*
f. as subst. *oratory*; adv. **ōrātōrĭē.**
ōrātrix -īcis, f. *a female suppliant.*
ōrātū, abl. sing. m. *by request.*
orbātor -ōris, m. *one who deprives
another of children or parents.*
orbis -is, m. *a circle, ring, disk; orbit,
coil*; orbis signifer, *the Zodiac*; orbis
lacteus, *the Milky Way*; orbis terrae,
terrarum, *the world.* Transf., *rotation, round;* of style, *roundness.*
orbĭta -ae, f. *a wheel-rut.*
orbĭtās -ātis, f. *bereavement, loss of
children or parents.*
orbo -are, *to bereave, deprive of parents
or children.*
orbus -a -um, *deprived of parents or
children;* as subst. *an orphan;* in
gen., *deprived, destitute.*
orca -ae, f. *a pot or jar with a large belly.*
orchās -ādis, f. *a species of olive.*
orchestra -ae, f. *the part of a Roman
theatre reserved for senators;* meton.,
the senate.
Orcus i-, m. *Orcus, the infernal regions.*
Transf., *the god of the lower world;
death.*
ordĕum = hordeum; q.v.
ordĭa prīma = primordia; q.v.
ordĭnārĭus -a -um, *according to order,
regular, ordinary.*
ordĭnātim, *in good order, regularly,
properly.*
ordĭnātĭo -ōnis, f. *setting in order,
arrangement.*
ordĭno -are, *to set in order, settle,
arrange, appoint; to govern a country.*

Hence partic. **ordĭnātus** -a -um,
arranged, orderly.
ordĭor ordīri orsus, dep. *to begin;* esp.
to begin speaking. N. pl. of partic. as
subst. **orsa** -orum, *beginnings, undertaking;* esp. *words uttered, speech.*
ordo -ĭnis, m. *a series, line, row, order;*
milit., *a line, rank, file;* ordinem
ducere, *to be a centurion;* polit. and
socially, *an order, rank, class;* in gen.,
order, arrangement; ordine, *in turn,
in due order, regularly;* extra ordinem,
in an unusual, irregular manner.
Ŏrĕās -ădis, f. *a mountain-nymph.*
Ŏrestes -ae and -is, m. *son of Agamemnon and Clytemnestra, who killed
his mother to avenge his father.*
ōrexis -is, f. *desire, appetite.*
orgănĭcus -i, m. *a musician.*
orgănum -i, n. *an instrument;* esp., *a
musical instrument.*
orgĭa -orum, n. pl. *a secret festival;
mysteries; orgies.*
ŏrĭchalcum -i, n. *yellow copper ore;
brass.*
ōrĭcŭla = auricula; q.v.
ŏrĭens -entis, m. partic. from orior; q.v.
ŏrīgo -ĭnis, f. *origin, source, beginning;
an ancestor.*
Ŏrīōn -ōnis, m. *the constellation Orion.*
ŏrĭor orīri ortus, dep. *to rise; to spring
up, be born, proceed from a source or
cause.* Hence partic. **ŏrĭens** -entis,
rising. M. as subst. *the rising sun; the
east; the morning.*
ŏrĭundus -a -um, *arising from, springing
from.*
ornāmentum -i, n. *equipment, trappings, furniture; ornament, decoration;
honour, distinction.*
ornātrix -īcis, f. *a female hairdresser,
tire-woman.*
¹ornātus -ūs, m. *dress, attire, equipment;
embellishment, ornament.*
²ornatus -a -um, partic. from orno; q.v.
orno -are, *to equip, furnish, fit out;* also
*to adorn, decorate, embellish; to honour,
distinguish.*

Hence partic. **ornātus** -a -um,
*furnished, equipped, provided; adorned,
decorated, embellished.* Adv. **ornātē,**
splendidly, elegantly.
ornus -i, f. *the mountain-ash.*
ōro -are, *to speak;* esp. *to speak as an
orator;* with acc., *to treat, argue,
plead;* *to beg, pray, entreat, beseech.*
Ŏrontes -is and -ae, m. *chief river of
Syria.*
Orphēus -ĕi and -ĕos, *a mythical
minstrel, husband of Eurydice.*
orsa -orum, from ordior; q.v.
orsus -ūs, m. *a beginning, undertaking.*
¹ortus -ūs, m.: of heavenly bodies,
rising; of persons, *origin, birth;* in
gen., *origin, source.*
²ortus -a -um, partic. from orior; q.v.
ŏryx -ȳgis, m. *a wild goat or gazelle.*
ŏrȳza -ae, f. *rice.*
¹ōs ōris, n. (1) *the mouth;* hence *voice,
talk;* uno ore, *unanimously;* in gen.,
mouth, opening, source. (2) *the face,
countenance; presence, sight; ex-*

pression; boldness of expression, impudence; a mask.

²ōs ossis, n. *a bone.*

oscen -inis, m. *a bird from whose note auguries were taken (e.g., raven, owl, crow).*

Osci -orum, *an ancient people of Italy.*

oscillum -i, n. *a little mask.*

oscĭtātĭo -ōnis, f. *gaping, yawning.*

oscĭto -are, *to gape, yawn;* partic. **oscĭtans** -antis, *yawning, sleepy, listless;* adv. **oscĭtantĕr.**

oscŭlātĭo -ōnis, f. *kissing.*

oscŭlor -ari, dep. *to kiss; to caress, make much of.*

oscŭlum -i, n. *a little mouth; a kiss.*

ōsor -ōris, m. *a hater.*

Ossa -ae, m. and f. *a mountain range in Thessaly.*

ossĕus -a -um, *bony.*

ossĭfrăgus -i, m. and **ossĭfrăga** -ae, f. *the sea-eagle, osprey.*

ostendo -tendĕre -tendi -tentum and -tensum, *to hold out, show, reveal, present;* in speech, *to make plain, declare.* N. of partic. as subst. **ostentum** -i, *a prodigy, portent.*

ostentātĭo -ōnis, f. *showing, revealing; showing off, display; deceitful show, pretence.*

ostentātor -ōris, m. *one who shows; esp., a boaster.*

ostento -are, *to hold out, present, offer; to show, reveal; to show off, display;* in speech, *to declare, make known.*

ostentŭi, dat. sing. m. *for a show; merely for show; as a sign or proof.*

ostentum -i, n., subst. from ostendo; q.v.

Ostĭa -ae, f. and **Ostĭa** -orum, n. *the harbour and port of Rome, at the mouth of the Tiber;* adj. **Ostĭensis** -e.

ostĭārĭum -i, n. *a door-tax.*

ostĭātim, *from door to door.*

ostĭum -i, n. *door;* in gen., *entrance;* fluminis, *mouth.*

ostrĕa -ae, f. and **ostrĕum** -i, n. *an oyster.*

ostrĭfer -fĕra -fĕrum, *producing oysters.*

ostrīnus -a -um, *purple.*

ostrum -i, n. *purple dye prepared from a shell-fish; a purple dress.*

Ŏtho -ōnis, m. *a Roman cognomen.*

ōtĭor -ari, dep. *to be at leisure.*

ōtĭōsus -a -um, *at leisure, esp. free from public duties; calm, quiet, undisturbed, neutral.* Adv. **ōtĭōsē,** *at leisure; quietly, easily.*

ōtĭum -i, n. *free time, leisure, ease; peace, repose.*

ŏvans -antis, partic. *rejoicing, exulting; esp. celebrating the minor triumph (the ovatio).*

ŏvātĭo -ōnis, f. *an ovation, a kind of lesser triumph.*

Ŏvĭdĭus -a, *name of a Roman gens; esp. the poet P. Ovidius Naso (43 B.C.-17 A.D.).*

ŏvīle -is, n. *a sheepfold, an enclosure.*

ŏvillus -a -um, *of sheep.*

ŏvis -is, f. *a sheep.*

ōvum -i, n. *an egg.*

P, p, the fifteenth letter of the Latin Alphabet.

pābŭlātĭo -ōnis, f. *procuring fodder, foraging.*

pābŭlātor -ōris, m. *a forager.*

pābŭlor -ari, dep. *to forage, seek fodder.*

pābŭlum -i, n. *food, nourishment, fodder.*

pācālis -e, *peaceful.*

pācĭfer -fĕra -fĕrum, *peace-bringing.*

pācĭfĭcātĭo -ōnis, f. *making of peace, pacification.*

pācĭfĭcātor -ōris, m. *a peacemaker.*

pācĭfĭcātōrĭus -a -um, *peacemaking, pacific.*

pācĭfĭco -are, *to make peace; to appease, pacify.*

pācĭfĭcus -a -um, *peacemaking, pacific.*

pāciscor pācisci pactus, dep. *to make a bargain or agreement, to covenant, contract;* transit., *to stipulate for, bargain for; also to give in exchange.* Perf. partic. in pass. sense, **pactus** -a -um, *agreed upon, stipulated; betrothed.* N. as subst. **pactum** -i, *an agreement, treaty, pact;* quo pacto? *how?* alio pacto, *in another way.*

pāco -are, *to pacify, make peaceful;* poet., *to make fruitful.* Hence partic. **pācātus** -a -um, *peaceful, quiet;* n. as subst. *a peaceful country.*

pactĭo -ōnis, f. *a bargain, contract, agreement, treaty.*

pactor -ōris, m. *one who makes a contract or treaty, negotiator.*

pactum -i, n., and **pactus** -a -um, from paciscor; q.v.

Pācŭvĭus -i, m. *a Roman tragic poet.*

Pădus -i, m. *the river Po.*

paeān -ānis, m. (1) *the Healer, a surname of Apollo.* (2) *a hymn, paean.*

paedăgōgus -i, m. *a slave who accompanied children to and from school.*

paedor -ōris, m. *dirt, filth.*

paelex (pellex) -lĭcis, f. *a mistress, concubine.*

paelĭcātus -ūs, m. *concubinage.*

Paelĭgni -orum, m. pl. *an Italian tribe.*

paenĕ, *nearly, almost.*

paenīnsŭla -ae, f. *a peninsula.*

paenĭtentĭa -ae, f. *repentance, regret.*

paenĭtĕo -ēre, *to repent, regret, be sorry;* impers. **paenĭtet** hominem, *a person feels regret, is sorry;* gerundive **paenĭtendus** -a -um, *regrettable, unsatisfactory.*

paenŭla -ae, f. *a travelling-cloak, greatcoat.*

paenŭlātus -a -um, *wearing the paenula;* q.v.

paeōn -ōnis, m. *a metrical foot, consisting of three short syllables and one long.*

Paestum -i, n. *a town in Lucania famous for roses.*

paetŭlus -a -um, *with a slight cast in the eye.*

paetus -a -um, *with a cast in the eyes, squinting.*

pāgānus -a -um, *belonging to a village,*

rural; rustic; m. as subst. *a villager, countryman.*

păgātim, *in villages, by villages.*

păgella -ae, f. *a little page.*

păgĭna -ae, f. *a page of a letter, book, etc.*

păgĭnŭla -ae, f. *a little page.*

păgus -i, m. *a village or country district; a canton.*

păla -ae, f. *a spade; the bezel of a ring.*

Pălaestīna -ae, and **Pălaestīnē** -ēs, f. *Palestine.*

pălaestra -ae, f. *a gymnasium or wrestling school; wrestling.* Transf., *training in rhetoric.*

pălaestrĭcus -a -um, *of the palaestra, gymnastic;* adv. **pălaestrĭcē.**

pălaestrīta -ae, m. *the superintendent of a palaestra* (q.v.).

pălam: adv. *openly, publicly;* prep., with abl., *in the presence of.*

Pălātĭum -i, n. *the Palatine Hill in Rome:* in plur., *a palace;* adj. **Pălātīnus** -a -um.

pălātum -i, n. and **pălātus** -i, m. *the roof of the mouth, palate; taste; critical judgment.*

pălĕa -ae, f. *chaff.*

pălĕar -āris, n. *the dewlap of an ox.*

Pălēs -is, f. *tutelary goddess of herds and shepherds;* adj. **Pălīlis** -e; n. pl. as subst. **Pălīlia** -ĭum, *the feast of Pales on the 21st of April.*

pălimpsestus -i, m. *a palimpsest.*

Pălĭnūrus -i, m. *the pilot of Aeneas; a promontory on the coast of Lucania.*

pălĭūrus -i, m. *a plant, Christ's thorn.*

palla -ae, f. *a long outer garment, esp. as worn by women and actors.*

Pallas -ādis and -ādos, f. *Athene, the Greek goddess of wisdom, identified with Minerva;* adj. **Pallădĭus** -a -um; n. as subst. **Pallădĭum** -i *an image of Pallas.*

palleo -ēre, *to be pale or yellow;* partic. **pallens** -entis, *pale, wan, yellow, pale green; causing paleness; drooping, weak.*

pallesco pallescĕre pallui, *to grow pale or yellow;* with acc., *to turn pale at.*

pallĭātus -a -um, *clad in a pallium, i.e. as a Greek* (opp. togatus).

pallĭdŭlus -a -um, *somewhat pale.*

pallĭdus -a -um, *pale, wan; causing paleness.*

pallĭŏlum -i, n. *a little Greek cloak; a hood.*

pallĭum -i, n. *a coverlet; a Greek mantle.*

pallor -ōris, m. *paleness; fading.*

palma -ae, f. (1) *the palm of the hand; a hand; the blade of an oar.* (2) *the palm-tree; a date; a palm broom; a palm-branch as token of victory; hence, victory, honour, glory.*

palmāris -e, *deserving the palm or prize, excellent.*

palmārĭum -i, n. *a masterpiece.*

palmātus -a -um, *embroidered with palm-branches.*

palmēs -ĭtis, m. *a young branch esp. of a vine.*

palmētum -i, n. *a palm-grove.*

palmĭfer -fĕra -fĕrum, *abounding in palm-trees.*

palmōsus -a -um, *full of palms.*

palmŭla -ae, f. *the blade of an oar.*

pālor -ari, dep. *to wander, stray.*

palpebra -ae, f. *eyelid.*

palpĭto -are, *to move quickly, tremble, throb.*

palpo -are and **palpor** -ari, dep. *to stroke; to coax, flatter, wheedle.*

pălūdāmentum -i, n. *the military cloak.*

pălūdātus -a -um, *clad in the military cloak.*

pălūdōsus -a -um, *marshy, boggy.*

pălumbes -is, m. and f. *a wood-pigeon, ring-dove.*

¹pālus -i, m. *a pale, stake.*

²pălūs -ūdis, f. *a swamp, marsh, bog.*

păluster -tris -tre, *marshy, boggy.*

pampĭnĕus -a -um, *attached to or consisting of vine-tendrils.*

pampĭnus -i, m. and f. *a vine-tendril or vine-leaf.*

Pān Pānos, m. *the god of flocks, woods, and shepherds.*

pănăcĕa -ae, f. and **pănăcĕs** -is, n. *a plant, supposed to heal all diseases; panacea, heal-all.*

pānārĭum -i, n. *a bread-basket.*

panchrestus (panchristus) -a -um, *good for everything.*

pancrātĭum (-ŏn) -i, n. *a gymnastic contest.*

pando pandĕre pandi pansum and passum, (1) *to stretch out, spread out, extend;* crines passi, *dishevelled hair.* (2) *to throw open, lay open, reveal, disclose.* Hence partic. **passus** -a -um, *spread out, esp. spread out to dry;* n. as subst. *raisin-wine.*

pandus -a -um, *bent, curved, crooked.*

pango pangĕre panxi, *to fasten, fix, drive in.* Transf., *to compose, write.* In perf. **pĕpĭgi** and supine **pactum,** *to fix, settle, agree upon* (cf. paciscor).

pānĭcum -i, n. *a kind of wild millet.*

pānis -is, m. *bread;* in plur., *loaves.*

pannĭcŭlus -i, m. *a little garment.*

Pannŏnia -ae, f. *Pannonia, a district on the middle Danube.*

pannōsus -a -um, *ragged, tattered.*

pannūcĕus (-ĭus) -a -um, *ragged; wrinkled, shrivelled.*

pannus -i, m. *a piece of cloth; garment; rag.*

Pănormus -i, f. and **Pănormum** -i, n. *a town in Sicily* (modern Palermo).

pansa -ae, *splay-footed.*

panthēra -ae, f. *a panther or leopard.*

pantŏmīmus -i, m. and **pantŏmīma** -ae, f. *a dancer, mime.*

păpae, interj. *wonderful! indeed!*

păpās -ae and -ātis, m. *a tutor.*

păpāver -ĕris, n. *poppy.*

păpāvĕrĕus -a -um, *of the poppy.*

păpĭlio -ōnis, m. *butterfly.*

păpilla -ae, f. *nipple, teat, breast.*

Păpīrĭus -a -um, *name of a Roman gens.*

pappo -are, *to eat.*

pappus -i, m. *the woolly seed of certain plants.*

păpŭla -ae, f. *a pimple.*

păpȳrĭfer -fĕra -fĕrum, *producing papyrus.*

păpȳrus -i, m. and f. and **păpȳrum** -i, n. *the plant papyrus; clothing or paper made from papyrus.*

păr păris, *equal, like, a match*; m. and f. as subst., *a companion*; n. as subst., *the like, the equivalent*, or *a pair*; par impar ludere, *to play at odd and even*; par est, *it is appropriate.* Hence adv. **părĭtĕr**, *equally, alike; together, at the same time.*

părābĭlis -e, *easily procured.*

părăbŏla -ae and **părăbŏlē** -ēs, f. *a comparison.*

părăsītus -i, m. and **părăsīta** -ae, f. *a guest*; in bad sense, *a toady, parasite.*

părātĭo -ōnis, f. *preparing, preparation.*

¹părātus -a -um, partic. from paro; q.v.

²părātus -ūs, m. *preparation, fitting out, equipment.*

Parca -ae, f. *a goddess of fate*; pl. Parcae, *the three Fates.*

parco parcĕre pĕperci (and parci) parsum, *to be sparing, economize; to spare, refrain from injuring* (with dat.); *to refrain from, keep oneself from*; with infin., *to forbear to.*

parcus -a -um, *sparing, thrifty, economical; moderate, sparing*; of things, *scanty, small, meagre.* Adv. **parcē**, *sparingly, economically, moderately.*

pardus -i, m. *a panther or leopard.*

¹părens -entis, partic. from pareo; q.v.

²părens -entis, c. *a parent*; sometimes *grandfather or ancestor; author, cause, origin.*

părentālis -e, *parental, of parents (or ancestors)*; n. pl. as subst. **părentālĭa** -ĭum, *a festival in honour of the dead.*

părento -are, *to celebrate the parentalia.* Transf., *to avenge the dead.*

părĕo -ere, *to appear, become evident.* Transf., *to obey, give way to; to be subject to, serve* (with dat.); partic. **părens** -entis, *obedient.*

părĭēs -ĕtis, m. *a wall, properly the wall of a house.*

părĭĕtīnae -arum, f. pl. *old walls, ruins.*

Părĭlĭa = Palilia; see Pales.

părĭlis -e, *similar, like, equal.*

părĭo părĕre pĕperi partum; fut. partic. părĭtūrus; *to bring forth, bear, produce.* Transf., *to occasion, create, make, get.*

Păris -ĭdis, m. *a Trojan prince who carried off Helen.*

parma -ae, f. *a small round shield, a buckler.*

parmātus -a -um, *armed with the parma.*

parmŭla -ae, f. *a small round shield, buckler.*

Parnāsus (-ŏs) -i, m. *a mountain in Phocis, sacred to Apollo and the Muses*; f. adj. **Parnāsis** -ĭdis, and adj. **Parnāsĭus** -a -um.

păro -are, *to set, put; to prepare, provide, furnish, obtain; to buy.* Hence partic. **părātus** -a -um, *prepared, ready; provided, equipped*;

of persons, *skilled.* Adv. **părātē**, *with preparation, readily.*

părŏcha -ae, f. *a supplying of necessaries.*

părŏchus -i, m. *an officer who looked after travelling ambassadors and magistrates.* Transf., *a host.*

părŏpsis -ĭdis, f. *a dessert-dish.*

Părus (-ŏs) -i, f. *an island in the Aegean Sea, famous for marble*; adj. **Părĭus** -a -um.

parra -ae, f. *a bird of ill omen, perhaps owl.*

parrĭcīda -ae, f. *a parricide, one who murders a parent or near relative*; polit., *an assassin, traitor.*

parrĭcīdĭum -i, n. *the murder of a parent or any near relative*; polit., *assassination, treason.*

pars partis, *a part, piece, share; a direction, region; a side, party; an actor's role*; in gen., usually plur., *office, function, duty*; pars . . . pars, *some . . . others*; pro (sua) parte, pro virile parte, *to the best of one's ability*; magna ex parte, *to a great extent*; multis partibus, *many times, much.* Adv. **partim**, *partly*; used like a noun, *some.*

parsĭmōnĭa -ae, f. *thrift, economy.*

Parthi -orum, m. pl. *the Parthians*; adj. **Parthĭcus** and **Parthus** -a -um; subst. **Parthĭa** -ae, *Parthia.*

partĭceps -cĭpis, *sharing, participating in* (with genit.); as subst., *partner, comrade.*

partĭcĭpo -are, *to share with a person; to cause a person to share.*

partĭcŭla -ae, f. *a small part, particle.*

partim, adv. from pars; q.v.

partĭo -ire and **partĭor** -iri, dep. *to share out, distribute, divide*; perf. partic. in pass. sense **partītus** -a -um, *divided*; adv. **partītē**, *with proper divisions.*

partītĭo -ōnis, f. *division, sharing, distribution.*

partūrĭo -ire, *to desire to bring forth, have the pains of labour; to teem with anything, be full of.*

¹partus -a -um, partic. from pario; q.v.

²partus -ūs, m. *bearing, bringing forth, birth.* Transf., *young, offspring.*

părum, *too little, not enough* (as adv. or subst.); parum habere, *to think too little, be dissatisfied with.* Compar. **mĭnus**, *less*; sometimes = *not, not at all*; sin minus, *but if not.* Superl. **mĭnĭmē** (**mĭnŭmē**), *in the least degree, very little, least of all*; sometimes *not at all, by no means.*

părumper, *for a little while.*

Părus = Paros; q.v.

parvĭtās -ātis, f. *littleness, smallness.*

parvŭlus -a um, *very small*; of age, *young, little.*

parvus -a -um, *little, small; slight, weak*; of time, *short*; of age, *young*; of value, *poor, insignificant*; n. as subst. *a little.* Compar. **mĭnor**, *smaller, less*; of time, *shorter*; of age, *minor* (natu), *younger*; of value, *inferior.* Superl. **mĭnĭmus**, *smallest, least*;

n. as adv., minimum, *very little*.
Rare superl. **parvissimus** -a -um.

pasco pascĕre pāvi pastum. (1)
transit., *to feed, lead to pasture; to
keep, support; to nourish*; also *to give
as pasture*. Transf., *to feast, gratify*.
Pass. as middle, *to graze on*; also *to
feast upon, delight in*. (2) intransit.,
of animals, *to graze, browse*.

pascŭus -a -um, *for pasture or grazing*;
n. as subst. *a pasture*.

Pāsīthĕa -ae and **Pāsīthĕē** -ēs, f. *one
of the three Graces*.

passer -ĕris, m. *a sparrow or other
small bird; a sea-fish, a plaice or
flounder*.

passercŭlus -i, m. *a little sparrow*.

passim, *here and there, far and wide;
indiscriminately*.

passum -i, n., subst. from pando; q.v.

¹**passus** -a -um, partic. from pando; q.v.

²**passus** -a -um, partic. from patior; q.v.

³**passus** -ūs, m. *a step, stride, pace*;
esp. as a measure of length = five
Roman feet. Transf., *footstep, track*.

pastillus -i, m. *a lozenge*.

pastio -ōnis, f. *pasture, pasturing*.

pastor -ōris, m. *a herd*; esp. *a shepherd*.

pastōrālis -e, **pastōrīcīus** -a -um and
pastōrius -a -um, *of shepherds,
pastoral*.

¹**pastus** -a -um, partic. from pasco; q.v.

²**pastus** -ūs, m. *pasture, feeding; food,
sustenance*.

Pătăvium -i, n. *a town in North Italy,
birthplace of Livy (now Padua)*;
adj. **Pătăvīnus** -a -um.

pătĕfăcio -făcĕre -fēci -factum; pass.
pătĕfīo -fīĕri -factus sum; *to open,
throw open, open up, make accessible;
to bring to light, disclose, reveal*.

pătĕfactio -ōnis, f. *throwing open,
disclosing*.

pătella -ae, f. *a dish, platter, plate*.

pătĕo -ēre, *to be open, stand open, be
accessible or exposed; to be revealed,
disclosed, clear; to stretch out, extend*.
Hence partic. **pătens** -entis, *open,
unobstructed, accessible, exposed*; also
evident. Compar. adv. **pătentius**,
more openly.

păter -tris, m. *father, sire; founder,
head*; pater familias, *or* familiae,
head of a household; plur., patres,
forefathers; also as a title of the
senators, patres, *or* patres conscripti;
pater patriae, *father of his country, a
national hero*.

pătĕra -ae, f. *a shallow dish, saucer*.

păternus -a -um, *of a father, paternal;
native*.

pătesco pătescĕre pătŭi, *to be opened,
lie open; to be revealed; to spread out*.

pătībilis -e: pass, *endurable, bearable*;
act., *sensitive*.

pătībŭlum -i, n. *a yoke as an instrument
of punishment, a pillory*.

pătientia -ae, f. *endurance, resignation*;
in bad sense, *want of spirit*.

pătina -ae, f. *a dish*.

pătior păti passus, dep. *to suffer,
undergo, experience; to permit, allow*.
Hence partic. **pătiens** -entis,

enduring, capable of enduring, with
genit.; *patient*; in bad sense, *stubborn*.
Adv. **pătienter**.

patrātor -oris, m. *accomplisher, achiever*.

patria -ae, f. *fatherland*; see patrius.

patricius -a -um. *of the patres,
patrician, noble*; m. as subst., *a
patrician*.

patrimōnium -i, n. *property inherited
from a father, patrimony*.

patrimus -a -um, *having a father still
living*.

patrītus -a -um, *inherited from one's
father*.

patrius -a -um, *of a father, fatherly,
paternal; hereditary; ancestral;
native*. F. as subst. **patria** -ae, f.
(sc. terra), *fatherland, native land*.

patro -are, *to accomplish, execute,
achieve*.

patrōcinium -i, n. *the services of a
patron*; esp. *defence in a court of
law*; in gen., *defence, protection*;
plur., **patrōcinia**, *clients*.

patrōcinor -ari, dep. *to protect, defend*.

patrōna -ae, f. *a protectress, patroness*.

patrōnus -i, m. *a protector, defender,
patron*; esp. *an advocate in a court of
law*.

patruēlis -e, *descended from a father's
brother*; as subst., *a cousin*.

¹**patrŭus** -i, m. *a father's brother,
paternal uncle*.

²**patrŭus** -a -um, adj. *of an uncle*.

pătŭlus -a -um, *open, standing open,
spreading, extended*.

paucĭtās -ātis, f. *fewness, scarcity*.

paucŭlus -a -um, *very small*; plur.,
very few.

paucus -a -um, oftener plur. **pauci** -ae
-a, *few, little*; as subst., m. pl. **pauci**,
a few, the select few, the oligarchs; n.
pl. **paucă**, *a few words*.

paulātim (paullātim), *gradually, little
by little*.

paulispĕr (paullispĕr), *for a little
while*.

paulŭlus (paullŭlus) -a -um, *very
little*; n. as subst. **paulŭlum** -i, *a very
little*; acc. and abl., as adv., *a little*.

¹**paulus (paullus)** -a -um, *little, small*;
as subst., **paulum**, *a little*; acc., and
abl. **paulo**, *like adv., a little*.

²**Paulus (Paullus)** -i, m. *the name of a
family of the gens Aemilia*.

pauper -ĕris, *poor*; of things, *scanty,
meagre*.

paupercŭlus -a -um, *poor*.

pauperiēs -ēi, f. *poverty*.

paupĕro -are, *to make poor, to deprive*.

paupertās -ātis, f. *poverty*.

pausa -ae, f. *cessation, end*.

pausĭa -ae, f. *a species of olive*.

pauxillŭlus -a -um, *very little, very
small*.

pauxillus -a -um, *small, little*: n. as
subst. *a little*.

păvĕfactus -a -um, *frightened, terrified*.

păvĕo păvēre păvi: intransit., *to quake
with fear, panic*; transit., *to quake at*.

păvesco -ĕre: intransit., *to begin to
quake, take fright*; transit., *to be
alarmed by*.

păvĭdus -a -um, *trembling, quaking, fearful; causing fear.* Adv. **păvĭdē,** *fearfully.*

păvīmento -are, *to pave.*

păvīmentum -i, n. *a pavement of tiles, brick, stone, etc.*

păvĭo -ire, *to beat.*

păvĭto -are: intransit., *to shiver, tremble, quake with fear;* transit., *to quake at.*

păvo -ōnis, m. *peacock.*

păvor -ōris, m. *trembling, quaking; fear, panic.*

pax pācis, f. *peace; calm, quiet; of the gods, grace, favour;* pace tua, *with your good leave.*

pecco -are, *to make a mistake, go wrong, err or sin;* n. of partic. as subst. **peccātum** -i, *an error, fault, sin.*

pĕcŏrōsus -a -um, *rich in cattle.*

pectĕn -inis, m. *a comb; a weaver's comb; a rake; clasped hands; a quill,* for striking the strings of the lyre; *a shell-fish, the scallop.*

pecto pectĕre pexi pexum, *to comb; to card; to thrash;* partic. **pexus** -a -um, *with the nap on, woolly.*

pectus -ōris, n. *breast; heart, soul; mind.*

pĕcu, n. plur. pĕcŭa, *sheep, flocks;* also *pastures.*

pĕcŭārĭus -a -um *of sheep or cattle;* as subst., m. *a breeder of cattle, grazier;* n. pl. *herds of sheep or cattle.*

pĕcūlātor -ōris, m. *one who embezzles public money.*

pĕcūlātus -ūs, m. *embezzlement of public money.*

pĕcūlĭāris -e, *of one's private property; one's own, special, peculiar;* adv. **pĕcūlĭārĭtĕr,** *specially.*

pĕcūlĭum -i, n. *small property, savings;* esp. *the savings of slaves or sons.*

pĕcūnĭa -ae, f. *property, wealth;* esp. *money, cash.*

pĕcūnĭārĭus -a -um, *of money, pecuniary.*

pĕcūnĭōsus -a -um, *wealthy, rich; lucrative.*

¹pĕcus -ōris, n. *cattle, a herd, flock, esp. of sheep.*

²pĕcus -ūdis, f. *a single head of cattle; a beast, animal;* esp. *a sheep.*

pĕdālis -e, *a foot long* (or *wide*).

pĕdārĭus -a -um, *of a foot;* (senatores) pedarii, *senators of inferior rank.*

pĕdĕs -ĭtis, m.: adj., *going on foot;* subst., *a foot soldier;* coll., *infantry.*

pĕdester -tris -tre, *on foot, pedestrian;* copiae, *infantry;* sometimes, *on land.* Transf., *simple, ordinary, prosaic:* of style, *written in prose.*

pĕdĕtemptim, *feeling one's way; gradually, cautiously.*

pĕdĭca -ae, f. *a fetter; a trap, snare.*

pĕdĭcŭlōsus -a -um, *lousy.*

pĕdis -is, c. *a louse.*

pĕdĭsĕquus -i, m. and **pĕdĭsĕqua** -ae, f. *a follower, attendant, lackey.*

pĕdĭtātus -ūs, m. *infantry.*

pĕdum -i, n. *a shepherd's crook.*

Pēgăsus (-os) -i, m. *the winged horse which produced the fountain Hippo-* crene; adj. **Pēgăsēĭus** and **Pēgăsēŭs** -a -um; **Pēgăsĭdes,** *the Muses.*

pegma -ātis, n. *a bookcase; a stage, scaffolding.*

pēĭĕro and **periūro** -are, *to commit perjury, forswear oneself;* with acc., *to swear falsely by.*

pēior, compar. of malus; q.v.

pĕlăgus -i, n., Greek plur. pelage, *the open sea, the main.*

pēlămўs -ўdis, f. *the young tunnyfish.*

Pĕlasgi -orum, m. pl. *the Greeks.*

Pēlēus -ĕi and -ĕos, m. *king of Thessaly, husband of Thetis, father of Achilles;* **Pēlīdēs** -ae, m. *son or grandson of Peleus.*

Pēlĭon -i, n. *mountain range in Thessaly;* adj. **Pēlĭăcus** and **Pēlĭus** -a -um.

pellācĭa -ae, f. *enticing, allurement.*

pellax -ācis, *deceitful, seductive.*

pellĕgo = perlego; q.v.

pellex = paelex; q.v.

pellĭcĭo -lĭcĕre -lexi -lectum, *to entice, decoy, seduce.*

pellĭcŭla -ae, f. *a little skin or hide.*

pellĭo -ōnis, m. *a furrier.*

pellis -is, f. *a hide, skin; dressed hide, leather, felt;* milit., *a hut covered with skins.*

pellītus -a -um, *clothed in skins.*

pello pellĕre pĕpŭli pulsum, *to strike, knock, beat; to impel, propel, move, affect; to drive away, dislodge, banish.*

pellūcĕo = perluceo; q.v.

Pĕlŏponnesus -i, f. *the Peloponnese.*

Pĕlops -ŏpis, m. *the father of Atreus and Thyestes.*

pĕlōris -ĭdis, f. *an edible shell-fish, a clam.*

pelta -ae, f. *a small shield.*

peltastes or **-a** -ae, m. *a soldier armed with the pelta.*

peltātus -a -um, *armed with the pelta.*

pelvis -is, f. *a basin.*

pēnārĭus -a -um, *of or for provisions.*

Pēnātes -ĭum, m. pl., *the Penates, Latin deities of the household and family.* Transf., *home, dwelling.*

pēnātĭger -gĕra -gĕrum, *carrying the Penates.*

pendĕo pendēre pĕpendi, *to hang; to hang upon, depend on; to hang loose, hover; to be suspended, discontinued; to be in suspense, uncertain, undecided.*

pendo pendēre pĕpendi pensum:
transit., *to cause to hang down; to weigh; to pay out money; to weigh, consider, judge, value, esteem;* poenas, supplicia, *to pay a penalty, suffer punishment;* intransit., *to weigh.*
Hence partic. **pensus** -a -um, *weighed; esteemed, valued, prized;* nihil pensi habere, *to put no value upon, be indifferent about.* N. as subst. **pensum** -i, *wool weighed out to a spinner;* hence, *a day's work, task, duty.*

pendŭlus -a -um, *hanging; in suspense, undecided.*

Pēnĕlŏpa -ae, and **Pēnĕlŏpē** -ēs, f. *the wife of Ulysses.*

pĕnĕs, prep. with acc. *in the possession*

of, in the power of, belonging to; penes
se esse, to be in one's senses.

pĕnetrābilis -e: pass., that can be
passed through, penetrable; act.,
penetrating, piercing.

pĕnetrālis -e. (1) passing through,
penetrating. (2) inward, internal. N.
as subst. inner chambers, interior, esp.
of a temple.

pĕnetro -are: transit., to put into; to
pass through or into, to penetrate;
intransit., to make one's way in, to
penetrate.

pēnĭcillus -i, m. a painter's brush or
pencil; style.

pēnĭcŭlus -i, m. a brush; a sponge.

pēnis -is, m. a tail.

¹pĕnĭtus -a -um, adj. inward, internal.

²pĕnĭtus, adv. internally, inwardly,
inside; deeply, through and through;
widely.

penna -ae, f. a feather; a wing.

pennātus -a -um, feathered, winged.

pennĭger -gĕra -gĕrum, feathered,
winged.

pennĭpēs -pĕdis, wing-footed.

pennĭpŏtens -entis, able to fly, winged;
plur. as subst., birds.

pennŭla -ae, f. a little wing.

pensĭlis -e, hanging, pendent.

pensĭo -ōnis, f. a weighing out; hence
paying, payment, day of payment;
rent.

pensĭto -are, to weigh carefully, weigh
out; hence, to pay; to ponder,
consider.

penso -are, to weigh carefully; to
estimate, ponder, consider; to counter-
balance, requite; to pay for, purchase
one thing with another.

pensum -i, n. subst., from pendo; q.v.

Penthēus -ĕi and -ĕos, a king of Thebes.

pēnūrĭa -ae, f. lack, want, penury.

pĕnus -ūs and -i, c., **pĕnum** -i, n.,
pĕnus -ŏris, n. provisions, victuals.

peplum -i, n. and **peplus** -i, m. a robe
of state.

per, prep. with acc.: of space, through,
along, over; sometimes before, in the
presence of; of time, throughout,
during; in the course of, in a time of;
of means or instrument, through, by,
by means of, with, by way of; of cause,
because of, on account of; per me licet,
you may as far as I am concerned; in
entreaties, oaths, etc., in the name of.

pēra -ae, f. bag, wallet.

pĕrabsurdus -a -um, excessively absurd.

pĕraccommŏdatus -a -um, very
convenient.

pĕrācer -cris -cre, very sharp.

pĕrācerbus -a -um, very sour, very
harsh.

pĕractĭo -ōnis, f. finishing, completion.

pĕrăcūtus -a -um, very sharp; very
shrill; very sharp-witted. Adv.
pĕrăcūtē.

pĕrădŭlescens -entis, very young.

pĕraequē, quite equally.

pĕrăgĭto -are, to drive about violently,
harass.

pĕrăgo -ăgĕre -ēgi -actum. (1) to
pass through; in words, to go over,

mention. (2) to drive about, harass,
disturb. (3) to carry through, complete, accomplish; legal, to prosecute
till conviction.

pĕragrātĭo -ōnis, f. wandering through.

pĕragro -are, to wander through, travel
through.

pĕrāmans -antis, very loving; adv.
pĕrămantĕr.

pĕrambŭlo -are, to walk through, pass
through.

pĕrāmoenus -a -um, very pleasant.

pĕramplus -a -um, very large.

pĕrangustus -a -um, very narrow;
adv. **pĕrangustē**.

pĕrantiquus -a -um, very old.

pĕrappŏsĭtus -a -um, very suitable.

pĕrardŭus -a -um, very difficult.

pĕrargūtus -a -um, very witty.

pĕrāro -are, to plough through; to
furrow the brow; to scratch letters,
to write, write on.

pĕrattentus -a -um, very attentive;
adv. **pĕrattentē**.

perbacchor -ari, dep. to revel throughout.

perbĕātus -a -um, very happy.

perbellē, very prettily.

perbĕnē, very well.

perbĕnĕvŏlus -a -um, very well
disposed.

perbĕnignē, very kindly.

perbĭbo -bĭbĕre -bĭbi, to drink up,
absorb; mentally, to imbibe, take in.

perblandus -a -um, very charming.

perbŏnus -a -um, very good.

perbrĕvis -e, very short; perbrevi, in a
very short time; adv. **perbrĕvĭtĕr**.

perca -ae, f. a fish, the perch.

percălĕfactus -a -um, thoroughly
heated.

percălesco -călescĕre -călŭi, to become
very warm.

percallesco -callescĕre -callŭi: intransit., to lose sensibility, become
callous; transit., to get a good knowledge of.

percārus -a -um. (1) very dear, very
costly. (2) very dear, much loved.

percautus -a -um, very cautious.

percĕlebro -are, to speak of commonly;
pass., to be much mentioned.

percĕler -is -e, very swiftly; adv.
percĕlĕrĭtĕr.

percello -cellĕre -cŭli -culsum, to
strike, push; to beat down, overturn,
shatter, ruin; mentally, to daunt,
unnerve.

percensĕo -censēre -censŭi, to count
over, reckon; to survey, review; to
travel through.

perceptĭo -ōnis, f. a receiving, grasping,
gathering together.

perceptus -a -um, partic. from percipio;
q.v.

percĭo -cīre -cīvi -cītum and **percĭĕo**
-cĭēre, to stir up, set in motion; partic.
percĭtus -a -um, aroused, excited;
of character, excitable.

percĭpĭo -cĭpĕre -cēpi -ceptum, to lay
hold of, seize; to collect, gather,
harvest, gain; with the senses, to
feel, take in; mentally, to learn,

grasp, understand. N. pl. of partic. as subst. **percepta** -orum, *principles, rules.*

percitus -a -um, partic. from percio; q.v.

¹**percõlo** -are, *to strain, as through a sieve.*

²**percõlo** -cõlĕre -cõlŭi -cultum, *to adorn, decorate; to honour a person, revere greatly; to complete.*

percõmis -e, *very friendly.*

percommõdus -a -um, *very fit;* adv. **percommõdē.**

percontãtio (percunct-) -õnis, f. *inquiry, interrogation.*

percontãtor (percunct-) -õris, m. *an inquirer, asker of questions.*

percontor (percunctor) -ari, dep. *to sound; hence to inquire, interrogate, investigate.*

percõquo -cõquĕre -coxi -coctum, *to cook or heat thoroughly; to ripen; to scorch, blacken.*

percrẽbresco -brescĕre -brŭi and **percrẽbesco** -bescĕre -bŭi, *to become prevalent, get well known.*

percrẽpo -crẽpare -crẽpŭi -crẽpĭtum, *to resound, ring.*

percunct-; see percont-.

percũpĭdus -a -um, *very fond.*

percũpĭo -cũpĕre, *to desire exceedingly.*

percũrĭõsus -a -um, *very inquisitive.*

percũro -are, *to cure, heal thoroughly.*

percurro -currĕre -cŭcurri or -curri -cursum, *to run through, hasten through, travel through; in words, to run over, mention in passing; to run over in the mind or with the eye; to pass through stages.*

percursãtio -õnis, f. *travelling through.*

percursĭo -õnis, f. *running through; rapid consideration.*

percurso -are, *to ramble over, rove about.*

percussĭo -õnis, f. *striking, beating; esp. beating time; hence time, rhythm.*

percussor -õris, m. *a striker; esp. a murderer, assassin.*

percussus -ũs, m. *beating, knocking, striking.*

percũtĭo -cũtĕre -cussi -cussum, *to strike hard; to strike through, pierce, transfix; to strike down, cut down; mentally, to strike, shock; colloq., to deceive.*

perdẽcõrus -a -um, *very comely.*

perdẽlĩrus -a -um, *senseless.*

perdifficĭlis -e, *very difficult;* adv. **perdifficĭlĭtĕr.**

perdignus -a -um, *very worthy.*

perdĭlĭgens -entis, *very diligent;* adv. **perdĭlĭgentĕr.**

perdisco -discĕre -dĭdĭci, *to learn thoroughly.*

perdĭsertē, *very eloquently.*

perdĭtor -õris, m. *destroyer.*

perdĭtus -a -um, partic. from perdo; q.v.

perdĭũ, *for a very long time.*

perdĭũturnus -a -um, *lasting a very long time.*

perdĭvĕs -vĭtis, *very rich.*

perdix -dĭcis, c. *partridge.*

perdo -dĕre -dĭdi -dĭtum (in pass., usually pereo, perire), *to destroy, do away with, ruin; to lose; to waste, squander.*

Hence partic. **perdĭtus** -a -um, *miserable, ruined; morally lost, abandoned, profligate.* Adv. **perdĭtē,** *desperately, immoderately; in an abandoned manner.*

perdõcĕo -dõcẽre -dõcŭi -doctum, *to teach or instruct thoroughly;* partic. **perdoctus** -a -um, *very learned, very skilful;* adv. **perdoctē.**

perdõmo -dõmare -dõmŭi -dõmĭtum, *to tame or subdue thoroughly.*

perdũco -dũcĕre -duxi -ductum, *to lead through, bring along; conduct; to carry or construct buildings, from one point to another; to bring over to an opinion, to induce; in time, to continue, prolong; to smear over with a substance.*

perductor -õris, m. *a guide; a pimp, pander.*

perdũdum, *a long time ago.*

perdŭellĭo -õnis, f. *treason.*

perdŭellis -is, m. *a public enemy.*

perdŭim -is -it, alternative pres. subj. of perdo; q.v.

perdũro -are, *to last long, endure.*

pĕrĕdo -esse -ēdi -ēsum, *to eat up, devour; to consume, destroy.*

pĕrĕgrē, adv. *in, to or from a foreign country; abroad, from abroad.*

pĕrĕgrĩnãbundus -a -um, *travelling about.*

pĕrĕgrĩnãtĭo -õnis, f. *travelling or staying in foreign countries; roaming.*

pĕrĕgrĩnãtor -õris, m. *one who travels about.*

pĕrĕgrĩnĭtãs -ãtis, f. *the condition of a foreigner or alien; foreign manners.*

pĕrĕgrĩnor -ari, dep. *to stay or to travel in foreign countries; to roam, wander, ramble; to be strange, foreign.*

pĕrĕgrĩnus -a -um, *foreign, of a foreigner, strange;* m. and f. as subst. *a foreigner, stranger, esp. a foreigner resident in Rome.* Transf., *inexperienced.*

pĕrẽlĕgans -antis *very elegant;* adv. **pĕrẽlĕgantĕr.**

pĕrẽlõquens -entis, *very eloquent.*

pĕremnĭa, n. pl. *the auspices taken on crossing any running water.*

pĕrendĭē, *the day after tomorrow.*

pĕrendĭnus -a -um, *relating to the day after tomorrow.*

pĕrennis -e, *lasting throughout the year; durable, perennial.*

pĕrennĭtãs -ãtis, f. *duration, perpetuity.*

pĕrenno -are, *to last many years.*

pĕrĕo -ire -ĭi and -ĭvi -ĭtum, (often as pass. of perdo), *to go to waste, be ruined or lost, pass away, perish, die.*

pĕrĕquĭto -are, *to ride through, ride round.*

pĕrerro -are, *to wander through, ramble over; to look over, scan.*

pĕrẽrũdĭtus -a -um, *very learned.*

pĕrexĭgŭus -a -um, *very small, very scanty; of time, very short.* Adv.

pĕrexigŭē, *very scantily very sparingly.*

perfăcētus -a -um, *very witty, brilliant;* adv. **perfăcētē.**

perfăcĭlis -e, *very easy; very courteous.* N. acc. as adv. **perfăcĭle,** *very easily; very readily.*

perfămĭlĭāris -e *very familiar, intimate;* m. as subst. *a very great friend.*

perfectĭo -ōnis f. *completion; perfection.*

perfector -ōris, m. *a perfecter, finisher.*

perfectus -a -um, partic. from perficio; q.v.

perfĕro -ferre -tŭli -lātum, *to carry through, bear to the end;* se perferre, *to betake oneself;* of news, etc., *to deliver, convey;* of tasks, *to bring to an end;* of trouble, *to bear, suffer, endure.*
  Hence partic. **perfĕrens** -entis, *enduring, patient.*

perfĭca -ae, f. adj *accomplishing, perfecting.*

perfĭcĭo -fĭcĕre -fēci -fectum, *to bring to an end, complete, finish, achieve;* of time, *to live through;* of a pupil, *to make perfect.*
  Hence partic. **perfectus** -a -um, *perfect, complete, finished;* adv. **perfectē.**

perfĭdēlis -e, *very faithful.*

perfĭdĭa -ae, f. *faithlessness, treachery, falsehood.*

perfĭdĭōsus -a -um, *faithless treacherous;* adv. **perfĭdĭōsē.**

perfĭdus -a -um, *faithless treacherous, false.*

perfĭgo -fīgĕre -fixi -fixum, *to pierce through, stab.*

perflābĭlis -e, *able to be blown through.*

perflāgĭtĭōsus -a -um, *very shameful.*

perflo -are, *to blow through, blow over.*

perfluctŭo -are, *to surge over.*

perflŭo -flŭĕre -fluxi -fluxum, *to stream through, run away.*

perfŏdĭo -fŏdĕre -fōdi -fossum, *to dig through, pierce through; to excavate, make by digging.*

perfŏro -are, *to pierce through; to form by boring.*

perfrĕquens -entis, *much visited.*

perfrĭco -frĭcāre -frĭcŭi -frĭcātum and -frictum, *to rub over;* os, frontem, etc., *to put on a bold face.*

perfrĭgesco -frĭgescĕre -frixi, *to catch a chill.*

perfrĭgĭdus -a -um, *very cold.*

perfringo -fringĕre -frēgi -fractum, *to break through; to break in pieces, shatter.*

perfrŭor -frŭi -fructus, dep. *to enjoy to the full; to execute completely.*

perfŭga -ae, m. *a deserter.*

perfŭgĭo -fŭgĕre -fūgi -fūgĭtum, *to flee away, take refuge; esp. to desert to the enemy.*

perfŭgĭum -i, n. *a place of refuge, shelter.*

perfunctĭo -ōnis, f. *performing, discharging.*

perfundo -fundĕre -fūdi -fūsum, *to pour over; to steep in a fluid, to dye;* in gen., *to steep in, fill with.*

perfungor -fungi -functus, dep. *to perform fully, execute, discharge; to go through, endure.*

perfŭro -ere, *to rage furiously.*

Pergămum -i, n. and **Pergămus** -i, f., also plur. **Pergăma** -orum, n. *the citadel of Troy; Troy.*

pergaudĕo -ēre, *to rejoice exceedingly.*

pergo pergĕre perrexi perrectum, *to continue, proceed, go on with.*

pergrandis -e, *very large, very great.*

pergrātus -a -um, *very pleasant.*

pergrăvis -e, *very weighty, very important;* adv. **pergrăvĭtēr.**

pergŭla -ae, f., *a balcony, outhouse; a shop, workshop; a school.*

perhĭbĕo -ēre -ŭi -ĭtum, *to bring forward, cite; to maintain, assert, hold, say.*

perhīlum, *a very little.*

perhŏnōrĭfĭcus -a -um, *very honourable; very respectful;* adv. **perhŏnōrĭfĭcē,** *very respectfully.*

perhorresco -horrescĕre -horrŭi, *to begin to shudder or tremble, esp. with fear;* transit., *to shudder at.*

perhorrĭdus -a -um, *very dreadful.*

perhūmānus -a -um, *very friendly, very civil;* adv. **perhūmānĭtēr.**

Pĕrĭclēs -is, m. *Athenian statesman.*

pĕrĭclĭtātĭo -ōnis, f. *trial, experiment.*

pĕrĭclĭtor -ari, dep.: intransit., *to try, make a trial, venture; to take a risk, be in danger;* transit., *to try, test, prove; to endanger, risk.*

pĕrĭcŭlōsus -a -um, *dangerous, perilous;* adv. **pĕrĭcŭlōsē.**

pĕrĭcŭlum (pĕrĭclum) -i, n. *a trial, proof, test, attempt; danger, peril, hazard;* at law, *a trial, action, suit;* hence, *a legal record or register.*

pĕrĭdōnĕus -a -um, *very suitable.*

pĕrillustris -e *very evident; very distinguished.*

pĕrimbēcillus -a -um, *very weak.*

pĕrĭmo (pĕrĕmo) -ĭmĕre -ēmi -emptum, *to do away with, destroy, kill, annihilate.* Transf., *to thwart, frustrate.*

pĕrincommŏdus -a -um, *very inconvenient;* adv. **pĕrincommŏdē.**

pĕrindĕ, adv. *in like manner;* perinde ac, ut, or quam, *just as;* perinde ac si, *just as if.*

pĕrindulgens -entis, *very indulgent, very tender.*

pĕrinfirmus -a -um, *very weak.*

pĕringĕnĭōsus -a -um, *very clever.*

pĕrinīquus -a -um, *very unfair; very discontented or unwilling.*

pĕrinsignis -e, *very remarkable.*

pĕrinvītus -a -um, *very unwilling.*

pĕrĭŏdus -i, m. *a sentence, period.*

Pĕrĭpătētĭcus -a -um, *belonging to the Peripatetic or Aristotelian school of philosophy.*

pĕrĭpetasma -ātis, n. *curtain, hanging.*

pĕrĭrātus -a -um, *very angry.*

pĕriscĕlis -ĭdis, f. *garter or anklet.*

pĕristrōma -ătis, n. *curtain, coverlet, carpet, hanging.*

pĕristȳlĭum -ĭ, n. *a court with a colonnade round it.*

pĕristȳlum -ĭ, n. *a peristyle, a colonnade round a building.*

pĕrītĭa -ae, f. *experience, skill.*

pĕrītus -a -um, *experienced, skilful, practised, expert;* adv. **pĕrītē.**

pĕriūcundus -a -um, *very pleasant;* adv. **pĕriūcundē.**

pĕriūrĭum i-, n. *false swearing, perjury.*

pĕriūro = peiero; q.v.

pĕriūrus -a -um, *perjured; lying.*

perlābor -lābi -lapsus, dep. *to glide through, glide along.*

perlaetus -a -um, *very joyful.*

perlātē, adv. *very widely.*

perlectĭo -ōnis, f. *perusal.*

perlĕgo (pellĕgo) -lĕgĕre -lēgi -lectum, *to survey thoroughly, scan; to read through;* senatum, *to call over the roll of senators.*

perlĕvis -e, *slight;* adv. **perlĕvĭtĕr.**

perlĭbens (perlŭbens) -entis, from perlibet; q.v.

perlĭbērālis -e, *well-bred, very liberal;* adv. **perlĭbērālĭtĕr.**

perlĭbet (perlŭbet) -ere, *it is very pleasing;* partic. **perlĭbens (perlŭb-)** -entis, *very willing;* adv. **perlĭbentĕr (perlŭb-).**

perlĭcĭo = pellicio; q.v.

perlĭto -are, *to offer an auspicious sacrifice.*

perlongus -a -um, *very long, tedious;* adv. **perlongē,** *very far.*

perlŭbet, etc. = perlibet, etc.; q.v.

perlūcĕo (pellūcĕo) -lūcēre -luxi, *to shine through; to be transparent.*

perlūcĭdŭlus -a -um, *transparent.*

perlūcĭdus (pellūcĭdus) -a -um, *shining, bright; transparent.*

perluctŭōsus -a -um, *very mournful.*

perlŭo -lŭĕre -lŭi -lūtum, *to wash, bathe.*

perlustro -are, *to traverse, pass through; to survey, examine.*

permagnus -a -um, *very great very large.*

permănĕo -mănēre -mansi -mansum, *to remain, stay, last, continue.*

permāno -are, *to flow through, trickle through; to penetrate, extend.* Adv. from partic. **permanantĕr,** *by flowing through.*

permansĭo -ōnis, f. *a remaining, abiding.*

permārīnus -a -um, *going over the sea.*

permātūresco -mātūrescĕre -mātūrŭi, *to become thoroughly ripe.*

permĕdĭocris -e, *very moderate.*

permĕo -are, *to go through, traverse.*

permētĭor -mētiri -mensus, dep. *to measure out; to traverse.*

permīrus -a -um, *very wonderful.*

permiscĕo -miscēre -miscŭi -mixtum, *to mix together, mingle thoroughly to confuse, throw into confusion.* Hence partic. **permixtus** -a -um, *mixed; promiscuous;* adv. **permixtē.**

permissĭo -ōnis, f. *yielding, surrender; permission, leave.*

permissū, abl. sing. m. *by permission.*

permītĭālis -e, *destructive, annihilating.*

permītĭēs -ēi, f. *destruction, annihilation.*

permitto -mittĕre -mīsi -missum, *to let go;* esp. of weapons, *to hurl; to give up, yield, surrender, concede, sacrifice; to make allowance for; to allow, permit.*

permixtē, adv. from permisceo; q.v.

permixtĭo -onis, f. *mixture; confusion.*

permŏdestus -a -um, *very modest, very moderate.*

permŏlestus -a -um, *very troublesome;* adv. **permŏlestē,** *with much difficulty.*

permŏlo -ĕre, *to grind thoroughly.*

permōtĭo -onis, f. *movement, agitation.*

permŏvĕo -mŏvēre -mōvi -mōtum, *to move* or *stir up thoroughly; excite, agitate; to persuade, induce, influence a person.*

permulcĕo -mulcēre -mulsi -mulsum, *to stroke; to charm, soothe, soften.*

permultus -a -um, sing., *very much;* plur., *very many;* n. sing. as subst. *very much.*

permūnĭo -ire -īvi -ītum, *to fortify completely,* or *finish fortifying.*

permūtātĭo -ōnis, f. *complete change; exchange, interchange.*

permūto -are, *to change completely; to exchange, interchange.*

perna -ae, f. *ham.*

pernĕcessārĭus -a -um, *very necessary; very intimate.*

pernĕcessē, indecl. adj. *very necessary.*

pernĕgo -are, *to deny flatly; to persist in denying* or *refusing.*

pernĭcĭābĭlis -e, *deadly, destructive.*

pernĭcĭēs -ēi, *destruction, disaster, ruin, bane.*

pernĭcĭōsus -a -um, *destructive, ruinous;* adv. **pernĭcĭōsē.**

pernĭcĭtās -ātis, f. *swiftness, agility.*

pernix -nīcis, *swift, nimble, agile;* adv. **pernīcĭtĕr.**

pernōbĭlis -e, *very famous.*

pernocto -are, *to pass the night.*

pernosco -noscĕre -nōvi -nōtum, *to investigate* or *find out thoroughly;* in perf., *to know thoroughly.*

pernōtŭit -uisse, *it has become well known.*

pernox -noctis, adj. *all-night.*

pernŭmĕro -are, *to count out, reckon up.*

pēro -ōnis, m. *a boot of untanned hide.*

pĕrobscūrus -a -um, *very obscure.*

pĕrōdĭōsus -a -um, *very troublesome.*

pĕroffĭcĭōsē, *very attentively.*

pĕrŏlĕo -ēre, *to emit a strong smell.*

pĕrōnatus -a -um, *wearing leather boots.*

pĕropportūnus -a -um, *very convenient;* adv. **pĕropportūnē.**

pĕroptāto, abl. sing. n. *just as one would wish.*

pĕrōrātĭo -ōnis, f. *conclusion of a speech, peroration.*

pĕrornātus -a -um, *very ornate.*

pĕrorno -are, *to adorn greatly.*

pĕrōro -are, *to speak from beginning to end, to plead a cause throughout, explain* or *state thoroughly; to conclude a speech, wind up, close.*

pĕrōsus -a -um, *hating, detesting.*

perpāco -are, *to pacify thoroughly.*
perparvŭlus and **perparvus** -a -um, *very little.*
perpaucŭli and **perpauci** -ae, -a, *very few.*
perpaulum (perpaullum) i, -n. *a very little.*
perpauper -ĕris, *very poor.*
perpello -pellĕre -pŭli -pulsum, *to push hard, drive along; to urge, compel, constrain.*
perpendĭcŭlum -i, n. *plumbline, plummet;* ad perpendiculum, *in a straight line.*
perpendo -pendĕre -pendi -pensum, *to weigh carefully; to consider, examine.*
perpĕram, *wrongly, falsely.*
perpēs -pĕtis, *continuous, unbroken.*
perpessĭo -ōnis, f. *suffering, endurance.*
perpessū, alb. sing. m. *in the enduring.*
perpĕtior -pĕti -pessus, dep. *to bear to the end, endure.*
perpetro -are, *to complete, accomplish, perform.*
perpĕtŭĭtās -ātis, f. *uninterrupted succession, continuity;* ad perpetuitatem, *for ever.*
[1]**perpĕtŭō**, adv. from perpetuus; q.v.
[2]**perpĕtŭo** -are, *to make continual, continue, perpetuate.*
perpĕtŭus -a -um, *continuous, uninterrupted* (in space or time). Transf., *universal, general.* Abl. as adv. **perpĕtŭō**, *uninterruptedly.*
perplăcĕo -ēre, *to please greatly.*
perplexābĭlis -e, *intricate, obscure.*
perplexor -ari, dep. *to perplex.*
perplexus -a -um, *confused, intricate; obscure, ambiguous.* Adv. **perplexē** and **perplexim.**
perplĭcātus -a -um, *entangled, involved.*
perplŭit -ĕre, *to let the rain through; to run away or pour in like rain.*
perpŏlĭo -ire, *to polish thoroughly; perfect, complete.*
Hence partic. **perpŏlītus** -a -um, *polished, accomplished, refined.*
perpŏpŭlor -ari, dep. *to lay waste, devastate completely.*
perpŏtātĭo -ōnis, f. *continued drinking, drinking-bout.*
perpŏto -are, *to continue drinking; to drink up.*
perprimo -prīmĕre -pressi -pressum, *to press hard.*
perpugnax -ācis, *very pugnacious.*
perpurgo (perpūrĭgo) -are, *to clean thoroughly.* Transf., *to explain thoroughly, clear up.*
perpŭsillus -a -um, *very small.*
perpŭto -are, *to explain fully.*
perquam, *very much, extremely.*
perquīro -quīrĕre -quīsivi -quīsitum, *to search for eagerly; to inquire carefully into.* Compar. adv. from perf. partic. **perquīsītĭus** *more accurately.*
perrārus -a -um, *very uncommon;* abl. as adv. **perrārŏ.**
perrĕcondĭtus -a -um, *very abstruse.*
perrēpo -rēpĕre -repsi -reptum, *to crawl through, creep over.*

perrepto -are, *to crawl through, crawl about.*
perrĭdĭcŭlus -a -um, *very laughable;* adv. **perrĭdĭcŭle.**
perrŏgo -are, *to ask in succession, to ask one after another.*
perrumpo -rumpĕre -rūpi -ruptum, *to break through, burst through; to shatter, burst.*
Persae -arum, m. pl. *the Persians;* sing. **Persa** and **Persēs** -ae, m. *a Persian;* **Persĭa** -ae, f. *Persia;* **Persis** -ĭdis, f., as adj., *Persian,* as subst., *Persia;* adj. **Persĭcus** -a -um.
persaepe, *very often.*
persalsus -a -um, *very witty;* adv. **persalsē.**
persălūtātĭo -ōnis, f. *a general greeting.*
persălūto -are, *to greet in succession, greet all round.*
persăpĭens -entis, *very wise;* adv. **persăpĭentĕr.**
perscĭentĕr, *very discreetly.*
perscindo -scindĕre -scĭdi -scissum, *to tear to pieces.*
perscĭtus -a -um, *very clever.*
perscrībo -scrībĕre -scripsi -scriptum, *to write in full; to note down officially, enter; to make over or assign in writing.*
perscriptĭo -ōnis, f. *entry, noting down; assigning by written document.*
perscriptor -ōris, m. *one who makes an entry.*
perscrūto -are and **perscrūtor** -ari, dep. *to search through, look through, examine, investigate.*
persēco -sĕcare -sĕcŭi -sectum, *to cut through, cut away, dissect.*
persector -ari, dep. *to pursue eagerly; to investigate.*
persĕcūtĭo -ōnis, f. *prosecution.*
persĕdĕo (persĭdĕo) -sĕdēre -sēdi -sessum, *to remain sitting.*
persegnis -e, *very languid.*
persentĭo -sentire -sensi -sensum, *to perceive distinctly, feel deeply.*
persentisco -ĕre, *to begin to perceive distinctly or feel deeply.*
Persĕphŏnē -ēs, f. *Greek name of Proserpina;* q.v.
persĕquor -sĕqui -sĕcūtus, dep. *to follow constantly, pursue to the end, hunt out, overtake; to strive after; to imitate; to proceed against an offender, punish, avenge; to accomplish an action, perform, execute; to treat a subject, expound, describe.*
[1]**Persēs** -ae and **Persēus** -ĕi, m. *the last king of Macedonia, defeated by the Roman general Aemilius Paulus in* 169 B.C.; adj. **Persĭcus** -a -um.
[2]**Persēs** -ae, m. *a Persian; see* Persae.
Persēus -ĕi and -ĕos, m. *Perseus, who killed Medusa, and rescued Andromeda.*
persĕvērantĭa -ae, f. *persistence.*
persĕvēro -are, *to persist, persevere, continue.*
Hence partic. **persĕvērans** -antis, *enduring, persistent;* adv. **persĕvērantĕr.**
persĕvērus -a -um, *very strict.*
Persĭa; see Persae.
Persĭcus; see Persae and Perses.

persīdo -sīdĕre -sēdi -sessum, *to sink in,
settle down.*

persigno -are, *to note down, record.*

persĭmĭlis -e, *very like.*

persimplex -ĭcis, *very simple.*

persisto -ĕre, *to remain constant, persist.*

Persĭus -i, m. A. Persius Flaccus,
a satirist in the reign of Nero.

persolvo -solvĕre -solvi -sŏlūtum,
to unloose; hence *to explain,
expound; to pay, pay off, deal out.*

persŏna -ae, f. *a mask,* esp. *as worn by
actors;* hence *role, part, character,
personality.*

persōnātus -a -um, *masked; disguised;
counterfeit.*

persŏno -sŏnare -sŏnŭi -sŏnĭtum:
intransit., *to resound, sound forth; to
shout; to perform upon a musical instrument;* transit., *to make, resound; to
proclaim loudly.*

perspergo -ĕre, *to sprinkle, moisten.*

perspĭcax -ācis, *sharp-sighted.*

perspĭcĭentĭa -ae, f. *full awareness or
knowledge.*

perspĭcĭo -spĭcĕre -spexi, -spectum,
*to see through, look through; to look
at attentively, survey, examine;* mentally, *to regard, investigate, ascertain.*
Hence partic. **perspectus** -a -um,
ascertained, fully known.

perspĭcŭĭtās -ātis, f. *clearness, perspicuity.*

perspĭcŭus -a -um, *transparent, bright;
clear, evident.* Adv. **perspĭcŭē.**

persterno -sternĕre -strāvi -strātum,
to pave thoroughly.

perstĭmŭlo -are, *to goad on violently.*

persto -stare -stĭti -stātum, *to stand
firm, remain standing; to remain unchanged, last, endure; to stand firm,
persist, persevere.*

perstringo -stringĕre -strinxi -strictum.
(1) *to press tight, bind tight; to deaden,
dull the senses.* (2) *to graze, scratch;
to touch upon a subject; to scold,
blame, reproach a person.*

perstŭdĭōsus -a -um, *very eager;*
adv. **perstŭdĭōsē.**

persuādĕo -suādēre -suāsi -suāsum,
to persuade. (1) *to convince of a fact;
sibi persuadere, to satisfy oneself, be
convinced.* (2) *to persuade, prevail
upon a person to do a thing.*

persuāsĭo -ōnis, f. *persuasion; a conviction, belief.*

persuāsū, abl. sing. m. *by persuasion.*

persubtĭlis -e, *very fine; very subtle.*

persulto -are, *to leap, gambol, skip
about, skip over.*

pertaedet -taedĕre -taesum est, *to
cause weariness or disgust;* cf. taedet.

pertempto -are, *to prove, test, try;
to weigh, consider, examine; to assail.*

pertendo -tendĕre -tendi, *to push on,
proceed, continue.*

pertĕnŭis -e, *very slight.*

pertĕrebro -are, *to bore through.*

pertergĕo -tergēre -tersi -tersum *to
wipe over; to brush.*

perterrĕo -ēre, *to terrify.*

perterricrĕpus -a -um, *rattling terribly.*

pertexo -texĕre -texŭi -textum, *to
weave throughout; to complete,
accomplish.*

pertĭca -ae, f. *a long pole or rod.*

pertĭmesco -tĭmescĕre -tĭmŭi, *to
become very much afraid.*

pertĭnācĭa -ae, f. *firmness, obstinacy,
stubbornness.*

pertĭnax -ācis, adj., *tenacious; tight-
fisted, mean; firm, persistent, stubborn,
obstinate.* Adv. **pertĭnācĭtĕr.**

pertĭnĕo -tĭnēre -tĭnŭi, *to reach to,
extend to; to tend towards, have as
object or result; to relate to, belong to,
apply to, attach to.*

pertingo -ĕre, *to stretch out, extend.*

pertŏlĕro -are, *to endure to the end.*

pertorquĕo -ēre, *to twist, distort.*

pertractātĭo -ōnis, f. *thorough handling, detailed treatment.*

pertracto -are, *to handle, feel; to treat,
study, work upon.*

pertrăho -trăhĕre -traxi -tractum, *to
drag, forcibly conduct; to entice, allure.*

pertrecto = pertracto; q.v.

pertristis -e, *very sorrowful or austere.*

pertŭmultŭōsē, *in an agitated manner.*

pertundo -tundĕre -tŭdi -tūsum, *to
bore through, perforate.*

perturbātĭo -ōnis, f. *confusion, disorder, disturbance;* philosoph. *a passion,
emotion.*

perturbātrix -icis, f. *she that disturbs.*

perturbo ⸄-are, *to disturb thoroughly,
confuse, disquiet, upset.*
Hence partic. **perturbātus** -a -um,
confused, disturbed; adv. **perturbātē.**

perturpis -e, *very disgraceful.*

pertūsus -a -um, partic. from pertundo;
q.v.

pĕrungo -ungĕre -unxi -unctum, *to
anoint thoroughly, besmear.*

pĕrurbānus -a -um, *very polite or
witty; over-sophisticated.*

pĕruro -urĕre -ussi -ustum, *to burn up,
consume, inflame; to gall, chafe;
to pinch, nip with cold.*

pĕrūtĭlis -e, *very useful.*

pervādo -vādĕre -vāsi -vāsum. (1) *to
go through, pass through, pervade.*
(2) *to reach, arrive at.*

pervăgor -ari, dep. *to wander through,
to rove about; to be widely spread,
pervade.* Hence partic. **pervăgātus**
-a -um, *widespread, well known;
common, general.*

pervăgus -a -um, *wandering everywhere.*

pervărĭē, *very variously.*

pervasto -are, *to lay waste completely.*

pervĕho -vĕhĕre -vexi -vectum, *to
carry, lead, conduct, bring* (to or
through *a place);* pass. pervehi,
to travel to or through.

pervello -vellĕre -velli, *to pluck, pull,
twitch; to stimulate; to pain, to
disparage.*

pervĕnĭo -vĕnire -vēni -ventum, *to
come through to, arrive at, reach,
attain to, be passed to.*

perversĭtās -ātis, f. *perversity.*

perverto (**pervorto**) -vertĕre -verti
-versum, *to turn upside down, overturn,*

overthrow; to *undermine, subvert,*
pervert; in speech, *to trip up.*
  Hence partic. **perversus** -a -um,
crooked, awry, askew; distorted,
perverse. Adv. **perversē.**
pervespĕrī, *very late in the evening.*
pervestīgātio -ōnis, f. *examination,*
investigation.
pervestīgo -are, *to track out, investigate,*
search into.
pervĕtus -ĕris, *very old.*
pervĕtustus -a -um, *very old.*
pervīcācīa -ae, f. *firmness, persistence;*
stubbornness, obstinacy.
pervīcax -ācis, *firm, persistent; stubborn,*
obstinate; compar. adv. **pervīcācīus,**
more stubbornly.
pervīdĕo -vīdēre -vīdi -vīsum, *to look*
over, survey; to see through, discern,
distinguish.
pervīgĕo -ēre, *to flourish, bloom con-*
tinually.
pervīgil -ilis, *always watchful.*
pervīgīlātio -ōnis, f. and **pervīgīlium**
-i, n. *a vigil, religious watching.*
pervīgīlo -are, *to remain awake all night.*
pervīlis -e, *very cheap.*
pervinco -vincĕre -vīci -victum, *to*
conquer completely; to surpass, outdo;
to induce, prevail upon; to carry one's
point; to achieve, effect; to prove,
demonstrate.
pervīus -a -um, *passable, accessible;*
as subst., *a passage.*
pervolgo = pervulgo; q.v.
pervŏlĭto -are, *to fly round, flit about.*
¹**pervŏlo** -are, *to fly through, fly round.*
²**pervŏlo** -velle -vŏlŭi, *to wish greatly.*
pervŏlūto -are, *to roll round; esp. to*
unroll and read a book.
pervolvo -volvĕre -volvi -volutum,
to roll about; to unroll and read
a book.
perversē, etc., = perverse, etc.; q.v.
pervulgo (pervolgo) -are, *to publish,*
make publicly known; to make
generally available; to frequent, haunt
a place. Hence partic. **pervulgātus**
-a -um, *very usual or well known.*
pēs pĕdis, m. *the foot;* pedem referre,
to return; pedibus, *on foot, also by*
land; servus a pedibus, *an attendant,*
lackey; pedibus ire in sententiam,
to support a proposal; milit., pedibus
merere, *to serve in the infantry;*
pedem conferre, *to fight hand to hand.*
Transf., *a foot of a table, chair, etc.;*
a metrical foot; a measure of length;
pes (veli), *a rope or sheet, attached to*
the lower edge of a sail.
pessīmus, pessime; see malus.
pessŭlus -i, m. *a bolt.*
pessum *to the ground, to the bottom,*
downwards; pessum ire, *to sink, be*
ruined, perish; pessum dare, *to*
destroy, ruin, put an end to.
pestīfer -fĕra, -fĕrum, *pestilential,*
destructive, injurious; adv. **pestīfĕrē.**
pestīlens -entis, *unhealthy, fatal,*
noxious.
pestīlentīa -ae, f. *an unhealthy con-*
dition; a plague, infectious disease,
pest.

pestīlĭtās -ātis, f. = pestilentia; q.v.
pestis -is, f. *pest, pestilence, plague;*
destruction, ruin; curse, bane.
pĕtăsātus -a -um, *wearing the* petasus;
hence, *equipped for a journey.*
pĕtăso -ōnis, m. *a fore-quarter of pork.*
pĕtăsus -i, m. *a broad-brimmed felt hat,*
used by travellers.
pĕtaurum -i, n. *a spring-board.*
pĕtesso (pĕtisso) -ĕre, *to long for,*
strive after.
pĕtītio -ōnis, f. *an attack, thrust, blow;*
a request, application; standing for
office, candidature; at law, *a suit,*
a right of claim, right to bring an action.
pĕtītor -ōris, m. *a seeker;* polit., *a*
candidate; legal, *a plaintiff.*
pĕtītūrio -ire, *to desire to stand for*
election.
pĕtītus -ūs, m. *an inclining towards.*
pĕto -ĕre -īvi and -ii -itum, *to make for,*
go to; to attack, assail; to seek, strive
after; to ask for, beg, request, demand;
polit., *to stand for, canvas for;* legal,
to sue for; sometimes *to fetch, derive.*
pĕtorrītum (petŏrītum) -i, n. *an open*
four-wheeled carriage.
Petrōnius -i, m. *name of a Roman* gens;
esp. *of a satirist under Nero.*
pĕtŭlans -antis, *impudent, pert, wanton;*
adv. **pĕtŭlantĕr.**
pĕtŭlantīa -ae, f. *impudence, pertness,*
wantonness.
pĕtulcus -a -um, *butting with the head.*
pexātus -a -um, *wearing a garment with*
the nap on.
Phaedra -ae, f. *daughter of Minos,*
wife of Theseus.
Phaedrus -i, m. *a freedman of Augustus,*
author of Latin fables.
Phăĕthōn -ontis, m. *the son of Helios,*
killed trying to drive the chariot of his
father.
phălangae (pălangae) -arum, f. pl.
rollers.
phălangītae -arum, m. pl. *soldiers*
belonging to a phalanx.
phălanx -angis, f. *an array of soldiers*
in close formation.
Phălāris -ĭdis, m. *a tyrant of Agri-*
gentum.
phălĕrae -arum, f. pl. *metal bosses;*
military decorations; horses' trappings.
phălĕratus -a -um, *wearing phalerae;*
q.v.
Phălērum -i, n. *the oldest port of Athens.*
phantasma -ātis, n. *an apparition.*
phăretra -ae, f. *a quiver.*
phăretrātus -a -um, *wearing a quiver.*
pharmăceutrīa -ae, f. *sorceress.*
pharmăcŏpōla (-es) -ae, m. *a seller of*
drugs; a quack.
Pharsālus (-ŏs) -i, f. *a town in Thessaly,*
where Pompey was defeated by Caesar
in 48 B.C.
Phărus (-ŏs) -i, f., rarely m., *an island*
off Alexandria, with a lighthouse;
hence in gen. *a lighthouse.*
phăsēlus -i, m. and f. *the kidney-bean*
or French bean; a light bean-shaped
boat.
Phāsis -ĭdis and -ĭdos, m. *a river in*
Colchis, flowing into the Black Sea;

f. adj. **Phāsis** -ĭdis, and **Phāsiānus** -a -um, *Colchian*.

phasma -ātis, n. *a ghost, spectre*.

phĭăla -ae, f. *a drinking-vessel; a bowl, saucer*.

Phīdĭās -ae, m. *an Athenian sculptor*.

Phĭlippi -orum, m. pl. *a city in Macedonia, where Octavian and Antony defeated Brutus and Cassius*.

Phĭlippus -i, m. *the name of several kings of Macedon*; adj. **Phĭlippēus** and **Phĭlippĭcus** -a -um; f. as subst. **Phĭlippĭca** -ae, *one of the speeches of Demosthenes against Philip, or of Cicero against Antony*.

phĭlŏlŏgĭa -ae, f. *love of learning, study of literature*.

phĭlŏlŏgus -a -um, *learned, literary*; m. as subst. *a scholar*.

Phĭlŏmēla -ae, f. *the daughter of Pandion, turned into a nightingale*.

phĭlŏsŏphĭa -ae, f. *philosophy*.

phĭlŏsŏphor -ari, dep. *to philosophize, apply oneself to philosophy*.

phĭlŏsŏphus -a -um, *philosophical*; m. and f. as subst. *a philosopher*.

philtrum -i, n. *a love-potion, philtre*.

phĭlȳra -ae, f. *the inner bark of the linden-tree*.

phimus -i, m. *a dice-box*.

Phlĕgĕthōn -ontis, m. *a river in the infernal regions*.

phōca -ae, f. and **phōcē** -ēs, f. *a seal*.

Phōcis -ĭdis, f. *a district in the north of Greece*; adj. **Phōcēus** -a -um.

Phoebē -ēs, f. *the sister of Phoebus, the Moon-goddess, Diana*.

Phoebĭgĕna -ae, m. *the son of Phoebus, Aesculapius*.

Phoebus -i, m. *Apollo, the Sun-god*; hence subst. **Phoebăs** -ădis, f. *a priestess of Phoebus, a prophetess*; adj. **Phoebēius** and **Phoebēus** -a -um, *of Phoebus*.

Phoenīcē -ēs, f. *Phoenicia*; m. subst. **Phoenīces** -um, *the Phoenicians*; f. subst. **Phoenissa** -ae, f. *a Phoenician woman*.

phoenīcoptĕros -i, m. *the flamingo*.

phoenix -īcis, m. *the phoenix, a fabulous bird of Arabia*.

phōnascus -i, m. *a teacher of music*.

phrĕnēsis -is, f. *madness, frenzy*.

phrĕnētĭcus -a -um, *mad, frantic*.

Phrixus -i, m. *brother of Helle*.

Phrȳges -um, m. pl. *the Phrygians*; sing. **Phryx** -ȳgis; **Phrȳgĭa** -ae, f. *the country of Phrygia in Asia Minor*; adj. **Phrȳgĭus** -a -um, *Phrygian*; poet. = *Trojan*.

phthĭsis -is, f. *consumption*.

phy, interj. *pish! tush!*

phȳlarchus -i, m. *the head of a tribe, an emir*.

physĭca -ae, and **physĭcē** -ēs, f. *physics, natural science*.

physĭcus -a -um, *relating to physics, physical*; m. as subst. *a scientist*; n. pl. **physĭca** -orum, *physics*; adv. **physĭcē**, *in the manner of the scientists*.

physĭognōmōn -onis, m. *a physiognomist*.

physĭŏlŏgĭa -ae, f. *natural science*.

pĭābĭlis -e, *able to be atoned for*.

pĭācŭlāris -e, *atoning, expiating*; n. pl. as subst. *expiatory sacrifices*.

pĭācŭlum -i, n. *a means of expiating or appeasing; sacrifice; remedy; punishment; a victim; an act needing expiation, a sin, crime*.

pĭāmen -ĭnis, n. *means of atonement or expiation*.

pīca -ae, f. *a jay or magpie*.

pīcārĭa -ae, f. *a place where pitch is made*.

pīcĕa -ae, f. *the spruce-fir*.

Pīcēnum -i, n. *a district in central Italy*.

pīcĕus -a -um, *of pitch; pitch-black*.

pīco -are, *to smear with pitch*.

pictor -ōris, m. *a painter*.

pictūra -ae, f. *the art of painting; a painting, picture*; pictura textilis, *embroidery*.

pictūrātus -a -um, *painted*; vestes, *embroidered*.

pīcus -i, m. *a woodpecker*.

Pīĕris -ĭdis or -ĭdos, f. *a Muse*; plur. **Pīĕrĭdes**, *the Muses*; adj. **Pīĕrĭus** -a -um, *Pierian, poetic*.

pĭĕtās -ātis, f. *dutifulness, dutiful conduct; piety; patriotism; devotion; kindness*.

pĭger -gra -grum, *sluggish, unwilling, slow*; campus, *unfruitful*. Adv. **pĭgrē**.

pĭget -gēre -gŭit -gĭtum est, impers., it causes annoyance (or regret or shame); it disgusts; piget me, with genit., *I am disgusted with*.

pigmentārĭus -i, m. *a seller of paints and unguents*.

pigmentum -i, n. *paint, pigment*; of style, *ornament, decoration*.

pignĕrātor -ōris, m. *a mortgagee*.

pignĕro -are, *to give as a pledge, pawn, mortgage*.

pignĕror -ari, dep. *to take as a pledge; to claim*.

pignus -nŏris and -nĕris, n. *a pledge, pawn, security; a wager, bet, stake; a token, assurance, proof*; in plur., *persons as pledges of love*.

pĭgrĭtĭa -ae, and **pĭgrĭtĭes** -ēi, f. *sluggishness, indolence*.

pĭgro -are and **pĭgror** -ari, dep. *to be sluggish*.

¹**pĭla** -ae, f. *a mortar*.

²**pĭla** -ae, f. *a pillar, pier; a bookstall*.

³**pĭla** -ae, f. *a ball; a game of ball*.

pīlanus -i, m. = triarius; q.v.

pīlātus -a -um, *armed with the pilum or javelin*.

pīlentum -i, n. *a carriage, coach*.

pillĕātus (pĭlĕ-) -a -um, *wearing the felt cap*.

pillĕŏlus (pĭlĕ-) -i, m. *a little cap, skull-cap*.

pillĕus (pĭlĕus) -i, m. and **pillĕum** -i, n. *a felt cap, esp. as worn by manumitted slaves*.

pĭlo -are, *to deprive of hair*.

pĭlōsus -a -um, *covered with hair, hairy*.

pīlum -i, n. *the heavy javelin of the Roman infantry*.

¹**pĭlus** -i, m. *a single hair; a trifle*.

²**pĭlus** -i, m. *a division of the triarii in the Roman army*; primus pilus, *the*

chief centurion of the triarii *and of the legion.*

Pindārus -i, m. *a lyric poet of Thebes.*

pīnētum -i, n. *a pine-wood.*

pīnĕus -a -um, *made of pine-wood or deal.*

pingo pingĕre pinxi pictum, *to paint, to draw; to embroider; to stain, dye; to decorate, adorn;* in speech or writing, *to embellish, depict.*

pinguesco -ĕre, *to become fat, grow fertile.*

pinguis -e, *fat; oily; rich, fertile;* n. as subst. *fatness, fat.* Transf., *thick, dense; heavy, stupid; easy, quiet.*

pinguitūdo -inis, f. *fatness, broadness.*

pīnifer -fĕra -fĕrum and **pīnigĕr** -gĕra -gĕrum, *producing pines.*

¹**pinna** -ae, f. *a feather; a feathered arrow; a wing; a battlement along the top of a wall.*

²**pinna** (pīna) -ae, f. *a species of mussel.*

pinnātus -a -um, *feathered, winged.*

pinnĭger -gĕra -gĕrum, *feathered, winged;* piscis, *having fins.*

pinnīrăpus -i, m. *a crestsnatcher,* i.e. *a kind of gladiator.*

pinnŭla -ae, f. *a small feather or wing.*

pinso, pinsĕre; pinsi and pinsŭi; pinsum pinsĭtum and pistum, *to stamp, pound, crush.*

pīnus -i and -ūs, f. *a fir or pine; anything made of pine-wood, e.g. a torch, oar, ship.*

pīo -are, *to appease, propitiate; to venerate; to make good, atone for.*

pīper pīpĕris, n. *pepper.*

pīpĭlo -are, *to twitter, chirp.*

pīpŭlus -i, m. and **pīpŭlum** -i, n. *outcry.*

Pīraeēus and **Pīraeus** -i, m. *the Piraeus, the main port of Athens.*

pīrāta -ae, m. *pirate.*

pīrāticus -a -um, *piratical;* f. as subst. *piracy.*

pīrum -i, n. *a pear.*

pīrus -i, f. *a pear-tree.*

piscātor -ōris, m. *a fisherman; a fishmonger.*

piscātōrius -a -um, *of fishermen or fishing.*

piscātus -ūs, m. *fishes; fishing, a catch.*

piscĭcŭlus -i, m. *a little fish.*

piscīna -ae, f. *a fish-pond; a swimming-bath.*

piscīnārius -i, m. *one fond of fish-ponds.*

piscis -is, m. *a fish.*

piscor -ari, dep. *to fish.*

piscōsus -a -um, *abounding in fish.*

pistillum -i, n. *a pestle.*

pistor -ōris, m. *a grinder, miller; a baker.*

pistrīnum -i, n. *a mill; a bakery.*

pistris -is, and **pistrix** -trīcis, f. *a sea monster; a whale, shark, saw-fish.* Transf., *a small fast ship.*

pītuīta -ae, f. *phlegm, rheum.*

pītuītōsus -a -um, *full of phlegm.*

pius -a -um, *dutiful; godly, holy; patriotic; devoted, affectionate;* in gen., *honest, upright, kind.*

pix pĭcis, f. *pitch.*

plācābĭlis -e; pass., *easy to appease;* act., *appeasing.*

plācābĭlĭtās -ātis, f. *placability.*

plācāmen -ĭnis, and **plācāmentum** -i, n. *means of appeasing.*

plācātĭo -ōnis, f. *soothing, appeasing.*

plăcĕo -ēre -ŭi and -itus sum, -itum, *to please, be agreeable to;* impers. **plăcet,** *it seems good, it is agreed or resolved.*

Hence partic. **plăcĭtus** -a -um, *pleasing, agreeable; agreed upon.* N. as subst. *what is agreeable;* plur., *opinions, teaching.*

plăcĭdus -a -um, *quiet, still, gentle;* adv. **plăcĭdē.**

plăcĭtus -a -um, partic. from placeo; q.v.

plāco -are, *to soothe, calm; to reconcile, appease.*

Hence partic. **plācātus** -a -um, *soothed, appeased; calm, gentle, quiet;* adv. **plācātē.**

¹**plāga** -ae, f. *a blow, stroke; a wound.*

²**plăga** -ae, f. *a district, zone, region.*

³**plăga** -ae, f. *a net for hunting; a trap, snare.*

plăgiārius -i, m. *a kidnapper; a plagiarist.*

plăgōsus -a -um, *fond of flogging.*

plăgŭla -ae, f. *a bed-curtain.*

planctus -ūs, m. *beating;* esp. *beating of the breast, lamentations.*

plango plangĕre planxi planctum, *to beat, strike,* esp. *noisily; to strike the breast, head,* etc., as a sign of grief; hence plangere and pass. plangi, *to bewail.*

plangor -ōris, m. *loud striking or beating;* esp. *beating of the head and breast, loud lamentations.*

plānĭpēs -pĕdis, m. *an actor who wore no shoes.*

plānĭtās -ātis, f. *plainness, distinctness.*

plānĭtĭa -ae, and **plānĭtĭēs** -ēi, f. *a level surface, a plain.*

planta -ae, f. (1) *a green twig, cutting, graft; a plant.* (2) *the sole of the foot.*

plantārĭa -ĭum, n. pl. *young trees, slips.*

¹**plānus** -a -um, *even, flat;* n. as subst. *a plain, level ground;* de plano, *off-hand, easily.* Transf., *plain, clear, intelligible.* Adv. **plānē,** *distinctly, intelligibly; wholly, quite, thoroughly;* in answers, *certainly.*

²**plānus** -i, m. *a vagabond, a charlatan.*

plătălĕa -ae, f. *a water-bird, the spoonbill.*

plătănus -i, f. *the plane-tree.*

plătĕa -ae, f. *a street.*

Plătō (-ōn) -ōnis, m. *the Greek philosopher, disciple of Socrates.*

plaudo (plōdo) plaudĕre plausi plausum, *to strike, beat, clap together; to make a clapping noise, clap, applaud.*

plausĭbĭlis -e, *worthy of applause.*

plausor -ōris, m. *an applauder at the theatre.*

plaustrum (plostrum) -i, n. *a waggon, cart; Charles's Wain.*

plausus -ūs, m. *a noise of clapping; approbation, applause.*

Plautus -i, m., T. Maccius, *the Roman comic poet, born about* 254 B.C. Adj. **Plautīnus** -a -um.

plēbēcŭla -ae, f. *the common people, mob, rabble.*

plēbēĭus -a -um, *of the plebs or people, plebeian; common, low, mean.*

plēbēs -ēi and -i, f. = plebs; q.v.

plēbĭcŏla -ae, m. *a friend of the common people.*

plēbiscītum -i, n. *a decree of the people.*

plebs plēbis, f. *the plebeians, the common people, lower orders.*

¹**plecto;** see plexus.

²**plecto** -ĕre, *to punish;* usually pass., **plector** -i, *to be punished* (with blows).

plectrum -i, n. *a stick with which the strings of a stringed instrument were struck; a quill.* Transf., *the lyre; lyric poetry.*

Plēĭās -ădis, f. *a Pleiad;* usually plur. **Plēĭădes** -ădum, f. *the Pleiads, the Seven Stars.*

plēnus -a -um, *full, full of* (with genit. or abl.); *complete; plump; thick; pregnant; filled, satisfied; well-stocked, rich;* of age, *mature:* of the voice, *strong, loud;* of style, *full, copious.* Adv. **plēnē,** *fully, completely.*

plērusquĕ -raque -rumque and plur. **plērīquĕ** -raeque -raque, *very many, a large part, the most part;* n. sing. as subst., *the greater part;* acc. as adv. *for the most part, mostly, commonly.*

plexus -a -um, partic. as from plecto, *braided, plaited.*

Plīas = Pleias; q.v.

plīco -āre, -ŭi and -āvi, -ātum and ītum, *to fold.*

Plīnius -a -um, *name of a Roman gens;* esp. of C. Plinius Secundus (Maior, *the Elder*), *author of a Natural History,* and C. Plinius Caecilius Secundus (Iunior, *the Younger*), *author of letters,* etc.

plōdo = plaudo; q.v.

plōrābĭlis -e, *deplorable.*

plōrātor -ōris, m. *a lamenter.*

plōrātus -ūs, m. *weeping, lamenting.*

plōro -āre, *to lament, wail;* transit., *to weep over, deplore.*

plostellum -i, n. *a little waggon.*

plostrum = plaustrum; q.v.

plŭit plŭĕre, plŭit or plŭvit, *it rains, a shower falls.*

plūma -ae, f. *a small, soft feather; down* (esp. in pl.); meton. *bolster, featherbed; the first down on the chin.*

plūmātus -a -um, *covered with feathers.*

plumbĕus -a -um, *leaden, of lead.* Transf., *dull, stupid; heavy, oppressive; bad.*

plumbum -i, n. *lead; a bullet; a leaden pipe;* plumbum album, *tin.*

plūmĕus -a -um, *downy, of fine feathers.*

plūmōsus -a -um, *feathered, downy.*

plŭo; see pluit.

plūrĭmus and **plūs;** see multus.

pluscŭlus -a -um, *somewhat more, rather more.*

plŭtĕus -i, m. and **plŭtĕum** -i, n. *a shelter;* milit., *penthouse, shed, mantlet; breastwork, battlement.* Transf., *a board, couch, bookshelf.*

Plūtō (-ōn) -ōnis, m. *the king of the lower world;* adj. **Plūtōnĭus** -a -um.

plŭvĭālis -e, *of* or *from rain; bringing rain.*

plŭvĭus -a -um, *of* or *from rain, bringing rain;* as subst. **plŭvĭa** -ae, *rain.*

pōcillum -i, n. *a little cup.*

pōcŭlum -i, n. *a drinking-cup, goblet; a drink, draught.*

pŏdagra -ae, f. *gout in the feet.*

pōdex -icis, m. *fundament, anus.*

pŏdĭum -i, n. *a balcony, esp. in the amphitheatre.*

pŏēma -ătis, n. *a poem.*

poena -ae, f. *money paid as atonement, a fine;* in gen., *punishment, penalty; loss, hardship;* poenas dare, *to be punished.*

Poeni -orum, m. pl. *the Carthaginians;* sing. **Poenus** -i, m. adj. **Poenus, Pūnĭcus, Poenĭcĕus** -a -um, *Punic, Carthaginian.*

poenĭo = punio; q.v.

poenĭtet; see paenitet.

pŏēsis -is, acc. -in, f. *poetry.*

pŏēta -ae, m. *a maker;* esp. *a poet.*

pŏētĭcus -a -um, *poetical;* f. as subst. **pŏētĭca** -ae and **pŏētĭcē** -ēs, *the art of poetry;* adv. **pŏētĭcē.**

pŏētrĭa -ae, f. *a poetess.*

pŏl! interj. *by Pollux! truly! really!*

pŏlenta -ae, f. *pearl-barley, barley-groats.*

pŏlĭo -ire, *to polish, file, make smooth;* esp. *to cover with white, whiten; to adorn, to finish off.* Hence partic. **pŏlītus** -a -um, *polished, refined, accomplished;* adv. **pŏlītē.**

pŏlītĭa -ae, acc. -an. f. *the Republic* (Plato's work).

pŏlītĭcus -a -um *of the state, political.*

pŏlītus -a -um, partic. from polio; q.v.

pollen -inis, n. and **pollis** -inis, c. *fine flour, meal.*

pollentĭa -ae, f. *power, might.*

pollĕo -ēre, *to be strong, powerful, able;* partic. **pollens** -entis, *powerful, mighty.*

pollex -ĭcis, m. *the thumb;* also *the big toe.*

pollĭcĕor -cēri -cĭtus, dep. *to offer, promise;* perf. partic. in pass. sense, **pollĭcĭtus** -a -um, *promised.* N. as subst. *a promise.*

pollĭcĭtātĭo -ōnis, f. *an offer, promise.*

pollĭcĭtor -ari, dep. *to keep promising.*

pollinctor -ōris, m. *an undertaker.*

pollŭcĕo -lūcēre -luxi -luctum, *to offer, serve up.*

pollŭo -ŭĕre -ŭi -ūtum, *to defile, pollute, dishonour;* partic. **pollūtus** -a -um, *defiled, polluted; unchaste.*

Pollux -ŭcis, m. *the twin-brother of Castor.*

pŏlus -i, m. *the end of an axis, a pole; the sky, heaven.*

Pŏlýhymnĭa -ae, f. *one of the Muses.*

pŏlýpus -i, m. *polypus.*

pōmārĭus -a -um, *of fruit*; m. as subst., *a fruiterer*; n. as subst., *a fruit-garden, orchard.*

pōmērĭdĭānus = postmeridianus; q.v.

pōmērĭum or pōmoerĭum -i, n. *a clear space beside the walls of a town.*

pōmĭfer -fĕra -fĕrum, *fruit-bearing.*

pōmōsus -a -um, *abounding in fruit.*

pompa -ae, f. *a solemn procession; a suite, retinue; display, parade, ostentation.*

Pompēii -orum, m. pl. *a town in Campania, destroyed by an eruption of Vesuvius*; adj. Pompēiānus -a -um.

Pompēius (trisyl.) or Pompēius -a -um, *name of a Roman gens*; esp. of Cn. Pompeius, *Pompey the Great* (106-48 B.C.); adj. Pompēiānus -a -um, *belonging to Pompey.*

Pompilĭus -a -um, *name of a Roman gens*; esp. of Numa Pompilius, *second king of Rome.*

pompĭlus -i, m. *the pilot-fish.*

Pomptīnus -a -um, *Pomptine* or *Pontine*: palus or paludes, *a marshy district in Latium.*

pōmum -i, n. *any kind of fruit; a fruit-tree.*

pōmus -i, f. *a fruit-tree.*

pondĕro -are, *to weigh, consider, ponder.*

pondĕrōsus -a -um, *heavy, weighty; significant.*

pondo (abl.) *in weight*; as indecl. subst. *a pound, pounds.*

pondus -ĕris, n. *weight; a weight, burden, mass; balance; authority, influence.*

pōnĕ: adv. *behind, at the back*; prep. with acc., *behind.*

pōno pōnĕre pŏsŭi (pŏsīvi) pŏsĭtum (postum), *to lay, put, place, set; to put in place, settle; to put aside, lay down, discard; to lay to rest, lay out for burial*; milit., *to post, station; of money, etc., to store, deposit, invest; to stake, wager; of food, to put on table, to serve; of buildings, to found, set up; of laws, etc. to establish, ordain; of persons, to appoint; of an artist, to represent, picture; to reckon, count, regard; to lay down, assert, cite.*
Hence partic. pŏsĭtus -a -um, *in place; nix, fallen snow; of places, situated.*

pons pontis, m. *a bridge, gangway; the deck of a ship.*

pontĭcŭlus -i, m. *a little bridge.*

pontĭfex -fĭcis, m. *a pontiff, member of a Roman guild of priests.*

pontĭfĭcālis -e, *pontifical.*

pontĭfĭcātus -ūs, m. *the office of pontiff.*

pontĭfĭcus -a -um, *pontifical.*

Pontĭus -a -um, *name of a Roman* (originally Samnite) *gens.*

ponto -ōnis, m. *a flat-bottomed boat, punt.*

¹pontus -i, n. *the sea.*

²Pontus -i, m. *the Black Sea*; also *the country on the shores of the Black Sea*; adj. Pontĭcus -a -um.

pōpa -ae, m. *a junior priest or temple-servant.*

pŏpănum -i, n. *a sacrificial cake.*

pōpellus -i, m. *common people, rabble.*

pōpīna -ae, f. *a cook-shop, eating-house; the food sold there.*

pōpīno -ōnis, m. *a glutton.*

poplēs -ĭtis, m. *the ham, hough; the knee.*

pŏpŭlābĭlis -e, *that can be laid waste, destructible.*

pŏpŭlābundus -a -um, *laying waste, devastating.*

pŏpŭlāris -e. (1) *belonging to the same people or country, native*; as subst. *fellow-countryman, adherent, partner.* (2) *of the people or state; popular; democratic*; m. pl. as subst. *the popular party, the democrats.* Adv. pŏpŭlārĭtĕr, *after the manner of the people, vulgarly; in a popular manner, like a demagogue.*

pŏpŭlārĭtās -ātis, f. *fellow-citizenship; an attempt to please the people.*

pŏpŭlātĭo -ōnis, f. *laying waste, devastating, plundering.*

pŏpŭlātor -ōris, m. *a devastator, plunderer.*

pŏpŭlĕus -a -um, *of the poplar.*

pŏpŭlĭfer -fĕra -fĕrum, *producing poplars.*

pŏpŭlo -are and pŏpŭlor -ari, dep. *to lay waste, devastate, plunder; to ruin, spoil, rob.*

¹pŏpŭlus -i, m. *a people, political community, nation; as a section of the community, the people; in gen., the people, the public; hence any crowd, host, multitude.*

²pōpŭlus -i, f. *a poplar-tree.*

porca -ae, f. *a sow.*

porcīnus -a -um, *of a swine or hog.*

Porcĭus -a -um, *name of a Roman gens.*

porcus -i, m. *a pig, hog.*

porgo = porrigo; q.v.

porrectĭo -ōnis, f. *stretching out, extension.*

porrĭcĭo -rĭcĕre -rectum, *to offer as a sacrifice.*

¹porrĭgo -rĭgĕre -rexi -rectum, *to stretch out, extend; to offer, grant*; pass., porrigi, *to lie stretched out*; partic. porrectus -a -um, *stretched out, extended, long.*

²porrĭgo -gĭnis, f. *scurf, dandruff.*

porro, *forward, further; next, again, in turn*; in time, *far back, long ago, or in future.*

porrus -i, m. and porrum -i, n. *a leek.*

porta -ae, f. *a gate.*

portātĭo -ōnis, f. *carrying, conveying.*

portendo -tendĕre -tendi -tentum, *to indicate, predict, presage.*

portentĭfĭcus -a -um, *marvellous, miraculous.*

portentōsus -a -um, *extraordinary, monstrous, unnatural.*

portentum -i, n. subst. from portendo; q.v.

porthmĕus, acc. -ĕă, m. *ferryman.*

portĭcŭla -ae, f. *a little gallery or portico.*

portĭcus -ūs, f. *a portico, colonnade, arcade, gallery.* Transf., *the Stoic school* of philosophers.

portĭo -ōnis, f. *a part, section;* pro portione, *in proportion.*

¹**portītor** -ōris, m. *a customs-officer.*

²**portĭtor** -ōris, m. *a carrier;* usually *a boatman, ferryman.*

porto -are, *to bear, carry, convey, bring.*

portōrĭum i, n. *customs, harbour-dues; any toll, tax.*

portŭla -ae, f. *a little gate, postern.*

portŭōsus -a -um, *having many harbours.*

portus -ūs, m. *harbour, port; haven, refuge.*

posco poscĕre pŏposci, *to ask earnestly, request, call upon;* poscimur, *we are asked to sing;* esp. *to demand for punishment,* or *challenge to fight;* of things, *to demand, require.*

pŏsĭtĭo -ōnis, f. *placing, putting, posture;* caeli, *situation, climate.*

pŏsĭtor -ōris, m. *founder, builder.*

pŏsĭtūra -ae, f. *placing; situation, posture; ordering, formation.*

pŏsĭtus -ūs, m. *position, place, arrangement.*

possessĭo -ōnis, f. *a getting possession* or *possessing; occupation, enjoyment.* Transf., *a thing possessed, possession, property.*

possessĭuncŭla -ae, f. *a small property.*

possessor -ōris, m. *a possessor, occupier.*

possĭdĕo -sīdēre -sēdi -sessum, *to possess, have, hold.*

possīdo -sīdĕre -sēdi sessum, *to take possession of, occupy.*

possum posse pŏtŭi, *to be able; one may, one can; to avail, have influence.*
Hence partic. **pŏtens** -entis, *able, powerful, capable; influential, efficacious;* with genit., *master of.* Adv. **pŏtentĕr**, *strongly, efficaciously; according to one's power.*

post (older **postĕ**). Adv. *behind, in the rear;* of time, *afterwards;* multo post, *much later.* Prep., with acc., *behind;* of time, *after;* in rank, etc., *next after.*

postĕā, *thereafter, afterwards, next.*

postĕāquam, conj. *after.*

postĕrĭtas -ātis, f. *future generations, posterity.*

postĕrus (**postĕr**) -a -um, *subsequent, following, next, future;* in posterum, *for the next day* or *for the future;* m. pl. as subst. *posterity.* Compar. **postĕrĭor** -us, *next, later; inferior, worse;* n. acc. as adv., posterius, *later.* Superl. **postrēmus** -a -um, *hindmost, last; lowest, worst.* N. abl. as adv., postremo, *at last;* n. acc. postremum, *for the last time;* ad postremum, *at last.* Superl. **postŭmus** -a -um, *the last, last-born* (esp. of children born after the father's will or death).

postfĕro -ferre, *to consider of less account.*

postgĕnĭti -ōrum, m. pl. *posterity, descendants.*

posthăbĕo -ēre -ŭi -ĭtum, *to consider of less account, put after.*

posthāc, *hereafter, in future, afterwards.*

posthinc, *next.*

posthŏc, *afterwards.*

postīcus -a -um, *hinder, back;* n. as subst. **postīcum** -i, *a back-door.*

postilēna -ae, f. *a crupper.*

postillā, *afterwards.*

postis -is, m. *a door-post;* plur., *a door, doorway.*

postlīmĭnĭum -i, n. *the right to return home.*

postmĕrīdĭānus -a -um, *of the afternoon.*

postmŏdŏ and **postmŏdum**, *presently, soon.*

postpartor -ōris, m. *heir.*

postpōno -pōnĕre -pŏsŭi -pŏsĭtum, *to consider of less account, put after.*

postquam (or **post quam**), conj. *after, when.*

postrēmo, etc.; see posterus.

postrīdĭē, *the day after, on the next day.*

postscaenĭum -i, n. *the theatre behind the scenes.*

postscrībo -scrībĕre -scripsi -scriptum, *to write after.*

postŭlātĭo -ōnis, f. *a claim, demand, application; a complaint.*

postŭlātum -i, n. subst. from postulo; q.v.

postŭlātus -ūs, m. *a legal complaint, accusation, suit.*

postŭlo -are, *to claim, demand, request;* legal, *to demand a writ,* or *to impeach, accuse* a person; of things, *to demand, require.* N. of partic. as subst. **postŭlātum** -i, *a demand.*

postŭmus -a -um, superl. of posterus; q.v.

pōtātĭo -ōnis, f. *a drinking-bout.*

pŏtĕ; see potis.

pŏtens -entis, partic. from possum; q.v.

pŏtentātus -ūs, m. *political power, supremacy.*

pŏtentĭa -ae, f. *power, might, ability; efficacy, potency;* esp. *(unofficial) political power.*

pŏtestās -ātis, f. *power, ability, control.* Esp. *political supremacy, dominion; the authority of a magistrate, office command;* concr., *an officer, magistrate.* Transf., *opportunity, possibility, occasion;* facere potestatem, *to give opportunity* or *permission;* potestas est, *it is possible.*

¹**pōtĭo** -ōnis, f. *drinking; a drink, a draught;* esp. *a love-draught, philtre.*

²**pōtĭo** -ire, *to put in the power of.*

¹**pŏtĭor** -iri, dep., *to get possession of, to obtain; to possess, be master of.*

²**pŏtĭor;** see potis.

pŏtis, pŏtĕ; *able, capable;* potis (or pote) est, *can, is able* (or *possible*). Compar. **pŏtĭor** -us, *preferable, better;* n. acc. as adv. **pŏtĭus, rather, preferably.* Superl. **pŏtissĭmus** -a -um, *best of all, chief, principal;* n. as adv. **pŏtissĭmum**, *chiefly, above all.*

pōto pōtare pōtāvi pōtātum and pōtum, *to drink;* esp. *to drink heavily;* of things, *to absorb.*
Hence partic. **pōtus** -a -um: pass., *drunk, drained;* act., *having drunk, drunken.*

pōtor -ōris, m. *a drinker*; esp. *a tippler, drunkard*.

pōtŭlentus (**pōcŭlentus**) -a -um, *drinkable*; *drunk, intoxicated*.

¹**pōtŭs**, partic. from poto; q.v.

²**pōtus** -ūs, m. *a drinking, draught*.

prae. Adv. *before, in front*; prae quam, *in comparison with*. Prep. with abl., *before*; prae se ferre, *to show, exhibit*; *in comparison with*; *on account of, because of*.

praeăcūtus -a -um, *sharpened to a point, pointed*.

praealtus -a -um, *very high or deep*.

praebĕo -bēre -bŭi -bĭtum, *to offer, hold out*; *to provide, supply, allow*; with reflex., *to present or show oneself in a certain character, behave as*.

praebĭbo -bĭbĕre -bĭbi, *to drink before, drink to*.

praebĭtor -ōris, m. *a furnisher, supplier*.

praecălĭdus -a -um, *very hot*.

praecantrix -īcis, f. *a witch*.

praecānus -a -um, *prematurely grey*.

praecăvĕo -cāvēre -cāvi -cautum: intransit., *to take precautions, be on one's guard*; transit., *to beware of, guard against beforehand*.

praecēdo -cēdĕre -cessi -cessum, *to go before, precede*, in space or time; in rank, etc., *to surpass, excel*.

praecello -ĕre, *to surpass, extel*; genti, *to rule over*; partic. **praecellens** -entis, *excellent, distinguished, surpassing*.

praecelsus -a -um, *very high*.

praecentio -ōnis, f. *a musical prelude*.

praeceps -cĭpĭtis; *of motion, headlong, fast-falling, quick*; *of character, hasty, rash, blind*; *of places, steep, precipitous*; hence *dangerous*. N. as subst., *a steep place, precipice*; *danger*; as adv., *headlong*.

praeceptĭo -ōnis, f. *a pre-conception*; *a precept*; *the right to receive in advance*.

praeceptor -ōris, m. and **praeceptrix** -trīcis, f. *a teacher, instructor*.

praeceptum -i, n. subst. from praecipio; q.v.

praecerpo -cerpĕre -cerpsi -cerptum, *to pluck prematurely*; *to intercept*.

praecīdo -cīdĕre -cīdi -cīsum, *to cut short, lop, mutilate*; ancoras, *to cut the cables*; of speech, brevi praecidam, *I will put it briefly*. Hence partic. **praecīsus** -a -um, *broken off*; of places, *steep, precipitous*; of speech, *brief*. Adv. **praecīsē**, *briefly, in few words; absolutely, decidedly*.

praecingo -cingĕre -cinxi -cinctum, *to gird in front, surround with a girdle*.

praecĭno -cīnĕre -cīnŭi -centum: intransit. *to sing or play before*; *to sing an incantation*; transit. *to prophesy, predict*.

praecipes -is = praeceps; q.v.

praecĭpĭo -cĭpĕre -cēpi -ceptum, *to take before, receive in advance*; iter, *to get the start*; mentally, *to anticipate*; *to instruct, advise, warn*. N. of partic. as subst. **praeceptum** -i, *a command, rule, injunction*.

praecĭpĭto -are: transit., *to cast headlong down*; *to hurry along*; intransit., *to fall headlong, rush down*. Adv. from pres. partic., **praecĭpĭtantĕr**, *headlong*.

praecĭpŭus -a -um, *peculiar, special*; *excellent, distinguished, extraordinary*, as legal term *received beforehand*. N. as subst. **praecĭpŭum** -i, *pre-eminence, superiority*. Adv. **praecĭpŭē**, *especially, chiefly, particularly*.

praecīsus -a -um, partic. from praecido; q.v.

praeclārus -a -um, *very bright, very clear*; *striking, beautiful*; *remarkable, excellent, famous*; in bad sense, *notorious*. Adv. **praeclārē**, *very clearly*; *admirably, excellently*.

praeclūdo -clūdĕre -clūsi -clūsum, *to close in front, shut up, make inaccessible*.

praeco -ōnis, m. *a public crier, herald*.

praecōgĭto -are, *to consider carefully beforehand*.

praecognosco -cognoscĕre -cognĭtum, *to learn beforehand*.

praecŏlo -cŏlĕre -cultum, *to cultivate before*; partic. **praecultus** -a -um, *cultivated, adorned*.

praecompŏsĭtus -a -um, *composed beforehand, studied*.

praecōnĭus -a -um, *belonging to a* praeco *or crier*. N. as subst. **praecōnĭum** -i, *the office of a crier*; hence, *publishing, making known*; *a public commendation*.

praeconsūmo -sūmĕre -sumptum, *to use up beforehand*.

praecontrecto -are, *to handle beforehand*.

praecordĭa -ōrum, n. pl. *the midriff, diaphragm*; *the stomach*; *the breast, heart* (as seat of passions).

praecorrumpo -rumpĕre -ruptum, *to bribe beforehand*.

praecox -cōcis and **praecŏquis** -e, *ripe before the time, premature*.

praecultus -a -um, partic. from praecolo; q.v.

praecurro -currĕre -cŭcurri and -curri -cursum, *to run before, go on ahead*; in time, *to precede*; in quality, *to surpass*. N. pl. of partic. as subst. **praecurrentia** -ĭum, *antecedents*.

praecursĭo -ōnis, f. *going before, running ahead*; rhet., *preparation of the hearer*.

praecursor -ōris, m. *a forerunner*; milit., *vanguard, advance-guard*; *spy, scout*.

praecursōrĭus -a -um, *sent in advance*.

praecŭtĭo -cŭtĕre -cussi -cussum, *to shake before, brandish before*.

praeda -ae, f. *spoils of war, plunder, booty*; of animals, *prey*; in gen., *plunder, gain*.

praedābundus -a -um, *plundering*.

praedamno -are, *to condemn before*; spem, *to give up hope*.

praedātĭo -ōnis, f. *plundering, pillaging*.

praedātor -ōris, m. *plunderer, robber*; *poet, hunter*.

praedātōrĭus -a -um, *plundering, predatory.*

praedēlasso -are, *to weary beforehand.*

praedestĭno -are, *to appoint beforehand.*

praedĭātor -ōris, m. *a buyer of landed estates.*

praedĭātōrĭus -a -um, *relating to the sale of land.*

praedĭcābĭlis -e, *praiseworthy.*

praedĭcātĭo -ōnis, f. *making publicly known, proclamation; praising, commending.*

praedĭcātor -ōris, m. *a praiser, commender, public eulogist.*

¹praedĭco -are, *to make publicly known, publish, proclaim, declare; to praise, commend; to boast.*

²praedīco -dīcĕre -dixi -dictum, *to say or name beforehand; to predict, foretell, prophesy; to warn, admonish, instruct.* Hence n. of partic. as subst. **praedictum** -i, *a prophecy, prediction; an order, command; a previous agreement.*

praedictĭo -ōnis, f. *prophesying, predicting; rhet. premising.*

praedictum -i, n. subst. from praedico; q.v.

praedĭŏlum -i, n. *a small estate, little farm.*

praedisco -ĕre, *to learn before.*

praedispōsĭtus -a -um, *arranged at intervals beforehand.*

praedĭtus -a -um, *endowed, furnished, provided.*

praedĭum -i, n. *a farm, landed estate.*

praedīvĕs -ĭtis, *very rich.*

praedo -ōnis, m. *robber, plunderer.*

praedŏcĕo -dŏcēre -doctum *to teach before.*

praedor -ari, dep. *to plunder, rob; to carry off.*

praedūco -dūcĕre -duxi -ductum *to lead forward, bring in front.*

praedulcis -e, *very sweet.*

praedūrus -a -um, *very hard, very strong.*

praeēmĭnĕo -ēre, *to project; to excel.*

praeĕo -īre -ivi and -ĭi -ĭtum, *to go before, precede; hence to go over beforehand verbally, say in advance, dictate; to order, command.*

praefātĭo -ōnis, f. *saying beforehand; a religious or legal form of words, formula; a preface, introduction.*

praefectūra -ae, f. *the office of superintendent; esp. a subordinate provincial command.* Transf., *a town or district governed by a praefectus.*

praefectus -a -um, partic. from praeficio; q.v.

praefĕro -ferre -tŭli -lātum. (1) *carry in front; to show, display; to prefer; to anticipate.* (2) *to carry by; praeferri, to ride by.*

praefĕrox -ōcis, *very bold, impetuous.*

praeferrātus -a -um, *tipped with iron.*

praefervĭdus -a -um, *burning hot, very hot.*

praefestīno -are, *to hasten prematurely; to hasten by.*

praefĭcĭo -fĭcĕre -fēci -fectum, *to set over, appoint as superintendent.* M. of partic. as subst. **praefectus** -i, *an overseer, superintendent, civil or military officer;* praefectus urbis, *governor of the city (Rome).*

praefīdens -entis, *over-confident.*

praefīgo -fīgĕre -fixi -fixum, *to fix in front, fasten before; to tip, point with; to pierce through, transfix.*

praefīnĭo -ire, *to fix, prescribe, appoint beforehand.*

praeflōro -are, *to deprive of blossom;* fig., *to diminish, lessen.*

praeflŭo -flŭĕre, *to flow past.*

praefōco -are, *to choke, suffocate.*

praefŏdĭo -fŏdĕre -fōdi -fossum, *to dig in front of; to bury previously.*

praefor -fāri -fātus, dep. *to speak before, to say beforehand, esp. of prayers; divos, to invoke.*

praefrīgĭdus -a -um, *very cold.*

praefringo -fringĕre -frēgi -fractum, *to break off in front;* partic. **praefractus** -a -um, *of style, abrupt, disconnected; of character, stern, harsh;* adv. **praefractē**.

praefulcĭo -fulcire -fulsi -fultum, *to support, prop up; to use as a prop.*

praefulgĕo -fulgēre -fulsi, *to gleam, shine forth;* with dat., *to outshine.*

praegĕlĭdus -a -um, *very cold.*

praegestĭo -ire, *to desire exceedingly.*

praegnans -antis, *pregnant; full.*

praegrācĭlis -e, *very slim, lank.*

praegrăvis -e, *very heavy; unwieldy, wearisome; stupefied.*

praegrăvo -are, *to press heavily upon, to weigh down, oppress; to outweigh.*

praegrĕdĭor -grĕdi -gressus, dep. *to go before, precede; to outstrip; to pass by, march by.*

praegressĭo -ōnis, f. *going before, precedence.*

praegustātor -ōris, m. *one who tastes before, a taster.*

praegusto -are, *to taste before.*

praeĭăcĕo -ēre, *to lie before.*

praeiŭdĭcĭum -i, n. *a previous judgment, preliminary decision or examination; a premature decision; an example, precedent.*

praeiŭdĭco -are, *to decide beforehand, give a preliminary judgment.* Hence partic. **praeiŭdĭcātus** -a -um, *previously decided;* opinio praeiudicata, *a prejudice.*

praeiŭvo -iŭvare -iŭvi, *to assist before.*

praelābor -lābi -lapsus, dep. *to glide past, before or along.*

praelambo -ĕre, *to lick before, taste before.*

praelĕgo -lĕgĕre -lēgi -lectum. (1) *to read out as a teacher, to lecture upon.* (2) *to sail past, coast along.*

praelīgo -are, *to bind in front; to bind up.*

praelongus -a -um, *very long.*

praelŏquor -lŏqui -lōcūtus, dep. *to speak beforehand or first.*

praelūcĕo -lūcēre -luxi, *to shine or carry a light before;* with dat., *to outshine, surpass.*

praelūsĭo -ōnis, f. *prelude.*

praelustris -e, *very fine.*

praemando -are, *to order beforehand;* n. pl. of partic. as subst. **praemandāta** -orum, *a warrant of arrest.*

praemātūrus -a -um, *too early, premature.*

praemĕdĭcātus -a -um, *protected by medicine or charms.*

praemĕdĭtātĭo -ōnis, f. *considering beforehand.*

praemĕdĭtor -ari, dep. *to practise or consider beforehand;* perf. partic., in pass. sense, **praemĕdĭtātus** -a -um, *considered beforehand.*

praemĕtŭo -ĕre, *to fear beforehand, be apprehensive;* adv. from partic. **praemĕtŭentĕr**, *apprehensively, anxiously.*

praemitto -mittĕre -mīsi -missum, *to send before, send on ahead.*

praemĭum -i, n. *that which is taken first, the pick; a gift, award, reward, recompense;* poet., *notable exploit.*

praemŏlestia -ae, f. *trouble beforehand.*

praemōlior -iri, dep. *to prepare beforehand.*

praemŏnĕo -ēre, *to warn, advise beforehand; to foretell, presage.*

praemŏnĭtus -ūs, m. *prediction, warning.*

praemonstro -are, *to point out the way; to prophesy, predict.*

praemordĕo -mordēre -mordi -morsum, *to bite off; to pilfer.*

praemŏrior -mŏri -mortŭus, dep. *to die prematurely.*

praemūnĭo -ire, *to fortify in front; to secure, make safe.*

praemūnītĭo -ōnis, f. *fortifying beforehand;* rhet., *preparation of one's hearers.*

praenăto -are, *to swim before or past.*

praenĭtĕo -ēre, *to outshine.*

praenōmen -ĭnis, n. *the first name, usually standing before the gentile name* (e.g., Marcus, in M. T. Cicero).

praenosco -ĕre, *to get to know beforehand.*

praenōtĭo -ōnis, f. *a preconception, innate idea.*

praenūbĭlus -a -um, *very cloudy or dark.*

praenuntĭo -are, *to announce beforehand, foretell.*

praenuntĭus -a -um, *foretelling;* as subst. *a harbinger, token, omen.*

praeoccŭpo -are, *to seize beforehand, to preoccupy; to anticipate, prevent.*

praeopto -are, *to choose before, to prefer.*

praepando -ĕre, *to open wide in front, extend before.*

praepărātĭo -ōnis, f. *preparation.*

praepăro -are, *to make ready, prepare;* ex praeparato, *by arrangement.*

praepĕdĭo -ire, *to entangle, shackle, fetter; to hinder, impede, obstruct.*

praependĕo -ēre, intransit., *to hang before, hang in front.*

praepĕs -pĕtis, *rapidly flying, swift;* m. and f. as subst., *a bird, esp. a bird of good omen.*

praepĭlātus -a -um, *having a button in front* (of foils, etc.).

praepinguis -e, *very fat or rich.*

praepollĕo -ēre, *to be very or more powerful.*

praepondĕro -are, *to outweigh, to turn the scale.*

praepōno -pōnĕre -pŏsŭi -pŏsĭtum, *to put before; to put over, set over as commander,* etc.; *to prefer.* Hence m. of partic., as subst. **praepŏsĭtus** -i, *a commander.*

praeporto -are, *to carry before.*

praepŏsĭtĭo -ōnis, f. *placing before; preferring, preference;* gram., *a preposition.*

praepossum -posse -pŏtŭi, *to have the chief power.*

praepostĕrus -a -um, *having the last first, inverted, perverse;* adv. **praepostĕrē.**

praepŏtens -entis, *very powerful.*

praeprŏpĕrantĕr, *very hastily.*

praeprŏpĕrus -a -um, *over-hasty, precipitate;* adv. **praeprŏpĕrē.**

praequam; see prae.

praequĕror -quĕri -questus, dep. *to complain beforehand.*

praerădĭo -are, *to outshine.*

praerăpĭdus -a -um, *very rapid.*

praerĭgesco -rĭgescĕre -rĭgŭi, *to grow very stiff.*

praerĭpĭo -rĭpĕre -rĭpŭi -reptum, *to snatch before somebody else; to carry off before the time; to anticipate, forestall.*

praerōdo -rōdĕre -rōdi -rōsum, *to gnaw off, bite through.*

praerŏgātīvus -a -um, *asked before others* (for vote, opinion, etc.); f. as subst. **praerŏgātĭva** -ae, f. *the tribe or century voting first in the comitia; hence the first century's vote;* in gen., *a previous choice; a sure sign, indication.*

praerumpo -rumpĕre -rūpi -ruptum, *to break off in front.* Hence partic. **praeruptus** -a -um, *broken off; of places, steep, precipitous;* of character, *headstrong, hasty.*

[1]**praes** praedis, m. *a surety, security, one who stands bail.*

[2]**praes,** adv. *at hand.*

praesaepes (**praesaepis**) -is, f. **praesaepe** -is, n. and **praesaepium** -i, n. *an enclosure; a crib, manger, stall; a hive; a haunt, lodging, tavern.*

praesaepĭo, *to block up in front.*

praesāgĭo -ire, *to presage, forebode, have a presentiment of.*

praesāgītĭo -ōnis, f. *foreboding, presentiment.*

praesāgĭum -i, n. *presage, presentiment, foreboding; prediction.*

praesāgus -a -um, *foreboding; predicting.*

praescisco -ĕre, *to find out beforehand.*

praescĭus -a -um, *knowing beforehand, prescient.*

praescrībo -scrībĕre -scripsi -scriptum, *to write before, set out in writing; to put forward or use as a pretext; to outline; dictate; to prescribe, ordain, direct beforehand.* Hence n. partic. as subst. **praescriptum** -i, *a prescribed limit, regulation, rule.*

praescriptĭo -ōnis, f. *a title, inscription, introduction; a precept, rule; a pretext; legal, an objection, demurrer.*

praesēco -sĕcare -sĕcŭi -sectum, *to cut in front, cut short.*

praesens -entis, partic. from praesum; q.v.

praesensĭo -ōnis, f. *a presentiment, foreboding; preconception.*

praesentĭa -ae, f. *presence; animi, presence of mind; in praesentia, for the present; sometimes power, effect.*

praesentĭo -sentire -sensi -sensum, *to feel beforehand, have a presentiment of.*

praesertim, *especially, chiefly.*

praesĕs -sĭdis, *sitting before, protecting. As subst. a protector; also a chief, ruler, president.*

praesĭdĕo -sĭdere -sēdi -sessum, *to sit before; to watch over, protect, guard; to preside over, manage, direct. M. of partic. as subst.* **praesĭdens** -entis, *a president, ruler.*

praesĭdĭārĭus -a -um, *on guard.*

praesĭdĭum -i, n. *sitting before; protection, help, support.* Milit., *guard, escort; a garrison; a post.*

praesignĭfĭco -are, *to indicate beforehand.*

praesignis -e, *distinguished, remarkable.*

praesŏno -sōnare -sŏnŭi, *to sound forth.*

praespargo -ĕre, *to scatter in front.*

praestābĭlis -e, *distinguished, pre-eminent; in compar., preferable.*

praestans -antis, partic. from praesto; q.v.

praestantĭa -ae, f. *superiority, excellence.*

praestĕs -stĭtis, *protecting.*

praestīgĭae -ārum, f. pl. *deception, illusion, juggling.*

praestĭtŭo -stĭtŭĕre -stĭtŭi -stĭtūtum, *to prescribe, appoint beforehand.*

¹**praesto**, adv. *present, at hand ready; with esse, to be at hand, be ready to help.*

²**praesto** -stare -stĭti -stĭtum. (1) *to stand before; to be outstanding, surpass, excel;* impers., praestat, *it is better, preferable.* (2) transit., *to become surety for, answer for, be responsible for.* Transf., *to perform, execute, fulfil; to show, manifest, exhibit; to offer, present;* with se and acc. *to show oneself, behave as.*
    Hence partic. **praestans** -antis, *excellent, distinguished, eminent.*

praestōlor -ari, dep., *to wait for, expect.*

praestringo -stringĕre -strinxi -strictum, *to bind up, in front.* Transf., *to make blunt or dull.*

praestrŭo -strŭĕre -struxi -structum. (1) *to build in front; to block up, make impassable.* (2) *to build beforehand, to prepare.*

praesŭl -sŭlis, c. and **praesultātor** -ōris, m. *a dancer.*

praesulto -are, *to leap or dance before.*

praesum -esse -fŭi, *to be before; to be over, preside over; to take the lead.*
    Hence partic. (with compar.) **praesens** -entis, *present, at hand, in*

space or time; in praesens (tempus), *for the present time;* esp. *immediate, ready; effective, powerful, helpful, resolute, determined.*

praesūmo -sūmĕre -sumpsi -sumptum, *to take beforehand; to anticipate; to take for granted.*
    Hence partic. **praesumptus** -a -um, *taken for granted, presumed.*

praesūtus -a -um, *sewn over in front.*

praetempto -are, *to try, test beforehand.*

praetendo -tendĕre -tendi -tentum, *to stretch or hold out;* pass., praetendi, of places, *to lie before or in front.* Transf., *to hold out as a pretext, allege in excuse.*

praetento = praetempto; q.v.

praetĕpesco -tĕpescĕre -tĕpŭi, *to glow beforehand.*

praeter. Adv., *except.* Prep. with acc., *beyond, past; beside, contrary to, beside; more than; except; in addition to.*

praetĕrăgo -ĕre, *to drive past, drive by.*

praetĕrĕā, *besides, further; after this, hereafter.*

praetĕrĕo -ire -ivi and oftener -ĭi -ĭtum, *to go by, pass by.* Transf., *to escape the notice of a person; to pass by, pass over, omit; to surpass, outstrip; to transgress.*
    Hence partic. **praetĕrĭtus** -a -um, *past, gone by.*

praetĕrĕquĭto -are, *to ride past, ride by.*

praeterfĕro -ferre -tŭli -lātum, *to carry past.*

praeterflŭo -flŭĕre, *to flow past, flow by.*

praetergrĕdĭor -grĕdi -gressus, dep. *to pass by, go beyond.*

praetĕrĭtus -a -um, partic. from praetereo; q.v.

praeterlābor -lābi -lapsus, dep. *to glide by, flow by, slip away.*

praetermĕo -are, *to pass by.*

praetermissĭo -ōnis, f. *leaving out, omission; passing over, neglecting.*

praetermitto -mittĕre -misi -missum, *to let pass, let go by; to neglect, omit; to pass over, overlook.*

praeterquam or **praeter quam**, *more than, beyond;* after neg., *except;* with quod, *apart from the fact that.*

praetervectĭo -ōnis, f. *a passing place.*

praetervĕhor -vĕhi -vectus sum, *to ride by, be carried past, march past, pass by.*

praetervŏlo -are, *to fly past; to slip by, escape.*

praetexo -texĕre -texŭi -textum, *to weave in front, form a border; to adorn; to cover, conceal; to put forward as a pretext.*
    Hence partic. **praetextus** -a -um, *bordered,* esp. *of the toga.* F. as subst. **praetexta** -ae, f. *a toga bordered with purple, worn by magistrates and boys;* also praetexta (fabula), *a tragedy with Roman characters.* N. as subst. **praetextum** -i, *a pretence, pretext.*

praetextātus -a -um, *wearing the toga praetexta; veiled; licentious.*

praetextū, abl. sing. m. *in outward appearance; under a pretext.*

praetinctus -a -um, *moistened beforehand.*

praetor -ōris, m. *leader, chief; a magistrate,* esp. one who helped the consuls by administering justice, commanding armies, etc.

praetōriānus -a -um, *belonging to the imperial body-guard, praetorian.*

praetōrius -a -um. (1) *relating to the praetor, praetorian.* (2) *relating to any general* or *commander;* praetoria navis, *flagship;* cohors, *the general's body-guard.* As subst.: m. **praetōrius** -i, *an ex-praetor* or *man of praetorian rank;* n. **praetōrium** -i, *the official residence of the praetor* or propraetor; *a palace;* also *the headquarters in a Roman camp.*

praetrĕpĭdo -are, *to be hasty* or *impatient.*

praetūra -ae, f. *the office of praetor.*

praeumbro -are, *to overshadow;* *to obscure.*

praeustus -a -um, *burnt at the end* or *tip; frost-bitten.*

praevălĕo -vălēre -vălŭi, *to be very strong; to prevail, get the upper hand.*

praevălĭdus -a -um, *very strong;* terra, *too productive.*

praevārĭcātĭo -ōnis, f. *collusion.*

praevārĭcātor -ōris, m. *an advocate guilty of collusion.*

praevārĭcor -ari, dep. of an advocate, *to have a secret understanding with the other side, to be guilty of collusion.*

praevĕhor -vĕhi -vectus sum, *to ride* (or *run) before* or *past.*

praevĕnĭo -vĕnire -vēni -ventum, *to come before, anticipate, get the start of.*

praeverro -ĕre, *to sweep before.*

praeverto (**praevorto**) -vertĕre -verti -versum, and **praevertor** -verti -versus sum; of preference, *to put first, take first, turn first to;* of early action, *to anticipate, outstrip, forestall; to surprise, preoccupy.*

praevĭdĕo -vĭdēre -vĭdi -vīsum, *to see before, foresee.*

praevĭtĭo -are, *to corrupt beforehand.*

praevĭus -a -um, *going before, preceding.*

praevŏlo -are, *to fly before.*

pragmătĭcus -a -um, *skilled in business;* m. as subst. *a person who supplied speakers with material.*

prandĕo prandēre prandi pransum, *to take lunch; to lunch upon;* perf. partic. in act. sense **pransus** -a -um, *having lunched; well-fed.*

prandĭum -i, n. *a late breakfast* or *lunch.*

pransus -a -um, partic. from prandeo; q.v.

prăsĭnus -a -um, *leek-green.*

prātensis -e, *of a meadow.*

prātŭlum -i, n. *a little meadow.*

prātum -i, n. *a meadow; meadow-grass.*

prāvĭtās -ātis, f. *crookedness, deformity; perversity, depravity.*

prāvus -a -um, adj. *crooked, deformed; perverse; depraved.* Adv. **prāvē**.

Praxĭtĕlēs -is and -i, m. *a sculptor of Athens.*

prĕcārĭus -a -um, *begged for,* or *got by entreaty; uncertain, precarious.* N. abl. as adv. **prĕcārĭo**, *by entreaty.*

prĕcātĭo -ōnis, f. *begging, request prayer.*

prĕces; see prex.

prĕcĭae -arum, f. *a kind of vine.*

prĕcor -ari, dep. *to beg, entreat, pray, invoke.*

prĕhendo prĕhendĕre prĕhendi prehensum and prendo prendĕre prendi prensum, *to lay hold of, seize, grasp; to catch, detain, arrest; to take in,* mentally or by the senses.

prĕhenso and **prenso** -are, *to lay hold of, clutch at.* Transf., *to canvass for votes.*

prēlum -i, n. *a wine* or *olive-press.*

prĕmo prĕmĕre pressi pressum, *to press; to step on, lie on; to hug, keep close to; to press hard, squeeze; to pursue closely, press upon; to press down, strike down; to disparage, slander; to press together, close; to check, curb.*
Hence partic. **pressus** -a -um, *subdued, measured;* of style, *compressed, concise.* Adv. **pressē**, *accurately, precisely, distinctly;* of style, *briefly, concisely.*

prendo = prehendo; q.v.

prensātĭo -ōnis, f. *canvassing for office.*

prenso = prehenso; q.v.

pressĭo -ōnis, f. *leverage* or *means of leverage.*

presso -are, *to press.*

¹pressus -a -um, partic. from premo; q.v.

²pressus -ūs, m. *pressing, pressure.*

prestēr -ēris, m. *a fiery whirlwind* or *a waterspout.*

prĕtĭōsus -a -um, *costly, precious, dear;* of persons, *extravagant.* Adv. **prĕtĭōsē**.

prĕtĭum -i, n. *worth, value, price;* esse in pretio, *to be prized;* operae pretium, *worth while.* Transf., *prize, reward; a ransom; a bribe; punishment.*

prex prĕcis (usually plur.) f. *request, entreaty;* esp. *prayer to a god;* sometimes *a curse, execration.*

Prĭāmus -i, m. *the last king of Troy;* adj. **Prĭāmēĭus** -a -um.

Prĭāpus -i, m. *the god of gardens and vineyards.*

prĭdem, *long ago, long since.*

prĭdĭē, *on the day before.*

prīmaevus -a -um, *young, youthful.*

prīmāni -orum, m. pl. *soldiers of the first legion.*

prīmārĭus -a -um, *in the first rank, distinguished.*

prīmĭgĕnus -a -um, *original, primitive.*

prīmĭpīlāris -is, m. *the centurion of the first maniple of the triarii, the chief centurion of a legion.*

prīmĭpīlus; see pilus.

prīmĭtĭae -arum, f. *first-fruits.*

prīmĭtĭus, *first, for the first time.*

prīmordĭum -i, n. *first beginning, origin;* plur. often = atoms.

prīmōris -e, *first, foremost; at the tip;* primoribus labris, *superficially;* of rank, *first, most distinguished.*

prīmus; see prior.

princeps -cĭpis, adj. *first, foremost.* As subst., *leader;* polit., *often as a title of the Roman emperor;* milit., plur., principes, *the second line in a Roman army, between* hastati *and* triarii.

princĭpālis -e. (1) *first, in time or rank.* (2) *of a prince.* (3) *of the principia in a Roman camp.*

princĭpātus -ūs, m. (1) *first place, pre-eminence; rule, dominion.* (2) *beginning, origin.*

principĭālis -e, *original.*

principĭum -i, n. *beginning, origin; groundwork, foundation;* in plur., *elements, first principles;* polit., *the tribe* or *curia which voted first;* milit., in plur., *the front ranks* or *the head-quarters in a camp.*

prĭŏr prĭus, genit. -ōris, compar. adj., *fore, former,* of place or time; *higher in importance;* m. pl. as subst., *ancestors.* N. acc. as adv. **prĭus,** *before, previously; formerly; sooner, rather;* **prĭus quam,** or **prĭusquam,** conj., *before.* Superl. **prīmus** -a -um, *first, foremost,* of place or time; *of rank, etc., first, most distinguished;* (partes) primae, *the leading part;* in primis, *especially.* N. acc. as adv. **prīmum,** *at first* or *for the first time.* N. abl. **prīmō,** *at first.*

priscus -a -um, *ancient, antique; of the old school, venerable; former, previous.* Adv. **priscē,** *in the old-fashioned way.*

pristĭnus -a -um, *former, previous, earlier.*

prĭus; see prior.

prīvātim, *privately, as a private person, in private life; at home.*

prīvātĭo -ōnis, f. *freeing, release.*

prīvigna -ae, f. *stepdaughter.*

prīvignus -i, m. *stepson.*

prīvilēgĭum i, n. *a special law, private law.*

prīvo -are, *to strip, deprive; to free, release.*
Hence partic. **prīvātus** -a -um, as adj., *private, unofficial;* in privato, *in private;* (vir) privatus, *a private person.*

prīvus -a -um, *single, every;* distributively, *one each; particular, special, one's own;* with genit., *deprived of.*

¹prō, prep., with abl., *before, in front of; for, on behalf of, in favour of; in place of; like, as good as;* se pro cive gerere, *to behave as a citizen; as a reward for; in proportion to, according to, by virtue of;* pro virili parte, *to the best of one's abilities;* pro eo quantum, *in proportion as.*

²prō! (proh!), interj. *oh! ah!*

prōăvĭa -ae, f. *a great-grandmother.*

prōăvītus -a -um, *ancestral.*

prōăvus -i, m. *a great-grandfather; an ancestor, forefather.*

prŏbābĭlis -e, (1) *probable, credible.* (2) *acceptable, good.* Adv. **prŏbābĭlĭtĕr,** *probably, credibly.*

prŏbābĭlĭtās -ātis, f. *probability, credibility.*

prŏbātĭo -ōnis, f. *proving, trial, examination; approval, proof, demonstration.*

prŏbātor -ōris, m. *one who approves, an approver.*

prŏbĭtās -ātis, f. *honesty, uprightness.*

prŏbo -are, *to make* or *find good; to approve, pronounce good;* with dat., *to recommend to;* with abl., *to judge by a standard;* in gen., *to show, prove, demonstrate.*
Hence partic. **prŏbātus** -a -um, *found good, approved; acceptable.*

prŏbrōsus -a -um, *shameful, disgraceful, infamous.*

probrum -i, n. *abuse, reproach; ground for reproach, disgrace; infamous conduct,* esp. *unchastity.*

prŏbus -a -um, *good, excellent, fine; morally good, upright, virtuous.* Adv. **prŏbē,** *well, rightly, properly.*

prŏcācĭtās -ātis, f. *shamelessness, impudence.*

prŏcax -cācis, *shameless, bold, impudent;* adv. **prŏcācĭtĕr.**

prōcēdo -cēdĕre -cessi -cessum, *to go ahead, proceed, advance, continue; to come out, go out;* of actions, etc., *to turn out, result;* sometimes *to turn out well, prosper.*

prŏcella -ae, f. *a storm, tempest, gale;* in fighting, *charge, onset, wave.*

prŏcellōsus -a -um, *stormy, tempestuous.*

prŏcer -ēris, m. *a chief noble, prince.*

prōcērĭtās -ātis, f. *height, length.*

prōcērus -a -um, *tall, long;* compar. adv. **prōcērĭus,** *farther forward.*

prōcessĭo -ōnis, f. *a (military) advance.*

prōcessus -ūs, m. *advance, progress.*

prōcĭdo -cīdĕre -cĭdi, *to fall forwards.*

prōcinctū, abl. sing. m. *being girded* or *equipped; readiness for battle.*

proclāmātor -ōris, m. *a bawler.*

proclāmo -are, *to call out, cry out.*

prōclīno -are, *to bend over, incline forwards.*

prōclīvis -e and **prōclīvus** -a -um, *inclined forwards, sloping downwards;* proclive, or per proclive, *downwards.* Transf., *inclined, ready, prone; easy to do.*

prōclīvĭtās -ātis, f. *a slope.* Transf., *inclination, tendency.*

prōclīvus = proclivis; q.v.

Procnē (Prognē) -ēs, f. *wife of Tereus; changed into a swallow.*

prŏco -are and **prŏcor** -ari, dep. *to ask, demand.*

prōconsul -sŭlis, m. (also **prō consŭlĕ**), *a proconsul, one who serves as a consul, in command of any army, or as governor of a province.*

prōconsŭlāris -e, *proconsular.*

prōconsŭlātus -ūs, m. *the office of proconsul.*

prōcrastĭnātĭo -ōnis, f. *procrastination.*

prōcrastĭno -are, *to put off till tomorrow, defer.*

prōcrĕātĭo -ōnis, f. *begetting, procreation.*

prōcrĕātor -ōris, m. *begetter, creator.*

prōcrĕātrix -īcis, f. *mother.*

prōcrĕo -are, *to beget; to produce, cause make.*

prōcresco -ĕre, *to come forth, arise; to increase.*

Procrustēs -ae, m. *a robber killed by Theseus.*

prōcŭbo -are, *to lie stretched out.*

prōcūdo -cūdĕre -cūdi -cūsum, *to hammer out, forge; to form, produce.*

prŏcŭl, *far; at, to, or from a distance.*

prōculco -are, *to tread on, trample down.*

prōcumbo -cumbĕre -cŭbŭi -cŭbĭtum, *to lean or bend forward; to fall down, sink down, be laid low.*

prōcūrātĭo -ōnis, f. *taking care, management, administration.* Esp. (1) *the office of imperial procurator.* (2) *an attempt to propitiate a deity.*

procūrātor -ōris, m. *a manager, bailiff, agent, factor;* regni, *a viceroy;* under the empire, *a financial agent or undergovernor.*

procūrātrix -tricis, f. *she that governs.*

prōcūro -are, *to take care of, look after; to manage, administer; to be a procurator; to sacrifice in order to avert evil.*

prōcurro -currĕre -curri and -cŭcurri -cursum, *to run forward;* of places, *to project, jut out.*

prōcursātĭo -ōnis, f. *running forward, skirmishing.*

prōcursātor -ōris, m. *a skirmisher.*

prōcurso -are, *to run forward;* milit. *to skirmish.*

prōcursus -ūs, m. *running forward;* milit., *advance, charge.*

prōcurvus -a -um, *bent forward.*

¹prŏcus -i, m. = procer; q.v.

²prŏcus -i, m. *a wooer, suitor; a canvasser.*

prōdĕo -ire -ĭi -ĭtum, *to advance, go forward; to project; to come out, appear.*

prōdĭco -dicĕre -dixi -dictum, *to put off.*

prōdictātor -ōris, m. *one who acts as dictator.*

prōdĭgentĭa -ae, f. *profusion, prodigality.*

prōdĭgĭālis -e, *dealing in wonders;* adv. prōdĭgĭālĭtĕr, *wonderfully.*

prōdĭgĭōsus -a -um, *unnatural, wonderful.*

prōdĭgĭum -i, n. *a prodigy, portent; an enormity, an unnatural thing; a monster.*

prōdĭgo -ĭgĕre -ēgi -actum, *to drive forth; to spend, waste.*

prōdĭgus -a -um, *profuse, extravagant; rich, abound in.* Adv. prōdĭgē.

prōdĭtĭo -ōnis, f. *betrayal, treason.*

prōdĭtor -ōris, m. *a betrayer, traitor.*

prōdo -dĕre -dĭdi -dĭtum. (1) *to put forth, bring forth; to show, publish; to appoint.* (2) *to forsake, betray.* (3) *to hand over, deliver, transmit.*

prōdŏcĕo -ēre, *to teach, inculcate.*

prōdrŏmus -i, m. *forerunner.*

prōdūco -dūcĕre -duxi -ductum, *to bring forward, bring out, extend; to produce, bring up, advance, promote; to divulge, bring to light;* in pronunciation, *to lengthen out, make long;* in time, *to prolong, continue;* also *to put off, postpone.*

Hence partic. prōductus -a -um, *extended, lengthened, prolonged;* of syllables, *pronounced long;* n. pl. as subst. *preferable things* (in the Stoic philosophy). Adv. prōductē, *long* (of pronunciation).

prōductĭo -ōnis, f. *extending, lengthening, prolonging.*

proelĭātor -ōris, m. *warrior.*

proelĭor -ari, dep. *to give battle, fight, strive.*

proelĭum -i, n. *battle, fight, strife.*

prŏfāno -are, *to profane, desecrate.*

prŏfānus -a -um, *not sacred; uninitiated; ordinary, common, profane; impious.*

prŏfectĭo -ōnis, f. *departure; source, origin.*

prŏfecto, *truly, really, indeed.*

prōfĕro -ferre -tŭli -lātum. (1) *to bring forth, bring forward, offer to publish, bring to light, reveal; to produce, cite, mention.* (2) *to advance, bring forward, impel.* (3) *to enlarge, extend;* in time, *to lengthen;* also *to put off, postpone.*

prŏfessĭo -ōnis, f. *declaration, profession.* Transf., *a register of persons and property; an occupation, art, profession.*

prŏfessor -ōris, m. *an authority, expert.*

prŏfessōrĭus -a -um, *authoritative.*

prŏfestus -a -um, *not kept as a festival, common.*

prōfĭcĭo -fĭcĕre -fēci -fectum:* of persons, *to make progress, advance;* of things, *to be of use, assist, help.*

prŏfĭciscor -fĭcisci -fectus, dep. *to start forward, set out, depart; to arise or spring from an origin.*

prŏfĭtĕor -fĭtēri -fessus, dep. *to acknowledge, confess; to profess or declare oneself anything; to profess a science, art, etc.; to make any public statement; to offer, promise.*

prōflīgātor -ōris, m. *a spendthrift.*

prōflīgo -are, *to overthrow, overcome, ruin; to lower, debase; to bring almost to an end, nearly finish.*

Hence partic. prōflīgātus -a -um, *ruined, degraded.*

prōflo -are, *to blow forth, breathe forth.*

prōflŭentĭa -ae, f. *fluency.*

prōflŭo -flŭĕre -fluxi fluxum, *to flow forth; to proceed.*

Hence partic. prōflŭens -entis, *flowing;* f. as subst. (sc. aqua), *running water;* of style, *flowing, fluent.* Adv. prōflŭentĕr.

prōflŭvĭum -i, n. *flowing forth.*

prōfor -fari -fatus, dep. *to say, speak, declare.*

prŏfŭgĭo -fŭgĕre -fūgi:* intransit., *to flee away, escape;* transit., *to flee away from.*

prŏfŭgus -a -um, *fleeing, fugitive; banished; migratory.*

prŏfundo -fundĕre -fūdi -fūsum, *to pour forth, shed, cause to flow;* pass., profundi, *to stream forth.* Transf., *to stretch at full length; to release, discharge; to utter; to spend, sacrifice, give up; to lavish, squander.* Hence partic. **prŏfūsus** -a -um, *lavish, extravagant.* Adv. **prŏfūsē**, *in disorder; lavishly, extravagantly.*

prŏfundus -a -um, *deep, profound; high; thick, dense; boundless.* N. as subst. **prŏfundum** -i, *depth, abyss;* poet., *the sea.*

prŏfūsus -a -um, partic. from profundo; q.v.

prŏgĕner -i, *a grand-daughter's husband.*

prōgĕnĕro -are, *to engender, produce.*

prōgĕnĭes -ēi, f. *descent, lineage; progeny, offspring, descendants.*

prōgĕnĭtor -ōris, m. *founder of a family, ancestor.*

prōgigno -gignĕre -gĕnŭi -gĕnĭtum, *to engender, bring forth.*

prōgnātus -a -um, *born, sprung from;* m. as subst., *a son.*

Prognē = Procne; q.v.

prōgrĕdĭor -grĕdi -gressus, dep., *to go forth, go out; to go forwards, advance, proceed.*

prōgressĭo, f. *advance, progress; increase;* rhet., *climax.*

prōgressus -ūs, m. *going forwards, advance, progress; increase.*

proh! = pro!; q.v.

prŏhĭbĕo -ēre, *to hold back, restrain, hinder; to forbid, prohibit; to preserve, defend, protect.*

prŏhĭbĭtĭo -ōnis, f. *hindering, prohibition.*

prōĭcĭo -icĕre -iēci -iectum, *to throw forth; to fling forward; to put forward, cause to project* (pass., *to project); to fling out, throw away, abandon; to defer, put off.* Hence partic. **prōĭectus** -a -um, *jutting forward, prominent; stretched out, prostrate; hence abject, contemptible, downcast;* with ad, *addicted to.*

prōĭectĭo -ōnis, f. *throwing forward, stretching out.*

prōĭectū, abl. sing. m. *by jutting out.*

prŏinde and **prŏin** (o and i sometimes scanned as one syllable), *consequently, therefore;* foll. by ut or quam, *just as;* foll. by quasi, ac, ac si, *just as if.*

prōlābor -lābi -lapsus dep. (1) *to glide forward, slip along or out.* (2) *to fall forward, fall down.*

prōlapsĭo -ōnis, f. *slipping, sliding.*

prōlātĭo -ōnis, f. *bringing forward, mentioning; an extension; putting off, deferring.*

prōlāto -are, *to extend, enlarge, lengthen; to put off, defer.*

prōlecto -are, *to entice, allure.*

prōlēs -is, f. *offspring, descendants, posterity; the young men of a race; of plants, fruit.*

prōlētārĭus -i, m. *a citizen of the lowest class, serving the state only by begetting children.*

prōlĭcĭo -lĭcĕre -lixi, *to lure forth, entice.*

prōlixus -a -um, *wide, broad, long.* Transf., *willing, obliging; favourable.* Adv. **prōlixē**, *freely; willingly.*

prōlŏgus -i, m. *prologue.*

prōlŏquor -lŏqui -lŏcūtus, dep. *to speak out, say openly.*

prōlūdo -lūdĕre -lūsi -lūsum, *to play beforehand, to prelude.*

prōlŭo -lŭĕre -lŭi -lūtum, *to wash away or off; to wash clean.*

prōlūsĭo -ōnis, f. *a prelude, preliminary exercise.*

prōlŭvĭes -ēi, f. *an inundation; scourings, discharge.*

prōmĕrĕo -ēre -ŭi -ĭtum and **prō-mĕrĕor** -ēri -ĭtus, dep. *to deserve;* n. of partic. as subst. **prōmĕrĭtum** -i, *deserts, merit.*

Prōmētheūs -ĕi and -ĕos, m. *Prometheus, punished for stealing fire from heaven and giving it to mankind;* adj. **Prōmētheūs** -a -um.

prōmĭnĕo -ēre -ŭi, *to stand out, jut out, project, extend;* partic. **prōmĭnens** -entis, *jutting out, projecting;* n. as subst. *a projection.*

prōmiscus and **prōmiscŭus** -a -um, *mixed, indiscriminate, promiscuous; commonplace, usual.* Adv. **prōmiscē** and **prōmiscŭē.**

prōmissĭo -ōnis, f. *a promise.*

prōmissor -ōris, m. *a promiser.*

prōmitto -mittĕre -mīsi -missum, *to let go forward, send forth; to let grow; to promise, undertake.* Hence partic. **prōmissus** -a -um, *let grow, long, hanging down.* N. of partic. as subst. **prōmissum** -i, *a promise.*

prōmo prōmĕre prompsi promptum, *to bring out, produce; to bring forward, disclose, express.* Hence partic. **promptus** -a -um, *ready, at hand; easy; visible, apparent;* of persons, *prepared, resolute, prompt.* Adv. **promptē.**

prōmontŏrĭum -i, n. *a mountain ridge; a promontory.*

prōmŏvĕo -mŏvēre -mōvi -mōtum, *to move forwards, push onwards, make to advance; to extend; to postpone.*

promptū, abl. sing. m.: in promptu esse, *to be ready, easy, or manifest;* in promptu ponere, *to make manifest;* in promptu habere, *to have ready or have on show.*

promptus -a -um, partic. from promo; q.v.

prōmulgātĭo -ōnis, f. *publication, promulgation* (of a proposed law).

prōmulgo -are, *to publish, promulgate* (esp. a proposed law).

prōmulsis -ĭdis, f. *hors d'oeuvres.*

prōmuntŭrĭum = promontorium; q.v.

prōmus -i, m. *a steward, butler.*

prōmūtŭus -a -um, *advanced, paid beforehand.*

prōnĕpōs -pōtis, m. *great-grandson.*

prōneptis -is, f. *great-granddaughter.*
prōnoea -ae, f. *providence.*
prōnŭba -ae, f. (1) *a matron attending a bride.* (2) *epithet of Juno, as the goddess presiding over marriage.*
prōnuntiātio -ōnis, f. *public declaration; the decision of a judge, a judgment;* in logic, *a proposition;* in rhetoric, *delivery.*
prōnuntiātor -ōris, m. *a relater.*
prōnuntio -are, *to make publicly known, declare;* in the senate, *to announce a resolution;* at a sale, *to make a statement as to defects;* rhet. *to declaim, recite, deliver.* N. of partic. as subst. prōnuntiātum -i, in logic, *a proposition.*
prōnŭrus -us, f. *a grandson's wife.*
prōnus -a -um, *inclined forward, stooping forward; rushing down or past; precipitous, steep.* Transf., *inclined, well-disposed, favourable; easy.* Adv. prōnē, *on a slope.*
prŏoemĭum -i, n. *preface, introduction, prelude.*
prōpāgātio -ōnis, f. *spreading, propagation; extension, enlargement.*
prōpāgātor -ōris, m. *an extender, enlarger.*
¹prōpāgo -are, *to spread, propagate plants; to extend, enlarge, prolong.*
²prōpāgo -inis, f. *a layer, slip or shoot* (esp. of the vine); *of men and animals, offspring, race, posterity.*
prōpālam, *publicly, in public.*
prōpātŭlus -a -um, *open, uncovered;* n. as subst. *an open place, unroofed space;* in propatulo, *publicly.*
prŏpē, adv. and prep; comparⁱ prŏpĭus; superl. prŏxĭmē. Adv. *near,* in space or time; *nearly;* propius, *more nearly, more closely;* proxime, of time, *just now.* Prep. with acc. *near to,* in space or time; in gen., *approximating to, not far from.*
prōpĕdĭem, *at an early date, very soon.*
prōpello -pellĕre -pŭli -pulsum, *to drive before one, drive forth or away.*
prŏpĕmŏdŏ and prŏpĕmŏdum, *almost, nearly.*
prōpendĕo -pendēre -pendi -pensum. *to hang down; to preponderate; to incline, be favourable.*
Hence partic. prōpensus -a -um, *weighty; tending, inclined, disposed;* esp. *favourably disposed.* Adv. prōpensē, *readily, willingly.*
prōpensio -ōnis, f. *inclination, propensity.*
prŏpĕrantĕr, adv. from propero; q.v.
prŏpĕrantĭa -ae, f. *haste, rapidity.*
prŏpĕrātĭo -ōnis, f. *haste.*
prŏpĕro -are: intransit., *to hasten;* transit., *to hasten something, to accelerate, complete quickly.* Adv. from pres. partic. prŏpĕrantĕr, *hastily.* Past. partic. prŏpĕrātus -a -um, *hasty;* n. as subst. prŏpĕrātum -i, *haste;* abl. prŏpĕrātō, *in haste.*
Prŏpertius -i, m., Sex. Aurelius. *a poet of the Augustan age.*

prŏpĕrus -a -um, *quick, rapid, hasty;* adv. prŏpĕrē.
prōpexus -a -um, *combed forwards, hanging down.*
prōpīno -are, *to drink to anyone.*
prōpinquĭtās -ātis, f. *nearness, proximity; friendship or relationship.*
prōpinquo -are: intransit., *to come near, draw near, approach;* transit. *to bring near, hasten on.*
prōpinquus -a -um, *near, close, neighbouring; similar; nearly related, closely connected;* as subst., *a kinsman.* Adv. prōpinquē.
prŏpĭor -us, genit. -ōris, *nearer,* in space or time (cf. prope); *more like; more closely connected; more suitable.* Superl. prŏxĭmus (proxŭmus) -a -um, *very near, nearest;* in time, *next, following,* or *most recent;* in rank, etc., *next, next best; most like; most nearly connected;* m. pl. as subst. *near relations or close friends.*
prōpĭtio -are, *to soothe, appease.*
prōpĭtĭus -a -um, *favourable, gracious.*
prŏpĭus, compar. of prope; q.v.
prōpōla -ae, m. *a retailer, huckster.*
prōpolluo -ŭĕre, *to pollute worse.*
prōpōno -pōnĕre -pōsŭi -pŏsĭtum, *to put on view, expose, display; to publish, relate, tell; to propose, promise, offer as a reward or hold over as a threat; to imagine, put before the mind; to propose to oneself, purpose, intend.* N. of partic. as subst. prōpŏsĭtum -i, *a design, purpose; the subject or theme of a discourse; the first premiss of a syllogism.*
prōporrō, adv. *further, moreover,* or *altogether.*
prōportĭo -ōnis, f. *proportion, analogy, similarity.*
prōpŏsĭtĭo -ōnis, f. *a purpose; the subject of a discourse;* in logic, *the first proposition of a syllogism.*
prōpŏsĭtum -i, n. subst. from propono; q.v.
prōpraetor -ōris, m. (and prō praetōre) *a praetor's deputy; an ex-praetor,* sent as governor to a province or given a military command.
proprĭĕtās -ātis, f. *a property, peculiarity; ownership.*
proprĭtim, *peculiarly, specially.*
proprĭus -a -um, *one's own, special, peculiar characteristic; lasting, permanent.* Hence adv. propriē, *exclusively, peculiarly, characteristically; in a proper sense.*
propter. Adv., *near, close by.* Prep. with acc. *near; on account of, because of.*
proptĕrĕā, adv. *on that account, therefore.*
prōpŭdĭum -i, n. *a shameful action; a wretch, villain.*
prōpugnācŭlum -i, n. *a fortification rampart, defence.*
prōpugnātĭo -ōnis, f. *defence.*
prōpugnātor -ōris, m. *a defender.*
prōpugno -are, *to skirmish in front; fight in defence, defend.*

prŏvěnĭo -věnire -věni -ventum, *to come on, appear*; of corn, *to come up, grow*; of events, *to result, come about*: esp. *to turn out well, succeed.*

prŏventus -ūs, m. *coming forth, growing; product, crop; result, issue, success.*

prŏverbĭum -i, n. *a proverb.*

prŏvidentĭa -ae, f. *foresight, fore-knowledge; forethought, providence.*

prŏvĭděo -vīděre -vīdi -vīsum, *to look forward to, see at a distance; to see beforehand, foresee; to take pre-cautions for* or *against, provide for, make preparation for.*
   Hence partic. **prŏvĭdens** -entis, *provident, prudent*; adv. **prŏvĭdentěr.** N. abl. of perf. partic. **prŏvīsō,** *with forethought.*

prŏvĭdus -a -um, *foreseeing; providing, taking measures for*; in gen., *cautious, prudent.*

prŏvincĭa -ae, f. *employment, sphere of duty, office,* esp. *that of a magistrate.* Transf., *a country governed by a Roman magistrate, a province.*

prŏvincĭālis -e, *of a province*; m. as subst., esp. plur., *inhabitants of provinces, provincials.*

prŏvīsĭo -ōnis, f. *foresight*; hence *provision, planning.*

prŏvīso -ěre, *to look out for, go to see.*

prŏvīsor -ōris, m. *one who provides for* or *against.*

prŏvīsū, abl. sing. m. *by foreseeing; by providing for* or *against.*

provixisse, perf. infin. *to have lived on.*

prŏvŏcātĭo -ōnis, f. *a challenge*; esp. *an appeal to a higher court.*

prŏvŏcātor -ōris, m. *a challenger; a kind of gladiator.*

prŏvŏco -are, *to call out; to excite, rouse, provoke; to challenge to a contest*; legal, *to appeal to a higher court.*

prŏvŏlo -are, *to fly forth, to rush out.*

prŏvolvo -volvěre -volvi -vŏlūtum, *to roll forward, roll over and over*; provolvere se, and provolvi, *to throw oneself down,* hence *to abase oneself.*

prŏvŏmo -ěre, *to vomit forth.*

prŏxĭmĭtās -atis, f. *nearness close connexion; similarity.*

prŏxĭmus -a -um, superl.; see propior.

prūdens -entis, *foreseeing, aware; skilled, experienced, practised; prudent, discreet, judicious.* Adv. **prūdentěr.**

prūdentĭa -ae, f. *foresight; knowledge; sagacity, discretion.*

prŭīna -ae, f. *hoar-frost, rime.*

prŭīnōsus -a -um, *frosty.*

prūna -ae, f. *a live coal.*

prūnĭtĭus -a -um, *of plum-tree wood.*

prūnum -i, n. *a plum.*

prūnus -i, f. *plum-tree.*

prūrīgo -ĭnis, f. *the itch.*

prūrĭo -ire, *to itch.*

prўtănēum -i, n. *the town-hall in a Greek city.*

prўtănis -is, acc. -in, m. *chief magistrate in a Greek state.*

psallo psallěre psalli, *to play on* or *sing to a stringed instrument.*

psaltērĭum -i, n. *a stringed instrument.*

psaltrĭa -ae, f. *a female player on the cithara.*

psēcăs -ădis, f. *an anointer of hair.*

pseudŏthўrum -i, n. *a secret door.*

psīthĭa (vitis) -ae, f. *a kind of Greek vine.*

psittācus -i, m. *parrot.*

psўchŏmantĭum or **-ěum** -i n. *a place of necromancy*

-ptě, suffix, *self, own.*

ptĭsănārĭum -i, n. *a decoction of crushed barley* or *rice.*

pūbens -entis, of plants, *in full growth luxuriant.*

pūběr -běris = pubes; q.v.

pūbertās -ātis, f. *puberty, the age of maturity; signs of puberty, growth of hair,* etc.

[1]pūbes -is, f. *the signs of puberty, growth of hair,* etc.; *the youth, adult male population.*

[2]pūbes and **pūběr** -ěris, *arrived at the age of puberty, adult, ripe*; m. pl. as subst. **pūběres** -um, *the men, the adult male population.*

pūbesco -bescěre -bŭi, *to grow up, arrive at maturity.*

pūblĭcānus -a -um, *of the farming of the public taxes*; m. as subst. *a farmer of the Roman taxes.*

pūblĭcātĭo -ōnis, f. *confiscation.*

pūblĭcĭtŭs, *at the public expense, in the public service; publicly.*

pūblĭco -are, *to confiscate; to make public, throw open, publish.*

pūblĭcus -a -um, *belonging to the people, public*; res publica, or respublica, *the state.* Transf., *uni-versal, general; common, ordinary.* M. as subst. **pūblĭcus** -i, *a state official*; N. **pūblĭcum** -i, *public territory; the public revenue, the treasury; an open place, the open street.* Adv. **pūblĭcē,** *for the people, publicly, at the public expense; all together.*

Pūblĭus -i, m. *a Roman praenomen,* abbrev. P.

pŭděo -ěre, *to be ashamed*; usually 3rd person, *to cause shame, fill with shame*; often impers., **pŭdet**; te huius templi pudet, *you are ashamed of.* Hence gerundive **pŭdendus** -a -um, *shameful, disgraceful.* Partic. **pŭdens** -entis, *modest, shamefaced*; adv. **pŭdentěr,** *modestly, bashfully.*

pŭdĭbundus -a -um, *modest, bashful.*

pŭdĭcĭtĭa -ae, f. *modesty, chastity, virtue.*

pŭdĭcus -a -um, *modest chaste virtuous*; adv. **pŭdĭcē.**

pŭdor -ōris, m. *feeling of shame bashfulness, decency, honour; chastity, purity; that which causes shame, a disgrace.*

pŭella -ae, f. *a girl, maiden; a young woman, young wife,* or *sweetheart.*

pŭellāris -e, *girlish, maidenly.* Adv. **pŭellārĭtěr.**

pŭellŭla -ae, f. *a little girl.*

pŭellus -i, m. *a little boy.*

pŭer -i, m. *a child*; in plur., *children*; esp. *a boy, lad*; a puero, a pueris, *from boyhood.* Transf., *a serving-lad, page, slave.*

pŭĕrīlis -e, *youthful, boyish; puerile, silly, childish.* Adv. **pŭĕrīlĭtĕr**, *boyishly; childishly.*

pŭĕrĭtĭa -ae, f. *boyhood.*

pŭerpĕrīum -i, n. *childbirth, labour.*

pŭerpĕrus -a -um, *of childbirth*; f. as subst. *a woman in labour.*

pŭertĭa = pueritia; q.v.

pŭĕrŭlus -i, m. *a little boy, young slave.*

pūga (pȳga) -ae, f. *the rump, buttocks.*

pŭgil -ilis, m. *a boxer, fighter with the caestus.*

pŭgĭlātĭo -ōnis, f. *fighting with the caestus; boxing.*

pŭgillāris -e, *that can be grasped with the fist*; m. pl. as subst. **pŭgillāres** -ium (sc. libelli), *writing-tablets.*

pŭgĭo -ōnis, m. *a dagger, dirk, poniard.*

pŭgĭuncŭlus -i, m. *a little dagger.*

pugna -ae, f. *a fight, battle; battle-line, array*; in gen., *contest.*

pugnācĭtās -ātis, f. *desire to fight, pugnacity.*

pugnācŭlum -i, n. *a fortress.*

pugnātor -ōris, m. *a fighter, combatant.*

pugnax -ācis, *fond of fighting, combative; obstinate, contentious.* Adv. **pugnācĭter.**

pugno -are, *to fight, give battle; to struggle, contend, fight, to strive, exert oneself.*

pugnus -i m. *the fist.*

pulchellus -a -um, *pretty.*

pulcher -chra -chrum and **pulcer** -cra -crum, *beautiful, lovely*; morally *excellent, fine.* Adv. **pulchrē** (**pulcrē**), *beautifully, finely*; as exclamation, *bravo! well done!*

pulchrĭtūdo -ĭnis, f. *beauty, excellence.*

pūlēĭum (pūlēgĭum) -i, n *fleabane, penny-royal.*

pūlex -ĭcis, m. *a flea.*

pullārĭus -i, m. *feeder of sacred chickens.*

pullātus -a -um, *clad in dirty or black garments.*

pullŭlo -are, *to shoot up, sprout, burgeon, luxuriate.*

¹**pullus** -i, m. *a young animal*; esp. *a chicken, chick.*

²**pullus** -a -um, *dark-coloured, blackish*; poet., *sad, gloomy.* N. as subst. *a dark garment.*

pulmentārĭum -i, n. *a relish.*

pulmentum -i. n. *a relish*; in gen., *food, victuals.*

pulmo -ōnis, m. *the lung* (usually plur.).

pulpa -ae, f. *flesh.*

pulpāmentum -i, n. *flesh, esp. tit-bits.*

pulpĭtum -i, n. *a platform or stage.*

puls pultis, f. *porridge, pulse.*

pulsātĭo -ōnis, f. *knocking, beating.*

pulso -are, *to strike, beat, knock; to stir, move, affect.*

pulsus -ūs, m. *beating, blow, push; influence, impulse.*

pulto -are, *to knock, strike.*

pulvĕrĕus -a -um, *full of dust, dusty.*

pulvĕrŭlentus -a -um, *full of dust, dusty.*

pulvillus -i, m. *a little pillow.*

pulvīnar -aris, n. *a couch*, esp. *one carrying images of the gods at the* Lectisternium (q.v.).

pulvīnārĭum -i, n. *anchorage.*

pulvīnus -i, m. *pillow, cushion; a seat of honour.*

pulvis -ĕris, m. (rarely f.) *dust, powder.* Transf., *arena, scene of action*; sine pulvere palmae, *prize without effort.*

pūmex -ĭcis, m. *pumice-stone; any soft, porous stone.*

pūmĭcĕus -a -um, *made of pumice-stone.*

pūmĭco -are, *to polish with pumice-stone.*

pūmĭlĭo -ōnis, c. and **pūmĭlus** -i, m. *a dwarf.*

punctim, *by stabbing, by thrusting* (opp. caesim).

pungo pungĕre pŭpŭgi punctum, *to prick, puncture, stab; to touch, move, penetrate; to sting, vex, annoy.* N. of partic. as subst. **punctum** -i, *a prick, a little hole, small puncture; a point, spot.* Hence *a vote; a moment of time*; in speech, etc., *a short clause, section.*

pūnĭcĕus -a -um, *purple, red.*

Pūnĭcus; see Poeni.

pūnĭo (poenĭo) -ire and **pūnĭor** -iri, dep. *to punish; to avenge.*

pūnĭtor -ōris, m. *punisher, avenger.*

pūpa -ae, f. *a little girl; a doll.*

pūpilla -ae, f. (1) *an orphan girl, ward, minor.* (2) *the pupil of the eye.*

pūpillāris -e, *of an orphan or ward.*

pūpillus -i, m. *an orphan or ward.*

puppis -is, f. *the poop or stern of a vessel*; poet., *the whole ship.*

pūpŭla -ae, f. *the pupil of the eye.*

purgāmen -ĭnis, n. (1) *sweepings, filth.* (2) *a means of purgation.*

purgāmentum -i, n. *sweepings, rubbish, filth.*

purgātĭo -ōnis, f. *cleaning out, cleansing; excusing, justification.*

purgo -are. (1) *to clean, cleanse, purify.* Hence *to excuse, defend, justify; to allege in defence.* (2) *to clear away, wash off.*

purpŭra -ae, f. *the purple-fish.* Transf., *purple dye; purple cloth; 'the purple',* = *high rank,* etc.

purpŭrātus -a -um, *clad in purple.* M. as subst., *a man of high rank, a courtier.*

purpŭrĕus -a -um, *purple-coloured; dark-red, dark-brown.* Transf., *clad in purple*; in gen., *gleaming, bright, beautiful.*

pūrus -a -um, *clean, pure, cleared.* Transf., *without addition, simple, plain*; morally, *upright, pure*; of style, *pure, faultless*; legally, *without conditions, absolute.* N. as subst. *the clear sky.* Adv **pūrē** and poet. **pūrĭtĕr**, *purely, cleanly*; of style, *faultlessly.*

pūs pūris, n. *corrupt matter; bitterness.*

pŭsillus -a -um, *tiny; puny; petty, mean.*

pŭsĭo -onis, m. *little boy.*

pŭtāmen -ĭnis, n. *cutting, paring, shell*

pŭtātor -ōris, m. *pruner.*

pŭtĕal -ālis, n. *stone curb round the mouth of a well or sacred place.*

pŭtĕālis -e, *of a well.*

pŭtĕo -ēre, *to stink.*

pŭter -tris -tre and putris -e, *rotten, putrid; loose, crumbling, friable, flabby.*

pŭtesco pūtescĕre, *to decay.*

pŭtĕus -i, m. *a well, pit.*

pŭtĭdus -a -um, *rotten, stinking, foul; of style, affected, in bad taste;* adv. pŭtĭdē, *affectedly.*

pŭto -are, *to cleanse, clear;* of trees, *to lop.* Transf., *to clear up, settle,* esp. of accounts; hence *to weigh up, ponder, reckon, estimate; to consider, believe, think;* parenthetically, puto or ut puto, *I suppose.*

putrĕfăcĭo -făcĕre -fēci -factum. *to make rotten or soft.*

putresco -ĕre, *to become rotten.*

putrĭdus -a -um, *rotten, decayed.*

pŭtus -a -um, *pure, unmixed, unadulterated.*

pȳga = puga; q.v.

Pygmaei -orum, m. *the Pygmies, a race of dwarfs in Africa.*

pȳra -ae, f. *funeral pyre.*

pȳrămis -ĭdis, f. *pyramid;* hence *a cone.*

pȳrōpus -i, m. *bronze.*

Pyrrhus -i, m. (1) *son of Achilles.* (2) *a king of Epirus, enemy of the Romans.*

Pȳthăgŏras -ae, m. *Greek philosopher of Samos* (about 540 B.C.).

Pȳtho -ūs, f. *the old name of Delphi;* adj. Pȳthĭcus, Pȳthĭus -a -um, *Delphic, relating to Apollo;* f. as subst., *the priestess of Apollo;* n. pl., *the Pythian games, celebrated every fourth year in honour of Apollo.*

pyxis -ĭdis, f. *a little box, casket.*

Q

Q, q, *the sixteenth letter of the Latin Alphabet,* only used before u and another vowel.

quā, abl. f. of qui, as adv.: relat., *by which way, where;* also *whereby,* or *as far as;* qua . . . qua, *partly . . . partly;* interrog., *by what way? how?;* indef., *in any way, at all.*

quācumque (-cunque), *wherever; by whatever way.*

quādamtĕnŭs, *to a certain point.*

quadra -ae, f. *a square;* used of any square object or square piece.

quadrāgēni -ae -a, *forty at a time, forty each.*

quadrāgēsĭmus (-ensĭmus) -a -um, *fortieth;* f. as subst. *the fortieth part,* esp. *as a tax.*

quadrāgĭes (-ĭens), *forty times.*

quadrāgintā, *forty.*

quadrans -antis, m. *a fourth part, quarter;* as a coin, *the fourth part of an as.*

quadrantārĭus -a -um, *of a quarter;* of price, *costing a quarter of an as.*

quadrīdŭum (quatrīdŭum) -i, n. *a space of four days.*

quadrĭennĭum -i, n. *a period of four years.*

quadrĭfārĭam, *in four parts.*

quadrĭfĭdus -a -um, *split into four.*

quadrīgae -arum, f. *a team of four horses abreast,* esp. drawing a chariot.

quadrīgārĭus -a -um, *of a racing charioteer.*

quadrīgātus -a -um, *stamped with the figure of a four-horse chariot.*

quadrīgēni -ae -a, *four years old.*

quadrĭgŭlae -arum, f. *a little team of four horses.*

quadrĭiŭgis -e, *in a team of four.*

quadrĭiŭgus -a -um, *in or with a team of four.*

quadrīmus -a -um, *four years old.*

quadringēnārĭus -a -um, *of four hundred each.*

quadringēni -ae -a, *four hundred at a time, four hundred each.*

quadringentēsĭmus (-ensĭmus) -a -um, *four hundredth.*

quadringenti -ae -a, *four hundred.*

quadringentĭens (-ĭēs), *four hundred times.*

quadrĭpertītus -a -um, *divided into four parts, fourfold.*

quadrĭrēmis -e, *with four banks of oars;* f. as subst., *a quadrireme.*

quadrĭvĭum -i, n. *a crossroads, place where four roads meet.*

quadro -are: transit., *to make square; to join properly together;* intransit., *to be square; to fit exactly, to suit;* esp. of accounts, *to agree.* Partic. quadrātus -a -um, *squared, square;* n. as subst., *a square.*

quadrum -i, n. *a square.*

quadrŭpĕdans -antis, *going on four feet, galloping;* plur. as subst., *horses.*

quadrŭpēs -pĕdis, *four-footed, on four feet;* as subst., *a quadruped.*

quadruplātor -ōris, m. *a multiplier by four; an exaggerator; an informer.*

quadruplēx -plĭcis, *fourfold, quadruple.*

quadruplor -ari, dep. *to be an informer.*

quadruplus -a -um, *fourfold;* n. as subst., *four times the amount.*

quaerĭto -are, *to seek* or *enquire about eagerly.*

quaero quaerĕre quaesĭi or quaesĭvi quaesĭtum, *to seek, search for;* sometimes *to obtain, get; to miss, want; to seek to know, ask, enquire into* a matter. Partic. quaesītus -a -um, *sought out; unusual, select;* in bad sense, *far-fetched, affected;* n. as subst., *a question* or *a gain.*

quaesĭtĭo -ōnis, f. *an interrogation.*

quaesĭtor -ōris, m. *investigator, inquirer,* esp. judicial.

quaeso -ĕre, *to seek for, ask for;* first person, quaeso, *I beg.*

quaestĭo -ōnis, f. *seeking, searching; inquiry, investigation;* esp. *judicial inquiry;* quaestiones perpetuae, *standing courts of justice.*

quaestĭuncŭla -ae, f. *a little question.*

quaestor -ōris, m. *one of the quaestors, magistrates in Rome, occupied with matters of law and finance.*

quaestōrius -a -um, *belonging to a quaestor.* N. as subst., *the quaestor's tent in camp, or residence in a province.* M. as subst., *an ex-quaestor.*

quaestuōsus -a -um, *profitable; fond of gain; having gained much, rich.*

quaestūra -ae, f. *the office of quaestor, quaestorship.*

quaestus -ūs, m. *gaining, getting, profit; a source of profit, occupation, business.*

quālibet (quālŭbet) *wherever you like; in any way you please.*

quālis -e: interrog., *of what kind?*; relat. (with or without antecedent talis), *of the kind that, such as;* indef., *having some quality or other.* Adv. **quālĭtĕr**, *as, just as.*

quāliscumque (-cunque) qualecumque: relat., *of whatever kind;* indef., *any whatever.*

quālislĭbet, quălēlĭbet, *of what sort you will.*

quālĭtās -ātis, f. *quality, property.*

quālus -i, m. and **quālum** -i, n. *wicker-basket.*

quam, adv. *how, in what way:* interrog., *how much? how?*; exclam., *how!*; relat., *of correspondence, as* (often with tam); with superl. adj. or adv., *as . . . as possible* (with or without possum); quam primum, *as soon as possible;* of comparison, *than, as.*

quamlĭbet (quamlŭbet), *as much as you please.*

quamobrem (quam ob rem): interrog., *wherefore? why?*; relat., *for which reason, wherefore.*

quamquam (quanquam), *although, though;* at the beginning of a sentence, *nevertheless, and yet.*

quamvīs, *as much as you please, ever so much;* as conj., *however much, although.*

quānam, *by what way?*

quandō, *when:* interrog., *when?*; indef., *at any time, ever;* relat., *at the time when;* sometimes causal, *since, because.*

quandōcumque (-cunque): relat., *whenever, as often as;* indef., *at some time or other.*

quandōquĕ: relat., *whenever, as often as;* indef., *at some time or other.*

quandŏquĭdem, *since, because.*

quantŏpĕrĕ (quantō ŏpĕrĕ), *with what great trouble; how much.*

quantŭlus -a -um, *how little, how small.*

quantŭluscumque -ăcumque -um-cumque, *however small.*

quantus -a -um: interrog., *how great?*; exclam., *how great!*; relat. (with or without tantus), *(as great) as;* quantus quantus, *however great.* N. as subst. **quantum:** interrog., *how much?*; exclam., *how much!*; relat., *as much as;* quantum in me est, *as far as in me lies.* Neuter in genit. (or locative) of price, **quantī**, *for how much, at what price;* in abl., **quantō**, *(by) how much,* with compar. adj. or adv.

quantuscumque -acumque -um-cumque, *however great.*

quantuslĭbet -tālĭbet -tumlĭbet, *as great as you will, however great.*

quantusvīs -āvīs -umvīs, *as great as you please, however great.*

quāpropter, *wherefore.*

quārē (quā rē), *wherefore.*

quartădĕcŭmāni -orum, m. *soldiers of the fourteenth legion.*

quartānus -a -um, *of the fourth;* f. as subst. (sc. febris) *a quartan fever;* m. pl. as subst., *the soldiers of the fourth legion.*

quartārius -i, m. *the fourth part of a sextarius.*

quartus -a -um, *the fourth;* f. as subst., *the fourth hour;* n. acc. or abl. **quartum, quartō**, *for the fourth time.*

quartusdĕcĭmus -a -um, *fourteenth.*

quăsĭ, *as if, just as,* esp. in hypothetical comparisons; also with descriptions, *as it were, a sort of;* with numerals, *about.*

quăsillus -i, m. and **quăsillum** -i, n. *little basket.*

quassātio -ōnis, f. *a shaking.*

quasso -are: transit., *to shake violently; to shatter, break in pieces;* intransit., *to shake.*

quătĕfăcĭo -făcĕre -fēci, *to shake, weaken.*

quătēnŭs, *how far, to what extent; in so far as, since.*

quătĕr, *four times;* hence *again and again.*

quăterni -ae -a, *four at a time, four each.*

quătio quătĕre quassi quassum, *to shake, brandish, agitate;* sometimes *to shatter.*

quattŭor, *four.*

quattŭordĕcim, *fourteen.*

quattŭorvĭrātus -ūs, m. *the office of the quattuorviri.*

quattŭorvĭri -ōrum, m. *a board of four magistrates.*

-quĕ, enclitic conj., *and;* repeated, -que . . . -que, *both . . . and . . .*

queis = quibus; *see* qui.

quĕmadmŏdum (quem ad mŏdum), *in what manner, how* (interrog. or relat.); esp. corresponding with sic, ita, item, etc., *as, just as.*

quĕo quīre quīvi and quĭi quĭtum, *to be able.*

quercētum -i, n. *an oak-wood.*

quercĕus -a -um, *oaken.*

quercus -ūs, f. *the oak;* sometimes *a crown of oak leaves.*

quĕrēla (querella) -ae, f. *a complaint, complaining.*

quĕrĭbundus -a -um, *complaining, plaintive.*

quĕrĭmōnĭa -ae, f. *a complaining, complaint.*

quĕrĭtor -ari, dep., *to complain excessively.*

quernus -a -um, *of oak, oaken.*

quĕror quĕri questus, dep. *to complain, lament, bewail;* of animals, *to make a plaintive sound.*

querquētŭlānus -a -um, *of an oak-wood.*

quĕrŭlus -a -um, *complaining, plaintive.*

questus -ūs, m. *complaint, lament.*

¹quī quae quod: interrog. adj., *which? what? what kind of?*; exclam., *what!*; indef., (with f. quae or qua) *any, some*; relat., *who, which, what, that.* Acc. n. sing., **quod**, as adv.: quod sciam, *as far as I know.* Abl. **quō**, with comparatives: quo celerius, eo melius, *the faster the better.*

²quī (old abl. of ¹qui): interrog., *in what manner? how?*; relat., *wherewith, wherefrom*; indef., *somehow.*

quĭă, *because.*

quĭănam, quĭănĕ, *why?*

quīcum, *with whom, with which.*

quīcumque (-cunque) quaecumque quodcumque: relat., *whoever, whichever, whatever*; indef., *any available.*

quīdam quaedam quoddam (subst. quiddam), *a certain person or thing* (known but not necessarily named). Transf., *a kind of.*

quĭdem, *indeed*; ne . . . quidem *not, even . . .*

quidnī? *why not?*

quĭēs -ētis, f. *rest, quiet; peace; sleep; a dream; a resting-place.*

quĭesco -escĕre -ēvi -ētum, *to rest; to be at peace; to sleep; to cease* from action.

quiētus -a -um, *resting; sleeping; at peace, undisturbed, neutral*; of character, *quiet, calm.* Adv. **quiētē.**

quīlĭbĕt quaelĭbet quodlĭbet (subst. quidlibet), *any you will, anyone, anything.*

quīn: in questions, *why not?*; in commands, to encourage, *but come now*; in statements, *rather, but indeed*; in subordinate clauses, with subjunctive, *but that, without, that not, who not.*

quīnam quaenam quodnam, *which, what?*

quincunx -cuncis, *five-twelfths.*

quindĕcĭens (-ĭēs), *fifteen times.*

quindĕcim, *fifteen.*

quindĕcimprīmi -orum, m. *the fifteen chief senators of a municipium.*

quindĕcimvir -i, m. *one of a board of fifteen magistrates.*

quindĕcimvĭrālis -e, *of the quindecimviri.*

quindēni or **quīni dēni** -ae -a, *fifteen at a time, fifteen each.*

quingēni -ae -a, *five hundred at a time, five hundred each.*

quingentēsĭmus (-ēnsĭmus) -a -um, *five hundredth.*

quingenti -ae -a, *five hundred.*

quingentĭens (-ĭēs), *five hundred times.*

quīni -ae -a, *five at a time, five each.*

quīnīvīcēni -ae -a, *twenty-five each.*

quinquāgēni -ae -a, *fifty at a time, fifty each.*

quinquāgēsĭmus (-ensĭmus) -a -um, *fiftieth*; f. as subst. (*a tax of*) *a fiftieth part.*

quinquāgintā, *fifty.*

quinquātrūs -ūum, f. pl., and **quinquātrĭa** -ōrum and -ĭum, n. pl. *a festival of Minerva.*

quinquĕ, *five.*

quinquennālis -e, *happening every five years, or lasting for five years.*

quinquennis -e, *of five years; five years old.*

quinquennĭum -i, n. *a period of five years.*

quinquĕpertītus -a -um, *in five portions, fivefold.*

quinquĕprīmi -orum, m. *the five chief senators in a municipium.*

quinquĕrēmis -e, *having five banks of oars*; f. as subst., *a quinquereme.*

quinquĕvir -i, m., *one of a board of five.*

quinquĕvĭrātus -ūs, m. *the office of quinquevir.*

quinquĭēs (-ĭens), *five times.*

quinquĭplĭco -are, *to multiply by five.*

quintădĕcĭmāni -ōrum, m. *soldiers of the fifteenth legion.*

quintānus -a -um, *of the fifth*; f. as subst. (sc. via), *a road in a Roman camp*; m. pl., *soldiers of the fifth legion.*

Quintĭlĭānus (Quinct-) -i, m. M. Fabius Quintilianus, *head of a school of rhetoric at Rome.*

Quintīlis (Quinctīlis) -is, m. (with or without mensis), *the fifth month afterwards called Iulius.*

¹quintus -a -um, *fifth*; quintum, quinto, *for the fifth time.*

²Quintus (abbrev. Q.) and f. **Quinta.** *a Roman praenomen.*

quintusdĕcĭmus -a -um, *fifteenth.*

quippĕ, *certainly, indeed, to be sure of course.*

quippĭnī, *why not?*

Quirīnus -i, m. *the name of Romulus after his apotheosis*; adj. **Quirīnus** -a -um, and **Quirīnālis** -e, *of Romulus*: collis, *the Quirinal Hill at Rome*; n. pl. **Quirīnālia** -ium, *a festival in honour of Romulus.*

¹Quīris -itis and pl. **Quirītēs** -ĭum and -um, m. *the inhabitants of the Sabine town Cures*; also used of *the citizens of Rome in their civil capacity.*

²quīris or **cŭris**, *a spear.*

quĭrītātĭo -ōnis, f. *a shriek, scream.*

quĭrīto -are, *to shriek, scream, cry out.*

¹quis quid, pron.: interrog., *who? what? which?*; indef., *anyone, anybody, anything.* N. nom. and acc. **quĭd?** *what?*; with genit., *how much? how many?* sometimes *why?*; quid ita? *why so?*

²quis = quibus; see qui.

quisnam quaenam quidnam, pron. *who? what?*

quispĭam quaepĭam quodpĭam (subst. quidpĭam, quippĭam), *anyone, anything; someone, something*; n. acc. as adv. *at all.*

quisquam quaequam quidquam (quicquam), *anybody, anyone, anything*, esp. in negative sentences and questions.

quisque quaeque quidque (adj. quodque), *each, every, everyone, everything,*

quisquĭliae -arum, f. pl. *rubbish, sweepings, refuse.*

quisquis quaequae quidquid (quicquid), and adj. quodquod: relat., *whoever, whatever, whichever*; indef., *anyone, anything.*

quīvīs quaevīs quidvīs (adj. quodvīs), *whoever or whatever you will, anyone, anything.*

quīvīscumque quaeviscumque quodviscumque, *whosoever, whatsoever.*

¹quō: interrog., *where? to what place? whither? how far? to what extent? to what end?*; indef., *to any place, anywhither*; relat., *to the end that, in order that.*

²quō, *because, whereby*; see also quominus.

quoad, *how far; as far as, as long as;* also *until.*

quōcircā, *wherefore, on which account.*

quōcumque, *whithersoever*

quod, conj.; *the fact that, the point that; as to the fact that, whereas; because, on the ground that; why, on which account;* with temporal clause, *since; as far as, to the extent that;* introducing a fresh sentence, *and, but, now,* esp. foll. by si.

quōdammŏdo, *in a certain way in a certain measure.*

quōiās = cuias; q.v.

quōlĭbet, *whithersoever you please.*

quōmĭnŭs, *by which the less, so that not.*

quōmŏdo, *in what manner, how.*

quōmŏdocumquĕ, *in whatever way; somehow.*

quōmŏdonam, *how then?*

quōnam, *whither then?*

quondam, *in the past, formerly, once;* in the future, *sometime;* in gen., *at times, sometimes.*

quŏnĭam, *since, whereas, because.*

quōpĭam, and **quōquam,** *to any place at all.*

quŏquĕ, placed after the word which it emphasizes, *also, too.*

quōquō or **quō quō,** *whithersoever, to whatever place.*

quōquōversŭs (-versum, -vorsum), *in every direction.*

quorsum (quorsŭs), *whither? to what place? to what purpose?*

quŏt, indecl., *how many* (interrog. and exclam.); relat. (often with tot) *as many;* quot annis, *every year.*

quŏtannīs = quot annis; see quot.

quotcumquĕ, *as many as, however many.*

quŏtēni -ae -a, *how many each.*

quŏtīdiānus (cottīdiānus, cŏtīd-), *daily, of every day; everyday, common, ordinary.*

quŏtīdiē (cottīdiē, cŏtīd-), *daily, every day.*

quŏtiēs (quŏtiens), *how often* (interrog. and exclam.); relat. (often with toties) *as often as.*

quŏtiescumquĕ (-cunquĕ), *however often.*

quotquŏt, indecl., *however many.*

quŏtus -a -um, *which in number?* quota pars, *how small a fraction?;* quotus quisque, *one in how many? how rare?*

quŏtuscumquĕ (-cunquĕ) -ācumquĕ -umcumquĕ, *whatever in number;* pars quotacumque, *however small a fraction.*

quŏtusquisquĕ; see quotus.

quŏusquĕ (quō usquĕ), *how long? how far?*

quōvīs, *to whatever place you will.*

quum = ²cum; q.v.

R, r, seventeenth letter of the Latin Alphabet.

răbĭdus -a -um, *raging, mad, savage;* adv. **răbĭdē.**

răbĭēs -ēi, f. *madness, rage, fury, frenzy.*

răbĭōsŭlus -a -um, *rather furious.*

răbĭōsus -a -um, *raging, mad, savage;* adv. **răbĭōsē.**

Răbīrius -a -um, *name of a Roman gens.*

răbŭla -ae, m. *a bawling advocate.*

răcēmĭfer -fĕra -fĕrum, *bearing clusters.*

răcēmus -i, m. *a cluster,* esp. *of grapes.*

rădiātus -a -um, *provided with spokes or rays.*

rādīcĭtŭs, *with or by the root; utterly.*

rādīcŭla -ae, f. *a little root.*

rădĭo -are and **rădĭor** -ari, dep. *to gleam, radiate.*

rădius -i, m. *a staff, rod; the spoke of a wheel; the radius of a circle;* in weaving, *a shuttle;* in botany, *a kind of long olive.* Transf., *a ray, beam of light.*

rādix -īcis, f. *a root; the foot of a mountain;* in gen., *foundation, basis, origin.*

rādo rādĕre rāsi rāsum, *to scrape, shave graze; to erase; to hurt, offend.*

raeda -ae, f. *a travelling carriage.*

raedārius -i, m. *coachman.*

rāmālĕ -is, n. usually plur., *sticks, brushwood.*

rāmentum -i, n., usually plur., *shavings, splinters, chips.*

rāmĕus -a -um, *of branches.*

rāmex -īcis, m. *a rupture;* plur.,*the lungs.*

Ramnes and **Ramnenses** -ium, m. pl. *one of the three tribes into which the early Roman citizens were divided.*

rāmōsus -a -um, *full of boughs, branching.*

rāmŭlus -i, m. *a little branch, twig.*

rāmus -i, m. *a bough, branch, twig.*

rāna -ae, f. *a frog.*

rancens -entis, *stinking, putrid.*

rancĭdŭlus -a -um, *rather putrid.*

rancĭdus -a -um, *stinking, rank, offensive.*

rānuncŭlus -i, m. *a little frog, tadpole.*

răpācĭtās -ātis, f. *greediness.*

răpax -ācis, *snatching, grasping, greedy.*

răpĭdĭtās -ātis, f. *rapid flow, rapidity.*

răpĭdus -a -um, *rushing, swift, violent;* adv. **răpĭdē.**

răpīna -ae, f. *robbery, pillage; booty, plunder.*

răpĭo răpĕre răpŭi raptum, *to seize, snatch, tear away; to plunder a place, to hurry along a person or thing;* se rapere, *to rush off.* Transf., *to pervert, lead astray.* N. of partic. as subst. **raptum** -i, *plunder.*

raptim, *violently, hastily, hurriedly.*

raptĭo -ōnis, f. *carrying off, abduction.*

rapto -are, *to seize and carry off, to hurry away; to rob, plunder* a place

raptor -ōris, m. *a robber, plunderer.*

raptus -ūs, m. *tearing off, rending away; carrying off, abduction, rape; plundering.*

rāpŭlum -i, n. *a little turnip.*

rārĕfăcĭo -făcĕre -fēci -factum *to make thin, rarefy.*

rāresco -ĕre, *to become thin, to lose density; to widen out; to grow less.*

rārĭtās -ātis, f. *thinness, looseness of texture; fewness, rarity.*

rārus -a -um, *loose, thin; scattered, scanty, far apart;* milit., *in loose order;* in gen., *rare, infrequent;* sometimes *extraordinary, distinguished.* Adv. rārō, rārē, *seldom, rarely*

rāsĭlis -e, *scraped, smooth.*

rastrum -i, n., plur. gen. rastri -orum, *a hoe, rake, mattock.*

rătĭo -onis, f. *a reckoning, account, consideration, calculation;* rationem ducere, *to compute; any transaction, affair, business; a reason, motive, ground; a plan, scheme, system; reasonableness, method, order; a theory, doctrine, science; the reasoning faculty.*

rătĭōcĭnātĭo -ōnis, f. *reasoning;* esp. *a form of argument, syllogism.*

rătĭōcĭnātīvus -a -um, *argumentative; syllogistic.*

rătĭōcĭnātor -ōris, m. *a calculator, accountant.*

rătĭōcĭnor -ari, dep. *to compute, calculate; to argue, infer, conclude.*

rătĭōnālis -e, *reasonable, rational.*

rătĭōnārĭum -i, n. *a statistical account*

rătis -is, f. *a raft;* poet., *a ship, boat.*

rătĭuncŭla -ae, f. *a little reckoning, account; a poor reason; a petty syllogism.*

rătus -a -um, partic. from reor; q.v.

raucĭsŏnus -a -um, *hoarsely sounding.*

raucus -a -um, *hoarse, harsh-sounding.*

raudus (rōdus, rūdus) -ĕris, n. *a rough mass, lump,* esp. *of copper money.*

raoduscŭlum -i, n. *a small sum of money.*

Răvenna -ae, f. *a town in Gallia Cispadana, near the Adriatic.*

rāvus -a -um, *tawny or greyish.*

rĕa; *see* reus.

rĕapsĕ, *in truth, really.*

rĕbellātĭo = rebellio; q.v.

rĕbellātrix -īcis, f. *renewing war, rebellious.*

rĕbellĭo -ōnis, f. *a renewal of war,* esp. *by the conquered; a revolt.*

rĕbellis -e, *renewing war, insurgent.*

rĕbellĭum = rebellio; q.v.

rĕbello -are, *to renew war, revolt, fight back.*

rĕbŏo -are, *to echo, resound; to make to resound.*

rĕcalcitro -are, *to kick back;* fig., *to deny access.*

rĕcălĕo -ēre, *to be warm again.*

rĕcălesco -ĕre, *to become warm again.*

rĕcalfăcĭo -făcĕre -fēci -factum, *to make warm again.*

rĕcandesco -candescĕre -candŭi, *to grow white; to become hot, begin to glow.*

rĕcanto -are: intransit., *to resound echo;* transit., *to recall, recant; to charm away.*

rĕcēdo -cēdĕre -cessi -cessum, *to go back, retreat, retire; to disappear.*

rĕcello -ere, *to spring back, fly back.*

rĕcens -entis, *new, fresh, young, recent; vigorous.* As adv. rĕcens, *lately, recently.*

rĕcensĕo -censēre -censŭi -censum, *to review, muster, examine; to recount.*

rĕcensĭo -ōnis, f. *reviewing, mustering.*

rĕceptăcŭlum -i, n. *a reservoir, receptacle; a place of refuge, shelter, retreat.*

rĕcepto -are, *to draw back, receive back take in; to receive frequently, harbour.*

rĕceptor -ōris, m. and receptrix -tricis, f. *a receiver, harbourer.*

rĕceptus -ūs, m. *drawing back; withdrawal, recantation; retiring, retreat, return;* poet., *a place of retreat.*

rĕcessim, *backwards.*

rĕcessus -ūs, m. *going back, retreat, withdrawal; a place of retreat, quiet place.*

rĕcĭdīvus -a -um, *returning, repeated.*

[1]rĕcĭdo -cĭdĕre -ccĭdi -cāsūrus, *to fall back; to relapse, recoil, descend, sink, fall.*

[2]rĕcīdo -cīdĕre -cīdi -cīsum, *to cut back, lop away.*

rĕcingo -cingĕre -cinxi -cinctum, *to ungird, loosen.*

rĕcino -ĕre, *to resound, echo;* transit. *to cause to resound.*

rĕcĭpĭo -cĭpĕre -cēpi -ceptum, *to hold back, retain; to take back, fetch back;* se recipere, *to withdraw, retreat; to regain, recover; to receive, accept, take to oneself; to receive hospitably.* Transf., *to accept, admit, allow; to accept an obligation;* hence *to guarantee, promise, be responsible for.* N. of partic. as subst., receptum -i, *an engagement, guarantee.*

rĕcĭprŏco -are, *to move backwards and forwards;* animam, *to breathe.*

rĕcĭprŏcus -a -um, *going backwards and forwards; mare, ebbing.*

rĕcĭtātĭo -ōnis, f. *a reading aloud.*

rĕcĭtātor -ōris, m. *a reader aloud.*

rĕcĭto -are, *to read aloud, read out, recite.*

reclāmātĭo -ōnis, f. *loud disapprobation.*

reclāmĭto -are, *to cry out against.*

reclāmo -are, *to cry out against, contradict loudly;* poet., *to re-echo, resound.*

reclīnis -e, *leaning backwards.*

reclīno -are, *to bend back, cause to lean back.*

reclūdo -clūdĕre -clūsi -clūsum, *to open; to reveal; fata, to relax.*

rĕcōgĭto -are, *to think again, reconsider.*

rĕcognĭtĭo -ōnis, f. *inspection, examination.*

rĕcognosco -noscĕre -nōvi -nītum, to recognize, know again, recall; to review, inspect, investigate.

rĕcŏlo -cŏlĕre -cŏlŭi -cultum, to cultivate or work again; to resume; to set up again, rehabilitate; to reflect upon, to recall.

rĕcompōno -pōnĕre -pŏsĭtum, to readjust.

rĕconcĭlĭātĭo -ōnis, f. winning back, restoration.

rĕconcĭlĭātor -ōris, m. a restorer.

rĕconcĭlĭo -are, to restore, repair; of persons, to reunite, reconcile.

rĕconcinno -are, to restore, renovate, repair.

rĕcondo -dĕre -dĭdi -dĭtum to put away, put back, store, hide. Hence partic. **rĕcondĭtus** -a -um, put away, concealed; abstruse, profound; of character, reserved, mysterious.

rĕconflo -are, to rekindle.

rĕconlĭgo -lĭgĕre -lēgi -lectum, to collect again, recover.

rĕcŏquo -cŏquĕre -coxi -coctum, to boil again, heat up again, remould.

rĕcordātĭo -ōnis, f. recollection, remembrance.

rĕcordor -ari, dep. to remember, recollect; to think of, ponder over.

rĕcrĕo -are, to restore, refresh, invigorate, revive.

rĕcrĕpo -are, to echo, resound.

rĕcresco -crescĕre -crēvi -crētum, to grow again.

rĕcrūdesco -crūdescĕre -crūdŭi, to become raw again, break out afresh.

rectĭo -ōnis, f. ruling, direction.

rector -ōris, m. ruler, governor, director, guide; navis, steersman; of animals, driver or rider.

rectus; see rego.

rĕcŭbo -are, to lie back, recline.

rĕcumbo -cumbĕre -cŭbŭi, to lie back, recline (esp. at table); in gen., to sink down, fall down.

rĕcŭpĕrātĭo -ōnis, f. recovery.

rĕcŭpĕrātor (**rĕcĭpĕrātor**) -ōris, m. a recoverer; pl., recuperatores, a board of arbiters appointed by the praetor.

rĕcŭpĕrātōrĭus -a -um, of the recuperatores (q.v.).

rĕcŭpĕro (**rĕcĭpĕro**) -are, to regain, recover.

rĕcūro -are, to restore, refresh.

rĕcurro -currĕre -curri -cursum, to run back; to revert, return.

rĕcurso -are, to run back, return.

rĕcursus -ūs, m. return, retreat.

rĕcurvo -are, to bend or curve backwards.

rĕcurvus -a -um, bent or curved backwards; winding.

rĕcūsātĭo -ōnis, f. refusal; legal, a protest, counter-plea.

rĕcūso -are, to object to, protest against, refuse; legal, to take exception, plead in defence.

rĕcŭtĭo -cŭtĕre -cussi -cussum, to strike back, cause to rebound.

rĕda -ae, f. = raeda; q.v.

rĕdămo -are, to love in return.

rĕdargŭo -gŭĕre -gŭi, to refute, disprove, contradict.

reddo -dĕre -dĭdi -dĭtum. (1) to give back, restore; reddi, or se reddere, to return; in words, to repeat, recite; to reproduce by imitation, to represent, reflect. (2) to give in return; hence to answer; to translate, render interpret; to make, render, cause to be. (3) to give as due; to pay up, deliver; fulfil; reddere ius, to administer justice.

rĕdemptĭo -ōnis, f. a buying up, bribing; farming of taxes; buying back, ransoming, redemption.

rĕdempto -are, to ransom, redeem.

rĕdemptor -ōris, m. buyer, contractor, farmer (of taxes).

rĕdemptūra -ae, f. contracting, farming (of taxes, etc.).

rĕdĕo -īre -ĭi (-īvi) -ĭtum. (1) to go back, come back, return; ad se, to come to one's senses; redit, the matter comes up again. (2) of revenue, income, etc., to come in. (3) to fall back upon, be reduced or brought to.

rĕdhālo -are, to breathe out again.

rĕdhĭbĕo -ēre -ŭi -ĭtum, to take back.

rĕdĭgo -ĭgĕre -ēgi -actum, to drive back, bring back; of money, etc., to draw in, call in; in gen., to bring or reduce to a condition; to reduce in number, value, etc.; to lessen, bring down.

rĕdĭmĭcŭlum -i, n. a fillet, chaplet.

rĕdĭmĭo -īre -ĭi -ĭtum, to bind round, wreathe, crown.

rĕdĭmo -ĭmĕre -ēmi -emptum, to buy back, redeem; to ransom, recover; in gen., to buy up, contract for, farm, hire, procure.

rĕdintĕgro -are, to restore, renew, repair.

rĕdĭpiscor -i, dep. to get back.

rĕdĭtĭo -ōnis, f. going back, return.

rĕdĭtus -ūs, m. going back, return; in gratiam, reconciliation; of money, etc., returns, income, revenue.

rĕdĭvĭa = reduvia; q.v.

rĕdĭvīvus -a -um, renewed, renovated; n. as subst., old building materials used again.

rĕdŏlĕo -ēre -ŭi, to emit an odour, smell of.

rĕdŏmĭtus -a -um, tamed again.

rĕdŏno -are, to give back; to give up.

rĕdūco -dūcĕre -duxi -ductum, to draw backwards, bring back, lead home; also to bring to a state or condition. Hence partic. **rĕductus** -a -um, drawn back; withdrawn, retired, remote, sequestered.

rĕductĭo -ōnis, f. bringing back, restoration.

rĕductor -ōris, one who brings back.

rĕduncus -a -um, bent back, curved.

rĕdundantĭa -ae, f. overflowing; redundancy.

rĕdundo -are, to overflow, stream over; to be in excess, be copious, diffuse, to abound in (with abl.); to be left over, overflow, spread.

prōpulso -are, *to drive back, repel, ward off.*

prŏ-quaestōre, *an ex-quaestor who helped to govern a province.*

prōquam (or **prō quam**), *in proportion as, according as.*

prōra -ae, f. *the prow, bow of a ship;* poet., *a ship.*

prōrēpo -rēpĕre -repsi, *to creep forward, crawl forth.*

prōrēta -ae, and **prōrēus** -i, m. *a look-out man.*

prōrĭpĭo -rĭpĕre -rĭpŭi -reptum, *to snatch, tear, drag forth;* se proripere, *to rush forward.*

prōrŏgātĭo -ōnis, f. *prolongation of a term of office; deferring.*

prōrŏgo -are, *to prolong; to defer, put off.*

prorsum and **prorsŭs**, *forwards, straight ahead.* Transf., *utterly, wholly; in a word, to sum up.*

prorsus (**prōsus**) -a -um, *straight-forward;* of style, *in prose.*

prōrumpo -rumpĕre -rūpi -ruptum: transit., *to cause to break out, to thrust out;* prorupta audacia, *unbridled;* intransit., *to burst forth, break out.*

prōrŭo -rŭĕre -rŭi -rŭtum: intransit., *to rush forth, to fall down;* transit., *to fling forward or down, overthrow, destroy.*

prōsāpĭa -ae, f. *family, race, stock.*

proscaenĭum -i, n. *the stage of a theatre.*

proscindo -scindĕre -scĭdi -scissum, *to tear up; to break up fallow land, plough up.* Transf., *to censure, defame, satirize.*

proscrībo -scrībĕre -scripsi -scriptum, *to make publicly known, publish; to offer publicly for sale or hire, advertise; to confiscate; to proscribe, outlaw.*

proscriptĭo -ōnis, f. *an advertisement of sale; a proscription, outlawry.*

proscriptŭrĭo -ire, *to desire a proscription.*

prōsĕco -sĕcare -sĕcŭi -sectum, *to cut off; to plough up.* N. of partic. as subst. **prōsectum** -i, *part of a victim cut out to be offered to a god; the entrails.*

prōsēda -ae, f. *a prostitute.*

prōsēmĭno -are, *to sow or scatter as seed; to disseminate.*

prōsĕquor -sĕqui -sĕcūtus, dep. *to follow or accompany out, to 'see off';* in hostile sense, *to attack, pursue;* in gen., *to attend; to go on with, continue; to imitate.*

Prŏserpĭna -ae, f. *the daughter of Ceres, carried off by Pluto to the lower world.*

prōseucha -ae, f. *a (Jewish) house of prayer, a conventicle.*

prōsĭlĭo -ire -ŭi (-ĭvi or -ĭi), *to spring up, leap forth.*

prōsŏcer -ĕri, m. *a wife's grandfather.*

prospecto -are, *to look forward, look out upon, survey; to look forward to, expect.*

prospectus -ūs, m. *outlook, view, prospect; sight, gaze.*

prospĕcŭlor -ari, dep. intransit., *to explore, reconnoitre;* transit., *to look out for, wait for.*

prosper (**prospĕrus**) -a -um, *fortunate favourable, lucky, prosperous;* n. pl. as subst. *prosperity, good fortune.* Adv. **prospĕrē.**

prospĕrĭtās -ātis, f. *prosperity, good fortune.*

prospĕro -are, *to make fortunate, cause to succeed.*

prospĕrus = prosper; q.v.

prospĭcĭentĭa -ae, f. *foresight, precaution.*

prospĭcĭo -spĭcĕre -spexi -spectum: intransit., *to look forward, look out; to take care, exercise foresight;* transit., *to see ahead, make out in the distance; to look towards; to foresee; to look out for, provide, procure.*

prosterno -sternĕre -strāvi -strātum, *to cast down; to debase; to overthrow, destroy, ruin.*

prostĭtŭo -stĭtŭĕre -stĭtŭtum, *to prostitute.*

prosto -stare -stĭti, *to stand out, project; to be exposed for sale; to prostitute oneself.*

prōsŭbĭgŏ -ĕre, *to dig up, root up.*

prōsum prōdesse prōfŭi, *to be useful, do good, benefit* (with dat.).

prōtĕgo -tĕgĕre -texi -tectum, *to cover in front; to cover over, protect; to furnish with a roof.*

prōtēlum -i, n. *a team of oxen; a series, succession.*

prōtendo -tendĕre -tendi -tentum, *to stretch forward, stretch out.*

prōtĕnus = protinus; q.v.

prōtĕro -tĕrĕre -trīvi -trītum, *to trample under foot, tread down; to overthrow, rout, defeat; to drive away, push aside.*

prōterrĕo -ĕre, *to scare away.*

prōtervĭtās -ātis, f. *boldness, impudence; pertness.*

prōtervus -a -um, *bold, impudent;* in milder sense, *pert;* of things, *violent.* Adv. **prōtervē.**

Prōtĕus -ĕi and -ĕos, m. *a god of the sea, with the power of changing himself into different shapes.*

prōtĭnam, *immediately, at once.*

prōtĭnus (**prōtĕnŭs**), adv. *forward, further on;* of time, *continuously or immediately.*

prōtollo -ĕre, *to put forward; to lengthen, prolong.*

prōtrăho -trăhĕre -traxi -tractum, *to draw, forward, drag out; to bring to light, reveal, make known; to compel, force; to protract, defer.*

prōtrūdo -trūdĕre -trūsi -trūsum, *to push forward, thrust out; to put off, defer.*

prōturbo -are, *to drive forward, drive away; to throw down, overcome.*

prŏūt, *just as, according as.*

prōvĕho -vĕhĕre -vexi -vectum, *to carry forward; to carry on; to advance, promote;* pass., provehi, *to ride forward, drive, sail, and* fig. *to be carried away.*

　Hence partic. **prōvectus** -a -um, *advanced, esp. in age.*

rĕdŭvĭa (rĕdīvĭa) -ae, f. *a hangnail, whitlow.*

rĕdux -dŭcis, adj.: act., *bringing back, restoring;* pass., *brought back, returned.*

rĕfectĭo -ōnis, f. *repairing, restoring.*

rĕfello -fellĕre -felli, *to refute, disprove.*

rĕfercĭo -fercire -fersi -fertum, *to stuff, to cram;* partic. **rĕfertus** -a -um, *stuffed, crammed, filled.*

rĕfērĭo -ire, *to strike back, strike again.* Transf., *to reflect.*

rĕfĕro rĕferre rettŭli rĕlātum. (1) *to carry back, bring back;* referre pedem, or se, or pass., referri, *to return, go back.* (2) *to bring again, restore, repeat; to echo; to reproduce, recall.* (3) *to say back, answer.* (4) *to bring as expected, pay up, deliver; to bring back a message, report; to refer a matter to authority; to enter in a record,* etc., *register, put down, enter; to assign to a cause.*

rĕfert -ēre, *to form anew.*, impers., *it matters, it concerns, it makes a difference;* meā, illorum refert, *it matters to me, to them.*

rĕfertus -a -um, partic. from refercio; q.v.

rĕfervĕo -ēre, *to boil over.*

rĕfervesco -ēre, *to boil up, bubble up.*

rĕfĭcĭo -fĭcĕre -fēci -fectum. (1) *to make again, restore, repair, re-establish, refresh, revive.* (2) *to get back, receive, get.*

rĕfīgo -fīgĕre -fixi -fixum, *to unfasten, demolish, remove;* of laws, *to repeal, abrogate.*

rĕfingo -ĕre, *to form anew.*

rĕflāgĭto -are, *to ask back, demand again.*

rĕflātŭ, abl. sing. m. *by a contrary wind.*

rĕflecto -flectĕre -flexi -flexum, *to bend back, turn back, divert;* intransit., *to yield, retreat.*

rĕflo -are: intransit., *to blow back, blow contrary;* transit., *to blow out.*

rĕflŭo -flŭĕre -fluxi -fluxum, *to flow back; to overflow.*

rĕflŭus -a -um, *flowing back.*

rĕformātŏr -ōris, m. *a reviver.*

rĕformīdātĭo -ōnis, f. *dread, terror.*

rĕformīdo -are, *to dread, fear, shun, avoid.*

rĕformo -are, *to form again, mould anew.*

rĕfŏvĕo -fŏvēre -fōvi -fōtum, *to warm again, revive, restore, refresh.*

refractārĭŏlus -a -um, *somewhat contentious, stubborn.*

refrāgor -ari, dep. *to oppose, withstand, thwart.*

refrēno -are, *to rein back, hold in, restrain, curb.*

refrīco -frĭcare -frĭcŭi -frĭcatum, *to rub again; to excite again, renew.*

refrīgĕrātĭo -ōnis, f. *cooling, coolness.*

refrīgĕro -are, *to cool off;* pass., refrigerari, *to cool oneself, grow cool, grow languid.*

refrīgesco -frĭgescĕre -frixi, *to grow cold, cool down; to flag, fail, grow stale.*

refringo -fringĕre -frēgi -fractum, *to break up, break open; to curb check.*

rĕfŭgĭo -fŭgĕre -fūgi: intransit., *to flee back, run away; to shrink;* of places, *to recede;* transit., *to fly from, avoid.*

rĕfŭgĭum -i, n. *refuge.*

rĕfŭgus -a -um, *fugitive, receding, recoiling.*

rĕfulgĕo -fulgēre -fulsi, *to gleam back, shine brightly, glitter.*

rĕfundo -fundĕre -fūdi -fūsum, *to pour back, to make overflow.*

rĕfūtātĭo -ōnis, f. *refutation.*

rĕfūtātŭ, abl. sing. m. *by refutation.*

rĕfūto -are, *to drive back, check, repress; to refute, disprove.*

rēgālis -e, *of a king, royal, regal;* adv. **rēgālĭtĕr**, *regally, tyrannically.*

rēgĕlo -are, *to thaw, warm.*

rēgĕro -gĕrĕre -gessi -gestum, *to carry back, throw back.*

rēgĭa; see regius.

rēgĭficus -a -um, *princely, splendid.*

rēgigno -ĕre, *to bring forth again.*

Rēgillus -i, m. *a lake in Latium, scene of a victory of the Romans over the Latins,* 496 B.C.

rēgĭmen -ĭnis, n. *control, guidance, rule, direction, government; a ruler, governor;* poet., *rudder.*

rēgīna -ae, f. *queen; princess; lady, mistress, sovereign.*

rēgĭo -ōnis, f. (1) *a direction, line;* esp. *a boundary line, boundary;* e regione, *in a straight line,* also *opposite, over against* (with genit. or dat.). (2) *a region, district, province.* Transf., *sphere, department.*

rēgĭōnātim, *according to districts.*

Rēgĭum (Rhēgĭum) -i, n. (1) *a town in Gallia Cispadana.* (2) *a town in Calabria.*

rēgĭus -a -um, *of a king, royal, regal; splendid, magnificent.* F. as subst. **rēgĭa** -ae, *palace, court, the royal family; capital city.* Adv. **rēgĭē**, *royally; tyrannically.*

regnātŏr -ōris, m. *ruler, king.*

regnātrix -trīcis, f. adj., *ruling.*

regno -are; intransit., *to be a king, reign; to be master, be a tyrant; to prevail;* transit., in pass., regnari, *to be ruled by a king.*

regnum -i, n. (1) *royal power, monarchy, supremacy; tyranny.* (2) *a realm, kingdom, estate.*

rēgo rĕgĕre rexi rectum, *to guide, direct, to rule, govern, administer.* Hence partic. **rectus** -a -um, *ruled;* as adj. *straight; upright.* Transf., *right, correct, proper; honest, upright; natural, plain, straightforward;* n. as subst., *right.* Adv. **rectē**, *in a straight line; rightly, properly;* recte est, *all is well.*

regrĕdĭor -grĕdi -gressus, dep. *to step back, go back;* milit., *to retire, retreat.*

ꞌregressus -ūs, m. *a going back, return; retreat; refuge, recourse.*

rēgŭla -ae, f. *a ruler, a plank.* Transf., *a rule, pattern, model.*

ꞌrēgŭlus -i, m. *a petty king,* or *king's son, prince.*

²**Rĕgŭlus,** *a surname in the* gens Atilia.

rĕgusto -are, *to taste again or repeatedly.*

rĕĭcĭo -icĕre -iēci -iectum, *to throw back, throw behind, throw away; to drive off;* of a storm, *to drive back, cast up.* Transf., *to throw off, reject; to refer;* in time, *to put off;* legal, *to challenge* a juror.

rĕĭectĭo -ōnis, f. *throwing back, rejection;* legal, *the challenging of a juror.*

rĕĭecto -are, *to throw back.*

rēlābor -lābi -lapsus, dep. *to glide back, fall back.*

rĕlanguesco -languescĕre -langŭi, *to become faint; to slacken.*

rĕlātĭo -ōnis, f. *carrying back, bringing back;* polit., *a report;* gram., *repetition.*

rĕlātor -ōris, m. *one who makes a report.*

rĕlātus -ūs, m. *a narrative; a report.*

rĕlaxātĭo -ōnis, f. *relaxation, easing.*

rĕlaxo -are, *to loosen, enlarge; to ease, lighten, relax.*

rĕlēgātĭo -ōnis, f. *banishment.*

¹**rĕlēgo** -are, *to send away; to put aside, reject; to banish.*

²**rĕlĕgo** -lĕgĕre -lēgi -lectum, *to gather up again;* of places, *to pass again;* of topics, *to go over again.*

rĕlentesco -ĕre, *to become languid again.*

rĕlĕvo -are, *to lift again; to lighten; to relieve, alleviate.*

rĕlictĭo -ōnis, f. *leaving, deserting.*

rĕlĭcŭos and **rĕlĭcus** = reliquus; q.v.

rĕlĭgātĭo -ōnis, f. *tying up.*

rĕlĭgĭo (rellĭgĭo) -ōnis, f. of persons, *scrupulousness, conscientious exactness;* esp. *religious scruple, awe, superstition, strict observance;* in gen., *moral scruples, conscientiousness;* of gods, etc., *sanctity; an object of worship, holy thing* or *place.*

rĕlĭgĭōsus (rellĭgĭōsus) -a -um, of persons, *scrupulous, conscientious; holy, strict, superstitious;* of actions, either *required* or *forbidden by religion;* of gods, etc., *holy, sacred.* Adv. **rĕlĭgĭōsē,** *conscientiously, scrupulously; religiously.*

rĕlĭgo -are, *to tie on, fasten behind.*

rĕlĭno -lĭnĕre -lēvi -lĭtum, *to unseal.*

rĕlinquo -linquĕre -līqui -lictum, *to leave behind;* at death, *to bequeath; to leave unchanged;* pass., *to remain; to omit, leave out, pass over; to desert, abandon, forsake.*

rĕlĭquĭae (rellĭquĭae) -ārum, f. pl. *remains, relics, remnant.*

rĕlĭquus (rĕlĭcus) -a -um, *left behind, remaining, other;* of a debt, *outstanding;* of time, *remaining, future.* N. as subst., sing. and plur., *the rest; the remainder;* in reliquum, *for the future.*

relli-; see **reli-.**

rĕlūcĕo -lūcēre -luxi, *to glitter.*

rĕlūcesco -lūcēscĕre -luxi, *to become bright again.*

rĕluctor -ari, dep. *to struggle against, resist.*

rĕmănĕo -mănēre -mansi -mansum, *to remain behind, stay, continue.*

rĕmāno -are, *to flow back.*

rĕmansĭo -ōnis, f. *remaining in a place.*

rĕmĕdĭum -i, n. *means of healing, cure, remedy, medicine.*

rĕmĕo -are, *to go back, return.*

rĕmētĭor -mētiri -mensus, dep. *to measure again, go back over;* perf. partic. sometimes pass. in meaning.

rēmex -mĭgis, m. *a rower.*

rēmĭgātĭo -ōnis, f. *rowing.*

rēmĭgĭum -i, n. *rowing.* Transf. *oars; crew.*

rēmĭgo -are, *to row.*

rēmĭgro -are, *to wander back, come back, return.*

rĕmĭniscor -i, dep. *to call to mind, recollect, remember.*

rĕmiscĕo -miscēre -mixtum, *to mix up, mingle.*

rĕmissĭo -ōnis, f. *letting go back, letting fall, lowering; breaking off, interrupting; remitting;* animi, *relaxation, quiet.*

rĕmitto -mittĕre -misi -missum. (**1**) *to send back, send again; throw back; echo.* (**2**) *to let go back, relax, loosen; to relieve, abate;* with infin., *to give up doing;* intransit., *to ease off.* (**3**) *to give up, yield; abandon, sacrifice; to forgive* an offence, *remit* punishment.

Hence partic. **rĕmissus** -a -um, *relaxed, mild, gentle;* in bad sense, *negligent, remiss.* Adv. **rĕmissē.**

rĕmōlĭor -iri, dep. *to push back.*

rĕmollesco -ĕre, *to become soft again.*

rĕmollĭo -ire, *to make soft again, to weaken.*

rĕmŏra -ae, f. *delay, hindrance.*

rĕmŏrāmen -ĭnis, n. *delay.*

rĕmordĕo -mordēre -morsum. *to worry, harass.*

rĕmŏror -ari, dep.: intransit., *to remain behind, linger, loiter;* transit., *to obstruct, hinder.*

rĕmōtĭo -ōnis, f. *putting away, removing.*

rĕmŏvĕo -mŏvēre -mōvi -mōtum. *to move back, withdraw.*

Hence partic. **rĕmōtus** -a -um, *removed, withdrawn, distant, far off, remote;* adv. **rĕmōtē,** *far off, at a distance.*

rĕmūgĭo -ire, *to bellow again, bellow back.*

rĕmulcĕo -mulcēre -mulsi *to stroke back.*

rĕmulcum -i, n. *a tow-rope.*

rĕmūnĕrātĭo -ōnis, f. *a recompense, return.*

rĕmūnĕror -ari, dep. *to repay, reward.*

rĕmurmŭro -are, *to murmur back.*

¹**Rēmus** -i, m. *an oar.*

²**Rēmus** -i, m. *twin brother of Romulus.*

rēnarro -are, *to relate again.*

rēnascor -nasci -nātus, dep. *to be born again, grow again.*

rēnāvĭgo -are, *to sail back.*

rĕnĕo -nēre, *to unravel.*

rēnes -um, m. pl. *the kidneys.*

rĕnīdĕo -ēre, *to shine back, glitter; to beam with joy, laugh, smile.*

rĕnītor -i, dep. *to oppose, withstand, resist.*

¹**rĕno** -nare, *to swim back.*

²rēno (rhēno) -onis, m. *a garment made of fur.*

rēnōdo -are, *to tie back.*

rēnōvāmen -ĭnis, n. *renewal.*

rēnŏvātĭo -ōnis, f. *renewal, renovation;* renovatio singulorum annorum, *compound interest.*

rēnŏvo -are, *to renew, restore, repair; to repeat.*

rēnŭmĕro -are, *to count over again; to pay back.*

rēnuntĭātĭo -ōnis, f. *a formal report, public announcement.*

rēnuntĭo -are. (1) *to bring back word, report, announce.* (2) *to disclaim, refuse, renounce.*

rēnŭo -nŭĕre -nŭi, *to deny, refuse, reject.*

rēnŭto -are, *to refuse, decline.*

rĕor rēri rătus, dep. *to think suppose, judge;* partic., in pass. sense, **rătus** -a -um, *determined, settled;* ratum facere, *to ratify, confirm, make valid;* pro rata, *in proportion.*

rĕpāgŭla -orum, n. pl. *bars or bolts; restraints, limits.*

rĕpandus -a -um, *bent backwards, turned up.*

rĕpārābĭlis -e, *that can be restored.*

rĕparco = reperco; q.v.

rĕpăro -are, *to restore, renew, make good; to get in exchange, purchase.*

rĕpastĭnātĭo -ōnis, f. *digging up again.*

rĕpecto -pectĕre -pexum, *to comb back.*

rĕpello rĕpellĕre reppŭli, rĕpulsum, *to drive back, drive away; to banish, repel;* a spe, *to disappoint;* criminationes, *to refute.*

rĕpendo -pendĕre -pendi -pensum, *to weigh back again; to ransom; to repay, requite.*

rĕpens -entis, *sudden, unexpected; fresh, recent.* Adv. **rĕpentĕ,** *suddenly, unexpectedly.*

rĕpentīnus -a -um, *sudden, unexpected;* n. abl. as adv. **rĕpentīnō,** *suddenly.*

rĕperco (rĕparco) -percĕre -persi or -pĕperci, *to spare, be sparing, abstain.*

rĕpercussus -ūs, m. *reverberation; echo, reflection.*

rĕpercŭtĭo -cŭtĕre -cussi -cussum, *to strike back, make rebound;* perf. partic. **rĕpercussus** -a -um, *rebounding, reflected.*

rĕpĕrĭo rĕpĕrīre reppĕri rĕpertum, *to get again; to find, discover, ascertain, invent.*

rĕpertor -ōris, m. *discoverer, inventor.*

rĕpĕtentĭa -ae, f. *recollection, remembrance.*

rĕpĕtītĭo -ōnis, f. *repetition.*

rĕpĕtītor -ōris, m. *one who demands back.*

rĕpĕto -ĕre -īvi *and* -ĭi -ītum, *to seek again, go back for or to; to ask back;* res repetere, *to demand satisfaction;* (pecuniae) repetundae, *money claimed back, as having been extorted; to return to, renew, begin again; to trace back, deduce; to recollect, recall.*

rĕpĕtundae: see repeto.

rĕplĕo -plēre -plēvi -plētum, *to fill again, fill up; to make full, fill, satisfy.* Hence partic. **replētus** -a -um, *filled, full.*

rĕplĭcātĭo -ōnis, f. *rolling again, folding round.*

rĕplĭco -are, *to unroll; to turn over, review.*

rēpo rēpĕre repsi reptum, *to creep, crawl.*

rĕpōno -pōnĕre -pŏsŭi -pŏsĭtum, *to lay back; to put aside, lay up, deposit, store; mentally, to reckon, place; to replace, restore; to replace by a substitute; to requite.*

rĕporto -are, *to bring back, carry back;* of reports, *to deliver.*

rĕposco -ĕre, *to ask back again; to demand as a right, claim.*

rĕpostor -ōris, m. *a restorer.*

rĕpōtĭa -ōrum, n. *an after-party, second entertainment.*

repraesentātĭo -ōnis, f. (1) *vivid presentation, lively description.* (2) *payment in cash.*

repraesento -are, *to bring back, reproduce; to perform immediately, hasten on;* pecuniam, *to pay cash.*

rĕprĕhendo -prĕhendĕre -prĕhendi -prĕhensum, *and* **reprendo** -prendĕre -prendi -prensum, *to catch, hold fast, detain, check; to blame, reprove; to refute.*

rĕprĕhensĭo -ōnis, f. *stopping, check; blame, censure; refutation.*

rĕprĕhenso -are, *to hold back, hold fast.*

rĕprĕhensor -ōris, m. *a censurer, reprover; an improver, reformer.*

repressor -ōris, m. *a restrainer.*

rĕprimo -primĕre -pressi -pressum, *to hold back, restrain, hinder, repress.*

rĕprōmissĭo -ōnis, f. *a counterpromise.*

rĕprōmitto -mittĕre -mīsi -missum, *to promise in return.*

repto -are, *to creep, crawl along.*

rĕpŭdĭātĭo -ōnis, f. *refusal, rejection.*

rĕpŭdĭo -are, *to refuse, reject, disdain; to divorce.*

rĕpŭdĭum -i, n. *divorce.*

rĕpŭĕrasco -ĕre, *to become a boy again, to frolic.*

rĕpugnantĭa -ae, f. *incompatibility.*

rĕpugno -are *to fight against, oppose, resist; to be opposed, repugnant, inconsistent, incompatible.* Hence partic. **rĕpugnans,** *contrary, opposed;* n. pl. as subst. *contradictions;* adv. **rĕpugnantĕr,** *unwillingly.*

rĕpulsa -ae, f. *repulse, rejection; denial, refusal.*

rĕpulsans -antis, partic., *beating back;* colles verba repulsantes, *echoing.*

repulsū, abl. sing. m. *by striking back, by reflection, by echoing.*

rĕpungo -ĕre, *to prick again.*

rĕpurgo -are, *to clean again; to purge away.*

rĕpŭtātĭo -ōnis, f. *re-appraisal.*

rĕpŭto -are. (1) *to reckon back, count, compute.* (2) *to think over, reconsider.*

rĕquĭes -ētis, f. *rest, repose.*

rĕquĭesco -quĭescĕre -quĭēvi -quĭētum, *to rest, repose*; pass. partic. **rĕquĭētus** -a -um, *rested, refreshed*; *ager, fallow.*

rĕquīro -quīrĕre -quīsĭi *and* -quīsīvi -quisitum, *to ask for, look for, enquire after; to demand, desire; to miss, feel the want of.*

rēs rēi, f. *a thing, object, matter, affair, circumstance*; natura rerum, *the world, the universe, nature*; pro re, *according to circumstance*; esp. *the real thing, fact, truth, reality*; rē verā, *in truth*; *possessions, property, wealth; interest, advantage, benefit*; in rem, *to one's advantage; cause, ground, reason*; qua re, quam ob rem, *wherefore; a matter of business; a law-suit, action*; res publica or respublica, *the republic, state, commonwealth*; e republicā, *in the public interest.*

rĕsacro = resecro; q.v.

rĕsaevio -ire, *to rage again.*

rĕsălūto -are, *to salute back, greet in return.*

rĕsānesco -sānescĕre -sānŭi, *to become sound again.*

rĕsarcio -sarcire -sartum, *to patch up, mend, repair, restore.*

rescindo -scindĕre -scĭdi -scissum, *to tear back, cut away, break open*; vulnus, *to reopen*; *of laws, etc., to rescind, repeal.*

rescisco -sciscĕre -scīvi *and* -scĭi -scītum, *to find out, ascertain.*

rescrībo -scrībĕre -scripsi -scriptum, *to write again, rewrite; to enrol again, transfer; to write back, answer in writing; in book-keeping, to pay, repay.*

rĕsĕco -sĕcare -sĕcŭi -sectum, *to cut back, cut short.*

rĕsēmino -are, *to produce again.*

rĕsĕquor -sĕqui -sĕcūtus, dep. *to follow again*; dictis, *to answer.*

rĕsĕro -are, *to unbolt, open up, disclose, reveal.*

rĕservo -are, *to lay up, keep back, reserve; to save, preserve, keep.*

rĕsĕs -sĭdis, *sitting; inactive, calm, quiet.*

rĕsĭdĕo -sĭdĕre -sēdi -sessum, *to remain sitting, stay, rest.*

rĕsīdo -sĭdĕre -sēdi, *to sit down, settle, sink, subside, abate.*

rĕsĭdŭus -a -um, *remaining, outstanding*; pecuniae, *arrears.*

rĕsigno -are, *to unseal, open, reveal; to cancel, annul; to transfer, give back, resign.*

rĕsĭlio -silire -sĭlŭi -sultum, *to leap back, rebound; to shrink, contract.*

rĕsīmus -a -um, *bent backwards, turned up.*

rēsīna -ae, f. *resin.*

rĕsĭpĭo -sipere, *to have a flavour of anything.*

rĕsĭpisco -sĭpiscĕre -sĭpĭi, also -sĭpīvi, *to recover one's senses; to become rational again.*

rĕsisto -sistĕre -stĭti. (1) *to stay, still, stop, continue; to recover one's footing.* (2) *to resist, oppose, withstand*; usually with dat.

rēsolvo -solvĕre -solvi -sŏlūtum, *to untie, loosen, open; to melt; to dissipate; to dispel; to release; to reveal; to weaken.*

rĕsŏnābĭlis -e, *resounding.*

rĕsŏno -are; intransit., *to resound, echo*; transit., *to make resound.*

rĕsŏnus -a -um, *resounding, echoing.*

rĕsorbĕo -ēre, *to swallow again, suck back.*

respecto -are, *to look eagerly back (at); to have a regard for, give thought to.*

respectus -ūs, m. *looking back*; hence *care, regard, consideration; looking around one*; meton., *refuge, retreat.*

respergo -spergĕre -spersi -spersum, *to sprinkle, splash.*

respersio -ōnis, f. *sprinkling.*

respĭcĭo -spĭcĕre -spexi -spectum, *to look behind, look back (at); to look back upon; to look to, provide for; to look to, depend upon; to have a regard for, care for, consider.*

respīrāmen -ĭnis, n. *windpipe.*

respīrātĭo -ōnis, f. *taking breath, respiration; exhalation.*

respīrātus -ū, m. *taking breath.*

respīro -are. (1) *to breathe back, blow in a contrary direction.* (2) *to breathe again, to take breath; to recover from fear, etc.; of things, to abate, decline.*

resplendĕo -ēre, *to glitter back, gleam again.*

respondĕo -spondĕre -spondi -sponsum: intransit., *to match, correspond to, answer to; to resemble; legal, to answer to one's name, appear, be present*; transit., *to give an answer to person or thing, to answer, reply.* N. of partic. as subst. **responsum** -i, *an answer, reply*; *a lawyer's opinion.*

responsĭo -ōnis, f. *a reply, answer.*

responsito -are, *to keep giving an answer or opinion.*

responso -are, *to keep answering; to re-echo*; with dat., *to defy, withstand.*

responsum -i, n. subst. from respondeo; q.v.

respublica; see res.

respŭo -spŭĕre -spŭi, *to spit out, reject, refuse, repel.*

restagno -are, *to overflow, be swamped.*

restauro -are, *to restore, rebuild.*

resticŭla -ae, f. *a thin rope.*

restinctĭo -ōnis, f. *slaking, quenching.*

restinguo -stinguĕre -stinxi -stinctum, *to put out again, extinguish, quench, slake, destroy.*

restĭo -ōnis, m. *a rope-maker.*

restĭpŭlātĭo -ōnis, f. *a counter-engagement.*

restĭpŭlor -ari, dep. *to obtain a promise in return.*

restis -is, *a rope, cord.*

restĭto -are, *to remain behind, linger.*

restĭtŭo -ŭĕre -ŭi -ūtum, *to put back, replace, restore; to reinstate, re-establish; to repair, make good.*

restĭtūtĭo -ōnis, f. *restoration, reinstatement.*

restĭtūtor -ōris, m. *restorer.*

resto -stare -stĭti. (1) *to make a stand, resist, oppose.* (2) *to stand still, stay behind; to be left over, survive; to remain available* or *possible;* of the future, *to await, be in store.*

restringo -stringĕre -strinxi -strictum, *to bind back, draw back; to confine, restrict, restrain.*
Hence partic. **restrictus** -a -um, *close, tight; stingy; strict, severe.*
Adv. **restrictē,** *sparingly; strictly.*

rĕsulto -are *to spring back, rebound; to echo, resound;* of style, *to go jerkily.*

rĕsūmo -sūmĕre -sumpsi -sumptum, *to take again, resume; to renew, repeat.*

rĕsŭpĭno -are, *to throw down, prostrate.*

rĕsŭpīnus -a -um, *bent backwards, on one's back;* also *with head thrown back.*

rĕsurgo -surgĕre -surrexi -surrectum, *to rise up again, appear again.*

rĕsuscĭto -are, *to revive, resuscitate.*

rĕtardātĭo -ōnis, f. *hindering.*

rĕtardo -are, *to slow down, retard, impede.*

rētē -is, n. *a net.*

rĕtĕgo -tĕgĕre -texi -tectum, *to uncover, reveal, open, disclose.*

rĕtempto -are, *to attempt again.*

rĕtendo -tendĕre -tendi -tensum *and* -tentum, *to slacken, unbend.*

rĕtentĭo -ōnis, f. *keeping back; withholding.*

[1]**rĕtento** -are, *to hold firmly; to preserve maintain.*

[2]**rĕtento** = retempto; q.v.

rĕtentus -a -um, partic. from retendo or from retineo; q.v.

rĕtexo -texĕre -texŭi -textum, *to unravel, undo, reverse; to cancel, annul; to retract; to revise.*

rētĭārĭus -i, m. *a gladiator using a net.*

rĕtĭcentĭa -ae, f. *keeping silent.*

rĕtĭcĕo -ēre: intransit., *to keep silence, say nothing:* transit., *to keep silent about.*

rētĭcŭlum -i, n. *a little net; a net-bag; a hair-net.*

rĕtĭnācŭla -ōrum, n. pl. *a rope, cable.*

rĕtĭnentĭa -ae, f. *recollection.*

rĕtĭnĕo -tĭnēre -tĭnŭi -tentum, *to hold back, detain; to restrain; to keep, reserve, maintain.*
Hence partic. **rĕtĭnens** -entis, *tenacious.*

rĕtinnĭo -ire, *to resound, ring again.*

rĕtōno -are, *to thunder back, resound.*

rĕtorquĕo -torquēre -torsi -tortum, *to twist back, bend back.*

rĕtractātĭo -ōnis, f. (1) *refusal, denial.* (2) *reconsideration.*

retracto (retrecto) -are. (1) *to handle again, undertake anew, reconsider.* (2) *to draw back, refuse, be reluctant; dicta, to withdraw.*

retrăho -trăhĕre -traxi -tractum, *to draw back; to hold back, withdraw; to draw on again, induce.*
Hence partic. **retractus** -a -um, *withdrawn; distant, remote.*

retrĭbŭo -trĭbŭĕre -trĭbŭi -trĭbūtum, *to give again* or *give as due.*

retrō, *backwards, back, behind.*

retrŏăgo -ăgĕre -ēgi -actum, *to drive back, reverse.*

retrorsum, *backwards, behind, in return, in reversed order.*

retrūdo -trūdĕre -trūsum, *to push back;* perf. partic. retrūsus, *remote, obscure.*

rĕtundo rĕtundĕre rĕtŭdi (rettŭdi) rĕtūsum (rĕtunsum), *to hammer back, blunt, dull; to check* or *weaken;* partic. **rĕtūsus (rĕtunsus)** -a -um, *dull, blunt.*

rĕus -i, m. and **rĕa** -ae, f. *a party in a law-suit, whether plaintiff* or *defendant;* esp. *a defendant, accused person;* in gen., *one bound* or *answerable.*

rĕvălesco -vălescĕre -vălŭi, *to become well again, be restored, recover.*

rĕvĕho -vĕhĕre -vexi -vectum, *to carry back;* pass., *to drive back, ride back, sail back.*

rĕvello -vellĕre -velli -vulsum, *to tear back, pull away; to remove, banish.*

rĕvēlo -are, *to unveil, lay bare.*

rĕvĕnĭo -vĕnire -vēni -ventum, *to come back, return.*

rĕvērā, adv. from res; q.v.

rĕvĕrentĭa -ae, f. *respect, fear, awe.*

rĕvĕrĕor -vĕrēri -vĕrĭtus, dep. *to revere, respect, fear;* partic. **rĕvĕrens** -entis, *respectful, reverent;* adv. **rĕvĕrenter;** gerundive, **rĕvĕrendus** -a -um, *awesome, venerable.*

rĕversĭo (rĕvorsĭo) -ōnis, f. *turning back, return, recurrence.*

rĕverto (rĕvorto) -vertĕre -verti, and pass. **rĕvertor (rĕvortor)** *to return, come back, revert.*

rĕvincĭo -vincire -vinxi -vinctum, *to tie back, bind fast.*

rĕvinco -vincĕre -vīci -victum, *to beat back, subdue; to refute.*

rĕvĭresco -virescĕre -virŭi, *to grow green* or *strong again; to revive.*

rĕvīso -ĕre: intransit., *to pay a fresh visit, return;* transit., *to come to see again, revisit.*

rĕvīvisco -vīviscĕre -vixi, *to come to life again, revive.*

rĕvŏcābĭlis -e, *able to be called back.*

rĕvŏcāmen -ĭnis, n. *calling back, recall.*

rĕvŏcātĭo -ōnis, f. *calling back; withdrawing, revocation.*

rĕvŏco -are, *to call again* or *back; to recall; to bring* or *get back, recover; to refer;* to revoke.

rĕvŏlo -are, *to fly back.*

rĕvŏlūbĭlis -e, *able to be rolled back.*

rĕvolvo -volvĕre -volvi -vŏlūtum, *to roll backwards;* esp. *to unroll* or *open a book;* hence *to go over again;* pass., *to roll back, come round again in due course.*

rĕvŏmo -vŏmĕre -vŏmŭi, *to vomit up, disgorge.*

rĕvor-; see rever-.

rex, rēgis, m. *ruler, king, prince, chief; monarch, tyrant.*

Rhădămanthus -i, m. *brother of Minos, a judge in the lower world.*

¹Rhĕa (Rēa) Silvĭa, *mother of Romulus and Remus.*

²Rhĕa -ae, f. *old name of Cybele.*

rhēda = raeda; q.v.

Rhēnus -i, m. *the Rhine.*

rhētor -ōris, m. *a teacher of rhetoric, a rhetorician.*

rhētŏrĭcus -a -um, *rhetorical*; subst., f. **rhētŏrĭca** -ae and **rhētŏrĭcē** -ēs, *the art of oratory*; m. pl. **rhētŏrĭci** -ōrum, *teachers of rhetoric*; adv. **rhētŏrĭcē**, *rhetorically.*

rhīnŏcĕrōs -ōtis, m. *a rhinoceros.*

rhō, n. indecl. *the Greek name of the letter R.*

Rhŏdănus -i, m. *the Rhone.*

Rhŏdus (-ŏs) -i, f. *Rhodes*; adj. **Rhŏdĭus** -a -um, and **Rhŏdĭensis** -e.

rhombus (-ŏs) -i, m. (1) *a magician's circle.* (2) *the turbot.*

rhomphaea (rumpĭa) -ae, f. *a long javelin.*

rhythmĭcus -i, m. *one who teaches rhythm.*

rhythmus (-ŏs) -i, m. *rhythm, time, harmony.*

rhýtĭum -i, n. *a drinking-horn*

rīca -ae, f. *a veil.*

rīcĭnum -i, n. *a small veil.*

rictus -ūs, m. and **rictum** -ī, n. *the open mouth.*

rĭdĕo rĭdēre risi rīsum: intransit., *to laugh, smile, look cheerful*; with dat., *to please*; transit., *to laugh at.*

rĭdĭcŭlārĭus and **rĭdĭcŭlōsus** -a -um, *laughable, droll.*

rĭdĭcŭlus, *exciting laughter; droll, humorous; absurd, ridiculous*; m. as subst., *a joker, jester*; n., *a joke, jest.* Adv. **rĭdĭcŭlē**, *humorously; absurdly.*

rĭgĕo -ēre, *to be stiff* (esp. with cold); *of hair, to stand on end*; partic. **rĭgens** -entis, *stiff.*

rĭgesco rĭgescēre rĭgŭi, *to grow stiff; of hair, to stand on end.*

rĭgĭdus -a -um, *stiff, unbending, hard; stern, inflexible.* Adv. **rĭgĭdē.**

rĭgo -are, *to lead or conduct water; to wet, moisten, bedew.*

rĭgor -ōris, m. *stiffness, hardness*, esp. *from cold.* Transf., *sternness.*

rĭgŭus -a -um; act., *watering*; pass., *well-watered, irrigated.*

rīma -ae, f. *a crack, fissure, leak.*

rīmor -ari, dep. *to cleave; to probe, pry into, examine.*

rīmōsus -a -um, *full of cracks, leaky.*

ringor -i, dep. *to show the teeth; to snarl, be angry.*

rīpa -ae, f. *bank, shore.*

rīpŭla -ae, f. *a little bank.*

riscus -i, m. *a box, trunk.*

rīsĭo -ōnis, f. *laughter.*

rīsor -ōris, m. *a laugher, mocker.*

rīsus -ūs, m. *laughing, laughter; ridicule; an object of laughter.*

rītĕ, *in due form, with proper ceremonies, properly, fitly, rightly.*

rītus -ūs, m. *usage, ceremony, rite*; abl., ritu, with genit., *after the manner of.*

rīvālis -is, m. *a rival in love.*

rīvālĭtās -ātis, f. *rivalry* (in love).

rīvŭlus -i, m. *small brook, rivulet.*

rīvus -i, m. *stream.*

rixa -ae, f. *quarrel, brawl, contention.*

rixor -ari, dep. *to quarrel brawl contend.*

rōbīgīnōsus -a -um, *rusty.*

rōbīgo (rūbīgo) -inis, f. *rust; blight, mildew; inaction, mental rust.* Personif. **Rōbīgo (Rūb-)** -inis, f. or **Rōbigus (Rūb-)** -i, m. *a deity invoked to preserve grain from mildew;* **Rōbīgālĭa** -ĭum, n. *the festival of Robigo.*

rōbŏrĕus -a -um, *oaken.*

rōbŏro -are, *to strengthen, make firm.*

rōbur -ōris, n. *hard wood; esp., oak, oak-wood; a dungeon at Rome, also called the Tullianum; as a quality, hardness, strength; in gen., the pick flower, of anything.*

rōbustus -a -um, *of hard wood; esp. of oak, oaken; strong, powerful, firm.*

rōdo rōdĕre rōsi rōsum, *to gnaw, nibble at; to corrode, consume; to disparage, backbite, slander.*

rŏgālis -e *of the funeral pile.*

rŏgātĭo -ōnis, f. *asking; a question; a request; a proposed law, a bill.*

rŏgātĭuncŭla -ae, f. *a minor question or bill.*

rŏgātor -ōris, m. *one who asks; the proposer of a bill; a polling-clerk.*

rŏgātū, abl. sing. m. *at the request.*

rŏgito -are, *to ask eagerly.*

rŏgo -are, *to ask, inquire; to ask for, request;* polit., rogare aliquem sententiam, *to ask a person his opinion*; rogare populum or legem, *to propose a law, introduce a bill*; rogare magistratum, *to offer a person for election.*

rŏgus -i, m. *funeral pile.*

Rōma -ae, f. *Rome*; adj. **Rōmānus** -a -um.

Rōmŭlus -i, m. *son of Mars, founder and first king of Rome*; adj. **Rōmŭlĕus** and **Rōmŭlus** -a -um.

rōrārii -ōrum, m. pl. *light-armed troops skirmishers.*

rōrĭdus -a -um, *bedewed.*

rōrĭfer -fēra -fērum, *dew-bringing.*

rōro -are: intransit., *to drop dew, drip, be moist*; transit., *to bedew, moisten, water; to drip, let fall in drops.*

rōs rōris, m. *dew, moisture*; ros marinus, rosmarinus, *rosemary.*

rōsa -ae, f. *a rose; a garland of roses; a rose-tree.*

rŏsārĭus -a -um, *of roses*; n. as subst. *a rose-garden.*

rŏscĭdus -a -um, *bedewed, dewy; dripping like dew; moistened.*

Roscius -a -um, *name of a Roman gens.*

rŏsētum -i, n. *a garden of roses.*

rŏsĕus -a -um, *of roses; rose-coloured, rosy.*

rosmărīnus; see ros.

rostrātus -a -um, *having a beak, beaked curved*; columna rostrata, *a pillar in the forum, adorned with ships' prows.*

rostrum -i, n. *beak, snout; a ship's prow*; plur. **rostra** -ōrum, *the speaker's platform in the Forum* (ornamented with prows of ships).

rŏta -ae, f. *a wheel*; poet., *a chariot.*

rŏto -are, *to whirl round, swing, brandish*; pass. rotari, *to revolve, to roll round.*

rŏtundo -are, *to round, make round.*

rŏtundus -a -um, *round circular*; sometimes *spherical; rounded, complete, self-contained.* Adv. **rŏtundē,** of style, *elegantly, smoothly.*

rŭběfacio -făcěre -fēci -factum, *to redden, make red.*

rŭbellus -a -um, *reddish.*

rŭběo -ēre, *to be red; to blush*; partic. **rŭbens** -entis, *red, blushing.*

rŭber -bra -brum, *red, ruddy.*

rŭbesco -bescěre -bŭi, *to become red.*

¹rŭbēta -ae, f. *a species of toad.*

²rŭbēta -ōrum, n. pl. *bramble-thickets.*

rŭběus -a -um, *of bramble.*

Rŭbico -ōnis, m. *a river, once the boundary between Italia and Gallia Cisalpina.*

rŭbĭcundus -a -um, *red, ruddy.*

rŭbīgo = robigo; q.v.

rŭbor -ōris, m. *redness; a blush; modesty; shame, disgrace.*

rubrīca -ae, f. *red earth; red ochre; a law with its title written in red.*

rŭbus -i, m. *a bramble-bush; a blackberry.*

ructo -are, and **ructor** -ari, dep. *to belch.*

ructus -ūs, m. *belching.*

rŭdens -entis, m. *a rope, halyard.*

rŭdīmentum -i, n. *a trial, attempt, essay.*

¹rŭdis -e, *rough, raw, uncultivated; unrefined, unskilled, awkward.*

²rŭdis -is, f. *a small stick; a foil (given to gladiators on their discharge).*

rŭdo rŭděre rŭdīvi rŭdītum, *to bellow, roar.*

¹rŭdus (rōdus) -ěris, n. *broken fragments of stone.*

²rŭdus = raudus; q.v.

rūfus -a -um, *red, ruddy.*

rūga -ae, f. *a wrinkle.*

rūgōsus -a -um, *wrinkled.*

rŭina -ae, f. *falling down, collapse, ruin, destruction; the ruins of a building, debris.*

rŭinōsus -a -um, *going to ruin.*

rūmex -īcis, f. *sorrel.*

Rūmīna -ae, f. *a Roman goddess*; **Rūmīnālis ficus,** m. *a fig-tree under which the she-wolf had suckled Romulus and Remus.*

rūmĭnātĭo -ōnis, f. *chewing the cud; ruminating.*

rūmĭno -are, *to chew the cud, ruminate.*

rūmor -ōris, m. *report, rumour, common talk, hearsay; general opinion, popular judgment.*

rumpo rumpěre rūpi ruptum, *to break, shatter, burst open; to cause to break forth; to destroy, violate, annul; to break off, interrupt.*

rūmuscŭlus -i, m. *trifling rumour, idle talk, gossip.*

rūna -ae, f. *a dart.*

runco -are, *to weed, thin out.*

rŭo rŭěre rŭi rŭtum; fut. partic. **rŭĭtūrus;** intransit., *to rush down, fall,*

collapse, be ruined; to rush along; to be precipitate; transit., *to hurl down;* also *to cast up.*

rūpēs -is, f. *rock, cliff.*

ruptor -ōris, m. *breaker, violator.*

rūrĭcŏla -ae, *inhabiting* or *cultivating the country.*

rūrĭgěna -ae, m. *one born in the country, a rustic.*

rūro -are and **rūror** -ari, dep. *to live in the country.*

rursus and **rursum,** *backward, back; on the other hand, in return; again, afresh.*

rūs rūris, n. *the country, a country-seat, farm, estate*; acc., rus, *to the country;* locative, ruri (or rure), *in the country.*

russus -a -um, *red, russet.*

rustĭcānus -a -um, *of the country, rustic.*

rustĭcātĭo -ōnis, f. *living in the country.*

rustĭcĭtās -ātis, f. *rustic manners, rusticity.*

rustĭcor -ari, dep. *to live in the country.*

rustĭcŭlus -a -um, *countrified*; m. as subst., *a rustic.*

rustĭcus -a -um, *of the country, rural, rustic; plain, simple; awkward, boorish*; m. as subst. *a countryman, a boor.* Adv. **rustĭcē.**

rūta -ae, *the herb rue; bitterness, unpleasantness.*

rŭtĭlo -are: intransit., *to shine reddish;* transit., *to make red.*

rŭtĭlus -a -um, *red, golden, auburn.*

rutrum -i, n. *a spade, shovel.*

rŭtŭla -ae, f. *a little bit of rue.*

Rŭtŭli -ōrum, m. pl. *an ancient people of Latium.*

S

S, s, the eighteenth letter of the Latin alphabet.

Săba -ae, f. *a town in Arabia, famous for perfumes.*

sabbăta -ōrum, n. pl. *the Sabbath, the Jewish day of rest.*

Săbelli -ōrum, m. *poetic name of the Sabines.*

Săbīni -orum, m. pl. *an ancient people of Italy, northerly neighbours of the Latins.*

săbŭlum -i, n. *gravel, sand.*

săburra -ae, f. *sand used as ballast.*

sacco -are, *to strain* or *filter.*

saccŭlus -i, m. *a small bag.*

saccus -i, m. *a sack, bag*; esp. *a purse.*

săcellum -i, n. *a small shrine, chapel.*

săcer -cra -crum, *sacred, holy, consecrated;* in bad sense, *accursed, devoted to destruction, horrible.* N. sing. as subst. **sacrum** -i, *a holy thing* or *place; a sacrifice* or *victim;* n. pl. *sacred rites, worship.*

săcerdōs -dōtis, c. *a priest, priestess.*

săcerdōtālis -e, *priestly.*

săcerdōtĭum -i, n. *priesthood.*

săcrāmentum -i, n.: legal, *money deposited by the parties in a suit; hence a civil suit, legal process;* milit., *oath of allegiance;* hence *an oath* or *solemn promise.*

sacrārĭum -i, n. (1) *a place where sacred things are kept, sacristy.* (2) *a place of worship, chapel, shrine.*

sacrĭcŏla -ae, c. *a sacrificing priest or priestess.*

sacrĭfer -fĕra -fĕrum, *carrying sacred things.*

sacrĭfĭcālis -e, *of sacrifices.*

sacrĭfĭcātĭo -ōnis, f. *sacrificing.*

sacrĭfĭcĭum -i, n. *sacrifice.*

sacrĭfĭco -are, *to sacrifice.*

sacrĭfĭcŭlus -i, m. *a sacrificing priest.*

sacrĭfĭcus -a -um, *sacrificial, sacrificing.*

sacrĭlĕgĭum -i, n. *stealing of sacred things, sacrilege, profanation.*

sacrĭlĕgus -a -um, *stealing sacred things, sacrilegious, impious.*

sacro -are. (1) *to dedicate to a god, consecrate; to devote, allot; to doom, curse.* (2) *to make holy, make inviolable; to immortalize.*
Hence partic. sacrātus -a -um, *holy, consecrated.*

sacrōsanctus -a -um, *consecrated, holy, sacred, inviolable.*

sacrum; see sacer.

saecŭlāris -e, *relating to a saeculum or age;* ludi, *secular games* (celebrated at intervals of about 100 years).

saecŭlum (poet. saeclum) -i, n. *a generation; the spirit of the age, the times; a hundred years, a century, an age.*

saepĕ, *often, frequently;* saepĕnŭmĕrō, *repeatedly, again and again.*

saepes (sēpes) -is, f. *hedge, fence.*

saepīmentum -i, n. *hedge, enclosure.*

saepĭo saepire saepsi saeptum, *to hedge in, enclose, surround, confine;* n. *of partic. as subst.* saeptum -i, *barrier, wall, enclosure;* in plur., *the enclosure where the Romans voted at the comitia.*

saeta -ae, f. *a bristle, stiff hair; part of an angler's line.*

saetĭger -gĕra -gĕrum, *having bristles, bristly;* m. *as subst. a boar.*

saetōsus -a -um, *bristly.*

saevĭdĭcus -a -um, *angrily spoken.*

saevĭo -ire -ĭi -ītum, *to rage, be furious, take violent action.*

saevĭtĭa -ae, f. *rage, ferocity.*

saevus -a -um, *raging, fierce, furious, violent, savage, cruel;* adv. saevē and saevĭtĕr.

săga -ae, f., *a prophetess, fortune-teller.*

săgācĭtās -ātis, f. *keenness, acuteness, shrewdness.*

săgātus -a -um, *clothed in a sagum;* q.v.

săgax -ācis, *keen, acute;* esp. *keen-scented; mentally acute, shrewd, clever.* Adv. săgācĭtĕr.

săgīna -ae, f. *fattening, cramming; food, nourishment.*

săgīno -are, *to fatten, cram.*

săgitta -ae, f. *arrow.*

săgittārĭus -a -um, *of an arrow;* m. *as subst. an archer.*

săgittĭfer -fĕra -fĕrum, *carrying arrows.*

săgitto -are, *to shoot arrows.*

sagmen -ĭnis, n. *a bunch of sacred herbs.*

săgŭlum -i, n. *a small military cloak.*

săgum -i, n. *a cloak of coarse wool, as worn by servants, and esp. by soldiers,* saga sumere, *to take up arms, prepare for war.*

Săguntum -i, n. and Săguntus (-ŏs) -i, f. *a town on the coast of Spain.*

săl, sălis, m. *salt; brine, sea-water;* fig., sing. and plur., *wit.*

sălăco -ōnis, m. *a swaggerer, braggart.*

Sălămis -minis, f. (1) *an island in the Saronic Gulf.* (2) *a town in Cyprus.*

sălăpūtĭum -i, n. *a little man, manikin.*

sălārĭus -a -um, *of salt;* n. *as subst. salt money, an allowance, pay.*

sălax -ācis, *lustful, lecherous.*

sălebra -ae, f. *jolting; a rough patch of road;* of style, *ruggedness.*

sălebrōsus -a -um, *rugged, rough.*

Sălĭātus -ūs, m. *the office of a priest of Mars;* see Salii.

sălictum -i, n. *a plantation of willows.*

sălignus -a -um, *of willow-wood.*

Sălĭi -ōrum, m. *a college of 12 priests of Mars Gradivus;* adj. Sălĭāris -e, *relating to the Salii; splendid, magnificent.*

sălillum -i, n. *a little salt-cellar.*

sălīnae -arum, f. *salt-works, brine-pits.*

sălīnum -i, n. *a salt-cellar.*

sălĭo sălire sălŭi saltum, *to spring, leap, bound;* f. pl. *of partic. as subst.* sălĭentēs -ium, *fountains.*

sălĭunca -ae, f. *wild nard.*

sălīva -ae, f. *spittle, saliva; appetite, taste.*

sălix -ĭcis, f. *a willow.*

Sallustĭus -i, m.: C. Sallustius Crispus, *the Roman historian Sallust, contemporary of Cicero.*

salpa -ae, f. *a kind of stock-fish.*

salsāmentum -i, n. *fish-pickle, brine; salted or pickled fish.*

salsūra -ae, f. *salting, pickling.*

salsus -a -um, *salted, salty;* hence *sharp, biting, witty;* adv. salsē.

saltātĭo -ōnis, f. *a dancing, dance.*

saltātor -ōris, m. *a dancer.*

saltātōrĭus -a -um, *of dancing.*

saltātrix -trīcis, f. *a dancing-girl.*

saltātus -ūs, m. *a dancing, dance.*

saltem, *at least, at all events.*

salto -are, *to dance, esp. with gesticulation;* with acc., *to represent in pantomime, to sing with gestures.*

saltŭōsus -a -um, *wooded.*

¹saltus -ūs, m. *a spring, leap, bound.*

²saltus -ūs, m. *a forest or mountain pasture; a pass, dale, ravine, glade.*

sălūbris and sălūber -bris -bre, *healthful, healthy, wholesome; sound, useful; healthy, vigorous.* Adv. sălūbrĭtĕr, *wholesomely, advantageously.*

sălūbrĭtās -ātis, f. *wholesomeness; soundness, health.*

sălum -i, n. *the open sea.*

sălūs -ūtis, f. *health, soundness; safety, welfare, well-being, salvation; a wish for a person's welfare, salutation, greeting.*

sălūtāris -e, *healthful, wholesome, advantageous*; n. pl. as subst. *remedies, medicines.* Adv. **sălūtārĭtĕr.**

sălūtātĭo -ōnis, f. *greeting, salutation; a call, ceremonial visit*; concr., *visitors.*

sălūtātŏr -ōris, m. *a visitor, caller.*

sălūtātrix -trīcis, f. adj. *greeting, paying a visit.*

sălūtĭfer -fĕra -fĕrum, *health-bringing.*

sălūto -are, *to wish well, greet, call upon, pay respect to, reverence.*

salvĕo -ēre, *to be well, be in good health;* salve, salvete, as a greeting, *Good day! Good morning!,* used also in bidding farewell.

salvus -a -um, *safe, unhurt, well, all right;* salvo iure, *without infraction of law.* Adv. **salvē.**

sambūca -ae, f. *a species of harp.*

sambūcistrĭa -ae, f. *a female harpist.*

Samnĭum -i, n. *a region of central Italy*; adj. and subst. **Samnīs** -ītis, *Samnite, a Samnite.*

Sămŏs (**-ŭs**) -i, f. *an island in the Aegean Sea*; adj. **Sămĭus** -a -um.

Sămŏthrācē -ēs, **Sămothrāca** -ae, and **Sămŏthrācĭa** -ae, f. *Samothrace, an island in the northern Aegean.*

sānābĭlis -e, *curable.*

sānātĭo -ōnis, f. *healing, curing.*

sancĭo sancire sanxi sanctum (sancītum), *to consecrate, hallow, make inviolable, confirm, ratify, decree;* also *to forbid on pain of punishment, provide against.* Hence partic. **sanctus** -a -um. *consecrated, holy, sacred; pure, virtuous.* Adv. **sanctē,** *solemnly, conscientiously.*

sanctĭmōnĭa -ae, f. *sanctity, sacredness; purity, chastity, virtue.*

sanctĭo -ōnis, f. *a clause in a law defining a penalty.*

sanctĭtās -ātis, f. *inviolability, sanctity; purity, chastity.*

sanctĭtūdo -ĭnis, f., *sanctity.*

sanctŏr -ōris, m., *an enacter.*

sanctus -a -um, partic. from sancio; q.v.

sandālĭum -i, n. *a slipper, sandal.*

sandāpĭla -ae, f. *a bier used for poor people.*

sandyx -dȳcis, f. *vermilion.*

sanguĭnans -antis, *bloodthirsty.*

sanguĭnārĭus -a -um, *of blood; blood-thirsty, savage.*

sanguĭnĕus -a -um, *of blood, bloody; blood-red.*

sanguĭnŏlentus -a -um, *stained with blood, bloody; wounding, injuring; blood-red.*

sanguis -ĭnis, m. (and **sanguen,** n.) blood. Transf. *blood-relationship, race, family, progeny; life-blood, strength, vigour.*

sănĭēs -ēi, f. *corrupted blood, matter; slaver, venom, poison.*

sānĭtās -ātis, f. *health, soundness; good sense, sanity;* of style, *correctness, purity.*

sanna -ae, f. *a mocking grimace.*

sannĭo -ōnis, m. *a buffoon.*

sāno -are, *to heal, cure, restore, repair.*

sānus -a, -um, *sound, healthy, uninjured; of sound mind, rational, sane;* of style, *correct.* Hence adv. **sanē,** *rationally, sensibly.* Transf., *really, indeed, to be sure;* with imperatives, *then, if you will;* sane quam, *exceedingly, extremely.*

săpa -ae, f. *must or new wine.*

săpĭentĭa -ae, f. *wisdom, good sense, discernment;* esp. *proficiency in philosophy, science,* etc.

săpĭo săpĕre săpīvi or săpĭi. (1) *to taste;* with acc., *to taste of* or *smell of.* (2) *to have taste, be able to taste.* (3) mentally, *to discern, be sensible, be wise, think.* Hence partic. **săpĭens** -entis, *wise, sensible, judicious;* as subst., *a sensible, judicious person;* also *wise man, philosopher, sage.* Adv. **săpĭentĕr.**

săpor -ōris, m. *taste, flavour, flavouring; sense of taste; taste in style* or *conduct.*

Sapphō -ūs, f. *a lyric poetess of Mytilene in Lesbos.*

sarcĭna -ae, f. *a bundle, pack, burden, load.*

sarcĭnārĭus -a -um, *of burdens* or *baggage.*

sarcĭnātŏr -ōris, m. *cobbler.*

sarcĭnŭla -ae, f. *a little bundle.*

sarcĭo sarcire sarsi sartum, *to mend, patch, repair, make good.* Hence partic. **sartus** -a -um; sartus (et) tectus, *in good condition, well-preserved.*

sarcŏphăgus -i, m. *coffin, grave.*

sarcŭlum -i, n. *a light hoe.*

Sardēs (**Sardis**) -ĭum, f. pl. *Sardis, the old capital of Lydia;* adj. **Sardĭānus** -a -um.

Sardi -ōrum, m. *the Sardinians;* adj. **Sardus, Sardōnĭus, Sardōus** -a -um, *Sardinian;* subst. **Sardīnĭa** ae, f. *Sardinia.*

sardŏnyx -nȳchis, m. and f. *a precious stone, sardonyx.*

sargus -i, m. *a salt-water fish, the sargue.*

sărīsa -ae, f. *the long Macedonian pike.*

sărīsŏphŏrus -i, m. *a Macedonian pikeman.*

Sarmăta -ae, m. *a Sarmatian;* subst. **Sarmătĭa** -ae, f. *Sarmatia;* adj. **Sarmătĭcus** -a -um, *Sarmatic;* adv. **Sarmătĭcē;** f. adj. **Sarmătĭs** -ĭdis.

sarmentum -i, n. *twigs, brushwood.*

sarrācum -i, n. = serracum; q.v.

sarrĭo (**sărĭo**) -ire -ŭi and -ĭvi, *to hoe, weed.*

sartāgo -ĭnis, f. *frying-pan.*

sartus -a -um, partic. from sarcio; q.v.

săt, sătăgĭto, sătăgo; see satis.

sătellĕs -ĭtis, c. *a guard, attendant; an accomplice;* plur., *escort, suite, train.*

sătĭās -ātis, f. *sufficiency, abundance; satiety.*

sătĭĕtās -ātis, f. *sufficiency, abundance; satiety.*

sătĭnĕ, sătĭn = satisne; see satis.

¹**sătĭo** -are, *to satisfy, fill; to cloy, satiate.*

²**sătĭo** -ōnis, f. *a sowing* or *planting;* in plur. *sown fields.*

sătĭra; see satur.

sătĭs or **săt**, *enough, sufficient; as adv., enough, sufficiently, fairly, quite*; compar. **sătĭus**, *better, more advantageous*; **sătĭnē**, **sătĭn** = satisne, *introducing questions*; **sătĭs** (or **săt**) **ăgo** or **sătăgo** -ăgĕre, *to satisfy or pay a creditor; to have enough to do, have one's hands full*; **sătĭs do** dare, *to give bail or security*; **sătĭs accĭpĭo** accĭpĕre, *to take bail or security*; **sătĭs făcĭo** or **sătĭsfăcĭo** -făcĕre, *to give satisfaction, satisfy, pay up, make amends*; *also to prove sufficiently.*

sătĭsdătĭo -ōnis, f. *a giving bail or security.*

sătĭsfactĭo -ōnis, f. *amends, reparation, apology.*

sătĭus, compar. of satis; q.v.

sător -ōris, m. *a sower, planter, begetter, father, producer.*

sătrăpes -is; plur. satrapae -arum; m., *the governor of a Persian province, viceroy.*

sătur -ūra -ŭrum, *full, sated, rich, copious.* F. as subst. **sătŭra** -ae, *a dish of various ingredients, a medley*; per saturam, *indiscriminately*; **sătŭra** (or **sătĭra**), '*satire*', *as a literary form.*

sătŭrēia -ae, f., plur. **sătŭrēia** -ōrum, n.; *the herb savory.*

sătŭrĭtās -ātis, f. *satiety, abundance.*

Sāturnālĭa, etc.; see Saturnus.

Sāturnus -i, m. (1) *the planet Saturn.* (2) *a mythical king of Latium.* Hence adj. **Sāturnĭus** -a -um, and **Sāturnālĭs** -e; n. pl. as subst. **Sāturnālĭa** -ĭum and -ĭorum, *a festival of Saturn beginning on the 17th of December.*

sătŭro -are, *to satisfy, fill.*

¹sătus -a -um, partic. from sero; q.v.

²sătus -ūs, m. *sowing, planting; begetting, origin.*

sătўrus -i, m. *a satyr.* Transf., *Greek Satyric drama.*

saucĭātĭo -ōnis, f. *wounding.*

saucĭo -are, *to wound, hurt.*

saucĭus -a -um, *wounded, hurt, stricken, distressed.*

sāvĭor -ari, dep. *to kiss.*

sāvĭum (suāvĭum) -i, n. *a kiss.*

saxētum -i, n. *a rocky place.*

saxĕus -a -um, *of rock, stony.*

saxĭficus -a -um, *petrifying.*

saxōsus -a -um, *full of rocks, rocky.*

saxŭlum -i, n. *a little rock.*

saxum -i, n. *a rock, stone; esp. the Tarpeian rock.*

scăbellum (scăbillum) -i, n. *footstool; a musical instrument played with the foot.*

scăber -bra -brum, *scabby; rough.*

scăbĭes -ēi, f. *scab, mange, itch; roughness; itching desire.*

scăbĭōsus -a -um, *scabby; rough.*

scăbo scăbĕre scăbi, *to scratch.*

scaena (scēna) -ae, f. *stage, scene, theatre; natural background; publicity, the public eye.*

scaenālĭs -e, *theatrical.*

scaenĭcus -a -um, *of the stage, theatrical*; m. as subst. *a stage-hero, an actor.*

Scaevŏla -ae, m. *the left-handed, a surname of the gens Mucia.*

scaevus -a -um, *left, on the left.* Transf., *awkward.*

scālae -arum, f. pl. *a flight of stairs, ladder*; milit., *scaling-ladders.*

scalmus -i, m. *a thole-pin, rowlock.*

scalpellum -i, n. *a lancet, scalpel.*

scalpo scalpĕre scalpsi scalptum, *to carve, scrape, scratch.*

scalprum -i, n. *a chisel; a penknife.*

scammōnĕa (-mōnĭa) -ae, f. *the plant scammony.*

scamnum -i, n. *a bench, stool.*

scando scandĕre scandi scansum, *to climb, mount, rise.*

scăpha -ae, f. *a small boat, skiff.*

scăphĭum -i, n. *a pot, bowl, drinking-vessel.*

scăpŭlae -ārum, f. pl. *the shoulder-blades; the shoulders, back.*

scăpus -i, m. *a weaver's beam, or perhaps leash-rod.*

scărus -i, m. *a salt-water fish; perhaps parrot-fish.*

scătebra -ae, f. *a spouting up, bubbling up.*

scătĕo -ēre and **scăto** -ĕre, *to gush, spout up; to teem, abound.*

scăturrīgo -gĭnis, f. *a bubbling spring.*

scăturrĭo -ire, *to gush, bubble over.*

scaurus -a -um, *with swollen ankles.*

scazŏn -ontis, m. *an iambic trimeter with a spondee or trochee in the last foot.*

scĕlĕro -are, *to pollute with guilt.* Partic. **scĕlĕrātus** -a -um, *polluted with guilt; impious, wicked; tiresome, noxious*; adv. **scĕlĕrātē**, *impiously, wickedly.*

scĕlĕrōsus -a -um, *guilty, wicked.*

scĕlestus -a -um, *guilty, wicked, accursed*; adv. **scĕlestē**.

scĕlus -ĕris, n. *a crime.* Transf., *misfortune, calamity.* As a term of abuse, *scoundrel, rascal.*

scēn-; see scaen-.

sceptrĭfer -fĕra -fĕrum, *sceptre-bearing.*

sceptrum -i, n. *a sceptre*; poet., *dominion, kingdom.*

sceptūchus -i, m. *wand-bearer, a court official.*

schĕda and **scĭda** -ae, f. *a strip of papyrus bark; a leaf of paper.*

schēma -ae, f. and -ătis, n. *shape, figure, form.*

schoenŏbătēs -ae, m. *a rope-walker.*

schŏla -ae, f. *learned leisure; conversation, debate; a lecture, dissertation; a school; a sect.*

schŏlasticus -a -um, *of a school; esp. rhetorical*; m. as subst. *a student or teacher of rhetoric.*

scĭda = schida; q.v.

scĭentĭa -ae, f. *knowing, knowledge, acquaintance, skill.*

scīlĭcĕt, *evidently, certainly, of course; ironically, no doubt; in answers, certainly; explanatory, namely.*

scilla (squilla) -ae, f. *a sea-leek, squill; a crayfish or prawn.*

scīn = scisne; see scio.

scindo scindĕre scīdi scissum, *to cut,
rend, split; to divide, separate.* Partic.
scissus -a -um, *torn, rent;* of the
voice, *harsh.*

scintilla -ae, f. *a spark; a glimmer.*

scintillo -are, *to sparkle, glitter.*

scintillŭla -ae, f. *a little spark.*

scio scire scivi or scii scitum, *to know,
understand;* with infin., *to know how
to;* with adv., scire Graece, *to understand Greek.*
   Hence partic. **sciens** -entis, *knowing, aware; understanding; versed in,
acquainted with* (with genit.); adv.
scientĕr; for **scitus** -a -um, see
scisco.

¹scīpĭo -ōnis, m. *a staff, wand.*

²Scīpĭo -ōnis, m. *a family of the gens
Cornelia;* **Scīpĭădēs** -ae, *one of the
family of the Scipios, a Scipio.*

scirpĕus (sirpĕus) -a -um, *of rushes;*
f. as subst. *basket-work.*

scirpĭcŭlus (sirpĭcŭlus) -a -um, *of
rushes;* m. and f. as subst. *a rush-
basket.*

scirpus (sirpus) -i, m. *a rush, bulrush.*

sciscĭtor -ari, dep. and **sciscĭto** -are,
to inquire, examine, interrogate.

scisco sciscĕre scivi scitum, *to investigate, inquire;* polit. *to vote, ordain,
resolve.*
   Hence partic. **scitus** -a -um,
*knowing, shrewd, judicious; pretty,
fine;* adv. **scitē,** *skilfully;* n. of
partic. as subst., *a decree, statute;*
plebis scitum, *a decree of the people of
Rome.*

scissus -a -um, partic. from scindo;
q.v.

scītor -ari, dep., *to seek to know, inquire,
ask.*

scītū, abl. sing. m. *by a decree.*

scītus -a -um, partic. from scisco;
q.v.

sciūrus -i, m. *a squirrel.*

scŏbis -is, f. *filings, chips, shavings,
sawdust.*

scomber -bri, m. *a mackerel.*

scōpae -ārum, f. pl. *a besom, broom.*

scōpŭlōsus -a -um, *rocky, craggy.*

scŏpŭlus -i, m. *a rock, crag, cliff,
danger, ruin.*

scorpĭo -ōnis, and **scorpĭus** (-ŏs) -i,
m. *a scorpion;* milit., *an engine for
throwing missiles;* a *salt-water fish,
perhaps the sculpin.*

scortēus -a -um, *leathern, made of
leather;* f. as subst. *a leathern garment.*

scortor -ari, dep. *to whore, go with
harlots.*

scortum -i, n. *a harlot, prostitute.*

scrĕo -are, *to clear the throat, hawk,
hem.*

scrība -ae, m. *a clerk, secretary, notary.*

scrĭblīta -ae, f. *a kind of pastry.*

scrībo scrībĕre scripsi scriptum, *to
engrave, draw lines, write, write on,
write about;* polit., *to draw up laws,
etc.;* legal, dicam scribere, *to bring an
action;* with double acc., *to appoint in
writing;* milit., *to enrol.* N. of partic.

as subst. **scriptum** -i *a mark or line;
a composition, piece of writing;* esp.
a decree, law.

scrīnĭum -i, n. *a case for books or
papers.*

scriptĭo -ōnis, f. *the act of writing;
authorship, composition; wording.*

scriptĭto -are, *to write often.*

scriptor -ōris, m. *a scribe, clerk, secretary; a writer, author, composer.*

scriptŭla -ōrum, n. *the lines on a draught-
board.*

scriptum -i, n., subst. from scribo;
q.v.

scriptūra -ae, f. *a piece of writing,
composition; a testamentary disposition; a rent paid on public pastures.*

scrīpŭlum (scrūpŭlum, scriptŭlum)
-i, m. *a small weight or measure.*

scrŏbis -is, c. *a ditch; a grave.*

scrōfa -ae, f. *a breeding sow.*

scrūpĕus and **scrūpōsus** -a -um, *of
sharp stones, rugged, rough.*

scrūpŭlōsus -a -um, *full of stones, rough,
rugged.* Transf., *exact, scrupulous,
precise.*

scrūpŭlum = scripulum; q.v.

scrūpŭlus -i, m. *a small stone.* Transf.,
an anxiety, doubt, scruple.

scrūpus -i, m. *a sharp stone.* Transf.,
a worry, anxiety.

scrūta -ōrum, n. pl. *frippery, trash.*

scrūtor -ari, dep. *to search through,
investigate, examine.*

sculpo sculpĕre sculpsi sculptum, *to
carve, cut, chisel.*

sculptĭlis -e, *carved.*

sculptor -ōris, m. *sculptor.*

scurra -ae, m. *a dandy, man-about-
town; a jester, buffoon.*

scurrīlis -e, *like a buffoon; mocking,
jeering.*

scurrīlĭtās -ātis, f. *buffoonery.*

scurror -ari, dep. *to play the buffoon.*

scŭtāle -is, n. *the thong of a sling.*

scŭtātus -a -um, *armed with a shield.*

scŭtella -ae, f. *a flat dish, saucer.*

scŭtĭca -ae, f. *a whip.*

¹scŭtŭla -ae, f. *a little square-shaped
dish.*

²scŭtŭla -ae, f. *a roller, cylinder.*

scŭtŭlāta -ōrum, n. pl. *checked cloths,
checks.*

scŭtŭlum -i, n. *a little shield.*

scūtum -i, n. *a large quadrangular
shield.*

Scylla -ae, f. *a rock at the straits between
Sicily and Italy, opposite to Charybdis;*
adj. **Scyllaeus** -a -um.

scymnus -i, m. *cub, whelp.*

scўphus -i, m. *a drinking-cup, goblet.*

scўtāla -ae and **scўtălē** ēs, f. = scutula;
q.v.

Scўthēs (Scўthă) -ae, m. *a Scythian;*
Scўthia -ae, f. *Scythia.*

sē or **sēsē,** acc. sing. and plur.; **suī,**
genit.; **sĭbī,** dat.; **se** or **sēsē,** abl.;
strengthened forms, **sēpse, sēmet;**
reflexive pronoun of third person,
himself, herself, itself, themselves; sibi
velle, *to mean;* secum = cum se;
inter se, *reciprocally.*

sēbum -i, n. *tallow, fat.*

sēcēdo -cēdĕre -cessi -cessum, *to go apart, withdraw.*

sēcerno -cernĕre -crēvi -crētum, *to separate, part, sunder; to distinguish; to set aside, reject.* Hence partic. **sēcrētus** -a -um, *separate, alone, special; retired, solitary; hidden, secret;* with abl., *deprived of.* N. as subst. **sēcrētum** -i, *retirement, solitude; a secret, mystery.* Abl. as adv. **sēcrētō**, *apart, separately.*

sēcessĭo -ōnis, f. *a going apart, withdrawal, secession.*

sēcessus -ūs, m. *a going apart, withdrawal, retirement; a retreat, recess.*

sēcĭus; see secus.

sēclūdo -clūdĕre -clūsi -clūsum, *to shut off; to confine, to separate from others.*

sēco sĕcare sĕcŭi sectum, *to cut, amputate, to wound, hurt; to divide, part;* hence *to settle disputes; to cut out, make by cutting.*

sēcrētus -a -um, partic. from secerno; q.v.

secta -ae, f. *a way, mode of life, procedure; a school of thought.*

sēctātor -ōris, m. *a follower, hanger-on;* plur., *train, retinue.*

sectĭlis -e, *cut; able to be cut.*

sectĭo -ōnis, f. *cutting.* Transf., *the buying up of state property;* concr., *auctioned property, a lot.*

¹sector -ōris, m. *a cutter.* Transf., *a buyer of state property.*

²sector -ari, dep. *to follow eagerly; to accompany, attend;* of enemies, *to run after, chase;* in gen., *to strive after, try to get or find.*

sectūra -ae, f. *cutting;* aerariae secturae, *copper-mines.*

sēcŭbĭtus -ūs, m. *lying alone.*

sēcŭbo -are, -ui, *to sleep alone.*

sēcŭl-; see saecul-.

sēcum = cum se; see se.

sēcundāni -ōrum, m. pl. *soldiers of the second legion.*

sēcundārĭus -a -um, *second-rate.*

sēcundo -are, *to favour, assist.*

sēcundum: adv., *after, behind;* prep., with acc., *following, after, along beside; during; in addition to; next after, next to; according to; in favour of.*

sēcundus -a -um. (1) *going after, second, following; inferior, second-rate.* (2) *going the same way, attending, favouring;* secundo flumine, *downstream;* res secundae, *prosperity, success.* As subst.: n. abl. sing. **sēcundō**, *secondly;* f. pl. **sēcundae** -ārum, *the second role, second fiddle;* n. pl. **sēcundā** -ōrum, *prosperity, success.*

sēcŭrĭfer -fĕra -fĕrum, and **sēcŭrĭger** -gĕra -gĕrum, *carrying an axe.*

sēcŭris -is, f. *an axe, hatchet;* esp. *the headsman's axe;* hence *supreme power, Roman supremacy.*

sēcūrĭtās -ātis, f. *freedom from care; peace of mind, composure; careless-*

ness, false confidence. Transf., *freedom from danger, security.*

sēcūrus -a -um, *free from care, unconcerned, fearless, tranquil; careless;* objectively, *safe, secure.* Adv. **sēcūrē.**

¹sēcŭs, n. indecl., *sex.*

²sēcŭs, adv. *otherwise, not so;* foll. by atque (ac), or quam, *otherwise than, differently from;* non secus, haud secus, *just so.* Transf., *not as one would wish,* i.e. *wrongly, badly.* Compar. **sĕquĭus** or **sētĭus**, *otherwise, not so; less; rather badly.*

sēcūtor -ōris, m. *a gladiator armed with sword and shield.*

sĕd (sĕt), *but, however;* sed enim, *but in fact;* confirming, *and indeed, and what is more.*

sēdātĭo -ōnis, f. *allaying, soothing.*

sēdĕcim, *sixteen.*

sēdēcŭla -ae, f. *a low seat, stool.*

sĕdĕo sĕdēre sēdi sessum, *to sit; to sit in council or judgment; to sit about, be inactive;* milit. *to remain encamped;* of things, *to be settled, stay fixed;* of resolves, *to be firmly determined.*

sēdēs -is, f. *a seat; a chair, throne; an abode, home;* of things, *place, seat, base, foundation.*

sēdīle -is, n. *a seat, bench.*

sēdītĭo -ōnis, f. *insurrection, rising, mutiny; dissension, quarrel.*

sēdītĭōsus -a -um, *quarrelsome, turbulent, restless;* adv. **sēdītĭōsē.**

sēdo -are, *to settle, soothe, calm, allay;* partic. **sēdātus** -a -um, *calm, composed;* adv. **sēdātē.**

sēdūco -dūcĕre -duxi -ductum, *to lead apart, turn aside, separate;* partic. **sēductus** -a -um, *remote, distant.*

sēductĭo -ōnis, f. *leading aside.*

sēdŭlĭtās -ātis, f. *zeal, application.*

sēdŭlus -a -um, *busy, diligent;* in bad sense, *officious.* N. abl. as adv. **sēdŭlō**, *busily; purposely, designedly.*

sĕgĕs -ĕtis, f. *a cornfield; standing corn, a crop;* in gen., *field, ground, soil; source, origin; profit.*

segmentātus -a -um, *adorned with borders or patches.*

segmentum -i, n. *a cutting, shred;* plur., *borders or patches of purple or gold.*

segnĭpēs -pēdis, *slow-footed.*

segnis -e, *slow, tardy, sluggish, lingering.* N. acc. as adv. **segnĕ**, and adv. **segnĭtĕr**, *slowly, sluggishly.*

segnĭtĭa -ae, and **segnĭtĭēs** -ēi, f. *sluggishness, slowness.*

segrĕgo -are, *to segregate, separate, remove.*

sēiŭgātus -a -um, *separated.*

sēiŭgis -is, m. *a chariot drawn by six horses.*

sēiunctim, *separately.*

sēiunctĭo -ōnis, f. *separation.*

sēiungo -iungĕre -iunxi -iunctum, *to separate, sever, disjoin.*

sēlectĭo -ōnis, f. *choosing out, selection.*

Sēleucus -i, m. *name of several kings of Syria.*

sēlībra -ae, f. *half a pound.*

sēlīgo -līgĕre -lēgi -lectum, *to choose, select.*

sella -ae, f. *a seat, chair, stool;* sella (curulis), *a magistrate's seat;* sella (gestatoria), *a sedan-chair.*

sellisternĭa -ōrum, n. pl. *religious banquets in honour of goddesses.*

sellŭla -ae, f. *a little chair.*

sellŭlārĭus -i, m. *a sedentary worker.*

sēmĕl, *once, a single time; for the first time; once for all;* indef., *once, ever, at any time.*

Sĕmĕla -ae, and **Sĕmĕlē** -ēs, f. *mother of Bacchus.*

sēmen -ĭnis, n. *seed; a seedling, scion, shoot; a stock, race; an element; a cause, origin; an author, instigator.*

sēmentĭfer -fēra -fērum, *seed-bearing, fruitful.*

sēmentis -is, *a sowing* or *planting;* plur., sementes, *young growing corn.*

sēmentīvus -a -um, *of seed-time.*

sēmestris (**sēmenstris**) -e, *of six months, lasting six months.*

sēmēsus -a -um, *half-eaten.*

sēmĭădāpertus -a -um, *half-open.*

sēmĭănĭmis -e and **sēmĭănĭmus** -a -um, *half-alive, half-dead.*

sēmĭăpertus -a -um, *half-open.*

sēmĭbōs -bŏvis, m. *half-ox.*

sēmĭcāper -pri, m. *half-goat.*

sēmĭcrĕmātus and **sēmĭcrĕmus** -a -um, *half-burnt.*

sēmĭcŭbĭtālis -e, *half a cubit long.*

sēmĭdĕus -a -um, *half-divine;* as subst., *a demigod.*

sēmĭdoctus -a -um, *half-taught.*

sēmĭermis (**sēmermis**) -e and **sēmĭermus** (**sēmermus**) -a -um, *half-armed, half-equipped.*

sēmĭēsus = semesus; q.v.

sēmĭfactus -a -um, *half-done, half-finished.*

sēmĭfer -fēra -fērum, *half-animal; half-savage.*

sēmĭgermānus -a -um, *half-German.*

sēmĭgrăvis -e, *half-overcome.*

sēmĭgro -are, *to go away, depart.*

sēmĭhĭans -antis, *half-open.*

sēmĭhŏmo -hŏmĭnis, m. *half-man; half-wild.*

sēmĭhora -ae, f. *half an hour.*

sēmĭlăcer -cēra -cērum, *half-mangled.*

sēmĭlĭber -bĕra -bĕrum, *half-free.*

sēmĭlixa -ae, m. *half a sutler.*

sēmĭmārīnus -a -um, *half in the sea.*

sēmĭmas -măris, m. *half-male, hermaphrodite; castrated.*

sēmĭnārĭum -i, n. *a plantation, nursery.*

sēmĭnātor -oris, m. *begetter, author.*

sēmĭnex -nĕcis, *half-dead.*

sēmĭnĭum -i, n. *a begetting; a race* or *breed.*

sēmĭno -are, *to sow, plant; to beget, produce.*

sēmĭnūdus -a -um, *half-naked; ill-protected.*

sēmĭplēnus -a -um, *half-full, half-manned.*

sēmĭpŭtātus -a -um, *half-pruned.*

sēmĭrēductus -a -um, *half bent back.*

sēmĭrĕfectus -a -um, *half-repaired.*

sēmĭrŭtus -a -um, *half-ruined, half pulled down.*

sēmis -issis, m. *the half of anything,* e.g. of an as or iuger; *as a rate of interest* = 6 *per cent per annum.*

sēmĭsĕpultus -a -um, *half-buried.*

sēmĭsomnus -a -um and **sēmĭsomnis** -e, *half-asleep, drowsy.*

sēmĭsŭpīnus -a -um, *half on the back.*

sēmīta -ae, f. *a narrow way, footpath.*

sēmĭtālis -e, and **sēmĭtārĭus** -a -um, *of the footpaths.*

sēmĭustŭlātus = semustulatus; q.v.

sēmĭustus (**sēmustus**) -a -um, *half-burnt.*

sēmĭvir -vĭri, m. adj., *half-man half-animal; hermaphrodite; castrated, effeminate.*

sēmĭvīvus -a -um, *half-dead, very faint.*

sēmŏdĭus -i, m. *half a modius.*

sēmŏvĕo -mŏvēre -mōvi -mōtum, *to move away, set aside, separate;* partic. **sēmōtus** -a -um, *remote, distant.*

semper, *always, at all times.*

sempĭternus -a -um, *continual, ever-lasting.*

Semprōnĭus -a -um, *name of a Roman gens.*

sēmuncĭa -ae, f. *half an uncia.*

sēmuncĭārĭus -a -um, *of the fraction* 1/24: faenus, 1/24 *per cent monthly,* i.e. ½ *per cent per annum.*

sēmustŭlātus (**sēmĭustŭlātus**) -a -um *half-burnt.*

sēnācŭlum -i, n. *an open space in the Forum, used by the Senate.*

sēnārĭŏlus -i, m. *a trifling senarius.*

sēnārĭus -a -um, *composed of six in a group;* senarius (versus), m. *a senarius, a verse of six feet.*

sĕnātor -ōris, m. *a member of the senate, a senator.*

sĕnātōrĭus -a -um, *of a senator, senatorial.*

sĕnātus -ūs, (or -i), m *a council of elders, the Senate;* senatus (senati) consultum, *a formal resolution of the senate.*

Sĕnĕca -ae, m. M. Annaeus Seneca, *a rhetorician from Corduba in Spain;* L. Annaeus Seneca, *his son, a Stoic philosopher, tutor of Nero.*

¹sĕnectus -a -um, *old, aged;* f. as subst. **sĕnecta** -ae, *old age.*

²sĕnectūs -ūtis, f. *old age;* concr., *old men.*

sĕnĕo -ēre, *to be old.*

sĕnesco senescĕre sĕnŭi, *to grow old; to flag, wane.*

sĕnex sĕnis; ·compar. **sĕnĭor:** adj., *old, aged;* subst., *an old person.*

sēni -ae -a, *six at a time,* or *six each.*

sĕnīlis -e, *of an old man, senile;* adv. **sĕnīlĭtĕr.**

sēnĭo -ōnis, m. *the number six upon dice.*

sĕnĭor, compar. of senex; q.v.

sĕnĭum -i, n. *old age; decline, decay; gloom, grief.*

sensĭcŭlus -i, m. *a little sentence.*

sensĭfer -fĕra -fĕrum, *producing sensation.*

sensĭlis -e, *having sensation, sensitive.*

sensim, *just perceptibly, gradually, by degrees.*

sensus -ūs, m. *sense, sensation; feeling, attitude; judgment, perception, understanding; sense, meaning of words, etc.; a sentence.*

sententĭa -ae, f. *a way of thinking, opinion, thought, meaning, purpose; a decision, vote; meaning, sense of words, etc.; a sentence, period; esp., a maxim, aphorism.*

sententĭŏla -ae, f. *a short sentence, maxim, aphorism.*

sententĭōsus -a -um, *pithy, sententious;* adv. **sententĭōsē.**

sentĭcētum -i, n. *a thorn-brake.*

sentīna -ae, f. *bilge-water; rabble, dregs of the population.*

sentĭo sentīre sensi sensum, *to feel, perceive; to experience, feel the force of a thing; to realize a truth; to hold an opinion, judge, suppose; legal, to decide, to vote.* N. pl. of partic. as subst. **sensa** -ōrum, *thoughts, sentiments.*

sentis -is, c. *a thorn-bush, briar.*

sentisco -ĕre, *to begin to perceive*

sentus -a -um, *neglected, rough.*

sĕorsum, sorsum, sorsus, *apart, separately.*

sēpărātim, *apart, separately, differently.*

sēpărātĭo -ōnis, f. *separation, severance.*

sēpăro -are, *to sever, separate; to consider or treat separately.* Hence partic. **sēpărātus** -a -um, *separate, distinct;* compar. adv. **sēpărātĭŭs,** *less closely.*

sēpĕlĭo -pelīre -pēlīvi and -pēlĭi -pultum, *to bury; to ruin, destroy;* partic. **sepultus,** *buried, sunk, immersed.*

sēp-; see also **saep-.**

sēpĭa -ae, f. *cuttle-fish.*

sēpōno -pōnĕre -pŏsŭi -pŏsĭtum, *to put on one side, place apart, reserve; to put out of the way, banish; to distinguish, divide.* Partic. **sēpŏsĭtus** -a -um, *distant, remote; choice, select.*

sepse = se ipse; see ipse.

septem, *seven.*

September -bris, *of September;* (mensis) *September, the seventh month of the Roman year, September.*

septemdĕcim, *seventeen.*

septemflŭus -a -um, *with seven mouths.*

septemgĕmĭnus -a -um, *sevenfold.*

septemplex -plĭcis, *sevenfold.*

septemtrĭōnālis -e, *northern.*

septemtrĭōnēs (septen-) -um, m. pl. *the seven stars of either the Great Bear or the Little Bear;* in gen., *the north; the north wind.*

septemvir -vīri, m. *one of the septemviri, a college or guild of seven persons;* adj. **septemvīrālis** -e, *of septemviri;* subst. **septemvīrātus** -ūs, m. *the office of a septemvir.*

septēnārius -a -um, *containing seven;* m. pl. as subst. **septēnārii,** *verses containing seven feet, heptameters.*

septendĕcim = septemdecim; q.v.

septēni -ae, -a, *seven at a time or seven each.*

septentrĭo = septemtrio; q.v.

septĭes (-ĭens), *seven times.*

septĭmānus -a -um, *of the seventh;* m. pl. as subst. *soldiers of the seventh legion.*

septĭmus (septŭmus) -a -um, *seventh;* **septĭmum,** *for the seventh time.*

septĭmus dĕcĭmus -a -um, *seventeenth.*

septingentēsĭmus (-ensĭmus) -a -um, *seven hundredth.*

septingenti -ae -a, *seven hundred.*

septŭāgēsĭmus (-ensĭmus) -a -um, *seventieth.*

septŭāgintā, *seventy.*

septŭennis -e, *of seven years.*

septum = saeptum; q.v.

septunx -uncis, m. *seven-twelfths.*

sĕpulcrālis -e, *of a tomb, sepulchral.*

sĕpulcrētum -i, n. *a burial-place, cemetery.*

sĕpulcrum -i, n., *a place of burial, grave, tomb.*

sĕpultūra -ae, f. *burial, interment; also the burning of a dead body.*

Sēquăna -ae, m. *a river of Gaul (now the Seine).*

sĕquax -ācis, *following, attending, pursuing.*

sĕquester -tri or -tris, m. *a depositary; a go-between, agent, mediator.*

sĕquestra -ae, f. *a mediator.*

sĕquĭus = secius, compar. of secus; q.v.

sĕquor sĕqui sĕcūtus, dep. *to follow, accompany, attend; to pursue, chase; in time, to follow, ensue; to follow logically, follow as a consequence;* of property, *to go to, fall to; to conform to; to strive after, aim at.*

sēra -ae, f. *a bar or bolt.*

sĕrēnĭtās -ātis, f. *clear weather.*

sĕrēno -are, *to make clear, make bright.*

sĕrēnus -a -um, *clear, bright, fair;* n. as subst. *fair weather.*

Sērēs -um, m. *the Chinese, famous for their silks;* adj. **Sērĭcus** -a -um, *Chinese; silken.*

sĕresco -ĕre, *to become dry.*

sērĭa -ae, f. *a large jar.*

sērĭes, acc. -em, abl. -e, f. *a row, chain, series; a line of descent, lineage.*

sērĭus -a -um, *serious, earnest;* n. as subst. *earnest, seriousness;* abl. as adv. **sērĭō,** *in earnest, seriously.*

sermo -ōnis, m. *talk, conversation; discussion; common talk, report, rumour; a subject of conversation; a conversational style,* or *prose; any manner of speaking, style, expression, diction, language, dialect.*

sermōcĭnor -ari, dep. *to converse, talk, discuss.*

sermuncŭlus -i, m. *rumour, tittle-tattle.*

¹sĕro sĕrĕre sēvi sătum, *to sow, set, plant;* n. pl. of partic. as subst., **săta** -ōrum, *standing corn, crops; to beget, engender, bring forth;* partic. **sătus** -a -um, *sprung, born;* in gen., *to produce, give rise to.*

²**sĕro** sĕrĕre sĕrŭi sertum, *to join together, put in a row, connect*, partic. **sertus** -a -um, *linked, connected*; n. as subst. **sertum** -i, and plur. **serta** -orum, *a garland, wreath*; also f. **serta** -ae.

serpens -entis, c. *a snake, serpent.*

serpentĭgĕna -ae, m. *sprung from a serpent.*

serpentĭpēs -pēdis, *snake-footed.*

serpĕrastra -orum, n. *bandages* or *knee-splints.*

serpo serpĕre serpsi serptum, *to creep, crawl, advance slowly.*

serpyllum (-pillum, -pullum) -i, n. *wild thyme.*

serra -ae, f. *a saw.*

serrācum (**sarr-**) -i, n. *a kind of waggon.*

serrātus -a -um, *toothed like a saw, serrated*; m. pl. as subst. (sc. nummi), *milled coins.*

serrŭla -ae, f. *a little saw.*

sertum; see sero.

sĕrum -i, n. *whey.*

sērus -a -um, *late, too late*; n. as subst. **serum** -i, *a late hour*; n. abl. sing. as adv. **sērō**, *late, too late.*

serva -ae, f. see servus.

servābĭlis -e, *able to be saved.*

servātor -ōris, m. and **servātrix** -īcis, f., *a preserver, saviour; a watcher.*

servīlis -e, *of a slave, servile*; adv. **servīlĭtĕr.**

Servīlĭus -a -um, *name of a Roman gens.*

servĭo -ire, (with dat.), *to be a slave, to serve, help, gratify*; legal, of buildings, etc., *to be subject to certain rights*, e.g. *to be mortgaged.*

servĭtĭum -i, n. *slavery, servitude, subjection*; concr., *slaves, servants, a household.*

servĭtūdo -ĭnis, f. *slavery, servitude.*

servĭtūs -ūtis, f. *slavery, servitude*; in gen., *subjection, obedience*; legal, of houses, etc., *liability to certain burdens*, e.g. *a right of way*; concr., *slaves.*

servo -are, *to watch over, observe*; *to keep, protect, save; to lay up, reserve; to keep, retain* a promise, etc.; *to keep to, stay in* a place. Partic., in superl., **servantissĭmus** -i, *most careful, most observant.*

servŭlus (**servŏlus**) -i, m. and **servŭla** (**servŏla**) -ae, f. *a young slave.*

servus -a -um, adj., *serving, servile, subject*; legal, of lands, etc., *subject to other rights*; m. and f. as subst., *a slave, servant.*

sescēnāris -e, *a year and a half old.*

sescēnārĭus -a -um, *consisting of six hundred.*

sescēni -ae -a, *six hundred at a time* or *six hundred each.*

sescentēsĭmus (-ensĭmus) -a -um, *six hundredth.*

sescenti -ae -a, *six hundred*; in gen., *countless.*

sescentiēs (-iens), *six hundred times.*

sĕsĕlis -is, f. *a plant, hartwort.*

sesquī, *one half more, half as much again.*

sesquĭalter -altĕra -altĕrum, *one and a half.*

sesquĭhōra -ae, f. *an hour and a half.*

sesquĭmŏdĭus -i, m. *a modius and a half.*

sesquĭoctāvus -a -um, *containing 9/8 of a thing.*

sesquĭpĕdālis -e, *a foot and a half long.*

sesquĭpēs -pĕdis, m. *a foot and a half long, wide*, etc.

sesquĭplāga -ae, f. *a blow and a half.*

sesquĭplex -plĭcis, *one and a half times as much.*

sesquĭtertĭus -a -um, *containing 4/3 of anything.*

sessĭbŭlum -i, n. *a seat, stool, chair.*

sessĭlis -e, *fit for sitting*; of plants, *low, dwarf.*

sessĭo -ōnis, f. *the act of sitting; loitering, idling; a session; a place for sitting, seat.*

sessĭto -are, *to sit much, sit often.*

sessĭuncŭla -ae, f. *a little company* or *assembly.*

sessor -ōris, m. *a sitter; an inhabitant.*

sestertĭus -a -um, *consisting of two and a half*; m. as subst. **sestertĭus** -i, *a sesterce, a silver coin*, = ¼ denarius, = 2½ asses.

Sestĭus -a -um, *name of a Roman gens.*

sĕt = sed; q.v.

sēta = saeta; q.v.

seu; see sive.

sĕvērĭtās -ātis, and **sĕvērĭtūdo** -ĭnis, f. *gravity, sternness.*

sĕvērus -a -um, *grave, serious, strict, stern, hard*; adv. **sĕvērē.**

sēvŏco -are, *to call aside, withdraw, separate.*

sēvum = sebum; q.v.

sex, *six.*

sexāgēnārĭus -a -um, *containing sixty; sixty years old.*

sexāgēni -ae -a, *sixty at a time*, or *sixty each.*

sexāgēsĭmus (-ensĭmus) -a -um. *sixtieth.*

sexāgiēs (-iens), *sixty times.*

sexāgintā, *sixty.*

sexangŭlus -a -um, *hexagonal.*

sexcen-; see sescen-.

sexdĕcim = sedecim; q.v.

sexennis -e, *six years old.*

sexennĭum -i, n. *a period of six years.*

sexiēs (-iens), *six times.*

sexprīmi -ōrum, m. *a board of six magistrates in a provincial town.*

sextādĕcĭmāni -orum, m. pl. *soldiers of the 16th legion.*

sextans -antis, m. *one sixth.*

sextārĭus -i, m. *one sixth, esp.* of a congius (about a pint).

Sextīlis -e, *of the sixth month of the old Roman year*; **sextilis** (mensis), *the sixth month*, afterwards called *Augustus.*

sextŭla -ae, f. *1/72.*

sextus -a -um, *sixth*; **sextum**, *for the sixth time.*

sextusdĕcĭmus -a -um, *sixteenth.*

sexus -ūs, m. *sex.*

sī, if, supposing that; quod si, and if, but if; si modo, if only; si quis, if anybody; si non, si minus, nisi, if not, unless.

sĭbĭla -ōrum, n. pl.: as adj., hissing; as subst., = plur. of sibilus (q.v.).

sībĭlo -are,: intransit., to hiss, whistle; transit., to hiss at.

sībĭlus -i, m. (poet. plur. sibila; q.v.), a hissing, whistling.

Sĭbylla -ae, f. a prophetess of Apollo, a Sibyl; adj. **Sĭbyllīnus** -a -um, of the Sibyl, Sibylline.

sīc, so, thus, in this way; like this, as follows; in that case, with this limitation; leading up to consecutive clause, so much, to such a degree; interrog. **sīcĭne,** is it thus that?

sīca -ae, f. dagger, dirk, poniard.

Sīcāni -ōrum, m. pl. an ancient people of Sicily; adj. **Sīcānus** and **Sīcānĭus** -a -um, Sicanian; subst. **Sīcānĭa** -ae, f. Sicania = Sicily.

sīcārĭus -i, m. an assassin, murderer.

siccĭtās -ātis, f. dryness, drought; sound health; of style, plainness, simplicity.

sicco -are, to make dry, to dry; to stanch; to drain.

siccus -a -um, dry; thirsting, thirsty; of health, sound; sober, temperate; of style, plain, simple; adv. **siccē.**

Sĭcĭlĭa -ae, f.; see Siculi.

sīcĭnĕ; see sic.

sĭcŭbĭ, if anywhere.

Sĭcŭli -ōrum, m. pl., the Sicilians; adj. **Sĭcŭlus** -a -um, Sicilian; subst. **Sĭcĭlĭa** -ae, f. Sicily.

sīcundĕ, if from anywhere.

sīcŭt and **sīcŭti,** as, just as; as for example; as it were; with verb in subj., just as if.

Sĭcyōn -ōnis, f. a city in the Peloponnese; adj. **Sĭcyōnĭus** -a -um, Sicyonian; n. pl. as subst. a kind of soft shoes from Sicyon.

sīdĕrĕus -a -um, of the stars starry; gleaming.

sīdo sīdĕre sīdi and sēdi sessum, to sit or sink down, settle, alight; to remain lying or fixed; naut. to stick fast, be stranded; of feelings, to subside.

Sīdōn -onis, f. a city of Phoenicia; adj. **Sīdōnĭus** -a -um; f. adj. **Sīdōnis** -ĭdis.

sīdus -ĕris, n. a constellation, or a single star; any luminary, heavenly body; time of year, season, weather; in astrology, star, destiny; plur., the heavens. Transf., pride, glory.

sĭgilla -ōrum, n. pl. small figures, images; a seal.

sĭgillātus -a -um, adorned with small figures.

sigma -ātis, n. the Greek letter sigma; a semicircular dining-couch.

signātor -ōris, m. one who seals; a witness.

signĭfer -fĕra -fĕrum, bearing signs or figures; covered with constellations. M. as subst. **signĭfer** -fĕri a standard-bearer; a leader.

signĭfĭcātĭo -ōnis, f. indication, sign, token; sign of assent, approbation; emphasis; meaning, signification.

signĭfĭco -are, to indicate, show; to foreshow; to mean, signify; partic. **signĭfĭcans** -antis, distinct, clear; adv. **signĭfĭcantĕr.**

signo -are, to mark, inscribe; to seal, seal up; to coin, stamp money. Transf., to impress, indicate; to observe, notice.

signum -i, n. a sign, mark, token; a warning, symptom; milit., a standard, banner, ensign, or a signal, order, command, or a watchword, password; a figure, image, statute; a seal, signet; a group of stars, constellation.

sĭlānus -i, m. a fountain.

sĭlentĭum -i, n. silence, stillness, quiet; repose; obscurity.

sĭlĕo -ēre -ŭi, to be still, silent; with acc., to be silent about; to be still, rest, be inactive; partic. **sĭlens** -entis, silent, still; pl. as subst. the dead.

sĭler -ĕris, n. the brook-willow.

sĭlesco -ere, to become silent, grow still.

sĭlex -ĭcis, m. (rarely f.), any hard stone, such as flint; crag, rock, cliff.

sĭlĭcernĭum -i, a funeral feast.

sĭlīgo -ĭnis, f. wheat; wheaten flour.

sĭlĭqua -ae, f. a husk, pod, shell; in plur., pulse.

Sīlĭus -a -um, name of Roman gens.

Sĭlūres -um, pl. a British people.

sīlus -a -um, snub-nosed, pug-nosed.

silva, a wood, forest; bush; a plantation, grove; a mass, plenty, abundance.

Silvānus -i, m. god of woods and forests.

silvesco -ĕre, of a vine, to run wild, run to wood.

silvestris -e, of woods; wooded; wild, rural.

silvĭcŏla -ae, m. and f. and **silvĭcultrix** -trīcis, f. inhabiting woods.

silvifrăgus -a -um, shattering the woods.

silvōsus -a -um, well wooded.

sīmĭa -ae, f. ape, monkey.

sĭmĭlis -e; compar. similior, superl. simillimus; like, resembling, similar (with genit. or dat.); veri similis, probable; n. as subst. a resemblance or comparison; adv. **sĭmĭlĭtĕr,** similarly.

sĭmĭlĭtūdo -ĭnis, f. likeness, resemblance; veri similitudo, probability; intended likeness, imitation; a metaphor, simile· uniformity, monotony.

sĭmĭlo = simulo; q.v.

sĭmĭŏlus -i, m. little ape.

sĭmĭtū, together.

sīmĭus -i, m. ape, monkey.

simplex -plĭcis; simple, single; un-mixed, pure, plain, absolute; morally simple, straightforward. Adv. **simplĭcĭtĕr,** simply, plainly; artlessly; frankly.

simplĭcĭtās -ātis, f. simplicity; straight-forwardness, honesty, candour.

simplum -i, m. the simple sum or number (opp. double, etc.).

simpŭlum -i, n. a ladle.

simpŭvĭum -i, n. a sacrificial bowl.

sĭmul, *at once, at the same time, together;* simul atque (ac), *as soon as.*

sĭmŭlacrum -i, n. *an image, likeness, portrait; effigy, a shade, ghost, imitation, phantom, appearance.*

sĭmŭlāmen -ĭnis, n. *an imitation.*

sĭmŭlātĭo -ōnis, f. *assumed appearance, pretence, feint.*

sĭmŭlātor -ōris, m. *an imitator; a pretender, feigner.*

sĭmŭlo -are, *to make like, cause to resemble; to make a copy of, to represent; to play the part of; to pretend a thing is so, simulate, feign;* partic. **sĭmŭlans** -antis, *imitating, imitative;* adv. from perf. partic. **sĭmŭlātē,** *feignedly.*

sĭmultās -ātis, f. *a clash, rivalry, feud.*

sĭmŭlus -a -um, *rather snub-nosed.*

sīmus -a -um, *snub-nosed.*

sĭn, conj. *but if, if however.*

sĭnāpī -is, n. and **sĭnāpis** -is, f. *mustard.*

sincērĭtās -ātis, f. *purity, soundness, integrity.*

sincērus -a -um, *pure, whole, sound, genuine, uncorrupt;* adv. **sincērē,** *honestly, frankly.*

sinciput -pĭtis, n. *half a head; the smoked chap of a pig.*

sindōn -ōnis, f. *fine cotton cloth, muslin.*

sĭnē, prep. with abl., *without.*

singillātim, *singly, one by one.*

singŭlāris -e, *alone, single individual, singular; unique, extraordinary.* Adv. **singŭlārĭter,** *singly; in the singular number; particularly, extraordinarily.*

singŭli; see singulus.

singultim, *with sobs.*

singulto -are: intransit., *to gasp, sob;* transit., *to sob out, gasp out.*

singultus -ūs, m. *a sobbing, gasping.*

singŭlus -a -um, more freq. plur. **singŭli** -ae, -a, *single, separate, one at a time; distributive, one each.*

sĭnister -tra -trum, *left, on the left hand; wrong, perverse; unfavourable, adverse;* sometimes, in augury, *favourable.* F. as subst. **sĭnistra** -ae, *the left hand;* also *the left side.* Adv. **sĭnistre,** *wrongly, unfavourably.*

sĭnistrorsus (-orsum), *to the left.*

sĭno sĭnĕre sīvi sĭtum, *to let alone, leave; to let, allow, permit;* partic. **sĭtus** -a -um, *placed, laid down; lying, situated.*

Sĭnōpa -ae, and **Sĭnōpē** -ēs, f. *a town on the Black Sea.*

sĭnum; see `sinus.

sĭnŭo -are, *to bend, curve.*

sĭnŭōsus -a -um, *winding, sinuous.* Transf., *roundabout, diffuse.*

¹sĭnus -i, m. and **sĭnum** -i, n. *a large bowl.*

²sĭnus -ūs, m. *a curve, fold, winding; of dress, a fold, pocket, lap;* in a coastline, *a bay, gulf.* Transf., *heart, secret feelings.*

sīpārĭum -i, n. *a curtain; a drop-scene at a theatre.*

sīpho (sīfo) -ōnis, m. *a siphon; a fire-engine.*

sīquando, *if ever.*

sīquĭdem, *if indeed;* sometimes *since, because.*

Sīrēn -ēnis, f., usually plur. **Sīrēnes** -um, *the Sirens, nymphs who by their song lured mariners to destruction.*

Sīrĭus -i, m. *the Dog-Star Sirius.*

sīs = (1) si vis; see volo. (2) second sing. of pres. subj. of sum; q.v. (3) dat. or abl. plur. of suus; q.v.

sisto sistĕre stĭti stătum: transit., *to cause to stand, set, place; legal, to cause to appear in court;* vadimonium sistere, *to appear on the appointed day; to stop, check; to establish firmly;* intransit., *to place oneself, stand; legal, to present oneself in court; to stand still, to halt; to stand firm.* Hence partic. **stătus** -a -um, *fixed, determined, regular.*

sistrum -i, n. *a sort of rattle used in the worship of Isis.*

sīsymbrĭum -i, n. *an aromatic herb, perhaps mint.*

Sĭsyphus -i, m. *a robber, condemned in the lower world to roll a stone uphill for ever.*

sĭtella -ae, f. *an urn for drawing lots.*

sĭtĭcŭlōsus -a -um, *very dry, parched.*

sĭtĭo -ire: intransit., *to thirst, to be thirsty, dry, parched;* transit., *to thirst for, thirst after;* partic. **sĭtĭens** -entis, *thirsty, dry, parched; eager, desirous;* adv. **sĭtĭentĕr.**

sĭtis -is, f. *thirst; dryness, drought; eager desire.*

sĭtĭtor -ōris, m. *a thirster.*

sittўbus -i, m. *a strip of parchment showing the title of a book.*

sĭtŭla -ae, f. *a jar.*

¹sĭtus -a -um, partic. from sino; q.v.

²sĭtus -ūs, m. (1) *layout, site, position, situation.* (2) *being left; neglect, dirt, decay; mental rusting, dullness.*

sīvĕ and **sĕu,** *or if;* sive (seu) . . . sive (seu), *whether . . . or.*

smăragdus -i, m. and f. *emerald.*

sŏbŏles, sŏbŏlesco = suboles, subolesco; q.v.

sŏbrīnus -i, m. and **sŏbrīna** -ae, f. *a cousin on the mother's side.*

sōbrĭus -a -um, *sober; without wine; moderate, frugal; sober-minded, reasonable, sensible.* Adv. **sōbrĭē.**

soccŭlus -i, m. *a little soccus;* q.v.

soccus -i, m. *a light shoe or slipper, esp. as worn by comic actors.*

sŏcer -ĕri, m. *father-in-law;* plur., **sŏceri,** *father- and mother-in-law.*

sŏcĭa -ae, f., see socius.

sŏcĭābĭlis -e, *easily united, compatible.*

sŏcĭālis -e, *of partners or allies; conjugal; sociable.* Adv. **sŏcĭālĭtĕr,** *sociably.*

sŏcĭĕtās -ātis, f. *partnership, fellowship, association, alliance.*

sŏcĭo -are, *to unite, combine, associate.*

sŏcĭus -a -um, *sharing, associated, allied.* M. and f. as subst. *a partner comrade, associate, ally.*

sōcordĭa (sēcordĭa) -ae, f. *folly, stupidity; negligence, indolence.*

sŏcors -cordis, *weak-minded, stupid; negligent, slothful, careless;* compar. adv. **sŏcordĭus,** *too feebly.*

Sŏcrătēs -is, m. *the Athenian philosopher, put to death in* 399 B.C. Adj. **Sŏcrătĭcus** -a -um, *Socratic;* m. pl. as subst., *followers of Socrates.*

socrus -ūs, f. *mother-in-law.*

sŏdālĭcĭum -i, n. *an association; esp. a secret society;* in gen., *comradeship.*

sŏdālĭcĭus -a -um, *of companionship.*

sŏdālis -is, c. *member of an association, esp. of a priesthood* or *a secret society;* in gen., *a comrade;* of things, *companion, attendant on.*

sŏdālĭtās -ātis, f. *an association; comradeship, intimacy.*

sŏdēs, *if you please, with your leave.*

sōl sōlis, m. *the sun;* poet., *a day;* personif., *the Sun-god.*

sōlācĭŏlum -i, n. *a small consolation.*

sōlācĭum -i, n. *consolation, comfort, relief.*

sōlāmen -ĭnis, n. *consolation comfort.*

sōlāris -e, *of the sun, solar.*

sōlārĭum -i, n. *a sundial; a terrace exposed to the sun.*

sōlātor ōris, m. *a consoler, comforter.*

soldūrĭi -ōrum, m. pl. *retainers, vassals.*

soldus = solidus; q.v.

sŏlěa -ae, f. *a sandal; a kind of fetter; a shoe for an animal; a fish, the sole.*

sŏlěātus -a-um, *wearing sandals.*

sōlennis = sollemnis; q.v.

sŏlěo sŏlēre sŏlĭtus sum, *to be accustomed;* ut solet, *as usual;* partic. **sŏlĭtus** -a -um, *accustomed, habitual, usual;* n. as subst. *that which is usual.*

sōlers = sollers; q.v.

sŏlĭdĭtās -ātis, f. *solidity.*

sŏlĭdo -are, *to make firm* or *solid.*

sŏlĭdus (soldus) -a -um, *dense, solid; whole, complete, entire; firm, enduring, real;* n. as subst., *firm ground, solid substance, entirety.* Adv. **sŏlĭdē,** *firmly;* scire, *to know for certain.*

sōlĭferrěum -i, n. *a javelin entirely of iron.*

sōlistĭmus -a -um; *see* tripudium.

sōlĭtārĭus -a -um, *alone, lonely.*

sōlĭtūdo -ĭnis, f. *solitude, loneliness; desertion, deprivation, want.*

sōlĭtus -a -um, partic. from soleo; q.v.

sōlĭum -i, n. (1) *a chair of state, throne;* hence *dominion, regal power.* (2) *a bath-tub.*

sōlĭvăgus -a -um, *wandering alone; solitary, lonely.*

sollemnis -e, *yearly, annual, recurring; solemn, festive, religious; usual, customary.* N. as subst. **sollemne** -is. *a solemn feast, religious rite; a custom.* Adv. **sollemnĭtěr.**

sollers -ertis, *clever, skilful;* adv. **sollertěr.**

sollertĭa -ae, f. *cleverness, skill.*

sollĭcĭtātĭo -ōnis, f. *inciting, instigation.*

sollĭcĭto -are, *to move violently, disturb, agitate; to rouse, vex, disquiet; to incite, instigate, tamper with.*

sollĭcĭtūdo -ĭnis, f. *uneasiness, disquiet, anxiety.*

sollĭcĭtus -a -um, *disturbed, agitated, restless; anxious, uneasy, worried;* of animals, *watchful;* in act. sense, *disquieting.* Adv. **sollĭcĭtē,** *anxiously, carefully.*

sōlo -are, *to make solitary.*

sōloecismus -i, m. *a grammatical error.*

Sōlōn -ōnis, m. *a famous Athenian legislator, active about* 600 B.C.

sōlor -ari, dep. *to comfort, console; to assuage, relieve troubles, etc.*

solstĭtĭālis -e, *of the summer solstice; of summer; of the sun.*

solstĭtĭum -i, n. *solstice, esp. the summer solstice; summer.*

sŏlum -i. n. *bottom, floor, foundation; the sole of the foot,* or *shoe; soil, ground, earth, land, country.*

sōlus -a -um, *alone, only, sole;* of places, *solitary, uninhabited.* N. acc. as adv. **sōlum,** *alone, only.*

sŏlūtĭo -ōnis, f. *a loosening; a paying, payment; a solution, explanation.*

solvo solvěre solvi sŏlūtum, *to loosen; to untie, release, free; to dissolve, break up; to exempt; to break up, weaken, bring to an end; to pay off, discharge a debt;* solvendo non esse, *to be insolvent; to meet* engagements, *perform* duties; *to break down a* restraining influence; *to solve a* problem, *explain* a difficulty.
Hence partic. **sŏlūtus** -a -um, *loosened, unbound, free, unencumbered, independent;* in bad sense, *unrestrained, unbridled; lax, lazy, negligent:* of style, *fluent* or *in prose.* Adv. **sŏlūtē,** *loosely, freely; carelessly.*

somnĭcŭlōsus -a -um, *sleepy, drowsy;* adv. **somnĭcŭlōsē.**

somnĭfer -fěra -ferum, *sleep-bringing; narcotic, deadly.*

somnĭo -are, *to dream;* with acc., *to dream of; to imagine foolishly.*

somnĭum -i, n. *a dream; a fancy, day-dream; foolishness, nonsense.*

somnus -i, m. *sleep, slumber; drowsiness, laziness, inactivity; night.*

sŏnābĭlis -e, *resounding.*

sŏnĭpēs -pědis, *sounding with the feet;* m. as subst., *a horse.*

sŏnĭtus -ūs, m. *a sound, noise.*

sŏnĭvĭus -a -um, *sounding;* sonivium tripudium, *the noise of the food falling from the beaks of the sacred chickens.*

sŏno sŏnare sŏnŭi sŏnĭtum, *to sound, resound, make a noise; to sing of, to celebrate;* of words, *to mean.*

sŏnor -ōris, m. *sound, noise, din.*

sŏnōrus -a -um, *sounding, resonant, loud.*

sons sontis, *guilty.*

sontĭcus -a -um, *important, serious.*

sŏnus -i, m. *noise, sound; tone, character, style.*

sŏphĭa -ae, f. *wisdom.*

sŏphistēs -ae, m. *a sophist.*

Sŏphoclēs -is and -i, m. *the Greek tragic poet;* adj. **Sŏphoclēus** -a -um.

¹**sŏphŏs** (-ŭs) -i, m. *wise*; as subst., *a wise man*.

²**sŏphōs**, adv. *bravo! well done!*

sōpio -ire, *to put to sleep, lull to sleep, quieten; to stun, render senseless.*

sŏpor -ōris, m. *deep sleep; laziness; a sleeping draught.*

sŏpōrātus -a -um, *full of sleep.*

sŏpōrĭfer -fĕra -fĕrum, *causing deep sleep.*

sŏpōrus -a -um, *sleep-bringing.*

Sōractĕ -is, n. *a mountain in Etruria.*

sorbĕo -ēre, *to suck in, drink, swallow.*

sorbĭlo, *by sipping; drop by drop.*

sorbum -i, n. *a service-berry.*

sordĕo -ēre, *to be dirty; to appear vile.*

sordēs -is, f. *often plur.* **sordēs** -ĭum, *dirt, filth; shabby or dirty garments; low rank; sordid conduct, meanness.*

sordesco sordescĕre sordŭi, *to become dirty.*

sordĭdātus -a -um, *wearing shabby or dirty clothes.*

sordĭdŭlus -a -um, *somewhat dirty or mean.*

sordĭdus -a -um, *dirty, filthy, shabby; low, base in rank; mean in conduct.* Adv. **sordĭdē,** *meanly; stingily.*

sōrex -ĭcis, m. *a shrew-mouse.*

sŏror -ōris, *a sister.*

sŏrōrĭcīda -ae, m. *one who murders a sister.*

sŏrōrĭus -a -um, *of a sister, sisterly.*

sors sortis, f. *a lot; a casting of lots; an oracular response, prophecy; official duty as allotted; with genit., share, part; fate, fortune, destiny; money, capital out at interest.*

sortĭlĕgus -a -um, *prophetic, oracular;* m. as subst., *a soothsayer, fortune-teller.*

sortĭor -iri, dep., and **sortĭo** -ire: instransit., *to cast lots;* transit., *to allot, cast lots for; share out;* also *to obtain by lot; to choose.*
Hence partic. **sortītus** -a -um; dep., *having obtained* (by lots) or *cast lots for;* pass. *gained by lot;* n. abl. as adv., **sortītō,** *by lot, by fate.*

sortītĭo -ōnis, f. *casting lots, deciding by lot.*

¹**sortītus** -ūs, m. *casting lots, deciding by lot.*

²**sortītus** -a -um, partic. from sortior, q.v.

sospĕs -ĭtis, *safe, unhurt, uninjured; lucky, favourable.*

Sospĭta -ae, f. *the Saviour;* epithet of Juno.

sospĭto -are, *to keep safe, preserve.*

sōtēr -ēris; acc. -ēra; m. *a saviour.*

sōtēria -ōrum, n. pl. *presents given on recovery from sickness.*

spādix -dīcis, *chestnut-coloured.*

spādo -ōnis, m. *a eunuch.*

spargo spargĕre sparsi sparsum, *to scatter, sprinkle, throw about; to spread, circulate, distribute; to disperse, dissipate;* with abl. *to besprinkle with.*
Hence partic. **sparsus** -a -um, *spread out, scattered; speckled, spotted.*

sparsĭo -ōnis, f. *a sprinkling.*

Sparta -ae, and **Spartē** -es, f. *Sparta, the capital of Laconia;* adj. **Spartānus** -a -um, *Spartan.*

spartum -i, n. *Spanish broom.*

spărŭlus -i, m. *a fish, sea-bream.*

spărus -i, m. *a spear with a curved blade.*

spătha -ae, f. *a broad two-edged sword.*

spătĭor -ari, dep. *to walk about, take a walk;* of things, *to spread out, expand.*

spătĭōsus -a -um, *ample, wide;* of time, *long;* adv. **spătĭōsē.**

spătĭum -i, n. *space, extent, room; distance, interval; dimensions, size; a tract, course, esp. in a race; an open space, a walk.* Transf., *a space of time, period; leisure, opportunity; metrical time, measure, quantity.*

spĕcĭālis -e, *individual, particular, special.*

spĕcĭēs -ēi, f.: act., *a seeing, view;* pass., *sight, look; shape, form, outward appearance; beauty; a vision, phantom; a representation, image, statue.* Transf., *pretext, pretence; notion, idea; kind, species.*

spĕcillum -i, n. *a surgeon's probe.*

spĕcĭmen -ĭnis, n. *a visible mark, example, model; a pattern, ideal.*

spĕcĭo (**spĭcĭo**) spĕcĕre spexi, *to look at, see.*

spĕcĭōsus -a -um, *beautiful, handsome, imposing;* in bad sense, *plausible, specious.* Adv. **spĕcĭōsē.**

spectābĭlis -e, *visible; worth seeing, notable.*

spectācŭlum -i, n. *sight, show, spectacle; the seats in the theatre or circus.*

spectātĭo -ōnis, f. *looking, watching, viewing; inspection of money.*

spectātor -ōris, m. and **spectātrix** -trīcis, f. *a watcher, spectator, observer; an examiner, critic.*

spectĭo -ōnis, f. *the right to observe auspices.*

specto -are, *to look at, contemplate, watch; to test, examine;* of places, *to look towards, face.* Transf., *to consider, contemplate, look for; to bear in mind, have in view;* of things, *to tend, incline.*
Hence partic. **spectātus** -a -um, *tried, approved;* hence *esteemed, respected.*

spectrum -i. n. *a spectre, apparition.*

¹**spĕcŭla** -ae, f. *a look out, watch-tower.*

²**spĕcŭla** -ae, f. *a little hope, ray of hope.*

spĕcŭlābundus -a -um, *watching, on the watch.*

spĕcŭlāris -e, *like a mirror; transparent;* n. pl. **spĕcŭlāria** -ōrum, *window-panes.*

spĕcŭlātor -ōris, m.: milit., *scout, spy;* in gen., *observer, investigator.*

spĕcŭlātōrius -a -um, *of a scout;* f. as subst. *a spy-boat.*

spĕcŭlātrix -īcis, f. *a (female) observer, watcher.*

spĕcŭlor -ari, dep. *to look out, spy, watch.*

spĕcŭlum -i, n. *a mirror;* fig., *image, copy.*

spĕcus -ūs, m., f., and n. *a cave, hole, hollow.*

spēlaeum -i, n. *a cave, den.*

spēlunca -ae, f. *a cave, den.*

sperno spernĕre sprēvi sprētum, *to remove; to reject, scorn, spurn.*

spēro -are, *to look for, expect;* of good things, *to hope, hope for;* of bad, *to anticipate, forebode.*

spēs -ĕi, f. *expectation;* of good things, *hope;* of bad, *anticipation, foreboding.*

sphaera -ae, f. *a globe, sphere.*

sphaeristērium -i, n. *a place for playing ball.*

Sphinx Sphingis, f. *the Sphinx, a mythical monster at Thebes.*

spīca -ae, f. *a spike; an ear of corn; a tuft.*

spīcĕus -a -um, *of ears of corn.*

spīcifer -fĕra -fĕrum, *carrying ears of corn.*

spīcŭlum -i, n. *sharp point; sting; spear, dart.*

spīna -ae, f. *a thorn, prickle; a thorn-bush;* in pl., *anxieties, difficulties, perplexities.*

spīnētum -i, n. *thorn-hedge, thorn-brake.*

spīnĕus -a -um, *of thorns, thorny.*

spīnōsus -a -um, *of thorns, thorny, prickly;* of style, *crabbed, obscure;* of feeling, *anxious.*

spīnus -i, m. *blackthorn.*

spīra -ae, f. *a coil, twist.*

spīrābĭlis -e, *that may be breathed.*

spīrācŭlum -i, n. *an air-hole.*

spīrāmen -ĭnis, n. *an air-hole; a breath, puff.*

spīrāmentum -i, n. *an air-hole; a breathing-space, pause, interval.*

spīrĭtŭs -ūs, m. *breathing, breath, exhalation; a sigh, the breath of life; life; inspiration; spirit, disposition; a high spirit, pride.*

spīro -are: intransit., *to breathe, blow, draw breath; to be alive; to have inspiration, be inspired;* transit., *to breathe out, exhale.*

spissesco -ĕre, *to become thick.*

spisso -are, *to make thick, thickness.*

spissus -a -um, *close, dense, thick, crowded; slow, tardy, difficult;* adv. spissē.

splendĕo -ēre, *to shine, glitter, be bright.*

splendesco -ĕre, *to become bright.*

splendĭdus -a -um, *shining, bright, brilliant; distinguished, outstanding; showy, specious;* of sound, *clear.* Hence adv. splendĭdē, *splendidly, finely, nobly.*

splendor -ōris, m. *brilliance, brightness, lustre, distinction;* of sound, *clarity.*

splēnĭum -i, n. *an adhesive plaster.*

spŏlĭātĭo -ōnis, f. *plundering, stripping.*

spŏlĭātor -ōris, m. and spŏlĭātrix -trĭcis, f. *plunderer.*

spŏlĭo -are, *to strip, despoil, plunder, rob.*

spŏlĭum -i, n. usually plur., *skin or hide stripped from an animal; arms, clothing,* etc., *taken from an enemy;* in gen., *spoils, plunder, booty.*

sponda -ae, f. *a bedstead, bed, sofa, bier.*

spondālĭum -i, n. *a sacrificial hymn.*

spondĕo spondēre spŏpondi sponsum, *to pledge oneself to, promise solemnly, vow; to be a security, go bail for a person.* Partic. as subst.: sponsus -i, m. *a betrothed man, bridegroom;* sponsa -ae, f. *a betrothed woman, bride;* sponsum -i, n. *a covenant.*

spondēus -i, m. *a spondee (— —).*

spondȳlus -i, m. *a kind of mussel.*

spongĭa (-ĕa) -ae, f. *a sponge; an open-worked cuirass.*

sponsa -ae, f. subst. from spondeo; q.v.

sponsālis -e, *of betrothal;* n. pl. as subst. sponsālĭa -ĭum or -iōrum, *a betrothal, betrothal feast.*

sponsĭo -ōnis, f. *a solemn promise, engagement, guarantee; a wager.*

sponsor -ōris, m. *a surety, bail.*

sponsū, abl. sing. m. *by an engagement.*

sponsus -i, m. and sponsum -i, n. subst. from spondeo; q.v.

spontĕ, abl. f.: of persons, *willingly, of one's own accord; unaided;* of things, *by itself, automatically; in itself, alone.*

sporta -ae, f. *a basket, hamper.*

sportella -ae, f. *a little basket.*

sportŭla -ae, f. *a little basket; a dole, given by the great to their clients.*

sprētĭo -ōnis, f. *contempt, disdain.*

sprētor -ōris, m. *a despiser.*

spūma -ae, f. *foam, froth.*

spūmesco -ĕre, *to begin to foam.*

spūmĕus -a -um, *foaming, frothy.*

spūmifer -fĕra -fĕrum, and spūmĭger -gĕra -gĕrum, *foaming.*

spūmo -are, *to foam, froth.*

spūmōsus -a -um, *foaming, frothy.*

spŭo spŭĕre spŭi spūtum, *to spit out;* n. of partic. as subst. spūtum -i, *spittle.*

spurcĭtĭa -ae, f. and spurcĭtĭēs -ēi, f. *filthiness, dirt.*

spurco -are, *to make dirty, defile;* partic. spurcātus -a -um, *foul.*

spurcus -a -um, *dirty, filthy, unclean;* adv. spurcē.

spūto -are, *to spit, spit out.*

spūtum -i, n. subst. from spuo; q.v.

squālĕo -ēre, *to be rough, stiff; to be overgrown* or *dirty from neglect; to wear mourning.*

squālĭdus -a -um, *rough, stiff, scaly; squalid, dirty; in mourning;* of style, *rough;* adv. squālĭdē.

squālor -ōris, m. *roughness, stiffness; dirt caused by neglect; mourning;* of style, *roughness.*

squālus -i, m. *a kind of fish.*

squāma -ae, f. *a scale; scale armour; a fish.*

squāmĕus -a -um, *scaly.*

squāmĭger -gĕra -gĕrum, *scale-bearing, scaly;* m.pl. as subst. *fishes.*

squāmōsus -a -um, *covered with scales, scaly.*

st! *hush! hist!*

stăbĭlīmentum -i, n. *a stay, support.*

stăbĭlĭo -ire, *to make firm; to establish.*

stăbĭlis -e, *firm, steady, stable*; adv.
stăbĭlĭtĕr.

stăbĭlĭtās -ātis, f. *firmness, stability;
durability.*

stăbŭlo -are: transit., *to stable cattle;*
intransit., *to have a stall.*

stăbŭlum -i, n. *standing-room, quarters,
habitation; a pothouse, brothel.*

stacta -ae, and stactē -ēs, f. *oil of
myrrh.*

stădĭum -i, n. *a stade, a Greek measure
of length; a race-course.*

stagno -are: intransit. *to be stagnant,
stagnate;* of places, *to lie under water;*
transit., *to overflow, inundate.*

stagnum -i, n. *standing water; a pond,
marsh, swamp; a lake, strait.*

stāmen -ĭnis, n. *the warp on a loom;
the thread hanging from a distaff;*
stamina ducere, *to spin; any thread
or woven cloth.*

stāmĭnĕus -a -um, *full of threads.*

stannum -i, n. *an alloy of silver and
lead.*

stătārĭus -a -um, *steady, stable,
stationary;* f. as subst. stătārĭa -ae,
a quiet kind of comedy; m. pl. stătārĭi
-ōrum, *the actors in this.*

stătēra -ae, f. *a steelyard, a balance.*

stătim, *firmly, steadfastly; on the spot,
at once.*

stătĭo -ōnis, f. *a standing still; a place
of abode;* milit., *post, station, or
picket;* naut., *roadstead, anchorage.*

Stătĭus -m.: Caecilius Statius, *a comic
poet, born* 168 B.C.: P. Papinius
Statius, *a poet of Domitian's time.*

stătīvus -a -um, *standing still, fixed;*
n. pl. as subst. *a permanent camp.*

¹stător -ōris, m. *a magistrate's attendant.*

²Stător -ōris, m. *stayer of flight, a
surname of Jupiter.*

stătŭa -ae, f. *a statue, image.*

stătŭārĭus -a -um, *of statues;* f. as
subst. *the art of sculpture;* m. *a
statuary.*

stătūmen -ĭnis, n. *stay, support;* in
pl., *the ribs of a ship.*

stătŭo -ŭĕre -ŭi -ūtum *to cause to
stand, place, set up; to establish, settle
a point; to give a ruling, make arrangements; to decide* (on a course of
action or matter of fact).

stătūra -ae, f. *stature, height.*

¹stătus, partic. from sisto; q.v.

²stătus -ūs, m. *a standing posture,
position, condition, state;* rhet. *the
answer to an action.*

stella -ae, f. *a star;* stella comans, *a
comet.*

stellans -antis, *starry, set with stars,
bright.*

stellātus -a -um, *set with stars, starry,
bright.*

stellĭfer -fĕra -fĕrum and stellĭger
-gĕra -gĕrum, *star-bearing, starry.*

stellĭo (stēlĭo) -ōnis, m. *a spotted
lizard.*

stemma -ătis, n. *a garland, chaplet; a
genealogical tree.*

stercŏro -are, *to dung, manure.*

stercus -ŏris, n. *dung, manure.*

stĕrĭlis -e *barren; bare, empty; fruitless, vain.*

stĕrĭlĭtās -ātis, f. *barrenness.*

sternax -ācis, *throwing to the ground.*

sterno sternĕre strāvi strātum, *to
stretch out, spread;* se sternere, *to
lie down; to strike down, lay down,
overthrow; to make smooth; to calm,
allay; to strew, spread a thing* (with
something else); lectum, *to make,
make up;* equos, *to saddle;* viam,
to pave. N. of partic. as subst.
strātum -i, *a coverlet, blanket; a
bed; a saddle-cloth, saddle; a pavement.*

sternŭmentum -i, n. *a sneeze.*

sternŭo -ŭĕre -ŭi, *to sneeze;* of a light,
to sputter.

sterquĭlīnĭum -i, n. *a dung-heap.*

sterto -ĕre, *to snore.*

stĭbădĭum -i, n. *a semicircular seat.*

stigma -ătis, n. *a brand put upon slaves;*
in gen., *a branded mark, stigma.*

stigmătĭās -ae, m. *a branded slave.*

stilla -ae, f. *a drop.*

stillĭcĭdĭum -i, n. *dripping moisture;
rain-water falling from the eaves of
houses.*

stillo -are: intransit., *to drip, drop;*
transit., *to drop, let drop; to instil*
feelings or ideas

stĭlus, *a stake, pale; the pointed instrument with which the Romans wrote on
waxen tablets; hence writing, composition; mode of writing, style.*

stĭmŭlātĭo -ōnis, f. *spurring on,
stimulating.*

stĭmŭlo -are *to goad, prick; to vex,
annoy; to incite, stir up.*

stĭmŭlus -i, m. *a goad; a sting, torment;
spur, incentive;* milit., *a pointed stake.*

stinguo -ĕre, *to extinguish, annihilate.*

stĭpātĭo -ōnis, f. *a crowd of attendants,
retinue.*

stĭpātor -ōris, m. *an attendant, follower;*
in plur., *train, retinue.*

stĭpendĭārĭus -a -um. (1) *liable to
taxes, tributary;* m. pl. as subst.
tributaries. (2) *of soldiers, serving for
pay.*

stĭpendĭum -i, n. (1) *a tax, tribute,
contribution.* Transf., *punishment.* (2)
*the pay of a soldier; military service;
a year's service, campaign.*

stĭpēs -ĭtis, m. *a log, stump, tree-trunk;
a branch, post, club; a blockhead.*

stīpo -are, *to press closely, compress; to
crowd* a place; *to press round a
person, accompany, attend.*

stips stĭpis, f. *a small coin, gift, ee.*

stĭpŭla -ae, f. *stalk, haulm, stubble; a
reed-pipe.*

stĭpŭlātĭo -onis, f. *agreement, covenant,
stipulation.*

stĭpŭlor -ari, dep. *to make demands,
bargain, stipulate.*

stīrĭa -ae, f. *icicle.*

stirpĭtŭs, *root and branch, thoroughly.*

stirps (stirpes, stirpis), stirpis, f.
rarely m., *the stock or stem of a
plant; a young shoot;* of men,
stock, source, origin; of things, *root,
foundation.*

stīva -ae, f. *a plough-handle.*

stlātārius -a -um, *brought by sea;* hence *costly.*

stlis, archaic, = lis; q.v.

sto stare stĕti stătum, *to stand, stand still, remain standing; to stand up stiffly;* milit., *to be stationed, or to stand firm;* naut., *to lie at anchor;* of abstr. things, *to remain, be fixed, stand firm, persist; to be resolved;* with ab, cum, pro, *to stand by, support, favour;* with abl. of price, *to cost;* per hominem stare, *to happen through a person's fault, be due to a person.*

Stŏĭcus -a -um, *Stoic;* m. as subst., *a Stoic;* n. pl. *the Stoic philosophy;* adv. **Stŏĭcē,** *like a Stoic, stoically.*

stŏla -ae, f. *a long outer garment, worn by Roman matrons and musicians.*

stŏlĭdus -a -um, *stupid, dull, obtuse;* adv. **stŏlĭdē.**

stŏmăchor -ari, dep. *to be angry.*

stŏmăchōsus -a -um, *angry, peevish, cross;* compar. adv. **stŏmăchōsius.**

stŏmăchus -i, m. *the gullet, oesophagus; the stomach;* stomachus bonus, *a good digestion,* hence *good humour; taste, liking; distaste, chagrin, anger.*

stŏrĕa (stŏria) -ae, f. *a rush mat.*

strābo -ōnis, m. *a squinter.*

strāgēs -is, f. *an overthrow; debris; slaughter, massacre, carnage.*

strāgŭlus -a -um, *covering, serving as a cover;* n. as subst. **strāgŭlum** -i, *a covering, carpet, mattress.*

strāmen -inis, n. *straw, litter.*

strāmentum -i, n. *straw, litter; a saddle, housing* (for mules).

strāmĭnĕus -a -um, *made of straw.*

strangŭlo -are, *to choke, strangle, throttle.*

strangūrĭa -ae, f. *strangury.*

strătēgēma -ătis, n. *a piece of generalship, a stratagem.*

strātum -i, n., subst. from sterno; q.v.

strēna -ae, f. *a favourable omen; a new year's gift.*

strēnŭĭtās -ātis, f. *briskness.*

strēnŭus -a -um, *brisk, active, vigorous;* in bad sense, *turbulent, restless;* adv. **strēnŭē.**

strĕpĭto -are, *to rustle, rattle, clatter.*

strĕpĭtus -ūs, m. *clattering, crashing, creaking, rumbling.*

strĕpo -ĕre -ŭi -ĭtum, *to clatter, creak, clash, rumble;* of persons *to cry out;* of places, *to resound.*

strictim, *so as to graze; superficially, slightly, summarily.*

strictūra -ae, f. *a mass of iron.*

strictus -a -um, partic. from stringo; q.v.

strīdĕo strīdēre strīdi and **strīdo** strīdĕre, *to make a harsh noise; to creak, grate, hiss.*

strīdor -ōris, m. *a creaking, grating* or *hissing noise.*

strīdŭlus -a -um, *creaking, hissing, grating.*

strĭgĭlis -is, f. *a scraper used at the baths.*

strĭgo -are, *to halt, stop.*

strĭgōsus -a -um, *lean, thin;* of style, *dry, meagre.*

stringo stringĕre strinxi strictum.
(1) *to draw tight together, to bind, tie.*
(2) *to strip off, pluck, prune;* esp. *to draw a weapon from its sheath.*
(3) *to graze, touch lightly; to affect, injure;* in speech, *to touch upon.*
Hence partic. **strictus** -a -um, *close, tight; strict;* of style, *brief, concise.*

stringor -ōris, m. *a shock, a twinge.*

strix strīgis, f. *a screech-owl.*

strŏpha -ae, f. *a trick, artifice.*

strŏphĭum -i, n. *a breast-band; a headband, chaplet.*

structĭlis -e, *used in building.*

structor -ōris, m. (1) *a builder, mason, carpenter.* (2) *a waiter, carver.*

structūra -ae, f. *the act of building;* concr. *a building;* of style, *arrangement, putting together.*

strŭēs -is, f. *a heap.*

strūma -ae, f. *a scrofulous tumour.*

strūmōsus -a -um, *scrofulous.*

strŭo strŭĕre struxi structum, *to put together, arrange; to pile up; to build, erect, construct; to devise, contrive.*

stŭdĕo -ēre -ŭi, *to be eager, take pains, strive after* (usually with dat.); *to side with, support, favour a person; to study a subject.*

stŭdĭōsus -a -um, *eager, zealous, keen; favouring a person or side, partial, devoted;* esp. *devoted to learning, studious.* Adv. **stŭdĭōsē,** *eagerly.*

stŭdĭum -i, n. *zeal, eagerness, application, enthusiasm; devotion to, goodwill towards a person or cause; application to learning, study.*

stultĭtĭa -ae, f. *foolishness, silliness.*

stultus -a -um, *foolish, silly;* m. as subst., *a simpleton, fool;* adv. **stultē.**

stūpa = stuppa; q.v.

stŭpĕfăcĭo -făcĕre -fēci -factum, pass. **stŭpĕfīo** -fiĕri, *to make senseless, benumb, stun.*

stŭpĕo -ere -ŭi, *to be stunned, astounded, amazed;* of inanimate things, *to stand still, halt, cease.*

stŭpesco stŭpescĕre stŭpŭi, *to become amazed, astounded.*

stŭpĭdĭtās -ātis, f. *dullness, senselessness.*

stŭpĭdus -a -um, *senseless, stunned; stupid, dull.*

stŭpor -ōris, m. *senselessness, insensibility; astonishment; dullness, stupidity.*

stuppa (stūpa) -ae, f. *tow, oakum.*

stuppĕus -a -um, *of tow.*

stupro -are, *to ravish, defile, pollute.*

stuprum -i, n. *disgrace, defilement;* esp. *ravishing, violation.*

sturnus -i, m. *a starling.*

Stўgĭālis, Stўgĭus; see Styx.

stўlus; see stilus.

Styx, Stўgis and Stўgos; acc. Stўgem and Stўga; f. *a river in Arcadia;* also *a river in the infernal regions;* adj. **Stўgĭālis** -e, and **Stўgĭus** -a -um, *Stygian, infernal.*

suādēla -ae, f. *persuasion.*

suădĕo suādēre suāsi suāsum, *to recommend, advise* (a course of action to a person).

suādus -a -um, *persuasive*; f. as subst. *persuasion.*

suāsĭo -ōnis, f. *advice, recommendation; persuasive eloquence.*

suāsor -ōris, m. *an adviser, recommender; one who advocates a law.*

suāsōrĭus -a -um, *of persuasion*; as subst. *persuasive discourse.*

suāsus -ūs, m. *persuasion.*

suāvĕŏlens -entis, *sweet-smelling.*

suāvĭdĭcus -a -um, *sweetly speaking.*

suāvĭlŏquens -entis, *sweetly speaking.*

suāvĭlŏquentĭa -ae, f. *sweetness of speech.*

suāvĭŏlum, suāvĭor; see sav-.

suāvis -e, *sweet, pleasant*; adv. **suāvĭtĕr.**

suāvĭtās -ātis, f. *sweetness, pleasantness.*

suāvĭum = savium; q.v.

sŭb, prep. (1) with abl.: *underneath, under; close under, at the foot of;* in time, *at, near to; in the power of, under; under cover of.* (2) with acc., *to* (or *along*) *the underside of; up under, down under, along under; close up to;* in time, *towards, just before;* also *immediately after; into the power of.*

sŭbabsurdus -a -um, *somewhat absurd*; adv. **sŭbabsurdē.**

sŭbaccūso -are, *to accuse a little.*

sŭbactĭo -ōnis, f. *preparation, discipline.*

sŭbadrōganter, *somewhat arrogantly.*

sŭbagrestis -e, *somewhat rustic or boorish.*

sŭbămārus -a -um, *somewhat bitter.*

sŭbausculto -are, *to listen secretly.*

subc-; see succ-.

subdifficĭlis -e, *somewhat difficult.*

subdiffīdo -ĕre, *to be somewhat distrustful.*

subdĭtīcĭus and **subdĭtīvus** -a -um, *supposititious, substituted, counterfeit.*

subdo -dĕre -dĭdi dĭtum, *to put, place or lay under; to subject, subdue; to put in the place of another, substitute; to counterfeit.*

subdŏcĕo -ēre, *to teach as an assistant, help in teaching.*

subdŏlus -a -um, *with secret guile; sly, crafty;* adv. **subdŏlē.**

subdŭbĭto -are, *to doubt or hesitate a little.*

subdūco -dūcĕre -duxi -ductum, *to draw up from under, pull up, raise, remove; to take away stealthily, steal;* naut., *to draw a ship up on shore;* milit., *to withdraw;* of accounts, *to balance, cast up.*

subductĭo -ōnis, f. *the drawing up of a ship on dry land; a reckoning, computing.*

sŭbĕdo -esse -ēdi, *to eat from under, wear away.*

sŭbĕo -īre -ĭi or -īvi -ĭtum. (1) *to go under, pass under;* of a bearer, *to to under and support; to undergo, submit to, take upon oneself.* (2) *to come from under, approach, advance, mount, climb;* of thoughts, etc., *to*

come into, or *come over, the mind.* (3) *to come on after, to follow;* sometimes *to come and support.*

Hence partic. **sŭbĭtus** -a -um, as adj., *sudden; coming suddenly, taking by surprise;* pass., *suddenly done, hastily contrived, improvised.* N. as subst. *a sudden occurrence, emergency.* N. abl. as adv. **sŭbĭtō,** *suddenly.*

sŭber -ĕris, n. *cork-tree; cork.*

subf-; see subff-.

subg-; see sugg-.

sŭbhorrĭdus -a -um, *somewhat rough.*

sŭbĭăcĕo -ēre -ŭi, *to lie under; to be subject to, be connected with.*

sŭbĭcĭo -icĕre -ĭēci -ĭectum, (1) *to throw* or *place under; to submit, subject;* in speech or writing, *to append, reply.* (2) *to throw up from below, raise, lift; to put into a mind, suggest.* (3) *to substitute, insert by guile, counterfeit.*

Hence partic. **sŭbĭectus** -a -um, *subjected;* of places, *lying near, adjacent;* superl. adv. **sŭbĭectissĭmē,** *most submissively.*

sŭbĭectĭo -ōnis, f. *a laying under, placing under; a counterfeiting, forging.*

sŭbĭecto -are, *to put under;* also *to throw up from below.*

sŭbĭector -ōris, m. *forger, counterfeiter.*

sŭbĭgo -ĭgĕre -ēgi -actum, *to drive under; to subject, constrain, subdue, compel; to drive up from below, to propel; to work the soil;* in gen., *to work at; to train, discipline.*

sŭbimpŭdens -entis, *somewhat impudent.*

sŭbĭnānis -e, *somewhat vain.*

sŭbindĕ, *immediately afterwards; repeatedly.*

sŭbinsulsus -a -um, *somewhat insipid.*

sŭbinvĭdĕo -ēre, *to envy somewhat;* partic. **sŭbinvīsus** -a -um, *somewhat hated.*

sŭbinvīto -are, *to invite mildly.*

sŭbīrascor -īrasci -īrātus, dep. *to get a little angry.*

sŭbĭtārĭus -a -um, *hastily contrived, improvised.*

sŭbĭto, sŭbĭtus; from subeo; q.v.

subiungo -iungĕre -iunxi -iunctum, *to yoke beneath; to join on, attach; to subdue, subjugate.*

sublābor -lābi -lapsus, dep. *to glide up; to glide from beneath, slip away.*

sublātĭo -ōnis, f. *lifting up, elevation.*

sublātus -a -um, partic. from tollo; q.v.

sublĕgo -lĕgĕre -lēgi -lectum, *to gather from below, pick up; to carry off secretly; to choose in the place of another.*

sublĕvātĭo -ōnis, f. *a relieving, lightening.*

sublĕvo -are, *to raise, lift, support; to encourage a person; to alleviate troubles.*

sublīca -ae, f. *a pile, stake.*

sublīcĭus -a -um, *resting upon piles.*

sublĭgācŭlum -i, and **sublĭgar** -āris, n. *a loincloth, kilt.*

subligo -are, *to bind below, bind on.*

sublimis -e (archaic **sublimus** -a -um), *high, raised, lofty; elevated, sublime.* N. acc. sing. as adv. **sublime**, *on high, aloft.*

sublimitās -ātis, f. *loftiness height, sublimity.*

sublimus; see sublimis.

sublūceo -ēre, *to gleam faintly, glimmer.*

sublūo -lŭere -lūtum, *to wash below; of rivers, to flow beneath.*

sublustris -e, *gleaming faintly, glimmering.*

subm -; see summ-.

subnascor -nasci -nātus, dep. *to grow up out of or after.*

subnecto -nectĕre -nexŭi -nexum, *to tie on, bind on beneath.*

subnĕgo -are, *to deny a little, partly refuse.*

subnixus (**subnīsus**) -a -um, *propped up, supported.*

subnŏto -are, *to mark beneath, write underneath; to notice secretly.*

subnūba -ae, f. *a rival.*

subnūbĭlus -a -um, *somewhat cloudy.*

sŭbo -are, *to be in heat.*

sŭbobscēnus -a -um, *somewhat obscene.*

sŭbobscūrus -a -um, *somewhat obscure.*

sŭbŏdiōsus -a -um, *rather unpleasant.*

sŭboffendo -ĕre, *to give some offence.*

sŭbŏlĕo -ēre (only in 3 pers.), *to emit a smell; hence to make itself felt.*

sŭbŏlēs -is, f. *a sprout, shoot, offspring, progeny.*

sŭbŏlesco -ĕre, *to grow up.*

sŭbŏrior -ŏriri, dep. *to arise after or in succession.*

sŭborno -are. (1) *to furnish, equip, provide.* (2) *to instigate secretly, suborn.*

sŭbortus -us, m. *an arising after or in succession.*

subp -; see supp-.

subrancĭdus -a -um, *somewhat putrid.*

subraucus -a -um, *somewhat hoarse.*

subrectus (**surr-**), partic. from subrigo; q.v.

subremigo (**surr-**) -are, *to row underneath.*

subrēpo (**surr-**) -rēpĕre -repsi, *to creep or crawl up to from below.*

subreptĭcius = surrepticius; q.v.

subrīdĕo (**surr-**) -rīdēre -rīsi -rīsum, *to smile.*

subrīdĭcŭlē, *somewhat laughably.*

subrigo (**surr-**) -rigĕre -rexi -rectum, *to raise, lift up.*

subringor -i, dep. *to make a wry face.*

subrĭpĭo = surripio; q.v.

subrŏgo (**surr-**) -are, *to suggest that a person be chosen as substitute for another.*

subrostrāni -ōrum, m. *loungers about the rostra, idlers.*

subrŭbĕo -ēre, *to blush slightly, be rather red.*

subrŭo -rŭĕre -rŭi -rŭtum, *to undermine, overthrow, destroy.*

subrustĭcus -a -um, *somewhat clownish.*

subscrĭbo -scrībĕre -scripsi -scriptum, *to write under, write beneath; to sign a document; to complete an indict-* ment, hence *to prosecute, accuse;* with dat., *to support, assent to; to note down, make a note of.*

subscriptio -ōnis, f. *a writing beneath, signature; the completion of an indictment; a record, register.*

subscriptor -ōris, m. *the signer of an indictment; an accuser.*

subsĕcīvus = subsīcīvus; q.v.

subsĕco -sĕcare -sĕcŭi -sectum, *to cut away below.*

subsellĭum -i, n. *a bench, seat, esp. in the courts.*

subsentĭo -sentire -sensi, *to notice secretly.*

subsĕquor -sĕqui -sĕcūtus, dep. *to follow after; to support a cause, etc.*

subservio -ire, *to be subject to, comply with.*

subsĭcīvus (**subsec-**) -a -um, *left over; extra, superfluous, spare.*

subsĭdĭārĭus -a -um, *in reserve.*

subsĭdĭum -i, n.: milit., *reserve troops, auxiliary forces;* in gen., *support, help, assistance.*

subsĭdo -sīdĕre -sēdi -sessum, *to crouch down, settle, sink, subside; to stay, remain; to lie in wait, lurk in ambush.*

subsignānus -a -um, *serving beneath the standard;* milites, *reserve legionaries.*

subsigno -are, *to write under, endorse; to enter on a list, to register.*

subsĭlio -sĭlire -sĭlŭi, *to leap up, spring up.*

subsisto -sistĕre -stĭti, *to stand; to make a stand, to withstand; to come to a stand, stop, halt, cease; to stay, remain.*

subsortĭor -iri, dep. *to choose by lot as a substitute.*

subsortītĭo -ōnis, f. *the choice of a substitute by lot.*

substantĭa -ae, f. *substance, essence; property, means of subsistence.*

substerno -sternĕre -strāvi -strātum, *to spread beneath, lay under; to set out, provide.*

substĭtŭo -ŭĕre -ŭi -ūtum, *to put next; to put under, to put in the place of another, to substitute.*

substo -stare, *to stand firm.*

substringo -stringĕre -strinxi -strictum, *to draw together, bind up;* partic. **substrictus** -a -um, *narrow, contracted, small.*

substructĭo -ōnis, f. *a base, foundation.*

substrŭo -strŭĕre -struxi -structum, *to build beneath, lay a foundation.*

subsŭlto -are, *to spring up, leap up.*

subsum -esse -fŭi, *to be near, be close at hand; to be under; to be subject; to be there, to exist.*

subsūtus -a -um, *fringed, edged below.*

subtēmen -ĭnis, n. *the weft or woof in weaving.*

subter (**supter**), adv. and prep., *beneath, below, underneath.*

subterfŭgĭo -fŭgĕre -fūgi, *to escape.*

subterlābor -lābi -lapsus, dep. *to glide under, flow under; to slip away, escape.*

subtĕro -tĕrĕre -trīvi -trītum, *to wear away underneath.*

subterrānĕus -a -um, *underground, subterranean.*

subtexo -texĕre -texŭi -textum, *to weave beneath; to connect, join on; to cover, darken.*

subtīlis -e, *finely woven, slender, fine;* of senses, etc., *discriminating, nice;* of style, *plain, simple, unadorned.* Hence adv. **subtīlĭtĕr,** *by fine links* or *passages;* of judgment, *with discrimination;* of style, *plainly, simply.*

subtīlĭtās -ātis, f. *fineness, minuteness;* of judgment, *discrimination;* of style, *plainness, simplicity.*

subtĭmĕo -ēre, *to be a little afraid.*

subtrăho -trăhĕre -traxi -tractum, *to draw up from beneath; to draw away secretly, remove, steal away.*

subturpĭcŭlus -a -um, *rather on the disgraceful side.*

subturpis -e, *rather disgraceful.*

subtŭs, adv. *beneath, below, underneath.*

subtūsus -a -um, *somewhat bruised.*

sŭbūcŭla -ae, f. *a shirt.*

sŭbŭla -ae, f. *a shoemaker's awl.*

sŭbulcus -i, m. *a swineherd.*

Sŭbūra -ae, f. *a part of Rome, north-east of the Forum.*

sŭburbānĭtās -ātis, f. *nearness to the city.*

sŭburbānus -a -um, *near the city* (Rome), *suburban;* n. as subst. *an estate near Rome.*

sŭburbĭum -i, n. *a suburb.*

sŭburgŭĕo -ēre, *to drive close.*

subvectĭo -ōnis, f. *carrying up, conveyance, transport.*

subvecto -are, *to carry up, convey, transport.*

subvectus -ūs, m. *a carrying up.*

subvĕho -vĕhĕre -vexi -vectum, *carry up, convey, transport.*

subvĕnĭo -vĕnīre -vēni -ventum, *to come up to aid, to succour, relieve.*

subvĕrĕor -ēri, dep. *to be rather anxious.*

subversor -ōris, m. *overthrower.*

subverto (-vorto) -vertĕre -verti -versum, *to overthrow, overturn, destroy.*

subvexus -a -um, *sloping upwards.*

subvŏlo -are, *to fly up.*

subvolvo -ĕre, *to roll up.*

succāvus -a -um, *hollow underneath.*

succēdo -cēdĕre -cessi -cessum. (1) *to go under; to submit to.* (2) *to go from under, ascend, mount.* (3) *to come after; to succeed, relieve, follow;* of things, *to turn out well, prosper, succeed.*

succendo -cendĕre -cendi -censum, *to set on fire from below; to kindle, inflame.*

succensĕo = suscenseo; q.v.

¹**succentŭrĭo** -are, *to put in the place of another, to substitute.*

²**succentŭrĭo** -ōnis, m. *an under-centurion.*

successĭo -ōnis, f. *succeeding, succession.*

successor -ōris, m. *a successor, follower, heir.*

successus -ūs, m. (1) *an advance uphill, approach.* (2) *success.*

succīdĭa -ae, f. *a flitch of bacon.*

¹**succīdo** -cidĕre -cidi, *to fall under; to sink, flag, fail.*

²**succīdo** -cidĕre -cīdi -cīsum, *to cut from under, cut down.*

succĭdŭus -a -um, *sinking, failing.*

succingo -cingĕre -cinxi -cinctum, *to gird below, gird up; to equip, arm, provide, surround;* partic. **succinctus** -a -um, as adj., *concise, succinct.*

succingŭlum -i, n. *a girdle.*

succino -ĕre, *to sing to, accompany;* in speech, *to chime in.*

succlāmātĭo -ōnis, f. *shouting in reply.*

succlāmo -are, *to shout back.*

succontŭmēliōsē, *somewhat insolently.*

succresco -crescĕre -crēvi, *to grow up, increase; to grow up to, match.*

succrispus = subcrispus; q.v.

succumbo -cumbĕre -cŭbŭi -cŭbĭtum, *to lie down under, sink down, give way, succumb, surrender.*

succurro -currĕre -curri -cursum· (1) *to run beneath, go under; to undergo;* of ideas, *to come into the mind.* (2) *to come to aid, succour, help, assist.*

succŭtĭo -cŭtĕre -cussi -cussum, *to shake from beneath, fling aloft.*

sūcĭdus -a -um, *juicy, full of sap.*

sūcĭnus -a -um, *of amber.*

sūco -ōnis, m. *a sucker.*

sūcus (succus) -i, m. *juice, sap; a draught; flavour, taste; sap, vigour, energy.*

sūdārĭum -i, n. *handkerchief, towel.*

sūdātōrĭus -a -um, *of sweating;* n. as subst. *a sweating-room.*

sūdātrix -trīcis, f. *causing perspiration.*

sūdis -is, f. *a stake, pile; a spike, point.*

sūdo -are: intransit., *to sweat, perspire; to make a great effort; to drip with moisture; to drip from, distil;* transit., *to sweat out, to exude; to soak with sweat.*

sūdor -ōris, m. *sweat, perspiration; great exertion; any moisture.*

sūdŭs -a -um, *dry;* of weather, *bright, cloudless;* n. as subst. *fine weather.*

Suēbi (Suēvi) -orum, m. *a Germanic tribe.*

suemus, I plur. as from sueo, *we are accustomed.*

suesco -suescĕre suēvi suētum: intransit., *to become accustomed;* transit., *to accustom.* Hence partic. **suētus** -a -um, *accustomed; customary, usual.*

Suētōnĭus -i, m. C. Suetonius Tranquillus, *author of the* Lives of the Caesars.

suētus -a -um, partic. from suesco; q.v.

Suēvi = Suebi; q.v.

sūfes (suffes) -fĕtis, m. *the chief magistrate at Carthage.*

suffarcĭno -are, *to stuff, cram.*

suffĕro sufferre, *to hold up, support; to endure, suffer.*

suffĭcĭo -fĭcĕre -fēci -fectum: transit., to put under; hence, to stain, steep, suffuse; to provide, supply; to put in place of another, to substitute, choose as a substitute; intransit., to be adequate, suffice; with infin., to be able.

suffīgo -fīgĕre -fixi -fixum, to fix up, fasten.

suffīmen -ĭnis and **suffīmentum** -i, n. incense.

suffĭo -ire, to fumigate, perfume; to warm.

sufflāmen -ĭnis, n. a brake, drag, hindrance.

sufflo -are: intransit., to blow; transit., to blow up, inflate.

suffōco -are, to strangle, choke, suffocate.

suffŏdĭo -fŏdĕre -fōdi -fossum, to pierce underneath, excavate, undermine.

suffrāgātĭo -ōnis, f. voting in favour, support.

suffrāgātor -ōris, m. a voter in favour; a (political) supporter.

suffrāgātōrĭus -a -um, relating to the support of a candidate.

suffrāgĭum -i, n. a voting tablet, a vote; the right to vote, franchise; in gen., judgment; approval, support.

suffrāgor -ari, dep. to vote for; to favour, approve, support.

suffringo -ĕre, to break underneath.

suffŭgĭo -fŭgĕre -fūgi, to flee, escape.

suffŭgĭum -i, n. a shelter, place of refuge.

suffulcĭo -fulcire -fulsi -fultum, to support beneath, undergo, underprop.

suffundo -fundĕre -fūdi -fūsum, to pour over, spread through, suffuse; to steep, stain, cover.

suffuscus -a -um, brownish, dark.

Sŭgambri (**Sӯg-**, **Sĭg-**) -ōrum, m. pl. a Germanic tribe.

suggĕro -gĕrĕre -gessi -gestum, to bring up, supply, provide; to add, attach; to place next.

suggestus -i, n. and **suggestus** -ūs, m. a raised place, height, elevation; esp., a platform.

suggrandis -e, somewhat large.

suggrĕdĭor -grĕdi -gressus, dep. to go up to, approach, attack.

sŭgillātĭo -ōnis, f. a bruise; mockery, insult.

sŭgillo -are, to beat, to insult.

sūgo sūgĕre suxi suctum, to suck.

sŭillus -a -um, of swine.

sulcātor -ōris, m. a plougher.

sulco -are, to furrow, plough; to wrinkle.

sulcus -i, m. a furrow; ploughing; a trench or ditch; a track, path.

sulfur (**sulpur**) -ŭris, n. sulphur; lightning.

sulfŭrātus -a -um, containing sulphur.

sulfŭrĕus -a -um, sulphurous.

Sulla (**Sylla**) -ae, m. a name of a family in the gens Cornelia; adj. **Sullānus** -a -um; verb **sullātŭrĭo** -ire, to wish to imitate Sulla.

Sulmo -ōnis, m. birth-place of Ovid; adj. **Sulmōnensis** -e.

sulpur = sulfur; q.v.

sultis = si vultis; see volo.

sum, esse, fŭi, to be, to exist, be there, be so; with dat., to be in one's possession; copulative, to be so and so, with complement; fut. partic. **fŭtūrus** -a -um, future, about to be; n. as subst. the future.

sūmen -ĭnis, n. the udder of a sow; a sow.

summa -ae; see summus.

summātim, adv. summarily, briefly.

summātus -ūs, m. supremacy, chief authority.

summergo -mergĕre -mersi -mersum, to plunge under, to sink.

summĭnistro -are, to help by supplying.

summissĭo (**subm-**) -ōnis, f. a letting down, lowering.

summitto (**subm-**) -mittĕre -misi -missum. (1) to let down, send under, lower; subject, subordinate; with animum, or se, to condescend, submit. (2) to send up from below, to raise, rear, make to grow. (3) to send as help. (4) to send secretly. Hence partic. **summissus** (**subm-**) -a -um, let down, lowered; mild, gentle, humble; in bad sense, mean, abject. Adv. **summissē**, softly, calmly; modestly, humbly.

summŏlestus (**subm-**) -a -um, somewhat troublesome; adv. **summŏlestē**, with some vexation.

summŏnĕo (**subm-**) -ēre, to remind secretly.

summŏpĕrĕ (**summō ŏpĕrĕ**), very much, exceedingly.

summŏrosus (**subm-**) -a -um, somewhat peevish.

summŏvĕo (**subm-**) mŏvĕre -mōvi -mōtum, to move up from below; to move away, drive off, expel; esp. of the lictor, to clear a way for a magistrate, to keep back the crowd; to force away from, compel, to give up; pass. partic., **summōtus**, lying out of the way, remote.

summūto (**subm-**) -are, to exchange.

sūmo sūmĕre sumpsi sumptum, to take, choose, obtain, buy; of clothes, etc., to put on; to exact a punishment; to take upon oneself, claim; to take for granted, assume.

sumptĭo -ōnis f. the premiss of a syllogism.

sumptŭārĭus -a -um, relating to expense, sumptuary.

sumptŭōsus -a -um: of things, costly, expensive; of persons, lavish, extravagant; adv. **sumptŭōsē**, expensively, sumptuously.

sumptus -ūs, m. cost, expense.

sŭo sŭĕre sŭi sūtum, to sew, stitch together, join together.

sŭōmet and **sŭōpte**; see suus.

sŭŏvĕtaurīlĭa -ĭum, n. pl., a sacrifice of a pig, sheep and bull.

sŭpellex -lectĭlis, f. household furniture.

¹sŭper -a -um; see superus.

²**sŭper.** Adv., *over, above; besides, beyond, moreover; remaining, over and above.* Prep.: with abl., of place *over, above;* of time, *at; concerning, about; besides, beyond;* with acc., of place, *over, above, upon; besides, beyond;* of time, *during;* of superiority, *above, more than.*

sŭpĕrā; see supra.

sŭpĕrābĭlis -e, *that can be surmounted; conquerable.*

sŭpĕraddo -addĕre -addĭtum, *to add as well, put on besides.*

sŭpĕrātor -ōris, m. *a conqueror.*

sŭpĕrbĭa -ae, f. *pride; haughtiness, arrogance.*

sŭpĕrbĭo -ire: of persons, *to be proud, pride oneself;* of things, *to be splendid, superb.*

sŭpĕrbus -a -um, *haughty, exalted, proud; arrogant, overbearing; brilliant, splendid.* Adv. **sŭpĕrbē,** *haughtily, proudly.*

sŭpercĭlĭum -i, n. *an eyebrow; the eyebrows; a nod* (as expression of will); *arrogance, censoriousness;* of things, *ridge, summit.*

sŭpĕrēmĭnĕo -ēre, *to overtop.*

sŭperfĭcĭēs -ēi, f. *top, surface.*

sŭperfĭo -fĭĕri, *to be left over.*

sŭperfĭxus -a -um, *fixed on the top.*

sŭperflŭo -flŭĕre, *to flow over, overflow, be superfluous.*

sŭperfundo -fundĕre -fūdi -fūsum, *to pour over, pour upon;* pass., *to overflow;* in gen., *to spread about, spread over.*

sŭpergrĕdĭor -grĕdi -gressus, dep. *to step beyond, overstep; to exceed, surpass.*

sŭpĕrĭăcĭo -ĭăcĕre -ĭēci -ĭectum or -ĭactum, *to throw over, throw upon; to overtop, exceed, go beyond.*

sŭpĕrimmĭnĕo -ēre, *to overhang.*

sŭpĕrimpendens -entis, *overhanging.*

sŭpĕrimpŏsĭtus -a -um, *laid over, placed upon.*

sŭpĕrincĭdens -entis, *falling on top.*

sŭpĕrincŭbans -antis, *lying over or upon.*

sŭpĕrincumbo -cumbĕre -cŭbŭi *to lie on, lie over.*

sŭpĕrinĭcĭo -inĭcĕre -inĭēci -inĭectum, *to throw upon.*

sŭpĕrinsterno -sternĕre -strāvi, *to spread over, lay over.*

sŭpĕrĭor -oris, compar. of superus, q.v.

sŭperlātĭo -ōnis, f. *exaggeration, hyperbole.*

sŭperlātus -a -um, *exaggerated, hyperbolical.*

sŭpernus -a -um, *above, upper, high;* adv. **sŭpernĕ,** *above or from above.*

sŭpĕro -are: intransit., *to go above, overtop, project; to prevail, conquer; to abound; to remain, be over;* esp. *to remain alive, survive; to be too much, to exceed;* transit., *to rise above, surmount, overtop, pass; to surpass, excel, exceed; to overcome, conquer.* Compar. of pres. partic. **sŭpĕrantĭor** -oris, *more dominant.*

sŭpĕrobrŭo -ŭĕre, *to overwhelm.*

sŭperpendens -entis, *overhanging.*

sŭperpōno -pōnĕre -pŏsŭi -pŏsĭtum, *to place over,* or *upon; to put in authority.*

sŭperscando -ĕre, *to climb over.*

sŭpersĕdĕo -sĕdĕre -sēdi -sessum, *to sit above, sit out;* hence *to forbear, refrain.*

sŭperstagno -are, *to spread out into a lake.*

sŭpersterno -sternĕre -strāvi -strātum, *to spread over* or *upon.*

sŭperstĕs -stĭtis, *standing over* or *near; present, witnessing; surviving, living on.*

sŭperstĭtĭo -ōnis, f. *superstition, fanaticism.*

sŭperstĭtĭōsus -a -um, *superstitious;* adv. **sŭperstĭtĭōsē.**

sŭpersto -are, *to stand over* or *upon.*

sŭperstrŭo -strŭĕre -struxi -structum, *to build upon.*

sŭpersum -esse -fŭi -fŭtūrus, *to be over and above; to be left, remain, survive; to be plentiful, to abound; to be superfluous, be redundant.*

sŭpĕrurgĕo -ēre, *to press from above.*

sŭpĕrus (rarely **sŭper**) -a -um, *situated above; upper, higher;* m. pl. as subst. *the gods above;* also *men on earth;* n. pl. *heights* or *heavenly bodies.* Compar. **sŭpĕrĭor** -ĭus, *higher, upper;* of time, *earlier, former, past;* of rank, etc., *higher, greater.* Superl. **sŭprēmus** -a -um, of place, *highest, uppermost;* in time, *last, final;* of degree, *highest, greatest;* of rank, *highest;* n. sing. as subst., *the end;* n. pl., **sŭprēma** -ōrum, *death, funeral rites, last will and testament.* Used as another superl. **summus** -a -um, *highest, uppermost, at the top;* **summa urbs,** *the highest part of the city;* of the voice, *highest, loudest;* of time, *last;* of rank, etc., *greatest, highest, most distinguished.* F. as subst. **summa** -ae *the highest place, the main thing, most important point; a summary, the gist, the sum total of an amount.* N. as subst. **summum** -i, *surface, top;* acc. as adv., *at most.* Adv. **summē,** *in the highest degree, extremely.*

sŭpervācănĕus and **sŭpervācŭus** -a -um, *superfluous, unnecessary, extra.*

sŭpervado -ĕre, *to go over, surmount.*

sŭpervĕhor -vĕhi -vectus sum, *to ride* or *sail past.*

sŭpervĕnĭo -vĕnire -vēni -ventum, *to come upon, rise above; to arrive, come up,* esp. *unexpectedly.*

sŭperventus -ūs, m. *coming up, (unexpected) arrival.*

sŭpervīvo -ĕre, *to survive.*

sŭpervōlĭto -are, and **sŭpervōlo** -are, *to fly over, fly above.*

sŭpīno -are, *to put face upwards, throw on the back.*

sŭpīnus -a -um, *lying on the back, face-upwards;* manus, *with palm upwards;* of streams, *flowing up, returning;* of ground, *sloping upwards;* of character, *negligent, lazy.*

suppaenĭtet -ēre, *to cause slight regret.*

suppār -pāris, *almost equal.*

suppĕdĭtātĭo -ōnis, f. *abundant provision.*

suppĕdĭto -are: intransit., *to be at hand, be ready, suffice;* transit., *to provide, supply, give.*

suppernātus -a -um, *lamed in the hip.*

suppĕtĭae -ārum, f. pl. *help, aid.*

suppĕtĭor -ari, dep. *to help, assist.*

suppĕto -ēre, -īvi and -ĭi, -ĭtum, *to be in store, be at hand; to suffice, be enough.*

supplanto -are, *to trip up.*

supplēmentum -i, n. *filling up, completion;* milit., *a body of recruits, reinforcements.*

supplĕo -plēre -plēvi -plētum, *to fill up, make complete.*

supplex -plĭcis, *kneeling; entreating, suppliant;* adv. **supplĭcĭtĕr.**

supplĭcātĭo -ōnis, f. *solemn public prayer* or *thanksgiving; a religious festival* or *fast.*

supplĭcĭum -i, n. (1) *a humble entreaty, supplication, prayer.* (2) *punishment;* esp. *capital punishment.*

supplĭco -are, *to kneel, beseech, entreat;* esp. *to pray to the gods.*

supplōdo -plōdĕre -plōsi, *to stamp.*

supplōsĭo -ōnis, f. *a stamping.*

suppōno -pōnĕre -pŏsŭi -pŏsĭtum. (1) *to put under; to subject.* (2) *to put next to, to add.* (3) *to put in the place of; to substitute, counterfeit, forge.*

supporto -are, *to carry up.*

suppŏsĭtīcĭus -a -um, *substituted, spurious.*

suppressĭo -ōnis, f. *embezzlement.*

supprĭmo -prĭmĕre -pressi -pressum, *to press under; to hold down, check, restrain; to keep back, suppress, conceal;* pecuniam, nummos, *to embezzle.* Partic. **suppresssus** -a -um, *checked, restrained;* of the voice, *low, subdued.*

suppŭdet -ēre, *to cause some shame.*

suppus -a -um, *head-downwards.*

suppŭto -are, *to count up, compute.*

suprā. Adv. *over, on the top;* of time, *before, previously;* in writing, *above;* of amount, etc., *over, more, beyond;* supra quam, *more than.* Prep., with acc., *above, over;* of time, *before;* of amount, *more than, above, beyond.*

suprascando -ĕre, *to climb over, surmount.*

suprēmus, etc.; see superus.

sūra -ae, f. *the calf of the leg.*

surcŭlus -i, m. *a young shoot, sprout, twig; a slip, sucker.*

surdaster -tra -trum, *somewhat deaf.*

surdĭtās -ātis, f. *deafness.*

surdus -a -um, *deaf; unwilling to hear, insensible; not heard, still, silent;* of sounds, etc., *indistinct, faint.*

surēna -ae, m. *a Parthian grand vizier.*

surgo surgĕre surrexi surrectum, *to rise, get up; to spring up, arise.*

surpŭit, etc., forms from surripio; q.v.

surr-; see also subr-.

surreptīcĭus (subr-) -a -um, *stolen, secret, surreptitious.*

surrĭpĭo -rĭpĕre -rīpŭi -reptum, *to take away secretly; to steal, filch.*

sursum (sursus), *upwards, on high;* sursum deorsum, *up and down, backwards, and forwards.*

sus sŭis, c. *a sow, swine, pig, hog; a kind of fish.*

suscensĕo -ēre -ŭi, *to be angry, bear a grudge.*

susceptĭo -ōnis, f. *undertaking.*

suscĭpĭo -cĭpĕre -cēpi -ceptum, *to take up, catch up; to support, raise; to accept, receive,* esp. *to acknowledge a child as one's own; to take upon oneself, undertake, begin; to maintain a point, be ready to prove.*

suscĭto -are, *to stir up, arouse, excite.*

suspecto -are, *to keep looking at, gaze upon; to look upon with suspicion, suspect.*

¹**suspectus** -a -um, partic. from suspicio; q.v.

²**suspectus** -ūs, m. *looking upwards; respect, esteem.*

suspendĭum -i, n. *a hanging of oneself.*

suspendo -pendĕre -pendi -pensum, *to hang up; to prop up, support; to keep in suspense, leave undecided; to check, break off.* Hence partic. **suspensus** -a -um, *hovering, hanging, suspended; dependent; ambiguous, doubtful, in suspense.*

suspĭcax -ācis: act., *suspicious, suspecting;* pass., *suspicious, suspected.*

¹**suspĭcĭo** -spĭcĕre -spexi -spectum, *to look from below, look upwards; to look up to, esteem, respect; to look askance at, suspect.* Hence partic. **suspectus** -a -um, *suspected.*

²**suspĭcĭo** -ōnis, f. *mistrust, suspicion; a faint idea, imperfect conception.*

suspĭcĭōsus -a -um, *feeling suspicion, suspecting; exciting suspicion, suspicious;* adv. **suspĭcĭōsē,** *in a suspicious manner, suspiciously.*

suspĭcor -ari, dep. *to suspect; to conjecture, suppose, surmise.*

suspīrātus -ūs, and **suspīrĭtus** -ūs, and **suspīrĭum** -i, n. *a deep breath, a sigh.*

suspīro -are: intransit., *to draw a deep breath, to sigh;* transit., *to sigh for, long for.*

susque dequĕ, *up and down.*

sustentācŭlum -i, n. *a prop, support.*

sustentātĭo -ōnis, f. *forbearance.*

sustento -are, *to hold up, support, sustain; to maintain; to put off, hinder, delay.*

sustĭnĕo -tĭnēre -tĭnŭi -tentum, *to hold up, support, sustain;* with infin., *to endure to, have the heart to; to maintain; to put off, delay; to hold back, check, restrain.*

sustollo -ĕre, *to lift up, raise; to take away, remove, destroy.*

sŭsurrātor -ōris, m. *a mutterer.*

sŭsurro -are, *to murmur, mutter, whisper;* of bees, *to hum.*

¹**sŭsurrus** -i, m. *a murmur, muttering, whisper, hum, buzz.*

²**sŭsurrus** -a -um, *whispering, muttering.*

sūtĭlis -e, *stitched together, fastened together.*

sūtor -ōris, m. *a shoemaker, cobbler.*

sūtōrĭus and sūtrīnus -a -um, *of a shoemaker.*

sūtūra -ae, f. *a seam, suture.*

sŭus -a -um, reflexive possessive pronoun of 3rd person, *his, her, its, their* (*own*); often strengthened by -pte or -met; sometimes *proper, due, suitable; favourable; independent.* As subst., *one's own people, property,* etc.

Sybāris -ris, f. *a town in Lucania, famous for luxury.*

sycŏphanta -ae, f. *an informer, trickster.*

Sylla = Sulla; q.v.

syllăba -ae, f. *a syllable;* in plur., *verses, poems.*

syllăbātim, *syllable by syllable.*

syllŏgismus (or -ŏs) -i, m. *a syllogism.*

symbŏla -ae, f. *a contribution towards a common feast.*

symphōnĭa -ae, f. *a concert, musical performance.*

symphōnĭăcus -a -um, *of or for a concert.*

sўnedrus -i, m. *a Macedonian councillor.*

syngrăpha -ae, f. *a bond, agreement to pay.*

sўnŏdūs -ontis, m. *a fish, perhaps bream.*

synthĕsis -is, f. *a dinner-service; a suit of clothes; a dressing-gown.*

Syrācūsae -ārum, f. pl. *the chief town of Sicily.*

Syrĭa -ae, f. *Syria;* adj. Syrĭus, Sўrus, Sўrĭăcus -a -um, *Syrian;* subst. Sўri -orum, *the Syrians.*

syrma -mătis, n. *a long robe, worn by tragic actors.*

syrtis -is, f. *a sandbank, quicksand;* esp. *one on the coast of Northern Africa.*

T

T, t, the nineteenth letter of the Latin Alphabet.

tăbella -ae, f. *a small flat board or tablet; a writing-tablet; a document, letter, record; a votive tablet; a voting-ticket, ballot; a picture.*

tăbellārĭus -a -um, *of letters* or *of voting.* M. as subst. *a letter-carrier.*

tābĕo -ere, *to waste away; to drip, run.*

tăberna -ae, f. *a booth, hut; a cottage, hovel; a stall, shop; an inn, tavern; a block of seats in the Circus.*

tăbernāculum -i, n. *a hut, tent.*

tăbernārĭus -i, m. *a shopkeeper.*

tābes -is, f. *wasting away, decay, melting; disease, pestilence; demoralization; decayed matter, corruption.*

tābesco tābescĕre tābŭi, *to melt, waste away; to pine, be spoiled.*

tābĭdŭlus -a -um, *wasting, consuming.*

tābĭdus -a -um: pass., *melting, wasting, dissolving;* act., *consuming.*

tābĭfĭcus -a -um, *consuming.*

tābŭla -ae, f. *a board, plank; a draughtboard; a painted panel, a painting; a votive tablet; a map; a writing-tablet; a document;* in plur., *a record, register; a catalogue; an auction.*

tăbŭlārĭum -i, n. *archives, records.*

tăbŭlātĭo -ōnis, f. *flooring, planking; a storey.*

tăbŭlātus -a -um, *floored, boarded;* n. as subst., *a floor, storey; a row* or *layers of vines.*

tābum -i, n. *corrupt moisture, matter; a plague, pestilence.*

tăcĕo -ēre -ŭi -ĭtum, *to be silent,* say *nothing; to be still, quiet;* transit., *to be silent about, pass over in silence.*

Hence partic. tăcĭtus -a -um: pass., *passed over in silence, unmentioned; implied, tacit; secret, concealed;* act., *silent, mute, still, quiet.* Adv. tăcĭtē.

tăcĭturnĭtās -ātis, f., *silence, taciturnity*

tăcĭturnus -a -um, *silent, still, quiet.*

tăcĭtus -a -um, partic. from taceo; q.v.

Tăcĭtus -i, m., Cornelius, *the historian of the early Empire.*

tactĭlis -e, *able to be touched.*

tactĭo -ōnis, f. *touching, sense of touch.*

tactus -ūs, m. *touch, touching; influence, operation; the sense of touch.*

taeda -ae, f. *pine-wood; a board, a torch,* esp. as used at weddings.

taedet taedēre taedŭit, and taesum est, impers., *it causes weariness* or *boredom.*

taedĭfer -fĕra -fĕrum, *torch-bearing.*

taedĭum -i, n. *disgust, weariness, boredom.*

taenĭa -ae, f. *a fillet, head-band.*

taeter -tra -trum, *foul, hideous, offensive; disgraceful, abominable;* adv. taetrē.

tăgax -ācis, *thievish, given to pilfering.*

tālāris -e, *of* or *stretching to the ankles;* n. pl. as subst. *wings on the ankles, winged sandals,* or *a robe reaching to the ankles.*

tālārĭus -a -um, *of dice.*

tālĕa -ae, f. *a cutting, slip; a short stake* or *bar.*

tălentum -i, n. *a (Greek) weight;* also *a sum of money.*

tālĭo -ōnis, f. *retaliation.*

tālis -e, *of such a kind, such.*

talpa -ae, f. or m. *a mole.*

tālus -i, m. *the ankle, ankle-bone; the heel; a die* (made originally of anklebones of animals).

tam, *so, so far, to such a degree.*

tămărix -ĭcis, f. *the tamarisk.*

tamdĭū, *so long.*

tămĕn, *however, yet, nevertheless.*

Tămĕsis -is, m. and Tămĕsa -ae, *the Thames.*

tămetsi, *even if, although.*

tamquam (tanquam), *as, just as, like as; just as if.*

tandem, *at length, at last;* in questions, *after all, may I ask?*

tango tangĕre tĕtĭgi tactum, *to touch, strike, push, hit; to border on, to reach; to steal; to defile; to taste; to affect the feelings; to touch upon a subject.*

Tantălus i-, m. *a son of Jupiter, who offended the gods and was " tantalised "* in Hades.

tantillus -a -um, *so little, so small*

tantispĕr, *just so long.*

tantŏpĕrĕ, *so greatly, so much.*

tantŭlus -a -um, *so small, so little;* n. as subst. *such a trifle.*

tantum; see tantus.

tantummŏdo, *only just.*

tantus -a -um, *of such a size, so great.* N. as subst. **tantum** -i, *so much;* acc. as adv., *so far,* or *only;* tantum non, *all but;* genit. **tanti,** *for so much, worth so much;* abl. **tanto,** *by so much.*

tantusdem tantādem tantundem, *just so much, just so great.*

tăpēta -ae, m. **tăpēta** -ōrum, n. pl., and **tăpētĭa** -ĭum, n. pl., *drapery, tapestry.*

tardesco -ĕre, *to become slow.*

tardĭpēs -pĕdis, *slow-footed, limping.*

tardĭtās -ātis, f. *slowness, tardiness; dullness, stupidity.*

tardo -are: intransit., *to loiter, be slow;* transit., *to slow down, hinder, delay.*

tardus -a -um, adj. *slow, tardy; dull, stupid;* poet., *making slow;* of speech, *measured, deliberate.* Adv. **tardē,** *slowly.*

Tărentum -i, n. *a coastal town of southern Italy* (now Taranto); adj. **Tărentīnus** -a -um.

Tarpēius -a -um, *name of a Roman family;* mons Tarpeius, *the Tarpeian rock, from which criminals were thrown.*

Tarquinĭi -orum, m. pl. *an old town in Etruria, whence came the Tarquin family, including two kings of Rome.*

Tarrāco -ōnis, f. *a town in Spain.*

Tartărus (-ŏs) -i, m.; plur. **Tartără** -ōrum, n. *the infernal regions;* adj. **Tartărĕus** -a -um.

taurĕus -a -um, *of a bull;* f. as subst. *a whip of bull's hide.*

taurĭformis -e, *shaped like a bull.*

taurīnus -a -um, *of* or *like a bull.*

taurus -i, m. *a bull.*

Taurus -i, m. *a mountain range in Asia Minor.*

taxātĭo -onis, f. *rating, valuing, appraising.*

taxillus -i, m. *a small die.*

taxus -i, f. *yew-tree.*

¹**tē;** see tu.

²**-tē,** *suffix added to tu,* etc.

techna -ae, f. *a cunning trick, artifice.*

tector -ōris, m. *a plasterer.*

tectōrĭŏlum -i, n. *plaster* or *stucco work.*

tectōrĭus -a -um, *used for covering, of* or *for plastering;* n. as subst. *plaster, stucco, fresco painting, cosmetic.*

tectus -a -um, partic. from tego; q.v.

tĕgēs -ĕtis, f. *a mat, rug, covering.*

tĕgĭmen, tĕgŭmen, tegmĕn -ĭnis, n. *a cover, covering.*

tĕgĭmentum, tĕgŭmentum, tegmentum -i, n. *a covering.*

tĕgo tĕgĕre texi tectum, *to cover; to bury; to conceal; to shield, protect.* Hence partic. as adj. **tectus** -a -um, *covered, concealed; close, reserved, cautious.* N. as subst. **tectum** -i, *a roof* or *ceiling; a shelter, dwelling.* Adv. **tectē,** *covertly.*

tegu-; see also tegi-.

tēgŭla -ae, f. *a roof-tile.*

tela -ae, f. *a web in weaving; a warp; a spider's web; a loom; a design.*

Tēlĕmăchus -i, m. *son of Penelope and Ulysses.*

tellūs -ūris, f. *earth, soil, land; a country; the world.*

tēlum -i, n. *a missile; a dart, javelin, spear; any weapon; a beam of light.*

tĕmĕrārĭus -a -um, *accidental; inconsiderate, thoughtless, rash.*

tĕmĕrē, adv. *blindly, by chance, casually, heedlessly;* non temere, *not for nothing, not lightly, not easily.*

tĕmĕrĭtās -ātis, f. *chance, accident; rashness.*

tĕmĕro -are, *to darken; to defile, dishonour.*

tēmētum -i, n. *intoxicating drink; wine,* etc.

temno temnĕre tempsi temptum, *to despise.*

tēmo -ōnis, m. *a pole; the pole of a waggon; a waggon; Charles's Wain.*

Tempē, n. pl., indecl. *a valley in Thessaly.*

tempĕrāmentum -i, n. *a right proportion, middle way, mean, moderation.*

temperantĭa -ae, f. *temperance moderation, self-control.*

tempĕrātĭo -ōnis, f. *moderation, just proportion; an organizing principle.*

tempĕrātor -ōris, m. *one who arranges* or *governs.*

tempĕri; see tempus.

tempĕriēs -ēi, f. *a proper mixture, tempering;* of climate, *mildness.*

tempĕro -are: intransit., *to be moderate, control oneself;* with dat. *to control, use with moderation,* or *to spare;* with ab, or with abl., *to keep from, refrain from;* transit., *to mix properly, temper, mitigate, regulate.* Hence partic. as adj. **tempĕrans** -antis, *moderate, temperate, restrained;* adv. **tempĕranter:** perf. partic. **tempĕrātus** -a -um, *tempered, ordered, moderate;* adv. **tempĕrātē.**

tempestās -ātis, f. *a period of time, a season; weather; esp. bad weather, storm, tempest;* fig., *attack, fury.*

tempestīvĭtās -ātis, f. *fit time, proper season.*

tempestīvus -a -um, *opportune, fit, appropriate; early; ripe, mature.* Adv. **tempestīvē,** *seasonably.*

templum -i, n. *a section, a part cut off; a space marked out by the augur for auspices; consecrated ground, esp. a sanctuary, asylum; a place dedicated to a deity, a shrine, temple; any open space, quarter, region; a rafter, crossbeam.*

tempŏrālis -e, *temporary, lasting for a time.*

tempŏrārĭus -a -um, *temporary; seasonable.*

tempŏri; see tempus.

temptābundus -a -um, *trying, attempting.*

temptāmĕn -ĭnis, and **temptāmentum** -i, n. *a trial, attempt, essay.*

temptātĭo -ōnis, f. *a trial, test; an attack.*

temptātor -ōris, m. *an assailant.*

tempto -are, *to prove, try, test, attempt; to test by attack, to assail; to work upon, tamper with, excite, disturb.*

tempus -ŏris, n. *a division, section; of the temples of the head; of time, a space, period, moment; time, in gen.; a fit time, occasion, opportunity; the state, condition of things (esp. bad); time in pronouncing a syllable, quantity; time in grammar, tense.* As adv. **tempŏrĕ, tempŏrī,** and **tempĕrī,** *at the right time,* or *for the occasion;* **in tempŏrĕ,** *at the right moment;* **ex tempŏrĕ,** *on the spur of the moment.*

tēmŭlentus -a -um, *drunken, tipsy.*

tĕnācĭtās -ātis, f. *tenacity; stinginess.*

tĕnax -ācis, *holding fast, clinging, tenacious; sparing, frugal, stingy; firm, steady; obstinate.* Adv. **tĕnācĭtĕr,** *firmly, steadily.*

tendĭcŭla -ae, f. *a snare, trap.*

tendo tendĕre tĕtendi tentum and tensum: transit., *to stretch, extend, spread; to direct, present, give;* barbiton, *to string;* praetorium, *to pitch;* intransit., *to direct one's course, tend, make towards; to be inclined, aim at, strive after;* with infin., *to try, attempt;* milit., *to pitch one's tent, encamp.*

tĕnebrae -arum, f. pl. *darkness; night; blindness; obscurity.*

tĕnebrĭcōsus -a -um, *dark, gloomy, obscure.*

tĕnebrōsus -a -um, *dark, gloomy.*

tĕnĕo tĕnēre tĕnŭi tentum, *to hold; to possess, keep, preserve, maintain; to understand, grasp, know, remember; to contain, comprise;* milit. *to occupy, garrison; to master, restrain, keep back; to charm, amuse;* intransit., *to keep on, persevere, persist, endure.*

tĕner -ĕra -ĕrum, *tender, delicate, soft; young;* adv. **tĕnĕrē.**

tĕnĕrasco -ĕre, *to grow tender.*

tĕnĕrĭtās -ātis, f. *tenderness, softness.*

tĕnor -ōris, m. *course, continued movement; duration, career.*

tensa -ae, f. *a car on which images of the gods were carried.*

tento, etc.; see tempto, etc.

tentīgo -ĭnis, f. *lecherousness.*

tentōrĭum -i, n. *a tent.*

tentus -a -um, partic. from tendo and teneo; q.v.

tĕnŭĭcŭlus -a -um, *very mean, slight.*

tĕnŭis -e, *thin, slight, slender; refined, subtle; little, trivial, feeble; mean, low.* Adv. **tĕnŭĭtĕr,** *thinly; subtly; slightly, poorly.*

tĕnŭĭtās -ātis, f. *thinness; refinement, subtlety; slightness, poverty.*

tĕnŭo -are, *to make thin, attenuate; to weaken, diminish.*

tĕnŭs, prep. after noun or pronoun in abl. or genit., *up to, down to, as far as.*

tĕpĕfăcĭo -făcĕre -fēci -factum, *to make warm.*

tĕpĕo -ēre, *to be warm,* or *lukewarm.*

tĕpesco tĕpescĕre tĕpŭi, *to grow warm* or *lukewarm.*

tĕpĭdus -a -um, *warm, lukewarm, tepid;* compar. adv. **tĕpĭdĭus.**

tĕpor -ōris, m. *lukewarmness, moderate heat.*

tĕr, *three times, thrice.*

terdĕcĭēs (-ĭens) *thirteen times.*

tĕrĕbinthus -i, f. *the terebinth-tree.*

tĕrebro -are, *to bore through, pierce, perforate.*

tĕrēdo -ĭnis, f. *a worm that gnaws wood.*

Tĕrentĭus -a -um, *the name of a Roman gens;* esp. of M. Terentius Afer, *the comic dramatist.*

tĕrĕs -rĕtis, *rounded, polished, well-turned, smooth; refined, elegant.*

tergĕmĭnus = trigeminus; q.v.

tergĕo -ēre and **tergo** -ĕre, tersi tersum, *to wipe, scour, clean;* partic. **tersus** -a -um, *clean, neat, correct.*

tergĭversātĭo -ōnis, f. *backwardness, reluctance, evasion.*

tergĭversor -ari, dep. *to be backward and reluctant, shuffle, find excuses, evade.*

tergo = tergeo; q.v.

tergum -i, n. *the back;* terga dare, *to flee;* a tergo, *in the rear; a hide, skin;* meton., *a thing made out of hide.*

tergus -ŏris, n. *the back; skin, hide, leather.*

termĕs -ĭtis, m. *a branch,* esp. of olive.

Termĭnālĭa -ĭum and -ĭōrum, n. *the Festival of Terminus (god of boundaries).*

termĭnātĭo -ōnis, f. *limiting, determining, termination.*

termĭno -are, *to limit, set bounds to, restrict, define, close.*

termĭnus -i, m. *a boundary-mark, limit, end;* personif., *the god of boundaries.*

terni -ae -a, *three at a time,* or *three each.*

tĕro tĕrĕre trīvi trītum, *to rub; to whet, smooth; to grind, thresh; to wear out, use up, spend.* Hence partic. as adj. **trītus** -a -um, *worn; frequented; practised;* of words, etc., *trite, well-known.*

Terpsĭchŏrē -ēs, f. *the Muse of dancing;* in gen., *poetry.*

terra -ae, f. *earth, land, ground, soil; a country, land, region;* orbis terrarum, *the whole world.*

terrēnus -a -um, *belonging to the earth, terrestrial; made of earth, earthen;* n. as subst. *land, ground.*

terrĕo terrēre, *to frighten, terrify; scare away; to deter.*

terrestris -e, *of the earth, terrestrial.*

terrĕus -a -um, *of earth, earthly.*

terrĭbĭlis -e, *terrible, dreadful.*

terrĭcŭla -ōrum, n. pl. *a bogey.*

terrĭfĭco -are, *to frighten, terrify.*

terrĭfĭcus -a -um, *frightful, terrible.*

terrĭgĕna -ae, m. and f. *earth-born.*

terrĭlŏquus -a -um, *terror-speaking.*

territo -are, *to frighten, intimidate, scare.*

territōrĭum -i, n. *land belonging to a town, district, territory.*

terror -ōris, m. *fright, fear, terror; a frightening object.*

tersus -a -um, partic. from tergeo; q.v.

tertiădĕcĭmāni -ōrum, m. pl. *soldiers of the thirteenth legion.*

tertiānus -a -um. (1) *of the third day;* f. as subst., *a tertian fever.* (2) *belonging to the third legion;* m. pl. as subst., *soldiers of the third legion.*

tertĭus -a -um, *third;* acc. n. sing. **tertĭum**, *for the third time;* abl. **tertĭō**, *for the third time,* or *thirdly.*

tertĭusdĕcĭmus -a -um, *thirteenth.*

tĕruncĭus -i, m. *one quarter;* ne teruncius quidem, *not a farthing.*

tesqua (tesca) -ōrum, n. pl. *wastes, deserts.*

tessella -ae, f. *a small cube of stone.*

tessĕra -ae, f. *a cube; a piece of mosaic paving; a die* (with numbers on all six sides); *a token; a watchword.*

tessĕrārĭus -i, m. *the officer who received the watchword.*

testa -ae, f. *an earthen vessel, pot, jug, urn,* etc.; *a potsherd; a brick or tile; the shell of shell-fish; any shell, covering.*

testāmentārĭus -a -um, *relating to a will;* m. as subst., *a forger of wills.*

testāmentum -i, n. *a last will, testament.*

testātĭo -onis, f. *calling to witness,* or *bearing witness.*

testĭfĭcātĭo -onis, f. *bearing witness, testifying; evidence, proof.*

testĭfĭcor -ari, dep. *to bear witness to, give evidence of; to show, bring to light; to call to witness.*

testĭmōnĭum -i, n. *witness, evidence; proof, indication.*

¹testis -is, c. *one who gives evidence, a witness; an eye-witness, spectator.*

²testis -is, m. *a testicle.*

testor -ari, dep. (1) *to bear witness to, give evidence of; to make known, publish, declare;* as pass., *to be attested, declared.* (2) *to make a will.* (3) *to call to witness.*

testūdĭnĕus -a -um, *of a tortoise; of tortoise-shell.*

testūdo -ĭnis, f. *a tortoise; tortoise-shell; a lyre, cithara,* etc.; *an arch or vault;* milit. *a shed, to protect soldiers while attacking fortifications, also a formation with shields held over the soldiers' heads and interlocking.*

testŭla -ae, f. *a potsherd.*

testum -i, n. with abl. testo and testu, *an earthen pot.*

teter; see taeter.

Tēthys -thўos; acc. -thyn; f. *a marine goddess.*

tetrachmum or **tetradrachmum** -i, n. *a Greek coin of four drachmae.*

tetrarchēs -ae, m. *ruler over one-fourth of a country, tetrarch.*

tetrarchĭa -ae, f. *a tetrarchy.*

tetrĭcus -a -um, *harsh, gloomy, severe.*

Teucer -cri, and **Teucrus** -i, m. (1) *son of Telamon,* and *brother of Ajax.* (2) *first king of Troy;* hence adj. **Teucrus** -a -um, *Trojan;* m. pl. as subst. *the Trojans;* **Teucrĭa** -ae, f. *Troy.*

Teutŏni -ōrum, and **Teutŏnes** -um, m. pl. *the Teutons, a Germanic people.*

texo texĕre texŭi textum, *to weave; to twine together, plait; to put together, construct, build;* of speech or writing, *to compose.* N. of partic. as subst.

textum -i, *woven cloth, a web, fabric;* of composition, *style.*

textĭlis -e, *woven, textile, plaited.* N. as subst. *a woven fabric, piece of cloth.*

textor -ōris, m. and **textrix** -trīcis, f. *a weaver.*

textrīnum -i, n. *weaving.*

textum -i, n. subst. from texo; q.v.

textūra -ae, f. *a web, texture; putting together, construction.*

textus -ūs, m. *a web; texture, structure;* of speech or writing, *connexion.*

thălămus -i, m. *a room,* esp. *a woman's bedroom; a marriage-bed; any abode, dwelling.*

thălassĭnus -a -um, *sea-green.*

Thālĭa -ae, f. *the Muse of comic poetry.*

thallus -i, m. *a green branch.*

Thapsus (-ŏs) -i, f. *a town in Africa, where Caesar conquered the Pompeians.*

thĕātrālis -e, *of a theatre, theatrical.*

thĕātrum -i, n. *a theatre.*

Thēbae -arum, f. pl. *Thebes.* (1) *a city of Upper Egypt.* (2) *the chief city of Boeotia.* Adj. **Thēbānus** -a -um, *belonging to Thebes in Boeotia.*

thēca -ae, f. *a case, envelope, covering.*

thēma -ătis, n. *a topic, subject.*

thĕŏlŏgus -i, m. *a theologian.*

thermae -arum, f. pl. *warm springs, warm baths.*

thēsaurus -i, m. *a treasure, store, hoard; a treasury, store-house.*

Thēsēus -ĕi and -ĕos, m. *a king of Athens, conqueror of the Minotaur;* adj. **Thēsēus** and **Thēsēĭus** -a -um, *of Theseus.*

thĕsis -is, f. *a proposition, thesis.*

Thessălĭa -ae, f. *Thessaly, a region in the north of Greece;* adj. **Thessălĭcus** and **Thessălus** -a -um, *Thessalian;* f. adj. **Thessălis** -ĭdis, *Thessalian.*

Thĕtis -ĭdis or -ĭdos, f. *a sea-nymph, mother of Achilles;* poet., *the sea.*

thĭăsus -i, m. *a Bacchic rout, band of revellers.*

Thisbē -ēs, f. *a Babylonian maiden, loved by Pyramus.*

thŏlus -i, m. *a cupola, dome.*

thōrax -ācis, m. *a breastplate, cuirass.*

Thrācĭa -ae; also **Thrāca** -ae and **Thrācē** -ēs; f. *the country of Thrace;* adj. **Thrācĭus** and **Thrēĭcĭus** -a -um, *Thracian;* **Thrax** -ācis and **Thrēx** -ēcis, m. *Thracian, a Thracian.*

Thūcўdĭdēs -is, m. *the Athenian historian of the Peloponnesian war.*

Thūlē (Thўlē) -ēs, f. *an island in the extreme north of Europe.*

thunnus (thynnus) -i, m. *a tunny-fish.*

thūs, thūrārĭus, etc. = tus, turarius, etc.; q.v.

Thўestēs -ae and -is, m. *son of Pelops, brother of Atreus.*

Thўĭās and **Thўăs** -ădis, f. *a Bacchante.*

Thўlē = Thule; q.v.

thymbra -ae, f. *the herb savory.*

thўmum -i, n. *the herb thyme.*

thynnus = thunnus; q.v.

thyrsus -i, m. *the stalk of a plant; a wand, as carried by Bacchus and his attendants.*

tiāra -ae, f. and **tiārus** -ae, m. *a turban.*

Tĭbĕris -bĕris, m.; also poet. **Tĭbris** or **Thĭbris** -brĭdis, m. *the river Tiber*; adj. **Tĭbĕrīnus** -a -um, *of the river Tiber*; m. as subst. *the river-god of the Tiber.*

Tĭbĕrĭus -i, m. *a Roman praenomen,* abbreviated Ti.

tĭbĭa -ae, f. *the shin-bone, tibia; a pipe, flute* (originally made of a hollow bone).

tĭbīcĕn -ĭnis, m. *a flute-player, piper; a pillar, prop.*

tĭbīcīna -ae, f. *a female flute-player.*

tĭbīcĭnĭum -i, *playing on the flute.*

Tĭbris = Tiberis; q.v.

Tĭbullus -i, m.; Albius, *a Roman elegiac poet.*

Tĭbŭr -būris, n. *an old town in Latium*; adj. **Tĭburs** -burtis, **Tĭburtīnus** and **Tĭburnus** -a -um.

tĭgillum -i, n. *a small beam.*

tĭgnārĭus -a -um, *of beams*; faber, *a carpenter.*

tignum -i, n. *a beam.*

Tĭgrānēs -is, m. *a king of Armenia.*

tigris -ĭdis and -is, c. *a tiger.*

tĭlĭa -ae, f. *linden or lime-tree.*

tĭmĕfactus -a -um, *frightened, alarmed.*

tĭmĕo -ēre, *to be afraid, fear, dread*; partic. **tĭmens** -entis, *fearing, fearful.*

tĭmĭdĭtās -ātis, f. *fearfulness, timidity.*

tĭmĭdus -a -um, *fearful, timid*; adv. **tĭmĭdē.**

tĭmor -ōris, m. *fear, dread; an object exciting fear.*

tinctĭlis -e, *in which something is dipped.*

tĭnĕa -ae, f. *a grub, larva, worm.*

tingo tingĕre tinxi tinctum, *to wet, moisten; to dye, colour, imbue.*

tinnĭo -ire, *to ring, tinkle; to talk shrilly; to make to chink*; hence *to pay money.*

tinnītus -ūs, m. *ringing, tinkle, jingle.*

tinnŭlus -a -um, *ringing, tinkling, jingling.*

tintinnābŭlum -i, n. *a bell.*

tintinno (tintĭno) -are, *to ring, tinkle.*

tīnus -i, f. *a shrub, the laurustinus.*

Tĭrĭdātēs -dātis, m. *name of several kings of Armenia.*

tīro -ōnis, m. *a young soldier; a recruit, beginner, learner.*

tīrōcĭnĭum -i, n. *the state of a recruit, rawness, inexperience; beginning, apprenticeship*; concr. *a body of recruits.*

tĭruncŭlus -i, m. *a young beginner.*

Tĭryns -nthis or -nthos, f. *an Argive town where Hercules was brought up*; adj. **Tĭrynthĭus** -a -um.

Tīsĭphŏnē -ēs, f. *one of the Furies.*

Tītān -tānis, and **Tītānus** -i, m.; usually plur. **Tītānes** -um and **Tītāni** -ōrum, *the Titans, who warred against Jupiter and were by him cast into Hades.*

Tīthōnus -i, m. *husband of Aurora.*

Tĭtĭes -ĭum and **Tĭtĭenses** -ĭum, m. pl., *one of the three original tribes at Rome.*

tĭtillātĭo -ōnis, f. *a tickling.*

tĭtillo -are, *to tickle.*

tĭtŭbātĭo -ōnis, f. *a staggering, reeling; uncertainty.*

tĭtŭbo -are, *to totter, stagger; to stammer; to falter, waver, hesitate*; adv. from partic. **tĭtŭbantĕr,** *hesitatingly, uncertainly.*

tĭtŭlus -i, m. *an inscription, label, notice; a title, honour; pretence, pretext.*

Tĭtus -i, m. *a Roman praenomen,* abbreviated T.

tŏcŭlĭo -ōnis, m. *a usurer.*

tōfus (tōphus) -i, m. *tufa.*

tŏga -ae, f. *the white woollen upper garment worn by Roman citizens.*

tŏgātŭlus -i, m. *a little client.*

tŏgātus -a -um, *wearing the toga*; m. as subst. *a Roman citizen*; f. as subst. *the national drama of the Romans.*

tŏgŭla -ae, f. *a little toga.*

tŏlĕrābĭlis -e; pass., *bearable*; act., *tolerant, patient*; compar. adv. **tŏlĕrābĭlĭus,** *rather patiently.*

tŏlĕrantĭa -ae and **tŏlĕrātĭo** -onis, f. *bearing, endurance.*

tŏlĕro -are, *to carry, bear, endure, sustain; to sustain; to support, keep up, maintain.* Hence pres. partic. **tŏlĕrans** -antis, *enduring, patient*; adv. **tŏlĕrantĕr**; perf. partic. **tŏlĕrātus** -a -um, *endurable.*

tollēno -ōnis, m. *a machine for raising weights, a crane.*

tollo tollĕre sustŭli sublātum. (1) *to lift up, raise, elevate*; in crucem, *to crucify*; tollere ancoras, *to weigh anchor*; laudibus, *to extol*; of children, *to acknowledge as one's own, to bring up.* (2) *to take away, remove, carry off, steal; to destroy, abolish.*

tŏmācŭlum (-aclum) -i, n. *a kind of sausage.*

tōmentum -i, n. *the stuffing of a pillow, mattress,* etc.

Tŏmi -ōrum, m. pl. and **Tŏmis** -is, f. *a town on the Black Sea, Ovid's place of exile.*

tōmus -i, m. *a cutting, chip, shred.*

tondĕo tondēre tŏtondi tonsum, *to shave, shear, clip; to mow, reap, prune; to browse on, crop; to fleece a person.*

tŏnĭtrus -ūs, m. and **tŏnĭtruum** -i, n. *thunder.*

tŏno -are -ŭi -ĭtum, *to thunder.* Transf.: instransit., *to make a loud noise*; transit., *to thunder forth.*

tonsa -ae, f. *an oar.*

tonsĭlis -e, *shorn, clipped, cut.*

tonsillae -arum, f. *the tonsils.*

tonsor -ōris, m. *a hair-cutter, barber.*

tonsōrĭus -a -um, *of or for clipping.*

tonstrĭcŭla -ae, f. *a little female barber.*

tonstrīna -ae, f. *a barber's shop.*

tonstrix -īcis, f. *a female barber.*

tonsūra -ae, f. *clipping, shearing, shaving.*

tophus, etc. = tofus, etc.; q.v.

tŏpĭārĭus -a -um, *of ornamental gardening*; m. as subst. *a landscape gardener*; f. as subst. *the art of landscape gardening.*

tŏrăl -ālis, n. *the valance of a couch.*

tŏreuma -ătis, n. *carved or embossed work.*

tormentum -i, n. *an instrument for twisting or pressing; a windlass; the rack; any instrument of torture;* hence *suasion, pressure; torture, torment;* milit., *a piece of artillery, or a missile.*

tormĭna -um, n. pl. *the colic, gripes.*

tormĭnōsus -a -um, *suffering from colic.*

torno -are, *to turn in a lathe; to round, make round.*

tornus -i, m. *a lathe.*

tŏrōsus -a -um, *muscular, brawny.*

torpēdo -ĭnis, f. (1) *lethargy, sluggishness.* (2) *a fish, the electric ray.*

tŏrpĕo -ēre, *to be sluggish, numb, inert, inactive.*

torpesco -pescĕre -pŭi, *to become sluggish or numb.*

torpĭdus -a -um, *numb, sluggish.*

torpor -ōris, m. *numbness, sluggishness, dullness, inactivity.*

torquātus -a -um, *wearing a twisted collar or necklace.*

torquĕo torquēre torsi tortum, *to twist, wind, curl, wrench; to distort; to hurl violently, whirl; to rack, torture, torment, plague, try, test.* Hence partic. **tortus** -a -um, *twisted, crooked, intricate;* adv. **tortē.**

torquis (torquēs) -is, m. and f. *a twisted collar or necklace; a ring, wreath, chaplet.*

torrĕo torrēre torrŭi tostum, *to burn, parch, dry up.* Hence partic. as adj. **torrens** -entis, *burning, hot, parched; rushing, seething.* M. as subst. *a torrent.*

torresco -ĕre, *to become parched.*

torrĭdus -a -um, *parched, burnt, dry.* Transf., *pinched, nipped with cold.*

torris, is, m. *a firebrand.*

tortĭlis -e, *twisted, twined.*

torto -are, *to torture, torment.*

tortor -ōris, m. *a torturer, tormentor; a wielder.*

tortŭōsus -a -um, *tortuous, intricate, involved.*

¹tortus -a -um, partic. from torqueo; q.v.

²tortus -ūs, m. *a twisting, curve.*

tŏrus -i, m. *any round protuberance; a muscle; a bed, sofa; a marriage couch; a bier; a mound;* fig., *an ornament.*

torvĭtās -ātis, f. *savageness, wildness.*

torvus -a -um, *savage, grim, fierce.*

tŏt, indecl. *so many.*

tŏtĭdem, indecl. *just as many.*

tŏtĭes (-ĭens), *so often, so many times.*

tōtus -a -um, genit. tōtīus, dat. tōtī; *whole, complete, entire; whole-hearted, absorbed.* N. as subst. **tōtum** -i, *the whole;* ex toto, in toto, *on the whole.*

toxĭcum -i, n. *poison (for arrows).*

trăbālis -e, *of beams of wood; like a beam.*

trăbĕa -ae, f. *a white robe with scarlet stripes and a purple seam, worn by kings and knights.*

trăbĕātus -a -um, *clad in the trabea;* q.v.

trabs trăbis, f. *a beam of wood; a tree-trunk; a ship; a roof; a table.*

tractābĭlis -e, *that can be handled, manageable; yielding, compliant.*

tractātĭo -ōnis, f. *handling, management.*

tractātor -ōris, m. *a masseur.*

tractātrix -īcis, f. *a masseuse.*

tractātus -ūs, m. *handling, management, treatment.*

tractim, *gradually, by degrees.*

tracto -are, *to drag along, haul, pull about; to handle, manage, treat; to behave towards a person.*

¹tractus -a -um, partic. from traho; q.v.

²tractus -ūs, m. *a dragging process;* verborum, *drawling;* belli, *extension;* concr., *a track, trail; extent, position; a tract, district.*

trāditĭo -ōnis, f. *giving up, surrender; instruction, relation.*

trāditor -ōris, m. *traitor.*

trādo (transdo) -dĕre -dĭdi -dĭtum, *to hand over, give up, surrender, betray; to hand down to posterity;* esp. *to report, relate, teach;* with reflex., *to commit, surrender, devote oneself.*

trādūco (transdūco) -dūcĕre -duxi -ductum, *to lead over, bring over or across; to lead past in front of others; to transpose, transfer;* of time, *to pass, spend, lead; to show, display; to expose to ridicule, " show up ".*

trāductĭo -ōnis, f. *transferring;* rhet., metonymy; temporis, *passage* or *lapse of time.*

trāductor -ōris, m. *a transferrer.*

trādux -ŭcis, m. *vine-layer.*

trăgĭcus -a -um, *tragic; lofty, sublime; awful, fearful.* M. as subst. *a tragic poet.* Adv. **trăgĭcē,** *tragically.*

trăgoedĭa -ae, f. *tragedy; a dramatic scene.*

trăgoedus -i, m. *tragic actor, tragedian.*

trăgŭla -ae, f. *a species of javelin.*

trăhĕa -ae, f. *sledge, drag.*

trăho trăhĕre traxi tractum, *to trail, pull along; to drag, pull violently; to draw in, take up;* of air, *to breathe; to draw out,* hence *to lengthen; to draw together, contract.* Transf., *to draw, attract; to take in or on, assume, derive; to prolong, spin out; to ascribe, refer, interpret.* Hence partic. **tractus** -a -um, *of speech, fluent, flowing.* N. as subst., *a flock of wool.*

trāĭcĭo (transĭcĭo) -ĭcĕre -ĭēci -ĭectum, (1) *to throw a thing (or person) across something; to convey over, transport.* (2) *to pass through or across a thing (or person); to cross, penetrate, pierce.*

trāĭectĭo -ōnis, f. *a passing over, crossing over; transferring, transposition; hyperbole.*

trāĭectus -ūs, m. *crossing over, passage.*

tralat- = translat-; q.v.

trālūcĕo = transluceo; q.v.

trāma -ae, f. *the woof in weaving.*

trāmĕo = transmeo; q.v.

trāmĕs -itis, m. *by-way, foot-path.*

trāmigro = transmigro; q.v.

trāmitto = transmitto; q.v.

trānăto (transnăto) -are, *to swim across, pass through.*

tranquillĭtās -ātis, f. *quiet, calm.*

tranquillo -are, *to calm.*

tranquillus -a -um, *quiet, calm.* N. as subst. *a calm, quietness.* Adv. **tranquillē.**

trans, prep. with acc., *over, across, on* or *to the other side of.*

transăbĕo -ire -ĭi, *to go through or past.*

transactor -ōris, m. *manager, accomplisher.*

transădīgo -ĭgĕre -ēgi -actum, *to drive a thing through* something else; also *to pierce, penetrate.*

Transalpīnus -a -um, *beyond the Alps, transalpine.*

transcendo (transscendo) -scendĕre -scendi -scensum, *to climb over, pass over;* *to step over, transgress.*

transcrībo (transscribo) -scrībĕre -scripsi -scriptum, *to copy, transcribe.* Transf., *to transfer, convey, assign.*

transcurro -currĕre -cŭcurri and -curri -cursum, *to run across or over, hasten past.*

transcursus -ūs, m. *a running past, hastening through.*

transdo = trado; q.v.

transdūco = traduco; q.v.

transenna -ae, f. *lattice-work, grating.*

transĕo -īre -ĭi -ĭtum, *to go over, cross, pass over, go past.* Transf., *to be changed; to pass time; to pass beyond, transgress; to pass over, ignore, or touch lightly on.*

transfĕro transferre transtŭli translātum and trālātum, *to carry over or across;* *to transfer, transport, convey.* Transf., *to put off, defer; to change;* in writing, *to copy; to translate into another language; to use* a word *figuratively or metaphorically.*

transfīgo -fīgĕre -fixi -fixum, *to pierce through, or thrust through.*

transfŏdio -fŏdĕre -fōdi -fossum, *to stab through, transfix.*

transformis -e, *changed, transformed.*

transformo -are, *to change, transform.*

transfŭga -ae, *deserter.*

transfŭgio -fŭgĕre -fūgi -fūgĭtum, *to desert to the enemy.*

transfŭgĭum -i, n. *desertion.*

transfundo -fundĕre -fūdi -fūsum, *to pour from one vessel into another, to transfer.*

transfūsio -ōnis, f. *a pouring out, pouring off.*

transgrĕdĭor -grĕdi -gressus, dep. *to go across, pass over.*

transgressĭo -ōnis, f. *going over, passage; transposition of words.*

transgressus -ūs, m. *going over, passage.*

transĭgo -ĭgĕre -ēgi -actum, *to stab, pierce through;* of time, *to pass, spend;*

of business, *to finish, complete, accomplish, transact;* of a difference or dispute, *to settle.*

transĭlĭo (transsĭlĭo) -sĭlire -sĭlŭi, *to spring over, leap across; to pass over* a thing, or *to pass beyond, transgress.*

transĭtĭo -ōnis, f. *going across, passing over; communication, infection, contagion;* concr., *a passage.*

transĭtus -ūs, m. *passing over or across, transit; changing over, transition.*

translātīcĭus (trālātīcĭus) -a -um, *customary, prescriptive; common, usual.*

translātĭo (trālātĭo) -ōnis, f. *transferring, handing over;* of plants, *grafting; a translation; a metaphor, trope.*

translātīvus -a -um, *transferable.*

translātor -ōris, m. *transferrer.*

translūcĕo (trālūcĕo) -ēre, *to shine through or across.*

transmărīnus -a -um, *from beyond the sea, foreign.*

transmĕo (trāmĕo) -mĕare, *to go over or through.*

transmigro -are, *to migrate.*

transmissĭo -ōnis, f. and **transmissus** -ūs, m. *passage.*

transmitto (trāmitto) -mittĕre -mīsi -missum. (1) *to send across, send over, transmit; to convey, make over, entrust;* of time, *to let pass.* (2) *to go across, pass through or over; to leave unnoticed.*

transmontāni -ōrum, m. pl. *dwellers beyond the mountains.*

transmŏvĕo -mŏvēre -mōvi -mōtum, *to remove, transfer.*

transmūto -are, *to change, transmute.*

transnăto = tranato; q.v.

transpădānus -a -um, *beyond (i.e. north of) the Po, transpadane.*

transpectus -ūs, m. *a looking through, seeing through.*

transpĭcĭo (transspĭcĭo) -spĭcĕre, *to look through, see through.*

transpōno -pōnĕre -pŏsŭi -pŏsĭtum, *to put over, remove, transfer.*

transporto -are, *to convey across, transport.*

transrhēnānus -a -um, *beyond the Rhine.*

transtĭbĕrīnus -a -um, *beyond the Tiber.*

transtrum -i, n. *cross-beam; thwart.*

transulto (transsulto) -are, *to spring across.*

transŭo (transsŭo) -sŭĕre, *to sew through;* hence *to pierce through.*

transvectĭo (trāvectĭo) -ōnis, f. *a carrying across or past; esp. the riding of a Roman knight past the censor at the periodical muster.*

transvĕho (trāvĕho) -vĕhĕre -vexi -vectum, *to carry over or past; pass., to ride, sail,* etc., *across;* of a knight, *to ride past the censor at a muster;* of time, *to pass by.*

transverbĕro -are, *to pierce through, transfix.*

transversārĭus -a, -um, *lying across, transverse.*

transversus, trăversus and **transvorsus** -a -um, *transverse, oblique, athwart;* transverso itinere, *obliquely;* transversum digitum, *a finger's breadth;* de transverso, *unexpectedly.*

transvŏlĭto -are, *to fly across.*

transvŏlo (trăvŏlo) -are, *to fly over* or *across; to hasten through* or *past.*

trăpētus -i, m. **trăpētum** -i, n. and plur. **trăpētes** -um, m. *an oil-press.*

Trăsŭmēnus (also **Trasy-** and **Trasi-;** also with double **n**) -i, m. *the Trasimene lake, where Hannibal conquered the Romans under Flaminius* (217 B.C.).

trav- = transv-; q.v.

trēcēni -ae, -a, *three hundred at a time* or *each.*

trĕcentēsĭmus -a -um, *three-hundredth.*

trĕcenti -ae -a, *three hundred.*

trĕcentiēs (-iens) *three hundred times.*

trĕchĕdĭpnum -i, n. *a light garment worn at table.*

trēdĕcim, *thirteen.*

trĕmĕbundus -a -um, *trembling.*

trĕmĕfăcĭo -făcĕre -fēci -factum, *to cause to tremble.*

trĕmesco (-isco) -ĕre, *to tremble, quake;* with acc., *to tremble at.*

tremi-; see treme-.

trĕmo -ĕre -ŭi, *to tremble, quake;* with acc. *to tremble at;* gerundive as adj. **trĕmendus** -a -um, *fearful, terrible.*

trĕmor -ōris, m. *a trembling, quaking.*

trĕmŭlus -a -um, *trembling, quaking;* poet., *that causes trembling.*

trĕpĭdātĭo -ōnis, f. *agitation, anxiety.*

trĕpĭdo -are, *to be agitated, be busy, bustle about;* with acc., *to be anxious about;* with infin., *to be in a hurry to* do a thing; of flame, *to flicker.* Adv. from partic. **trĕpĭdantĕr,** *anxiously, hurriedly.*

trĕpĭdus -a -um, *agitated, restless, disturbed, in an emergency;* adv. **trĕpĭdē.**

trēs trĭa, *three.*

tresvĭri = triumviri; q.v.

Trēvĕri (Trēvĭri) -ōrum, m. *a Germanic people.*

trĭangŭlus -a -um, *three-cornered, triangular.* N. as subst. *a triangle.*

trĭārii -ōrum, m. pl. *experienced Roman soldiers, drawn up in the third rank, behind the others.*

trĭbŭārĭus -a -um, *relating to a tribe.*

trĭbŭlis -is, m. *a fellow-tribesman.*

trĭbŭlum -i, n. *threshing machine.*

trĭbŭlus -i, m. *a thorny plant, the caltrop.*

trĭbūnăl -ālis, n. *the tribunal, a raised platform* used by magistrates and generals.

trĭbūnātus -ūs, m. *tribuneship.*

trĭbūnĭcĭus -a -um, *of a tribune, tribunicial;* m. as subst. *an ex-tribune.*

trĭbūnus -i, m. *a tribune;* tribuni aerarii, *paymasters who assisted the quaestors;* tribuni militum, or militares, *military officers, of whom there were six to every legion;* tribuni plebis, *tribunes of the people, magistrates who protected the plebeians.*

trĭbŭo -ŭere -ŭi -ūtum, *to divide out, allot, assign; to grant, give, allow, yield, ascribe, attribute.*

trĭbus -ūs, f. *a tribe, a division of the Roman people.*

trĭbūtārĭus -a -um, *relating to tribute.*

trĭbūtim, *tribe by tribe.*

trĭbūtĭo -ōnis, f. *a distribution.*

trĭbūtum -i, n. *tax, tribute.* Transf., *a gift, present.*

trĭbūtus -a -um, *arranged according to tribes.*

trīcae -ārum, f. pl. *trifles, nonsense; vexations, troubles.*

trĭcēni -ae -a, *thirty at a time* or *each.*

trĭceps -cĭpĭtis, *three-headed.*

trĭcēsĭmus (-ensĭmus) *thirtieth.*

trĭchĭla -ae, f. *summer-house, arbour.*

trĭcĭēs (-iens) *thirty times.*

trĭclīnĭum -i, n. *dining-couch;* hence *dining-room.*

trĭcor -ari, dep. *to make difficulties, shuffle, trifle.*

trĭcorpŏr -pŏris, *having three bodies.*

trĭcuspis -ĭdis, *having three points.*

trĭdens -entis, *having three teeth* or *prongs.* M. as subst. *a trident, a three-pronged spear.*

trĭdentĭfer and **trĭdentĭger** -ĕri, m. *the trident-bearer* (of Neptune).

trĭdŭum -i, n. *a space of three days.*

trĭennĭa -ĭum, n. pl. *a festival celebrated every three years.*

trĭennĭum -i, n. *a space of three years.*

trĭens -entis, m. *a third part, one-third.*

trĭentābŭlum -i, n. *the equivalent in land for the third part of a sum of money.*

trĭērarchus -i, m. *the commander of a trireme.*

trĭĕtērĭcus -a -um, *recurring every three years, triennial.*

trĭĕtēris -ĭdis, f. *a space of three years* or *a triennial festival.*

trĭfārĭam, *in three places, on three sides.*

trĭfaux -faucis, *having three throats.*

trĭfĭdus -a -um, *split in three parts, three-forked.*

trĭformis -e, *having three forms.*

trĭgĕmĭnus (tergĕmĭnus) -a -um, *threefold, triple.*

trĭgintā, *thirty.*

trĭgon -ōnis, m. *a ball for playing.*

trĭlĭbris -e, *of three pounds' weight.*

trĭlinguis -e, *having three tongues.*

trĭlix -īcis, *having three threads.*

trĭmetrŏs (-us) -a -um, *containing three double feet.* M. as subst., *a trimeter.*

trīmus -a -um, *three years old.*

Trīnacrĭa -ae, f. *the triangular land,* i.e. *Sicily;* adj. **Trīnacrĭus** -a -um, and f. **Trīnacris** -ĭdis, *Sicilian.*

trīni -ae, -a; *three at a time, three together.*

Trinobantes -um, m. *a people in east Britain.*

trĭnōdis -e, *having three knots.*

trĭōnēs -um, m. pl. *the ploughing oxen; the constellations Great Bear and Little Bear.*

trĭpart-; see tripert-.

trĭpectŏrus -a -um, *having three breasts.*

trĭpĕdālis -e, *of three feet in measure.*
trĭpertītus (-partītus) -a -um, *three-fold, triple.* N. abl. sing. trĭpertītō (-partītō), *in three parts.*
trĭpēs -pĕdis, *having three feet.*
trĭplex -līcis, *threefold, triple.* M. pl. as subst. *a writing tablet with three leaves.*
trĭplus -a -um, *threefold, triple.*
trĭpudio -are, *to beat the ground with the feet, to dance,* esp. *as a religious rite.*
trĭpŭdĭum -i, n. (1) *a religious dance.* (2) *a favourable omen, when the sacred chickens ate fast.*
trĭpūs -pŏdis, m. *three-legged seat, tripod,* esp. *that at Delphi.*
trĭquetrus -a -um, *three-cornered, triangular.*
trĭrēmis -e, *having three banks of oars;* f. as subst., *a trireme.*
triscurrĭa -ōrum, n. pl. *gross buffooneries.*
tristĭcŭlus -a -um, *somewhat sorrowful.*
tristis -e, *sad, gloomy, dismal, forbidding, harsh;* *of taste or smell,* *harsh, bitter.* N. acc. tristĕ used like adv. *harshly.*
tristĭtĭa -ae and tristĭtĭēs -ēi, f. *sadness, gloom, harshness.*
trĭsulcus -a -um, *three-pointed, three-pronged.*
trĭtĭcĕus -a -um, *wheaten.*
trĭtĭcum -i, n. *wheat.*
Trītōn -ōnis or -ōnos, m. (1) *Triton, son of Neptune, a god of the sea.* (2) *a lake in Africa, supposed birth-place of Minerva;* adj. Trītōnĭācus, Trītōnĭus -a -um, and f. Trītōnis -ĭdis or -ĭdos, esp. *in connexion with Minerva.*
trĭtūra -ae, f. *threshing.*
trĭumphālis -e, *triumphal.* N. pl. as subst. *the distinctions of a triumphing general.*
trĭumpho -are, *to triumph, to have a triumph;* hence, fig., *to exult;* pass., *to be triumphed over, be completely conquered.*
trĭumphus (old form trĭumpus) -i, m., *triumphal procession, triumph.*
trĭumvir -vĭri, m. *a triumvir;* usually plur. trĭumvĭri (also trēsvĭri), *a board or commission of three.*
trĭumvĭrālis -e, *of a triumvir.*
trĭumvĭrātus -ūs, m. *the office of a triumvir.*
trĭvĭālis -e, *ordinary, trivial.*
trĭvĭum -i, n. *a place where three roads meet, crossroads, public place.*
trĭvĭus -a -um, *of three ways, of cross-roads;* esp. *of deities worshipped at crossroads;* f. as subst. Trīvia -ae, *Diana or Hecate.*
Trōās -ădis; see Tros.
trŏchaeus -i, m. *a trochee, a metrical foot* (— ◡).
trochlĕa -ae, f. *a set of blocks and pulleys for raising weights.*
trŏchus -i, m. *child's hoop.*
Trōes; see Tros.
Trōia, Trōĭădes, Trōĭcus; see Tros.
Trōĭŭgĕna -ae, *born in Troy, Trojan.*

trŏpaeum, -i, n. *a trophy, monument of victory.* Transf., *any memorial.*
Trōs Trōis, m. *a king of Phrygia, after whom Troy was named;* Trōĭă or Trōĭă -ae, f. *the town of Troy, besieged and finally captured by the Greeks;* adj. Trōus, Trōĭus, Trōĭcus, Trōĭānus -a -um, *Trojan;* subst. Trōs Trōis, m. *a Trojan;* f. adj. and subst. Trōăs -ădos, *Trojan, a Trojan woman.*
trŭcīdātĭo -onis, f. *slaughtering, massacre.*
trŭcīdo -are, *to slaughter, massacre;* *to demolish, destroy.*
trŭcŭlentĭa -ae, f. *roughness, ferocity.*
trŭcŭlentus -a -um, *rough, ferocious, cruel, wild;* compar. adv. trŭcŭlentĭus.
trūdis -is, f. *pointed staff, stake.*
trūdo trūdĕre trūsi trūsum, *to push, thrust;* *to press, urge on, force.*
trulla -ae, f. *ladle, pan or basin.*
trunco -are, *to shorten, maim, mutilate.*
truncus -a -um, *maimed, mutilated, cut short.* M. as subst. truncus -i, *a lopped tree, the trunk of a tree; the trunk of the human body.* Transf., *dolt, blockhead.*
trŭtĭna -ae, f. *a balance, pair of scales.*
trux trŭcis, *savage, fierce, grim.*
tū; pron. *of the 2nd person;* strengthened forms in -te, -met, temet; *thou, you;* plur. vos, etc. *ye, you.*
tŭba -ae, f. *the straight war-trumpet of the Romans.*
¹tŭber -ĕris, n. *swelling, hump.* Transf., *truffle.*
²tŭber -ĕris; m. *a kind of apple-tree;* f. *the fruit of this tree.*
tŭbĭcĕn -ĭnis, m. *a trumpeter.*
tŭbĭlustrĭum -i, n. *a feast of trumpets.*
tŭdĭto -are, *to strike often.*
tŭĕor (or tŭor) tŭĕri tŭĭtus and tūtus, dep., and tŭĕo -ēre, *to look at, regard;* esp. *to look after, watch over, guard.* Perf. partic. as pass. adj. tūtus -a -um, *watched over;* hence *safe, secure, out of danger; watchful, cautious.* N. as subst. tūtum -i, *a safe place, safety.* N. abl. tūtō and adv. tūtē, *safely.*
tŭgŭrĭum -i, n. *peasant's hut, cottage.*
tŭĭtĭo -ōnis, f. *a protecting, preservation.*
Tullĭus -a -um, *the name of a Roman gens;* esp. *of Servius Tullius, sixth king of Rome,* and *of M. Tullius Cicero, the Roman orator and statesman.* Hence adj. Tulliānus -a -um, *Tullian;* n. as subst. Tulliānum, -i, *part of a Roman state prison.*
tum, *then, at that time; next, thereupon, afterwards;* cum . . . tum, *both . . . and especially,* or *not only . . . but also.*
tŭmĕfăcĭo -făcĕre -fēci -factum, *to cause to swell; to puff up with pride.*
tŭmĕo -ēre, *to swell, be swollen, be puffed up; to swell with pride, anger or excitement;* *of style, to be pompous, tumid.*

tŭmesco tŭmescĕre tŭmŭi, *to begin to swell; to swell with anger or excitement.*

tŭmĭdus -a -um, adj. *swollen, puffed up; swollen with pride, anger or excitement; of style, pompous, tumid, bombastic.*

tŭmor -ōris, m. *swelling, protuberance; excitement of the mind, esp. in pride or anger; in gen., ferment, commotion; of style, turgidity, bombast.*

tŭmŭlo -are, *to bury.*

tŭmŭlōsus -a -um, *full of mounds, hilly.*

tŭmultŭārĭus -a -um; *of troops, hastily brought together, suddenly levied; in gen., sudden, hasty, improvised.*

tŭmultŭātĭo -ōnis, f. *confusion, bustle.*

tŭmultŭor -ari, dep. and **tŭmultŭo** -are, *to be confused, be in an uproar.*

tŭmultŭōsus -a -um, adj. *alarmed, disturbed, confused; disquieting, turbulent;* adv. **tŭmultŭōsē,** *confusedly, tumultuously.*

tŭmultus -ūs, m. *confusion, uproar, bustle; esp. of political commotion, insurrection, rebellion.* Transf., *mental disturbance, excitement.*

tŭmŭlus -i, m. *mound of earth, hillock, hill; esp. a sepulchral mound.*

tunc, *then, at that time; next.*

tundo tundĕre tŭtŭdi tunsum and tūsum, *to thump, pound, strike repeatedly; to deafen, importune.*

tŭnĭca -ae, f. *a sleeved garment, tunic; a jacket, coat, covering.*

tŭnĭcātus -a -um, *clothed in a tunic.*

tŭor = tueor; q.v.

turba -ae, f. *tumult, disturbance;* hence *a mob, throng, crowd.*

turbāmentum -i, n. *means of disturbance.*

turbātĭo -ōnis, f. *disturbance, confusion.*

turbātor -ōris, m. *disturber, troubler.*

turbĕn -ĭnis, n. = ²turbo; q.v.

turbĭdus -a -um, *confused, disordered, wild;* adv. **turbĭdē.**

turbĭnĕus -a -um, *shaped like a top.*

¹turbo -are, *to disturb, throw into disorder or confusion; to upset; esp. to cause political disturbance, to unsettle.*

Hence partic. as adj. **turbātus** -a -um, *disturbed, disordered, restless, troubled; sometimes angered, exasperated;* adv. **turbātē.**

²turbo -ĭnis, m. *an eddy, whirling round; a mental or political disturbance; a child's top; a reel; a spindle.*

turbŭlentus -a -um: pass., *confused, restless, stormy, boisterous;* act., *turbulent, causing disturbance;* adv. **turbŭlentē** and **turbŭlentĕr,** *in confusion, tumultuously.*

turdus -i, m. and **turda** -ae, f. *a thrush.*

tūrĕus -a -um, *of incense.*

turgĕo turgēre tursi, *to swell up, be swollen; of style, to be pompous, turgid.*

turgesco -ĕre, *to begin to swell, swell up; to swell with passion; of style, to be pompous.*

turgĭdus -a -um, *swollen; of style, turgid, bombastic.*

tūrĭbŭlum -i, n. *a censer for burning incense.*

tūricrĕmus -a -um, *burning incense.*

tūrĭfer -fĕra -fĕrum, *producing incense.*

tūrĭlĕgus -a -um, *collecting incense.*

turma -ae, f. *a troop of cavalry, a squadron; any troop, throng.*

turmālis -e, *of a troop or squadron.*

turmātim, *troop by troop, in troops.*

Turnus -i, m. *a king of the Rutuli, killed by Aeneas.*

turpĭcŭlus -a -um, *somewhat ugly or deformed.*

turpĭfĭcātus -a -um, *corrupted.*

turpis -e, *ugly, foul; morally foul, disgraceful;* n. as subst. **turpĕ,** *a disgrace;* adv. **turpĭtĕr,** *foully, disgracefully.*

turpĭtūdo -ĭnis, f. *ugliness; moral baseness, disgrace.*

turpo -are, *to make ugly, befoul; to disgrace, dishonour.*

turrĭger -gĕra -gĕrum, *tower-bearing.*

turris -is, f. *tower; esp. as used in military operations; sometimes howdah.* Transf., *dove-cote.*

turrītus -a -um, *turreted, furnished with towers; towering.*

turtur -ŭris, m. *turtle-dove.*

tūs (thūs) tūris, n. *incense, frankincense.*

Tusci -ōrum, m. *the Tuscans, Etruscans, inhabitants of Etruria;* adj. **Tuscus** -a -um, *Etruscan.*

tussĭo -ire, *to have a cough, to cough.*

tussis -is, f. *a cough.*

tūtāmen -ĭnis, and **tūtāmentum** -i, n. *a defence, protection.*

tūtēla -ae, f. *protection, guard, charge, esp. of wards, etc., guardianship, tutelage;* concr., act. *protector, guardian;* pass., *the person or thing protected.*

¹tūtor -ōris, m. *a watcher, protector; esp. the guardian of a woman, minor, or imbecile.*

²tūtor -ari dep.: also **tūto** -are; *to protect, watch, keep.* Transf., *to guard against.*

tūtus -a -um, partic. from tueo; q.v.

tŭus -a -um, possess. pron. of the 2nd pers. sing., *thy, thine, your.*

Tȳdēus -ĕi and -ĕos, m. *the son of Oeneus;* hence **Tȳdīdes** -ae, m. *son of Tydeus, i.e. Diomedes.*

tympănum (tўpănum) -i, n. *a tambourine, kettle-drum; a drum or wheel for raising weights.*

Tyndărēus -ĕi, and **Tyndărus** -i, m. *king of Sparta, father of Castor and Pollux, Helen and Clytemnestra;* adj. **Tyndărĭus** -a -um; subst. m. **Tyndărĭdēs** -ae, *a male descendant,* and f. **Tyndăris** -ĭdis, *a female descendant of Tyndareus.*

tȳpus -i, m. *a figure on a wall.*

tȳrannĭcīda -ae, m. *the slayer of a tyrant.*

tȳrannĭcus -a -um, *tyrannical;* adv. **tȳrannĭcē.**

tȳrannis -ĭdis, f. *despotism, tyranny.*

tўrannoctŏnus -i, m. *the slayer of a tyrant.*

tўrannus -i, m. *an absolute ruler, prince, lord; a usurper, despot, tyrant.*

Tўrīus, see Tyrus.

tўrŏtărichŏs -i, m. *a dish of cheese and salt-fish.*

Tyrrhēni -ōrum, m. pl. *a Pelasgian people;* subst. **Tyrrhēnia** -ae, f. *their country, Etruria;* adj. **Tyrrhēnus** -a -um, *Etruscan.*

Tўrus (-ŏs) -i, f. *Tyre, a city of Phoenicia, famous for its purple;* adj. **Tўrius** -a -um.

U

U, u, originally written V, v, the 20th letter of the Latin Alphabet.

¹ūber -ĕris, n. *an udder, teat, breast; richness, abundance, fertility.*

²ūber -eris, adj., *rich, fertile, fruitful, copious;* adv. in compar. **ūbĕrius** and superl. **ūberrĭmē,** *more and most abundantly.*

ūbertās -ātis, f. *fruitfulness, abundance.*

ūbertim, *abundantly, copiously.*

ŭbĭ, *where* (interrog. and relat.); *of time, when, as soon as; of other relations, wherein, whereby, with whom.*

ŭbĭcumquĕ (-cunquĕ): relat., *wherever;* indef., *anywhere, everywhere.*

Ubii -ōrum, m. *a Germanic people.*

ŭbīquĕ, *everywhere.*

ŭbĭvīs, *wherever you will, anywhere.*

ūdus -a -um, *wet, moist.*

ulcĕro -are, *to make sore, ulcerate, wound.*

ulcĕrōsus -a -um, *full of sores, ulcerous, wounded.*

ulcīscor ulcisci ultus, dep. (1) *to take vengeance for, to avenge.* (2) *to take vengeance on, to punish.*

ulcus -ĕris, n. *a sore, ulcer, wound.*

ūlīgo -ĭnis, f. *moisture, damp.*

Ūlixēs -is or ei, m. *Latin name for Ulysses* or *Odysseus, husband of Penelope, king of Ithaca.*

ullus -a -um; genit. ullius, dat. ulli; *any;* as subst., *anyone, anything.*

ulmĕus -a -um, *of elm-wood.*

ulmus -i, f. *elm.*

ulna -ae, f. *elbow, arm; an ell.*

ultĕrĭor -ius, compar. as from ulter, *farther, more distant, more advanced, more remote.* Superl. **ultĭmus** -a -um, *most distant, farthest, extreme;* in time or succession, either *original* or *last, final;* ad ultimum, *to the last;* ultimum, *for the last time;* in rank, etc., *either highest, greatest,* or *meanest, lowest.*

ultĭo -ōnis, f. *avenging, punishment, revenge.*

ultor -ōris, m. *avenger, punisher.*

ultrā, adv. and prep. *beyond, on the far side (of), farther (than), more (than).*

ultrix -īcis, f. *avenging.*

ultrō, adv. *to the far side, beyond;* ultro et citro, *up and d wn.* Transf.,

besides, moreover; of one's own accord, spontaneously, gratuitously.

ŭlŭla -ae, f. *an owl.*

ŭlŭlātus -ūs, m. *howling, wailing, yelling.*

ŭlŭlo -are, *to howl, yell;* transit., *to howl to;* of places, *to resound with howling.*

ulva -ae, f. *sedge.*

umbella -ae, f. *a parasol.*

umbĭlicus -i, m. *the navel; middle, centre; the end of the roller of a scroll; a kind of sea-snail.*

umbo -ōnis, m. *a boss, round projection;* esp. *the centre of a shield; a shield; the elbow.*

umbra -ae, f. *a shade, shadow; a shady place; protection; idleness, pleasant rest; a phantom, ghost, shade, semblance; an uninvited guest; a fish, perhaps grayling.*

umbrāculum -i, n. *a shady place, arbour; quiet, retirement; a parasol.*

umbrātilis -e, *retired, contemplative.*

Umbri -ōrum, m. pl. *a people of central Italy;* **Umbria** -ae, f. *Umbria.*

umbrĭfer -fĕra -fĕrum, *shady.*

umbro -are, *to shade, over-shadow.*

umbrōsus -a -um, *shady.*

ūmecto (hū-) -are, *to wet, moisten.*

ūmectus (hū-) -a -um, *moist.*

ūmĕo (hū-) -ēre, *to be moist;* partic. **ūmens** -entis, *moist.*

ūmĕrus (hū-) -i, m. *the upper arm or shoulder.*

ūmesco (hū-) -ĕre, *to become moist.*

ūmĭdŭlus (hū-), -a -um, *moist.*

ūmĭdus (hū-) -a -um, *wet, moist, damp;* ligna, *unseasoned;* n. as subst. *a wet place.*

ūmor (hū-) -ōris, m. *moisture, fluid.*

umquam (unquam), *at any time, ever.*

ūnā, adv. from unus; q.v.

ūnănĭmĭtās -ātis, f. *concord, unanimity.*

ūnănĭmus -a -um, *of one mind, agreeing, unanimous.*

uncia -ae, f. *a twelfth; an ounce.*

unciārĭus -a -um, *of a twelfth part;* faenus, 8⅓%.

unciātim, *little by little.*

uncīnātus -a -um, *hooked.*

unciŏla -ae, f. *a mere twelfth.*

unctĭo -ōnis, f. *anointing.*

unctĭto -are, *to anoint, besmear.*

unctor -ōris, m. *an anointer.*

unctūra -ae, f. *anointing of the dead.*

unctus -a -um, partic. from ungo; q.v.

¹uncus -i, m. *a hook.*

²uncus -a -um, *hooked, curved.*

unda -ae, f. *water, fluid,* esp. as *a wave;* fig. *a stream of people,* etc.

undĕ, *whence, from where* (interrog. and relat.). Transf., *how, from whom.*

undĕcĭēs (-ĭens) *eleven times.*

undĕcim, *eleven.*

undĕcĭmus -a -um, *eleventh.*

undĕcumquĕ (-cunquĕ), *from whatever place.*

undēni -ae -a, *eleven at a time* or *eleven each.*

undēnōnāgintā, *eighty-nine.*

undeoctōgintā, *seventy-nine.*

undēquadrāgintā, *thirty-nine.*

undēquinquāgēsĭmus -a -um, *forty-ninth.*

undēquinquāgintā, *forty-nine.*

undēsexāgintā, *fifty-nine.*

undētrĭcēsĭmus -a -um, *twenty-ninth.*

undēvĭcēsĭmus, *nineteenth.*

undēvīgintī, *nineteen.*

undĭquĕ, *from or on all sides, from everywhere, everywhere; altogether, in every respect.*

undĭsŏnus -a -um, *resounding with waves.*

undo -are: intransit., *to surge, wave, undulate;* transit., *to flood.*

undōsus -a -um, *surging, billowy.*

ūnetvĭcēsĭmāni -ōrum, m. pl. *soldiers of the twenty-first legion.*

ūnetvĭcēsĭmus -a -um, *twenty-first.*

ungo (unguo) ungĕre unxi unctum, *to anoint, besmear;* partic. **unctus** -a -um, *besmeared, anointed, greasy; rich, copious;* n. as subst. *a sumptuous repast.*

unguĕn -ĭnis, n. *fatty substance, ointment.*

unguentārĭus -a -um, *of ointment;* m. as subst. *a dealer in unguents.*

unguentātus -a -um, *anointed.*

unguentum -i, n. *salve, ointment, perfume.*

unguĭcŭlus -i, m. *a finger or toe-nail.*

unguis -is, m. *a finger- or toe-nail; of animals, claw, hoof;* de tenero ungui, *from childhood;* ad (or in) unguem, *to a hair, nicely, perfectly.*

ungŭla -ae, f. *a hoof, claw, talon.*

unguo = ungo; q.v.

ūnĭcŏlor -oris, *of one colour.*

ūnĭcus -a -um, *one, only, sole; singular, unique;* adv. **ūnĭcē,** *singly, especially.*

ūnĭformis -e, *having one form, simple.*

ūnĭgĕna -ae, *of the same race; only-begotten, unique.*

ūnĭmănus -a -um, *having but one hand.*

ūnĭo -ōnis, m. *a large pearl.*

ūnĭtās -ātis, f. *unity, oneness.*

ūnĭtĕr, *in one, together.*

ūnĭversālis -e, *general, universal.*

ūnĭversĭtās -atis, f. *the whole, total; the universe, the world.*

ūnĭversus (archaic **ūnĭvorsus**) -a -um, *combined in one, whole, entire;* plur. **ūnĭversi** -ae -a, *all together;* n. as subst. **ūnĭversum** -i, *the whole; the world, the universe;* phrase, in universum, and adv. **ūnĭversē,** *generally, in general.*

ūnus -a -um, genit. ūnīus, dat. ūni, *one; only one; one and the same; any one;* ad unum omnes, *all to a man;* in unum, *into one place;* uno tempore, *at the same time.* Adv. **ūnā,** *in one, together.*

ūpĭlio (ōpĭlio) -ōnis, m. *a shepherd.*

Ŭrănĭa -ae and **Ŭrănĭē** -ēs, f. *the Muse of Astronomy.*

urbānĭtās -ātis, f. *city life, esp. life in Rome.* Hence *politeness, urbanity, refinement; wit, pleasantry.*

urbānus -a -um, *of a city* (esp. Rome); *urban;* hence *refined; elegant; witty, pleasant;* m. pl. as subst. *the inhabitants of a city, the townsfolk.* Adv.

urbānē, *politely, courteously; wittily, elegantly.*

urbs -bis, f. *a walled town or city;* esp. *the city of Rome.*

urcĕŏlus -i, m. *a small jug or pitcher.*

urcĕus -i, m. *a jug, pitcher.*

ūrēdo -ĭnis, f. *a blight on plants.*

urgĕo urgēre ursi, *to push, press, drive, urge; to beset, oppress; to stress;* of work, *to press on with, ply hard; follow up.*

ūrīna -ae, f. *urine.*

ūrīnātor -ōris, m. *a diver.*

ūrīno -are and **ūrīnor** -ari, dep. *to dive.*

urna -ae, f. *a jug, pitcher, jar, pot.*

ūro ūrĕre ussi ustum, *to burn; to dry up, parch; chafe, gall; to disturb, harass.*

ursa -ae, f. *a she-bear.*

ursus -i, m. *a bear.*

urtīca -ae, f. *a nettle.* Transf., *desire.*

ūrus -i, m. *a kind of wild ox.*

ūsĭtātus -a -um, *customary, usual;* adv. **ūsĭtātē.**

uspĭam, *anywhere.*

usquam, *anywhere; at all, in any way; in any direction.*

usquĕ, *through and through, all the way, continuously; always;* usque Romam, *as far as Rome;* usque a Romulo, *ever since Romulus.*

usquĕquāquĕ, *always.*

ustor -ōris, m. *a burner of corpses.*

ustŭlo -are, *to burn, scorch, singe.*

¹ūsŭcăpĭo -căpĕre -cēpi -captum, *to acquire ownership by long use.*

²ūsŭcăpĭo -ōnis, f. *ownership acquired by long possession or use.*

ūsūra -ae, f. *use, enjoyment;* esp. *use of borrowed capital; interest paid for money borrowed.*

ūsurpātĭo -ōnis, f. *using, use; undertaking.*

ūsurpo -are, *to use, bring into use; to take possession of, acquire, appropriate, usurp; to perceive, to notice; to use a word, to mention;* hence *to call, name.*

ūsus -ūs, m. *use, application, practice, exercise; social intercourse, familiarity; legal,* usus et fructus, ususfructus, *the use of others' property.* Transf., *practice, skill; experience; utility, usefulness, profit;* usui esse, ex usu esse, *to be useful, be of use;* usus est, *there is need of, occasion for;* usu venit, *it happens.*

ūsusfructus; see usus.

ŭt or ŭtī. (1) with indic. verb: *how* (interrog. and exclam.); relat., *as,* esp. with corresponding sic or ita; ut ut, *in whatever way;* explanatory, *as, as being* (sometimes without verb); temporal, *as when, while, since;* of place, *where.* (2) with subjunctive: *in indirect questions, how;* in wishes, *o that;* concessive, *granted that;* consecutive, *so that,* often preceded by ita, tam, etc.; explaining or defining, *namely that;* final, *in order that* (negat. ne or ut ne); in " indirect command " *that, to;* after verbs of fearing (= ne non), *that . . . not.*

utcumquĕ (-cunquĕ), *in whatever manner, however; whenever.*

ūtensĭlĭa -ĭum, n. pl., *useful things, utensils.*

¹ūter ūtris, m. *the skin of an animal used as bag or bottle.*

²ūter utra utrum; genit. utrīus, dat. utri; interrog., *which of the two?;* plur., *which side? which set?;* relat., *that (of two) which;* indef., *either of the two.*

ŭtercumquĕ (-cunquĕ) utrăcumquĕ utrumcumquĕ, *whichever of the two.*

ŭterlĭbet utrālĭbet utrumlĭbet, *whichever of the two you please.*

ŭterquĕ utrāquĕ utrumquĕ; genit. utrīusquĕ, dat. utrīquĕ; *each of two;* in plur., usually, *each side, each set;* sometimes of individuals, *both.*

ŭtĕrus -i, m. and **ŭtĕrum** -i, n. *womb; belly.*

ŭtervīs utrăvīs utrumvīs; genit. utri-usvīs, dat. utrīvīs; *whichever of the two you please.*

ūtī = ut; q.v.

Ūtĭca -ae, f. *a town in Africa where Cato the younger killed himself;* adj. **Ūtĭcensis** -e.

ūtĭlis -e, *useful, fit, profitable;* adv. **ūtĭlĭtĕr.**

ūtĭlĭtās -ātis, f. *usefulness, profit, advantage.*

ŭtĭnam, *would that! oh that!*

ŭtĭquĕ, *at any rate, certainly, at least.*

ūtor ūtī ūsus, dep. *to use, employ; to possess, enjoy;* of persons, *to associate with,* or, with a predicate, *to find.* Hence partic. **ūtens** -entis, *possessing.*

utpŏtĕ, *seeing that, inasmuch as.*

utrārĭus -i, m. *a water-carrier.*

utrimquĕ (-inquĕ) *from* or *on both sides.*

utrō, *to which of two places? to which side?*

utrŏbĭquĕ (utrŭbĭquĕ), *on each of two sides; both ways.*

utrŏquĕ, *to both sides, in both directions; at each point, both ways.*

utrum, *whether;* used mainly in alternative questions, direct or indirect.

ŭtŭt, *however;* see ut.

ūva -ae, f. *a bunch of grapes;* meton., *vine.* Transf., *a cluster.*

ūvesco -ĕre, *to become moist.*

ūvĭdŭlus -a -um, *moist.*

ūvĭdus -a -um, *moist, damp, wet.* Transf., *drunken.*

uxor -ōris, f. *a wife;* uxorem ducere, *to marry a wife.*

uxōrĭus -a -um. (1) *of a wife.* (2) *too devoted to one's wife, uxorious.*

V

V, v, the twenty-first letter of the Latin Alphabet.

văcātĭo -ōnis, f. *freedom, immunity, exemption.* Transf., *money paid for exemption from military duties.*

---

vacca -ae, f. *a cow.*

vaccīnĭum -i, n. *the blueberry, whortleberry;* according to some, *the hyacinth.*

văcēfĭo -fĭĕri, *to be made empty.*

văcillātĭo -ōnis, f. *rocking, reeling.*

văcillo (vaccillo) -are, *to totter, reel, stagger.*

văcīvus (vŏcīvus) -a -um, *empty.*

văco -are, *to be empty;* of property, *to be vacant, to have no master;* in gen., *to be free from anything, be without; to be free from work, be at leisure;* with dat., *to have time for;* impers., vacat, *there is time (for).*

văcŭēfăcĭo -făcĕre -fēci -factum, *to make empty.*

văcŭĭtās -ātis, f. *freedom, exemption, immunity; a vacancy in a public office.*

văcŭo -are, *to make void, to empty.*

văcŭus -a -um, *empty, void; empty-handed; vacant; devoid, exempt, without* (with abl. or *ab*); *free, at leisure;* with dat., *free for; worthless, useless, vain.* N. as subst. **văcŭum** -i, *an empty place, vacuum.*

vădĭmōnĭum -i, n. *bail, security, recognizance.*

vādo -ĕre, *to go, hasten, rush.*

vădor -ari, dep. *to bind over by bail.*

vădōsus -a -um, *shallow.*

vădum -i, n. *a shallow, shoal, ford in river or sea;* in gen., *water, river, sea;* fig., *shallows,* typical either of *safety* or of *danger.*

vae, interj. *alas! woe!*

văfer vafra vafrum, *artful, sly, crafty;* adv. **vafrē.**

văgīna -ae, f. *a scabbard, sheath, case; the husk of grain.*

văgĭo -ire, *to whimper as a child.*

văgītus -ūs, m. *whimpering, crying.*

văgor -ōris, m. = vagitus; q.v.

văgor -ari, dep. *to wander, ramble, rove.*

văgus -a -um, *wandering, roaming; fickle; diffuse, aimless.* Adv. **văgē**, *dispersedly.*

vah (vaha), interj. *ah! oh!*

valdē, *intensely, very much;* in replies *certainly, very much so.*

vălēdico -ĕre, *to say good-bye.*

vălĕo -ēre, *to be strong, vigorous, in good health, well; to have force, avail, prevail, be able; to be worth;* of words, *to mean, signify;* as a farewell greeting, vale, or valeas, *farewell, good-bye;* valere iubere, *to bid farewell, say good-bye to.* Hence partic. **vălens** -entis, *strong, powerful, healthy;* adv. **vălentĕr.**

Vălĕrĭus -a -um, *name of a Roman gens.*

vălesco -ĕre, *to grow strong.*

vălētūdo -ĭnis, f. *state of health;* sometimes either *ill-health, weakness,* or *good health.*

vălĭdus -a -um, *strong, powerful, healthy, well; mighty, influential;* of medicines, *efficacious.* Adv. **vălĭdē**, *strongly, powerfully;* in replies, *certainly to be sure.*

vallāris -e, *relating to the* vallum;
q.v.

vallēs (vallis) -is, f. *a vale, valley,
hollow.*

vallo -are, *to fortify with a palisade;
to strengthen.*

vallum -i, n. *a palisade of stakes; a
fortification, defence.*

vallus -i, m. *a post, stake;* collectively,
a palisade, stockade.

valvae -ārum, f. pl. *folding-doors.*

vānesco -ěre, *to pass away, disappear.*

vānilŏquentĭa -ae, f. *idle talk, vaunting.*

vānilŏquus -a -um, *lying; boastful.*

vānĭtās -ātis, f. *emptiness; worthlessness, unreality; boasting, ostentation.*

vannus -i, f. *winnowing-fan.*

vānus -a -um, *empty, void; vain, idle,
worthless, meaningless;* of persons,
ostentatious, boastful, unreliable.

văpĭdus -a -um, *spiritless, spoiled, flat.*

văpor (văpōs) -ōris, m. *vapour, steam;
warm exhalation, warmth.*

văpōrārĭum -i, n. *a steam flue.*

văpōro -are; intransit., *to steam, reek;*
transit., *to fill with vapour, heat,
warm.*

vappa -ae, f. *flat wine.* Transf., *a
worthless fellow.*

văpŭlo -are, *to be flogged, beaten,
knocked about;* of things, *to be
wasted.*

vărĭantĭa -ae, and **vărĭātĭo** -ōnis, f.
difference, variation.

vārĭco -are, *to stand with feet apart.*

vārĭcōsus -a -um, *having varicose
veins.*

vārĭcus -a -um, *straddling.*

vărĭĕtās -ātis, f. *variety, difference,
diversity.*

vărĭo -are: transit., *to vary, diversify,
change, alter, do or say differently;*
pass., variari, *to waver, be divided,
vary;* intransit., *to be different, vary.*

¹**vărĭus** -a -um, *various, manifold,
changeable, diverse;* of persons, in
bad sense, *fickle, changeable;* adv.
vărĭē, *diversely, variously.*

²**Vărĭus** -a -um, *name of a Roman gens.*

vārix -ĭcis, c. *a varicose vein.*

Varro -ōnis, m. *a surname in the gens
Terentia.*

¹**vărus** -a -um, *knock-kneed;* in gen.,
crooked, bent; diverse, different.

²**Vărus** -i, m. *a Roman surname.*

¹**văs** vădis, m. *a bail, surety.*

²**văs** vāsis, n. *a vessel, receptacle;* plur.
milit., *war materials, equipment.*

vāsārĭum -i, n. *an outfit allowance.*

vascŭlārĭus -i, m. *a maker of vessels,*
esp. *in metal.*

vascŭlum -i, n. *a small vessel.*

vastātĭo -ōnis, f. *devastating, laying
waste.*

vastātor -ōris, m. *devastator, ravager.*

vastĭfĭcus -a -um, *devastating.*

vastĭtās -ātis, f. *a waste, emptiness,
desolation;* concr. in plur., *devastators.*

vasto -are, *to empty; to lay waste,
ravage, devastate, prey upon.*

vastus -a -um, *empty, waste, desolate;
laid waste, devastated.* Transf., *vast,*

enormous; rough, rude. Adv. **vastē,**
widely, extensively; rudely, roughly.

vātēs -is, c. *a prophet, seer; a bard, poet.*

Vātĭcānus -a -um, *Vatican:* mons,
collis, *the Vatican Hill on the west
side of the Tiber.*

vātĭcĭnātĭo -ōnis, f. *soothsaying,
prophecy.*

vātĭcĭnātŏr, ōris, m. *soothsayer, prophet.*

vātĭcĭnor -ari, dep. *to prophesy; to
talk wildly, to rave.*

vātĭcĭnus -a -um, *soothsaying, prophetic.*

vătillum (băt-) -i, n. *a chafing-dish or
shovel.*

Vătĭnĭus -a -um, *the name of a Roman
gens.*

-**vě,** enclitic, *or, or perhaps.*

vēcordĭa (vae-) -ae, f. *folly, madness.*

vēcors (vae-) -cordis, *senseless, mad.*

vectīgăl -gālis, n. *revenue, income;* esp.
a tax, impost, duty.

vectīgālis -e, *relating to income or to
taxes; liable to tax, tributary.*

vectĭo -ōnis, f. *carrying, conveyance.*

vectis -is, m. *a lever, crow-bar; a bar,
bolt.*

vecto -are, *to carry, convey;* pass., *to
ride or be driven.*

vector -ōris, m.: act., *a carrier, bearer;*
pass., *a passenger, rider.*

vectōrĭus -a -um, *for carrying;* navigia,
transports.

vectūra -ae, f. *conveying, transportation;
passage-money, fare.*

věgěo -ēre, *to stir up, excite.*

věgětus -a -um, *lively, vigorous, fresh.*

věgrandis -e, *diminutive.*

věhěmens (poet. **vēmens**) -entis,
violent, furious, impetuous; adv.
věhěmentěr, *violently; forcibly,
exceedingly.*

věhĭcŭlum -i, n. *vehicle, conveyance.*

věho věhěre vexi vectum, *to carry,
convey;* pass., *to sail, ride, drive,* etc.;
so also pres. partic., vehens, *riding.*

Vēii -ōrum, m. pl. *an old town in
Etruria;* adj. **Vēiens** -entis.

věl: conj., *singly, or;* doubled, *either
... or;* adv. *even, actually; for
example.*

vēlāmen -ĭnis, n. *covering, garment.*

vēlāmentum -i, n. *a covering, veil;*
in plur., *olive-branches wrapped in
wool, carried by suppliants.*

vēlārĭum -i, n. *an awning in a theatre.*

vēlāti -ōrum, m. pl., milit. *the reserve,
supernumary troops.*

vēlēs -ĭtis, m. usually plur., velites,
light-armed infantry, skirmishers.

vēlĭfer -fěra -fěrum, *carrying sail.*

vēlĭfĭcātĭo -ōnis, f. *sailing.*

vēlĭfĭco -are and **vēlĭfĭcor** -āri, dep.
to sail. Transf., *to work for an end.*

vēlĭtāris -e, *of light-armed troops.*

vēlĭvŏlans -antis, and **vēlĭvŏlus** -a
-um, *flying with sails.*

vellĭco -are, *to pluck, twitch; to taunt,
criticize.*

vello vellěre velli (vulsi, volsi) vulsum
(volsum), *to pull, twitch; to pluck out;*
partic. **vulsus** -a -um, *plucked, smooth.*

vellus -ěris, n. *a fleece; skin, hide.*

vēlo -are, *to cover, veil, hide.*

vēlōcĭtās -ātis, f. *quickness, rapidity.*

vēlox -ōcis, *quick, rapid, swift;* adv. **vēlōcĭtĕr.**

vēlum -i, *a sail;* vela dare, *to sail; a covering, awning, curtain.*

vĕlŭt (vĕlŭtī), *as, just as; even as; as for instance;* with subjunctive, velut, or velut si, *as if, just as if.*

vēmens = vehemens; q.v.

vēna -ae, f. *a blood-vessel, vein, artery; a water-course; a vein of metal; a vein of talent, disposition, natural inclination.*

vēnābŭlum -i, n. *a hunting-spear.*

Vēnăfrum -i, n. *a Samnite town in Campania.*

vēnālīcĭus -a -um, *of the sale of slaves;* m. as subst. *a slave-dealer.*

vēnālis -e, *on sale, to be sold; venal;* m. as subst. *a slave put up for sale.*

vēnātīcus -a -um, *of or for the chase.*

vēnātĭo -ōnis, f. *the chase, hunting; game.*

vēnātor -ōris, m. *a hunter, sportsman.*

vēnātōrĭus -a -um, *of or for the chase.*

vēnātrix -īcis, f. *huntress.*

vēnātus -ūs, m. *the chase, hunting.*

vendĭbĭlis -e, *on sale, saleable; popular, acceptable.*

vendĭtātĭo -onis, f. *a putting up for sale; hence boasting, vaunting.*

venditātor -ōris, m. *vaunter, boaster.*

vendĭtĭo -ōnis, f. *selling, sale.*

vendĭto -are, *to offer for sale, try to sell; to praise, advertise.*

venditor -ōris, m. *seller, vendor.*

vendo -dĕre -dĭdi -dĭtum (pass. usually veneo; q.v.), *to put up for sale, sell; to betray; to recommend, advertise.*

vĕnēfĭcĭum -i, n. *poisoning; magic, sorcery.*

vĕnēfĭcus -a -um, *poisonous, magical;* m. as subst., *a poisoner, sorcerer; a sorceress, witch.*

vĕnēnĭfer -fĕra -fĕrum, *poisonous.*

vĕnēno -are, *to poison, drug;* partic. **vĕnēnātus** -a -um, *poisoned, drugged; enchanted.*

vĕnēnum -i, n. *a drug; poison* (fig. *ruin, destruction); a love-potion; colouring matter, dye; rouge.*

vēnĕo vēnīre vēnĭi vēnum, *to go for sale, to be sold* (used as pass. of vendo).

vĕnĕrābĭlis -e, *venerable, reverend.*

vĕnĕrābundus -a -um, *reverent, respectful.*

vĕnĕrātĭo -ōnis, f. *reverence, respect.*

vĕnĕrātor -ōris, m. *a venerator, reverer.*

vĕnĕrĭus; see venus.

vĕnĕror -ari, dep. *to ask reverently; to revere, respect, worship.*

vĕnĭa -ae, f. *grace, indulgence, favour, permission; pardon, forgiveness.*

vĕnĭo vĕnīre vēni ventum, *to come;* in course of time, *to happen, come, arrive; to grow, arise.*

vēnor -ari, dep, *to hunt.*

venter -tris, m. *the belly, stomach; the womb.*

ventĭlo -are, *to wave, brandish, fan.*

ventĭto -are, *to come often, resort.*

ventōsus -a -um, *full of wind, windy; swift* or *light as wind; puffed up, vain; changeable, inconstant.*

ventrĭcŭlus -i, m. *the belly; a ventricle.*

ventŭlus -i, m. *a slight wind.*

ventus -i, m. *wind; rumour, favour.*

vēnūcŭla (venn-) -ae, f. *a kind of grape.*

vēnum and **vēno,** acc. and dat. n., *for sale.*

vēnumdo (vēnundo) -dăre -dĕdi -dătum, *to offer for sale, to sell.*

vĕnus -ĕris, f. *charm, loveliness; love; a loved one;* personif., **Vĕnus,** *goddess of love; the Venus throw, highest throw of the dice;* adj. **Vĕnĕrĕus (-ĭus)** -a -um, *of Venus or of love.*

Vĕnŭsĭa -ae, f. *a town on the borders of Lucania and Apulia, birthplace of Horace.*

vĕnustās -ātis, f. *loveliness, charm, attractiveness.*

vĕnustus -a -um, *charming, lovely, graceful;* adv. **vĕnustē.**

vēpallĭdus -a -um, *very pale.*

veprēcŭla -ae, f. *a thorn-bush.*

veprēs -is, m. *a thorn-bush, briar-bush.*

vēr vēris, n. *spring;* primo vere, *in the beginning of spring;* ver sacrum, *an offering of the firstlings.*

vērātrum -i, n. *hellebore.*

vērax -ācis, *speaking the truth, truthful.*

verbēna -ae, f., often in pl., *sacred boughs carried by the Fetiales.*

verber -ĕris, n. *a lash; a whip, scourge, thong; a blow, stroke; whipping.*

¹verbĕro -are, *to beat, whip, thrash;* with words, *to assail, lash.*

²verbĕro -ōnis, m. *a rascal.*

verbōsus -a -um, *copious, diffuse, wordy;* adv. **verbōsē.**

verbum -i, n. *a word;* verbum facere, *to speak;* uno verbo, *in a word, briefly;* ad verbum, *word for word;* verbi causa, *for example;* grammat., *a verb; an expression, saying; mere words, mere talk;* verba dare homini, *to cheat a person.*

Vercingĕtŏrix -rīgis, m. *a Gallic chief.*

vĕrēcundĭa -ae, f. *modesty, diffidence, bashfulness;* with genit., *respect for, scruple about.*

vĕrēcundor -ari, dep. *to be bashful, ashamed, shy.*

vĕrēcundus -a -um, *bashful, modest, shy, diffident;* adv. **vĕrēcundē.**

vĕrēdus -i, *a swift horse, hunter.*

vĕrĕor -ēri -ĭtus, dep. *to be afraid, fear; to have respect for, revere;* gerundive **verendus** -a -um, *venerable, reverend.*

Vergĭlĭus -i, m. P. Vergilius Maro, *author of the Aeneid, Georgics, and Eclogues.*

Vergĭnĭus -a -um, *the name of a Roman gens.*

vergo vergĕre versi: intransit., *to bend, be inclined, verge;* of time, *to draw to an end;* transit., *to bend, turn, incline.*

vērĭdĭcus -a -um, *truthful.*

vĕrĭlŏquĭum -i, n. *etymology.*

vĕrīsĭmĭlis -e, *probable, likely.*

vĕrīsĭmĭlĭtūdo ĭnis, f. *probability.*

vērĭtās -ātis, f. *the truth, reality; truthfulness, telling of truth;* in gen., *honesty.*

vermen -ĭnis, n. *a griping pain.*

vermĭcŭlus -i, m. *little worm, grub.*

vermis -is, m. *worm.*

verna -ae, c. *a slave born in the master's house; a native.*

vernācŭlus -a -um, *of a slave born in the house; native, domestic.*

vernīlis -e, *like a slave; mean, abject; pert, forward;* adv. **vernīlĭtĕr,** *like a slave.*

verno -are, *to flourish, grow green.*

vernŭla -ae, c. *a little slave born in the house;* as adj. *native, indigenous.*

vernus -a -um, *of spring, vernal.*

Vērōna -ae, f. *a town of northern Italy, birthplace of Catullus.*

¹verrēs -is, m. *a boar.*

²Verrēs -is, m. *C. Cornelius, praetor in Sicily, prosecuted by Cicero;* adj. **Verrĭus** and **Verrīnus** -a -um.

verrīnus -a -um, *of a boar.*

verro verrĕre verri versum, *to drag, pull, sweep, sweep up; to sweep clean, brush, scour.*

verrūca -ae, f. *a wart; blemish.*

verrunco -are, *to turn out;* bene verruncare, *to turn out well.*

versābundus -a -um, *whirling round, revolving.*

versātĭlis -e, *turning round, revolving; versatile.*

versĭcŏlor -ōris, *of various colours.*

versĭcŭlus -i, m. *a little line; a poor little verse.*

versĭfĭcātĭo -ōnis, f. *making of verses.*

versĭfĭcātor -ōris, m. *versifier.*

versĭfĭco -are, *to write verse.*

verso (vorso) -are, *to turn about, turn this way and that; to bend, ply, twist; to influence, agitate; to turn over in the mind, think of.* Pass., *to be about, hover, resort;* *to be engaged, take part, be employed.*

versum = versus; q.v.

versūra -ae, f. *turning; the borrowing of money to pay a debt; hence a loan.*

¹versus (vors-) and **versum** (vors-), *towards;* used esp. after an accusative or prep. and acc.; sursum versus, *upwards.*

²versus (vors-) -a -um, partic. from verro or verto; q.v.

³versus (vors-) -ūs, m. *a row, line; a line of writing,* esp. of poetry.

versūtĭa -ae, f. *wile, stratagem.*

versūtus -a -um, *dexterous; cunning, crafty, sly;* adv. **versūtē.**

vertex (vortex) -ĭcis, m. (1) *a whirl, eddy, whirlwind, gust.* (2) *the crown of the head;* in gen., *head, summit, elevation.* (3) *the pole* of the heavens.

vertĭcōsus (vortĭc-) -a -um, *eddying.*

vertīgo -ĭnis, f. *whirling round, revolution; giddiness, vertigo.*

verto (vorto) vertĕre verti versum, *to turn, turn round, turn up;* intransit., *to turn oneself;* milit., vertere in fugam, *to put to flight, rout;* terga vertere, *to flee; to interpret, construe, understand in a certain way, to impute; to*

alter, change; to translate; to change for another, exchange; vertere solum, *to go into exile; to upset, overthrow;* pass. or intransit., of time, *to roll round;* pass., *to move in a certain sphere, to depend on, centre in.*

Vertumnus (vor-) -i, m. *god of the changing year.*

vĕrū -ūs, n. *a spit; a javelin.*

vērus -a -um, *true, real, genuine; truthful, veracious; just, reasonable.* N. as subst. *truth, reality; right, duty;* veri similis, *likely, probable.* N. nom. as adv. **vērum,** *but yet, still, however;* strengthened, **vērun-tāmen** (vērum-), *notwithstanding, nevertheless.* N. abl. as adv. **vērō,** *in truth, indeed, in fact;* in a climax, *even, indeed;* ironically, *to be sure;* adversative, *but indeed, but in fact.* Adv. **vērē,** *truly, really, rightly.*

vĕrutum -i, n. *javelin.*

vĕrūtus -a -um, *armed with a javelin.*

vervex -vēcis, m. *a wether; a sheep, dolt.*

vēsānĭa -ae, f. *madness, insanity.*

vēsānĭens -entis, *raging.*

vēsānus -a -um, *mad, insane;* of things, *furious, wild.*

vescor -i, dep. *to eat, feed on; to use, enjoy.*

vescus -a -um: act., *consuming;* pass., *wasted, thin.*

vēsīca -ae, f. *the bladder; a purse, a lantern* of style, *bombast.*

vēsīcŭla -ae, f. *a little bladder.*

vespa -ae, f. *wasp.*

Vespăsĭānus -i, m., T. Flavius, *Roman emperor,* A.D. 69-79.

vesper -ĕris or -ĕri, m. *evening; the west; the evening star;* vespere, vesperi, *in the evening.*

vespĕrasco -ĕre, *to become evening.*

vespertīnus -a -um, *of evening; western.*

vespillo -ōnis, m. *a corpse-bearer for the poor.*

Vesta -ae, f. *goddess of the hearth and domestic life;* adj. **Vestālis** -e, *Vestal;* f. as subst. *a Vestal virgin, priestess of Vesta.*

vester (voster) -tra -trum, *your, yours.*

vestĭbŭlum -i, n. *entrance-court, court-yard;* in gen., *entrance; beginning.*

vestīgĭum -i, n. *a foot-step, track; a trace, mark;* in plur., *the foot;* in vestigio, e vestigio, *at that moment.*

vestīgo -are, *to track, trace.*

vestīmentum -i, n. *clothing, a garment.*

vestĭo -ire, *to dress, clothe; to cover, adorn.*

vestis -is, f. *a covering* or *garment, clothing; a blanket, carpet, tapestry.*

vestītus -ūs, m. *clothing, clothes; a covering.*

Vĕsŭvĭus -i, m. *Vesuvius, the volcano in Campania.*

vĕtĕrānus -a -um, *old;* m. pl. *old soldiers, veterans.*

vĕtĕrasco -ascĕre -āvi, *to grow old.*

vĕtĕrātor -ōris, m. *an old hand, old stager.*

vĕtĕrātŏrĭus -a -um, *cunning, crafty*; adv. **vĕtĕrātŏrĭē.**

vĕtĕrīnus -a -um, *of draught*; bestia, *a beast of burden.*

vĕternōsus -a -um, *lethargic, sleepy, dull.*

vĕternus -i, m. *age; lethargy, inactivity, sloth.*

vĕto (vŏto) vĕtare vĕtŭi vĕtĭtum, *to forbid, prohibit*; n. of perf. partic. as subst. **vĕtĭtum** -i, *that which is forbidden; a prohibition.*

vĕtŭlus -a -um, *little old, poor little old*; as subst., *an old man or woman.*

vĕtus -ĕris; superl. vĕterrĭmus; *old, ancient, of long standing; experienced.* M. pl. as subst. *the ancients.*

vĕtustās -ātis, f. *age; antiquity, past time; long duration, length of time* (including future time).

vĕtustus -a -um, *old, ancient, of long standing; old-fashioned, antiquated.*

vexāmen -ĭnis, n. *shaking, upheaval.*

vexātĭo -ōnis, f. *shaking, jolting, shock; ill-treatment.*

vexātor -ōris, m. *one who shakes, harasses, disturbs.*

vexillārĭus -i, m. *a standard-bearer*; in plur. *a corps of veterans, a reserve.*

vexillum -i, n. *a standard, flag; a company, troop.*

vexo -are, *to shake, toss, jostle; to harass, annoy.*

vĭa -ae, f. *a way, passage; a highway, road, street; a course, march, journey; means, way, method*; abl. vĭā, *methodically.*

vĭātĭcus -a -um, *relating to a journey*; n. as subst., *journey money; also savings* or *prize-money.*

vĭātor -ōris, m. (1) *a traveller, wayfarer.* (2) *an apparitor, messenger.*

vĭbro -are: transit., *to cause to vibrate, brandish, shake; to brandish and hurl* a weapon; *to curl, frizzle* hair; intransit., *to shake, tremble, quiver, vibrate.*

vĭburnum -i, n. *the wayfaring-tree.*

vīcānus -a -um, *dwelling in a village*; m. pl. as subst. *villagers.*

vĭcārĭus -a -um, *substituted, vicarious*; m. as subst., *a substitute*; esp. *an under-servant.*

vīcātim, *from street to street; in villages.*

vĭcĕ, vĭcem,; see vicis.

vīcēni -ae -a, *twenty at a time* or *twenty each.*

vīcēsĭmāni -ōrum, m. pl. *soldiers of the twentieth legion.*

vīcēsĭmārĭus -a -um, *relating to the* vicesima.

vīcēsĭmus (vīcens-) -a -um, *twentieth*; f. as subst. **vīcēsĭma (vīcens-)** -ae, *the twentieth part, as a toll or tax.*

vĭcĭa -ae, f. *vetch.*

vĭcĭēs (-ĭens), *twenty times.*

vīcīnālis -e, *neighbouring, near.*

vīcīnĭa -ae, and **vīcīnĭtās** -ātis, f. *neighbourhood; vicinity; likeness*; concr., *the neighbours.*

vīcīnus -a -um, *near, neighbouring*; m. and f. as subst., *a neighbour*; n. as subst., *neighbourhood, vicinity.*

vĭcis (genit. nom. not found), *change, interchange, alternation*; per vices, in vices, *alternately, reciprocally; recompense, retaliation; the vicissitude of fate, lot, destiny; one's place, office, duty*; vicem, vice, in vicem, ad vicem, *in place of, instead of, like.*

vĭcissim, *in turn.*

vĭcissĭtūdo -ĭnis, f. *change, alteration.*

victĭma -ae, f. *an animal offered in sacrifice, victim.*

victĭmārĭus -i, m. *to live on, feed on.*

victor -ōris, m. and **victrix** -trīcis, f. *conqueror, victor*; as adj., *victorious.*

victōrĭa -ae, f. *victory, conquest.*

victōrĭātus -i, m. *a silver coin stamped with a figure of Victory.*

victōrĭŏla -ae, f. *a small statue of Victory.*

victrix -trīcis, f.; see victor.

victus -ūs, m. *living; manner of life; nourishment, food.*

vīcŭlus -i, m. *a little village, hamlet.*

vīcus -i, m. *part of a town, a street; a village, hamlet; an estate, country-seat.*

vĭdēlĭcet, *it is clear*; as adv. *clearly, plainly, manifestly; namely*; iron-ically, *of course, to be sure.*

vĭdĕo vĭdēre vĭdi vīsum, *to see; to perceive, notice, observe; to look into* a matter, *see to, provide for.* Pass., *to be seen; to seem, appear, be thought; also to seem good, seem right.* N. of perf. partic. as subst. **vīsum** -i, *a sight, appearance, vision.*

vĭdŭĭtās -ātis, f. *want; widowhood.*

vĭdŭo -are, *to deprive*; f. of perf. partic. **vĭdŭāta** -ae, *widowed.*

vĭdŭus -a -um, *deprived, bereaved, widowed*; f. as subst. **vĭdŭa** -ae, *a widow*, or *an unmarried woman.*

Vienna -ae, f. *town in Gallia Narbonensis* (now Vienne).

vĭĕo -ēre, *to weave together*; partic. **vĭētus** -a -um, *shrivelled, shrunken.*

vĭgĕo -ēre, *to be vigorous, thrive, flourish.*

vĭgesco -ĕre, *to become vigorous, begin to thrive.*

vĭgēsĭmus = vicesimus; q.v.

vĭgĭl -ĭlis, *wakeful, watchful*; m. as subst., *a watchman.*

vĭgĭlantĭa -ae, f. *watchfulness, vigilance.*

vĭgĭlax -ācis, *watchful, wakeful.*

vĭgĭlĭa -ae, f. *wakefulness, sleeplessness, watch; a watch of the night; the watch, sentinels*; fig. *watchfulness, vigilance, care.*

vĭgĭlo -are: intransit., *to keep awake, watch; to be vigilant, watchful, careful*; transit. in pass, *to be watched through, watched over.* Pres. partic. **vĭgĭlans** -antis, *watch ul, vigilant*; adv. **vĭgĭlantĕr.**

vĭgĭnti, *twenty.*

vĭgintĭvĭrātus -ūs, *the office of the* vigintiviri.

vĭgintĭvĭri -ōrum, m. pl. *a commission of twenty.*

vĭgor -ōris, m. *force, energy.*
vīlĭco -are, *to manage an estate as bailiff.*
vīlĭcus -i, m. *a bailiff, steward, overseer of an estate;* f. vīlĭca -ae, *a bailiff's wife.*
vīlis -e, *cheap, worth little;* adv. **vīlĭtĕr.**
vīlĭtās -ātis, f. *cheapness, low price;* in gen., *worthlessness.*
villa -ae, f. *a country-house, estate, farm.*
villĭc-; see vilic-.
villōsus -a -um, *shaggy, hairy.*
villŭla -ae, f. *a small country-house, little farm.*
villum -i, n. *a sup of wine.*
villus -i, m. *shaggy hair.*
vīmen -ĭnis, n. *an osier, twig; a basket.*
vīmentum = vimen; q.v.
Vīmĭnālis collis, *one of the seven hills of Rome.*
vīmĭnĕus -a -um, *of osiers, wicker.*
vīn = visne; see volo.
vīnācĕus -a -um, *belonging to wine or a grape.*
vīnālĭa -ium and -iōrum, n. pl. *wine festivals, one in April, one in August.*
vīnārĭus -a -um, *of wine;* as subst. m. *a vintner;* n. *a wine-jar.*
vincĭbĭlis -e, *easily gained.*
vincĭo vincire vinxi vinctum, *to bind, tie up; to surround, encompass; to restrain, confine, secure.*
vinco vincĕre vici victum, *to conquer, overcome, master, surpass; to prove successfully, win one's point.*
vincŭlum (vinclum) -i, n. *a band, cord, chain, fetter, tie;* plur., *imprisonment.*
Vindĕlĭci -ōrum, m. pl. *a Germanic people.*
vindēmĭa -ae, f. *vintage; grapes, wine.*
vindēmĭātor -ōris, m. *a harvester of grapes.*
vindēmĭŏla -ae, f. *a little vintage; a perquisite.*
vindex -ĭcis, c. *a claimant or protector; an avenger, punisher.*
vindĭcātĭo -ōnis, f. *defending, protecting; avenging.*
vindĭcĭae -ārum, f. pl. *things or persons claimed as property; the making of a claim.* Transf., *protection.*
vindĭco -are, *to claim; to arrogate, assume; appropriate; to claim as free;* hence *to liberate, deliver or protect; to avenge, punish.*
vindicta -ae, f. *a rod used in manumitting slaves.* Transf., *deliverance; vengeance, punishment.*
vīnĕa -ae, f. *a vineyard;* milit. *a mantlet, penthouse.*
vīnētum -i, n. *vineyard.*
vīnĭtor -ōris, m. *a vinedresser.*
vīnŏlentĭa -ae, f. *wine-drinking, intoxication.*
vīnŏlentus -a -um, *mixed with wine; drunk, intoxicated.*
vīnōsus -a -um, *full or fond of wine.*
vīnum -i, n. *wine, wine-drinking.*

vĭŏla -ae, f. *a violet or stock; the colour violet.*
vĭŏlābĭlis -e, *able to be injured.*
vĭŏlārĭum -i, n. *a bed of violets.*
vĭŏlātĭo -ōnis, f. *injury, violation, profanation.*
vĭŏlātor -ōris, m. *injurer, violator, profaner.*
vĭŏlens -entis, *violent, furious, impetuous;* adv. **vĭŏlentĕr.**
vĭŏlentĭa -ae, f. *violence, impetuosity.*
vĭŏlentus -a -um, *violent, vehement, furious, impetuous.*
vĭŏlo -are, *to violate, outrage, injure.*
vīpĕra -ae, f. *a viper; a snake, serpent.*
vīpĕrĕus -a -um, *of a viper or snake; snaky.*
vīpĕrīnus -a -um, *of a viper or snake.*
vir, vĭri, m. *a man, male person;* esp. *a grown man; a husband; a man of character or courage, "he-man";* milit. *a soldier, esp. an infantryman; a single man, individual.*
vĭrāgo -ĭnis, f. *a female warrior, heroine.*
vĭrectum (-ētum) -i, n. *greensward, turf.*
vĭrĕo -ēre, *to be green, vigorous, healthy, fresh.*
vīres -ĭum, f. pl.; see vis.
vĭresco -ĕre, *to grow green.*
vĭrētum = virectum; q.v.
virga -ae, f. *a green twig, a slip; a rod; a wand; a broom; a streak, stripe;* in plur., virgae, *the lictors' rods.*
virgātus -a -um. (1) *made of twigs.* (2) *striped.*
virgētum -i, n. *an osier-bed.*
virgĕus -a -um, *of twigs or rods.*
Virgĭlius = Vergilius; q.v.
virgĭnālis -e, **virgĭnārĭus, virgĭnĕus** -a -um, *maidenly.*
virgĭnĭtās -ātis, f. *virginity.*
virgo -ĭnis, f. *a maiden, virgin, girl.*
virgŭla -ae, f. *a little bough, twig; a rod, staff.*
virgultum -i, n. (1) *a thicket, copse.* (2) *a slip for planting.*
virguncŭla -ae, f. *a little girl.*
vĭrĭdans -antis, *green;* hence verb **vĭrĭdor** -ari, *to become green.*
vĭrĭdārĭum -i, n. *a pleasure-garden.*
vĭrĭdis -e, *green.* Transf., *fresh, young, vigorous.*
vĭrĭdĭtās -ātis, f. *greenness; freshness, bloom.*
vĭrīlis -e, *manly, male, virile; of a grown man, adult; courageous, spirited;* pro virili parte, *to the best of one's ability.* Adv. **vĭrīlĭtĕr,** *manfully.*
vĭrīlĭtās -ātis, f. *manhood, virility.*
vĭrītim, *man by man, individually.*
vĭrōsus -a -um, *stinking, fetid.*
virtūs -ūtis, f. *manliness; excellence, worth, goodness, virtue; bravery, courage.*
vīrus -i, n. *slimy liquid, slime; poison,* esp. *of snakes, venom; any harsh taste or smell.*
vīs, acc. vim, abl. vī; plur. **vīrēs** -ĭum, f. *force, power, strength; might, influence;* in sing. also *violence; a large number, quantity; the force,*

nature, meaning of a thing; plur., milit., *troops, forces.*

viscātus -a -um, *smeared with bird-lime.*

viscĕrātĭo -ōnis, f. *public distribution of meat.*

viscum -i, n. and **viscus** -i, m. *mistletoe; bird-lime.*

viscus -ĕris, usually plur. **viscĕra** -um, n. *flesh;* also *internal organs, entrails; inmost part* or *heart of anything.*

vīsĭo -ōnis, f. *seeing, view; appearance; notion, idea.*

vīsĭto -are, *to see often; to visit.*

vīso vīsĕre vīsi vīsum, *to look at, look into, see after; to go to see, visit, call upon;* gerundive **vīsendus** -a -um, *worth seeing, notable.*

vīsum -i, n. subst. from video; q.v.

vīsus -ūs, m. *seeing, sight; an appearance.*

vīta -ae, f. *life.*

vītābĭlis -e, *that can* or *should be avoided.*

vītābundus -a -um, *trying to avoid.*

vītālis -e, *of life, vital; living, surviving;* adv. **vītālĭtĕr,** *vitally.*

vītātĭo -ōnis, f. *avoiding, shunning.*

Vītellius -a -um, *the name of a Roman gens;* Aulus Vitellius, *the Roman emperor who succeeded Otho* (A.D. 69).

vītellus -i, m. *the yolk of an egg.*

vītĕus -a -um, *of a vine.*

vītĭcŭla -ae, f. *a little vine.*

vītĭfer -fĕra -fĕrum, *vine-bearing.*

vītĭgĕnus -a -um, *produced from the vine.*

vītĭo -are, *to injure, damage, corrupt; to forge, falsify.*

vītĭōsĭtās -ātis, f. *viciousness, corruption.*

vītĭōsus -a -um, *faulty, corrupt, bad, wrong;* adv. **vītĭōsē.**

vītis -is, f. *a vine; a centurion's staff.*

vītĭsător -ōris, m. *one who plants vines.*

vītĭum -i, n. *a fault, defect, blemish; crime, vice;* relig., *a defect in auguries* or *auspices.*

vīto -are, *to avoid, shun.*

vītrĕus -a -um, *of glass; glassy, transparent, glittering.*

vītrĭcus -i, m. *stepfather.*

vītrum -i, n. (1) *glass.* (2) *woad.*

vitta -ae, f. *a ribbon, band, fillet.*

vittātus -a -um, *bound with a fillet.*

vītŭla -ae, f. *calf, heifer.*

vītŭlīnus -a -um, *of a calf;* assum, *roast veal;* f. as subst. **veal.**

vītŭlus -i, m. *a bull-calf;* also *of the young of other animals.*

vītŭpĕrābĭlis -e, *blamable.*

vītŭpĕrātĭo -ōnis, f. *blaming, scolding, censure;* meton., *blameworthy conduct.*

vītŭpĕrātor -ōris, m. *a blamer.*

vītŭpĕro -are, *to blame, scold, censure.*

vīvārĭum -i, n. *a warren, preserve, fish-pond.*

vīvātus -a -um, *quickened, vivid.*

vīvax -ācis, *long-lived, lasting, enduring; brisk, lively, vigorous.*

vīvesco vīvescĕre vixi, *to grow lively.*

vīvĭdus -a -um, *full of life, animated, vigorous; life-like.*

vīvĭrādix -īcis, f. *a cutting with a root, a layer.*

vīvisco = vivesco; q.v.

vīvo vīvĕre vixi victum, *to live, be alive; to live well, to enjoy life; to survive; to live on* anything; *to dwell.*

vīvus (**vīvŏs**) -a -um, *alive, living; lifelike;* flumen, *running water;* ros, *fresh;* sulfur, *natural.*

vix, *with difficulty, scarcely, only just;* vix dum, or vixdum, *hardly yet*

vŏcābŭlum -i, n. *name, appellation;* grammat. *a noun.*

vŏcālis -e, *vocal; speaking, singing;* f. as subst. *a vowel.*

vŏcāmen -ĭnis, n. *name, appellation.*

vŏcātĭo -ōnis, f. *summons, invitation.*

vŏcātor -ōris, m. *an inviter.*

vŏcātus -ūs, m. *summons, invocation.*

vŏcīfĕrātĭo -ōnis, f. *loud calling, shouting.*

vŏcīfĕror -ari, dep. *to cry aloud, shout.*

vŏcĭto -are, *to be accustomed to name; to shout loudly* or *often.*

vŏco -are, *to call, summon, invoke, invite; to name, designate; to bring* or *put into any state* or *condition;* in dubium, *to call in question.*

vŏcŭla -ae, f. *a low, weak voice; a low tone; a petty speech.*

vŏlaema pĭra, n. pl. *a kind of large pear.*

vŏlātĭcus -a -um, *winged, flying; flighty, inconstant.*

vŏlātĭlis -e, *winged, flying; swift, rapid; fleeting, transitory.*

vŏlātus -ūs, m. *flying, flight.*

Volcānus (**Vulc-**) -i, m. *Vulcan, the god of fire, husband of Venus.*

volgo, volgus = vulgo, vulgus; q.v.

vŏlĭto -are, *to fly about, flit, flutter, rush around.*

volnĕro = vulnero; q.v.

¹**vŏlo** velle vŏlŭi (vīn = visne; sīs = si vis; sultis = si vultis); *to be willing, to wish, want; to will, ordain; to suppose, maintain that;* sibi velle. *to mean, signify.*

Hence partic. **vŏlens** -entis, *willing, favourable.*

²**vŏlo** -are, *to fly; to move rapidly, rush;* f. pl. of partic. volantes, -ium = *birds.*

vŏlōnes -um, m. pl. *volunteers (in the Second Punic War).*

Volsci -ōrum, m. pl. *a people in Latium.*

volsella -ae, f. *a pair of tweezers.*

volsus -a -um, partic. from vello; q.v.

volt-; see vult-.

vŏlūbĭlis -e, *rolling, revolving, turning round; changeable, inconstant;* of speech, *rapid, fluent;* adv. **vŏlūbĭlĭtĕr,** *fluently.*

vŏlūbĭlĭtās -ātis, f. *turning, revolution; roundness; inconstancy, flow of words, fluency.*

vŏlūcer volucris volucre, *flying, winged; fleet, swift, fleeting.* F. as subst. **vŏlucris** -is, *a bird* or *flying insect.*

vŏlūmen -ĭnis, n. *a scroll, book; a roll, wreath, fold.*

vŏluntārĭus -a -um, *voluntary, acting* or *done voluntarily;* m. pl. as subst. *volunteers.*

vŏluntās -ātis, f. *will, wish, inclination;* esp. *goodwill; last will, testament;* of words, etc., *meaning, sense.*

vŏlup, *agreeably, pleasantly.*

vŏluptārĭus -a -um, *pleasant; concerned with or devoted to pleasure.*

vŏluptās -ātis, f. *pleasure, delight, enjoyment;* in plur., *public shows.*

vŏluptŭōsus -a -um, *delightful.*

vŏlūtābrum -i, n. *a place for pigs, a slough.*

vŏlūtābundus -a -um, *rolling, wallowing.*

vŏlūtātĭo -ōnis, f. *rolling about, wallowing; disquiet.*

vŏlūto -are, *to roll round, tumble about;* partic. volutans, *rolling about.* Transf., *to turn over in the mind, consider;* to *busy, occupy.*

volva (vulva) -ae, f. *womb;* esp. *a sow's womb*

volvo volvĕre volvi vŏlūtum, *to wind, turn, roll, twist round;* in pass. *to roll.* Esp. *to unroll a book, to read.* Transf., of time, *to make roll by;* of persons, *to turn over in the mind, consider; to experience, go through.*

vōmer (vōmis) -ĕris, m. *ploughshare.*

vŏmĭca -ae, f. *an ulcer, sore, boil; a plague, curse.*

vōmis -eris, m. = vomer; q.v.

vŏmĭtĭo -ōnis, f. *vomiting, throwing up.*

vŏmo -ere -ŭi -ĭtum, *to vomit; to vomit forth, throw up.*

vŏrāgo -ĭnis, f. *pit, chasm, abyss.*

vŏrax -ācis, *gluttonous, voracious.*

vŏro -are, *to eat greedily, swallow up, consume, devour.*

vors-; see vers-.

vort-; see vert-.

vōs, *you,* plur. of tu; q.v.

vōtīvus -a -um, *of a vow, votive, vowed.*

vōtum -i, n. *a vow, promise to the gods; a votive offering;* in gen., *prayer, wish, desire.*

vŏvĕo vōvēre vōvi vōtum, *to vow, promise to a god; to pray for, wish.*

vox vōcis, f. *voice, cry, call; accent, language; sound, tone;* a *saying, utterance.*

Vulcānus = Volcanus; q.v.

vulgāris (volg-) -e, *common, ordinary, usual;* adv. **vulgārĭtĕr,** *in the ordinary way.*

vulgātus -a -um, partic. from vulgo; q.v.

vulgīvăgus -a -um, *wandering, vagrant.*

vulgo (volgo) -are, *to make common or accessible, spread, publish, impart;* partic. **vulgātus** -a -um, *common, commonly known.*

vulgus (volgus) -i, n. (occ. m.) *the people, the public;* a *mass, crowd, rabble, mob.* Abl. as adv. **vulgō,** *commonly, generally, in public.*

vulnĕrātĭo (voln-) -ōnis, f. *wounding, a wound.*

vulnĕro (voln-) -are, *to wound, injure.*

vulnĭfĭcus (voln-) -a -um, *inflicting wounds.*

vulnus (volnus) -ĕris, n. *a wound, injury.*

vulpēcŭla (volp-) -ae, f. *a little fox.*

vulpēs (volpēs) -is, f. *a fox.*

vulsus -a -um, partic. from vello; q.v.

vultĭcŭlus -i, m. *look, aspect.*

vultŭōsus -a -um, *grimacing, affected.*

vultur (voltur) -ŭris, m. *a vulture.*

vultŭrīnus (volt-) -a -um, *of or like a vulture.*

vultŭrĭus (volt-) -i, m. *a vulture.* Transf., *a rapacious man.*

Vulturnus (Volt-) -i, m. *a river in Campania.*

vultus (voltus) -ūs, m. *expression of face, countenance, look, aspect.* Transf., *face.*

X

X, x, the twenty-second letter of the Latin alphabet.

xĕnĭum -i, n. *a present to a guest.*

Xĕnŏphōn -ōntis, m. *an Athenian soldier and writer.*

xĕrampĕlīnae -ārum, f. pl. *dark-red garments.*

Xerxēs -is, m. *king of the Persians, defeated at Salamis.*

Xiphĭas -ae, m. *sword-fish.*

xystus -i, m. and **xystum** -i, n. *an open colonnade, a walk planted with trees.*

Y

Y, y, a letter borrowed from the Greek in order to represent the Greek upsilon.

Z

Z, z, representing the Greek zeta.

Zăma -ae, f. *a town in Numidia, where Scipio defeated Hannibal (201 B.C.).*

zēlŏtўpus -a -um, *jealous.*

Zēno (-ōn) -ōnis, m. *name of several Greek philosophers.*

zĕphўrus -i, m. *a warm west wind, zephyr.*

zm-; see sm-.

zōdĭăcus -i, m. *the zodiac.*

zōna -ae, f. *a girdle, money-belt;* in pl. zonae, *terrestrial zones.*

zōnārĭus -a -um, *of a girdle;* m. as subst. *girdle-maker.*

zōthēca -ae, f. *a private room.*

CASSELL'S ENGLISH-LATIN DICTIONARY

A

A, an; often not translated; sometimes *unus*; a certain, *aliquis, quidam.*

abandon, *relinquĕre, deserĕre, destituĕre*; of things, *omittĕre.*

abandoned, *perditus, nefarius.*

abase, *frangĕre, (de)minuĕre, comprimĕre.*

abasement, *demissio, deminutio.*

abash, *percellĕre, perturbare.*

abate: transit. *imminuĕre, remittĕre*: intransit. *cadĕre, imminui, decrescĕre*; of passion, *defervescĕre.*

abatement, *remissio, deminutio.*

abbreviate, *imminuĕre, contrahĕre.*

abbreviation, *compendium, contractio.*

abdicate, *(magistratu) se abdicare*; *(magistratum) eiurare.*

abdication, *abdicatio, eiuratio.*

abdomen, *abdomen.*

abduction, *raptus (-ūs), raptio.*

aberration, *error.*

abet, *adiuvare.*

abettor, *socius, adiutor.*

abeyance: to be in —, *in dubio esse, intermitti*; to leave in —, *rem integram relinquĕre.*

abhor, *abhorrēre ab, odisse, odio habēre.*

abhorrence, *odium.*

abhorrent, = inconsistent, *abhorrens, alienus, contrarius*; see also hateful.

abide, = linger, *(com)morari, manēre*; = last, *durare*; to abide by, *stare in.*

abiding, *diuturnus, stabilis, mansurus.*

ability, *potestas, vires, facultas*; = mental strength, *ingenium*; according to one's —, *pro sua parte, pro parte virili.*

abject, *abiectus, contemptus, humilis.*

abjure, *abiurare, recusare.*

ablative, *(casus) ablativus.*

able, *potens*; = mentally strong, *ingeniosus*; to be able, *posse, valēre.*

able-bodied, *firmus, robustus, validus.*

ablution, *lavatio, ablutio.*

abnegation, *temperantia.*

abnormal, *novus, inusitatus, singularis.*

aboard: to go —, *(navem) conscendĕre*; to be —, *in nave esse.*

abode: = sojourn, *habitatio*; see also house.

abolish, *abolēre, tollĕre, delēre, exstinguĕre.*

abolition, *dissolutio*; — of debts, *tabulae novae.*

abominable, *detestabilis, immanis.*

abominate, *odisse, detestari.*

aborigines, *indigenae, aborigines.*

abortive: of premature birth, *abortivus*; fig., = unsuccessful, *inritus.*

abound, *abundare, superesse*; — in, *(re) abundare.*

about: adv. of time or number, *fere, ferme, circiter*; prep., of place, *circa, circum*; of time, *circa*; of respect, = concerning, *de* with *abl.*

above, adv. of place, *supra*; from above, *desuper, superne*; prep., *super, supra.*

abreast, *pariter*; two horses yoked —, *equi biiugi* or *biiuges.*

abridge; see abbreviate.

abroad, adv.: = out of doors, *foras* (of motion), *foris* (of rest); = in a foreign land, *peregre*; to travel —, *peregrinari*; to spread —, = publish, *divulgare.*

abrogate, *abrogare, rescindĕre.*

abrupt: = steep, *abruptus, arduus, praeruptus*: of speech, *abruptus*; = sudden, *subitus, repentinus, improvisus*. Adv. *abrupte, praerupte*; *subito, de improviso, repente.*

abscess, *vomica.*

abscond, *delitescĕre, latēre, occultari.*

absence, *absentia*; in my —, *me absente.*

absent, adj. *absens*; to be —, *abesse.*

absent, v. to absent oneself, *se removēre, non comparēre.*

absolute, *absolutus, simplex*; absolute power, *dominatio, imperium singulare.* Adv. *plane, prorsus, omnino*; opp. to relatively, *per se, simpliciter.*

absolve, *(ab)solvĕre.*

absorb, *(com)bibĕre, absorbēre*; absorbed in a thing, *totus in re.*

abstain, *(se) re abstinēre.*

abstinence, *abstinentia, temperantia.* days of —, *ieiunium.*

abstinent, *abstinens, temperatus.*

abstract, subst. *epitome, epitoma.*

abstract, adj. *quod nullo sensu percipi potest.*

abstract, v. *abstrahĕre, sevocare*; see also steal.

abstracted, *omnium rerum (or sui) oblitus.*

abstraction, *oblivio.*

abstruse, *abstrusus, obscurus, reconditus.*

abstruseness, *obscuritas.*

absurd, *absurdus, ineptus, ridiculus*: adv. *absurde, inepte, ridicule.*

absurdity, *insulsitas, ineptia.*

abundance, *abundantia, ubertas, copia.*

abundant, *largus, amplus*; adv. *abunde abundanter, large.*

abuse, subst.: = wrong use, *usus (-ūs) perversus*; = abusive language, *convicium*; a bad custom, *mos pravus.*

abuse, v.: = to misuse, *(re) abuti*; = to speak abusively to, *(homini) maledicĕre.*

abusive, *maledicus, maledicens, contumeliosus*; adv. *maledice, contumeliose.*

abut, *adiacēre, attingĕre.*

abyss, *gurges, barathrum, vorago.*

academy; at Athens, *Academia*; = school, *ludus, schola.*

accede; see agree.

accelerate, *accelerare.*

accent, *vox, sonus (-ūs), tenor.*

accept, *accipĕre, recipĕre.*

acceptable, *iucundus, acceptus, gratus.*

acceptation; = significance, *significatio.*

access, *aditus (-ūs), accessus (-ūs).*

accessary, = accomplice *conscius, (culpae) socius.*

accessible, *facilis.*

accession; = increase, *accessio*; to the throne, *initium regni.*

accessory, = additional; use verb *accedo.*

accident, *casus* (*-ūs*).

accidental, *fortuitus*; adv. *forte, casu, fortuito.*

acclaim, subst., *clamor, acclamatio.*

acclaim, v. *acclamare.*

accommodate, *accommodare.*

accommodating, *obsequens, facilis.*

accommodation, *hospitium*; see also agreement.

accompaniment, *comitatus* (*-ūs*).

accompany, *comitari*; in a crowd, *stipare*; accompanied by, *cum* (with abl.); in music, *concinĕre.*

accomplice, *socius, sceleris conscius.*

accomplish, *conficĕre, perficĕre, absolvĕre, peragĕre, exsequi.*

accomplished, *politus, elegans, doctus, eruditus.*

accomplishment: = fulfilment, *confectio, perfectio, absolutio*; = skill, *ars.*

accord, subst.: of one's own —, *sponte* (*sua*), *ultro*; see also harmony.

accordance: in — with, *ex, de, pro,* with abl.; in — with circumstances, *ad tempus, pro re.*

according to; see accordance.

accordingly, *ergo, itaque.*

accost, *appellare, compellare, adoriri.*

account, subst. = reckoning, *ratio*; = account books, *tabulae* (*-arum*); to be of —, *magni habēri*; to be of no —, *nullo numero esse*; on my —, *mea de causa, meo nomine*; on — of, *propter, ob*; = narrative, *memoria, narratio.*

account, v.: = to think, *habēre, aestimare, ducĕre*; to — for, *rationem de re reddĕre.*

accountable; see responsible.

accountant, *scriba.*

accretion, *accessio, incrementum, cumulus.*

accumulate, (*co*)*acervare, exaggerare.*

accumulation, *cumulus, acervus.*

accuracy: = care taken, *cura, diligentia*; = truth, *veritas.*

accurate: = careful, *diligens, religiosus*; = carefully done, *accuratus*; = true, *verus.*

accusation, *accusatio, crimen.*

accusative, *accusativus* (*casus*).

accuse, *accusare, arguĕre, insimulare.*

accused, *reus.*

accuser: on a criminal charge, *accusator*; in a civil suit, *petitor*; = informer, *index, delator.*

accustom, *adsuefacĕre*; to grow accustomed, *adsuescĕre*; to be accustomed, *solēre.*

accustomed, *adsuetus, solitus.*

ache, subst., *dolor.*

ache, v. *dolēre.*

achieve: = to finish, *conficĕre, efficĕre, perficĕre*; = to gain, reach, *adsequi, consequi.*

achievement: = doing, *confectio*; = deed, *facinus* (*-oris*).

acid, adj., *acidus, acerbus, acer*; in temper, *acerbus, morosus.*

acknowledge: = to accept as one's own, *agnoscĕre*; to — a child, *suscipĕre, tollĕre*; = to admit, *fateri, confiteri*; = to give thanks, *gratias agĕre*; to — a payment, (*in*) *acceptum referre.*

acknowledged, *cognitus, probatus, spectatus.*

acknowledgement = confession, *confessio*; = thanks, *gratiae* (*-arum*).

acme, *fastigium*; or use *summus.*

acorn, *glans.*

acquaint; see inform.

acquaintance: = knowledge; of things, *scientia*; of persons, *usus, familiaritas*; = person known, *amicus, familiaris.*

acquainted, *notus, cognitus*; — with a person, *familiaris*; — with a thing, *peritus, sciens.*

acquiesce, *acquiescĕre, rem aequo animo ferre.*

acquiescence, *adsensus* (*-ūs*).

acquire; see gain.

acquirement, acquisition: = thing gained, see gain; = skill or knowledge, *ars, scientia*; the process of — *comparatio, adeptio.*

acquisitive, *lucri studiosus.*

acquit, *absolvĕre.*

acquittal, *absolutio liberatio*

acrid, *acer, acerbus.*

acrimonious, *mordax, acerbus amarus aculeatus.*

acrimony, *acerbitas.*

across: adv., use compound verb with *trans-*; prep., *trans.*

act, subst.: of a play, *actus* (*-ūs*); of Parliament, *lex*; = thing done, *factum.*

act, v.: = to behave, *agĕre, facĕre, se gerĕre*; of drugs, *efficax esse*; to act on the stage, *in scena esse*; to act the chief part, *primas partes agĕre.*

action: = doing, *actio*; = deed, *factum*; = battle, *pugna, proelium*; = part of a play, *actio*; = legal proceedings, *lis, actio*; to take (legal) —, *litem* or *actionem intendĕre. diem dicĕre, lege agĕre.*

actionable, (*res*) *cuius actio est.*

active: = quick, *celer, acer, promptus*; = industrious, *impiger,* (*g*)*navus, strenuus*; adv. actively, *impiger,* (*g*)*naviter, strenue.*

activity; = quickness, *celeritas, agilitas*; = industry, *industria,* (*g*)*navitas.*

actor, *qui agit* or *facit, actor*; on a stage, *histrio, actor*: comic —, *comoedus*: tragic —, *tragoedus.*

actress, *mima.*

actual, *verus*; adv. *vere, re vera.*

actuate, *movēre, impellĕre.*

acumen, *ingenii acies* or *acumen.*

acute: of pain, *acer, gravis, vehemens*; of intellect, *acutus, perspicax, sagax.* Adv., of feeling, *acute*; of intellect, *acriter, subtiliter.*

acuteness, *ingenii acies* or *acumen subtilitas.*

adage, *proverbium.*

adamant, subst. *adamas* (*-antis*), m.

adamantine, adj. *adamantinus.*

adapt, *accommodare, aptare.*

adaptation, *accommodatio.*

adapted, *aptus, idoneus.*

add, *addĕre, adicĕre;* to — up, *computare.*

adder, *vipera.*

addict, v.; to — oneself, *se dare, dedĕre, tradĕre.*

addicted, *deditus.*

addition: = adding, *accessio;* in arithmetic, *additio.*

additional, *novus, additus, adiectus.*

address, v. = to speak to, *adloqui, adfari, appellare, compellare;* to address a letter, *(homini) epistulam inscribere.*

address, subst.: speech, *contio, oratio;* the — of a letter, *inscriptio;* = place, *locus;* = adroitness, *dexteritas, sollertia.*

adduce, *adducĕre, proferre.*

adept, *callidus, peritus.*

adequate, *aptus, idoneus;* adv. *apte, satis.*

adhere, *(in)haerĕre.*

adherent, *socius, fautor, cliens.*

adhesive, *tenax.*

adieu! *vale!* plur. *valete;* to bid —, *(hominem) valēre iubēre.*

adjacent, *contiguus, vicinus, finitimus;* to be —, *adiacēre.*

adjective, *nomen adiectivum.*

adjoin; see adjacent.

adjourn, *ampliare, rem differre.*

adjournment, *dilatio.*

adjudge, *addicĕre, adiudicare.*

adjudicate; see judge.

adjunct; see addition.

adjure, = entreat, *obsecrare, obtestari.*

adjust; see arrange, adapt.

adjustment, *accommodatio.*

administer, *administrare, procurare;* to — medicine, *medicinam dare, adhibēre;* to — justice, *ius dicĕre.*

administration: the act, *administratio, procuratio;* = the government, *ei qui reipublicae praesunt.*

admirable, *(ad)mirabilis, praeclarus;* adv. *admirabiliter, mirum in modum, praeclare.*

admiral, *praefectus classis.*

admiration, *admiratio.*

admire, *(ad)mirari.*

admissible, *aequus;* or use verb.

admission: = leave to enter, *aditus (-ūs), accessus (-ūs);* = confession, *confessio;* in argument, *concessio.*

admit; to let in, *admittĕre, recipĕre;* in argument, *concedĕre, dare;* = to confess, *fateri, confiteri;* to — of, = allow, *recipĕre, pati.*

admonish, *(ad)monēre, commonēre.*

admonition, *(ad)monitio.*

ado: with much —, *vix, aegre;* see fuss.

adolescence, *adulescentia.*

adolescent, *adulescens.*

adopt, *adoptare;* = to choose, accept, *adsumĕre, accipĕre, recipĕre;* to — a resolution, *constituĕre.*

adoption, *adoptio.*

adoptive, *adoptivus.*

adorable, *sanctus, venerandus.*

adoration, *cultus (-ūs), veneratio.*

adore, *venerari, colĕre;* = to love. *diligĕre, amare.*

adorn, *(ex)ornare, decorare.*

adornment, *ornatus (-ūs), exornatio.*

adrift, to be, *fluctibus iactari.*

adroit, *callidus, sollers, dexter;* adv. *callide, dextere.*

adroitness, *dexteritas.*

adulation, *adulatio, adsentatio.*

adult, *adultus, pubes.*

adulterate, *corrumpĕre, vitiare.*

adulterer, *adulter, moechus.*

adultery, *adulterium.*

adults, subst. *puberes* (plur. only).

adumbrate, *adumbrare.*

adumbration, *adumbratio.*

advance, v.: intransit., *progredi, procedĕre;* to become advanced in years, *aetate provehi;* transit., *promovēre, provehĕre, adiuvare, augēre.*

advance-guard, *primum agmen.*

advantage, *commodum, lucrum, fructus (-ūs), utilitas, bonum;* to be of — *expedire, prodesse, usui esse.*

advantageous, *utilis, fructuosus, opportunus;* adv. *utiliter.*

advent, *adventus (-ūs).*

adventitious, *adventicius, externus.*

adventure, subst.: = exploit, *facinus (-oris), inceptum;* = happening, *casus (-ūs).*

adventure, v. *audēre, tentare, experiri, periclitari.*

adventurous, *audax;* adv. *audacter.*

adverb, *adverbium.*

adversary, *adversarius.*

adverse, *adversus, contrarius;* adv. *contra, secus.*

adversity, *res adversae, calamitas.*

advertise; = to make known, *praedicare, pronuntiare;* of goods, *proscribĕre, inscribĕre.*

advertisement, = notice of sale, *proscriptio.*

advice, *consilium;* by my —, *me auctore.*

advise, *suadēre, monēre;* see also inform.

advisedly, *consulte, considerate, de industria.*

adviser, *suasor, auctor.*

advocate, subst.; legal, *patronus;* in gen., *suasor, auctor.*

advocate, v. *suadēre.*

adze, *ascia.*

aerial, *aerius, aetherius.*

afar, *procul, longe.*

affability, *comitas.*

affable, *adfabilis, comis;* adv. *comiter.*

affair, *res, negotium.*

affect, v.: = to influence, *adficĕre, tangĕre, (com)movēre;* = to be fond of, *diligĕre, amare;* = to make a show of, *simulare, imitari.*

affectation, *simulatio.*

affected, *quaesitus, simulatus;* of style, *putidus, molestus;* adv. *putide, moleste.*

affection: in gen., *adfectio, adfectus (-ūs);* = friendly sentiment, *amor, caritas, studium;* dutiful —, *pietas.*

affectionate, adj. *amans;* dutifully — *pius;* adv. *amanter, pie.*

affiance, = betroth, (de)spondēre.

affidavit, testimonium per tabulas datum.

affinity, propinquitas, necessitudo; in gen., = close connexion, cognatio, coniunctio.

affirm, adfirmare, confirmare

affirmation, adfirmatio.

affirmative, use verb.

affix, adfigere, adligare, adnectĕre.

afflict, adflictare, vexare.

affliction, aegritudo, dolor, molestia.

affluence, divitiae, opes, copia.

affluent, dives.

afford, = supply, praestare praebēre, sufficĕre, suppeditare.

affray, rixa, pugna.

affright; see frighten.

affront, subst. contumelia.

affront, v. contumeliā adficĕre.

afloat: to be —, navigare, navi vehi.

afoot, pedibus.

aforesaid, quem (quod) supra scripsi.

afraid, timidus, pavidus, trepidus; to be —, timēre, metuĕre.

afresh; see again.

after, Prep.: of place or time, post, with acc.; of rank, etc., secundum, with acc.; of conformity, = according to, ad, with acc. Conj., postquam, cum, ubi.

afterwards, post, postea, dein(de), inde; = after this, posthac; some months —, paucis postea mensibus, aliquot post menses.

afternoon: in the —, post meridiem; adj. postmeridianus.

again, rursus, rursum, denuo; = a second time, iterum; again and again, identidem; = further, moreover, porro, autem.

against, contra, adversus, in, with acc.; — the stream, adverso flumine; — my will, me invito.

age: = time (esp. time of life), aetas; of the same —, aequalis; = old age, of persons, senectus; of things, vetustas.

aged, aetate provectus; an — man, senex (-is).

agency, = instrumentality, opera.

agent, procurator.

aggrandize, amplificare, augēre.

aggrandizement, amplificatio; or use verb.

aggravate: = to make worse, (ad)-gravare; = to annoy, exasperare, lacessĕre.

aggregate, summa.

aggression, impetus (-ūs), incursus (-ūs), iniuria.

aggressive, hostilis, infensus.

aggressor, qui prior oppugnat qui iniuriam facit.

aggrieve; see grieve.

aghast, stupefactus, perturbatus; to stand —, stupēre, obstupescĕre.

agile, agilis, velox, pernix.

agility, agilitas, pernicitas, velocitas.

agitate: = to shake, agitare, quatĕre, vibrare; mentally, = to disturb, percutĕre, perturbare, sollicitare; = to discuss, agitare, disputare, disserĕre.

agitated, sollicitus, trepidus.

agitation: physical, agitatio, iactatio; mental, animi motus (-ūs), commotio concitatio.

agitator, turbator.

ago, abhinc; long —, (iam) pridem, iam dudum.

agony, aegritudo, dolor.

agrarian, agrarius.

agree, concinĕre, consentire; it is agreed, constat; to — upon, = settle, componĕre, constituĕre.

agreeable: of things, acceptus, gratus, dulcis; of persons, commodus, lepidus.

agreement; = harmony, consensus (-ūs) concordia; = arrangement, compact pactum, pactio, conventum.

agricultural, rusticus.

agriculture, agri cultura, agri cultio.

agriculturist, agricola.

aground, to run, sidēre.

ague, febris.

ah! aha! interj. a, ah, aha.

ahead, use compound verb with prae- or pro-.

aid, subst. auxilium, adiumentum, subsidium, opem (nom. ops not used).

aid, adiuvare, subvenire, succurrĕre, opem ferre.

ailing, aeger; see sick.

aim, subst. finis, propositum, consilium.

aim, v. to take aim, telum dirigĕre or intendĕre; to aim at, telo petĕre; fig., adfectare, petĕre, quaerĕre, spectare.

air, subst. (1), aer, aether (upper air), aura (breeze), anima (= breath); in the open —, sub Iove, sub divo. (2), = look manner, vultus (-ūs), aspectus (-ūs), species. (3) = tune. modus, numeri.

air, v. ventilare.

airy, aerius.

akin: = related, consanguineus, propinquus, agnatus, cognatus; = similar, connected, finitimus, vicinus.

alacrity, alacritas, pernicitas.

alarm, subst.: = loud noise, clamor, strepitus (-ūs); = disturbance, turba, tumultus (-ūs); = fear, terror, trepidatio.

alas! heu! eheu! vae! ei!

alcove, zotheca.

alder, alnus; adj. alneus.

alert, vigil, alacer, promptus.

alias, nomen alienum.

alien, adj.: = foreign, peregrinus, externus; = adverse, alienus, aversus.

alien, subst. peregrinus, advena, alienigena.

alienate, (ab)alienare, avertĕre.

alienation, (ab)alienatio.

alight, v. descendĕre.

alike: adj. par, similis; adv. pariter, similiter, aeque.

alive, vivus; to be —, vivĕre.

all: = every single, omnis; = the whole, totus; all together, cunctus, universus; in —, omnino; not at —, minime; — but, tantum non.

allay, lenire, sedare, mitigare.

allegation, adfirmatio; see also accusation.

allege: see assert.

allegiance, *fides*; to swear — to, *in verba hominis iurare*.

allegory, *allegoria*.

alleviate, (*ad*)*levare*; see also allay.

alleviation, *levatio, mitigatio, levamen*.

alley, *angiportus* (-*ūs*).

alliance, *societas, foedus* (-*eris*).

allot: by lot, *sortiri*; in gen., *distribuĕre, adsignare, adiudicare*.

allotment, *adsignatio*; of land, *ager adsignatus, possessio*.

allow. (1) = permit, *sinĕre, pati; permittĕre, concedĕre*; I am —ed, *licet mihi*. (2) = admit, *concedĕre, confiteri*. (3) = grant; q.v.

allowable, *concessus, licitus*.

allowance: = indulgence, *indulgentia*; to make — for, *ignoscĕre, condonare*; an — of food, *diaria, demensum*.

alloy: without —, *sincerus, purus*.

allude to, = to refer to, *significare, designare*.

allure, *adlicĕre, inlicĕre, invitare, inescare*.

allurement, *invitamentum, blanditia, inlecebra*.

alluring, *blandus*.

allusion, *significatio, mentio*; or use verb.

ally, subst. *socius*.

ally, v.: = make an alliance, *foedus facĕre* (or *ferire*)*, societatem inire*; = join together as allies, *sociare*.

almanack, *fasti* (-*orum*)*, ephemeris*.

almighty, *omnipotens*.

almond, *amygdala*.

almost, *prope, paene*.

alms, *stips* (-*is,* f.: nom. not used).

aloft, *sublime, alte; sublimis,* adj.

alone: adj. *solus, unus;* adv. = only; q.v.

along: adv.*, porro, protinus;* prep.*, secundum, praeter;* — with, *una cum.*

aloof, *procul.*

aloud, *clara* or *magna voce.*

already, *iam.*

also, *etiam, praeterea, quoque, item.*

altar, *ara, altaria* (plur.).

alter: transit.*, mutare, commutare, immutare,* (*con*)*vertĕre;* intransit., use passive, e.g. *mutari.*

alterable, adj. *mutabilis.*

alteration, (*com*)*mutatio;* a sudden —, *conversio.*

altercation, *altercatio, iurgium, rixa.*

alternate, v.: transit.*, alternare, variare;* intransit.*, variare.*

alternate, adj. *alternus;* adv. *invicem.*

alternation, *vicissitudo.*

alternative: there is no alternative left except . . .*, nihil restat nisi ut . . . .*

although, *quamquam; etsi* (= even if); *quamvis* (= however much); *licet* (= granted that).

altitude, *altitudo.*

altogether, = wholly, *omnino.*

always, *semper.*

amalgamate, (*com*)*miscĕre.*

amalgamation, *coniunctio, mixtura.*

amanuensis, *librarius, servus a manu.*

amass, (*co*)*acervare, aggerare, accumulare.*

amaze, *obstupefacĕre.*

amazed, (*ob*)*stupefactus, stupidus;* to be —*, stupĕre,* (*ob*)*stupescĕre.*

amazement, *stupor.*

amazing, *mirus, admirabilis;* adj. *admirabiliter, mirum in modum.*

ambassador, *legatus.*

amber, *sucinum, electrum.*

ambiguity, *ambiguitas; ambages* (plur.; = riddle).

ambiguous, *anceps, ambiguus, dubius;* adv. *ambigue.*

ambition, *ambitio, gloria; laudis studium contentio honorum.*

ambitious, *gloriae* (or *laudis*) *cupidus.*

ambrosia, *ambrosia.*

ambush, *insidiae* (plur.).

ameliorate, *corrigĕre, emendare.*

amen! *fiat! esto!*

amenable, (*dicto*) *oboediens.*

amend, *emendare, corrigĕre.*

amendment, *correctio, emendatio.*

amends, *satisfactio, expiatio:* to make — for*, expiare, satisfacĕre.*

amenity, *amoenitas.*

amiability, *suavitas.*

amiable, *suavis, amabilis;* adv. *suaviter.*

amicable; see friendly.

amidst, *inter,* with acc.

amiss, *male, perperam, prave:* to take —*, aegre ferre.*

ammunition, *apparatus* (-*ūs*) *belli, arma* (-*orum*); see also bullet.

amnesty, use *venia,* or *ignoscĕre.*

among, *inter,* with acc.; *in,* with abl.; *apud,* with acc.

amorous, *amans;* in bad sense, *libidinosus.*

amount, *summa.*

amount to, v. *efficere:* what does it — to? *quae summa est?* it —s to the same thing, *idem est, nihil interest.*

amphitheatre, *amphitheatrum.*

ample, *amplus;* adv. *ample, abunde.*

amplify, *amplificare.*

amplitude, *amplitudo.*

amputate, *praecidĕre, amputare.*

amuse, *delectare, oblectare.*

amusement, *delectatio, oblectatio, oblectamentum.*

amusing, *facetus, festivus.*

anachronism; use phrase, e.g. *tempora miscĕre.*

analogous, *similis.*

analogy, *similitudo.*

analyse, *explicare; quasi in membra discerpĕre.*

analysis, *explicatio, enodatio.*

anarchy, *licentia.*

anatomy; refer to the structure of the body, = *compages* or *conformatio corporis.*

ancestor; sing. *auctor generis;* plur. *maiores.*

ancestral, *avitus, proavitus.*

ancestry, *origo, genus.*

anchor, subst. *ancora;* to cast —*, ancoram iacĕre;* to weigh —*, ancoram tollĕre.*

anchor, v. transit. (*navem*) *ad ancoras deligare.*

anchorage, *statio.*

ancient, *antiquus, vetus, vetustus, priscus;* the ancients, *veteres, antiqui.*

appetite, *appetentia, appetitio*; for food, *fames.*

applaud, v.: *(ap)plaudĕre.*

applause, *plausus (-ūs).*

apple, *malum*; — tree, *malus,* f.

appliance, *apparatus (-ūs), instrumentum.*

application: = request, *petitio*; of the mind, *animi intentio, diligentia.*

apply, v.: transit., = bring to bear, *adhibēre, admovēre*; to — oneself, *se conferre*; intransit., = refer, *pertinēre*; = make application, *adīre.*

appoint, *constituĕre, dicĕre, destinare*; of officials, *creare, facĕre*; to — to command, *praepōnĕre, praeficĕre.*

appointment: = office, *munus (-eris), magistratus (-ūs)*; = agreement to meet, *constitutum.*

apportion, *dividĕre, distribuĕre, adsignare.*

apposite, *aptus, accommodatus.*

appraise, *aestimare.*

appreciate, *aestimare; agnoscĕre.*

apprehend, *comprehendĕre*; = to grasp mentally, *comprehendĕre, complecti (animo or mente), intellegĕre*; = fear; q.v.

apprehension: = mental grasp, *intellegentia*; = fear, *timor.*

apprehensive; see timid.

apprentice, subst. *homo (homini) addictus.*

apprentice, v. *addicĕre.*

approach, subst. *adventus (-ūs), aditus (-ūs).*

approach, v. *accedĕre, appropinquare, adventare.*

approbation; see approval.

appropriate, adj. *idoneus, aptus, accommodatus*; adv. *apte, accommode.*

appropriate, v. *(ad)sumĕre, sibi adrogare, sibi vindicare.*

approval, *approbatio, comprobatio*; with your approval, *pace tua.*

approve, *(ap)probare, comprobare.*

approved, *probatus, spectatus.*

approximate, adj. *propinquus.*

approximate, v., see approach.

April, *Aprilis (mensis).*

apron, *subligaculum.*

apt: = appropriate; q.v.; = prone, *pronus, propensus*; adv. *apte.*

aptitude, *habilitas.*

aquatic, *aquatilis.*

aqueduct, *aquae ductus (-ūs).*

aquiline, *aduncus.*

arable; see plough.

arbiter, *arbiter, disceptator.*

arbitrarily, *libidinose.*

arbitrary: = capricious, *libidinosus*; of power, use *dominari* or *dominatio.*

arbitrate, v. *disceptare, diiudicare.*

arbitration, *arbitrium.*

arbour, *umbraculum.*

arc, *arcus (-ūs).*

arcade, *porticus (-ūs).*

arch, subst. *arcus (-ūs), fornix.*

arch, adj. *petulans, improbus, malus.*

arch, v. *arcuare*; see curve.

archaeology, *rerum antiquarum scientia.*

archaism, *verbum obsoletum.*

archer, *sagittarius.*

architect, *architectus.*

architecture, *architectura.*

archives, *tabulae publicae.*

arctic, *septentrionalis, arctous.*

ardent, *ardens, fervens, acer*; adv., *ardenter, acriter.*

ardour, *ardor, fevor, studium.*

arduous, *arduus, difficilis.*

area, *area, superficies.*

arena, *harena.*

argue: = to discuss, *disserĕre, disputare*; = conclude, seek to prove, *argumentari, conligĕre.*

argument: = dispute, *disputatio*; line of —, *argumentum.*

arid, *aridus, siccus.*

aright, *recte, bene.*

arise, *surgĕre, (ex)oriri, exsistĕre.*

aristocracy: = aristocrats, *optimates, patricii, nobiles*; as a form of government, *optimatium dominatus (-ūs).*

aristocrat, aristocratic; see aristocracy.

arithmetic, *arithmetica (-orum).*

arithmetical, *arithmeticus.*

ark, = chest, *arca.*

arm, subst. *bracchium*; upper —, *lacertus*; arms, = embrace, *complexus (-ūs)*; *manūs* (plur.); see also arms.

arm, v. transit. *armare*; intransit., *armari, arma capĕre.*

arm-chair, *sella.*

armed, *armatus.*

armistice, *indutiae (-arum).*

armour, *arma (-orum)*; armour-bearer, *armiger.*

armourer, *faber armorum.*

armpit, *ala.*

arms, *arma (-orum), tela (-orum)*, (offensive).

army, *exercitus (-ūs)*; in marching array, *agmen*; in battle array, *acies.*

aromatic, *odorus, odoratus.*

around: adv. and prep., *circa, circum.*

arouse, *excitare, suscitare.*

arraign; see accuse.

arrange, *ordinare, componĕre, disponĕre, digerĕre*; abstr., *constituĕre, componĕre.*

arrangement, *ordo, ratio, dispositio*; or use verb.

arrant, render by superl., or *summus.*

array: of battle, *acies*; = dress, *vestis.*

array, v. = dress, *vestire.*

arrears, *pecuniae residuae.*

arrest: = put under arrest, *comprehendĕre, in custodiam dare*; = stop; q.v.

arrival, *adventus (-ūs), accessus (-ūs).*

arrive, *advenire, pervenire, adventare.*

arrogance, *adrogantia, superbia.*

arrogant, *adrogans, superbus*; adv. *adroganter, superbe.*

arrogate, v. *sibi adrogare, (ad)sumĕre.*

arrow, *sagitta.*

arsenal, *armamentarium*; naval —, *navalia (-ium).*

art, *ars, artificium, peritia* (= acquired skill); the fine —s, *artes ingenuae* or *liberales.*

artful, *astutus, callidus*; adv. *astute, callide.*

artfulness *astutia, calliditas, dolus.*

article, *res*; = clause or item, *caput, condicio*.
articulate, adj. *clarus*.
articulate, v. *dicĕre*.
artificer, *artifex, opifex*.
artificial, adj. *artificiosus*; adv. *arte, manu, opere*.
artillery, *tormenta* (-*orum*).
artisan, *opifex, faber*.
artist, *artifex*; or *poeta, pictor*, etc.
artistic, adj. *artifex*; adv. *artificiose, summa arte*.
artless, adj. *simplex*; adv. *simpliciter, sine arte*.
as, adv. and conj.: see while, because, since, though; as . . . as., *tam . . . quam . . .*; such . . . as . . ., *talis . . . qualis . . .*; as great as . . ., *tantus . . . quantus*; as soon as, *simul ac*; the same as, *idem ac, atque, qui*; as far as, *tenus* (prep.), *usque* (adv., = all the way); as if, as though, *quasi, tamquam, velut*; as regards . . ., *quod ad . . . attinet*.
ascend, *scandĕre, ascendĕre*.
ascendency, render by *superior* or *summus*.
ascent, *ascensus* (-*ūs*).
ascertain, *explorare, cognoscĕre, comperire*.
ascetic, render by phrase (e.g. *cibo abstinēre*).
ascribe, *ascribĕre, adiudicare, attribuĕre*.
ash (tree), *fraxinus*; adj. *fraxineus*; mountain-ash, *ornus*.
ashamed, *pudore adfectus*; I am ashamed, *pudet me*.
ashes, *cinis, favilla*.
ashore: of rest, *in litore*; of motion, *in litus*; to put —, *exponĕre*.
aside, *seorsum*; see apart.
ask: of questions, *rogare, interrogare, quaerĕre*; of favours, etc., *rogare, petĕre, poscĕre*.
askance: to look — at, *limis oculis adspicĕre*.
aslant, *oblique, ex transverso*.
asleep, *dormiens, in somno, per somnum*.
asp, *aspis*.
aspect, *aspectus* (-*ūs*), *forma, facies, species*.
asperity, *asperitas, acerbitas*.
asperse, *infamiā aspergĕre, calumniari*.
aspersion, *calumnia, opprobrium*.
aspirate, *aspiratio*.
aspire, (*ad rem*) *aspirare, contendĕre*; (*rem*) *adfectare*.
aspiration, *appetitio, adfectatio*.
ass, *asinus*; a little —, *asellus*.
ass-driver, *asinarius*.
assail, *oppugnare, adoriri*.
assailant, *qui oppugnat*.
assassin, *sicarius, percussor*.
assassinate, *insidiis interficĕre*.
assassination, *caedes*; to accuse of —, *accusare inter sicarios*.
assault, *impetus* (-*ūs*), *incursus* (-*ūs*), *oppugnatio*; legal, *vis*.
assay, subst. *obrussa*.
assemble, v. transit., *convocare*; in-transit., *convenire, coire*.
assembly, *conventus* (-*ūs*), *concilium*.
assent, subst. *adsensio, adsensus* (-*ūs*).

assent, v. *adsentire, adnuĕre*.
assert: = to state, *dicĕre, adfirmare, confirmare*; to — a right, *ius retinēre, obtinēre*.
assertion: = statement, *adfirmatio*; = maintenance, *defensio, vindicatio*.
assess, *aestimare*.
assessment, *aestimatio, census* (-*ūs*).
assessor, *censor*; = a judge's assistant *adsessor*.
assets, *bona* (-*orum*).
assiduity, *adsiduitas, sedulitas*.
assiduous, *adsiduus, sedulus, industrius*; adv. *adsidue, sedulo, industrie*.
assign, *adsignare,* (*at*)*tribuĕre*.
assignation, *constitutum*.
assimilate: = to make like, (*ad*) *aequare, similem facĕre*; = to digest, *concoquĕre*.
assist, (*ad*)*iuvare, auxilium ferre, auxiliari, opitulari, subvenire*.
assistance, *opem* (nom. sing. not used), *auxilium, adiumentum*.
assistant, *adiutor*.
associate, subst. *socius, sodalis*.
associate, v. transit., (*con*)*iungĕre, (con*)*sociare, congregare*; intransit., use pass., or reflex.
association, *societas, sodalitas, sodalicum*.
assort, *digerĕre*.
assuage, *mitigare, lenire, sedare, levare*.
assume: = take to oneself, *sibi adrogare,* (*ad*)*sumĕre, occupare*; = take for granted, *ponĕre, sumĕre*.
assurance: = strong assertion, *confirmatio*; = confidence, *fiducia*.
assure, *homini* (*pro certo*) *adfirmare, confirmare*; = to secure; q.v.
assured: of things, *certus, exploratus*; to feel assured, *credĕre, confidĕre, pro certo habēre*.
assuredly, *profecto, certe*.
astern, *in* or *a puppi*.
astonish, *obstupefacĕre*.
astonished, *attonitus*; to be —, *obstupescĕre, stupēre*.
astonishing, *mirabilis, mirus*; adv. *mire, mirum in modum, mirabiliter*.
astonishment, *stupor,* (*ad*)*miratio*.
astray, use adj. *vagus*, or verb *vagari*.
astrologer, *astrologus, mathematicus*.
astrology, *astrologia*.
astronomy: treat as astrology; q.v
astute, *astutus, callidus*.
asunder, *seorsum*; see apart.
asylum: see refuge.
at: of place, *ad, apud, in*, or locative case; of time, *in, ad*, or abl. case.
atheism, *deum esse negare*.
athlete, *athleta*.
athwart: see across.
atmosphere, *aer, caelum*.
atmospheric, use genit. *aeris* or *caeli*.
atom, *atomus*.
atone, (*ex*)*piare*.
atonement, *piaculum*.
atrocious, *nefandus, nefarius, atrox*; adv. *nefarie*.
atrocity: as quality, *immanitas, atrocitas*; as deed, *res atrox, nefas*.
attach, *adfigĕre, adligare*; fig., *adiungĕre, applicare*.

attached, *aptus*; = fond, *studiosus*.

attachment, *studium, amor, caritas*.

attack, *impetus (-ūs), oppugnatio, incursus (-ūs)*.

attack, v. *oppugnare, adoriri, adgredi (ap)petĕre*; to be —ed by disease, *morbo corripi*.

attacker, *oppugnator*.

attain, *adsequi, consequi*.

attainment, *adeptio, comparatio*; = acquired skill, *ars, doctrina, eruditio*.

attempt, subst. *conatus (-ūs), inceptum*.

attempt, v. *conari, temptare*.

attend: of physical presence, (*hominem*) *comitari, prosequi, deducĕre*; as a servant, (*homini*) *famulari, ministrare*; at a gathering, *adesse, interesse, frequentare*; mentally, = to pay attention, *operam dare, curare, animadvertĕre, animum attendĕre, hoc agĕre*; not to attend, *aliud agĕre*.

attendance, *apparitio, adsectatio*; of large numbers, *frequentia*.

attendant: = escort, (*ad*)*sectator, stipator*; = servant, *servus, minister, famulus*.

attention, *animus attentus, animi intentio*; = an attentive act, *officium*.

attentive: = paying attention, *attentus, intentus, erectus*; adv. *attente, intente*; = helpful, kind, *officiosus, observans*.

attenuate, v. *attenuare, extenuare*.

attest: = vouch for, *testari, testificari*; = call to witness, *testari, testem facĕre*.

attestation, *testificatio*; = evidence, *testimonium*.

attire; see dress.

attitude: physical, (*corporis*) *habitus (-ūs), status (-ūs)*; mental, *animus*.

attract, *attrahĕre, allicĕre*.

attraction, *vis attrahendi*; = pleasant object, *oblectamentum*.

attractive, adj. *iucundus, suavis*.

attribute, subst.; use phrase with *natura* or *proprius*; gram., *attributio, attributum*.

attribute, v. (*at*)*tribuĕre, adsignare*.

attrition; render by verb *terĕre*.

attune; use phrase with *concinĕre* or *consonus*.

auburn, *fulvus*.

auction, *auctio*; to hold an —, *auctionari*.

auctioneer, *magister auctionis, praeco*.

audacious, *audax, protervus, confidens*.

audacity, *audacia, protervitas*.

audience: = hearing *admissio, aditus (-ūs)*; = hearers, *audientes, corona*; a large —, *audientium frequentia*.

audit, v. *rationes dispungĕre*.

augment, v. (*ad*)*augēre, amplificare*.

augmentation, *amplificatio*.

augur, subst. *augur*.

augur, v., = foretell, *praedicĕre, vaticinari, augurari*.

augury, *augurium, omen*.

August, (*mensis*) *Sextilis*; later *Augustus*.

august, adj. *augustus, inlustris, magnificus*.

aunt, *amita* (= father's sister); *matertera* (= mother's sister).

auspices, *auspicium*.

auspicious, *felix, prosper, faustus*; adv. *feliciter, prospere, fauste*.

austere, *austerus, severus, tristis*; adv. *austere, severe*.

austerity, *austeritas, severitas*.

authentic, *certus, verus*; adv. *certo auctore*.

authenticity, *fides, auctoritas*.

author: = originator, *auctor, inventor*; = writer, *scriptor*.

authoritative, *gravis*.

authority, *auctoritas, gravitas*; an — for speech or action, *auctor*; the —s, *magistratus, potestates*.

authorize, *auctor esse, potestatem facĕre, permittĕre*.

autocrat, *dominus*.

autumn, *autumnus*.

autumnal, *autumnalis*.

auxiliaries, *auxilia*, (*milites*) *auxiliares*.

auxiliary, adj. *auxiliaris, auxiliarus*.

avail, *valēre, prodesse*; to — oneself of, *uti*.

avarice, *avaritia*.

avaricious, *avarus*.

avaunt! *abi! apage!*

avenge, *vindicare, ulcisci*.

avenger, *ultor, vindex*.

avenue, *xystus*.

aver; see affirm, assert.

averse, *aversus, alienus*.

avert, *avertĕre, prohibēre*.

aversion, *odium, animus aversus*.

avoid, *vitare, declinare, aversari*.

avow, *profitēri, confitēri*.

avowal, *confessio*.

avowed, *apertus*; adj. *aperte*.

await, *exspectare, manēre, opperiri*.

awake, adj. *vigilans*; to be —, *vigilare*.

awake, v.: transit., (*e somno*) *excitare*; intransit., *expergisci, excitari*.

award, subst. *arbitrium, addictio*.

award, v. *addicĕre, adiudicare*; see give.

aware, *gnarus*; to be —, *scire, novisse*.

away, *procul*; often rendered by compound verb with *ab-*.

awe, subst. *formido, reverentia, veneratio*.

awe, v. *terrēre*; *formidinem inicĕre*.

awe-inspiring, awful, *dirus, formidolosus, terribilis*.

awhile, *aliquamdiu, paulisper, parumper*.

awkward, *agrestis, rusticus, rudis, inscitus*; adv. *inscite, rustice*.

awkwardness, *rusticitas, inscitia*.

awl, *subula*.

awning, *velum*.

awry; adj. *obliquus, perversus*; adv. *oblique, perverse*.

axe, *securis, dolabra*.

axis, axle, *axis*.

ay, aye, adv. *ita, certe, sane*; I say ay, *aio*.

azure, *caeruleus*.

B

baa, v. *balare*.

babble, v. *blaterare, garrire*.

babbler, *garrulus*.

babe, baby, *infans*.

baboon: see ape.

bachelor, *caelebs.*

back, subst. *tergum:* on one's back, *supinus* (adj.).

back, v.: transit., = move backwards, *retro movēre;* = support, *favēre;* intransit., = go back, *se recipēre, recedēre.*

back, backwards, *retro, retrorsum;* or use compound verb with *re-.*

backbite, *rodēre, absenti maledicēre.*

bacon, *lardum.*

bad, *malus, pravus* (= crooked), *turpis* (= ugly, foul); *improbus, perversus, nequam;* in — health, *aeger;* adv. *male, prave, turpiter, improbe.*

badge, *signum, insigne, nota.*

badger, *meles.*

badness, *pravitas, turpitas, nequitia.*

baffle, *eludēre, ad inritum redigēre.*

bag, *saccus, culeus.*

baggage, *sarcinae, impedimenta (-orum), vasa (-orum).*

bail, subst.: = security given, *vadimonium;* = person giving security, *vas, sponsor.*

bail, v. *spondēre.*

bailiff; on an estate, *procurator, vilicus;* at law courts, *apparitor.*

bait, subst. *esca.*

bait, v. = put bait on (a hook), *escam (hamo) imponēre;* = feed, *cibum praebēre;* = worry, *vexare, lacessēre.*

bake, *coquēre, torrēre.*

baker, *pistor.*

bakery, *pistrinum.*

balance, subst.: = scales, *trutina, libra;* = remainder, use adj. *reliquus.*

balance, v. *aequis ponderibus librare;* fig., *compensare;* the accounts —, *ratio constat.*

bald, *glaber, calvus;* of language, *incultus.*

baldness, *calvitium.*

bale, subst. *fascis.*

bale (out), v. *egerēre, exhaurire.*

baleful, *perniciosus, exitiosus.*

balk, v *frustrari, eludēre.*

ball: = round object, *globus;* a — to play with, *pila, follis* (= football); see also bullet; —, = dance, *saltatio.*

ballad, *carmen.*

ballast, *saburra.*

ballet, *pantomimus;* — dancer, *pantomimus.*

ballot, *suffragium, tabella.*

balm, *balsamum;* fig., *solatium.*

balustrade, *cancelli (-orum).*

ban; see forbid.

band, subst.: for binding, *fascia, ligamen;* = company, *manus, turba, grex, caterva.*

band (together), v.; see combine.

bandage; see band and bind.

bandit, *latro.*

bandy: to — words, *altercari.*

bandy, bandy-legged, *loripes.*

bane, *venenum, virus;* fig., *pernicies, pestis.*

baneful, *perniciosus, exitiosus.*

bang, subst., *crepitus (-ūs), sonitus (-ūs).*

bang, v.; see strike.

banish, v. (*homini*) *aqua et igni interdicēre;* (*hominem*) (*ex*)*pellēre, exterminare, relegare, deportare.* Transf., *exterminare,* (*ex*)*pellēre, amovēre.*

banishment, *interdictio aquae et ignis, relegatio, deportatio, exsilium.*

bank, subst.: of earth, *agger;* of a river, *ripa;* financial, *argentaria, mensa publica.*

banker, *argentarius.*

bankrupt, *decoctor;* to become —, (*rationes*) *conturbare, decoquēre.*

banner, *vexillum.*

banquet, *epulae (-arum), convivium, cena.*

banter, subst. *cavillatio, ludibrium.*

banter, v. *cavillari, iocari.*

bar, subst.; = a long piece, *asser, later;* = bolt, *claustrum, obex, sera;* legal, *forum;* to practise at the —, *causas agēre, dicēre, orare.*

bar, v. = bolt, *occludēre, obserare;* = hinder, *impedire, prohibēre.*

barbarian, *barbarus.*

barbaric, barbarous, *barbarus;* = savage, cruel, *immanis, saevus, crudelis;* adv. *barbare, saeve, crudeliter.*

barbarity, *immanitas.*

barbed, *hamatus.*

barber, n. *tonsor:* a —'s shop, *tonstrina.*

bard, *vates.*

bare, adj. *, nudus;* = mere, *merus.*

bare, v. *nudare, aperire.*

barefaced, *impudens.*

barefoot, *pedibus nudis.*

barely, *vix, aegre.*

bargain, subst. *pactio, pactum.*

bargain, v. *pacisci.*

bark, subst.: of trees, *cortex, liber;* of dogs, *latratus.*

bark, v. *latrare.*

barley, *hordeum.*

barn, *horreum.*

barracks, *castra (-orum).*

barrel, *cupa, seria, dolium, orca.*

barren, *sterilis, infecundus.*

barrenness, *sterilitas.*

barricade, subst. *munimentum.*

barricade, v. *praesepire, obstruēre, oppilare.*

barrier, *septum, cancelli (-orum), claustra (-orum).*

barrister; see advocate.

barrow, *ferculum.*

barter, subst. (*per*)*mutatio mercium.*

barter, v. *merces mutare.*

base, subst. *basis, fundamentum, radix.*

base, adj. *turpis;* — coin, *nummi adulterini;* — born, *ignobilis, humili loco natus.* Adv. *turpiter.*

baseness, *turpitudo.*

bashful, *pudens, pudicus, verecundus;* adv. *verecunde.*

bashfulness, *pudor, verecundia.*

basin, *pelvis, trulla.*

basis; see base.

bask, *apricari.*

basket, *corbis, qualus, sporta, calathus.*

bas-relief, *toreuma (-atis,* n.).

bass, (in music), *gravis.*

bastard, *nothus.*

bat: the flying creature, *vespertilio*; for games, *clava*.

batch, *numerus*.

bath, subst. *balineum, balneum, balneae* (-*arum*, plur.).

bath, bathe, v.: transit. *lavare, abluĕre, perfundĕre*; intransit., *lavari, perlui*.

bath-tub, *alveus*.

battalion, *cohors*.

batter, *pulsare, percutĕre, verberare*.

battering-ram, *aries*.

battery: = assault, *vis*; of artillery, *tormenta* (-*orum*).

battle, *proelium, pugna*.

battle-array, *acies*.

battle-axe, *bipennis, securis*.

battle-cry, *clamor*.

battle-field, *locus pugnae*; sometimes *acies*.

battlement, *pinna*.

bawl, *vociferari, clamitare*.

bay, subst.: the tree, *laurea, laurus*; of the sea, *sinus* (-*ūs*).

bay, adj. *spadix, badius*.

bay, v. *latrare*.

be, *esse; existĕre, exstare*.

beach, *litus*.

beacon: = lighthouse, *pharus*; = fire, *ignis*.

bead, *baca*.

beak, *rostrum*.

beaker, *poculum*.

beam, subst.: of wood, *tignum, trabs*; of light, *radius, iubar*.

beam, v. (*ad*)*fulgēre*.

bean, *faba*.

bear, subst.: the animal, *ursus, ursa*; the constellation, *arctos, septentriones*: the Great —, *ursa major*; the Little —, *ursa minor*.

bear, v.: = carry, *ferre, gestare, portare*; = endure, (*per*)*ferre, pati, sustinēre, tolerare*; = have, (feeling, etc.), *gerĕre*; = produce, bring forth, *parĕre, ferre*.

beard, subst. *barba*.

beard, v.; see defy.

bearer: = porter, *baiulus*; — of letters, *tabellarius*.

beast, *bestia* (wild); *belua; pecus* (-*udis*, tame); *fera* (wild); *iumentum* (— of burden).

beastliness, *spurcitia*.

beastly, *spurcus, immundus*.

beat, v.: = strike, *ferire, percutĕre, pulsare*; to be beaten, *vapulare*; to beat down, (*pro*)*sternĕre* —, = overcome, *vincĕre, superare*; intransit., *palpitare, salire*.

beating, subst. *ictus* (-*ūs*), *verbera* (-*um*, plur.).

beau, *homo bellus* or *elegans*.

beautiful, *pulcher, speciosus, formosus, bellus, amoenus* (of landscapes, etc.); adv. *pulchre, belle*.

beautify, (*ex*)*ornare*.

beauty, *pulchritudo, species, forma, amoenitas* (of places).

beaver, *castor, fiber*.

becalmed, *ventis destitutus*.

because, *quod, quia, quoniam*; because of, *propter, ob*.

beck, = nod, *nutus* (-*ūs*).

beckon, *digito innuĕre*.

become, v. *fieri, evadĕre*; = to suit, *decēre, convenire*.

bed: for sleeping, *lectus*: to make a —, *lectum sternĕre*; to go to —, *cubitum ire*: of a river, *alveus*.

bedaub, (*ob*)*linĕre, perungĕre*.

bed-clothes, bedding, *stragulum, lodix*.

bedew, *inrorare*.

bedizen, (*ex*)*ornare*.

bedroom, *cubiculum*.

bee, *apis*: — hive, *alvus, alveus*; a swarm of —s, *examen apium*.

beech, *fagus*; adj. *fageus, faginus*.

beef, (*caro*) *bubula*.

beetle, subst. *scarabaeus*.

befall, *accidĕre, contingĕre*.

befit, *convenire, aptum esse, decēre*.

before, Adv.: in space, *prae*; in time, *prius, ante*. Prep.: in space, =in presence of, *coram*; = in front of, *ante*; in time, *ante*. Conj., *antequam, priusquam*.

beforehand, *antea*.

befoul, *inquinare, foedare*.

befriend, *adiuvare, favēre*.

beg, *mendicare*; = to ask earnestly, *precari, orare, rogare*.

beget, *gignĕre, generare, procreare*.

beggar, *mendicus*.

beggarly, *miser, vilis*.

beggary, *egestas, paupertas, mendicitas*.

begin, *incipĕre, ordiri, inchoare*.

beginning, *initium, principium, primordium*; — of a speech, *exordium*; the —s of a science, *elementa* (-*orum*), *rudimenta* (-*orum*).

beginner, = novice, *tiro*.

begone! *abi! apage te!*

begrudge, *invidēre*.

beguile, *decipĕre, fallĕre*.

behalf: on — of, *pro*.

behave, *se gerĕre*.

behaviour, *mores* (-*um*, plur.).

behead, *detruncare, obtruncare*; in execution, *securi ferire*.

behind: adv. *pone, post, retro, a tergo*; prep. *pone, post*.

behold, v. *adspicĕre, intueri, contemplari, spectare*.

behold! *en! ecce!*

beholden, = indebted, *obnoxius*.

behove: it behoves, *decet, convenit, oportet*.

being, *natura*; a human being, *homo*.

belated, *serus*.

beleaguer, *obsidēre*.

belie: = misrepresent, *criminari, calumniari*; = refute, *refellĕre, refutare*.

belief, *fides, opinio, persuasio*.

believe, *credĕre, fidem habēre*; = to think, *credĕre, putare, arbitrari, opinari*; I firmly —, *mihi persuasum est*.

bell, *tintinnabulum*; sometimes *aes*.

bellow, subst. *mugitus* (-*ūs*).

bellow, v. *mugire*.

bellows, *follis*.

belly, *venter, alvus, abdomen*.

belong, *esse*, with genit. or possess. adj.; *attinēre, pertinēre*.

below: adv., *subter, infra*; prep., *infra, subter, sub.*

belt, *cingulum, zona, balteus.*

bench, *scamnum, subsellium*; for rowers, *transtrum.*

bend: transit., (*in*)*flectĕre, inclinare*; intransit., pass. or reflex.

bending, *flexus* (*-ūs*), *flexio, inclinatio.*

beneath; see below.

beneficence, *beneficentia, liberalitas.*

beneficent, *liberalis, beneficus.*

beneficial, *utilis, salutaris.*

benefit, subst. *beneficium.*

benefit, v.: transit., *prodesse,* (*ad*)*iuvare*; intransit., *proficĕre.*

benevolence, *benevolentia.*

benevolent, *benevolus.*

benign, *benignus.*

benignity, *benignitas.*

bent, subst. *animi inclinatio, voluntas.*

bent, adj. *curvus*; bent on a thing, *rei* (genit.) *studiosus, cupidus.*

benumb; to be —ed, *obtorpescĕre, torpēre.*

bequeath, *legare.*

bequest, *legatum.*

bereave, *orbare.*

bereaved, *orbus.*

bereavement, *orbitas.*

berry, *baca, bacula, acinus.*

beseech, *orare, implorare, obtestari.*

beset, *obsidēre, urgēre, premĕre.*

beside, prep.: = near, *prope, iuxta*; = except, *praeter*; — the point, *nihil ad rem*; — oneself, *sui impotens.*

besides, *praeter* (*quam*); as adv. = in addition, *praeterea, ultro.*

besiege, *obsidēre, circumsedēre.*

besmear, (*ob*)*linĕre.*

bespatter, *adspergĕre, conspergĕre.*

bespeak, *imperare.*

best, *optimus*; see good.

bestir: to bestir oneself, *se* (*com*)*movēre, excitare.*

bestow; see give.

bet, subst. *pignus* (*-oris*).

betake: to betake oneself, *se conferre.*

betimes, *mature.*

betoken, *significare.*

betray, *prodĕre.*

betrayal, *proditio.*

betrayer, *proditor.*

betroth, (*de*)*spondēre.*

betrothal, *sponsalia* (*-ium* or *-iorum*).

better, adj. *melior, potior* (= preferable); I am getting better, *convalesco.*

better, adv. *melius.*

better, v. transit. *meliorem facĕre, corrigĕre, emendare.*

between, *inter,* with acc.

beverage, *potio, potus* (*-ūs*).

bevy, *grex.*

bewail, *deplorare, deflēre,* (*con*)*queri.*

beware, v. *cavēre.*

bewilder, (*con*)*turbare.*

bewitch, *fascinare*; see also charm.

beyond: adv., *ultra, supra*; prep., *trans, ultra, extra, praeter.*

bias, subst. *inclinatio animi.*

bias, v. *inclinare* (*animum*).

bibulous, *bibulus.*

bid, subst. (at a sale), *licitatio.*

bid, v.: = command, *iubēre, imperare*; = invite, *invitare*; at a sale, *liceri.*

bide, *manēre.*

bier, *feretrum, sandapila.*

big, *magnus, grandis, vastus.*

bile, *bilis.*

bilge-water, *sentina.*

bill: of a bird, *rostrum*; = a proposed law, *rogatio*; to bring forward a —, *rogationem ferre*; to reject a —, *antiquare*; to carry a —, *perferre.*

billet, subst., = letter, *epistula.*

billet, v.: to billet troops, *milites per domos disponĕre.*

billow, *fluctus* (*-ūs*).

billowy, *fluctuosus.*

bind, v. (*ad*)*ligare, vincire*; fig., *obligare, adstringĕre*; to — together, *conligare, constringĕre*; to — over, *vadari.*

biographer; see historian.

biped, *bipes.*

birch, *betula.*

bird, *avis, volucris, ales*; — catcher, *auceps*; — lime, *viscum.*

birth, *ortus* (*-ūs*); of noble —, *nobili genere natus.*

birthday, *dies natalis.*

bishop, *episcopus.*

bit: of a horse, *frenum*; = piece, *frustum.*

bitch, *canis* (*femina*).

bite, subst., *morsus* (*-ūs*).

bite, v. *mordēre.*

biting, *mordens, mordax, acidus.*

bitter, *amarus, acerbus, acidus*; adv. *amare, acerbe.*

bitterness, *acerbitas.*

bivouac, subst. *excubiae* (*-arum*).

black, *ater, niger*; dressed in —, *sordidatus, pullatus, atratus*; a black man, *Aethiops.*

blackberry, *rubus.*

blackbird, *merula.*

blacken, v.: transit., *nigrum facĕre*; intransit., *nigrescĕre.*

Black Sea, *Pontus Euxinus.*

blacksmith, *faber* (*ferrarius*).

bladder, *vesica.*

blade: of grass, *herba*; of an oar, *palma*; of a knife, *lamina.*

blame, subst. *culpa, reprehensio, vituperatio.*

blame, v. *reprehendĕre, culpare, vituperare.*

blameless, *innocens, integer, sanctus.*

blamelessness, *innocentia, integritas sanctitas.*

bland, *blandus, lenis, mitis*; adv. *blande.*

blandishment, *blanditia, blandimentum.*

blank, *vacuus.*

blanket, *lodix.*

blast, subst. *flamen, flatus* (*-ūs*).

blast¹ v. transit.; see blight.

blaze, subst. *flamma.*

blaze, v. *ardēre,* (*con*)*flagrare.*

bleach, *candidum facĕre.*

bleak; see cold.

blear-eyed, *lippus*; to be —, *lippire.*

bleat, subst. *balatus* (*-ūs*).

bleat, v. *balare.*

bleed, v. *sanguinem dare* or *effundĕre.*

blemish, subst. *vitium, mendum, macula.*

blemish, v. (*com*)*maculare.*

blend, (com)miscēre.

bless: in words, *bonis ominibus prosequi:* in gen., *beare, fortunare.*

blessed, *beatus, fortunatus.*

blessedness, *felicitas.*

blight, subst. *robigo.*

blight, v. *robigine adficĕre;* of hopes, *frustrari.*

blind, adj. *caecus, oculis captus;* adv., = rashly, *temere.*

blind, v. *(oc)caecare, oculis privare.*

blindfold, *oculis opertis.*

blindness, *caecitas.*

blink, *connivēre, nictare.*

bliss, *felicitas.*

blister, *pustula.*

blithe, *laetus, hilaris.*

bloated, *turgidus, tumidus.*

block, subst. *stipes, truncus, caudex.*

block, v. *claudĕre, occludĕre, opplēre, obstruĕre.*

blockade, subst. *obsessio, obsidio.*

blockade, v. *obsidēre, obsĭdēre, circumvallare.*

blockhead; see block.

blood, *sanguis, cruor;* = birth, race, *sanguis, genus.*

bloodless, *exsanguis, incruentus.*

blood-red, *cruentus, sanguineus.*

blood-relation, *consanguineus.*

bloodshed, *caedes.*

bloodshot, *sanguine suffusus.*

blood-stained, *cruentus.*

blood-thirsty, *sanguinarius.*

bloody, *cruentus, sanguineus.*

bloom, subst. *flos.*

bloom, v. *florēre, vigēre.*

blossom; see bloom.

blot, subst.; on paper, *litura;* in gen. *macula, labes.*

blot, v. *(com)maculare;* to — out, *delēre, exstinguĕre.*

blow, subst. *ictus (-ūs), plaga.*

blow, v. *flare;* to — into, *inflare;* to — on, *adflare.*

blowing, subst. *flatus (-ūs).*

bludgeon, *fustis.*

blue, *caeruleus.*

blunder, subst. *error, erratum, mendum.*

blunder, v. *errare.*

blunt, adj. *hebes;* fig., = rude, *agrestis, rusticus;* adv., of speech, *libere, liberius.*

blunt, v. transit. *hebetare, obtundĕre.*

blush, subst. *rubor.*

blush, v. *erubescĕre, rubēre.*

bluster, subst. *declamatio.*

bluster, v. *declamare, declamitare.*

boar, *verres;* a wild —, *aper.*

board, subst.: = plank, *tabula;* = food, *victus (-ūs), alimentum;* = body of officials, *conlegium.*

board, v.: to — over, *contabulare;* to — a ship, *navem conscendĕre;* to — with anyone, *apud hominem habitare.*

boast, *gloriari, (se) iactare.*

boaster, *iactator, homo gloriosus.*

boasting, subst. *gloriatio, iactatio.*

boastful, *gloriosus;* adv. *gloriose.*

boat, *linter, scapha, navicula.*

boatman, *nauta.*

bodily, *corporeus.*

body, *corpus (-oris);* a — of men, *manus, numerus, grex.*

bodyguard, *stipatores, satellites.*

bog, *palūs (-ūdis).*

boggy, *uliginosus, paluster.*

bogy, *terricula (-orum, plur.).*

boil, subst. *vomica.*

boil, v. transit., *coquĕre;* intransit., *fervēre, (ef)fervescĕre, (ex)aestuare.*

boisterous, *turbidus;* of weather, *turbulentus.*

bold, *audax, confidens, ferox, animosus;* adv. *audacter, confidenter, ferociter, animose.*

boldness, *audacia, confidentia.*

bole, *truncus, stirps.*

bolster, *cervical, culcita, pulvinus.*

bolt, subst.: = fastening, *obex, sera, pessulus;* = weapon, *telum.*

bolt, v. *claudĕre, occludĕre, obserare.*

bombast, *(verborum) tumor, inflata oratio.*

bombastic, *inflatus.*

bond, *vinculum, ligamentum, compes, catena;* = legal document, *chirographum, syngrapha.*

bondage, *servitūs (-ūtis), servitium.*

bone, *os (ossis).*

bony, *osseus.*

book, *liber, volumen, codex.*

bookseller, *bibliopola.*

boon, *beneficium.*

boorish, *agrestis, inurbanus, rusticus;* adv. *rustice, inurbane.*

boot, *calceus;* an army —, *caliga.*

bootless, *inutilis, inritus;* adv. *frustra.*

booty, *praeda.*

border, *margo;* of a stream, *ripa;* of a country, *finis.*

border, v.; to border on, *adiacere, attingĕre.*

bore, subst. *homo importunus* or *odiosus.*

bore, v.: = perforate, *perforare, terebrare;* = weary, *obtundere, defatigare, vexare;* I am bored, *taedet me.*

boredom, *taedium.*

born: to be —, *nasci.*

borrow, *mutuari, mutuum sumĕre.*

borrowed, *mutuus, alienus.*

bosom, *sinus (-ūs), pectus (-oris), gremium.*

boss, *umbo, bulla.*

botany, *(ars) herbaria.*

both, *ambo; uterque* (= each); both ... and ..., *et ... et ..., cum ... tum ...*

bother, subst. *molestia, incommodum.*

bother, v.; see annoy; = to take trouble, *curare.*

bottle, *lagena, ampulla.*

bottom, *fundus, solum;* the bottom of the sea, *imum mare.*

bough, *ramus.*

bounce, *resilire.*

bound, subst.: = limit, *finis, modus, terminus;* = jump, *saltus (-ūs).*

bound, v.: = limit, *(de)finire, terminare;* = jump, *salire.*

boundary, *finis, terminus, confinium.*

boundless, *infinitus, immensus.*

bountiful, *largus, liberalis;* adv. *large, liberaliter.*

bounty, *largitas, liberalitas, munificentia.*

bout, *certamen;* a drinking —, *comissatio.*

bow, subst.: the weapon, *arcus (-ūs)*; of a ship, *prora*; = movement of the body, *corporis inclinatio.*

bow, v. *flectĕre, demittĕre, inclinare*; to bow to, *salutare*; fig., *obsequi, obtemperare.*

bowman, *sagittarius.*

bowstring, *nervus.*

bowels, *viscera (-um), alvus.*

bower, *umbraculum.*

bowl, subst. *crater, cratera, patera.*

bowl, v. *volvĕre.*

box, subst.: = receptacle, *arca, cista, pyxis*; the shrub, *buxus*; adj. *buxeus.*

box, v. intransit. *pugnis certare.*

boxer, *pugil.*

boy, *puer.*

boyhood, *aetas puerilis, pueritia.*

boyish, *puerilis*; adv. *pueriliter.*

brace, subst.: = strap, *fascia, vinculum*; = stay (rigid), *fibula*; = a pair, *par.*

brace, v. *(ad)ligare*; mentally, *(con)firmare.*

bracelet, *armilla.*

brackish, *amarus.*

brag; see boast.

braid, subst. *limbus*; of hair, *gradus.*

braid, v. *texĕre, nectĕre.*

brain, *cerebrum.*

bramble, *rubus, vepris.*

branch, subst. *ramus.*

branch, v. *dividi.*

brand, subst.: = firebrand, *torris, fax*; = a mark, *nota.*

brand, v. *notam inurĕre, notare.*

brandish, *vibrare, iactare.*

brass, *orichalcum.*

bravado, *iactatio.*

brave, *fortis, strenuus, animosus*; adv. *fortiter, strenue.*

bravery, *fortitudo.*

bravo! *euge! factum bene! macte!*

brawl, subst. *rixa, iurgium.*

brawl, v. *rixari.*

brawny, *robustus, lacertosus.*

brazen, *a(h)eneus, aereus*; fig., = shameless, *impudens*; — face, *os durum.*

breach, subst.: to make a —, *perfringĕre, discutĕre*; a — of treaty, *foedus ruptum* or *violatum.*

bread, *panis*; = subsistence, *victus (-ūs).*

breadth, *latitudo.*

break, subst. *intervallum*; — of day, *prima lux, diluculum.*

break, v. (1) transit. *frangĕre, confringĕre, rumpĕre*; to — open, *refringĕre*; fig., = to weaken, subdue, *domare, frangĕre, infringĕre*; to — a treaty, *foedus violare*; — a promise, *fidem fallĕre.* (2) intransit. *frangi, confringi, rumpi*; to break in, *inrumpĕre*; to — out, *erumpĕre*, fig. *exoriri, exardescĕre, gliscĕre.*

breaker, *fluctus (-ūs).*

breakfast, *ientaculum.*

breakwater, *moles.*

breast, *pectus, animus* (fig.).

breast-plate, *lorica, thorax.*

breastwork, *pluteus, lorica.*

breath, *spiritus (-ūs), anima*; to put out of —, *exanimare.*

breathe, *spirare*; to — again, *respirare*; to — upon, *adflare*; to — out, *exhalare.*

breathless, *exanimatus, exanimis.*

breeches, *bracae*; wearing —, *bracatus.*

breed, subst. *genus (-eris, n.).*

breed, v. transit. *gignĕre, generare parĕre, procreare*; intransit., *nasci.*

breeding, *cultus (-ūs).*

breeze, *aura.*

brevity, *brevitas.*

brew, *coquĕre*; of trouble, *imminēre, impendēre.*

briar; see brier.

bribe, subst. *pretium.*

bribe, v. *(pretio, pecuniā, etc.) corrumpĕre.*

briber, *corruptor.*

bribery, *largitio*; or use verb.

brick, *later*; adj. *latericius.*

bridal, adj. *nuptialis.*

bride, bridegroom, *(nova) nupta, (novus) maritus.*

bridge, *pons.*

bridle, *frenum.*

bridle, v. *(in)frenare.*

brief, *brevis*; in —, *ne longus sim.* Adv. *breviter, paucis (verbis).*

brier, briar, *vepris, dumus, frutex.*

brigade, *legio.*

brigand, *latro.*

bright, *clarus, lucidus, splendidus, fulgens*; of weather, *serenus*; to be —, *clarēre.* Adv. *clare, lucide.*

brighten, v.: transit., *inlustrare, inluminare*; intransit., *clarescĕre.*

brightness, *candor, splendor, nitor, fulgor*; of weather, *serenitas.*

brilliant, *splendidus, inlustris, luculentus, praeclarus.*

brim, *ora, margo, labrum.*

Brindisi, *Brundisium.*

brine, *muria, salsamentum.*

bring: by carrying, *(ad)ferre, (ap)portare*; by leading, etc., *(ad)ducĕre*; to — back, *referre, reducĕre*; to — together, *cogĕre*; to — about, *efficĕre (ut)*; to — forward, *in medium proferre*; to — in, yield, *reddĕre*; to — up, *educare.*

brink, *margo, ripa.*

brisk, *alacer, vegetus.*

briskness, *alacritas.*

bristle, subst. *saeta.*

bristle, v. *horrēre.*

bristly, *saetosus.*

brittle, *fragilis.*

broach, *aperire.*

broad, *latus, amplus*; adv. *late.*

broil, subst. *rixa.*

broil, v. *torrēre.*

bronze, subst. *aes.*

bronze, adj. *a(h)eneus, aereus.*

brooch, *fibula.*

brood, subst. *fetus (-ūs).*

brood, v. *incubare.*

brook, subst. *rivus, rivulus.*

brook, v. *ferre, tolerare.*

broom: the plant, *genista*; for sweeping, *scopae (-arum, plur.).*

broth, *ius (iuris).*

brother, *frater.*

brotherhood, = association, *societas, sodalitas.*

brotherly, *fraternus.*

brow: = eyebrow, *supercilium*; = forehead, *frons*; of a hill, *summus collis.*

brown, *fuscus, fulvus.*

bruise, v. *contundĕre.*

bruit, v. *(di)vulgare.*

brush, subst. *penicillus*; see broom.

brush, v. transit. *verrĕre, (de)tergĕre.*

brush-wood, *virgultum, sarmentum.*

brutal, *ferus, inhumanus, immanis*; adv. *inhumane, immaniter.*

brutality, *immanitas.*

brute, *pecus, belua*; see beast.

bubble, subst. *bulla.*

buccaneer, *pirata, praedo.*

bucket, *situla, hama.*

buckle, *fibula.*

buckler, *scutum, clipeus, parma.*

bud, subst. *gemma, germen.*

bud, v. *gemmare.*

budge, *loco cedĕre.*

buff, *luteus.*

buffalo, *bos.*

buffet, = blow, *alapa, colaphus.*

buffoon, *sannio, scurra.*

buffoonery, *scurrilitas.*

bug, *cimex (-icis).*

bugbear; see bogy.

bugle, *bucina.*

build, *aedificare, (ex)struĕre.*

builder, *aedificator, structor.*

building, subst.: the process, *aedificatio, exstructio*; the thing built, *aedificium.*

bulb, *bulbus.*

bulk, *magnitudo, amplitudo, moles.*

bulky, *amplus, ingens.*

bull, *taurus.*

bullock, *iuvencus.*

bullet, *glans.*

bullion, *aurum, argentum.*

bulrush, *iuncus, scirpus.*

bulwark, *propugnaculum.*

bump, subst.: = swelling, *tumor, tuber*; = bang, *ictus (-ūs).*

bump, v.: to bump into, *offendĕre.*

bumper; see cup.

bunch, of fruit, *racemus, uva*; see bundle.

bundle, *fascis, manipulus, sarcina.*

bung, *obturamentum.*

buoyant, *levis.* Transf., *hilaris.*

burden, subst. *onus (-eris)*: beast of —, *iumentum.*

burden, v. *onerare, opprimĕre.*

burdensome, *gravis, molestus.*

bureau, *scrinium.*

burgess, burgher, *municeps, civis.*

burglar, *fur.*

burglary, *furtum.*

burial, *sepultura, humatio.*

burial-ground, *sepulturae locus, sepulcrum.*

burn, v. transit., = set on fire, *incendĕre*; to burn up, *comburĕre, (con)cremare*; intransit., = to blaze, *ardēre, flagare.*

burnish, *polire.*

burrow, *cuniculus.*

burst, v. transit. *(di)rumpĕre.*

bury, *humare, sepelire.*

bush, *frutex, dumus.*

bushy, *ruticosus.*

bushel, *medimnus.*

business, *res, negotium.*

buskin, *cothurnus.*

bust, *effigies.*

bustle, subst. *festinatio, trepidatio.*

bustle, v. *festinare, trepidare.*

busy, *occupatus, negotiosus*; adv. *sedulo, industrie.*

busy-body, *ardelio.*

but: = except, *praeter*; all but, *tantum non*; = only, *modo, tantum, solum*; as adversat. conj., *sed, verum, at*; *atqui* (= and yet); *tamen* (= however); but if, *sin, quodsi.*

butcher, *lanius.*

butcher, v. *caedĕre*; of persons, *trucidare.*

butchery, *caedes.*

butler, *cellarius, promus.*

butt, = object of ridicule, *ludibrium.*

butt, v. *arietare, cornu petĕre.*

butterfly, *papilio.*

buttocks, *clunes (-ium), nates (-ium), pyga.*

buttress, v. *fulcire.*

buxom, *hilaris.*

buy, v. *(co)emĕre, mercari.*

buyer, *emptor.*

by: of place, *ad, apud, iuxta, prope*; to go —, *praeterire*; to stand —, *adesse*; of time, — night, *noctu, nocte*; — moonlight, *ad lunam*; of means or manner, *per* with acc.; of agency, *ab (homine)*; in adjuration, *per* with acc.; of distribution, one — one, *singuli, singillatim.*

by-way, *trames (-itis), semita, deverticulum.*

by-word: to become a —, *contemptui esse.*

C

cabbage, *brassica, caulis.*

cabin, *casa, tugurium.*

cabinet: = room, *conclave*; = cupboard, desk, etc., *armarium, thesaurus, scrinium.*

cable, *ancorale, funis ancorarius.*

cackle, *strepĕre.*

cadaverous, *exsanguis.*

cadence, *numerus.*

cadet, *tiro.*

Cadiz, *Gades (-ium, plur.).*

cage, *cavea.*

cajolery, *blanditiae (-arum).*

cake, subst. *placenta.*

cake, v., = stick together, *concrescĕre.*

calamitous, *calamitosus, luctuosus.*

calamity, *calamitas, clades.*

calculate, *computare.*

calculated, *accommodatus, aptus, idoneus.*

calculation, *ratio.*

caldron, *a(h)enum, cortina.*

calendar, *fasti (-orum).*

calf, *vitulus, vitula*; — of the leg, *sura.*

call, subst.: = cry, *vox*; = visit, *salutatio.*

call, v.: = cry out, *clamare*; = name, *vocare, nominare, appellare*; = summon, *(ad)vocare*; to — together.

convocare; to — for, = to demand, (*de*)*poscere, flagitare*; to — on, = visit, *salutare, visĕre*.

caller, = visitor, *salutator*.

callous, *callosus*. Transf., *durus*.

calm, subst. *quies, tranquillitas, otium, pax*; — at sea, *malacia*.

calm, adj. *quietus, tranquillus, placidus*; adv. *tranquille, placide; aequo animo*.

calm, v. *sedare, lenire, tranquillare*.

calumniate, *calumniari, criminari*.

calumniator, *obtrectator*.

calumny, *criminatio, calumnia*.

camel, *camelus*.

camp, *castra (-orum)*.

campaign, *stipendium*.

can, subst.; see jug.

can, v. *posse*; see able.

canal, *fossa*.

cancel, *delēre, tollĕre*.

candid, *liber, apertus, verus, simplex*; adv. *libere, aperte*.

candidate, *candidatus*.

candour, *libertas, candor*.

candle, *candela*.

candlestick, *candelabrum*.

cane, subst. *harundo, calamus*; for walking, *baculum*; for correction, *ferula*.

cane, v. (*ferulā*) *verberare*.

canine, *caninus*.

canker, v. *corrumpĕre*.

cannon, *tormentum*.

canoe, *cymba*.

canon, = a rule, *lex, regula, norma*.

canopy, *aulaeum*.

canton, *pagus*.

canvas, in a sail, *carbasus, velum*.

canvass, *ambire*.

canvassing, *ambitio, ambitus (-ūs)*.

cap, *pileus, galerus*.

capability, *facultas*.

capable, *aptus, idoneus*; often rendered by *posse*.

capacious, *capax, amplus*.

caparison, *phalerae (-arum,* plur.).

capital, subst.: = chief city, *caput*; or use *urbs* with adj.: of a pillar, *capitulum*; of money, *sors, caput*.

capital, adj., *capitalis*; see excellent, etc.

capitulate; see surrender.

caprice, *libido, levitas*.

capricious, *inconstans, levis*.

captain, *princeps, dux*; of a ship, *navarchus, magister*.

captious, *morosus, difficilis*.

captivate, *capĕre*.

captive, *captus, captivus*.

captivity, *captivitas*.

capture, *capĕre, comprehendĕre*.

car, *carrus, cisium, plaustrum, vehiculum*.

caravan, *comitatus (-ūs)*.

carcase, *cadaver*.

card, subst. *charta*.

card, v. *pectĕre*.

care, subst.: = attention, caution, *cura, diligentia*; = anxiety, *cura, sollicitudo*; = management, *cura, curatio*.

care, v.; to — for, — about, *curare*.

career, *curriculum, cursus (-ūs)*.

careful, *diligens, accuratus, attentus*; adv. *diligenter, accurate*.

careless, *neglegens*.

carelessness, *imprudentia, neglegentia, incuria*.

caress, subst. *complexus (-ūs)*.

caress, v. *blandiri, permulcēre*.

caressing, *blandus*.

cargo, *onus (-eris)*.

carnage, *caedus, strages*.

carnal, render by genit. *corporis*.

carnival, *feriae (-arum)*.

carousal, *comissatio, potatio*.

carouse, v. *comissari, potare*.

carp, v.: to — at, *carpĕre, vellicare*.

carpenter, *faber (tignarius)*.

carpet, *tapeta (-ae), tapeta (-orum), tapetia (-ium)*.

carriage: = act of carrying, *gestura*; = bearing, *habitus*; = vehicle, *vehiculum*.

carrier, *gerulus*; letter —, *tabellarius*.

carry, *ferre, portare, vehĕre, gerĕre*; to — out (= perform), *conficĕre, exsequi*.

cart, *plaustrum*.

carve, *caelare, scalpĕre, sculpĕre*: to — meat, *scindere, secare*.

carver, *caelator, sculptor*.

carving, *caelatura, scalptura, sculptura*.

cascade, *aquae ex alto desilientes*.

case: = receptacle, *theca, involucrum*; gram., *casus (-ūs)*; judicial, *causa*; = chance, *res, casus (-ūs)*.

casement, *fenestra*.

cash, subst. *pecunia praesens* or *numerata*.

cash, v. *praesenti pecunia solvĕre*.

cashier, v. = discharge, *exauctorare*.

cask, *dolium, cupa*.

casket, *arcula, capsula*.

casque, *galea, cassis*.

cast, subst., = throw, *iactus (-ūs)*.

cast, v. *iacĕre, conicĕre, iactare, mittĕre*; to — in metal, *fundĕre*; to be — down, *adfligi*.

castaway, *perditus, profligatus*; by ship-wreck, *naufragus*.

castigate; see punish.

castle, *castellum*.

casual, *fortuitus, forte oblatus*; adv. *forte, casu, fortuito*.

cat, *feles* (or *felis*).

catalogue, *index*.

catapult, *catapulta*.

cataract, in the eye, *glaucoma*; see also cascade.

catarrh, *gravedo, pituita*.

catastrophe; see disaster.

catch, *capĕre, excipĕre, deprehendĕre, comprehendĕre*; to — up, *adsequi, consequi*; to — fire, *ignem concipĕre*.

categorical, *simplex, definitus*.

category, *genus (-eris), numerus*.

cater, *obsonare*.

caterpillar, *eruca*.

cattle, *boves*; coll., *pecus (-oris)*; a head of —, *pecus (-udis)*.

cauldron; see caldron.

cause, subst. *causa; materia* (= occasion, ground); *res* (= case, affair).

cause, v. transit., *facĕre, efficĕre* (*ut*); *movēre, excitare*.

causeway, *agger*.

caustic, *mordax, acerbus.*
cauterize, *adurĕre.*
caution, = *care, cautio, cura, prudentia.*
caution, v. *monēre.*
cautious, *providus, prudens, cautus;* adv. *prudenter, caute.*
cavalcade, = *comitatus (-ūs).*
cavalier, = horseman, *eques.*
cavalierly, *adroganter, insolenter.*
cavalry, *equitatus, equites (-um,* plur.*).*
cave, *caverna, specus, spelunca, antrum.*
cavil; see carp.
cavity; see hole.
cease, *desinĕre, desistĕre.*
ceaseless, *perpetuus, adsiduus;* adv. *perpetuo, adsidue.*
cedar, *cedrus.*
cede, *concedĕre.*
ceiling, *tectum.*
celebrate, *celebrare.*
celebrated, *celeber, clarus, inlustris.*
celebration, *celebratio.*
celebrity, *gloria, laus;* = celebrated person, *vir insignis.*
celerity, *celeritas.*
celestial, *caelestis, divinus.*
cell, *cella, cubiculum.*
cellar, *cella;* a wine—, *apotheca.*
cement, subst. *gluten.*
cemetery, *sepulchra (-orum).*
censor, *censor.*
censorious, *severus.*
censure, subst. *reprehensio, vituperatio.*
censure, v. *reprehendĕre, vituperare.*
census, *census (-ūs);* to take a census, *censēre.*
centaur, *centaurus.*
centre, subst. *media pars;* or use *medius* (e.g. the — of the city, *media urbs*).
centurion, *centurio.*
century, *centum anni, saeculum.*
ceremonious, *sollemnis.*
ceremony, *ritus (-ūs), caerimonia.*
certain, *certus, stabilis, fidus* (= trustworthy); a — person, *quidam;* to know for —, *certo scire.*
certainly, *certo;* in answers, *profecto, sane;* = admittedly, *certe, quidem, sane.*
certify, *confirmare.*
cessation, *intermissio.*
chafe, v.: transit., *calefacĕre;* intransit., *stomachari, aestuare.*
chaff, *palea.*
chagrin, *aegritudo, stomachus, dolor.*
chain, subst., *catena, vinculum;* = series, *series.*
chain, v. *vincire.*
chair, *sella, sedile, cathedra.*
chalice, *calix.*
chalk, *creta.*
challenge, (*ad pugnam) provocare*
chamber, *cubiculum.*
champ, *mandĕre.*
champion, *propugnator, defensor.*
chance, *casus (-ūs), fors;* by —, *forte, casu.*
chance, v. *accidĕre;* see also happen, risk.
change, subst. *(com)mutatio, vicissitudo.*
change, v.: transit., *(com)mutare, convertĕre;* intransit., *(com)mutari.*

changeable, *mutabilis, inconstans, varius.*
changeableness, *mutabilitas, varietas.*
changeling, *puer subditus.*
channel, *fossa, canalis, fretum.*
chant, v. *canĕre, cantare.*
chaos, *chaos, confusio, perturbatio.*
chaotic, *confusus, perturbatus.*
chapel, *aedicula, sacellum.*
chapter, of a book, *caput.*
character: = symbol, letter, *littera;* = disposition, nature, *natura, ingenium, mores (-um);* = part played, *persona, partes (-ium);* = reputation, *fama, existimatio.*
characteristic, subst. *proprietas.*
characteristic, adj. *proprius;* adj. *proprie, more suo.*
characterize, *notare, designare.*
charcoal, *carbo.*
charge, subst.: = price, *pretium;* = command, *mandatum;* = care (of), *cura, custodia;* = accusation, *accusatio, crimen;* = attack, *impetus (-ūs), incursus (-ūs).*
charge, v. to — to a person, *homini imputare;* to — with a duty, (*homini) committĕre, mandare;* = accuse, *accusare, insimulare;* = attack, *invadĕre, impetum facĕre, incurrĕre.*
charger: = dish, *lanx;* = horse, *equus.*
chariot, *currus (-ūs).*
charioteer, *auriga.*
charitable, *benignus, liberalis, beneficus;* adv. *benigne, liberaliter.*
charity, *benignitas;* as conduct, *beneficentia, liberalitas.*
Charles, *Carolus.*
charm, subst.: = magic formula, *carmen;* = amulet, *fascinum;* = attraction, *blandimentum, dulcedo, lepor.*
charm, v.: by magic, *fascinare;* see delight.
charming, *suavis, lepidus;* of country, *amoenus.*
chart, *tabula.*
chary, *parcus.*
chase, subst. *venatio, venatus (-ūs).*
chase, v. *venari;* = engrave, *caelare.*
chasm, *hiatus (-ūs), specus (-ūs).*
chaste, *castus, pudicus.*
chastise, *castigare;* see punish.
chastisement, *castigatio, animadversio.*
chastity, *castitas, pudicitia.*
chat, subst. *sermo.*
chat, v. *fabulari, garrire.*
chatter, *garrulitas.*
chattering, *garrulus, loquax.*
cheap, *vilis.*
cheat, subst.: = deception, *fraus, dolus;* = deceiver, *circumscriptor, fraudator.*
cheat, v. *fallĕre, decipĕre, fraudare.*
check, subst. *impedimentum, mora.*
check, v. *continēre, impedire, reprimĕre.*
cheek, *gena;* puffed out, *bucca.*
cheer, subst.: = shout, *clamor;* to be of good —, *bono animo esse.*
cheer, v. = shout, *clamare;* = gladden *exhilarare, erigĕre.*
cheerful, *hilaris, laetus;* adv. *hilare laete.*
cheering, subst. *favor.*
cheerless, *tristis, maestus.*

cheese, *caseus.*
chequered, *varius.*
cherish, *fovēre, colēre, tuēri.*
cherry, *cerasus.*
chest, *pectus (-oris)*; = receptacle, *arca, cista.*
Chester, *Deva.*
chestnut, *castanea.*
chew, *mandēre.*
chicanery, *dolus, calumnia.*
chicken, *pullus (gallinaceus).*
chide, *obiurgare, increpare.*
chiding, *obiurgatio.*
chief, subst. *caput, princeps, dux.*
chief, adj. *primus, praecipuus*; adv. *praecipue.*
chieftain, *regulus.*
child: male, *filius*; female, *filia*: a small —, *infans*; children, *pueri, liberi.*
child-birth, *partus (-ūs).*
childhood, *pueritia, aetas puerilis.*
childish, *puerilis*; adv. *pueriliter.*
childless, *(liberis) orbus.*
chill, subst. *horror, frigus (-oris).*
chill, v. *refrigerare.*
chin, *mentum.*
china, use *murra*; adj. *murrinus.*
chink, *rima.*
chip, *assula.*
chirp, *pipilare.*
chisel, subst. *scalprum, caelum.*
chivalrous, *magnanimus.*
chivalry, as an institution, *ordo equester*; as a spirit, *magnanimitas.*
choice, subst. *delectus (-ūs), magnanimitas.*
choice, adj. *electus, eximius.*
choir, *chorus.*
choke, v. *suffocare, animam intercludēre.*
choler; see anger.
choose, v. *eligēre, diligēre.*
chop, *abscidēre, praecidēre.*
chord, *nervus.*
chorus, *chorus.*
Christ, *Christus.*
Christian, *Christianus.*
chronic, *longinquus, diuturnus.*
chronicle, subst. *annales (-ium).*
chronicle, v. transit., *in annales referre.*
chronicler, *annalium scriptor.*
chronology, *temporum (or rerum) ordo.*
church, *ecclesia.*
churlish, *agrestis, rusticus, inurbanus.*
cinder, *cinis.*
cipher, subst.: = a secret writing, *notae*; = a nobody, *numerus.*
cipher, v. *computare.*
circle, *orbis, circulus*; of people, *corona.*
circuit, *circuitus (-ūs), orbis, circulus.*
circular, *rotundus.*
circulate, v. transit. *circumagēre, dispergēre*; of news, etc., *divulgare.*
circumlocution, *circumitio verborum.*
circumnavigate, *circumvehi (navi).*
circumscribe, *circumscribēre, definire.*
circumspect, *cautus, providus, prudens.*
circumspection, *cautio, prudentia.*
circumstance, *res, tempus*: according to —s, *pro re (natā)*; in these —s, *quae cum ita sint.*
circumvallation, *circummunitio.*

circumvent, *circumvenire, circumscribēre.*
cistern, *cisterna, lacus, puteus.*
citadel, *arx.*
cite, v. *proferre, memorare*; before a court, *citare, in ius vocare.*
citizen, *civis.*
citizenship, *civitas.*
city, *urbs.*
civic, *civilis, civicus.*
civil: = civic, *civilis, civicus*: — war, *bellum civile, intestinum, domesticum*; = polite, *urbanus*; adv. *urbane.*
civilization, *cultus (-ūs), humanitas.*
civilize, *expolire.*
civilized, *humanus.*
clad, *vestitus.*
claim, v. *postulare, vindicare*; to — back, *repetēre.*
claimant (at law), *petitor.*
clammy, *lentus.*
clamour, subst. *vociferatio, clamor.*
clamour, v. *(con)clamare, vociferari.*
clan, *gens, tribus (-ūs).*
clandestine, *clandestinus, furtivus*; adv. *clam, furtim.*
clang, subst. *sonus (-ūs), sonitus (-ūs).*
clang, v. *strepēre, (re)sonare.*
clank, subst. *crepitus (-ūs), strepitus (-ūs).*
clank, v. *crepare, crepitare.*
clap, subst.: of hands, *plausus (-ūs)*; of thunder, *tonitrus (-ūs).*
clap, v. *(manibus) plaudēre.*
clash, subst.: = collision, *concursus (-ūs)*; = loud noise, *crepitus (-ūs), strepitus (-ūs).*
clash, v. *concrepare*; = disagree, *inter se (re)pugnare, dissidēre, discrepare.*
clasp, subst.: = fastener, *fibula*; see also embrace, grasp.
class, *genus (-eris), classis, ordo.*
classical, from the Roman point of view, *Graecus.*
classify, *in genera describēre.*
clatter, subst. *crepitus (-ūs), strepitus (-ūs).*
clatter, v. *crepare, strepēre.*
clause, *pars, membrum, caput.*
claw, *unguis.*
clay, *argilla.*
clean, adj. *purus, mundus.*
clean, v. *purgare.*
cleanliness, *munditia, mundities.*
clear, adj. *clarus*; of weather, *serenus, lucidus*; of style, *lucidus*; = evident, intelligible, *planus, manifestus*; it is —, *apparet, liquet.* Adv. *clare, plane, manifeste, lucide.*
clear, v. *expedire, purgare*; to — up a matter, *expedire, explicare.*
clearness, *claritas*; of weather, *serenitas.*
cleave: = split, *(dif)findēre, scindēre*; = stick, *(ad)haerēre.*
cleaver, *culter.*
cleft, *rima.*
clemency, *clementia, mansuetudo.*
clement, *clemens, mansuetus, indulgens, lenis.*
clench: to — the fist, *digitos comprimēre.*

clerk, *scriba.*
clever, *sollers, callidus, astutus;* adv. *sollerter, callide, astute.*
cleverness, *sollertia, calliditas.*
client, *cliens, consultor.*
cliff, *scopulus, cautes.*
climate, *caelum.*
climax, *gradatio.*
climb, subst. *ascensus (-ūs).*
climb, v. *scandĕre, ascendĕre, eniti.*
cling, *(ad)haerēre, amplecti.*
clip, *tondēre, praecīdĕre, resecare.*
cloak, subst. *amiculum, pallium;* for journeys, *lacerna;* a soldier's —, *sagum.*
cloak, v. *dissimulare, tegĕre.*
clod, *glaeba.*
clog, v. *impedire.*
cloister, *porticus (-ūs).*
close, subst., = end, *finis, exitus.*
close, adj.: = reserved, *taciturnus, tectus;* = niggardly, *parcus;* = near, *propinquus, vicinus, finitimus;* = closely packed, *densus, confertus, artus;* adv. *arte, dense.*
close, adv. *prope, iuxta.*
close, v.: transit., = shut, *claudĕre, occludĕre;* = finish, *finire;* intransit., = be shut, *claudi;* = come to an end, *finiri.*
closeness, = nearness, *propinquitas, vicinitas.*
closet, *cubiculum.*
clot, subst., of blood, *sanguis concretus.*
clot, v. *concrescĕre.*
cloth, *textum, textile.*
clothe, v. *vestire, amicire.*
clothes, clothing, *vestis, vestimenta (-orum).*
cloud, subst. *nubes, nimbus.*
cloud, v. *obscurare.*
cloudless, *serenus.*
cloudy, *nubilus.*
clownish, *rusticus, agrestis.*
cloy, *satiare, saturare.*
club, subst.: = cudgel, *clava, fustis;* = association, *circulus, sodalitas.*
clubfooted, *scaurus.*
clue, *glomus (-eris), filum;* = indication, *indicium.*
clump, *globus.*
clumsiness, *inscitia.*
clumsy, *inhabilis, ineptus, inscitus;* adv. *inepte, inscite.*
cluster, = bunch, *racemus, uva.*
clutch, *comprehendĕre, adripĕre.*
coach; see carriage.
coachman, *raedarius, auriga.*
coagulate, v. *coire, concrescĕre.*
coal, *carbo;* a live —, *pruna.*
coalesce, *coalescĕre, coire.*
coalition, *coniunctio, consociatio.*
coarse, *crassus;* of behaviour, etc., *incultus, inurbanus.* Adv. *crasse; inculte.*
coarseness, *crassitudo; mores inculti.*
coast, subst. *litus (-oris), ora;* on the —, adj., *maritimus.*
coast, v. *oram legĕre, praetervehi.*
coat, *toga, tunica;* = hide, *vellus (-eris), pellis.*
coax, *blandiri, permulcēre.*
cobble, *(re)sarcire.*

cobbler, *sutor.*
cock, *gallus (gallinaceus).*
code, *leges.*
coerce, *coercēre, cohibēre, cogĕre.*
coercion, *coercitio, vis.*
coffer, *cista, arca.*
coffin, *arca, capulus.*
cog, of a wheel, *dens.*
cogency, *pondus (-eris), vis.*
cogent, *firmus, validus, gravis.*
cogitate, *cogitare.*
cognizance, *cognitio.*
cognizant, *conscius.*
coheir, *coheres.*
cohere, *cohaerēre.*
coherent, *cohaerens, contextus, congruens.*
cohort, *cohors.*
coin, *nummus.*
coin, v. transit. *cudĕre, signare.*
coinage, *res nummaria.*
coincide, *congruĕre, eodem tempore fieri.*
coincidence, = chance; q.v.
Colchester, *Camulodunum.*
cold, subst. *frigus (-oris), algor;* in the head, *gravedo.*
cold, *frigidus, gelidus:* to be —, *frigēre, algēre;* adv. *frigide, gelide.*
collapse, v. *conlabi, concidĕre, corruĕre.*
collar, subst. *monile, torques.*
collate, v. transit. *conferre.*
collation: = comparison, *conlatio;* = meal, *cena.*
colleague, *conlega.*
collect, v.: transit. *conligĕre, congerĕre;* to — money, etc., *exigĕre;* intransit., *convenire, coire.*
collection, *conlatio, congeries.*
college, *conlegium, societas, sodalitas.*
collide, *confligĕre.*
collision, *concursus (-ūs), concursio.*
collocation, *conlocatio.*
colloquial; — speech, *sermo humilis.*
colloquy, *conloquium.*
collusion, *conlusio, praevaricatio.*
Cologne, *Colonia Agrippina.*
colonel, *tribunus militum, praefectus.*
colonist, *colonus.*
colonnade, *porticus (-ūs).*
colony, *colonia.*
colossal, *vastus, ingens.*
colour, subst. *color;* = paint, *pigmentum.*
colour, v. *colorare, tingĕre, inficĕre;* intransit., see blush.
colt, *eculeus.*
column: = pillar, *columna;* milit., *agmen.*
comb, *pecten;* of a cock, *crista.*
comb, v. *(de)pectĕre.*
combat, subst. *pugna, certamen.*
combat, v.: see fight.
combination *(con)iunctio, societas.*
combine, v. transit. *(con)iungĕre, consociare.*
come, *venire, pervenire, advenire, accedĕre;* to — about, *fieri;* to — back, *redire;* to — together, *convenire;* to — upon, *invenire.*
comedy, *comoedia.*
comeliness, *venustas, decor, pulchritudo.*
comely, *bellus, venustus, pulcher.*
comet, *cometes (-ae).*

comfort, subst.; = consolation, *solatium, consolatio*; —s, *commoda (-orum)*.
comfort, v. (*con*)*solari, adlevare*.
comfortable, *commodus*.
comforter, *consolator*.
comic, comical: = of comedy, *comicus*; = ridiculous, *ridiculus, faeetus*; adv. *ridicule, facete*.
coming, subst. *adventus (-ūs)*.
command, subst.; = right to give orders, *imperium*; supreme —, *summa imperii*; = an order given, *imperium, iussum, mandatum*; a — of the senate, *decretum*.
command, v. (*hominem*) *iubēre*, (*homini*) *imperare*; of places, = dominate, *imminēre, despectare*.
commander, *dux, imperator, praefectus*.
commemorate, *celebrare*.
commemoration, *celebratio*.
commence, *incipēre*; see begin.
commend: = commit, entrust, *commendare, committēre, credēre*; = praise, *laudare, commendare, probare*.
commendable, *laudabilis*.
commendation, *commendatio, laus*.
commendatory, *commendaticius*.
comment, subst. *dictum*.
comment, v. *sententiam dicēre, censēre*.
commentator, *interpres, explanator*.
commerce, *commercium, negotia (-orum), mercatura*.
commiserate, (*com*)*miserari*; see pity.
commissariat, *res frumentaria, commeatus (-ūs)*.
commission, subst. = allotted task, *mandatum*; = position of trust, *munus (-eris)*.
commission, v. *mandare*.
commit: = entrust, *mandare, commendare, committēre, credēre*; = do, perpetrate, *facēre, committēre, patrare*; = oblige, engage, *obligare, obstringēre*.
committee, *consilium*.
commodious, *commodus, opportunus, aptus*; adv. *commode, opportune, apte*.
commodity, *res, merx*.
common, subst. *ager publicus*.
common, adj.: = belonging to several or all, *communis*; = belonging to people or state, *publicus*; = commonplace, ordinary, *vulgaris, quotidianus*; the — people, *plebs*. Adv., = usually, *fere, ferme, plerumque*.
commonplace, subst. *locus communis*.
commonwealth, *respublica, civitas*.
commotion, *tumultus (-ūs), motus (-ūs)*.
commune, *conloqui*.
communicate, *communicare*; see false share, tell.
communication, *communicatio*.
communicative, *loquax*.
communion, *commercium, societas*.
community, = state, society, *civitas, respublica*.
commute; see exchange.
compact, subst. *pactio, pactum, conventus (-ūs)*.
compact, adj. *densus, crassus, confertus*; adv. *confertim*.
companion, *comes, socius, sodalis*.
companionable, *adfabilis, facilis*.
company, *societas*; milit., *manipulus*.

comparable, *comparabilis*.
comparative, *comparativus*.
compare, *comparare, componēre, conferre*.
comparison, *comparatio, conlatio*; in — with, *prae, ad*.
compass, subst.: = extent, *ambitus (-ūs), circuitus (-ūs)*; a pair of —es, *circinus*.
compass, v.; see encompass, accomplish.
compassion, *misericordia*.
compassionate, *misericors*.
compatible, *congruens, conveniens*.
compatriot, *civis*.
compel, *cogēre, compellēre, adigēre*.
compendious, *brevis*.
compensate; to — for, *compensare, rependēre*.
compensation, *compensatio*.
compete, *contendēre, certare*.
competent: see able: to be —, *competēre*.
competition, *contentio, certamen, certatio*.
competitor, *competitor*.
compile, *componēre*.
complacent, *qui sibi placet*.
complain, (*con*)*queri*.
complaint, *questus (-ūs), querimonia, querela*; = illness, *morbus*.
complaisance, *obsequium, obsequentia, indulgentia*.
complaisant, *indulgens, facilis, obsequens*.
complement, *complementum*.
complete, adj. *absolutus, perfectus, iustus*; adv. *omnino, prorsus*.
complete, v. *complēre, explēre, absolvēre, conficēre*.
completion, *confectio, absolutio, finis*.
complex, *multiplex*.
complexion, *color*.
compliance, *obsequium*.
complicate, *impedire*.
complicated, *involutus, impeditus*.
complication, *implicatio*.
compliment, *laus*; to pay —s, *laudare*.
complimentary, *honorificus*.
comply, v. *obsequi*, (*con*)*cedēre, morem gerēre*.
components, *partes (-ium)*.
compose: = make up, constitute, *componēre, efficēre*; of literature, *componēre, scribēre*.
composed, = calm, *tranquillus*.
composer, *scriptor*.
composition: the act, *compositio*; literary, *scriptio, scriptura*; the product, *scriptum*.
composure, *tranquillitas, aequus, animus*.
compound, adj. *compositus, multiplex*.
compound, v. *miscēre, confundēre*.
comprehend: = contain, *continēre, complecti*; = understand, (*mente*) *comprehendēre, complecti, intellegēre*.
comprehension, *comprehensio, intellegentia*.
comprehensive, *late patens*.
compress, *comprimēre, condensare*.
compression, of style, *compressio*.
compromise, v.: = to settle, *componēre*,

compromittĕre; = to embarrass, *impedīre*.

compulsion, *vis, necessitas*; under —, *coactus -a -um*.

compunction, *paenitentia*.

compute, *computāre*.

comrade, *socius, comes, sodalis*.

comradeship, *sodalitas, contubernium*.

concave, *(con)cavus*.

conceal, *celāre, occulĕre, occultāre, abdĕre*.

concede, *(con)cedĕre, permittĕre*.

conceit; render by *sibi placēre*.

conceive: physically, *concipĕre*; mentally, *concipĕre, intellegĕre, comprehendĕre*.

concentrate: = bring together, *conligĕre, contrahĕre*; to — on, = attend to, *(animum) attendĕre*.

conception: physical, *conceptio, conceptus (-ūs)*; mental, *notio, opinio*.

concern, subst.: = affair, *res, negotium*; = anxiety, *cura, anxietas, sollicitudo*.

concern, v. *pertinēre, attinēre*; it —s, *interest, refert*.

concerning, = about, *de*.

conciliate, *conciliāre*.

conciliation, *conciliatio*.

conciliatory, *pacificus, blandus*.

concise, *brevis, pressus, adstrictus*; adv. *adstricte, breviter*.

conciseness, *brevitas*.

conclave; see assembly.

conclude: = finish, *finire, conficĕre*; = draw a conclusion, *concludĕre, conligĕre*.

conclusion, *finis, conclusio*.

conclusive, *gravis, certus*.

concoct, *miscēre*; fig., *fingĕre, excogitare, conflare*.

concoction, *potus (-ūs)*.

concord, *concordia, consensus (-ūs)*.

concordant, *concors*.

concourse, *concursus (-ūs), concursio*.

concrete, = solid, *solidus*.

concur, *consentire, congruĕre*.

concurrence, *consensio, consensus (-ūs)*.

concurrently, *una, simul*.

condemn, *damnare, condemnare*.

condemnation, *damnatio, condemnatio*.

condense, v. transit., *densare, spissare*; intransit., *concrescĕre*.

condensed, *densus, spissus, concretus*; of style, *pressus, densus*.

condescend, *se submittĕre, descendĕre*.

condescending, *comis, facilis*.

condescension, *comitas, facilitas*.

condign, = due, *debitus, meritus*.

condiment, *condimentum*.

condition: = state, *condicio, status (-ūs)*; = stipulation, *condicio, pactum, lex*.

conditioned, adj. *adfectus*.

condole, *casum (hominis) dolēre*.

conduce, *conducĕre (ad rem)*.

conducive, *utilis*.

conduct, subst.: = behaviour, *vita, mores (-um, plur.)*; = management, *administratio*.

conduct, v.: = lead, *(de)ducĕre*; = manage, *gerĕre, administrare*.

conductor, *dux*.

conduit, *canalis*.

cone, *conus, meta*.

confederacy, *foedus (-eris, n.), societas*.

confederates, *socii, foederati*.

confer: = give, *conferre, tribuĕre*; = talk, *conloqui, consultare*.

conference, *conloquium*.

confess, *fateri, confiteri*.

confession, *confessio*.

confidant, *conscius (f. conscia)*.

confide: = entrust, *committĕre, mandare, credĕre*; to — in, *(con)fidere*.

confidence, *fides, fiducia, confidentia*.

confident, *(con)fidens*; adv. *(con)fidenter*.

confidential; see secret.

confiding, adj. *credulus*.

confine, subst. *finis, terminus, confinium*.

confine, v. *includĕre, coercēre, cohibēre*.

confined, adj. *artus*.

confinement, *inclusio*; = imprisonment, *custodia*.

confirm, *(con)firmare*; = ratify, *sancire, ratum facĕre*.

confiscate, *publicare*.

confiscation, *publicatio*.

conflagration, *incendium, ignis*.

conflict, subst. *certamen, pugna*.

conflict, v.: = fight, *pugnare, certare, contendĕre*; = differ, *dissentire, discrepare, repugnare*.

confluence, *confluens* or plur. *confluentes*.

conform, *obsequi, obtemperare*.

conformable, *accommodatus, congruens*.

conformation, *conformatio, forma, figura*.

conformity, *convenientia*; in — with, *ex, secundum*.

confound; = confuse, *confundĕre*; = astonish, *obstupefacĕre*; = frustrate, *frustrari*.

confront, v. *obviam ire, se opponĕre*.

confuse, *confundĕre, (per)miscēre, (per)turbare*.

confused, *confusus, perplexus*; adv. *confuse, perplexe*.

confusion, *confusio, perturbatio*.

confute, *refellĕre, redarguĕre, confutare*.

congeal: transit. *congelare*; intransit. *concrescĕre*.

congenial, *gratus, concors*.

congratulate, *gratulari*.

congratulation, *gratulatio*.

congregate, *congregari, convenire, confluĕre*.

congregation, *conventus (-ūs), coetus (-ūs)*.

congress, *conventus (-ūs), concilium*.

conjecture, subst. *coniectura, opinio*.

conjecture, v. *augurari, conicĕre, coniectare*.

conjugal, adj. *coniugalis*.

conjugate, gram., *declinare*.

conjugation, gram., *declinatio*.

conjure, v.: transit., = entreat, *obtestari, obsecrare*; to — up, *(mortuorum) animas elicĕre*; intransit., = perform tricks, *praestigiis uti*.

conjurer, *magus, praestigiator*.

connect, *adligare, (con)iungĕre, connectĕre*.

connexion, *coniunctio*; between persons, *societas, necessitudo*; by marriage, *adfinitas*.

connive, *connivēre,* (*rem*) *dissimulare.*

connivance, *indulgentia.*

connoisseur, *iudex, existimator.*

conquer, (*de*)*vincĕre, superare.*

conqueror, *victor.*

conquest, *victoria.*

consanguinity, *consanguinitas.*

conscience, *conscientia.*

conscientious, *religiosus, sanctus;* adv. *religiose, sancte.*

conscientiousness, *religio, sanctitas, fides.*

conscious, = aware, *gnarus, conscius;* adv., render by adj. *prudens.*

consciousness, *sensus* (-ūs).

conscript: see recruit.

conscription, *delectus* (-ūs).

consecrate, *consecrare, dedicare.*

consecrated, *sacer.*

consecration, *consecratio, dedicatio.*

consecutive, *continens, continuus;* adv. *continenter.*

consent, subst. *consensus* (-ūs).

consent, v. *velle.*

consequence: = result, *exitus* (-ūs), *eventus* (-ūs); in — of, *ex, propter;* = importance, *momentum, auctoritas.*

consequently, *itaque, ergo, igitur.*

conserve, (*con*)*servare;* of fruit, *condire.*

conservative, polit., *qui nihil in republica immutari vult.*

consider: = think about, *considerare, expendĕre, delibare, contemplari;* = take into account, *respicĕre;* to — that, *arbitrari, ducĕre;* = to regard as, *ducĕre, habĕre, existimare.*

considerable, *magnus, gravis;* adv. *aliquantum.*

considerate, *humanus, officiosus, benignus.*

considerateness, *humanitas, benignitas.*

consideration: = thought, *consideratio, deliberatio, contemplatio;* = proper regard, *ratio, respectus* (-ūs).

consign, *committĕre, credĕre, mandare.*

consist, *consistĕre, constare.*

consistent: = with, *consentaneus, congruens;* = unchanging, *constans;* adv. *constanter.*

consolation, *solatium, consolatio.*

console, (*con*)*solari.*

consoler, *consolator.*

consonant, subst., gram., *consonans.*

consonant, adj. *consentaneus, congruens.*

consort, subst. *comes, socius;* = husband or wife, *coniunx.*

consort, v.; to — with, *familiariter uti.*

conspicuous, *conspicuus, clarus, insignis;* adv. *clare.*

conspiracy, *coniuratio.*

conspirator, *coniuratus.*

conspire, *coniurare, conspirare.*

constable, *lictor.*

constancy, *constantia, fides, fidelitas.*

constant, *constans, firmus;* = incessant, *continuus, perpetuus;* = faithful, *fidelis, fidus.* Adv. *constanter; semper, perpetuo.*

constellation, *sidus* (-eris, n.), *signum.*

consternation, *pavor, terror.*

constitute; = to make up, *componĕre, efficĕre;* = to establish, *statuĕre, constituĕre, designare;* = to appoint, *creare, facĕre.*

constitution, *constitutio, habitus* (-ūs); of a state, *civitatis status* (ūs).

constitutional: = natural, *innatus, insitus;* = legal, *legitimus.* Adv. *naturā; legitime, e republica.*

constrain, *cogĕre, compellĕre.*

constraint, *vis.*

construct, *facĕre, fabricari.*

construction: as an act, *fabricatio, aedificatio;* = form, plan, *structura, figura, forma;* = interpretation, *interpretatio;* to put a good — on, *rem in bonam partem accipĕre.*

construe, *interpretari, accipĕre.*

consul, *consul;* ex-consul, *vir consularis.*

consulship, *consulatus* (-ūs).

consult, *consultare, deliberare;* to — a person, *hominem consulĕre.*

consume, *consumĕre, conficĕre, absumĕre.*

consummate, adj. *summus, absolutus, perfectus;* adv. *summe, absolute, perfecte.*

consummation, *absolutio, perfectio.*

contact, (*con*)*tactus* (-ūs).

contagion, *contagio.*

contain, *capĕre, habĕre, continēre.*

contaminate, *contaminare, inquinare, polluĕre.*

contamination, *macula, labes.*

contemplate, *contemplari, intuēri.*

contemplation, *contemplatio.*

contemporary, *aequalis.*

contempt, *contemptus* (-ūs), *fastidium.*

contemptible, *contemptus, turpis.*

contend: = to struggle, *contendĕre,* (*de*)*certare;* = to maintain, *contendĕre, confirmare, adfirmare.*

content, subst. *animus contentus.*

content, adj. *contentus.*

content, v. *satisfacĕre* (with dat.); to — oneself with saying, *satis habēre dicĕre.*

contentedly, *aequo animo;* or use adj. *contentus.*

contentious, *pugnax.*

conterminous, *confinis.*

contest, subst. *certatio, certamen, contentio.*

contest, v. *contendĕre.*

context, *argumentum.*

contiguity, *vicinitas, propinquitas.*

contiguous, *confinis, continens.*

continence, *continentia, temperantia.*

continent, subst. *continens.*

continent, adj. *continens, castus;* adv. *continenter, caste.*

contingency, *casus* (-ūs).

contingent, subst. *auxilia* (-orum).

contingent, adj. *fortuitus, forte oblatus.*

continual, *continuus, perpetuus, adsiduus;* adv. *continenter, adsidue, perpetuo.*

continuance, continuation, *perpetuitas, adsiduitas, diuturnitas.*

continue, v.: transit. *extendĕre, producĕre, continuare;* intransit., = to persevere, *pergĕre, perseverare;* = to last, *durare,* (*per*)*manēre.*

continuity, *continuatio, perpetuitas.*

contort, *depravare, distorquēre.*

contortion, *distortio, depravatio.*

contour, *forma, figura.*

contract, subst. *pactum, conductio, locatio, redemptio.*

contract, v.: = draw in, *contrahĕre, adducĕre;* = incur, *contrahĕre;* to — for, *locare, conducĕre,* or *redimĕre;* intransit., = become smaller, *se contrahĕre, minui.*

contracted, *contractus, angustus, brevis.*

contraction, *contractio.*

contractor, *conductor, redemptor.*

contradict, *obloqui, contradicĕre;* fig., *repugnare, discrepare.*

contradictory, *contrarius, repugnans, diversus.*

contrary, subst.: on the —, *contra;* in answers, *immo.*

contrary, adj. *adversus, contrarius.*

contrary to, *contra, praeter,* with acc.

contrast, subst. *diversitas, dissimilitudo.*

contrast, v. transit. *comparare, conferre;* intransit. *discrepare.*

contravene, *violare, frangĕre.*

contribute, v.: = give, *contribuĕre, conferre;* = help, *prodesse, adiuvare.*

contrite, adj.; see penitent.

contrivance, = contriving, *inventio, excogitatio;* = thing contrived, *machina.*

contrive, *excogitare, invenire, fingĕre, efficĕre.*

control, subst. *potestas, imperium, dicio;* self —, *moderatio, temperantia.*

control, v. *moderari, temperare, coercĕre.*

controversial, = disputed, *controversus.*

controversy, *controversia, contentio.*

controvert, *refellĕre, refutare.*

contumacious, *contumax, pertinax;* adv. *contumaciter, pertinaciter.*

contumacy, *pertinacia, contumacia.*

contumelious, *contumeliosus, probrosus.*

contumely, *contumelia.*

convalescent, use verb *convalescĕre.*

convene, *convocare.*

convenience, *commoditas, opportunitas.*

convenient, *commodus, opportunus, accommodatus;* adv. *commode, opportune, accommodate.*

convention: = assembly, *conventus (-ūs);* = agreement, *foedus (-eris, n.), pactio;* = custom, *mos.*

conventional, *translaticius, usu receptus.*

converge, *coire, in unum vergĕre.*

conversant, *versatus, exercitatus, peritus.*

conversation, *sermo, conloquium.*

converse, v. *conloqui, sermonem conferre.*

conversion, *(com)mutatio, conversio.*

convert, v. *(com)mutare, convertĕre;* — to an opinion, *ad sententiam traducĕre.*

convex, *convexus.*

convey: see carry; legal, *transcribĕre, abalienare.*

convict, v. *condemnare, convincĕre.*

conviction, *damnatio;* = belief, *opinio, sententia.*

convince, *persuadĕre.*

convivial, *hilaris.*

conviviality, *hilaritas.*

convoke, *convocare.*

convoy, subst. *praesidium.*

convoy, v. *deducĕre, comitari.*

convulse, *agitare, percutĕre. (com)movēre.*

convulsion, *motus (-ūs), turba;* medical, *convulsio.*

cook, subst. *coquus.*

cook, v. *coquĕre.*

cool, subst. *frigus (-oris, n.).*

cool, adj. *frigidus;* of temper, etc., *lentus* (= phlegmatic), *impavidus* (= undismayed), *impudens* (= impudent). Adv. *frigide; lente.*

cool, v.: transit., *refrigerare;* intransit., *refrigerari, defervescĕre.*

co-operate, *una agĕre;* to — with, *adiuvare.*

co-operation, *opera, auxilium.*

cope, v. *resistĕre, certare;* able to —, *par.*

coping, *fastigium.*

copious, *copiosus, abundans, largus;* adv. *copiose, abundanter, large.*

copiousness, *copia, abundantia.*

copper, subst. *aes.*

copper, adj. *a(h)enus.*

coppice, copse, *silva.*

copy, subst. *exemplum, exemplar.*

copy, v. *imitari;* to — out, *transcribĕre, describĕre.*

cord, *restis, funis.*

cordial, *benignus, comis;* adv. *benigne, comiter.*

cordiality, *benignitas, comitas.*

core, *nucleus, granum.*

cork, subst. *cortex.*

corn, *frumentum;* the price of —, *annona;* — field, *seges.*

corner, *angulus.*

cornet, *cornu, buccina.*

corporal, subst. *decurio.*

corporal, corporeal, adj. *corporeus,* or genit. of *corpus.*

corporation, *municipium, conlegium.*

corps, *manus (-ūs).*

corpse, *cadaver.*

corpulent, *obesus, pinguis.*

correct, adj.; of conduct, *honestus, rectus;* of style, *emendatus, purus;* = true, *verus.* Adv. *recte, honeste; pure; vere.*

correct, v. *corrigĕre, emendare;* see also punish.

correction, *correctio, emendatio;* see also punishment.

correspond, v. *respondēre, congruĕre;* letter, *litteras dare et accipĕre.*

correspondence: = agreement, *congruentia, convenientia;* = letters, *litterae, epistulae.*

corresponding, *par.*

corroborate, *confirmare, comprobare.*

corroboration, *confirmatio.*

corrode, *rodĕre.*

corrupt, adj. *corruptus, impurus, pravus;* adv. *corrupte, impure, prave.*

corrupt, v. *corrumpĕre, depravare, vitiare.*

corrupter, *corruptor.*

corruptible, = venal, *venalis.*

corruption, *corruptio, depravatio, corruptela.*

corsair, *pirata.*

corslet, *thorax, lorica.*

cortege, *comitatus (-ūs).*

cosmetic, *fucus.*

and, *et; -que* (enclitic); *atque, ac;* — so, *itaque;* — yet, *tamen;* — not, *et non, neque, nec.*

anecdote, *fabula, fabella.*

anew, *denuo, ab integro.*

anger, subst. *ira, iracundia, indignatio.*

anger, v. *lacessĕre, inritare.*

angle, *angulus.*

angle, v. *piscari.*

angler, *piscator.*

angry, adj. *iratus, iracundus;* to be (or become) angry, *irasci;* adv. *iracunde.*

anguish, *cruciatus (-ūs), dolor, angor.*

angular, *angulatus.*

animadvert, *animadvertĕre.*

animal, subst. *animal, animans;* = a beast, *bestia, pecus (-udis,* domestic); *belua* (large), *fera* (wild).

animal, adj. *animalis;* or genit. of *animal, corpus,* etc.

animate, v. *animare;* fig., *excitare, incitare.*

animate, adj. *animalis, animatus.*

animated, *animatus, animans, animalis;* = lively, *vegetus, alacer.*

animation, *alacritas, vigor.*

animosity, *odium, invidia.*

ankle, ankle-bone, *talus.*

annals, *annales (-ium,* plur.).

annex, v.: = add, *(ad)iungĕre, addĕre;* = conquer, *sibi subicĕre.*

annihilate, *delēre, exstinguĕre.*

annihilation, *exstinctio, excidium.*

anniversary, *festus dies anniversarius.*

annotate, *adnotare.*

annotation, *adnotatio.*

announce, *(re)nuntiare, praedicare.*

annoy, *lacessĕre, inritare, vexare.*

annoyance, *molestia, vexatio.*

annual, *annuus, anniversarius;* adv. *quotannis.*

annuity, *annua pecunia.*

annul, *tollĕre, delēre, abrogare, abolēre.*

anoint, *(in)unguĕre.*

anointing, subst. *unctio.*

anon, *brevi (tempore), mox.*

anonymous, *sine nomine.*

another, pron. and adj. *alius; alter* (= a second); they fear one —, *alius alium timet, inter se timent.*

answer, subst. *responsum;* to a charge, *defensio, excusatio.*

answer, v. *respondēre;* to a charge, se *defendĕre, excusare;* of an oracle, *responsum dare;* to — for, *(rem) praestare.*

answerable: to be — to a person, *homini rationem reddĕre.*

ant, *formica.*

antagonist, *adversarius.*

antagonistic, *contrarius, adversus, infensus.*

antecedent, adj. *antecedens, prior.*

antecedents, subst. *antecedentia (-ium).*

antechamber, *vestibulum, atriolum.*

antelope; see deer.

anterior, *antecedens, prior.*

anthem, *cantus (-ūs).*

anticipate: = to act first, forestall, *occupare, praevertĕre, antevertĕre;* = to expect, *exspectare.*

anticipation: see anticipate; = expectation, *exspectatio, spes.*

antics, *ludi, ioca.*

antidote, *remedium.*

antipathy: of things, *(rerum) discordia, repugnantia;* of persons, *odium.*

antiquary, antiquarian, *rerum antiquarum studiosus.*

antiquated, *obsoletus, priscus.*

antique, *antiquus.*

antiquity, *antiquitas, vetustas.*

antithesis: rhet. *contentio;* = the opposite, *contrarium.*

antler, *cornu.*

anvil, *incus (-udis).*

anxiety, *anxietas, cura, sollicitudo.*

anxious, *anxius, sollicitus, trepidus;* adv. *anxie, sollicite.*

any, anyone: with negative, or in questions, *ullus* (adj.) *quisquam* (substantival); after *si, nisi,* or *ne,* use *qui, qua, quod* (adj.), *quis* (subst.); — you like, — you please, *quivis, quilibet.*

anywhere, *usquam; ubivis* (= anywhere you please); *quoquam* (= to any place).

apace, *celeriter.*

apart, *seorsum;* or use compound verbs with *dis-* and *se-.*

apartment; see room.

apathetic, *hebes, lentus.*

apathy, *stupor, lentitudo.*

ape, *simia, simius.*

ape, v. *imitari.*

Apennines, *Apenninus.*

aperture; see opening.

apex, *cacumen, apex.*

aphorism, *sententia, dictum, elogium.*

apiece, use distrib. num.

apologise, *excusare.*

apology: = defence, *defensio;* = excuse, *excusatio.*

apophthegm, *elogium, sententia, dictum.*

apostrophize; see address.

apothecary, *medicus.*

appal, *(ex)terrēre;* see frighten.

apparatus, *apparatus (-ūs).*

apparel, *vestis, vestimentum.*

apparent: = evident, *manifestus, apertus;* to be —, *apparēre;* = not real, *fictus, simulatus;* adv. *ut videtur.*

apparition: = appearing, *adventus(-ūs);* = spectre, *simulacrum, species.*

appeal, subst.: legal, *appellatio, provocatio;* = entreaty, *obsecratio, preces.*

appeal, v.: legal, to a magistrate, *(hominem) appellare;* to the people, *ad populum provocare;* appeal to, = entreat, *obtestari, obsecrare;* appeal to, = please, *placēre.*

appealing, *supplex.*

appear: = become visible, be evident, *apparere, conspici;* to appear in public, *in publicum prodire;* —, = be present, put in an appearance, *comparēre, adesse;* to —, = seem, *videri.*

appearance: = arrival, *adventus (-ūs);* or use verb; = looks, *species, facies, habitus (-ūs);* = semblance, *species.*

appease, *placēre;* of hunger etc., *sedare.*

appeasement, *placatio.*

appellant; see appeal.

append, *addĕre, adiungĕre.*

appendage, *appendix, accessio.*

cost, subst. *pretium, sumptus (-ūs);*
— of living, *annona.*
cost, v. *(con)stare, venire.*
costly, *carus, pretiosus.*
costume, *vestitus (-ūs), habitus (-ūs).*
cot, *lectulus.*
cottage, *casa, tugurium.*
cottager, *rusticus.*
couch, subst. *lectus, lectulus, cubile.*
couch, v. *cubare, latēre, delitescĕre.*
cough, subst. *tussis.*
cough, v. *tussire.*
council, *concilium;* a — of war,
consilium, praetorium.
councillor, *senator, decurio.*
counsel, = advice, *consilium, auctoritas.*
counsel, v.; see advise.
count: = to number, *(e)numerare, per-*
censēre, computare; = to consider,
habēre, ducĕre; to — upon, *confidĕre.*
countenance, subst.: = face, *vultus*
(-ūs), os; = favour, *favor.*
countenance, v.: = approve, *appro-*
bare; = allow, *permittĕre.*
counter, subst.: for counting, *calculus;*
in a shop, *mensa.*
counter, adv.: — to, *contra;* to run —
to, *adversari.*
counteract, *resistĕre.*
counter-balance, *(ex)aequare, com-*
pensare.
counterfeit, adj. *falsus.*
counterfeit, v. *simulare.*
counterpane, *lodix.*
countless, *innumerabilis, innumerus.*
country: opp. to town, *rus:* in the —,
ruri; = native land, *patria;* = region,
terra, regio.
country-house, *villa.*
countryman, *(homo) rusticus.*
country-town, *municipium, oppidum.*
couple, subst. *par, bini -ae -a.*
couple, v. transit. *(con)iungĕre, copulare.*
courage, *fortudo, virtus, animus.*
courageous, *fortis, strenuus, animosus;*
adv. *fortiter, strenue.*
courier, *nuntius, tabellarius.*
course, *cursus (-ūs);* — of life, *vitae*
curriculum; a — of action, *ratio;* of
—, *scilicet, sane;* a — at dinner,
ferculum.
court, subst.: = enclosed space, *area;*
a royal —, *aula, regia;* a — of justice,
forum, basilica.
court, v. transit., *petĕre, colĕre, captare.*
courteous, *comis, urbanus;* adv. *comiter,*
urbane.
courtesy, *urbanitas, comitas.*
courtier, *aulicus.*
cousin, *(con)sobrinus, patruelis.*
covenant, subst. *pactio, pactum, con-*
ventio.
covenant, v. *pacisci.*
cover, subst.: = lid, *operimentum;* =
shelter, *perfugium.*
cover, v.: to — up, *(con)tegĕre, operire,*
velare; = to protect, *protegĕre, de-*
fendĕre.
covering, *tegmen.*
covert, subst., = thicket, *dumetum.*
covert, adj.: see secret.
covet, *adpetĕre, concupiscĕre.*

covetous, *avarus, avidus;* adv. *avare,*
avide.
covetousness, *avaritia, aviditas.*
cow, subst. *vacca.*
cow, v. *domare.*
coward, *homo ignavus* or *timidus.*
cowardice, *ignavia, timiditas.*
cowardly, *ignavus, timidus.*
cowl, *cucullus.*
coy, *verecundus.*
crab, *cancer.*
crabbed: in temper, *acerbus, morosus;*
of style, *implicatus, impeditus.*
crack, subst.: = noise, *crepitus (-ūs),*
fragor; = fissure, *rima.*
crack, v.: transit., *frangĕre, findĕre,*
rumpĕre; intransit., = break open,
dissilire, dehiscĕre; = make a noise,
crepare.
cradle, *cunae (-arum), cunabula*
(-orum).
craft: = cunning, *dolus, astutia;* =
skill, trade, *ars, artificium;* = boat,
cymba, scapha.
craftsman, *artifex, opifex.*
crafty, *astutus, callidus, dolosus;* adv.
astute, callide, dolose.
crag, *scopulus, rupes.*
cram, *farcire, refercire, stipare.*
cramp; see confine.
crane: the bird, *grus;* the machine,
trochlea, tolleno.
crank, of a machine, *uncus.*
cranny, *rima.*
crash, subst. *fragor, strepitus (-ūs).*
crash, v. *strepĕre.*
crater, *crater.*
crave; see beg, need.
craving, *desiderium.*
crawl, *repĕre, serpĕre.*
crazy: = decrepit, *decrepitus, imbecil-*
lus; = deranged, *cerritus.*
creak, v. *stridĕre, crepĕre.*
creaking, subst. *stridor, crepitus (-ūs).*
crease, v. *rugare.*
crease, subst. *ruga.*
create, *creare, gignĕre, generare, facĕre.*
creator, *creator, fabricator, auctor.*
creature, *animal.*
credibility, *fides, auctoritas.*
credible, *credibilis.*
credit, subst. *fides.*
credit, v.: = to believe, *credĕre;* to — a
thing (to a person), *rem acceptam*
(homini) referre.
creditable, *honestus, honorificus;* adv.
honeste.
creditor, *creditor.*
credulity, *credulitas.*
credulous, *credulus.*
creek, *sinus (-ūs), aestuarium.*
creep, see crawl.
crest, *crista, iuba.*
crested, *cristatus, iubatus.*
crestfallen, *demissus.*
crevice; see crack.
crew: on a ship, *nautae (-arum);* in
gen., *grex.*
crib, *praesepe.*
crime, *scelus (-eris), delictum, facinus*
(-oris).
criminal, *scelestus, sceleratus, nefarius;*
adv. *nefarie.*

crimson, coccineus.
cringe, adulari.
cringing, abiectus.
cripple, debilitare, frangĕre, infringĕre.
crippled, claudus, mancus, debilis.
crisis, discrimen.
crisp: = curled, crispus; = brittle, fragilis.
criterion, norma, obrussa.
critic, iudex, criticus, existimator.
critical: = discriminating, elegans, subtilis; = of a crisis, anceps, dubius.
criticism, iudicium.
criticize; = to judge, iudicare; = to find fault with, reprehendĕre, culpare.
croak, v. crocire, queri.
crockery, fictilia (-ium).
crocodile, crocodilus.
crocus, crocus.
crone, vetula, anus (-ūs), anicula.
crook, a shepherd's, pedum.
crooked, pravus; adv. prave.
crookedness, pravitas.
crop, subst.: of corn, etc., messis, fruges (-um); of birds, ingluvies.
crop, v.: = to browse on, (at)tondĕre; = to cut short, praecīdĕre, amputare.
cross, subst. crux.
cross, adj.: = transverse, transversus, obliquus; = annoyed, difficilis, morosus.
cross, v.: = to go across, transire, transgredi; = to oppose, obsistĕre, adversari; to — out, delēre.
cross-examine, interrogare.
crossing, subst. transitus (-ūs).
crouch, se demittĕre.
crow, subst. cornix.
crow, v. canĕre.
crowd, subst. turba, vulgus, multitudo.
crowd, v.: transit., stipare, cogĕre; intransit., concurrĕre, congregari.
crown, subst.: = garland, corona; a king's diadema (-atis); fig., = sovereignty, regnum; the — of the head, vertex.
crown, v. coronare, diadema (regi) imponĕre.
crucifixion, crucis supplicium.
crucify, cruci adfigĕre.
crude: = raw, unripe, crudus; = rough, informis, incultus, rudis; adv. inculte.
cruel, crudelis, saevus, atrox; adv. crudeliter, atrociter.
cruelty, crudelitas, saevitia.
cruise, v. (per)vagari, circumvectari, navigare.
crumb, mica.
crumble: transit., comminuĕre, conterĕre; intransit., render by pass.
crumple, (con)rugare.
crush, v. opprimĕre, contundĕre, conterĕre; fig., adfligĕre.
crust, crusta.
crutch, baculum.
cry, subst. clamor, vociferatio; of distress, ploratus (-ūs).
crystal: subst. crystallus; adj. crystallinus.
cub, catulus.
cube, tessera, cubus.
cuckoo, cuculus.

cucumber, cucumis.
cud: to chew the cud, ruminare, remandĕre.
cudgel, subst. baculum, fustis.
cue, = hint, signum, indicium.
cuff, subst.: = blow, alapa, colaphus; = sleeve, manica extrema.
cuirass, thorax, lorica.
culmination, fastigium.
culpable, culpandus.
culprit; see criminal.
cultivate, (ex)colĕre, exercēre.
cultivation, culture, cultus (-ūs), cultura; = education, etc., humanitas, litterae (-arum).
cultivator, cultor.
cumber, impedire, (prae)gravare, onerare.
cumbrous, gravis, incommodus.
cunning, subst. calliditas, astutia, dolus.
cunning, adj. callidus, astutus, dolosus; adv. callide, astute.
cup, poculum, scyphus, calix.
cup-bearer, minister, servus.
cupboard, armarium.
cupidity, cupiditas, avaritia.
curb, subst. frenum.
curb, v. frenare, coercēre, cohibēre.
curdle, v.: transit., coagulare; intransit., concrescĕre.
cure, subst. medicina, sanatio.
cure, v. sanare, medēri.
curiosity, noscendi studium.
curious: = inquisitive, curiosus; = strange, insolitus, novus, mirus.
curl, v. transit. crispare.
curling-irons, calamister.
curly, crispus.
currency, nummi (-orum).
current, subst.: in a river, flumen; at sea, aestus (-ūs).
current, adj.: = this, hic; = common, usitatus, vulgaris; adv. vulgo.
curse, subst.: of speech, exsecratio, imprecatio; = malign influence, pernicies, pestis.
curse, v. exsecrari, detestari.
cursory; see brief.
curt, brevis, abruptus; adv. breviter, praecise.
curtail, (co)artare, (im)minuĕre.
curtain, velum, aulaeum.
curve, subst. flexus (-ūs), sinus (-ūs).
curve, v. transit. (in)curvare, (in)flectĕre.
cushion, pulvinus, pulvinar.
custody, custodia, vincula (-orum).
custom, consuetudo, mos, usus (-ūs).
customary, usitatus, quotidianus, solitus.
custom-duty, vectigal, portorium.
customer, emptor.
cut, v. secare, caedĕre; to — corn, etc., (de)metĕre; to — down, succīdĕre; to — off, = destroy, absumĕre, exstinguĕre; to — short, praecīdĕre, amputare.
cutlery, cultri (-orum).
cut-throat, sicarius.
cutting, adj., of speech, mordax.
cuttlefish, sepia, lolligo.
cycle, orbis, circulus.
cylinder, cylindrus.
cymbal, cymbalum.
cynic, cynicus.

cynical, *mordax*.
cypress, *cupressus*.

D

dabble: to — in, *attingĕre*.
daffodil, *narcissus*.
dagger, *pugio, sica*.
daily: adj., *quotidianus*; adv., *quotidie*.
daintiness: = fussiness, *cuppedia*;
= elegance, *venustas*.
dainty: = particular, *fastidiosus*; =
elegant, *elegans, delicatus*.
dale, *vallis*.
dalliance, *lascivia, ludus*.
dally: = to linger, *morari*; = to
sport, *lascivire, ludĕre*.
dam, subst.: = mother, *mater*; =
breakwater, *moles, agger*.
dam, v. *obstruĕre, coercĕre*.
damage, subst. *damnum, incommodum,
noxa*.
damage, v. *laedĕre, nocĕre*.
dame, *matrona, domina*.
damn, *damnare, condemnare*.
damp, subst. *umor*.
damp, adj. *umidus, udus*.
damp, v. *umectare*; fig., *comprimĕre,
restinguĕre*.
damsel, *puella, virgo*.
dance, subst. *saltatio, saltatus (-ūs)*.
dance, v. *saltare*.
dancer, *saltator* (f. *saltatrix*).
dandy, *homo elegans*.
danger, *periculum, discrimen*.
dangerous, *periculosus, infestus, lubricus*;
adv. *periculose*.
dangle, (*de*)*pendĕre*.
dank, *umidus*.
Danube, *Danubius*.
dapper, *nitidus*.
dappled, *maculosus*.
dare, *audēre*; = to challenge, *provocare*.
daring, subst. *audacia*.
daring, adj. *audax*.
dark, subst.; see darkness.
dark, adj. *obscurus*; in colour, *fuscus,
pullus*. Adv. *obscure*.
darken, v. *obscurare, occaecare*.
darkness, *obscuritas, tenebrae (-arum),
caligo*.
darling, subst. *deliciae (-arum)*.
darling, adj. *suavissimus, mellitus*.
darn, *sarcire*.
dart, subst. *telum, iaculum*; to throw
—s, *iaculari*.
dart, v. = to dash, *provolare, se
conicĕre*.
dash, subst., = rush, *impetus (-ūs)*.
dash, v.: transit., to — one thing
against another, *adfligĕre, offendĕre*;
to — down, *proruĕre*; intransit., see
dart.
dastardly, *ignavus*.
date, subst.: the fruit, *palmula*;
= a particular time, *dies, tempus
(-oris)*; out of —, *obsoletus*.
date, v.; to — a letter, *diem in epistula
ascribĕre*.
dative, (*casus*) *dativus*.
daub, (*ob*)*linĕre*, (*per*)*ungĕre*.

daughter, *filia*: — -in-law, *nurus (-ūs)*.
dauntless, *impavidus*.
dawdle, *cessare*.
dawn, *diluculum, prima lux, aurora*
(poet.); it is —, *lucescit*.
day, *dies*: at break of —, *prima luce*;
good —, *salve*(*te*); a period of two
—, *biduum*; on the — before, *pridie*;
on the — after, *postridie*.
day-break; see dawn.
dazzle, *perstringĕre, caecare*.
dead, *mortuus*. Transf., = dull, *languidus*; at — of night, *nocte intempesta*.
deaden, *hebetare, enervare, debilitare*.
deadly, *mortifer, exitialis, perniciosus*.
deaf, *surdus, auribus captus*.
deafen, *exsurdare, obtundĕre*.
deafness, *surditas*.
deal, v.: to — out, *dividĕre, distribuĕre*;
to — with, see treat.
dealer, *mercator, negotiator*; a retail —,
institor, propola.
dealing, *commercium, negotium, usus
(-ūs)*.
dear: = expensive, *carus, pretiosus*;
= beloved, *carus*.
dearly, = at a high price, *care, magno
pretio*.
dearness, *caritas*.
dearth, *inopia, caritas, penuria*.
death, *mors, letum, obitus (-ūs)*.
debar, *excludĕre, prohibēre*.
debase, *corrumpĕre, vitiare*.
debasement, *ignominia*.
debate, subst. *disceptatio, disputatio*.
debate, v. *disceptare, disputare*.
debauch, subst. *comissatio*.
debauch, v. *corrumpĕre, depravare,
vitiare*.
debauchery, *stuprum*.
debenture, *syngrapha*.
debility, *infirmitas, imbecilitas, debilitas*.
debit, v.: to — a thing to a person,
homini rem expensam ferre.
debt, *aes alienum*.
debtor, *debitor, obaeratus*.
decade, *decem anni*.
decamp, *discedĕre*.
decant, *diffundĕre*.
decanter, *lagena*.
decapitate; see behead.
decay, *tabes, defectio virium*.
decay, v. *marcescĕre, senescĕre, tabescĕre*.
decease, *obitus (-ūs)*.
deceit, *fallacia, fraus, dolus*.
deceitful, *fallax, dolosus, fraudulentus*;
adv. *fallaciter, dolose*.
deceive, *decipĕre, fallĕre, circumvenire*.
deceiver, *fraudator*.
December, (*mensis*) *December*.
decency, *honestas, decentia, decorum*.
decent, *honestus, decens, decorus*; adv.
honeste, decenter, decore.
deception, *fraus, dolus, fallacia*.
decide, *statuĕre, constituĕre*.
decided, *certus*; of persons, *constans,
firmus*. Adv. *firme, constanter*; in
answers, *vero, plane, sane*.
decimate, *decimare*.
decipher, *explanare, explicare*.
decision: = settlement, *arbitrium*,

sententia; of character, *constantia, firmitas.*

deck, subst. *pons.*

deck, v.; see adorn; a decked ship, *navis constrata.*

declaim, *pronuntiare, declamare.*

declamation, *declamatio, pronuntiatio.*

declaration, *declaratio, praedicatio*; — of war, *belli denuntiatio.*

declare, *declarare, praedicare, pronuntiare*; to — war, *bellum denuntiare* or *indicĕre.*

declension, *declinatio.*

decline, subst. *deminutio.*

decline, v.: = refuse, *recusare, renuĕre*; to — battle, *pugnam detrectare*; = fail, *deficĕre, (de)minui, decrescĕre.*

declivity, *declivitas, clivus.*

decompose: transit., *(dis)solvĕre, resolvĕre*; intransit., *dissolvi, tabescĕre, putrescĕre.*

decomposition, *(dis)solutio, tabes.*

decorate, *(ex)ornare, decorare.*

decoration, *ornatus (-ūs), ornamentum.*

decorous, *decorus*; adv. *decore.*

decoy, subst. *inlex.*

decoy, v. *inlicĕre, adlicĕre, inescare.*

decrease, subst. *deminutio, imminutio.*

decrease, v.: transit., *(de)minuĕre, imminuĕre, extenuare*; intransit., *decrescĕre, (de)minui.*

decree, subst. *decretum, edictum.*

decree, v. *decernĕre, edicĕre, sancire.*

decrepit, *decrepitus.*

decry, *vituperare, obtrectare.*

dedicate, *(de)dicare, consecrare.*

deduce: = derive, *(de)ducĕre*; = infer, *conligĕre, concludĕre.*

deduct, *detrahĕre, deducĕre.*

deduction: = decrease, *deductio, deminutio*; = inference, render by verb.

deed: = action, *factum, res gesta*; = document, *tabula, syngrapha.*

deep, subst. *altum, pontus.*

deep, adj. *altus, profundus*; of sounds, *gravis*; fig., *summus, gravis.* Adv. *alte, penitus; graviter.*

deer, *cervus* (f. *cerva*).

deface, *deformare, foedare.*

defame, *calumniari, obtrectare.*

default: = error, *culpa, peccatum*; = lack, *defectio, inopia*; legal, to let judgment go by —, *vadimonium deserĕre.*

defeat, subst. *clades.*

defeat, v.: see conquer, baffle.

defect, *labes, vitium, mendum.*

defection, *defectio.*

defective, *imperfectus, mendosus, vitiosus*; adv. *imperfecte, mendose, vitiose.*

defence, *defensio, tutela, praesidium.*

defenceless, *inermis.*

defend, *defendĕre, tuĕri.*

defendant, *reus.*

defensive: — weapons, *arma (-orum).*

defer, *differre, proferre, procrastinare*; to — to, *cedĕre, obsequi.*

deference, *observantia, obsequium.*

deferential, *submissus, observans*; adv. *submisse.*

defiance, *provocatio.*

deficiency, *defectio, inopia.*

deficient; see defective.

defile, subst. *angustiae (-arum), fauces (-ium).*

defile, v. *contaminare, maculare, foedare, polluĕre.*

defilement, *macula, labes.*

define, *(de)finire, circumscribĕre.*

definite, *certus, status, definitus*; adv. *certe, certo, definite.*

definition, *(de)finitio.*

deflect, v.: transit., *deflectĕre*; intransit., *declinare, errare.*

deform, *deformare.*

deformed, *distortus, deformatus.*

deformity, *deformitas, pravitas.*

defraud, *(de)fraudare, circumvenire.*

defray, *suppeditare, solvĕre.*

defunct, *mortuus.*

defy, = challenge, *provocare.*

degenerate, adj. *degener.*

degenerate, v. *degenerare, depravari, peior fieri.*

degradation, *ignominia, dedecus (-oris, n.).*

degrade, = lower in rank, *in ordinem cogĕre* (of soldiers), *ex loco movere*; see also disgrace.

degrading, *indignus, indecorus.*

degree: = amount, *gradus (-ūs)*; by —s, *gradatim, sensim*; = rank, *gradus, ordo.*

deify, *consecrare, in deorum numerum, referre.*

deign, *dignari, velle,* with infin.

deity, *deus, numen.*

dejected, *maestus, perculsus, adflictus*; adv. *maeste.*

dejection, *maestitia, tristitia, maeror.*

delay, subst. *mora, cunctatio.*

delay, v.: transit., *(re)morari, detinĕre*; intransit., *(com)morari, cunctari.*

delegate, subst. *legatus.*

delegate, v.: = to depute, *legare, adlegare*; = to entrust, *committĕre, mandare.*

deleterious, *noxius.*

deliberate, adj. *consideratus, cogitatus*; adv. *considerate, cogitate, consulto.*

deliberate, v. *deliberare, consulĕre, considerare.*

deliberation, *deliberatio, consultatio*; see also slowness.

deliberative, *deliberativus*; a — body, *consilium.*

delicacy: of taste, etc., *elegantia, subtilitas, humanitas*; of health, *suavitas.*

delicate: = tender, *tener, mollis, delicatus*; in taste, etc., *elegans, subtilis, humanus*; in health, *imbecillus, infirmus*; of tasks, *difficilis.* Adv. *molliter, delicate, eleganter, subtiliter.*

delicious, *suavis, dulcis*; adv. *suaviter.*

delight, subst. *delectatio, voluptas.*

delight, v.: transit., *delectare, oblectare*; intransit., *gaudēre, delectari, oblectari.*

delightful, *iucundus, suavis, gratus*; adv. *iucunde, suaviter, grate.*

delightfulness, *suavitas, incunditas.*

delineate, *describĕre, adumbrare.*

delineation, *adumbratio, descriptio.*

delinquency, *delictum, scelus (-eris, n.).*

delirious, *delirus.*

delirium, *delirium, furor.*
deliver: = to hand over, *prodĕre, dedĕre, tradĕre;* = to utter, *pronuntiare;* see also free.
deliverance, *liberatio, salūs (-ūtis).*
deliverer, *liberator, vindex.*
delivery, *actio, elocutio, dictio.*
dell, *vallis.*
delude, *deludĕre.*
deluge, subst. *eluvio.*
deluge, v. transit. *inundare.*
delusion, *fraus, dolus, fallacia; error.*
delusive, *falsus, fallax, vanus.*
delve, *fodĕre.*
demagogue, *plebicola, plebis dux.*
demand, subst. *postulatio, flagitatio.*
demand, v. *poscĕre, postulare, flagitare.*
demarcation: a line of —, *finis, confinium.*
demean, v.; to — oneself; = to behave, *se gerĕre;* = to stoop, *descendĕre, se demittĕre.*
demeanour, *mores (-um), habitus (-ūs).*
demerit, *culpa.*
demigod, *heros.*
demise, subst. *obitus (-ūs).*
democracy, *reipublicae forma popularis.*
democrat, *plebicola, popularium fautor.*
democratic, *popularis.*
demolish, *demoliri, evertĕre.*
demolition, *demolitio, eversio.*
demonstrate, *demonstrare, docĕre, probare.*
demonstration: =proof, *demonstratio;* = display, *ostentatio.*
demoralize: = corrupt, *mores corrumpĕre;* = unnerve, *percellĕre.*
demur: legal, *exceptionem facĕre;* = to hesitate, *dubitare, haesitare.*
demure, *verecundus.*
demurrer, legal, *exceptio.*
den, *specus (-ūs), latibulum.*
denial, *negatio, repudiatio.*
denizen, *incola.*
denominate, *(de)nominare.*
denotation, *significatio.*
denote, *designare, indicare, significare.*
denounce, *increpare, vituperare;* in court, *accusare, nomen deferre.*
dense, *densus, confertus, crassus;* adv. *dense, confertim.*
dent, subst. *nota, vestigium.*
denunciation, *delatio, accusatio.*
deny: = say that . . . not, *negare, infitias ire;* = refuse to give, *negare.*
depart, *abire, discedĕre, digredi.*
department: = office, *munus (-eris, n.), provincia;* = branch, *pars, genus (-eris, n.).*
departure, *abitus (-ūs), discessus (-ūs).*
depend: = to be dependent, *pendĕre (ex), positum* or *situm esse (in);* = to rely on, *(con)fidĕre;* — upon it, *mihi crede.*
dependence, *clientela;* = reliance, *fiducia.*
dependent, subst. *cliens.*
dependent, adj. *obnoxius.*
depict, *depingĕre, describĕre.*
deplorable, *flebilis, miserabilis.*
deplore, *deplorare, deflĕre.*
deploy, *explicare, dilatare.*
deport, = to remove, *deportare.*

deportment, *gestus (-ūs), habitus (-ūs), mores (-um).*
depose, *loco movēre;* as a witness, *testari, testificari.*
deposit, v., *(de)ponĕre.*
deposition: = evidence, *testimonium.*
depravation, *depravatio, corruptio.*
deprave, *depravare, corrumpĕre, vitiare.*
depravity, *pravitas, mores corrupti.*
deprecate, *deprecari.*
depreciate, = disparage, *elevare, obtrectare.*
depreciation, *obtrectatio.*
depredation, *latrocinium.*
depress, *premĕre, deprimĕre;* mentally, *animum frangĕre, infringĕre.*
depression, = low spirits, *tristitia.*
deprivation, *privatio, spoliatio.*
deprive, *privare, (de)spoliare.*
deprived, *orbus.*
depth, *altitudo.*
deputation, *legatio, legati (-orum).*
depute, *(ad)legare.*
deputy, *legatus, vicarius.*
derange, *perturbare, conturbare.*
deranged, *demens, insanus.*
derangement, *perturbatio;* =insanity, *dementia, insania.*
deride, *deridēre, inridēre.*
derision, *inrisio.*
derive, *(de)ducĕre, trahĕre.*
derogate, to — from, *derogare, detrahĕre.*
descend, *descendĕre;* of property, *pervenire (ad hominem).*
descendant, *prognatus;* plur. *posteri.*
descent: = movement, *descensus (-ūs);* = slope, *declivitas;* = origin, *origo, genus (-eris, n.).*
describe, *describĕre, depingĕre, explicare.*
description, *descriptio.*
desecrate, *profanare, polluĕre, violare.*
desecration, *violatio.*
desert, subst. *dignitas, meritum.*
desert, subst., = wilderness, *solitudo, vastitas.*
desert, adj. *desertus, solus, vastus.*
desert, v.: = abandon, *deserĕre, (de)relinquĕre, destituĕre;* = change sides, *transfugĕre.*
deserter, *desertor, transfuga.*
desertion, *(de)relictio; transitio ad hostem.*
deserve, *(com)merēre, (com)merēri; dignum esse (re).*
deservedly, *merito, pro meritis, iure.*
deserving, *(re) dignus.*
design, subst.: = outline, form, *descriptio, forma;* = purpose, *consilium.*
design, v. = delineate, *designare, describere;* = intend, *in animo habēre, cogitare.*
designate, *designare, notare, nominare.*
designedly, *consulto, de industria.*
designing, *callidus, astutus, vafer.*
desirable, *optabilis.*
desire, subst. *appetitio, cupiditas, cupido.*
desire, v. *appetĕre, cupĕre, avēre.*
desirous, *cupidus, studiosus.*
desist, *desistĕre, absistĕre.*
desk, *mensa, scrinium.*

desolate, adj. *vastus, desertus.*

desolate, v. *vastare, populari.*

despair, subst. *desperare, spem abicĕre.*

despatch, *litterae (-arum), epistula.*

despatch, v.: = send, *mittĕre*; = complete, finish, *conficĕre, perficĕre*; = hasten, haste, *maturare*; = kill, *interficĕre, interimĕre.*

desperate: = hopeless, *desperatus, exspes*; = dangerous, *periculosus.* Adv. *desperanter.*

desperation, *desperatio.*

despicable, *contemptus.*

despise, *contemnĕre, despicĕre, spernĕre.*

despite: in — of, *contra.*

despond, v. *desperare, animum demittĕre.*

despondency, *animus demissus.*

despot, *tyrannus, dominus.*

despotic, *imperiosus, superbus*; adv. *superbe, tyrannice.*

despotism, *dominatus (-ūs), tyrannis, regnum.*

dessert, *mensa secunda.*

destine, *destinare, constituĕre.*

destiny, *fatum, sors.*

destitute, *inops, egens, privatus.*

destitution, *inopia, egestas.*

destroy, *perdĕre, delĕre, exstinguĕre.*

destruction, *excidium, exstinctio, pernicies.*

destructive, *perniciosus, exitiosus*; adv. *perniciose.*

desuetude, *desuetudo*; to fall into —, *obsolescĕre.*

desultory, *inconstans, levis.*

detach, *separare, seiungĕre, disiungĕre.*

detachment, of troops, *manus (-ūs).*

details, *singula (-orum).*

detail, v. *(singula) explicare, exsequi.*

detain, *tenēre, retinēre.*

detect, *invenire, deprehendĕre.*

detention, *retentio; custodia.*

deter, *deterrēre, absterrēre.*

deteriorate: transit., *depravare, corrumpĕre*; intransit., *in peius mutari.*

deterioration, *deterior condicio.*

determination: = intention, *institutum, consilium*; of character, *constantia, firmitas animi.*

determine, *statuĕre, constituĕre.*

determined, *certus* = resolute, *constans, firmus.*

detest, *odisse, detestari.*

detestable, *detestabilis.*

detestation, *odium.*

dethrone, *regno expellĕre.*

detract; see derogate, depreciate.

detriment, *damnum, detrimentum.*

detrimental, *perniciosus, iniquus.*

devastate, *(per)vastare, (de)populari.*

devastation, *vastatio; vastitas.*

develop, v. transit., *educare, excolĕre, alĕre*; intransit., *crescĕre, adulescĕre, augeri.*

development, *auctus (-ūs), progressus (-ūs).*

deviate, *declinare, decedĕre, aberrare.*

deviation, *declinatio, digressio.*

device: = emblem, *insigne*; = plan, *machina, dolus.*

devil, *diabolus* (eccl.); go to the —! *abi in malam crucem.*

devious, *devius, vagus.*

devise, *excogitare, fingĕre, machinari*; see also bequeath.

devoid, *vacuus, liber.*

devolve, v.: transit., *deferre, permittĕre, mandare*; intransit., *(per)venire, permitti.*

devote, *devovēre, consecrare, (de)dicare*; fig., *dedĕre, conferre.*

devoted, *deditus, studiosus*; adv. *studiose.*

devotion, = zeal, *studium*; plur., see prayers.

devour, *(de)vorare, consumĕre.*

devouring, *edax.*

devout, *pius (erga deos)*; adv. *pie, sancte.*

dew, *ros.*

dewy, *roscidus.*

dexterity, *dexteritas, sollertia.*

dexterous, *dexter, sollers*; adv. *dext(e)re sollerter.*

diadem, *diadema (-atis, n.).*

diagonal, *diagonalis.*

diagram, *descriptio, forma.*

dial, *solarium.*

dialect, *lingua.*

dialectics, *dialectica.*

dialogue, *dialogus*; in plays, *diverbium*; = conversation, *sermo, conloquium.*

diamond, *adamas.*

diaphragm, *praecordia (-ium, plur.).*

diary, *commentarii diurni.*

dice, die, *talus, tessera*; — box, *fritillus.*

dictate, *dictare*; see also order.

dictator, *dictator.*

dictatorial, *dictatorius, imperiosus.*

dictatorship, *dictatura.*

diction, *dicendi* or *scribendi genus (-eris).*

die, v. *mori, (mortem) obire*; of wind, *cadĕre.*

diet, *victus (-ūs), diaeta.*

differ, *discrepare, differre.*

difference, *varietas, diversitas, dissensio.*

different, *alius, diversus, varius*; adv. *aliter, diverse, varie.*

difficult, *difficilis, arduus, impeditus.*

difficulty, *difficultas*; to be in difficulties, *laborare*; with —, *vix, aegre.*

diffidence, *verecundia, diffidentia.*

diffident, *verecundus, diffidens*; adv. *verecunde, diffidenter.*

diffuse, v.: transit., *diffundĕre*; intransit., *diffundi, permeare.*

diffuse, adj. *verbosus, fusus*; adv. *verbose, fuse.*

dig, *fodĕre*; to — up, *effodĕre.*

digest, v. *concoquĕre.*

digger, *fossor.*

dignified, *gravis, augustus.*

dignify, *honestare, honorare.*

dignity, *dignitas, amplitudo, auctoritas, maiestas.*

digress, *digredi, aberrare.*

digression, *digressio.*

dike: = earthwork, *moles, agger*; = ditch, *fossa.*

dilapidated, *ruinosus.*

dilapidation, *ruina.*

dilate: = to extend, *dilatare*; in speech, *latius dicĕre.*

dilatory, *tardus, lentus.*

dilemma, in logic, *complexio.*
diligence, *diligentia, industria.*
diligent, *diligens, industrius;* adv. *diligenter, industrie.*
dilute, *aquā miscēre, diluēre.*
dim, adj. *obscurus, hebes;* to grow —, *hebescēre.*
dim, v. transit., *obscurare, hebetare.*
diminish, v.: transit., *(im)minuēre, deminuēre;* intransit., render by passive.
din, subst. *strepitus (-ūs).*
din, v.: to — into (a person), *(hominis) aures obtundēre.*
dine, *prandēre, cenare.*
dingy, *fuscus, sordidus.*
dining-room, *triclinium.*
dinner, *prandium* (morning), *cena* (evening).
dint: by — of, *per*, or abl.
dip, v.: transit., *tingēre, mergēre;* intransit., *tingi, mergi, vergēre;* to — into a book, *librum attingēre.*
diploma, *diploma (-atis, n.).*
diplomat, *legatus.*
diplomatic, = clever, *astutus, callidus.*
dire, *dirus, atrox.*
direct, adj. *rectus.* Adv. *recte;* = immediately, *statim, confestim.*
direct, v. *regēre, dirigēre, intendēre; gubernare, administrare;* = to show the way, *viam monstrare;* to — a letter, *epistolam inscrībēre.*
direction: = course, *cursus (-ūs), via, regio;* = management, *cura, regimen, administratio.*
director, *magister, curator, praefectus.*
dirge, *nenia.*
dirt, *caenum, sordes.*
dirty, adj. *spurcus, sordidus, turpis;* to be —, *sordēre.* Adv. *spurce.*
dirty, v. *inquinare, polluēre.*
disable, *enervare, debilitare.*
disadvantage, *incommodum, iniquitas.*
disadvantageous, *incommodus, iniquus;* adv. *incommode, inique.*
disaffected, *(ab)alienatus, aversus.*
disaffection, *animus alienus* or *aversus.*
disagree, *dissentire, dissidēre.*
disagreeable, *ingratus, gravis, molestus;* adv. *ingrate, graviter, moleste.*
disagreement, *discrepantia, dissensio, dissidium.*
disallow, *vetare.*
disappear, *e conspectu abire, evanescēre.*
disappoint, *frustrari, spem fallēre, spe depellēre.*
disapproval, *improbatio.*
disapprove, *improbare, condemnare.*
disarm, *armis exuēre.*
disarrange, *(per)turbare, confundēre.*
disarrangement, *perturbatio.*
disaster, *clades, calamitas.*
disastrous, *calamitosus, funestus;* adv. *calamitose, funeste.*
disavow, *infitiari, abnuēre.*
disavowal, *infitiatio.*
disband, *exauctorare, dimittēre.*
disbelieve, *non credēre.*
disburden, *exonerare liberare, expedire.*
disc, *orbis.*
discern, *(dis)cernēre, dispicēre.*

discerning, *perspicax, sagax, subtilis, prudens.*
discernment, *prudentia, iudicium, subtilitas.*
discharge, subst., *(di)missio;* = shooting, *emissio, coniectio, coniectus (-ūs).*
discharge, v.: from service, *missum facēre, dimittēre;* = to shoot, *(e)mittēre, conicēre;* = to perform, *(per)fungi.*
disciple, *discipulus, auditor.*
discipline, subst. *disciplina;* sense of —, *modestia.*
discipline, v. *instituēre, exercēre.*
disclaim, *repudiare.*
disclose, *detegēre, aperire, patefacēre.*
disclosure, *patefactio, indicium.*
discolour, *decolorare.*
discomfit, *profligare, adfligēre.*
discomfiture, *clades.*
discomfort, *incommodum.*
disconcert, *percellēre, perturbare.*
disconsolate, *maestus.*
discontent, *molestia, taedium.*
discontinue, *interrumpēre, intermittēre, omittēre.*
discord, = disagreement, *dissensio, dissidium, discordia.*
discordant: in music, *dissonus, absonus, = disagreeing, discors, discrepans.*
discount, subst. *deductio, decessio.*
discountenance, *improbare, condemnare.*
discourage, *animum frangēre, infringēre;* to — from, *deterrēre, dissuadēre.*
discourse, subst., = conversation, *sermo, conloquium;* = set speech, *oratio, contio.*
discourse, v.: = to converse, *confabulari, conloqui;* = to make a speech, *orationem habēre, contionari.*
discourteous, *inurbanus, inlepidus;* adv. *inurbane, inlepide.*
discourtesy, *inurbanitas.*
discover, *invenire, reperire, cognoscēre;* see also disclose.
discoverer, *inventor.*
discovery, *inventio, investigatio;* = thing discovered, *inventum.*
discredit, subst., = disgrace, *dedecus (-oris, n.), ignominia.*
discreditable, *inhonestus, turpis.*
discreet, *prudens, cautus;* adv. *prudenter, caute.*
discretion, *prudentia, iudicium.*
discriminate, *diiudicare, discernēre, distinguēre.*
discrimination, *distinctio, discrimen.*
discursive, *varius, vagus.*
discuss, *disceptare, disputare, disserēre.*
discussion, *disceptatio, disputatio.*
disdain, subst. *fastidium, contemptio.*
disdain, v. *spernēre, fastidire, aspernari.*
disdainful, *fastidiosus.*
disease, *morbus.*
diseased, *aeger, aegrotus.*
disembark, v.: transit., *exponēre;* intransit., *egredi.*
disembarkation, *egressus (-ūs).*
disengage, *solvēre, liberare.*
disengaged, *otiosus, vacuus.*
disentangle, *expedire, explicare.*
disfavour, *invidia, offensa.*

disfigure, *deformare.*

disfranchise, *civitatem adimĕre, suffragio privare.*

disgrace, *dedecus* (-oris, n.), *infamia, ignominia.*

disgrace, v. *dedecorare, dehonestare.*

disgraceful, *turpis, inhonestus, flagitiosus*; adv. *turpiter, inhoneste, flagitiose.*

disguise, *vestis mutata, persona* (= mask); fig., *simulatio.*

disguise, v. *aliena veste occultare*; fig., *dissimulare.*

disgust, subst. *fastidium, taedium, satietas.*

disgust, v. *fastidium* (or *taedium*) *movēre.*

disgusting, *foedus, molestus*; adv. *foede, moleste.*

dish, subst. *patina, lanx.*

dish, v.: to — up, *adponĕre.*

dishearten, *animum frangĕre.*

dishonest, *malus, improbus*; adv. *male, improbe.*

dishonesty, *improbitas, fraus.*

dishonour: see disgrace.

dishonourable, *inhonestus.*

disinclination, *declinatio, animus aversus.*

disinclined, *aversus*; to be —, *nolle.*

disinherit, *exheredare.*

disinherited, *exheres.*

disintegrate, v. transit. *dissolvĕre.*

disinter, *effodĕre, eruĕre.*

disinterested, *suae utilitatis immemor.*

disjoin, *disiungĕre, seiungĕre.*

disjointed, *incompositus*; adv. *incomposite.*

disk, *orbis.*

dislike, subst. *odium, fastidium.*

dislike, v. *fastidire, abhorrēre.*

dislocate, *extorquēre, luxare.*

dislodge, (de)*pellĕre, expellĕre, deicĕre.*

disloyal, *improbus, infidus, infidelis.*

disloyalty, *infidelitas.*

dismal, *maestus, miser*; adv. *maeste, misere.*

dismantle, *nudare, diruĕre.*

dismast, *malo privare.*

dismay, *consternatio, pavor, terror.*

dismay, v. *consternare, pavefacĕre,* (per)*terrēre.*

dismember, *discerpĕre.*

dismiss, *dimittĕre, ablegare.*

dismissal, *dimissio.*

dismount, *ex equo desilire.*

disobedience, *contumacia.*

disobey, *non parēre.*

disoblige, *offendĕre.*

disorder, subst. *confusio, turba.*

disorder, v. (per)*turbare, miscēre, confundĕre.*

disordered, =sick, *aeger.*

disorderly: =confused, *confusus,* (per)*turbatus, perplexus, incompositus*; = insubordinate, *turbidus, turbulentus.*

disown, *repudiare, infitiari.*

disparage, *extenuare, elevare, obtrectare.*

disparagement, *obtrectatio.*

disparity, *dissimilitudo, differentia.*

dispassionate, *placidus, placatus, tranquillus.*

dispatch: see despatch.

dispel, *discutĕre, dissipare, dispellĕre.*

dispense, *distribuĕre, dividĕre*; to — with, (di)*mittĕre.*

dispersal, *dissipatio, diffugium.*

disperse, v.: transit., *dissipare, dispergĕre, dispellĕre*; intransit., *dilabi, diffugĕre.*

displace, *loco* (suo) *movēre.*

display, subst. *ostentatio.*

display, v. *ostentare, ostendĕre.*

displease, *displicēre, offendĕre.*

displeasure, *offensio, offensa.*

disposal, *arbitrium*: at the — of, *penes* (with acc.).

dispose: = to arrange, *ordinare, constituĕre*; = to incline, *inclinare*; see also sell, use, and rid.

disposed, *inclinatus, propensus, pronus.*

disposition: = arrangement, *conlocatio, ordinatio*; = character, *ingenium, indoles, natura.*

dispossess, *possessione depellĕre.*

disproportion, *dissimilitudo.*

disproportionate, *impar.*

disprove, *refellĕre, redarguĕre.*

dispute, subst. *controversia, altercatio, rixa.*

dispute, v. *ambigĕre, disputare*; contendĕre, *rixari.*

disqualify, = hinder, *impedire.*

disquieted, *inquietus, sollicitus.*

disregard, subst., *neglegentia, incuria.*

disregard, v. *neglegĕre, omittĕre.*

disreputable, *infamis.*

disrepute, *infamia.*

disrespect, *insolentia.*

disrespectful, *insolens.*

dissatisfaction, *molestia, offensa, offensio.*

dissatisfied: I am —, *paenitet me* (with genit.).

dissatisfy, *displicēre.*

dissect, *persecare.*

dissemble, *dissimulare.*

dissembler, *dissimulator.*

disseminate, *spargĕre, dispergĕre*

dissension, *discordia.*

dissent, subst. *dissensio.*

dissent, v. *dissentire, dissidēre.*

dissimilar, *dissimilis, dispar.*

dissimulation, *dissimulatio.*

dissipate, *dissipare.*

dissipated, *dissolutus, luxuriosus.*

dissipation, *luxuria, licentia.*

dissolute; see dissipated.

dissolution, *dissolutio.*

dissolve, v.: transit., *liquefacĕre,* (dis)*solvĕre*; intransit., *liquescĕre,* (dis)*solvi.*

dissonant, *dissonus, absonus.*

dissuade, *dissuadēre, dehortari, deterrēre.*

dissuasion, *dissuasio.*

distaff, *colus.* f.

distance, subst. *spatium, intervallum*; at a —, *procul, longe*; from a —, *eminus.*

distance, v. *superare.*

distant, *remotus, longinquus*; to be —, *distare, abesse.*

distaste, *fastidium.*

distasteful, *molestus, ingratus.*

distemper, *morbus.*

distend, *distendĕre.*

distil, v. *stillare.*

distinct: = separate, *separatus, disiunctus;* = clear, *distinctus, clarus, perspicuus.* Adv. *distincte, clare, perspicue.*

distinction, *discrimen, distinctio;* honourable —, *honor, dignitas;* a mark of —, *insigne.*

distinctive, *proprius;* adv. *proprie.*

distinguish, *distinguěre, secerněre, diiudicare;* see also honour.

distinguished, *insignis (prae)clarus.*

distort, *detorquěre, distorquěre.*

distorted, *pravus.*

distract: = to make inattentive, *distrahěre, distiněre;* = to agitate, *(per)turbare.*

distracted, distraught, *(per)turbatus, amens, vecors.*

distraction: see agitation, frenzy.

distrain, v. *bona venděre.*

distress, subst. *miseria, aerumna, labor.*

distress, v. *angěre, vexare, sollicitare, adflictare.*

distressed, *sollicitus, anxius, adflictus;* to be —, *laborare.*

distressing, *gravis, acerbus.*

distribute, *distribuěre, dividěre.*

distribution, *distributio.*

district, *ager, regio, terra.*

distrust, subst. *diffidentia.*

distrust, v. *diffiděre.*

distrustful, *suspiciosus, diffidens.*

disturb, *(per)turbare, commověre.*

disturbance, *turba, turbatio, tumultus (-ūs).*

disturber, *turbator.*

disunion, *dissensio, dissidium, discordia.*

disunite, *seiungěre, secerněre, disiungěre.*

disused, *desuetus.*

ditch, *fossa.*

ditcher, *fossor.*

ditty, *nenia, carmen.*

diurnal, *diurnus.*

dive, *urinari, se (de)mergěre.*

diver, *urinator.*

diverge, *deceděre, disceděre;* of roads, *in diversas partes ferre.*

divergence, *declinatio.*

diverse, *alius, diversus, dissimilis;* adv. *aliter, diverse, dissimiliter.*

diversify, *variare, distinguěre.*

diversion: = turning aside, *derivatio, deductio;* = distracting, *avocatio;* = recreation, *oblectatio, oblectamentum.*

diversity, *diversitas, discrepantia.*

divert: = turn aside, *avertěre;* = amuse, *delectare, oblectare;* see also distract.

divest, *nudare, spoliare, privare;* to — oneself of a thing, *exuěre.*

divide: transit., *dividěre, partiri, distribuěre;* intransit., *dividi, disceděre.*

divination, *divinatio, vaticinatio, auguratio.*

divine, adj. *divinus, caelestis;* adv. *divine, divinitus.*

divine, v. *divinare, vaticinari, augurari, coniectare.*

diviner, *haruspex, hariolus.*

divinity, *divinitas, numen.*

divisible, *dividuus.*

    vision, *partitio, divisio;* = part, *pars;* milit., *legio.*

divorce, subst. *divortium, repudium.*

divorce, v. *divortium facěre.*

divulge, *(di)vulgare, (in medium) proferre, aperire, patefacěre.*

dizziness, *vertigo.*

dizzy, *vertiginosus.*

do, *facěre, efficěre, agěre, gerěre:* how do you —? *quid agis?* he is done for, *de eo actum est.*

docile, *docilis.*

docility, *docilitas.*

dock, subst.: for ships, *navale;* in the —, *reus.*

dock, v.; see curtail.

doctor, subst. *medicus.*

doctor, v. *curare.*

doctrine, *dogma (-atis, n.), disciplina.*

document, *litterae (-arum), instrumentum.*

dodge, v. *eluděre.*

doe, *cerva.*

doer, *actor, auctor.*

doff, *exuěre.*

dog, subst. *canis;* of a —, *caninus.*

dog, v. *indagare, investigare.*

dogged, *pervicax, pertinax;* adv. *pertinaciter.*

dogma, *dogma, placitum.*

doing; see action.

dole, subst. *stips, diaria (-orum), sportula.*

dole, v.; see distribute.

doleful, *tristis, flebilis, maestus;* adv. *flebiliter, maeste.*

dolphin, *delphinus.*

dolt, *stipes, caudex, baro.*

domain: = kingdom, *regnum;* = estate, *possessio.*

dome, *tholus.*

domestic, subst.; see servant.

domestic, adj.; = of the home, *domesticus, familiaris, privatus;* = not foreign, *intestinus, domesticus.*

domesticate; see tame.

domicile, *domicilium, domus.*

dominate, *dominari, regnare.*

domination, *dominatio, dominatus (-ūs).*

domineer, *dominari.*

domineering, *imperiosus, superbus.*

dominion, *potestas, imperium, dicio;* of a king, *regnum.*

Don, *Tanais.*

donation, *donum.*

doom, subst. *fatum, sors.*

doom, v. *condemnare, damnare.*

door, *ostium, ianua;* back —, *posticum;* out of —s, *foras, foris.*

doorkeeper, *ianitor (f. ianitrix).*

doorpost, *postis.*

dormant: to lie —, *iacěre.*

dormitory, *cubiculum.*

dormouse, *glis.*

dose, subst. *potio, medicamentum.*

dose, v. *medicamentum dare.*

dot, *punctum.*

dotage, *senium.*

dotard, *senex, delirus.*

dote, v.: to — upon, *deamare, deperire.*

double, adj. *duplex* (=twofold), *duplus* (=twice as much), *geminus* (=twin).

double, v. *duplicare;* = to sail round. *flectěre, circumvehi.*

doublet, *tunica.*

double-tongued, *bilinguis.*
doubly, *bis, dupliciter.*
doubt, subst. *dubitatio, scrupulus.*
doubt, v. *dubitare, animi pendēre.*
doubtful, adj. *dubius, incertus;* adv. *dubie, ambigue, dubitanter* (= doubt-ingly).
doubtless, *sine dubio.*
dough, *farina.*
doughty, *fortis, strenuus.*
dove, *columba.*
Dover, *Portus Dubris.*
dower, dowry, *dos.*
down, subst.: of feathers, etc., *pluma, lanugo;* = hill, *collis, clivus.*
down: prep., — from, *de;* — stream, *secundo flumine;* adv. rendered by compound verb with *de* —; see down-wards.
downcast, *demissus, tristis, maestus.*
downfall, (*oc*)*casus* (-*ūs*), *ruina.*
downpour, *imber.*
downright, adj.: = complete, *merus, summus;* = straight-forward, *simplex.*
downright, adv. *prorsus, omnino.*
downtrodden, *adflictus.*
downwards, *desuper, deorsum.*
downy, *plumeus.*
doze, v. *dormitare.*
dozen, *duodecim.*
drab, *ravus;* see brown.
drag, v. *trahēre.*
dragon, *draco, serpens.*
drain, subst. *fossa, cloaca.*
drain, v. *siccare,* (*ex*)*haurire.*
drama, *fabula.*
dramatic, *scaenicus.*
draper, *qui pannos vendit.*
draught; of drink, *haustus* (-*ūs*), *potio;* of air, *spiritus* (-*ūs*), *aura.*
draw, v. (1) transit., *trahēre, ducēre;* of fluids, *haurire:* to — a sword, *gladium* (*de*)*stringēre;* to — tight, *adducēre, adstringēre;* = to portray by drawing, *describēre,* (*de*)*pingēre;* = to induce, *movēre;* to — up (a docu-ment), *concipēre;* to — up (troops) *instruēre.* (2) intransit.: to — near, *accedēre, appropinquare;* to — back, *recedēre,* se *recipēre.*
draw-bridge, *pons, ponticulus.*
drawer: of water, *aquarius;* chest of drawers, *armarium.*
drawing, *pictura.*
dray, *carrus, plaustrum.*
dread: see fear.
dream, subst. *somnium;* in a —, *in somno.*
dream, v. *somniare;* to — of, *vidēre in somnis.*
dreamy, *somniculosus.*
dreary, *tristis, miser;* adv. *misere.*
dregs, *faex.*
drench, *madefacēre, perfundēre.*
dress, subst. *vestis, vestitus* (-*ūs*), *ornatus* (-*ūs*).
dress, v. *vestire;* of food, *coquēre;* of wounds, *curare.*
dressed, *vestitus;* — in black, *sordida-tus;* — in white, *albatus.*
dressing, medic., *fomentum.*
drift, subst. = aim, *consilium, ratio.*
drift, v. *ferri, fluitare.*

drill, subst.: the tool, *terebra;* of troops, *exercitatio.*
drill, v.; = to bore, *perforare, terebrare;* = to train, *exercēre, exercitare.*
drink, subst. *potio, potus* (-*ūs*).
drink, v. *bibēre, potare, haurire* (= drink up); to — to a person, *homini propinare.*
drinker, *potor, potator* (habitual).
drinking-bout, *potatio, comissatio.*
drip, *stillare.*
drive, subst. *gestatio.*
drive, v. (1) transit., *agēre, pellēre;* to — out, *expellēre, exturbare;* = to force, *cogēre, compellēre.* (2) intran-sit.: in a carriage, etc., (*in*)*vehi, gestari;* to — at, *petēre.*
drivel: see nonsense.
driver, *raedarius, auriga;* of animals, *agitator.*
drizzle, v. *leniter pluēre.*
droll, *lepidus, ridiculus, facetus;* adv. *lepide, ridicule, facete.*
drone, *fucus.*
droop, v.: transit., *demittēre;* intran-sit., (*de*)*pendēre;* = wither, *langues-cēre, flaccescēre.*
drop, subst. *gutta, stilla.*
drop, v.: transit., *demittēre, deicēre;* intransit., = fall in drops, (*de*)*stillare;* = fall to the ground, *delabi, decidēre.*
dropsy, *hydrops.*
dross, = refuse; q.v.
drought, *siccitas.*
drove, *grex, armentum.*
drover, *pecuarius, armentarius.*
drown, (*in aquam*) *summergēre;* with noise, *obstrepēre.*
drowsy, *somniculosus, semisomnus.*
drudge, subst. *servus, mediastinus.*
drudge, v. *servire.*
drudgery, *opera servilis.*
drug, subst. *medicamentum;* poisonous —, *venenum.*
drum, *tympanum.*
drunk, *ebrius, temulentus.*
drunkenness, *ebrietas;* as habit, *ebriositas, vinolentia.*
dry, adj. *siccus, aridus, sitiens* (= thirsty). Transf., *exilis, ieiunus, aridus.* Adv., of style, *exiliter, ieiune.*
dry, v. transit. *siccare;* to — tears, *abstergēre lacrimas;* intransit., *siccari, arescēre.*
dryness, *siccitas.*
dubious; see doubtful.
duck, subst. *anas.*
duck, v. (*sub*)*mergēre;* to — the head, *caput demittēre.*
dudgeon, *ira, stomachus.*
due, adj. *ius* (*iuris*), *debitum;* —s, *vectigal;* harbour —s, *portorium.*
due, adj. *debitus; meritus, iustus, idoneus.*
duel, *certamen.*
dulcimer, *sambuca.*
dull, adj. *hebes, obtusus, tardus;* = uninteresting, *aridus, frigidus.* Adv. *tarde, frigide.*
dull, v. *hebetare, obscurare, obtundēre.*
dulness, of mind, (*ingenii*) *tarditas, stupor.*
dumb, *mutus;* to become —, *obmutes-cēre.*

dumbfounder, *obstupefacĕre.*
dun, adj. *fucus, suffuscus.*
dunce, *stipes.*
dung, *stercus (-oris), fimus.*
dungeon, *carcer, robur.*
dunghill, *sterquilinium.*
dupe, subst. *homo credulus.*
duplicate; see copy.
duplicity, *allacia, fraus.*
durable, *firmus, stabilis, perpetuus;* adv. *firme, stabiliter.*
duration, *temporis spatium.*
during, *per* with acc.; *in* with abl.; *inter* with acc.
dusk, *crepusculum.*
dusky, *fuscus;* see dark.
dust, subst. *pulvis.*
dust, v. *detergĕre.*
dusty, *pulverulentus.*
dutiful, *pius, officiosus;* adv. *pie, officiose.*
dutifulness, *pietas.*
duty, *officium, munus;* sense of —, *pietas, religio;* —tax, *vectigal.*
dwarf, *nanus, pumilio.*
dwarfish, *pusillus.*
dwell, *habitare, (in)colĕre.*
dweller, *incola.*
dwelling, *domicilium, sedes, domus.*
dwindle, *(de)minui, decrescĕre.*
dye, v. *tingĕre, inficĕre.*
dyer, *infector.*
dynasty; use phrase with *domus.*
dyspepsia, *cruditas.*
dyspeptic, *crudus.*

E

each: of two, *uterque;* of three or more, *unusquisque, quisque, omnis;* — other, *inter se, alius alium.*
eager, *cupidus, studiosus, acer;* adv. *cupide, studiose, acriter.*
eagerness, *cupiditas, studium, ardor.*
eagle, *aquila.*
ear, *auris;* of corn, *spica, arista.*
early, adj. *matutinus* (= in the morning), *novus* (= fresh), *maturus, tempestivus* (= in good time).
early, adv. *mane* (in the morning); *mature, tempestive.*
earn, *merēre* and *merēri.*
earnest, adj. *intentus, gravis, serius;* in —, *serio.* Adv. *intente, impense.*
earnestness, *studium, contentio.*
earnings, *quaestus (-ūs), lucrum.*
earth: = soil, *terra, solum;* = the globe, *terra, orbis (terrarum).*
earthen, *terrenus.*
earthenware; adj., *fictilis;* subst., *fictilia (-ium).*
earthly, *terrestris; humanus.*
earthquake, *terrae motus (-ūs).*
earthwork, *agger.*
ease, subst. = rest, *tranquillitas, quies, otium, pax;* to be at ease, *quiescĕre;* = readiness, *facilitas.*
ease, v. *exonerare, expedire.*
easiness, *facilitas.*
east, subst. *oriens, orientis (solis) partes.*
eastern, easterly, *orientis; ad orientem versus.*

easy, *facilis;* = tranquil, *tranquillus, quietus, otiosus.*
eat, *ĕdĕre, (re)vesci;* to — away, *rodĕre.*
eatable, *esculentus.*
eating-house, *popina.*
eaves-dropper, *auceps.*
ebb, subst. *aestūs decessus (-ūs).*
ebb, v. *recedĕre.*
ebony, *hebenus.*
Ebro, *Hiberus.*
ebullition: use *effervescĕre;* of passions, *impetus (-ūs), aestus (-ūs).*
eccentric, *inusitatus.*
echo, subst. *imago vocis.*
echo, v. *vocem reddĕre, resonare;* see also *imitate.*
eclipse, subst. *defectio, defectus (-ūs).*
eclipse, v. transit. *obscurare.*
economical, *frugi, parcus;* adv. *parce.*
economy: = management, in gen., *rei familiaris administratio;* = frugality, *parsimonia.*
ecstasy: = frenzy, *insania, furor;* = bliss, *elatio voluptaria.*
ecstatic, *fanaticus, furens, insanus.*
eddy, *vertex.*
edge, a cutting —, *acies;* = margin, *margo, ora.*
edible, *esculentus.*
edict, *edictum, decretum, iussum*
edify, *docēre.*
edit, *(librum) ĕdĕre.*
educate, *instituĕre, erudire, educare.*
education, *educatio, disciplina, eruditio.*
eel, *anguilla.*
efface, *delēre, abolēre.*
effect, subst. (1), = consequence, *effectus (-ūs), eventus (-ūs), consecutio.* (2), = influence, *vis, effectus (-ūs);* without —, *frustra;* in —, *revera, reapse.* (3), —s, = property, *res, bona (-orum).*
effect, v. *facĕre, efficĕre, conficĕre.*
effective, effectual, *efficiens, efficax;* adv. *efficienter, efficaciter.*
effeminacy, *mollitia, mollities.*
effeminate, *mollis, effeminatus;* adv. *molliter, effeminate.*
effervesce, *effervescĕre.*
effete, *effetus, obsoletus.*
efficacy, *efficientia, vis.*
effigy, *effigies, imago, simulacrum.*
effort, *opera, labor, conatus (-ūs);* to make an —, *operam dare, contendĕre.*
effrontery, *impudentia, os (impudens).*
effulgence, *splendor, fulgor.*
egg, *ovum.*
egoism, egotism, *sui ostentatio, sui amor.*
egoist, egotist, *qui sibi soli studet.*
egregious, *singularis, praeclarus.*
egress, *egressus (-ūs), exitus (-ūs).*
eight, adj. *octo;* — each, *octoni;* — times, *octies.*
eighteen, *duodeviginti.*
eighteenth, *duodevicesimus.*
eighth, *octavus;* an —, *octava pars.*
eightieth, *octogesimus.*
eighty, *octoginta;* — each, *octogeni;* — times, *octogies.*
either, *alteruter, utervis, uterlibet;* either . . . or, *aut . . . aut, vel. . . . vel.*

ejaculate, *vocem emittĕre.*
ejaculation, *vox.*
eject, *expellĕre, eicĕre, deicĕre.*
ejection, *expulsio, eiectio, deiectio.*
eke, v.: to — out, *rei* (dat.) *parcĕre.*
elaborate, adj. *elaboratus, exquisitus;* adv. *exquisite.*
elaborate, v. *elaborare, expolire.*
elapse, *intercedĕre, praeterire.*
elated, *elatus.*
elation, *animus elatus; gaudium.*
Elbe, *Albis.*
elbow, *cubitum.*
elder, *maior (natu).*
elderly, *aetate provectus.*
elect, adj. *designatus.*
elect, v. *creare, legĕre, eligĕre.*
election, *electio;* as an occasion, *comitia (-orum).*
electioneering, subst. *ambitio.*
elective, *suffragiis creatus.*
elector, *qui ius suffragii habet.*
elegance, *elegantia, venustas.*
elegant, *elegans, venustus, nitidus;* adv. *eleganter, venuste, nitide.*
elegy, *elegia (-orum).*
element: scientific, *elementum;* =part, *membrum; pars;* the —s of a subject, *elementa (-orum), principia (-orum).*
elementary, *primus.*
elephant, *elephantus, elephas.*
elevate, *(at)tollĕre, extollĕre.*
elevated, of places, *editus, altus;* of spirits, *elatus.*
elevation: = raising, *elatio;* of spirits, *elatio, altitudo;* = rising ground, *locus editus* or *superior.*
eleven, *undecim;* — each, *undeni;* — times, *undecies.*
eleventh, *undecimus.*
elicit, *elicĕre, evocare.*
eligible, *opportunus, idoneus, dignus.*
elk, *alces.*
ell, *ulna, cubitum.*
elm, *ulnus.*
elocution, *pronuntiatio.*
elongate; see lengthen.
elope, *clam fugĕre.*
eloquence, *eloquentia, facundia.*
eloquent, *eloquens, facundus;* adv. *facunde, diserte.*
else, adj. *alius.*
else, adv.: = besides, *praeterea;* = otherwise, *aliter, alioqui(n).*
elsewhere, *alibi.*
elucidate; see explain.
elude, *(e)vitare, declinare.*
elusive, *fallax.*
Elysian, *Elysius.*
Elysium, *Elysium.*
emaciate, *attenuare, macerare.*
emaciated, *macer.*
emaciation, *macies.*
emanate, *emanare, effundi.*
emancipate, *liberare;* of slaves, *manumittĕre.*
emancipation, *liberatio;* of slaves, *manumissio.*
emancipator, *liberator.*
embalm, *condire.*
embankment, *agger, moles.*
embark, v.: transit., *imponĕre in navem;* intransit. *conscendĕre (navem).*

embarrass, *(con)turbare, impedire.*
embarrassing, *difficilis.*
embarrassment, *implicatio, conturbatio;* financial —, *angustiae (-arum).*
embassy, *legatio, legati (-orum).*
embellish, *(ex)ornare, decorare.*
embellishment, *decus (-oris, n.), ornamentum.*
embers, *cinis, favilla.*
embezzle, *avertĕre, supprimĕre.*
embezzlement, *peculatus (-ūs), suppressio.*
embezzler, *pecuniae aversor.*
embitter, *exacerbare.*
emblem, *insigne, signum.*
embody: to — troops, *milites conscribĕre;* = to include, *includĕre.*
emboss, *caelare.*
embrace, subst. *amplexus (-ūs), complexus (-ūs).*
embrace, v. *amplecti, amplexari, complecti;* = to contain, *comprehendĕre;* to — an opportunity, *occasionem capĕre;* to — an opinion, *in sententiam transire.*
embrocation, *fomentum.*
embroider, *(acu) pingĕre.*
embroil, *conturbare;* to — in a matter, *re implicare.*
emend, *emendare, corrigĕre.*
emendation, *emendatio.*
emerald, *smaragdus.*
emerge, *emergĕre, exsistĕre.*
emergency, *casus(-ūs), discrimen.*
emigrate, *(e)migrare, demigrare.*
emigration, *(e)migratio.*
eminence: = high ground, *locus editus, tumulus;* = distinction, *praestantia, fastigium.*
eminent, *insignis, (prae)clarus, egregius.* Adv. *egregie, praecipue, imprimis.*
emissary, *legatus, emissarius.*
emit, *(e)mittĕre, iacĕre.*
emolument, *emolumentum, lucrum.*
emotion, *animi motus (-ūs)* or *adfectus (-ūs).*
emperor, *imperator, princeps.*
emphasis, *vis.*
emphatic, *gravis, vehemens;* adv. *graviter, vehementer.*
empire, *imperium, principatus (-ūs).*
employ, *(re) uti; (rem) usurpare, exercĕre, adhibĕre;* of persons, to be —ed, *detineri, versari.*
employment: as an act, *usus (-ūs), usurpatio;* = business, *res, negotium.*
emptiness, *inanitas.*
empty, adj. *inanis, vacuus, vanus, cassus.*
empty, v. *vacuefacĕre, exinanire.*
emulate, *aemulari.*
emulation, *aemulatio.*
emulous, *aemulus;* adv. *certatim.*
enable, *homini rei* (genit.) *facultatem facĕre.*
enact, *(legem) sancire, iubĕre, statuĕre, constituĕre.*
enactment; see law.
enamoured; see love.
encamp, v. *castra ponĕre, considĕre.*
enchant, *(ef)fascinare.* Transf., *capĕre, delectare.*
enchantment; see charm.
enchantress, *venefica.*

encircle, *cingĕre, circumdare.*

enclose, *includĕre, saepire, continĕre.*

enclosure, *saeptum, saepimentum.*

encomium, *laus, laudatio.*

encompass; see encircle.

encounter, subst. *congressus (-ūs), concursio.*

encounter, v. *concurrĕre, congredi, obviam fieri;* = to face unwelcome things, *obire, oppetĕre.*

encourage, *(ad)hortari, confirmare, erigĕre.*

encouragement, *confirmatio, (ad)hortatio.*

encroach, v.: to — on, *occupare, invadĕre.*

encroachment, *iniuria.*

encumber, *onerare, praegravare, impedire.*

encumbrance, *onus (-eris, n.), impedimentum.*

end, subst.: = termination, *finis, exitus (-ūs);* in the —, *tandem, denique;* = aim, object, *finis, consilium, propositum.*

end, v.: transit., *finire, conficĕre, terminare;* intransit., *finem habĕre, desinĕre;* to — well, *bene evenire.*

endanger, *in periculum adducĕre, periclitari.*

endear, *devincire.*

endearments, *blanditiae (-arum, plur.).*

endeavour, subst. *conatus (-ūs), nisus (-ūs).*

endeavour, v. *conari, (e)niti.*

endless, *infinitus, aeternus, perpetuus;* adv. *sine fine, perpetuo.*

endorse; see allow, sanction.

endow: to — a daughter, *dotem filiae dare;* see also give.

endowed, *ornatus, praeditus, instructus.*

endurable, *tolerabilis, patibilis.*

endurance, *patientia, perpessio.*

endure: = to bear, *(per)ferre, sustinēre, pati, perpeti;* = to last, *(per)manēre, durare.*

enemy, *hostis* (public), *inimicus* (personal or private); *adversarius.*

energetic, *acer, strenuus, impiger;* adv. *acriter, strenue, impigre.*

energy, *vis, impetus (-ūs), contentio.*

enervate, *enervare, debilitare, (e)mollire.*

enervation, *debilitatio, languor.*

enforce, *exsequi.*

enfranchise, *in civitatem adscribĕre; civitate donare.*

enfranchisement, *civitas, civitatis donatio.*

engage: = to bind, make liable, *obligare, obstringĕre;* = to promise, undertake, *spondēre, promittĕre, recipĕre;* = to join battle, *confligĕre, congredi.*

engaged: = busy, *occupatus;* — to be married, *sponsus, pactus.*

engagement: = promise, *sponsio, pactum, pactio, promissum;* an — to marry, *pactio nuptialis;* = piece of business, *negotium;* = battle *pugna, proelium.*

engaging, *blandus, suavis.*

engender, *gignĕre, generare.*

engine, *machina, machinatio, machinamentum.*

engineer, *machinator, faber.*

England, *Anglia; Britannia* (= Britain).

English, *Anglus, Anglicus; Britannus, Britannicus.*

engrave, *incidĕre, insculpĕre, scalpĕre.*

engraver, *scalptor.*

engross, = occupy exclusively, *occupare, tenēre.*

engulf, *absorbēre, (de)vorare, (ex)haurire.*

enhance, *augēre, amplificare.*

enhancement, *amplificatio.*

enigma, *aenigma (-atis, n.), ambages (-um).*

enigmatic, *obscurus, ambiguus;* adv. *ambigue, per ambages.*

enjoin; see command.

enjoy, *(re) frui, gaudēre;* = to have, *uti, habēre.*

enjoyment, *gaudium, voluptas.*

enlarge, *amplificare, dilatare, augēre;* to — upon, *pluribus (verbis) disputare.*

enlighten, *inlustrare, inluminare.* Transf., *docēre, erudire.*

enlightenment, *humanitas.*

enlist, v.: transit., of troops, *(con)-scribĕre;* in gen., = win over, *conciliare;* intransit., *nomen dare.*

enliven, *excitare, exhilarare.*

enmity, *inimicitia, odium, simultas.*

ennoble, *nobilium ordini adscribĕre; ornare, honestare.*

ennui, *taedium.*

enormity, *immanitas;* = monstrous action, *scelus (-eris, n.), flagitium.*

enormous, *ingens, immanis;* adv. *praeter modum.*

enough, *sat, satis, adfatim;* more than —, *nimis;* not —, *parum.*

enquire; see ask; to — into, *quaerĕre, inquirĕre, cognoscĕre.*

enquiry, *quaestio, inquisitio, cognitio.*

enrage, *inritare, exasperare.*

enrich, *locupletare, ditare.*

enroll, *(ad)scribĕre;* see enlist.

enshrine, *dedicare, consecrare.*

ensign: = banner, *signum, vexillum;* = banner-bearer, *signifer, aquilifer.*

enslave, *(hominem) in servitutem redigĕre.*

enslaved, *servus.* Transf., *addictus, emancipatus.*

ensnare, *capĕre, inretire, inlicĕre.*

entail, *adferre, inferre;* see cause.

entangle, *impedire, implicare.*

entanglement, *implicatio.*

enter, *intrare, introire, inire, ingredi;* to — upon an undertaking, *ingredi, inire, suscipĕre, incipĕre;* to — public life, *ad rempublicam accedĕre;* to — an alliance, *societatem facĕre.*

enterprise, *inceptum, opus (-eris, n.).*

enterprising, *promptus, acer, audax.*

entertain: = to have, *habēre;* = to amuse, *delectare, oblectare;* = to receive hospitably, *hospitio accipĕre, excipĕre.*

entertaining; see amusing.

entertainment: = hospitality, *hospitium;* = banquet, *epulae (-arum) convivium.*

enthusiasm, *studium, fervor, ardor.*

enthusiastic, *fanaticus, ardens, fervidus;* adv. *ardenter, acriter.*

entice, *adlicĕre, adlectare, inlicĕre.*

enticement, *inlecebrae, esca.*

enticing, *blandus.*

entire, *totus, integer, solidus.* Adv. *omnino, plane, prorsus, penitus.*

entitle: = to name, *appellare, nominare;* = to give a title to, *ius* or *potestatem dare.*

entrails, *intestina (-orum), viscera (-um).*

entrance, subst.: as act, *ingressio, introitus (-ūs);* = place of —, *aditus (-ūs), introitus (-ūs), ostium.*

entrap; see ensnare.

entreat, *precari, rogare, orare, obsecrare.*

entrench, *fossā (com)munire, vallare.*

entrenchment, *vallum, munitio, munimentum.*

entrust, *(con)credĕre, committĕre, mandare, commendare.*

entry; see entrance; in accounts, *nomen.*

entwine, *(in)nectĕre, implicare, redimire.*

enumerate, *(di)numerare, enumerare.*

enunciate, *edicĕre, pronuntiare, enuntiare.*

enunciation, *enuntiatio.*

envelope, subst. *involucrum.*

envelope, v. *involvĕre, obducĕre.*

envenom, *venenare, veneno imbuĕre.*

enviable, *fortunatus, beatus.*

envious, *invidus, lividus.*

environs, render by phrase with *loca* and *circum.*

envoy, *legatus.*

envy, subst. *invidia, livor.*

envy, v. *invidēre.*

ephemeral, *unius diei, caducus, brevis.*

epic, *epicus, heroicus;* an — poem, *epos.*

Epicurean, *Epicureus;* = hedonist, *voluptarius.*

epidemic, *morbus, pestilentia.*

epigram, *epigramma (-atis,* n.).

epigrammatic, *salsus.*

epilepsy, *morbus comitialis.*

epilogue, *epilogus.*

episode, *embolium, excursus (-ūs).*

epistle, *epistula, litterae (-arum).*

epitaph, *titulus, elogium.*

epitome, *epitome, summarium.*

epoch, *tempus (-oris,* n.), *aetas, saeculum.*

equability, *aequus animus, aequabilitas.*

equable, *aequus, aequabilis;* adv. *aequo animo, aequabiliter.*

equal, subst. *par, compar.*

equal, adj. *aequus, aequalis, par, compar;* adv. *aeque, aequaliter, pariter.*

equal, v. *(ad)aequare, aequiparare.*

equality, *aequalitas, aequabilitas.*

equalize, *(ex)aequare, adaequare.*

equanimity, *aequus animus, aequitas animi.*

equestrian, subst. *eques (-itis).*

equestrian, adj. *equester* or *equestris.*

equidistant, to be, *pari intervallo inter se distare.*

equilateral, *aequis lateribus.*

equilibrium, *aequilibrium;* to hold in —, *librare.*

equinox, *aequinoctium.*

equip, *armare, instruĕre, ornare.*

equipment, *arma (-orum), armamenta (-orum), armatura.*

equitable, adj. *aequus, iustus, meritus.*

equity, *aequitas, aequum, iustitia.*

equivalent; see equal.

equivocal, *ambiguus, anceps, dubius.*

equivocate, *tergiversari.*

equivocation, *ambiguitas.*

era, *tempus.*

eradicate, *extirpare, evellĕre, eruĕre.*

erase, *delĕre, inducĕre.*

erasure, *litura.*

ere; see before.

erect, adj. *(e)rectus.*

erect, v. *erigĕre, tollĕre;* = build, *aedificare, exstruĕre.*

erection: as act, *aedificatio, exstructio;* = a building, *aedificium.*

erotic, *amatorius.*

err, *errare, vagari; falli* (= be mistaken); *peccare* or *delinquĕre* (= do wrong).

errand, *mandatum.*

erratic, *vagus, inconstans.*

erroneous, *falsus;* adv. *falso, perperam.*

error, *error, erratum; peccatum* (= sin).

erst, *quondam, olim.*

erudite, *litteratus, doctus, eruditus.*

erudition, *doctrina, eruditio.*

eruption, *eruptio.*

escape, subst. *fuga, effugium.*

escape, v. *(ef)fugĕre, elabi, evadĕre.*

escarpment, *vallum.*

eschew, *vitare;* see avoid.

escort, *comitatus (-ūs);* under a person's —, *homine comitante.*

escort, v. *comitari, deducĕre, prosequi.*

esoteric, *arcanus, occultus.*

especial, *praecipuus;* adv. *praesertim, praecipue, maxime.*

espouse; see betroth and marry.

essay, subst.: = attempt, *conatus (-ūs);* = treatise, *libellus.*

essay, v. *conari.*

essence, *natura, vis.*

essential, *verus, proprius;* adv. *reapse, vere, necessario.*

establish: = set up, *statuĕre, instituĕre;* = make strong, *confirmare, stabilire;* = prove, *probare, vincĕre.*

establishment, *constitutio, confirmatio;* = household, *familia.*

estate: = condition, *status (-ūs), habitus (-ūs), condicio, sors;* = property, *res, fundus, praedium.*

esteem, subst. *opinio, existimatio.*

esteem, v.: = think, *existimare, putare;* = respect, *diligĕre, vereri.*

estimable, *bonus, gravis, probus.*

estimate, subst. *aestimatio;* in gen., = judgment, *iudicium.*

estimate, v., = value, *aestimare, censere.*

estimation; see esteem.

estrange, *(ab)alienare.*

estrangement, *alienatio, discidium.*

estuary, *aestuarium.*

eternal, *aeternus, sempiternus, perpetuus;* adv. *in aeternum, perpetuo.*

eternity, *aeternitas.*

ether, *aether.*

ethereal, *aetherius.*

ethical, *moralis;* or use phrase with *mores.*

ethics, *philosophia moralis*; see ethical.
etiquette, *mos, usus (-ūs)*.
eulogy, *laudatio, laus*.
euphemism; render by phrase, such as *mitiorem in partem vertĕre dicendo*.
euphony, *sonus dulcis*.
evacuate, *vacuefacĕre, (de)relinquĕre*; *loco discedĕre*.
evade, *(ef)fugĕre, subterfugĕre*.
evaporate, *in vaporem vertĕre*.
evasion, *ambages (-um), tergiversatio*.
evasive, *ambiguus*; adv. *ambigue*.
even, adj. *aequus, planus*; of numbers, *par*. Adv. *aequaliter, pariter*.
even, adv. *etiam, vel, adeo*: not —, *ne . . . quidem*; — if, *etsi, etiamsi*.
evening, subst. *vesper (-eris or -eri)*; in the —, *vesperi*.
evening, adj. *vespertinus*; the — star, *Hesperus, Vesper*.
evenness, *aequalitas*; of temper, *aequus animus*.
event: = result, *eventus (-ūs), exitus (-ūs)*; = occurrence, *factum, casus (-ūs)*: at all —s, *certe, saltem*.
eventful, *memorabilis*.
ever, adv.: = always, *semper*; = at any time, *umquam (unquam), quando* (after *num* and *si*); for —, *in aeternum, in perpetuum*.
everlasting; see eternal.
every, *quisque, omnis*: — ŏne, *unus-quisque*; one in — ten, *decimus quisque*; — body, *omnes (-ium), nemo non*; — day, *quotidie*; — thing, *omnia (-ium)*; — where, *ubique, passim*.
evict, *(ex)pellĕre, detrudĕre*.
evidence, legal, *testimonium, indicium*; in gen., *argumentum*.
evident, *manifestus, apertus*; it is —, *apparet, liquet*. Adv. *aperte, manifesto*.
evil, subst. *malum, incommodum*.
evil, adj. *malus, pravus, improbus*.
evil-doer, *maleficus*.
evil-speaking, *maledicus*.
evince, *ostendĕre, probare, praestare*.
evoke, *evocare, elicĕre, excitare*.
evolution: — of soldiers, *decursus (-ūs)*; in nature, *rerum progressio*.
ewe, *ovis femina*; — lamb, *agna*.
ewer, *urceus, hydria, urna*.
exact, *exactus, subtilis, diligens*; adv. *diligenter, accurate, subtiliter*.
exacting, *rapax*.
exaction, *exactio*.
exactitude, *subtilitas, diligentia*.
exaggerate, *augĕre, in maius extollĕre*.
exaggeration, *superlatio, traiectio*.
exalt, *augĕre, amplificare, (ex)tollĕre*.
exaltation: of feeling, *elatio*; in rank, *dignitatis accessio*.
exalted, *altus, (ex)celsus, elatus*.
examination, *investigatio, inquisitio*.
examine, *investigare, inquirĕre*.
example, *exemplum, exemplar, documentum*; for —, *verbi causa, exempli gratia, vel*.
exasperate, *irritare, exasperare*.
exasperation, *ira*.
excavate, *(ex)cavare, effodĕre*.
excavation, *cavum*.

exceed, *excedĕre, egredi*.
excel, *excellĕre, praestare* (with dat.).
excellence, *excellentia, praestantia*.
excellent, *excellens, praestans, egregius, optimus*; adv. *excellenter, egregie, optime*.
except, prep. *praeter, extra*; except you, *te excepto*.
except, v. *excipĕre, eximĕre*.
exception, *exceptio*; all without —, *omnes ad unum*.
exceptional, *rarus*; adv. *praeter modum*.
excess: — in quantity, *nimium*; in conduct, *intemperantia, licentia*.
excessive, *nimius, immodicus*; adv. *nimis, immodice, praeter modum*.
exchange, subst. *permutatio*; of money, *collybus*.
exchange, v. *(per)mutare*.
exchequer, *aerarium, fiscus*.
excitable, *irritabilis, fervidus*.
excite, *excitare, concitare, (com)movĕre, incendĕre*.
excited, *trepidus*.
excitement, *concitatio, commotio*.
exclaim, *(ex)clamare, vociferari*.
exclamation, *exclamatio, vox*.
exclude, *excludĕre, prohibĕre, arcēre*.
exclusive: of persons, *rari aditūs*; of properties, = belonging to one only, *proprius*.
excrescence, *tuber*.
excruciating, *acerbissimus*.
exculpate, *excusare, (ex)purgare*.
exculpation, *purgatio*.
excursion, *iter (-ineris)*.
excuse, subst. *excusatio*.
excuse, v.: = make excuses for, *excusare*; *(ex)purgare*; = pardon, *ignoscĕre, veniam dare*.
execrable; see abominable.
execrate, *exsecrari, detestari, abominari*.
execute: = carry out, *exsequi, persequi efficĕre*; = punish by death, *necare, securi ferire*.
execution: = carrying out, *effectio*; = capital punishment, *supplicium*; = slaughter, in gen., *strages, caedes*.
executioner, *carnifex*.
executive: use phrase with *administrare*.
exegesis, *explanatio, interpretatio*.
exemplary, adj.; see excellent.
exempt, adj. *immunis, liber, solutus*.
exempt, v. *excipĕre, eximĕre, liberare*.
exemption, *immunitas*.
exercise, subst. *exercitatio*; = literary task, *thema (-atis)*.
exercise, v.: = carry on, *exercēre, facĕre, efficĕre*; = work, train, *exercēre*.
exert, v. *contendĕre, intendĕre*; to — oneself, *niti, eniti, conari*.
exertion, *contentio, conatus (-ūs)*.
Exeter, *Isca (Dumnoniorum)*.
exhale, *(ex)halare*.
exhalation, *exhalatio*.
exhaust, *exhaurire*; = wear out, *consumĕre, conficĕre*.
exhausted, *confectus, defessus, fatigatus*.
exhaustion; see fatigue.
exhibit, v. *proponĕre, exhibēre*; see show.

exhibition, *spectaculum, ludi (-orum).*
exhilarate, *(ex)hilarare, hilarem facĕre.*
exhilaration, *hilaritas.*
exhort, *(ad)hortari.*
exigence, *necessitas, angustiae (-arum).*
exile, subst.: = banishment, *exsilium, relegatio;* to be in —, *exsulare;* = person banished, *exsul.*
exile, v. *eicĕre, relegare, (ex)pellĕre.*
exist, *esse, exsistĕre, exstare.*
existence; use *esse.*
exit: = going out, *exitus (-ūs);* = way out, *exitus (-ūs), ostium.*
exonerate, *(culpa) liberare.*
exorbitant, *immodicus;* adv. *immodice.*
exordium, *exordium, prooemium.*
exotic, *peregrinus, externus.*
expand, v. transit. *(ex)pandĕre, extendĕre, laxare.*
expanse, *spatium.*
expatiate, *pluribus (verbis) disputare.*
expatriate; see banish.
expect, *exspectare, sperare.*
expectant, *adrectus, suspensus.*
expectation, *exspectatio, spes.*
expectorate, *exscreare, exspuĕre.*
expediency, *utilitas.*
expedient, subst. *ratio, consilium.*
expedient, adj. *commodus, utilis:* it is —, *expedit.*
expedite, *expedire, maturare.*
expedition: = speed, *celeritas;* milit., *expeditio.*
expeditious, *celer, promptus;* adv. *celeriter, prompte.*
expel, *(ex)pellĕre, eicĕre.*
expend, *expendĕre, impendĕre.*
expense, *impensa, impendium.*
expensive, *sumptuosus, carus, pretiosus;* adv. *sumptuose, pretiose.*
expenditure, of public money, *erogatio;* see also expense.
experience, subst. *rerum usus (-ūs), experientia;* I speak from —, *expertus dico.*
experience, v. *experiri, pati.*
experienced, *(rerum) peritus.*
experiment, *experimentum, periculum.*
expert, *sciens, callidus, peritus.*
expertness, expertise, *calliditas, peritia.*
expiate, *luere, expiare.*
expiation, *expiatio, poena, piaculum.*
expiatory, *piacularis.*
expire, *exspirare;* of time, *exire.*
explain, *exponĕre, explicare, interpretari.*
explanation, *explicatio, interpretatio.*
explicit, *apertus, definitus;* adv. *plane, definite.*
explode: = to discredit (a theory), *explodĕre, refellĕre, confutare;* intransit., = to burst, *dirumpi.*
export, *exportare.*
exportation, *exportatio.*
exports, *merces (quae exportantur).*
expose, *exponĕre;* to danger, etc., *obicĕre, offerre;* = to unmask, *detegĕre.*
exposition, *expositio.*
expound; see explain.
express, (in words), *significare, declarare;* to — oneself, *loqui, dicĕre.*

expression: = thing said, *verbum, sententia, dictum, vox;* of the features, *vultus (-ūs).*
expressive, *significans;* adv. *significanter.*
expressiveness, *vis.*
expulsion, *exactio, expulsio.*
expunge, *delēre, oblitterare.*
expurgate, *(ex)purgare.*
exquisite, *exquisitus, venustus;* adv. *exquisite, venuste.*
extant: to be —, *exstare.*
extempore, *subitus;* to speak —, *ex tempore dicĕre.*
extend, v.; transit., *extendĕre, augēre, amplificare;* intransit., *patēre, extendi.*
extensive, *magnus, amplus, latus;* adv. *late.*
extent, *ambitus (-ūs), spatium;* to this —, *hactenus;* to a certain —, *aliqua ex parte.*
extenuate, *levare, mitigare, minuĕre.*
extenuation, *imminutio.*
exterior, subst. *forma, species.*
exterior, adj.; see external.
exterminate, *ad unum interficĕre; eradicare, exstirpare.*
extermination, *internecio, occidio.*
external, *externus exter(us), exterior;* adv. *extrinsecus.*
extinct, *exstinctus, obsoletus.*
extinction, *exstinctio.*
extinguish, *exstinguĕre, restinguĕre.*
extirpate, *exstirpare, eradicare, excidĕre.*
extol, *laudibus, (ef)ferre, (con)laudare.*
extort, *exprimĕre, extorquēre.*
extortion, *res repetundae.*
extortionate, *rapax, avarus.*
extra, adv. *praeterea.*
extract, v. *extrahĕre, evellĕre, exprimĕre;* from a book, *excerpĕre.*
extraction: as act, *evulsio;* = origin, *origo, genus (-eris, n.).*
extraneous; see external.
extraordinary, *inusitatus, insolitus, novus, mirus.* Adv. *extra ordinem, praeter morem, mire.*
extravagance: in expenditure, *sumptus (-ūs);* in gen., = excess, *intemperantia, immoderatio.*
extravagant: = lavish, *prodigus, sumptuosus;* in gen., = excessive, *nimius, immoderatus, intemperans.* Adv. *prodige, sumptuose; immoderate, intemperanter.*
extreme, subst.; see extremity.
extreme, adj. *extremus, ultimus, summus.* Adv. *summe;* often rendered by superl.
extremity: = top, *cacumen, fastigium;* = farthest part, or extreme degree, render by adj. *extremus.*
extricate, *expedire, (ex)solvĕre.*
extrude, *extrudĕre, eicĕre.*
exuberance, *ubertas, luxuria.*
exuberant, *luxuriosus, laetus;* adv. *uberrime.*
exude, *(ex)sudare, manare.*
exult, *exsultare, gestire, laetari.*
exultant, *laetus.*
exultation, *laetatio, exsultatio.*
eye, subst. *oculus, ocellus.*
eye, v. *adspicĕre, contemplari, intueri.*

eye-ball, *pupula.*
eye-brow, *supercilium.*
eye-lid, *palpebra* (usually plur.)
eyesight, *acies.*
eye-witness, *arbiter.*

F

fable, *fabula (commenticia).*
fabled, fabulous, *fabulosus, fictus, commenticius.*
fabric: built, *aedificium*; woven, *textum, textile*; fig., *compages.*
fabricate, *fabricari, texĕre.*
fabrication: = making, *fabricatio*; = falsehood, *commentum, mendacium.*
fabricator, *auctor.*
face, subst. *facies, vultus (-ūs); os (oris); — to —, coram.*
face, v.: = to be opposite, *(a)spectare*; = to encounter, *obire, obviam ire.*
facetious, *iocosus, facetus*; adv. *iocose, facete.*
facetiousness, *facetiae (-arum).*
facilitate, *faciliorem reddĕre.*
facility, *facilitas.*
facing, *contra, adversus.*
facsimile, *descriptio imagoque.*
fact, *res, factum*; in —, *reapse, sane.*
faction, *factio, pars.*
factious, *factiosus, seditiosus*; adv. *per factionem, seditiose.*
factiousness, *factio, studium partium.*
factitious; see false.
factory, *fabrica, officina.*
faculty, *vis, facultas.*
fade, *pallescĕre.*
faded; see pale.
fading, = transient, *caducus, fluxus.*
fagot, *fascis, sarmenta (-orum,* plur.).
fail, subst.: without —, *certo, omnino.*
fail, v.: = to give out, *deficĕre, deesse*; = not to succeed, *concidĕre, cadĕre*; transit., *deficĕre, deserĕre, destituĕre.*
failing, *peccatum, vitum.*
failure, *defectio.*
fain: I would — do, *velim facĕre, libens faciam.*
faint, adj. *languidus, defessus.*
faint, v. *conlabi, (animo) linqui.*
faint-hearted, *timidus.*
faintness, *languor.*
fair, subst. *nundinae (-arum).*
fair, adj.: = beautiful, *pulcher, venustus, formosus*; of weather, *serenus*; = favourable, *secundus, idoneus*; morally, *aequus, iustus*; = moderately good, *mediocris.* Adv., *aeque, iuste*; *mediocriter.*
fairness: = beauty, *pulchritudo, forma, venustas*; = justice, *iustitia, aequitas.*
fairy, *nympha.*
faith: = fidelity, *fides, fidilitas, pietas*; = belief, *opinio, persuasio, fides*; to have — in, *credĕre, confidĕre.*
faithful, *fidelis, fidus*; adv. *fideliter.*
faithfulness, *fidelitas, fides, constantia.*
faithless, *perfidus*; adv. *perfide.*
faithlessness, *perfidia, infidelitas.*
fall, subst. *casus (-ūs), lapsūs (-us)*; = ruin, *ruina, excidium*; = lessening, *deminutio.*

fall, v. *cadĕre, decidĕre, ruĕre*; to — dead, *cadĕre, concidĕre, occidĕre*; of a city, *expugnari, capi*; to — back, = retreat, *pedem referre*; to — back on, *recurrĕre* or *confugĕre ad*; to — upon, = attack, *invadĕre, incurrĕre*; to — out, = happen, *evenire*; = disagree, *dissentire, dissidēre.*
fallacious, *fallax, falsus*; adv. *fallaciter, falso.*
fallacy, *vitium, captio.*
fallible, *errori obnoxius.*
fallow: the field lies —, *ager cessat*; — ground, *novalis.*
false, *falsus*; *fictus, commenticius* (= made up), *subditus* (=forged), *perfidus* (=treacherous); to play —, *deesse.* Adv. *falso, perperam.*
falsehood, *mendacium, commentum.*
falsify, *vitiare, corrumpĕre.*
falter, *haesitare, haerēre, titubare.*
falteringly, *titubanter.*
fame, *laus, gloria, fama.*
familiar: = well known, *familiaris, notus*; = acquainted, *sciens, gnarus, peritus.* Adv. *familiariter.*
familiarity, *familiaritas, consuetudo.*
family, subst. *familia* (= household); *domus; gens* (= clan); *genus (-eris,* = race, stock); of good —, *nobilis.*
family, adj. *familiaris, domesticus; gentilis; privatus* (opp. to *publicus*).
famine, *fames, cibi inopia.*
famish, *fame enecare, conficĕre.*
famous, *(prae)clarus, inlustris, celeber.*
fan, subst.: for winnowing, *vannus*; for fanning oneself, *flabellum.*
fan, v. *ventilare.*
fanatical, *fanaticus.*
fancied, *opinabilis, opinatus.*
fancy, subst.: as a faculty, *inventio, cogitatio*; = idea, notion, *opinio*; = liking, preference, *libido.*
fancy, v.: = to imagine, *fingĕre*; = to think, *opinari, putare.*
fang, *dens.*
fanged, *dentatus.*
far: in space, *procul, longe*: from — off *eminus*; farther, *longius, ultra*; as — as, *tenus* (prep.), *usque* (adv. = all the way); — and wide, *longe lateque*; in degree, — better, *longe* or *multo melior*; — from it, *minime*; so —, *hactenus.*
farce, *mimus.*
farcical, *mimicus, ridiculus*; adv. *mimice, ridicule.*
fare, subst.: = food, *cibus, victus (-ūs)*; = money for journey, *vectura, naulum.*
fare, v. *se habēre,* with adv.
farewell! *valē! valēte!*; to bid — *valēre iubēre.*
far-fetched, *longe repetitus, arcessitus.*
farm, subst. *fundus, praedium, ager.*
farm, v.: = till, *arare, colĕre*; = hire, *redimĕre, conducĕre*; — out, = let out on contract, *(e)locare.*
farmer, *agricola, colonus*; a — of revenues, *publicanus.*
farming, *agricultura, res rusticae*; = hiring, *redemptio, conductio.*
farthing, *quadrans, teruncius*; I do not care a — for, *haud flocci facio.*

fascinate, *fascinare*; see charm.

fascination, *fascinum.* Transf., *blanditia, dulcedo.*

fashion, subst.: = custom, way, *mos, consuetudo, ritus (-ūs)*; = style of dress, *habitus (-ūs), ornatus (-ūs)*; = what is fashionable, *saeculum*; out of —, *obsoletus.*

fashion, v. *fabricari, (ef)fingĕre.*

fashionable, *elegans*; adv. *eleganter.*

fast, subst. *ieiunium.*

fast, adj.: = quick, *celer, citus, rapidus*; = fixed, firm, *firmus, stabilis*; to make —, *firmare, stabilire.*

fast, adv.: = quickly, *celeriter, rapide*; = firmly, *firme, firmiter.*

fast, v. *ieiunium servare.*

fasten, *(ad)figĕre, (ad)ligare, adnectĕre*; to — together, *connectĕre.*

fastening, *vinculum, claustra (-orum).*

fastidious, *fastidiosus, delicatus*; adv. *fastidiose, delicate.*

fat, subst. *adeps, sebum.*

fat, adj. *pinguis, obesus.*

fatal, *perniciosus, funestus.*

fatality: = power of fate, *fatum*; = accident, *casus (-ūs).*

fate, *fatum, necessitas, sors*; the Fates, *Parcae.*

fated, *fatalis.*

father, subst. *pater, parens.*

father, v.: to — upon, *ascribĕre, tribuĕre.*

father-in-law, *socer.*

fatherless, *orbus.*

fatherly, *paternus.*

fathom, subst. *ulna.*

fathom, v. *explorare.*

fatigue, subst. *(de)fatigatio, lassitudo.*

fatigue, v. *(de)fatigare.*

fatigued, *(de)fatigatus, (de)fessus.*

fatten: transit., *saginare*; intransit., *pinguescĕre.*

fatuity, *fatuitas, ineptia.*

fatuous, *fatuus, ineptus*; adv. *inepte.*

fault, *culpa, vitium, delictum*; to find — with, *culpare, accusare.*

faultless, *integer, innocens*; adv. *integre, innocenter.*

faulty, *mendosus, vitiosus*; adv. *mendose, vitiose.*

favour, subst.; as position, *gratia*; as disposition, goodwill, *favor, benevolentia*; an act of —, *beneficium*; to do a —, *gratificari.*

favour, v. *favēre, studēre, suffragari.*

favourable, *propitius* (of gods), *commodus, secundus*; adv. *benigne, commode.*

favourer, *fautor* (f. *fautrix*).

favourite, subst. *deliciae (-arum).*

favourite, adj. *carus, gratiosus.*

fawn, subst. *hinnuleus.*

fawn, v.: to — upon, *adulari.*

fawning, subst. *adulatio.*

fealty, *fides, fidelitas.*

fear, subst. *metus (-ūs), timor, pavor.*

fear, v. *metuĕre, timēre, verēri.*

fearful: = afraid, *timidus, pavidus*; = dreadful, *dirus, terribilis.* Adv. *timide, pavide; dire.*

fearless, *impavidus, intrepidus*; adv. *sine timore, impavide.*

feasible, *quod fieri potest.*

feast, subst.: = feast-day, *dies festus*; = banquet, *convivium, epulae (-arum).*

feast, v.: transit., *pascĕre*; intransit., *epulari, convivari.*

feat, *facinus (-oris, n.), factum.*

feather, subst. *penna (pinna).*

feature, of the face, *lineamentum*; the —s, *vultus (-ūs).*

February, *(mensis) Februarius.*

fecund, *fecundus.*

fecundity, *fecunditas, fertilitas.*

federal, *foederatus, foedere, sociatus.*

fee, subst. *merces.*

fee, v. *mercedem dare.*

feeble, *infirmus, invalidus, debilis*; adv. *infirme.*

feebleness, *debilitas, infirmitas.*

feed, v.: transit., *pascĕre, alĕre*; intransit., *vesci, (de)pasci.*

feel: = to touch, handle, *temptare, tangĕre*; to — an emotion, *laetitiam, etc., capĕre, percipĕre, sentire.*

feeler, *crinis, corniculum.*

feeling, subst. *sensus (-ūs), tactus (-ūs)*; = emotion, *animus, animi motus (-ūs)* or *adfectus (-ūs).*

feeling, adj. *humanus, misericors.*

feign, *fingĕre, simulare.*

feigned, *fictus, simulatus*; adv. *ficte, simulate.*

feint, *simulatio.*

felicitate, *gratulari.*

felicitation, *gratulatio.*

felicitous, of style, *venustus.*

felicity: = happiness, *vita beata*; of style, *venustas.*

fell, adj. *dirus, saevus.*

fell, v. *caedere, excidĕre*; in gen., = knock down, *(con)sternĕre.*

fellow: = associate, *socius, comes*; = equal, *par*; = person, *homo.*

fellow-citizen, **fellow-countryman,** *civis.*

fellow-heir, *coheres.*

fellow-servant, *conservus.*

fellowship, *societas*; = corporation, *conlegium.*

fellow-soldier, *commilito.*

felon: see criminal.

felt, *coactum.*

female, subst. *femina, mulier.*

female, **feminine,** *muliebris, femineus*; gram., *femininus.*

fen, *palūs (-ūdis, f.), uligo.*

fence, subst. *saepes, saepimentum.*

fence, v.: = enclose, *saepire*; = fight with swords, *batuĕre.*

fencer, *gladiator.*

fenny, *uliginosus, paluster.*

ferment, *fermentum.* Transf., *frevor, aestus (-ūs).*

ferment, v. *fervēre.*

fern, *filix.*

ferocious, *ferus, saevus, atrox.*

ferocity, *saevitia, atrocitas.*

ferret, subst. *viverra.*

ferry, subst. *traiectus (-ūs)*; — -boat, *scapha, cymba*; —-man, *portitor.*

ferry, v. *traicĕre, transmittĕre.*

fertile, *fecundus, fertilis, uber.*

fertility, *fertilitas, ubertas, fecunditas.*

fervent, fervid, *fervidus, fervens; ardens;* adv. *ardenter, ferventer.*
fervour, *ardor, fervor.*
festival, *dies festus, feriae (-arum).*
festive, *hilaris, festus.*
festivity: see festival; = mirth, *festivitas, hilaritas.*
festoon, subst. *serta (-orum).*
fetch, *adferre, adducĕre.*
fetid, *teter, foetidus, gravis.*
fetter, subst. *compes, catena, vinculum.*
fetter, v. *vincula inicĕre.* Transf., *impedire.*
feud, *simultas; inimicitia.*
fever, *febris;* to be in a — (fig.), *trepidare, aestuare.*
feverish, *febriculosus.* Transf., *trepidus;* — excitement, *summa trepidatio.*
few, *pauci, rari.*
fib, *mendaciunculum.*
fibre, *fibra.*
fickle, *inconstans, levis.*
fickleness, *inconstantia, levitas.*
fiction, *res ficta, fabula, commentum.*
fictitious, *commenticius, fictus.*
fiddle, *fides (-ium).*
fiddler, *fidicen.*
fidelity, *fidelitas, fides.*
fidget, v. *trepidare.*
fidgety, *inquietus.*
field: = piece of land, *ager, arvum, campus* (= plain); — of battle, *acies;* fig., = sphere, *campus, locus, area.*
fiendish, *nefandus, immanis, atrox.*
fierce, *ferox, ferus, saevus;* adv. *ferociter, saeve.*
fierceness, *ferocitas, saevitia.*
fiery, *igneus, flammeus.* Transf., *ardens, fervidus, ferox.*
fife, *tibia.*
fifteen, *quindecim:* — each, *quini deni;* — times, *quindecie(n)s.*
fifteenth, *quintus decimus.*
fifth, *quintus.*
fiftieth, *quinquagesimus.*
fifty, *quinquaginta;* — each, *quinquageni.*
fig, *ficus.*
fight, subst. *pugna, certamen.*
fight, v. *(de)pugnare, dimicare, proeliari.*
fighter, *pugnator, proeliator.*
figment: see fiction.
figurative, *translatus;* adv. *per translationem.*
figure, subst.: = form, shape, *figura, forma, species;* = image, representation, *signum, figura, imago;* a — of speech, *conformatio, figura.*
figure, v. *fingĕre;* see imagine.
figured, *sigillatus, caelatus.*
filament, *fibra, filum.*
file, subst.: the tool, *lima, scobina;* milit., *ordo;* rank and —, *milites.*
file, v. *limare, polire.*
filial, *pius (erga parentes);* adv. *pie.*
filings, *scobis.*
fill, v. *implēre, complēre.*
fillet, *vitta, infula* (religious).
film, *membrana.*
filter, subst. *colum.*
filter, v. *(per)colare, liquare.*
filth, *impuritas;* see dirt.
filthy, *impurus, obscenus;* adv. *impure.*
fin, *pinna.*

final, *ultimus, extremus;* adv. *ad extremum, postremo.*
finance, finances: domestic, *res familiaris;* of a state, *vectigalia (-ium), aerarium.*
find, v. *invenire, reperire;* to — out, *cognoscere, invenire.*
finder, *inventor, repertor.*
fine, subst. *multa.*
fine, adj. *praeclarus, pulcher;* the — arts, *artes liberales;* = thin, *tenuis, subtilis;* of weather, *serenus, sudus.* Adv. *praeclare; tenuiter, subtiliter.*
fine, v. *multare.*
fineness, *elegantia;* = thinness, *tenuitas, subtilitas;* of weather, *serenitas.*
finery, *munditia, apparatus (-ūs).*
finesse, *artificium.*
finger, subst. *digitus.*
finger, v. *tangĕre, attrectare.*
finish, subst. *absolutio, perfectio.*
finish, v.: = complete, *conficĕre, absolvĕre, peragĕre;* = put an end to, *finire, terminare.*
finished, *absolutus, perfectus.*
finite, *finitus, circumscriptus.*
fir, *abies, pinus.*
fire, subst. *ignis, flamma, incendium;* to be on —, *ardēre, flagrare;* to set on —, *incendĕre.* Transf., = ardour, *(animi) vis, ardor, fervor;* of missiles, *telorum coniectus (-ūs).*
fire, v.: transit., *incendĕre;* intransit., to — up, *exardescĕre.*
fire-brand, *fax, torris.*
fire-brigade, *vigiles.*
fire-engine, *sipho(n).*
fire-place, fire-side, *caminus, focus.*
fire-wood, *lignum* (usually plur.).
firm, *firmus, stabilis, solidus;* adv. *firmiter, firme, solide.*
firmness, *firmitas, stabilitas;* of mind, *constantia.*
first, adj. *primus, prior* (of two).
first, adv. *primum, primo.*
first-born, *natu maximus* (of two, *maior*).
first-fruits, *primitiae (-arum).*
fish, subst. *piscis.*
fish, v. *piscari;* fig., to — for, *captare.*
fisherman, *piscator.*
fishhook, *hamus.*
fishing, *piscatus (-ūs);* of —, adj., *piscatorius.*
fishing-line, *linum.*
fishing-net, *rete, iaculum.*
fishing-rod, *harundo.*
fishmonger, *cetarius.*
fissure, *rima.*
fist, *pugnus.*
fisticuffs, *pugilatio.*
fit, subst. *impetus (-ūs).*
fit, fitted, adj. *aptus, idoneus, commodus;* adv. *apte, commode.*
fit, v.: transit. *aptare, accommodare;* to — out, *(ex)ornare, instruĕre;* intransit. *convenire.*
fitness, *habilitas, opportunitas.*
five, *quinque;* — each, *quini;* a period of — years, *lustrum, quinquennium;* — times, *quinquie(n)s.*
fix, v. *(ad)figĕre.*
fixed, *certus.*

flabby, flaccid, *marcidus, fluidus.*

flag, subst. *signum, vexillum;* — ship, *navis praetoria.*

flagon, *lagena.*

flagrant, *impudens;* adv. *impudenter.*

flail, *pertica.*

flame, subst. *flamma.*

flame, v. *ardēre, flagrare.*

flaming, *flammeus.*

flank, *latus (-eris, n.).*

flap, subst. *lacinia.*

flap, v.: to — the wings, *alis plaudēre;* in gen., *fluitare.*

flare, v. *flagrare.*

flash, subst. *fulgor.*

flash, v. *fulgēre, splendēre.*

flask, *ampulla.*

flat: = level, *planus, aequus, pronus* (= lying —); of wine, *vapidus;* of jokes, etc., *frigidus.* Adv. *plane.*

flatter, *adulari, blandiri.*

flatterer, *adsentator.*

flattering, *blandus.*

flattery, *adulatio, blandimentum.*

flaunt, *iactare, ostentare.*

flavour, subst. *sapor, sucus.*

flavour, v. *condire.*

flaw, *vitium, mendum.*

flawless, *emendatus.*

flax, *linum, carbasus.*

flaxen, *lineus;* of colour, *flavus.*

flay, *pellem detrahēre (corpori).*

flea, *pulex.*

fledged, *plumatus.*

flee, *(ef)fugĕre.*

fleece, subst. *vellus (-eris, n.).*

fleece, v. *tondēre;* = rob, *expilare, spoliare.*

fleecy, *laniger.*

fleet, subst. *classis.*

fleet, adj. *velox, celer, pernix.*

fleeting, *fugax, caducus, fluxus.*

fleetness, *velocitas, pernicitas.*

flesh, *caro* (= meat), *viscera (-um), corpus (-oris, n.).*

flexible, *flexibilis, lentus, facilis.*

flicker, *trepidare, micare.*

flight: = fleeing, *effugium, fuga;* to put to —, *fugare;* = flying, *lapsus (-ūs), volatus (-ūs);* of stairs, *scalae (-arum).*

flightiness, *mobilitas, levitas.*

flighty, *mobilis, levis, inconstans.*

flimsiness, *tenuitas.*

flimsy, *tenuis.* Transf., *inanis.*

flinch, *refugēre.*

fling, *iacĕre, conicĕre.*

flint, *silex.*

flippancy, *petulantia.*

flippant, *petulans.*

flirt, v., perhaps *subblandiri.*

flit, *volitare.*

flitch, *succidia.*

float, *innare, fluitare;* in the air, *pendēre, volitare.*

flock, subst. *grex.*

flock, v. *adfluĕre, confluĕre;* to — together, *concurrĕre.*

flog, *verberare;* to be flogged, *vapulare.*

flogging, *verbera (-um).*

flood, subst. *eluvio;* — tide, *aestus accessus (-ūs).* Transf., *vis magna, flumen.*

flood, v. transit. *inundare.*

floor, *solum, pavimentum* (of stone).

floral, *floreus* (poet).

Florence, *F orentia.*

florid, *rubicundus.* Transf., *floridus.*

flounder, *fluitare.* Transf., *titubare.*

flour, *farina.*

flourish, subst., in style, *calamister.*

flourish, v.: intransit., *florēre, vigēre;* transit., *vibrare.*

flout, *ludificari, deridēre.*

flow, subst. *fluxio, lapsus (-ūs);* of words, *volubilitas, copia (verborum).*

flow, v. *fluĕre, labi* (= glide), *manare* (= ooze).

flower, subst. *flos, flosculus;* = best part, *flos, robur.*

flower, v. *florēre, (ef)florescĕre.*

flowery, *floreus, floridus.*

flowing, of speech, *fluens, volubilis, fusus.*

fluctuate, *fluctuare, pendēre.*

fluency, *facundia, volubilitas.*

fluent, *volubilis, disertus;* adv. *volubiliter.*

fluid, subst. *liquor, humor.*

fluid, adj. *liquidus.*

flush, subst. *rubor.*

flush, v. *rubescĕre.*

fluster, *agitare, sollicitare.*

flute, *tibia, harundo.*

flute-player, *tibicen.*

fluted, *striatus.*

flutter, subst. *trepidatio.*

flutter, v. *trepidare, volitare.*

fly, subst. *musca.*

fly, v. *volare, volitare,* see also **flee.**

flying, *volatilis, volucer.*

foal, *eculeus, pullus equinus.*

foam, subst. *spuma.*

foam, v. *spumare, (ex)aestuare.*

foamy, *spumeus, spumosus.*

fodder, *pabulum.*

foe, *hostis* (public), *inimicus* (private).

fog, *nebula, caligo.*

foggy, *nebulosus, caliginosus.*

foible, *vitium.*

foil, subst.: a fencer's —, *rudis;* of metal, *lamina.*

foil, v. *ad inritum redigĕre, eludĕre.*

foist, *supponĕre, subdĕre.*

fold, subst.: in fabric, etc., *sinus (-ūs);* for animals, *ovile, stabulum.*

fold, v. *(com)plicare;* with -ed hands, *compressis manibus.*

folding-doors, *valvae (-arum).*

foliage, *frons,* plur. *frondes.*

folk; see **people.**

follow, *(con)sequi, insequi, persequi* (to the end); to — after, succeed, *succedĕre.*

follower, *(ad)sector.*

following, subst. *secta.*

following, *(in)sequens, proximus, posterus.*

folly, *stultitia, ineptia.*

foment, *fovēre.* Transf., *excitare.*

fond: = loving, *amans, studiosus;* = foolish, *stultus.* Adv. *amanter; stulte.*

fondle, *(per)mulcēre, amplexari.*

fondness: = love, *studium, amor, caritas;* = folly, *stultitia.*

food, *cibus, victus (-ūs), alimentum;* of animals, *pabulum.*

fool, subst. *homo stultus;* to play the —, *ineptire, desipĕre.*

fool, v. (e)ludĕre, ludificare.
foolery, ineptiae (-arum), nugae (-arum).
foolhardy, temerarius.
foolish, stultus, ineptus, insulsus; adv. stulte, inepte, insulse.
foot, pes; on — (adj.), pedes, pedester; the — of the mountain, infimus mons; as a measure, pes; a — in size, pedalis; a metrical —, pes.
footing, ratio, status (-ūs).
footman, pedisequus, servus a pedibus.
footpad, latro.
foot-path, semita, callis.
foot-print, vestigium.
foot-soldier, pedes.
footstool, scamnum, scabillum.
for, prep.: = on behalf of, instead of, in return for, pro, with abl.; — this reason, propter hoc; — a sum of money, render by genit. or abl. of price; of time, to last for, for the purposes of, in with acc.: = during, render by acc., or per with acc.
for, conj. nam(que), etenim, enim (second word in clause).
forage, subst. pabulum.
forage, v. pabulari, frumentari.
forager, pabulator, frumentator.
foraging, subst. pabulatio, frumentatio.
forbear, parcĕre, temperare, (se) abstinēre.
forbearance, abstinentia, patientia.
forbid, vetare, interdicĕre; it is forbidden, non licet.
force, subst. vis; to be in —, valēre; milit., forces, copiae (-arum).
force, v.; see compel.
forced, of language, arcessitus; a — march, magnum iter.
forcible: = done by force, per vim factus; = strong, validus, gravis, vehemens. Adv. vi, per vim; valide, vehementer.
ford, subst. vadum.
ford, v. vado transire.
forearm, subst. bracchium.
forebode: = to prophesy, portendĕre; = to expect, praesagire, praesentire.
foreboding, subst. praesensio.
forecast, v. praevidēre, prospicĕre.
forefather, avus, proavus; —s, maiores (-um).
forefinger, digitus index.
forego, dimittĕre, (con)cedĕre.
forehead, frons (-ntis).
foreign, peregrinus, externus, adventicius; = incompatible, abhorrens, alienus.
foreigner, peregrinus, advena.
foremost, primus, princeps.
forenoon, dies antemeridianus.
forensic, forensis.
forerunner, praenuntius.
foresee, praevidēre, prospicĕre.
foresight, providentia.
forest, silva.
forestall, praevenire.
foretell, praedicĕre.
forethought, providentia.
forewarn, praemonēre.
forfeit, subst. poena, multa.
forfeit, v. amittĕre; multari.
forge, subst. fornax, officina.

forge, v. procudĕre, fabricari. Transf.: = make, in gen., fabricari, fingĕre; =counterfeit, subicĕre, supponĕre.
forged, of money, adulterinus.
forger, (of documents) subiector.
forgery, (of documents) subiectio.
forget, oblivisci, dediscĕre: to be forgotten, e memoria excidĕre.
forgetful, obliviosus, immemor.
forgetfulness, oblivio.
forgive, ignoscĕre; veniam dare.
forgiveness, venia.
forgiving, clemens, exorabilis.
fork, (for hay-making), furca, furcilla.
forked, bifurcus.
forlorn, relictus, destitutus.
form, subst.: = shape, figura, forma, facies; in proper —, rite; = bench, scamnum.
form, v.: = shape, make, (ef)fingĕre (con)formare, fabricari; milit., to — (up) troops, instruĕre, ordinare.
formality, ritus (-ūs).
formation, conformatio, forma.
former, prior, pristinus, superior; the — . . . the latter, ille . . . hic. Adv. antea, olim, quondam.
formidable, metuendus, terribilis, formidolosus; adv. formidolose.
formless, informis, rudis.
formula, formula, carmen, verba (-orum).
forsake, deserĕre, destituĕre.
forsooth! scilicet, sane.
forswear, = swear falsely, periurare. See also abjure.
fort, arx, castellum, castrum.
forth, of place, foras; often rendered by compound verb with e- or ex- or pro; and so —, et cetera.
forthcoming, express by future tense.
forthwith, extemplo, statim.
fortification, munitio, munimentum.
fortify, (com)munire.
fortitude, fortitudo, virtūs (-ūtis, f.).
fortuitous, fortuitus, forte oblatus; adv. forte, fortuito, casu.
fortunate, felix, fortunatus, beatus; adv. feliciter, fortunate.
fortune, fortuna, fors, casus (-ūs); = wealth, divitiae (-arum), res (familiaris), bona (-orum).
fortune-teller, sortilegus; female, saga.
forty, quadraginta; — each, quadrageni; — times, quadragie(n)s.
forward, adj., = pert, protervus.
forward, adv. porro, ante; to go —, pergĕre.
forward, v.; of letters, perferendum curare; = help, promote, adiuvare.
foster, nutrire, alĕre.
foster-child, alumnus, f. alumna.
foster-father, nutricius.
foster-mother, nutrix.
foul, foedus, turpis, immundus; adv., foede, turpiter.
foulness, foeditas.
found: of cities, etc., condĕre, fundare; = cast in metal, fundĕre.
foundation, fundamenta (-orum); from the —s, funditus.
founder, subst. conditor, auctor.
founder, v. submergi, deperire

fount, fountain, _fons, caput._ Transf., _fons, principium, origo._

four, _quattuor:_ — each, _quaterni;_ — times, _quater;_ a period of — years, _quadriennium;_ — fold, _quadruplex._

fourteen, _quattuordecim:_ — each, _quaterni deni;_ — times, _quater decie(n)s._

fourteenth, _quartus decimus._

fourth, _quartus:_ for the — time, _quartum._

fowl, subst. _avis, volucris, ales;_ = hen, _gallina._

fowl, v. _aucupari._

fowler, _auceps._

fowling, _aucupium._

fox, _vulpes;_ of a —, adj. _vulpinus._

fraction, _pars._

fractious, _morosus, difficilis_

fracture, v. _frangĕre._

fragile, _fragilis._

fragility, _fragilitas._

fragment, _fragmentum._

fragrance, _odor suavis._

fragrant, _suavis; suaveolens_ (poet).

frail, adj. _infirmus, debilis._

frailty, _infirmitas._

frame, subst. _compages;_ — of mind, _animus._

frame, v. _fingĕre, fabricari;_ — draw up in words, _concipĕre, componĕre._

framework, _compages, contignatio._

France, _Gallia._

franchise, _civitas, iūs (iūris, n.)._

frank, _candidus, apertus;_ adv. _candide, aperte._

frankincense, _tūs (tūris, n.)._

frankness, _simplicitas, libertas._

frantic, _insanus, amens;_ adv. _insane._

fraternal, _fraternus;_ adv. _fraterne._

fraternity, _germanitas, fraternitas;_ = society, _sodalitas, sodalicium._

fratricide: as act, _parricidium fraternum;_ as person, _fratricida._

fraud, _fraus, dolus (malus), fallacia._

fraudulent, _fraudulentus, dolosus;_ adv. _fraudulenter, dolo malo, dolose._

fraught, _refertus, repletus._

fray, _pugna._

free, adj.: = unrestricted, _liber, solutus, vacuus;_ to be — from, _(re) carēre;_ of space, = unoccupied, _patens, apertus;_ = without cost, _gratuitus;_ = generous, _largus, liberalis._ Adv. _libere, solute;_ = generously, _large._

free, v. _liberare, eximĕre, solvĕre;_ of slaves, _manumittĕre._

freebooter, _latro, praedo._

free-born, _ingenuus._

freedman, _libertus, libertinus._

freedom, _libertas, licentia;_ — of choice, _arbitrium;_ — from punishment. _impunitas._

freehold, _praedium liberum._

freeholder, _possessor._

freewill, _voluntas._

freeze, transit., _glaciare,_ (con)_gelare._

freight, _onus (oneris, n.)._

French, _Gallicus;_ a — man, _Gallus._

frenzied, _furens, insanus, amens._

frenzy, _furor, insania, amentia._

frequency, _frequentia, crebritas._

frequent, adj. _frequens, creber;_ adv. _frequenter, crebro, saepe._

frequent, v. _celebrare, frequentare._

frequented, _frequens, celeber._

fresh: = new, _recens, novus;_ = refreshed, _untired, recens, integer, vegetus;_ = cold, _frigidus._

freshen, _recreare, reficere;_ intransit., of wind, _increbrescere._

freshness, _viriditas._

fret: transit., = chafe, _atterĕre,_ = distress, _sollicitare, vexare;_ intransit., _dolere, macerari._

fretful, _morosus, stomachosus;_ adv. _morose, stomachose._

fretfulness, _morositas, stomachus._

friable, _puter or putris._

friction, _tritus (-ūs)._

friend, _amicus_ (f. _amica_), _sodalis._

friendliness, _comitas, adfabilitas._

friendly, _amicus, comis._

friendship, _amicitia, familiaritas._

frieze, (the cloth), _gausape_ or _gausapum_.

fright, _terror, pavor._

frighten, (ex)_terrēre._

frightful, _terribilis, formidolosus;_ adv. _terribilem in modum, formidolose._

frigid, _frigidus._

frill, _segmenta (-orum)._

fringe, _fimbriae (-arum), limbus._

frisk, _salire, lascivire._

frisky, _lascivus._

fritter, subst., _laganum._

fritter, v. (con)_terĕre, dissipare._

frivolity, _nugae (-arum), levitas._

frivolous, _levis, inanis._

fro: to and —, _huc (et) illuc, ultro citro(que)._

frog, _rana._

frolic, subst. _ludus, lascivia._

frolic, v. _ludĕre, lascivire._

frolicsome, _lascivus, ludibundus, iocosus._

from, _a, ab; ex_ (= out of); _de_ (=down from).

front, subst. _frons, pars prior;_ in — of, _pro,_ with abl.

front, v., = look towards, _aspectare._

frontier, _finis, terminus, confinium._

fronting, _adversus, oppositus._

frost, _gelu, pruina; frigus (-oris,_ n. = frosty weather).

frosty, _frigidus._

froth, subst. _spuma._

froth, v. _spumare._

frothy, _spumosus, spumeus._

froward, _contumax, pertinax;_ adv. _contumaciter, pertinaciter._

frowardness, _contumacia, pertinacia._

frown, subst. _frontis contractio._

frown, v. _frontem contrahĕre._

frozen, _rigidus._

frugal, _parcus, frugi_ (indecl.); adv. _parce, frugaliter._

frugality, _parsimonia, frugalitas._

fruit, _fructus (-ūs), frux_ and plur. _fruges_ (esp. of grain), _pomum_ (esp. = fruit of trees), _baca_ (= berry).

fruitful, _fecundus, fertilis, uber;_ adv. _fecunde._

fruitfulness, _fecunditas, fertilitas._

fruition, _fructus (-ūs)._

fruitless, *inutilis, cassus, inritus;* adv. *incassum, frustra, re infecta.*

fruit-tree, *pomum.*

frustrate, *ad inritum redigĕre.*

fry, v. *frigĕre.*

frying-pan, *sartago.*

fuel, *ligna (-orum).*

fugitive, subst. *fugitivus, profugus.*

fugitive, adj. *fugax, fugitivus.*

fulfil, *explēre, exsequi, conficĕre.*

fulfilment, *confectio.*

full: = filled, *plenus, repletus;* — of food, *satur;* = complete, *plenus, integer;* of a writer or speaker, *copiosus.* Adv. *plene; copiose, abundanter.*

fuller, *fullo.*

full-grown, *adultus.*

fulminate, *fulminare, intonare.*

fulsome, *putidus;* adv. *putide.*

fumble; see feel.

fume, subst. *vapor, halitus (-ūs).*

fume, v. *(ex)aestuare.*

fumigate, *suffire.*

fun, *iocus, ludus.*

function, *munus (-eris, n.), officium.*

fund, *pecunia.*

fundamental, *primus, principalis;* adv. *penitus.*

fundamentals, *elementa (-orum), principia (-orum).*

funeral, subst. *funus (-eris, n.), exsequiae (-arum).*

funeral, adj. *funebris;* — pile, *rogus, pyra.*

funereal, *funebris, lugubris.*

funnel, *infundibulum.*

funny, *ridiculus, iocularis;* adv. *ridicule.*

fur, *pellis.*

furbish, *interpolare, expolire.*

furious, *rabidus, furens;* adv. *rabide.*

furl, *(vela) contrahĕre.*

furlong, *stadium.*

furlough, *commeatus (-ūs).*

furnace, *fornax.*

furnish: = equip, *(ad)ornare, instruere;* = supply, give, *suppeditare, praebere.*

furnished, *instructus, praeditus.*

furniture, *supellex; apparatus (-ūs).*

furrow, subst. *sulcus.*

furrow, v. *sulcare.*

further: adj. *ulterior;* adv. *ulterius, amplius; praeterea.*

furthest, *ultimus.*

furtive, *furtivus;* adv. *furtim, furtive.*

fury, *furor, rabies.*

fuse, *liquefacĕre, fundĕre.*

fuss, subst. *trepidatio, tumultus (-ūs).*

fuss, v. *trepidare.*

fusty; see mouldy.

futile, *futilis, inanis, vanus.*

futility, *futilitas.*

future, subst. *futura (-orum);* for the —, *in futurum.*

future, adj. *futurus, posterus.*

G

gabble, *garrire, blaterare.*

gable, *fastigium.*

gadfly, *asilus, tabanus.*

gage, *pignus (-oris, n.).*

gaiety, *hilaritas, laetitia.*

gain, subst. *lucrum, quaestus (-ūs;* = profit), *commodum* (= advantage).

gain, v. *lucrari, lucri facĕre, consequi, capĕre;* to — over, *conciliare.*

gainful, *quaestuosus, lucrosus.*

gait, *incessus (-ūs).*

gala; see festival.

galaxy, *orbis lacteus.*

gale, *ventus, aura* (= breeze).

gall, subst. *fel, bilis.*

gall, v. *terĕre;* = annoy, *mordĕre, urĕre.*

gallant, *amator.*

gallant, adj.: = brave, *fortis, animosus;* adv. *fortiter, animose;* = attentive to females, *officiosus.*

gallantry, *virtus (-utis, f.), fortitudo;* in love, *amores (-um).*

gallery, *porticus (-ūs).*

galley, *navis longa, triremis.*

gallon, *congius.*

gallop, subst. *gradus (-ūs) citatus:* at a —, *equo admisso.*

gallop, v. *equo admisso vehi* or *currĕre.*

gallows, *crux.*

gamble, v. *aleā ludĕre.*

gambler, *aleator.*

gambling, *alea.*

gambol, subst. *lusus (-ūs).*

gambol, v. *ludĕre, lascivire.*

game, susbt.: as played, *ludus;* a — of chance, *alea;* as hunted, *ferae (-arum)*; on table, *(caro) ferina.*

gammon, *perna.*

gammon, interj. *gerrae!*

gander, *anser (mas* or *masculus).*

gang, *grex, caterva.*

gangway, *forus.*

gaol, *carcer; vincula (-orum).*

gaoler, *custos.*

gap, *lacuna, hiatus (-ūs).*

gape, *(in)hiare, (de)hiscĕre.*

garbage, *purgamentum, quisquiliae (-arum).*

garble, *corrumpĕre, vitiare.*

garden, subst. *hortus.*

garden, v. *in horto fodĕre, hortum colĕre.*

garish, *clarus, splendidus.*

garland, *corona, sertum* (usually plur.).

garlic, *alium.*

garment, *vestimentum.*

garner, subst. *horreum.*

garner, v. *condĕre.*

garnish, *(ex)ornare, instruĕre, decorare.*

garret, *cenaculum.*

garrison, subst. *praesidium.*

garrison, v. *(urbi) praesidium imponĕre.*

garrulity, *garrulitas, loquacitas.*

garrulous, *garrulus, loquax, verbosus;* adv. *loquaciter.*

gas, *spiritus (-ūs), vapor.*

gash, subst. *vulnus (-eris, n.).*

gash, v. *vulnerare.*

gasp, subst. *anhelitus (-ūs).*

gasp, v. *anhelare.*

gasping, adj. *anhelus.*

gate, *ianua, ostium;* of a city, *porta.*

gate-keeper, *ianitor.*

gate-post, *postis.*

gather, v.: transit., *legĕre, conligĕre.*

conferre; = conjecture, *conĭcĕre*; intransit., *convenīre, congregāri*.

gathering, subst.: as act, *collectio*; = assembly, *coetus (-ūs)*; = a sore, *suppuratio.*

gaudy, *fucatus, magnificus.*

gauge, v. *metiri.*

gaunt, *macer.*

gauntlets, *manicae (-arum).*

gay: of spirits, *hilaris, laetus*; adv. *hilare, laete*; of colour, etc., *splendidus, nitidus.*

gaze, subst. *obtutus (-ūs).*

gaze, v.: to — at, *intueri, contemplari.*

gazelle, *dorcas.*

gazette, *acta (diurna).*

gear, *ornatus (-ūs), supellex, apparatus (-ūs).*

gem, *gemma.*

gender, *genus (-eris, n.).*

genealogy, render by *origo* or *stirps.*

general, subst. *dux, imperator*; a lieutenant—, *legatus*; the —'s tent, *praetorium.*

general, adj. *generalis, communis, vulgaris*; often rendered by genit. plur. *omnium.* Adv., = in —, *ad summam, in universum, generatim*; = usually, *fere, vulgo, plerumque.*

generalship, *ductus (-ūs)*; under the — of Caesar, *Caesare duce.*

generate, *gignĕre, generare, parĕre.*

generation, *saeculum, aetas.*

generosity, *benignitas, liberalitas.*

generous, *benignus, liberalis*; of birth, *generosus, nobilis.* Adv. *benigne, liberaliter, large.*

genial, *comis, benignus*; adv. *comiter.*

geniality, *comitas.*

genitive, *(casus) genitivus.*

genius, = ability, *ingenium* or *indoles*, with adj. such as *praeclarus*; a man of —, *homo ingeniosus* or *praeclaro ingenio (praeditus).*

genteel, *elegans, urbanus*; adv. *eleganter, urbane.*

gentility, *elegantia, urbanitas.*

gentle: = well-born, *generosus, ingenuus, nobilis*; = mild, *lenis, mitis, mansuetus*; adv. *leniter, mite, mansuete.*

gentleman: by birth, see gentle; in behaviour, etc., *homo liberalis.*

gentlemanly, *liberalis, urbanus, honestus.*

gentleness, *mansuetudo, lenitas.*

gentlewoman: see lady.

gentry, *nobilitas, nobiles (-ium).*

genuine, *sincerus, merus, germanus*; adv. *reapse, sincere, vere.*

geography, *geographia, terrarum descriptio.*

geometrical, *geometricus.*

geometrician, *geometres (-ae).*

geometry, *geometria.*

George, *Georgius* (late Latin).

germ, *germen, semen.*

German, *Germanus, Germanicus.*

germane, *adfinis.*

Germany, *Germania.*

germinate, *germinare.*

germination, *germinatio.*

gesticulate, *se iactare, gestum facĕre.*

gesticulation, gesture, *iactatio, gestus (-ūs).*

get, v.: transit., *capĕre, adipisci, (com)parare, consequi*; to — anything done, *rem faciendam curare*; intransit., = become, *fieri*; to — along, *procedĕre*; — at, *attingĕre*; — away, *effugĕre*; — down, *descendĕre*; — in, *introire*; — out, *egredi, exire*; — up, *surgĕre.*

ghastliness, *pallor.*

ghastly, *exsanguis, pallidus.*

ghost, *manes (-ium), lemures (-um)*; the Holy Ghost, *Spiritus Sanctus*; to give up the —, *exspirare.*

giant, *vir maior quam pro humano habitu*; myth., *gigas.*

gibe, subst. *cavillatio.*

gibe, v. *cavillari.*

giddiness, *vertigo.*

giddy, *vertiginosus.* Transf., *levis, inconstans.*

gift, *donum.*

gig, *cisium.*

gild, *inaurare.*

gills, *branchiae (-arum).*

gimlet, *terebra.*

gingerly, *pedetemptim, sensim.*

giraffe, *camelopardalis.*

gird, *(suc)cingĕre, accingĕre*: to — on, *accingĕre*; to — oneself, *(suc)cingi* or *accingi.*

girdle, *zona, cingulum.*

girl, *puella, virgo.*

girlhood, *aetas puellaris.*

girlish, *puellaris.*

girth, *ambitus (-ūs), circuitus (-ūs)*; of a horse, *cingula.*

give, *dare, tribuĕre, donare*; to — back, *reddĕre*; to give up, = surrender, *tradĕre, dedĕre*; = cease, *desistĕre*; to — in, — way, *cedĕre.*

gizzard, *ingluvies, guttur.*

glad, *laetus, hilaris*; adv. *laete, libenter.*

gladden, *(ex)hilarare.*

glade, *silva, saltus (-ūs).*

gladiator, *gladiator*; a trainer of —s, *lanista.*

gladiatorial, *gladiatorius.*

gladness, *laetitia, hilaritas.*

glance, subst. *aspectus (-ūs).*

glance, v. *aspicĕre.*

glare, subst.: of light, *fulgor*; = fierce look, *oculi torvi.*

glare, v., of light, *fulgĕre*; = look fiercely, *torvis oculis intueri.*

glass, subst. *vitrum*; a looking- —, *speculum.*

glass, adj., or **glassy,** *vitreus.*

gleam, subst. *fulgor.*

gleam, v. *fulgĕre.*

gleaning, subst. *spicilegium.*

glee, *hilaritas, laetitia, gaudium.*

glen, *(con)vallis.*

glib, *loquax, volubilis*; adv. *loquaciter, volubiliter.*

glibness, *loquacitas, volubilitas.*

glide, *(pro)labi.*

glimmer, *sublucĕre.*

glimmering, adj. *sublustris.*

glitter, subst. *fulgor.*

glitter, v. *fulgĕre, nitĕre, lucĕre.*

glittering, *lucidus, nitidus*; — white, *candidus.*

gloat, *aspectu se delectare.*
globe, *globus, sphaera*; = the earth, *orbis terrarum.*
globular, *globosus.*
gloom, *obscuritas, caligo, tenebrae (-arum)*; = sadness, *tristitia, maestitia.*
gloomy: = dark, *obscurus*; = sad, *tristis, maestus*; adv. *maeste.*
glorify, *laudare, celebrare.*
glorious, *(prae)clarus, amplus, inlustris*; adv. *(prae)clare, ample.*
glory, subst. *gloria, honor, decus (-oris, n.).*
gloss, subst.: = shine, *nitor*; = explanation, *interpretatio.*
gloss, v.: to — over, *extenuare.*
glossary, *glossarium.*
glossy, *nitidus.*
Gloucester, *Glevum.*
gloves, *manicae (-arum, = long sleeves).*
glow, subst. *ardor, fervor.*
glow, v. *ardēre, flagrare.*
glow-worm, *cicindela.*
glue, subst. *gluten.*
glue, v. *glutinare.*
glut, subst. *satietas.*
glut, v. *satiare, explēre.*
glutinous, *lentus, glutinosus.*
glutton, *helluo.*
gluttonous, *edax, vorax.*
gluttony, *gula, edacitas.*
gnarled; see knotty.
gnash; to — the teeth, *(dentibus) (in)frendēre.*
gnat, *culex.*
gnaw, *(ad)rodēre.*
gnawing, adj. *mordax.*
go, v. *ire, vadĕre* (esp. fast), *gradi* (= to step), *proficisci* (= set out) *discedĕre* (= depart); to — back, *redire, reverti*; — beyond, *excedĕre*; — down, *descendĕre*; — forward, *procedĕre*; — in, *inire, intrare, ingredi*; — off, *abire*; — on, = continue, *pergĕre*, = happen, *fieri, agi*; — out, *exire, egredi*; — up, *ascendĕre*; — without, *carēre*; to —, = to become, *fieri.*
goad, subst. *stimulus.*
goad, v. *stimulare, incitare.*
goal, *meta, calx.*
goat, m. *caper, hircus*; f. *capra, capella.*
gobble, *(de)vorare.*
go-between, *conciliator, interpres.*
goblet, *poculum, scyphus.*
god, *deus, divus, numen (divinum)*; the —s, *di (dii), divi, numina, caelestes, superi*; —s of the household, *lares, penates*; so help me —, *ita me deus (ad)iuvet.*
goddess, *dea, diva.*
godhead, *numen.*
godless, *impius.*
godlike, *divinus.*
godliness, *pietas (erga deos).*
godly, *pius (erga deos).*
godsend, *res quasi divinitus oblata.*
gold, *aurum.*
golden, *aureus.*
gold-mine, *aurifodina.*
goldsmith, *aurifex.*
good, subst. *bonum, salus (-utis, f.)*; to do —, *prodesse*; —s, = property,

possessions, *bona (-orum)*; = merchandise, *merx.*
good, adj. *bonus, probus*; morally —, *bonus, probus, honestus*; = kind, *bonus, benignus*; = useful, *utilis*; = convenient, *commodus*; = wholesome, *saluber, salutaris*; — day! *salve!* good!, interj., *euge! bene habet.*
goodbye, *vale* (plur. *valete*).
good-for-nothing, *nequam.*
good-humour, *comitas, facilitas.*
good-humoured, *comis, facilis.*
good-looking, *pulcher, venustus.*
good-nature, *facilitas, comitas, benignitas.*
good-natured, *facilis, comis, benignus.*
goodness, *bonitas*; moral —, *probitas, virtūs (-ūtis, f.)*; = kindness, *benignitas, bonitas.*
good-tempered, *mitis, lenis.*
goose, *anser.*
gore, subst. *cruor.*
gore, v. *(cornibus) transfigĕre.*
gorge, subst.: = throat, *gula, guttur, fauces (-ium)*; = narrow pass, *angustiae (-arum), fauces (-ium).*
gorge, v. *(ex)satiare.*
gorgeous, *splendidus, magnificus*; adv. *splendide, magnifice.*
gorgeousness, *splendor, magnificentia.*
gory, *cruentus, cruentatus.*
gospel, *evangelium.*
gossamer, *aranea.*
gossip, subst.; = talk, *sermo, rumor*; = talker, *garrulus* or *loquax*; = friend, *familiaris.*
gossip, v. *sermonem conferre, garrire.*
gourd, *cucurbita.*
gout, *articulorum dolor*; — in the hands, *chiragra*; — in the feet, *podagra.*
gouty, adj. *arthriticus.*
govern: politically, *gubernare, administrare, curare*; in gen., = restrain, guide, *moderari, temperare, regēre.*
government, *administratio, gubernatio*; = supreme power, *imperium, regnum*; = those in power, render by relative clause.
governor, *gubernator, rector*; with delegated powers, *praefectus, legatus.*
governorship, *praefectura.*
gown: man's, *toga*; woman's, *stola, palla.*
grace, subst.: = favour, goodwill, *gratia, favor*; by the — of god, *deo favente*; = gracefulness, charm, *lepos (lepor), venustas, elegantia*; myth., the Graces, *Gratiae (-arum).*
grace, v. *(ad)ornare, decorare.*
graceful, *venustus, elegans*; adv. *venuste, eleganter.*
gracious, *propitius*; see also kind.
grade, *gradus (-ūs).*
gradually, *paullatim, gradatim, sensim.*
graft, subst. *surculus.*
graft, v. *inserĕre.*
grain: = particle, *granum, mica*; = corn, *frumentum.*
grammar, *grammatica (-ae,* f., or *-orum,* n. pl.).

grammarian, *grammaticus.*
grammatical, *grammaticus.*
granary, *horreum, granaria* (-orum).
grand, *grandis, magnificus, amplus.*
granddaughter, *neptis.*
grandees, *nobiles, proceres.*
grandeur, *amplitudo, magnificentia.*
grandfather, *avus.*
grandiloquent, *grandiloquus.*
grandmother, *avia.*
grandson, *nepos.*
grant, subst. *donum;* = act of granting, *concessio.*
grant, v.: = bestow, *permittĕre, concedĕre;* = admit, *concedĕre, dare;* —ed that, *ut* with subj.
grape, *acinus;* bunch of grapes, *uva.*
graphic, *expressus.*
grapple, *luctari.*
grappling-iron, *ferrea manus* (-ūs), *harpago.*
grasp, subst.: physical, *complexus* (-ūs), *manūs* (plur.); mental, *captus* (-ūs).
grasp, v.: physically, *(ap)prehendĕre, comprehendĕre, prensare;* mentally, *intellegĕre, animo comprehendĕre;* to — at, *captare, adfectare, appetĕre.*
grasping, *avarus, appetens.*
grass, *gramen, herba.*
grasshopper, *gryllus.*
grassy, *gramineus, herbidus.*
grate, subst. *focus, caminus.*
grate, v.: = rub, *(con)terĕre;* = make a grating noise, *stridĕre.*
grateful: = thankful, *gratus;* adv. *grate, grato animo;* = pleasant, *gratus, acceptus.*
gratification: as act, *expletio, delectatio;* = pleasure, *voluptas.*
gratify: see please.
grating, subst.: = bars, *cancelli* (-orum), *clatri* (-orum); = harsh noise, *stridor.*
gratitude, *gratus animus.*
gratuitous, *gratuitus;* adv. *gratis, gratuito.*
gratuity; see alms, gift.
grave, subst.: = place of burial, *sepulcrum;* = place of cremation, *bustum;* = state of death, *mors.*
grave, adj. *gravis, serius, tristis.*
gravel, *glarea.*
gravity, *gravitas.*
gravy, *ius* (iuris, n.), *sucus.*
graze: of animals, transit. *pascĕre,* intransit. *pasci;* = to touch in passing, *radĕre, stringĕre.*
grazier, *pecuarius.*
grazing, subst. *pascua* (-orum, plur.).
grease, subst. *adeps, lardum.*
grease, v. *ung(u)ĕre.*
greasy, *unctus, pinguis.*
great, *magnus, grandis, amplus; clarus, summus, ingens;* as plur., the great, *nobiles* (-ium); greater, *maior;* greatest, *maximus;* how —, *quantus;* so —, *tantus;* too —, *nimius.* Adv., greatly, *magnopere.*
greaves, *ocreae.*
Greece, *Graecia.*
greed, *aviditas, cupiditas.*
greedy, *avidus, cupidus;* adv. *avide, cupide.*
Greek, adj. and subst. *Graecus.*

green, subst.: = greenness, *viriditas, color viridis:* = grassy space, *campus.*
green, adj. *viridis, virens;* to be — *virēre;* = fresh, *viridis, recens.*
greens, *holus* (-eris, n.).
greet, *salutare, salvere iubēre.*
greeting, *(con)salutatio.*
grey, *canus* (= hoary); *caesius* or *glaucus* (grey-blue).
greyness, *canities.*
gridiron, *craticula.*
grief, *dolor, aegritudo, maeror, luctus* (-ūs); = mourning).
grievance, *iniuria; querimonia* (=complaint).
grieve, v.: transit., *dolore adficĕre, angĕre;* intransit., *dolēre, maerēre, lugēre.*
grievous, *acerbus, gravis;* adv. *acerbe, graviter.*
grill, v. *torrēre.*
grim, *torvus, saevus.*
grimace, subst. *os distortum.*
grimness, *saevitia, torvitas.*
grimy; see dirty.
grin, subst. *rictus* (-ūs).
grin, v. *ridēre.*
grind, v. *molĕre;* to — the teeth, *dentibus frendĕre.*
grinder, (of teeth) *dens genuinus.*
grindstone, *cos.*
grip; see grasp.
grisly, *foedus, horrendus.*
grist, *farina.*
groan, subst. *gemitus* (-ūs).
groan, v. *gemĕre.*
groin, *inguen.*
groom, subst. *agaso.*
groom, v. *curare.*
groove, *canalis.*
grope, *praetemptare.*
gross: = great, too great, *magnus, nimius;* = disgraceful, *turpis, foedus.* Adv. *nimium; turpiter, foede.*
grot, grotto, *antrum.*
grotesque, *mirus; ridiculus.*
ground, subst.: = earth, soil, *humus* (f.), *solum, terra;* on the —, *humi;* = place, position, *locus;* = reason, basis, *causa, ratio:* on the — that, *quod.*
ground, v. of a ship, *sidĕre.*
groundless, *vanus, falsus;* adv. *temere, falso.*
groundlessness, *vanitas.*
groundwork, *fundamentum.*
group, subst. *caterva, globus, circulus.*
group, v. *disponĕre.*
grouping, *dispositio.*
grove, *lucus, nemus* (-oris, n.).
grovel, *humi iacēre.*
grovelling, *abiectus, humilis, submissus.*
grow: intransit., *crescĕre, augeri;* to — up, *adolescere;* = to become, *fieri;* transit., *alĕre, colĕre.*
grower, *cultor.*
growl, subst. *fremitus* (-ūs).
growl, v. *fremĕre.*
grown, grown-up, *adultus, pubes.*
growth, *auctus* (-ūs), *incrementum.*
grub, subst. *vermiculus.*
grub, v.: to — up, *eruĕre.*
grudge, subst. *simultas, invidia.*

grudge, v. (*rem homini*) *invidĕre.*
gruff, *asper*; adv. *aspere.*
grumble, *murmurare, fremĕre.*
grunt, subst. *grunnitus (-ūs).*
grunt, v. *grunnire.*
Guadalquivir, *Baetis.*
guarantee, subst.: as a thing, *fides, sponsio, vadimonium*; = guarantor, *vas, sponsor.*
guarantee, v. *praestare, fidem dare.*
guard, subst. *custodia, praesidium*; to mount —, *excubare, excubias* or *vigilias agĕre*; to be on one's —, *(prae)cavĕre*; off one's —, *incautus, imprudens*; = persons on guard, *custodes (-um), custodia, praesidium.*
guard, v. *custodīre, tueri.*
guarded, *cautus, circumspectus*; adv. *caute.*
guardian, *custos, defensor*; of a ward, *tutor.*
guardianship, *custodia*; of a ward, *tutela.*
guess, subst. *coniectura.*
guess, v. *conicĕre, divinare, augurari.*
guest, *hospes (-itis),* f. *hospita*; at a party, *conviva.*
guidance, *ductus (-ūs), consilium.*
guide, *dux.*
guide, *ducĕre.* Transf., *regĕre, gubernare, moderari.*
guild, *conlegium.*
guile, *dolus, astutia.*
guileless, *simplex, apertus*; adv. *simpliciter.*
guilelessness, *simplicitas.*
guilt, *vitium, culpa, noxia.*
guiltless, *innocens, insons.*
guilty, *sons, sceleratus, nocens*; adv. *scelerate.*
guise, *habitus (-ūs), species.*
gulf, *sinus (-ūs,* = bay); *gurges* (= abyss).
gullet, *gula, guttur.*
gullible, *credulus.*
gully, *alveus.*
gulp, subst. *haustus (-ūs).*
gulp, v. *haurire, obsorbĕre.*
gum: of the mouth, *gingiva*; of plants, *gummi.*
gun: use *tormentum.*
gurgle, *murmurare.*
gush, v. *effundi.*
gust, *flabra (-orum,* n. plur.).
gusty, *turbidus, procellosus.*
gut, subst. *intestinum.*
gut, v. *exinanire.*
gutter, *canalis, cloaca.*
guttural, of sounds, *gravis.*
gymnasium, *gymnasium, palaestra.*
gymnastic, *gymnicus, palaestricus.*

H

ha! *ha!*
habit: = custom, *consuetudo, mos, usus (-ūs)*; = state, *habitus (-ūs).*
habitable, *habitabilis.*
habitation, *domicilium, sedes, domus.*
habitual, *inveteratus, usitatus*; adv. *de* or *ex more.*
habituate, *adsuefacĕre.*

hack, v. *caedĕre.*
hackneyed, *tritus.*
haft, *manubrium.*
hag, *anus (-ūs), anicula.*
haggle, *de pretio ambigĕre.*
hail, subst. *grando.*
hail, v.: it —s, *grandinat*; = to greet, *salutare, appellare.*
hail, interj. *salve!* plur. *salvete!*
hair: single, *pilus, capillus, saeta* (= bristle); coll., use plur., or *crinis, comae (-arum), caesaries* (flowing).
hairdresser, *tonsor.*
hairpin, *crinale.*
hairsplitting, *disserendi spinae (-arum).*
hairy, *pilosus, capillatus.*
halcyon, subst. *alcedo, (h)alcyon.*
halcyon, adj. *serenus.*
hale, adj. *sanus, validus, robustus.*
hale, v. *rapĕre, trahĕre.*
half, subst. *dimidium.*
half, adj. *dimidius, dimidiatus.*
half-asleep, *semisomnus, semisopitus.*
half-burnt, *semiustus.*
half-hour, *semihora.*
half-open, *semiapertus.*
half-pound, *selibra.*
hall, *atrium.*
hallo! *heus! ohe!*
halloo, subst. *clamor.*
halloo, v. *clamare, vociferari.*
hallow, *consecrare, dedicare.*
hallowed, *sacer, sanctus.*
hallucination, *error.*
halm, *calamus.*
halt, adj. *claudus.*
halt, v.: = limp, *claudicare*; = stop *consistĕre.*
halter, *capistrum, laqueus* (= noose).
halve, *ex aequo dividĕre.*
halved, *dimidiatus.*
ham, *poples*; salted, smoked, etc., *perna.*
hamlet, *vicus, viculus.*
hammer, subst. *malleus.*
hammer, v. *malleo (con)tundĕre.*
hamper, subst. *corbis.*
hamper, v. *implicare, impedire.*
hamstring, v. *poplitem succidĕre.*
hand, subst. *manus (-ūs,* f.), *palma* (= palm); right —, *(manus) dextra* or *dextera*; left —, *(manus) sinistra* or *laeva*; to give a person one's —, *homini dextram porrigĕre*; = workman, *opera* (usually plur.); an old —, *veterator*; to be at —, *praesto esse, adesse*; in —, on —, *in manibus*; — to — (in fighting), *comminus.*
hand, v. *dare, tradĕre, porrigĕre.*
handcuffs, *manicae (-arum).*
handful, *manipulus.*
handicraft, *artificium.*
handiwork, *opus (-eris,* n.), *opificium.*
handkerchief, *sudarium.*
handle, subst. *manubrium, capulus, ansa* (lit. and fig.).
handle, v. *tractare, contrectare.*
handling, *tractatio.*
handsome, *formosus, venustus, pulcher.* Transf., *liberalis*; adv. *praeclare, liberaliter.*
handwriting, *manus (-ūs,* f.), *chirographum.*

handy, *habilis, promptus.*

hang, v.: intransit., *pendēre*; to — over, *imminēre*; to — back, *cessare*; transit., *suspendĕre*; to — the head, *caput demittĕre.*

hanger-on, *adsecla.*

hanging, subst. *suspendium.*

hangman, *carnifex.*

hanker; to — after, *desiderare.*

haphazard, adv. *temere.*

hapless, *miser, infelix.*

haply, *fortasse, forsitan.*

happen, *fieri, accidĕre, contingĕre.*

happiness, *vita beata, felicitas.*

happy, *beatus, felix, fortunatus*; of language, *aptus.* Adv. *beate, feliciter.*

harangue, *contio*; to deliver a —, *contionari.*

harass, *vexare, sollicitare.*

harbinger, *praenuntius, antecursor.*

harbour, subst. *portus (-ūs)*; — -dues, *portorium*; full of —s, *portuosus.*

harbour, v. *(hospitio) excipĕre.*

hard, adj. *durus*; = difficult, *difficilis, arduus.*

hard, adv. *summa vi, enixe.*

harden, v.: transit., *durum facĕre*; intransit., *obdurescĕre.*

hard-hearted, *durus, ferreus.*

hardihood, *audacia.*

hardly, = scarcely, *vix, aegre.*

hardness, *duritia (or durities)*; = severity, *iniquitas, crudelitas.*

hardship, *labor, incommodum, molestia.*

hardware, *ferramenta (-orum).*

hardy, *robustus.*

hare, *lepus (leporis, m.).*

hark! interj. *heus!*

harlequin, *sannio.*

harm, subst. *damnum, detrimentum.*

harm, v. *nocēre, laedĕre.*

harmful, *nocens, noxius.*

harmless, *innocens, innoxius.*

harmlessness, *innocentia.*

harmonious, *concors* (lit. and fig.); *congruens, conveniens.* Adv. *concorditer, congruenter, convenienter.*

harmonize, v.: transit. *concordes facĕre, componĕre, (re)conciliare*; intransit., *concinĕre, consentire.*

harmony, *concordia* (lit. and fig.); *consensus (-ūs), convenientia.*

harness, subst. *ornamenta equi.*

harness, v. *(equum) ornare.*

harp, subst. *lyra.*

harp, v. *psallĕre.*

harpist: m. *fidicen psaltes (-ae)*; f. *fidicina, psaltria.*

harpy, *harpyia.*

harrow, subst. *(h)irpex, crates.*

harrow, v. *occare*; to — the feelings, *(ex)cruciare.*

harrowing, *terribilis, atrox.*

harry, *vexare, cruciare.*

harsh: in sound, *raucus, asper*; in taste, *acer, asper*; in temper, *asper, morosus, durus.* Adv. *aspere.*

harshness, *asperitas.*

hart, *cervus.*

harvest, subst. *messis.*

harvester, *messor.*

haste, subst. *festinatio, celeritas*; nervous —, *trepidatio.*

haste, hasten, v.: intransit., *properare, festinare, maturare*; transit., *accelerare, maturare, properare.*

hastiness, of temper, *iracundia.*

hasty: = hurried, *(prae)properus, citus, praeceps*: = irritable, *iracundus, stomachosus.* Adv. *propere, properanter, raptim.*

hat, *petasus.*

hatch, v. *(ex ovis) excludĕre*: = to concoct, *moliri, machinari.*

hatches, *claustra (-orum).*

hatchet, *securis, ascia, dolabra.*

hate, hatred, *odium, invidia.*

hate, v. *odisse*; to be hated, *odio esse.*

hateful, *odiosus, invisus*; adv. *odiose.*

haughtiness, *superbia, insolentia, adrogantia.*

haughty, *superbus, insolens, adrogans*; adv. *superbe, insolenter, adroganter.*

haul, v. *trahĕre, ducĕre.*

haulm; see stalk.

haunch, *clunis.*

haunt, subst. *latebrae (-arum), latibulum, lustra (-orum).*

haunt, v. *frequentare, (con)celebrare*; of spirits, cares, etc., *agitare, sollicitare.*

have, *habēre, tenēre*; to — to do *debēre facĕre.*

haven, *portus (-ūs).*

havoc, *vastatio, strages.*

hawk, subst. *accipiter (-tris, m.).*

hawk, v. = sell, *venditare.*

hay, *faenum.*

hay-fork, *furca.*

hazard, subst. *fors, casus (-ūs), periculum* (= risk), *alea* (= gambling).

hazard, v.; see dare or endanger.

hazardous, *periculosus*; adv. *periculose.*

haze, *nebula, caligo.*

hazel, *corylus.*

hazy, *nebulosus.*

he, *hic, ille, is*; = himself, *ipse.*

head, subst. *caput, vertex*; the back of the —, *occipitium*; = understanding or memory, *mens, animus, iudicium*; = chief, leader, *caput, princeps, dux*; to be at the —, *praeesse*; to put at the —, *praeficere*; = point, heading, *caput.*

head, adj. *primus, primarius, princeps.*

head, v. *ducĕre, praeesse.*

head-band, *infula, vita, redimiculum.*

head-dress, *mitra.*

headland, *promontorium.*

headlong, *praeceps.*

headquarters, *praetorium, principia (-orum).*

headstrong, *pervicax, temerarius.*

head-wind, *ventus adversus.*

heady, = intoxicating, *fervidus.*

heal, v.: transit., *sanare, medēri, curare*; intransit., *consanescĕre.*

healing, subst. *sanatio.*

healing, adj. *saluber, salutaris.*

health, *sanitas, valetudo.*

healthful, *saluber, salutaris.*

healthy, *sanus, salvus, saluber* (of places); adv. *salubriter.*

heap, subst. *acervus, agger.*

heap, v. *cumulare, coacervare, congerĕre.*

hear, *audire, auscultare* (= listen to). Transf., = find out, learn, *cognoscĕre accipĕre.*

hearer, auditor.

hearing, subst.: as sense, auditus (-ūs); as process, auditio; = an audience, audientia; a judicial —, cognitio.

hearken, auscultare.

hearsay, rumor, auditio.

heart: physical, cor; = seat of feeling, etc. animus, mens, pectus (-oris, n.); from the —, ex animo; = courage, animus; = memory: to know by —, memoria tenēre; to learn by —, ediscēre; dear —, (mea) vita.

heart-breaking, miserabilis, maestus, flebilis.

heart-broken, animo fractus or adflictus.

heartfelt, verus.

hearth, focus.

heartiness, studium, alacritas.

heartless, crudelis, saevus; adv. crudeliter, saeve.

heartlessness, crudelitas, saevitia.

heart-sick, animo aeger.

hearty, verus (= true), alacer (= brisk), benignus (=kind). Adv. summo studio.

heat, subst. calor, ardor, fervor, aestus (-ūs); of passion, etc., ardor, fervor, aestus.

heat, v. calefacěre, fervefacěre. Transf., accenděre.

heath: as plant, erice(-es, f.); as a place, loca inculta.

heathen, adj. paganus.

heave, v.: transit., (at)tollěre, extollěre; to — a sigh, gemitum dare, or ducěre; intransit., aestuare, fluctuare, tumescěre.

heaven: = sky, caelum; = gods, di (dei), superi; the will of —, numen divinum; for —'s sake! per deos immortales! — forbid, di meliora.

heavenly, caelestis, divinus.

heaviness, gravitas, pondus(-eris, n.); of atmosphere, crassitudo; = sadness, tristitia, maestitia.

heavy, gravis, ponderosus; of air, crassus; of soil, spissus; of rain, magnus; abstr., = oppressive, gravis, molestus; = downcast, tristis, adflictus, maestus. Adv. graviter.

heavy-armed; — troops, gravior armatus (-ūs).

Hebrew, adj. Hebraeus, Hebraicus.

hectic, febriculosus.

hector, se iactare.

hedge, subst. saepes, saepimentum.

hedge, v. saepire.

hedgehog, ericus, echinus.

heed, subst.: to take —, cavēre.

heed, v. curare, observare; = obey, parēre, obedire.

heedless, neglegens, temerarius; adv. neglegenter, temere.

heedlessness, neglegentia, temeritas.

heel, subst. calx.

heel, v. in latus labi or inclinari.

heifer, iuvenca.

height, altitudo, proceritas; the — of glory, summa gloria; = high place, locus editus, altitudines (-um, plur.).

heighten; render by altior; = increase, augēre, amplificare, exaggerare.

heinous, foedus, nefarius, atrox; adv. foede, nefarie, atrociter.

heinousness, atrocitas.

heir, heres; sole —, heres ex asse.

heirloom, res hereditaria.

Helen, Helena.

hell, inferi (-orum), Tartarus, or n. plur. Tartara.

hellebore, (h)elleborus, veratrum.

Hellenic, Graecus.

hellish, infernus, nefandus.

helm, gubernaculum.

helmet, cassis, galea.

helmsman, gubernator.

help, subst. auxilium, subsidium.

help, v. (ad)iuvare, subvenire, succurrěre; so — me God, ita me di ament; I can't — saying, facěre non possum quin dicam.

helper, adiutor; f. adiutrix.

helpful, utilis.

helpless, inermis, inops.

helplessness, inopia.

hem, subst. limbus, instita.

hem, v.: = sew, suěre; to — in, circumsedēre, obsidēre.

hemp, cannabis.

hen, gallina.

hence, hinc; as interj., apage; a few days —, paucis diebus, post paucos dies.

henceforth, posthac.

Henry, Henricus.

her, possessive, eius, illius; — own, suus -a -um.

herald, subst., caduceator, fetialis, praeco; = forerunner, praenuntius.

herald, v. nuntiare.

herb, herba, olus (oleris, n.).

herd, subst. grex; of large cattle, armentum; of a —, gregalis, gregarius; in —s, gregatim; of people, the common —, vulgus (-i, n.).

herd, v. intransit. congregari.

herdsman, pastor, armentarius.

here: = at this place, hic; to be —, adesse; = to this place, hither, huc; from — (hence), hinc; — and there. rarus (adv. raro).

hereafter, posthac, aliquando.

hereditary, hereditarius, paternus.

herein, in hac re.

hereupon, hic.

heritage, hereditas, patrimonium.

hermit, homo solitarius.

hero: = demigod, heros; = brave man, vir fortissimus; in a play, persona prima.

heroic, heroicus; = brave, valiant, fortis; adv. fortiter.

heroine: = demi-goddess, heroina, herois; = brave woman, femina fortissima.

heroism, eximia virtus (-utis), animus fortis.

heron, ardea.

hers; see her.

herself, reflex., se; otherwise ipsa.

hesitate, dubitare, cunctari, haesitare.

hesitation, dubitatio, haesitatio, cunctatio.

heterogeneous, diversus, dissimilis.

hew, caeděre, dolare.

hewn; hewn stone, saxum quadratum.

hexameter, hexameter (or -trus).

heyday, flos aetatis.

hiatus, *hiatus (-ūs).*

hibernate, *per hiemen dormire* or *quiescĕre.*

hiccough, hiccup, *singultus (-ūs).*

hidden, *occultus*; to lie —, *latēre.*

hide, subst. *corium, pellis.*

hide, v.: transit., *abdĕre, celare*; of feelings, etc., *dissimulare*; intransit., render by reflex.

hideous, *foedus, turpis*; adv. *foede.*

hideousness, *foeditas, deformitas.*

hiding-place, *latibulum, latebra.*

higgledy-piggledy, *confuse.*

high, adj. *altus,* (ex)celsus, *procerus* (= tall), *sublimis* (= raised aloft); in rank, *amplus*; of prices, *magnus*; of sound, *acutus*; of meat, *rancidus.* Adv. *alte*; to value —, *magni aestimare.*

high-born, *generosus, nobili loco ortus.*

high-flown, *tumidus.*

high-handed, *superbus, imperiosus.*

highlander, *homo montanus*

highlands, *loca montuosa (-orum)*

high-minded, *magnanimus. generosus.*

high-priest, *Pontifex Maximus.*

high-spirited, *ferox, animosus.*

high-tide *plurimus aestûs accessus (-ūs).*

highway, *via.*

highwayman, *latro, grassator.*

hilarity, *hilaritas, laetitia.*

hill, *collis, tumulus*; up —, *adverso colle*

hilly, *montuosus, clivosus.*

hilt, *capulus.*

him; see he.

himself, reflex., *se*; otherwise *ipse.*

hind, subst.: = female stag, *cerva*; = servant, *verna, servus*; = peasant, *rusticus, agrestis.*

hind, adj. *aversus, posterior.*

hinder, *impedire, obstare, officĕre.*

hindmost, *postremus, ultimus, novissimus.*

hindrance, *impedimentum.*

hinge, subst. *cardo.*

hint, subst. *significatio.*

hint, v. *significare.*

hip, *coxendix.*

hire, subst. *merces.*

hire, v. *conducĕre.*

hired, *conductus, mercenarius*

hireling, *mercenarius.*

hirer, *conductor.*

his, *eius, illius, huius*; — own. *suus -a -um.*

hiss, subst. *sibilus* (plur. *sibila*).

hiss, v. *sibilare*; to — off the stage, *exsibilare, explodĕre.*

hist! *st!*

historian, *rerum* (gestarum) *scriptor.*

historic, historical, *historicus*; — writings, *libri ad historiam pertinentes.*

history, *historia, rerum gestarum memoria, annales*; ancient —, *antiquitatis memoria.*

histrionic, *scaenicus.*

hit, subst. *plaga, ictus (-ūs).*

hit, v. *ferire, tundĕre, percutĕre*; to — it off = agree, *convenire*; to — upon, *offendĕre, incidĕre.*

hitch, subst. *impedimentum* (= hindrance), *mora* (= delay).

hitch, v. *(ad)iungĕre, adnectĕre.*

hither, adj. *citerior.*

hither, adj. *huc*; — and thither, *huc illuc.*

hitherto, *adhuc, hactenus.*

hive, *alvearium, alvus.*

ho! *heus!*

hoard, subst. *copia, acervus.*

hoard, v. *conquirĕre, coacervare.*

hoar-frost, *pruina.*

hoarse, *raucus*; adv. *rauca voce.*

hoary, *canus.*

hoax, subst. *ludificatio.*

hoax, v. *ludificari, inludĕre.*

hobble, *claudicare.*

hobby, *studium.*

hock, *poples.*

hoe, subst. *sarculum, marra*

hoe, v. *sarire.*

hog, *sus, porcus.*

hoggish, *suillus.*

hogshead, *dolium.*

hoist, *sublevare, tollĕre.*

hold, subst.: = grasp *manus (-ūs)*; of a ship, *caverna.*

hold, v.: = to have, possess, *tenēre, obtinēre, possidēre, habēre*; = to contain, *capĕre, continēre*; = to conduct, *agĕre, habēre*; to — an opinion = that, *censēre, ducĕre*; = to check, *cohibēre*; to — out (= endure), *durare, sustinēre.*

holding, subst. *possessio.*

hole, *cavum, foramen; rima* (= chink); *lacuna* (= pit).

holiday, *dies festus, feriae(-arum).*

holiness, *sanctitas, religio.*

Holland, *Batavia.*

hollow, subst., = valley, *convallis, valles* (vallis); see also hole.

hollow, adj. *(con)cavus*; of sounds, *fuscus, raucus*; = insincere, *vanus, simulatus.*

hollow, v. *(ex)cavare.*

holm-oak, *ilex.*

holy, *sacer, sanctus*; adv. *sancte.*

homage, *cultus (-ūs), observantia.*

home, subst. *domus, domicilium*; at — *domi*; from —, *domo*; —wards *to* one's —, *domum.*

home, adj. *domesticus, familiaris.*

homeless, *domo carens.*

homeliness, *simplicitas.*

homely, *simplex, rudis.*

homewards, *domum.*

homicide; see murder.

homily, *oratio.*

homogeneous, *eiusdem generis.*

honest, *probus, sincerus, frugi,* adv. *probe, sincere.*

honesty, *probitas, sinceritas, fides.*

honey, *mel*

honeycomb, *favus.*

honeyed, honied, *mellitus, suavis. dulcis.*

honour, subst.: = official distinction, *dignitas, honos* (honor); = moral integrity, *honestas, fides*; sense of — *pudor*; an — to, = a credit to, *decus.*

honour, v. *colĕre, honorare, celebrare.*

honourable: = honoured, *honoratus, amplus*; = bring honour, *honestus, honorificus.* Adv. *honeste, honorifice.*

hood, *cucullus.*

hoodwink, *ludificari, inludĕre.*

hoof, *ungula.*

hook, subst. *hamus, uncus.*

hook, v. *hamo capĕre.*

hooked, *aduncus, hamatus.*

hoop, *circulus;* a child's —, *trochus.*

hoopoe, *upupa.*

hoot, hooting, subst.: of owls, *cantus* (-ūs); of persons, *vociferatio.*

hoot, v.: of owls, *canĕre;* of persons, *vociferari, obstrepĕre.*

hop, v. *salire.*

hope, subst. *spes;* a gleam of —, *specula;* to have no —, *desperare.*

hope, v. *sperare.*

hopeful, hopefully; render by phrase with *spes.*

hopeless: = despairing, *spe carens;* = despaired of, *desperatus.*

hopelessness, *desperatio; res desperatae.*

horde, *grex, caterva.*

horizon, *orbis finiens;* = sky, in gen., *caelum.*

horizontal, *aequus, libratus;* adv. *ad libram.*

horn, *cornu;* as a drinking-cup, *poculum.*

horned, *corniger, cornutus.*

hornet, *crabro.*

horny, *corneus.*

horoscope, *horoscopus, genesis;* to cast a —, *sidera natalicia notare.*

horrible, horrid, *horribilis, foedus, atrox;* adv. *foede.*

horrify, *(ex)terrēre, obstupefacĕre.*

horror, *horror, timor, pavor;* a —, = a monster, *monstrum.*

horse, *equus;* = cavalry, *equites* (-*um*), *equitatus* (-ūs).

horseback; to ride on —, *in equo vehi, equitare;* to fight on — *ex equo pugnare.*

horse-fly, *tabanus.*

horse-hair, *pilus equinus.*

horseman, *eques.*

horse-race, *curriculum equorum*

horse-shoe, *solea.*

horticulture, *hortorum cultus* (-ūs).

hospitable, *hospitalis;* adv. *hospitaliter, comiter.*

hospitality, *hospitium, hospitalitas.*

host, *hospes;* at a feast, *convivator;* at an inn, *caupo;* = multitude; army, *exercitus* (-ūs).

hostage, *obses.*

hostelry, *caupona.*

hostess, *hospita.*

hostile, *hostilis, inimicus, infestus.*

hostility, *animus infestus, inimicitia, odium;* hostilities, *hostilia* (-ium), *bellum.*

hot, *calidus, fervidus, fervens, ardens;* to be —, *calēre, fervēre, aestuare;* to make —, *calefacĕre.* Adv. *ardenter.*

hotel, *deversorium, hospitium.*

hotheaded, *fervidus, temerarius.*

hound, subst. *canis (venaticus).*

hound, v. *instigare, urgēre.*

hour, *hora;* half an —, *semihora;* what — is it? *quota hora est?*

hourly, *singulis horis, in horas.*

house, subst. *domus, aedes, aedificium, domicilium;* = race, clan, *gens, genus;* at my —, *apud me, domi meae*

house, v. = store, *condĕre.*

housebreaker, *fur.*

household, subst. *domus, familia.*

household, adj. *domesticus;* —-gods, *lares* (-um), *penates* (-ium).

householder, *paterfamilias.*

house-keeper, *promus.*

house-maid, *ancilla.*

house-wife, *materfamilias, hera.*

hovel, *tugurium, gurgustium.*

hover, *(circum)volitare, imminēre.*

how. (1) interrog. *quomodo? quemadmodum? qui?;* with adj. or adv., *quam?;* how great? *quantus?;* how small? *quantulus?;* how many? *quot?;* how often? *quotie(n)s?.* (2) in exclamation, *ut, quam;* also *quantus, quantulus,* etc.

howbeit, *(at)tamen.*

however: adv. *quamvis, quamlibet;* — great, *quantuscunque, quantus quantus;* — many, *quotquot;* — often, *quotienscunque;* conj., *sed, autem, (at)tamen, nihilominus.*

howl, subst. *ululatus* (-ūs), *eiulatus* (-ūs).

howl, v. *ululare, fremĕre, eiulare.*

hubbub, *tumultus* (-ūs), *turba.*

huckster, *caupo, institor.*

huddled, *conferti.*

hue, *color.*

hug, subst. *complexus* (-ūs).

hug, v. *amplecti, complecti;* to — the shore, *litus premĕre* or *legĕre.*

huge, *immanis, ingens.*

hulk, *alveus navis.*

hum, subst. *fremitus* (-ūs), *murmur, susurrus.*

hum, v. *fremĕre, murmurare;* = sing softly, *secum canĕre.*

human, *humanus, hominum* (= of men); — feelings, *humanitas;* — being, *homo.* Adv. *humano modo.*

humane, *misericors, clemens;* adv. *clementer, humane.*

humanity: = nature of man, *humanitas, natura humana;* = mankind, *homines* (-um), *gens humana;* = kindly feeling, *clementia, misericordia.*

humble, adj.: = obscure, *humilis, obscurus:* of — origin, *humili loco natus;* = modest, unassuming, *summissus, verecundus.* Adv. *summisse.*

humble, v. *infringĕre, comprimĕre;* to — oneself, *se* or *animum summittĕre.*

humid, *humidus.*

humidity, *humor.*

humiliation, *dedecus* (-oris, n.).

humility, *animus summissus.*

humorous: of situations, *ridiculus;* of persons, *iocosus, lepidus, facetus.*

humour: = fluid, *humor;* = disposition, *ingenium, natura, animus;* = fancy, caprice, *voluptas, libido;* I am in the — to do, *libet mihi facere;* = sense of fun, *festivitas, facetiae(-arum).*

humour, v. *indulgēre, morem gerĕre* (with dat.).

hump, *gibbus, gibba.*

humpbacked, *gibber.*

hundred, adj. *centum;* a — at a time, *centeni -ae -a;* a — times, *centie(n)s*

hundred-fold, *centuplex.*

hunger, subst. *fames.*

hunger, v. *esurire.*

hungry, *esuriens, ieiunus*; adv. *avide.*

hunt, v. *venari, consectari.*

hunt, subst. *venatio, venatus (-ūs).*

hunter, huntsman, *venator.*

huntress, *venatrix.*

hurdle, *crates.*

hurl, *iacĕre, iaculari, conicĕre.*

hurling, subst. *coniectus (-ūs).*

hurrah! *io!*

hurricane, *tempestas, procella.*

hurried, *citatus, praeceps*; adv. *festinanter, propere, raptim.*

hurry, subst. *festinatio, trepidatio.*

hurry, v.: transit. *accelerare, incitare, rapĕre; maturare* (= to hurry on); instransit., *festinare, properare, maturare.*

hurt, subst. *vulnus (-eris, n.).*

hurt, adj.: physically, *saucius*; in feelings, *offensus.*

hurt, v. *laedĕre, nocĕre*; to — a person's feelings, *hominem offendĕre*; to be — at a thing, *rem aegre ferre*; it —s, *dolet.*

hurtful, *nocens, noxius, molestus.*

husband, subst. *maritus, vir, coniunx.*

husband, v. *parcĕre.*

husbandman, *agricola, colonus.*

husbandry, *res rustica, agricultura.*

hush! interj. *st! tacē* (plur. *tacēte*).

hush, v. *comprimĕre.*

husk, *folliculus.*

hustings, *suggestus (-ūs), comitium.*

hustle, v. *offendĕre, pulsare.*

hut, *casa, tugurium.*

hutch, *cavea* (= cage).

hyacinth, *hyacinthus (hyacinthos).*

hymeneal, *nuptialis.*

hymn, subst. *carmen, hymnus* (ecclesiastical).

hymn, v. *canĕre, cantare, celebrare.*

hyperbole, *hyperbole, veritatis superlatio.*

hyperbolical, *superlatus.*

hypercritical, *nimium severus.*

hypochondria, *atra* (or *nigra) bilis.*

hypochondriacal, *melancholicus.*

hypocrisy, *(dis)simulatio, fraus.*

hypocrite, *(dis)simulator.*

hypocritical, *simulatus, fictus*; adv. *simulate, ficte.*

hypothesis, *opinio, sententia, coniectura.*

I

iambic, subst. *iambus.*

iambic, adj. *iambeus.*

ice, *glacies, gelu.*

icicle, *stiria.*

icy, *glacialis, gelidus, frigidus.*

idea: = notion, conception, *notio, notitia, imago*; in gen., = thought, *cogitatio, opinio, sententia*; = purpose, *consilium.*

ideal, subst., = perfect type, *exemplar, specimen.*

ideal, adj.: = perfect, *perfectus, optimus, summus*; = existing only in the mind, *commenticius.*

identical, *idem.*

identify: = recognize, *agnoscĕre.*

identify; render by *idem* (= same), or phrase like *quis sit* (= who he is).

ides, *idūs (-uum).*

idiocy, *fatuitas.*

idiom, *propria loquendi ratio.*

idiotic, *fatuus.*

idle, adj.: = inactive, lazy, *otiosus, vacuus, piger, segnis*; = useless, *inutilis, vanus, irritus.* Adv. *segniter*; = in vain, *frustra, incassum.*

idle, v. *cessare, nihil agĕre.*

idleness: = inactivity, *cessatio, otium*; = laziness, *segnitia, pigritia.*

idler, *homo deses; cessator.*

idol, *idolum* (ecclesiastical); *fictus deus.*

idolize, *(tamquam deum) colĕre.*

idyl, *bucolica (-orum, n.*; = pastoral poetry).

if, *si*; and —, *quodsi*; but —, *sin*; — only, *si modo* (or *dum modo* with subj.); even —, *etsi, etiamsi*; as —, *quasi, tamquam*; in indirect questions, if (= whether) is *num.*

igneous, *igneus.*

ignite, v.: transit., *accendĕre, incendĕre*; intransit., *exardescĕre, accendi, incendi.*

ignoble: by descent, *ignobilis, obscuro loco natus*; in character, *inliberalis, abiectus, turpis*; adv. *trupiter.*

ignominious, *turpis*; adv. *turpiter, cum ignominia.*

ignominy, *ignominia, dedecus (-oris).*

ignorance, *inscientia, ignoratio.*

ignorant, *inscius, ignarus, imperitus* (= inexperienced), *indoctus* (= untaught); to be —, *nescire, ignorare.* Adv. *inscienter, imperite*; or render by adj.

ignore, *praeterire, neglegĕre.*

ill, subst. *malum.*

ill, adj.: = sick, *aeger, aegrotus*: to be —, *aegrotare*; = evil, *malus*; —-fame, *infamia.*

ill, adv. *male, prave.*

ill-advised, *inconsultus, temerarius.*

ill-bred, *inhumanus, inurbanus.*

ill-disposed, *malevolus.*

illegally, *contra leges.*

illegitimate: of actions, *non legitimus*; of persons, *nothus.*

ill-fated, *infelix, miser.*

ill-gotten, *male partus.*

ill-health, *valetudo infirma.*

illiberal, *inliberalis, sordidus, malignus.*

illicit, *inlicitus, vetitus*; see illegally.

illiterate, *indoctus.*

ill-matched, *impar.*

ill-natured, *malevolus, malignus.*

illness, *aegrotatio, valetudo infirma.*

illogical, *absurdus.*

ill-omened, *dirus, tristis.*

ill-starred, *infelix.*

ill-tempered, *acerbitas, morositas, iracundia.*

illume, illuminate: = throw light on, *inlustrare, inluminare*; = enlighten the mind, *docēre, erudire*; = adorn with pictures, *varie pingĕre, coloribus distinguĕre.*

illusion, *error, opinio vana.*

illusory, *vanus, falsus.*

illustrate *(librum) picturis ornare*; see also explain.

illustration; in a book, *pictura, tabula;* = example, *exemplum.*

illustrious, *(prae)clarus, inlustris, insignis.*

ill-will, *malevolentia.*

image, *imago, simulacrum, species.*

imaginary, *opinabilis, commenticius; fictus, falsus.*

imagination, *cogitatio.*

imagine, *animo concipĕre, (cogitatione) fingĕre, excogitare; =* to think, *putare, opinari.*

imbecile, *fatuus, stultus.*

imbecility, *imbecillitas animi, stultitia.*

imbibe, *(com)bibĕre, imbibĕre.*

imbue, *inficĕre, imbuĕre, tingĕre.*

imitable, *imitabilis.*

imitate, *imitari; =* portray, *exprimĕre, effingĕre; =* emulate, *aemulari.*

imitation, *imitatio, aemulatio; =* a copy, *effigies, imago, simulacrum.*

imitator, *imitator* (f. *imitatrix); aemulus, aemulator.*

immaculate, *purus, integer;* adv. *pure.*

immaterial, *sine corpore, expers corporis; =* unimportant, *nullius momenti, levis.*

immature, *immaturus, crudus.*

immeasurable, *immensus, infinitus.*

immediate: = direct, *proximus;* = without delay, *praesens.* Adv., = directly, render by *ipse;* —before, or —after, *sub* with acc.; = at once, *statim, confestim, extemplo.*

immemorial; render by *antiquus.*

immense, *ingens, vastus, immensus.* Adv. *in immensum; =* very much *maxime, valde.*

immensity, *immensitas.*

immigrate, *(im)migrare.*

immigrant, *advena.*

imminent, *praesens;* to be —, *instare, imminēre, impendēre.*

immoderate, *immodicus, nimius, intemperans;* adv. *immodice, intemperanter, praeter modum, nimis.*

immodest, *impudicus, impudens;* adv. *impudenter.*

immodesty, *impudicitia.*

immolate, *immolare.*

immolation, *immolatio.*

immoral, *pravus, inhonestus, turpis;* adv. *prave, inhoneste, turpiter.*

immorality, *mores corrupti; turpitudo.*

immortal, *immortalis, aeternus, sempiternus* (of things).

immortality, *immortalitas, aeternitas, sempiterna gloria.*

immoveable, *immobilis, stabilis.*

immune, *immunis;* see also free.

immunity, *vacatio, immunitas.*

immure, *includĕre.*

immutability, *immutabilitas, constantia.*

immutable, *immutabilis, constans, stabilis;* adv. *constanter.*

impair, *(im)minuĕre, debilitare, infringĕre.*

impale, *(hasta* or *palo) transfigĕre.*

impart, *impertire, communicare, dare.*

impartial, *aequus;* to be —, *neutri favēre.*

impartiality, *aequitas.*

impassable, *invius, impeditus.*

impassioned, *ardens, vehemens.*

impassive, *lentus.*

impassivity, *lentitudo, lentus animus.*

impatience, *festinatio.*

impatient, *impatiens morae, ardens acer;* adv. *ardenter, acriter.*

impeach, *accusare.*

impeachment, *accusatio.*

impede, *impedire.*

impediment, *impedimentum;* in speech. *haesitantia linguae.*

impel, *impellĕre, urgēre.*

impend, *impendēre, imminēre.*

impenetrable, *impenetrabilis impervius, impeditus.*

impenitent, *obstinatus, offirmatus.*

imperative, gram., *imperativus* (adj.).

imperfect: gram., *imperfectus* (adj.); = unfinished, *imperfectus, rudis; =* faulty, *vitiosus, mendosus;* adv. *vitiose, mendose, male.*

imperfection, *vitium, mendum, culpa.*

imperial, render by· genit., e.g. *imperatoris, principis.*

imperil, *in discrimen adducĕre.*

imperious, *superbus, adrogans;* adv. *superbe, adroganter.*

imperishable, *immortalis, aeternus.*

impersonate; see imitate.

impertinence, *insolentia.*

impertinent: = rude, *insolens;* adv. *insolenter; =* not to the point, *nihil ad rem.*

imperturbable, *stabilis, firmus, gravis;* adv. *firme, graviter.*

impervious; see impenetrable.

impetuosity, *violentia, impetus (-ūs).*

impetuous, *violentus, rapidus, vehemens;* adv. *violenter, vehementer.*

impetus, *impetus (-ūs), vis.*

impiety, *impietas (erga deos), nefas.*

impious, *impius (erga deos) nefarius;* adv. *impie, nefarie.*

impinge, *incidĕre, impingi.*

implacable, *implacabilis, inexorabilis:* adv. *atrociter, saeve.*

implant, *inserĕre, ingenerare.*

implement, *instrumentum.*

implicate, *implicare, admiscēre, inligare.*

implicated, *implicatus, conscius.*

implicit: = implied, *tacitus; =* complete, *totus, summus.* Adv. *tacite;* see also altogether.

implore, *implorare, rogare, orare.*

imply: = to mean, indicate, *significare;* = to involve, *(in se) habēre;* to be implied, *(in re) inesse.*

impolite, *inurbanus;* adv. *inurbane.*

impoliteness, *inhumanitas, rusticitas.*

import, subst.; in plur., = imported goods, *res quae importantur; =* meaning, *vis, significatio.*

import, v.: = bring into a country, *invehĕre, importare; =* signify, *significare, valēre.*

importance: of things, *momentum, pondus (-eris), vis;* of persons, = position, etc., *amplitudo, dignitas, auctoritas.*

important, *gravis, magnus;* to be —, *magni momenti esse, multum valēre.*

import-duty, *portorium.*
importunate, *molestus, improbus.*
importune, *fatigare; flagitare.*
importunity, *flagitatio.*
impose, *imponĕre;* see also cheat.
imposing, *speciosus, magnificus.*
imposition, = deception, *fallacia, fraus.*
impossible, *quod fieri non potest.*
impost, *vectigal, tributum.*
impostor, *fraudator.*
impotence, *imbecillitas, infirmitas.*
impotent, *invalidus, infirmus, imbecillus.*
impound, = confiscate, *publicare.*
impoverish, *in egestatem redigĕre.*
impoverishment, *egestas, inopia.*
impracticable, *quod fieri non potest.*
imprecate, *(im)precari;* see also curse.
imprecation, *preces (-um), exsecratio.*
impregnable, *inexpugnabilis.*
impress, *imprimĕre, inculcare.*
impression, *impressio;* = copy, *exemplum, imago expressa;* = footstep, *vestigium.* Transf., = effect on the mind, *animi motus (-ūs);* to make an —, *animum (com)movēre;* = thought, idea, *opinio;* to be under an —, *putare, opinari.*
impressive, *gravis;* adv. *graviter.*
impressiveness, *gravitas.*
imprint; see impress.
imprison, *in custodiam* (or *carcerem) conicĕre.*
imprisonment, *custodia, carcer, vincula (-orum).*
improbable, *non verisimilis.*
impromptu, *ex tempore.*
improper, *indecorus, indignus;* adv. *indecore, indigne, perperam.*
improve, v.: transit., *meliorem facĕre, emendare, corrigĕre;* intransit., *meliorem fieri, proficĕre.*
improvement, *correctio, emendatio:* or render by *melior.*
improvidence, *imprudentia.*
improvident, *improvidus, imprudens;* adv. *improvide, imprudenter.*
improvised, *subitarius, ex tempore.*
imprudence, *imprudentia, temeritas.*
imprudent, *imprudens, temerarius;* adv. *imprudenter, temere.*
impudence, *impudentia, os impudens.*
impudent, *impudens, procax, improbus;* adv. *impudenter.*
impugn, *impugnare, improbare.*
impulse, *impulsio, impulsus (-ūs);* or render by verb.
impulsive, *vehemens, acer.*
impunity, *impunitas;* with —, *impune.*
impure, *impurus, obscenus, foedus, turpis;* adv. *impure, obscene, foede, turpiter.*
impurity, *impuritas, obscenitas, turpitudo.*
imputation, = charge, *crimen, culpa, accusatio.*
impute, *adsignare, ascribĕre, attribuĕre.*
in: of place, render by locative, or *in* with abl., or plain abl.; when = into, *in* with acc.; of time, render by abl., or by *in* and abl.; in the case of, *in* with abl.; in the hands of, *penes* with acc.; in the writings of, *apud* with acc.

inability, *infirmitas, inopia;* or render by *non posse.*
inaccessible, *inaccessus;* of persons, *rari aditūs.*
inaccurate: of a person, *indiligens;* of reports, etc., *falsus.*
inaction, inactivity, *otium, quies;* = laziness, *desidia, inertia.*
inactive, *quietus, iners; segnis.*
inadequate, *impar;* adv. *parum, haud satis.*
inadmissible, *inlicitus.*
inadvertence, *imprudentia.*
inadvertent, *imprudens;* adv. *imprudenter, temere.*
inalienable, *quod abalienari non potest.*
inane, *inanis.*
inanimate, *inanimus, inanimatus.*
inanition, *inanitas.*
inapplicable, to be, *non valēre.*
inapposite; see inappropriate.
inappropriate, *non idoneus.*
inaptitude, *inutilitas.*
inarticulate, *parum distinctus.*
inasmuch as, *quandoquidem.*
inattention, *neglegentia, incuria.*
inattentive, *non attentus;* to be — *aliud agĕre.*
inaugurate, *inaugurare, dedicare, consecrare.*
inauguration, *dedicatio, consecratio.*
inauspicious, *infelix, nefastus;* adv. *infeliciter, malis ominibus.*
incalculable, *immensus, ingens.*
incandescent, *candens.*
incantation, *carmen, cantio.*
incapable; render by *non posse.*
incarcerate; see imposing.
incarnate, *incarnatus* (ecclesiastical); *specie humana* (or *corpore) indutus.*
incautious, *incautus, inconsultus;* adv. *incaute, inconsulte, temere.*
incendiary, *incendiarius, incendiorum auctor.*
incense, subst. *tus (turis).*
incense, *accendĕre, incendĕre.*
incentive, *stimulus, incitamentum.*
inception, *initium.*
inceptive, *incipiens.*
incessant, *perpetuus, adsiduus, continuus;* adv. *perpetuo, adsidue.*
inch, *uncia.*
inchoate, *inchoatus.*
incident, *casus (-ūs), res.*
incidental, *fortuitus, forte oblatus;* adv. *casu, forte, fortuito.*
incipient, render by *initium* or *incipio.*
incisive, *mordax;* adv. *praecise.*
incite, *incitare, stimulare, impellĕre.*
incivility, *inurbanitas, inhumanitas.*
inclement: of persons, *severus, saevus;* of weather, *gravis, asper.*
inclination: physical, *inclinatio;* = slope, *fastigium, clivus;* mental, = propensity, *inclinatio, studium.*
incline, v.: transit., *inclinare;* intransit., *inclinari, (se) inclinare, propendĕre.*
inclined, *inclinatus, propensus, pronus.*
inclose; see enclose.
include, *comprehendĕre, complecti, adscribĕre;* to — among the accused, *in reos referre.*
including, *cum* with abl.

incognito, *alieno* or *dissimulato nomine*.

incoherent, *interruptus*; adv. *interrupte*; to speak —, *haud cohaerentia dicĕre*.

income, *vectigal, reditus* (*-ūs*, = returns), *pecunia, quaestus* (*-ūs*).

incommode, *incommodum* or *molestum esse*.

incomparable, *unicus, singularis, egregius*; adv. *unice, egregie*.

incompatibility, *repugnantia, diversitas*.

incompatible, *alienus, contrarius*; to be —, *abhorrēre, repugnare*.

incompetence, *inscitia*.

incompetent, *inscitus, inhabilis*; adv. *inscite*. Legally, render by phrase with *ius* or *potestas*.

incomplete, *imperfectus*; adv. *imperfecte*.

incomprehensible, *quod comprehendi non potest*.

inconceivable, *quod (mente) comprehendi non potest*; sometimes *incredibilis*. Adv. *incredibiliter, mirum in modum*.

inconclusive, (*argumentum*) *quo nihil efficitur*.

incongruity, *repugnantia*.

incongruous, *alienus, non aptus*.

inconsiderable, *levis, tenuis, exiguus*.

inconsiderate, = unthinking, *inconsideratus, inconsultus*; adv. *inconsiderate, nullo consilio, temere*.

inconsistency, *inconstantia, repugnantia*.

inconsistent, *inconstans, contrarius, repugnans*; adv. *inconstanter*.

inconsolable, *inconsolabilis*; *qui nullo solacio levari potest*.

inconspicuous, *obscurus*.

inconstancy, *inconstantia, levitas, varietas*.

inconstant, *inconstans, levis, varius*.

incontinence, *incontinentia, intemperantia*.

incontinent, *incontinens, intemperans*; adv. *incontinenter*; = immediately, *statim*.

incontrovertible, *quod refutari non potest*.

inconvenience, *incommodum*; to cause —, *negotium exhibēre*.

inconvenient, *inopportunus, incommodus*; adv. *incommode*.

incorrect, *falsu⟨, mendosus*; = morally wrong, *improbus, iniustus*. Adv. *perperam, falso, mendose*.

incorrigible, *perditus*; *qui corrigi non potest*.

incorruptibility, *integritas, sanctitas*.

incorruptible, *incorruptus, integer, sanctus*; adv. *incorrupte, integre, sancte*.

increase, subst. *incrementum, auctus* (*-ūs*).

increase, v.: transit., *augēre, amplificare*; intransit., *crescĕre, augēri, gliscĕre*.

incredible, *incredibilis*; adv. *incredibiliter*.

incredulous, *incredulus*.

increment, *incrementum*.

incriminate, *suspectum reddĕre*; to — oneself, *se scelere adligare*.

inculcate, *inculcare; docēre*.

incumbent; see ought, must.

incur, *suscipĕre, contrahĕre*; to — disgrace, *dedecus in se admittĕre*.

incurable, *insanabilis*.

incursion, *incursio*; see attack.

indebted: = owing money, *obaeratus*; = obliged, *obnoxius, obligatus*.

indecency, *turpitudo, obscenitas*.

indecent, *indecorus, turpis*; adv. *indecore, turpiter*.

indecision, *dubitatio, haesitatio*.

indecisive, *dubius, anceps*; adv. (of fighting), *aequo marte*.

indecorous, *indecorus*.

indeed: emphatic, *vere, profecto, sane*; and —, *atque adeo*; then —, *tum vero*; concessive, *quidem*; interrogative, *ain tu? itane est?*; ironical, *scilicet, nimirum, videlicet*.

indefatigable, *adsiduus, impiger*; adv. *adsidue, impigre*.

indefensible, *quod defendi non potest*.

indefinable, *quod (verbis) definiri non potest*.

indefinite, *incertus, dubius, anceps, ambiguus*: for an — period, *in incertum*; gram., *infinitus, indefinitus*.

indelible, *quod deleri non potest*.

indelicate, *impudicus, impurus*.

indemnify, *damnum restituĕre*.

independence, *libertas*.

independent, *liber, solutus, sui iuris* from taxes, etc., *immunis*; adv *libere, suo arbitrio*.

indescribable, *inenarrabilis, singularis*; adv. *inenarrabiliter, singulariter*.

indestructible, *quod everti non potest*; *perennis, perpetuus*.

indeterminate, *incertus*.

index, *index*; of a dial, *gnomon, horarum index*.

India, *India*.

Indian: subst. *Indus*; adj. *Indicus*.

indicate, *indicare, significare*.

indication, *indicium, significatio, signum*.

indicative: render by *indicium* or *indico*; gram., the — mood, *modus indicativus*.

indict, *accusare, nomen deferre*.

indictment; bill of —, *crimen, accusatio*.

indifference: = neglect, *neglegentia, incuria*; = calmness, *aequus animus, securitas*; = apathy, *lentitudo*.

indifferent: = negligent, *neglegens, remissus*; = calm, *securus*, or render by *aequo animo*; = apathetic, *lentus*; = mediocre, *mediocris*. Adv. *neglegenter, lente, aequo animo*; = without discrimination, *promiscue*.

indigence, *inopia, egestas*.

indigenous, *vernaculus*; applied to persons, *indigena*.

indigent, *inops, egens*.

indigestible, *gravis*.

indigestion, *cruditas*.

indignant, *indignans, (sub)iratus*.

indignation, *indignatio, stomachus, ira*.

indignity, *ignominia, contumelia*.

indirect: physically, *non rectus, devius*; of speech, *obliquus*; gram., *obliquus*; adv. *oblique*.

indirectness; in speech, *circumitio.*
indiscreet, *inconsultus.*
indiscretion, see imprudence.
indiscriminate, *promiscuus*; adv. *promiscue, sine ullo discrimine, temere.*
indispensable, *necessarius.*
indispose, *abstrahĕre, avocare.*
indisposed: = unwell, *aegrotus, infirma valetudine*; = disinclined, *aversus, alienus.*
indisputable, *certus, manifestus*; adv. *certe, haud dubie.*
indissoluble, *indissolubilis; aeternus.*
indistinct: *parum clarus, obscurus*; adv. *parum clare, obscure.*
indistinguishable, *quod discerni non potest.*
indite, *scribĕre.*
individual, subst.; see man, person.
individual, adj. *proprius, singularis; singuli -ae -a.*
individuality, *propria natura.*
individually, *singillatim, viritim; in singulos.*
indivisible, *individuus, quod dividi non potest.*
indoctrinate, *erudire, docĕre, instituĕre.*
indolence, *ignavia, desidia, segnities.*
indolent, *ignavus, deses, segnis*; adv. *ignave, segniter.*
indomitable, *invictus, indomitus.*
indoor, adj. *umbratilis.*
indoors, *domi, intus.*
indorse; see endorse.
indubitable, *haud dubius, certus.*
induce, *inducĕre, impellĕre, inlicĕre, persuadēre.*
inducement, *incitamentum, inlecebra.*
induct, *inaugurare.*
induction, in logic, *inductio.*
indulge, v. *indulgēre, morem gerĕre, (in)servire.*
indulgence, *indulgentia, venia* (= pardon).
indulgent, *indulgens, benignus*; adv. *indulgenter, benigne.*
industrious, *industrius, sedulus, strenuus*; adv. *industrie, strenue.*
industry, *industria, sedulitas.*
indwelling, *insitus, innatus.*
inebriated, *ebrius, temulentus.*
inebriation, *ebrietas.*
ineffable, *inauditus, incredibilis*; adv. *incredibiliter.*
ineffective, *inritus, inutilis*; to be —, *effectu carēre*; adv. *frustra, nequicquam.*
inelegant, *invenustus, inelegans, inurbanus*; adv. *ineleganter, inurbane.*
ineligible, = unsuitable, *inopportunus.*
inept, *ineptus.*
inequality, *inaequalitas, dissimilitudo.*
inequitable, *iniquus, iniustus*; adv. *inique, iniuste.*
inert, *iners, tardus, segnis*; adv. *tarde, segniter.*
inestimable, *inaestimabilis, singularis, unicus*; adv. *singulariter, unice.*
inevitable, *necessarius, haud dubius, inevitabilis*; adv. *necessario.*
inexact, *haud accuratus* (of things), *indiligens* (of persons).
inexcusable, *quod nihil excusationis habet.*

inexhaustible, *quod exhauriri non potest; infinitus.*
inexorable, *inexorabilis, severus, durus.*
inexpediency, *inutilitas.*
inexpedient, *inutilis, inopportunus.*
inexperience, *imperitia, inscientia.*
inexperienced, *imperitus, ignarus, rudis.*
inexpiable, *inexpiabilis.*
inexplicable, *inexplicabilis.*
inexpressible, *inauditus, inenarrabilis.*
inextinguishable, *quod exstingui non potest.*
inextricable, *inexplicabilis, inextricabilis.*
infallible, *certus, haud dubius*; to be —, *omni errore carēre.* Adv. *certo.*
infamous, *infamis, turpis, flagitiosus*; adv. *turpiter, flagitiose.*
infamy, *infamia, dedecus, ignominia.*
infancy, *infantia, pueritia.*
infant: subst. *infans*; adj. *infans, puerilis.*
infantine, *puerilis.*
infantry, *pedites (-um), peditatus (-ūs).*
infatuate, *infatuare, occaecare, pellicĕre.*
infatuated, *amens, demens.*
infatuation, *amentia, dementia.*
infect, *inficĕre, contaminare.*
infection, *contagio, contactus (-ūs).*
infectious, an — disease, *pestilentia.*
infelicity, *infelicitas, malum.*
infer, *concludĕre, coligĕre.*
inference: as a process, *argumentatio, coniectura*; = conclusion, *conclusio, coniectura.*
inferior, adj. *inferior, deterior, minor.*
infernal, *infernus*; the — regions, *inferi (-orum)*; = diabolical, *nefandus, nefarius.*
infertility, *sterilitas.*
infest, *infestum reddĕre.*
infested, *infestus.*
infidelity, *infidelitas, perfidia.*
infinite, *infinitus, immensus.* Adv., = very much, *incredibiliter, sane quam.*
infinitesimal, *minimus, (per)exiguus.*
infinity, *infinitas.*
infirm, *infirmus, invalidus, debilis.*
infirmity: = weakness, *infirmitas, imbecillitas, debilitas*; = a failing, *vitium.*
inflame, *inflammare, accendĕre, incendĕre.*
inflammable, *facilis ad exardescendum.*
inflammatory, *seditiosus, turbulentus.*
inflate, *inflare.*
inflated, *inflatus, tumidus, turgidus.*
inflation, *inflatio.*
inflect, gram., *declinare.*
inflection, gram., *declinatio, flexus (-ūs).*
inflexibility, *obstinatio, pertinacia.*
inflexible, *obstinatus, pertinax*; adv. *obstinate, pertinaciter.*
inflict, (*rem homini*) *adferre, infligĕre, imponĕre*; (*re hominem*) *adficĕre.*
infliction, = trouble, *malum, incommodum.*
influence, subst. *vis, pondus (-eris), momentum*: divine —, *adflatus (-ūs) divinus*; personal —, *auctorita* (= prestige), *potentia* (= unofficial power), *gratia* (= interest); to have — *valēre, pollēre, posse.*

influence, v. *movēre, impellēre.*
influential, *potens, gravis, gratiosus.*
influx; render by *influere.*
inform: = to form, shape, (*ef*)*fingĕre,* (*con*)*formāre;* = to tell, *certiorem facĕre, docēre;* to — against a person, *hominis nomen deferre.*
informality, at auspices, etc., *vitium;* otherwise phrase, e.g. *res haud sollemni more facta.*
information: = news, *nuntius;* = knowledge, *scientia, doctrina;* = accusation, *delatio, indicium.*
informer, *delator, index.*
infrequency, *raritas.*
infrequent, *rarus.*
infringe, *rumpĕre, frangĕre, violare.*
infringement, *immunitio, violatio.*
infuriate, *efferare, exasperare.*
infuriated, *furens.*
infuse, *infundĕre; inicĕre, incutĕre.*
ingenious, *sollers, callidus, artificiosus;* adv. *sollerter, callide, artificiose.*
ingenuity, *ars, sollertia, subtilitas.*
ingenuous, *apertus, simplex, liber;* adv. *aperte, simpliciter, libere.*
ingenuousness, *libertas.*
inglorious, *inglorius, inhonestus;* adv. *sine gloria, inhoneste.*
ingraft, *inserĕre.*
ingrained, *insitus, inveteratus.*
ingratiate: to — oneself, *favorem sibi conciliare.*
ingratitude, *animus ingratus.*
ingredient, *pars.*
ingress, *ingressus (-ūs).*
inhabit, *incolere, habitare;* thickly —ed, *frequens.*
inhabitable, *habitabilis.*
inhabitant, *incola, habitator;* of a city, *civis.*
inhale, *spiritu ducĕre.*
inharmonious, *discors, absonus, dissonus.*
inhere, *inesse, inhaerēre.*
inherent, *insitus, innatus, proprius;* adv. *naturā, per se.*
inherit, (*rem*) *hereditate accipĕre;* see also heir.
inheritance, *hereditas.*
inherited, *hereditarius, patrius.*
inhibit, *interdicĕre.*
inhibition, *interdictum.*
inhospitable, *inhospitalis.*
inhospitality, *inhospitalitas.*
inhuman, *inhumanus, crudelis;* adv. *inhumane, crudeliter.*
inhumanity, *inhumanitas, crudelitas.*
inimical, *inimicus;* see also hostile.
inimitable, *haud imitabilis.*
iniquitous, *iniustus, iniquus;* adv. *iniuste, inique, improbe.*
iniquity, *iniustitia, iniquitas.*
initial, adj. *primus.*
initiate, *initiare; imbuĕre, instituĕre;* see also begin.
initiative: to take the —, *occupare.*
injudicious, *inconsultus, temerarius;* adv. *inconsulte, temere.*
injunction; see command.
injure, *laedĕre, violare, nocēre.*
injurious, *noxius, damnosus, gravis, malus;* adv. *male.*

injury, *detrimentum, incommodum, damnum, malum, iniuria.*
injustice, *iniustitia;* = unjust act, *iniuria.*
ink, *atramentum.*
inkling, *odor.*
inland, *mediterraneus.*
inlay, *inserĕre, variare, distinguĕre.*
inlet, of the sea, *aestuarium.*
inmate, *deversor, inquilinus;* see inhabitant.
inmost, *intimus;* — being, *viscera (-um), medulla.*
inn, *deversorium, hospitium, caupona.*
innate, *innatus, insitus, proprius.*
inner, *interior, intestinus, domesticus.*
innkeeper, *caupo.*
innocence, *innocentia, integritas;* = simplicity, *simplicitas.*
innocent, *innocens, insons; integer, sanctus;* adv. *integre, caste.*
innocuous, *innocuus;* adv. *sine fraude.*
innovate, (*res*) *novare, mutare.*
innovation; political —s, *res novae* (plur.).
innumerable, *innumerabilis.*
inoffensive, adj. *innocens.*
inopportune, *inopportunus.*
inordinate, *immodicus, nimius;* adv. *praeter modum, immodice, nimis.*
inquire: = ask questions, *quaerĕre, sciscitari, percontari, rogare;* = hold an inquiry, *quaerĕre, inquirĕre, cognoscĕre.*
inquiry, *percontatio, interrogatio;* a judicial —, *quaestio, inquisitio, cognitio.*
inquisitive, *audiendi cupidus, curiosus;* adv. *curiose.*
inquisitiveness, *studium audiendi, curiositas.*
inquisitor, *quaesitor.*
inroad, *incursio, incursus (-ūs), inruptio.*
insane, *insanus, amens* (= distracted), *demens* (= deranged), *furiosus* (= raving); adv. *insane, dementer, furiose.*
insanity, *insania, furor, amentia, dementia.*
insatiable, *insatiabilis inexplebilis.*
inscribe, *inscribĕre, ascribĕre.*
inscription, *inscriptio, index, titulus, epigramma (-atis,* n.).
inscrutable, *obscurus, occultus, tectus.*
insect, *insectum, bestiola.*
insecure, *instabilis, incertus, lubricus,* or neg. with *tutus* or *firmus.*
insensibility, *torpor.* Transf., *lentitudo.*
insensible, *sensūs expers.* Transf., *lentus.* Adv. *sensim, paulatim.*
insert, *inserĕre, includĕre, intericĕre, addĕre, adscribĕre* (in writing).
insertion, *interpositio;* or render by verb.
inside, subst. *pars interior.*
inside, adv. *intus, intro.*
inside, prep. *in* (with abl.), *intra* (with acc.).
insidious, *fallax, dolosus;* adv. *fallaciter, dolose.*
insidiousness, *fallacia, dolus, fraus.*
insight: = knowledge, *cognitio, intellegentia, perspicientia;* = intelligence, *iudicium, consilium.*

insignia, *fasces (-ium), insignia (-ium).*

insignificance, *exiguitas.*

insignificant, *exiguus, minutus, levis, nullius momenti.*

insincere, *falsus, simulatus;* adv. *falso, simulate.*

insincerity, *fallacia, simulatio.*

insinuate: to — oneself, *se insinuare, adrepĕre;* = to suggest, hint, *significare.*

insinuating, *blandus.*

insinuation, *significatio.*

insipid, *insulsus, ineptus, frigidus;* adv. *insulse, inepte, frigide.*

insist: = state positively, *confirmare, declarare, dictitare;* = demand, *flagitare, (ex)poscĕre.*

insolence, *insolentia, impudentia, adrogantia.*

insolent, *insolens, impudens, adrogans;* adv. *insolenter, impudenter, adroganter.*

insoluble, *quod liquefieri non potest.* Transf., *inexplicabilis.*

insolvent, to be, *non esse solvendo.*

insomuch, . . . that, *sic, ita,* or *adeo . . . ut.*

inspect, *inspicĕre, intuēri, contemplari.*

inspection, *cura, custodia.*

inspector, *custos, curator.*

inspiration, = breathing in, *spiritus (-ūs);* divine —, *divinus adflatus (-ūs);* by divine —, *divinitus;* = suggestion, in gen., *monitus (-ūs), consilium.*

inspire, *inspirare;* = instil, *inicĕre, incutĕre;* = excite, *excitare, incendĕre.*

inspired, *divino spiritu inflatus.*

inspirit, *animum addĕre.*

instability, *inconstantia.*

install, *inaugurare.*

instalment, *pensio, pars, portio.*

instance, subst.: = urgent request, *preces (-um);* = example, *exemplum, specimen;* for —, *verbi causa, velut, vel.*

instant, subst. *punctum* or *momentum temporis;* at the very —, *(in) tempore ipso.*

instant, adj.; = urgent, *vehemens, intentus, impensus;* = immediate, *praesens.*

instantaneous, *subitus, praesens;* adv. *momento temporis, e vestigio.*

instantly: = immediately, *statim, confestim, extemplo;* = urgently, *intente, vehementer, impense.*

instead, adv. *potius, magis.*

instead of, prep., *pro* with abl., *(in) loco* with genit.; — fighting he sleeps, *non pugnat sed dormit,* or *cum possit pugnare, dormit.*

instep, *pes superior.*

instigate, *incitare, impellĕre, stimulare.*

instigation, *stimulus;* at your —, *impulsu tuo.*

instigator, *auctor, impulsor, suasor.*

instil, *instillare;* see also inspire.

instinct, subst. *natura;* = natural appetite, *appetitus (-ūs).*

instinct, adj. *imbutus.*

instinctive, *naturalis;* adv. *naturā, naturaliter.*

institute, institution: as act, *initium;* or render by verb; = custom,

institutum, *lex, mos;* = corporation, *conlegium, sodalitas.*

institute, v. *condĕre, instituĕre, constituĕre.*

instruct: = teach, *erudire, docēre, instituĕre;* = order, *mandare, praecipĕre.*

instruction: = teaching, *institutio, eruditio, doctrina;* = direction, *praeceptum, mandatum.*

instructor, *magister, praeceptor.*

instrument, *instrumentum, machina;* steel —s, *ferramenta (-orum);* a stringed —, *fides (-ium);* legal, =deed, *instrumentum, tabula.*

instrumental, *utilis, aptus;* — music, *cantus nervorum et tibiarum.*

instrumentality, *opera, ministerium.*

insubordinate, *seditiosus, turbulentus.*

insubordination, *immodestia.*

insufferable, *intolerabilis.*

insufficient, *haud sufficiens, impar;* adv. *parum, haud satis.*

insult, subst. *contumelia, probrum.*

insult, v. *contumeliam imponĕre.*

insulting, *contumeliosus, maledicus;* adv. *contumeliose, maledice.*

insuperable, *in(ex)superabilis;* = invincible, *invictus.*

insurgent, subst. and adj., *rebellis.*

insurrection, *rebellio, seditio, motus (-ūs).*

intact, *integer, salvus, incolumis.*

intangible, *intactilis; quod tangi non potest.*

integral, *necessarius.*

integrity, *integritas, probitas.*

intellect, *mens, ingenium, intelligentia.*

intelligence; see intellect; = news *nuntius.*

intelligent, *mente praeditus, intellegens; sapiens, prudens.* Adv. *intellegenter, sapienter, prudenter.*

intelligible, *quod facile intellegi potest; planus, perspicuus;* adv. *perspicue, plane.*

intemperance, *intemperantia, impotentia;* in drink, *ebrietas.*

intemperate, *intemperans, impotens, immodicus;* — in drink, *ebriosus.* Adv. *intemperanter, immodice.*

intend, *(facĕre) in animo habēre; cogitare, destinare, intendĕre.*

intense, *acer, magnus, summus, nimius;* adv. *valde, magnopere, acriter, summe.*

intensify, *maiorem reddĕre, augēre.*

intent, *intentus, attentus;* to be —, *animum intendĕre, incumbĕre, studēre.*

intention, *consilium, propositum, institutum.*

intentionally, *consulto, de industria.*

inter, *sepelire, humare.*

intercalary, *intercalaris, intercalarius.*

intercede, *(de)precari.*

intercession, *deprecatio.*

intercessor, *deprecator.*

intercept, *intercipĕre, excipĕre;* in gen., = cut off, *intercludĕre.*

interchange, subst. *permutatio, vicissitudo.*

interchange, v. *(com)mutare, permutare.*

interchangeably, *invicem.*

intercourse, in gen. *usus (-ūs)*, *commercium*; sexual, *concubitus (-ūs)*, *consuetudo*, *coitus (-ūs)*.

interdict; subst. *interdictum*.

interdict, v. *interdicĕre*.

interest, subst.: = attention, *studium*; = advantage, *bonum*, *utilitas*, *usus (-ūs)*; it is in my —, *interest meā*, *refert meā*, *expedit mihi*; = influence, *gratia*; — on money, *faenus (-oris)*, *usura*; compound —, *anatocismus*; simple —, *perpetuum faenus*; to lend out money on —, *faenerari*.

interest, v.: = to hold the attention, *tenēre*; sometimes *placēre*; to — oneself in, *studēre*, *operam dare*.

interested: = attentive, *attentus*, *erectus*; *studiosus*, with genit.; = concerned, see interest, subst.

interfere, *intervenire*, *se interponĕre*, *se immiscēre*; to — with, = to hinder, *impedire*.

interim, *temporis intervallum*; an — decree, *edictum ad tempus propositum*.

interior, subst. *pars interior*.

interior, adj. *interior*, *internus*.

interject, *interponĕre*, *intericĕre*.

interjection, *interiectio*.

interlace, *implicare*.

interlude, *embolium*.

intermarriage, *connubium*.

intermediate, *medius*.

interment, *sepultura*, *humatio*.

interminable, *infinitus*; adv. *infinite*, *sine fine*.

intermingle, *(inter)miscēre*.

intermission, *intermissio*.

intermittently, *aliquando*, *nonnumquam*, *interdum*.

internal; see inner; adv. *intus*, *penitus*.

international: — law, *ius (iuris*, n.) *gentium*.

internecine, *internecivus*.

interpellation, *interpellatio*.

interpolate, *addĕre*, *inserĕre*; = to falsify, *corrumpĕre*, *interpolare*.

interpose, *interponĕre*, *intericĕre*; = to intervene, *se interponĕre*.

interposition, *interiectus (-ūs)*, *interventus (-ūs)*; = mediation, intervention, *interventus (-ūs)*.

interpret, *interpretari*; to — favourably, *in bonam partem interpretari* or *accipĕre*.

interpretation, *interpretatio*, *explanatio*.

interpreter, *interpres*.

interregnum, *interregnum*.

interrogate, *(inter)rogāre*, *quaerĕre*, *exquirĕre*.

interrogation, *percontatio*, *quaestio*, *interrogatio*.

interrogative, gram., *interrogativus*.

interrupt, *interrumpĕre*, *interpellare*, *interfari*.

interruptedly, *interrupte*.

interruption: in speaking, *interpellatio*, *interfatio*; in gen., = pause, *intermissio*, *intervallum*.

intersect, *secare*, *scindĕre*; so as to form the figure X, *decussare*.

intersection, = the figure X, *decussatio*, *decussis*.

intersperse, *(in)miscēre*.

interstice, *rima*, *foramen*.

interval, *intervallum*, *spatium*; in the —, *interim*; at —s, *aliquando*, *nonnumquam*.

intervene: = be between, *interiacēre*, *intercedĕre*; = come between, *intercedĕre*, *intervenire*.

intervention, *interventus (-ūs)*.

interview, subst. *congressio*, *congressus (-ūs)*, *conloquium*.

interweave, *intexĕre*.

intestate, *intestatus*; adv. *intestato*.

intestine, adj. *intestinus*.

intestine(s), subst. *intestina*, *viscera*, *exta* (all plur.).

intimacy, *familiaritas*, *consuetudo*, *necessitudo*.

intimate, adj. *familiaris*, *intimus*, *coniunctus*; adv. *familiariter*, *intime*, *penitus*.

intimate, v. *significare*, *indicare*.

intimation, *significatio*, *nuntius*.

intimidate, *(de)terrēre*, *timorem inicĕre*.

intimidation, = threats, *minae (-arum)*.

into, *in* with acc.

intolerable, *intolerabilis*; adv. *intoleranter*.

intolerance, *superbia*, *adrogantia*.

intolerant, *immitis*, *difficilis*, *superbus*.

intone, *canēre*.

intoxicate, *ebrium reddĕre*.

intoxicated, *ebrius*, *temulentus*.

intoxication, *ebrietas*.

intractable, *indocilis*, *difficilis*.

intrepid, *intrepidus*, *impavidus*.

intrepidity, *animus intrepidus* or *impavidus*; *fortitudo*.

intricacy, *contortio*.

intricate, *contortus*, *implicatus*, *perplexus*, *impeditus*.

intrigue, subst.; = plot, *dolus*, *fallacia*; = amour, *adulterium*.

intrigue, v. = plot, *dolis* or *fallacia contendĕre*; see also interest.

intrinsic, *verus*, *in re ipsa positus*; adv. *per se*, *vere*.

introduce, *introducĕre*, *inducĕre*, *invehĕre*; of persons, = make one known to another, *introducĕre*, *commendare*.

introduction, *introductio*, *inductio*, *invectio*; an — to a book, etc., *prooemium*, *exordium*, *praefatio*.

introspection, *ipsum se inspicĕre*.

intrude, *se interponĕre* or *offerre*.

intrusion, *importunitas*.

intrusive, *molestus*, *importunus*; adv. *moleste*.

intuition, *cognitio*, *perceptio*; as a quality, *ingenii*, *acumen* or *acies*.

inundation, *eluvio*, *diluvium*.

inure, *adsuefacĕre*.

invade, *invadĕre*, *incurrĕre*, *incursionem facĕre*.

invader, *hostis*.

invalid, subst. *aeger*, *aegrotus*.

invalid, adj. *inritus*, *infirmus*, *vitiosus*.

invalidate, *inritum facĕre*, *tollĕre*, *rescindĕre*.

invasion, *incursio*, *inruptio*.

invective, *convicium*, *probrum*.

inveigh, *invehi*, *insectari*, *increpare*.

inveigle; see mislead.

invent, *invenire, reperire, excogitare.*
invention, *inventio, excogitatio;* = thing invented, *inventum, reperta* (*-orum,* plur.); = falsehood, *commentum, mendacium.*
inventor, *inventor, repertor, auctor.*
inventory, *tabula, index.*
inverse, *inversus, conversus.*
inversion, *conversio.*
invert, (con)*vertĕre, invertĕre.*
invest: to — with an office, *magistratum mandare, deferre;* to — with a quality, *addĕre, impertire;* to — money, *pecuniam conlocare, occupare;* = to besiege, *circumsedĕre, obsidēre.*
investigate, *exquirĕre,* (per)*scrutari, investigare;* judicially, *quaerĕre, cognoscĕre.*
investigation, *investigatio, inquisitio;* a judicial —, *quaestio, cognitio.*
investigator, *investigator, indagator.*
inveterate, *inveteratus;* to become —, *inveterascĕre.* Adv. *penitus.*
invidious, *invidiosus;* adv. *invidiose.*
invidiousness, *invidia.*
invigorate, *corroborare,* (con)*firmare.*
invincible, *invictus, in(ex)superabilis.*
inviolability, *sanctitas.*
inviolable, *inviolabilis, inviolatus; sanctus, sacrosanctus;* adv. *inviolate.*
inviolate, *integer; inviolatus, intactus.*
invisible, *caecus;* to be —, *sub oculos non cadĕre.*
invitation, *invitatio;* at your —, *invitatus* (or *vocatus*) *a te.*
invite, *invitare, vocare;* = to allure, *adlectare, invitare.*
inviting, *blandus, gratus, amoenus.*
invocation, of help, *imploratio;* of witnesses, *testatio.*
invoice, *libellus.*
invoke, *invocare, implorare;* as a witness, *testari, invocare testem.*
involuntary, *invitus, coactus;* adv. *non sponte,* or render by adj. *invitus.*
involve: = to envelop, *involvĕre;* = to implicate, *implicare, adligare, admiscēre;* to be —d in debt, *aere alieno laborare;* = to imply, comprise, *continēre, habēre.*
invulnerable, *invulnerabilis.*
inward, *interior;* adv. *introrsus, intus, intrinsecus.*
inweave, *intexĕre.*
inwrought, *intextus.*
irascibility, *iracundia.*
irascible, *iracundus, in iram praeceps, stomachosus.*
ire; see anger.
Ireland, *Hibernia.*
irk: it —s, *piget, taedet, molestum est.*
irksome, *gravis, molestus, odiosus.*
irksomeness, *taedium, molestia.*
iron, subst.: *ferrum;* of —, adj. *ferreus;* tipped with —, *ferratus;* —s, = fetters, *vincula, compedes.*
iron, adj. *ferreus;* — tools, *ferramenta* (*-orum*).
ironically, *per ironiam.*
ironmongery, *ferramenta* (*-orum,* plur.).
irony, *ironia, dissimulatio.*
irradiate, *inlustrare, conlustrare.*

irrational, *absurdus, rationis expers, stultus;* adv. *absurde.*
irreconcilable; of persons, etc. *implacabilis, inexorabilis;* of ideas, (*res*) *inter se repugnantes, contrariae.*
irrecoverable, *inreparabilis.*
irrefragable, *certus, firmus; quod refelli non potest.*
irregular, *enormis* (= shapeless), *incompositus* (= rough), *inusitatus* (= unusual); *inaequalis* (= not uniform); gram., *anomalus;* at elections, *vitiosus;* of troops, *tumultuarius.* Adv. *enormiter, incomposite, praeter morem; vitio.*
irregularity, *enormitas;* gram., *anomalia;* of conduct, *licentia;* at an election, *vitium.*
irrelevant, *alienus;* it is —, *nihil ad rem pertinet.*
irreligion, *impietas* (*erga deos*), *deorum neglegentia.*
irreligious, *impius* (*erga deos*); adv. *impie.*
irremediable; see incurable.
irremovable, *immobilis, immutabilis.*
irreparable, *inreparabilis.*
irreproachable; see blameless.
irresistible, *invictus, in(ex)superabilis cui nulla vi resisti potest.*
irresolute, *dubius, incertus;* to be —, *dubitare, haesitare.* Adv. *dubitanter.*
irresolution, *dubitatio, haesitantia.*
irrespective, *sine ullo discrimine.*
irreverence, *impietas* (*erga deos*).
irreverent, *inverecundus, impius* (*erga deos*); adv. *impie.*
irrevocable, *inrevocabilis.*
irrigate, *inrigare.*
irrigation, *inrigatio, inductio aquarum.*
irritable, *stomachosus, iracundus;* adv. *stomachose.*
irritate: to — a wound, *inflammare;* mentally, *inritare.*
irritation, = annoyance, *stomachus.*
irruption, *inruptio, incursio.*
island, *insula.*
islander, *insulanus, insulae incola.*
isle; see island.
isolate, *secernĕre, seiungĕre, separare.*
isolated, *remotus, solus.*
isolation, *solitudo.*
issue, subst.: = outcome, *exitus* (*-ūs*), *eventus* (*-ūs*); = subject, *res, causa;* = offspring, *liberi* (*-orum*), *progenies, stirps.*
issue, v.: transit., = give out, of orders, etc. *edĕre, proponĕre, pronuntiare;* of stores, etc., *dispensare, distribuĕre;* intransit., = come out, *egredi, erumpĕre;* = end up, turn out, *evadĕre, exire, evenire.*
isthmus, *isthmus* or *isthmos.*
it, *hic, haec, hoc; is, ea, id; ille, illa, illud.*
Italian, *Italicus, Italus.*
Italy, *Italia.*
itch, subst.: as disease, *scabies;* as sensation, *prurigo, pruritus* (*-ūs*).
itch, v. *prurire;* to — to do a thing, *gestire facĕre.*
item, in a list, *pars, res.*
iterate, *iterare.*

itinerant, *circumforaneus.*
itinerary, *itineris descriptio.*
ivory, subst. *ebur.*
ivory, adj. *eburneus.*
ivy, *hedera.*

J

jabber, v. *blaterare, garrire.*
jabbering, subst. *clamor, strepitus -ūs).*
jackass, *asinus.*
jackdaw, *graculus.*
jacket, *tunica.*
jade: of a horse, *caballus;* of a woman, *mulier importuna.*
jaded, *fatigatus, (de)fessus.*
jagged, *serratus;* of rocks, *asper, praeruptus.*
jail, *carcer.*
jailbird, *furcifer.*
jamb, *postis.*
James, *Iacobus.*
janitor, *ianitor, ostiarius.*
January, *Ianuarius (mensis).*
jar, subst. *olla, cadus, urceus, urna, amphora;* on the —, of a door, *semiapertus.*
jar, v. *discrepare.*
jargon, *sermo barbarus.*
jarring, *dissonus, absonus, discors.*
jasper, subst. *iaspis.*
jaundice, *morbus regius* or *arquatus.*
jaundiced, *arquatus.* Transf., *lividus, invidus.*
jaunt, *iter, excursio;* to take a —, *excurrĕre.*
javelin, *pilum, iaculum;* to throw a —, *iaculari.*
jaw, *mala;* the —s of death, etc., *fauces (-ium).*
jealous, *invidus, lividus;* to be —, *aemulari, invidĕre.*
jealousy, *invidia, aemulatio.*
jeer, subst. *cavillatio, ludibrium, inrisio.*
jeer, v. *cavillari, inridēre, in ludibrium vertēre.*
jejune, *ieiunus, aridus, exilis;* adv. *ieiune.*
jeopardize, *in periculum adducĕre.*
jeopardy; see danger.
jerkin, *tunica.*
jerky, of style, *salebrosus.*
Jerusalem, *Hierosolyma (-orum).*
jest, subst. *iocus, ridiculum;* in —, *ioco, per iocum.*
jest, v. *iocari, ioculari, cavillari.*
jester, *scurra.*
jet, *gagates;* — black, *niger;* a — of water, *aqua saliens.*
jetsam, *res naufragio eiectae.*
jetty, *moles.*
Jew, *Iudaeus.*
jewel, *gemma.*
jewelled, *gemmeus, gemmatus.*
jeweller, *aurifex.*
Jewish, *Iudaicus.*
jig; see dance.
jilt, *repudiare.*
jingle, *tinnire.*
jingling, subst. *tinnitus (-ūs).*
job, *opus (-eris, n.);* a put-up —, *fraus.*
jockey, *agaso* (= groom).

jocose, jocular, *iocosus, ridiculus, facetus;* adv. *iocose, per iocum, facete.*
jocularity, *iocus, facetiae (-arum).*
jog, subst. *impulsus (-ūs).*
jog, v.: transit., *fodicare, impellĕre;* intransit., to — on, — along, *lente progredi.*
John, *Ioannes.*
join, v.: transit., = connect, *(con)-iungĕre, conectĕre, copulare;* to — battle, *proelium* or *pugnam committĕre;* intransit., *(con)iungi, conecti;* to — in, *interesse.*
joiner, *faber.*
joint, subst.: in a body, *commissura, articulus;* in a plant, *nodus;* in other things, *coagmentum, compages compactura.*
joint, adj. *communis;* adv. *coniuncte, coniunctim, una, communiter.*
jointed, *geniculatus.*
joint-heir, *coheres.*
joist, *tignum transversum.*
joke; see jest.
joker, *homo ridiculus.*
jollity, *hilaritas, lascivia.*
jolly, *hilaris, lascivus.*
jolt, v. *iactare, concutĕre, quassare.*
jolting, subst. *iactatio, quassatio.*
jostle, *fodicare.*
jot, subst.: not a —, *nihil, minime;* not to care a — for, *non flocci facĕre.*
jot, v.: to — down, *adnotare, scribĕre.*
journal: = diary, *ephemeris;* = news-paper, *acta diurna (-orum).*
journey, subst. *iter, cursus (-ūs), via;* a — abroad, *peregrinatio;* a — by sea, *navigatio.*
journey, v. *iter facĕre;* to — abroad, *peregrinari.*
journeyman, *opifex.*
Jove, *Iuppiter;* by —! *mehercle!*
jovial, *hilaris, lascivus;* adv. *hilare, lascive.*
joviality, *hilaritas, lascivia.*
joy, *gaudium, laetitia;* = pleasure, *voluptas.*
joy, v. *gaudēre, laetari, exsultare.*
joyful, *laetus, hilaris.* Adv. *laete, libenter, hilare;* often rendered by adj. *laetus* or *libens.*
jubilant, *gaudio exsultans* or *triumphans.*
judge, subst.: in court, *iudex, quaesitor, praetor;* in gen., *iudex, aestimator, existimator.*
judge, v., *iudicare; existimare, censēre:* to — between *diiudicare.*
judgment: in court, *iudicium;* to pronounce —, *ius dicĕre;* a — seat, *tribunal;* in gen., = considered opinion, *iudicium, sententia;* in my —, *meo iudicio, me iudice;* = discernment, *iudicium, consilium.*
judicature, *iurisdictio.*
judicial, *iudicialis, forensis;* a — decree, *edictum;* a — investigation, *iudicium.* Adv. *iure, lege;* to proceed —, *lege agĕre.*
judicious, *sagax, sapiens, prudens:* adv. *sagaciter, sapienter, prudenter.*
jug, *urceus, urceolus.*
juggle, *praestigias agĕre.*
juggler, *praestigiator.*

juggling, subst. *praestigiae* (*-arum*); = trickery, *dolus, fraus.*

juice, *sucus.*

July, *Quinctilis* or *Iulius* (*mensis*).

jumble, subst. *congeries, turba, farrago.*

jumble, v. (*per*)*miscēre.*

jump, subst. *saltus* (*-ūs*).

jump, v. *salire*; to — for joy, *exsultare gaudio*; to — in, *insilire*; to — over, *transilire.*

junction, (*con*)*iunctio.*

juncture, *tempus, tempestas.*

June, (*mensis*) *Iunius.*

jungle, *loca virgultis obsita.*

junior, *iunior,* (*natu*) *minor.*

juniper, *iuniperus.*

jurisconsult, *iuris* or *iure peritus.*

jurisdiction, *iurisdictio.*

jurisprudence, *iuris prudentia.*

jurist; see jurisconsult.

juror, *iudex.*

jury, *iudices* (*-um*).

just, adj. *iustus, aequus, meritus* (= deserved); adv. *iuste, iure, legitime, merito.*

just, adv.: of time, *commodum*; — now, *in praesentia*; — lately, *modo, nuperrime, recens*; in gen., = exactly, *admodum*, or render by *ipse*, esp. with numerals; — as, *ita* (or *sic*) *ut, perinde ac*; in replies, — so, *ita vero, admodum*; = only, *modo, solum, tantum.*

justice, *iustitia, aequitas*; = rights, just treatment, *ius* (*iuris*, n.).

justifiable, *iustus, legitimus*; adv. *recte, iure.*

justification, *purgatio, excusatio.*

justify, *purgare, excusare.*

jut: to — out, *exstare, eminēre*; of geographical features, *excurrēre.*

juvenile, *puerilis, iuvenilis.*

K

keel, *carina.*

keen: physically, *acer*; of perception, *acutus, perspicax, sagax*; = enthusiastic, *acer, studiosus.* Adv. *acriter; acute, sagaciter; studiose, summo studio.*

keenness: = poignancy, *acerbitas*; = penetration, *sagacitas, perspicacitas*; — of vision, *acies*; = enthusiasm, *studium.*

keep, v. Transit., (*con*)*servare, custodire, tenēre, habēre*: of animals = to support, *alēre*; to — in, *includēre, continēre*; to — apart, *distinēre*; to — back, *retinēre, cohibēre*; to — off, *arcēre*; to — faith, *fidem servare*; to — watch, *custodias agēre*; to — a secret, *rem celare* or *occultam tenēre*: Intransit.: = to remain, (*re*)*manere*: to — silent, *tacēre*; to — on doing a thing, *pergēre, perseverare.*

keeper, *custos, curator.*

keeping, subst. *custodia, tutela*

keg, *dolium.*

ken, *conspectus* (*-ūs*).

kennel, *stabulum* (*canis*).

Kent, *Cantium.*

kerb, *crepido.*

kerchief, *sudarium.*

kernal, *nucleus.* Transf., *medulla, flos, robur.*

kettle, *cortina, lebes, a(h)enum.*

kettle-drum, *tympanum.*

key, *clavis.*

kick, subst. *pedis* or *calcis ictus* (*-ūs*).

kick, v. *calcitrare, calce petēre*; to — back, *recalcitrare.*

kid, *haedus, haedulus.*

kidnap; see steal.

kidney, *renes* (*renum*).

kidney-bean, *phaselus.*

kill, *interficēre, caedēre, occidēre, necare* (violently), *trucidare* (= butcher, massacre); to — oneself, *mortem sibi conciscēre, se interimēre*; to — time, *horas fallēre.*

kiln, *fornax.*

kin; see kindred.

kind, subst. *genus* (*-eris*, n.); *modus*; of such a —, *talis*; a — of, render by *quasi* or *quidam*; every — of, *omnis* or plur., *omnes.*

kind, adj. *benignus, beneficus* (in action), *benevolus* (in disposition), *humanus, indulgens, clemens*; a — action, *beneficium, officium.* Adv. *benigne, clementer, indulgenter, humane.*

kindle, v.: transit., *accendēre, incendēre, inflammare*; intransit., *accendi,* (*ex*)*ardescēre.*

kindness, *bonitas, benignitas, benevolentia, humanitas*; an act of —, *beneficium, officium.*

kindred, subst., abstr. *consanguinitas, cognatio, necessitudo*; = relatives, *consanguinei, cognati, necessarii* (*-orum*).

king, *rex*; a petty —, *regulus.*

kingdom, *regnum.*

kingfisher, n. (*h*)*alcedo,* (*h*)*alcyon.*

kingly, *regius, regalis.*

kingship, *regia potestas, regnum.*

kinsman; see relative.

kiss, subst. *osculum, suavium.*

kiss, v. *osculari, suaviari.*

kissing, subst. *osculatio.*

kitchen, *culina.*

knapsack, *mantica, sarcina.*

knave, *homo nequam* or *sceleratus*; colloquially, *scelestus, furcifer.*

knavery, *nequitia, fraus, dolus.*

knavish, *nequam, fraudulentus*; adv. *fraudulenter.*

knead, *depsēre, subigēre*

knee, *genu.*

kneel, *genibus niti.*

knife, *culter*; small —, *cultellus.*

knight, *eques.*

knighthood, *ordo equester; dignitas equestris.*

knit, *texēre*; to — the brow, *frontem contrahēre.*

knob, *bulla, nodus* (in plants).

knobbed, knobbly, *nodosus.*

knock, v. *pulsare*; to — against, *offendēre*; to — down, *sternēre*; to — up, = arouse, *suscitare*; -ed up, = exhausted, (*de*)*fessus.*

knocking, subst. *pulsatio.*

knock-kneed, *varus.*

knot, subst. *nodus;* = group of people, *circulus.*

knot, v. *nodare, nectĕre.*

knotty, *nodosus.* Transf., *difficilis, spinosus;* a — point, *nodus.*

know, *scire, cognitum* or *compertum habĕre;* to get to —, *(cog)noscĕre;* not to —, *nescire, ignorare;* = be acquainted with, *novisse* (perf. of *noscere*); to — again, = recognize, *agnoscĕre, noscitare.*

knowing, adj. *sciens, prudens;* = clever, *callidus, astutus.* Adv. *consulto, de industria;* or render by adj. *sciens* or *prudens.*

knowledge, *scientia, notitia, cognitio;* as imparted and acquired, *doctrina, disciplina;* without the — of a person, *clam homine.*

known, *notus;* to make —, *declarare.*

knuckle, *articulus (digiti).*

L

laborious, *laboriosus, operosus;* adv. *laboriose, operose.*

labour, subst. *labor, opus (-eris, n.), opera;* in childbirth, *partus (-ūs);* to be in —, *parturire.*

labour, v.: = work, toil, *laborare, niti, contendere;* = be distressed, *laborare* (with abl.); to — under a delusion, *decipi, falli.*

laboured, *adfectatus, nimis exquisitus.*

labourer, *operarius, opera.*

labyrinth, *labyrinthus.*

labyrinthine, *perplexus, impeditus.*

lacerate, *lacerare, laniare.*

laceration, *laceratio, laniatus (-ūs).*

lachrymose, *lacrimabundus.*

lack, subst. *inopia, penuria, egestas.*

lack, v. *carēre, egēre, indigēre.*

lackey, *pedisequus.*

lack-lustre, *decolor.*

laconic, = concise, *brevis, adstrictus;* adv. *breviter, adstricte.*

lad, *puer.*

ladder, *scalae (-arum).*

lade, = to load, *onerare.*

laden, *onustus, oneratus, gravis.*

lading, subst. *onus (-eris, n.).*

ladle, subst. *trulla, cyathus.*

ladle, v. *haurire.*

lady, in gen., *femina, mulier, matrona;* the — of the house, *domina, hera, materfamilias.*

lady-like, *liberalis; quod matronā dignum est.*

lady's-maid, *famula, ornatrix.*

lag, *cessare, morari, cunctari.*

laggard, *cessator, cunctator.*

lagoon, *lacus (-ūs), lacuna.*

lair, *latibulum, cubile.*

laird, *dominus, possessor.*

lamb, *agnus,* f. *agna;* as meat, *(caro) agnina.*

lame, adj. *claudus;* = feeble, *debilis;* to be —, *claudicare;* a — excuse, *excusatio vana.*

lameness, *claudicatio.*

lament, lamentation, *lamentum*

(usually plur.), *lamentatio, ploratus (-ūs).*

lament, v. *lamentari, deflēre, (de)plorare.*

lamentable, *lamentabilis, flebilis;* adv. *flebiliter.*

lamented, *flebilis.*

lamp, *lucerna, lychnus.*

lamp-black, *fuligo.*

lampoon, *carmen famosum.*

lance, subst., *lancea, hasta, sarisa.*

lance, v. *incidĕre.*

lancet, *scalpellum.*

land, subst.: opp. to sea, *terra;* — as possessed, cultivated, etc., *ager, solum, terra;* = a particular country, *terra, regio, ager, fines (-ium).*

land, adj. *terrestris, terrenus.*

land, v.: transit., *(in terram) exponĕre;* intransit., *(ex nave) egredi.*

landed: — property, *ager, possessio* (usually plur.); a — proprietor, *agrorum possessor.*

landing, subst. *egressus (-ūs).*

landlord, *agrorum possessor; caupo* (= innkeeper).

landmark, *lapis, terminus.*

landslide, *terrae lapsus (-ūs).*

lane, *angiportum;* a country — *semita.*

language, *oratio;* the — of a people, tongue, *lingua, sermo;* = diction, style, *oratio, sermo;* = things said, *verba* or *dicta (-orum).*

languid, *languidus;* to be —, *languēre;* adv. *languide.*

languish, *languere, languescĕre; tabescĕre.*

languor, *languor.*

lank, lanky, *prolixus.*

lantern, *lanterna.*

lap, subst. *gremium* (= bosom), *sinus (-ūs);* = fold of the gown); on a race-course, *spatium.*

lap, v. *lambĕre.*

lap-dog, *catellus.*

lapse, subst.: = error, *lapsus (-ūs), error, peccatum;* of time, *fuga;* after the — of a year, *interiecto anno.*

lapse, v.: = go wrong, *errare, peccare;* of property, *reverti.*

lard, *adeps, lar(i)dum.*

larder, *cella penaria, carnarium.*

large, *magnus, grandis, amplus.* Adv., = to a great extent, *magna ex parte.*

large-hearted, *magnanimus, liberalis, benignus.*

largeness, *magnitudo, amplitudo;* — of mind, *magnanimitas.*

largess, *largitio, congiarium.*

lark, *alauda.*

larynx, *guttur.*

lascivious, *impudicus;* adv. *impudice.*

lash, subst.: = whip, *flagrum, flagellum, scutica;* = blow (lit. and fig.). *verber.*

lash, v.: = whip, *flagellare, verberare;* = tie, bind, *(ad)nectĕre, (ad)ligare.*

lassitude, *lassitudo, languor.*

last, subst.: let the cobbler stick to his —, *ne sutor supra crepidam.*

last, adj.: = final, *ultimus, extremus, postremus, novissimus;* = most recent, *proximus.* At last, *tandem, postremum.* Adv. **lastly,** *postremo, denique.*

last, v. *durare,* (*per*)*manēre.*
lasting, *stabilis, diuturnus, perennis.*
latch, *pessulus* (=bolt).
late, adj.: = coming —, *serus;* = recent, *recens;* the —, = the dead, *demortuus;* of an emperor, *divus.* Adv. **lately, of late,** *nuper, recens, modo.*
late, adv.: = too —, *sero;* rather —, *serius;* = at night, *multa nocte.*
lateness, render by adj.
latent, *occultus, abditus.*
lateral, *a latere.*
lathe, *tornus;* to work at the —, *tornare.*
Latin, adj. *Latinus;* the — tongue, *lingua Latina, sermo Latinus;* to translate into —, *Latine reddere.*
latinity, *latinitas.*
latitude, = freedom, *libertas, licentia.*
latter, *posterior:* the former . . . the —, *hic . . . ille.*
lattice, *cancelli* (-*orum*).
laud; see praise.
laudable, *laudabilis, laude dignus;* adv. *laudabiliter.*
laudatory, *honorificus.*
laugh, laughter, *risus* (-*ūs*), *cachinnus* (loud), *cachinnatio;* to be a —ing stock, *ludibrio* or *irrisui esse;* to raise a —, *risum movēre.*
laugh, v.: intransit., *ridēre;* loudly, *cachinnare;* to — at, transit., (*de*)*ridēre, inridēre.*
laughable, *ridiculus.*
laughter; see laugh.
launch, v.: transit., of ships, *deducēre;* intransit., to — out, *in aequor efferri.* Transf., *exspatiari.*
laurel, *laurus* (-*i* and -*us*), *laurea;* adj., of —, *laureus;* decked with —, *laureatus.*
lava, *massa ardens, saxa* (-*orum,* pl.) *liquefacta.*
lavish, adj. *prodigus, profusus;* a — giver, *largitor.* Adv. *large, prodige, effuse.*
lavishness, *effusio, largitas, munificentia.*
law, *lex, ius* (*iuris,* n.); *fas* (= divine —); *norma, regula* (= rule, standard); to carry a —, *legem perferre;* to go to —, *lege agĕre.*
lawful, *legitimus;* it is —, *licet.* Adv. *legitime, lege, per leges.*
lawgiver; see legislator.
lawless, *effrenatus;* adv. *effrenate, licenter, contra legem.*
lawlessness, (*effrenata*) *licentia.*
lawn: = fine linen, *sindon;* of grass, *pratum, herba.*
lawsuit, *lis, controversia.*
lawyer, *iurisconsultus, iurisperitus.*
lax, (*dis*)*solutus, remissus, neglegens;* adv. (*dis*)*solute, remisse, neglegenter.*
lay, subst.; see song.
lay, v. *ponĕre,* (*con*)*locare;* to — foundations, *fundamenta iacĕre;* to — an ambush, *insidiari;* to — siege, *obsĭdēre;* to — eggs, (*ova*) *parĕre;* to — aside, (*de*)*ponĕre;* to — before, *proponĕre;* to — down an office, *magistratu se abdicare;* to — down arms, *ab armis discedĕre;* to — up, *condĕre, reponĕre;* to — waste, *vastare.*

layer, of a plant, *propago.*
laziness, *ignavia, segnitia.*
lazy, *piger, ignavus, segnis;* adv. *pigre, ignave, segniter.*
lead, subst. *plumbum.*
lead, v.: = conduct, *ducĕre;* to — past, *traducĕre;* to — back, *reducĕre;* to — the way, *praeire;* = command, *ducĕre, praeesse;* = induce, *adducĕre, persuadēre;* = pass, spend, *agĕre;* of roads, to — in a certain direction, *ferre, ducere.*
leaden, *plumbeus.*
leader, *dux, ductor, auctor.*
leadership, *ductus* (-*ūs*); under my —, *me duce.*
leading, *princeps, primarius, summus.*
leaf: of a tree, *folium, frons;* of a book, *scheda, pagina, charta;* of metal, *bractea, lamina.*
leafy, *frondosus, frondeus, frondifer.*
league, subst. *foedus* (-*eris,* n.), *pactum, societas.*
leak, subst. *rima;* to spring a —, *rimam agĕre.*
leak, v.; to — away, *perfluĕre.*
leaky, *rimosus, rimarum plenus.*
lean, adj. *macer, exilis; strigosus* (of horses, etc.).
lean, v. (*se*) *inclinare;* to — upon, (*re*) (*in*)*niti.*
leanness, *macies.*
leap, subst. *saltus* (-*ūs*).
leap, v. *salire:* to — down, *desilire;* — forward, *prosilire;* — for joy, *gestire, exsultare.*
leap-year, *annus bisextus.*
learn, *discĕre, ediscĕre* (by heart), *perdiscĕre* (thoroughly); *cognoscĕre* (= get to know, in gen.).
learned, *doctus, eruditus;* adv. *docte, erudite.*
learner, *discipulus.*
learning, *doctrina, eruditio.*
lease, subst. *conductio.*
lease, v. *conducĕre* (= take a — of), *locare* (= give a — of).
leash, *lorum, copula.*
least, adj. *minimus.*
least, adv. *minime;* at —, *saltem, certe;* not in the —, *nihil omnino.*
leather, *corium, aluta* (tanned); adj., of —, *scorteus.*
leave, subst.: = permission, *permissio, licentia;* to give —, *potestatem facĕre;* with your —, *pace tua;* I have —, *mihi licet;* to take — of, *valēre iubēre;* — of absence, *commeatus* (-*ūs*).
leave, v.: = desert, abandon, *relinquĕre, deserĕre, destituĕre;* to — property, *relinquĕre, legare;* = to depart, *discedĕre, proficisci;* to — off, *desistĕre;* to — out, *omittĕre, praetermittĕre.*
leaven, subst. *fermentum.*
leaven, v. *fermentare.*
leavings, *reliquiae* (-*arum*).
lecture, *schola, acroasis.*
lecture-room, *schola, auditorium.*
ledge; — of rock, *dorsum.*
ledger, *codex* (*accepti et expensi*).
leech, *hirudo, sanguisuga.*
leek, *porrum, porrus.*
leer, *oculis limis intuēri.*

leering, *limus.*

lees, *faex.*

left, = remaining, *reliquus;* to be —, *restare.*

left, (opp. right) *sinister, laevus;* the — hand, *sinistra;* on the —, *a sinistra.*

leg, *crus (cruris,* n.); — of a table, *pes.*

legacy, *legatum.*

legal, *legitimus;* adv. *legitime, lege.*

legate, *legatus, nuntius.*

legation, *legatio.*

legend: on coins, etc., *inscriptio, titulus;* = myth, fable, *fabula.*

legendary, *fictus, fabulosus.*

leggings, *ocreae (-arum).*

legible, *quod facile legi potest.*

legion, *legio.*

legionary, *legionarius.*

legislate, *leges facĕre* or *constituĕre.*

leisure, *otium;* to be at —, *vacare, otiari, cessare;* at —, *otiosus, vacuus.*

leisurely, *lentus;* adv. *otiose.*

lend, = to allow, *sinĕre, pati, permittĕre;* — us go, *eamus;* to — alone, *omittĕre;* to — down, *demittĕre,* to — fly, *emittĕre;* to — go, *(di)mittĕre;* to — in, *admittĕre;* to — off, *absolvĕre;* to — slip, *omittĕre;* see also lease.

lend, *mutuum dare, commodare;* to — at interest, *faenerari.*

length, *longitudo;* in time, *longinquitas, diuturnitas:* at —, *tandem.*

lengthen, v. *longiorem facĕre;* in time, *producĕre, prorogare.*

length-wise, *in longitudinem.*

lengthy, in words, *verbosus, longus.*

leniency, *clementia, lenitas.*

lenient, *clemens, lenis;* adv. *clementer.*

lentil, *lens.*

less: adj. *minor;* adv. *minus;* much —, *nedum.*

lessee, *conductor.*

lessen, *(de)minuĕre, imminuĕre.*

lessening, *deminutio, imminutio.*

lesson: to give —s, *docēre;* = warning or example, *documentum.*

lest, conj., *ne* with subj.

lethal, *mortifer, exitialis.*

lethargic, *torpidus;* a — person, *lethargicus.*

lethargy, *lethargus, torpor.*

letter: of the alphabet, *littera;* to the —, *ad verbum;* = epistle, *litterae (-arum), epistula.*

letter-carrier, *tabellarius.*

lettered, *litteratus.*

letters, = learning, *doctrina, litterae (-arum);* a man of —, *homo doctus.*

lettuce, *lactuca.*

levee, *salutatio.*

level, adj. *aequus, planus;* — ground, *planities.*

level, v.: = make even, *(ex)aequare;* = bring to the ground, *solo aequare, sternĕre;* to — a weapon, *librare.*

lever, *vectis.*

leveret, *lepusculus.*

levity, *inconstantia, levitas; iocus, iocatio.*

levy, subst. *dilectus (-ūs);* to hold a —, *dilectum habēre.*

levy, v.: to — soldiers, *milites (con)-scribĕre;* to — tribute, *tributum imponĕre, vectigal exigĕre.*

lewd, *impudicus, impurus;* adv. *impure.*

liable, *obnoxius.*

liar, *(homo) mendax.*

libation, *libamentum;* to make a —, *libare.*

libellous, *famosus, probrosus.*

liberal, *liberalis, largus, munificus;* too —, *prodigus, profusus;* the — arts, *artes liberales* or *ingenuae.* Adv. *liberaliter, large, munifice;* to give —ly, *largiri.*

liberate, *liberare;* to — a slave, *manumittĕre.*

liberation, *liberatio;* of a slave, *manumissio.*

liberator, *liberator.*

libertine, *homo dissolutus, ganeo.*

liberty, *libertas;* excessive —, *licentia:* at —, *liber.*

library, *bibliotheca.*

licence, subst.: = permission, *copia, potestas;* = liberty, *licentia.*

license, v. *potestatem dare.*

licentious, *dissolutus, impudicus;* adv. *dissolute, impudice.*

licentiousness, *libido, impudicitia.*

lick, *lingĕre, lambĕre;* to — up, *ligur(r)ire.*

lid, *operculum, operimentum.*

lie, subst. *mendacium.*

lie, v. = tell a lie, *mentiri.*

lie, v. = be situated, *iacēre, cubare, positum esse;* to — between, *interiacēre;* to — down, *procumbĕre;* to — hid, *latēre;* to — in wait, *insidiari.*

lief; I had as —, *malim.*

lieu; in — of, *pro, loco, vice.*

lieutenant, *legatus.*

life, *vita, anima;* to come to — again, *reviviscĕre;* the necessaries of —, *victus (-ūs);* time of —, *aetas;* the prime of —, *flos aetatis, aetas integra.* Transf., = liveliness, *vis, vigor, alacritas;* full of — *vividus, vegetus, alacer.*

life-guards, *(milites) praetoriani.*

lifeless, *exanimis;* of style, *frigidus, exilis, ieiunus;* adv. *frigide.*

life-time, *aetas;* in my —, *me vivo.*

lift, v. *(at)tollĕre, extollĕre, (sub)levare.*

ligament, *ligamentum, ligamen.*

light, subst. *lumen, lux;* to bring to —, *in lucem proferre, patefacĕre;* source of —, *lumen, lucerna* (= lamp), *candela* or *cereus* (= taper or torch); to work by lamp-—, *lucubrare.*

light, adj.: opp. to dark, *clarus, inlustris, candidus* (in colour); opp. to heavy, *levis;* — soil, *solum tenue;* —-hearted, *hilaris, curis vacuus.* Adv. *leviter;* — clad, *expeditus.*

light, v.: = set light to, *accendĕre;* = illuminate, *inlustrare;* to — upon, *incidĕre, offendĕre.*

lighten: = make less heavy, *exonerare;* = cause lightning, *fulgurare, fulgēre.*

lighthouse, *pharus.*

lightness, *levitas.*

lightning, *fulmen, fulgur;* struck by —, *fulmine ictus, de caelo tactus.*

like, adj. *similis, par.*
like, adv. *similiter; instar, modo, ritu* (all with genit.).
like, v. *amare, diligĕre;* I — this, *hoc mihi placet* or *cordi est;* I — to do it, *iuvat me facĕre.*
likelihood, *veri similitudo, probabilitas.*
likely, *veri similis, probabilis.*
like-minded, *concors.*
liken, *comparare.*
likeness: = resemblance, *similitudo;* = portrait, *effigies, imago.*
likewise, *item, itidem.*
liking, *amor, voluptas* (= pleasure), *libido* (= caprice); to one's —, *gratus, iucundus.*
lily, *lilium.*
limb, *membrum, artus (-uum,* plur.).
lime, subst.: the mineral, *calx;* bird- —, *viscum;* the tree, *tilia.*
lime, v. (with bird- —), *visco inlinĕre.*
lime-kiln, (*fornax*) *calcaria.*
limit, subst. *terminus, finis, modus.*
limit, v. *finire, terminare.*
limitation, *determinatio;* = exception, *exceptio.*
limited, *parvus, angustus, brevis.*
limp, adj. *languidus.*
limp, v. *claudicare, claudum esse.*
limpet, *lepas.*
limpid, *limpidus, pellucidus.*
limpness, *languor.*
Lincoln, *Lindum.*
linden-tree, *tilia.*
line, *linea;* in a straight —, *e regione, rectā lineā, ad lineam;* a — of poetry, *versus (-ūs), versiculus;* milit., — of battle, *acies;* — of march, *agmen;* the front —, *prima acies, hastati (-orum);* second —, *principes (-um);* third —, *triarii (-orum);* in plur., lines (= entrenchments, etc.), *muni-tiones (-um), munimenta (-orum), vallum;* = cord, thin rope, *funis, funiculus;* a fishing —, *linea;* plumb- —, *perpendiculum.*
line, v. *complēre.*
lineage, *stirps, genus (-eris,* n.), *origo.*
lineaments, *lineamenta (-orum).*
linen, *linum;* — cloth, *linteum;* adj., of —, *linteus.*
linger, *cessare, morari, cunctari.*
lingerer, *cunctator, cessator.*
lingering, subst. *mora, cunctatio, cessatio.*
lingering, adj. *tardus, lentus.*
liniment, *unguentum.*
link, subst.: = torch, *fax, taeda, funale;* = bond, *vinculum, necessi-tudo;* — of a chain, *annulus.*
link, v. *connectĕre, (con)iungĕre.*
lint, *linamentum.*
lintel, *limen superum.*
lion, *leo;* adj., of a —, *leoninus.*
lioness, *leaena.*
lion-hearted, *magnanimus.*
lip, *labrum, labia.*
liquid, subst. *liquor, umor, latex.*
liquid, adj. *liquidus;* to become —, *liquescĕre, liquefieri;* to make —, *liquefacĕre.*
Lisbon, *Olisipo.*
lisp, *balbutire.*
lisping, *blaesus.*

list, *tabula, libellus, index.*
listen; see hear.
listless, *socors, deses, languidus;* adv. *languide.*
listlessness, *languor, socordia, desiaia.*
literal: the — sense. *propria vis.* Adv. *ad verbum;* to translate —ly, *ad verbum transferre.*
literary, *litteratus, litterarum studiosus;* — tastes, *studia (-orum) litterarum.*
literature, *litterae (-arum), litterarum monumenta (-orum).*
lithe, *mollis, flexibilis.*
litigate, *litigare, rem lite persequi.*
litigation, *lis.*
litigious, *litigiosus.*
litter, subst.: = the vehicle, *lectica;* = brood, *fetus (-ūs), suboles;* of straw, *stramentum.*
little, a little, as subst., *paulum, nonnihil, parum* (= too little); just a —, *paululum;* a — better, *paulo melior;* a — before, sub (with acc.); a — sad, *subtristis;* — by —, *sensim, gradatim;* he said —, *pauca dixit.*
little, adj. *parvus, parvulus, exiguus;* often rendered by diminutive of subst; so —, *tantulus;* how —, *quantulus;* for a — while, *parumper, paulisper.*
little, adv. *paulum;* see also little, subst.
littleness, *parvitas, exiguitas.*
live, adj = living; q.v.
live, v. *esse, spirare, vivĕre;* to — on a thing, *re vivĕre* or *vesci;* to — in a place, *locum incolĕre* or *habitare.*
livelihood, *victus (-ūs).*
liveliness, *alacritas.*
lively, *alacer, vegetus, vehemens.*
liver, *iecur.*
livid, *lividus;* — colour, *livor;* to be —, *livēre.*
living, adj. *vivus.*
lizard, *lacerta, lacertus, stellio.*
lo! *en, ecce.*
load, subst. *onus (-eris,* n.).
load, v. *onerare, onus imponĕre;* of firearms (*arma*) *parare, instruĕre.*
loaded, *onustus, oneratus.*
loaf, *panis.*
loam, *lutum.*
loan, *mutuum, res commodata;* of money, *pecunia mutua.*
loath, *invitus:* I am —, *piget me, nolo.*
loathe, v. *fastidire, odisse, aspernari.*
loathing, *fastidium odium.*
loathsome, *teter, foedus.*
lobby, *vestibulum.*
lobster, *cancer* (= crab).
local, render by genitive *loci* or *regionis.*
locality, *locus, loci natura.*
loch, *lacus (-ūs).*
lock, subst.: on a door, *claustra (-orum);* see also hair.
lock, v. *obserĕre, occludĕre;* to — up, *concludĕre.*
locker, *armarium.*
lock-jaw, *tetanus.*
locust, *locusta.*
lodge, v.: intransit., = stay, *deversari, devertĕre;* = stick, *haerēre;* transit., *hospitio excipĕre.*

lodger, *deversor, inquilinus.*
lodgings, *deversorium, deverticulum, meritoria (-orum).*
loft, *cenaculum.*
loftiness, *altitudo, elatio, excelsitas.*
lofty, *altus, (ex)celsus, editus, sublimis;* of speech, *grandis.* Adv. *alte, excelse.*
log, *lignum, stipes* (= tree-trunk).
logic, *logica (-orum), dialectica (-ae, f. or -orum, n.); disserendi ratio.*
logical, *logicus, dialecticus;* a — consequence, *consequens.* Adv. *dialectice;* often *ratione.*
logician, *dialecticus.*
loin, *lumbus.*
Loire, *Liger.*
loiter, *cessare.*
loll, *recumbĕre, recubare.*
London, *Londinium.*
lone, lonely, *solus, solitarius.*
loneliness, *solitudo.*
long, adj.: in space, *longus, procerus* (= tall): very —, *praelongus;* — hair, *capillus promissus;* six feet —, *longus pedes sex;* a — way, *longe, procul;* in time, *longus, diuturnus;* for a — time, *diu;* a — time ago, *iam pridem.*
long, adv. of time, *diu;* how —?, *quamdiu?* so —, *tam diu;* see also long, adj.
long, v. *avēre, cupĕre, gestire.*
longer, of time, *diutius, longius, amplius;* no —, *non iam, non diutius.*
longing, *appetitus (-ūs), appetitio, cupido.*
look, subst. *aspectus (-ūs), conspectus (-ūs), obtutus (-ūs, = gaze);* = expression, *vultus (-ūs);* = appearance, in gen., *species, facies.*
look, v.: to — at, *aspicĕre, intuēri, contemplari, spectare;* to — about, *circumspicĕre;* to — back, *respicĕre;* to — down, *despicĕre;* to — up, *suspicĕre;* of position, to — in a certain direction, *spectare;* = to appear, seem, *vidēri.*
looking-glass, *speculum.*
loom, subst. *tela.*
loop, subst. *laqueus.*
loophole, *foramen, fenestra.*
loose, adj.: = slack, *laxus, fluxus, remissus;* of soil, *rarus;* at liberty, *liberatus, liber;* of morals, *(dis)solutus, effrenatus.* Adv. *laxe, (dis)solute.*
loose, v. *(re)laxare, remittĕre, (re)solvĕre.*
lop; to — off, *amputare, praecidĕre.*
lopsided; see uneven.
loquacious, *loquax, verbosus;* adv. *loquaciter.*
loquacity, *loquacitas.*
lord, *dominus.*
lordly, = proud; q.v.
lordship, *imperium, potestas, dominatus (-ūs).*
lore, *eruditio, doctrina.*
lose, *amittĕre, perdĕre* (wilfully); to — a battle, *vinci;* to — colour, *pallescĕre;* to — heart, *animo cadĕre* or *deficĕre;* to — one's way, *errare;* = to be bereft of, *privari, orbari.*
losing, subst. *amissio.*

loss, *damnum, detrimentum, iactura;* I am at a —, *dubius sum, haereo dubito.*
lost, to be, *perire;* — in thought, *in cogitatione defixus.*
lot, *sors;* casting of —s, *sortitio, sortitus (-us);* to decide by —, *sortiri.*
loth; see loath.
lottery, *sors, sortitio, alea.*
loud, *clarus, magnus;* adv. *magna voce.*
lounge, v. *nihil agĕre, desidĕre.*
louse, *pediculus.*
loutish, *rusticus, agrestis.*
love, subst. *amor, caritas* (= affection), *pietas* (= devotion), *studium* (= enthusiasm); a — affair, *amor;* god of —, *Cupido, Amor;* goddess of —, *Venus;* my —! *mea voluptas! deliciae meae!*
love, v. *amare, diligĕre, studēre* (with dat.).
loved, *carus.*
loveliness, *venustas, amoenitas.*
lovely, *venustus; amoenus* (esp. of scenery).
lover, *amator, amans,* and f. *amatrix.*
loving, adj. *amans, studiosus;* adv. *amanter.*
low, adj. *humilis, demissus;* of voice, *summissus;* of price, *vilis;* of character or standing, *humilis, ignobilis, obscurus;* of spirits, *tristis, maestus.*
low, adv. *humiliter, demisse;* to speak —, *submissa voce dicĕre.*
low, v., of cattle, *mugire.*
low-born, *obscuro* (or *humili*) *loco natus.*
lower, adj. *inferior.*
lower, v. *demittĕre;* to — the voice, *vocem submittĕre;* to — oneself = condescend, *se submittĕre, descendĕre.*
lowering, see dark, threatening.
lowest, *infimus, imus.*
lowing, of cattle, *mugitus (-ūs).*
lowlands, *loca (-orum) plana.*
lowliness, *humilitas, obscuritas;* as a virtue, *modestia.*
lowly: of rank, *humilis, obscurus;* = unassuming, *modestus.*
lowness, *humilitas* (lit. and fig.); of price, *vilitas.*
loyal, *fidelis, fidus;* adv. *fideliter.*
loyalty, *fides, fidelitas.*
lubricate, *ung(u)ĕre.*
lucid, *(pel)lucidus, dilucidus, perspicuus;* adv. *(di)lucide, perspicue.*
lucidity, *perspicuitas.*
luck, *fortuna, fors, casus (-ūs);* good —, *res secundae, felicitas;* good — to it! *bene vertat!*
lucky, *felix, fortunatus, faustus;* adv. *feliciter, fauste.*
lucrative, *quaestuosus, lucrosus.*
lucre, *lucrum, quaestus (-ūs).*
ludicrous, *ridiculus.*
lug, *trahĕre.*
luggage, *impedimenta (-orum), vasa (-orum), sarcinae (-arum,* = knapsacks).
lugubrious, *lugubris, flebilis, maestus.*
lukewarm, *tepidus;* = unenthusiastic, *languidus, frigidus.*

lull, v.: transit., *sedare*; to — to sleep, *sopire*; intransit., the wind —s, *venti vis cadit.*
lullaby, *cantus (-ūs).*
lumber, *scruta (-orum).*
luminary, = heavenly body, *sidus (-eris, n.).*
luminous, *lucidus, inlustris*; see also *lucid.*
lump, *massa, glaeba (gleba).*
lumpy, *crassus, glebosus.*
lunar, *lunaris.*
lunatic; see mad, madman.
lunch, subst. *prandium.*
lunch, v. *prandēre.*
lung, *pulmo*; —s, *pulmones, latera.*
lurch, see roll; to leave in the —, *deserēre, destituēre.*
lure, subst. *inlex, inlecebra.*
lure, v. *adlicēre, inlicēre, pellicēre.*
lurid, *obscurus, caliginosus.*
lurk, *latēre, latitare, delitescēre.*
luscious, *(prae)dulcis.*
lust, subst. *libido, cupiditas.*
lust, v. *concupiscēre.*
lustful, *libidinosus, impudicus.*
lustily, *valide.*
lustre, = brightness, *nitor, splendor*; = a space of five years, *lustrum.*
lusty, *validus, vegetus.*
lute, *lyra, fides (-ium), cithara* (poet.).
luxuriant, *laetus, luxuriosus.*
luxuriate, *luxuriare.*
luxurious, *luxuriosus, mollis, delicatus*; adv. *luxuriose, molliter, delicate.*
luxury, *luxus (-ūs), luxuria.*
lynx, *lynx.*
lynx-eyed, *lynceus.*
Lyons, *Lugdunum.*
lyre; see lute.
lyric, lyrical, *melicus, lyricus.*

M

Maas or **Meuse**, *Mosa.*
mace, *fasces (-ium).*
Macedonia, *Macedonia*; a —n, *Macedo*; —n, adj., *Macedonius, Macedonicus.*
macerate, *macerare.*
machination, *machina, dolus.*
machine, *machina, machinatio, machinamentum.*
mackerel, *scomber.*
mad, *insanus, furiosus, demens*; to be —, *furēre, insanire.* Adv. *insane, furiose, dementer.*
madden, *(homini) furorem incutēre, mentem alienare*; fig., *exacerbare, exasperare.*
madness, *insania, dementia, furor.*
magazine, = store, *horreum, receptaculum, armamentarium*; see also journal.
maggot, *vermis, vermiculus.*
magic, subst. *ars magica, magice.*
magic, adj. *magicus; mirabilis, mirus.*
magician, *magus.*
magistracy, *magistratus (-ūs).*
magistrate, *magistratus (-ūs).*
magnanimity, *magnanimitas, magnus animus.*

magnanimous, *magnanimus.*
magnet, (*lapis*) *magnes.*
magnificence, *magnificentia, splendor.*
magnificent, *magnificus, splendidus, amplus*; adv. *magnifice, splendide, ample.*
magnify, *augēre, amplificare, exaggerare.*
magniloquence, *magniloquentia.*
magniloquent, *magniloquus.*
magnitude, *magnitudo, spatium* (= extent).
magpie, *pica.*
maid: = virgin, *virgo*; = any girl, *puella*; = servant-girl, *ancilla, famula.*
maidenhood, *virginitas.*
maidenly, *virgineus, virginalis.*
mail: = armour, *arma (-orum)*; = letters, *litterae (-arum).*
maim, *mutilare, truncare.*
maimed, *mancus, truncus.*
main, subst. = sea, *pelagus, altum.*
main, adj. *primus, praecipuus, princeps*; the — point, *caput, res (summa).* Adv. *praecipue, potissimum.*
mainland, *terra (continens).*
maintain: = preserve, *sustinēre, sustentare, (con)servare, retinēre*; = keep alive, *alēre*; to — in argument, *contendēre, confirmare, adfirmare.*
maintenance, *conservatio, salus*; = livelihood, *victus (-ūs).*
maize, *far.*
majestic, *augustus, sanctus, magnificus*; adv. *auguste.*
majesty, *maiestas, dignitas, amplitudo*; divine —, *numen.*
major, subst.: milit., *tribunus militum*; in law, (*homo*) *sui iuris.*
major, adj. *maior.*
majority, *maior pars, maior numerus, plures* (= more people), *plurimi* (= most).
make, subst. *figura, forma, conformatio.*
make: = form, create, *facĕre, efficĕre, fabricari, aedificare*; to — one's way, *iter facĕre*; to — render, cause to be, *facĕre, reddĕre*; to — good, *reparare, resarcire*; = to appoint, *facĕre, creare, instituĕre*; in valuing, to — much of a thing, *rem magni facĕre*; = cause, compel, *facĕre* or *efficĕre* (with ut and subj.), *cogĕre* (with infin.); in arithmetic, = form, come to, *efficĕre, esse*; to — away with, *interficĕre, tollĕre*; to — for, *petĕre*; to — up a story, *fingĕre, comminisci*; to — way, *cedĕre.*
maker, *fabricator*; or use verb.
makeshift, adj. *subitarius.*
maladministration, *prava rerum administratio.*
malady; see illness.
malapropos, adv. *intempestive.*
malaria, *caelum grave et pestilens.*
malcontent, *homo rerum novarum cupidus.*
male, adj. *virilis, mas, masculus*; the — sex, *virilis sexus (-ūs).*
malediction, *exsecratio, dirae (-arum).*
malefactor, *homo maleficus or sceleratus.*
malevolent, *malevolus.*

malice, *malignitas, invidia, malevolentia.*

malicious, *malevolus, malignus, invidus.*

malign, v.; see slander.

maligner, *obtrectator.*

malignity, *malevolentia;* of a disease, *vis (morbi).*

malleable, *lentus, mollis.*

mallet, *fistuca, malleus.*

mallow, *malva, malache.*

Malta, *Melita.*

maltreat, *male tractare, vexare.*

mammal, *animal.*

man, *homo* (= human being); *vir* (i.e. not woman or child); men, plur., *mortales, homines, genus humanum;* all to a —, *omnes ad unum;* — by —, *viritim;* no —, *nemo.* Transf., in draughts, *calculus;* in chess, *latro, latrunculus;* of ships, merchant- —, *navis mercatoria;* —of-war, *navis longa.*

man, v. = furnish with men, *complēre.*

manacle, subst. *compes, catena.*

manacle, v. *vincire.*

manage, *tractare, administrare, gerĕre, (pro)curare.*

manageable, *habilis, docilis, facilis.*

management, *administratio, tractatio, cura, (pro)curatio.*

manager, *administrator, (pro)curator.*

mandate, *iussum, mandatum.*

mandible, *maxilla.*

mane, *iuba;* with a —, *iubatus.*

mange, *scabies.*

manger, *praesepe* or *praesepis.*

mangle, v. *(di)laniare, lacerare.*

mangled, *truncus, lacer.*

manhood, *aetas adulta;* to reach —, *togam virilem sumĕre.*

mania, *insania.*

manifest, adj. *apertus, manifestus, perspicuus,* it is —, *patet, apparet;* adv. *aperte, manifesto.*

manifest, v. *aperire, patefacĕre, manifestum facĕre.*

manifestation, *demonstratio, indicium.*

manifesto, *edictum.*

manifold, *multiplex, varius.*

manipulate, *tractare.*

mankind, *homines (-um), genus humanum.*

manliness, *virtūs (-ūtis);* animus virilis.*

manly, *virilis, fortis.*

manner, *ratio, modus, via;* = sort, kind, *genus (-eris, n.);* — of writing, *oratio, sermo.*

manners, *mores (-um);* a person of good —, *homo bene moratus.*

mannikin, *homuncio, homunculus, homullus.*

manoeuvre, *decursus (-ūs), decursio;* = trick, stratagem, *artificium, dolus.*

manoeuvre, v. *(in armis) decurrĕre, evagari.*

manor, *fundus, praedium.*

mansion, *aedes (-um), domus.*

manslaughter, *hominis caedes, homicidium.*

mantelet, *vinea, pluteus, testudo.*

mantel-piece, *mensa, abacus, tabula.*

mantle, *amiculum, palla* (for women), *pallium; lacerna* or *paenula* (for travelling); *sagum* (= soldier's —).

manual, subst. *libellus.*

manual, adj., render by *manu.*

manufacture, subst. *fabrica.*

manufacture, v. *fabricari* or *fabricare.*

manufacturer, *opifex, artifex, fabricator.*

manumission, *manumissio.*

manumit, *manu mittĕre,* or *manumittĕre.*

manure, *stercus (-oris, n.), fimus.*

manure, v. *stercorare.*

manuscript, *chirographum.*

many, *multi;* a good —, *complures, plerique;* very —, *permulti, plurimi;* — times as great, *multiplex;* — a time, *saepe, saepenumero;* as — as, *tot . . . quot;* just as —, *totidem;* so — times, *totie(n)s.*

many-coloured, *variis coloribus distinctus.*

map, *tabula.*

map, v., to — out, *designare, describĕre.*

maple, *acer;* adj., of —, *acernus.*

mar, *foedare, deformare, corrumpĕre.*

marauder, *praedator, direptor.*

marauding, *praedatorius, praedabundus.*

marble, subst. *marmor.*

marble, adj. *marmoreus.*

March, *(mensis) Martius.*

march, subst. *iter;* a regular day's —, *iustum iter;* to make forced —es, *magnis itineribus contendĕre;* troops on the —, *agmen.*

march, v.: intransit., *iter facĕre, incedĕre;* — off, *proficisci;* — fast, *contendĕre;* — in the rear, *agmen cogĕre;* transit., *ducĕre;* — back, *reducĕre;* to — across, *tra(ns)ducĕre.*

marches, *fines (-ium), confinium.*

mare, *equa.*

margin, *margo.*

marginal, *in margine scriptus* or *positus.*

marine, adj. *marinus, ad mare pertinens.*

mariner, *nauta.*

marines, *classiarii, classici milites.*

maritime, *maritimus.*

marjoram, *amaracus.*

mark, subst. *nota, signum, indicium;* it is the — of a wise man to do so, *est sapientis facĕre;* to make one's —, *clarum fieri.*

mark, v. *(de)signare, notare;* = take notice of, *observare, animadvertĕre;* to — out, *metiri, designare.*

marked, *inlustris, insignis.*

market: the place, *macellum, forum;* cattle —, *forum boarium;* the business, *mercatus (-ūs), nundinae (-arum).*

marketable, *venalis.*

marriage, *coniugium, matrimonium, nuptiae (-arum), conubium.*

marriageable, *nubilis, adultus.*

marriage-contract, *pactio nuptialis.*

marriage-settlement, *dos.*

marrow, *medulla.*

marry, v.; = give in marriage, *in matrimonium dare;* of a man, to — a woman, *ducĕre (in matrimonium);* of a woman, to — a man, *nubĕre* (with dat.); to — out of her station, *enubere*; to — beneath her, *denubĕre*; of a couple, to — each other, *matrimonio* or *nuptiis* (*con*)*iungi*.

marry! interj. *medius fidius, mehercle.*

Marseilles, *Massilia.*

marsh, *palūs,* (*-ūdis,* f.).

marshal, subst. *dux.*

marshal, v. *instruĕre, disponĕre.*

marshy, *paluster, uliginosus.*

martial, *militaris, bellicosus.*

martyr: to become a — for a cause, *pro re mortem occumbĕre.*

marvel, subst. *miraculum, portentum.*

marvellous, (*per*)*mirus, mirificus,* (*ad*)*mirabilis*; adv. *mire mirifice,* (*ad*)*mirabiliter.*

masculine, *virilis, masculus.*

mask, subst., *persona, larva.* Transf., *persona, species, simulatio.*

mask, v. *tegĕre, occultare, dissimulare.*

mass, *massa, moles*; a great —, *magna copia* or *vis*; — of people, *multitudo.*

massive, *solidus, magnus gravis.*

massacre, subst. *caedes, strages, trucidatio.*

massacre, v. *caedĕre, trucidare.*

mast: on ships, *malus*; = acorns, etc., *glans.*

master, subst.: = owner, ruler, *dominus*; — of a house, *pater familias, herus*; — of property, *possessor*; to become —, *potiri*; a school- —, *magister*; one's own —, *sui potens, sui iuris*; = expert, *artifex, homo peritus.*

master, v.: = subdue, *domare, vincĕre, superare*; to — passions, *continēre, coercēre*; to — a subject, = understand, *intellegĕre,* (*per*)*discĕre, comprehendĕre.*

masterful, *superbus, imperiosus, adrogans.*

masterly, *artificiosus, artifex* (of persons); or render by *ars.*

mastery, = victory, *victoria.*

masticate, *manducare, mandĕre.*

mat, subst. *storea* or *storia, teges.*

mat, v.: to — together, *implicare.*

match, subst.: = one's equal, *par* (with dat.); no — for, *impar*; = contest, *certamen*; = marriage, *condicio, nuptiae* (*-arum*).

match, v.: = equal, suit, *parem esse, aequare*; = bring together as opponents, *componĕre, conferre*; to — oneself with *congredi, certare.*

matchless, *singularis, unicus, egregius.*

match-maker, (*nuptiarum*) *conciliator* (f. *-trix*).

mate, subst. *socius* (= companion), *coniunx* (= husband or wife).

mate, v.: in chess, *ad incitas redigĕre*; = be united, *coniungi.*

material, subst. *materies* or *materia, copia rerum.*

material, adj., *corporeus*; see also important. Adv.; see much.

maternal, *maternus.*

mathematical, *mathematicus.*

mathematician, *mathematicus.*

mathematics, *mathematica.*

matricide, *matricidium* (the crime); *matricida* (the person).

matrimonial; see conjugal.

matrimony, *matrimonium*; see marriage.

matron, = married woman, *matrona.*

matronly, *matronalis.*

matter, subst. (1), = physical substance, *corpus, res corporeae.* (2) in discussion, etc.: — available, *materies* or *materia, silva, copia rerum*; subject—, the — in hand, *res, propositum, institutum.* (3), = affair, in gen., *res, causa*; how do —s stand? *quo loco res est?*; a business —. *negotium.* (4), = trouble: what's the —? *quid* (*rei*) *est?* (5), = pus, *pus* (*puris*).

it matters, *interest, refert*; — to me, *meā*; — to him, *eius*; — a great deal, *magnopere* or *multum* or *magni.*

mattock, *dolabra.*

mature, *maturus, adultus.*

maturity, *maturitas.*

matutinal, *matutinus.*

maudlin; see drunken, silly.

maul; see injure.

maw, *ingluvies, venter.*

mawkish, *putidus*; adv. *putide.*

maxim, *praeceptum, regula, institutum, sententia.*

maximum, *quod maximum est.*

May, (*mensis*) *Maius.*

may, v., I may do: = I can, *possum facĕre*; = I have permission, *licet mihi facĕre*; = perhaps I will do *fortasse faciam.*

mayor, *urbis praefectus.*

maze, *labyrinthus.*

mead, as a drink, *mulsum.*

mead, meadow, *pratum*; adj., of the —, *pratensis.*

meagre, *ieiunus, exilis, exiguus*; adv. *ieiune, exiliter.*

meagreness, *ieiunitas, exilitas.*

meal: = flour, *farina*; of food, in gen. *cibus, epulae* (*-arum,* = banquet); a morning —, *prandium*; the main — of the day, *cena.*

mean, subst. *modus, mediocritas.*

mean, adj.: = central, *medius*; = low in rank, *humilis, ignobilis, obscurus*; = morally low, *inliberalis, abiectus sordidus.* Adv. *inliberaliter, abiecte sordide.*

mean, v.: = intend, *in animo habēre, cogitare velle*; = signify, indicate, *significare, sibi velle, valēre*; = refer to, allude to, *significare, dicĕre, intellegĕre.*

meaning: = signification, *significatio, vis, sententia*; see also purpose.

meanness: moral, *inliberalitas, animus abiectus, sordes* (plur.); of rank, *humilitas, obscuritas.*

means: = instrument, method, way, *via, ratio, consilium*; by all — *omnino*; by no —, *minime, nullo modo*; by — of, render by abl. or *per*; = resources, *res familiaris, fortuna, opes* (*-um,* plur.).

meantime, in the, *interea, interim.*

measure, subst. *mensura, modus*; in full —, *pleno modio, cumulate*; according to the — of, *pro,* with abl.; beyond —, *praeter modum,* *immodice, nimis*; in some —, *aliqua-tenus, aliqua ex parte*; = steps taken, course of action, *ratio, consilium*; in music, *modi, numeri (-orum)*.

measure, v.: transit., *(di)metiri*; intransit., *esse*, with genit.

measured; see moderate.

measureless, *immensus, infinitus*.

measurement, *mensio, mensura*.

measurer, *mensor*.

measuring-rod, *decempeda*.

meat, *cibus*; = flesh, *caro*.

mechanic, *faber, opifex*.

mechanical, *mechanicus*.

mechanism, *machina, machinatio*.

medallion, *clipeus* or *clipeum*.

meddle, *se interponĕre, (rem) attingĕre*.

meddler, *ardelio, homo importunus*.

mediate, v. *se interponĕre*; to — a peace, *pacem conciliare*.

mediator, *deprecator, arbiter, con-ciliator*.

medical, *medicus*.

medicinal, *saluber, salutaris*.

medicine: = remedy, *medicina, medicamentum, remedium*: = medical science, *medicina, ars medendi*.

mediocre, *mediocris*.

mediocrity, *mediocritas*.

meditate, *cogitare, meditari commentari*.

meditation, *cogitatio, commentatio, meditatio*.

meditative, *in cogitatione defixus*.

Mediterranean Sea, *Mare Internum, mare nostrum*.

medium; see mean and means.

medley, *farrago; conluvies, conluvio*.

meek, *demissus, verecundus*; adv. *verecunde*.

meekness, *animus demissus verecundia*.

meet, adj.; see fit, proper.

meet, v.: transit., *obviam fieri, incidĕre, offendĕre*; to go to —, *obviam ire, occurrĕre*; to — death, *mortem obire* or *oppetĕre*; intransit., to — together, *(inter se) congredi, convenire, coire; confluĕre* (in large numbers), *convolare* (in haste).

meeting, *congressio, concursus (-ūs)*; = assembly, *conventus (-ūs), coetus (-ūs)*; a crowded —, *frequentia*.

melancholy, subst.: = hypochondria, *atra bilis*; = sorrow, *tristitia, maestitia*.

melancholy, adj. *tristis, maestus*.

melee, *pugna, proelium*.

mellow, adj. *maturus, mitis*; of wine, *lenis, mollis*.

mellow, v.: transit., *coquĕre*; intransit., *maturescĕre*.

melodious, *canorus, numerosus*; adv. *numerose*.

melody, *melos, cantus (-ūs)*.

melt, v.: transit., *liquidum facĕre, liquefacĕre, dissolvĕre*; intransit., *liquescĕre, liquefieri, dissolvi, tabescĕre*.

member: of the body, *membrum*; a — of a nation, *civis*; of the senate, *senator*; of a corporation, *sodalis*.

membrane, *membrana*.

memoirs, *historiae (-arum), commentarii (-orum)*.

memorable, *memorabilis, memoriā dignus*.

memorandum, *libellus, index*

memorial, *monumentum*.

memory, *memoria, recordatio* (= recollection): to keep in —, *memoria tenēre*; from —, *ex memoria, memoriter*; to commit to —, *ediscĕre*; in the — of man, *post hominum memoriam*.

menace; see threat.

mend, v.: transit., *reficĕre, reparare, reconcinnare, (re)sarcire*; fig., *emendare, corrigĕre*; intransit., = improve; q.v.

mendacious, *mendax*; adv. *falso, per mendacium*.

mendacity, *mendacium*.

mendicancy, *mendicitas, egestas*.

mendicant, *mendicus*.

menial, adj. *servilis*.

mensuration, *ars metiendi*.

mental, render by genit. *animi, ingenii, mentis*. Adv. *mente, animo, cogitatione*.

mention, subst. *mentio, commemoratio*.

mention, v. *mentionem facĕre, commemorare*; above— —ed, render by *supra*, with *commemorare* or *dicĕre*.

mentor; see adviser.

mercenary, subst. *miles mercennarius* or *conducticius*.

mercenary, adj. *mercennarius, conducticius; venalis* (= readily bribed).

merchandise, *merx, res (rerum) venales*.

merchant, *mercator, negotiator*.

merchant-ship, *navis mercatoria* or *oneraria*.

merciful, *misericors, clemens, mansuetus*; adv. *clementer, mansuete*.

merciless, *immitis, inclemens, inhumanus, crudelis*; adv. *inclementer, inhumane, crudeliter*.

mercilessness, *inclementia, inhumanitas, crudelitas*.

mercurial, *mobilis, levis*.

mercury; the god, *Mercurius*; the metal, *argentum vivum*.

mercy, *misericordia, clementia, mansuetudo*.

mere, subst. *lacus (-ūs)*.

mere, adj. *merus, solus, unus*; often *ipse*. Adv. *tantum, modo, solum*.

meretricious, *fucatus*.

merge; see dip or mingle.

meridian, adj. *meridianus*.

merit, subst. *meritum, dignitas, virtus*; according to —, *pro merito*.

merit, v.; see deserve.

merited, *meritus, debitus*.

meritorious, *laude dignus, laudabilis*; adv. *bene, optime*.

merriment, *hilaritas, festivitas*.

merry, *hilarus, hilaris, festivus*; adv. *hilariter, festive*.

mesh, *macula*.

mess, subst.: = common meal, *convivium*; = dirt, *squalor, conluvio*; = confusion, *turba, perturbatio rerum*.

message, *nuntius, mandatum*.

messenger, *nuntius (f. nuntia)*.

messmate, *conviva, sodalis*.

metal, *metallum*.

metaphor, *translatio, verba (-orum) translata*.

metaphorical, *translatus*; adv. *per translationem, translatis verbis*.

metaphysics; render by *philosophia*.

mete; see measure.

meteor, *fax (caelestis)*.

method, *ratio, via, modus, ars*.

methodical, render by phrase; adv., *ratione et via*.

metonymy, *immutatio*.

metre, *numerus, metrum*.

metrical, *numerosus, metricus*.

metropolis, *caput*.

mettle, *animus, audacia, ferocitas*.

mettlesome, *animosus, audax, ferox*.

Meuse; see Maas.

midday, subst. *meridies, tempus meridianum*.

midday, adj. *meridianus*.

middle, subst. *medium*; the — of the road, *media via*.

middle, adj. *medius*; the — way, *mediocritas*.

middling, *mediocris*.

midland, adj. *mediterraneus*.

midnight, subst. *media nox*.

midst, render by adj. *medius*; in the — of, *inter, in*.

midsummer, *summa aestas*.

midway, render by adj. *medius*.

midwife, *obstetrix*.

midwinter, *bruma*.

mien, *habitus (-ūs), vultus (-ūs)*.

might, subst. *vis, robur, nervi (-orum, plur.)*; with all one's —, *summa vi, summa ope*.

mighty, *potens, validus*; adv. *magnopere, valde, summa vi*.

migrate, *abire, discedēre, migrare*.

migration, *profectio*.

Milan, *Mediolanum*.

mild, adj. *lenis, mitis*; to make —, *mitigare, lenire*; to grow —, *mitescēre*; of character, etc., *mitis, clemens, mansuetus*. Adv. *leniter, clementer, mansuete*.

mildew, *robigo* or *rubigo, mucor, situs (-ūs)*.

mildness, of character, *lenitas, mansuetudo, clementia*.

mile (Roman), *mille*, plur. *milia (passuum)*.

milestone, *miliarium*.

military, adj. *militaris, bellicus*; — service, *militia*; — stores, *apparatus (-ūs) belli*; — skill, *rei militaris peritia*.

militate, to — against, *obstare, adversari*.

milk, subst. *lac*; new —, *lac recens*; curdled —, *lac concretum*.

milk, v. *mulgēre*.

milk-pail, *mulctra, mulctrum*.

milk-white, milky, *lacteus*; the — Way, *lacteus orbis, via lactea*.

mill, *mola, pistrinum*.

miller, *pistor*.

millet, *milium*.

million, *decies centena mil(l)ia*.

mimic, v. *imitari*.

mimicry, *imitatio*.

minaret, *turris*.

mince, v. *concidēre, consecare*.

mince, mincemeat, subst. *minutal*.

mincing, *putidus*.

mind, subst. *animus, mens, ingenium* (= intellect or character); to show presence of —, *praesenti animo uti*; to be in one's right —, *sanae mentis esse*; to be out of one's —, *insanire*; to bear in —, *meminisse*; to call to —, *recordari*; to make up one's —, *statuēre, constituēre*.

mind, v.: = attend to, *animum (ad rem) advertēre, (rem) animadvertēre, curare, agēre*; mind you come, *cura (ut) venias*; object to, *aegre ferre*.

mindful, *memor*.

mine, subst., *metallum*; milit., *cuniculus*.

mine, possess. pron., *meus*.

mine, v. *(ef)fodēre*; milit., *cuniculos agēre*.

mineral, subst. *metallum*.

mingle; see mix.

minimum, *minimum, pars minima*.

minion, *minister, servus*.

minister, subst., *minister, servus*; a — of state, *principis socius et administer omnium consiliorum, ille penes quem est cura administrandae reipublicae*.

minister, *conducēre, prodesse*.

ministry, *ministerium, administratio*.

minor, subst., *filius (f. filia) familias*.

minor, adj.; see little, small.

minority, *aetas nondum adulta*; = smaller number, *pars* or *numerus minor*.

minstrel, *citharoedus*.

mint, subst.: the plant, *ment(h)a*; where money is coined, *moneta*.

mint, v.; see coin.

minute, subst., = moment, *punctum* or *momentum temporis*.

minute, adj.: = very small, *exiguus, pusillus, minutus*; = exact, *subtilis, accuratus*; adv. *subtiliter, accurate*.

minutes, plur. subst. *libellus, commentarii (-orum)*.

miracle, *res mira, miraculum*.

miraculous, *mirus, mirificus, mirabilis*; in a — manner, *mirum in modum*.

mire, *lutum*.

mirror, *speculum*.

mirth, *hilaritas, laetitia, gaudium*.

mirthful, *hilaris (hilarus), laetus*.

miry, *luteus, lutulentus*.

misadventure, *casus (-ūs), incommodum*.

misanthrope, *qui genus humanum odit*.

misapply, *abuti, perverse uti*.

misapprehend; see misunderstand.

misbehave, *male se gerēre*.

miscalculate, *male computare; errare, falli, decipi*.

miscalculation, *error*.

miscarriage, *abortus (-ūs), abortio*; a — of justice, *iudicium perversum*.

miscarry, *abortum facēre*; in gen. = fail, *cadēre, secus procedēre*.

miscellaneous, *varius, diversus*.

miscellany, as a literary form, *satura*.

mischance; see misfortune.

mischief; = damage, *malum, incommodum, damnum;* = wrongdoing, *maleficium.*

mischief-maker, *mali auctor.*

mischievous; = harmful, *noxius, perniciosus;* = playful, *lascivus.*

misconceive, *perperam accipĕre.*

misconception, *opinio falsa, error.*

misconduct, *delictum, peccatum.*

misconstrue; see misinterpret.

miscreant, (*homo*) *scelestus* or *sceleratus.*

misdeed, *scelus* (-*eris*, n.), *maleficium.*

misdemeanour, *delictum.*

misdirect, (*epistulam*) *perperam inscribĕre;* = to misuse, *abuti, peram uti.*

miser, *homo avarus.*

miserable, *miser, infelix, adflictus;* adv. *misere.*

miserliness, *avaritia, sordes* (-*ium*).

miserly, *avarus, tenax.*

misery, *miseria, aerumna, tristitia.*

misfortune, *fortuna adversa, res adversae, calamitas, incommodum;* he had the — to, *accidit ei ut.*

misgive; see distrust, doubt.

misgiving, *timor, sollicitudo, praesagium.*

misgovern, *male regĕre* or *administrare.*

misguide, *in errorem inducĕre.*

mishap; see misfortune.

misinform, *falso docēre.*

misinterpret, *male* or *perperam interpretari.*

misjudge, *male iudicare.*

mislead, *decipĕre, fallĕre, in errorem inducĕre.*

mismanage; see misgovern.

misogynist, *qui mulieres odit.*

misplace, (*in*) *alieno loco conlocare;* misplaced, fig., can be rendered by *male* or *perperam,* e.g. with —*d* humour, *male salsus.*

misprint, *mendum.*

mispronounce, *male pronuntiare.*

misquote, render by phrase, such as *verba* (*auctoris*) *vitiose proferre.*

misrepresent, *calumniari, depravare.*

misrule; see misgovern.

miss, subst.; render by verb.

miss, v.: = feel the loss of *desiderare, requirĕre;* = fail to meet or find, (*de*)*errare;* — out, = omit, *omittĕre, praetermittĕre.*

misshapen, *deformis, distortus.*

missile, subst. *telum,* (*telum*) *missile.*

missile, adj. *missilis.*

missing, to be, *desiderari, deesse.*

mission, *missio;* = delegation, *legatio.*

misspend, *perdĕre;* see also waste.

misstatement, *quod falsum est; mendacium.*

mist, *nebula. caligo.*

mistake, subst. *error, erratum;* to make a —, *errare, peccare;* a — in writing, *mendum.*

mistaken, to be, *errare, falli.*

mistakenly, *per errorem, perperam.*

mistress, *domina;* — of a house, *materfamilias, hera;* a school- —, *praeceptrix, magistra;* = sweetheart, *amica.*

misty, *nebulosus, caliginosus;* fig. *obscurus.*

misunderstand, *perperam. intellegĕre.*

misunderstanding, *error;* between persons, *offensio, dissidium.*

misuse, subst. *usus* (-*ūs*) *perversus.*

misuse, v. *abuti, male uti.*

mitigate, *lenire, mitigare.*

mitigation, *mitigatio, levatio.*

mix, v.: transit., *miscēre, admiscēre, temperare;* to — up, = confuse, *confundĕre, permiscēre;* intransit., use transit. verb in pass. or with reflex.

mixed, (*per*)*mixtus, promiscuus.*

mixture, *mixtura, temperatio; permixtio;* a — of good and evil, *bona mixta malis.*

moan, subst. *gemitus* (-*ūs*).

moan, v. *gemĕre.*

moat, *fossa.*

mob, *turba, multitudo; vulgus, plebs.*

mobile, *mobilis.*

mobility, *mobilitas, agilitas.*

mock, adj. *simulatus, fictus, falsus.*

mock, v. *deridēre, inludēre, ludibrio habēre;* see also disappoint.

mocker, *derisor.*

mockery, *ludibrium.*

mockingly, *per ludibrium.*

mode, *ratio, modus;* — of dress, *habitus* (-*ūs*).

model, subst. *exemplar, exemplum.*

model, adj. *optimus.*

model, v. *fingĕre, formare.*

moderate, adj.: = restrained, *moderatus, modestus, temperatus;* = middling, *modicus, mediocris.* Adv. *moderate, modeste, temperate; modice, mediocriter.*

moderate, v. *moderari, temperare coercēre.*

moderation, *modus, modestia, temperantia.*

modern, *recens, novus; huius aetatis.*

modest, *pudens, verecundus;* = moderate, slight, *mediocris, modicus.* Adv. *pudenter, verecunde.*

modesty, *pudor, verecundia.*

modify, (*im*)*mutare;* see also change.

modulate, *modulari.*

modulation, *flexio, flexus* (-*ūs*).

moiety; see half.

moist, *humidus.*

moisten, *conspergĕre* (= sprinkle), *rigare* (= water).

moisture, *humor.*

molar, subst. *dens genuinus.*

mole: = mound, *moles, agger;* the animal, *talpa;* = mark on the body, *naevus.*

molest, *sollicitare, vexare.*

mollify, *mollire, mitigare, lenire.*

molten, *liquefactus.*

moment: of time, *punctum* or *momentum temporis;* for the —, *in praesens;* at the —, *hoc tempore, in praesentia;* = importance, *momentum.*

momentary, *brevissimus.*

momentous, adj. *magni momenti.*

momentum, *momentum, vis.*

monarch, *rex, princeps, dominus.*

monarchical, *regius;* a — form of government, *genus reipublicae regium,*

monarchy, *imperium singulare, potestas regia, regnum.*

monetary, *pecuniarius, nummarius, argentarius.*

money, *pecunia, argentum;* ready —, *pecunia praesens* or *numerata;* a piece of —, *nummus.*

money-bag; see purse.

mongrel, *hibrida.*

monk, *monachus* (eccl.).

monkey, *simia.*

monotheist, *qui unum modo deum esse credit.*

monotonous, *canorus;* or render by *idem* and *semper.*

monsoon, *ventus (qui certo tempore flare consuevit).*

monster, *monstrum, portentum, belua.*

monstrous, *immanis, monstruosus;* adv. *monstruose, praeter naturam.*

month, *mensis.*

monthly: adj. *menstruus;* adv. *singulis mensibus, in singulos menses.*

monument, *monumentum.*

monumental, = important, *gravis, magni momenti.*

mood, *animus;* gram., *modus.*

moody, *morosus.*

moon, *luna;* —light *lunae lumen;* a —light night, *nox luna inlustris.*

moor, moorland, *loca (-orum) fruticetis obsita.*

moor, v. *religare, deligare.*

moot point; it is a —, *incertum* or *dubium est.*

mop subst. *peniculus.*

mop, v. *detergere.*

moping, *tristis, maestus.*

moral, adj.: = relating to morals, *moralis;* — teaching, *morum praecepta (-orum);* = morally correct, *honestus, probus.*

morale, *animus.*

morality, morals, *mores (-um).*

moralize, = *de moribus praecipere.*

morass, *palūs (-ūdis).*

morbid, *aeger, aegrotus.*

more, subst. = a greater amount, *plus.*

more, adj.: sing., *plus* or *amplius* with genit.; plur., *plures.*

more, adv., render by compar. of adj. or adv.; otherwise by *magis* or *potius* (= rather); no — (= no longer), *non iam;* the — . . . the — . . ., *quo* (with compar.), *eo* (with compar.).

moreover, *praeterea, ultro.*

moribund, *moribundus.*

morn, morning, subst. *tempus matutinum;* in the —, *mane, matutino tempore;* early in the —, *multo mane, prima luce;* good —! *salve!*

morning, adj. *matutinus.*

morning-star, *Lucifer.*

morose, *morosus, acerbus, difficilis;* adv. *morose, acerbe.*

moroseness, *morositas, acerbitas.*

morrow, *posterus dies; crastinus dies* (= tomorrow).

morsel, *offa, mica, pars exigua.*

mortal, adj. *mortalis;* see also fatal.

mortality *condicio mortalis, mortalitas;* see also death.

mortar: for mixing, *pila;* for binding together, *arenatum.*

mortgage, subst. *pignus (-oris, n.).*

mortgage, v. *pignori dare, obligare.*

mortification, *offensio, dolor.*

mortify, v.: intransit., *putrescere;* transit., fig., *offendere, vexare.*

mosaic, subst. *pavimentum* or *opus tessellatum.*

mosaic; adj. *tessellatus.*

mosquito, *culex.*

moss, *muscus.*

mossy, *muscosus, musco circumlitus.*

most, adj. *plurimus;* for the — part, *plerumque, maximam partem;* at the —, *summum.*

most, adv., render by superl. of adj. or adv.; otherwise *maxime; plurimum.*

mostly, *fere, plerumque; maximam partem.*

moth, *blatta.*

mother, *mater;* of a —, adj., *maternus.*

mother-in-law, *socrus (-ūs).*

motherly, *maternus.*

mother-tongue, *patrius sermo.*

motion, subst.: = movement, *motus (-ūs);* to be in —, *moveri;* = proposal, *sententia, rogatio.*

motion, v. = to gesture, *adnuere, significare.*

motionless, *immotus, immobilis.*

motive, *causa, ratio.*

mottled, *maculosus.*

motto, *sententia, dictum, praeceptum.*

mould, subst.: = shape, *forma;* = soil, *terra.*

mouldy, *mucidus.*

moult, *plumas ponere.*

mound, *tumulus, agger.*

mount, subst.; see horse.

mount, v.: intransit., see rise; transit., = ascend, *scandere, ascendere;* to — a horse, *conscendere equum;* = furnish with horses, *(milites) equis imponere:* —ed, *equo vectus.*

mountain, *mons;* of a —, *montanus.*

mountainous, *montuosus.*

mountebank, *circulator, planus.*

mourn, *maerere, lugere;* see also lament.

mournful, *tristis, maestus, flebilis;* adv. *maeste, flebiliter.*

mourning, subst. *maeror, maestitia, luctus (-ūs); vestis lugubris;* in —, adj. *sordidatus.*

mouse, *mus (muris).*

mouse-trap, *muscipula.*

mouth, *os;* with open —, *hians.*

movable, *mobilis, agilis.*

move: transit., *(com)movere;* to — rapidly, *agitare;* to — round *versare;* to — to action, *impellere;* intransit., *moveri, se movere, ferri.*

movement, *motus (-ūs).*

mow, *demetere, secare.*

mower, *faenisex.*

much, subst. *multum* or *multa.*

much, adj. *multus;* sometimes *magnus* (= great); too —, adj. *nimius.*

much, adv. *multum, valde:* very —, *plurimum;* with compar. or superl., *multo;* too —, adv., *nimium, nimis;* — less, *nedum, ne dicam.*

mud, *lutum, caenum.*
muddle, subst. *turba, confusio.*
muddle, v. *confundĕre, (per)miscēre, turbare.*
muddy, *lutulentus, luteus.*
muffle, *velare, obvolvĕre.*
muggy, *humidus* (= damp), *calidus* (= warm).
mulberry, *morum*; — -tree, *morus.*
mulct, *multare.*
mule, *mulus.*
mull: —ed wine, *vinum fervidum.*
mullet, *mullus, mugil(is).*
multifarious, *multiplex, varius.*
multiform, *multiformis.*
multiply, *multiplicare.*
multitude, *multitudo, vis, vulgus.*
multitudinous, *creber, frequens, multus.*
munch, *manducare.*
mundane, *humanus, quotidianus.*
municipality, *municipium.*
munificence, *munificentia, liberalitas.*
munificent, *munificus, liberalis.*
munition, *belli instrumenta (-orum)* or *apparatus (-ūs).*
mural *muralis.*
murder, subst. *caedes, occisio, homicidium*; — of a near relative, *parricida.*
murderous, *sanguinarius, cruentus.*
murmur, subst. *murmur, susurrus, fremitus (-ūs)*; = complaint, *querela.*
murmur, v. *murmurare, fremĕre, mussare*; = complain, *fremĕre, queri.*
muscle, in anatomy, *musculus, torus*; —s, = strength, *lacerti (-orum), nervi (-orum).*
muscular, *lacertosus.*
muse, *Musa, Camena.*
mushroom, *fungus, boletus.*
music, *(ars) musica*; a piece of —, *modi (-orum), cantus (-ūs).*
musical, *musicus, symphoniacus*; — understanding music, *artis musicae peritus*; = melodious, *canorus, numerosus.*
musician, *musicus*; or *fidicen, tibicen,* etc.
muslin, *sindon.*
must, subst. *mustum.*
must, v.: I — go, *eundum est mihi, ire debeo, ire me oportet, necesse est eam.*
mustard, *sinapi.*
muster, v.: transit., *recensēre*; = assemble, *convocare*; to — up courage, *animum sumĕre*; intransit., *congregari, coire, convenire.*
musty, *mucidus.*
mutability, *mutabilitas.*
mutable, *mutabilis, inconstans, mobilis.*
mute, adj. *mutus.*
mutilate, *mutilare, truncare.*
mutilated, *mutilus, mutilatus, truncatus.*
mutinous, *seditiosus*; adv. *seditiose.*
mutiny, subst. *seditio, motus (-ūs).*
mutiny, v. *seditionem facĕre.*
mutter, *mussare, mussitare, murmurare.*
muttering, subst. *murmur.*
mutton, *caro (ovilla).*
mutual, *mutuus*; adv. *mutuo*
my, *meus,* sometimes *noster.*
myriad, *decem millia*; = an indefinitely large number, *sescenti.*

myrmidon, *satelles, adsecula.*
myrrh, *murra*; of —, *murrinus.*
myrtle, *myrtus*; of —, adj. *myrteus*; —berry, *myrtum*; — grove, *myrtetum.*
myself; see self.
mysterious, *occultus, secretus, arcanus.*
mystery: religious, *mysteria (-orum)*; in gen., *res occulta.*
mystic, *mysticus*; see also secret, strange.
mystification, *ambages (-um).*
mystify, *tenebras (homini) offundĕre.*
myth, *fabula.*
mythical, *fabulosus.*
mythology, *fabulae (-arum), historia fabularis.*

N

nail, subst.: on finger or toe, *unguis*; for hammering, *clavus.*
nail, v. *(clavis) adfigĕre.*
naive, *simplex.*
naked, *nudus*; adv. *aperte.*
nakedness, *nudatum corpus*; of style, *ieiunitas, exilitas.*
name, subst. *nomen, vocabulum, cognomen* (= family name); in — (only) *verbo*; good — (= reputation) *nomen, fama, existimatio.*
name, v. *nominare, appellare, dicĕre*; = mention, *nominare*; = appoint q.v.
nameless, *nominis expers.*
namely; render by simple apposition, or relative clause or *dico* (= I mean).
namesake (*homo*) *eodem nomine appellatus.*
nap, subst.: = sleep, *somnus (brevis)*; of cloth, *villi (-orum).*
nap, v.; see sleep; Homer is caught —ping, *dormitat Homerus.*
napkin, *mappa, mantele.*
Naples, *Neapolis.*
narrate, *(e)narrare, referre, memorare.*
narration, *narratio, expositio.*
narrative, subst. *narratio, historia.*
narrator, *narrator.*
narrow, adj. *angustus, artus* (= tight), *contractus* (= narrowed); to have a — escape, *aegre periculum effugĕre.* Adv.: = scarcely, *aegre, vix*; = carefully, *accurate, diligenter.*
narrowness, *angustiae (-arum)*; — of mind, *animus angustus.*
narrows, *augustiae (-arum), fauces (-ium).*
nasal, *narium* (genit.).
nastiness: = unpleasantness, *amaritudo, gravitas*; = foulness, *foeditas.*
nasty: = disagreeable, *amarus, gravis*; = foul, *foedus, spurcus.*
natal, *natalis, natalicius.*
nation, *populus, gens* (= people), *civitas* (= body of citizens), *respublica* (= state).
national, render by genit.; in the — interest, *e republica.*
native, subst. *indigena*; a — of Rome, *homo Romae natus.*
native, adj. *indigena*; — land, *patria*; — language, *patrius sermo.*

natural, *naturalis, nativus, innatus* or *insitus* (= inborn); *simplex* or *candidus* (= unaffected); — ability or disposition, *indoles, ingenium, natura*; — death, *mors necessaria*; — science or philosophy, *physica, naturae investigatio*. Adv. *secundum naturam, naturaliter*; *sponte* (= without compulsion); *simpliciter* (= unaffectedly).

naturalize: to — a person, *homini civitatem dare*; to — an animal or plant, *importare*.

nature, *natura*; the realm of —, *rerum natura*; the — of a person (or thing), *natura, ingenium, indoles*.

naught, *nihil*; to set at —, *neglegĕre*.

naughtiness, *improbitas, petulantia, malitia*.

naughty, *improbus, petulans, malus*.

nausea, *nausea, fastidium* (= disgust).

nauseous: see loathsome, disgusting.

nautical, naval, adj. *navalis, nauticus*.

navigable, *navigabilis, navium patiens*.

navigate, *navigare*.

navigation, *navigatio, res nauticae*.

navigator: see sailor.

navy, *classis*.

nay; = no, *non*; — rather . . . , *immo* (*vero*), *atque adeo*.

near, adj. *propinquus*: —er, *propior*; —est, *proximus*; *vicinus* (= neighbouring).

near, adv. *prope, iuxta, propter*.

nearly, *prope, paene, fere* or *ferme*.

nearness, *propinquitas*.

neat: = clean, tidy, *nitidus, mundus, concinnus*; = undiluted, *merus*. Adv. *nitide, concinne*.

neatness, *munditia, concinnitas*.

nebulous, *nebulosus*.

necessaries, *res necessariae*.

necessary, adj. *necessarius*: this is —, *hoc est necessarium, opus est hoc*; adv. *necessarie, necessario*.

necessitate, *cogĕre*; see compel.

necessity: = what must be, *necessitas, res necessaria*; = want, *necessitas, egestas*.

neck, *collum, cervix* (often plur., *cervices*).

necklace, *monile, torques*.

need, subst. *necessitas*: there is — of, *opus est* (with nom. or abl.).

need, v. *requirĕre, egēre*.

needful, *necessarius*.

needle, *acus* (-*ūs*).

needless: see unnecessary.

needlework, *opus acu factum*.

needy, *egens, indigens, inops*.

nefarious, *nefarius*.

negation, *negatio, infitiatio*.

neglect, negligence, *neglegentia, incuria*.

negotiate, *agĕre, conloqui*; to — a peace, *pacem componĕre*.

negotiation, *conloquium*; —s are in progress, *agitur* (*de re*).

negotiator, *legatus, orator, internuntius*.

Negro, *Aethiops*.

neigh, *hinnire*.

neighbour, *vicinus* (f. *vicina*); —s, *vicini, finitimi vicinia*; = fellow man, *alter, ceteri* (plur., = others).

neighbourhood, *vicinia, vicinitas*.

neighbouring, *vicinus, propinquus, finitimus*.

neighbourly, *ut decet vicinum*.

neighing, *hinnitus* (-*ūs*).

neither, pron. *neuter*; in — direction, *neutro*.

neither, conj. *nec* (or *neque*); — . . . nor, *nec . . . nec*; in commands, wishes, etc., *neve* (or *neu*).

nephew, *filius fratris* or *sororis*.

nereid, *Nereis*.

nerve, = vigour, etc., *nervi* (-*orum*).

nervous, = vigorous, *nervosus*; see also timid.

nervousness, *timiditas, trepidatio*.

nest, *nidus*.

nestling, *pullus*.

net, subst. *rete, plaga* (usually plur.).

nettle, *urtica*.

nettled, adj. *offensus, subiratus*.

network, *reticulum*.

neuter, gram., *neuter, neutralis*.

neutral, *medius, neutrius partis*.

never, *nunquam*.

nevertheless, *nihilominus*, (*at*)*tamen*.

new, *novus, recens, insolitus* (= unaccustomed). Adv. *nuper, modo, recens*.

new-comer, *advena*.

new-fangled, *mirus, novus*.

newness, *novitas, insolentia*.

news, *res, nuntius*; what —? *quid novi?*

newspaper, *acta* (-*orum*) *diurna* or *publica*.

newt, *lacertus, lacerta* (= lizard).

next, adj. *proximus*; the — year, *proximus* or *insequens annus*; the — day, *posterus dies*; on the — day, *postero die, postridie*.

next, adv. *deinceps, deinde, postea*.

nibble, (*ad*)*rodĕre, gustare* (= to taste).

nice: = pleasant, *suavis, dulcis*; = fastidious, *delicatus*; = discerning, *diligens, subtilis*. Adv. *bene, probe; diligenter, subtiliter*.

nicety: = fastidiousness, *fastidium*; = precision, *subtilitas*.

niche, *aedicula* (for statues).

nick; in the — of time, *in ipso articulo* (*temporis*).

nickname, *nomen per ludibrium datum*.

niece, *fratris* or *sororis filia*.

niggardly; see miserly.

night, *nox*; by —, *nocte, noctu*; in the dead of —, *intempesta nocte*.

nightfall; at —, *sub noctem*.

nightingale, *luscinia*.

nightly, adj. *nocturnus*.

nightmare, *insomnium*.

Nile, *Nilus*.

nimble, *agilis*.

nine, *novem*; — times, *novie*(*n*)*s*; — each, *noveni*.

nineteen, *undeviginti*; — each, *undeviceni*.

nineteenth, *undevicesimus, nonus decimus*.

ninety, *nonaginta*; — each, *nonageni*.

ninth, *nonus*.

no, adj. *nullus*; often *nihil*, with partitive genit.; by — means, *minime, haudquaquam*.

no, adv.: in answers, *non, minime (vero)*; — but, *immo (vero)*; to answer yes or —, *aut etiam aut non respondēre*; to say —, *negare*; with comparatives *non, nihilo.*

nobility: of birth, *nobilitas, genus nobile*; of character, *ingenuus.*

noble, subst. *homo nobilis*; —s, plur., *nobiles, proceres.*

noble, adj.: by birth, *nobilis, generosus*; morally, *ingenuus, honeꞌtus, liberalis*; adv. *ingenue, honeste.*

nobody, *nemo*; and —, *nec quisquam.*

nocturnal, *nocturnus.*

nod, subst. *nutus (-ūs).*

nod, v. *nutare*; to — assent, *adnuēre*; = doze, *dormitare.*

noise, subst. *sonitus (-ūs); strepitus (-ūs;* loud); *crepitus (-ūs;* = clattering, creaking); *fragor (=* — of breaking); to make a —, *strepēre, (con)crepare.*

noise, v.: see publish.

noiseless, *tacitus*; adv. *tacite, (cum) silentio.*

noisily, noisy; *tumultuosus*; adv. *cum strepitu.*

nomadic, *vagus.*

nominally, *nomine, verbo.*

nominate, *nominare. dicĕre, creare.*

nomination, *nominatio.*

nominative, *casus (-ūs) nominativus.*

none, *nemo, nullus.*

nonentity, *nihil*; = obscure person, *terrae filius.*

nonsense, *ineptiae (-arum), nugae (-arum)*; as interj., *nonsense! gerrae!, fabulae!*; to talk —, *garrire.*

nonsensical, *absurdus, ineptus.*

nook, *angulus.*

noon, *meridies*; of —. adj. *meridianus.*

noose, *laqueus.*

nor, *nec* or *neque*; in commands, *neve* or *neu.*

normal; see regular.

north, subst. *septentrio (or pl. septentriones.*

northern, northerly, *septentrionalis, aquilonaris*; — wind, *aquilo.*

north pole, *polus glacialis, arctos.*

North Sea, *Oceanus Germanicus.*

northwards, *(ad) septentrionem versus.*

nose, *nasus, nares (-ium* = nostrils).

nostrils, *naris* (usually plur.).

not, *non, haud*; — at all, *minime, nullo modo, haudquaquam*; — enough, *parum, minus*; not even . . ., *ne . . . quidem*; and —, = nor, *nec* or *neque*; to say that . . . —, *negare.*

notable; see remarkable.

notary, *scriba.*

notch, v. *incidĕre.*

note, subst. *adnotatio*; in music, *sonus, vox*; = letter, *epistula.*

note, v. *adnotare*; see also write, notice.

note-book, *adversaria (-orum), commentarius.*

noted; see famous.

nothing, *nihil (nil), nulla res*; — of the kind, *nihil tale*; — new, *nihil novi*; good for —, *nequam*; — but, *nihil aliud nisi.*

notice, subst.: = act of noticing, *animadversio, notatio*; = announcement, warning, *promulgatio, denuntiatio*; as a visible object, *proscriptio, titulus.* .

notice, v. *animadvertĕre.*

noticeable; see remarkable.

notification, *promulgatio, denuntiatio.*

notify; see inform.

notion, *notio, suspicio.*

notoriety, *infamia.*

notorious, *notus, infamis.*

notwithstanding, as adv. *nihilominus, tamen*; as prep. see spite.

nought; see nothing.

noun, *nomen.*

nourish, *alĕre, nutrire.*

nourishment, *alimentum, cibus.*

novel, subst. *fabula.*

novel, adj. *novus.*

novelty: = newness, *novitas, insolentia*; = new thing, *res nova.*

November, *(mensis) Novembris* or *November.*

novice, *tiro.*

now: as adv. of time, *nunc, iam, hoc tempore, in praesentia*; now . . . now . . ., *modo . . . modo . . .*; = and then, *interdum, nonnunquam*; as a particle of transition, *autem, vero, quidem.*

nowadays, *nunc, hodie.*

nowhere, *nusquam.*

nude, *nudus.*

nudge, *fodicare.*

nuisance, render by adj. *molestus* or *gravis.*

null, *vanus, inritus, inanis.*

nullify, *ad inritum redigĕre.*

numb, adj. *torpens*; to be —, *torpēre*; to grow —, *torpescĕre.*

number, subst. *numerus*; a large —, *multitudo, copia.*

number, v. *(di)numerare.*

numbering: a — of the people, *census (-ūs).*

numberless, *innumerus, innumerabilis.*

numbness, *torpor.*

numerical, render by subst. *numerus.*

numerous, plur. *multi, plurimi, frequentes, crebri.*

nuptial, *nuptialis*; a — song, *epithalamium, hymenaeus.*

nuptials, subst. *nuptiae (-arum).*

nurse, subst. *nutrix* (= children's —).

nurse, v. *nutrire, fovēre*; to — the sick, *curare (hominem), adsidēre (homini).*

nursery, for plants, *seminarium.*

nursling, *alumnus.*

nurture, *educatio.*

nut, *nux.*

nutriment, nutrition; see food.

nutshell, *putamen.*

nymph, *nympha*; water- —, *Naias*; wood- —, *Dryas, Hamadryas*; sea- —, *Nereis.*

O

O! Oh! interj. *o! pro! heu!* — that (in wishes), *utinam, o si.*

oak, *quercus (-ūs), aesculus (=* winter- —*), ilex (=* holm- —*)*; adj., of —, *quernus*; the wood of the —, *robur*; an — -wood, *quercetum.*

oakum, *stuppa.*

oar, *remus.*

oath, *iusiurandum, sacramentum* (military).

oats, *avena.*

obdurate; see obstinate.

obedience, *oboedientia, obtemperatio.*

obedient, *obediens, dicto audiens, obtemperans*; adv. *oboedienter.*

obeisance; see bow.

obelisk, *obeliscus.*

obey, *parēre, oboedire, obtemperare, obsequi.*

object, subst. *res*; to be an — of hatred, *odio esse*; = purpose, aim, *consilium, propositum, finis*; my —, *quod volo* or *sequor.*

object, v.: = feel annoyance, *gravari, moleste ferre*; = make objections, *contra dicĕre, recusare, repugnare.*

objection, *quod contra dicitur, contradictio.*

objective, adj. *externus, verus* (= true).

oblation; see offering.

obligation, *officium* (= duty), *religio* (= sense of —); under —, adj., *obnoxius.*

oblige: = compel, *cogĕre*; = to put under obligation, *obligare, obstringĕre*; = do a favour to, *gratum facĕre, commodare.*

obliging, *comis, officiosus*; adv. *comiter, officiose.*

oblique, *obliquus.* Adv., *oblique, in obliquum*; fig., *per ambages.*

obliquity, *obliquitas*; moral —, *pravitas, iniquitas.*

obliterate, *delēre, abolēre.*

oblivion, *oblivio, oblivium.*

oblivious, *immemor, obliviosus.*

oblong, *oblongus.*

obloquy, *odium; opprobrium,* (= abuse).

obnoxious: = subject, liable, *obnoxius*; = objectionable, *noxius, invisus.*

obscene, *obscenus, turpis*; adv. *obscene, turpiter.*

obscenity, *obscenitas, turpitudo.*

obscure, *obscurus; reconditus* (= abstruse), *ambiguus* (= uncertain); *humilis* (= undistinguished). Adv. *obscure; ambigue, per ambages.*

obscure, v. *obscurare, tenebras offundĕre.*

obscurity, *obscuritas; tenebrae* (= *arum*; = dark).

obsequies; see funeral.

obsequious, *(nimis) obsequens.*

obsequiousness, *obsequentia.*

observance, *mos, ritus (-ūs)*; religious —, *cultus (-ūs) deorum.*

observant, *attentus*; — of, *diligens,* with genit.

observation, *observatio, animadversio, notatio*; = remark, *dictum.*

observe: = watch, notice, *observare, animadvertĕre, contemplari*; = keep up, maintain, *(ob)servare, conservare.*

observer, *spectator* (f. *spectatrix*); *speculator* (f. *speculatrix*).

obsolete, *obsoletus*; to become —, *obsolescĕre.*

obstacle, *impedimentum, obex* (= barrier).

obstinacy, *pertinacia, pervicacia, obstinatio.*

obstinate, *pertinax, pervicax, obstinatus*; adv. *pertinaciter, pervicaciter, obstinate.*

obstreperous, *tumultuosus.*

obstruct, *obstruĕre, obstare* (with dat.)

obstruction, *impedimentum, obstructio.*

obtain, v.: transit., *adipisci, consequi*; to — by asking, *impetrare, exorare* intransit., see prevail.

obtrude, *ingerĕre, inculcare.*

obtuse, *hebes, obtusus.*

obviate, *occurrĕre, obviam ire.*

obvious, *apertus, manifestus*; adv. *aperte, manifesto.*

occasion, subst.: = time, *tempus*; = suitable time, opportunity, *occasio.*

occasion, v. *auctorem esse* (with genit.) *creare, movēre.*

occasionally, *raro, interdum.*

occult, *occultus.*

occupation: = taking, *occupatio*; = business, *occupatio, negotium.*

occupy: = take, *capĕre, occupare*; = hold, *habēre, tenēre, obtinēre, possidēre*; = engage, keep busy, *occupare, tenēre, detinēre.*

occur: = come to mind, *in mentem (homini) venire, subire*; = be found in books, *reperiri, legi*; = happen, *fieri, accidĕre.*

occurrence, *casus (-ūs), res (gesta).*

ocean, *oceanus.*

October, *(mensis) October.*

octogenarian, *homo octoginta annos natus.*

odd: = not even, *impar*; see also strange, extraordinary.

ode, *carmen.*

odious, *invisus, invidiosus.*

odium, *invidia*; causing —, *invidiosus.*

odour, *odor.*

of, render by genitive; of, = composed of, *ex*, or use special adj. (e.g. of marble, *marmoreus*); of = concerning, *de.*

off, adv. render by compound verbs in *ab- (au-), de-, ex-*; far —, *longe* or *procul.*

off, prep., *contra* (= opposite).

offence: = displeasure, *offensio, offensa*; = fault, *peccatum, delictum.*

offend: = hurt, displease, *offendĕre, laedĕre*; to be —ed, *aegre ferre*; = commit an offence, *peccare.*

offensive: = giving offence, *odiosus, molestus, gravis*; opp. to defensive, render by *bellum inferre.*

offer, subst. *condicio*; or use verb.

offer, v.: transit., *offerre, praebēre, porrigĕre* (= hold out); to — violence, *vim adferre*; intransit., = present itself, *offerri, dari, incidĕre.*

office: = duty, function, *munus (-eris,* n.), *officium*; = official position, *magistratus (-ūs), honor, provincia*; a good —, = a kindness, *beneficium, officium.*

officer, official, praefectus.

official, adj. publicus; adv. publice.

officiate, munere (or officio) fungi.

officious, molestus; adv. moleste.

officiousness, nimium studium.

offspring, progenies, stirps, liberi (-orum; = children).

oft, often, saepe, saepenumero; how —? quotie(n)s?; so —, totie(n)s.

ogle, oculis limis intueri.

ogre, larva.

oil, subst. oleum; of —, adj., olearius.

oil, v. oleo ungere or perfundere.

ointment, unguentum.

old. (1), in gen., = not new, vetus, vetustus; an — soldier, veteranus. (2), = having lived long, grandis (natu); an — man, senex, vetulus; an — woman, anus, anicula, vetula; to grow —, senescere. (3), = no longer existing, antiquus, priscus, pristinus; in the — days, olim, quondam.

old age, senectūs (-ūtis).

older, grandior, maior (natu).

oldest, natu maximus.

old-fashioned, obsoletus, antiquus, priscus.

oligarchy, paucorum dominatio.

olive, (tree or fruit), oliva, olea; an — grove, olivetum.

omen, omen, auspicium.

ominous, render by phrase, such as omen infaustum.

omission, praetermissio.

omit, omittere, praetermittere, praeterire.

omnipotent, omnipotens.

on, adv. porro; or render by compound verb in pro-: to go —, pergere, procedere; — to, in with acc.

on, prep.: of place, in with abl.; sometimes a, ab (of sides, etc.), or abl. alone; of time when, abl. alone; = immediately after, e (ex) or abl. absol.; on, = about, concerning, de.

once: as numeral, semel; = at one time, aliquando, olim, quondam; at —, simul (= at the same time), statim, continuo (= immediately).

one, unus, unicus; — of two, alter; — at a time, — by —, singuli (-orum) or adv. singillatim; — or two, unus vel alter; it is all — to me, nihil mea interest; indef., = a person, homo, or render by verb in second pers. sing. (esp. subj.); — another, render by inter, with acc. of plur. pron.; — day, aliquando.

one-eyed, luscus, altero oculo captus.

onerous, gravis.

oneself, ipse.

one-sided, iniquus, impar.

onion, caepa or caepe.

only, adj. unus, unicus, solus.

only, adv. solum, tantum, modo (esp. after si and dum); not — . . . but also, non solum . . . sed etiam.

onset, onslaught, impetus (-ūs), incursio.

onward; see on, adv

ooze, subst. uligo.

ooze, v. manare, sudare.

open, adj. (ad)apertus; patens or hians (= wide —); to stand —, patēre; an — space, propatulum; in the —

air, sub divo, sub Iove. Transf., = candid, apertus, simplex, candidus; of questions, = undecided, integer. Adv. aperte, palam, manifesto.

open, v.: transit., aperire, patefacere; to — a book, librum (e)volvere; to — one's mouth, hiscere; intransit., aperiri, se aperire, patefieri, dehiscere (= to gape —).

opening, = aperture, foramen, fenestra; = opportunity, occasio, opportunitas, ansa; = beginning, initium, exordium.

operate, vim or effectum habēre; in war, rem agere or gerere; in surgery, secare.

operation, effectio; res (gesta or gerenda); a business —, negotium.

operative, adj. efficax.

opinion, opinio, iudicium, sententia.

opponent, adversarius; in a lawcourt, my —, iste.

opportune, opportunus; adv. opportune, commode.

opportuneness, opportunitas, commoditas.

opportunity, occasio, facultas, copia.

oppose: = to set against, opponere, obicere; = to resist, adversari, resistere, obsistere, obstare.

opposed, adversus, adversarius, contrarius.

opposite, adj. adversus, oppositus, contrarius; — to (or —), as prep., contra, e regione (with genit. or dat.).

opposition: = difference, repugnantia, discrepantia; = body of opponents, factio adversa.

oppress, premere, opprimere, vexare.

oppression, vexatio, iniuria.

oppressive, gravis, iniquus (= unjust); adv. graviter, inique.

oppressor, tyrannus; or render by verb.

opprobrious, probrosus, turpis.

opprobrium, dedecus, opprobrium.

optical, render by oculorum (= of eyes).

option, optio; see also choice.

opulence, opulentia; see wealth.

opulent, opulentus; see rich.

or, aut; — perhaps, — if you like, vel, -ve; — else, aut, vel; — rather, vel (potius); either . . . or, aut . . . aut, vel . . . vel; in conditions, whether . . . or . . ., sive (or seu); in alternative questions, an; — not, direct, an non, indirect, necne.

oracle, oraculum, sors, responsum (oraculi); to give an —, or oracular response, oraculum dare.

oral, render by verb dicere or loqui.

oration, oratio, contio; to deliver an —, orationem (or contionem) habēre.

orator, orator.

oratorical, oratorius.

oratory, doctrina dicendi, ars oratoria.

orb, globus, sphaera, orbis.

orbit, orbis, circulus, ambitus (-ūs).

orchard, pomarium.

orchid, orchis.

ordain; see decree, appoint.

ordeal; see danger, trial.

order: = methodical arrangement, ordo; to arrange in —, ordinare, disponere, digerere; in —, ordine;

out of —, extra ordinem; = class, group, ordo; = fraternity, conlegium; = a command, iussum; by — of the consul, consulis iussu; in — that, render by ut with subj. (neg. ne), or by ad with gerund or gerundive, etc.

order, v.: = arrange, ordinare, digerěre, disponěre; = command, iuběre, imperare; = demand, imperare (with acc.).

orderly, adj. compositus, dispositus; = well-behaved, modestus.

ordinal, adj.: an — number, numerus ordinalis.

ordinance, edictum.

ordinary, adj. = usual, usitatus, quotidianus, communis; = mediocre, mediocris, vulgaris. Adv. ferme, fere, plerumque.

ore, aes.

organ; see instrument, means; musical, organum.

organic; render by animal or corpus.

organization, descriptio, temperatio; political —, reipublicae forma.

organize, ordinare, constituěre, describěre, temperare.

orgies; see revelry.

Orient, Oriental; see east, eastern.

origin, origo, fons.

original, subst. = pattern, exemplum, exemplar.

original, adj.: = primary, primus, principalis; antiquus, pristinus; = one's own, proprius, (sui) ipsius, novus (= new). Adv., = at first, primum, primo, initio.

originate, v., intransit. (ex)oriri.

originator, auctor.

ornament, subst. ornamentum, decus (-oris, n.).

ornament, v. (ex)ornare, decorare.

ornate, (per)ornatus; adv. ornate.

orphan, orbus (subst. and adj.).

oscillate, agitari; mentally, dubitare.

oscillation, agitatio; mental, dubitatio.

osier; subst. vimen; adj. vimineus.

ostensible, simulatus, fictus; adv. specie, per speciem.

ostentation, iactatio, ostentatio.

ostentatious, gloriosus, iactans; adv. gloriose.

ostler, agaso.

ostracism, at Athens, testarum suffragia (-orum); or render by expellěre.

ostrich, struthiocamelus.

other: as adj. = different, alius, diversus; as pron., alius; the — (of two), alter; all the —s, ceteri, reliqui; belonging to —s, adj., alienus; on the — hand, contra, autem.

otherwise, aliter, alioqui(n).

ought, v.: I — to go, eundum est mihi, ire debeo, ire me oportet.

ounce, uncia: half- —, semuncia.

our, ours, noster; — people, nostri (-orum); of — country, nostras.

out, adv. foras (of going out), foris (of being out), extra.

out of, prep.: = away from, outside, e (ex), extra; — one's mind, sui or mentis non compos; = arising from,

because of, propter, per, or rendered by participle with abl., e.g. — fear, metu coactus.

outbid, licitatione vincěre.

outbreak, eruptio; = beginning, initium, principium; = disturbance, seditio.

outcast, exsul, extorris, profugus.

outcry, clamor, vociferatio, convicium.

outdo, superare, vincěre.

outer, exterior.

outflank, circumire, circumvenire.

outlandish, peregrinus, barbarus.

outlast, diutius durare (with quam or abl.).

outlaw, subst. proscriptus.

outlaw, v. proscriběre, (homini) aqua et igni interdicěre.

outlawry, proscriptio.

outlay, sumptus (-ūs), impensa.

outlet, exitus (-ūs); see also mouth.

outline, subst. (extrema) lineamenta (-orum); in a sketch, adumbratio.

outline, v. describěre, adumbrare.

outlive, (homini) superesse.

outlook: physical, render by spectare; = prospects, spes; = attitude, animus.

outlying, longinquus.

outnumber, numero (or multitudine) superare.

outpost, statio.

outrage, subst. iniuria, indignitas.

outrage, v. violare, iniuriā adficěre.

outrageous, immanis, indignus; adv. indigne.

outright: = at once, statim, ilico; = completely, plane, prorsus, omnino.

outrun, cursu superare.

outset, initium.

outside, superficies (= surface), species; on the —, extrinsecus.

outside, adj. exter (exterus), externus.

outside, adv. extra, extrinsecus, foris (of rest), foras (of motion).

outskirts; see suburb.

outspoken; see frank.

outspread, patulus, passus.

outstanding, reliquus; see also debt.

outstrip, (cursu) superare.

outvote, suffragiis vincěre.

outward, adj. exter (exterus), externus; — show, species; adv. extra, extrinsecus.

outweigh, praeponderare, vincěre superare.

outwit, circumvenire.

outworks, munimenta (exteriora).

oval, adj. ovatus.

ovation, ovatio; fig., to receive an —, magnis clamoribus excipi.

oven, furnus.

over, adv. super, insuper, supra; to be — (= remain), superesse, superare; — and done with, confectus, peractus; it is all — with us, actum est de nobis.

over, prep.: = across, super, trans; = above, super, supra; = more than, super, amplius (with numerals), plus quam.

overawe, (de)terrēre.

overbalance, praeponderare.

overbearing, adrogans, superbus.

overboard: to throw —, *iacturam facĕre*; with genit., to fall —, *in mare excidĕre*.

overcast, of sky, *nubilus*.

overcharge, v. *nimium exigĕre, nimio vendĕre*.

overcome, *(de)vincĕre, superare*.

overdone, *(nimis) elaboratus*.

overdraw; to — an account, *aes alienum contrahĕre* (= incur debt).

overdressed, *nimis splendide ornatus*.

overdue, *debitus;* see owing.

overeat, *nimis edĕre, helluari*.

overfill, *supra modum implĕre*.

overflow, subst.; see flood.

overflow, v. *redundare, effundi:* to — on to, *inundare*.

overgrown, = covered with foliage, etc., *obitus;* see also huge, enormous.

overhang, *imminĕre, impendĕre*.

overhasty, *praeproperus, praeceps;* adv. *praepropere*.

overhaul; see examine; also overtake.

overhead, adv. *supra, insuper:* from —, *desuper*.

overhear, *subauscultare, exaudire*.

overjoyed, *laetitiā exsultans*.

overland, adv. *terrā* (opp. *mari*).

overlap, *imminĕre, impendĕre*.

overlay, *inducĕre, inlinĕre;* with gold, *inaurare*.

overload, *nimis onerare*.

overlook: = watch, examine, *observare, inspicĕre, intuēri;* = pardon, *ignoscĕre, condonare;* = miss, fail to notice, *praeterire, omittĕre*.

overmuch, adv. *nimis, nimium*.

overpower, *superare, vincĕre, debellare*.

overpowering; see overwhelming.

overrate, *nimis magni facĕre*.

overreach, *circumvenire, circumscribĕre*.

overrule, *vincĕre;* of providence, *gubernare*.

overrun, *(per)vagari*.

overscrupulous, *diligentior, religiosior*.

oversee, *(pro)curare*.

overseer, *custos, (pro)curator*.

oversight: = failure to notice, error, *incuria;* = superintendence, *curatio, procuratio, cura*.

oversleep, *diutius dormire*.

overspread, *obducĕre, inducĕre*.

overstate; see exaggerate.

overt, *apertus, manifestus*.

overtake: = catch up with, *consequi;* = surprise, *opprimĕre, deprehendĕre*.

overtax, *iniquis oneribus premĕre*.

overthrow, subst. *clades, ruina, excidium*.

overthrow, v. *deicĕre, adfligĕre, evertĕre*.

overture: diplomatic, *condicio;* musical, *exordium*.

overturn, *evertĕre, subvertĕre*.

overweening, *superbus, insolens*.

overwhelm, *obruĕre, opprimĕre*.

overwork, subst. *labor nimius*.

overwrought, *nimis intentus*.

overzealous, *nimis studiosus*.

owe, v. *debēre*.

owing to, prep. *propter, ob, per;* it was — you that . . . not, *per te stetit quominus*.

owl, *ulula, noctua, strix*.

own: one's —, *proprius;* my —, *meus;* your —, *tuus, vester;* his —, *suus, ipsius* (genit.), *ipsorum*.

own, v.: = confess, *fatēri, confitēri;* = possess, *habēre, possidēre*.

owner, *possessor, dominus*.

ownership, *dominium*.

ox, *bos;* of oxen, adj. *bubulus;* a driver of oxen, *bubulcus*.

oxherd, *armentarius*.

oyster, *ostrea;* — shell, *ostreae testa*.

P

pace, subst.: = a step, *gradus (-ŭs), passus (-ŭs);* as a measure = *passus (-ŭs);* = speed, *velocitas, gradus (-ŭs);* at a quick —, *pleno* or *citato gradu*.

pace, v. *gradi, incedĕre, ambulare, spatiari;* = measure by pacing, *passibus metiri*.

pacific, *pacificus,* or *pacis* (genit.).

pacify, *placare, pacare, sedare*.

pack, subst.: = bundle, *sarcina;* = crowd, *turba, grex*.

pack, v. *stipare, co(artare);* of luggage, etc., *conligĕre, componĕre*.

packet, *fasciculus*.

pack-horse, *equus clitellarius*.

pack-saddle, *clitellae (-arum)*.

pact, *pactio, pactum*.

paddle; see oar, row.

Padua, *Patavium*.

page, of a book, *pagina*.

pageant, *spectaculum, pompa*.

pail, *hama, situla*.

pain, subst. *dolor;* violent — *cruciatus (-ŭs)*.

pain, v. transit. *dolore adficĕre, cruciare, angĕre*.

painful, *gravis, acerbus, molestus;* adv. *graviter, acerbe, dolenter*.

painless, *sine dolore, doloris expers*.

pains, = exertion, *opera, labor, studium;* to take —, *operam dare*.

painstaking, *operosus, laboriosus*.

paint, subst. *pigmentum, fucus*.

paint, v.: as an artist, *pingĕre;* = to colour, *inficĕre, fucare*.

paint-brush, *penicillus*.

painter, *pictor*.

painting, *pictura; ars pingendi*.

pair, subst. *par;* of horses or oxen, *iugum;* often *bini* (= two at a time).

pair, v.: transit., *(con)iungĕre;* in-transit., *(con)iungi, coire*.

palace, *(domus) regia*.

palatable, *iucundus, suavis, dulcis*.

palate, *palatum*.

palatial, *regius*.

palaver, *nugae (-arum)*.

pale, subst.: = stake *palus, sudis;* = fence, *saepes*.

pale, adj. *pallidus, luridus;* to be —, *pallēre*.

Palermo, *Panormus*.

palfrey, *equus* or *caballus*.

palimpsest, *palimpsestus*.

palisade, *vallum, vallus*.

pall, v. or render by *taedet*.

pallet, *lectulus, grabatus*.

palliate, *excusare, extenuare*.

pallid; see pale.
pallor, *pallor.*
palm, subst. *palma;* adorned with —, *palmatus.*
palm, v.: to — off, *imponĕre, supponĕre.*
palmer; see pilgrim.
palmy, *florens, optimus.*
palpable, *tractabilis quod tangi potest;* = obvious, *manifestus, apertus;* adv. *manifesto, aperte.*
palpitate, *palpitare, micare.*
paltry, *vilis, minutus, pusillus.*
pamper, *nimis indulgēre.*
pamphlet, *libellus.*
pan, *patina;* frying- —, *sartago.*
panacea, *panchrestum medicamentum.*
pander, subst. *leno.*
pander, v. *lenocinari;* see flatter, indulge.
panegyric, *laudatio, laudes.*
panegyrist, *laudator, praedicator.*
panel, *tympanum;* a panelled ceiling, *lacunar.*
pang, *dolor.*
panic, subst. *pavor, terror.*
panic, v. *pavēre.*
panic-stricken, *pavidus.*
pannier, *clitellae (-arum).*
panoply; see armour.
panorama; see prospect, view.
pant, v. *anhelare.*
pantheism, *deum in universa rerum natura situm esse credĕre.*
panther, *panthera.*
panting, subst. *anhelitus (-ūs).*
pantomime, *mimus.*
pantry, *cella penaria.*
paper, subst. *charta, papyrus;* a written (printed) —, *charta, scriptum, libellus;* public —s, *tabulae publicae;* a news —, *acta (diurna).*
papyrus, *papyrus* or *papyrum.*
par: on a — with, *aequus, par.*
parable, *parabola, similitudo.*
parade, subst.: = show, *ostentatio;* milit., *decursus (-ūs).*
parade, v.: = display, *ostentare;* milit., intransit., *decurrĕre.*
paradise, *sedes beatorum* or *piorum.*
paradox; render by *admirabilis* or *contra opinionem.*
paragon, *specimen.*
paragraph, *caput* (= section).
parallel, adj.: — to, *e regione,* with genit. or dat.; = similar, *par,* (con)*similis, congruens.*
paralyse, *debilitare, enervare, adfligĕre.*
paralysed, *pede, manu,* etc., *captus.* Transf., *debilis, torpens torpidus;* to be —, *torpēre.*
paralysis, *nervorum remissio.* Transf., *debilitas, torpedo.*
paramount, *summus.*
paramour; see lover.
parapet, *pluteus, lorica.*
paraphernalia, *apparatus (-ūs).*
paraphrase, subst., *interpretatio, paraphrasis.*
paraphrase, v. *interpretari.*
parasite, *parasitus; adsecula* (=hanger-on).
parasitic, *parasiticus.*
parasol, *umbella,* or *umbraculum.*

parcel, *fascis, fasciculus;* see part, portion.
parcel out, v. *partiri, dividĕre, distribuĕre.*
parch, *torrēre,* (ex)*urĕre.*
parched, *aridus, torridus.*
parchment, *membrana.*
pardon, subst. *venia.*
pardon, v., (*homini rem*) *ignoscĕre* or *condonare.*
pardonable, *excusabilis.*
pare, (*re*)*secare, subsecare.*
parent, *parens.*
parentage, *stirps, genus (-eris,* n.).
parental, *parentum* (genit.).
parenthesis, *interpositio, interclusio.*
Paris, *Lutetia.*
parity; see equality.
park, subst. *vivarium* (= preserve), *horti (-orum,* = pleasure-gardens).
parley, subst. *conloquium, sermo.*
parley, v. *conloqui, sermones conferre.*
parliament, *senatus (-ūs);* act of — *senatūs consultum;* house of — *curia;* member of —, *senator.*
parliamentary, *senatorius.*
parody, subst. *ridicula imitatio.*
parole, *fides* (data).
paroxysm, *febris accessio.* Transf., *vis, impetus (-ūs).*
parricide: as person, *parricida;* as act, *parricidium.*
parrot, *psittacus.*
parry, v. = check, ward off, *propulsare, defendĕre, arcēre.*
parsimonious, *parcus, sordidus, tenax;* adv. *parce, sordide.*
parsimony, *parsimonia, tenacitas.*
parsley, *apium.*
part, subst., *pars, membrum;* in two, three —s, *bifariam, trifariam* or *bipartito, tripartito;* for the most —, *maximam partem, fere, plerumque;* to do one's — *officio* or *munere fungi;* to take — in, *partem capĕre* or *participem esse; —,* = side, cause, *partes (-ium);* to take a person's —, *homini adesse, favēre; —* in a play, role, *partes (-ium), persona;* to play the chief —, *primas (partes) agĕre.*
part, v. transit., *separare, dividĕre, dissociare;* intransit., *digredi, discedĕre.*
partake, *participem esse;* of food, *gustare.*
partaker, *particeps, socius, adfinis.*
partial, = favouring, *studiosus, cupidus.*
partiality, *studium, cupiditas.*
partially, *per studium;* see also partly.
participate, (*rei,* genit.) *esse participem;* (*rei,* dat.) *interesse.*
participation, *societas.*
participator, *particeps, socius, adfinis.*
participle, *participium.*
particle, *particula, frustum* (esp. of food); gram., *particula.*
particoloured, *versicolor, varius.*
particular, adj.: = individual, *proprius, separatus;* = special, outstanding, *singularis, praecipuus;* = exacting, fussy, *elegans, delicatus.* Adv., *magnopere, praesertim, praecipue.*

particularize, *nominare* (= name), *enumerare* (= enumerate).

particulars, subst. *singula* (*-orum*).

parting, subst. *digressus* (*-ūs*), *discessus* (*-ūs*).

partisan, *fautor, homo studiosus.*

partisanship, *studium, favor.*

partition, *partitio*; = wall, barrier, *paries.*

partly, *partim, parte, (aliqua) ex parte.*

partner, *socius, consors*; in marriage *coniunx.*

partnership, *consortio, societas.*

partridge, *perdix.*

party, *partes* (*-ium*), *factio* (esp. polit.) *secta* (of philosophers, etc.); to belong to a —, *partes sequi*; —, = social gathering, *convivium.*

party-wall, *paries.*

parvenu, *novus homo.*

pass, v. (1) ⇒ go along, go past, *transgredi, transire, praeterire*; to — over, let —, *praeterire, transire, omittĕre*; to — off, *abire, decedĕre*; (2) of time: to — time, *agĕre, degĕre, (tra)ducĕre, consumĕre*; of time itself, to —, *transire, abire, praeterire.* (3) to — a law, get a law —ed, *legem perferre.* (4) to — down, — along, *tradĕre, porrigĕre, traicĕre.* (5) to — a test, be approved, *(ap)probari, satisfacĕre.*

passable, = tolerable, *tolerabilis, mediocris*; adv. *tolerabiliter, mediocriter.*

passage, *transitus* (*-ūs*), *transitio, transgressio*; = way, road, *iter, via*; in a book, *locus.*

passenger, *viator; vector* (on horseback, etc.).

passing; in —, *praeteriens* (partic.), *obiter.*

passion, = suffering, *perpessio, toleratio*; = emotion, *animi motus* (*-ūs*) *commotio*; = uncontrolled emotion, *libido, cupiditas*; = anger, *ira, iracundia*: to fly into a —, *exardescĕre*; = extreme fondness, *studium.*

passionate, adj. *cupidus, concitatus, vehemens, ardens*; = hot-tempered, *iracundus, cerebrosus.* Adv. *cupide, vehementer, effuse; iracunde.*

passionless, *cupiditatis expers.*

passive: to remain —, *quiescĕre*; gram. *passivus.* Adv. *aequo animo, patienter.*

passiveness, *patientia.*

password, *tessera.*

past, subst. *praeteritum tempus.*

past, adj. *praeteritus, ante actus*; = immediately preceding, *prior, superior, proximus.*

past, adv., render by compound verbs in *praeter-* or *trans-*

past, prep., *praeter, trans.*

pastime, *ludus oblectamentum.*

pastoral, *pastoralis, pastoricius; agrestis, rusticus*: — poetry, *bucolica* (*-orum*).

pastry, *crustum, crustulum.*

pasture, subst. *pascuum, ager pascuus.*

pasture, v.: transit., *pascĕre*; intransit., *pabulari, pasci.*

patch, subst. *pannus.*

patch, v. *(re)sarcire.*

patchwork, *cento.*

patent, = open, plain, *manifestus, apertus.*

paternal, *paternus, patrius.*

path, *via, iter, semita, trames.*

pathetic, *flebilis, maestus*; adv. *flebiliter, maeste.*

pathless, *invius.*

pathos, *maestitia, tristitia.*

patience, *patientia, tolerantia, perseverantia* (at work), *aequus animus* (= calmness).

patient, subst. *aeger, aegrotus.*

patient, adj. *patiens, tolerans*; adv. *patienter, toleranter, aequo animo.*

patrician, *patricius.*

patrimony, *patrimonium.*

patriot, *civis bonus.*

patriotic, *patriae* (or *reipublicae*) *amans*; adv. *pro patria.*

patriotism, *patriae amor.*

patrol, v. *circumire, lustrare.*

patron, *patronus, praeses.*

patronage, *patrocinium* (from the patron's side), *clientela* (from the client's); in gen., *praesidium.*

patroness, *patrona.*

patronize, *favēre* (with dat.).

patter, subst. *crepitus* (*-ūs*).

patter, v. *crepare, crepitare.*

pattern, *exemplum, exemplar, specimen, documentum.*

paucity, *paucitas*, or render by adj.

paunch, *abdomen, venter.*

pause, subst. *mora, intervallum, intermissio.*

pause, v. *intermittĕre, subsistĕre, morari.*

pave, *(viam) sternĕre* or *munire.*

pavement, *pavimentum, via strata.*

paving, *stratura.*

paving-stone, *saxum quadratum.*

paw, subst. *pes* (= foot), *ungula* (= claw).

paw, v. *(solum) pedibus ferire.*

pawn, subst. *pignus* (*-oris*, n.); at chess, *latrunculus, latro.*

pawn, v. *(op)pignerare, pignori dare.*

pay, subst. *stipendium, merces.*

pay, v.: transit., *(per)solvĕre, pendĕre, numerare*; to — a penalty *poenam dare* or *luĕre*; intransit., = be profitable, *prodesse, lucro esse.*

paymaster, *dispensator*; milit., *tribunus aerarius.*

payment, *solutio, repraesentatio* (in cash).

pea, *pisum, cicer.*

peace, subst. *pax, otium, concordia.*

peaceful, *pacatus, placidus, quietus, tranquillus*; adv. *placide, quiete, tranquille.*

peace-offering, *piaculum, placamen.*

peach, *(malum) persicum.*

peacock, *pavo.*

peak, *cacumen, apex*; or rendered by adj. *summus.*

peal, subst.: — of laughter, *cachinnus*; — of thunder, *tonitrus* (*-ūs*).

peal, v. *sonare.*

pear, *pirum;* — tree, *pirus.*
pearl, *margarita.*
peasant, *rusticus, agrestis.*
pebble, *calculus, lapillus.*
peccadillo, (*leve*) *delictum.*
peck, as measure, *modius.*
peck, v. *vellicare.*
peculation, *peculatus* (*-ūs*).
peculiar: = of one only, *proprius, peculiaris;* = remarkable, *singularis, praecipuus, mirus.* Adv., = especially, *praecipue, praesertim.*
peculiarity, *proprietas.*
pecuniary, *pecuniarius.*
pedagogue, *paedagogus;* = schoolmaster, *magister.*
pedant, pedantic; render by (*nimis*) *diligens.*
pedestal, *basis.*
pedestrian, subst. *pedes.*
pedestrian, adj. *pedester.*
pedigree, *stemma* (*-atis* n.)
pedlar, *institor.*
peel, subst. *cutis, corium.*
peel, v.: transit., *cutem detrahĕre;* intransit., *cutem* (*de*)*ponĕre.*
peep, subst. *aspectus* (*-ūs*), *conspectus* (*-ūs*).
peep, v. (*strictim*) *prospicĕre inspicĕre.*
peer, subst.: = equal, *par;* = noble, *unus e patriciis* or *nobilibus.*
peer, v.: to — into, *rimari, scrutari.*
peerless, *unicus, singularis.*
peevish, *stomachosus, morosus, difficilis;* adv. *stomachose, morose.*
peevishness, *stomachus, morositas.*
peg, *clavus* (= nail).
pell-mell, *effuse, confuse, passim.*
pellucid; see transparent.
pelt, v.: transit., see throw; of rain, *ferri, descendere;* —ing rain, *maximus imber.*
pen, subst.: for writing, *calamus, stilus;* = fold, *saeptum.*
pen, v.: = write, *scribĕre, litteris mandare;* = fold, *saeptis includĕre.*
penalty, *poena, multa, supplicium.*
penance, *piaculum, poena, satisfactio.*
pence; see penny.
pencil: for drawing *penicillus;* for writing, *stilus.*
pending; adj., the matter is still —, *adhuc sub iudice iis est.*
pending, prep.: = during, *per;* = until, *dum* with subj.
pendulous, *pendulus.*
penetrable, *penetrabilis.*
penetrate, *penetrare, pervadĕre;* by stealth, (*se*) *insinuare;* into a mind, *descendĕre.*
penetrating, adj., of cold, etc., *acutus, acer;* mentally, *sagax, perspicax, subtilis.*
penetration, *acies, acumen.*
peninsula, *paeninsula.*
penitence, *paenitentia.*
penny, *as, nummus* (*sestertius*).
pension, *annua* (*-orum*).
pensive, *in cogitatione defixus.*
penthouse, milit., *vinea.*
penurious, *parcus, sordidus, avarus;* adv. *sordide.*
penury, *inopia, egestas.*

people, subst. (1), = persons, *homines, mortales;* our —, *nostri;* young —, *pueri, adulescentes.* (2), = a community, *populus;* adj., of the —, *publicus;* (3), = race, tribe, *gens, natio.* (4) common —, *plebs, vulgus, multitudo.*
people, v. *frequentare, complēre.*
pepper, *piper.*
perambulate, *perambulare, peragrare, pervagari.*
perceive, *sentire, percipĕre; vidēre* (= see), *audire* (= hear), *intellegĕre* (= understand).
percentage, *pars, portio.*
perceptible, *manifestus; quod percipĕre possis.*
perception; render by verb; = discernment, *iudicium, sagacitas.*
perch, subst., as fish, *perca.*
perch, v. *insidēre.*
percolate, *permanare.*
percussion, *ictus* (*-ūs*; = blow).
perdition, *exitium, pernicies.*
peremptory, *adrogans.* Adv. *adroganter;* in refusals, *praecise.*
perennial, *perennis, iugis.*
perfect, adj. *plenus, absolutus, perfectus, integer* (= sound intact), *merus* (= sheer). Adv. *plene, absolute, perfecte; plane* (= wholly).
perfect, v. *perficĕre, absolvĕre.*
perfection, *absolutio, perfectio.*
perfidious, *perfidus, perfidiosus;* adv. *perfidiose.*
perfidy, *perfidia.*
perforate, *perforare,* (*per*)*terebrare.*
perforce, *vi, per vim, necessario;* or adj. *invitus* (= unwilling).
perform, (*per*)*fungi, exsequi, perficĕre, conficĕre, peragĕre;* on the stage, *partes agĕre.*
performance, (*per*)*functio, confectio;* on the stage, *fabula.*
performer, *actor, auctor, confector;* on the stage, *actor, histrio* (= actor), *acroama* (*-atis*, n.; musical).
perfume, subst. *odor, unguentum.*
perfume, v. *odorare, odore adficĕre.*
perfunctory, *neglegens.*
perhaps, *fortasse, forsitan;* unless —, *nisi forte,* lest —, *ne forte.*
peril; see danger, risk.
period: of time, *tempus, spatium temporis;* = end, *finis, terminus;* rhet. or gram., *periodus,* (*verborum* or *orationis*) *circuitus* (*-ūs*).
periodical, adj. *sollemnis;* adv. *certis* (or *statis*) *temporibus.*
perish, *perire, interire, occidĕre.*
perishable, *fragilis, caducus, fluxus.*
perjure, *periurare* (or *peierare*); *periurium facĕre.*
perjured, *periurus.*
perjury, *periurium.*
permanence, *perennitas, stabilitas.*
permanent, *perennis, stabilis;* adv. *perpetuo.*
permissible, *licitus;* it is —, *licet.*
permission, *facultas, potestas, copia, venia;* with your —, *pace tua.*
permit, v. (*hominem*) *sinĕre;* (*homini*) *permittĕre, concedĕre, copiam facĕre.*

permutation, *(per)mutatio.*

pernicious, *perniciosus, exitiosus;* adv. *perniciose, exitiose, funeste.*

peroration, *peroratio, conclusio.*

perpendicular, *directus;* adv. *ad lineam, rectâ lineâ.*

perpetrate, *committĕre, in se admittĕre.*

perpetrator, *auctor; qui facinus in se admisit.*

perpetual, *sempiternus, perennis, adsiduus;* adv. *adsidue, perpetuo.*

perpetuity, *perpetuitas.*

perplex, *distrahĕre, sollicitare.*

perplexed, *dubius, inops consilii.*

perplexing, *difficilis, perplexus impeditus.*

perplexity, *dubitatio.*

persecute, *insectari, vexare.*

persecution, *insectatio, vexatio.*

persecutor, *vexator, insectator.*

perseverance, *perseverantia, constantia, pertinacia.*

persevere, *perseverare, perstare, persistĕre.*

persevering, *perseverans, constans, pertinax;* adv. *perseveranter, constanter.*

persist; see persevere.

person: = human being, *homo, caput;* in person, *ipse, praesens, coram;* = body, form, *corpus, species, forma;* gram. *persona.*

personal, *privatus, proprius;* to make a — appearance, *ipse adesse.*

personality, *persona, hominis natura, ingenium* (= disposition).

personate, *(hominis) partes agĕre.*

personification, *prosopopoeia, personarum fictio.*

personify, *humana specie induĕre.*

perspicacious, *perspicax, sagax, acutus;* adv. *perspicaciter.*

perspicacity, *perspicacitas, acies ingenii.*

perspicuity, *perspicuitas.*

perspicuous, *(di)lucidus, perspicuus, apertus;* adv. *(di)lucide, perspicue, aperte.*

perspiration, *sudor.*

perspire, *sudare.*

persuade, *persuadĕre adducĕre;* to try to —, *suadĕre.*

persuasion, *persuasio.*

persuasive; render by verb.

pert, *protervus, procax;* adv. *proterve.*

pertain, *pertinēre, attinēre.*

pertinacious, *pertinax, obstinatus;* adv. *pertinaciter, obstinate.*

pertinacity, *pertinacia, obstinatio.*

pertness, *protervitas, procacitas.*

perturbation, *perturbatio.*

Perugia, *Perusia.*

perusal, *lectio, perlectio.*

peruse, *(per)legĕre, evolvĕre.*

pervade, *permanare.*

perverse, *perversus, pravus;* adv. *perverse, perperam, prave.*

perversion, *corruptio, depravatio.*

perversity, *perversitas, pravitas.*

pervert, v. *depravare, corrumpĕre, detorquēre.*

pest, *pestis, pernicies, lues.*

pester, *sollicitare, vexare.*

pestilence, *pestilentia, pestis lues, morbus.*

pestilential, *pestilens, foedus.*

pestle, *pilum, pistillum.*

pet, subst. *deliciae (-arum), amores (-um).*

pet, v. *fovēre, in deliciis habēre.*

Peter, *Petrus* (late Latin).

petition; see prayer, request; a formal —, *libellus;* to grant a —, *petenti satisfacĕre.*

petition, v. *petĕre, rogare, implorare.*

petrify, *in lapidem (con)vertĕre.* Transf., *obstupefacĕre:* to be petrified, *obstupescĕre, stupēre.*

pettifogger, *leguleius, rabula.*

petty, *minutus, tenuis.*

petulance, *petulantia, protervitas.*

petulant, *petulans, protervus.*

phantom, *simulacrum, imago.*

phase, *status (-ūs), ratio;* different —s, *vices* (plur.).

pheasant, *(avis) Phasiana, Phasianus.*

phenomenon; = remarkable event, *prodigium, portentum, miraculum.*

phial; see bottle.

philanthropic, *hominibus amicus, humanus.*

philanthropy, *benevolentia, humanitas.*

Philip, *Philippus.*

philological, *grammaticus.*

philologist, *grammaticus, philologus.*

philology, *grammatica (-ae* or *-orum), philologia.*

philosopher, *philosophus, sapiens.*

philosophical, *philosophus;* = wise, *sapiens.* Adv. *philosophorum more, sapienter;* = calmly, *aequo animo.*

philosophize, *philosophari; ratiocinari, disputare.*

philosophy, *philosophia.*

philtre, *philtrum.*

phlegm, *pituita;* = coolness, *patientia, lentitudo.*

phlegmatic, *tardus, patiens, lentus;* adv. *patienter, lente, aequo animo.*

phrase, *locutio; verbum.*

phrase, v.; see express, say.

phraseology, *locutio, dicendi genus (-eris,* n.).

physic, subst.; see medicine.

physical: = natural, render by genit. *naturae* or *corporis;* = of physics, *physicus.* Adv. *naturâ;* = in the manner of physics, *physice.*

physician; see doctor.

physics, *physica (-orum).*

physiognomy, *oris habitus (-ūs)* or *lineamenta (-orum).*

physiology, *physiologia.*

Piacenza, *Placentia.*

pick: = pluck, gather, *legĕre, carpĕre, conligĕre;* to — up, *tollĕre;* to — out, *eligĕre.*

pick-axe, *dolabra.*

picked, *delectus, electus.*

picket, *statio, custodia.*

pickle, subst. *salsura, muria.*

pickle, v. *muriâ condire.*

picture, subst. *tabula (picta), pictura.*

picture, v., = imagine, *cogitatione fingĕre, depingĕre, ante oculos proponĕre.*

picturesque, *amoenus, venustus.*

pie, *crustum.*

piebald, *bicolor.*

piece, *pars, fragmentum* (broken off), *frustum* (esp. of food), *mica* (= crumb); — of cloth, *pannus*; a piece of money, *nummus*; to break into —s, *confringĕre, comminuĕre*; to tear to —s, *discerpĕre, dilacerare, dilaniare*; to fall to —s, *dilabi,* (dis)solvi.

piecemeal, *membratim, minutatim.*

piece together, v. *consuĕre, fabricari.*

pied, *maculosus, versicolor.*

pier, *pila, moles, agger.*

pierce, *pungĕre;* to — through, *perforare, perfodere, transfigĕre.*

piercing, adj. *acer, acutus.*

piety, *pietas* (erga deos), *religio* (= religious feeling), *sanctitas* (= holiness).

pig, *porcus, sus.*

pigeon, *columba, columbus, palumbes* (= wood- —).

piggish, *suillus, porcinus.*

pigment; see paint.

pigmy; see Pygmy.

pigsty, *hara.*

pike: the weapon, *hasta, sarissa;* the fish, *lupus.*

pile, subst., *strues, cumulus, acervus;* a — driven into the ground, *sublica, sudis;* a bridge built on —s, *pons sublicius.*

pile, v. *(co)acervare, cumulare, congerĕre, exstruĕre.*

pilfer, *surripĕre, furari.*

pilgrim, *viator, peregrinator.*

pilgrimage, *iter, peregrinatio* (sacra).

pill, *pilula.*

pillage, subst. *rapina, direptio, compilatio, expilatio.*

pillage, v. *diripĕre, compilare, expilare, praedari.*

pillager, *praedator, direptor, expilator.*

pillar, *columna, pila;* fig., = support, stay, *columen.*

pillow, *pulvinus, cervical.*

pilot, subst. *gubernator.*

pilot, v. *gubernare.*

pimple, *pustula.*

pin, subst. *acus* (-ūs; = needle).

pin, v. *(ad)figĕre.*

pincers, *forceps.*

pinch, subst. *aculeus* (= sting), *morsus* (-ūs; = bite).

pinch; v.: = nip, *urĕre;* = stint, confine, *coartare, urgēre.*

pinching, of poverty, *angustus.*

pine, subst. *pinus;* of —, adj. *pineus.*

pine, v. *tabescĕre, confici;* to — for, *desiderare.*

pining, subst. *tabes.*

pinion, subst. of a bird, *penna.*

pinion, v. *(re)vincire.*

pink, *puniceus.*

pinnace, (navis) actuaria lembus.

pinnacle, *fastigium.*

pint, perhaps *sextarius;* half a —, *hemina.*

pioneer, *praecursor, explorator;* or render by *primus.*

pious, *pius, religiosus* (= scrupulous), *sanctus* (= saintly). Adv. *pie, religiose, sancte.*

pip, in fruit, *acinus, granum.*

pipe, subst.: = tube, *tubus, canalis, fistula;* = musical instrument, *fistula, tibia, calamus* (= reed- —).

pipe, v. *fistulā* (or *tibiā*) *canĕre.*

piper, *fistulator, tibicen.*

pipkin, *olla.*

piquancy, *sal, vis.*

piquant, *acer;* = stimulating, humorous, *salsus, facetus.*

pique, subst. *offensio, ira.*

pique, v. *vexare, sollicitare.*

piracy, *latrocinium* (maritimum).

pirate, *praedo* (maritimus).

piratical, *piraticus, praedatorius.*

pit, subst. *fovea, puteus, fossa* (= ditch); in the theatre, *cavea* (media or summa).

pit against, v. *opponĕre.*

pitch, subst.: the substance, *pix;* of —, adj. *piceus;* = degree, *fastigium, gradus* (-ūs); to such a — of madness, *eo amentiae;* in music, *sonus, vox;* = slope, *fastigium.*

pitch, v.: of tents, etc., *ponĕre, constituĕre;* = throw, *iacĕre, conicĕre.*

pitcher, *urceus.*

pitchfork, *furca.*

piteous, pitiable, *miser, miserabilis;* adv. *misere, miserabiliter.*

pitfall, *fovea.*

pith, *medulla.*

pithy, *medullosus.* Transf., *sententiosus, nervosus.*

pitiful: = full of pity, *clemens, misericors;* = mean, *abiectus, humilis, vilis;* see also piteous. Adv. *clementer; abiecte, humiliter.*

pitifulness, *clementia, misericordia;* = meanness, *humilitas.*

pitiless, *immisericors, inexorabilis, inhumanus, crudelis;* adv. *immisericorditer, inhumane, crudeliter.*

pitilessness, *crudelitas, inhumanitas, saevitia.*

pittance, *mercedula, stips, pecunia exigua.*

pity, subst. *misericordia, miseratio.*

pity, v. *misereri, miserari,* or impers. *miseret.*

pivot, *cardo* (= hinge).

placability, *placabilitas.*

placable, *exorabilis, placabilis.*

placard, *libellus, titulus.*

place, subst. (1), = position, spot, *locus, regio;* at, to, from this —, *hic, huc, hinc;* at, to, from that —, *ibi, eo, inde.* (2), = proper position *locus, sedes, statio;* in — of, (in) loco with genit., or *pro* with abl. (3), = situation, office, *munus* (-eris, n.), *officium.* (4) in the first —, *primo, primum;* in the next —, *deinceps.*

place, v. *ponĕre, (con)locare;* to — oneself, *consistĕre;* to — here and there, *disponĕre.*

placid, *placidus, quietus, tranquillus.*

plagiarism, *furtum.*

plagiarize, *furari.*

plague, subst. *pestis, pestilentia.* Transf., *pernicies, lues, malum.*

plague, v. *vexare, sollicitare, exagitare*

plain, subst. *campus, planities;* of the —, adj. *campestris.*

plain, adj.: = clear, *clarus, perspicuus, manifestus;* = candid, *simplex, apertus, liber;* = unadorned, *simplex, inornatus;* = not beautiful, *invenustus.* Adv.: = clearly, *clare, perspicue, manifesto;* = candidly, simply, *simpliciter, aperte, libere.*

plainness: = clearness, *perspicuitas;* = candour, simplicity, *simplicitas.*

plaint; see complaint.

plaintiff, *petitor.*

plaintive, *miserabilis, flebilis, queribundus;* adv. *miserabiliter, flebiliter.*

plait, subst.: = fold, *sinus (-ūs), ruga;* = braid of hair, *gradus (-ūs).*

plait, v. *plicare, intexēre.*

plan, subst.: as drawn, *descriptio;* = layout, scheme, *forma, figura, conformatio;* a — of action, *consilium, propositum, institutum.*

plan, v.: = design, mark out, *designare, describēre;* = form a — of action, *intendēre, consilium capēre* or *inire.*

plane, subst.: = flat surface, *planum, libramentum;* the tool, *runcina;* the tree, *platanus.*

planet, *stella errans* or *vaga.*

plank, *tabula, axis;* to cover with —s, *contabulare.*

plant, subst. *herba, planta.*

plant, v. *serēre, conserēre, obserēre;* in gen., = put in position, *ponēre, statuēre, constituēre.*

plantation, *plantarium* or *seminarium* (= nursery garden), *arbustum, locus arboribus consitus.*

planter, *sator, qui serit.*

planting, subst., as act, *satio, satus (-ūs).*

plash, subst. *murmur, sonus.*

plash, v. *murmurare.*

plaster, subst. *gypsum tectorium;* in medicine, *emplastrum.*

plaster, v. *gypsare, gypso inlinēre.*

plasterer, *tector.*

plate, subst.: = thin layer of metal, *lam(i)na, bractea;* = wrought metal, at table, *vasa argentea* or *aurea;* = platter, *catillus, patella.*

plate, v.: to — with silver, *argento inducēre.*

platform, *suggestus (-ūs), tribunal.*

Platonic, *Platonicus;* the — philosophy, *Academia.*

platter, *catillus, patella.*

plaudit, *plausus (-ūs).*

plausibility, *verisimilitudo; simulatio, species.*

plausible: = probable, *veri similis, probabilis;* in bad sense, *speciosus.* Adv. *probabiliter;* in bad sense, *in speciem, simulate.*

play, subst.: = amusement, *ludus, lusus (-ūs), lusio;* at the theatre, *fabula, ludus scaenicus;* = scope, free action, *campus, area;* = movement, *motus (-ūs), gestus (-ūs);* fair —, *aequum (et) bonum.*

play, v.: on an instrument, *modulari;* on a stringed instrument, *psallēre;* = amuse oneself, *ludēre;* to — a part, *partes agēre, personam gerēre;*

to — the fool, *ineptire, desipēre;* to — into the hands of an opponent, *praevaricari.*

player: on strings, *fidicen* (f. *fidicina*), *psaltes, citharista;* on a wind instrument, *tibicen* (f. *tibicina*); see also gambler and actor.

playfellow, playmate, *conlusor.*

playful, *lascivus, iocosus;* adv. *iocose.*

playfulness, *lascivia.*

plaything, *ludibrium.*

playwriter, playwright, *fabularum scriptor.*

plea: at law, *petitio, exceptio, defensio;* in gen., = excuse, *excusatio.*

plead: at law, *causam agēre, dicēre, orare;* to — as an excuse, *causari, obtendēre;* = to beg, entreat, *orare, obsecrare, implorare.*

pleader, *orator, causidicus.*

pleasant, pleasing, *gratus, iucundus, suavis, dulcis;* of places, *amoenus;* of manner, *comis, urbanus.* Adv. pleasantly, *iucunde, suaviter;* = affably, *comiter, urbane.*

pleasantness, *iucunditas, dulcedo, suavitas;* of places, *amoenitas;* of manner, *comitas, urbanitas.*

pleasantry, *facetiae (-arum), iocus.*

please, v.: = to give pleasure to, *placēre, delectare,* or impers. *libet;* = to see fit, be disposed, *velle;* if you please, *si placet;* colloq., please! *sis, amabo.*

pleasing; see pleasant.

pleasure: = enjoyment, delight, *voluptas, delectatio, oblectamentum;* fond of —, *voluptarius;* = liking, inclination, *arbitrium, libido.*

plebeian, adj. *plebeius* (opp. *patricius*).

pledge, subst. *pignus (-eris* or *-oris), cautio, arrabo.*

pledge, v. *(op)pignerare, obligare;* to — one's word, *fidem interponēre, promittēre, recipēre.*

plenary; see full, complete.

plenipotentiary, *legatus.*

plenteous, plentiful, *uber, abundans, copiosus;* adv. *abunde, abundanter, copiose.*

plenty, *ubertas, copia, abundantia;* sometimes *satis* with genit.

pliable, pliant, *lentus, flexibilis, mollis.*

pliancy, pliability, *mollitia.*

plight; see condition, and pledge.

plod, *repēre, tarde progredi.*

plot, subst.: of ground, *agellus, area;* = scheme, conspiracy, *coniuratio;* of a play, etc., *argumentum (fabulae).*

plot, v.: intransit., *coniurare;* transit. *machinari.*

plotter; see conspirator.

plough, subst. *aratrum;* — -man, — -boy, *arator, bubulcus;* — -share, *vomer;* — -handle, *stiva.*

plough, v. *arare;* to — up, *exarare;* to — round, *circumarare.*

ploughing, subst. *aratio.*

pluck, subst. *animus, virtūs (-ūtis).*

pluck, v. *(e)vellēre;* to — flowers, *flores carpēre, decerpēre;* to — up courage, *animum recipēre.*

plum, *prunum.*

plumage, *plumae, pennae (pinnae).*
plumb-line, plummet, *linea, perpendiculum.*
plume, subst. *pluma, penna (pinna).*
plump, *pinguis.*
plum-tree, *prunus.*
plunder, subst. *praeda, rapina.*
plunder, v. *praedari, diripĕre, expilare, (de)spoliare.*
plunderer, *direptor, praedator.*
plunge, v.: transit., *(sub)mergĕre, immergĕre;* intransit., *se mergĕre,* etc.
plural, *pluralis;* in the —, *pluraliter.*
ply, v. *exercēre.*
Po, the river, *Padus.*
poacher, *fur.*
pocket, subst. *sinus (-ūs);* = fold in the toga; *sacculus* (= a small bag), *crumena* (= purse).
pocket, v. *intercipĕre, avertĕre.*
pocket-book, *pugillares (-ium).*
pod, *siliqua.*
poem, *carmen, poema (-atis, n.).*
poet, *poeta, carminum auctor, vates* (= bard).
poetess, *poetria.*
poetical, *poeticus;* adv. *poetice, poetarum more.*
poetry, *poetice or poetica, poesis.*
poignant, *acer.*
point, subst.: = sharp end, *acumen, cuspis, spiculum, mucro;* geograph., *promontorium;* = spot, *locus;* on the — of doing, render by *in eo est ut,* or fut. partic.; the — at issue, *res, caput;* to the —, *ad rem.*
point, v.: = make sharp, *(prae)acuĕre;* to — out, indicate, *(digito) monstrare, indicare.*
point-blank, *directus:* to refuse —, *praecise negare.*
pointed, adj. *(prae)acutus;* = significant, *salsus, aculeatus;* adv. *salse.*
pointless, *insulsus, frigidus, ineptus.*
poise, v. *librare.*
poison, subst. *venenum, virus, toxicum.*
poison, v.: = render poisonous, *venenare, veneno imbuĕre;* = attack with —, *veneno necare, venenum dare.*
poisoner, *veneficus (f. venefica).*
poisoning, subst. *veneficium.*
poisonous, *venenatus, veneno imbutus.*
poke, v. *(hominem) fodĕre;* to — the fire, *ignem excitare;* to — about, *rimari, perscrutari.*
polar, *septentrionalis* (= northern).
pole, *contus, pertica, longurius;* of the earth, *axis, cardo, polus;* south —, *axis meridianus;* north —, *axis septentrionalis.*
polecat, *feles.*
polemics, *disputationes (-um), controversiae (-arum).*
police; render by *aediles (-ium);* —men, *vigiles (-um).*
policy, *ratio rei publicae gerendae, consilia (-orum);* = prudence, *prudentia, consilium.*
polish, subst., = polished state, *nitor.*
polish, v. *(per)polire, expolire.*
polished, *nitidus, mundus, (per)politus.*
polite, *urbanus, comis, humanus;* adv. *urbane, comiter, humane, humaniter*

politeness, *urbanitas, comitas, humanitas.*
politic, *prudens, circumspectus, providus.*
political, *publicus, civilis;* a — discussion, *sermo de republica habitus;* — science, *ratio civilis, reipublicae gerendae ratio.*
politician, *vir rerum civilium* (or *reipublicae) peritus.*
politics, *civilis ratio, respublica;* to take up —, *ad rempublicam accedĕre.*
polity, *reipublicae forma.*
poll, subst. = voting, *suffragium, comitia (-orum).*
pollard, *amputatus.*
polling-booth, *saeptum, ovile.*
poll-tax, *exactio capitum.*
pollute, *polluere, inquinare, contaminare.*
pollution, = filth, *conluvio, impuritas.*
polygamy, *plures uxores habēre.*
polytheism, *multorum deorum cultus (-ūs).*
pomade, *capillare, unguentum.*
pomegranate, *malum granatum* or *Punicum.*
pomp, *apparatus (-ūs).*
pompous, *magnificus, gloriosus;* of style, *tumidus.* Adv. *magnifice, gloriose.*
pomposity, *magnificentia.*
pond, *stagnum, piscina, lacus (-ūs).*
ponder, *considerare, ponderare, secum reputare.*
ponderous, *ponderosus, gravis.*
pontiff, *pontifex.*
pony, *mannus, mannulus.*
pool; see pond.
poop, *puppis.*
poor: = not rich, *pauper; inops, egens, mendicus* (= destitute); = inferior, *mediocris, tenuis;* of language, or of soil, *exilis, ieiunus;* = pitiable, *miser, infelix;* = little, *misellus.* Adv. *tenuiter, mediocriter, misere.*
pop, v. *crepare;* to — out, *evadĕre, exsilire.*
poplar, *populus;* of the —, adj. *populeus.*
poppy, n. *papaver (-eris, n.).*
populace, *multitudo, plebs.*
popular: = belonging to the people, *popularis;* the — party, *populares (-ium);* = liked, *gratiosus, (in vulgus) gratus or acceptus.*
popularity, *gratia, populi favor.*
populate; see people, v.
population, *civium or incolarum numerus, cives (-ium), incolae (-arum).*
populous, *frequens, celeber.*
porch, *vestibulum.*
pore, subst. *foramen.*
pore, v. *(totum) se abdĕre (re or in re).*
pork, *porcina.*
porker, *porcus.*
porous, *rarus.*
porridge, *puls.*
port, = harbour, *portus (ūs).*
portcullis, *cataracta.*
portend, *portendĕre, denuntiare.*
portent, *portentum, prodigium, monstrum, omen.*
portentous, *portentosus, monstr(u)osus;* adv. *monstr(u)ose.*

porter: at a gate, *ianitor*; for luggage, *baiulus*.
portfolio, *scrinium*.
portico, *porticus (-ūs)*.
portion, *pars, portio*; a marriage —, *dos*.
portmanteau, *vidulus, mantica*.
portrait, *imago (picta)*.
portray, *depingĕre*.
position: = place, *locus, situs (-ūs)*, *sedes*; = state, *locus, status (-ūs)*, *condicio*.
positive; = certain, *certus*; a — statement, *adfirmatio*; adv. *adfirmate* (of assertion), *certe, certo* (of knowing).
possess: = to have, *possidēre, habēre, tenēre*; or render by *esse*, with dat. of possessor; of feelings, etc., = to overwhelm, *invadĕre, occupare*.
possession, *possessio*; to take —, *occupare, capĕre, potiri*.
possessive, *tenax (suorum)*; gram., *possessivus*.
possessor, *possessor, dominus*.
possibility: render by *posse*; see also opportunity.
possible; render *posse*; it is — for me to live, *vivĕre possum*; it is — that, *fieri potest ut*; as quickly as —, *quam celerrime*. Adv.; see perhaps.
post, subst.; = stake, *palus*; door —, *postis*; milit., *statio, praesidium*; = office, *locus, munus (-eris, n.)*; for letters, *tabellarii (-orum*; = letter-carriers).
post, v.: milit., *(dis)ponĕre*; to — a letter, *litteras tabellario dare*.
postage, *vecturae pretium*.
posterior, adj. *posterior*.
posterity, *posteritas, posteri (-orum)*.
postern, *posticum*.
posthaste, *quam celerrime*.
posthumous; *post patrem mortuum natus*.
postman, *tabellarius*.
postpone, *differre, proferre, prorogare*.
postulate, subst. *sumptio*.
posture: of body, *status (-ūs), habitus (-ūs)*; of affairs, *status (-ūs), condicio, ratio*.
pot; *olla*.
potent; see powerful, efficacious.
potentate, *res, tyrannus, princeps*.
potential; see possible.
pothouse, *caupona*.
potion, *potio*; see also *philtre*.
potsherd, *testa*.
potter, *figulus*; —'s workshop, *figlina*.
pottery, = pots, etc., *fictilia (-ium)*.
pouch, *sacculus, saccus*.
poultice, *emplastrum*.
pounce: to — upon, *involare*.
pound, subst.: as measure of weight, *libra*; = enclosure, *saeptum (publicum)*.
pound, v. *(con)tundĕre, (con)terĕre*.
pour, v.: transit., *fundĕre*; to — in, *infundĕre*; to — out, *effundĕre*; intransit. *fundi, fluĕre, ferri*.
pouring, adj. (of rain), *effusus*.
poverty, *paupertas*; extreme —, *egestas, inopia, mendicitas*.
powder, subst. *pulvis*.

power. (1), = force, vigour, *vis* (plur. *vires*), *robur, lacerti (-orum*, physical); military —, *opes (-um)*. (2), = authority, *imperium, potestas, ius (iuris*, n.); unofficial —, *potentia*; in the — of, *penes (hominem)*, *in manu (hominis)*; to have great —, *multum posse* or *valēre*.
powerful, *validus, valens, potens, robustus* (physically); of speech, *gravis, nervosus*. Adv. *graviter, vehementer, valde*.
powerless, *invalidus, impotens*; to be —, *nihil posse*.
practicable; see possible.
practical, of a person, (*rerum*) *usu peritus*; — knowledge, *usus (-ūs)*.
practice: = experience, *usus (-ūs)*, *tractatio*; = custom, *mos, consuetudo*; = deed, *factum*.
practise: = do, engage in, *facĕre, exercēre, tractare*; = rehearse, *meditari*.
praetor, *praetor*.
praetorship, *praetura*.
prairie, *campus*.
praise, subst. *laus, laudatio* (= laudatory oration).
praise, v. *(con)laudare, laude adficĕre, praedicare*.
praiseworthy, *laudabilis, laude dignus*.
prance, *exsilire, exsultare*.
prank, *iocus*.
prate, prattle, *garrire*.
pray, *precari, rogare, orare, supplicare*.
prayer, *preces (-um), precatio, votum*.
prayerful, *supplex*.
preach, *docēre, orationem habēre*.
preamble, *exordium*.
precarious, *incertus, dubius*.
precaution; to take —s, *providēre, praecavēre*.
precede, *anteire, antegredi, antecedĕre*.
precedence, *prior locus*; to take —, *(homini) antecedĕre*.
precedent, *exemplum*.
preceding, *prior, superior*; = immediately before, *proximus*.
precept, *praeceptum, mandatum*.
preceptor, *magister, praeceptor*.
preceptor, *magister, praeceptor*.
precincts, *termini (-orum), fines (-ium)*.
precious, *magni pretii, splendidus, egregius*; a — stone, *gemma*.
precipice, *locus praeceps*.
precipitate, adj. *temerarius, praeceps, inconsultus*. Adv. *temere*.
precipitate, v. *praecipitare, deicĕre, deturbare*.
precipitous, *praeceps, praeruptus*.
precise: of things, *definitus, accuratus*; of persons, *diligens*. Adv. *subtiliter*; see also just.
precision, *subtilitas*; of persons, *diligentia*.
preclude, *prohibēre*.
precocious, *praecox*.
preconceived, *praeiudicatus*.
preconception, *praeiudicata opinio*.
preconcerted, *ex composito factus*.
precursor, *praecursor, praenuntius*.
predatory, *praedatorius, praedabundus*.
predecessor, in an office, *decessor*.

predetermine, *praefinire, praestituĕre.*
predicament, *difficultas, angustiae* (*-arum*).
predicate, subst. *attributio, attributum.*
predicate, v. *praedicare, dicĕre.*
predict, *praedicĕre.*
prediction, *praedictio, praedictum.*
predilection, *studium.*
predispose, (*animum*) *inclinare.*
predisposed, *propensus, proclivis.*
predisposition, (*animi*) *proclivitas, studium.*
predominance, *potentia, principatus* (*-ūs*).
predominant, *potens, praepollens;* = more numerous, *plures.*
predominate, (*prae*)*pollēre;* = be more numerous, *plures esse.*
preeminence, *praestantia, eminentia.*
preeminent, *praestans, praecipuus, egregius;* adv. *praecipue.*
preexist, *antea exstare* or *esse.*
preface, *prooemium, praefatio.*
prefatory; to make a few — remarks, *pauca praefari.*
prefect, *praefectus.*
prefecture, *praefectura.*
prefer, *anteponĕre, anteferre, praeferre;* with infin., *malle.*
preferable, *potior, melior;* adv. *potius.*
preferment, *honor* (= office).
prefix, v. *praeponĕre.*
pregnant, *praegnans, gravida;* of language, *pressus;* of events, *magni momenti.*
prejudge, *praeiudicare.*
prejudice, subst.: = premature judgment, *opinio praeiudicata;* = damage, *detrimentum.*
prejudice, v.: to be —d about a matter, *rem praeiudicatam habēre;* see also harm.
preliminary, adj.: a — inquiry, *praeiudicium;* — remarks, *praefatio.*
prelude, *prooemium.* Transf., *prolusio.*
premature, *immaturus, praeproperus;* adv. *ante tempus.*
premeditate, *praemeditari, cogitare.*
premeditation, *praemeditatio.*
premise, premises: in logic, —s, *principia* (*-orum*); minor —, *adsumptio;* major —, *propositio;* —s, = building, *aedificium, domus.*
premise, v. *praefari, ponĕre.*
premium, *praemium.*
premonition, *monitio, monitum.*
preoccupation, *animus rei* (dat.) *deditus.*
preoccupy, = seize beforehand, (*prae*)*occupare;* to be preoccupied about a thing, *totum in re versari.*
preparation, *praeparatio, apparatus* (*-ūs*), *meditatio* (of a lesson, etc.); to make —s, *parare.*
prepare, (*ap*)*parare, praeparare, instruĕre;* to — for war, *bellum* (*ap*)*parare;* to — a speech, lesson, etc., *meditari, commentari.*
preponderate; see predominance.
prepossess, = win over, *delenire, permulcĕre.*
prepossession; see prejudice.
preposterous, *praeposterus.*

prerogative; see right.
presage, subst. *praesagium, augurium.*
presage, v.: = foreshow, *portendĕre, significare;* = forebode, *praesagire, augurari.*
prescient, *praesciens, sagax.*
prescribe, *praescribĕre.*
presence, *praesentia;* in my —, *coram me* (abl.); — of mind, *praesens animus.*
present, subst. *donum, munus.*
present, adj.: physically, *praesens;* to be —, *adesse;* of time, *praesens, hic;* at —, *nunc, hoc tempore;* for the —, *in praesentia, in praesens* (*tempus*); gram. *praesens.* Adv., soon, *mox, brevi.*
present, v.: = bring forward, *offerre, obicĕre, praebēre;* to — oneself, *occurrĕre, obvenire;* = give, *donare, munerari, dare;* = introduce, *introducĕre, inducĕre.*
presentiment, *praesagitio, augurium;* to have a —, *praesagire.*
preservation, *conservatio;* = safety *salūs* (*-ūtis*).
preserve, v. (*con*)*servare, tuēri* (=watch over), *sustinēre* (= uphold).
preserver, (*con*)*servator* (f. *servatrix*).
preside, *praesidēre, praeesse.*
presidency, *praefectura.*
president, *praefectus;* or use verb.
press, subst. *prelum, torcular* (for wine, etc.).
press, v.: transit., *premĕre, comprimĕre;* to — out, *exprimĕre;* = urge, harry, *premĕre, urgēre, instare;* intransit., to — on, *pergĕre, contendĕre.*
pressing; see urgent.
pressure, *pressus* (*-ūs*) *vis, pondus* (*-eris,* n.).
prestige, *nomen, gloria, fama.*
presume: = take liberties, *sibi adrogare* or *sumĕre, audēre;* = to suppose, *sumĕre, credĕre.*
presumption: = presumptuousness, *adrogantia;* = supposition, *coniectura, opinio.*
presumptuous, *adrogans;* adv. *adroganter.*
pretence, *simulatio, species;* without —, *sine fuco ac fallaciis.*
pretend, *simulare, fingĕre.*
pretender, *simulator;* to the throne, *qui regnum sibi adrogat.*
pretension: = claim, *postulatio;* = display, *ostentatio.*
preterite, gram., *praeteritum* (*tempus*).
preternaturally, *praeter naturam, mirabili quodam modo.*
pretext, *causa, simulatio species;* to use as a —, *praetendĕre.*
prettiness, *concinnitas, venustas.*
pretty, adj. *bellus, pulcher, concinnus, lepidus;* adv. *belle, concinne, lepide.*
pretty, adv. *satis, admodum.*
prevail: = be prevalent, *esse, obtinēre;* = win, *vincĕre, superare;* to — upon, = persuade, *persuadēre, adducĕre.*
prevalent, (*per*)*vulgatus;* to become —, *increbrescĕre.*
prevaricate, *tergiversari.*
prevarication, *tergiversatio.*

prevent, *prohibēre, impedire.*
previous; see preceding.
prey, subst. *praeda:* a beast of —, *fera.*
prey, v. *praedari;* fig., to — upon, *(animum)* (ex)*edĕre, consumĕre.*
price, subst. *pretium;* — of corn, *annona;* at a high —, *magni (pretii);* to set a — on, *(rei,* dat.) *pretium constituĕre.*
priceless, *inaestimabilis.*
prick, v. *pungĕre, stimulare;* to — up one's ears, *aures erigĕre.*
prickle, *aculeus, spina.*
prickly, *aculeatus, spinosus.*
pride, *superbia, insolentia, adrogantia;* source of —, *decus (-oris).*
priest, *sacerdos, flamen;* high —, *pontifex maximus.*
priestess, *sacerdos.*
priesthood, *sacerdotium.*
prim, *(nimis) diligens.*
primal, primeval; see ancient, first.
primary, *primus, principalis;* = chief, *praecipuus.* Adv. *initio, primo; prae-cipue.*
prime, subst.: of life, *integra aetas;* to be in one's —, *vigēre, florēre;* — of anything, *flos, robur.*
prime, adj.: = first, *primus;* = ex-cellent, *eximius, optimus.*
primitive, *priscus, antiquus.*
prince: = king's son, *filiu. regis, regulus;* = king, *rex.*
princess, *mulier regii generis, filia regis.*
principal, subst.: of a school, *magister;* = capital, *caput, sors.*
principal, adj., *primus, princeps, prae-cipuus* (= chief). Adv. *maxime, praecipue.*
principle, *principium, elementum, ratio;* of conduct, *institutum, praeceptum;* a man of —, *homo constans* or *gravis;* want of —, *levitas.*
print, v. *imprimĕre.*
prior, adj. *prior;* see also preceding.
prison, *carcer, vincula (-orum,* =chains), *custodia* (=confinement).
prisoner: a — of war, *captivus* (f. *captiva);* in gen. (*homo) captus, comprehensus;* = a person on trial, render by *reus.*
pristine, *pristinus, priscus, antiquus.*
prithee! *quaeso, cedo.*
privacy, *solitudo.*
private, *privatus, proprius, domesticus;* = secret, *arcanus, secretus;* a — soldier, *miles gregarius, manipularis.* Adv. *clam, secreto, occulte, privatim* (= in a private capacity).
privateer, *navis praedatoria.*
privation, *inopia, egestas.*
privet, *ligustrum.*
privilege, *ius (iuris,* n.), *praecipuum, beneficium.*
privy, adj.: see private; — to, *conscius rei* (genit.); — council, *consilium regis;* — purse, *fiscus.*
prize, subst.: = reward, *praemium, palma;* = prey, *praeda.*
prize, v. *magni aestimare.*
pro and con, *in utramque partem.*
probability, *veri similitudo, probabilitas.*

probable, *veri similis; probabilis* (of guesses, etc.); adv. *probabiliter.*
probe, v. *scrutari, rimari.*
probity, *probitas.*
problem, *quaestio.*
problematical, *dubius, incertus.*
proceed, *pergere, procedĕre, progredi;* = to act, *agĕre, facĕre;* to — from, *emanare, oriri;* to — against, in the courts, *litem intendĕre.*
proceeding, proceedings, in gen., *acta (-orum);* legal, *lis, actio.*
proceeds, *reditus (-ūs), fructus (-ūs).*
process, *ratio;* legal, *lis, actio.*
procession, *pompa.*
proclaim, *declarare, pronuntiare, edicĕre* (by decree).
proclamation, *pronuntiatio, declaratio, praedicatio;* = thing proclaimed, *edictum.*
proconsul, *pro consule.*
proconsular, *proconsularis.*
procrastinate, *differre, procrastinare.*
procrastination, *procrastinatio.*
procreate, *procreare.*
procreation, *procreatio.*
procure, (*com)parare;* to — in addition, *adquirĕre.*
prodigal, subst. *nepos.*
prodigal, adj. *prodigus, profusus, effusus.*
prodigality, *effusio, prodigentia.*
prodigious, *ingens, immanis.*
prodigy, *prodigium, portentum, miraculum.*
produce, subst. *fructus (-ūs).*
produce, v.: = bring forward, *pro-ferre, exhibēre, producĕre;* = bring into existence, (*pro)creare, gignĕre, parĕre;* = cause, bring about, *facĕre, efficĕre.*
product, production, *opus (-eris* = work); an artistic —, *artificium.*
productive, *ferax, uber.*
productiveness, *ubertas.*
proem, *prooemium.*
profanation, *violatio, nefas.*
profane, adj.: = not sacred, *profanus;* = impious, *impius;* adv. *impie.*
profane, v. *violare, polluĕre.*
profanity, *impietas.*
profess, *profiteri.*
professed, *manifestus, apertus.*
profession: = declaration, *professio;* = employment, *munus (-eris,* n.), *ars.*
proffer, v. *promittĕre;* see offer.
proficiency, *scientia, peritia.*
proficient, *peritus, sciens.*
profit, subst. *lucrum, quaestus (-ūs), fructus (-ūs).*
profit, v.: = be of service, *prodesse;* = gain advantage, *proficĕre, lucrum facĕre.*
profitable, *utilis, fructuosus;* adv. *utiliter.*
profitless, *inutilis, vanus.*
profligacy, subst. *homo perditus* or *profligatus.*
profligate, adj. *perditus, flagitiosus, profligatus;* adv. *perdite.*
profound, *altus.* Adv. *penitus* (= com-pletely).
profundity, *altitudo.*
profuse, *effusus, profusus.*

profusion, *largitas, effusio.*

progenitor, *parens.*

progeny, *progenies.*

prognostic, *signum.*

prognosticate; see forebode.

programme, *libellus.*

progress, subst.: = journey, *iter*; = advance, *progressus (-ūs)*; to make much —, *multum proficĕre.*

progress, v. *progredi, proficĕre.*

progression, *progressus (-ūs).*

prohibit, *vetare, interdicĕre.*

prohibition, *interdictum.*

project, subst. *consilium, propositum.*

project, v. *prominēre, eminēre, exstare.*

projectile, *(telum) missile.*

proletariat, *proletarii (-orum).*

prolific; see fruitful.

prolix, *longus, verbosus.*

prologue, *(pro)ducĕre, prorogare, extendĕre.*

prolongation, *productio, prorogatio.*

prolonged, *longus, diuturnus.*

promenade, *ambulatio.*

prominence, *eminentia;* = importance *dignitas, auctoritas.*

prominent: = projecting, *prominens,* or render by verb; = distinguished, *praestans, egregius, inlustris.*

promiscuous, *promiscuus;* adv. *promiscue, temere.*

promise, subst., *promissum, fides.*

promise, v.: = to make a —, *promittĕre, pollicēri, fidem dare;* = to show —, *bonam spem ostendĕre.*

promising, adj. *bonae spei* (genit.).

promissory; a — note, *chirographum.*

promontory, *promontorium;* small —, *lingua, li(n)gula.*

promote, of person, *provehĕre, producĕre;* of causes, etc., *(ad)iuvare, amplificare; consulĕre, prodesse,* with dat.

promoter, *auctor, adiutor, fautor.*

promotion: = rise to higher position, *dignitatis accessio;* = furthering, *amplificatio.*

prompt, *promptus;* adv. *cito.*

prompt, v., = suggest, *subicĕre.*

prompter, *qui rem homini subicit.*

promptitude, *celeritas.*

promulgate, *promulgare.*

promulgation, *promulgatio.*

prone: = face-down, *pronus;* =liable, inclined, *pronus, proclivis, propensus.*

proneness, *proclivitas.*

prong, *dens.*

pronoun, *pronomen.*

pronounce, *enuntiare, exprimĕre, dicĕre;* formally, *pronuntiare, declarare.*

pronunciation, *appellatio, locutio.*

proof, subst.: = act of proving, *probatio, demonstratio;* = means of proving, *argumentum, signum, indicium;* = trial, *experimentum;* to put to the —, *experiri, temptare.*

prop, subst. *adminiculum.*

prop, v. *fulcire;* see support.

propagate: of plants, *propagare, inserĕre;* of living creatures, *gignĕre, procreare;* abstr., *vulgare, serĕre.*

propagation: *propagatio;* abstr., use verb.

propel, *propellĕre, impellĕre.*

propensity, *proclivitas, animus proclivis.*

proper: = peculiar, characteristic, *proprius;* = genuine, *verus, germanus;* = becoming, *decorus, honestus;* it is —, *decet;* = suitable, *aptus, idoneus.* Adv. *proprie, vere; apte.*

property: = characteristic, *proprietas;* = what one owns, *bona (-orum), res;* private —, *res familiaris;* inherited —, *patrimonium.*

prophecy: the act, *praedictio, vaticinatio;* = what is prophesied, *praedictum.*

prophesy, *praedicĕre, praenuntiare, vaticinari.*

prophet, *vates.*

prophetic, *divinus, fatidicus, vaticinus;* adv. *divinitus.*

propinquity; see nearness.

propitiate, *placare, propitiare.*

propitiation, *placatio;* means of —, *piaculum.*

propitious, *propitius, faustus;* adv. *fauste.*

proportion: = portion, *pars, portio;* = relationship, *ratio;* in —. *pro portione, pro rata parte;* in — to, *pro,* with abl.

proposal, *condicio, sententia, consilium.*

propose: = bring forward for consideration, *ponĕre;* to — a law, *legem ferre* or *rogare;* = intend, *cogitare, in animo habēre.*

proposer: of a law, *legis lator;* in gen., *auctor.*

proposition, in logic, *pronuntiatum, propositio.*

proprietor, *possessor, dominus.*

propriety, *convenientia, decorum, honestas.*

prorogation, *prorogatio.*

prorogue, *prorogare.*

prosaic, *ieiunus, frigidus.*

proscribe, *proscribĕre.*

proscription, *proscriptio.*

prose, *(soluta) oratio.*

prosecute: = carry out, *exsequi, perficĕre;* = bring action against, *iudicio persequi, accusare.*

prosecution: = carrying out, *exsecutio;* at law, *accusatio, actio, lis.*

prosecutor, *accusator.*

proselyte, *discipulus.*

prospect: = view, *prospectus (-ūs);* = hope, *spes.*

prospective, *futurus;* adv. *in futurum.*

prosper: transit., *fortunare, secundare;* intransit., *florēre, vigēre.*

prosperity, *res* (plur) *secundae* or *prosperae; prosperitas.*

prosperous, *secundus, prosper(us);* adv. *bene, prospere.*

prostitute, subst. *meretrix, scortum.*

prostrate, v. *(pro)sternĕre;* to — oneself before a person, *ad pedes hominis procumbĕre;* to be —d by grief, *in maerore iacēre.*

protect, *tuēri, defendĕre, (pro)tegĕre, custodire.*

protection, *tutela, praesidium, custodia;* to take under one's —, *in fidem recipĕre.*

protector, *defensor, propugnator, custos.*

protest, subst. *recusatio.*

protest, v.: = state positively, *ad-severare, adfirmare;* to — against, *recusare, intercedĕre.*

prototype, *exemplum, exemplar.*

protract, (*pro*)*ducĕre, prorogare, trahĕre.*

protrude: transit., *protrudĕre;* intransit., *protrudi, prominēre.*

protuberance, *tuber, gibber.*

proud, *superbus, adrogans, fastidiosus;* adv. *superbe, adroganter.*

prove: = show clearly, *probare ostendĕre, docēre;* to — oneself, *se praestare* or *praebēre;* intransit., = to turn out, *fieri, evadĕre, exire.*

provender, *pabulum.*

proverb, *proverbium;* according to the —, *ut aiunt.*

proverbial, proverbially, *proverbii loco* (= as a proverb).

provide: = supply, furnish, (*com*)*par-are, praebēre, suppeditare;* to — for, *consulĕre* or *providēre,* with dat.; of laws, = require, order, *iubēre.*

provided that, *dum, dummodo* (with subj.).

provided with, adj. *instructus, ornatus, praeditus.*

providence, *providentia.*

provident, *providus, diligens.* Adv. *diligenter.*

providentially, *divinitus.*

province: = duty, *provincia, officium;* = district, *regio, provincia.*

provincial, *provincialis;* = countrified, *rusticus, agrestis, inurbanus.*

provision, = stipulation, *condicio, cautio.*

provision, v. (*oppidum*) *cibo instruĕre.*

provisional, render by phrase, *ad* or *in tempus.*

provisions, *cibus, cibaria* (*-orum*), *alimentum;* for an army, *commeatus* (*-ūs*).

provoke: = call forth, (*com*)*movēre, ciēre;* = make angry, *incitare, lacessĕre;* to — to action, *incitare, concitare, impellĕre.*

provoking, *molestus.*

prow, *prora.*

prowess, *virtūs* (*-ūtis*).

prowl, *vagari, peragrare.*

proximity; see nearness.

proxy, *procurator, vicarius.*

prudence, *prudentia, cautio, circum-spectio.*

prudent, *prudens, cautus, circumspectus;* adv. *caute, considerate.*

prudish, *rusticus, severus, tetricus.*

prune, (*am*)*putare, recidĕre.*

pruner, of trees, *putator.*

pruning, subst. *putatio.*

pruning-hook, *falx.*

pry, *rimari, investigare, scrutari.*

pshaw! *phy!*

public, subst. *homines* (*-um,* plur.), *populus, vulgus.*

public, *publicus, communis* (= not private); to show oneself in —, *in publicum prodire;* — life, *respublica, forum;* the — interest, *respublica;* at the — expense, *sumptu publico,*

publice; in a — capacity, *publice;* — opinion, *vulgi opinio.* Adv. publicly, in —, *aperte, palam, coram omnibus.*

publican, *publicanus;* = inn-keeper, *caupo.*

publication, *praedicatio;* of a book, *editio libri;* = book, *liber.*

publicity, *celebritas, lux.*

publish, *proferre, ēdĕre.*

pudding, *placenta.*

puddle, *stagnum.*

puerile, *puerilis, ineptus.*

puff, v. *anhelare;* to — out, = inflate, *inflare.*

pugilism, *pugilatus* (*-ūs*), *pugilatio.*

pugilist, *pugil.*

pull, v.: = twitch, tweak, *vellĕre, vellicare;* = drag, *trahĕre;* to — out, (*e*)*vellĕre, eripĕre.*

pullet, *pullus* (*gallinaceus*).

pulley, *trochlea.*

pulsate, *palpitare, agitari, moveri.*

pulse: of the blood, *venarum pulsus* (*-ūs*); the vegetable, *legumen.*

pulverize, *in pulverem redigĕre.*

pumice, *pumex;* of —, adj., *pumiceus.*

pump, subst. *antlia.*

pump, v. *exhaurire.*

pun, subst. *facetiae* (*-arum*), *logos* (or *-us*).

punch, subst., the drink, *calidum;* — bowl, *cratera;* see also blow.

punch, v. *tundĕre.*

punctilious, *diligens;* in religious matters, *religiosus;* adv. *diligenter, accurate.*

punctual, *diligens;* adv. *diligenter, ad tempus.*

punctuality, *diligentia* (= care).

punctuate, *distinguĕre, interpungĕre.*

punctuation, *distinctio, interpunctio;* — mark, *interpunctum.*

puncture, subst. *punctum.*

puncture, v. (*com*)*pungĕre.*

pungent, *acer, acutus;* adv. *acriter, acute.*

punish, *punire, poenā adficĕre, ulcisci;* to be —ed, *puniri, poenas dare.*

punisher, *vindex, ultor.*

punishment, *castigatio, animadversio;* = what is inflicted, *poena, supplicium, multa.*

puny, *pusillus, exiguus.*

pupil: of the eye, *pupula;* at school, *alumnus* (f. *alumna*), *discipulus* (f. *discipula*).

puppy, *catulus, catellus.*

purchasable, *venalis.*

purchase, subst.: as act, *emptio;* = thing bought, *merx, quod emptum est.*

purchase, v. (*co*)*emĕre, mercari.*

purchaser, *emptor.*

pure: physically, *purus;* pure and simple, *merus, sincerus;* morally, *purus, integer, sanctus, castus.* Adv.: = wholly, *prorsus, plane;* morally, *pure, integre, caste.*

purgation, *purgatio, lustratio.*

purge, *purgare.*

purification, *purgatio;* ceremonial —, *lustratio.*

purify, (*ex*)*purgare, purum facĕre; lustrare* (with ceremonial).

purity: moral, *integritas, sanctimonia, sanctitas;* of language, *integritas, sinceritas.*

purloin, *avertĕre, surripĕre, furari.*

purple, subst. *purpura, ostrum conchylium, color purpureus.*

purport; see meaning, mean.

purpose, subst. *propositum, consilium, animus, voluntas;* for the — of, (*eo consilio*) *ut;* on —, *consulto, de industria;* to no —, *frustra, nequiquam;* to the —, *ad rem.*

purpose, v. *statuĕre, cogitare, in animo habēre.*

purposeless, *vanus, inanis, irritus.*

purposely; see purpose.

purse, *marsupium, zona, crumena.*

pursuant to, *ex* (with abl.), *secundum* (with acc.).

pursue, (*per*)*sequi, insequi, insectari.*

pursuit: = search, *consectatio;* = occupation, *negotium, occupatio, artificium.*

push, subst. (*im*)*pulsus* (-*ūs*), *impetus* (-*ūs*).

push, v. (*im*)*pellĕre,* (*pro*)*trudĕre, urgēre;* intransit., to — on, *contendĕre, instare, pergĕre.*

pushing, adj. *protervus, confidens.*

pusillanimity, *timiditas; animus timidus.*

pusillanimous, *timidus, abiectus;* adv. *timide, abiecte.*

put, *ponĕre,* (*con*)*locare;* — away, *abdĕre;* — back, *reponĕre;* — down, *deponĕre, demittĕre; comprimĕre* (= suppress); — on, of clothes, *induĕre, sumĕre;* — off, of clothes, *exuĕre,* (*de*)*ponĕre;* — off, = postpone, *differre;* — out, *eicĕre, extrudĕre, expellĕre; exstinguĕre* (= quench); — together, *conferre, componĕre;* — up, *erigĕre, statuĕre;* — up with (= tolerate), *ferre, tolerare.*

putative, *falsus; qui dicitur esse.*

putrefy, *putescĕre;* to cause to —, *putrefacĕre.*

putrid, *putridus, putidus.*

puzzle, *quaestio, aenigma, nodus.*

puzzle, v. *dubium facĕre, impedire;* to be —d, *dubitare, haerēre.*

puzzling, *difficilis, ambiguus.*

Pygmy, *pygmaeus;* = any dwarf, *nanus, pumilio, pumilus.*

pyramid, *pyramis.*

pyre, *rogus, pyra.*

Pyrenees, *Pyrenaei montes, Pyrenaeum.*

Q

quadripartite, *quadripartitus.*

quadruped, *quadrupes.*

quadruple, *quadruplex.*

quaff, v. *ducĕre, haurire.*

quag(mire), *palūs* (-*ūdis*).

quail, subst. *coturnix.*

quail, v. *animo deficĕre, pavēre.*

quaint, *lepidus, facetus, concinnus* = odd, *insolitus, novus.*

quake, *tremĕre, contremiscĕre.*

qualification: = right, *ius* (*iuris*, n.); = limitation, *exceptio, condicio.*

qualified, *idoneus, aptus, dignus.*

qualify, v.: transit., = make fit, *idoneum reddĕre, instituĕre;* = modify, restrict, *circumscribĕre, deminuĕre;* intransit., *idoneum esse* (or *habēri*).

quality: = nature, character, *natura, ingenium, indoles;* of what —? *qualis?;* of such a —, *talis;* good —, *virtūs* (-*ūtis*); bad —, *vitium;* = kind, sort, *genus* (-*eris*, n.), *nota* (of wine); a lady of —, *generosa femina.*

qualm, *fastidium* (= disgust), *nausea, nauseola* (= squeamishness); — of conscience, *conscientia* (*mala*).

quantity, = number, *numerus;* a certain —, *aliquot, aliquantum;* a large —, *multitudo, copia, vis;* — in scansion, *mensura, quantitas.*

quarrel, subst. *iurgium, altercatio, rixa.*

quarrel, v. *iurgare, altercari, rixari.*

quarrelsome, *litigiosus, pugnax.*

quarry, subst.: a stone —, *lapicidinae* (-*arum*), *lautumiae* (-*arum*); = prey, *praeda.*

quart, (as measure) *duo sextarii.*

quartan, adj. *quartanus.*

quarter: = fourth part, *quarta pars, quadrans;* = district, *vicus, regio;* = mercy, *venia.*

quarter, v. *quadrifariam dividĕre;* to — troops, *milites per hospitia disponĕre.*

quarterly, *trimestris;* adv. *tertio quoque mense.*

quarters, *hospitium, habitatio, tectum;* milit., winter — (for troops), *hiberna* (-*orum*), summer —, *aestiva* (-*orum*); at close —, *comminus;* to come to close —, *manum conserĕre.*

quash, *rescindĕre, infirmare.*

quaver; see tremble.

quay, *margo, crepido.*

queen, *regina.*

queer, *novus, insolitus, mirus.*

quell, *opprimĕre, comprimĕre.*

quench, *exstinguĕre, restinguĕre.*

querulous, *queribundus, querulus.*

query; see question.

quest; see seek, search.

question, subst.: = inquiry, *quaestio, interrogatum;* to ask —s, (*inter*)-*rogare;* = doubt, dispute, *controversia, dubium;* there is no — that, *haud dubium est quin.*

question, v.: = to ask questions, (*inter*)*rogare, percontari, quaerĕre;* = to doubt, *dubitare.*

questionable, *incertus, ambiguus, dubius.*

questioning, subst. (*inter*)*rogatio, percontatio.*

quibble, subst. *captio, cavillatio.*

quibble, v. *cavillari.*

quibbling, adj. *captiosus.*

quick, = prompt, active, *promptus, alacer, expeditus;* — witted, *astutus, sagax, catus.* Adv., = fast, *cito, celeriter.*

quicken: = accelerate, *accelerare maturare;* in gen., = stimulate *incitare, stimulare, incendĕre.*

quicklime, *calx viva.*
quickness, *velocitas*; of intellect, *ingenii acumen, sagacitas.*
quicksand, *syrtis.*
quicksilver, *argentum vivum.*
quiet, subst. *tranquillitas, pax, otium, silentium.*
quiet, adj. *quietus, tranquillus, taciturnus* (= not talking); to be —, *quiescĕre, silēre, tacēre.* Adv. *quiete, tranquille, silentio* (= in silence).
quiet, quieten, v. *tranquillare, pacare.*
quill, *penna; spina;* for striking strings, *plectrum.*
quinquennial, *quinquennalis.*
quintessence, *flos.*
quip, *dictum.*
quit, *decedĕre (de loco).*
quite, adv.: = completely, *admodum, prorsus, omnino, funditus;* = fairly, moderately, *satis.*
quiver, subst. *pharetra.*
quiver, v. *tremĕre, micare.*
quivering, adj. *tremulus.*
quoit, *discus.*
quotation, *prolatio, commemoratio;* = passage quoted, *locus adlatus.*
quote, *adferre, proferre, (com)memorare.*
quoth he, or she, *inquit, ait.*

R

rabbit, *cuniculus.*
rabble, *multitudo, turba, plebecula.*
rabid, *rabidus;* adv. *rabide.*
race, subst.: = family, people, *genus (-eris, n.), gens;* = contest of speed, *cursus (-ūs), certamen, curriculum.*
race, v. *(cursus) certare.*
race-course, *curriculum, stadium, circus.*
race-horse, *equus, celes.*
raciness, *sucus, sapor.*
rack, subst., for torture, *eculeus, tormentum.*
rack, v. *torquēre, (ex)cruciare, vexare.*
racket: = noise, *strepitus (-ūs).*
racy, *salsus.*
radiance, *fulgor, candor, splendor.*
radiant, *clarus, candidus, splendidus.*
radiate, *fulgēre, radiare.*
radical, adj.: = innate, *insitus, innatus;* = complete, *totus;* in politics, *novarum rerum cupidus* or *studiosus.* Adv. *radicitus, funditus, prorsus, omnino.*
radish, *raphanus, radix.*
raft, *ratis.*
rafter, *tignum, trabs.*
rag, *pannus.*
rage, subst. *rabies, furor, ira* (= anger).
rage, v. *furĕre, saevire.*
raging, *furens, furibundus, saevus.*
ragged: of people, *pannosus;* of clothes, *lacer.*
rail, subst. *tignum transversum.*
rail, v.: to — off, *(con)saepire;* to — at, *maledicĕre, conviciari.*
railing, subst. *saepimentum, saepes.*
raillery, *iocus, cavillatio.*
raiment, *vestis, vestitus (-ūs).*
rain, subst. *pluvia, imber.*
rain, v.: it —s, *pluit.*

rainbow, *arcus (-ūs) pluvius.*
rain-cloud, *nimbus.*
rainy, *pluvius, pluvialis.*
raise: = lift, *(ex)tollĕre, (e)levare, erigĕre;* = increase, *augēre;* = promote, elevate, *producĕre, provehĕre;* = arouse, *excitare, erigĕre, tollĕre.*
rake, subst. *rastellus, pecten;* =prodigal roué, *ganeo, nepos, vappa.*
rake, v. *radĕre, pectine verrĕre.*
rakish, *profligatus, dissolutus.*
rally, v.: transit.; to — troops, *ordines restituĕre;* = banter, *ludĕre, irridēre;* intransit., = recover, *se conligĕre, convalescĕre* (from illness).
ram, subst. *aries.*
ramble, subst. *ambulatio.*
ramble, v. *errare, vagari, ambulare* (= walk about).
rambling, *vagus.*
rampant, *ferox, superbus;* to be —, *superbire.*
rampart, *vallum, agger; praesidium.*
rancid, *rancidus.*
rancorous, *malevolus, malignus, invidus;* adv. *maligne, infeste.*
rancour, *odium, invidia, malevolentia.*
random: at —, *temere.*
range, subst.: = row, *ordo, series;* a — of mountains, *montes perpetui;* of a missile, *(teli) coniectus (-ūs).*
rank, subst.: of soldiers, *ordo;* = degree, station, *ordo, gradus (-ūs), locus.*
rank, adj.: of plants, *luxuriosus;* of smell, *foetidus, graveolens;* = great, extreme, *maximus, summus.*
rank, v. *numerare, habēre.*
rankle, v. *mordēre, pungĕre.*
ransack: = plunder, *diripĕre, spoliare;* = search thoroughly, *rimari, (per)scrutari.*
ransom, subst.: = money paid, *pretium, pecunia;* = the arrangement, *redemptio.*
ransom, v. *redimĕre.*
rant, v. *declamare, ampullari.*
rap, subst. *pulsatio.*
rap, v. *pulsare.*
rapacious, *rapax, avidus.*
rapacity, *rapacitas, aviditas.*
rapid, subst. *vertex, gurges.*
rapid, *rapidus, citus, celer;* adv. *rapide, cito, celeriter.*
rapidity, *rapiditas, celeritas.*
rapine, *rapina.*
rapture, *(summa) voluptas, exsultatio.*
rare: = uncommon, *rarus, inusitatus;* = thin, *rarus, tenuis;* = exceptional, *singularis, eximius.* Adv. *raro.*
rarefy, *extenuare.*
rarity, = fewness, *raritas, paucitas.*
rascal, *homo scelestus, lucrifer, verbero.*
rascality, *scelestus, nequam.*
rash, *praeceps, inconsultus, temerarius;* adv. *inconsulte, temere.*
rashness, *temeritas.*
rat, *mus.*
rate, subst.: = price, *pretium;* — of interest, *usura;* — of exchange, *collybus;* = tax, *vectigal, tributum;* at any —, *certe, utique.*

rate, v., = value, *aestimare.*
rather: = in preference, *potius,*
libentius, prius; I would —, *malo;*
= somewhat, *aliquantum.*
ratification, *sanctio;* or use verb.
ratify, *sancire, ratum facĕre, confirmare.*
ration, *demensum, cibaria (-orum).*
rational, *ratione praeditus;* (rationi)
consentaneus; to act —ly, *prudenter
agĕre.*
rationality; see *ratio.*
rattle, subst.: = noise, *crepitus (-ūs),*
strepitus (-ūs); a child's —, *crepi-
taculum, crepitacillum.*
rattle, v. *crepare, strepĕre.*
ravage, (*per*)*vastare,* (*de*)*populari.*
ravaging, *vastatio, populatio.*
rave, *furĕre, insanire.*
raven, *corvus.*
ravening, ravenous, *rapax, vorax.*
ravine, *fauces (-ium).*
raving, *furens, furibundus, insanus.*
ravish: = carry off, *rapĕre, abducĕre;*
= debauch, (*con*)*stuprare.*
ravishing; see *delightful.*
raw, *crudus;* = inexperienced, *rudis,*
imperitus; of weather, *frigidus,*
humidus.
ray, *radius, iubar.*
raze, *solo (ad)aequare.*
razor, *novacula.*
reach, subst.: = grasp, capacity,
captus (-ūs).
reach, v. = touch, get to, *tangĕre,*
contingĕre, attingĕre; (*ad locum*)
(*per*)*venire, accedĕre.*
react: to — upon, = affect, *adficĕre;*
to — to, (*rem*) *ferre* or *accipere,*
with adv.
reactionary, *qui* (*rempublicam*) *ad
pristinum statum revocare vult.*
read, *legĕre, evolvĕre;* to — through,
perlegĕre; to — aloud, *recitare;*
well —, of a person, *litteratus.*
reader, *legens, qui legit.*
readiness, *animus promptus* or *paratus;*
— of speech, *volubilitas linguae,
lingua prompta.*
reading, subst. *lectio;* a — aloud,
recitatio.
ready, *paratus, promptus;* — money,
pecunia praesens or *numerata;* to
make —, (*com*)*parare, instruĕre;* to
be —, *praesto esse.* Adv., = willingly,
prompto or *parato animo, libenter.*
real, *verus, sincerus;* — estate, *fundus,
praedium.* Adv. *revera, vere.*
realistic, to be, *veritatem imitari.*
reality, *res (vera), veritas.*
realization, = completion, *effectus*
(*-ūs*).
realize: = effect, *efficĕre, perficĕre;*
= understand, *intellegĕre, comprehendĕre;* of money, *pecuniam redigĕre.*
realm, *civitas, respublica, regnum.*
reap, (*de*)*metĕre, messem facĕre;* fig.,
fructum capĕre, percipĕre.
reaper, *messor.*
reaping-hook, *falx.*
reappear, *redire, rursus apparēre.*
rear, subst.; use adj. *extremus* or
novissimus, with *agmen* or *acies;* to

form the — guard, *agmen claudĕre* or
cogĕre.
rear, v. = bring up, *alĕre, educare.*
reason, subst.: = cause, *causa, ratio;*
for this (or that) —, *ideo, idcirco;*
by — of, *propter, ob;* there is no —
why, *non est cur,* with subj.; for
no —, *temere;* as a faculty, *ratio,
mens, consilium.*
reason, v. *ratiocinari, reputare;* to
— with another person, *disceptare,
disputare.*
reasonable: of persons, *rationis particeps, prudens;* = fair, (*rationi*)
consentaneus, aequus, iustus. Adv.
ratione; = adequately, *satis.*
reasonableness: = rationality, *ratio;*
= fairness, *aequitas, moderatio.*
reasoner, *disputator.*
reasoning, *ratio, ratiocinatio.*
reassert, *iterare* (= repeat).
reassure, (*animum*) *confirmare, erigĕre.*
rebel, subst. *homo seditiosus, hostis
patriae.*
rebel, v. *seditionem* (*com*)*movēre, deficĕre, desciscĕre.*
rebellion, *seditio, defectio, motus (-ūs).*
rebellious, *seditiosus, turbulentus,
novarum rerum cupidus;* adv.
seditiose, turbulente(r).
rebound, v. *repelli, resilire.*
rebuff, subst. *repulsa.*
rebuff, v. *repellĕre, reicĕre.*
rebuild, *restituĕre, reficĕre.*
rebuke, subst. *reprehensio, vituperatio,
obiurgatio.*
rebuke, v. *reprehendĕre, vituperare,
obiurgare.*
rebuker, *obiurgator.*
rebut, *redarguĕre, repellĕre, refellĕre.*
recall, subst. *revocatio.*
recall, v. *revocare;* to — to mind,
recordari, in memoriam revocare.
recant, *recantare.*
recantation, *receptus (-ūs).*
recapitulate, *enumerare, commemorare.*
recapitulation, *enumeratio.*
recapture, v. *recipĕre.*
recast, *reficĕre.*
recede, *recedĕre, retro cedĕre.*
receipt, = act of receiving, *acceptio,*
or use verb; in a ledger, a —,
acceptum; to enter as a —, *acceptum
referre.*
receive, *accipĕre, excipĕre, recipĕre.*
receiver, *receptor* (f. *receptrix*).
recent, *recens, novus;* adv. *nuper,
recens.*
receptacle, *recaptaculum, cella, horreum.*
reception, *acceptio, hospitium* (in a
house).
receptive, *docilis.*
receptiveness, *docilitas.*
recess, *recessus (-ūs), latibulum.*
reciprocal, *mutuus;* adv. *mutuo,
invicem.*
reciprocate, *inter se dare.*
recital, *narratio, commemoratio.*
recitation, *recitatio.*
recite, *recitare;* = narrate, (*com*)-
memorare, dicĕre, (*e*)*narrare.*

reckless, *neglegens, temerarius, imprudens;* adv. *neglegenter, temere, imprudenter.*

recklessness, *imprudentia, neglegentia, temeritas.*

reckon, = count, calculate, *computare;* see also consider.

reckoning, subst. *ratio, computatio.*

reclaim, v.: = ask back, *repetĕre; reposcĕre;* = reform, *corrigĕre, emendare.*

recline, v. *se reclinare, recumbĕre.*

recluse, *homo solitarius.*

recognizance, *sponsio, vadimonium.*

recognize: = know again, *agnoscĕre, cognoscĕre, noscitare;* = acknowledge, *noscĕre;* = approve, *(com)probare.*

recoil, *resilire, recellĕre;* to — in horror, *refugĕre.*

recollect, *(com)meminisse, reminisci, recordari.*

recollection, *memoria, recordatio.*

recommence, v.: transit., *redintegrare, renovare;* intransit., *renasci, renovari.*

recommend, *commendare, probare.*

recommendation, *commendatio, laus, laudatio.*

recommendatory, *commendaticius.*

recompense, subst. *remuneratio, praemium.*

recompense, v. *remunerari.*

reconcile, *placare, reconciliare, in gratiam reducĕre;* = make congruous, *accommodare.*

reconciliation, *reconciliatio gratiae.*

recondite, *reconditus, exquisitus.*

reconnoitre, *explorare, (pro)speculari.*

reconsider, *denuo considerare.*

record, v. *perscribĕre, in tabulas referre.*

record-office, *tabularium.*

records, *tabulae (-arum), historia; annales (-ium,* = chronicles).

recount, *referre, (e)narrare, (com)memorare.*

recourse: to have — to, *confugĕre, se conferre (ad);* = stoop to, *descendĕre (ad).*

recover, v.: transit., *recuperare, recipĕre, reparare;* intransit., *refici, convalescĕre, se colligĕre.*

recovery, *recuperatio;* in health, *salus* or *sanitas restituta.*

recreant; see coward.

recreate, *renovare, recreare.*

recreation, *requies, (animi) remissio.*

recrimination, *(mutua) accusatio.*

recruit, subst. *tiro.*

recruit, v. *recreare, reficĕre;* milit., = enrol, *conscribĕre, delectum habĕre.*

recruiting, subst. *delectus (-ūs), conquisitio.*

rectification, *correctio, emendatio.*

rectify, *corrigĕre, emendare.*

rectilinear, *(di)rectus.*

rectitude, *probitas, integritas, honestas.*

recumbent, *(re)supinus, recubans.*

red, *ruber;* of the hair, *rufus, rutilus;* to be —, *rubĕre;* the — Sea, *Sinus Arabicus.*

redden, v.: transit., *rubefacĕre;* intransit., *rubescĕre.*

redeem, *redimĕre, liberare* (= set free).

redeemer, *liberator, vindex.*

redemption, *redemptio, liberatio.*

red-hot, *candens, fervens.*

redness, *rubor.*

redolent, *redolens* (with acc.).

redouble, *ingeminare.*

redound, *redundare;* it —s to my credit, *est mihi honori.*

redress, subst. *satisfactio.*

redress, v. *restituĕre, compensare, sarcire.*

reduce: = to bring, *redigĕre, revocare* — to order, *in integrum reducĕre;* to be —ed to, *redire;* = diminish, *(im)minuĕre, deminuĕre;* = conquer, *vincĕre, expugnare.*

reduction, = diminution, *deminutio.*

redundancy, of style, *redundantio.*

redundant, *supervacaneus.*

re-echo, v.: transit., *referre;* intransit. *resonare.*

reed, *harundo, calamus.*

reedy, *harundineus.*

reef, = rocks, *scopuli, saxa.*

reef, v.: to — sails, *contrahĕre vela.*

reek, *fumare.*

reel, subst., = dance, *saltatio.*

reel, v. *titubare, vacillare.*

reestablish, *restituĕre.*

reestablishment, *restitutio.*

refer: to — a matter, *referre, deferre;* — to, = mention, *mentionem facĕre;* — to, = mean, be speaking of, *dicĕre, spectare.*

referee, *arbiter.*

reference, render by verbs; with — to, *quod attinet ad.*

refill, *replēre.*

refine: of liquids, *liquare;* of metals, *purgare.*

refined, *(ex)politus, urbanus, humanus.*

refinement, *urbanitas, humanitas;* of language, etc., *subtilitas.*

reflect, v.: transit., of light, *repercutĕre;* in gen., = show, *ostendĕre;* this —s credit on you, *hoc tibi est honori;* intransit., = think, *considerare, reputare, cogitare.*

reflection: of light, *repercussus (-ūs),* = image reflected, *imago;* = thought, *cogitatio, consideratio;* = blame, *reprehensio, vituperatio.*

reform, v.: of troops, *restituĕre, reficĕre;* = amend, *corrigĕre, emendare;* intransit., = get better, *se corrigĕre.*

reformation, *correctio, emendatio.*

reformer, *corrector, emendator.*

refract, *infringĕre.*

refractory, *contumax.*

refrain, subst. *carmen.*

refrain, v. *(se) abstinēre, temperare.*

refresh, *recreare, reficĕre.*

refreshment: abstr., *refectio;* = food, *cibus.*

refrigerate, *refrigerare.*

refuge, *perfugium, refugium, asylum;* to seek — at, *confugĕre ad.*

refugee, *fugitivus* (= runaway), *exsul* (= exile).

refund, *reddĕre, dissolvĕre.*

refusal, *recusatio, repudiatio.*

refuse, subst. *purgamentum, faex, quisquiliae (-arum).*

refuse, v.: to — to give, (de)negare; to — to accept, recusare, respuĕre, repudiare; to — battle, pugnam detrectare; to — to do, nolle, recusare.

refutation, refutatio, dissolutio.

refute, refellĕre, redarguĕre, refutare, convincĕre.

regain, recipĕre, reciperare.

regal; see royal.

regale; see entertain, feast.

regalia, insignia (-ium) regia.

regard, subst.: = consideration, respectus (-ūs), cura; = esteem, studium, amor; Cicero sends his —s, Cicero tibi salutem plurimam dicit; see also reference.

regard, v.: = look at, observare, intuĕri; = bear in mind, respicĕre, spectare; = consider, ducĕre, habĕre; = concern, relate to, attinĕre or pertinĕre ad.

regardless, neglegens, incuriosus.

regency, regni administratio, interregnum.

regent, interrex.

regicide, regis caedes (= deed); regis interfector (= person).

regiment, legio; of cavalry, turma (equitum).

region, regio, tractus (-ūs), locus.

register, liber, tabulae (-arum), album.

register, v. perscribĕre, in album referre.

regret, subst. dolor, desiderium (= longing), paenitentia (= repentance).

regret, v.: = grieve, dolĕre; = feel loss of, desiderare, requirĕre; = repent of an action, impers. paenitet; I — having done it, paenitet me fecisse.

regular: = correct, iustus, legitimus, rectus; — troops, milites legionarii; = constant, even, certus, constans, aequabilis. Adv., = correctly, ordine, iuste, legitime, recte; = constantly, evenly, constanter, aequabiliter.

regularity, ordo, constantia, aequabilitas.

regulate, ordinare, dirigĕre, moderari.

regulation, administratio; = an order, iussum, praeceptum, lex.

rehabilitate, restituĕre.

reign, subst., regnum; in your —, te regnante or rege.

reign, v. regnare (as king), imperare (as emperor).

reimburse, (rem homini) reddĕre.

rein, subst. habena, frenum; to pull in the —s, habenas adducĕre; to loosen the —s, frenos dare.

rein, v. frenare.

reinforce, (con)firmare, augĕre.

reinforcement, supplementum, novae copiae (-arum), subsidium.

reinstate, restituĕre.

reiterate, iterare.

reject, reicĕre, repudiare, respuĕre; to — a bill, legem antiquare.

rejection, reiectio, repudiatio repulsa (of a candidate).

rejoice, gaudĕre, laetari; transit., laetificare, exhilarare.

rejoicing, gaudium, laetitia.

rejoin; see return or answer.

relapse, v. recidĕre, relabi.

relate, v. (e)narrare, (com)memorare, referre; — to, = concern, spectare, pertinere, attinere ad.

related, propinquus, cognatus, consanguineus, adfinis (by marriage).

relation, ratio; in — to, ad, pro, erga; —s, familiaritas, necessitudo, amicitia; see also relative and narrative.

relationship, propinquitas, cognatio, adfinitas (by marriage).

relative, subst.; see related.

relative, adj.; render by spectare ad (= relate to) or comparare (= compare).

relax, v.: transit. (re)laxare, remittĕre; intransit., (re)languescĕre, relaxari.

relaxation, (animi) relaxatio, remissio.

relay, subst. equi per viam dispositi.

release, subst. liberatio, missio.

release, v. liberare, (ex)solvĕre, missum facĕre; to — a slave, manu mittĕre.

relent, molliri, iram remittĕre.

relentless, immisericors inexorabilis, crudelis; adv. crudeliter.

relevant, to be, ad rem attinĕre.

reliance, fides, fiducia.

relic, **relics**, reliquiae (-arum).

relict, vidua.

relief: = alleviation, (ad)levatio, sublevatio, levamen(tum); = aid, auxilium, subsidium; in art, asperitas; to engrave in —, caelare.

relieve: = lighten, ease, (ad)levare, sublevare; = take another's place, excipĕre, succedĕre (with dat.).

religion, religio, cultus (-ūs) deorum.

religious: of persons, erga deos pius, sanctus, religiosus; — observances, ritūs (-uum), religiones (-um). Adv. pie, sancte, religiose.

relinquish, relinquĕre.

relish, subst.; = liking, fondness, studium.

relish, v.; see enjoy.

reluctant, invitus, coactus; to be —, nolle.

rely, (con)fidĕre, fidem habĕre, niti; —ing upon, fretus.

remain: = stay, endure, (per)manēre, remanēre, durare, morari (= linger); = be left over, restare, superesse.

remainder, residuum, quod restat.

remaining, reliquus, superstes.

remains, reliquiae (-arum).

remand, subst. comperendinatio.

remand, v., remittĕre; legal, (reum) ampliare, comperendinare.

remark, subst. dictum.

remark, v.; see observe, say.

remarkable, singularis, insignis, mirus; adv. singulariter, insigniter, mire.

remedial, salutaris.

remedy, remedium, medicina, medicamen(tum).

remember, meminisse, reminisci, recordari, memoriā tenēre.

remembrance, memoria, recordatio.

remind, (ad)monēre, commonēre, commonefacĕre.

reminiscence, recordatio; —s, written up, commentarii (-orum).

remiss, neglegens.

remit: = send back, *remittĕre*; = let off (debts, etc.), *remittĕre, condonare.*

remittance, *pecunia.*

remnant; see remainder.

remonstrance, *reclamatio, (ad)monitio.*

remonstrate, *reclamare, reclamitare.*

remorse, *conscientia mala, paenitentia.*

remorseless; see pitiless.

remote, *remotus, disiunctus, longinquus.*

remoteness, *longinquitas.*

removal, *amotio;* to a new home, *(de)migratio.*

remove, v.: transit., *amovēre, sub-movēre, tollĕre, auferre;* = lead away, *abducĕre;* intransit., *se movēre, dis-cedĕre, abire, migrare.*

remunerate, *remunerari.*

remuneration, *remuneratio, praemium.*

rend, *(di)scindĕre, divellere.*

render: = give (back), *reddĕre, referre, tribuĕre;* to — thanks, *gratias agĕre;* = make, cause to be, *facĕre, reddĕre.*

rendezvous, perhaps *locus ad con-veniendum constitutus.*

renegade, *transfuga.*

renew: = make new, *(re)novare, reficĕre;* = begin again, repeat, *renovare, redintegrare, iterare.*

renewal, *renovatio, instauratio.*

renounce, *renuntiare, repudiare se (re) abdicare.*

renovate: see renew.

renown, *fama, gloria, laus.*

renowned, *clarus, inlustris.*

rent, subst., *reditus (-ūs), vectigal merces (-edis).*

renunciation, *abdicatio, repudiatio.*

reopen, *iterum aperire.*

repair, v., *reficĕre, reparare, restituĕre;* see also go.

reparation, *satisfactio.*

repast; see meal.

repay, *reddĕre, reponĕre, solvĕre.*

repayment, *solutio;* or use verb.

repeal, subst. *abrogatio.*

repeal, v. *rescindĕre, tollĕre, abrogare.*

repeat, *iterare, redintegrare.*

repeatedly, *identidem, saepenumero, etiam atque etiam.*

repel, *repellĕre, propulsare, reicĕre.*

repent, impers. *paenitet;* I — of having done that, *paenitet me id fecisse;* I — of the crime, *paenitet me sceleris.*

repentance, *paenitentia.*

repentant, *paenitens.*

repetition, *iteratio, repetitio.*

repine, *(con)queri.*

repining, *querela* (= complaint).

replace: = put back, *reponĕre, restit-uĕre;* to — by another, *substituĕre.*

replenish, *replēre, supplēre.*

replete; see full.

repletion, *satietas.*

reply, subst. *responsum, responsio.*

reply, v. *respondēre;* — by letter, *rescribĕre.*

report, subst.: official, *relatio, renuntia-tio;* = rumour, *fama, rumor;* = loud noise, *fragor, crepitus (-ūs).*

report, v. *(re)nuntiare, referre;* it is —ed, *ferunt, traditur, dicitur.*

repose, subst. *(re)quies, otium.*

repose, v.: transit., *(re)ponĕre;* in-transit., *quiescĕre.*

repository, *thesaurus, receptaculum.*

reprehend, *reprehendĕre.*

reprehensible, *culpā dignus.*

represent: = portray, *exprimĕre, (ef)fingĕre, (de)pingĕre, adumbrare* (= sketch); = state, *dicĕre, monēre;* = play a part, *personam gerĕre, partes agĕre.*

representation, = image, likeness, *imago, effigies.*

representative, subst. *vicarius, pro-curator.*

repress, *comprimĕre, cohibēre.*

reprieve, *supplicium differre.*

reprimand, subst. *reprehensio.*

reprimand, v. *reprehendĕre.*

reprisals, *talio;* to make —s, *par pari respondēre.*

reproach, subst. *exprobratio, obiectatio;* in words, *probrum, convicium.*

reproach, v. *increpitare, obiurgare.*

reproachful, *obiurgatorius.*

reprobate, adj. *perditus, profligatus.*

reproduce, *regignĕre, denuo generare.*

reproof, *vituperatio, reprehensio, obiur-gatio.*

reprove, *vituperare, reprehendĕre.*

reprover, *reprehensor, obiurgator.*

reptile, *bestia serpens.*

republic, *respublica (libera); civitas.*

republican, *vir liberae reipublicae studiosus.*

republican, adj. *popularis;* or genit. *reipublicae liberae.*

repudiate; see reject.

repudiation, *repudiatio.*

repugnance, *repugnantia, odium* (= hatred).

repugnant, *repugnans, diversus, alienus.*

repulse, subst., of a candidate, *repulsa.*

repulse, v. *repellĕre, propulsare, reicĕre.*

repulsive, *odiosus, foedus.*

reputable, *honestus.*

reputation, *fama, opinio;* good —, *existimatio, gloria;* bad —, *infamia.*

repute; to be in good —, *bene audire.*

request, subst. *preces (-um), rogatio;* at my —, *rogatu meo, me rogante.*

request, v. *precari, orare, rogare.*

require: = demand, *poscĕre, postulare, imperare;* = need, *egēre, requirĕre, desiderare.*

requirement, *postulatio;* or use verb.

requisite, adj. *necessarius.*

requisition, *postulatio;* or render by *imperare.*

requite, *compensare, rependĕre.*

rescind, *rescindĕre, abrogare, tollĕre.*

rescript, *responsum, rescriptum.*

rescue, subst. *liberatio;* or use verb.

rescue, v. *liberare, servare, eripĕre.*

research, *eruditio, investigatio.*

resemblance, *similitudo;* bearing a —, *similis.*

resemble, *similem esse* (with genit. or dat.).

resent, *aegre* or *moleste ferre.*

resentful, *iracundus.*

resentment, *ira, stomachus.*

reservation, *exceptio, condicio.*

reserve, subst.: = store, *copia*; milit., —s, *subsidia* (*-orum*); in —, adj. *subsidiarius*; — of manner, *taciturnitas*; without —, *aperte*.

reserve, *retinēre, reponēre*.

reserved, *taciturnus, occultus, tectus*.

reservoir, *lacus* (*-ūs*), *cisterna* (underground).

reside, v. *habitare*. Transf., *residēre, inesse*.

residence: act, *habitatio, mansio, commoratio*; place of —, *domus, domicilium, sedes*.

resident, subst. *habitator, incola*.

residue, *quod reliquum est*.

resign, (*magistratu*) *abire or se abdicare*; in gen., = give up, (*con*)*cedēre, deponēre*; to — oneself, *animum submittēre*.

resignation, *abdicatio*; = resigned attitude, *animus submissus or aequus*.

resin, *resina*.

resist, *resistēre, repugnare, adversari*.

resolute, *fortis, firmus, constans*; adv. *fortiter, firme, firmiter, constanter*.

resolution: = determination, *constantia, firmitudo*; = a purpose, *sententia, consilium, propositum*.

resolve, v.: = break down, *dissolvēre, dissipare*; = determine, *statuēre, constituēre, decernēre*; of a deliberative body, *sciscēre, iubēre*.

resolved, *certus*.

resonant, *resonans*.

resort, subst. = place, *locus*.

resort, v.: to a place, *celebrare, frequentare*; — to, = have recourse to, *confugēre, decurrēre, descendēre*.

resound, *resonare, personare*.

resource, resources, *facultates* (*-um*), *opes* (*-um*); = wealth or power).

respect, subst.: = esteem, *observantia, reverentia*; to pay one's —s to, *salutare*; in all —s, *omnino*; in — of, *ad, de, ab*.

respect, v. *observare*, (*re*)*vereri, colēre*; see also concern, relate.

respectability, *honestas*.

respectable, *honestus*; adv. *honeste, bene*.

respectful, *observans, verecundus*; adv. *verecunde*.

respecting, *de* with abl.

respective, *proprius, suus* (often with *quisque*).

respiration, *respiratio, spiritus* (*-ūs*).

respite; see reprieve.

resplendent, *splendidus*.

respond, response; see answer.

respondent, legal, *reus*.

responsibility, responsible; render by *rationem reddēre* (= give an account); to make oneself —, (*rem*) *praestare, in se recipēre, promittēre*.

responsive, *apertus* (= open), *facilis* (= tractable).

rest, subst.: = repose, (*re*)*quies, otium, tranquillitas*; = remainder, *reliquum, quod restat*.

rest, v., intransit., (*re*)*quiescēre, conquiescēre*; — upon, (*re*) (*in*)*niti*.

restless, *inquietus, turbidus, sollicitus* (= anxious).

restoration, *refectio*; or use verb.

restorative, subst. *medicina*.

restore: = give back, *reddēre*; = reinstate, replace, *restituēre, redintegrare, reficēre*; to — to health, *sanare*.

restrain, *coercēre, continēre, cohibēre, inhibēre*.

restraint, *moderatio, modus*; = hindrance, *impedimentum*.

restrict, *coercēre, circumscribēre*, (*de*)*finire*.

restriction, *modus, finis*; see restraint.

result, subst. *exitus* (*-ūs*), *eventus* (*-ūs*); the — is that, *evenit ut*; without —, *nequiquam*.

result, v. *fieri, evenire, evadēre, oriri*.

resume, *repetēre, recolēre*.

resuscitate, *ab inferis excitare*; see also revive.

retail, *divendēre*.

retailer, *caupo*.

retain, *tenēre, retinēre*, (*con*)*servare*.

retainer: = attendant, *cliens, adsectator, satelles*; = retaining fee, *arrhabo*.

retaliate, *par pari respondēre, ulcisci*.

retaliation, *ultio* (= revenge).

retard, (*re*)*morari*, (*re*)*tardare*.

retire, v. *abire*, (*re*)*cedēre, se removēre*, milit., *pedem referre, se recipēre*.

retired, adj. *secretus, remotus, solitarius*.

retirement, *solitudo, otium*.

retiring; see modest.

retort; see reply.

retrace, *repetēre*; — one's steps, *pedem referre*.

retract, *renuntiare*.

retreat, subst. *reditus* (*-ūs*), *recessus* (*-ūs*), *receptus* (*-ūs*), *fuga*; see also refuge.

retreat, v. *se recipēre, pedem referre, fugēre* (= flee).

retrench, *sumptūs minuēre*.

retribution, *poena*.

retrieve; see recover.

retrograde; render by *retro* (= backwards), or *in deteriorem partem* (= for the worse).

retrogression, *recessus* (*-ūs*), *regressus* (*-ūs*).

retrospect, (*praeteritorum*) *memoria*.

retrospective, render by *retro* (= backwards) or by *praeterita* (*-orum*; = the past).

return, subst.: = journey back, *reditus* (*-ūs*), *regressus* (*-ūs*); = giving back, *remuneratio*; = official declaration, *renuntiatio, professio*.

return, v.: transit., *reddēre, referre*; intransit., *redire, reverti* (= turn back).

returned, adj. *redux*.

reunion, *reconciliatio*; see also assembly.

reunite, *iterum coniungēre; reconciliare*.

reveal, *patefacēre, aperire, evulgare*.

revel, revelry, *comissatio, bachatio*.

revel, v. *comissari*, (*per*)*bacchari*; *luxuriare, exsultare*.

reveller, *comissator*.

revenge, subst. *ultio, vindicta, vindicatio*.

revenge, v. *ulcisci, vindicare*.

revengeful, *ulciscendi cupidus*.

revenue, *vectigal, reditus* (-*ūs*).

reverberate, = resound, *resonare*.

reverberation, *repercussus* (-*ūs*).

revere, (*re*)*verēri, venerari*.

reverence, subst. *reverentia, veneratio, verecundia; religious* —, *religio, pietas erga deos*.

reverend, *venerabilis, reverendus*.

reverent, *verecundus*; in religious sense, *religiosus, pius.* Adv. *verecunde; religiose*.

reverie, *cogitatio*.

reverse, subst.: = change, *conversio*, (*com*)*mutatio, vicissitudo*; = the opposite, *contrarium*; = defeat, *clades*; = hind part, *pars aversa*.

reverse, v. *invertĕre,* (*com*)*mutare, con-vertĕre*.

reversion, legal, *hereditas*.

revert, *redire, revolvi*.

review, subst. *recognitio*; milit., *recen-sio, lustratio*.

review, v. *inspicĕre, contemplari*; milit., *recensēre, lustrare*.

revile, *conviciari, insectari, maledicĕre*.

reviler, *conviciator*.

reviling, subst. *maledictio, probrum, convicium*.

revise, *retractare*; see also correct.

revision, *emendatio*.

revisit, *revisĕre*.

revive, v.: transit., *recreare, excitare*; fig. *redintegrare*; intransit., *revirescĕre, recreari*; fig. *renasci*.

revocation, *revocatio, abrogatio*.

revoke, *abrogare, rescindĕre*.

revolt, subst. *defectio, seditio*; of a conquered people, *rebellio*.

revolt, v. *deficĕre, desciscĕre*; of a conquered people, *rebellare*.

revolting, adj. *taeter, foedus, turpis*.

revolution, *conversio, orbis, ambitus* (-*ūs*); politica l —, *res* (*rerum*, plur.) *novae*.

revolutionary, adj. *seditiosus, turbulentus, novarum rerum cupidus*.

revolutionize, *novare, commutare*.

revolve, *se* (*re*)*volvĕre* or (*re*)*volvi, circumverti*.

revulsion; see disgust.

reward, subst. *praemium, merces*.

reward, v. *remunerari, compensare, praemium dare*.

rewrite, *iterum scribĕre*.

rhetoric, *rhetorica, ars dicendi*.

rhetorical, *rhetoricus, oratorius*; adv. *rhetorice*.

rheumatism, *dolor artuum*.

Rhine, river, *Rhenus*.

Rhone, river, *Rhodanus*.

rhythm, *numerus, modus*.

rhythmical, *numerosus*; adv. *numerose, modulate*.

rib, *costa*; of a ship, *statumen*.

ribald, *obscenus*.

ribbon, *redimiculum, taenia, vitta*.

rich: = possessing wealth, *dives, locuples, opulentus*; to grow —, *ditescĕre*; = costly, sumptuous, *opimus, pretiosus, lautus*; = copious, fertile, *copiosus, abundans, uber, ferax.* Adv. *copiose, abundanter, pretiose*.

riches, *divitiae* (-*arum*, plur.), *opes* (-*um*, plur.); *pecunia* (= money).

richness, *abundantia, ubertas*.

rid, *liberare*; to get — of, — oneself of, *deponĕre, dimittĕre*.

riddance, *liberatio*.

riddle, subst. *aenigma* (-*atis*, n.), *ambages* (-*um*, plur.).

riddled, e.g. with wounds, *confossus*.

ride, v.: on a horse, *equitare, equo* (*equo*) *vehi*; in a chariot, *ire curru*; at anchor, *in ancoris consistĕre*.

rider, *eques*.

ridge, *iugum, montis dorsum*.

ridicule, subst. *ridiculum*.

ridicule, v. *inridēre, deridēre,* (*in*)*ludĕre*.

ridiculous, *ridiculus*; adv. *ridicule*.

riding, *equitatio*; or use verb.

rife; to become —, *percrebescĕre*.

rifle; see plunder.

rift, *rima*.

rig, subst. *habitus* (-*ūs*).

rig, v. *armare, ornare*.

rigging, *armamenta* (-*orum*), *rudentes* (-*um*).

right, subst. *fas, ius* (*iuris*, n.).

right, adj.: opp. to left, *dexter*; — hand, (*manus*) *dextra*; at — angles *ad pares angulos*; morally —, *rectus, iustus, aequus*; = suitable, proper, *rectus, verus*; at the — time, *ad tempus*; you are —, *ita est ut dicis*; it is all —, *bene habet.* Adv. *recte, iuste, iure, merito* (= deservedly) *bene* (=well).

righteous, *probus, aequus, iustus*; adv. *probe, iuste*.

righteousness, *probitas*.

rightful, *legitimus, iustus*; adv. *legitime, iuste, iure*.

rigid, *rigidus, durus*; adv. *rigide, dure*.

rigidity, *rigor*.

rigour, *severitas, duritia*.

rill, *rivus, rivulus*.

rim, *ora*.

rime, *pruina*.

Rimini, *Ariminum*.

rind, *cortex, liber* (= inner bark).

ring, subst. *orbis, anulus*; a — of people, *corona*.

ring, v. *tinnire*; = resound, *resonare*.

ringing, subst. *tinnitus* (-*ūs*).

ringing, adj. *tinnulus, canorus*.

ringleader, *auctor, princeps, dux*.

ringlet, *cincinnus, cirrus*.

rinse, *eluĕre*.

riot, subst. *seditio, motus* (-*ūs*), *tumultus* (-*ūs*).

riot, v. *seditionem movēre*; = revel, *comissari, luxuriare*.

rioter, *homo turbulentus*.

riotous, adj. *turbulentus*; = wild, in gen., *luxuriosus*; — living, *luxuria.* Adv. *turbulente*.

rip, *scindĕre, divellĕre*.

ripe, *maturus, tempestivus*.

ripen: transit., *maturare*; intransit., *maturari, maturescĕre*.

ripeness, *maturitas*.

ripple, subst., *unda*.

rise, subst.: = origin, *ortus* (-*ūs*); to give — to, *parĕre, efficĕre*; = increase, *incrementum*; = rising ground, *clivus, collis.*

rise, v.: = get up, (*ex*)*surgĕre, se erigĕre, se levare*; of sun, stars, etc., *oriri*; = originate, start, (*co*)*oriri, surgĕre, nasci*; = increase, *increbescĕre, crescĕre*; to — in dignity, etc., *crescĕre, emergĕre, ascendĕre*; = rebel, *consurgĕre, cooriri.*

rising, subst. *ortus* (-*ūs*); see also rebellion.

rising, adj.: — ground, *clivus, collis.*

risk, subst. *periculum, discrimen.*

risk, v. *in periculum adducĕre* or *vocare.*

rite, ritual, subst. *ritus* (-*ūs*).

rival, subst. *aemulus* (f. *aemula*), *competitor* (f. *competitrix*); in love, *rivalis.*

rival, adj. *aemulus.*

rival, v. *aemulari, certare* (*cum*).

rivalry, *aemulatio, certamen*; in love, *rivalitas.*

river, *flumen, fluvius, amnis*; adj. *fluviatilis, fluvialis.*

river-bed, *alveus.*

road, *via, iter*; on the —, *in itinere, obiter.*

roadstead, *statio.*

roam, *palari, vagari, errare.*

roaming, *vagus, errabundus.*

roar, subst. *fremitus* (-*ūs*), *mugitus* (-*ūs*).

roar, v. *mugire, fremĕre, vociferari* (of persons).

roast, v. *torrēre, frigĕre.*

roasted, *assus*; — meat, *assum.*

rob, (*ex*)*spoliare, compilare, latrocinari.*

robber, *praedo, latro, fur.*

robbery, *latrocinium, spoliatio, rapina.*

robe, subst.: = *vestis, vestimentum*; woman's —, *palla, stola*; — of state, *trabea.*

robe, v. *vestire.*

robust, *robustus, validus.*

rock, subst. *saxum, rupes, scopulus.*

rock, v.: transit., *agitare, quatĕre*; intransit., *agitari, nutare, vacillare.*

rocky, *scopulosus, saxeus.*

rod, *virga, ferula, decempeda* (for measuring).

roe: of fish, *ova* (-*orum*); = female deer, *caprea.*

roebuck, *capreolus.*

rogue, (*homo*) *nequam* or *scelestus; veterator.*

roguery, *fraus, dolus, nequitia.*

role, *partes* (-*ium*), *persona.*

roll, subst. *volumen*; = list of names, *album.*

roll, v.: transit., *volvĕre, volutare, versare*; intransit., *volvi, volutari.*

roll-call; to answer a —, *ad nomina respondēre.*

roller, *cylindrus, phalangae* (-*arum*).

rolling, adj. *volubilis.*

Roman, *Romanus.*

romance, subst. *fabula.*

romance, v. *fabulari.*

romantic, *fictus, commenticius* (= imaginary); *mirus, novus* (= strange).

Rome, *Roma.*

roof, subst. *tectum, culmen.*

roof, v. (*tecto*) *tegĕre.*

room: = space, *locus, spatium*; to make —, *locum dare*; = apartment, *conclave, cubiculum.*

roomy, *laxus, spatiosus.*

root, subst. *radix, stirps*: by the —s, *radicitus.*

root, v. to —, or become —ed, *radices agĕre, inveterascĕre*; to be —ed, *inhaerēre*; —ed, *inveteratus*; for — up, see uproot.

rope, *funis, restis.*

rose, *rosa.*

rosemary, *ros marinus*

rosy, *roseus.*

rot, subst. *tabes.*

rot, v. *putescĕre, tabescĕre.*

rotate, *volvi, circumagi.*

rotation, *ambitus* (-*ūs*); in —, *ordine.*

rotatory, *versatilis.*

rotten, *putrefactus, putridus.*

rotundity, *figura rotunda.*

rouge, subst. *fucus.*

rouge, v. *fucare.*

rough, *asper, horridus, atrox, hirsutus* (= shaggy). Adv. *aspere.*

roughen, (*ex*)*asperare.*

roughness, *asperitas*; of style, *salebra.*

round, subst. *orbis*; in fighting, *congressus* (-*ūs*).

round, adj. *rotundus, globosus.*

round, adv. and prep., *circum, circa.*

round, v.: = make round, *rotundare, tornare*; = sail round, *flectĕre*; — off, = complete, *concludĕre, absolvĕre.*

roundabout, *devius*; a — way, *ambages* (-*um*), *circuitus* (-*ūs*).

rounded, *teres.*

roundly, *plane, praecise.*

rouse, *excitare.*

rout, subst. *fuga*; see also mob.

rout, v. *fugare, dissipare, fundĕre.*

route; see way, road, journey.

routine, *usus* (-*ūs*), *ordo.*

rove; see wander.

row, subst.: = line, *ordo, versus* (-*ūs*); in a row, (*ex*) *ordine*; see also quarrel and noise.

row, v. *remigare*; to — a boat, *lintrem remis propellĕre*; to — hard, *remis contendĕre.*

royal: = of a king, *regius*, or *regis* (genit); = like a king, *regalis.* Adv. *regie, regaliter.*

royalty, *regnum, regia potestas.*

rub, *terĕre, conterĕre*; to — down, (*de*)*fricare*; to — out, *delēre.*

rubbish, *rudus* (-*eris*, n.), *quisquiliae* (-*arum*).

rubble, *rudus* (-*eris*, n.).

rudder, *gubernaculum, clavus.*

ruddy, *rubicundus.*

rude: = unfinished, *rudis, inconditus*; = ill-mannered, *importunus, inhumanus, insolens.* Adv. *incondite; insolenter.*

rudeness, *inhumanitas, importunitas, insolentia.*

rudimentary, *inchoatus.*

rudiments, *elementa* (-*orum*).

ruffian, *latro, sicarius.*

ruffianly, *nefarius, nequam, sceleratus.*

ruffle, v. *agitare*: to be —d, *inhorrescĕre.* Transf., see irritate.

rug, *stragulum.*
rugged, *asper, horridus, praeruptus.*
ruin, subst.: = collapse, *ruina, exitium, pernicies;* concr., —s, *parietinae (-arum), ruinae (-arum).*
ruin, v. *perdĕre, pessum dare, conficĕre.*
ruinous, *exitiosus;* = in ruins, *ruinosus.*
rule, subst = ruler, *regula, decempeda;* = regulation, *lex, praeceptum;* = government, *imperium, regnum.*
rule, v. *dominari, regĕre, praeesse, imperare;* to — as a king, *regnare;* to — passions, etc., *temperare,* with dat.
ruler, *rector, dominus, rex* (= king); see also rule.
rumble, subst. *murmur.*
rumble, v. *(in)sonare, murmurare.*
ruminate, *ruminare.*
rumination, *ruminatio.*
rumour, subst. *rumor, fama, sermo.*
rumour, v.: it is —ed, *fertur, fama est.*
run, subst. *cursus (-ūs) citatus.*
run, v. *currĕre, cursu ferri;* of fluids, = flow, *fluĕre;* — about, *cursare;* — into, *incurrĕre;* — through, *percurrĕre.*
runaway, *fugitivus.*
runner, *cursor.*
running, of water, *vivus.*
rupture, v. *frangĕre, confringĕre, rumpĕre.*
rural, *rusticus, rusticanus, agrestis.*
ruse, *dolus.*
rush, subst.: the plant, *iuncus, scirpus;* of —es, adj., *iunceus, scirpeus;* = dash, *impetus (-ūs).*
rush, v. *ruĕre, ferri, currĕre.*
russet, *fulvus* (poet).
rust, subst. *robigo, ferrugo* (of iron only).
rust, v. *robiginem trahĕre;* fig. *torpescĕre.*
rustic, *rusticus, agrestis.*
rustle, subst. *crepitus (-ūs), sonus.*
rustle, v. *crepare, crepitare.*
rusty, *robiginosus.*
rut, *orbita.*

S

sable, adj. *niger, ater.*
sabre, *gladius, ensis, acinaces.*
sack, subst.: = bag, *saccus, culeus;* — of a city, *direptio.*
sack, v. *diripĕre, spoliare.*
sacker, *direptor.*
sacred, *sacer, sanctus;* to declare —, *sancire.* Adv. *sancte.*
sacredness, *sanctitas, religio.*
sacrifice, subst. *sacrificium, sacra (-orum);* = victim, *victima, hostia.* Transf., = loss, *iactura.*
sacrifice, v. *sacrificare, immolare.* Transf., = give up, *iacturam facĕre,* with genit.; *dedĕre.*
sacrilege, *sacrilegium.*
sacrilegious, *sacrilegus.*
sad, *maestus, tristis;* = causing sadness, *gravis, acerbus, luctuosus.*
sadden, *dolore adficĕre.*
saddle, subst. *ephippium.*
saddle, (*equum*) *sternĕre.*
sadness, *maestitia, tristitia, dolor.*
safe, subst. *armarium, arca.*

safe, adj.: = protected, *tutus;* feeling —, *securus;* = and sound, *incolumis, salvus;* —, = reliable, *fidus.* Adv. *tuto.*
safe-conduct, *fides (publica).*
safeguard, *propugnaculum, munimentum.*
safety, *salūs (-ūtis), incolumitas.*
saffron, *crocus;* adj., *croceus.*
sagacious, *sagax, prudens* ; adv. *sagaciter, prudenter.*
sagacity, *sagacitas, prudentia.*
sage, subst. and adj. *sapiens.*
sail, subst. *velum;* to set —, *vela dare;* to furl one's —s, *vela contrahĕre.*
sail, v. *navigare;* to — past, *praetervehi;* — out, *enavigare.*
sailing, subst. *navigatio.*
sailor, *nauta.*
saintly, *sanctus.*
sake: for the — of, *causā, gratiā* (with genit.); *pro* (with abl.); *ob* or *propter* (with acc.).
salaam, v. *corpus humi prosternĕre.*
salad, *acetaria (-orum).*
salary, *merces, salarium.*
sale, *venditio, hasta* (= auction); to offer for —, *venum dare* for —, adj., *venalis.*
salesman, *venditor.*
salient, *praecipuus.*
saline, *salsus.*
sallow, *pallidus, luridus.*
sally, *eruptio.*
sally, v. *erumpĕre, eruptionem facĕre.*
salt, subst. *sal.*
salt, adj. *salsus.*
salt, v. *sale condire.*
salt-cellar, *salinum.*
salt-mine, **salt-works**, *salinae (-arum).*
salubrious, *saluber* or *salubris;* adv. *salubriter.*
salutary, *salutaris, utilis.*
salutation, *salutatio.*
salute, *salutare.*
salvation, *salūs (-ūtis).*
salve, *unguentum;* for eyes, *collyrium.*
same, *idem, eadem, idem;* the — as, *idem qui, idem ac (atque);* in the — place, *ibidem;* at the — time, *simul, eodem tempore;* it is all the — to me, *meā nihil interest.*
sample, *exemplum, specimen.*
sanctify, *(con)secrare, dedicare.*
sanction, subst. *confirmatio, auctoritas;* with the — of a person, *hominis iussu.*
sanctity, *sanctitas, sanctimonia.*
sanctuary: = holy place, *templum, delubrum, fanum;* = refuge, *asylum, receptaculum.*
sand, *harena, saburra.*
sandal, *crepida, solea;* wearing —s, *crepidatus, soleatus.*
sandy, *harenosus.*
sane, *sanus, mentis compos.*
sanguinary, *cruentus, sanguineus, sanguinarius.*
sanguine; see hopeful.
sanity, *mens sana.*
sap, subst. *sucus.*
sap, v. *cuniculos agĕre.* Transf. *corrumpĕre, haurire.*

scour, (de)tergēre, (ex)purgare; to — the land, agrum pervagari, percurrēre.
scourge, subst. flagrum, flagellum. Transf., pestis.
scourge, v. virgis caedēre, verberare.
scourging, subst. verbera (-um).
scout, subst. explorator, speculator.
scout, v. explorare, speculari.
scowl, v. frontem contrahēre.
scramble, v.; to — up, scandēre, escendēre.
scrap, frustum, fragmentum.
scrape, subst. angustiae (-arum), difficultas.
scrape, v. radēre: to — off, abradēre; to — together, corradēre.
scraper, (for flesh) strigil, strigilis.
scratch, v. scabēre, radēre; to — out, delēre.
scream, subst. vociferatio, ululatus (-ūs).
scream, v. clamitare, vociferari, ululare.
screech, v. ululare.
screeching, subst. ululatus (-ūs).
screen, umbraculum.
screen, v. (pro)tegēre, tueri, defendēre.
screw, subst. clavus (= nail).
scribe, scriba, librarius.
scroll, volumen.
scrub, (de)tergēre.
scruple, religio, scrupulus.
scruple, v. dubitare.
scrupulous, religiosus; adv. religiose.
scrutinize, (per)scrutari.
scrutiny, (per)scrutatio.
scuffle, rixa, turba.
scull, subst., = oar, remus.
scull, v. remigare.
sculptor, sculptor.
sculpture, subst.: the art, ars fingendi, sculptura; a work of —, opus (-eris, n.) or signum (= statue).
sculpture, v. sculpēre.
scum, spuma. Transf., faex, sentina.
scurrilous, contumeliosus, probrosus, scurrilis; adv. contumeliose.
scutcheon, insigne (or in plur.).
scythe, falx.
sea, subst. mare, pelagus (-i, n.), aequor (poet.), pontus (poet.), altum (= 'the deep'); on the —, of the —, adj. maritimus, marinus.
sea-gull, gavia.
seal, subst.: on a letter, signum; the animal, phoca.
seal, v. (con)signare, obsignare.
sealing-wax, cera.
seam, sutura.
seaman, nauta.
seamanship, ars navigandi.
sear, v. (ad)urēre.
search, subst. investigatio, inquisitio.
search, v.: = a place, investigare, explorare; a person, excutēre; to — for, quaerēre, exquirēre, petēre.
seasickness, nausea.
season, subst., tempus, tempestas, hora; in due —, tempore, ad tempus; for a —, in tempus.
season, v.: = flavour, condire; = harden, durare.
seasonable, tempestivus, opportunus; adv. tempore, tempestive, opportune.

seasoning, condimentum.
seat, subst. sedes, sella; a row of — subsellium; = abode, dwelling, domicilium, sedes.
seat, v. ponēre, conlocare.
seaweed, alga.
secede, abire, decedēre, secedēre.
secession, secessio.
seclude, secludēre, segregare, removēre.
secluded, secretus, seclusus.
seclusion, solitudo.
second, subst., of time, momentum (temporis).
second, adj. secundus, alter; for the — time, iterum. Adv. secundo, deinde.
second, v., = support, adesse, auxilio esse, suffragari (all with dat.).
secondary, secundarius, inferior.
seconder, suasor, auctor.
second-rate, inferior.
secrecy, secretum.
secret, subst. res occulta or arcana; in —, clam.
secret, adj. occultus, arcanus, secretus; = underhand, clandestinus, furtivus. Adv. clam, in occulto, occulte, furtim.
secretary, scriba, servus a manu.
secrete, celare, occultare, abdēre.
sect, secta, schola.
section, pars, portio.
secure, = carefree, securus; = safe, tutus; adv. tuto.
secure, v.: = make safe, munire, confirmare; = arrest, comprehendēre.
security: = safety, salūs (-ūtis, f.); = pledge, pignus (-eris, n.), cautio, vadimonium (= bail).
sedan, lectica.
sedate, sedatus, gravis; adv. sedate, graviter.
sedentary, render by sedēre.
sedge, ulva.
sediment, faex, sedimentum.
sedition, seditio, motus (-ūs).
seditious, seditiosus, turbulentus; adv. seditiose.
seduce, corrumpēre.
seducer, corruptor, corruptela.
seduction, corruptela, stuprum.
sedulity, sedulitas, adsiduitas, diligentia.
sedulous, sedulus, adsiduus, diligens; adv. sedulo, adsidue, diligenter.
see, vidēre, cernēre conspicēre (= catch sight of), aspicēre (= look at), spectare (= watch); to go to —, visēre, visitare; = to understand, vidēre, intellegēre; to — to, curare, providēre.
seed, semen.
seed-time, sementis.
seedling, arbor novella.
seek, quaerēre, exquirēre, (ex)petēre; — to do, = endeavour, conari, tendēre.
seem, vidēri; to — good, vidēri.
seeming, adj. fictus, falsus; adv. in speciem, ut videtur.
seemliness, decorum.
seemly, decorus, honestus; it is —, decet, convenit.
seer, vates.
seethe, v.: transit., fervefacēre, coquēre; intransit., fervēre, aestuare.

...gregate, segregare, seponēre, seiungēre.
...eine, river, Sequana.
..., (ap)prehendēre, rapēre, corripēre, occupare.
...eldom, raro.
select, adj. (e)lectus, delectus, exquisitus.
select, v. legēre, eligēre, deligēre.
selection, electio, res selectae = things chosen, ipse; reflexive, render
self: = emphatic, ipse; reflexive, render by personal pronoun with ipse (third person se or sese); by one —, solus; beside one —, mente captus; in it —, per se.
self-confidence, fiducia sui.
self-confident, confidens.
self-control, imperium sui, continentia, temperantia.
self-evident, manifestus, apertus.
self-indulgence, intemperantia, impotens sui, intemperans.
self-indulgent, ...perans.
self-love, amor sui.
self-satisfied, to be, sibi placēre.
self-seeking, cupiditas.
self-willed, pertinax, pervicax.
selfish, to be, sibi (soli) consulēre.
sell, vendēre, venum dare; to try to —, venditare; to be sold, venire.
seller, venditor, institor, propola.
semblance, species, imago.
senate, senatus (-ūs); = house, curia.
senator, senator.
senatorial, senatorius.
send, mittēre; — away, relegare; — for, arcessēre, accire; — forward, praemittēre; ...
senior, = older, (natu) grandior or maior.
sensation, sensus (-ūs); = excitement, (animi) commotio; to create a —, admirationem movēre.
sensational, mirificus, mirus; adv. mirifice, mire.
sense: = sensation, feeling, intelligence, sensus (-ūs); = understanding, intelligence, iudicium, prudentia; out of one's —s, mentis compos; = meaning (of a word), vis, significatio, sententia.
senseless, = unconscious, (omni) sensu carens; = foolish, rationis expers.
sensible, = intelligent, prudens; adv. prudenter.
sensitive, patibilis, sensilis; mollis.
sensual, libidinosus.
sensuality, libido.
sentence, subst. sententia, enuntiatio, sententia; in court, iudicium, decretum, sententia; v. damnare, condemnare.
sentiment: = opinion, sententia, opinio; = feeling, sensus (-ūs), animus.
sentimental, mollis, effeminatus.
sentimentality, mollitia (animi).
sentry, sentinel, excubitor, vigil; —s, plur., stationes, vigiliae, excubiae.
separable, separabilis, dividuus.
separate, adj. separatus, singuli, disiunctus. Adv. separatim, (adj., = one by one).
separate, v. separare, seiungēre, dividēre.
separation, separatio, disiunctio.

sepulchral, sepulc...
sepulchre, sepulc...
sequel, eventus (-ūs...
sequence, ordo, ser...
serene, serenus, tran...
serf, servus.
serious: of persons, ...things, serius, grav...; Adv. serio, graviter, grav...
seriousness, ...tristitia.
serpent, serpens, anguis...
serried, densus, confertus...
servant, servus, famulus,... ancilla (= maid).
serve, servire, praesto es...famulari, ministrare; to ...apponēre; as a soldier... merēre, militare; —...
service, opera, ministerium; —...ful action, officium; —...militia, stipendia (-orum...
serviceable, utilis, opportunus. Transf...
servile, servilis. abiectus.
servility, adulatio.
servitude, servitus (-ūtis), servit...
session, conventus (-ūs); see company, collect...
set, subst. status, constitutus.
set, adj. status. ...
set, v.: transit. ponēre, statuēre, sepo...locare; — apart, secernēre, praefi... — forth, exponēre; — over, intran... — up, statuēre, constituēre; — of sun, etc., occidēre; to — of sun, etc., occasus (-ū... proficisci.
setting, subst., of sun, etc., conlocare, ac... ...transit., conlocare, compositio...
settle, v.: statuēre, componēre, conficēre; ...stituēre, rationes putare or ...counts, rationes solvēre, expedire; intransit...; — a debt, solvēre, ...(con)sidēre, se conlocare, compositio...
settlement, pactum, of a colony, deductio.
settler, advena, colonus.
seven, septem; — at a time, septie(n)s; — at ...times, septeni; — times, septingenti.
seven hundred, septemdecim (septen-); — times...
seventeen, septemdecim (septen-); — each, septeni deni; — times, septie(n)s decie(n)s.
seventeenth, septimus decimus.
seventh, septimus.
seventieth, septuagesimus.
seventy, septuaginta; — at a time, septuageni; — each, septuageni; — times, septuagie(n)s.
sever, dividēre, dirimēre, disiungēre.
several: = some, nonnulli, (com)plures; = respective, suus, proprius; aliquot; adv. singillatim.
severe, severus, austerus, gravis; adv. severe, austere, —ly wounded, graviter ictus.
severity, severitas, gravitas.
Seville, Hispalis.
sew, suēre.
sewer, cloaca.
sex, sexus (-ūs).
shabbiness, sordes (-ium). Transf., sordidus...
shabby, obsoletus. Transf., ...turpis. Adv. obsolete; sordide.

showy, *speciosus, magnificus.*

shred, *frustum.*

shrew, *oblatratrix, mulier importuna.*

shrewd, *acutus, perspicax, sagax*; adv. *acute, sagaciter.*

shrewdness, *(ingenii) acumen* or *acies*; *sagacitas.*

shriek, subst. *ululatus (-ūs), clamor.*

shriek, v. *ululare, clamare.*

shrill, *acutus, argutus*; adv. *acute.*

shrine, *aedicula, delubrum, sacellum.*

shrink; transit., *contrahēre*; intransit., *se contrahēre*; to — from, *refugēre, abhorrēre.*

shrivelled, *rugosus, vietus* (=shrivelled).

shroud, v. *involvēre, velare, tegēre.*

shrub, *frutex.*

shrubbery, *arbustum.*

shudder, subst. *horror, tremor.*

shudder, v. *horrēre, tremēre.*

shuffle, *claudicare* (= limp), *tergiversari* (= be evasive).

shuffling, subst. *tergiversatio.*

shun, *(de)fugēre, vitare, declinare.*

shutter, *foricula, valvae (-arum, plur.).*

shuttle, *radius.*

shy, adj. *timidus, verecundus*; adv. *timide, verecunde.*

shy, v., of a horse, *consternari.*

shyness, *timor, verecundia, pudor.*

Sicily, *Sicilia.*

sick, *aeger, aegrotus*; to be —, *aegrotare* (= to vomit, *vomēre*); to feel —, *nauseare.* Transf., of boredom, render by *taedet.*

sickle, *falx.*

sickly, *infirmus.*

sickness: = nausea, *vomitus (-ūs), nausea*; = illness, *morbus aegrotatio.*

side, subst. *latus (-eris, n.), pars* (= part or faction); on this —, *hinc*; on this — of, *citra, cis*; on (or from) all —s, *undique*; on both —s, *utrinque.*

side, adj. *obliquus, transversus.*

side, v.: to — with, *(ab homine) stare*; *(homini) favēre* or *studēre.*

sideboard, *abacus.*

sidelong, *obliquus, transversus, limus.*

sideways, *oblique*; or use *obliquus* as adj.

siege, *oppugnatio* (= attack), *obsidio* (= blockade).

sieve, *cribrum.*

sift, *cribrare.* Transf., *investigare.*

sigh, subst. *suspirium.*

sigh, v. *suspirare, suspiria ducēre.*

sight, subst. *visus (-ūs), aspectus (-ūs)*; to catch — of, *conspicēre, conspicari*; = view, range of —, *conspectus (-ūs)*; = thing seen, *species, facies, spectaculum.*

sign, subst. *signum, indicium, vestigium* (= foot-mark), *insigne* (= badge); a good —, *omen faustum*; a bad —, *omen sinistrum.*

sign, v.; to — a document, *(con)signare, subscribēre*; see also signal.

signal, subst. *signum*; to give a —, *signum dare.*

signal, adj. *insignis, maximus, egregius*; adv. *insigniter, egregie.*

signal, v. *significare, signum dare.*

signalize, v. *insignire.*

signature, *nomen (subscriptum).*

signet, *signum* (= seal).

significance, *significatio, vis.*

significant: see expressive.

signify, *significare*; of words, *valēre.*

silence, subst. *silentium*; to keep —, *tacēre, silēre.*

silence, v. *in silentium redigēre, comprimēre, confutare.*

silent, *silens, tacitus, mutus*; to be —, *silēre* (= make no noise), *tacēre* (=not speak). Adv. *tacite, silentio.*

silk, *bombyx, vestis serica.*

silken, *sericus bombycinus.*

silk-worm, *bombyx.*

sill, *limen inferum.*

silliness, *stultitia, fatuitas, infacetiae (-arum).*

silly, *stultus, fatuus, infacetus.*

silt, subst. *limus.*

silver, subst. *argentum*; adorned with —, *argentatus.*

silver, **silvery**, adj. *argenteus*; — mine, *argenti metalla (-orum).*

silver, **silvery**, adj. *argenteus.*

silver, v. *argento inducēre.*

similar, *similis, par*; adv. *similiter, pariter.*

similarity, *similitudo.*

simile, *similitudo, translatio.*

similitude, *similitudo.*

simmer, *fervescēre, lente fervēre.*

simper, v. *subridēre, inepte ridēre.*

simple, *simplex*; *sincerus* (= guileless), *inconditus* (= artless), *ineptus* (= silly); adv. *simpliciter.*

simplicity, *simplicitas, natura simplex*; *stultitia* (= folly).

simplify, *simplicem reddēre.*

simulate, *simulare.*

simulation, *simulatio.*

simultaneously, *eodem tempore, simul, una.*

sin, subst. *peccatum, delictum, nefas.*

sin, v. *peccare, delinquēre.*

since, adv. *postea, abhinc*; long —, *iamdudum, iampridem.*

since, prep. *ex, ab, post*; — the foundation of the city, *post urbem conditam.*

since, conj.: of time, *cum, postquam, ex quo (tempore)*; causal, *cum, quandoquidem, quia, quoniam.*

sincere, *sincerus, simplex, candidus, verus*; adv. *sincere, ex animo, simpliciter.*

sincerity, *animus sincerus, veritas, simplicitas.*

sinew, *nervus.*

sinewy, *nervosus.*

sinful, *impius, improbus, pravus, malus.*

sing, *canere, cantare, modulari.*

singe, *amburēre, adurēre.*

singer, *cantor, cantator.*

singing, subst. *cantus (-ūs), concentus (-ūs).*

single, adj. *unus, solus, unicus, singularis*; = unmarried, *caelebs*; not a — one, *ne unus quidem.* Adv. *singillatim, viritim*; or adj. *singuli* (= one by one).

singular: opp. to plural, *singularis*; = outstanding, *singularis, unicus,*

egregius, maximus; = strange, mirus, mirabilis. Adv. singulariter, unice, egregie, maxime, mire, mirabiliter.

sinister, sinister; infaustus (= unlucky), pravus (= wrong).

sink, v.: transit., (sub)mergĕre, demergĕre, deprimĕre; intransit. (con)sidĕre, desidĕre, submergi, demergi; of prices, courage, etc., cadĕre.

sinuous, sinuosus.

sip, v. (primis labris) degustare.

sir, in addresses, bone vir, vir optime.

sire, pater, genitor.

sister, soror, germana.

sit, v.: transit., to — a horse, in equo haerĕre; intransit., sedēre; to — down, considĕre, adsidĕre; of a court, habēri.

site, situs (-ūs).

sitting, subst. sessio, consessus (-ūs).

situated, situs, positus, conlocatus.

situation: situs (-ūs), locus; = state of affairs, (rerum) status (-ūs); = office, munus (-eris, n.).

six, sex; — at a time, — each, seni; — times, sexie(n)s.

sixteen, sedecim; — at a time, — each, seni deni; — times, sedecie(n)s.

sixteenth, sextus decimus.

sixth, sextus; for the — time, sextum.

sixtieth, sexagesimus.

sixty, sexaginta; — at a time, — each, sexageni; — times sexagie(n)s.

size: magnitudo, amplitudo; = glue, gluten.

skeleton, ossa (-ium, n.), ossium compages.

sketch, subst. adumbratio, descriptio.

sketch, v. describĕre, designare, adumbrare.

skiff, scapha, cymba, navicula.

skilful, sollers, peritus, callidus; adv. sollerter, perite, callide.

skill, sollertia, peritia, ars, calliditas.

skim, despumare, spumam eximĕre; to — over a thing, perstringĕre, percurrĕre, transcurrĕre.

skin, subst. cutis, pellis, membrana (thin).

skin, v. pellem or corium detrahĕre.

skip, salire (= leap); to — for joy, exsultare; = pass over, transilire, praeterire.

skipper, navis magister.

skirmish, subst. proelium.

skirmisher, veles.

skirt, v. tangĕre; — the coast, oram legĕre.

skittish, protervus; to be —, lascivire; adv. proterve.

skittishness, protervitas, lascivia.

skulk, latēre, delitescĕre.

skull, caput.

sky, caelum; under the open —, sub divo.

slack: = loose, laxus, remissus; = careless, remissus, segnis, neglegens; adv. laxe, neglegenter.

slacken, v.: transit., (re)laxare, remittĕre; intransit., laxari, remitti.

slackness, remissio, neglegentia.

slake, v., of thirst, restinguĕre, exstinguĕre, explēre.

slander, subst. calumnia, (falsa) criminatio.

slander, v. calumniari, criminari, obtrectare.

slanderer, obtrectator.

slanderous, maledicus, famosus; adv. falso, per calumniam.

slanting, obliquus, transversus.

slash, v. caedĕre, incidĕre; see cut.

slate: for writing, tabula; = tile, tegula.

slaughter, subst. caedes, occidio, strages.

slaughterer, lanius.

slaughterhouse, laniena.

slave, subst. servus, ancilla (female), verna (home-born), famulus; fellow——, conservus; of a —, adj., servilis; to be a —, servire.

slave-dealer, venalicius, mango.

slavery, servitūs (-ūtis), servitium.

slavish, servilis; adv. serviliter.

slay, interficĕre, occidĕre, necare.

slayer, interfector; of a man, homicida; of a close relative, parricida.

sledge, trahea.

sleek, lēvis, nitidus (= shining); to be —, nitēre.

sleep, subst. somnus, sopor; want of —, vigilia.

sleep, v. dormire.

sleepiness, veternus, somni cupido.

sleepless, insomnis, vigilans.

sleeplessness, insomia, vigilia.

sleepy, semisomnus, somniculosus, somno gravis.

sleet, nix grandine mixta.

sleeves, manicae (-arum).

slender, tenuis, gracilis, exilis.

slenderness, tenuitas, gracilitas.

slice, v. concidĕre, secare.

slide, v. labi.

slight, adj. levis, tenuis, exiguus.

slight, v. neglegĕre, contemnĕre.

slim, exilis.

slime, limus.

slimy, limosus.

sling, subst.: the weapon, funda; for the arm, fascia.

sling, v. (fundā) mittĕre, torquēre.

slink, v.: to — away, sese subducĕre.

slip, subst. lapsus (-ūs), culpa (= fault), error (= mistake); of a plant, surculus.

slip, v. labi; — away, se subducĕre, elabi; to let —, amittĕre, omittĕre.

slipper, crepida, solea.

slippery, lubricus.

slit, subst. rima.

slit, v. incidĕre, findĕre, scindĕre.

slope, subst. clivus, fastigium; upward, acclivitas; downward, declivitas.

slope, v. vergĕre.

sloping, acclivis, declivis, pronus.

sloth, inertia, segnitia, desidia, ignavia.

slothful, iners, segnis, ignavus; adv. segniter, ignave.

slough, palūs (-ūdis); of a snake, vernatio, exuviae (-arum).

slovenliness, sordes (-ium), neglegentia.

slovenly, sordidus, discinctus, neglegens.

slow, tardus, lentus; adv. tarde, lente, sensim (= gradually).

slowness, tarditas, segnitas, pigritia.

slug, *limax.*
sluggish, *segnis, piger, ignavus;* adv. *segniter, ignave.*
sluggishness, *pigritia, ignavia, inertia.*
sluice, *emissarium.*
slumber; see **sleep**.
slur; see **disgrace**.
slur over, v. *extenuare.*
sly, *vafer, subdolus;* adv. *vafre, subdole.*
slyness, *dolus, astutia.*
smack, subst.: = flavour, *sapor, gustus (-ūs);* = blow, *alapa;* = small ship, *lenunculus;* fishing- —, *horia.*
smack, v.; to — of, *sapĕre, (red)olēre.*
small, *parvus, parvulus, exiguus, minutus;* a — mind, *animus pusillus;* so —, *tantulus;* how —? *quantulus?*
smallness, *parvitas, exiguitas.*
smart, subst. *dolor, cruciatus (-ūs).*
smart, v. = to feel pain, *dolere, plecti.*
smart, adj.: = active, *acer, alacer;* = witty, *salsus;* = elegant, *lautus, mundus, nitidus.*
smear, v. *(in)linĕre, oblinĕre.*
smell, subst. *odor, odoratus (-ūs);* = the sense), to have a bad —, *male olēre.*
smell, v.: = perceive a —, *olfacĕre;* = give off a smell, *olēre;* to — of, *redolēre.*
smelt, *fundĕre, coquĕre.*
smile, subst. *risus (-ūs);* with a —, *subridens.*
smile, v. *(sub)ridēre, renidēre.*
smite, v. *ferire, percutĕre.*
smith, *faber;* black—, *faber ferrarius.*
smithy, *officina, fabrica.*
smoke, subst. *fumus.*
smoke, v. *fumare.*
smoky, *fumosus.*
smooth, adj. *levis, teres;* of style, *lenis;* of manner, *blandus;* of temper, *aequus.* Adv. *leniter.*
smoothness, *levitas, aequabilitas.*
smother, *suffocare, animam intercludĕre.* Transf., *opprimĕre, comprimĕre.*
smuts, *fuligo.*
snail, *cochlea.*
snake, *anguis, serpens, vipera.*
snaky, *vipereus, anguineus.*
snap, v.: transit., = break, *frangĕre;* — the fingers, *digitis concrepare;* — up, *adripĕre, corripĕre;* intransit., *dissilire, frangi.*
snappish, *morosus, difficilis, mordax.*
snare, subst. *laqueus, plaga, insidiae (-arum).*
snare, v. *inlaqueare.*
snarl, subst. *gannitus (-ūs).*
snarl, v. *(og)gannire, (sub)ringi.*
snatch, *rapĕre, corripĕre;* — at, *captare;* — away, *eripĕre, avellĕre.*
sneak, = go stealthily, *(cor)repĕre;* — in, *inrepĕre;* — away, *(furtim) se subducĕre.*
sneer, subst., *rhonchus.*
sneer, v. *deridēre, inridēre.*
sneeze, *sternuĕre.*
sneezing, *sternumentum.*
snore, *stertĕre.*
snort, v. *fremĕre.*
snout, *rostrum.*
snow, subst. *nix.*
snow, v.: it —s, *ningit.*

snowy, *nivosus, niveus.*
snub; see **rebuke**.
snub-nosed, *silus, simus.*
snuff, of a candle, *fungus.*
so: adv., = thus, *sic, ita;* = to such an extent, *sic, ita, adeo, tam;* so . . . as, *tam . . . quam;* so that (final), *ut;* so great, *tantus;* so many, *tot;* so many times, *totie(n)s;* so far as, *quantum;* so long as, *dum (modo),* with subjunc.; as conj., so, and so, *itaque, ergo, igitur.*
soak, *madefacĕre;* — up, *bibĕre;* — through, *permanare.*
soap, *sapo.*
soar, *sublime ferri, subvolare.*
sob, subst. *singultus (-ūs).*
sob, v. *singultare.*
sober, *sobrius, temperans, temperatus;* adv. *sobrie, temperate.*
sobriety, *sobrietas, temperantia.*
sociable, *comis, facilis, socialis;* adv. *socialiter.*
social, *communis, civilis;* — life, *vitae societas, vita communis.*
socialism, *bona communia habēre.*
society, *homines (-um), hominum conventus (-ūs);* more limited, *societas, sodalitas, conlegium, factio* (political); the — of an individual, *convictus (-ūs), consuetudo.*
sock; see **stocking**.
socket, *cavum.*
sod, *caespes.*
soda, *nitrum.*
sodden, *madidus.*
sofa, *lectulus, grabatus.*
soft, *mollis, tener, lenis, effeminatus;* adv. *molliter, leniter.*
soften, v.: transit., *(e)mollire, mitigare, lenire;* intransit., *molliri, mitescĕre.*
softness, *mollitia, mollities.*
soil, subst. *solum, terra, humus.*
soil, v. *inquinare, polluĕre, maculare.*
sojourn, subst. *commoratio, mansio.*
sojourn, v. *(com)morari, manēre.*
sojourner, *hospes, peregrinus, advena.*
solace, subst. *solatium, consolatio.*
solace, v. *(con)solari.*
solar, render by genit. *solis.*
soldier, *miles;* fellow —, *commilito;* foot —, *pedes;* horse —, *eques.*
soldierly, *militaris.*
soldiery, *milites (-um),* or coll. sing. *miles.*
sole, subst.: of the foot, *solum, planta;* the fish, *solea.*
sole, adj. *solus, unus, unicus;* adv. *solum, tantum.*
solemn, *sanctus, religiosus;* see also **serious**. Adv. *sancte, graviter.*
solemnization, *celebratio.*
solemnize, *celebrare.*
solicit: = ask for, *petĕre, poscĕre, captare;* = incite, *sollicitare.*
solicitation, *preces (-um).*
solicitous, *sollicitus, anxius;* adv. *sollicite, anxie.*
solicitude, *sollicitudo, cura, anxietas.*
solid, *solidus, stabilis, firmus;* adv. *firme, firmiter.*
solidity, *soliditas.*

solitary, *solus, solitarius;* of places, *desertus.*

solitude, *solitudo.*

solstice: the summer —, *solstitium;* winter —, *bruma.*

solution, *(dis)solutio;* of problems, *explicatio.*

solve, *(dis)solvĕre, expedire, explicare.*

solvent; to be —, *solvendo esse.*

some, somebody, someone, *aliquis -quid,* pron., and *aliqui -qua -quod,* adj.; *quis, quid,* pron., and *qui, qua, quod,* adj. (indef., usually after *si, nisi, ne* or *num*); *nescioquis,* pron., and *nescioqui,* adj.; *nonnullus* (esp. plur., = — few); *aliquot* (plur., indecl.); distributively, — . . . others, *alii . . . alii;* to — degree, *aliquantum;* at — time, *aliquando.*

somehow, *nescio quomodo, nescio quo pacto.*

something, *aliquid, nonnihil.*

sometimes, *aliquando, nonnunquam, interdum.*

somewhat, *aliquantum, aliquantulum.*

somewhere, *alicubi.*

son, *filius, natus;* — -in-law, *gener;* step- —, *privignus.*

song, *carmen, cantus (-ūs), canticum.*

sonorous, *canorus, clarus;* adv. *canore, clare.*

soon, *mox, brevi (tempore);* too —, *ante tempus;* as — as possible, *quam primum;* as — as, *simul ac.*

sooner, *maturius;* = for preference, *potius, libentius.*

soot, *fuligo.*

soothe, *mulcĕre, lenire, placare, sedare.*

soothing, *blandus.*

soothsayer, *haruspex, hariolus, auspex.*

soothsaying, subst. *haruspicina, auspicium.*

sop, *frustum, offa (panis).*

sophism, sophistry, *captio, sophisma.*

sophistical, *captiosus.*

soporific, adj. *soporifer, soporus.*

sorcerer, *veneficus.*

sorceress, *venefica, maga, saga.*

sorcery, *ars magica.*

sordid, *sordidus, abiectus;* adv. *sordide.*

sordidness, *sordes (-ium).*

sore, subst. *ulcus (-eris,* n.).

sore, *adj.,* = painful, *gravis, acerbus;* adv. *graviter.*

sorrow, subst. *dolor, maestitia, tristitia, luctus (-ūs).*

sorrow, v. *dolēre, maerēre, lugēre.*

sorrowful, *tristis, maestus, lugubris;* adv. *maeste.*

sorry; see sorrowful; I am —, = I regret, *me paenitet;* = I pity, *me miseret.*

sort, subst., = kind, *genus;* of what —? *qualis? cuiusmodi?* of that —, *talis, eiusmodi;* he is not the — of man to, *non is est qui,* with subjunc.

sort, v. *digerĕre.*

sortie, *excursio, eruptio;* to make a —, *erumpĕre.*

sot, *potator, homo ebriosus.*

soul, *anima, animus* (rational or emotional); not a —, *nemo, ne unus quidem.*

sound, subst. *sonus, sonitus (-ūs), strepitus (-ūs).*

sound, adj. *sanus, integer;* safe and —, *incolumis, salvus;* of sleep, *altus, artus;* of arguments, *gravis.* Adv., of sleep, *arte;* of beating, etc., *graviter.*

soundness, *sanitas, integritas;* of arguments, *gravitas.*

sour, adj. *acerbus, amarus.*

sour, v. *exacerbare.*

source, *fons, caput, origo, principium.*

sourness, *acerbitas, amaritudo.*

south, subst. *meridies, regio meridiana.*

south, southern, adj. *meridianus, australis;* — wind, *auster;* — -west wind, *Africus.*

southwards, *in* or *ad meridiem.*

sovereign, subst. *rex, dominus, princeps.*

sovereign, adj. *sui iuris;* — remedy, *remedium efficacissimum.*

sovereignty, *summa imperii, (summum) imperium, dominatio, regnum.*

sow, subst. *sus.*

sow, v. *serĕre, semen spargĕre.*

sower, *sator.*

sowing, subst. *satio, satus (-ūs).*

space, *spatium, locus.*

spacious, *amplus.*

spaciousness, *amplitudo, laxitas.*

spade, *pala.*

Spain, *Hispania.*

span, subst., as measure, *palmus;* the — of life, *vitae summa.*

span, v.; see measure; of bridges, *iungĕre.*

spangled, *distinctus.*

Spanish, *Hispanus, Hispanicus, Hispaniensis.*

spar, subst. *asser, longurius.*

spare, v. *parcĕre* (with dat.).

sparing, *parcus;* adv. *parce.*

spark, *scintilla, igniculus.*

sparkle, v. *scintillare, fulgĕre, nitĕre.*

sparrow, *passer.*

spatter, *spargĕre, aspergĕre.*

speak, *dicĕre, loqui, fari;* — out, — up, *eloqui;* — to, *adfari, appellare, adloqui;* — together, *conloqui.*

speaker, *orator, is qui dicit.*

spear, subst. *hasta.*

spear, v. *hastā transfigĕre.*

special, *praecipuus, proprius, peculiaris;* adv. *praecipue, imprimis, praesertim.*

species, *genus (-eris,* n.), *species.*

specific, adj.: = peculiar, *proprius, peculiaris;* = explicit, *disertus;* adv. *diserte.*

specify, *denotare, enumerare.*

specimen, *specimen, documentum exemplum.*

specious, *speciosus.*

speck, *macula.*

speckled, *maculis distinctus, maculatus.*

spectacle, *spectaculum.*

spectator, *spectator, is qui spectat.*

spectre; see ghost.

speculate, = consider, *cogitare, quaerĕre.*

speculation: = thought, *cogitatio;* scientific —, *rerum contemplatio;* = guess, *coniectura.*

speculative, = conjectural, *coniecturalis.*

speech, *oratio*; a — before the people, *contio*; to deliver a —, *orationem* (or *contionem*) *habēre*.

speechless; see dumb.

speed, subst. *celeritas, velocitas*.

speed, v.: transit., *maturare*; ι = make prosperous, *fortunare*; intransit., = hasten, *properare, festinare*.

speedy, *citus, celer, velox*; adv. *cito, celeriter, velociter*.

spell, subst. *carmen*.

spellbound, *defixus, stupens, stupefactus*.

spend: of money, *insumĕre*; of time, *agĕre, degĕre, consumĕre*.

spendthrift, *nepos, homo prodigus*.

sphere, *sphaera, globus*; = field of activity, *provincia*.

spherical, *globosus*.

spice, *condimentum*.

spicy, *conditus*; fig. *salsus*.

spider, *aranea*; —'s web, *aranea*.

spike, *clavus, cuspis*.

spikenard, *nardus*.

spill, *effundĕre*.

spin, *nēre*; — round, transit., *versare, circumagĕre*; intransit., use pass.; to — out, = prolong, *ducĕre*.

spindle, *fusus*.

spine, *spina*.

spinster, *virgo, innupta*.

spiral, adj. *tortuosus*.

spire, *turris*.

spirit: = character, *animus, ingenium, indoles, natura*; = animation, courage, *animus, spiritus (-ūs), ferocia*; a disembodied —, *anima*, plur. *manes (-ium)*; = intention, meaning, *consilium, sententia*.

spirited, *animosus, ferox, acer*.

spiritless, *ignavus*.

spiritual, render by genit., *animi* or *ingenii*.

spit, subst. *veru*.

spit, v. *spuĕre*; — out, *respuĕre*.

spite, subst. *malignitas, malevolentia, invidia, odium*.

spite, v.; see vex, annoy.

spiteful, *malignus, malevolus*; adv. *maligne*.

splash, v. transit., *aspergĕre*.

splendid, *splendidus, egregius, (prae)clarus*; adv. *splendide, (prae)clare*.

splendour, *splendor*; *apparatus (-ūs,* = pomp).

splinter, *fragmentum*.

split, subst. *fissura, scissura, rima*.

split, v.: transit., *(dif)findĕre, scindĕre*; intransit., *(dif)findi, dissilire*.

spoil, subst. *praeda*; —s of war, *spolia (-orum,* plur.).

spoil, v.: — plunder, *(ex)spoliare*; = to injure, mar, *corrumpĕre, perdĕre, vitiare*.

spoiler, *spoliator*.

spoiling, spoliation, *spoliatio*.

spoke, *radius*.

spondee, *spondeus*.

sponge, subst. *spongia*.

sponsor, of measures, etc., *auctor*.

spontaneous, *voluntarius*; adv. *(sua) sponte, ultro*.

spoon, *cocleare*.

sport, subst. *ludus, lusus (-ūs)*; = hunting, *venatio*; = mockery, *ludibrium, inrisio*.

sport, v. *ludĕre, lascivire*.

sportive, adj. *lascivus, iocosus, festivus*; adv. *per iocum, iocose*.

sportiveness, *lascivia, iocus*.

sportsman, *venator*.

spot, subst.: = mark, stain, *macula, nota*; = place, *locus*.

spot, v. *notare, maculare*.

spotless, *sine maculis, purus*.

spotted, *maculosus, maculis distinctus*.

spouse, *coniunx*.

spray, subst.: liquid, *aspergo*; on a tree, *virgula*.

spread, v.: transit. *(ex)pandĕre, explicare, extendĕre, spargĕre (= scatter), (di)vulgare (= publish)*; intransit., render by pass.

sprig, *surculus, virgula*.

sprightliness, *alacritas, facetiae (-arum,* = pleasantries).

sprightly, *alacer; facetus (= humorous)*.

spring, subst. *fons*; fig., *origo, principium*; the season, *ver, tempus vernum*.

spring, v. = leap, *salire*; to — from, *(ex re) nasci, (ex)oriri*; to — up, of plants, *crescĕre*; of winds, *surgĕre*.

spring-tide, *aestus (-ūs) maximus*.

sprinkle, *spargĕre, aspergĕre, conspergĕre*.

sprite, *faunus, nympha*.

sprout, v. *pullulare, germinare*.

spruce, adj. *comptus, bellus, nitidus, elegans*; adv. *belle, nitide, eleganter*.

spur, subst. *calcar*.

spur, v.: to — a horse, *equo calcaria subdĕre*.

spurious, *adulterinus, falsus*.

spurn, *fastidire, aspernari, repudiare*.

spy, subst. *explorator, speculator*.

spy, v. *explorare, speculari*.

squabble, subst. *rixa, altercatio, iurgium*.

squabble, v. *rixari*.

squadron, of cavalry, *(equitum) turma* or *ala*; of ships, *classis*.

squalid, *sordidus, spurcus*; adv. *sordide*.

squall, subst. *procella*; an infant's, *vagitus (-ūs)*.

squall, v. *vagire*.

squalor, *sordes (-ium)*.

squander, *profundĕre, perdĕre, dissipare*.

squanderer, *nepos*.

square, subst. *quadratum, quadra*.

square, adj. *quadratus*.

square, v. *quadrare*.

squash, v. *conterĕre, contundĕre*.

squat, v. *subsidĕre, considĕre*.

squeak, subst. *stridor*.

squeak, v. *stridĕre*.

squeamish, *fastidiosus, delicatus*.

squeamishness, *fastidium*.

squeeze, subst. *compressio*.

squeeze, v. *premĕre, comprimĕre*; — out, *exprimĕre*.

squint, v. *limis* or *perversis oculis esse*; one who —s, *strabo*.

squirrel, *sciurus*.

stab, v. *confodĕre*.

stability, *stabilitas, firmitas, constantia*.

stable, subst. *stabulum*.

stable, adj. *stabilis, firmus, constans*.

stable, v. *stabulare*.

stack, subst. *cumulus, acervus, strues.*
stack, v. *cumulare.*
staff: = stick, *baculum, scipio*; a herald's —, *caduceus*; = assistants, military, *legati (-orum)*, civil, *adiutores.*
stag, *cervus.*
stage, *proscaenium, scaena*; of the —, *scaenicus*; = degree, *gradus (-ūs).*
stagger, v. *titubare, vacillare.*
stagnant, *stagnans, piger, lentus.*
stagnate, *stagnare.* Transf., *hebescĕre, languēre.*
staid; see sober.
stain, subst. *macula, labes, nota.*
stain, v. *maculare, foedare, polluĕre.*
stainless, *purus, integer.*
stair, *gradus (-ūs)*; —case, *scalae (-arum).*
stake, subst.: = post, *palus, stipes, sudes*; = pledge, *pignus (-oris, n.)*; to be at —, *agi, in discrimine esse.*
stake, v. *(de)ponĕre.*
stale, subst. *culmus, caulis, calamus.*
stalk, v.; = strut, *incedĕre.*
stall, subst. *stabulum*; = shop, *taberna.*
stall, v. *stabulare.*
stammer, v. *balbutire, lingua haesitare.*
stammering, adj. *balbus.*
stamp, subst. *nota, signum, imago (impressa)*; of the foot, *pedis supplosio.*
stamp, v. *signare, notare*; with the foot, *pedem supplodĕre*; to — underfoot, *conculcare.*
stand, subst.: to come to a —, *consistĕre, subsistĕre*; to make a — against, *resistĕre* (with dat.).
stand, v. (1) = be upright, *stare, consistĕre*; to — by, *adesse*; — fast, *consistĕre, subsistĕre, restare*; — for office, *petĕre*; stand in the way, *obstare*; — out, *eminēre, extare*; — up, *surgĕre.* (2) = set upright, place, *statuĕre, constituĕre.* (3) = tolerate, *tolerare, perferre, sustinēre.*
standard: = flag, *vexillum, signum*; = measure, *regula, norma.*
standard-bearer, *vexillarius, signifer.*
standing, subst. *condicio, gradus (-ūs) locus*; of long —, *vetus.*
standstill: to be at a —, *haerēre.*
star, *stella, astrum.* Transf., *lumen.*
stare, subst. *obtutus (-ūs).*
stare, v. *spectare, intuēri*; in astonishment, *stupēre.*
stark, *rigidus.*
starling, *sturnus.*
start, subst.: = sudden movement, *saltus (-ūs)*; = beginning, *initium, principium*; = setting out, *profectio.*
start, v.: transit., = institutĕre, aggredi, incipĕre*; intransit., = move suddenly, *expavescĕre*; to — up, *exsilire*; = begin, *incipĕre, (ex)ordiri*; = set out, *proficisci.*
startle; see frighten.
startling, *terribilis*; = strange, *mirus.*
starve, v.: transit., *fame necare*; intransit., *fame confici* or *perire.*
state, subst.: = condition, *status (-ūs), condicio, locus*; polit., *respublica, civitas*; = grandeur, *apparatus (-ūs), magnificentia.*

state, adj. *publicus.*
state, v. *adfirmare, adseverare, dicĕre.*
stately, *lautus, magnificus.*
statesman, *vir reipublicae peritus.*
statesmanship, *ars reipublicae regendae*
station, subst. see position; v. see place, set.
stationary, *immobilis, immotus*; — camp, *(castra) stativa (-orum).*
statue, *signum, statua, effigies.*
stature, *statura.*
statute, *lex.*
staunch, adj. *firmus, certus, fidus.*
staunch, v. *(sanguinem) sistĕre* or *cohibēre.*
stay, subst.: = prop, *adminiculum*; = sojourn, *mansio, commoratio.*
stay, v.: transit., = prop, *fulcire*; = stop, *(de)morari, detinēre, cohibēre*; intransit., *(com)morari, manēre.*
stead: in— of, *pro*, with abl.: *loco* or *in vicem*, with genit.
steadiness, *stabilitas, firmitas, constantia.*
steady, *stabilis, firmus, constans*; adv. *firme, firmiter, constanter.*
steal, v.: transit., *furari, surripĕre*; intransit., = go stealthily, *subrepĕre*; — in, *inrepĕre*; — away, *se subducĕre.*
stealthy, *furtivus, clandestinus*; adv. *furtim, clam.*
steam, subst. *(aquae) vapor, nidor fumus.*
steam, v. *vaporare.*
steed, *equus.*
steel, subst. *chalybs*; = sword, *ferrum*
steel, v.: to — oneself, *obdurescĕre.*
steep, adj. *praeruptus, praeceps, arduus*
steep, v. *madefacĕre, imbuĕre.*
steer, subst. *iuvencus.*
steer, v. *gubernare, regĕre.*
steering, subst. *gubernatio.*
steersman, *gubernator, rector.*
stem, subst.: of a tree, *stirps, truncus*; of a plant, *caulis, calamus*; = race, *stirps, genus (-eris, n.).*
stem, v. = check, *cohibēre, coercēre.*
step, subst.: = stair, *gradus (-ūs)*; = pace, *gradus, passus, gressus* (all *-ūs)*; — by —, *gradatim, pedetentim*; = plan, measure, *ratio, consilium.*
step, v. *gradi*; — in, *ingredi*; — forwards, *progredi.*
step-brother, *filius vitrici,* or *novercae.*
step-daughter, *privigna.*
step-father, *vitricus.*
step-mother, *noverca.*
step-sister, *filia vitrici* or *novercae.*
step-son, *privignus.*
sterile, *sterilis.*
sterility, *sterilitas.*
sterling, *verus, bonus.*
stern, subst., *puppis.*
stern, adj. *durus, severus*; adv. *severe, dure.*
sternness, *severitas.*
steward, *procurator*; of an estate, *vilicus.*
stewardship, *cura, procuratio.*
stick, subst. *baculum, virga* (= rod), *fustis* (= cudgel).

stick, v.: transit., *(ad)figĕre*; intransit., *(ad)haerēre, adhaerescĕre*; = get stuck, *haerēre, haesitare, dubitare*.

sticky, *tenax, lentus*.

stiff, *rigidus, durus*; to be —, *rigēre*. Adv., *rigide, dure, duriter*.

stiffen, v.: transit., *rigidum facĕre*; intransit., *rigescĕre*.

stiffness, *rigor*.

stifle, *suffocare*.

stigma, *nota*.

stigmatize, *notare, notam inurĕre*.

still, adj. *tranquillus, quietus, placidus*.

still, adv. *adhuc, etiam*; see also nevertheless.

still, v. *sedare, placare*.

stilling, subst. *sedatio*.

stillness, *silentium, tranquillitas, quies*.

stimulate, *stimulare, excitare, incitare*.

stimulus, *stimulus, incitamentum*.

sting, subst. *aculeus*.

sting, v. *pungĕre, aculeos infigĕre*.

stinginess, *parsimonia, tenacitas*.

stinging, *mordax, acerbus, aculeatus*.

stingy, *parcus, sodidus, tenax*; adv. *parce, sordide*.

stink; see smell.

stint, v. *parce dare, parcĕre*.

stipend; see salary.

stipendiary, *mercenarius, stipendiarius*.

stipulate, *stipulari, (de)pacisci*.

stipulation, *pactum, condicio*.

stir, subst. *motus (-ūs), tumultus (-ūs)*.

stir, v.: transit., *(com)movēre, exagitare*; intransit., *se movēre, progredi*.

stitch, v. *(con)suĕre*.

stock, subst.: of a tree, *truncus, stirps*; = family, *genus, stirps*; = store, *copia, vis*.

stock, adj.; see common, trite.

stock, v. *instruĕre, ornare*.

stockade, *vallum*.

stoic, subst. and adj. *stoicus*.

stoical, *ferreus, rigidus, austerus*; adv. *austere, stoice*.

stoicism, *stoicorum ratio* or *doctrina*.

stomach, subst. *stomachus*.

stone, subst. *lapis, saxum*; of —, adj. *lapideus*; in fruit, *nucleus*; precious —, *gemma*.

stone, v. *lapides in hominem conicĕre*.

stony: = of stone, *lapideus, saxeus*; = full of stones, *lapidosus, saxosus*.

stony-hearted, *durus, ferreus*.

stoop, v. *se inclinare* or *demittĕre*.

stooping, adj. *pronus, inclinatus*.

stop, subst.: = stay, *mansio*; = pause, *intermissio, pausa*; as punctuation, *interpunctum*.

stop, v.: transit., *sistĕre, prohibēre, comprimĕre*; — up, *obturare, occludĕre*; intransit., = halt, *(con)sistĕre*; = stay, *manēre, (com)morari*; = cease, refrain, *desinĕre*.

stoppage, *obstructio, impedimentum*.

store, subst. *copia, vis*.

store, v. *coacervare, reponĕre, condĕre*.

store-house, *horreum, thesaurus, apotheca*.

store-room, *cella*.

storey, *tabulatio, tabulatum*.

stork, *ciconia*.

storm, subst. *tempestas, procella*.

storm, v.: transit., *expugnare, vi capĕre*; intransit., *furēre, saevire*.

storm-cloud, *nimbus*.

storming, subst. *expugnatio*.

stormy, *turbulentus, turbidus*; adv. *turbulente, turbide*.

story: = tale, *fabula, res, narratio*; to tell a —, *narrare*; = falsehood, *mendacium*; see also storey.

stout: = fat, *obesus, pinguis*; = thick, *crassus, densus*; = strong, *validus, robustus*; = brave, *fortis*. Adv. *fortiter, valide, robuste*.

stove, *focus, caminus*.

stow; see store.

straggle, *vagari, deerare, palari*.

straight: adj. *(di)rectus, erectus*; adv. *recta, recto itinere*.

straighten, *corrigĕre*.

straightforward, *simplex, apertus*.

strain, subst.: = exertion, *intentio, contentio*; of music, etc., *modus*; = manner, *modus*; in this —, *ita, sic*.

strain, v. *contendĕre*; see also filter.

strained; see far-fetched.

strait, subst.: = narrow sea, *fretum*; = any narrow passage, or difficulty, *angustiae (-arum, plur.)*.

strait, *artus, angustus*.

straiten, *in angustias adducĕre*.

strand, subst. *litus (-oris, n.), ripa*.

strand, v. *navem vadis inlidĕre*.

strange, adj.: = foreign, *peregrinus, externus*; = alien, not one's own, *alienus*; = unusual, *insolitus, novus, mirus, mirabilis*. Adv. *mirum in modum, mirabiliter*.

strangeness, *novitas, insolentia*.

stranger, *hospes, advena, peregrinus*.

strangle, *strangulare, gulam laqueo frangĕre*.

strap, subst. *lorum*.

strap, v. *loris (con)stringĕre*.

stratagem, *ars, dolus*.

strategy, *ars belli gerendi*.

straw, *stramentum*.

strawberry, *fragum*.

stray, adj. *errabundus*.

stray, v. *(ab)errare, vagari, palari*.

streak, subst. *linea, nota*.

streak, v. *lineis distinguĕre*.

stream, subst. *flumen, rivus*; up —, *adverso flumine*; down —, *secundo flumine*.

stream, v. *fluĕre, effundi*.

streamer, *vexillum*.

street, *via, vicus*.

strength, *vires (-ium, plur.), robur, nervi (-orum)*.

strengthen, transit., *(con)firmare, (con)roborare*.

strengthening, subst. *confirmatio*.

strenuous, *strenuus, impiger, (g)navus*; adv. *strenue, impigre*.

strenuousness, *(g)navitas, studium*.

stress, *momentum, vis*.

stretch, subst.: = effort, *contentio, nisus (-ūs)*; at a —, *uno tenore*; = expanse, *tractus (-ūs), spatium*.

stretch, v.: transit., *(ex)tendĕre, contendĕre*; to — out, *porrigĕre*; intransit., render by pass.

strew, *sternĕre, spargĕre*.

strict: = exact, *diligens, religiosus*; = severe, *severus, rigidus.* Adv. *accurate; severe, rigide.*

strictness: = carefulness, *accuratio, diligentia;* = severity, *severitas, rigor.*

stricture, *animadversio, reprehensio.*

stride, subst. *ingens gradus (-ūs).*

strife, *certamen, contentio, controversia.*

strike, v.: transit., *ferire, percutĕre, pulsare, caedĕre*; mentally, *percutĕre, percellĕre*; to be struck by lightning, *de caelo tangi*; to — down, *adfligĕre*; — out, *elidĕre, delēre*; intransit., to — against, *offendĕre, incurrĕre.*

striking; see remarkable.

string, subst. *linum, linea, filum*; bow—, *nervus*; of a musical instrument *nervus, fides* (usually plur.).

string, v. *nervos aptare* (of an instrument); see also bind.

stringent; see severe.

strip, subst.; of paper, *scidula chartae*; of cloth, *lacinia.*

strip, v.: transit., *spoliare, (de)nudare, exuĕre*; intransit., *vestem exuĕre* or *deponĕre.*

stripe; see streak and stroke.

stripling, *adulescens, adulescentulus.*

strive, *(e)niti, contendĕre.*

striving, *nisus (-ūs), certatio, contentio.*

stroke, subst. *ictus (-ūs), verber, plaga*; of lightning, *fulmen*; — of fortune, *eventus (-ūs).*

stroke, v. *(per)mulcēre, demulcēre.*

stroll, subst. *ambulatio.*

stroll, v. *ambulare, spatiari, reptare.*

strong, adj. *validus, firmus, robustus, fortis*; of flavours, *acer*; of winds, *vehemens*; of arguments, *gravis, firmus*; to be —, *valēre, pollēre.* Adv. *valide, firmiter, fortiter, vehementer.*

stronghold, *arx.*

structure: abstract, *ratio, forma, conformatio*; material, *aedificium, moles, compages.*

struggle, subst. *certamen, luctatio.*

struggle, v. *luctari, niti, contendĕre.*

strut, (superbe) *incedĕre.*

stubble, *stipulae (-arum,* plur.).

stubborn, *pertinax, pervicax, obstinatus*; adv. *pertinaciter, pervicaciter, obstinate.*

stubbornness, *pertinacia, pervicacia, obstinatio.*

stud, *bulla.*

studded, *distinctus.*

student; see scholar.

studied, *meditatus, commentatus.*

studious, *litterarum studiosus*; adv. *summo studio, studiose.*

study, subst., *studium, meditatio, commentatio, cognitio* (with genit.).

study, v. *rei* (dat.) *studēre; in rem inquīrere.*

stuff, subst. *materia, materies*; = gear, *impedimenta (-orum), supellex*; = fabric, *textile, tela*; — and nonsense! *nugae! gerrae!*

stuff, v. *farcire, refercire, replēre.*

stuffing, *fartum* (in food), *tomentum* (for cushions).

stultify, *ad inritum redigĕre.*

stumble, *offendĕre*; — upon, *incidĕre.*

stumbling, subst. *offensio.*

stump, *stipes (-itis), truncus.*

stun, *sensu privare.* Transf., *(ob)stupe-facĕre.*

stupefaction, *stupor, torpor.*

stupefy; see stun.

stupendous, *ingens, immanis; mirus.*

stupid, *stupidus, stolidus, stultus*; adv. *stolide, stulte.*

stupidity, *stupiditas, stupor, stultitia.*

stupor, *stupor, torpor.*

sturdy; see strong, firm.

sturgeon, *acipenser.*

stutter, v. *balbutire.*

sty, *hara, suile.*

style, subst., *genus (-eris,* n.), *ratio, modus*; — of dress, *habitus (-ūs)*; of language, *dicendi* or *scribendi genus, oratio, sermo.*

style, v. *appellare.*

stylish, *speciosus, elegans*; adv. *speciose, eleganter.*

suave, *suavis, urbanus, blandus.*

suavity, *suavitas, urbanitas.*

subdivide, *iterum dividĕre.*

subdivision, *pars.*

subdue, *in imperium redigĕre, domare.*

subject, subst.: of a person, *civis*; = a matter, *res, quaestio*; gram., *subiectum.*

subject, adj. *subiectus, obnoxius.*

subject, v. *subicere, obnoxium reddĕre.*

subject-matter, *materia, res.*

subjection, *servitus (-ūtis), officium.*

subjective, render by personal pronouns or by *opinio.*

subjoin, *subiungĕre, subicĕre.*

subjugate, *(per)domare, subigĕre.*

subjunctive, *(modus) subiunctivus.*

sublime, *elatus, excelsus*; adv. *elate, excelse.*

sublimity, *elatio, excelsitas.*

submerge, *submergĕre.*

submission, *obsequium, officium.*

submissive, *oboediens, submissus.*

submit, v.: transit., *referre (ad senatum,* etc.); — to, = endure, *perferre.*

subordinate, subst. *minister.*

subordinate, adj. *inferior, subiectus* (with dat.).

subordinate, v. *subicĕre, posthabēre.*

subordination, *obsequium, disciplina.*

suborn, *subornare, subicĕre.*

subscribe: = write underneath, *subscribĕre*; = contribute, *conferre.*

subscription, = contribution, *conlatio, conlecta.*

subsequent, *(in)sequens, posterior*; adv. *postea.*

subserve, *(in)servire, obtemperare, obsequi.*

subservience, *obtemperatio.*

subside, *residĕre, considĕre.*

subsidiary, *subsidiarius.*

subsidy, *subsidium, vectigal, tributum.*

subsist, *esse*; — on a thing, *re vesci.*

subsistence, *victus (-ūs).*

substance, *natura, corpus (-oris,* n.), *res*; = property, *res, bona (-orum,* plur.).

substantial, *verus* (= real), *solidus* (= firm), *gravis* (= important),

amplus (= large). Adv. *firmiter*
(=solidly), *magna ex parte* (=largely).
substantiate; see *prove, establish.*
substantive, gram., *nomen.*
substitute, subst. *vicarius.*
substitute, v. transit., *substituĕre,*
sufficĕre (esp. of the replacing of
magistrates).
subterfuge, *tergiversatio.*
subterranean, *subterraneus.*
subtle, *subtilis; argutus, acutus.* Adv.
subtiliter, argute, acute.
subtlety, *ingenii acumen, subtilitas,*
argutiae (-arum, plur.).
subtract, *deducĕre.*
suburban, *suburbanus.*
subvert, *subvertĕre, evertĕre.*
succeed, v.: transit., = come after,
(*sub)sequi, excipĕre, succedĕre* (with
dat.); intransit., = do well, of persons,
rem bene gerĕre, florēre; of things,
succedĕre, bene evenire.
success, *res secundae, successus (-ūs).*
successful, *felix;* of things, *secundus,*
prosper. Adv. *feliciter, prospere, bene.*
succession, *successio;* = series, *con-*
tinuatio, series; in —, *ex ordine.*
successive, *continuus;* adv. (*ex*) *ordine,*
deinceps.
successor, *successor.*
succinct, *brevis;* adv. *breviter.*
succour, subst. *auxilium, subsidium.*
succour, v. *subvenire, succurrĕre,* with
dat.
succumb, *succumbĕre.*
such, adj. *talis; huius modi, eius modi;*
such . . . as, *talis . . . qualis;* such
that, *talis ut,* with subj.; in — a way,
tali modo, ita, sic.
suck, v. *sugĕre;* — out, *exsorbēre.*
sucker, *surculus, planta.*
suckle, v. *mammam praebēre.*
suckling, (*infans*) *lactens.*
sudden, *subitus, repentinus, inopinatus;*
adv. *subito, repente.*
sue: = entreat, *rogare, orare;* at law,
(*hominem*) *in ius vocare.*
suet, *sebum.*
suffer: = endure, *pati,* (*per)ferre,*
tolerare, subire; = be in pain,
dolorem ferre, dolore adfici; = be ill,
aegrotare; = be punished, *plecti,*
poenas dare; = allow, *pati, sinere.*
sufferance, *patientia;* on —, *precarius,*
adj.
suffering, *dolor, miseria;* see pain.
suffice, *sufficĕre, satis esse.*
sufficient; render by adv. *satis.*
suffocate, *suffocare;* see strangle.
suffrage, *suffragium.*
suffuse, *suffundĕre.*
suggest, (*rem homini*) *subicĕre.*
suggestion, *admonitio, consilium.*
suicide: to commit —, *sibi mortem*
consciscĕre.
suit, subst.: at law, *actio, lis, causa;*
of clothes, *vestis, vestitus (-ūs).*
suit, v.: = adapt, *accommodare;* = fit,
be suitable, *convenire, congruĕre.*
suitable, *idoneus, aptus, accommodatus,*
opportunus; adv. *idonee, apte, accom-*
modate, opportune.
suitableness, *opportunitas.*

suite: = retinue, *comitatus (-ūs),*
comites (-um); of rooms, *conclavia*
(*-ium*).
suitor, = wooer, *procus.*
sulkiness, sullenness, *morositas.*
sulky, sullen, *morosus;* adv. *morose.*
sully, *maculare, inquinare.*
sulphur, *sulfur;* dipped in —,
sulfuratus.
sulphurous, *sulpureus.*
sultry, *aestuosus.*
sum, subst. *summa;* of money, *pecunia.*
sum up, v. *breviter repetĕre.*
summary, subst. *epitoma* or *epitome.*
summary, adj.: = brief, *brevis;*
= quick, *subitus, repentinus.* Adv.
breviter, summatim; statim.
summer, *aestas;* of —, adj., *aestivus.*
summit, *cacumen, culmen;* or render
by adj. *summus.*
summon, (*ad)vocare, accessĕre, accire;*
before a court, *appellare, in ius*
vocare; to — up courage, *animum*
colligĕre.
summons: at a person's —, *hominis*
accitu.
sumptuous, *sumptuosus, lautus;* adv.
sumptuose.
sumptuousness, *apparatus (-ūs),*
lautitia.
sun, subst. *sol;* rising —, *sol oriens;*
setting —, *sol occidens.*
sunburnt, *adustus.*
sunder, *separare, disiungĕre.*
sundial, *solarium.*
sundry, *diversus, varius.*
sunny, *apricus.*
sunrise, *solis ortus (-ūs).*
sunset, *solis occasus (-ūs).*
sunshine, *sol.*
sup, *cenare.*
superannuated, *emeritus, rude donatus.*
superb, *magnificus, lautus;* adv.
magnifice, laute.
supercilious, *superbus, fastidiosus, in-*
solens.
superciliousness, *superbia, insolentia.*
superficial, = exterior, *externus;* =
shallow, *levis;* adv. *strictim, leviter.*
superfluous, adj. *supervacaneus, super-*
vacuus; to be —, *superesse.* Adv. *ex*
supervacuo.
superhuman, *divinus, maior quam pro*
homine.
superintend, *administrare, praeesse.*
superintendent, *praefectus.*
superior, *superior, melior* (= better).
superlative, *optimus, egregius, singularis;*
gram., *superlativus.*
supernatural, *divinus, caelestis;* by —
agency, *divinitus.*
supernumerary, *praeter* (*iustum*)
numerum; of soldiers, *ascriptivus;*
in plur., *accensi.*
superscription, *inscriptio.*
supersede, *succedĕre* (with dat.).
superstition, *superstitio.*
superstitious, *superstitiosus;* adv. *super-*
stitiose.
supervene, *supervenire;* see also
follow.
supervise, (*pro)curare.*
supervision, (*pro)curatio.*

supine, subst. *supínum* (gram.).

supine, adj. *supinus.* Transf., *iners, neglegens;* adv. *neglegenter.*

supineness, *neglegentia, inertia.*

supper, *cena.*

supplant, *in alterius locum inrepĕre.*

supple, *mollis, lentus.*

supplement, *supplementum, incrementum.*

suppliant, *supplex.*

supplicate, *supplicare, obsecrare, obtestari.*

supplication, *obsecratio, obtestatio.*

supply, supplies, *copia, facultas;* milit. *commeatus (-ūs).*

supply, v. = provide, *suppeditare, ministrare.*

support, subst. *firmamentum;* = maintenance, *alimentum, victus (-ūs);* = help, *subsidium, auxilium.*

support, v.: = hold up, *sustinēre, fulcire;* = endure, *(per)ferre, tolerare;* = maintain, *alĕre;* = help, *adesse, suffragari,* with dat.

supporter, *adiutor, suffragator, fautor.*

suppose, = assume, *ponĕre, sumĕre;* = believe, *credĕre, putare, opinari.*

supposition, *opinio, coniectura.*

supposititious, *subditus, subditivus.*

suppress, *supprimĕre, comprimĕre.*

supremacy, *principatus (-ūs), dominatio, imperium.*

supreme, *supremus, summus;* adv. *unice, maxime.*

sure, *certus, tutus* (= safe), *firmus* (= trustworthy); I am —, *pro certo habeo.*

surely, *certe, profecto, scilicet;* in questions, *nonne?* — not? *num?*

surety, *vas, sponsor* (of a person).

surface, *superficies,* or render by adj. *summus.*

surfeit, subst. *satietas.*

surfeit, v.: to — oneself, *se ingurgitare.*

surge, subst. *fluctus (-ūs).*

surge, *fluctuare;* — forward, *proruĕre.*

surgeon, *medicus, chirurgus.*

surliness, *morositas, difficultas.*

surly, *morosus, difficilis.*

surmise, subst. *coniectura.*

surmise, v. *suspicari, coniecturam facĕre.*

surmount, *transcendĕre, (ex)superare.*

surmountable, *(ex)superabilis.*

surname, *cognomen, cognomentum.*

surpass, *vincĕre, (ex)superare, praestare* (with dat.).

surplus, subst. *residuum, quod superest.*

surprise, subst., *(ad)miratio;* or render by v. or adj.

surprise, v. *admirationem (homini) movēre;* to be —d, *(ad)mirari;* = take by —, *opprimĕre, necopinantem adoriri.*

surprising, *mirus, mirabilis.*

surrender, subst. *deditio, traditio.*

surrender, v. *dedere, tradere, (con)cedĕre;* intransit., *se dedĕre.*

surreptitious, *furtivus, clandestinus;* adv. *furtim, clam.*

surround, *cingĕre, circumdare, circumvenire.*

survey, subst. *contemplatio, conspectus (-ūs);* of land, *mensura.*

survey, v. *spectare, contemplari;* = measure land, *agrum metiri, mensuram agĕre.*

surveyor, (of land), *decempedator, metator.*

survive, *superesse, superstitem esse.*

surviving, survivor, *superstes.*

susceptible, *mollis.*

suspect, adj. *suspectus.*

suspect, v. *suspicari;* = think, fancy, *putare.*

suspend, *suspendĕre;* = break off, defer, *intermittĕre, differre;* from office, *loco movēre, magistratum abrogare.*

suspense, *dubitatio:* in —, adj., *suspensus.*

suspension, *dilatio* (= delay); — of hostilities, *indutiae (-arum).*

suspicion, *suspicio.*

suspicious, *suspiciosus, suspicax;* adv. *suspiciose.*

sustain, *sustinere, sustentare.*

sustenance, *alimentum, victus (-ūs).*

sutler, *lixa.*

swaddling-clothes, *fasciae (-arum), incunabula (-orum).*

swagger, *gloriari, se iactare.*

swallow, subst. *hirundo.*

swallow, v. *(ab)sorbēre, (de)vorare.*

swamp, subst. *palus (-udis).*

swamp, v. *(de)mergĕre, immergĕre.*

swampy, *paluster, paludosus.*

swan, *cygnus, olor;* of a —, *cygneus.*

swarm, subst. of bees, *examen.*

swarm, v. *congregari, confluĕre.*

swarthy, *fuscus, adustus.*

sway, subst. *imperium, dominatio, dicio.*

sway, v., = move to and fro, *agitare, motare;* see also govern.

swear, *iurare;* — falsely, *peierare* or *periurare.*

sweat, subst. *sudor.*

sweat, v. *sudare.*

sweep, subst., = expanse, *ambitus (-ūs), spatium.*

sweep, v. *verrĕre.*

sweepings, *quisquiliae (-arum).*

sweet, *dulcis, suavis;* adv. *dulciter, suaviter.*

sweeten, *dulcem reddĕre* or *facĕre.*

sweetheart, *deliciae (-arum), amores (-um).*

sweetness, *dulcedo, suavitas.*

swell, v.: transit., *tumefacĕre, augēre;* intransit., *tumēre, tumescĕre, crescĕre* (= grow).

swelling, subst. *tumor, tuber.*

swerve, subst. *declinatio.*

swerve, v. *declinare.*

swift, *citus, velox, celer, pernix;* adv. *cito, celeriter, perniciter.*

swiftness, *celeritas, velocitas, pernicitas.*

swim, v. *nare, natare;* — across, *tranare.*

swimmer, *natator.*

swimming, subst. *natatio.*

swindle, subst. *fraus.*

swindle, v. *fraudare, circumvenire.*

swindler, *fraudator.*

swine, *sus, porcus;* adj., of —, *suillus.*

swineherd, *subulcus, suarius.*

swing, v.: transit., *agitare, vibrare, iactare.*
switch, subst. *virga, virgula.*
Switzerland, *Helvetia.*
swoon, v. *animo linqui, conlabi.*
swoop, subst. *impetus (-ūs).*
swoop, v. *impetum facĕre, incurrĕre.*
sword, *gladius, ensis, ferrum.*
sycophancy, *sycophantia, adsentatio, adulatio.*
sycophant, *sycophanta, adsentator, adulator.*
syllable, *syllaba.*
sylvan, *silvestris.*
symbol, *symbolum, signum.*
symmetrical, *aequalis, congruens;* adv. *pariter, aequaliter.*
symmetry, *convenientia, congruentia, aequalitas.*
sympathetic, *concors, humanus, misericors.*
sympathize, *congruĕre, consentire, miserēri* (= pity).
sympathy, *consensus (-ūs), concordia; humanitas.*
symphony, *symphonia, concentus (-ūs).*
symptom, *(morbi) indicium* or *signum.*
syndicate, *societas.*
synonymous, *idem significans.*
synopsis, *epitome* or *epitoma; breviarium.*
syntax, *syntaxis* (gram.); *verborum constructio.*
Syracuse, *Syracusae (-arum,* plur.).
system, *ratio, disciplina.*
systematic, *accuratus, compositus;* adv. *ordine, accurate, composite.*

T

tabernacle, *tabernaculum.*
table, *mensa;* = fare, *cena, victus (-ūs)* = list, *index.*
table-napkin, *mappa.*
tablet, *tabula, tabella, album.*
tacit, *tacitus;* adv. *tacite.*
taciturn, *taciturnus.*
taciturnity, *taciturnitas.*
tack, subst., = small nail, *clavulus.*
tack, v., in sailing, *reciprocare;* see also nail and sew.
tackle, subst. *instrumenta (-orum), armamenta (-orum).*
tackle, v. *tractare, obviam ire.*
tact, *dexteritas.*
tactful, *dexter;* adv. *dextere, dextre.*
tactics, *res militaris, belli ratio.*
tactless, *ineptus, insulsus, infacetus.*
tactlessness, *ineptiae (-arum).*
tail, *cauda.*
tailor, *textor.*
taint, subst. *contagio, vitium.*
taint, v. *inficĕre, contaminare, corrumpĕre.*
take, *capĕre, sumĕre, accipĕre* (= receive); — away, *auferre, demĕre, adimĕre;* — down, in writing, *litteris mandare;* — in, mentally, *percipĕre, comprehendĕre;* — on, *suscipĕre;* to —, = to move, by carrying, *ferre;* by leading, *ducĕre;* to — in good part, *in bonam partem accipĕre;* intransit., to — to, *se conferre ad,* with acc.

taking, subst. *acceptio, expugnatio* (of a city).
tale, *narratio, fabula, historia.*
tale-bearer, *delator, sycophanta.*
talent: = weight or coin, *talentum;* = faculty, *ingenium, (ingenii) facultas.*
talented, *ingeniosus, eximii ingenii.*
talk, subst. *sermo, conloquium.*
talk, v. *(con)loqui, sermocinari;* to — to, *adloqui, adfari.*
talkative, *loquax, garrulus;* adv. *loquaciter.*
talkativeness, *loquacitas.*
tall, *longus, procerus, (ex)celsus.*
tallness, *proceritas, statura procera.*
tally, v. *convenire.*
talon, *unguis, ungula.*
tame, adj. *cicur, mitis, mansuetus;* to grow —, *mitescĕre.* Transf., *demissus;* of language, *frigidus.* Adv. *demisse; frigide.*
tame, v. *mansuefacĕre, domare.*
tamer, *domitor;* f. *domitrix.*
taming, *domitus (-ūs).*
tamper; see meddle.
tan, v.: to — skins, *conficĕre;* of the sun, *colorare.*
tangible, *tractabilis; quod tangi potest.*
tangle, subst. *implicatio, nodus.*
tank, *lacus (-ūs).*
tantalize; see tease.
tap, v. *leviter ferire;* to — a cask, *relinĕre.*
tape; see ribbon.
taper, subst. *cereus, funalis.*
tapestry, *pictura acu facta, stragulum pictum.*
tar, *pix (liquida).*
Taranto, *Tarentum.*
tardiness, *tarditas.*
tardy, *tardus, lentus;* adv. *tarde, lente.*
target, *scopu..*
tarnish, v. transit., *inquinare.*
Tarragona, *Tarraco.*
tarry, *(com)morari, cunctari, cessare.*
tart, adj. *acerbus, amarus;* adv. *acerbe.*
tartness, *acerbitas.*
task, subst. *pensum, opus (-eris, n.).*
task-master, *operis exactor.*
taste, subst.: = sense of —, *gustatus (-ūs), palatum;* = flavour, *sapor, gustatus (-ūs).* Transf., critical —, *iudicium, intellegentia;* = liking, *gustatus (-ūs), studium.*
taste, v.: transit., *(de)gustare, (de)libare;* intransit., *sapĕre.*
tasteful, *elegans, scitus, concinnus;* adv. *eleganter, scite.*
tasteless, *sine sapore, insulsus; inelegans;* adv. *insulse, ineleganter.*
tastelessness, *insulsitas.*
tatter, *pannus.*
tattered, *pannosus.*
taunt, subst. *probrum, convicium.*
taunt, v. *(rem homini) obicĕre.*
taunting, *contumeliosus;* adv. *contumeliose.*
tavern, *caupona, taberna.*
tavern-keeper, *caupo.*
tawdry, *fucosus.*
tawny, *fulvus.*
tax, taxation, *vectigal, tributum.*

tax, v., *vectigal* or *tributum* (*homini*) *imponĕre.*

taxable, *vectigalis, stipendiarius.*

tax-collector, (*vectigalium*) *exactor.*

teach, (*e*)*docēre, instituĕre, erudire.*

teachable, *docilis.*

teachableness, *docilitas.*

teacher, *doctor, magister* (with f. *magistra*).

teaching, subst. *doctrina, disciplina, eruditio.*

team, (of horses or oxen), *iugum.*

tear, subst. *lacrima, fletus* (*-ūs*, = weeping).

tear, v. transit. (*di*)*scindĕre*, (*di*)*lacerare*, (*di*)*vellĕre*; — away, *avellĕre*; — down, *rescindĕre, revellĕre*; — out, *evellĕre.*

tearful, *lacrimans, lacrimabundus*; adv. *multis cum lacrimis.*

tearing, tear, subst. *scissura.*

tease, *fatigare, vexare, obtundĕre.*

tedious, *lentus, longus, molestus*; adv. *lente, moleste.*

tediousness, *molestia.*

teem, *scatēre.*

tell: = relate, say, *dicĕre, narrare, referre* (*com*)*memorare, docēre* (= inform); = command, *iubēre, imperare*; = count, *numerare*; intransit., = have effect, *valēre.*

temerity, *temeritas.*

temper, subst. *ingenium, animus*; bad —, *iracundia, stomachus.*

temper, v. *temperare, miscēre, lenire.*

temperance, *temperantia, continentia, moderatio.*

temperate, *temperans, continens, moderatus*; adv. *continenter, moderate.*

temperateness, *temperantia.*

tempest, *tempestas, procella.*

tempestuous, *turbidus, violentus, vehemens*; adv. *turbide, violenter, vehementer.*

tempestuousness, *violentia.*

temple, *aedes, templum, fanum, delubrum*; of the head, *tempus* (*-oris*, n.).

temporal, *humanus.*

temporarily, *ad* or *in tempus.*

tempt, (*at*)*temptare, sollicitare, inlicere.*

temptation, *sollicitatio, inlecebra.*

ten, *decem*; — each, — at a time, *deni*; — times, *decie*(*n*)*s.*

tenacious, *tenax, pertinax*; adv. *tenaciter.*

tenacity, *tenacitas, pertinacia.*

tenant, *conductor, inquilinus, incola.*

tend: transit., *colĕre, curare*; intransit., *spectare, tendĕre.*

tendency, *inclinatio, proclivitas.*

tender, adj. *tener, mollis, indulgens* (= kind, fond); adv. *molliter, indulgenter.*

tender, v. *deferre.*

tenderness, *mollitia*; = affection, *indulgentia, amor.*

tendon, *nervus.*

tendril, *clavicula, pampinus.*

tenour, *tenor*; = drift, purport, *sententia.*

tense, subst. *tempus* (*-oris*, n.).

tense, adj. *intentus, attentus.*

tension, *intentio.*

tent, *tabernaculum*; general's —, *praetorium.*

tenth, *decimus.*

tenure, *possessio.*

tepid, *tepidus*; to become —, *tepescĕre*; to be —, *tepēre.*

term, subst.: = limited time, *spatium, dies*; = word, *verbum, vocabuium*; = condition, *condicio, lex*; to be on good —s with, *familiariter uti.*

term, v.: see call, name.

terminate; see end.

termination, *finis, exitus* (*-ūs*), *clausula.*

terrace, *solarium, ambulatio.*

terrestrial, *terrestris, terrenus, humanus.*

terrible, *terribilis, horribilis, atrox*; adv. *terribilem in modum, atrociter.*

terrific; see dreadful, terrible.

terrify, (*per*)*terrēre.*

territory, *fines, ager, regio, terra.*

terror, *terror, formido, metus* (*-ūs*).

terse, *pressus, brevis, angustus*; adv. *presse, breviter, anguste.*

terseness, *brevitas, oratio pressa.*

test, subst.; see trial, examination.

test, v. *temptare, experiri, explorare.*

testament, = will, *testamentum.*

testator, *testator.*

testify, *testari, testificari.*

testimonial, *litterae commendaticiae.*

testimony, *testimonium.*

testy, *morosus.*

text, *oratio, verba* (*-orum*).

textile, adj. *textilis.*

texture, *textura, textus* (*-ūs*).

Thames, *Tamesis* or *Tamesa.*

than, after comparative, *quam*, or abl. case.

thank, v. *gratias agĕre*: = feel gratitude, *gratiam habēre*; — you! or No — you! *benigne* (*dicis*).

thankful, *gratus*; adv. *grate, grato animo.*

thankfulness, *animus gratus.*

thankless, adj. *ingratus*; adv. *ingrate.*

thanks, subst. *gratia* or plur. *gratiae, grates.*

thanksgiving, *supplicatio.*

that, demonstr. pron. *ille, illa, illud*, or *is, ea, id*, or *iste, ista, istud.*

that, relat. pron. *qui, quae, quod.*

that, conj. in indirect statement, render by acc. and infin; after verbs of fearing, *ne* followed by subj.; in final clauses, = in order —, *ut* followed by subj.; in consecutive clauses, *ut* followed by subj.

thatch, *stramentum.*

thaw, v.: transit., (*dis*)*solvĕre, liquefacĕre*; intransit., (*dis*)*solvi, liquescĕre.*

the, no regular equivalent in Latin; — famous, *ille, illa, illud*; — more people have, — more they want, *homines quo plura habent eo ampliora cupiunt.*

theatre, *theatrum, scaena* (= stage).

theatrical, *scaenicus, theatralis*; adv. *more histrionum.*

theft, *furtum.*

their, theirs, *suus* (= — own); *eorum, illorum.*

theme, *res, propositum, quaestio.*

then, *tum, tunc*; = therefore, *ergo, igitur.*

thence, *inde, illinc, istinc.*

thenceforth, *inde, ex eo tempore.*

theory, *ratio, doctrina, ars, scientia.*

there, *ibi, illic, istic*; to be —, *adesse*; — is, *est*; — are, *sunt*; = to that place, *eo, illuc.*

thereabouts, *prope* (= near), *fere* (= nearly).

thereafter, thereupon, *inde, deinde, postea.*

therefore, *igitur, ergo, itaque, ideo.*

therein, *in eo, in ea re.*

they, when emphatic, is rendered by nom. plur. of *is, ea, id* or of *ille, illa, illud.*

thick: = stout, *crassus, pinguis*; = closely packed, *densus, artus, confertus.* Adv. *confertim, crebro.*

thicken, v.: transit., *densare*; intransit., *densari, concrescĕre* (= curdle).

thicket, *dumetum, fruticetum.*

thickness, *crassitudo, crebritas.*

thief, *fur.*

thigh, *femur.*

thin, adj.: = slim, *gracilis, exilis, macer*; = rare, *tenuis, rarus.*

thin, v. *attenuare, extenuare.*

thine, *tuus.*

thing, *res, negotium*; often rendered by neuter of adj. or pron.

think, *cogitare*; = believe, suppose, *opinari, credĕre, putare*; to — about, (rem) *reputare, (de re) cogitare.*

thinness, *tenuitas, gracilitas, raritas, macies.*

third, *tertius.*

thirst, subst. *sitis.*

thirst, v. *sitire.*

thirsty, *sitiens, siccus.*

thirteen, *tredecim*; — each, — at a time, *terni deni*; — times, *terdecie(n)s.*

thirteenth, *tertius decimus.*

thirtieth, *trice(n)simus.*

thirty, *triginta*; — each, — at a time, *triceni*; — times, *tricie(n)s.*

this, *hic, haec, hoc*; on — side (of), *citra*; of — kind, *huiusmodi.*

thistle, *carduus.*

thither, *eo, illuc, istuc*; hither and —, *huc (et) illuc.*

thong, *lorum.*

thorn, *sentis, spina.*

thorn-bush, *vepres, dumus, sentis.*

thorny, *spinosus.* Transf., *arduus, impeditus.*

thorough; see complete. Adv. *penitus, prorsus, omnino.*

thoroughbred, *generosus.*

thoroughfare, *transitus* (-*ūs*); = road through, *via (pervia).*

thou, *tu, tute, tutemet.*

though; see although.

thought, *cogitatio, animus* (= mind), *sententia* (= opinion), *opinio* (= supposition), *consilium* (= view, plan).

thoughtful, *in cogitatione defixus; prudens* (= sensible), *providus* (= far-sighted).* Adv. *prudenter.*

thoughtless, *neglegens, imprudens, temerarius* (= rash); adv. *neglegenter, imprudenter, temere.*

thoughtlessness, *neglegentia, temeritas* (= rashness).

thousand, *mille*; plur. *milia* (or *millia*); a — times, *millie(n)s.*

thousandth, *mille(n)simus.*

Thrace, *Thracia.*

thraldom, *servitūs* (-*ūtis*).

thrash: to — (or thresh) corn, *terĕre*; see also beat.

thrashing, threshing, *tritura.*

thrashing-floor, threshing-floor, *area.*

thrashing-machine, *tribulum.*

thread, subst. *filum, linea, linum.*

thread, v. *inserĕre.*

threadbare, *obsoletus, tritus.*

threat, *minae* (-*arum*), *(com)minatio.*

threaten, *(com)minari, minitari, de-nuntiare, intentare*; = impend, *(im)minĕre, instare*; = seem likely to do, render by *vidēri* with fut. infin.

threatening, *minax, minitabundus*; = impending, *instans, imminens.* Adv. *minaciter.*

three, *tres*; — times, *ter*; — each, — at a time, *trini* or *terni*; in — parts, adj. *tripertitus* or *tripartitus.*

threefold, *triplus, triplex.*

three hundred, *trecenti*; — each, — at a time, *treceni*; — times, *trecentie(n)s.*

three hundredth, *trecente(n)simus.*

threshold, *limen.*

thrice, *ter.*

thrift, *frugalitas, parsimonia.*

thrifty, *frugi, parcus*; adv. *frugaliter, parce.*

thrill, subst.: of pleasure, *voluptas, gaudium*; of fear, *horror.*

thrill, v. *commovēre*; intransit., of sounds, *resonare.*

thrilling, *mirificus, mirus.*

thrive, *vigēre, virēre, florēre.*

throat, *fauces* (-*ium*), *iugulum, guttur.*

throb, v. *salire, palpitare, micare.*

throne, *(regale) solium, sedes regia*; = royal power, *regnum, imperium.*

throng, subst. *multitudo, frequentia.*

throng, v. *celebrare, stipare, frequentare.*

throttle, *suffocare, spiritum intercludĕre.*

through, prep. *per,* with acc.; = on account of, *propter,* or *ob,* with acc.

through, adv., render by compound verb with *trans-* or *per-*; — and —, *penitus, prorsus, omnino.*

throw, throwing, subst. *iactus* (-*ūs*), *coniectus* (-*ūs*).

throw, v. *iacĕre, conicĕre, mittĕre* (esp. of weapons); — away, *abicĕre*; — back, *reicĕre*; — down, *deicĕre, deturbare, proruĕre.*

thrower, *iaculator.*

thrust, v. *trudĕre*; see push, drive.

thumb, *(digitus) pollex.*

thunder, subst. *tonitrus* (-*ūs*).

thunder, v. *(in)tonare.*

thunder-bolt, *fulmen.*

thunder-struck, *attonitus, obstupefactus.*

thus, *ita, sic.*

thwart, subst. *transtrum.*

thwart, v.: see hinder, prevent.

thy, *tuus.*

thyme, *thymum.*

Tiber, river, *Tiberis.*

ticket, *tessera.*

tickle, *titillare.*

tide, *(maritimus) aestus (-ūs)*; the turn of the —, *commutatio aestūs.*

tidiness, *munditia.*

tidings, *nuntius.*

tidy, *mundus*; adv. *munde.*

tie, subst. *vinculum, nodus.*

tie, v.; see bind; — a knot, *nodum facěre.*

tier, *ordo*; see row.

tiger, *tigris.*

tight, *strictus, a(d)strictus, artus*; — rope, *funis contentus.*

tighten, v. *stringěre, contenděre, adducěre.*

tile, *tegula, testa*; pan- —, *imbrex.*

till, prep. *(usque) ad*; — now, *hactenus.*

till, conj. *dum, donec, quoad.*

till, v. *colere, arare.*

tillage, *cultus (-ūs), cultura.*

tiller, *(gubernaculi) clavus.*

tilt, v. transit. *(in)vertěre.*

timber, *materia* or *materies.*

time, subst. *tempus (-oris, n.), dies, spatium* (= space of —), *saeculum* (= age), *otium* (= leisure), *occasio* (= opportunity); — of life, *aetas*; for a —, *ad* or *in tempus*; on —, *(in) tempore, temperi, tempestive*; from the — when, *ex quo (tempore)*; at —s, *interdum*; at the same —, *simul, eodem tempore*; — of day, *hora*; — in music, *tempus, numerus.*

timely; adj. *tempestivus, opportunus*; adv. *ad tempus, tempestive, opportune.*

timid, *timidus, verecundus* (= bashful), *ignavus* (= cowardly). Adv. *timide.*

timidity, *timiditas, verecundia* (= shyness).

tin, *plumbum album, stannum.*

tinder, *fomes.*

tinge, v. *imbuěre, colorare, inficěre, tingěre.*

tinkle, v. *tinnire.*

tinkling, subst. *tinnitus (-ūs).*

tinkling, adj. *tinnulus.*

tinsel, = metal leaf, *bractea.*

tip, subst. *cacumen, apex*; or render by adj. *extremus.*

tip, v., = head, point, *praefigěre*; — up, — over, *(in)vertěre, inclinare.*

tipple, *(per)potare.*

tipsy, *temulentus, ebrius.*

tiptoe, on, *suspenso gradu.*

tire, v. transit., *(de)fatigare.*

tired, *(de)fessus, fatigatus*; I am — of saying, *taedet me dicěre.*

tiresome, *importunus, molestus.*

tit-bits, *cuppedia (-orum), scitamenta (-orum).*

title, *titulus, index* (of a book), *nomen* (= name), *praescriptio* (= heading).

titled, *nobilis.*

titter, v.; see laugh.

Tivoli, *Tibur.*

to, commonly rendered by the Latin dative; for motion to, use *ad* with acc. (except with *domus* and *rus* and names of towns or small islands); —, or up —, a certain time, *ad* or *in* with acc.; to and fro, *huc (et) illuc.*

toad, *bufo.*

toadstool, *fungus.*

toast, v. *torrēre, frigěre*; = drink a health, *(homini) propinare.*

today: subst. *hodiernus dies*: of —, adj. *hodiernus*; adv. *hodie.*

toe, *(pedis) digitus.*

together, *una, simul*; all —, *cuncti, universi.*

toil, subst. *labor, opera.*

toil, v. *(e)laborare, sudare.*

toilsome, *laboriosus, operosus.*

token, *signum.*

Toledo, *Toletum.*

tolerable, *tolerabilis, patibilis*; = middling, *tolerabilis, mediocris, modicus*; adv. *mediocriter, modice, satis* (= sufficiently).

tolerance, toleration, *tolerantia; indulgentia, lenitas, facilitas.*

tolerate, *tolerare, (aequo animo) ferre.*

toll, subst. *vectigal, portorium.*

toll, v. *sonare.*

tomb, *sepulcrum.*

tomb-stone, *lapis, cippus, monumentum.*

tomorrow: subst. *crastinus dies*: of —, adj. *crastinus*; adv. *cras.*

tone, *sonus, sonitus (-ūs), vox.*

tongs, *forceps.*

tongue, *lingua.*

tonnage, expressed by numbers of *amphorae.*

too: = also, *etiam, quoque, praeterea*; = excessively, render by *nimis* or *nimium* or by comparative; — stupid to know, *stultior quam qui sciat*; — little, *parum.*

tool: an iron-, *ferramentum*; —s, plur., *instrumentum.*

tooth, *dens.*

top, subst.: = summit, *cacumen, culmen*; or render by adj. *summus*; a child's —, *turbo.*

top, adj. *summus.*

topic, *res.*

topical, *hodiernus, hic.*

topography, *locorum descriptio.*

torch, *fax, taeda.*

torment, subst. *cruciatus (-ūs), tormentum.*

torment, v. *(ex)cruciare, torquēre, vexare.*

tormenter, *vexator*; or render by verb.

tornado, *turbo, tempestas.*

torpid, *torpens, lentus, iners.*

torpor, *torpor.*

torrent, *torrens.*

torrid, *torridus.*

tortoise, *testudo.*

torture, *tormentum, cruciatus (-ūs), dolor, angor.*

torture, v. *(ex)cruciare, (ex)torquēre.*

torturer, *tortor, carnifex.*

toss, tossing, subst. *iactus (-ūs), iactatio.*

toss, v. *iactare.*

total, subst. *summa, universitas.*

total, adj. *totus, omnis*; adv. *omnino, funditus, penitus.*

totter, v. *labare, vacillare, titubare.*

touch, subst. *(con)tactus (-ūs), tactio.*

touch, v. *tangěre, attingěre, contingěre*; = influence, affect, *tangěre, (com)-movēre.*

touching, prep. *de,* with abl.

touchy, inritabilis, iracundus,

tough, lentus, durus.

toughness, duritia.

tour, subst. vestigium, indicium.

tow, subst. stuppa: of —, adj. stuppeus.

tow, v. trahĕre.

toward, towards, prep.: of motion, ad or adversus with acc.; of time, = near to, ad or sub, with acc.; of personal relations, adversus, erga, in, with acc.

towel, mantele.

tower, subst. turris; fig., arx, praesidium.

tower, v. eminēre, exstare; — over, imminēre, with dat.

towering, arduus.

town, urbs, oppidum; of a —, adj., urbanus.

town-hall, curia.

townsman, civis, oppidanus.

trace, subst. vestigium, indicium.

trace, v.: = draw, mark out, designare, describĕre, adumbrare; = follow up, track, (in)vestigare.

track, subst.; see path.

tract: = region, tractus (-ūs), regio; = treatise, libellus.

tractable, tractabilis, docilis, facilis.

tractableness, docilitas, facilitas.

trade, subst., = commerce, mercatura, commercium; = any occupation, ars, artificium.

trade, v. mercaturam facĕre, (com)mercari, negotiari.

trader, mercator; see also merchant.

tradition, memoria, litterae (-arum, documentary).

traditional, (a maioribus) posteris traditus.

tragedian: = writer, tragicus; = actor, tragoedus, tragicus actor.

tragedy, tragoedia; fig. casus (-ūs).

tragic, tragicus; = sad, tristis, miserabilis. Adv. tragice; miserabiliter.

train, subst.: a robe with a —, syrma; = procession, pompa; = any series, ordo, series.

train, v. (e)docēre, instituĕre; = drill, exercēre.

trainer, magister; of horses, equorum domitor.

training, disciplina, exercitatio.

traitor, proditor.

tramp; see walk, march.

trample, calcare, conculcare.

trance, render by animus a corpore abstractus.

tranquil, tranquillus, placidus, quietus.

tranquillity, tranquillitas, quies.

tranquillize, tranquillare, pacare, sedare.

transact, gerĕre, agĕre, conficĕre.

transaction, res, negotium.

transcend, (ex)superare, excellĕre.

transcendent, praestans, singularis, eximius.

transcribe, transcribĕre.

transcript, exemplum, exemplar.

transfer, subst. translatio, mancipium (of property).

transfer, v. transferre, traducĕre.

transference, translatio.

transfix, transfigĕre, traicĕre, confodĕre.

transform, (con)vertĕre, (com)mutare.

transgress, transcendĕre, violare; in-transit., delinquĕre, peccare.

transgression, delictum, peccatum.

transient, adj. brevis, fugax, caducus, fluxus.

transit, transitus (-ūs).

transition, transitio, transgressio.

transitive, transitivus (gram.).

translate, (con)vertĕre, reddĕre.

translator, interpres.

transmit, transmittĕre, tradĕre.

transparent, perlucidus (pell-), perspicuus; to be —, perlucēre, lucem transmittĕre. Trans., evidens, manifestus; adv. manifesto.

transpire, of secrets, etc., (di)vulgari, pervulgari, percrebrescĕre.

transplant, transferre, traducĕre.

transport, subst. as a ship, navigium vectorium, navis oneraria.

transport, v. transportare, transferre; for banishment, relegare; to be —ed with rage, iracundia exardescĕre, with delight, gaudio efferri or exsultare.

transpose, traicĕre.

transverse, transversus, transversarius.

trap, subst. laqueus; see also snare, net.

trap, v. inretire; see ensnare.

trappings, ornamentum, insignia (-ium); of horses, phalerae (-arum).

trash, quisquiliae (-arum), scruta (-orum).

trashy, vilis.

travail, v. parturire.

travel, subst. iter, peregrinatio (abroad); — through, see traverse.

traveller, viator, vector, peregrinator.

traverse, obire, peragrare, (per)lustrare.

tray, ferculum.

treacherous, perfidus, perfidiosus; adv. perfidiose.

treachery, perfidia, fraus.

tread, subst. (in)gressus (-ūs), gradus (-ūs).

tread, v. ingredi, incedĕre, insistĕre.

treason: in gen., perfidia, proditio; high —, maiestas, perduellio; to commit —, maiestatem minuĕre or laedĕre.

treasure, subst. thesaurus, gaza, opes (-um).

treasure, v.; see value: — up, (re)condĕre.

treasure-house, thesaurus.

treasurer, praefectus aerarii.

treasury, aerarium, fiscus.

treat, v.: = discuss, (rem) tractare, (de re) disputare; medically, curare; = entertain, invitare; = behave towards (with adv.), habēre, tractare; — with, = negotiate, agĕre (cum).

treatise, liber, libellus.

treatment, tractatio, curatio; kind —, comitas; cruel —, saevitia.

treaty, pactum, foedus (-eris, n.).

Trebizond, Trapezus (-untis).

treble, adj.; see triple: of voices, acutus.

treble, v. (rem) triplicem facĕre.

tree, arbor; genealogical —, stemma (-atis, n.).

tremble, tremĕre, contremiscĕre, micare (= flicker); to cause to —, tremefacĕre.

trembling, subst. tremor.

trembling, adj. tremebundus, tremulus.

tremendous, *terribilis;* = huge, *ingens, immanis.* Adv. *valde, magnopere, maxime.*

trench, subst. *fossa;* see also ditch.

trench, v. *fossam fodĕre* or *facĕre.*

Trent, *Tridentum.*

trepidation, *trepidatio.*

trial, *temptatio, experimentum, experientia;* = attempt, *conatus (-ūs);* in court, *iudicium, quaestio.*

triangle, *triangulum.*

triangular, *triangulus, triquetrus.*

tribe, at *Rome, tribus (-ūs);* by —s, *tributim;* in gen., *natio, gens.*

tribulation, *miseria, incommodum, aerumna.*

tribunal, *tribunal;* = law court, *iudicium.*

tribune, *tribunus.*

tributary, subst., render by verb *influĕre.*

tributary, adj. *vectigalis, stipendiarius.*

tribute, *tributum, vectigal, stipendium.*

trick, subst. *dolus, fraus, machina.*

trick, v.: see deceive.

trickery, *fallacia, astutia.*

trickle, v. *manare, rorare, stillare*

trident, *tridens.*

tried, *spectatus, cognitus, probatus.*

Trieste, *Tergeste.*

trifle, subst. *res parvi momenti; nugae (-arum).*

trifle, v. *nugari, ludĕre, ineptire.*

trifler, *nugator.*

trifling, subst. *iocus, ineptiae (-arum).*

trifling, adj. *levis, minutus, nugatorius.*

trim, v. *concinnare;* of hair, *comĕre;* = prune, *(am)putare.*

trimming, subst. *fimbriae (-arum).*

trio, = three together, *tres, tria.*

trip, v. transit., — up, *supplantare;* intransit., = stumble, *offendĕre.*

tripartite, *tripertitus* or *tripartitus.*

triple, *triplex.*

tripod, *tripūs (-podis).*

trite, *tritus, pervulgatus.*

triumph, subst. *triumphus;* = success, *victoria,* = rejoicing, *exsultatio.*

triumph, v. *triumphare, triumphum agĕre;* = exult, *exultare;* — over, = conquer, *superare, vincĕre.*

triumphal, *triumphalis.*

triumphant, *victor; elatus, exsultans.*

trivial, *levis.*

trochee, *trochaeus.*

Trojan, subst. *Tros;* adj. *Troianus.*

troop, subst. *caterva, grex, manus (ūs);* of horsemen, *turma;* —s, *copiae.*

trooper, *eques.*

trophy, *tropaeum.*

tropics, *regiones torridae.*

trot, subst. *gradus (-ūs) citatus* or *tolutilis.*

troth, *fides;* to plight —, *fidem dare.*

trouble, subst.: = adversity, *molestia, incommodum, calamitas;* of mind, *sollicitudo, anxietas;* — taken, = effort, *opera, negotium, labor.*

trouble, v. *vexare, agitare, sollicitare;* to — oneself, *laborare;* — about, *curare.*

troublesome, *molestus, gravis, incommodus.*

trough, *alveus.*

trousers, *brac(c)ae (-arum).*

truce, *indutiae (-arum).*

truckle, *morem gerĕre, obtemperare.*

trudge; see walk.

true, *verus, sincerus, germanus;* = loyal, *fidus, fidelis.* Adv. *vere, profecto, certe.*

trumpet, *tuba* (straight); *bucina, lituus, cornu* (curved); a — call, *classicum.*

trumpeter, *tubicen, bucinator.*

trump up, *fingĕre.*

truncheon, *scipio, fustis.*

trunk: of a tree, *truncus, stirps;* of the body, *truncus, corpus;* = chest, box, *arca;* of an elephant, *manus (-ūs), proboscis.*

trust, subst., = confidence, *fiducia, fides.*

trust, v.: = feel confidence, *(con)fidĕre, credĕre;* = entrust, *(con)credĕre, committĕre, mandare.*

trustee, *custos, procurator.*

trustworthiness, *constantia, fides.*

trustworthy, *certus, constans, fidus.*

truth, *veritas;* the —, = the fact(s), *verum, vera.*

truthful, *verus, verax, veridicus.*

truthfulness, *veritas.*

try, subst. *conatus (-ūs).*

try, v.: = make trial of, *temptare, experiri;* = attempt, *conari;* in court, to — a case, *iudicare, cognoscĕre, quaerĕre.*

trying, adj. *molestus, gravis, incommodus.*

tub, *dolium, labrum.*

tube, *tubus.*

tuck, v.: to — up, *succingĕre.*

tuft: of hair, *crinis;* of wool, *floccus;* of feathers, *crista.*

tufted, *cristatus.*

tug, v. *trahĕre.*

tumble, subst. *casus (-ūs), ruina.*

tumble, v. = disarrange, *(per)turbare, miscēre;* intransit., see fall.

tumid, *tumidus, inflatus, turgidus.*

tumour, *tumor, tuber.*

tumult, *tumultus (-ūs), motus (-ūs), turba.*

tumultuous, *tumultuosus, turbulentus, turbidus;* adv. *tumultuose, turbulente.*

tune, *cantus (-ūs), carmen, modi (-orum);* to keep in —, *concentum servare;* out of —, *absonus.*

tuneful, *canorus.*

tunic, *tunica.*

tunnel, *cuniculus.*

turban, *mitra.*

turbid, *turbidus.*

turbot, *rhombus.*

turbulent, *turbulentus, seditiosus, turbidus.*

turf, *caespes, herba.*

turgid, *tumidus.*

Turin, *Augusta Taurinorum.*

turmoil, *turba.*

turn, turning, *conversio, flexus (-ūs);* of events, *vicissitudo, commutatio;* to take a — for the better, *in melius mutari;* of alternation, *sors (= lot):* by —s, *alternis, invicem;* a good —, *officium;* a — of speech, *genus dicendi.*

turn, v.: transit., (con)vertĕre, advertĕre (= turn towards), versare, torquēre (= twist), flectĕre (= bend); — aside, deflectĕre; — away, avertĕre; — round, circumagĕre, rotare, volvĕre; — one's attention to, animum advertĕre, animadvertĕre; intransit., (con)verti, se (con)vertĕre; — out, = issue, end, evenire, evadĕre, cadĕre; — up, incidĕre.

turnip, rapum.

turpitude, turpitudo, dedecus (-oris, n.).

turret, turris, turricula.

turtle, turtle-dove, turtur.

Tuscany, Etruria.

tusk, dens.

tutelage, tutela; see also protection.

tutor, magister, praeceptor.

tweak, vellĕre, vellicare.

twelfth, duodecimus.

twelve, duodecim; — each, — at a time, duodeni; — times, duodecie(n)s.

twelvemonth, annus.

twentieth, vicesimus.

twenty, viginti; — each, — at a time, viceni; — times, vicie(n)s.

twice, bis.

twig, surculus, ramulus, virgula.

twilight; evening, crepusculum; morning, diluculum.

twin, subst. and adj., geminus.

twinge, dolor.

twinkle, micare, fulgĕre, coruscare.

twinkling, subst. fulgor; in the — of an eye, temporis puncto.

twist, v.: transit. (in)torquēre, (in)flectĕre.

twitch, v. vellĕre, vellicare.

two, duo; — each, — at a time, bini; in — parts, adj. bipartitus, adv. bipartito.

twofold, duplex.

two-footed, bipes.

two hundred., ducenti; — each, — at a time, duceni; — times, ducentie(n)s.

type: = model, exemplar, exemplum; = character, class, forma, figura, genus (-eris, n.).

tyrannical, adj. tyrannicus, superbus; adv. tyrannice, superbe, regie.

tyrannize, dominari.

tyranny, dominatio, tyrannis.

tyrant, tyrannus (= usurper or despot); dominus superbus.

U

udder, uber.

ugliness, deformitas, foeditas.

ugly, deformis, turpis, foedus.

ulcer, vomica, ulcus (-eris, n.).

ulterior, ulterior; see also further.

ultimate, extremus, ultimus; adv. ad extremum, ad ultimum, postremo.

umbrage: see shade, or offence.

umpire, arbiter, disceptator.

un-, as a negative prefix, is rendered by the Latin prefix in-, or else by non or haud or sine.

unabashed, = shameless, impudens.

unabated, integer (= whole).

unable, render by non posse.

unacceptable, ingratus, iniucundus.

unaccompanied, solus, sine comitatu.

unaccomplished, imperfectus, infectus.

unaccountable, inexplicabilis, inenodabilis.

unaccustomed, insuetus, insolitus.

unacquainted, ignarus, imperitus, inscius.

unadorned, inornatus, incomptus, simplex.

unadulterated, sincerus, merus, integer.

unadvised, imprudens, inconsultus; adv. imprudenter, inconsulte.

unaffected: = simple, simplex, candidus; = unmoved, immotus; to remain —, non adfici.

unafraid, impavidus, intrepidus, interritus.

unaided, sine ope, sine auxilio.

unalloyed, purus, sincerus, merus.

unalterable, immutatus.

unamiable, morosus, difficilis.

unanimity, unanimitas, consensio, concordia.

unanimous, unanimus, concors; adv. uno consensu, una voce.

unappeased, non satiatus, implacatus.

unapproachable: of place, invius; of persons, rari aditus.

unarmed, inermis, nudus.

unasked, (sua) sponte, ultro.

unassuming, modestus, modicus.

unattempted; to leave nothing —, nihil inexpertum omittĕre, omnia experiri.

unattended, incomitatus, sine comitibus.

unauthorized, inlicitus, inconcessus.

unavailing, inritus, futilis, vanus.

unavenged, inevitabilis; quod evitari non potest.

unaware, adj. inscius, nescius, ignarus.

unaware, unawares, adv. (de) improviso, (ex) inopinato; often by adj. agreeing with the person surprised, e.g. imprudens, necopinans.

unbar, reserare.

unbearable; see intolerable.

unbeaten, invictus.

unbecoming, indecorus, indignus, turpis; adv. indecore, turpiter.

unbeliever, qui non credit.

unbelieving, incredulus.

unbend, remittĕre, (re)laxare.

unbending, rigidus, durus.

unbewailed, in(de)fletus, indeploratus.

unbiassed, integer; neutro inclinatus.

unbidden, invocatus, iniussus.

unbind, (dis)solvere, laxare.

unblemished, adj. purus, integer, in(con)taminatus.

unblushing, impudens; — effrontery, os durissimum.

unborn, nondum natus.

unbosom: to — oneself, se patefacĕre, (rem) confiteri.

unbought, non emptus, inemptus.

unbound, of hair, passus, solutus.

unbounded, infinitus, immensus.

unbribed, incorruptus, integer.

unbridled, effrenatus.

unbroken, integer, sincerus; in time perpetuus; of horses, indomitus.

unbuckle; see unfasten, untie.

unburden, *exonerare, liberare.*

unburied, *inhumatus, insepultus.*

uncalled, *invocatus;* — for, see unnecessary.

uncared for, *neglectus.*

unceasing, *perpetuus, continuus, adsiduus.*

unceremonious, *simplex* (= natural), *inurbanus* (= rude); adv. *simpliciter, inurbane.*

uncertain, *incertus, ambiguus, dubius, anceps;* to be —, *dubitare, haesitare.*

uncertainty, *dubitatio, dubium;* or render by adj.

unchain, *e vinculis eximĕre;* see loose.

unchangeable, *immutabilis, certus, constans;* adv. *constanter.*

unchangeableness, *immutabilitas, constantia.*

unchanged, *immutatus, integer; idem* (= same).

uncharitable, *durus, inhumanus, iniquus;* adv. *inhumaniter.*

uncharitableness, *inhumanitas.*

unchaste, *incestus, impudicus.*

unchastity, *incestum, impudicitia.*

unchecked, *liber.*

uncivil; see rude.

uncivilized, *ferus, barbarus, incultus.*

unclasp, *refibulare;* see also loose.

uncle, *patruus* (= father's brother), *avunculus* (= mother's brother).

unclean, *impurus, inquinatus.*

unclouded, *serenus, tranquillus.*

uncoil, *evolvĕre, explicare.*

uncombed, *impexus, horridus, incomptus.*

uncomfortable, *molestus, incommodus, gravis;* adv. *incommode.*

uncommanded; see unbidden.

uncommon, *rarus, insolitus, inusitatus;* adv. *plus solito, praeter solitum.*

uncommunicative; see silent.

uncomplaining, *patiens.*

uncompleted, *imperfectus.*

unconcerned, *securus, neglegens, incuriosus.*

unconditional, *simplex, purus;* adv. *simpliciter, sine ulla pactione.*

unconfined, *liber.*

uncongenial; see unpleasant.

unconquerable; see invincible.

unconquered, *invictus.*

unconscious, = insensible, (*omni*) *sensu carens;* = ignorant, *inscius, ignarus.*

unconsecrated, *profanus.*

unconsidered, *neglectus.*

unconstitutional, *non legitimus;* adv. *contra legem, contra rempublicam.*

unconstrained, *liber.*

unconsumed, *inconsumptus.*

uncontaminated, *in(con)taminatus.*

uncontrollable, *impotens.*

uncontrolled, *liber, effrenatus.*

uncooked, *crudus, incoctus.*

uncorrupt, *incorruptus, purus.*

uncouth, *rudis, incultus, rusticus.*

uncouthness, *inhumanitas.*

uncover, *detegĕre, recludere, aperire.*

uncultivated; of soil, *incultus, vastus;* of manners, etc., *inhumanus, rudis, agrestis.*

uncurbed; see unbridled.

uncut, *intonsus* (of hair); *integer* (= whole).

undamaged, *inviolatus, integer.*

undaunted, *impavidus, intrepidus.*

undeceive, *errorem* (*homini*) *eripĕre.*

undecided, *incertus, dubius, ambiguus, anceps.*

undefended, *indefensus, nudus.*

undefiled, *incorruptus, purus.*

undefined, *infinitus.*

undeniable, *evidens, haud dubius;* adv. *certe, sine dubio.*

under, prep. *sub* (to be —, *sub* with abl.; to go —, or go along —, *sub* with acc.); *subter; infra* (with acc.); — Teucer's leadership, *Teucro duce;* in size or number, *infra* or *intra* (with acc.) or render as 'less than'; — these circumstances, *quae cum ita sint.*

underestimate, *minoris faːĕre* or *aetsimare.*

under-garment, *subucula.*

undergo, *subire, sustinēre, pati;* to — punishment, *poenas dare.*

underground, adj. *subterraneus.*

undergrowth, *virgulta* (-*orum*, plur.).

underhand, *clandestinus, insidiosus.*

undermine, (*cuniculis*) *subruĕre, labefactare.*

undermost, *infimus, imus.*

underneath, adv. *infra, subter.*

underrate, *minoris facĕre* or *aestimare.*

undersell, *minoris* (*quam ceteri*) *vendĕre.*

understand, *intellegĕre;* (*animo* or *mente*) *comprehendĕre.*

understanding, *mens, ingenium;* see also agreement.

undertake, *suscipĕre,* (*in se*) *recipĕre, incipĕre* (= begin).

undertaker, (of funerals), *libitinarius, vespillo.*

undertaking, subst. *inceptum, coeptum, res suscepta.*

undervalue, *minoris facĕre* or *aestimare.*

underwood; see undergrowth.

undeserved, *immeritus, iniustus* (= unjust); adv. *immerito.*

undeserving, *indignus, immerens.*

undesigned, *fortuitus.*

undesigning, *simplex, candidus.*

undesirable; see bad, worthless.

undeveloped, *immaturus, nondum adultus.*

undigested, *crudus, imperfectus.*

undiminished, *inlibatus, integer.*

undisciplined, *inexercitatus, inconditus.*

undisguised, *apertus;* adv. *palam.*

undistinguished, *mediocris, inglorius, ignobilis.*

undisturbed, *otiosus, tutus* (= safe).

undivided, *indivisus, totus, integer.*

undo: of knots, etc., (*dis*)*solvĕre, expedire;* see also ruin.

undone, *infectus;* to leave —, *omittĕre;* = ruined, *perditus.*

undoubted, *certus, haud dubius;* adv. *sine dubio.*

undress, v.: transit., *veste exuĕre* or *nudare;* intransit., *vestem exuĕre* or (*de*)*ponĕre.*

undressed, *nudus*; = unprocessed, *crudus, rudis.*

undue, *nimius, immodicus*; adv. *nimis, nimium.*

undulate, *fluctuare, vacillare.*

undutiful, *impius, officii immemor.*

unearth, *detegĕre, effodĕre.*

unearthly, *plus quam humanus.*

uneasiness, *sollicitudo*, *(animi) perturbatio.*

uneasy, in mind, *anxius, sollicitus, trepidus.*

uneducated, *indoctus, ineruditus, rudis.*

unemployed, *otiosus, vacuus.*

unencumbered, *liber, expeditus.*

unendowed, *indotatus.*

unenlightened, *indoctus, humanitatis expers.*

unenterprising, *iners, socors, piger.*

unenviable, *miser, tristis.*

unequal, *impar, dispar, dissimilis*; adv. *inaequaliter, impariter.*

unequalled, *summus, singularis.*

unerring, *certus.*

uneven, *iniquus, impar, inaequalis, asper* (= rough); adv. *inaequaliter.*

unevenness, *iniquitas, asperitas* (= roughness).

unexamined, *inexploratus.*

unexampled, *unicus, singularis, novus, inauditus.*

unexercised, *inexercitatus.*

unexhausted, *indefessus, integer* (= whole), *recens* (= fresh).

unexpected, *inexspectatus, insperatus, improvisus*; adv. *(ex) improviso, praeter spem, praeter opinionem.*

unexplored, *inexploratus.*

unfading, *immortalis, semper florens.*

unfailing, *perennis, perpetuus, certus.*

unfair, *iniquus, iniustus, immeritus*; adv. *inique, iniuste, iniuriā.*

unfairness, *iniquitas, iniuria.*

unfaithful, *infidelis, infidus, perfidus*; adv. *infideliter.*

unfaithfulness, *infidelitas, perfidia.*

unfamiliar; see unaccustomed.

unfasten, *(re)solvĕre, (re)laxare, refigĕre.*

unfathomable, *immensus, infinitus.*

unfavourable, *iniquus, adversus*; of omens, *tristis, infaustus.* Adv. *male.*

unfavourableness, *iniquitas*; or render by adj.

unfed, *impastus.*

unfeeling, *durus, ferreus, inhumanus*; adv. *inhumane.*

unfeigned, *verus, sincerus*; adv. *vere, sincere, ex animo.*

unfilial, *impius (erga parentes).*

unfinished, *imperfectus*; = crude, *rudis, impolitus.*

unfit, *inutilis, incommodus, indignus.*

unfitness, *inutilitas.*

unfix, *refigĕre.*

unfledged, *implumis.*

unfold, v. transit. *explicare, aperire.*

unforeseen, *improvisus.*

unforgiving, *implacabilis, inexorabilis.*

unforgotten, render by phrase with *oblivio* (= oblivion) or *memoria* (= memory).

unformed, *informis, imperfectus.*

unfortified, *immunitus.*

unfortunate; see unlucky.

unfounded, *vanus, fictus, falsus.*

unfrequented, *avius, devius, desertus.*

unfriendliness, *inimicitia, simultas.*

unfriendly, *inimicus, iniquus, alienus.*

unfruitful, *sterilis, infecundus.*

unfruitfulness, *sterilitas, infecunditas.*

unfulfilled, *inritus, vanus.*

unfurl, of sails, *pandĕre, explicare.*

unfurnished, *imparatus.*

ungainly, *inhabilis.*

ungenerous, *inliberalis, sordidus*; adv. *inliberaliter.*

ungentlemanly, *inliberalis, indecorus.*

ungodly; see impious.

ungovernable, *indomitus, effrenatus, impotens.*

ungraceful, *invenustus, inelegans.*

ungracious, *iniquus, morosus, asper*; adv. *morose, aspere.*

ungrateful, *ingratus, beneficii immemor.*

ungrudging; see liberal.

unguarded, *incustoditus, indefensus*; = imprudent, *incautus, imprudens*; adv. *incaute, temere.*

unguent, *unguentum.*

unhallowed, *profanus.*

unhappiness, *miseria, aegrimonia.*

unhappy, *infelix, infortunatus, miser*; adv. *misere, infeliciter.*

unharmed, *salvus, incolumis.*

unharness, *disiungĕre, solvĕre.*

unhealthy, *infirmae valetudinis, infirmus*; = unwholesome, *pestilens, gravis.*

unheard, *inauditus.*

unheeded, *neglectus.*

unhesitating, *strenuus, confidens*; adv. *strenue, confidenter.*

unhewn, *rudis.*

unhindered, *liber, expeditus.*

unhinged, in mind, *mente, captus.*

unhistorical, *commenticius, fictus.*

unholy, *profanus*; see also impious.

unhonoured, *inhonoratus.*

unhoped for, *insperatus.*

unhurt, *integer, incolumis, salvus.*

uniform, adj. *constans, aequabilis; unius generis.* Adv. *constanter, aequabiliter.*

uniformity, *aequabilitas, constantia.*

unimpaired, *integer, intactus, inviolatus.*

unimpeachable, *sanctus, integer, locuples.*

unimportant, *lĕvis; nullius momenti.*

uninformed, *indoctus.*

uninhabitable, *inhabitabilis.*

uninhabited, *desertus.*

uninitiated, *profanus.* Transf., *ignarus, imperitus.*

uninjured, *incolumis, integer, salvus.*

uninstructed, *indoctus, rudis.*

unintelligible, *obscurus*; adv. *obscure.*

unintentionally, *forte, non sponte*; or render by adj. agreeing with agent, such as *imprudens, insciens.*

uninteresting, *ieiunus, frigidus.*

uninterrupted, *continuus, perpetuus*; adv. *continenter, uno tenore.*

uninvited, *invocatus.*

union, *(con)iunctio, consociatio*; = united body, *societas, sodalitas.*

unique, *unicus, singularis.*

unison, *concordia vocum.*

unite, v.: transit., *(con)iungĕre, (con)-sociare* (as partners), *miscēre* (= mix); intransit., *coniungi, coire, consentire* (= agree).

united, *coniunctus, consociatus, socius.*

unity, =agreement, *consensio, concordia.*

universal, *universus, communis, omnium* (= of all); adv. *universe, in universum.*

universe, *mundus, rerum natura.*

unjust, *iniustus, iniquus;* adv. *iniuste, inique, iniuria.*

unkempt, *neglectus, incomptus.*

unkind, *inhumanus, severus;* adv. *inhumane, severe.*

unkindness, *inhumanitas, severitas.*

unknowing, *inscius, insciens, ignarus.*

unknown, *ignotus, incognitus, inexploratus;* a person — to me, *nescio quis.*

unlamented, *infletus, indefletus.*

unlawful, *non legitimus, inlicitus;* adv. *contra legem* or *leges.*

unlearn, *dediscĕre.*

unlearned, *indoctus, inlitteratus.*

unless, *nisi* (contracted *ni*).

unlike, *dissimilis, dispar, diversus.*

unlikely; see *improbable.*

unlimited, *infinitus, immensus.*

unload, *exonerare, onere liberare.*

unlock, *recludĕre, reserare.*

unlooked-for, *inexspectatus, insperatus.*

unloose, *solvĕre.*

unlucky, *infelix;* adv. *infeliciter, secus.*

unmanageable; see *ungovernable.*

unmanly, *viro indignus, effeminatus, mollis.*

unmannerly, *male moratus, inurbanus.*

unmarried, *caelebs.*

unmask, *detegĕre, patefacĕre.*

unmatched, *unicus, singularis.*

unmentioned; to leave —, *omittĕre, praetermittĕre.*

unmerciful, *immisericors, inclemens, immitis;* adv. *immisericorditer, inclementer.*

unmindful, *immemor.*

unmistakable; see *clear, certain.*

unmitigated, often to be rendered by the superl. of an adj., e.g. a war of — cruelty, *bellum atrocissimum;* see also *complete, absolute.*

unmixed, *merus, simplex.*

unmolested, *incolumis, inviolatus.*

unmoved, *immotus.*

unnatural, *monstruosus, portentosus;* of character, *immanis, impius.* Adv. *contra naturam, praeter naturam.*

unnavigable, *innavigabilis.*

unnecessary, *non necessarius, supervacuus, vanus.* Adv. *cum non opus, ex supervacuo, praeter necessitatem;* sometimes *nimis* or *nimium.*

unnerve, *enervare, debilitare.*

unobserved; see *unnoticed.*

unorganized, *inconditus.*

unostentatious; see *modest.*

unpaid, *non solutus, residuus.*

unpalatable, *amarus.*

unparalleled, *unicus, singularis.*

unpardonable, *quod excusari non potest.*

unpatriotic, *patriae immemor.*

unpitied, *immiserabilis.*

unpitying, *immisericors, immitis.*

unpleasant, *molestus, ingratus, odiosus;* adv. *moleste, ingrate, odiose.*

unpleasantness, *incommodum, molestia.*

unploughed, *inaratus.*

unpolished, *impolitus, rudis.*

unpolluted, *impollutus, intemeratus, integer.*

unpopular, *invidiosus, ingratus, offensus.*

unpopularity, *invidia, offensio.*

unpractised, *inexercitatus, rudis.*

unprecedented, *novus, inauditus.*

unprejudiced, *integer;* see *unbiassed.*

unpremeditated, *subitus;* or use phrase *ex tempore.*

unprepared, *imparatus.*

unprepossessing; see *unpleasant, ugly*

unprincipled, *improbus, nequam.*

unproductive, *infecundus, sterilis.*

unprofitably, *inutiliter, frustra, incassum.*

unprovoked, *non laccessitus;* or render by *ultro.*

unpublished, *nondum editus.*

unpunished, *impunitus, inultus;* or render by adv. *impune.*

unqualified; see *unsuitable* or *unconditional.*

unquenchable, *inexstinctus.*

unquestionable, *certus, haud dubius;* adv. *sine dubio.*

unravel, *retexĕre.* Transf., *explicare, enodare.*

unreasonable, *absurdus* (= irrational), *iniquus* (= unfair); adv. *absurde, inique.*

unremitting, *continuus, adsiduus.*

unreserved, = frank, *liber, apertus, simplex;* see also *unconditional.* Adv. *absolute, sine ulla exceptione.*

unrest; see *restlessness.*

unrestrained, *effrenatus, effusus, impotens.*

unrevenged, *inultus.*

unrewarded, *sine praemio, inhonoratus.*

unrighteous, *improbus, iniustus, iniquus;* adv. *improbe, inuste, inique.*

unrighteousness, *improbitas.*

unripe, *immaturus, crudus.*

unrivalled, *eximius, unicus, singularis.*

unroll, *evolvĕre, explicare.*

unruffled, *tranquillus, immotus.*

unruly, *effrenatus, ferox, turbidus.*

unsafe, *infestus, intutus, periculosus.*

unsaid, *indictus.*

unsatisfactory, *non idoneus, malus;* adv. *male, minus bene, secus.*

unseal, *resignare.*

unseasonable, *intempestivus, importunus, immaturus;* adv. *intempestive.*

unseasoned, of food, *non conditus;* of wood, *viridis, humidus.*

unseemly; see *indecorous.*

unseen, *invisus.*

unselfish, *suae utilitatis immemor, liberalis* (= generous).

unserviceable, *inutilis.*

unsettle, *labefacĕre, (per)turbare.*

unsettled, *inconstans, varius, incertus.*

unshaken, *immotus, inlabefactus.*

unshaved, *intonsus.*

unsheathe, *(de)stringĕre, e vagina educĕre.*

unshod, *pedibus nudis.*

unsightly; see ugly.
unskilful, unskilled, *inscitus, imperitus*; adv. *inscite, imperite.*
unskilfulness, *imperitia.*
unsociable, *insociabilis, difficilis.*
unsophisticated, *simplex.*
unsound, *vitiosus, infirmus*; of unsound mind, *insanus.*
unspeakable, *infandus, inenarrabilis.*
unspoiled, *incorruptus, integer.*
unstable, *inconstans, instabilis, incertus.*
unstained, *purus, in(con)taminatus, integer.*
unsteadiness, *inconstantia.*
unstring; to — a bow, *arcum retendĕre.*
unstrung, of nerves, etc., *fractus, debilitatus.*
unstudied, (of style) *simplex.*
unsubdued, *indomitus.*
unsuccessful, *infelix, infaustus*; adv. *infeliciter.*
unsuitable, unsuited, *incommodus, alienus*; adv. *incommode.*
untainted, *incorruptus, non infectus.*
untamed, *indomitus, ferus.*
untasted, *ingustatus.*
untaught, *indoctus.*
unteachable, *indocilis.*
unthankful; see ungrateful.
unthinking; see thoughtless.
untie, *(dis)solvĕre, laxare.*
until, prep. *ad* or *in*, with acc.
until, conj. *dum, donec, quoad.*
untilled, *incultus, inaratus.*
untimely, *immaturus, intempestivus.*
untiring, *adsiduus, indefessus.*
unto; see to.
untouched, *intactus, integer.*
untoward, *adversus.*
untried, *inexpertus, intemptatus.*
untroubled, *tranquillus, placidus, quietus.*
untrue, *falsus*; adv. *falso.*
untruth, *falsum, mendacium.*
unused, see unaccustomed; = not yet used, *recens, integer.*
unusual, *inusitatus, insuetus, insolitus*; in an — manner, *inusitate.*
unutterable, *infandus, inenarrabilis.*
unvarnished, *simplex.*
unveil, *detegĕre, aperire, patefacĕre.*
unversed, *rudis, imperitus.*
unviolated, *inviolatus.*
unwariness, *imprudentia.*
unwarlike, *imbellis.*
unwarrantable, *iniquus, iniustus.*
unwary, *incautus, imprudens*; adv. *incaute, imprudenter.*
unwashed, *inlotus.*
unwatched, *incustoditus.*
unwavering; see firm.
unwearied, *indefessus, integer.*
unweave, *retexĕre.*
unwelcome, *ingratus.*
unwell, *aeger, invalidus, infirmus.*
unwholesome, *pestilens, gravis.*
unwieldy, *inhabilis.*
unwilling, *invitus*; to be —, *nolle.*
unwind, *retexĕre, explicare.*
unwise, *insipiens, stultus*; adv. *insipienter, stulte.*
unwitting, *inscius, insciens.*
unwonted; see unusual.
unworthiness, *indignitas.*

unworthy, *indignus*; adv. *indigne.*
unwounded, *invulneratus, integer.*
unwrap, *evolvĕre, explicare.*
unwrought, *rudis, infectus.*
unyielding; see inflexible.
unyoke, *disiungĕre.*
up, prep.: — the river, *adverso flumine*; — the mountain, *in adversum montem.*
up, adv. *sursum*; — to, *usque ad* (with acc.), *tenus* (after an abl. or genit.); to go —, *ascendĕre.*
upbraid, *reprehendĕre, obiurgare, exprobrare.*
upbraiding, *obiurgatio, exprobratio.*
uphill; adj. *adclivis, arduus*; adv. *adverso colle, adversus collem.*
uphold, *sustinēre, sustentare.*
upland, adj. *editus.*
upon, prep.: in space, *super, in*; in time, = directly after, *e* or *ex* (with abl.); — this subject, *de hac re.*
upper, *superus, superior*; to get the — hand, *superare, vincĕre.*
uppermost, *summus, supremus.*
upright, *(e)rectus*; morally, *probus, honestus*; adv. *recte, probe, honeste.*
uprightness, *probitas, honestas.*
uproar, *tumultus (-ūs)*; see noise.
uproarious, *tumultuosus.*
uproot, *radicitus tollĕre, evellĕre.*
upset, adj. *adflictus, perculsus.*
upset, v. *evertĕre, subvertĕre.*
upshot, *exitus (-ūs), eventus (-ūs).*
upstart, *novus homo.*
upwards, *sursum.*
urbane, *urbanus.*
urbanity, *urbanitas.*
urge, v. *impellĕre, incitare, urgĕre.*
urgency, *gravitas, necessitas.*
urgent: of matters, *gravis, magni momenti*; of persons, *vehemens*; adv. *vehementer, magnopere.*
urn, *urna.*
usage, *mos, consuetudo.*
use, subst. *usus (-ūs), usurpatio, usura*; to make — of, *(re) uti.*
use, v.: = to make use of, *uti, usurpare, adhibēre*; = to treat, *tractare*; to — up, *consumĕre*; to — wrongly, *abuti.*
useful, *utilis, aptus, commodus*: to be —, *usui esse, prodesse.* Adv. *utiliter, apte, commode.*
usefulness, *utilitas, usus (-ūs), commoditas.*
useless, *inutilis, vanus, inritus*; adv. *frustra.*
usher, v.: to — in, *introducĕre.*
usual, *usitatus, solitus, consuetus*; more than —, *plus solito.* Adv. *ferme, fere, plerumque.*
usurer, *faenerator, toculio.*
usurp, *adsumĕre, occupare.*
usury, *faeneratio, usura*; to practise — *faenerari.*
utensils, *vasa (-orum), utensilia (-ium) supellex.*
utility; see usefulness.
utmost, *extremus, ultimus, summus*; to do one's —, *summis viribus contendĕre.*
utter, adj. *totus* (= whole). Adv. *omnino, penitus, funditus.*
utter, v. *dicĕre, pronuntiare, effari.*

utterance, *dictum* (= saying), *pronuntiatio* (= delivery).

V

vacancy: = empty space, *vacuum, inane, inanitas*; = unoccupied post, render by *vacuus*; — of mind, *stupiditas*.
vacant, *vacuus*.
vacate, *vacuefacĕre*; to — an office, *se magistratu abdicare*.
vacation, *feriae (-arum)*.
vacillate, *vacillare*.
vacillating, *dubius, incertus*.
vacillation, *dubitatio*.
vagabond, vagrant: subst. *grassator*; adj. *vagus*.
vagary, *ineptiae (-arum)*.
vague, *incertus, dubius, ambiguus*; adv. *incerte, dubie, ambigue*.
vain: = worthless, *inanis, levis*; = fruitless, *vanus, inritus*; = self-satisfied, *gloriosus*; to be —, *sibi placēre*. Adv. —ly, or in —, *frustra, nequiquam*.
vainglorious, *vaniloquus, gloriosus*.
vale; see valley.
valiant, *fortis, animosus, acer*; adv. *fortiter, animose, acriter*.
valid, *gravis, certus*; of laws, *ratus*.
validity, *gravitas, pondus (-eris, n.)*.
valley, *(con)vallis*.
valour, *virtus (-utis), fortitudo*.
valuable, *pretiosus, magni pretii*.
valuation, *aestimatio*.
value, subst. *aestimatio, pretium*.
value, v. *aestimare, ducĕre, pendĕre*; to — highly, *magni facĕre*.
valueless; see worthless.
van: of an army, *primum agmen*; as vehicle, see cart.
vanish, *(e)vanescĕre*.
vanity: = emptiness, *inanitas*; = self-satisfaction, *gloria, ostentatio*.
vanquish, *(de)vincĕre, superare*.
vanquisher, *victor (f. victrix)*.
vapid, *vapidus, ieiunus, insulsus*.
vapour, *vapor, nebula, exhalatio*.
variable, *varius, mutabilis, inconstans*.
variableness, *mutabilitas*; see change.
variance, *discordia, dissensio, discrepantia*; to be at —, *dissidēre, discordare, discrepare*.
variation, *varietas, vicissitudo*.
variegated, *varius, versicolor*.
variety, *varietas, diversitas*.
various, *varius, diversus*; adv. *varie, diverse*.
vary, v.: transit., *variare, mutare*; intransit., *variari, mutari*.
vase, *vas*.
vassal, *cliens*.
vassalage, *clientela*.
vast, *vastus, ingens, immanis*; adv. *magnopere, valde*.
vastness, *amplitudo, magnitudo*.
vat, *cupa, dolium*.
vault, subst., *fornix, camera*; a — underground, *hypogeum*.
vault, v., in building, *confornicare*; = leap, *salire*.

vaunt; see boast.
veal, *(caro) vitulina*.
veer, *se vertĕre, verti*.
vegetable, subst., *planta*; an edible —, *holus (-eris, n.)*; — market, *forum holitorium*.
vegetate, v., fig., *hebescĕre*.
vegetation, *herbae, plantae (-arum)*.
vehemence, *vis, contentio, impetus (-ūs), ardor*.
vehement, *vehemens, acer*; adv. *vehementer, acriter*.
vehicle: see carriage, waggon.
veil, subst. *rica*; bridal —, *flammeum, flammeolum*.
veil, v. *velare, tegĕre*.
vein, *vena*.
vellum, *membrana*.
velocity, *velocitas*.
venal, *venalis, nummarius*.
venality, *animus venalis*.
vend, *vendĕre*.
vendor, *venditor*.
venerable, *venerabilis*.
venerate, *colĕre, observare, venerari*.
veneration, *cultus (-ūs), veneratio*.
vengeance, *ultio, vindicta*; to take —, *ulcisci, vindicare*.
venial, *veniā dignus*.
venison, *(caro) ferina*.
venom, *venenum, virus*.
venomous, *venenatus*.
vent, subst. *foramen, spiramentum, emissarium*; to find —, *erumpĕre*.
vent, v.: to — anger, *stomachum effundĕre, evomĕre*.
ventilate, *ventilare* (= to fan); fig., *in medium proferre*.
venture, *periculum* (= risk); *alea* (= hazard); *facinus (-oris, = bold act)*.
venture, v.: = dare, *audēre, periclitari*; = endanger, *periclitari*.
venturesome, venturous, *audax, temerarius*; adv., *audacter*.
venturousness, *audacia, temeritas*.
veracious, *verus, verax, veridicus*.
veracity, *veritas*.
veranda, *subdialia (-ium), porticus (-ūs, f.)*.
verb, *verbum*.
verbal, render by *verbum* or *vox*.
verbatim, *ad verbum, totidem verbis*.
verbiage, *verba (-orum)*.
verbose, *verbosus*; adv. *verbose*.
verbosity, *copia* or *ubertas verborum*.
verdant, *viridis, viridans*.
verdict, *sententia, iudicium*; to pronounce a —, *iudicare, sententiam dicĕre*.
verdure, *viriditas*.
verge, subst. *margo, ora*; fig., on the — of, render by fut. partic., or *instare, or prope*.
verge, v. *vergĕre, inclinare, appropinquare*.
verification, *confirmatio*.
verify, *confirmare, probare*.
verily, *profecto, sane, certe*.
verisimilitude, *verisimilitudo*.
veritable, *verus*.
vermilion: subst. *minium*; adj. *miniatus*.

vernacular; — tongue, *sermo patrius.*

versatile, *versatilis, varius et multiplex.*

versatility, *facilitas, ingenium facile.*

verse, *versus (-ūs);* in sing. = line of poetry).

versed, *versatus, exercitatus, peritus.*

versification, *versuum ratio.*

versify, *versūs* (or *carmina*) *facĕre.*

vertex, *vertex,* or render by *summus.*

vertical, *(di)rectus;* a — line, *linea, perpendiculum;* adv. *recte, ad lineam, ad perpendiculum.*

vertigo, *vertigo.*

very, adj. *ipse;* see true, real.

very, adv.; render by superlative, or a special form with the prefix *per-,* or *maxime, summe, admodum;* not (so) —, *non ita, haud ita;* — much, with verbs, *magnopere, maxime, valde.*

vessel, *vas;* a blood —, *arteria, vena;* = ship, *navis.*

vest, v.: see clothe or invest.

vestal; a — virgin, *virgo vestalis.*

vestibule, *vestibulum.*

vestige, *vestigium, indicium.*

vetch, *vicia.*

veteran, subst. and adj. *veteranus.*

veto, subst. *intercessio* (of the tribunes).

veto, v. *intercedĕre, vetare.*

vex, *vexare, sollicitare;* to be —ed at, *aegre ferre,* or render by *piget.*

vexation, *indignatio, stomachus, molestia.*

vexatious, *molestus, gravis;* adv. *graviter.*

viands, *cibus.*

vibrate, *vibrare;* see also shake.

vibration, *motus (-ūs);* or render by verb.

vicarious, *vicarius;* adv. render by *loco* with genit., or *pro* with abl.

vice, *vitiositas, vitium, turpitudo.*

vicious, *vitiosus, turpis, flagitiosus;* adv. *turpiter, flagitiose.*

viciousness, *vitiositas;* see vice.

vicissitude, *vicissitudo, varietas, vices* (plur.).

victim, *victima, hostia.*

victor, *victor* (f. *victrix*).

victorious, *victor,* with f. *victrix;* adv., render by adj.

victory, *victoria;* to gain a —, *vincĕre, superare.*

victual, *rem frumentariam providĕre* (with dat.).

vie, *certare, contendĕre, aemulari.*

Vienna, *Vindobona.*

view, subst.: = vision, *conspectus (-ūs), prospectus (-ūs);* mental —, = judgment, *sententia, iudicium;* in my —, *meo iudicio, me iudice.*

view, v. *adspicĕre, intuĕri, contemplari.*

vigil, *vigilia, pervigilatio, pervigilium.*

vigilance, *vigilantia, diligentia.*

vigilant, *vigilans, intentus, diligens;* adv. *vigilanter, intente, diligenter.*

vigorous, *strenuus, impiger, acer;* adv. *strenue, impigre, acriter.*

vigour, *vis, nervi (-orum).*

vile, *abiectus, nequam, turpis;* adv. *abiecte, nequiter, turpiter.*

vileness, *turpitudo.*

vilify; see slander.

villa, *villa* (= country-house).

village, *pagus, vicus.*

villager, *paganus, vicanus.*

villain, *homo scelestus;* colloq., *verbero, scelus (-eris, n.).*

villainous, *scelestus, sceleratus, flagitiosus.*

villainy: as disposition, *improbitas, pravitas, nequitia;* as act, *scelus (-eris, n.), flagitium.*

vindicate: = maintain, *tenēre, obtinēre, defendĕre;* = justify, *probare, purgare.*

vindication, *vindicta, defensio.*

vindicator, *vindex, defensor.*

vindictive, *ulciscendi cupidus.*

vine, *vitis.*

vine-dresser, *vinitor.*

vinegar, *acetum.*

vineyard, *vinea, vinetum.*

vintage, *vindemia.*

vintner, *vinarius.*

violate, *violare, rumpĕre.*

violation, *violatio.*

violator, *violator, ruptor.*

violence, *violentia, vis; ardor* (of passion, etc.); *gravitas* (of weather, etc.).

violent, *violentus, vehemens, gravis* (of illness, weather, etc.): adv. *vi, per vim, violenter, vehementer, graviter.*

violet, subst. *viola;* a bed of —s, *violarium.*

viper, *vipera, aspis;* of a —, adj., *vipereus.*

virgin, subst. *virgo.*

virginity, *virginitas.*

virile, *virilis;* see manly.

virility, *virilitas;* see manhood.

virtual, virtually, *re non verbo.*

virtue: moral —, *virtus (-utis, f.), probitas;* = chastity, *pudicitia, sanctimonia;* = efficacy, *virtus, vis,* or use verb, e.g. *posse, prodesse;* by — of, *per, ex, pro.*

virtuous, *virtute praeditus, honestus, probus;* = chaste, *pudicus, castus;* adv. *honeste.*

virulence, *vis;* of diseases, *gravitas;* of hostility, *acerbitas.*

virulent, *gravis, acerbus;* adv. *graviter, acerbe.*

viscera, *viscera (-um), exta (-orum).*

viscous, *lentus, tenax.*

visible, *manifestus;* to be —, *apparēre, in conspectu esse:* adv., *manifesto, quod cernĕre possis.*

vision: = faculty of sight, *visus (-ūs); aspectus (-ūs);* = thing seen, *visus (-ūs), species;* = apparition, *simulacrum, imago.*

visionary: of things, *inanis, fictus, vanus;* of character, *fanaticus.*

visit, subst. *salutatio.*

visit, v.: = go to see, *(in)visĕre, visitare, salutare;* = punish, *animadvertĕre, punire.*

visitation; see punishment.

visitor, *salutator, hospes, advena.*

visor, *buccula* (= cheek-piece).

vista, *prospectus (-ūs);* see view.

vital, *vitalis;* adv. *vitaliter;* see also essential.

vitality, *vis, animus.*

vitiate, *depravare, corrumpĕre, inritum facĕre* (= invalidate).

vitiation, *corruptio, depravatio.*

vituperate, *vituperare, reprehendĕre.*

vituperation, *vituperatio, reprehensio.*

vivacious, *vividus, alacer, acer;* adv. *acriter.*

vivacity, *alacritas, vigor.*

vivid; see lively.

vixen, *vulpes;* of women, *canis.*

vocabulary, *index verborum* (= list of words), *copia verborum* (= stock or flow of words).

vocation, *officium, munus* (-eris, n.).

vociferate, *vociferari, clamare.*

vociferation, *vociferatio, clamor.*

vociferous, vociferously, *magno clamore.*

vogue, *mos.*

voice, subst. *vox.*

voice, v.; see utter, express.

void, subst. *inanitas, inane, vacuum.*

void, adj.: = empty, *inanis, vacuus;* = invalid, *inritus, vanus.*

volatile, *volaticus, levis, mobilis.*

volatility, *levitas, mobilitas.*

volcano, *mons flammas eructans;* or refer to some specific volcano.

volition, *voluntas.*

volley, *tela* (-orum) *coniecta.*

voluble, *volubilis;* see also fluent.

volume: = book, *liber, volumen;* = size, *magnitudo, amplitudo;* = quantity, *copia.*

voluminous, *copiosus, magnus, amplus.*

voluntary, *voluntarius;* adv., *ultro, (mea,* etc.) *sponte.*

volunteer, subst. *voluntarius* (*miles*).

volunteer, v. *operam suam profitēri.*

voluptuous, *voluptarius, luxuriosus, libidinosus.*

voluptuousness, *voluptas, luxuria.*

vomit, v. (*e*)*vomĕre.*

voracious, *edax,* (*cibi*) *avidus;* adv. *avide.*

voracity, *edacitas,* (*cibi*) *aviditas.*

vortex, *vertex, turbo.*

votary, *cultor.*

vote, subst. *suffragium, punctum, sententia.*

vote, v. *suffragium* or *sententiam ferre; censēre.*

voter, *suffragator, qui suffragium fert.*

voting-tablet, *tabella, suffragium.*

votive, *votivus.*

vouch, v.: to — for a thing, *rem in se recipĕre;* = assert, warrant, *adseverare, testari.*

vouchsafe, *concedĕre.*

vow, subst. *votum, devotio, sponsio.*

vow, v. (*de*)*vovēre;* = to undertake, promise, (*de*)*spondēre, promittĕre.*

vowel, *littera vocalis.*

voyage, subst. *navigatio, cursus* (-ūs).

voyage, v. *navigare.*

vulgar, *vulgaris, usitatus, plebeius.*

vulture, *vultur, vulturius.*

W

wade, *vado flumen transire.*

wag, subst. *ioculator, homo iocosus.*

wag, v. *movēre, quassare.*

wage; to — war, *bellum gerĕre.*

wager, subst. *sponsio, pignus* (-oris).

wager, v. *sponsionem facĕre, pignore certare.*

wages, *merces, stipendium.*

waggon, *plaustrum, vehiculum, carrus.*

wail, *plorare, plangĕre.*

wailing, subst. *ploratus* (-ūs).

wain, *plaustrum.*

wainscot, *paries* (= party-wall).

waist, *corpus* (-oris, n.) *medium.*

wait, subst. *mora* (= delay); to lie in — for, *aucupari, insidiari.*

wait, v. *manēre;* to — for, *opperiri, exspectare, praestolari;* to — at table, *ministrare.*

waiter, *famulus, minister, puer.*

waiting, subst.: = delay, *mora, commoratio;* at table, *ministerium.*

waive, (*rem*) *concedĕre,* (*de re*) *decedĕre.*

wake, subst. see watch; in the — of, *post.*

wake, v.: transit., *expergefacĕre, excitare;* intransit., *expergisci, excitari.*

wakefulness, *insomnia, vigilia.*

walk, subst.: a — as taken, *ambulatio;* to go for a —, *ire ambulatum;* = gait, *incessus* (-ūs), *ingressus* (-ūs).

walk, v. *pedibus ire, ambulare, ingredi, incedĕre.*

wall, subst. *murus, moenia* (-ium; of a town), *paries* (= partition).

wall, v. *muro cingĕre, munire.*

wallet, *saccus, crumena.*

wallow, *volutari.*

walnut, (fruit or tree), *iuglans.*

wan, *pallidus, exsanguis.*

wand, *virga, virgula.*

wander, *vagari, palari, errare:* to — through, *pervagari;* to — in mind, *delirare.*

wanderer, *erro, peregrinator.*

wandering, subst. *error, erratio.*

wandering, adj. *errabundus, vagus.*

wane, *decrescĕre, minui.*

want, subst. *penuria, inopia, egestas, desiderium* (— as felt), *defectio;* in —, adj. *inops, egenus, egens.*

want, v.: = lack, need, *egēre, indigēre, requirĕre, desiderare;* = wish, *velle, avēre, cupĕre.*

wanting, = defective, *vitiosus;* to be found —, *deesse, deficĕre.*

wanton, adj. *lascivus, petulans, protervus;* adv. *petulanter, proterve, ultro* (= without provocation).

wanton, v. *lascivire.*

wantonness, *lascivia, petulantia, protervitas.*

war, subst. *bellum;* civil —, *bellum intestinum, domesticum, civile;* a — of extermination, *bellum internecinum;* to declare —, *bellum indicĕre;* to make —, *bellum inferre;* to carry on a —, *bellum gerĕre.*

warble, *canĕre.*

war-cry, *clamor* (*bellicus*), *ululatus* (-ūs).

ward, subst.: = a quarter of a town, *regio, vicus;* = custody, *custodia;* = a minor, *pupillus.*

ward, v.: to — off, *arcēre, propulsare, avertere;* by prayers, *deprecari.*

warden, warder, *custos.*

wardrobe, *vestiarium.*

ware, wares, *merx.*

warehouse, *horreum, apotheca.*

warfare, *militia.*

wariness, *prudentia, cautio, circumspectio.*

warlike, *militaris, bellicus, ferox.*

warm, *calidus;* luke- —, *tepidus;* to be warm, *calēre.*

warm, v. *calefacĕre.*

warmth, *calor, fervor.*

warn, *(ad)monēre;* in advance, *praemonēre.*

warning, subst. *(ad)monitio, monitus* (*-ūs*), *exemplum* (= object-lesson).

warp, subst., in weaving, *stamen.*

warp, v.: of timber, intransit., *pandari.* Transf., *depravare, torquēre;* see also distort.

warrant, subst.: = authority, *auctoritas, potestas;* = written authorization, *mandatum, diploma* (*-atis,* n.).

warrant, v. *(con)firmare, promittĕre* (= promise).

warranty, *satisdatio;* see guarantee.

warrior, *miles, homo* (or *vir*) *militaris.*

wary, *providus, circumspectus, cautus.*

wash, subst. *lavatio;* a colour- —, *fucus* (esp. red).

wash, v.: transit., *lavare;* to — out, — away, *abluĕre;* intransit., *lavari.*

wasp, *vespa.*

waste, subst.: = unprofitable expenditure, *effusio, sumptus* (*-ūs*) *effusus, iactura;* = waste land, *vastitas, solitudo;* = discarded material, *ramenta* (*-orum*).

waste, adj. *vastus, incultus, desertus;* to lay —, *vastare, (de)populari.*

waste, v.: transit., = to spend unprofitably, *consumĕre, perdĕre;* intransit., to — away, *(con)tabescĕre, consumi, confici.*

wasteful, *profusus, effusus;* adv. *profuse, effuse.*

wastefulness, *profusio, effusio.*

watch, subst.: = watching, *excubiae* (*-arum*), *vigilantia, vigilia:* to keep —, *vigilare;* concrete, the —, *vigilia, statio;* = quarter of a night, *vigilia;* = timepiece, *horologium.*

watch, v.: = observe or guard, *(ob)servare, tuēri;* = stay awake, *vigilare, excubare.*

watchful, *vigilans;* adv. *vigilanter.*

watchfulness, *vigilantia, vigilia.*

watchman, *vigil, excubitor, custos.*

watchtower, *specula.*

watchword, *tessera, signum.*

water, subst. *aqua;* fresh —, *aqua dulcis;* rain —, *(aqua) pluvia, aqua caelestis;* to go for —, *aquari;* of the —, adj., *aquatilis, aquarius.*

water, v. *(in)rigare, conspergĕre* (= to sprinkle).

water-carrier, *aquator, aquarius.*

water-clock, *clepsydra.*

watering-place, *aquatio;* for bathing, etc., *aquae* (*-arum*).

water-jug, *hydria, urceus.*

water-snake, *hydrus.*

waterspout, *prester, typhon.*

waterworks, *aquae* or *aquarum ductu* (*-ūs*).

watery, *aquatilis, aquosus.*

wattle, subst.; = hurdle, *cratis;* of a cock, *palea.*

wave, subst. *fluctus* (*-ūs*), *unda.*

wave, v.: transit., *agitare, iactare vibrare;* intransit., *fluctuare undare.*

waver, *fluctuare, dubitare.*

wavering, subst. *dubitatio, fluctuatio.*

wavering, adj. *incertus, dubius.*

wax, subst. *cera.*

wax, v. = to cover with wax, *(in)cerare* intransit., = grow, *crescĕre.*

waxen, *cereus.*

way, (1), abstract: = journey, *via, cursus* (*-ūs*), *iter;* — up to, *aditus* (*-ūs*); = manner, *modus, ratio, via;* in this —, *sic, ita;* = custom, *mos, institutum;* —s and means, *opes* (*-um,* plur.). (2), concrete: = road, *via;* a bye- —, *trames, semita, callis;* in the —, adj. *obvius;* out of the —, *devius, avius, remotus;* the milky —, *orbis lacteus.*

wayfarer, *viator.*

waylay, *(homini) insidiari.*

wayward; see wilful.

we, *nos;* but often not expressed.

weak, *infirmus, debilis, imbecillus, invalidus; hebes* (= dull, faint, etc.); *levis* (of character, etc.); adv. *infirme.*

weaken, v. transit. *debilitare, enervare, infirmare.*

weakness, *imbecillitas, infirmitas, debilitas; levitas* (of arguments, etc.); *vitium* (= fault).

weal: the public —, *respublica.*

wealth, *divitiae* (*-arum*), *opes* (*-um*), *copia.*

wealthy, *dives, locuples, opulentus.*

weapon, *arma* (*-orum;* defensive) *telum* (offensive).

wear, subst. *usus* (*-ūs*).

wear, v.: to — away, *(con)terĕre;* = to have on the body, *gerĕre, gestare;* = to last, *durare;* to — off, *evanescĕre.*

weariness, *lassitudo, taedium.*

wearisome, *laboriosus, molestus.*

weary, adj. *(de)fatigatus, (de)fessus.*

weary, v.: transit., *(de)fatigare, obtundĕre* (= to bore); intransit., use impersonal *taedet.*

weasel, *mustela.*

weather, subst. *caelum, tempestas.*

weather, v.: to — a cape, *promontorium circumvehi;* to — a storm *vim tempestatis perferre.*

weave, *(con)texĕre.*

weaver, *textor.*

web, *tela, textum.*

wed; see marry.

wedding, *nuptiae* (*-arum*).

wedge, subst. *cuneus;* — -shaped, *cuneatus.*

week, *septem dies.*

week-days, *dies profesti.*

weep, *lacrimare, lacrimas fundĕre, flēre;* to — for, *(de)plorare, (de)flēre, lamentari.*

weeping, subst. *fletus* (*-ūs*), *lamentatio.*

weigh, v.: transit. (lit. and fig.), *(ex)pendĕre, pensare, examinare;* to

— down, *opprimĕre, gravare*; intransit., to — much, *magni ponderis
esse.*

weight, *pondus (-eris, n.), gravitas
momentum;* to have great —, *multum
valēre.*

weighty, *gravis* (lit. and fig.).

weir, *moles, agger.*

welcome, subst. *salutatio.*

welcome, adj. *acceptus, gratus.*

welcome! interj. *salve.*

welcome, v. *salutare, salvēre iubēre.*

welfare, *salūs (-ūtis, f.), commodum,
utilitas.*

well, subst. *puteus.*

well, adj. *salvus, sanus:* to be —,
(bene) valēre; to get —, *convalescĕre.*

well, adv. *bene, recte;* very —, *optime,
praeclare;* it is —, *bene est, bene habet.*

well, v.: to — up, *scatĕre.*

well-being, *salūs (-ūtis, f.).*

well-born, *nobilis.*

well-bred, *comis, urbanus.*

well-earned, *meritus.*

well-informed, *doctus, eruditus.*

well-known, *(omnibus) notus, celebratus.*

well-meaning, *benevolus, amicus.*

welter, subst. *congeries.*

west, subst. *occidens, solis occasus (-ūs).*

west, adj. *occidentalis;* — wind,
Zephyrus, Favonius.

westwards, *ad occasum, ad occidentem.*

wet, adj. *umidus, madidus;* to be —,
madēre.

wet, v. *madefacĕre, (in)rigare.*

wether, *vervex.*

whale, *balaena, cetus* or *cetos.*

wharf, *navale, crepido.*

what: interrog., as pronoun, *quid?,* as
adj. *qui, quae, quod?;* of — sort?
qualis?; of — size? *quantus?;*
relative, = that which, *(id) quod.*

whatever, whatsoever: relat. pronoun or adj., *quisquis, quicunque;*
indef., any —, *quivis.*

wheat, *triticum;* of —, adj., *triticeus.*

wheedle, *(e)blandiri.*

wheel, subst. *rota.*

wheel, v.: = turn round, transit.,
convertĕre, intransit., of troops, *signa
convertĕre;* = push forward on
wheels, *propulsare.*

wheeze, *anhelare;* see also pant.

whelp, *catulus.*

when: interrog., *quando?;* relat., *cum,
ubi, quando, ut, postquam* (= after).

whence, *unde.*

whenever, *quandocumque, quoties, cum*
(with indic).

where: interrog., *ubi?;* — from, *unde?;*
— to, *quo?;* relat., *ubi, qua.*

whereas, *quoniam, quod, cum.*

whereby; render by relative.

wherefore: interrog., *cur?;* relat.,
quare, quamobrem, quapropter.

wherein, *in quo, in quibus, ubi.*

whereof, render by genit. of relat.

whereupon, *quo facto.*

wherever, *ubicumque, quacumque.*

whet, *(ex)acuĕre.*

whether, conj. In single indirect
questions, *num, -ne* or *an,* followed
by subj.; in disjunctive indirect

questions, *utrum . . . an, -ne . . .an,*
followed by subj.; — . . . or not,
utrum . . . necne. In disjunctive
conditional sentences, when a thing
is so in either of two conditions,
— . . . or, is *sive* (or *seu*) . . . *sive*
(or *seu*).

whetstone, *cos.*

whey, *serum.*

which: interrog., *quis?;* — of the two
uter?; relat., *qui, quae, quod.*

whiff, *halitus (-ūs;* = breath).

while, subst.: for a —, *aliquamdiu;* in
a little —, *brevi, mox;* for a little —,
parumper, paulisper.

while, whilst, *dum, donec, quoad* (rare).

while, v.: to — away time, *tempus
fallĕre.*

whim, *libido.*

whimsical, *levis* (= fickle).

whine, v. *vagire* (esp. of children).

whining, subst. *vagitus (-ūs).*

whinny, *hinnire.*

whip, *flagrum, flagellum, scutica.*

whip, v. *verberare.*

whirl, v. transit., *(con)torquēre, rotare.*

whirlpool, *vertex, vorago, gurges.*

whirlwind, *turbo, vertex.*

whirr, subst. *stridor.*

whirr, v. *stridēre* or *stridĕre.*

whisht, interj. *st! tace, tacete.*

whisper, subst. *susurrus.*

whisper, v. *susurrare, insusurrare.*

whistle, v. *sibilare.*

whit, adj.; not a —, *ne minimum quidem,
minime.*

white, adj. *albus* (= dead —), *candidus*
(= shining —), *canus* (= hoary); to
be —, *albēre.*

whiten, whitewash, v. transit. *deal-
bare.*

whiteness, *candor.*

whither: interrog., *quo?;* relat., *quo.*

whithersoever, *quoquo, quocunque.*

who: interrog., *quis, quid;* relat., *qui,
quae, quod.*

whoever, *quicunque, quisquis.*

whole, subst.: the — of a thing,
tota res; on the —, *plerumque, ferme,
fere.*

whole, adj. *totus, omnis, universus,
integer* (= unhurt).

wholesome, *salutaris, utilis.*

wholesomeness, *salubritas, utilitas.*

wholly, *omnino, prorsus.*

whose, *cuius;* plur. *quorum, quarum,
quorum.*

why, *cur, quare, quamobrem.*

wicked, *improbus, malus, nefarius;* adv.
improbe, male, nefarie.

wickedness, *improbitas, scelus (-eris,
n.).*

wicker, *vimineus;* — work, *crates.*

wide, *latus, laxus, amplus;* adv. *late.*

widen, v.: transit., *amplificare, dilatare;*
intransit., *patescĕre.*

widow, *vidua.*

widowed, *viduus, orbus.*

width, *latitudo, amplitudo.*

wield, *tractare, uti* (with abl.).

wife, *uxor, coniunx.*

Wight, Isle of, *Vectis.*

wild, adj. *ferus, incultus, ferox;* a — beast, *fera;* adv. *ferociter, saeve.*

wilderness, wilds, *loca (-orum) deserta, solitudo, vastitas.*

wildness, *feritas, ferocia.*

wile, *ars, dolus.*

wilful, *contumax, pervicax;* adv. *contumaciter, pervicaciter;* see also *deliberately.*

wilfulness, *contumacia, pervicacia.*

will, subst.: = volition, *voluntas, animus, arbitrium;* against one's —, *invitus,* adj.; = testament, *testamentum.*

will, v.: = wish, *velle;* = leave property by will, *legare, relinquĕre.*

willing, *libens, volens, paratus;* adv. *libenter,* or use adj. *libens.*

willingness, *voluntas.*

willow, *salix.*

wily, *vafer, astutus, versutus.*

win, v.: transit., see get, gain; intransit., *vincĕre, superare.*

wind, subst. *ventus.*

wind, v. = turn, twist, *volvĕre, torquĕre.*

winding, subst. *sinus (-ūs), flexus (-ūs).*

winding, adj. *flexuosus, tortuosus.*

windlass, *sucula, tormentum.*

window, *fenestra.*

windy, *ventosus.*

wine, *vinum:* sour —, *vappa;* undiluted, *merum;* the — god, *Bacchus.*

wine-cellar, *apotheca.*

wine-merchant, *vinarius.*

wing, subst. *ala;* of an army, *cornu, ala.*

wing, v.; to — one's way, *volare.*

winged, *alatus, aliger, pennatus.*

wink, v. *conivēre, nictare.*

winner, *victor.*

winning, *venustus, suavis.*

winnow, *ventilare, evannēre.*

winnowing-fan, *ventilabrum, vannus.*

winter, subst. *hiems, bruma* (lit. = shortest day).

winter, adj. *hiemalis, hibernus.*

winter, v. *hiemare, hibernare.*

winter-quarters, *castra (-orum) hiberna.*

wipe, *(abs)tergĕre, detergĕre;* to — out, *abolēre, delēre.*

wire, *filum (ferreum).*

wisdom, *sapientia, prudentia, consilium.*

wise, *sapiens, prudens* (= sensible); to be —, *sapĕre.* Adv. *sapienter, prudenter.*

wish, subst. *optatio, desiderium* (= longing), *votum* (= prayer).

wish, v. *velle, cupĕre, (ex)optare;* not to —, *nolle.*

wistful, render by *desiderium* (= longing).

wit: as a quality, *ingenium, (ingenii) acumen, facetiae (-arum), sal* (with one's —s about one, *sanus;* = witty person, *(homo) facetus.*

wit, v.: to —, *videlicet, scilicet, dico.*

witch, *venefica, saga.*

witchcraft, *veneficium, ars magica.*

with, prep., *cum* (with abl.); sometimes plain abl.

withal, *simul.*

withdraw, v.: transit., *avertĕre, revocare, removēre;* intransit., *(re)cedĕre,*

discedĕre, se recipĕre; to — from office, *magistratu se abdicare.*

wither, v.: transit., *urĕre, corrumpĕre;* transit., *marcescĕre, marcēre.*

withered, *marcidus.*

withhold, *retinēre, recusare* (= to refuse).

within, prep. *intra* (with acc.), *in* (with abl.); — a period of time, render by plain abl.

within, adv. *intus, intro* (= to the inside).

without, prep. *sine* (with abl.), *extra* (with acc.); to be (or go) — a thing, *re carēre;* — going, — doing, etc., render by clause.

without, adv. *extra, foris* (= out of doors).

withstand, *resistĕre, obsistĕre* (with dat.).

witness, subst.: = one who gives evidence, *testis;* to call as a —, *testari, antestari;* = evidence, q.v.; = a party present, *arbiter, spectator;* before many —es, *coram multis.*

witness, v.: = give evidence, *testari;* = see, q.v.

witticism, *dictum, facetiae (-arum).*

witty, *dicax, facetus, salsus;* adv. *facete.*

wizard, *veneficus, magus.*

woad, *vitrum.*

woe, *dolor, luctus (-ūs);* interj., *vae!*

wolf, *lupus, lupa;* of a —, adj. *lupinus.*

woman, *femina* (opp. *vir*), *mulier* (esp. a grown —); an old —, *anus (-ūs);* a little —, *muliercula.*

womanish, *muliebris, mollis, effeminatus.*

womanly, *muliebris.*

womb, *alvus, uterus.*

wonder, subst.: as a feeling, *(ad)miratio;* = wonderful thing, *miraculum, res mira;* and no —, *nec mirum.*

wonder, v. *(ad)mirari;* I — whether, why, etc., *scire velim.*

wonderful, *mirus, mirificus, (ad)mirabilis;* adv. *mire, mirifice, (ad)mirabiliter.*

wont, subst. *mos, consuetudo.*

wont: to be —, *solēre, consuevisse.*

woo, *ambire, (in matrimonium) petĕre.*

wood: as substance, *lignum, materia (materies);* to get —, *lignari;* = collection of trees, *silva, nemus (-oris, n.).*

wooden, *ligneus.*

woodland, *silvae (-arum), nemora (-um).*

woodman, *lignator.*

wood-nymph, *(hama)dryas.*

wood-pecker, *picus.*

wood-pigeon, *palumbes.*

woody, wooded, *silvestris, silvosus.*

wooer, *procus.*

woof, *subtemen, trama.*

wool, *lana.*

woollen, woolly, *laneus.*

word, subst. *verbum;* = name, *vocabulum* or *nomen* (= name); *dictum* (= saying) = word of honour, *fides:* to keep one's —, *fidem servare;* to break one's —, *fidem fallĕre.*

word, v.; see express.

wordy, *verbosus.*

work, subst. *opus (-eris, n.);* = piece of —); *pensum* (= task); *opera,* *labor* (= effort); *liber* (= literary —); a small —, *opusculum.*

work, v.: intransit. (*e*)*laborare, operari*, to — at night, *lucubrare*; a —ing day, *dies profestus*; transit., = exercise, ply, *exercēre, exercitare*; = till, *colĕre*; = effect, do, *facĕre, efficĕre.*

workman, *opifex, operarius, artifex, faber.*

workmanship, *ars, opus* (*-eris*, n.).

workshop, *officina.*

world, *rerum natura, mundus*; *orbis terrarum* or *terrae* (= the globe); *terrae* (*-arum*; = all countries); *gentes, homines, omnes* (all plur., = mankind); the ancient —, *antiquitas, veteres* (*-um*, plur.); a man of the —, *homo rerum peritus*; the lower —, *inferi* (*-orum*).

worm, subst. *vermis, vermiculus, tinea* (in wood, books, etc.).

worm, v.: to — one's way in, (*se*) *insinuare.*

worry, subst.; see anxiety.

worry, v.: = tear, maul, (*di*)*lacerare*, (*di*)*laniare*; = harass, *vexare, sollicitare.*

worse, adj. *peior*; to grow —, *degenerare, ingravescĕre* (of troubles); adv. *peius, deterius.*

worship, subst. *veneratio, cultus* (*-ūs*): divine —, *cultus deorum*; to attend —, *sacris adesse.*

worship, v. *venerari, colĕre.*

worshipper, *cultor.*

worst: adj. *pessimus*; adv. *pessime.*

worst, v. *vincĕre.*

worth, subst., = merit, *virtūs* (*-ūtis*, f.), *dignitas.*

worth, adj.: render by genit. of value or by *valēre*; it is — while, *operae pretium est.*

worthless, *vilis, inutilis, nequam.*

worthy, *dignus* (with abl., or *qui* and subj.); adv. *digne.*

would; see will, wish; — that, in wishes, *utinam* and subj.

wound, subst. *vulnus* (*-eris*, n.), *cicatrix* (= scar).

wound, v. *vulnerare, sauciare.*

wounded, *vulneratus, saucius.*

wrangle; see quarrel.

wrap, *involvĕre, velare, amicire.*

wrapper, = cover, *involucrum, tegumentum.*

wrath, *ira, iracundia, indignatio.*

wrathful, *iratus, iracundus*; adv. *iracunde, per iram.*

wreath, *corona, serta* (*-orum*).

wreathe, *nectĕre, contorquēre* (= twist).

wreck, wreckage, *naufragium.*

wrecked, *naufragus.*

wrench, wrest, (*rem homini*) *extorquēre* or *eripĕre.*

wrestle, *luctari.*

wrestler, *luctator, athleta.*

wrestling, subst. *luctatio.*

wretch, *homo miser.*

wretched: = unfortunate, *miser, miserabilis*; = bad, *malus, nequam*; adv. *misere, miserabiliter*; *male* (= badly).

wretchedness, *miseria, aerumna.*

wriggle, *se torquēre, torquēri.*

wring; to — the neck, *gulam, frangĕre,*

wrinkle, subst. *ruga.*

wrinkle, v.; to — the forehead, *frontem contrahĕre.*

wrinkled, *rugosus.*

wrist; render by *manus* (= hand).

writ: Holy —, *Litterae* (*-arum*) *Sanctae*; a legal —, *mandatum, praescriptum.*

write, *scribĕre*; — out, *describĕre*; — back, *rescribĕre*; — often, *scriptitare.*

writer, *scriptor, scriba* (professional); *qui scribit.*

writhe, *torquēri.*

writing, subst.: as act, *scriptio, scriptura*; the art of —, *ars scribendi*; = thing written, *scriptum, litterae* (*-arum*).

writing-case, *scrinium.*

writing-tablet, *tabula, cera.*

wrong, subst.: = injury, *iniuria*; = wickedness, *nefas*; to do wrong, *peccare, delinquĕre.*

wrong, adj. *falsus* (= false), *pravus* (= perverse), *iniquus* (= unfair); to be — (i.e. mistaken), *falli, errare.* Adv. *male, perperam, prave, falso, inique, iniuriā.*

wrong, v. *iniuriā adficĕre.*

wroth, *iratus.*

wrought, *factus, confectus.*

wry, *distortus, perversus, pravus.*

Y

yacht, *celox.*

yard: the measure, *tres pedes* (*-um*); a — long, or wide, *tripedalis*: court —, *area*; sail—, *antenna.*

yawn, v. *oscitare*; = open wide, *scindi, hiare.*

ye; see you.

yea; see yes.

year, *annus, anni spatium*; lasting a —, adj. *annuus*; last —, *superiore* or *priore anno*; next —, *proximo anno*; every —, *singulis annis*; *quotannis*; every other —, *alternis annis*; a period of two —s, *biennium.*

yearly: adj., *annuus, anniversarius*; adv. *quotannis, singulis annis.*

yearn; to — for, *desiderare.*

yearning, *desiderium.*

yell, subst. *ululatus* (*-ūs*), *eiulatio.*

yell, v. *ululare, eiulare.*

yellow, *flavus, fulvus, aureus* (= golden), *croceus* (= saffron coloured).

yelp, yelping, subst. *gannitus* (*-ūs*).

yelp, v. *gannire.*

yes, *ita* (*est*), *certe, etiam, sane*; I say —, *aio.*

yesterday, adv. *heri*; of —, adj., *hesternus.*

yet: = nevertheless, (*at*)*tamen, at*; = even now, *etiamnunc, adhuc*; not —, *nondum*: with comparatives, = even, *etiam.*

yew, *taxus.*

yield, v.: transit., = produce, (*ef*)*ferre*; = give, *dare, praebēre*; = surrender, *dedĕre,* (*con*)*cedĕre*; intransit., (*con*)*cedĕre, obsequi.*

yielding, adj., *facilis, indulgens.*
yoke, subst. *iugum.*
yoke, v. *(con)iungĕre.*
yolk, (of an egg) *vitellus.*
yon, yonder, adj. *ille, iste.*
yonder, adv. *illic, istic* (= there, where you are).
yore: of —, *olim, quondam.*
York, *Eboracum.*
you, *tu, te,* etc. (sing.); *vos,* etc. (plur.); but often not expressed.
young, subst. *partus* (-*ūs*; = offspring), *fetus* (-*ūs*) or *proles* (= brood), *pullus* (= a single — animal).
young, adj. *parvus* or *parvulus* (= little), *adulescens* (= growing up), *novus* (= fresh, new); — child, *infans;* — lad, *puer;* — man, *adulescens, adulescentulus, iuvenis.*
younger, *iunior,* (*natu*) *minor.*
youngest, (*natu*) *minimus.*
your, yours, *tuus* (of a sing. owner; = thy), *vester* (of plur. owner); that of —s, *iste.*
yourself, *tu ipse, tute, tutemet.*
yourselves, *vos ipsi, vosmet* (*ipsi*).

youth, *pueritia, adulescentia, iuventūs* (-*ūtis,* f.); from one's — up, *ab ineunte aetate, a puero;* collective, = young people, *iuventus* (-*utis,* f.), *iuvenes* (-*um*); = a young man, *puer, adulescens, iuvenis.*
youthful, *iuvenilis iuvenalis, puerilis;* adv. *iuveniliter, iuvenum more.*

Z

zeal, *studium, ardor, fervor, industria.*
zealous, *studiosus, acer;* adv. *studiose, acriter.*
zenith, *vertex.*
Zephyr, *Zephyrus, Favonius.*
zero, render by *nihil.*
zest, *studium.*
zodiac: girdle, *cingulum;* = region *orbis, regio, plaga.*
zoology, *animantium descriptio.*

FINIS